The Oxford Dictionary of

Christian Art & Architecture

SECOND EDITION

PETER MURRAY
and LINDA MURRAY

Second Edition edited by
TOM DEVONSHIRE JONES

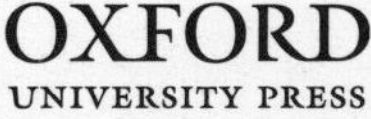

OXFORD
UNIVERSITY PRESS

Great Clarendon Street, Oxford, OX2 6DP,
United Kingdom

Oxford University Press is a department of the University of Oxford.
It furthers the University's objective of excellence in research, scholarship,
and education by publishing worldwide. Oxford is a registered trade mark of
Oxford University Press in the UK and in certain other countries

First published as *The Oxford Companion to Christian Art and Architecture* in 1996 by
Oxford University Press
First issued as an Oxford University Press paperback 1998
Unillustrated paperback edition published as *A Dictionary of Christian Art* 2001
Reissued with new covers 2004
Second Edition published as *The Oxford Dictionary of Christian Art and Architecture* 2013
Second Edition published as an Oxford University Press paperback 2014

Impression: 1

British Library Cataloguing in Publication Data
Data available

Library of Congress Cataloging in Publication Data
Data available

ISBN 978-0-19-969510-2

Printed in Great Britain by
Clays Ltd, St Ives plc

IN MEMORIAM
PETER JOHN MURRAY
23-4-1920
20-4-1992
Tu duca, tu signore, e tu maestro

Contents

Preface

More than thirty years' experience in teaching the History of Art and Architecture have taught us that simple lack of knowledge of the Bible, and of Christian doctrine, as well as something of church history and ritual, frequently prevents people from understanding—and even more, from appreciating—much of the greatest art which has ever been created.

Younger colleagues have told us that the problem is getting worse, and the same is true of English literature, where the words and cadences of the Authorized Version of the Bible, echoed by writers from Shakespeare to Hardy, no longer have the effect intended by the author and, because they are not recognized, their meaning and their relevance is lost. One of us, standing in London's National Gallery in front of Piero della Francesca's *Baptism of Christ*, heard someone ask his companion, 'What's the pigeon for?' The other caps this with the assertion that she heard an English couple, in front of Leonardo da Vinci's *Last Supper* in Milan—surely one of the most famous images ever created—say, 'I don't know what they are doing, but they seem to be having some sort of a meal.' A similar difficulty can arise when a student of the History of Art, who discourses freely on the technique, the style, the format, the authorship of a picture, and where and when it was painted, when asked to discuss the painter's management of the composition and disposition of the figures in the picture, and whether they properly express the subject, is unable to answer the question because the subject is not recognized as a biblical one.

This encyclopaedic dictionary is intended to help, but the problem is that anyone who does not know that a dove (not a pigeon) is a symbol of the Holy Ghost is not likely to find the answer to his problem by looking up 'pigeon'. So far as possible, therefore, we have provided a web of cross-references, so that individual definitions, not perhaps adequate in themselves, can be integrated into a larger scheme. Thus, given the title of the picture, *The Baptism of Christ*, it will be possible not only to learn that John in his Gospel (Ch. 1: 32) says specifically 'I saw the Spirit descending from heaven like a dove, and it remained on him', but also by following up the trail of cross-references to realize the significance of Baptism in the Gospels and in the life of the individual Christian, as well as its role in the planning and internal arrangements of churches. The whole book is intended to demonstrate the inspiration and creative drive provided by the Christian religion from its beginnings to the present century.

This, in fact, means that the Roman Catholic and Eastern Orthodox communities, from the Early Christian and Byzantine periods of the Roman and Byzantine Empires, and Europe generally, up to the Counter-Reformation period, are treated as fully as possible. This is followed by the expansion after the Counter-Reformation with the introduction of new ideas and practices in the context of Protestantism—but *only* in so far as they affected the arts. For example, Calvinism has been, on the whole, opposed to the visual arts and has affected architecture in so far as it provided gaunt auditory churches, adapted to sermons rather than to ritual. The growth of the symbolic still-life in Dutch 17th-century painting may also be due to Calvinist disapprobation of overt symbolism. It is also true that the popularity of Old Testament subjects in 17th-century Holland is because the Catholic subjects from the Lives of the Saints were now unacceptable. This also had repercussions outside the field of religious art in the growth of portrait, landscape, and genre painting, though that is not our concern here.

Because of our concern with religious art, the reader will find dogmas, rites, and liturgical matters are defined and explained *only* if they have bearing on the arts. Thus the doctrines of the Holy Trinity and the Immaculate Conception are iconographically important, whereas the theologically important doctrines of the Redemption and the Virgin Birth have had few artistic consequences. In architecture, differences in the design of churches, which are governed by the varied purposes which they were built to serve, are explained not only for themselves, but because they help the reader to understand the characteristics of styles nationally, regionally, and in the requirements of varying rites, as well as their evolution over the centuries. In liturgy, the actual vestments and vessels are often of great aesthetic significance, and we have tried especially to give an account of Eastern Orthodox usages, as well as Western, particularly in such controversial matters as Iconoclasm, and the use and abuse of images in general.

Some readers may feel that there is over-emphasis on the earliest ages of Christian art. But one should bear in mind that the first works of Christian art began in the Roman catacombs as early possibly as AD 290, and certainly by the very first years of the 4th century, over a decade before it was legally possible in Rome to be a Christian (the watershed date is 311–13), and that until about the end of the 17th century—that is, a time-span of roughly thirteen centuries—the Christian Church in the West was the stimulus to the building of churches and the commissioning of works of art. The invention and development of printing virtually ended the production of illuminated manuscripts by about 1500, but already etching and engraving had become important in the art of Dürer and Lucas van Leyden. Unfortunately, the Reformation in northern Europe was hostile to religious art, and the religious wars of the late 16th and 17th centuries were appallingly destructive. This destruction continued in the 18th century, with the rejection by the 'Age of Enlightenment' of art which was considered crude, peasant, and uncultured, if not mere folklore, so that in France the destruction of medieval sculpture was widespread, and the French Revolution continued the process on political and ideological grounds. There was, with the 18th century, accompanying the increasing popularity of subjects derived from antique classical literature, a slow but important change in the position of the artist, who no longer had the support of a Church amply supplied with excellent works from the past, while the Reformed Churches did not become patrons of painting or sculpture. Instead of painting and carving commissioned works, defined by the traditional subject-matter of religious art, and controlled by contract, convention, and orthodoxy enforced by the Catholic Church, the artist became a free-lance, sometimes executing commissions from lay patrons, but often relying on exhibitions (such as those of the French and British Royal Academies) where he exhibited pictures according to his personal taste and fancy, selling where he could to make a living. Only with difficulty can religious art survive, much less flourish, in such a climate, and only church architecture has had any real continuity of patronage. The absence of Church patronage also changed the character of art patronage itself; the new patrons wanted works of art which would reflect their worldly position and often their new wealth as well.

No one would be so foolish as to claim that the subject has been treated fully: vast libraries are devoted to it, and require it. This is an introduction only, which may help the enquirer to pursue a problem further, and—if its aims are successful—may encourage the reader and stimulate greater interest in, and understanding of, the purposes for which architects and artists have laboured, as well as perhaps a greater appreciation of their aesthetic achievements.

Authors with learned friends are much to be envied, for they so often prove their friendship by the help they so generously give; the Revd James Manock, the Revd John Maunsell, and the Revd Dr David Pym have given invaluable help with some of the problems that have arisen.

Our warmest thanks are due to the book's editor, Mrs Pam Coote, who has given constant and generous help and encouragement, particularly at moments of great despondency (no book is ever written without travail), and to her assistant, Miss Alysoun Owen. Our warmest thanks are also due to our copy-editor, Mrs Heather Watson, who has dealt with all the problems caused by a sometimes difficult text, and by our small divergencies from house style, with great patience and tact. Authors write with whatever abilities, knowledge, and perseverence they may possess, but it is upon the combined labours of a whole team that any successful outcome depends, and no author should ever forget it. We never will.

PETER AND LINDA MURRAY

Preface to the Second Edition

Bath Abbey, 'Lantern of the West', was the first 'monument' of Christian history I came to know and love, attending weekly in the pre-Second-World-War years, not least because my father was one of the church wardens. Growing up, I came to be at home in all manner of places of worship, enjoying first the works of art that adorned them or had adorned them, and later those created whether in sympathy or in conflict with the traditions of Christianity. It was not until Oxford University Press invited me, a continuing student of Christian art and architecture, to prepare this new edition of the Murrays' respected and loved *Companion* that I studied in a more systematic way the wide terrain their book encompassed. Wide though it was, it required—I was daunted to discover—much expansion. In the two decades that had elapsed between their writing and this revision, many changes and developments in art and architecture and in Christianity now need to be addressed.

During this interval, popular interest in arts of all kinds has expanded. Examples include the large and growing memberships of such bodies as the National Trust and Friends of the Royal Academy, the awareness of art in Britain's cathedrals, and the art coverage on television. I hope that readers will welcome the new outlook beyond Europe, not least in the substantial articles on North America, Australia, and the non-Western world, and also appreciate the place given to other traditions of Christianity alongside the devout Roman Catholic emphasis in the scholarship of Peter and Linda Murray. The bibliographic material to be found in some of the articles and in the online Bibliography alerts students and general readers to classic writings and also to recent controversial writers on movements and individual artists.

There are contributors to thank for a great part of the revising of original material and the writing of new entries and articles;, most of these are friends and colleagues in the work of Art and Christianity Enquiry (ACE) <acetrust.org>. Foremost among them has been Allan Doig whose *Liturgy and Architecture* (2008) is of the very content and quality I knew the *Dictionary*'s core articles would need if they were to be revised. These core articles taken together (Early Church, Byzantine, Pre-Romanesque, Romanesque, etc., through to Twentieth and Twenty-First Century Church Architecture) give a good introduction to the changing scene of Christian art and architecture. Doig himself contributed the bulk of the revision and introduced me to some specialist scholars for others. Graham Howes and Charles Pickstone skilfully and generously undertook the survey in Europe: Twentieth and Twenty-First Century Painting, Sculpture, and Stained Glass. These articles now appear in boxed shaded type together with other new articles that readers will enjoy discovering. I pride myself on the choice of able, willing, and patient contributing writers; these include Christopher Adams, Barbara Brend, Magdalen Evans, Elisabeth Flory, Peter Francis, Christian Frost, Pamela Hardesty, Geoffrey Hunter, Christopher Joby, Stephen Laird, Thomas P. Miller, Gordon Mursell, Peter Newby, Rod Pattenden, Manfred Richter, Aaron Rosen, Andrew Spira, Caroline Swash, Nicholas Temple, Dalibor Vesely, William Whyte, Joanna Yates, and Walter Zahner. Penny Dade gave helpful advice about the Bibliography and the websites.

The influence on me of Oxford University Press has been extensive over time and in its variety, chiefly in its history and reference books on art: among these, the *Oxford History of English Art* (Talbot Rice, Boase, Brieger, Evans, Mercer, Whinney and Miller, Burke, and Farr, the authors of its nine volumes); the reference dynasty of Osborne, Kemp, Chilvers, Farr, and Glaves-Smith; and in Christianity, Cross, Livingstone, Metzger, Coogan, Browning, and

Hastings are together a power of scholarship. Commissioning editors Rebecca Lane, Joanna Harris, and, chiefly, Jamie Crowther, have patiently guided me and enabled Elizabeth Bowen to assist me in a considerable number of practical ways over many months.

Through all the time of preparation my dear wife Susan has held together the editor's outer and inner man. This new edition is dedicated to her.

TOM DEVONSHIRE JONES

Peter and Linda Murray

A personal tribute

The key to the Murrays' success as a literary partnership rested in their commitment to teaching. They not only taught a whole generation of younger art historians in London—Peter at Birkbeck College, Linda mainly in the Extramural Department of the University—but they also wrote with pedagogic clarity for students and general readers around the world. (Their books were translated into numerous languages.) Best known for the *Penguin Dictionary of Art and Artists* and a number of titles in Thames & Hudson's World of Art series, they approached this *Oxford Companion* as their final joint publication. And so it proved to be. Following Peter's premature death in 1992, and with a daunting number of entries still unwritten, Linda completed the task with characteristic self-discipline and courage. She died much later, in 2004.

Peter Murray was educated at King Edward VI School, Birmingham, the Robert Gordon Academy, Aberdeen, the Slade School of Fine Art, London, and the Courtauld Institute, where he met Linda: they married in 1947. A translator of major Continental art historians and a brilliant Renaissance scholar with a passion for historiography, he was the author of *The Architecture of the Renaissance*, a book in which profound learning is lightly worn and complex technical matters are elegantly explained. He succeeded Pevsner as Professor of the History of Art at Birkbeck, and built up a talented department between 1967 and 1980. His love of fast cars found full expression most summers, when he and Linda drove to Italy.

Linda's education was more sporadic, as her family lived a peripatetic existence in Europe and further afield. As a writer her canvas was rather wider than Peter's: her books included studies of Michelangelo and a powerful novel, *The Dark Fire*, based on the turbulent life of Caravaggio—strangely, it was published only in the US as no British publisher would take it on. When she and Peter wrote jointly, as in the first edition of this *Companion*, the *Penguin Dictionary* and *The Art of the Renaissance* (Thames & Hudson), they claimed to be uncertain about who wrote which section of a particular article or chapter. Being Peter's cousin, however, and having worked with them for many years, I claim to be able to tell the difference in style! Both were gifted linguists who considered that no art historian could operate without at least three languages—Italian art historians would sometimes ask Peter to check their texts for grammatical slips.

As the Preface to this new edition makes clear, the Murrays wrote about Christian art and architecture from a traditional perspective and as devout Roman Catholics, but they would have welcomed the widening of their agenda in this new version and have thanked their successors as editors. They would also be pleased to see the book still in print, at a time when there is an increasing need for help on biblical and ecclesiastical matters that are slipping out of consciousness in our secularized culture in the West. At a time when five-year-olds are helping their grandparents to go online, eighteen-year-olds don't know who Moses is.

The Murray Bequest to Birkbeck College reflects these concerns in a sense, by supporting art history of earlier periods as traditionally taught. The bequest provides funds for postgraduate research, foreign travel, a Peter Murray Memorial Lecture every other year, and the acquisition of specialized books for a college library that already contains hundreds of items from the Murrays' own collection. In administering the bequest, the Trustees hope to fulfil Peter and Linda's wish to support work in the field to which they devoted their entire working lives.

PROFESSOR MICHAEL WHEELER
Chairman, the Murray Bequest

Contributors

Mr Christopher Adams, Estorick Collection of Modern Italian Art
Ms Elizabeth Bowen
Dr Barbara Brend
Mrs Penny Dade
The Revd Dr Allan Doig, Lady Margaret Hall, University of Oxford
Mrs Magdalen Evans
Elisabeth Flory, Spiritualité et Art
The Revd Peter Francis, Gladstone's Library
Professor Christian Frost, Kingston University
Ms Pamela Hardesty, Crawford College of Art & Design, Cork
Mr Graham Howes, Trinity Hall, University of Cambridge
Mr Geoffrey Hunter, London Diocesan House
Dr Christopher Joby, University of Manchester, and the Norwich Centre for Christian Learning
The Revd Dr Stephen Laird, Blean Vicarage, Canterbury
The Revd Canon Thomas P. Miller, Cathedral Church of St John the Divine, New York
The Rt Revd Gordon Mursell, former Bishop of Stafford
Canon Peter Newby, St Mary Moorfields Church, London
The Revd Dr Rod Pattenden
The Revd Charles Pickstone, St Laurence Church, Catford, London
Pastor Manfred Richter, Artheon (Society for Church and Contemporary Art)
Dr Aaron Rosen, King's College London
Mr Andrew Spira, Christie's Education, London
Mrs Caroline Swash, Central St Martins College of Arts and Design, London
Professor Nicholas Temple, University of Huddersfield
Professor Dalibor Vesely, Emmanuel College, University of Cambridge
The Revd Dr William Whyte, St John's College, University of Oxford
The Revd Joanna Yates, the United Society for Christian Literature
Dr Walter Zahner, Roman Catholic Diocese of Regensburg

Abbreviations

Collections, Museums

BL	British Library (London)
BM	British Museum (London)
BN	Bibliothèque Nationale (Paris)
CI	Courtauld Institute of Art (London)
Fitz.	Fitzwilliam Museum, Cambridge
Fogg	Fogg Art Museum (Cambridge, Mass.)
KHM	Kunsthistorisches Museum (Vienna)
Met. Mus	Metropolitan Museum of Art (New York)
NG	National Gallery (London)
NG of S.	National Gallery of Scotland (Edinburgh)
NPG	National Portrait Gallery (London)
V & A	Victoria and Albert Museum (London)

Other major collections are located as follows:

Hermitage	St Petersburg
Louvre	Paris
Prado	Madrid
Rijksmus.	Amsterdam
Uffizi	Florence

Books of the Bible

Old Testament (OT)

Chron.	Chronicles
Dan.	Daniel
Deut.	Deuteronomy
Exod.	Exodus
Ezek.	Ezekiel
Gen.	Genesis
Isa.	Isaiah
Jer.	Jeremiah
Josh.	Joshua
Judg.	Judges
Kgs.	Kings
Lam.	Lamentations
Lev.	Leviticus
Mic.	Micah
Neh.	Nehemiah
Num.	Numbers
Prov.	Proverbs
Ps(s).	Psalm(s)
Sam.	Samuel

New Testament (NT)

Col.	Colossians
Cor.	Corinthians
Eph.	Ephesians
Heb.	Hebrews
Matt.	Matthew
Pet.	Peter
Rev.	Revelation
Rom.	Romans
Thess.	Thessalonians
Tim.	Timothy

Apocrypha

Esd.	Esdras
Macc.	Maccabees

Biblical Translations

AV	Authorized Version (King James' Bible)
NRSV	New Revised Standard Version
Vg.	Vulgate

General

Acad.	Academy
Accad.	Accademia
Bib.	Bibliothèque, Biblioteca, Bibliothek
Cod.Grec.	Greek Codices
coll.	collection
Coll.	College
exhibition cat.	Exhibition catalogue
Gall.	Gallery
Inst.	Institute
Lib.	Library
Mus.	Museum
Nat.	National
Naz.	Nazional
Pal.	Palazzo
Paralip.	Paralipomenon
SJ	Society of Jesus (Jesuits)
Soc.	Society
S.	Saint
SS	Saints
St(e)	Saint (Sainte)
Sta	Santa

Note to the Reader

ENTRIES are arranged in letter-by-letter alphabetical order up to the first punctuation in the headword. Saints appear under the proper name by which they are known and not together under letter S.

Cross-references appear in two forms: within the body of the text a standard cross reference is denoted by an *asterisk in front of a word or series of words. A more explicit cross-reference may appear within the text and at the end of an entry in small capitals and indicate the entry headword to which attention is being directed. Cross-references appear only where reference is likely to amplify or increase understanding of the entry being read. They are not given automatically in all instances where a headword appears in the text.

Text Acknowledgements

Quotations in the text from the Bible are from the Authorized Version (Crown copyright) and from the New Revised Standard Version Bible, © 1989, by the Division of Christian Education of the National Council of the Churches of Christ in the USA. Used by permission. All rights reserved.

Please note that the final paragraph on page 626 in the entry 'twentieth and twenty-first century church architecture' is adapted from text in the *New Catholic Encyclopedia* (2011). © 2011 Gale, a part of Cengage Learning, Inc. Reproduced by permission. www.cengage.com/permissions

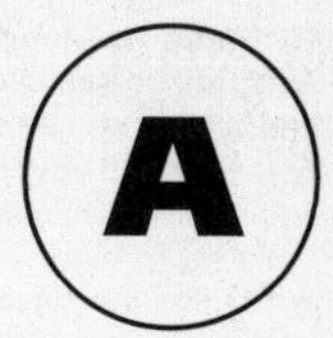

A *See* ALPHA AND OMEGA.

Aaron was the elder brother of *Moses. After the liberation of the Jews from their bondage in Egypt (Exod. 1: 8–14: 30), and after God had appeared to Moses on Mt. Sinai, Moses established the *tabernacle, and he made Aaron the first High Priest (Exod. 19: 3 ff. and 28: 1 ff.). This was of the Old Dispensation (*see* COVENANTS), that is, the establishment of Mosaic Law, where the coming of Christ created the New Dispensation. For this reason Aaron is sometimes represented as the precursor of Christ. He is usually shown with Moses, but the miracles he performed by himself (Exod. 7 and 8) when his rod turned into a serpent, swallowing the serpents produced by Pharaoh's magicians, or when he produced some of the *Plagues of Egypt, or the overnight flowering of his rod (Num. 17: *see* S. JOSEPH), are among the earliest subjects of religious art, e.g. in the 4th-century Roman *catacombs, though the subjects had been represented in the synagogue at *Dura-Europos (*c.*245/56). His part in the idolatry of the *golden calf (Exod. 32) was forgiven, and, as High Priest, he was the only person allowed to enter the Holy of Holies, the most sacred part within the tabernacle.

There is a long description of his priestly *vestments in Exod. 28, and he is often represented with a censer as a prototype of the Christian priesthood. *See also* KORAH, PUNISHMENT OF.

abacus A flat block of masonry on the top of a *capital, which is the transition from the capital to the architrave. In the Doric Order (*see* ORDER) the abacus is undecorated; in the Ionic and Corinthian Orders, the abacus has decorative mouldings.

abbey A monastery or religious community of monks or nuns, presided over by an *abbot or abbess. Normally the community began with twelve men or women, but often a newly founded community might have fewer, though a very large community might number from 100 to 200 members. The buildings are self-contained and male monasteries were often founded in desolate places (*see* CISTERCIANS, and *contrast* CLUNY), but some houses—especially *Benedictine ones—were in towns and served as schools, e.g. Westminster Abbey in London, San Giorgio Maggiore in Venice, or Ottobeuren in Bavaria. The essential layout of a male community consists of a church, a *cloister, usually surrounding a burial-ground, cells and dormitories for the monks, a guest-house for travellers, a *chapter-house, *scriptorium and library, and necessary domestic buildings—kitchen, refectory, infirmary, and so on. A plan drawn *c.*820, in the monastery of *Sankt Gallen in Switzerland, shows an ideal arrangement, variations of which remained the norm for centuries. A priory is a smaller community, usually dependent on an abbey, with a prior at its head, although for some Orders a priory is an independent unit—e.g. all *Dominican houses are priories. The great abbeys in England were major pre-*Reformation buildings, and many impressive ruins survive e.g. Fountains, Tintern, Rievaulx. In countries less affected by the Reformation—Austria, S. Germany, Italy—many old communities survive, but have often been rebuilt in the 17th or 18th centuries.

abbot, abbess (Aramaic *Abba*, father) The superior, usually elected for life, of a community of monks or nuns of certain religious Orders, principally *Benedictine. Abbots, like bishops, are distinguished by *mitre (*see* VESTMENTS), crozier (*see* CROSIER), and ring as well as the *habit of their *Order.

In the Middle Ages abbesses also exercised great power and were often entitled to mitre, crozier, and ring—the Abbess of Fontevrault, or of Romsey, for instance—although they had no spiritual jurisdiction, because, unlike abbots, they were not ordained. Their powers were somewhat circumscribed by the Council of *Trent, but some, such as *S. Theresa of Avila, exercised very considerable influence and they were often very formidable women. In the Eastern Church, an archimandrite is the equivalent of an abbot.

Abel was the second son of *Adam and Eve and was a shepherd, unlike his elder brother Cain, who was a tiller of the soil. Abel's offering of lambs as a sacrifice to God was accepted and Cain's, of the fruits of the earth, rejected (Gen. 4: 1–17). Genesis does not say why Cain's offering was rejected, but what God said implies that his offering had been inferior, or he himself unworthy—'sin is lurking at the door'. Out of jealousy, Cain murdered his brother—traditionally, with the jawbone of an ass—and Abel's blood cried out to Heaven. Christ Himself referred to 'righteous Abel' (Matt. 23: 35) and Abel was seen by the *Fathers of the Church as a *type of Christ, since he was a shepherd who offered an acceptable sacrifice and was an innocent victim. In Early Christian art Christ is often represented as the Good *Shepherd, as in the 3rd- or 4th-century statuette in the Vatican Museum, several 4th-century *sarcophagi, and the *Mosaic in the Mausoleum of Galla Placidia, *Ravenna, of *c.*440. Sheep, or lambs, were animals often used for sacrifices in the OT, and prefigure the reference by *John the Baptist to Christ as 'the Lamb of God' at the Baptism of Christ (John 1: 29).

Abgar, Legend of Abgar V (?4 BC–AD 50), was King of Edessa in Syria (now called Urfa and in Turkey). According to *Eusebius's 'Ecclesiastical History' (before 323), Abgar heard of Christ's miracles and wrote a letter to Him, asking to be cured of an illness. He was told that a disciple would come after the Ascension (Edessa was, in fact, a very early Christian community). Eusebius quoted the letters and claimed that they were preserved in Edessa: he does not mention any portrait. Later versions of the story claim that Hannan, Abgar's emissary to Jerusalem, actually painted a portrait of Jesus (*see* CHRIST, Portraits of), but was unable to catch a likeness so Christ Himself took the cloth and pressed it to His face, imprinting an image. Other versions omit Hannan's efforts and simply recount the creation of an image (a *vera icon*, true image) on a damp cloth. This is so close to the later story of *S. Veronica and the Vernicle that there must be some conflation. However, the story continues with the image (*see* MANDYLION, ACHEIROPOIETOS) being taken to Edessa, where *Etheria the Pilgrim saw, *c.*388, a statue of Abgar, but does not record the picture. Attempts have been made to identify this image with the Holy *Shroud of Turin, but it is more likely to be the prototype of the Byzantine full-face image of Christ with long hair, a full, pointed, beard, and heavy eyebrows, familiar in the *Pantocrator mosaics and paintings. The first definite mention of it is 6th century and by the 10th the image had been taken to the imperial palace in Constantinople, from which it was stolen by French Crusaders in 1207, and perhaps taken to the Sainte-Chapelle in Paris. It may have perished during the French Revolution, but what may be copies are in the Vatican (formerly in San Silvestro in Capite, Rome), Genoa (San Bartolommeo degli Armeni), and one said to be in Venice.

Abigail *See* DAVID.

Abiram *See* KORAH.

Abraham was the first of the *Patriarchs of the OT, the founder of the Hebrew nation and of other nations, since God promised that his descendants would be as innumerable as dust. He was originally called Abram, but his name was changed by God (similarly, his wife Sarai became Sarah). His story is told in Gen. 11–25, and three incidents in it have been subjects for Christian artists from the earliest times. He was born in Ur of the Chaldees, but was told by God to go to 'a land I will show you'. With his wife and his nephew *Lot he went first to Canaan and then to Egypt before returning to Canaan. Abram and Lot then separated, Lot choosing the plain of the Jordan, and settling in Sodom, Abram remaining in Canaan. In a local war, Sodom was captured and Lot was made captive with all his family and possessions. When Abram heard about it, he gathered all his trained men, defeated the forces of the local kings, and recaptured Lot, his family, and all his goods. Abram celebrated his victory with *Melchisedek, King of Salem and 'priest of God Most High', with an offering of bread and wine made by Melchisedek. This is seen by Christian interpreters as a *type of the *Eucharist. Lot returned to Sodom.

Abram's wife Sarai was barren, so she arranged for her maid *Hagar, who was a slave, to bear Abram a child, Ishmael. Three angels (Gen. 18: 1–15) visited Abram and Sarai at *Mamre—the three are held to symbolize the Holy Trinity—and they announced God's promise that Sarai would conceive a son, *Isaac. As she was then 90, Sarai 'laughed within herself'. This was when their names were changed to Abraham and Sarah. Nevertheless, Isaac was born, and Hagar and her son Ishmael were driven away. Before the destruction of Sodom and Gomorrah an angel was sent to warn Lot to escape, and he went to the land of Moab (*see* LOT). Later, God required Abraham, as proof of his obedience, to sacrifice his only son, Isaac: this is interpreted as a *type of the sacrifice of Christ, God's son. Isaac carrying the wood of the burnt offering (Gen. 22: 6) was a parallel to Christ carrying the cross. This is explicit in e.g. the **Biblia Pauperum*, as well as in the Epistle to the Hebrews (11: 17–19), but after an angel had restrained Abraham, a ram 'caught in a thicket' was sacrificed instead of Isaac. Later Isaac married Rebecca. Sarah died and was buried at Machpelah in Hebron, where Abraham himself, Isaac, Rebecca, and others were buried in a tomb near Hebron, which is traditionally believed to be theirs.

The three main episodes in Abraham's life represented in art are: (1) the meeting with *Melchisedek, which is shown in mosaics in Sta Maria Maggiore, Rome (5th cent.), and *Ravenna, Sant'Apollinare and San Vitale (6th cent.), as well as in the altarpiece of the *mystic meals by *D. Bouts in St Pieter, Leuven; (2) the Angels at Mamre, which are also shown in the mosaic cycle at Sta Maria Maggiore, Rome, and in San Vitale, Ravenna, and in a splendid fresco by Tiepolo in the Archbishop's palace at Udine (N. Italy) which shows Sarah openly sceptical of the angel's message; (3) the Sacrifice of Isaac, represented many times, beginning with *Dura-Europos (*c.*250) and the sarcophagus of *Junius Bassus (*c.*359), but perhaps best known as the subject of the competition for the doors of the Baptistery in Florence (1401), for which reliefs by Brunelleschi and *Ghiberti (the winner) still exist.

In addition to the story told in Genesis, the parable of *Dives and Lazarus (Luke 16: 22) refers to the souls of the just as 'in Abraham's bosom': *in sinum Abrahae* (*see* LIMBO), and this is sometimes represented as a number of figures held in a napkin or in a fold in Abraham's robe, e.g. the 12th/13th-century sculpture at *Saint-Denis, St-Trophime at Arles, and in the *Portal at Moissac. According to a Judaic-Christian apocryphal 'Testament of Abraham' of the 2nd century, the Archangel Michael appeared to the dying Abraham and showed him two roads, to Heaven and to Hell.

Abramtsevo *See* RUSSIAN ART AND ARCHITECTURE.

Absalom *See* DAVID.

acheiropoietos (Gk. not made by [human] hands) A term applied to images, usually portraits of Christ, which are claimed to be of miraculous origin. The earliest record of such an image, the *Mandylion, dates from 544. (*See also* SHROUD OF TURIN.) These images should not be confused with *icons purporting to be (or to be copies of) the portrait of the Virgin and Child said to have been painted by *S. Luke.

acolyte (server) Strictly, the highest of the four minor *orders of the priesthood, but in practice usually a layman or boy who serves the celebrant at the *altar and at other ceremonies by lighting and carrying candles, preparing the wine and water, and also the *censer, for the celebration of the Eucharist and serving the priest at Low Mass (a Mass without singing, and therefore simpler than the service of High Mass, at which the celebrant is normally served by a deacon). He (acolytes are normally male) also generally assists the celebrant at liturgical functions. The office existed in Rome by the 3rd century, and acolytes are often represented in paintings and mosaics. No special *vestment is prescribed, but for ceremonial occasions a *cassock and *cotta (or surplice) may be worn.

Acta Sanctorum (Lat. Lives of Saints) In general, the lives and deeds of saints; specifically, the vast volumes (64 so far, from 1643 to the present) published by a small group of Jesuit scholars working in Belgium. They are called Bollandists after their founder, Jan van Bolland, SJ (1596–1665), and their task is to publish a critical edition of all that is known of the lives of saints, arranged in order of their feast-days, from 1 January (the beginning of December has now been reached). When the pope suppressed the Society of Jesus in 1773, fifty volumes, up to 7 October, had been published: work was resumed in 1837. The 'Acta Sanctorum' (abbreviated AA.SS.) give such full details that they frequently provide evidence for identifying works of art connected with the obscurer saints.

'Acts of Pilate' An *Apocryphal Gospel, part of the 'Gospel of Nicodemus'.

Acts of the Apostles, the (Vg. **Actus Apostolorum**) The fifth book of the NT, written by *S. Luke, probably *c*.64/85, relates events of the first thirty-odd years of the Church, from the *Ascension and *Pentecost to *S. Paul's arrival in Rome after shipwreck in Malta. Many works of art illustrate subjects mentioned in Acts, including the Healing of the Lame Man (*see* PETER), the Death of Ananias, the Stoning of Stephen, the Conversion of S. Paul, the Martyrdom of S. James, and the Liberation of S. Peter. The tapestries designed for the *Sistine Chapel by *Raphael in 1515 (cartoons in London, V & A) are the best-known illustrations of the series.

Adam and Eve were, according to the first book of the OT of the Bible, the first humans, created directly by God (Gen. 1–4). Gen. 2: 7 tells how God formed man from the dust of the ground, and breathed into his nostrils the 'breath of life', to make him live. God then decided to give Adam a companion: vv. 21–2 tell how God caused a deep sleep to fall upon the man, and as he slept He took one of his ribs and made it into a woman. God did not name the man and woman 'Adam and Eve'; the names are said to derive from the Heb. for 'earth' and 'life', and Adam named her because she was the mother of mankind. They have been venerated as saints, especially in the East, though never formally so in the West; Christ is considered to be the 'Second Adam' and Mary the 'Second Eve' (cf. Rom. 5: 14; 1 Cor. 15: 45). They are also *Patron Saints of gardeners and tailors (as the first to wear clothes!). The parallel creation of Eve was early regarded as a *type of the Church, which sprang from the wound in Christ's side, as Eve had been created from Adam's rib (*Bible Moralisée). Nevertheless, the commonest subject is the *Fall of Man, i.e. Eve tempted by the Serpent, the eating of the forbidden fruit ('apple') of the *Tree of Knowledge, and the consequent Expulsion from Paradise. This was followed by the births of their three sons, Cain, *Abel, and *Seth. Adam and Eve occur frequently in Early Christian art, the earliest example probably being that in the San Gennaro Catacomb in Naples, of the first half of the 2nd century, followed by *Dura-Europos and many catacomb paintings and sarcophagi. Eve is often imitated from antique *Venus pudica* types (e.g. the *Junius Bassus sarcophagus, *c*.359), since this was one of the few opportunities for Early Christian artists to display their skill in rendering the nude (cf. the figure of *Temperance*, also derived from the *Venus pudica*, by Giovanni *Pisano in Pisa Cathedral, as late as 1310). The subject of Adam naming the animals (Gen. 2: 20) is much rarer, but occurs in the 6th-century *Vienna Genesis (Vienna Staats Bib.). The best-known image of the creation of Adam and Eve is in *Michelangelo's two frescoes on the *Sistine Chapel ceiling. Non-biblical scenes include the death of Adam (*see* SETH) and his burial on Golgotha, where the Cross was later to stand, and the rescue of Adam and Eve from *Limbo by Christ before His Resurrection, recounted in the *Apocryphal '*Gospel of Nicodemus' and repeated in the **Golden Legend*, and in countless Byzantine representations of the *Anastasis. *See also* ANASTASIS and FALL OF MAN.

Adonai *See* NOMEN SACRUM.

Adoration of the Blessed Sacrament *See* QUARANT'ORE.

Adoration of the Lamb A conflation of passages from the *Apocalypse (Rev. 5, 7, and 14) describing the *Lamb of God that was slain, worshipped by the four living creatures (AV has the Four Beasts)—probably the *Tetramorph, symbols of the Evangelists—and twenty-four Elders, martyrs in white robes with palms, and the 144,000 from the Twelve Tribes of Israel. The subject(s) occur in many illuminated MSS, and especially in *Dürer's Apocalypse woodcuts (1498), and the Ghent Altar (*see* EYCK). In the E. Orthodox Church the subject was less popular, and a Synod in Constantinople (692) condemned the representation of a lamb as a symbol of Christ, though this never took effect in the West and was later disregarded in the East.

Adoration of the Magi *See* MAGI, EPIPHANY.

Adoration of the Shepherds *See* NATIVITY OF CHRIST.

Adullam *See* DAVID.

Advent (Lat. *Adventus Domini*, the coming of the Lord) Advent is the first liturgical season of the year, the beginning of the Church's year. In antiquity an *adventus* was a formal entry into a city by a high official or the Emperor himself, and the word was taken over by the Christians as a name for the season before Christmas, beginning on the Sunday nearest to S. Andrew's Day (30 Nov.). It is a penitential season of preparation for the birth of Christ, as Lent is a preparation for the Resurrection, so the *liturgical colour is purple.

aedicule (Lat. *aedicula*, a small temple or shrine) A niche or opening framed by columns on either side, with an entablature and pediment above. Pagan aedicules were often set in temples and had a statue in the niche; Early Christian ones sometimes held funerary urns, but later also held statues. The aedicule discovered in the 1940s below *St Peter's in Rome is thought to be the Trophy or *Memoria* (*see* MARTYRIUM) of S. Peter himself. Immediately above the area are the four great piers supporting the dome, each of which contains a niche with a statue, carved under the supervision of *Bernini, of SS Longinus, Veronica, Andrew, and Helen (the Emperor Constantine's mother). In the aedicules above them, framed by the twisted columns (*Salomónicas) which survived from Old St Peter's, were relics—the lance, the veil, a fragment of the True Cross, and the head of S. Andrew (this last was returned to the Greeks, from whom it had been stolen, in 1965).

aer A large gold-embroidered veil used to cover the *discus and chalice in the E. Orthodox liturgy.

Africa *See* NON-WESTERN CHRISTIAN ART.

agape (Gk. love, charity; pl. *agapae*) In Apostolic times it seems to have been the custom for the congregation to eat a meal together on Sunday evening, before the celebration of the Eucharist. S. Paul (1 Cor. 11: 20–34) and S. Jude (5: 12) seem to be criticizing the obvious abuses this custom might lead to. There was also an ancient pagan custom of feasting at the graves of dead relatives on their anniversaries: the Christians took this over, particularly in celebrating the anniversaries of martyrs, and it is clear that such feasts were held in the *catacombs, where there are paintings of an agape in those of SS Peter and Marcellinus and of S. Callixtus. The custom died out after the 4th century, and certainly before the 8th.

Agatha (Agata), Saint She was a virgin martyred in Sicily, perhaps under the Emperor Decius in 251, but her largely legendary *Acta are 5th/6th century. She was venerated from an early date, and a church in Rome (Sant'Agata dei Goti) was dedicated to her by 593. It is said that the pagan Consul of Sicily, having failed to seduce her, had her consigned to a brothel run by an appropriately named Aphrodisia (*see* S. AGNES). Agatha was martyred by having her breasts cut off, and her gruesome attribute is a dish with two breasts on it. She is a *patron saint of the Knights of Malta, of Catania in Sicily, of wet-nurses, and of bell-founders, and is invoked against fire, eruptions of Etna, and diseases of the breast. Early representations are in Parenzo (Poreč in the former Yugoslavia) Cathedral (6th cent.), Palermo, and Monreale. She is often included in *Virgo inter Virgines pictures, and there is a tragic image by G. B. Tiepolo (1745–50: Berlin; 1735–40: Padua, Santo).

Aggeus The Vulgate form of Haggai, a minor OT *prophet.

Agnes, Saint She was a virgin martyred in Rome *c.*300/350. By *c.*354 the Basilica di Sant' Agnese fuori le Mura ('outside the walls'), which still exists, was dedicated to her near her tomb. Another church, Sant'Agnese in Agone, in Piazza Navona, in the centre of Rome, was erected on the site of her martyrdom: the present masterpiece of Baroque architecture is by G. Rainaldi and *Borromini, from 1652 onwards. Like *Agatha, S. Agnes was popular in both East and West as a virgin-martyr, and, again like Agatha, was said to have been forced into a brothel, where her hair grew miraculously to cover her nakedness (or, alternatively, an angel covered her with a robe so white that it blinded the lascivious). She was martyred by being stabbed in the neck. There are many early representations of her, from the gold glasses of the 4th century found in catacombs, the 6th-century mosaic in Sant'Apollinare Nuovo, Ravenna, or Duccio's *Maestà*, to the famous gold and enamel cup of 1381, with scenes from her life, now in the British Museum. She also appears frequently in *Virgo inter Virgines paintings. Because *Agnese* is so close to *agnus* (Lat. lamb) she is often shown with a lamb as in Ravenna and the *Duccio *Maestà*, where she holds a roundel with the image of the *Lamb and flag. The nuns of her convent in Rome still make *pallia for archbishops from the wool of lambs blessed on 21 January, her feast-day.

a

Agnus Dei (Lat. Lamb of God) There are two separate meanings for this. (1) The expression used by *John the Baptist when he first saw Jesus: 'Ecce agnus dei, ecce qui tollit peccata mundi . . .' i.e. 'Here is the Lamb of God, who takes away the sin of the world . . .' (John 1: 29). This is held to refer to Isaiah 53: 7, 'like a lamb that is led to the slaughter . . .' and identifies Jesus as the Messiah, the sacrificial lamb. Several references in the *Apocalypse are also relevant—*see* ADORATION OF THE LAMB. In this sense, an Agnus Dei is a representation of Christ as a lamb, usually with a *halo with a cross on it, and often carrying a flag, or pennant as a banner of victory, also with a cross on it. There is a mosaic in SS Cosma e Damiano, Rome, of *c.*530, which shows a lamb with a cruciform halo standing on a hillock, from which issue the four *Rivers of Paradise. Six lambs on either side represent the Apostles. A Synod in Constantinople held in 692 forbade the use of a lamb as a symbol of Christ, but it was ignored in the West and not much regarded in the East. The actual words *Ecce Agnus Dei* often appear on paintings of the Baptism of Christ.

(2) A *sacramental: a small wax medallion impressed with an Agnus Dei, made from the wax of the previous year's Paschal *candle and blessed by the pope in the first year of his pontificate and every seventh year afterwards. The custom was known in Rome in the 9th century, but may be older. There is an example of 1370 in the museum at Poitiers, France.

Agony in the Garden *See* CHRIST, GETHSEMANE.

agrapha (Gk. things not written) There are many sayings attributed to Christ that are not in the Gospels, and were probably passed on by word of mouth, which later appeared in non-canonical early writings and *Apocryphal Gospels, especially the 'Gospel of Thomas', but few are relevant to Early Christian or later art.

Ahab *See* ELIJAH.

Ahasuerus (Assuerus) *See* ESTHER.

aisle (Lat. *ala,* wing) describes the part or parts of a church parallel to the *nave, *choir, or *transepts and divided from them by piers, columns, or screens. It is also commonly used to describe the passage between seats or pews.

alabasters, Nottingham A generic name for a type of English sculpture, usually in relief, made as religious artefacts from *c.*1300 until the Reformation. Alabaster is a form of gypsum easily carved (and easily damaged), which can be painted and gilded. It was mined in the Midlands, and Nottingham was a centre of production and export—even to Iceland and S. Italy. Unsuitable for outdoor use, it was an excellent medium for tombs and *altarpieces, usually of scenes from the Life of Christ or the Virgin, with reliefs of the Holy Trinity or of the head of the Baptist on a charger being highly popular. It is not great art, but clearly met a need until the Reformation killed the trade, although tombs continued to be in demand. A very splendid 15th-century Nottingham alabaster relief with thirty-six figures, of scenes from the Life of the Virgin, is in the former collegiate church of Notre-Dame, Montréal, near Vézelay, Burgundy, where there are also fine choir stalls of 1522. The best collection of alabasters is in the Victoria and Albert Museum, London.

Alacoque *See* HEART, SACRED.

alb (Lat. *tunica alba,* a white tunic) A liturgical *vestment, deriving from Greek and Roman secular dress, worn by celebrant and ministers at Mass. It is a full-length, long-sleeved linen garment, usually belted at the waist with a girdle or cincture. It is sometimes ornamented with lace or embroidery; from the early Middle Ages 'apparels' were added—small patches or strips of coloured cloth or embroidery. *Clavi* are stripes, usually purple, from over each shoulder to hem and on sleeves, such as those seen in the mosaics of San Vitale, *Ravenna, of *c.*546. They were not used in later times. The cotta and surplice are versions of the alb.

Alban, Saint He was a Roman citizen martyred *c.*209/305 in what is now St Albans, near London. He is venerated as Protomartyr of Britain—i.e. the first Christian known to have been martyred in Britain. He is easily confused with S. Albino (or Albano) of Cologne and S. Albano of Mainz, both later saints, venerated in Germany. The great Abbey at St Albans, once the wealthiest in England, was founded in Saxon times, but the present building dates from 1077 to (mostly) the 19th century, when it was enthusiastically restored. The major works of art associated with S. Alban are the S. Alban's Psalter (*Albani Psalter*), with scenes from his life, dating from before 1123 and now in Hildesheim, Germany, and the *Life* by

Matthew Paris, of the 13th century, now in Trinity College, Dublin. Mary Adshead's painting of the patron saint was introduced into the newly consecrated St Alban's Church, Hemel Hempstead, Hertfordshire in 1958.

Alberti, Leon Battista (1404–72), was a Florentine architect and theorist, who like *Brunelleschi adapted ancient Roman models to Christian church-design. He is sometimes described as the purest type of the *Renaissance universal man—writer, painter, musician, sculptor, athlete, Latinist, trained in canon law, philosophy, mathematics. In 1428 he entered the papal civil service, and from 1447 to 1455 he was concerned with the restoration of ancient Roman monuments and of Old St Peter's and its enclave. He was an architect only in that he was a designer of buildings, a theorist who employed other men to do the actual construction. In the 1440s he began writing *De re aedificatoria*, of which a first version was completed by 1452. This first architectural treatise of the Renaissance was in direct emulation of the only surviving classical text on architecture, the *De architectura Libri X* by *Vitruvius, a 1st-century Roman architect. *De re* was written in Latin, circulating in MS during his lifetime, but was printed in Florence in 1485, probably just before the first printed edition of Vitruvius.

His buildings are few. Between 1446 and 1461 he designed and supervised, mostly by correspondence, the recasing of the Gothic San Francesco in Rimini (better known as the 'Tempio Malatestiano'), the first church to be organized—in such parts as survive—in a combination of the Classical Orders and a Roman *Triumphal Arch. In a letter of 1454 to his executant architect at Rimini he wrote: 'You can see where the sizes and proportions of the pilasters come from: if you alter anything you will spoil all that harmony . . .' In Mantua he planned two churches as examples of a Greek *cross and a Latin cross: San Sebastiano, begun in 1460, is the first modern use of the Greek cross plan, deriving from Roman tombs and Early Christian martyria and tombs, e.g. the so-called Mausoleum of Galla Placidia at *Ravenna, of a thousand years earlier. Sant'Andrea was begun in 1470, as a long-nave church, differing from the alternative modern *Basilical plan, established by Brunelleschi, since it was inspired by Roman baths. Where Brunelleschi was adapting the forms of Early Christian basilicas, Sant'Andrea is the first long-nave church of the Renaissance to have side chapels opening off the nave, instead of the aisles, and with an exceptionally wide coffered barrel-vault some 56 ft. across. The system of massive wall-elements upholding the barrel-vault derives from Roman baths and similar antique public buildings. Further, the nave arcade repeats the proportional system used for the façade and the *narthex, itself derived from the Arch of Septimius Severus in Rome, so that the interior and the exterior are governed by the same system of void and solid forms and harmonic proportions.

Although neither San Sebastiano nor Sant' Andrea was completed by Alberti, the basic forms remained as models and were used for centuries. Between them, Brunelleschi and Alberti laid the foundations of church design for the Renaissance and succeeding centuries.

Alexander VII, Pope (1655–67). Fabio Chigi, elected pope in 1655, was the second of *Bernini's two great papal patrons (the other being *Urban VIII). He succeeded Innocent X, who had favoured Bernini's great rival *Algardi, and at once gave grandiose commissions for the embellishment of Rome, beginning with the huge oval colonnade enclosing the piazza outside St Peter's and the scores of huge statues surmounting it. This was executed by Bernini and his assistants from 1656. Alexander also commissioned the *Cathedra Petri*, the focal point of the new St Peter's (1657–66), the Scala Regia of the Vatican (1663–6), and his own tomb in St Peter's (1672–8).

Algardi, Alessandro (1598–1654) He was an Italian sculptor, born in Bologna, who studied with the *Carracci, from whom he learned his classical restraint. After being court sculptor in Mantua, he moved to Rome in 1625, to be one of many minor sculptors overshadowed by *Bernini, and in his early Roman years worked as a supplier of designs and models for founders of decorative objects, and as a restorer of antiques. Cardinal Ludovisi, also Bolognese, brought him into contact with Domenichino, the only major artist from the Carracci circle still in Rome, who in 1628/9 secured him a commission for two stucco statues of the *Magdalene* and *S. John the Evangelist* in San Silvestro al Quirinale.

Friendship with Pietro da Cortona, architect of SS Luca e Martina, brought him a commission in 1634 for *Three martyr saints* in terracotta, now much damaged (in the church). His mastery of bronze was supreme, as he showed in 1633–5 in the *Urn for the Magdalene*, and the relief of the *Ecstasy of the Magdalene*, both in St-Maximin, southern France. His first major work in marble, the *Beheading of S. Paul*, made in 1634, was not erected in San Paolo Maggiore, Bologna, until 1644.

His only papal tomb followed, that of *Leo XI*, entirely in white marble (1634–44) in St Peter's, where it competed with Bernini's flamboyant *Urban VIII* in bronze, and white and coloured marble, the type of polychrome effect which Algardi always avoided. In 1635 he carved the marble *S. Philip Neri, with an angel* for Sta Maria in Vallicella, the saint's own church, relying for the resemblance on portraits by others. He executed many posthumous 'portraits' for tombs, such as the Mellini tombs (1633–4: Sta Maria del Popolo) and the Frangipani tombs (1637: San Marcello). His other major works are the huge white marble relief of *Pope S. Leo the Great repelling Attila from the gates of Rome* (1646–53: St Peter's), a masterpiece of carving, and his large bronze statue of *Pope Innocent X* in the Conservatori, Rome, of 1645–50.

In his last years he suffered severely from gout and corpulence and, his biographer records, from parsimony. He is, however, wonderfully subtle in his feeling for the character of a saint in his *S. Philip Neri*, or in the expression of ecstasy in the *Magdalene*, and forthright in his interpretation of a formidable and domineering woman like Pope Innocent's sister, Donna Olimpia Maidalchini, her headdress billowing around her like the sails of a war galleon.

allegory (Gk. *allegoria*, speaking otherwise) An allegory is a story or representation apparently about one thing but with a concealed meaning underlying the obvious one. It was a manner of interpreting the OT, used by Rabbis to make their teaching more memorable, and Saint Paul uses the method in his Epistle to the Galatians (4: 22 ff.): 'Abraham had two sons, one by a slave woman, the other by a free woman. One, the child of the slave, was born according to the flesh; the other, the child of the free woman, was born through the promise. Now this is an allegory; these women are two covenants . . .', i.e. Ishmael and Isaac represent the Synagogue and the Church. The allegorical interpretation of the OT as prefiguring the NT was common from S. Augustine onwards, throughout the Middle Ages—e.g. the Song of Solomon (AV Song of Songs, Vg. Canticle of Canticles) is an allegory of Christ's love for the Church, His bride. Allegory differs from *symbolism in that symbols are real things—a cross, or a lamb, symbolize Christ—while allegories may be of entirely invented examples. *See also* EXEGESIS.

Allerheiligenbild (Ger. All Saints picture) The title of an altarpiece by *Dürer (1511: Vienna, KHM), with the Trinity adored by All *Saints and the Christian community on earth.

All Saints *See* SAINTS.

All Souls *See* SOULS.

Allston, Washington (1779–1843) An American painter, poet, and composer, and a graduate of Harvard, his early works include biblical subjects: *The Head of Judas Iscariot* (1799), *Christ Looked at Peter* (1800), and *Moses and the Serpent* (1805). He studied with Benjamin West in London, where he was resident from 1810 to 1817; he became a lifelong friend of Coleridge, whose portrait he painted, and also travelled extensively to view the art of Europe. Returning to the United States, he produced epic allegories as well as lyric fantasies and neoclassical figure paintings. Biblical subjects of this period include *Jacob's Dream* (1817), *Miriam the Prophetess* (1821), and *The Prophet Jeremiah Dictating to the Scribe Baruch* (1820). He laboured over the problematic *Belshazzar's Feast* from 1817 to 1843. Allston's work embodied the translation of traditional subjects, form, and style from Europe to North America, and through his many students he continued to influence American art as it developed in the 19th century. *See also* NORTH AMERICA.

almond *See* MANDORLA.

alms *See* MERCY, WORKS OF.

almshouse A place of refuge for the aged poor, but not a hospital for the sick. In the Middle Ages almshouses were often built by rich merchants as works of charity, sometimes for indigent members of their own guilds. They usually consist of small houses of one, or at most two storeys, sometimes in a terrace, but often ranged round three or four sides of a court in a form clearly derived from collegiate buildings. Sometimes a separate house for the warden is provided.

almuce A medieval garment worn by canons, consisting of a hood and cape lined with fur, as a protection against cold. It later developed into a mark of rank, especially in France, but was never a liturgical *vestment, and should not be confused with an *amice, which is.

Alpha and Omega The first and last letters of the Greek alphabet (A, or A, Ω, or O), a *Nomen Sacrum for God, or, more usually, Christ. They are found in the Apocalypse (Rev. 1: 8; 21: 6; and 22: 13; e.g. 'I am the Alpha and the Omega, the beginning and the end, says the Lord'). The letters are found in the 3rd and 4th centuries, sometimes alone and sometimes with the *Chi-Rho monogram, in which case they usually appear below, or pendent from, the arms of the cross. In later years more specific symbols, such as the cross, became more common, but alpha and omega may still be found in such representations as the *Majestas Domini. During the period of *iconoclasm the only permitted representations of Christ were the cross, alpha and omega, and the chi-rho.

altar Altars are one of the oldest cult objects, indicating man's veneration and propitiation of supernatural forces. They are places of sacrifice, and have come to be an integral part of religious observance and hence of sacred places, temples, and churches.

Archaeology provides ample evidence of altars from remote antiquity, but in ancient Rome there was a distinction between *altare* and *ara*, the former usually being reserved to the cult of, and sacrifices to, one of the higher gods, while *ara* was normally used for lesser gods and offerings to the dead (but *see* ARA COELI). Despite this ancient distinction *ara* and *altare* became merged in Christian usage, especially when the funeral *agape became liturgical and connected intimately with the Eucharist. In the Bible, the first mention of sacrifice is in Genesis 4, where the offerings of Cain and *Abel had such disastrous consequences, but the first mention of an altar is in Gen. 8: 20, when *Noah built one after the Flood. There is a detailed description in Exod. 27: 1–8 of an altar to be built by Moses. There are comparatively few mentions of altars in the Bible—only two in the Gospels—and this has led to a major difference in the importance accorded to them by the various Churches. In the Eastern Orthodox, Western Catholic, and High Anglican traditions the stress on the sacrificial aspect of the Eucharist leads to the dominant position afforded to the altar in all churches and cathedrals, where it is usually the focal point of the building and situated in the *chancel or choir. In the Reformed Churches, and to some extent in Evangelical Anglicanism, the sacrificial aspects are replaced by emphasis on the community meal, so that the word 'altar' is often avoided and periphrases such as 'the Lord's Table' or 'Communion Table' are used. In such cases the altar/table is often subordinate to the *pulpit and *lectern and is placed in any convenient position (*see* CHARENTON, CHURCH ARCHITECTURE).

Obviously, the Last Supper itself was celebrated on an ordinary wooden table and this seems to have been the custom among the earliest Christians, but quite soon (certainly by the 4th cent.) stone altars were to be found where churches existed. They were simple slabs supported on stone columns, stone blocks, or stone *sarcophagi such as those found in the *catacombs, where the stone slab in an *arcosolium served as an altar. From this connection with the martyrs the rule arose of including a relic in an altar-slab, enclosed in what is called a sepulchre. In Early Christian churches the altar was always placed on the chord of the *apse, with the bishop's throne beyond it, in the centre of the apse, and with seats for the clergy on either side. The celebrant faced the congregation, a custom preserved at the papal altars in St Peter's and other Roman basilicas, and now revived generally. (This revival has resulted in moving old altars, thus ruining the spatial design of many medieval and later churches not designed for it. *See also* ALTARPIECE for further discussion of the position of altars.) Altars in churches of the Byzantine rite were, and still are, cubical blocks standing clear of the choir walls and usually covered by a *ciborium, like those in some surviving Early Christian churches in the West. They have altar-cloths reaching to the ground on all sides.

When the relics of the martyrs were transferred from the catacombs to churches in Rome and altars were dedicated to them, an opening or *confessio was frequently made in front of or below the altar, so that the faithful could reach down towards the relics below. This led to the practice of enclosing the altar within railings of wood or metal, or pierced and carved marble slabs called *transennae, and of placing a veil over the opening to exclude dust and prevent irreverent curiosity. In the course of time this simple curtain became an altar-frontal or *antependium. Famous examples of altars above a *confessio* are those of St Peter's and San Paolo fuori le Mura (St Paul's outside the Walls), in Rome. The original term '*altar-tomb' now has quite a different meaning.

Stone altars gradually replaced wooden ones, although wooden portable ones remained common. In 517 the Council of Epaone (Pamiers in France) forbade the continued use of wooden altars, but one was found in the Tomb of *S. Cuthbert (687) and their portability made them useful (*see also* ANTIMINSION). Old altars have a slab, called a *mensa* (Lat. table), with five crosses inscribed—one in each corner and one in the centre. Usually, the central cross is cut into a smaller slab which is the lid of the Sepulchre containing the relic, and it is this small part which is the altar-slab itself, all the rest being merely support. Metal altars are often very elaborate, one of the most famous being the High Altar of Sant'Ambrogio, Milan, over the tomb of *S. Ambrose and the two early martyrs, SS Gervase and Protase. It is of gold, silver, and gilt, with *cloisonné* enamels and jewels, with two doors at the back to give access to the saints' tomb. All sides have figurative panels, probably of N. Italian workmanship. Its creator Wolvinius is shown presenting it to Archbishop Angilbert (824–59), who commissioned it.

Eastern Orthodox churches have only one altar, enclosed within the *iconostasis, at which only one Mass may be said on any one day. In such churches, chapels containing altars are regarded as separate churches, even though they are part of the same building. Anglican, Lutheran, and other churches usually have only one altar, but most English cathedrals, and many of the larger parish churches, date from Pre-Reformation times and may still have subsidiary altars in chapels or in transepts and aisles; these are often used for weekday services, or in chapels for private prayer.

Churches of the Roman rite, except *oratories, have a high altar and at least one subsidiary altar, usually dedicated to the Virgin Mary ('Lady Altar'). Monastic churches have several altars, according to the size of the house, for each priest to say Mass daily: the 9th-century plan of *Sankt Gallen, in Switzerland, provides for seventeen altars. Churches also have subsidiary altars in chapels belonging to a family or a pious association, or dedicated to individual saints. The *Altar of Repose may be one of these. In larger churches the *sacristy often also contains an altar.

Altars in Catholic churches were usually covered with three linen altar-cloths (two are now allowed). These may be covered by an ornamental pall, to keep the altar-cloth clean. On or above the altar is a crucifix and at least two candles on the altar itself or on a shelf (**predella*), which forms part of the *reredos or dossal at the back of the altar. Since Counter-Reformation times the high altar has normally had six tall candles. There was also an *altarpiece, either carved or painted. The frontal or *antependium may be a simple cloth of the *liturgical colour of the season, or an elaborate permanent fixture. The *tabernacle may stand on the altar or be in a niche in the wall: in large churches and cathedrals it is common to have a separate Chapel of the Blessed Sacrament to contain it. Anglican and other Reformed churches may contain some or none of these accompaniments.

Canterbury Cathedral had a new altar in 2005 of *verde aosta chiesa* marble by Stephen *Cox in the St Anselm Chapel. (*See also* HORNS OF THE ALTAR.)

altar-cloth Since at least the 9th century it has been customary to cover the altar in a Catholic church with three linen cloths, the two lower ones being roughly the same size as the top of the altar, while the top one must be long enough to touch the ground on each side. It is held to symbolize Christ's shroud (*see* EPITAPHIOS). One under-cloth is now held to be sufficient.

altar-frontal *See* ANTEPENDIUM.

altar lights Originally, lighted candles were placed on the ground, or held by *acolytes behind the altar. Later, two candles and a crucifix were placed on the actual altar during Mass. This is referred to, *c.*1175, as 'the present custom' in the papal chapel. From the time of the Council of *Trent until recently it has been customary to have two candles for a Low Mass and six for High Mass, with seven for a Pontifical one. The candles are of beeswax, bleached for normal use but yellow—i.e. unbleached—for a Requiem Mass and Good Friday, and some other occasions in Lent. A sanctuary lamp is a small oil lamp kept burning on or near the *tabernacle when the Blessed Sacrament is reserved there. It usually has a red glass shade to distinguish it, but many Continental churches have numerous red lamps and the sanctuary one must also be accompanied by the tabernacle having a veil covering it. In 1549 the use of candles on the altar was prohibited in the Church of England, but, at least since 1890, two have been normal. Many Anglican churches following a High Anglican, or Anglo-Catholic, rite may well have as many candles and lamps as Catholic ones. *See also* QUARANT'ORE.

Altar of Repose The Catholic Easter rite in the West for Maundy Thursday concludes with the removal of the Blessed Sacrament to an Altar of Repose, separate from the High Altar, where it remains until Good Friday. The practice is first mentioned in the 15th century, and is one of the reasons why Catholic churches normally have at least two altars (*see also* EASTER SEPULCHRE).

altarpiece An altarpiece is basically a decorative adjunct to an *altar, not an essential part of it. It is an image, or images, which may be painted, carved in the round or relief, or any combination of them which identifies an altar dedicated to a particular saint (e.g. a Lady Altar), and since the Counter-Reformation it has become customary for the altar of a Catholic church to contain at least a representation of the titular saint. It may be convenient to distinguish between an altarpiece, or *retable, as one or more pictures or reliefs, and a *reredos which is a construction in wood or stone, often large and elaborate, containing carved figures. An altarpiece may hang on the wall behind the altar or be fixed to the back of the altar itself, or hang above it as e.g. Titian's *Assumption of the Virgin*: 1518, Venice, Frari; and may range from a single picture such as Caravaggio's *Madonna of Loreto*, 1603–5, Sant' Agostino, Rome, to a large *polyptych such as the Ghent Altar by van *Eyck (1432: Ghent, S. Bavo). In Italian the word *ancona* is often used to describe a large altarpiece with several panels in a single frame, while a *pala* is usually a single picture. The tendency in the first half of the 15th century in Italy to assemble all the saints, donors, and other figures in a single space, instead of each having its own panel, led to the development of the *Sacra Conversazione. Altarpieces may also be made of metal, like the *Pala d'Oro of St Mark's, Venice, which is made of gold and silver gilt, and decorated with *cloisonné* enamels and jewels.

In Early Christian times there were no altarpieces, because there was no place for them; the altar was free-standing and the celebrant stood behind it facing the congregation. By the 9th century, popular devotion to saints and the veneration of their relics led to changes in attitude towards the altar; it was no longer regarded as a structure so sanctified that it might be used only for the vessels required for the sacrifice of the Mass, and the Gospels and service books, but first reliquaries and then *shrines containing relics came to be placed on it. This led to three changes: the clergy originally seated in the apse moved to either side of the altar, the shrine became the focal point of the church instead of the altar, and the altar itself was moved further back in the choir, so that the celebrant officiated facing the shrine, with his back to the congregation.

By the 10th and 11th centuries the new system was consolidated by the removal of the shrine from the altar to a place where the veneration of the relics by pilgrims could no longer interfere with the services held at the altar, and the replacement of the shrine with an altarpiece or reredos which would combine several functions: to make room for a *tabernacle for the reservation of the Sacrament and for the crucifix placed over it; to incorporate a shelf (or *predella*) which extended the altar and provided a place for the candlesticks which, like the crucifix, were originally held by acolytes standing round the altar. It also enabled an image of the saint or saints to whom the altar was dedicated to be displayed above it, either alone or shown venerating Christ or perhaps the Virgin, and for a smaller series of images or scenes from the history or legend of the saint to be aligned below it on the *predella*. Eventually the size and importance of the altarpiece frequently overshadowed the altar itself and replaced it as the focal point of the church (e.g. Titian's *Assumption of the Virgin* in the Frari church in Venice).

Altarpieces may be of various types. At their simplest they consist of a single painted or carved image reflecting the dedication of the church or the altar, but if the dedication is to such events as the Resurrection, Ascension, or various incidents in the life of the Virgin, the altarpiece might well grow in complexity according to the number of incidents represented. The altarpiece known as the *Maestà* painted for Siena Cathedral (which is dedicated to the Virgin) in 1308–11 by *Duccio has a hieratic image of the Madonna and Child with Saints and Angels on the front, and the back has narrative scenes of the Life of Christ, centred round the Crucifixion, with a *predella* which had further scenes extending the narrative. The term *predella* came to have two meanings: strictly, it is the shelf which extends the altar surface, and is used for the candlesticks, but it also has come to mean the series of small pictures, carved scenes, or figures below the altarpiece or reredos. This extension of the altarpiece became essential if it had wings or shutters which closed over it, since it enabled it to be opened and shut more easily.

Many altarpieces are made up of more than one panel. A *diptych consists of two panels facing each other; it is a frequent form in devotional images but rare in altarpieces. A *triptych is of three panels, a central one flanked by two wings, which may be made to close over the central image, in which case the exterior of the wings is also painted, often in grisaille to simulate sculpture. Such altarpieces were often opened only on feast-days. A *polyptych consists of a number of panels, flanking a central one, and may also have a crowning element. Two of the most complex examples of polyptychs are the Ghent Altar, mentioned above, and the Isenheim Altar by *Grünewald where a series of shutters encloses a carved altarpiece called a *Schnitzaltar*. Another type is the Spanish 'retablo' (retable) such as the huge altar painted by El *Greco for Sto Domingo el Antiguo, Toledo, in 1577–9; a further Spanish form is the enormous carved and gilded wood screen filled with figures, which virtually fills the choir behind the altar, and in Toledo is enhanced by the *Transparente.

Reredoses range from simple carved reliefs of a single scene (*Last Supper*, *c.*1400: St James's, Somerton, Oxfordshire), of provincial workmanship (*see* ALABASTERS), to elaborate screens such as the 16th-century one in Winchester Cathedral, which reaches to the base of the *clerestory and consists of three tiers of niches, now filled with small figures of 1885–99. This type of reredos is also found in Oxford college chapels (All Souls, Magdalen, and New College). Perhaps the most magnificent of painted reredoses of the Late Gothic period is Veit Stoss's masterpiece in Cracow (1477–89), some 40 ft. high.

Carved altarpieces are a Baroque feature, from *Algardi's huge marble relief in St Peter's, Rome, of *Pope Leo the Great repelling Attila* of 1646–53, to *Bernini's *Ecstasy of S. Theresa*, in the Cornaro Chapel in Sta Maria della Vittoria, Rome, and to the *Asam brothers' similar exploitation of light combined with sculpture in Rohr, Munich, and Weltenburg. Nineteenth- and 20th-century churches have not developed any new types of altarpiece, since the trend, if not the rule, nowadays is towards a return to the Early Christian type of free-standing altar.

Anglican churches (and the Reformed churches) rarely have altarpieces, but where important reredoses exist they have survived, though their statuary is invariably Victorian replacements, the originals having been removed, or more probably smashed, either at the Reformation or during the Puritan ascendancy of the Commonwealth (1645–51). In some modern Anglican churches such as Coventry Cathedral, a tapestry takes the place of an altarpiece (*Christ in Majesty*, by Graham Sutherland, 1962, covers the entire windowless north wall), and modern tapestries have also been used in the choirs of medieval cathedrals such as Chichester, where the older reredos is now covered by tapestries by John Piper of 1966. In Orthodox churches of the Byzantine rite there are no altarpieces as such, all images being placed on the *iconostasis or incorporated in the *mosaic decorations.

altar-rails A low balustrade of wood, stone, or metal surrounding the altar, where worshippers kneel to receive Communion. Since they enclose the altar as a sacred place they were a cause of much controversy in the Church of England when they were made obligatory by Archbishop Laud in 1634, abolished by the Puritans, and finally re-established at the Restoration (1660). There has been a tendency in the present time, even in Roman Catholic churches, to remove them again. When they are made of pierced slabs of stone or marble they are called *transennae.

altar-tomb A tomb, often free-standing, with a flat stone slab on top. Many such tombs have been found in the Roman catacombs, and may have served for memorial celebrations of the Eucharist. The term is also used to describe flat-topped tombs, usually of medieval origin, many of which have, or once had, memorial brasses inserted into their surfaces. Some also have decorative or figurative memorial sculpture in their side panels. They are common in English country churchyards, and were used until the 19th century as family vaults.

ama, amula *See* AMPULLA.

Amannati (Ammanati), Bartolommeo (1511–92) He was a Florentine sculptor and architect. Almost all his work is secular; his sculpture—in particular, his female nudes—displaying sinuous grace and elegant elongation. In 1582 he published a letter to the Florentine Academy in which he publicly repudiated his use of the nude in sculpture, and, probably with his figures on the *Neptune Fountain* (Florence, Piazza della Signoria) in mind, expressed his contrition at having executed works which included 'nudes, Satyrs, Fauns, and similar things, exposing those parts which ought to be covered that cannot be looked at without shame'. He declared that a draped figure was as revealing of the sculptor's skill as a nude one, and claimed that Michelangelo's *Moses* was his finest work. He particularly enjoined upon his fellow-Academicians that their religious pictures should never offend against decency. His strictures, echoed by the writer Vincenzo Borghini in 1584, were most likely directed against altarpieces such as Bronzino's *Christ in Limbo* (1552: removed from Sta Croce, but not until 1821, now Uffizi depot), which contains notable displays of female semi-nudity. He also asserted that, in general, patrons accept what the artist creates, and rarely stipulate either subject or treatment; a fact which, if correct, shows how much the 16th-century patron differed from those of preceding centuries. Amannati's letter became one of the articles of Counter-Reformation artistic theory and influenced Late Mannerist art.

ambo (pl. *ambos* or *ambones*, Lat. from Gk.) An elevated lectern, usually of marble and often elaborately decorated, in an Early Christian church. It was used for reading the Gospel, and was larger than a *pulpit, because it had to accommodate the reader and his candle-bearing attendants. It was reached by a flight of steps on either side so that the procession might mount by one and descend by the other. The mounting of the steps was accompanied by the singing of the Gradual (from Lat. *gradus*, a step), chants based upon verses from the psalms or other biblical canticles. In San Clemente in Rome, two ambones, partly constructed from pieces recovered from the earlier 6th-century church which lies beneath the present 12th-century one, face each other across the later enclosed choir, or *schola cantorum; it is the best surviving example of the form, though a second ambo was often provided without a schola cantorum for the Epistles and other lessons. The Gospel ambo was placed on the north side of the nave, the Epistle ambo on the south. The ambo was not used for preaching, since in the early Church the bishop preached from his throne or from the altar steps, but it provided a model for the *pulpit which by the 13th century had superseded the earlier custom. In the nave of San Lorenzo, Florence, are two large ambones which Donatello left unfinished at his death in 1466. They are of bronze and bronzed wood, and stand on columns on either side of the nave, but although there are doors in them they are without means of access.

Ambrose, Saint, *Doctor of the Church (*c.*339–97) He was the son of the Praetorian Prefect of Gaul and himself became governor (*c.*370) of Aemilia-Liguria, based on *Milan. In 374 the *Arian Bishop of Milan died, and Ambrose was elected by the populace to succeed him, although he was not yet a baptized Christian. He was baptized, ordained, and consecrated Bishop, and became famous as a preacher and opponent of Arianism. He played a large part in the conversion of *S. Augustine of Hippo in 386 and excommunicated the Emperor Theodosius for permitting a massacre in Thessalonia in 390, forcing him to do public penance: this assertion of the authority of the Church over the State is the subject of an altarpiece by Rubens (Vienna, KHM) and a version of it by van Dyck (London, NG). Ambrose also drove the Arians out of N. Italy, for which reason he is sometimes represented with a scourge (roundel in Poldi-Pezzoli Mus., Milan). He usually appears as an elderly bearded bishop with a book, but is sometimes shown as a baby with a swarm of bees about to settle on his lips (e.g. Filippo Lippi, Berlin, formerly in Sant'Ambrogio, Florence): this was held to be a prophecy of his ability as a preacher, but the same story is told of Pindar and other ancient writers. The earliest representation of him, without a halo, is an early 5th-century mosaic in the chapel of San Vittore in Ciel d'Oro, in Sant'Ambrogio, Milan, the earliest part of the present church and a surviving part of the first church. He was buried in what is now the Basilica of Sant'Ambrogio in Milan, and his relics were placed under the High Altar in 835, but the present church, one of the earliest Romanesque churches in Italy, dates from *c.*950. The church contains his episcopal throne and the Golden Altar by Wolvinius (*c.*824/

59), in chased and enamelled goldsmith's work, which has scenes from the saint's life. Ambrose is also the patron saint of stonemasons, who adopted him because of his connection with Milan, the principal city of Lombardy, since many of them in the Middle Ages were Lombards.

ambulatory (Lat. *ambulare*, to walk) The passageway behind the choir of a medieval church, surrounding the area of the high altar, and designed usually as an extension from the aisles. It was of particular use in pilgrimage churches, since it gave easy access to shrines and to subsidiary chapels without disturbing services in the choir itself (*see* ALTARPIECE). An ambulatory with three, five, or occasionally seven (though this is rare) chapels projecting from it, so as to increase the number of side chapels and therefore the number of altars, was common from the 11th century onwards in monastic houses in the West and in *Romanesque and *Gothic churches. Ambulatories are not found in Eastern rite churches.

AMDG is an abbreviation for *ad maiorem Dei gloriam* (Lat. to the greater glory of God) occasionally found on works of art. It is particularly associated with the Jesuits.

American art *See* NORTH AMERICA.

Amiatinus Codex, the (Florence, Bib. Laurenziana) This is the earliest extant copy of *S. Jerome's Vulgate, made at the monastery of Monkwearmouth/Jarrow for Abbot Coelfrith between 680 and 715, and taken by him to present to Pope Gregory II for the shrine of S. Peter in Rome. Coelfrith died on the journey at Langres in 716, and his followers took the Bible to Rome; it was later given to the monastery at Monte Amiata in Tuscany. It is written in the distinctive Northumbrian round script, in two columns per page; the illustrations include a double-spread picture of the Tabernacle in Jerusalem, full-page pictures of Christ in Majesty, seven full-page diagrams of the Books of the Bible, and a full-page picture of the Prophet Ezra writing in his study. This picture typifies the priests and doctors of the Church upon whom rests the obligation to preserve and transmit Holy Writ, since Ezra, when the sacred books were burnt, was inspired by God to rewrite them from memory. The illustration is clearly inspired by one of the books Coelfrith had brought to Jarrow from a previous visit to Rome, which probably included a now lost *Codex grandior* by Cassiodorus (d. 580), which the Venerable Bede (d. 735), who was a monk in Jarrow, records seeing there. The Ezra picture is unlike any earlier Anglo-Saxon scribe-portrait, and is clearly of Mediterranean inspiration. The Amiatinus was used for the revision of the Vulgate made in 1590, and until 1886 it was thought to be Italian work, since it had a dedication from Petrus Langobardorum, but G. B. de' *Rossi discovered that this had been written over the dedication from Coelofridus Anglorum, thus restoring the work to its true origin.

amice A small rectangle of white linen worn round the neck and shoulders, with the *alb, by priests, deacons, and subdeacons. Its use in the West dates from the 8th century, and it counts as a *vestment, whereas in the East it is worn occasionally, simply to prevent sweat staining the vestments themselves. In some Orders it is worn as a hood during parts of the service. It should not be confused with *almuce.

Ammanati *See* AMANNATI.

Amnon *See* DAVID.

amnos (Gk. lamb) A Byzantine iconographical theme, representing the Christ Child lying on a paten, sometimes covered by an *Asteriskos, symbolizing the sacrifice of the Eucharist.

amphisbene (Gk. *amphis beinein*, to move both ways) A mythical reptile with a head at each end, so that it symbolized vigilance. It also appears as a sort of serpent swallowing its own tail, thus representing the powers of light and darkness in eternal conflict. This imaginary animal is typical of the allegorical interpretation of nature in a *Bestiary.

ampulla (ama, amula) Ampullae, or ampoules, are small flasks, a few inches high, made of earthenware, lead, pewter, or silver, which contained oil from lamps burning at the shrines of martyrs, or other material connected with martyrs. Sometimes they were used for chrism or other consecrated oils. Many have survived from Early Christian times, mostly from Egypt and the Holy Land: the most famous are the fifteen silver ones in Monza Cathedral, N. Italy, which were given, about the year 600, to Theodolinda, Queen of the Lombards, by Pope Gregory the Great.

They are thought to reproduce lost decorative cycles in churches in the Holy Land. Other examples are in Berlin and the British Museum. A secondary meaning is flasks used to hold the water and wine for the Eucharist, otherwise called cruets. The so-called 'Sainte Ampoule' was used for the coronation of the French kings, but was broken in 1793: a similar one was made for the coronation of the restored Charles II of Great Britain and Ireland in 1660 and is still in use. An ama or amula was a vessel in which unconsecrated wine was brought to the altar—i.e. a cruet. Very large ones, called flagons, were made for Anglican services, because in the Anglican rite Communion is given in both kinds and more wine is needed than is the case in Catholic churches (though this is now changing). Many splendid examples of late 17th- and 18th-century silversmiths' work are extant.

amulet A charm to avert evil spirits, and, therefore, forbidden to Christians, although common among the pagans. Nevertheless, the Jewish custom of wearing a phylactery combined with pagan usage to encourage their use among the earliest Christians. Some objects found in *catacombs are probably amulets, and much later examples can be found in e.g. Italian paintings of the Madonna and Child, where the Child wears a piece of coral round His neck: the *Senigallia Madonna* by *Piero Della Francesca (Urbino, Gall. Naz.) actually shows the Child as blessing, while at the same time wearing a large coral charm against the evil eye, which could also double as a teething ring.

Ananias Acts 5: 1–11 tell how Ananias and his wife Sapphira claimed to have sold their goods for the benefit of the Church, but retained part for themselves. On being questioned by S. Peter they fell dead. This is a rare subject in art, but both Masaccio (in Florence, Sta Maria del Carmine) and Raphael (in the Vatican tapestries) represented it.

Anargyroi (Gk. the healing saints) A name given to those saints who healed the sick without charge. The most famous in the West are *Cosmas and Damian, the patron saints of Cosimo de' Medici. The San Marco altarpiece by Fra *Angelico (*c.*1438–40: San Marco, Florence) includes the scene of Cosmas and Damian transplanting a leg from a dead negro to a white man whose leg had been severed.

Anastasis (Gk. Resurrection) In the West, the *Resurrection is normally represented by Christ rising from the Tomb, with sleeping soldiers at the sides. In the East, however, the term is used both for the Resurrection of Christ and also for the Resurrection of the Dead. The Eastern tradition is to represent the events of Easter Saturday as they are recounted in the *Apocryphal '*Gospel of Nicodemus'; events which, in the West, are known as the *Harrowing of Hell or Descent into *Limbo. Icons, wall-paintings, and mosaics of the Anastasis show Christ trampling on the Gates of Hell, driving out devils, and reaching for the hand of *Adam, who, with Eve and the Patriarchs, is rescued from the underworld; sometimes the personification of Hades is shown as an old man chained by angels. An Anglo-Saxon relief carving of the Harrowing of Hell is in Bristol Cathedral; Byzantine examples include mosaics in Hosios Lukas, Katholikon, *c.*1020, Daphni, Church of the Dormition, *c.*1100, and the apse painting in Constantinople, Church of the Chora (Kariye Camii), *c.*1315, and in a 12th-century mosaic of the *Last Judgement* in the Cathedral, Torcello (Venice).

The Church of the Holy Sepulchre in Jerusalem is dedicated to the Anastasis, and until the Turkish conquest, another in Constantinople had the same dedication.

anchor One of the most popular Early Christian symbols of hope (Heb. 6: 18–19, 'the hope set before us . . . a sure and steadfast anchor of the soul'). It occurs frequently on graves and also on *seals, having been recommended by S. Clement of Alexandria (*c.*200) as a suitable image for a seal-ring used by a Christian (others were doves, ships, fish, or fishermen). The crossbar of the anchor was also a symbol of the Cross, and occasionally it has a dolphin twined round it, which may be a symbol of Christ. After the Peace of the Church in the 4th century it was less used because the need for 'private' symbols of Christianity was no longer necessary. It was revived in the 17th to 19th centuries, especially on tombs. An anchor is also an attribute of several saints, including Pope S. Clement and S. John Nepomuk, both of whom were martyred by drowning.

ancona *See* ALTARPIECE.

Andachtsbild (pl. *Andachtsbilder*: Ger. devotional picture) A devotional image, of a type which arose in Germany in the 14th century, deriving from Italo-Byzantine works of the 12th/13th centuries, but much influenced by Northern mystical writers. The subjects are intended for contemplation and meditation, and are divorced from their biblical contexts. The most popular include scenes from the Passion—the *Schmerzensmann* or Man of Sorrows (*see* IMAGO PIETATIS), the *Pietà, the Dead Christ in the Tomb, and some types of Crucifix, as well as the Sorrows of Mary, and *Madonnas such as those of Humility, of Mercy, or the *Virgo inter Virgines. This Western form of devotional image is not the same as an *icon, which is to be venerated as a prototype of its original, whereas the *Andachtsbild* is a stimulus to devotion, and, because of its flexible iconography, developed into narrative cycles, whereas the icon remained almost unchanged for centuries.

Andrew, Saint (d. *c.*60) The first Apostle, he was originally a disciple of John the Baptist, but, convinced that Jesus was indeed the Messiah, he said to his brother Simon (i.e. *S. Peter), 'We have found the Messiah' (John 1: 35–42). Like Peter he was a fisherman, but little is known for certain of his life, although there are several spurious 'Acts' and a 'Passio', which passed into such collections as the **Golden Legend*. He is said to have worked in Greece and was crucified at Patras, traditionally on an X-shaped cross ('S. Andrew's cross'), but all the earliest representations show a normal cross and the X-shape is not common before the 14th/15th century. Nevertheless, his cult was universal by the 6th century and was very popular in the Middle Ages, especially in E. and N. Europe—there were said to be 637 pre-Reformation churches dedicated to him in Britain alone, and he was the patron saint of Greece, Russia, the Duchy of Burgundy (especially the Order of the Golden Fleece), and many other countries as well as Scotland. The connection with Scotland is said to have arisen from some of his relics being taken there, to what is now St Andrews in Fife. The most important relic, his head, stolen from Byzantium by the Crusaders after 1204, was taken to Amalfi in Italy and from there to Rome in April 1462, where it was received with great ceremony by Pius II, who recorded the event in his Autobiography (Bk. VIII). It remained in St Peter's until 1965, when it was returned to the Patriarch of Constantinople by Paul VI as a gesture of reconciliation with the E. Orthodox Church. Andrew is always represented in scenes of the Apostles and often as martyred, but rarely in other connections. He is shown as an old man with long grey hair and beard, usually with his cross or a fisherman's net. Sant'Andrea della Valle in Rome has vivid pictures of the martyrdom of S. Andrew, by Mattia Preti, 1650–51. *S. Andrew, Fisher of Men* is the title given to Norman Blamey's 1964 mural in St Andrew's Lutheran Church, Ruislip, Middlesex.

angel *See* ANGELS AND ARCHANGELS, and EVANGELIST SYMBOLS.

Angelico, Fra (*c.*?1387, or more probably, *c.*1400–55). Fra Giovanni da Fiesole, now beatified, is a rare example of a Renaissance artist who was exclusively a religious painter; no secular works are known. He was still a layman in 1417, and as Guido di Piero, active as a painter. He entered the Dominican Order and appears to have resumed painting in 1423; his first authenticated work is of 1429. As a member of the Order of Preachers, he used his art for didactic rather than mystic purposes and evolved—and perfected—a style based on the largeness of form, directness of narrative, and simplicity in iconography inherited from *Giotto and *Masaccio. His Order took over the convent of San Marco in Florence in 1436, and from 1441, when he was transferred there, he painted about fifty frescoes of NT subjects in the corridors and the friars' cells, designed as aids to meditation and devotion. These works concentrate on the essence of the subject, eschewing all the picturesque details which are the norm in devotional works for the laity; for instance, in the *Mocking of Christ* only the head of the man spitting, and the hands, one grasping a stick, of the mockers are shown; the *Christ in the Sepulchre* is surrounded by the Instruments of the *Passion—the column of the flagellation, the cross, the nails, the lance, the sponge—as well as by the kiss of Judas and the mocking; in the *Transfiguration* only the two heads of Moses and Elijah appear on either side of Christ, above the three astonished disciples. In many of these frescoes there are also two figures of a friar and a nun in meditation.

He also painted numerous altarpieces for San Marco and other convents, many of which, depicting the Madonna and Child in a group of saints, were important in the development of the type of altarpiece known as the *Sacra Conversazione. His paintings excel through their simple imagery, delicate colour, and a tender sweetness which in more worldly and sophisticated hands might have degenerated into cloying sentiment. From *c.*1445–7 he decorated a chapel in the Vatican, probably commissioned by Pope Eugenius IV, with scenes from the lives of SS Stephen and Laurence, which show his mastery of fashionable Florentine techniques in the use of bold perspective. A second chapel in the Vatican has been destroyed. He began to paint a small part of the huge fresco cycle of the *Last Judgement* at Orvieto Cathedral in 1447, which was completed by *Signorelli. His dedication to his art did not prevent his fulfilling his obligations to his Order in administrative offices (notably as Prior at Fiesole, 1450–2), and he is reputed to have used his influence with Pope Eugenius to divert to his friend, Fra *Antoninus (later canonized), the archbishopric of Florence to which the Pope wished to appoint him. His name of 'Fra Angelico' is really a name conferred on him through popular recognition of the deeply religious quality of his art, for he was already known as Fra Giovanni Angelico in the 15th century, and is recorded as such in Vasari's first Life of him, published in 1550.

angelic salutation *See* AVE MARIA.

angels and archangels Angels (Gk. *angeloi*, messengers) are frequently mentioned in both Old and New Testaments as spiritual beings, and are therefore common to both Judaism and Christianity. For artists the problem of finding a visual symbol for an immaterial spirit was solved by adapting the pagan winged figures of Victory or Genii, although the earliest known representations of angels, in the catacombs and elsewhere, following the Scriptures, are wingless (except for *cherubim and seraphim). These young men in long robes are easily confused with humans, and by *c.*350 winged figures are common, and are universal by the 6th century. (In 1983 a German court decided that angels as Christmas decorations must have wings to be tax-exempt.)

Archangels are sometimes distinguished by an orb and a long staff, as in the splendid ivory of S. Michael (London, BM: probably 5th cent.). A nimbus (*see* HALO) is also used to distinguish angels from men. The idea that there are several classes of angel arose partly from the various functions assigned to them in the Bible and partly from the names given to them by S. Paul (Eph. 1: 21; Col. 1: 16). They were arranged in hierarchies by Dionysius the Pseudo-Areopagite (i.e. not the Dionysius mentioned by S. Paul) in his *Celestial Hierarchy* of *c.*500, which, translated into Latin in the 9th century, became the standard text. He divided angels into three groups of three, starting with the highest: (1) Cherubim, Seraphim, Thrones, all of whom are red, the colour of love; (2) Dominations, Principalities (Authorities), and Powers, all blue, the colour of heaven and therefore of light and knowledge; (3) Virtues, Archangels, and Angels. A slightly different arrangement—followed by Dante (*Paradiso*, 28: 97–124)—is found in the 13th-century mosaics in the Florentine Baptistery. The passage in the Apocalypse (Rev. 8: 2) 'I saw the seven angels which stood before God' led to the belief that there are seven archangels, to whom names have been given: Gabriel, Michael, and Raphael are all mentioned in Scripture (e.g. Luke 1: 26; Jude 9; Tobit 12: 15), while Uriel is named in 2 Esd. 4: 1 and 5: 20 (2 Esd. in the Apocrypha of the AV only). Various Jewish writings give a variety of names for the other three, such as Raguel, Ramuel, Sariel, Jeramial, Chamuel, Jophiel, and Zadkiel.

In art, Gabriel is most frequently represented in Annunciation scenes, bearing a lily. Gabriel and Michael, as single figures, occur in 6th-century mosaics in Sant'Apollinare in Classe, Ravenna. Michael, described as Prince of Hosts (Dan. and Rev.), is often shown trampling on the defeated Lucifer or a dragon (e.g. B. Bermejo, Luton Hoo, Beds.; Epstein, Coventry Cathedral), or as weighing souls at the Last Judgement (e.g. Memlinc, Gdańsk Mus.), or, more rarely, as appearing at one of the shrines dedicated to him—Castel Sant'Angelo in Rome, Monte Gargano in S. Italy, Mont-Saint-Michel in Normandy, or St Michael's Mount in Cornwall. Raphael is always associated with the story of *Tobit and is shown as accompanying Tobias with his fish. There is a church dedicated to the Angelo Raffaele in Venice which has a cycle of paintings, attributed to G. A. Guardi, telling the whole story of Tobias. Because of this connection the idea of an angel—an *angelo custodes*—accompanying everyone, or at least every believer, became popular, especially in the 16th/17th centuries, and was made a universal feast by Clement X in 1670. Representations are very similar to Raphael and Tobias except for the fish, and the human soul for which the angel cares is often a much younger child, as in the painted statue by Ignaz Günther (1763: Munich, Bürgersaal). Many paintings of the subject exist, e.g. Guercino (Fano, Sant'Agostino). A painting by Botticini of the late 15th century

a

(Florence, Uffizi) shows Raphael and Tobias (with his fish), flanked by Michael and Gabriel. Another example on the same theme is Jackson Hlungwani's *Gabriel* carvings (1986) on the altar at the *New Jerusalem* site, Mbhokhota, Limpopo Province, South Africa.

Anglo-Saxon art and architecture

When the Roman Legions finally left Britain in the mid-5th century AD there ensued a long period of internecine strife accompanied by successive waves of invading Jutes, Angles, and Saxons, which cut off contacts between the North and the now declining power of Rome.

In Ireland (which had never been a Roman colony) rudimentary religious settlements became flourishing communities which developed a Celtic Christian art (*see* IRISH ART) independent of Roman example. Iona, off the west coast of Scotland, was colonized by Irish Christians, and from there Christianity spread across the north of England, and communities at Hexham, Durham, and Lindisfarne became important centres, their art having a strong Celtic cast to it. At the end of the 6th century Christianity was introduced (or reintroduced, since *Romano-British artefacts testify to its earlier existence), by *S. *Augustine at Canterbury, but it, together with the tiny enclave in Northumbria, was wiped out by the invasions, and did not begin to revive in earnest until Egbert, by force of arms, became the sole king in 802. The first incursion by the Danes had occurred in 787, but they then turned to Ireland, which they conquered. By 856 Viking invasions began, and when Alfred became king in 871 he had to contend both with the Danes and with Viking raids.

England became Christianized very slowly. The early forms of Christian artefacts are generally the same in design and techniques as those used almost simultaneously for pagan purposes. The pectoral cross of S. Cuthbert, who died in Lindisfarne in 687, is similar (though rather coarser in workmanship) to objects in the British Museum found in the Anglo-Saxon royal burial mound at Sutton Hoo (near Woodbridge, Suffolk) of 625–35. The more recent discovery of the Staffordshire Hoard, which probably dates from the early 8th century, also testifies to this syncretic development of pagan and Christian ornamentation where gold crosses and other items engraved with quotations from the Bible were discovered side by side with highly ornamented weaponry.

The influence of Irish manuscripts spread from Iona to Durham and Lindisfarne, while manuscripts from communities dependent on Canterbury show more influence from books imported from Gaul and Italy. Very roughly, the two sources are reflected in the types of scripts used, northern books using forms of letters and decorations which show the close affinity between their illuminations and Celtic manuscripts and metalwork, the southern ones written in forms closer to the uncial script emanating from the Mediterranean. The *Lindisfarne Gospels (London, BL) and the Durham Gospel Book (Cathedral Library) date almost certainly from either the end of the 7th century or the first years of the 8th, as may also a third manuscript, the Echternach Gospels (Paris, BN), all of which emanate from the Lindisfarne *scriptorium. The only surviving illustrated manuscript which predates these is the Book of Currow (Dublin, Trinity Coll. Lib.) which may have come from the same source or from Ireland. In terms of splendour the Book of *Kells (Dublin, Trinity Coll. Lib.) of the late 8th century bears comparison with the Lindisfarne Gospels. It was most probably made at Iona just before that monastery migrated to Kells for safety from increasingly devastating raids in the early years of the 9th century. The period from about 650 to 750 was one of great intellectual activity in Northumbria. The Codex *Amiatinus (Florence, Bib. Laurenziana), the oldest extant manuscript of the Latin Vulgate, was produced at the double monastery of Monkwearmouth/Jarrow. Also the Venerable Bede (*c.*673–735) whose many writings culminate in his famous history (*Historia Ecclesiastica Gentis Anglorum*) of 731, and Alcuin (735–804) who was one of the major figures in the Carolingian Renaissance at the court of Charlemagne, both came from the area. But the Norse invasions of the next two centuries and their eventual conquest of all northern England, meant that this fertile milieu could not last.

The major southern English manuscripts which have survived appear to be mid-8th century. The very grand Codex Aureus (Stockholm, Royal Lib.), the Barberini Gospels (Vatican Lib.), the Canterbury Bible (London, BL), like the Codex Aureus, a very rich manuscript with purple pages and gold lettering, probably all came from southeast England. The full-page Evangelist 'portrait' of S. Mark and the Canon Tables (*see* EUSEBIAN CANON) in the Canterbury Gospels blend clear influences from Mediterranean examples with interlacings of traditional Anglo-Saxon type, and may have been inspired by the Carolingian court school where Alcuin became active in the latter part of the 8th century. The Codex Aureus shows the emergence of a compromise between pattern-making and a more naturalistic rendering of the human figure in the Evangelist 'portrait' of S. John, and also an abandonment of the elongated beast-forms in favour of more compact animal forms, a stylistic change borne out in the metalwork of the period and also found in the stone sculpture surviving from the late 9th century.

The other important art of the period is sculpture. In the north, the only early survivors are the fragments of a wooden coffin, incised with effigies of Christ and the Virgin and Child, made for the translation of the body of S. Cuthbert in 698 from his tomb in Lindisfarne to Durham Cathedral (Cathedral Treasury) and some fragments of rudimentary carvings of the 7th century at Hexham (in the Abbey) which may in fact be Roman. The most notable pieces of monumental sculpture are the *standing crosses—though the dating of these is controversial and ranges from the 7th to the 9th centuries. The two major northern examples are the Ruthwell cross (Ruthwell, Dumfriesshire) and the Bewcastle cross (Bewcastle, Cumbria), which are dated between 750 and 850. Both have important figure sculpture, of which the Ruthwell cross is the finer, more extensive, and iconographically richer. Large numbers of such crosses survive, mostly in the north, some with scrolls, some with plants, or with fantastic birds or beasts entwined in their convoluted tails. Some have figure sculpture on one or two sides, the others having scroll decoration.

The Norse invasions, which began as early as 856 as devastating raids in search of plunder, finally became a settlement with York as its capital. The transition from paganism to Christianity is marked by such odd monuments as the late 9th- or early 10th-century Gosforth cross, Cumberland, which is carved with both the Crucifixion and with scenes from pagan mythology indicating some local syncretism. In the south there are few significant surviving sculptures that compare with these crosses or the manuscripts of the 9th century.

In 878 King Alfred's division of England with the Danes brought peace as well as greater support for learning, law, religion, and language, but unfortunately, except for the Alfred Jewel (Oxford, Ashmolean), no outstanding works of art from his reign (871–99) survive. The jewel is pear-shaped, of gold, enamel, and crystal, and its pierced gold frame is inscribed *Aelfred mec heht gewyrcan* ('Alfred had me made'). Within the frame is a crystal covering an enamel of a man holding two sceptres probably representing Christ in Majesty. The mount ends in a beast's mouth, gripping a socket, which may have held a staff. Alfred's three successors reconquered the Danelaw and achieved briefly a unified kingdom, which foundered under renewed Viking invasions, ending with the election of the Dane, Canute (1017–35) as king. During the 10th century Winchester had become the main cultural centre and capital, partially as a result of the religious revival and reorganization which began with the introduction into England of the monastic reforms emanating from *Cluny. The earliest important manuscript was a copy of Bede's *Life of S. Cuthbert* (Cambridge, Corpus Christi Coll.) which has a full-page painting of King Athelstan (Alfred's son) presenting the volume to S. Cuthbert, when he visited the new monastery at Chester-le-Street *c.*934. It is the earliest presentation picture in English art. The old interlacings and spiral patterns are now replaced with Carolingian-inspired acanthus leaf ornament that also appears on magnificent embroideries, such as the stole and maniple of S. Cuthbert (made between 909 and 916; Durham Cathedral Treasury).

The glory of the Winchester *scriptorium is the 10th-century *benedictional of S. Aethelwold (London, BL), which set standards of design and workmanship which spread into all the major scriptoria of the Anglo-Saxon world and influenced English illumination up to the 12th century in Winchester, Canterbury, and Peterborough; although in the 11th century draughtsmanship became more lively and fluid as is seen in the copies of the *Utrecht Psalter (London, BL), which was made in England. It appears that even the Norman Conquest in 1066 made little difference to the course of English manuscript production, though in some ways the upheaval impeded the more rapid spread of Continental Romanesque. Major pieces of sculpture are few; the little angels in St Lawrence, Bradford-on-Avon; the eroded Crucifixion at Romsey Abbey, Hampshire, where the hand of God the Father over Christ's head is possibly derived from Carolingian example. The most interesting carvings are the small ivories or whalebone reliefs, such as the whalebone 'Franks Casket' (Northumbrian, *c.*700, London, BM, and Florence, Mus. Naz.), which has a strange mixture of scenes such as the Adoration of the Magi, Romulus and Remus, the capture of Jerusalem by the Emperor Titus, and the story of Wayland the Smith, together with runic inscriptions. One of the most interesting ivories is of the *Last Judgement* (late 8th or early 9th cent., London, V & A), which is the earliest representation of the subject in the West, where the damned shown as being swallowed by *Leviathan in Hell - a form which became constant in English illumination but was not adopted on the Continent for a considerable time. A fine walrus ivory *Crucified Christ* (late 10th cent., London, V & A) which was made into part of a reliquary crucifix with enamels of the *Evangelist Symbols may be the one recorded as given by King Athelstan to the shrine of S. Cuthbert at Chester-le-Street.

Very little survives of Anglo-Saxon building—because the Normans replaced many of the churches in forms closer to the *Romanesque to which they were accustomed. Even the major Saxon cathedrals, established in rural areas, were rebuilt on urban sites following a canon of the Council of London in 1075 by the Norman Archbishop of Canterbury, Lanfranc. That there were once many Anglo-Saxon churches is shown by Domesday Book, where most of the settlements recorded in 1086 as having existed before the Conquest are mentioned as having a priest, and it may be assumed that therefore he had a church. The remains of excavated ground-plans (Reculver in north Kent, North Elmham in Norfolk, Old Winchester Cathedral) and fragments of surviving buildings suggest that even though many of the Saxon buildings were demolished by their Norman conquerors, Saxon architecture was already in the process of evolving towards the Romanesque of northern France. This is further evidenced by the rebuilding of Westminster Abbey in the 'Norman' style by King Harold before 1066. The earliest churches were probably of wood: the mid-7th-century Lindisfarne was built of logs and thatched with reeds; St Andrew's, Greenstead-juxta-Mare (Essex), is the only surviving wooden church (only the walls are original, the roof has been rebuilt) with walls of tree trunks rounded on the outside, flat inside, and tongue-and-grooved together. The ground-plan of the 6th-century Reculver shows that it began as a simple rectangular *nave with an *apsidal chancel; it may have had a narthex or porch at the entrance, and the *chancel was divided from the nave by two columns (or piers). In the 8th century it was enlarged by the addition of 'porticus'— these were not *aisles but tomb chambers ranged round the outside of the building. SS Peter and Paul, Canterbury, begun in 597, had a similar ground-plan with porticus, used for royal burials. The mid-7th century Bradwell-juxta-Mare (Essex) survived as a barn, and is probably the best pointer to what Anglo-Saxon churches were like in S. England—a rectangular nave, which excavation has shown once had an apsidal chancel and porticus. The grandest surviving church of the end of the 7th century is Brixworth (Northamptonshire), which has the same arrangement of a single nave and an apsidal east end, originally divided from the nave by triple arches borne on columns (now opened up and replaced by a single Gothic arch). The Saxons traded widely—as evidenced by garnets present in the Staffordshire Hoard that originate from Sri Lanka—and so it would be that this type of design may have been influenced by Byzantine churches more than local exemplars. Other more southerly Anglo-Saxon churches are Deerhurst (Gloucestershire, late 9th–10th cent.), Worth (Sussex, 11th cent.), the very grand St Mary, Stow (Lincolnshire, mid-11th cent.), once an abbey, and St Bene't, Cambridge, 11th cent.), though only fragments of the original churches have survived later rebuildings. The tower and chancel arch of Earls Barton (Northamptonshire, early 11th cent.) alone survive of the original church; the tower is remarkable for its characteristic Anglo-Saxon features: 'long-and-short' work—the stones of the quoins are set alternately horizontally and vertically—long pilaster strips, triangular 'arcading', and stumpy window balusters bulging in the middle. St Lawrence, Bradford-on-Avon (Wiltshire, 11th cent.), survived by being used as a cottage; it is stone built, consists of two chambers, the small rectangular chancel being divided from the high box-like nave by a narrow entrance arch. It is notable also for the round-headed blind arches on the outside, and for two fine carved angels high above the chancel arch, which may once have been part of a Crucifixion. The tower of St Mary's church at Sompting (Sussex) was built at the beginning of the 11th century and, although it may have been remodelled since, it is currently thought that the 'Rhenish helm' roof was retained from its original Anglo-Saxon form.

Of the northern group of churches only parts survive. Perhaps the best preserved are the porch and part of the tower of Monkwearmouth (Sunderland, built in 674), the late 7th-century crypts of S. Wilfred's two abbeys at Hexham (Northumberland) and Ripon (Yorkshire, now Cathedral), Escomb (Durham, late 7th cent.), and Barton-upon-Humber (North Lincolnshire, late 10th cent.), where the tower preserves the pilaster strips and arcading, both triangular and round-headed, and one of the two chapels once attached to it. The characteristics of Anglo-Saxon architecture are: 'long-and-short' work; narrow naves with projecting chambers; square-ended or apsidal chancels; few windows set high up; narrow doorways with very plain imposts; triangular-headed windows and 'arcading'; and the short bulging columns often placed in wall openings.

Anna The wife of *Tobit and mother of Tobias.

Anna, the prophetess The 84-year-old widow who witnessed the *Presentation of Christ in the Temple (Luke 2: 22–38). She is represented as a very old woman, along with *Simeon, in pictures of this subject: there is also a painting by Rembrandt (Amsterdam, Rijks.), which is thought to be a portrait of his mother as the Prophetess, studying the Scriptures.

Anna Selbdritt (Ger. Anna third part) There is no English equivalent for this (Ital. Anna metterza, Fr. Anne Trinitaire), which is a description of an image of *S. Anne with Mary seated on her lap, holding the Christ Child on hers. The iconography is distantly connected with Byzantine *Madonna types known as Nikopoia or Hodegetria and was developed naturalistically in Italy in e.g. Masaccio's *Madonna and Child with S. Anne* (Uffizi) or Leonardo da Vinci's versions in London (NG) and the Louvre. In turn these developed into a family group, such as the Holy Family, and extended family groups, known in German as *Die heilige Sippe.* (*see* KINSHIP OF CHRIST.)

Anne (Anna), Saint Anne and Joachim, traditionally the parents of the Virgin Mary, are not mentioned in the Bible, but a long account is given in various *Apocryphal Gospels, some of early date. The principal sources of the legend are the 'Protevangelium of James', the Pseudo-Matthew, and the 'Gospel of the Birth of Mary'; it is likely that they started from the story of the birth of Samuel (NRSV 1 Sam. 1: Vg. 1 Reg.; Douay 1 Kings) which tells how the childless Anna (Hannah) prayed for a son and promised to dedicate him to the Lord. The story of Joachim and Anne was very popular in the Middle Ages and later versions occur in the *Historiale* section of *Vincent of Beauvais's **Speculum Majus*, and also in the **Golden Legend.* Early representations of Anne with the child Mary as a kind of parallel to the Madonna and Child can be found in Sta Maria Antiqua in Rome (8th cent.) and the cult was known even earlier in the East—the Emperor Justinian dedicated a church to S. Anne *c.*550, and images are known to have existed in the 8th/9th century. Two paintings by Raniero di Ugolino, of 1285/90, in Pisa Museum are of Anne with the child Mary and of the Madonna and Child with small scenes from Anne's legend. The earliest cycle in the West is perhaps that on the capitals of the 12th-century west portal of Chartres Cathedral. The main elements of the story in the Apocryphal sources are: Joachim's offering rejected in the Temple because he was childless; his withdrawal to the wilderness with his flocks and shepherds; Anna's sorrow, and the angel who appeared to her and promised that she should have a child, and who also appeared to Joachim; their meeting at the Golden Gate of the Temple; the birth of Mary and her dedication to the Temple at the age of 3, where she was received by the High Priest Zacharias and walked alone up seven (later fifteen) steps to him; when she was about 14 the High Priest Zacharias was told by an angel to instruct widowers to bring rods to the Temple, to determine who should have responsibility for her; Joseph's rod blossomed (or had a dove fly from it) but he was reluctant to take charge of her. In the end he did, but would not live with her, and she was given the task of weaving the purple thread for the veil of the Temple. Then the *Annunciation occurred, and the rest of the Gospel narrative follows from there. Three major fresco cycles of the 14th century depict most of these scenes—they are Giotto's series in the Arena Chapel, Padua (*c.*1306–13), and its derivatives by Taddeo Gaddi and Giovanni da Milano, both in Sta Croce, Florence. Later accretions to the story include Anne teaching Mary to sew, or to read, which may be an English 13th-century invention, and was popular in the 17th century. The *Golden Legend*, following the *Speculum Historiale*, adds that Mary ascended fifteen steps in the Temple, that being the number of the 'Gradual Psalms' (119–33 in the Vg.: AV 120–34); and the extraordinary story that Anne was married

a

twice more after Joachim's death and had a daughter by each husband, each named Mary—i.e. the 'three Maries', the Virgin Mary, Mary Cleophas, and Mary Salome. The other Maries had children, thus producing a large number of relations for Christ, including many who became His *Apostles. Representations of all these people are known as the *Holy Kinship (Ger. 'Heilige Sippe') and are derived from the *Anna Selbdritt type: some have as many as fifteen or twenty figures. These ended abruptly in the 16th century, partly because *Luther attacked them specifically, but mainly because they were condemned by the Council of *Trent, as being inappropriate to the doctrine of the *Immaculate Conception. *See also* KINSHIP OF CHRIST.

Annunciation, the The name is used to refer to one of the most significant moments in the Christian story: the appearance of the angel to *Mary. The occasion of the *Incarnation is described in S. Luke's Gospel (1: 26–38): '. . . the angel Gabriel was sent by God . . . to a virgin . . . The virgin's name was Mary.' After greeting her, he said, '" . . . The Lord is with you". She was much perplexed . . . and wondered what sort of greeting this might be. The angel said, " . . . Do not be afraid, Mary, for you have found favour with God . . . you will conceive in your womb, and bear a son, and you will name him Jesus." . . . Mary said to the angel, "How can this be, since I am a virgin?" The angel said to her, "The Holy Spirit will come upon you and the power of the Most High will overshadow you" . . . Then Mary said, "Behold the handmaid of the Lord; let it be with me according to your word."'

When the date of Christmas was fixed in Rome at 25 December, in 336, it followed logically that the Feast of the Annunciation should be nine months earlier, on 25 March. It has always been a major Feast, whether regarded as the Incarnation of Christ or as a feast of Mary. It was celebrated in Constantinople *c.*430, and was universal by the 8th century. It is one of the most frequent subjects of Christian art, and probably goes back to the *catacombs: a very damaged wall-painting in the Catacomb of Priscilla may be the earliest representation (?4th cent.), but it is not certain that it is the Annunciation—*Bosio, who discovered it, did not recognize it as such. There is a similar painting in the Catacomb of SS Peter and Marcellinus, but a mosaic in Sta Maria Maggiore, Rome, of 432–40, certainly represents it. See the rendering in weft-faced compound twill in polychrome silk from 8th–9th-century-Egypt or Syria or Constantinople, in the Vatican Museums, Vatican City.

In the *Rabbula Gospels the figures of Mary and the angel occupy margins on either side of the composition given to the *Canon tables, the latter's contents as it were embodying the two principals' exchanges and their divine subject. A similar reliance on the Biblical text 'an angel sent from God' is seen in compositions showing the Court of Heaven first dispatching and later receiving back the angel messenger.

Later, however, various elements from the *Apocryphal Gospels (the *Protevangelium of James, the *Pseudo-Matthew) had been added to the Gospel account, giving rise to iconographical variations. The account in the Protevangelium describes how a council of Jewish priests decided to make a new veil for the temple, and various colours of thread were allocated to seven virgins, Mary being given 'the true purple and the scarlet', and she began to spin the scarlet. She went out to draw a pitcher of water and heard a voice saying, 'Hail, you that are highly favoured', but returned in fear to the house, and began to spin the purple thread. Then the angel appeared and delivered his message, after which 'she made the purple and the scarlet and brought them to the priest. And the priest blessed her and said: Mary, the Lord God has magnified your name . . . '.

These accretions were very popular in the East, and many icons show Mary with a spindle in her left hand. In the West, the apocryphal stories were officially frowned on (especially by *S. Jerome) and so Luke's narrative is the norm, with Mary frequently shown seated and reading. The text she reads is usually Isaiah (8: 14): 'Ecce virgo concipiet, et pariet filium . . . ' (Behold, a virgin shall conceive and bear a son . . .). In Eastern Byzantine and Russian icons Gabriel is usually on the right, whereas Western paintings have the opposite (it is an interesting fact that all but one of El Greco's Annunciation paintings have Gabriel on the 'wrong' side).

In the Arena Chapel in Padua, *Giotto painted a fresco cycle of the Life of Christ and of the Virgin which begins on the chancel arch with the sending of Gabriel by God, followed by two separate paintings of Gabriel, on the left of the arch, and Mary, on the right: the decision in Heaven to send Gabriel comes from yet another source, the **Meditationes Vitae Christi*. The presence of God is usually indicated by a small figure or just a hand

(*Dextera Dei), from which rays of light reach to the head of Mary (it was suggested that, as she heard the word of God, she conceived). From about 1300 the rays, which usually also have the dove of the Holy Spirit, may instead have a tiny figure of a child carrying a cross. This, which may derive from *S. Bonaventura, is theologically unacceptable and was discouraged, because it suggests that Christ did not take His human form from Mary. Nevertheless, German and Flemish examples continue into the 15th century at least (Master Bertram's Grabow Altar, 1379/83, Hamburg Kunsthalle; Master of Flémalle, Merode Altar, early 15th cent., New York, Met. Mus.). Other symbolic attributes include the lily (purity) in a pot, or held by Gabriel; the earliest example being perhaps the small panel by *Duccio (London, NG) from the *Maestà* painted for Siena Cathedral (1308–11). The *Annunciation* by Simone *Martini (1333: Uffizi) shows the lily in the centre of the picture, and is an early example of the Annunciation as the principal subject of a major altarpiece. In more realist pictures painted in the North in the 15th century, the lily appears with other symbols of virginity, such as the ray of light shining through a glass window (Jan van Eyck, Washington, NG), or a flask of pure water (Memlinc, Lehman Coll., New York; Fra Filippo Lippi, Florence, San Lorenzo), both of which symbolize the intact virginity of Mary. The large *Annunciation* of 1486 by Carlo Crivelli (London, NG) contains a rich collection of symbolical attributes, including the stoppered water-flask, the peacock of immortality, and the apple of the Fall.

The antithesis *Adam/Christ and Eve/Mary was also popular, and French cathedrals (Amiens, Chartres) have small reliefs of the *Fall of Man* below statues of the Annunciation—the beginning of Redemption with the reason for its need.

A late example of elaborate symbolism occurs in two early paintings by *Rossetti, *The Girlhood of Mary Virgin*, 1848–9, and *Ecce Ancilla Domini!*, 1850, both in London, Tate Gallery. The former was exhibited with two of Rossetti's sonnets explaining the symbolism.

Among more recent treatments note can be taken of David Jones (*c.*1903, National Museum of Wales, Cardiff); Paula Modersohn-Becker (1905, Vatican Collection of Modern Art, Rome); Oskar Kokoschka (1911, Museum am Ostwall, Dortmund, Germany); Maurice Denis (1913, Fine Art Museum, Tourcoing, France); Edward Meli (1950, Papua New Guinea); Brice Marden (1978, series of panels dispersed); Joseph Nuttgens (1986, St Matthew's, Addis Ababa); Clive Hicks-Jenkins (2004, Llandaff Cathedral, Wales). (*See also* MARY and *CHRIST.)

ansate *See* TABULA ANSATA.

antechapel The outer portion of a chapel, usually separated from the main portion by a screen, serving as an antechamber to the chapel itself. They are a frequent feature of college chapels.

antependium (Lat. hanging before) A veil or hanging in front of an *altar, with varying names: *pallium altaris*, *paramentum*, frontal, pall. Such hangings have been in use since about the 4th century in Rome, when the tombs of martyrs were removed from catacombs to basilicas. These altars gave access to the tombs beneath by an opening or *confessio*, and to protect them from dirt, dust, and irreverent curiosity a veil or hanging was attached to the front of the altar. By the 7th and 8th centuries rich stuffs were customary, often decorated with gold embroideries. From the 8th century onwards antependia were often made of metal—gold, silver-gilt, and enamels either with movable panels to give access to the tomb below, or merely as a more than usually magnificent ornament to the altar. One celebrated example is the mid-9th-century gold antependium made for St-Denis (outside Paris), which by the 15th century had been converted into a *reredos. It was destroyed during the French Revolution, but is known from a painting by the Master of S. Giles (*c.*1500, London, NG). Other golden altar frontals include the one made in 1022/4 for Basle Cathedral (now Paris, Cluny Mus.), the one in the Aachen Cathedral Treasury, the mid-14th-century one made for the cathedral at Monza (N. Italy), and the very grand Danish gilt-bronze ones—one from Lisbjërg of *c.*1140, consisting of an elaborate figured frontal, a low retable with a crucifix of *c.*1100, crowned by an arch supporting a cresting with a group of seven figures within it, two others with *repoussé* figures—one from Ølst of 1150/60 and the other from Odder of *c.*1200—all three in the Copenhagen Nationalmuseet. A further example of 1170 is in the church at Lyngsjö. The Silver Altar (Florence, Mus. dell'Opera), made for the Baptistery in Florence between 1366 and 1480 in silver, silver-gilt, and enamels, includes an antependium, and the *Pala d'Oro in Venice may have started as one before being transformed into a *reredos. The Golden Altar of Sant'Ambrogio, Milan, includes an antependium.

Antependia, or frontals, reached their present form in the 13th century, when they were made of materials which matched the vestments and other altar-furnishings, and were of the appropriate liturgical colour for the season. Their use declined in the 16th century, when carved or painted antependia came into vogue. In the 17th century in Italy, when the elaborate Neapolitan altars with their superb *pietra dura* decorations of inlaid marble intarsia work became fashionable, the permanent nature of the colourful decoration made any form of movable frontal unnecessary.

The Anglican rules of 1603 ordered that 'the altar should be covered during divine service with a carpet of silk or other decent stuff, as should be thought meet by the Bishop'. This was in fact a pall, which entirely covered the altar, hanging to the ground on all sides. Many Anglican churches, however, still use the frontal fixed to the altar.

Anthemios A 6th-century Greek geometer was born at Tralles, now Aydin in Turkey. In 532 the church of Hagia *Sophia in Constantinople was burned down in a riot and the Emperor Justinian commissioned Anthemios to rebuild it. This he did, with help from Isidoros of Miletus, between 532 and 537, producing the greatest masterpiece of Byzantine architecture and the inspiration of countless later Orthodox churches. The church of SS Sergius and Bacchus, also in Constantinople, may well have been a trial essay. Anthemios died sometime before 558.

Anthony *See* ANTONINUS, SAINT.

Antichrist This is the name given in the Bible to the false prophet who will lead many astray with false miracles until he is finally defeated by the Archangel Michael (*see* ANGELS AND ARCHANGELS), and his followers are consumed by fire. This will be followed by the Second Coming of Christ. The key passages in the NT are in Matt. 24; Mark 13; and Luke 21, but the actual name occurs only twice in the New Testament, in 1 John 2: 18–22, and 2 John 7. These references are confusing in that they refer to one and several Antichrists—'As you have heard that antichrist is coming, so now many antichrists have come . . .'. Other passages thought to refer to him are 2 Thess. 2: 3–12 and several in the book of Revelation. Sometimes he is equated with Satan, and sometimes with one of his angels, and, from early times, with humans such as the persecuting Emperors Nero and Caligula. About 1526 a series of woodcuts produced in *Cranach's shop under the influence of *Luther equated him with the Pope, an identification still current in some circles. The *Signs of the end of the world include his false miracles—raising the dead, rebuilding the Temple of Jerusalem—and the best-known example in painting is the fresco by *Signorelli in Orvieto Cathedral, which shows him as long-haired, in a parody of the traditional type of bearded Christ. In some medieval examples he is shown as one-eyed or with one eye larger than the other.

antiminsion or **antimension** (Gk. instead of a table) A consecrated altar-cloth used in the Eastern Church (*see* LITURGICAL OBJECTS). It is made of linen or silk and is about 18 inches square; on it are embroidered or painted representations of the Entombment, or scenes of the Passion, or the Instruments of the Passion. It is always consecrated by a bishop, in a rite similar to that used for the consecration of a fixed altar, and has sewn into it a relic or relics of a saint set in a type of cement so that it can serve as a portable altar on an unconsecrated table. Normally, it is used like a *corporal in the Western Church, but in that case it has a second corporal (*eileton*) under it, and when not in use it lies folded on the altar. Its use dates from the early 9th century.

antiphonal, an (antiphoner) This is the largest kind of *liturgical book, also called a chorale or office book. It is used to direct the choir, particularly when two or more choirs chant alternate verses. The introduction of antiphonal chanting has been credited to Pope Gregory the Great (590–604), but there is evidence of earlier use.

These books are often enormous, with huge illuminated initials. Many were produced in Italy from the 12th to the 15th centuries; few have been found outside Italy, and those that have are usually of Italian origin. Bologna was an important centre of book-production for about 150 years, and many antiphonals are in Bologna (Mus. Civico), or centres such as Modena, Venice, and Siena. Unfortunately, many of these magnificent books have been dismembered and the initials cut out to be treated as paintings in their own right.

antitype *See* TYPOLOGY.

Antoninus, Saint Archbishop of Florence (1389–1459), entered the Dominican Order at the age of 16. He worked in many parts of Italy, but returned to Florence in 1436, where he took over the abandoned convent of San Marco, which, between 1437 and 1452, was rebuilt by Michelozzo, an associate of Donatello, with the support of Cosimo de' Medici, to rehouse some Dominicans from their house in Fiesole, on the hill overlooking Florence. There he probably first met Fra *Angelico, who moved to San Marco in 1441 to direct the workshop responsible for the artistic work of the house, and to decorate it with an elaborate series of frescoes including some in a cell kept specially for Cosimo to retreat to. Antoninus was canonized in 1523, but 15th-century pictures often show him with a halo. There is a fresco cycle of his life in San Marco (16th–17th cent.), but two important paintings are non-Florentine—Lorenzo Lotto's altarpiece in the Dominican church of SS Giovanni e Paolo, Venice, and Luini's in London (Courtauld Gall.).

Antony Abbot, Saint (Antony of Egypt) (*c.*251/2–356), was born in Egypt. His *Life* was written by S. Athanasius, a contemporary. He retired to the desert *c.*285, but other hermits came to him and he is thus considered as the founder of monasticism, although he never actually founded an Order—the Antonites were founded about 750 years after his death (see below). The **Golden Legend* recounts that he was driven to flee to the desert by the fate of two Christian youths during the persecution by the Emperor Decius, and the fate of one of these youths has been transferred in greater elaboration to Antony. Thus in the desert he was tempted by demons, which form the subject-matter of most representations of him. These fall into two classes: horrible and fantastic subhuman creatures often physically assaulting him, as in works by *Bosch and *Grünewald; and more straightforward temptation by lewd women (who, however, reveal their true nature by a cloven hoof or two little horns sprouting from their foreheads). The former type was especially popular in N. Europe and lasted well into the 16th century. The second begins in the 13th century and, from the mid-15th, the women become progressively more nude. This type was current up to the 19th century. At the age of 90 Antony visited the even older *S. Paul the Hermit in the desert, guided by a centaur and a satyr, and a raven brought them bread; when Paul died Antony buried him, assisted by two lions. These two episodes occur frequently, and the visit is shown on the earliest known representation, a relief on the 8th-century Ruthwell cross in Scotland: many Irish High *crosses also have this and the *Temptation*. His relics are said to have been taken to Byzantium and thence to France, where they were in Vienne in Provence by *c.*960. In 1095 a French nobleman's son was cured of 'S. Anthony's fire' (erysipelas or a form of ergotism), and he and another man founded an Order, the Hospitallers of S. Antony or Antonites (Antonians), to provide hospitals for sufferers from this and other nervous and dermatological diseases. The Order was extremely successful and lasted until the 18th century, when it was absorbed into the Knights Hospitallers of *Malta, and the French branch was dissolved in the Revolution. The iconography of S. Antony is closely bound up with this Order, and he is usually represented in their habit of a black robe with a small cowl and a leather belt. He is shown as an old man with a T-shaped crutch, often made into a *Tau cross, and he also has a small bell and a pig (Pisanello in London, NG)—these last being taken over from the Antonites, who had the right to graze pigs freely and used a bell when seeking alms for their hospice. He is also shown with fire—S. Anthony's fire—but this is rarer. The greatest work of art associated with the Antonites is Grünewald's Isenheim Altar (Colmar, Mus.), but there are several panels from a dispersed polyptych by Sassetta in Berlin, Washington, New York, and elsewhere, and fragments of an altarpiece by Veronese are in Edinburgh (NG), London (Dulwich Gall.), and Ottawa.

Antony of Padua, Saint (1190/5–1231) The patron saint of Padua, he was a contemporary of *S. Francis. He was born in Lisbon, perhaps of Spanish parents. He joined the Augustinian Canons *c.*1210 (1214?), was ordained at Coimbra *c.*1219 and, deeply moved by relics of five Franciscans martyred in Morocco, he obtained permission to transfer to the Franciscans in 1220, and went to Africa as a missionary. Illness forced him to leave, and he returned to Europe via Sicily. He went to Assisi, and became a peripatetic

a

preacher in N. Italy, taught at Bologna, 1223–5, laying the foundations of the Franciscan theological school, and preached in S. France, 1225–7, against heresy. He was made his Order's Minister for the whole of Emilia, in N. Italy, from 1227 to 1230, settled in Padua in 1230 and continued to preach to huge crowds, notably from a platform in a walnut-tree (pictured in Lazzaro Bastiani: *S. Antony in the Walnut-tree*, Venice, Accad., 15th cent.). He died on his way back to Padua, and was canonized in 1232.

The huge basilica of Sant'Antonio in Padua, known as 'Il Santo', was built by *c.*1350, and modelled basically on St Mark's, Venice, with a central dome and six smaller domes, a Gothic choir with an ambulatory, and nine radiating chapels. Much of the detail is Venetian Gothic, particularly in the decorative pointed arches. The High Altar of the Santo is largely devoted to him and was one of the major works by *Donatello in Padua (1446–50), but has been much altered. It has a large statue of him, along with other Franciscan saints, and four large bronze reliefs of some of the many miracles attributed to him—a new-born infant testifying to its jealous father in favour of its mother, unjustly accused of adultery; restoring the foot of a boy who had cut it off in penitence for having kicked his mother; discovering the heart of a miser in his money-chest; and the conversion of an unbeliever, whose mule knelt in adoration of the Host borne by the saint. There is also a cycle of frescoes by Titian (1511) and a fresco by Mantegna, showing S. Antony and *S. Bernardino kneeling on either side of the flaming *IHS monogram (1452).

There is no contemporary image of him. His iconography stresses two aspects of his life: he is shown with a lily for purity and a book for wisdom, most notably in the bronze statue by Donatello; with the Christ Child, for his charity, as in a painting by Murillo (Seville Cath.), a subject much favoured in Counter-Reformation and Baroque art, which gave rise to hosts of popular images; and with a flaming heart, for eloquence and Divine Love. In pictures where S. Antony and S. Francis are shown together the only difference between them is in S. Francis's stigmata, but there is sometimes confusion in popular imagery between him and *S. Antony Abbot, particularly if he is shown with a beard and even with a piglet. S. Antony is invoked in Italy as a charismatic healer and a helper-saint, including help with the arrival of letters and in finding lost objects (the last of almost universal appeal), for all of which a thank-offering for charity—'S. Anthony's bread'—should be made.

apes and monkeys These have been interpreted in a bewildering number of ways as symbolic *beasts, but in general they represent lewdness, greed, and the *Devil. The identification with the Devil was first made in the Latin translation of *Physiologus (?*c.*400). When chained they may symbolize a penitent sinner and when shown in pictures of the procession of the Magi they represent the penitent sinner finding the way to Christ. This may explain the prominent pair in the *Adoration* by Gentile da Fabriano (1423: Uffizi), and also perhaps the one in Dürer's engraving of the *Madonna and Child with a chained Monkey*.

Apocalypse, the This is the Vulgate and Douay name for the last book in the Bible, called 'The Revelation of S. John' in the AV and NRSV, and traditionally written by the Evangelist on the island of Patmos during a persecution, perhaps that of the Emperor Domitian in 95; but believed by many to be the work of a different John. It is one of a group of about twenty Apocalypses, or visions foretelling the Last Things, but is the only one accepted into the *Canon of Scripture. This acceptance came only gradually, and it was still rejected in the East for centuries after it had become canonical in the West, where subjects from it occur from the late 4th century. There is a splendid, but much damaged mosaic in Sta Pudenziana, Rome, of *c.*400, as well as others in early Roman churches. The Spanish Abbot *Beatus (d. 798) wrote a Commentary which was popular and widely copied up to the 13th century: the MSS set the iconography for about eighty subjects derived from the text, including such familiar themes as the *Adoration of the Lamb, the *Majestas Domini, the *Hetoimasia, *Alpha and Omega, the *Apocalyptic Woman, and about seventy-five other subjects illustrating the text literally. Some of the great French *tympana of the 11th and 12th centuries are based on the Beatus group of MSS, e.g. Moissac (1110–20) and the Portail Royal at Chartres (1145–70). Another group of MSS, perhaps English in origin, influenced the Angers tapestries (1377–82: Angers, Musée), which originally had ninety scenes, and was still influencing the *block-books of the 15th century. The *Bible Moralisée also has many Apocalypse illustrations. In 1498 *Dürer published his woodcuts, which compress several scenes into one illustration and omit others, but they are the definitive type for the future, since his powerful imagery impressed itself on all his successors. The illustrations to *Luther's Bible (1522), made in *Cranach's shop, show this, as does the window in Milan Cathedral (1481–1545), and, when Greek and Russian Orthodox artists began to illustrate the Apocalypse in the 16th century even they were affected by Dürer's imagery. Apocalypse imagery has frequently been drawn on after wars and conflicts: see, for example, the sgraffito murals (1964) by the Polish immigrant artist Adam Kossowski in St Benet's Chaplaincy, Queen Mary, University of London.

Among the most popular of the ninety or so possible subjects the following are frequently represented in art, many of them in Dürer's etchings of the *Apocalypse*: the twenty-four Elders; *Tetramorphs; the Lamb with the Book and Seven Seals; the Four Horsemen; the Opening of the Fifth Seal; the Archangel Michael and the Dragon (*see* ANGELS AND ARCHANGELS); the Whore of Babylon; John eating the Book; Satan and the Beast, and the New Jerusalem. The Last *Judgement, always a popular subject, was usually derived from several sources and only partly from the text of the biblical Book of Revelation. See Blair Hughes-Stanton (1933) wood engravings; Georg Meistermann (1954 fresco) St Alphons, Würzburg, Germany.

Apocalyptic Woman (the Woman clothed with the Sun, *Mulier amicta sole*) In the Apocalypse (Rev. 12: 1 ff.) 'A great portent appeared in heaven: a woman clothed with the sun, with the moon under her feet, and on her head a crown of twelve stars. She was pregnant and was crying out in birth pangs... And she gave birth to a son, a male child, who is to rule all the nations...'. The woman is usually interpreted as either *Mary, the child being Jesus, or as the Church, including the Synagogue. The twelve stars (perhaps the Apostles) and the moon led to the iconographical merging of the Apocalyptic Woman with the *Immaculate Conception—compare the woodcut from *Dürer's 1498 *Apocalypse* with Velázquez's *Immaculate Conception* and its companion, *S. John on Patmos*, which shows the vision from Rev. 12, both of *c.*1618 (London, NG).

Apocrypha (Gk. hidden [writings]) This word can be used in two different senses with reference to the OT (for NT Apocrypha *see* APOCRYPHAL GOSPELS). In English Protestant versions of the Bible (AV, NRSV) there may be a section between the Old and New Testaments called Apocrypha: these are properly the *Deutero-Canonical books accepted since the 4th century by the Greek and Latin Churches as part of the Old Testament, but rejected by the Reformers in the 16th century as not part of the Hebrew Bible. In the Vulgate, and in English translations of it, the Deutero-Canonical books are printed as part of the OT, but 3 and 4 Esdras and the Prayer of Manasses are printed as an appendix, following a ruling by the Council of *Trent. Many stories from the OT Apocrypha feature in works of art, e.g. *Tobit, *Judith and Holofernes, and *Susanna and the elders. There are also writings accepted by neither Catholics nor Protestants, such as the 'Assumption of Moses', which may also have been illustrated—e.g. in the lost frescoes from the Moses cycle in the *Sistine Chapel.

Apocryphal Gospels (Acts, Apocalypses) are all non-canonical writings associated with the NT (*see* APOCRYPHA above): they can be grouped, like the NT itself, under Gospels, Acts, Epistles, and Apocalypses, as well as *agrapha, or sayings attributed to Christ. Some date from as early as the late 1st to early 3rd centuries, but they have all been rejected from the *Canon of Scripture (mostly by *S. Jerome, though parts of the 'Protevangelium of S. James' are accepted in the Eastern Church), and it is important to distinguish between their religious orthodoxy and their very great significance for the arts, especially in the late Middle Ages. Many of these accounts were intended to mislead and contain heretical elements, but others arose from the simple desire to possess more detailed accounts of the lives and actions of Christ Himself, Mary, and the Apostles. The accounts vary from the frankly incredible to the reasonably possible, and soon became intertwined with the NT itself as they were absorbed into popular devotional literature, e.g. the **Golden Legend*. They are extremely important for medieval art and even in the later centuries episodes from them feature in works of art. Some of the most important are the so-called Infancy Gospels (e.g. the 'Protevangelium of James', the 'Gospel of Thomas', the 'Pseudo-Matthew'), which give an account of the life of Mary, including the names of her parents, Joachim and *Anne, and her presentation in the Temple at the age of 3, as well as detailed descriptions of the *Nativity and the midwives

*Salome and Zelomi. Details in the narrative of the *Assumption include the miraculous gathering of the Apostles at her death-bed and the cutting off of the hands of the unbelieving Jephonias from her bier. Other apocryphal writings include the letters of *Abgar; the 'Acts of Peter', with the story of Peter meeting Christ outside Rome (*Quo vadis?) and his return to Rome to be crucified head-downwards; the 'Acts of Pilate' (or 'Gospel of Nicodemus'), a Passion narrative with the names of the two thieves, Dismas and Gestas, and the centurion Longinus; and the 'Apocalypse of Paul', which Dante drew on for his descriptions of the torments of Hell in the *Inferno* in his poem of *La Divina Commedia* (begun *c.*1306).

Apostles (Gk. *apostoloi*, messengers) Out of His many disciples, Christ chose twelve to be the principal bearers of His Word. The twelve, named in Matt. 10: 2–4, are Simon called *Peter, his brother *Andrew, *James and *John the sons of Zebedee, *Philip, *Bartholomew, *Matthew the tax-collector, *James son of Alphaeus, Thaddaeus, also called *Jude, *Simon Zelotes, *Thomas Didymus 'the twin', and *Judas Iscariot. After Judas's suicide, *Matthias was elected in his place (Acts 1: 26). Later both *Paul and *Barnabas were called Apostles, and certain missionaries have also been so called because they took Christianity into new territories, e.g. S. Patrick, Apostle of Ireland. The variations in names in the NT are variant names, not differences of persons, e.g. Thaddaeus/Jude. The twelve chosen by Christ were all present at the Last Supper (Mark 26: 20), the remaining eleven witnessed the Ascension (Mark 33: 16), and with the addition of Matthias were in the Upper Room when the Holy Spirit came down upon them (Acts 2: 1) (*see* PENTECOST). Only two of the Apostles—John and Matthew—were also *Evangelists.

Representations of Christ with the Apostles almost always show twelve, although after the conversion of S. Paul there were thirteen until the martyrdom of S. James, *c.*AD 44. Usually it is Matthias who is left out. The earliest representation of them is in the 3rd/4th-century *catacomb of S. Calixtus, where there is a Last Supper with Christ reclining on the left of a half-moon-shaped table, the Apostles in a row behind it, ending with one reclining on the right; the same arrangement is also found in one of the 5th/6th-century mosaics in the nave of Sant'Apollinare Nuovo in Ravenna. The Apostles are also found on 4th-century sarcophagi; on that of Theodosius in Sant'Ambrogio, Milan (389), Christ is seated as a teacher with six Apostles on either side; on that of Titus Julius Gorgonius in Ancona Cathedral, Christ has only five Apostles on either side of Him as He hands the scroll of the Law to S. Peter, in one of the earliest representations of the *Traditio Legis which becomes the norm for the subject.

The original apse mosaic in Old St Peter's is known only from copies, but the composition is central to the design and iconography of many later apse mosaics. The apse is divided into two registers: in the upper one Christ in Majesty is seated in the centre, flanked by S. Peter on His right and S. Paul on His left, both holding scrolls and identified by inscriptions. Above Christ is a semicircular canopy known as the 'tent of the tabernacle', and from beneath His throne flow the four *Rivers of Paradise with deer drinking (Ps. 42 AV, NRSV; Vg. 41). In the centre of the lower register is the Lamb and the Chalice, approached on either side by six sheep, representing the Apostles, issuing from Jerusalem on the left and Bethlehem on the right. The original mosaic was restored by Innocent III in the late 12th century, and he inserted, on either side of the Lamb, himself as Pope and a woman identified as Ecclesia Romana.

The model was not followed slavishly, but many of its features are constants. For instance, in the apse of SS Cosmas and Damian in Rome, *c.*520–30, one of the most beautiful and least restored mosaics, Christ stands on a brilliant sunset beneath a circle of light, instead of the more ornate 'tabernacle', and only five sheep approach from either side, the two central ones having been destroyed. In the superb mosaic on the triumphal arch and in the apse of Sant'-Apollinare in Classe, outside *Ravenna, made just before 549, Christ in Majesty is in a roundel in the upper register, flanked by the Evangelist Symbols, while the twelve sheep of the Apostles issue, six a side, from cities, which though not labelled are the Jerusalem and Bethlehem of the prototype. One of the finest 4th-century mosaics in Rome is the apse of Sta Pudenziana, where Christ is seated with the Apostles ranged on either side of Him, below representations of Jerusalem and Bethlehem. In the sky above are the symbols of the Evangelists, but unfortunately this majestic composition was badly mutilated in the 16th century, and two Apostle figures were destroyed and two of the Evangelist Symbols damaged.

Sometimes the Apostles are named, as in the procession circling the roundel with the Baptism of Christ in the mid-5th-century mosaic in the Baptistery of the Orthodox in Ravenna and in the procession of Apostles below the gigantic figure of the Virgin in the apse of the 12th-century Cathedral at Torcello. From the earliest times, the Apostles are characterized as upright, bearded figures in long robes, bearing scrolls, but S. Peter is not shown with his traditional key until the 5th century, and S. Paul's sword appears later still, perhaps in the 10th-century mosaic on the tomb of Otto III (983) in the crypt of St Peter's, and does not become common before the 12th century; e.g. in the two figures of S. Peter with a key and S. Paul with a sword in the portal of Vézelay, in Burgundy, of 1120–30. One of the more unusual symbolic representations of the Apostles is in the 12th-century apse mosaic of San Clemente in Rome, where the cross of the crucified Christ has twelve doves incorporated in it. Another unusual scene is in the 5th/6th-century *Rossano Gospels, where, at the Institution of the Eucharist (the *Communion of the Apostles), two groups of six Apostles each approach Christ separately, one group to receive bread, the other wine.

Many Italian polyptychs from the 14th century onwards contain series of heads or half-lengths of the Apostles incorporated in their frames, notably in the *Maestà* by *Duccio (1308–11). The series of tapestries designed by Raphael in 1515–16 for the Sistine Chapel (now Vatican Mus.) are of subjects drawn from the Acts of the Apostles. There is also a large series of half-length 'portraits' of the Apostles by Rubens, the originals being now in Madrid (Prado), but which were extensively copied, and of which two sets of engravings were also made in Rubens's lifetime. Others are by El *Greco and Ribera.

apotheosis (Gk.) The ancient pagan custom of deifying emperors and other important personages after their deaths; Domitian (81–96) demanded to be deified in his lifetime. The custom may have influenced the Christian idea of canonization, but certainly the iconography affected Christian art—the relief on the base of the Column of Antoninus Pius (d. AD 161), in Rome, shows the Genius of the emperor as a winged youth soaring upwards, remarkably like an angel bearing the souls of the righteous.

apparels Panels of embroidery on the front, back, and sleeves of a *dalmatic, *amice, or some similar *vestment.

Appearances, Post-Resurrection *See* CHRIST.

apple Although the account of the Fall of Man in Gen. 3 does not mention any particular fruit as that of the Tree of Knowledge from which *Adam and Eve were forbidden to eat, the fruit has always been regarded as the apple. In pagan mythology the apple was highly prized—cf. the golden apples dropped by Atalanta, or the apple awarded to Aphrodite by Paris—and it is held that the coincidence that the Latin word *malum*, meaning evil, also means apple, led to the identification. Certainly, apples are represented in Early Christian art in the catacombs and on sarcophagi in connection with Adam and Eve and they became the usual symbol of the Fall. Because Christ is the Second Adam and Mary the Second Eve, paintings of the Madonna and Child sometimes show one or the other with an apple as a symbol of Redemption, overcoming sin, although a pomegranate also has the same significance. *See also* FLOWERS AND FRUIT.

apse (Lat. *apsis*) A semicircular or polygonal section of a church, usually giving off the choir or transepts, covered by a semi-dome or a sectional vault. In some large German churches there is often a second apsidal end at the west end of the nave.

aquamanile Originally (*c.*525) a basin to hold the water proffered by the subdeacon for the priest's ablutions during the Mass, and therefore the symbol of the subdiaconate. Many are recorded, but none seems to have survived, and the term became transferred to the ewer from which the water was poured. Many of these survive from the 12th century onwards, but most were probably used at table—i.e. were secular—since the shapes are those of lions, griffins, or even knights on horseback. Most are of bronze or pewter.

Aquinas *See* THOMAS AQUINAS, SAINT.

Ara Coeli (Lat. Altar of Heaven) Sta Maria in Aracoeli is a church on the Capitoline Hill in Rome. It stands on the Arx Capitolina, the centre of ancient Rome, near where the augurs prophesied. There may also have been a temple dedicated to Tanit, the 'Virgo Coelestis'. A church was perhaps there in the 7th century, and there was certainly a monastery by 731. It is said to be the spot where the Emperor Augustus had a vision of the Madonna and Child and heard the words 'Haec est ara coeli'—This is the altar of Heaven. This version of the story is first recorded in the **Mirabilia Urbis Romae*, *c.*1130. *See also* AUGUSTUS AND THE SIBYL.

Arbor Vitae *See* TREE.

arca (Lat. coffer, chest, also coffin) This word is used in Italian for a richly decorated free-standing tomb-chest, usually borne either on columns or caryatid figures, which serves as both a tomb and a shrine, usually for a saint. Examples are the Arca of *S. Dominic in San Domenico, Bologna, and that of *S. Peter Martyr in the Portinari Chapel of Sant'Eustorgio, Milan. The Arca di San Domenico was begun by Nicola Pisano in 1264 and the body of the saint, who died in Bologna in 1221, was placed in it in 1267, most of the work on the tomb having been done by Arnolfo di Cambio. In 1492, Niccolò dell'Arca, so called because of his connection with it, was employed to elaborate the upper part of the tomb, but he died in 1494 leaving the work unfinished. The three missing figures of an angel bearing a candlestick, and two small figures of SS Petronius and Proculus, were made by the young *Michelangelo in 1494. The angel figure was made to conform to the one by Niccolò dell'Arca, and is the only angel figure by Michelangelo to have wings. The small figure of S. Proculus was badly damaged and has been rather clumsily repaired.

S. Peter Martyr was murdered on his way from Como to Milan in 1252 and was buried in Sant'Eustorgio. The grand tomb-shrine was made in 1336–9 by the Pisan sculptor Giovanni di Balduccio. In 1462–8 Pigello Portinari, the agent in Milan for the Medici bank, built the centrally planned Portinari Chapel at the far end of Sant'Eustorgio as a grand setting for the Arca and also as a burial chapel for himself.

arcade A row of arches borne on either *columns or *piers. Normally, in a long-nave church, arcades run the length of the nave, choir, or the transepts, and support the upper storeys of the *elevation. In some churches there may be arcades introduced for decorative purposes, running along the walls of the nave or transepts, and these are often in double rows, with mixtures of plain stone and—in England—*Purbeck marble. Lincoln Cathedral is an example. Single wall-arcades often stand on bases large enough to serve as a rudimentary bench (hence the expression 'the weakest to the wall', since in medieval churches the congregation stood), but in, for instance, the Lady Chapel (*see* CHAPEL) at Ely Cathedral each arch encloses a seat, since the Lady Chapel may have doubled as the *chapter-house.

arch The type of arch used in an arcade of the kind described above may be a round-headed shape or a pointed shape. The first type is characteristic of Roman Classical (as in a Roman Triumphal Arch) and Romanesque architecture (as in the north transept of Winchester Cathedral). Such arches are **semicircular** and the supports for such an arch have to be very strong, since all the weight of the arch and its superstructure presses directly downwards. The second type (in which the **pointed arch** may have many different profiles) is a characteristic of Gothic architecture. The principle behind the pointed arch is that as a consequence of each side of the arch abutting against the other at its apex, it has a greater self-supporting quality and avoids the dead-weight characteristic of the semicircular arch. This profile also helps the weight of the superstructure to be deflected from the arch into the supporting *piers or *columns. The varying profiles of pointed arches are a good indication of the type of *Gothic architecture and the period in which the church was built. Large windows in the superstructure, and the use of *ribbed *vaulting, instead of the massive barrel vaults used with the semicircular arch, also reduced the weight and encouraged the use of *buttresses, particularly the flying buttresses of French Gothic, to support the structure from outside the building. One of the most frequently found profiles of window is the *lancet window, usually simple, tall, and narrow; the use of *tracery in the window caused their shapes to change and they became much larger so as to allow more tracery to be introduced.

Other shapes of arch are the **horseshoe arch**, where the bases of the arch are turned inwards, a form introduced by Visigoth builders in Spain, but which came to be associated with Islamic buildings. The arch itself might be either semicircular or pointed (examples are the mosque known as La

Mezquita, Cordoba, or Sta Maria la Blanca, Toledo). The **ogee arch** has a very complex profile rising through a double concave and convex curve to a sharp point. It is rare in the structural elements of churches, but is often found in secular buildings, screens, elaborate tombs (Edward II's in Gloucester Cathedral, for example), or details such as the crest over the choir window of Gloucester. If the upper part of the arch is made to lean forwards it is a **nodding arch** (the Lady Chapel, Ely Cathedral, is a good example, a form not found in England before the 14th century. A **relieving arch** is one raised over á window or a doorway to reduce the pressure on the *lintel by deflecting the weight of the superstructure away from the opening. These are used extensively in the Pantheon, Rome, 2nd century AD, to deflect weight away from the great niches in the interior, and they have the same function in all later architecture. A **strainer arch** may, in fact, be an arch, but is often an almost straight or flat section of masonry, designed to prevent the walls or piers on either side from leaning inwards. The most famous examples are the huge double-strainer arches spanning the crossing at Wells Cathedral built after the tower was made taller and heavier; the large double one across the east transept at Salisbury; or the straight ones each sustained by an arch across the tower crossing at Canterbury and at Salisbury. These are almost straight bridges of masonry, made very decorative to disguise their utilitarian function.

archaeology, Christian There are many written documents for the early history of the Church, from the Acts of the Apostles to *Eusebius and many more for the period up to the 6th century; but for centuries nobody was interested in the recovery and interpretation of physical artefacts and works of art as testimonies to the early Church, and to the way in which the early Christians lived and worshipped. The actual forms of church buildings, sarcophagi, mosaics, ivories, frescoes in the catacombs, and other evidence were all ignored until the 16th century, when controversy with the Protestants encouraged investigation of the physical evidence of the earliest centuries. The first to use this non-documentary evidence were probably Onofrio Panvinio (1529–68), in connection with Old St Peter's, and Alfonso Ciacconio (1540–99), but the first serious investigation of the *catacombs, unvisited for a thousand years, was made in the 17th century by *Bosio, followed, after a two-hundred-year interval, by de' *Rossi. By then archaeology had ceased to be exclusively concerned with Greek and Roman antiquity, and the huge increase in knowledge of Christian antiquities dates from the mid-19th century (Smith and Cheetham, *Dictionary of Christian Antiquities*, 2 vols., 1875–80, or Cabrol-Leclercq, *Dictionnaire d'Archéologie chrétienne*, 15 vols., 1907–53), when scientific excavations began in the Near East, Syria, N. Africa, and the Holy Land itself, which are still continuing.

archangel *See* ANGELS AND ARCHANGELS.

archbishop The first use of the term is 4th century—S. Athanasius spoke of himself and his predecessor as archbishops of Alexandria. Originally, the term 'metropolitan' was used for a bishop (*see* ORDERS, HOLY) appointed to a see and having a number of suffragan or assistant bishops under him, but as more cities acquired metropolitan status, a new term had to be found for the old metropolitans, and the ranks of *patriarch, *exarch, and archbishop were created. The two specific insignia of a Catholic archbishop are the *pallium and a cross with two transverse arms. He also wears distinctive *vestments: a violet cassock, a rochet with crimson facings, a violet cape (also called *almuce or mozzetta), and *biretta, though at certain seasons (Advent, Lent) the violet is changed to black with violet trimmings. He is entitled to have his cross carried before him (except in the presence of the Pope or a Cardinal Legate) with the Crucifixion depicted on it, and turned to face him as he follows.

architrave The straight beam extending from the top of one *column or *pier to the next, or from one side of a doorway to the other. In a door this is also called a *lintel.

arcosolium An arched niche or recess in a *catacomb, where tombs or sarcophagi (often of martyrs) were placed, the flat tops of which could serve as an *altar for a Mass, or for an *agape.

Arianism A heresy promulgated by Arius (d. 336) and condemned by the Councils of *Nicaea (325) and Constantinople (381). It held that the Three Persons of the Holy *Trinity are not coequal and coeternal, but that the Father preceded the Son ('There was a time when He was not'), and the Holy Spirit was inferior to both. Few surviving works of art can be related to this doctrine, but of them the most important is the Arian Baptistery in *Ravenna. Later representations of the Holy Trinity as a bearded old man, a bearded younger man, and (with biblical authority) the Holy Ghost as a dove, can be interpreted improperly as implying degrees of seniority. Eleven hundred years after Arius, in S. France, there are representations of God the Father and God the Son as exactly identical, e.g. in *Quarton's *Coronation of the Virgin* (1454) in Villeneuve-lès-Avignon. Jean Fouquet, in *The Hours of Étienne Chevalier* (*c.*1450/60: Chantilly) portrayed the *Trinity* as three identical enthroned figures.

Ark *See* NOAH.

Ark of the Covenant, the The Ark of the Covenant, in the Holy of Holies, represented for the Jews the Presence of God among them, and was their most sacred religious object and symbol. When the Jews left Egypt, under the leadership of *Moses, they had no sacred objects, except, probably, the symbols of local pagan deities among whom they had lived ever since they had migrated to Egypt in the time of Joseph, several centuries before. The Divine purpose of the Exodus was to create a Jewish nation, worthy of *Abraham and *Isaac, and to redeem them from the idolatory into which they had fallen—and into which they at first so readily relapsed.

The Ark, and the Holy of Holies in which it was kept, were made according to the instructions given by God to Moses on Mount Sinai, and is described in Exod. 25: 10 ff. Its purpose was to give the Jews a centre for worship, a sacred symbol, a place for sacrifices and ceremonies, together with an established priesthood, which would provide them with a definite religious centre, and because they were then a nomadic tribe constantly on the move, one which could be easily transported. Later, when God had given Moses the Law, and by this means an ordered community had been established, the Tables of the Law were kept in the Ark, so that they too became part of the religious life of the community. The dimensions of the Ark were, approximately, four feet long by three feet wide by three feet high; it was covered with gold, and carried by gold-covered poles passed through rings at each corner of the Ark. On the top of the Ark was the golden *Seat of Mercy with golden *cherubim on either side facing each other and spreading their wings over the Mercy-Seat. There was also to be a table of acacia wood with a raised edge, all covered with gold, to hold the shew-bread—the bread of sacrifice—which was to be placed before the Ark together with a golden seven-branched candlestick and a gold-covered table to be an Altar of Incense. There was also (Exod. 39) an *altar covered with gold, for the burnt offering, and curtains round the *tabernacle (Exod. 26) and a veil to close the Holy of Holies where the Ark itself was kept. This part of the Tabernacle was to be entered only by the High Priest.

There is no mention of a Temple, suggesting a fixed structure, before 1 Sam. 1: 3–9 (Douay 1 Kgs. 1: 3–9; Vg. 1 Reg. 1: 3–9) with its account of Hannah coming to the Temple at Shiloh to pray for a son. 'Now Eli the priest was sitting on the seat beside the doorpost of the temple of the Lord.' Hannah's prayers were answered, as Eli had predicted, and the child was Samuel. Later, in 1 Sam. 4: 3–11 (Douay 1 Kgs. 4: 3–9; Vg. 1 Reg. 4: 3–9), faced with a battle with the Philistines, the Israelites took the Ark of the Covenant to be a talisman against defeat, but they lost the battle and the Ark was captured. The Philistines (1 Sam. 5: 1–5; Douay 1 Kgs. 5: 1–5; Vg. 1 Reg. 5: 1–5) took it to the temple of their god Dagon in Ashdod, but it destroyed the statue of the god; the Philistines then paraded it round the cities of Gath, but everywhere it was taken it wreaked such havoc that finally they sent it back with a peace offering. It was then taken to the house of Aminadab, where it remained for twenty years with Eleazar as its priest until David brought it to Jerusalem. While it was on the way there, the cart tipped and lest it should fall Uzzah put out his hand to steady it. For any unauthorized person to touch the Ark—even to preserve it from harm—was a sacrilege punishable by death. Uzzah was struck down by God immediately (2 Sam. 6: 7; Douay and Vg. 2 Reg./Kgs. 6: 7).

When David rejoiced and danced before the Ark (2 Sam. 6: 7; Douay and Vg. 2 Reg./Kgs. 6–7) there still was no Temple, so that it was once again in a tent, until Solomon (970–933 BC), after building the Temple, had the Ark brought into it (1 Kgs. 8; Douay and Vg. 3 Reg./Kgs. 8). According to these texts there was nothing in the Ark except the Mosaic Tables of the Law, but in Heb. 9: 4, S. Paul speaks of a pot of manna and *Aaron's 'rod which budded'. When Jerusalem was captured by Nebuchadnezzar (598 and 586 BC; 2 Kgs. 24: 10–16; Douay and Vg. 4 Reg./Kgs. 24: 10–16) the Ark was taken with the rest of the treasures of Solomon's *Temple to Babylon as spoil. Though the Jews were able to rebuild the Temple, because Cyrus, and after him Darius, kings of Persia, allowed the restoration of both city and Temple and returned to it much of the treasure taken by Nebuchadnezzar, there is no mention of a reconstruction of the Ark, although a Holy of Holies was apparently reconstituted. In art, representations of the Ark are rare, but there are paintings with imaginary reconstructions by *Poussin in the *Plague at Ashdod* and the *Destruction of Dagon's statue* (1630/1: Paris, Louvre); *The return of the Ark from captivity*, by the mid-17th-century French painter Sebastien Bourdon (London, NG); and *David dancing before the Ark* by the late 17th-century Neapolitan painter Luca Giordano (Lawrence, Univ. of Kansas).

The Ark of the Covenant is as rich in symbolism as *Noah's Ark. It is one of the symbols of Christ: the Seat of Mercy is a symbol of Christ as Judge, the Mosaic Tables of the Law are a symbol of Christ as Lawgiver and source of Justice, the offerings made before it symbolize the Eucharist. It is also a symbol of the Virgin, since she bore Christ within herself, as the Ark contained Divine Justice and the Covenant of Mercy.

Arma Christi (Lat. arms of Christ) Originally, this literally meant the weapons of Christ's victory over death, principally the Cross, Crown of Thorns, Nails, and Lance. A 4th-century sarcophagus (Vatican 171) has a *Chi-Rho monogram surrounded by the victor's laurel wreath over a cross, and an illustration in the *Utrecht Psalter (*c.*830) shows the Cross, Crown of Thorns, Lance, Scourge, and the Rod and Sponge. By about the 12th century the meaning of 'Arma' had become more heraldic and the Instruments of the Passion not only increase in number but also are shown on shields, sometimes borne by angels. The passion for relics caused an increase in number of Instruments, even including what was alleged to be the sword with which S. Peter cut off the ear of Malchus (cf. the column of the *Flagellation given to Sta Prassede in Rome in 1223). In addition to the Instruments, the Five Wounds of Christ also appear, often in the shorthand form of hands and feet and a heart pierced by a lance. Almost imperceptibly the Arma Christi image merges with the *imago pietatis, where several of the Instruments are shown distributed around the figure of the *Man of Sorrows, as in a painting by Lorenzo Monaco of 1404 (Florence, Accad.) or the fresco in Cell 26 of the friary of San Marco, Florence, by an assistant of Fra *Angelico (1440s). Mantegna's *Agony in the Garden* (*c.*1460/5: London, NG) is unusual in having five small angels bearing Instruments of the Passion, rather than the traditional chalice, in what is essentially a narrative scene.

Ars Moriendi (Lat. Art of Dying [Well]) A late 15th-century devotional work, designed to help the reader to make a good end. It is a variant on the *Dance of Death theme, probably derived mainly from a Netherlandish *block-book of *c.*1450 (London, BM) or from engravings by the Master E.S., who was active *c.*1450/67 in the Rhineland or Switzerland. Later, it was also produced as an ordinary printed book, with separate woodcuts, and was probably intended for priests (cf. BIBLIA PAUPERUM). Usually, there are eleven illustrations, five pairs of Faith, Despair, Impatience, Vainglory, and Avarice, with angels and devils contending for the dying man or woman's soul. The eleventh illustration shows the final triumph of the Guardian angel (*see* ANGELS AND ARCHANGELS) *'in the hour of death'*.

artophorion (Gk. bread-carrier) A small *tabernacle used in the E. Orthodox Church to contain the reserved Sacrament on or near the altar. Sometimes it takes the form of a silver dove suspended from the *ciborium, like some medieval *pyxes in the Western Church. *See also* AUMBRY, EUCHARIST, TABERNACLE.

Arts, the Liberal Secular education during the Middle Ages consisted of the Trivium, for the study of language (Grammar, Rhetoric, Dialectic), and the Quadrivium, for the study of the sciences (Geometry, Arithmetic, Music, Astronomy). Originally, there were nine subjects set out by Varro in the 1st century BC in his 'Disciplinarum Libri IX', an encyclopaedia of the Liberal Arts, which included architecture and medicine, but these were reduced to seven in the early 5th century AD by Martianus Capella who, between 410 and 429, wrote an allegory in which the seven Liberal Arts were personified. This became the basis of the medieval educational system. No student might proceed to study theology until the Trivium and the Quadrivium had been mastered.

The Trivium involved rather more than is implied by the bare names of the subjects; Grammar, for instance, extended to the classics and philosophy as well as the technical basis of correct language; in the Quadrivium, Mathematics underlay the study of all the other subjects, including Music.

Representations of the Liberal Arts are many. One of the oldest and most comprehensive series is in the mid-12th-century Portail Royal of Chartres Cathedral. The south door has a series of the Signs of the Zodiac with their usual accompaniment, the Labours of the Month, and fourteen figures for the Liberal Arts, each personification of an Art being accompanied by its classical authority, a commentary, on whose writings provided the text for the instruction. For the Trivium, Grammar is accompanied by a study of Priscian, the most considerable Latin grammarian of the early 6th century AD Rhetoric by Cicero, Dialectic by Aristotle, and in the Quadrivium, Geometry is accompanied by Euclid, Arithmetic by Nicomachus, whose *Introductio arithmetica* of the 1st century AD codified Pythagoras's systems of numbers, Music by Pythagoras, because of his correlation between mathematical and musical scales, and Astronomy by Ptolemy. The small figures of the Arts themselves are always female, and can sometimes be distinguished by attributes—Music by her harp and a peal of bells, Grammar with two small children at her feet. The reason for the presence of the Arts in the cathedral portal sculpture is that just as the Signs of the Zodiac mark the passage of time, and the Labours of the Months represent man's active life governed by work and the seasons, so the Arts represent his intellectual and spiritual life. The influential teacher and mystic, Hugh of St Victor, in his *De Sacramentis Christianae Fidei*, written between 1133 and his death in 1141, set out an Augustinian conception of the universe in which all creatures are the expression of Divine thought, and all human activity contributes to the possibility of man's progress towards God and is, therefore, dedicated to a theological end. This philosophy was dominant in the period when the programme for the Portail Royal was being elaborated and is not only entirely expressive of it, but remains current until the 13th century, so that the imagery of the Zodiac, the Labours, and the Arts becomes standard in this type of encyclopaedic programme.

All the Arts, plus philosophy, as well as the Zodiac and the Labours, are represented in the plaques around the base of the Fontana Maggiore in Perugia, by the Pisani (1278), all seven Arts in the reliefs surrounding the effigy of Pope Sixtus IV in Antonio Pollaiuolo's bronze monument in the crypt of St Peter's (1493), and even by inference among the philosophers grouped in Raphael's *School of Athens* in the Stanze of the Vatican, of 1509–11.

Asam, Cosmas Damian (1686–1739), and **Egid Quirin** (1692–1750) were brothers, and exponents of German Late *Baroque art. Both worked as architects and church decorators; Cosmas as a fresco painter, and Egid as a sculptor working mostly in stucco. Cosmas was in Rome *c.*1711–*c.*1714, and Egid probably acquired his experience of Bernini's grandiose Baroque at the same time in the architectural school of Carlo Fontana, one of Bernini's chief assistants. Together the Asam brothers created some of the most exuberant Baroque churches in S. Germany, using a scenographic style with light as an integral element, but always in a way both joyous and imbued with deep feeling. Their chief works are churches at Einsiedeln, Rohr, Weingarten, and Weltenburg (1717–21) with its famous figure of S. George on horseback, silhouetted against the light, and their own house in Munich with the adjoining church of St John Nepomuk (1733–46) and its Throne of Grace sculpture.

Ascension, the The name given to the last appearance of Christ on earth, after His Resurrection, and His departure to heaven. This dramatic event, central to, and the culmination of, the whole Gospel story, is treated very differently by the four Evangelists. Matthew and John do not mention it, Mark says merely 'So then the Lord Jesus, after he had spoken to them, was taken up into heaven . . . ' (Mark 16: 19, regarded by some as an interpolation). Only Luke gives a full account, divided between the last chapter of his Gospel and the first chapter of the Acts. 'Then He led them out as far as Bethany, and, lifting up his hands, he blessed them. While he was blessing, he withdrew from them, and was carried up into heaven' (Luke 24: 50–1). And again, 'When he had said this, as they were watching, he was lifted up, and a cloud took him out of their sight. While he was going up and they were gazing up toward heaven, suddenly two men in white robes stood by them. They said, "Men of Galilee, why do you stand looking up toward heaven? This Jesus, who has been taken up from you into heaven, will come in the same way as you saw him go into heaven." Then they returned to Jerusalem from the mount called Olivet, which is near Jerusalem, a sabbath's day journey away' (Acts 1: 9–11). The taking-up into Heaven is seen as the NT fulfilment of the OT *types of the taking-up of *Enoch, *Elijah, and *Moses. It is commemorated as the culmination of the Easter cycle, which begins with Ash Wednesday at the beginning of Lent, forty days before Easter, and ends with the Ascension, forty days after Easter, when the Paschal *candle is extinguished, symbolizing the completion of Christ's earthly mission.

The Ascension was slow to appear in art, and remains a less frequent subject than the Resurrection. It derives iconographically from pagan *apotheoses, rather as the *Sol Invictus is taken over from pagan prototypes. By the 5th century two types emerged, corresponding roughly to the idea of the Ascension as a positive act by Christ Himself, or as an Assumption, a taking-up into Heaven by action on the part of God the Father, as in the cases of Enoch, Elijah, and Moses. The vision of *Ezekiel, in Eastern art, inspired a treatment close to the *Majestas Domini, as in a 5th-century mosaic in Salonika, and the treatment as a Theophany, a divine manifestation, rather than as a historical event, led even to the inclusion of both Mary and Paul among the Apostles. Byzantine influence on the West can be seen in the mid-9th-century fresco in San Clemente, Rome, and strongly in the 12th-century mosaic of the main cupola of St Mark's, Venice, where Christ is seated on an arc of light in a star-studded sky, upheld by four angels. Immediately beneath Him stands the Virgin flanked by two angels, and round the dome are the twelve Apostles, S. Peter being the only one with a staff. At the base of the dome, below the Apostles, are figures representing Virtues and Beatitudes. Probably the figure of the Virgin is intended also to symbolize the Church. Among the earliest Western representations are those on an ivory relief (*c.*400: Munich, Bayerisches Nationalmus.) and on the doors of Sta Sabina, Rome, of *c.*432, where Christ is drawn up into heaven by two angels, while a third is near by, with the Apostles below in attitudes of astonishment and wonder. The Munich relief shows the three Maries approaching the sepulchre, and being greeted by the Angel. At the top Christ ascends into Heaven, his outstretched arm grasped by the hand of God (*dextrorum iunctio*, *see* DEXTERA DEI), while two Apostles crouch below. The representation in the *Rabbula Gospels, of 586, shows Christ in a *mandorla raised on the *Tetramorph with two angels presenting crowns; this is probably the earliest instance of the Virgin represented at the Ascension. A similar treatment of the scene is painted on the lid of a pilgrim's box of souvenirs brought back from the Holy Land, of the late 6th or early 7th century (Vatican, Museo Sacro). Twelve Apostles are shown, six on either side of the *Orant Virgin; above, Christ is raised up by four angels. The Virgin is usually shown as present from the 6th century onwards; see tusk fragment Egypt (AD 720–970, ivory, Metropolitan Museum, New York).

Sometimes a curious variation of Christ rising into heaven is found, which seems to be associated with the Winchester School of English illumination—in one of the illustrations of the Missal of Robert of Jumièges (1006 to 1023: Rouen, Bib. Municip.) and in the Cotton Psalter (1050: London, BL) the figure of Christ is reduced to no more than His feet disappearing into a cloud, and the same treatment is found in *Nicholas of Verdun's Klosterneuburg Altar of 1181.

Early Italian painted crosses (*see* CROCE DIPINTA) often show the Crucifixion, Resurrection, and Ascension in a close sequence. The damaged but impressive fresco, of *c.*1125/50, in San Pietro, in Tuscany, near Viterbo, represents the Ascension as its sole subject. Other representations include those on the tympanum of one of the west portal doors of Chartres Cathedral (mid-12th cent.), and paintings by *Giotto in the Arena Chapel, Padua (*c.*1306); Mantegna (1463/4: Uffizi); Correggio in the dome of San Giovanni Evangelista, Parma (1520–3); Tintoretto in the Scuola di San Rocco, Venice (1579–81); and Rembrandt (1636: Munich). It is notable that the subject was less popular in the Baroque period, and Rubens painted it only once, in a destroyed ceiling for the Jesuit church in Antwerp, known from a surviving sketch (1620: Vienna, Akad.). Hans *Feibusch painted Ascension murals in two English churches dedicated to the feast (1955 Welling, Kent and 1957 Wembley, Middlesex; also Castera Bazile painted an *Ascension* (1955 Holy Trinity Cathedral, Port-au-Prince, Haiti).

Ascension of Isaiah *See* ISAIAH.

Ashburnham Pentateuch, the (Paris, BN), is a Latin codex dating from the late 6th or 7th century. It is a version of the first five books of the OT, from the Creation to Moses, and consists of 142 pages of two-column text with many large initials. Nineteen pages have illustrations, some in water-colour, some in encaustic; 16 are full-page including a dramatic *Deluge* with the Ark at the top and bodies floating below. Some of the full-page illustrations are in two or three registers, and some illustrations occur irregularly on one side of the text. The origin of the MS is controversial, and it has been ascribed to S. France, N. Italy, and Spain, but its main links are with Egypt and the Near East. Its iconographic importance lies not only in the *Deluge*, but in its depiction of architectural settings, religious ceremonies, and domestic scenes, particularly in the inclusion of one which appears to be the Torah in a synagogue, showing the sacred books in a curtained tabernacle with their titles in Hebrew and Latin. This has led to the plausible suggestion that this Pentateuch is a Christian version of a Hebrew Bible.

Ashdod, Plague at *See* ARK OF THE COVENANT.

ashlar (from Old French *aisselier*, from Lat. *Axilla*) A smooth-cut stone, used in regular courses as a facing for a rougher construction in brick, or as a sustaining surface for rubble filling. The technique is of great antiquity.

asomatoi *See* ANGELS AND ARCHANGELS.

asperges, aspergillum An aspergillum is a *liturgical object used for the Asperges (Lat. sprinkling) with holy water which accompanies certain solemn ceremonies, such as the Easter Ceremonies. It is usually a short metal or wooden rod, with a brush or metal bulb at the end which is dipped in the holy water bucket (Aspersorium, *Situla). In early times a branch of hyssop (cf. Ps. 51; Vg. 50) or olive was used as an aspergillum, and today a sprig of rosemary or other herb may be used. The practice derives from Jewish ritual ablutions. It is rarely represented in art.

ass (NRSV consistently describes them as donkeys.) In AV Num. 22: 22–33 only *Balaam's ass saw the angel with a drawn sword barring her way, and after Balaam had beaten her for refusing to go on, she upbraided him, and Balaam then saw the angel and obeyed God's command.

The presence of the ox and the ass in the stable where Christ was born, so familiar from paintings and even Christmas *cribs, is not recorded in the NT but is first mentioned in the *Apocryphal Gospel of Pseudo-Matthew; the ass is also thought to have been the one on which Mary rode from Nazareth to Bethlehem, and on which she rode with the Christ Child on the flight into Egypt. Christ rode on an ass in His *Entry into Jerusalem (Matt. 21: 2–7), and, so legend has it, the dark cross-shaped markings on an ass's back come from that event.

As a symbol, the ass has contradictory meanings; it has been equated with lechery and sexual excess, with foolishness, obstinacy, and those who hear Christ's message but cannot, or will not, understand it, with dullness of mind, apathy, and sloth. On the good side, it is the symbol of meekness and humility, because Jesus Himself rode on one; of the ability of even the lowest understandings to recognize God, in that the ass knelt before the Blessed Sacrament which *S. Antony of Padua carried—a parallel in a saint's life with the Balaam story.

Assisi An Italian hill town in Umbria, in Central Italy, associated with *S. Francis, the founder of the *Franciscan Order, who began his mission to the poor there. He died in 1226 and was buried in what is now the Sacrament Chapel of Sta Chiara; in 1230 his body was translated to a tomb in the foundations of the new church which had been begun immediately after his canonization in 1228. The basilica of San Francesco consists of two churches built one above the other on arcades which support the terracing of the hillside on which stand the churches and the large convent, which is the mother-house of the Order. The saint's tomb was originally in the Lower Church under the High Altar of the Upper Church, and was apparently visible until the 15th century, but the threats from nearby Perugia to steal the body caused it to be moved and it was so well hidden that it was not rediscovered until 1818. It now lies in a deep crypt under the Lower Church.

The Upper Church is a simple Gothic structure, of four wide bays without aisles, a crossing giving on to transepts, and a shallow polygonal choir. It is cross-vaulted, and the walls are divided by a narrow gallery, above which are large traceried stained-glass windows, the earliest in Italy. Round the nave walls, below the gallery, is a series of twenty-eight frescoes of the Life of S. Francis, designed by *Giotto, but not necessarily executed by him alone (three are by the anonymous Master of S. Cecilia). The question of authorship is still much disputed. They date from *c.*1295 to the first years of the 14th century, and precede Giotto's work in the Arena Chapel in Padua.

The cycle is based on the *Legenda Maior* of *S. Bonaventura, written 1260–3, and is the first instance of a fresco-cycle of the life of a saint based on a biography using contemporary sources. It is, therefore, the fountain-head of all Franciscan iconography, since S. Bonaventura used the two *Lives* written by a contemporary of Francis, and his own was declared the official biography.

On either side of the windows, above the gallery, are further frescoes in poor state, attributed variously to *Cimabue, Roman late 13th-century painters, and even to the young Giotto. The walls of the transepts are also covered with frescoes in poor state, probably begun about 1277 by Cimabue and his studio; in the left transept is a dramatic *Crucifixion*, and a second one in the right transept, and there are scenes from the *Apocalypse, the Lives of the Virgin and of S. Peter. The vaults have frescoes of the Evangelists with views of cities representing parts of the Christian world; *S. Mark*, for instance, has recognizable views of buildings in Rome, possibly the earliest modern examples of topographical painting.

The Lower Church has been considerably enlarged from its original three bays to accommodate burial chapels. The vaults are frescoed throughout by a follower of Giotto, and most of the side chapels also have frescoes, notably those by Simone *Martini of the Life of S. Martin. Two staircases in the nave of the Lower Church lead down to the crypt, with the tomb of the saint. The piazza in front of the Upper Church is dominated by the façade with its large rose window, and from the piazza the main streets of the town run along the hillside, leading to the main square where a Roman temple of the late 1st century BC or early 1st century AD has a fine Corinthian hexastyle portico. This temple features prominently in the scene of *S. Francis and the Simpleton* in the Upper Church, presumably to give an authentic touch to the setting. Further along the hillside is the cathedral of San Rufino, its 8th- to 14th-century origins hidden by reworking in the 1570s. Further down the hillside from the cathedral is the basilica of Sta Chiara built (1257–65) on the model of San Francesco and notable for the huge late-14th-century buttresses arching out into the piazza. Under the church is a 19th-century crypt containing the body of *S. Clare, the friend of S. Francis and foundress of a parallel Order for women. Outside the town, at the bottom of the hill, is the church of Sta Maria degli Angeli, begun in 1569. It is a grandiose basilica in full early Baroque taste, finished in 1679, and rebuilt after an earthquake in 1832. Under the central dome is preserved the tiny chapel of the Portiuncula, where the saint began his religious life, and just behind it, built into one of the piers, is the cell where he died.

Assumption, the (Lat. *assumptio*, taking-up [into Heaven]) Assumption differs from Ascension (of Christ) in that *ascensio* is active and *assumptio* passive. The doctrine of the Assumption of the Blessed Virgin Mary was formally defined only in 1950 by Pope Pius XII ('the Immaculate Mother of God, Mary ever Virgin, when the course of her earthly life was finished, was taken up body and soul into the glory of Heaven'), but it is first mentioned in various *Apocryphal Gospels dating between the 2nd and 4th centuries, including one (perhaps 2nd cent.?) ascribed to S. John the Evangelist. According to some of them, Mary's body was taken up into Heaven on the way to her burial, or according to others, three days after her burial. In art, the Assumption forms part of a sequence from her death, or *Dormition, through several scenes up to her Assumption and *Coronation. The iconography was formulated in the West by 594, by S. Gregory of Tours, who records several apocryphal stories, and in the East by the 7th century. There is a fresco of the 9th century in San Clemente, Rome. The sequence of events leading up to the Assumption is set out in the 'Discourse of S. John the Divine concerning the Falling Asleep of the Holy Mother of God', perhaps of the 2nd century, and was later amplified in Vincent of Beauvais's **Speculum Majus* and the **Golden Legend*. The story begins with an angel, often named as Gabriel, bringing a palm branch from Paradise and announcing her forthcoming death to Mary; the difference between this scene and the Annunciation being that Gabriel carries a palm branch, not a lily. First, S. John the Evangelist miraculously returns from his mission, and then all the other Apostles are brought to her house in time to witness her death (except, in some versions, *Thomas, who was in India and returned later); at her death, her soul is received in the form of a child by Christ Himself. Her body is taken to burial when 'a certain Hebrew named Jephonias' tries to seize it and his hands stick to the bier (or are cut off) until he repents and Peter frees him. On the third day the Archangel Michael accompanies her body to Paradise, where it is reunited with her soul; she leaves behind an empty tomb, later found by the Apostles to be filled with roses and lilies. The actual scene of the Assumption often shows her in a *mandorla, borne upwards by angels, as in the Porta della Mandorla of Florence Cathedral, by Nanni di Banco (1414/21), which also shows S. Thomas receiving her girdle. This subject is rare outside Italy, but can be accounted for here because Prato Cathedral claimed to have the girdle itself. There is an obvious parallel with the OT *type of Elijah, who was taken up into Heaven on a whirlwind, leaving his mantle behind (2 Kgs. 2: 11–14; Vg. 4 Reg. 2: 11–14).

Immediately following the Assumption is the Coronation of Mary by Christ, and the two subjects are often treated together—the west front of Senlis Cathedral in France, of *c.*1170, is the first to have only one portal, and that representing the Coronation of the Virgin in the tympanum, with below it, her Death, and angels bearing her body to Heaven. Sens Cathedral in France (13th cent.) has a portal arranged in two tiers with the Death, Burial, and Assumption below and the Coronation above. Many other French cathedrals have 13th-century sculptures of the subject, and there is a very fine panel in the S. portal of Strasburg Cathedral. One of the best series of pictures is by Duccio, in his *Maestà* of 1308–11 (Siena, Opera del Duomo), with six scenes, of Gabriel announcing her death, S. John taking leave, the other Apostles doing so, the Dormition, the funeral (with Jephonias's hands stuck to the bier), and her burial. Important parts of the front of the *Maestà* are lost; almost certainly it included two large scenes of the Assumption and Coronation as the climax of the Marian series. An unusual treatment of the subject is by Aelbrecht Bouts (late 15th cent.: Brussels, Mus.), given by the artist himself to a chapel of the Virgin in Leuven. It shows Mary taken up to Heaven by two identical figures, who represent the Son and the Holy Ghost. *Molanus, the Counter-Reformation writer, records it in his guidebook to Leuven without surprise, so it must have seemed quite orthodox in the 16th century. Other major works are Titian's huge painting in the Franciscan church in Venice, Sta Maria Gloriosa de' Frari, of 1516–18, a landmark in Venetian High Renaissance art, and the large altarpiece by Annibale Carracci now in Bologna (Mus.), which was painted for San Francesco, Bologna, in 1592 and shows the astonished Apostles picking flowers from the empty tomb.

Assumption of Moses *See* MOSES.

Asteriskos (Gk. star) This is a liturgical object used in the E. Orthodox liturgy, consisting of two short strips of metal crossed and joined at the centre and then bent into a dome shape. It supports the veil which is placed over the consecrated bread on the *discus or paten (*see* *liturgical vessels).

astrology The irrational belief that human actions are influenced by the stars and planets is older than Christianity and contradicts the doctrine of free will. Nevertheless, it was widely believed during the Middle Ages and Renaissance and was formally condemned only in 1586, by Sixtus V. In the arts, personifications of the planets and signs of the Zodiac appear frequently in secular cycles (Cossa and others, in the Pal. Schifanoia, Ferrara; Perugino, Sala del Cambio, Perugia), and occasionally in a religious context, notably in illuminated MSS (the *Très Riches Heures*, by the Limbourg brothers, before 1416) and in portal sculptures, where the Labours of the Months are combined with the twelve Signs of the Zodiac (Paris, Notre-Dame, Amiens and Chartres cathedrals). The irrationality of the belief has done nothing to dim its popularity.

Athos, Mount, is the most easterly of three peninsulas projecting into the Aegean Sea from Macedonia and is joined to the Greek mainland by a narrow isthmus. The ridge, which runs down the centre of the isthmus, ends in the 'Holy Mountain' some 3,000 ft. high. The peninsula belongs to Basilian monasteries of the E. Orthodox rite. The earliest certain foundation is the Lavra monastery, established in 962 by S. Athanasius the Athonite, and the number of monasteries rose to twenty, plus many small dependencies. Once, Mt. Athos attracted monks from all the lands of the Orthodox rite, but a religious population which in 1901 numbered between 6,000 and 7,000 has dwindled to a handful and some monasteries are now abandoned. Access is difficult and no woman, or female animal even, is ever admitted.

The main architectural form of church is the so-called 'Athonite' triapsidal *cross-in-square with an extended *bema usually with a *narthex, as at the Lavra Katholikon, and sometimes, as at the 12th-century Serbian Chilandari monastery, a double narthex. The monasteries have no manuscripts earlier than the 9th century, earlier ones having been destroyed or sold, but a fine 10th-century Gospels with Evangelist 'portraits' against backgrounds of classical architecture is in the Stavronikita Library. There are paintings from *c.*1300 at Kariye and Vatopedi, and similar early 14th-century frescoes at Chilandari, and both there and at Vatopedi and Lavra there are portable mosaic icons of Constantinopolitan workmanship. A silver-gilt cover of a Gospel lectionary with a high relief figure of Christ *Pantocrator set with jewels and with two enamel bust figures of SS Gregory and Basil is in the Lavra treasury. The 'Painter's Manual of Mt. Athos', once thought to be a Byzantine manual, is actually by *Dionysius of Furna.

atrium (Lat., pl. *atria*) A large courtyard, usually surrounded by a cloister or wall, preceding the entrance to a major church or shrine. The form derives from Roman secular building. It served for the gathering and ordering of processions and pilgrims. A good surviving example is at Sant'Ambrogio, Milan, but the atrium of Old St Peter's in Rome, with its great bronze fountain in the shape of a pine-cone, which now stands on the staircase of the Belvedere in the Vatican, was especially famous.

attribute Most of the prophets, patriarchs, and the earlier saints have attributes or symbols—a sort of visual shorthand—by which they may be recognized. There are common attributes, such as martyrs' palms, prophets' books and scrolls, bishops' pastoral staffs, crowns or swords, which are too generalized to help in identification without some more specific attribute. This may reflect a significant episode, e.g. a chalice for *Melchisedech (Gen. 15: 18–20), a small boy for *Abraham (his son Isaac), a harp for King *David; or may be the instrument of martyrdom, e.g. *S. Laurence's gridiron, or *S. Catherine's wheel; or it may be a peculiar feature, such as *S. John the Baptist's camel-hair clothing (Matt. 3: 4); the Virgin's lily (for purity), or the stigmata of *S. Francis of Assisi. Many biblical figures have more than one attribute—David, for instance, also wears a crown, *S. Peter may have a key as well as a book or a scroll, and personifications such as *Ecclesia and Synagoga are also recognizable from their accompanying symbols. Sometimes two or more saints have the same symbol; *SS Hubert, *Eustace, and *Giles all have a deer; *SS Dorothy and *Elizabeth both have roses. Countries and cities often have *Patron saints whose attributes become part of their national or civic symbolism: for instance, *S. George of England and *S. Andrew of Scotland have their respective crosses in the flag of the Union, the arms of Venice are the Lion of *S. Mark, the *Evangelist's symbol. Even more important were the patron saints of the various trades and *Guilds. S. Joseph was an obvious choice for carpenters, but the Apostle Thomas was also a patron and is often shown with a carpenter's square as his attribute. S. Luke, 'the beloved physician', was clearly the patron of doctors, but he is also supposed to have painted the first *Madonna and Child*, and thus became the patron of painters. S. George the warrior was patron of armourers, as in the statue commissioned from Donatello by the Florentine Guild of Armourers for the Guild Church of Orsanmichele; and every other trade had at least one patron and often several.

In general, attributes can be found in the Bible for prophets and patriarchs, even if these are no more than texts from their prophecies, or symbols of events from their histories; the **Golden Legend* provides attributes for hundreds of early saints, while many later ones are distinguished by symbols derived from visions, devotions, or aspects of their life; for instance, the angel's lance which pierced the heart of *S. Theresa of Avila; the Sacred Heart of S. Margaret Mary Alacoque (*see* HEART); the black and white dog of *S. Dominic. Of major assistance in this are the specialized dictionaries of saints and their attributes, of which several exist, providing a greater range than can be included here.

auditory church A church designed for preaching, as well as for the celebration of the liturgy. In pre-Reformation times preaching was rarely associated with the liturgy and was concentrated on special occasions, particularly Lent, when long courses of sermons were delivered, separately from any rite and often in the open air to large crowds. Preachers like *Savonarola or *S. Bernardino used special platforms to speak to segregated audiences—women on one side, men on the other—as shown in e.g. Sano di Pietro's *S. Bernardino* (d.1444) *preaching in Siena* (Siena Cath.), where the saint is shown preaching from a rostrum in front of the Palazzo Pubblico to a large crowd gathered in the 'Campo'. Leonardo da Vinci, at the end of the 15th century, made notes on the design of buildings suitable for preaching, and there is a drawing inscribed 'teatro da predicare' (theatre for preaching) in his MS B (Paris, BN).

The typical auditory church was evolved in the mid-16th century by the Calvinists in Switzerland, France, and the northern Netherlands. They were often called temples, and the most famous was probably that at *Charenton, near Paris. Basically, they were centrally planned—circular, square, octagonal—so that the preacher's voice carried to all parts of the building. To increase the audience, galleries were used to enable twice as many people to hear: they may derive from the *gynaeceum in Early Christian and Byantine churches, but were not used to segregate the sexes—a painting of the Temple at Lyons shows men and women sitting together. In the 16th and 17th centuries preaching became an important part of the Counter-Reformation, especially among the *Jesuits, where the conflicting demands of audibility and the celebration of the liturgy had to be reconciled in their churches (*see* VIGNOLA). Anglicans had the same problem since, unlike Calvinists, they retained the altar as a focal point. The classic solution was arrived at by *Wren, who amalgamated the designs of the Temple at Charenton, Dutch Calvinist churches, and Belgian and Roman *Baroque churches in his own City churches and St Paul's Cathedral.

Augustine of Canterbury, Saint (d. 604/5). In 596 he was sent by Pope S. Gregory the Great to England with a group of Benedictine monks to convert the Anglo-Saxons, but when they reached Aix-en-Provence they heard such terrible stories that Augustine returned to Rome. He was sent back by the Pope and arrived in Thanet at Easter 597, where he was well received by King Ethelbert of Kent, whose wife was a Christian. The king restored the old church of Peter and Paul, and was later baptized with many of his followers. In 601 Augustine established the two metropolitan sees at Canterbury and York. He brought with him the Roman rite, and Roman diocesan organization, but Northumbria refused all co-operation, so that the differences resulted in great confusion, particularly over the date of Easter. It is probable that he brought with him the 6th-century *Gospels of S. Augustine* (Corpus Christi Coll., Cambridge), which is used at the enthronement of all Archbishops of Canterbury. He also introduced Roman forms of building (as at Reculver and Canterbury). *See also* ANGLO-SAXON ART.

Augustine of Hippo, Saint, *Doctor of the Church (354–430), was born at Thagaste, now in Algeria. His father was a pagan, but his mother Monica was a devout Christian (herself later canonized). Augustine was not baptized and for nine years of his adult life was a Manichaean heretic. He was educated in Carthage and taught in Rome and Milan, where his slow turn towards Christianity was confirmed by the influence of *S. Ambrose, who baptized him in 387. He returned to N. Africa in 388, where he founded a monastic community, becoming a priest in 391, and, from 396, was Bishop of Hippo, near his birthplace, where he died. He wrote many theological treatises and hundreds of letters and sermons, but his fame rests partly on his 'Confessions', an autobiography of *c.*400, and the 'City of God', written immediately after the sack of Rome in 410 to rebut the charge that the fall was caused by the abandonment of the pagan deities. His theological writings were of enormous importance and, after a thousand years, deeply influenced *Luther, *Calvin, and *Jansenism. He was made a Doctor of the Church in 1295, but his writings assumed their greatest importance in the controversies of the 16th and 17th centuries. His relics are in San Pietro in Ciel d'Oro, Pavia, where they were taken in the 8th century, and a tomb of 1362, attributed to Giovanni di Balduccio, contains them. Like S. Ambrose, he is usually represented as a bearded bishop in cope and mitre, but the earliest depiction of him is of *c.*600 and shows him as a classical philosopher (Rome, the Lateran). He is shown as a Doctor on the vault of the Upper Church of San Francesco, Assisi (13th cent.), and often thereafter as holding a book or engaged in study, as in the famous fresco by Botticelli (*c.*1480: Florence, Ognissanti). In groups of the Four Doctors he may be difficult to distinguish from Ambrose. Later, he appears in a black habit with a leather belt, because of his association with the later *Augustinian canons. Other attributes are a flaming heart, or a heart pierced by two or three arrows, referring to his treatise on the Holy Trinity. He may also hold a model of a city—the City of God. A much later legend tells how he met a child on the beach who was trying to collect the sea in a shell and drop it into a hole in the sand: when Augustine pointed out the inanity of this the child replied, 'No more than you trying to understand the mystery of the Trinity' (cf. the *predella* by Botticelli in the Uffizi). Apart from the reliefs of his life on his tomb there is a fresco cycle by Benozzo Gozzoli of 1465 in San Gimignano in Tuscany, and many others in Augustinian monasteries.

Augustinian canons, friars In the mid-11th century some priests began living a communal life and adapted a rule derived, probably correctly, from *S. Augustine for a community of women in 423. By the 12th century this had become widely adopted in Western Europe. In the early years of his reforms of 1059 and 1063, Pope S. Gregory VII, probably as a result of having been at *Cluny in 1047–9, established an Order of Regular Canons following this Augustinian Rule. Some independent Augustinian congregations were established, such as the *Premonstratensians, or White Canons, called after their house founded by S. Norbert at Prémontré near Laon in N. France, which was strongly influenced by the *Cistercians. In later years the ideal of living a communal life under vows while working in the world as religious gave rise to such Orders as the *Theatines and the *Jesuits. In England, Augustinian Canons were known as the Black Canons from their plain black habit, leather belt, and black cloak. At the Dissolution of the monasteries in 1539 there were about 195 houses in England and Scotland. The Order survives mainly as the Canons of the Lateran, in Rome, and the 'monks' of the Great St Bernard hospice in the Alps.

Another almost parallel Order of Augustinian Hermits, even more widespread than the Canons, had evolved by 1256. They were friars, not monks, and included Martin *Luther. By the 16th century there were about 3,000 friaries and 300 nunneries of the Order, of which thirty-two in England were destroyed at the Dissolution. A reminder of them survives in the street name, Austin Friars, in the City of London.

Augustus and the Tiburtine Sibyl In his fourth 'Eclogue', written between 42 and 37 BC, Virgil prophesied that a child would be born, under whose rule the world would be at peace. This was probably no more than normal flattery of the Emperor Augustus, but Christ was certainly born in Augustus's reign and it was soon seen as a foretelling of the Nativity—by the 6th century the story had been embellished and the child had become a Jewish boy, and, in the 12th century the **Mirabilia Urbis Romae* has a full story (Bk. *II, c. 1): 'While [Augustus] diligently listened to the [Tiburtine] *Sibyl, heaven opened, and a great brightness shone on him, and he saw in heaven a virgin exceedingly fair standing on an altar holding a manchild in her arms . . . and he heard a voice from heaven saying: "This is the Virgin who shall conceive the Saviour of the World". And again he heard another voice . . . "This is the altar of the Son of God" . . . The vision took place in his chamber, where the church of Sta Maria in Capitolio now is . . . Therefore it is called Sta Maria in Aracoeli.' It is in fact on the site of the Arx Capitolina, a particularly sacred place in ancient Rome. The **Golden Legend* and the **Speculum Humanae Salvationis* also have versions of the story, which soon became popular. The earliest representations were probably those in the church itself—a mosaic and a fresco by Cavallini (active 1273–1308), which is recorded by Vasari as comparatively well preserved, but both are now lost. In the account in the *Golden Legend* the story is linked with the three *Magi seeing the star in the form of a Child, and this is represented in Roger van der *Weyden's Bladelin Altarpiece (Berlin), where the left wing shows Augustus and the Sibyl and the right the Magi and the Child. It is likely that *mystery plays also influenced painters, as in the Master of the Tiburtine Sibyl's picture in Frankfurt (Städel, late 15th cent.).

aumbry (ambry) A cupboard or recess with a door in the wall of a church used for reservation of the Blessed Sacrament after the Eucharist or Mass, or for the Holy Oils (three types, used for anointing the sick and dying, and at Baptism, Confirmation, and Ordination). In Roman Catholic churches the Sacrament is now served in a *tabernacle on or near the *High Altar; Anglican churches, which reserve the Sacrament, normally have an Aumbry set into the wall of the *sanctuary or (more rarely) a tabernacle, *Sacrament house, or hanging *pyx.

aureole *See* HALO.

a

AUSTRALIA, NEW ZEALAND, AND THE PACIFIC

The Christian art and architecture of Australia, New Zealand, and the Pacific covers three broad phases of development over a period of some 200 years. The colonial period saw the implantation of mainly British cultural models to express the Christian faith in Australia and New Zealand. In the Pacific there is more diversity, with French interests in New Caledonia and French Polynesia, the best known being Tahiti. German interests in the Pacific, including New Guinea and Samoa, came to an end with the First World War. The 20th century saw the rise of a more nationalistic period of development that began to draw upon local modes of expression. This confidence has led into a third phase with a more fluid expression of context and culture that interacts with indigenous cultures and local landscapes. This also incorporates new patterns of migration within the Asian and Pacific regions with an attendant increase in religious and cultural diversity. Recent artistic and architectural examples indicate a more open and confident trust in the artistic vision to deliver a contextual and relevant expression of faith. They also reflect a certain critique of the colonial framework of missionary activity that at times still holds the Christian imagination captive to 19th-century models.

Colonial Developments

European colonial expansion in Asia and the Pacific brought with it an effort to establish an ordered culture, expressed partly through religious architecture and art, that in turn sought to convert local cultures to this imagined order of things. Settler cultures sought to establish these familiar signs through civic buildings and artefacts, including churches and their furnishings. The establishment of the firm models brought from 'home' was tempered by the vastly different religious and cultural forms of indigenous peoples. Faced with the mystery of the local religions and practices, settlers tended to strengthen their preference for models that expressed a connection with the history and cultural memory of Europe. Interaction with local customs, or any forms of innovation were considered as syncretic and in danger of diluting the purity of settler culture, and were rarely tolerated during this period driven by missionary concerns.

The first stage of settlement in the region drew on a taste for the 'Gothick' that was expressed through the ornamentation applied to the simple buildings in wood and stone that served as early churches and public buildings. In Australia, major public buildings were built following the prosperity of the 1850s gold rush, which led to and increased number of church projects such as those completed by William Wardell (1823–99) who designed the Roman Catholic cathedrals for Melbourne and Sydney. After a career in Britain, Wardell, a student of the influential Augustus *Pugin (1812–52), moved to Melbourne in 1858 as government architect. He later moved to Sydney and produced many fine public buildings in both cities. While these projects demonstrate the skills of local builders and include some local design work, they continue the larger taste for the *Gothic, advocated by Pugin, as the style of choice for church architecture, a choice that lasted well into the 20th century and is still often referenced in contemporary buildings.

This taste is also reflected in New Zealand and the Pacific where the Gothic style continued but with some adaptive use of local materials. Works by Frederick Thatcher (1814–90) and Benjamin Mountfort (1825–98) are significant—in particular, St Mary's in Auckland by Mountfort, which is the largest wooden Gothic church in existence. It was in the area of decoration where there was some attempt to allow for innovation with local cultures to occur. During the 1840s, churches were built by New Zealand Maori congregations that were adopted from the traditional form of the domestic 'whare'. This was a hybrid form that used indigenous and Western building techniques to achieve substantial wooden buildings with a central series of tree-like wooden columns supporting the roof. While decorative programmes of carving were met with some resistance, extant examples indicate an innovative programme of integrating Christian and Maori visual cultures. These efforts waned as Maori culture was much theatened in the face of expanding European settlement.

The Modern Period

The 20th century continued to see the favoured use of Gothic styles as cities and small towns were developed. Many projects begun in the 19th century continued to be added to; for example, the twin towers of St Mary's Cathedral, Sydney were only completed in 2000. In New Zealand an important exception was Francis Petre (1847–1918) who designed the impressive Cathedral of the Blessed Sacrament (1904) in Christchurch. It is held to be the finest Renaissance-style building in the region. Petre's other work included Wellington's Cathedral of the Sacred Heart in a Palladian style. His work was a radical break with the dominant Gothic, and he was also an innovator with materials, pioneering the use of steel and massed concrete well suited to achieving structural stability in a region prone to earthquakes.

In Western Australia, architect and priest John Cyril Hawes (1876–1956) designed a significant number of churches. His work was original in style while borrowing from a variety of sources such as *Romanesque and Renaissance. His churches demonstrate the use of natural materials such as local stone, and work towards an appropriate response to the otherwise warm climate. The Geraldton Cathedral (1916–38) is a distinctive landmark that blends several styles, including two towers based on Spanish mission design with a Renaissance-style dome. Hawes's later career was spent in the Bahamas, where he continued to build new churches in a variety of styles using local materials that respond well to the local climate.

It was in the period following the Second World War that modern design and construction methods began to be used in church building. In New Zealand, Ron Muston designed St James, Lower Hutt, built in 1953 as part of an urban design project providing civic and community buildings for a newly developing regional centre. It represents a shift to the clear lines of Modernist design and use of materials. Of particular significance is the Chapel of Futuna in Wellington, designed by John Scott (1924–92) and opened in 1961, which melds aspects of a cross floor plan with indigenous elements such as a central supporting pole and high-peaked roof lines reminiscent of Maori buildings. This provides an example of the reconsideration of Maori culture during a period that led to increasing bicultural policies within New Zealand national life. The extension of the nave to the Gothic Auckland Cathedral, developed by Richard Toy and begun in 1991, uses a canopy-like structure to provide a large space for religious and community gatherings that fulfills the contemporary needs of a cathedral and that also draws on Maori models.

In Australia, the Roman Catholic Cathedral, St Mary Star of the Sea in Darwin, designed by Ian Ferrier (1929–2000), features a series of parabolic curved concrete arches to sustain the overall form of the building. It was opened in 1962 and successfully responds to the tropical climate by allowing generous and open ventilation within a strong Modernist form. Ferrier also designed the Port Moresby Roman Catholic St Mary's Cathedral in New Guinea, which opened in 1969 and features on its façade elements based on a Sepik Spirit house. In Sydney, St Kevin's Roman Catholic Church, Dee Why, designed by Tom Gibbons, was opened in 1962. It is a ferro-concrete shell structure with seven peaked triangular forms that as a whole achieves a light tent-like structure. There are several tile floor decorations and ironwork details that were designed by the artist John Coburn.

Among the visual artists of the region the most influential figures have been those who worked with the Christian imagination and made it a point of dialogue in engaging with the local landscape and culture. Arthur Boyd (1920–99) is a major figure in Australian art who used biblical stories and placed them within the local environment in a manner that interpreted current events and themes in local culture. Works completed at the end of the Second World War display in apocalyptic mode the biblical dramas within the local landscape. In *The Mockers* (1945, Art Gallery of NSW, Sydney) a vast swathe of crowded humanity plays out acts of violence including a crucifixion. This unsettling scene is watched over by an ambiguous but wise figure.

Boyd drew on his respect for Rembrandt and Brueghel while reinventing the Australian landscape as the location for larger narratives taken from the Bible and Western mythology. This approach allowed him to play out stories of human power, lust, and love, and situate them within the context of Australian cultural tensions about race, belief, and ideology. Boyd took on a more prophetic edge in his use of the biblical material, and explored the nature of the human conscience. At times he used poetic means to sustain the beauty of human beings and their environment, while at other times his images are grotesque, filled with human anguish and suffering. Crippled figures, malevolent dogs, a chained artist with brush in hand, all serve to describe the condition of people with a meagre capacity for sympathetic imagination. This is not church art, but art that offers a perspective on what it means to be human, a central religious question for the art and culture of the 20th century.

In contrast with Boyd, John Coburn (1925–2006) approached the landscape and the religious imagination with an eye for its priestly and icon-like effects. His works often express a timeless silence that uses the natural environment to express an immanent sense of spiritual values. He reinterprets the symbols of the *Eucharist, for example, alongside natural forms such as birds and trees, to celebrate the rich, colourful environment of Australia as a paradise requiring a response of respect and reverence. Among designs for a completed set of tapestries that celebrate the seasons of nature and the seasons of life, *Maquette for Tapestry 'Hosanna'* (1986, Art Gallery of NSW, Sydney), Coburn demonstrates his capacity for rich colouration and symbolic depth. This is a Christian imagination alive to the rich colours and light of Australian landscape. It celebrates a spirituality that is open to the natural world and exults in its capacity to praise its creator and sustain human life. In many ways Coburn anticipates through rich imagery the concerns of recent trends in eco-theology that reconsider the presence of God as part of the human relationship with nature.

The Church in the region has not been a prolific source of commissions for artists and designers. This was partly the motivation for the development of the Blake Prize, first awarded in 1951 in Sydney. This began as a one-off event to inspire artists to attempt religious subject matter in the hope that some works would find their way into the many churches and synagogues being built in the post-war period. The Blake Prize quickly garnered the support of many younger and more innovative artists experimenting with ideas of colour and abstraction. This was due to its openness to subject matter not acknowledged in other art prizes that favoured portraiture or landscape. Within these first few years, tensions developed between innovation and tradition, as some of the organizers were looking to maintain certain figurative traditions of religious art. The now 60-year history of the Blake provides a helpful overview of the changing nature of religious expression within Australian culture. It also demonstrates the ongoing tensions between tradition and innovation that have marked that history.

In the latter part of the century, the Blake Prize continued to tolerate diversity as a stronger representation of women artists began to shift subject matter. It has also encompassed indigenous artists as well as the diverse experiences of an increasingly multicultural Australia. This broadened the religious themes to include Buddhism, Hinduism, and indigenous expressions of spirituality with strong connections to a sense of place. Christian themes continue to appear in both recognized and unexpected ways as contemporary artists search for new methods of addressing contemporary concerns. In more recent years, this has led to the inclusion of works that directly address social issues such as the environment, gender, and racial difference, as well as issues critical of religion such as recent response to sexual abuse by clergy. The Blake exhibition works both to affirm and to question the structures of the religious imagination in Australia. Another approach to the diverse challenges of contemporary art was developed through the Mandorla Art Prize. Awarded in Perth, Western Australia, since 1985, this prize is offered for a work that addresses a biblical theme chosen for each specific competition.

In New Zealand, Colin McCahon (1919–87) is a major figure who brought together a vision of the local landscape and the narrative of biblical stories. From a visual format with simple figures he began to include texts of biblical narrative or poetry, sometimes as cartoon-like speech bubbles. Through this approach, McCahon has built a form of visual theology that both affirms and negates the signs of God's presence. He poetically brought alive a sense of place within the New Zealand landscape and opened up questions of belief and doubt, and especially their capacity for creative interaction. His later work focused mainly on simple painterly gestures of inscribed words and numbers. In *Victory over Death 2* (1970, Australian National Gallery, Canberra) McCahon uses the words of the divine statement 'I am' to split open his vast canvas into light and dark areas, playing with negative and positive space. In many ways his works express the erasure of signs implied in the mystical tradition of the '*via negativa*' and foreshadow late modern theologies that deal with the absence of God. He has been an influential figure internationally as he links in his work the cultural process of seeing and the manner in which belief is structured and represented.

During this period, New Zealand saw the resurgence of pride in Maori tradition and the development of a more a bicultural national identity. Ralph Hotere (1931–2013) is an artist of significant influence in the development of a strong Maori visual culture from the 1960s. Hotere draws on his Maori heritage and on his education in a Maori Catholic community through his series of black paintings that will often incorporate cross forms and that can be understood against this background of the mystic in both traditions.

Many other contemporary artists refer to Christianity in New Zealand and the Pacific region. This, at times, has been focused on a more detached and critical reassessment of past colonial influences, and a positive reassessment of indigenous traditions. Within the region, the work of the Asian Christian Art Association and its publications have been of some influence as it has responded to the growing interest in cross-cultural theology and increasing respect for local cultures. It has also sponsored stronger links with Asia in a period of increasing Asian immigration into the region. (*See* NON-WESTERN CHRISTIAN ART).

With the rise of Australian interest in Aboriginal art, a number of Aboriginal artists have addressed Christian themes in their work. These include Miriam Rose Ungunmerr-Bauman, Jarinyanu David Downs, Julie Dowling, Queenie McKenzie, and other artists from Warmun in Western Australia. Some of these artists are from remote communities that have long contact with Christianity through church-run mission programmes. With the growth of the Aboriginal art movement from the 1970s, these works address the tradition of Christian themes as well as Aboriginal traditions of spirituality that centre on tribal and family relations with a clear responsibility for the environment. In this way they are 'two-way' works and have been considered at times as a form of syncretism, or more positively as works that address the tradition of Christianity with new insights from a culture finely attuned to its environment.

Post-Colonial Innovation

In the contemporary period, the religious context is one of an increased diversity of faiths alongside a wider social experimentation, with forms of spirituality sustained outside organized religious structures. Christian symbols now traffic in a marketplace driven by electronic and social media, where their effect comes not from any implicit authority but through their apparent usefulness to current needs. Church allegiance has moved in the last 50 years from being based on ideas of belonging to the more immediate need of finding hope within a culture marked by competing images of the future. The global impact of advertising and the media diversifies cultures, and, in turn, puts more demands on local traditions. Christianity is experiencing rapid change in its mode of communication and the points at which it engages with a society now more aware of the role of images.

This has given rise to a more open interest in inter-religious dialogue and a conversation with ideas outside the European imagination. It has also brought a more realistic assessment of the effects of colonialism on local cultures. European thinking wrote off local cultures as deviant, or as lacking in the qualities of civilization, or at worst of being anti-Christian, but is now itself under question. The image of Christ, therefore, appears more frequently in contemporary art as both a reference to the past and as an image to be critiqued as part of colonial power. Christianity is considered a problematic yet resourceful part of the region's cultural history. This critical engagement is not often reflected in the churches, which are frequently defensive about their authority and role within social life, with a tendency to hold on to favoured images and modes of expression. Christ, therefore, appears both as an irritant and as a source of comfort.

One of the positive areas of engagement has been with indigenous artists who address Christian stories. Once considered to be syncretistic, these artists exhibit spaces in their work that express both Aboriginal as well as Western Christian ideas. They offer possible new insights into the manner in which the Christian faith deals with history, racial difference, and the nature of the land, which local peoples hold as sacred. Rather than syncretistic, these new spaces are more hybrid in nature. They further offer novel conclusions to issues of faith in the context of the cultures of the region. The figure of Christ can therefore appear not simply as a form of translation but as the local face of freedom and renewal. This is a much more dynamic if not disruptive idea, particularly if Christianity is seen as a Western story only.

There have been various attempts to set up artists' networks in the region and to organize art exhibitions by artists who are Christian. These are usually sustained around major cities, and provide the basis of the Church constructively interacting with the arts and contemporary culture. Such initiatives will also reflect the tensions between different points of view on the purpose and value of the arts to Christian life and theological reflection. There has been some exploration of the use of the arts for evangelism, and several Christian tertiary education colleges offer courses in various art forms. There is a continuing diversity in the ways in which the contemporary Church understands its role within culture and how it might value the role of the artist and the ongoing development of the Christian imagination.

An important contemporary architectural project in this more complex period is St Patrick's Roman Catholic Cathedral (2003, Parramatta, near Sydney), designed by Romaldo Giurgola (1920–). This involved a renovation of the remains of the church Pugin designed that had been destroyed by fire in 1996, with the addition of a new liturgical space, incorporating a major art programme of sculptural work, windows, liturgical vessels, furniture, and vestments. Giurgola, who is well known for his work on Canberra's Parliament House, has achieved a sensitive renewal of the heritage elements of the site by creating a Blessed Sacrament Chapel within the fire-affected remnant. A new liturgical space for 800 people has been added, creating a contained space that enhances the movement of the liturgy in the centre of the gathered community. The overall space is beautifully lit by subtly filtering the strong Australian sun, in turn showing off the warm natural timbers and the spatial drama of the various art commissions.

One of Australia's foremost glass artists Klaus Zimmer (1928–2007) completed a major cycle of windows for this building, using a collage-like approach of gluing glass sheets on to a ground of opaque white glass, the result resembling painting rather than the heavy leaded windows typical of church decoration. The series of 78 windows uses a consistent set of organic-based vocabulary of symbols to express the liturgical meanings present in each physical space. The integration of the windows and the other art works offers a design approach focused on the movement of people, which at times might be a lone act of private devotion, while at other times involves large gatherings on special occasions. The interior of the building recalls a boat-like structure, which has successfully blended with the original 19th-century Gothic church. This cohesion of different elements is further addressed through the significant range of art commissions that punctuate the experience of navigating the spaces. Visual artists, sculptors, silversmiths, and metal workers have all added individual elements to sustain an engaging whole. This is a good example of attention to the given issues of the site, a respect for materials, and an appropriate collaboration with experts in art, music, liturgy, and local cultures.

The experiences of complexity noted above can also be seen in the history of the Blake Prize. This maintains a public space for debate about art and faith. Since the turn of the century, the Blake Prize has undergone a reinvigoration, in part due to the increased interest in the religious and spiritual imagination in the broader culture. Each year the prize sees over a thousand artists in all mediums submit works that range in subject matter from traditional religious ideas to a more critical engagement with ideas of spirituality. Owing to this open stance, controversy has erupted on a number of occasions concerning the works exhibited, because they addressed not only religious and spiritual ideas, but also matters of social justice and the wider cultural debate. This public interest is clear evidence that there is a growing curiosity about religion in the broader society, and that this is now expressed in increasingly diverse ways. Within this diversity, the Christian imagination remains alive and dynamic as it finds ways to respond to this field of competing images and ideas. The activity of image-making is important in renewing an ongoing relevance for the Christian faith, and in demonstrating its capacity to be contextualized in and through local cultures.

SEE WEB LINKS

- Official website of the Blake Prize, 60 years of Australia's premier religious art prize.
- Official website of the Mandorla Art Prize, Australia's art award inspired by Biblical quotations.

Auxiliary Saints *See* VIERZEHNHEILIGEN.

Ave Maria The opening words of the Angelic Salutation spoken by the Archangel Gabriel at the *Annunciation: 'Ave [Maria], gratia plena, Dominus tecum' (Hail, thou that art full of grace, the Lord is with thee, Vg. Luke 1; Hail, thou that art highly favoured, NRSV Luke 1: 28). The beginning of a prayer—the Hail Mary—addressed to the Virgin Mary is often found inscribed on representations of the Annunciation. Sometimes the words of Mary's reply 'Ecce ancilla Domini' (Behold the handmaid of the Lord) (NRSV has 'Here am I, the servant of the Lord', Luke 1: 38) are also included.

Averroes *See* THOMAS AQUINAS, S.

Avignon A town in Provence in SE France, which from 1309 to 1367, and again from 1370 to 1375, was the seat of the papacy during nearly seventy years of extreme unrest in Rome, and Italy generally. The papal 'exile' was provoked by struggles between Pope Boniface VIII and King Philip IV of France, during which Boniface was actually kidnapped at his castle of Anagni in 1303 by a French armed force, but he was released by the people of the town, though he died a month later in Rome.

When his successor Benedict XI died in 1304 in Perugia, the conclave elected Clement V 'in absentia'—the first of the seven French popes which followed. Clement never set foot in Italy and eventually settled in Avignon in 1309. He died in 1314, and was succeeded by John XXII (1316–34) and then by Benedict XII (1334–42), who began rebuilding the episcopal palace in Avignon into the Palace of the Popes. His successor, Clement VI (1342–52), bought Avignon and its immediate hinterland, the Comtat Venaissin, in 1348, and converted a gloomy fortress into a huge, lavish palace employing French architects for the building and artists from Italy, notably Simone *Martini and Matteo Giovanetti to decorate his palace and the cathedral of Ste-Marie-des-Doms. While it is possible, though unlikely, that Giotto might have been in Avignon (one early record of him lists Avignon among places where he worked), Simone Martini, who had been in Avignon from *c.*1340/1 and died there in 1344, was certainly the most considerable Italian artist who worked there. One of the panel pictures by Simone, known to have been painted in Avignon since it is dated 1342 (Liverpool, Walker Art Gall.), has the very unusual subject of the Christ Child returning to his parents after disputing with the Doctors in the Temple. Another unusual painting was done for his friend the poet Petrarch, also resident at the papal court, for whom he made a full-page illumination as a frontispiece for the poet's manuscript of Virgil (Milan, Ambrosiana). Although only the superb *sinopie* (underpainting in a reddish pigment) of his frescoes in the cathedral survive, the influence of these major works, and those by Giovanetti in the palace, helped to establish the Provençal school of painting. The frescoes by Giovanetti in the Tour de la Garderobe (the wardrobe tower)—a series of lively hunting and fishing scenes—the ceiling paintings in the audience chamber, and those in the palace chapel of St-Martial are all that now survive of his work in the Palais des Papes.

By the reign of Innocent VI (1352–62) Avignon had begun to suffer from marauding bands of mercenaries and was so unsafe that in 1357 the walls were rebuilt. His successor, Urban V (1362–70), realized that a return to Italy was essential if Rome were to remain the centre of Christianity and survive as an independent state instead of the papacy being an appanage of the French crown. After great difficulties he went to Italy in 1367, but by 1370 was forced to return to Avignon, where he died. His successor Gregory XI (1370–8), who was Clement VI's nephew, realized that continued residence in France was impossible and he left Avignon for good in 1376, arriving in Rome in 1377. Thus ended the so-called 'Babylonian Captivity' of the papacy, a title which refers to the Jewish seventy-year captivity, but wrongly since the decision to reside in Avignon was taken deliberately. When Gregory XI died, so great was the fear that yet another French pope might be elected, that Urban VI was forcibly enthroned by the Roman mob, but his behaviour alienated a large number of cardinals, who contested his election as invalid and elected Clement VII, who returned to Avignon. The scandal of two popes, one in France and one in Rome, was continued when Urban died and the Roman cardinals elected Boniface IX (1389–1402). When Clement died in Avignon in 1394 the Avignonese faction elected Benedict XIII. By this time the civil powers themselves were alarmed, and in 1398 efforts were made to depose Benedict. The papal palace was besieged until 1403, when the pope escaped dramatically to Spain, where he continued to insist on the legitimacy of his position until his death in 1423, when he was followed by two further Spanish schismatics until 1429. The Schism dragged on in Italy until 1417 when the Italian schismatics themselves abandoned the rival papal claimants and in 1417 elected Martin V, who returned to Rome in 1420.

The influence of the Italian art brought into Provence by the Avignonese papacies percolated more easily into Burgundy, Germany, and Bohemia than into the rest of France itself. The 14th-century painters of the Bohemian School show strong affinities with both Padua and Siena, and with German works of the so-called 'Soft Style', which was itself affected by Italian influence stemming from Provence as well as directly from N. Italy, and which contributed in the following century to the formation of the widely disseminated International Gothic style. Italian work in Avignon helped to establish the School of Provençal painters which flourished in the 15th century with such artists as Enguerrand *Quarton, whose major work contains two views of cities, purporting to be Rome and Jerusalem, which are probably largely of Avignon. To Quarton is now also attributed the anonymous *Pietà* of Villeneuve-lès-Avignon (Paris, Louvre) one of the grandest and most moving representations of the subject.

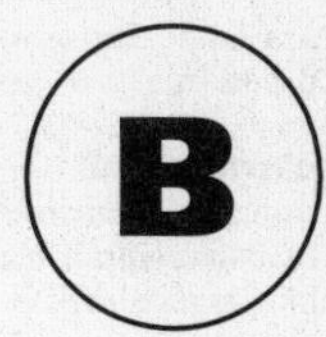

Baal, the Prophets of *See* ELIJAH (ELIAS).

Babel, Tower of According to Gen. 11: 1–9, the descendants of *Noah decided to build a huge tower at Babel (Babylon), to reach up to heaven. At that time all men spoke one language, and God punished their presumption by causing them all to speak different tongues, thus confusing the enterprise. Nimrod, 'the mighty hunter', is sometimes associated with the project. This is a very rare subject, and most of the known examples are Netherlandish, 16th or early 17th century, the most famous being the two paintings by Pieter *Bruegel the Elder: one in Vienna (1563: KHM), which includes Nimrod, and a later version in Rotterdam (Boymans Mus.), which does not. Both have an enormous round tower, clearly based on the forms of the Colosseum in Rome, which Bruegel had seen, but with ramps like the temple-tower, or *ziggurat*, in Babylon (6th cent. BC) which was probably the origin of the story.

Babylon, the Whore of *See* WHORE.

Balaam was an Eastern seer whose story is told in the OT (Num. 22–4). He was paid by the King of Moab to come and curse the Israelites, but was forbidden to do so by God. Later, he was permitted to go, provided he spoke only the words the Lord put into his mouth. On the way, he failed to see an angel barring his passage, but his ass saw it and refused to go on. Balaam beat her, but she lay down. 'Then the Lord opened the mouth of the ass, and she said to Balaam, "What have I done to you, that you have struck me these three times?"' At last, Balaam saw the angel. His blindness was sometimes compared to the incredulity of *S. Thomas. Eventually, Balaam blessed the Israelites instead of cursing them, to the fury of the king, saying: 'I see him, but not now: I behold him, but not near—a Star shall come out of Jacob, and a Sceptre shall rise out of Israel ...' (Num. 24: 17). The story of Balaam and his ass was known in East and West and is mentioned in the **Speculum Humanae Salvationis* and the **Biblia Pauperum*, but is not very common in art. In the 17th century Pieter Lastman, *Rembrandt's teacher, painted the incident of the indignant ass in 1622 (private coll., New York), and Rembrandt himself did so in 1626 (Paris, Mus. Cognacq-Jay). More important is the damaged wall-painting in the *Catacomb of Priscilla, of the early 3rd century, which is thought to be the earliest representation of the Madonna and Child, with a man pointing at a star. (It may, however, be the Prophecy of *Isaiah.) As an Eastern soothsayer, Balaam was held to foretell the *Magi led by a star to Jerusalem (Matt. 2: 2).

baldacchino (baldachin, baldaquin) Also sometimes referred to as a *ciborium, it may be a rich textile supported on four poles, held over the Blessed Sacrament (carried in a *monstrance) in processions, or over a bishop's throne. Such canopies are said to derive from those held over the Eastern emperors as a symbol of power. Like a ciborium, a baldacchino may also be a permanent structure of wood, metal, or stone over an altar, with four *columns or *piers supporting a dome-like top, or it may be hung on chains from the ceiling. The most famous baldacchino is the one by *Bernini, of gilt-bronze, which stands over the *confessio in St Peter's, Rome. It was made from bronze stripped from the Pantheon (1624–33). Sir Christopher *Wren seems to have intended a baldacchino for St Paul's Cathedral, and one was finally erected over the *High Altar when it was rebuilt after the Second World War. Baldacchinos are rare in Anglican churches.

Balthasar (Balthazar) was one of the *Magi.

bambino is Italian for baby boy and usually means the Christ Child, as in *Madonna col Bambino*. 'Il Santo Bambino' is a small statue, about 2 ft high, said to have been carved from olive-wood from the Garden of Gethsemane, perhaps *c.*1500. It is preserved in Sta Maria in

Ara Coeli, Rome, and is an object of popular devotion.

baptism All four Gospels relate how *John the Baptist, clad in a garment of camel-hair tied with a leather girdle (which makes him immediately recognizable in any image) preached repentance in the wilderness of Judaea and baptized penitents in the river Jordan, in a symbolic ritual cleansing. Jesus also came to him to be baptized; John demurred, but consented, proclaiming Him to be the Son of God, who would baptize with the Holy Ghost. All the Gospels say that 'the heavens opened, and he saw the Spirit of God descending like a dove and lighting upon him' (Matt. 3: 16–17). There are slight differences in the wording in the various Gospels, but the event, which was also witnessed by *John the Evangelist (as he afterwards became), was the moment when he was convinced that Jesus was the Messiah. *Andrew was probably also a witness. In Matt. 28: 19, after the Resurrection, Christ bade the Apostles to 'teach all nations, baptizing them', and in slightly different words the injunction is repeated in Mark 16: 15–16, and Luke 24: 47. Only in John 20: 21–3 do the words vary significantly, though the message remains the same.

In Acts 8: 36–8, *Philip baptized the believing eunuch in a nearby pool in one of the many references to baptism as the act which made the believer into a professed Christian. But once Christianity became established as a Church, and a legalized institution (*see* MILAN, EDICT OF), baptism became the first, and most important, rite for which special arrangements had to be made (*see* BAPTISTERY)—the Eucharist could be held in any convenient room. Because baptism was equated with a descent into the tomb (Rom. 7: 3–5) and a rebirth into a new Christian life, it was seen as a parallel with Christ's entombment and resurrection. Therefore the place where the rite was performed was often given a symbolic form, taking the shape of the type of tomb common in the area, or of a local *martyrium, as the most venerated kind of tomb. When partial immersion was superseded by affusion with water contained in a *font, the font itself often retained the symbolic shape.

Baptism in the early Church was performed by a bishop, and was combined with Confirmation (hence the provision of a chrismarion for the holy oils: see under BAPTISTERY), and the rite was originally performed only during the vigil of Easter, followed by the procession of the newly baptized and confirmed into the cathedral for the first Mass of Easter morning to receive their first Eucharist. Later, Pentecost and Christmas were added to the permitted dates, but with the spread of Christianity it became necessary to allow baptism to be performed by priests, so as to obviate long journeys to the nearest cathedral, and also because of the greater numbers desiring baptism. The spread of infant baptism resulted in the separation of the first Communion and Confirmation from Baptism, though Confirmation has always remained a sacrament reserved to a bishop, who now travels to the church, rather than the faithful to a cathedral.

Representations of the Baptism of Christ are legion, and follow the text in the Gospels. The dove—a physical manifestation of the same category of reality as the star of the *Magi—is always shown descending upon Christ, often amid rays of light. As late as the 9th century, while the Baptist is shown as a bearded man, at times appearing almost patriarchal, Christ is depicted as a beardless boy, despite the difference in their ages being no more than six months. This may well be an analogy with the representations of the Risen Christ as the Good Shepherd, in the Mausoleum of Galla Placidia, in *Ravenna (before 450) and in the small mosaic panels in the upper part of Sant' Apollinare Nuovo (493–early 6th cent.), also in Ravenna, where the post-Resurrection beardless Christ is differentiated from the bearded Christ of the Passion. The earliest representations of the Baptism of Christ are very damaged paintings in Rome, in the crypt of Sta Lucina at the entrance to the *catacomb of S. Calixtus on the Appian Way and in the vault of a room in the catacomb of SS Pietro e Marcellino (the Baptist is lost through damage), both of the late 3rd century; in a 3rd-century sarcophagus in Rome (Terme Museum), and in one of the ivory reliefs on the throne made in the 6th century, probably in Constantinople, for Archbishop Maximian of Ravenna (Ravenna, Mus. Arcivescovile). It appears also in the apex of the dome of the 6th-century Arian Baptistery in Ravenna, and its parallel in the Baptistery of the Orthodox was probably similar, though altered by later restorations.

By the 6th century, the scene closely follows the text in all the Gospels, with S. John baptizing Christ, who stands in the Jordan, and with the Holy Spirit descending upon him 'like a dove'. All later representations of the scene follow this iconography, with Christ resembling the bearded image of the *Mandylion, and generally with accompanying angels and other figures; see painted textile fragment (Egypt, 8th- to 11th-century tempera on linen ground, State Hermitage Museum, Saint Petersburg, Russia). The 11th- and 12th-century dome mosaics at Daphni and Hosios Lukas in Greece, are particularly fine examples. In Italy this traditional form was followed, for instance, by *Giotto in the Arena Chapel in Padua (*c.*1306), and in Renaissance examples such as the one by Piero della Francesca (*c.*1448/50: London, NG). Another example is the window (1905) by John La Farge (*see* NORTH AMERICA) in Harvard Chapel, Southwark Cathedral, London. Examples of murals overlooking the baptismal font are *The Baptism of Our Lord* (1952 in Chichester Cathedral) by Hans *Feibusch; anon. late 20th-century mural, Santa Trinidad Cathedral, Haiti; a fresco (2004) by Sergei Federov in Rochester Cathedral, Kent, reviewing the scene in Orthodox style.

Baptist *See* JOHN THE BAPTIST, S.

baptistery Once Christianity became an organized religion, after 313 (*see* MILAN, EDICT OF) instead of being a mission of preachers, it became convenient to have special buildings for its rites, instead of using *house-churches. The custom then arose of having a special arrangement—a vessel, a room, or a separate building—specifically designed for *baptism. This was even more necessary in that, in the early Church, neophytes were not admitted to the Eucharistic part of the service until after baptism. There is no literary or archaeological evidence for baptisteries before the early 3rd century; but, when special buildings began to be associated with community rites, it may be assumed that proper provision was made for the ceremony of initiation into the Church.

In the 3rd century, in the house-church at *Dura-Europos, used from soon after 200, a room seems to have been set aside as a place for baptisms, which at this time, and for long after, were by partial immersion and affusion. The earliest baptisteries, separate from the church or *basilica itself, were sometimes small domed structures, some with an *apse at one side, some with an *ambulatory round the baptismal pool (which rarely exceeded 3–4 ft in depth), and some were cruciform in shape. Ruins of such buildings have been found mainly in the Middle East, in areas surrounding the eastern and southern Mediterranean, and also in Greece, dating from as late as the 7th century, when the spread of Islam changed the religious character of the region. In places under Roman influence, such as France and Italy, there was a transition from a square to a circular, hexagonal, or octagonal form, as in the Lateran Baptistery (San Giovanni in Fonte, Rome), said to have been built by Constantine *c.*324 for the baptism of his sister and daughter, but perhaps of 432–40; and in the 5th century in Ravenna, where both the Baptisteries of the Orthodox and the *Arians are octagonal, as are the much later ones in Florence and Parma, to cite only the most famous. The choice of shape was dictated by association with the shape of a tomb—a cruciform shape stressed the parallel with the Crucifixion, the hexagonal shape alluded to the 'sixth day'—Friday, the day of the Crucifixion—and the octagonal refers to the Resurrection on the 'eighth day' (Rom. 6: 4) as the opening of a new dawn for the Christian soul. The circular plan also allowed references to the Anastasis Rotunda in Jerusalem, which was built on the site of Jesus's entombment. Because early baptisms were undertaken only by bishops and took place on particular days surrounding Easter and Whitsun, large numbers of catechumens entered the church at the same time, resulting in the need for large buildings designed for the purpose. These buildings took their shape from Roman mausolea, allowing the building form utilized for the commemoration of death to be harnessed for the representation of the Resurrection acted out in the baptismal rite. In the rite the bishop, who represented John the Baptist, immersed the catechumen three times, symbolizing the three days Christ spent in the tomb, and as such baptism was understood as the baptism into the death of Christ and so the allusion to Christ's own tomb was significant.

Because baptism was a ceremony for which the neophyte disrobed, casting aside his outer 'this-world' garments before entering the baptismal pool, and was then clothed in the white robe which was the outward symbol of his new Christian state, separate rooms or areas were required, particularly for the baptism of women. After baptism there was an anointing with holy oil or chrism, which in turn implies an area for a chrismarion in which the enthroned bishop performed this part of the rite. Frequently the chrismarion was *apsidal, or a rectangular projection from the baptistery, to admit of a cathedra, the throne of the bishop. Many Italian baptisteries have superb mosaic decorations, usually in their domes. Their relation to the basilica was always a close one, because of the nature of the ceremony, but once Christianity had become so general that it was, if only nominally, the religion of all the people, the practice of infant baptism superseded the earlier ritual of adult baptism, except among the Protestant Baptists, established in the 17th century, and among some charismatic sects, who still maintain the custom of total immersion. Even today, in cities such as Florence, most children born in the old city are brought to the ancient baptistery for baptism.

A few ancient baptisteries exist outside Italy. In France, at Fréjus, and at Poitiers, 6th- or 7th-century baptisteries have survived, though not in use; at Trier in Germany, the original 10th-century baptistery with its deep polygonal apse which served as a chrismarion was rebuilt in 1260 as the Marienkirche. In Italy, separate baptisteries continued to be built until the 10th century, and maintained in repair and use, and even rebuilt until the 14th century, after which baptism mostly took place in the church itself. English examples are rare, but one seems to have existed at Canterbury (*c*.740); it should not be confused with the early medieval water-tower which, during the 19th century, housed the font.

The baptism of infants led to the introduction of the *font, and to its placing within the church itself.

Barbara, Saint It is not certain whether Barbara ever existed, but she may have been an Egyptian martyr of the 3rd (?) century. Her legend was very popular in the Middle Ages and is known in various forms in both East and West by the 8th century, when the earliest known painting of her was made (Rome, Sta Maria Antiqua). Later, the **Golden Legend* spread her cult. She is supposed to have been the daughter of Dioscuros, a pagan ruler who shut her up in a tower. Barbara became a convert to Christianity and added a third window to her tower, in honour of the Holy Trinity. Her infuriated father brought her before the magistrate, who caused her to be tortured and, finally, beheaded by her own father. He was struck by lightning and no trace was left of him. As a result, Barbara became invoked against sudden death and especially against death by fire or lightning, and, therefore, patron saint of firemen, artillerymen, and miners. Later, she was thought to help those in danger of death to receive the Last Sacraments before death, and thus became one of the fourteen Holy Helpers (*see* VIERZEHNHEILIGEN). She has many attributes, but the usual ones are a tower (sometimes a small one held in her hands) or a cannon, and sometimes a pyx or chalice. In the unfinished painting by Jan van *Eyck (1434: Antwerp) she is shown reading, referring to her studies before her conversion. In the background, workmen are building a large tower. What were alleged to be her relics were brought from Constantinople to Venice, and were placed in the monastery of San Giovanni Evangelista on the island of Torcello in 1009.

Barnabas, Saint, was a Cypriot Jew whose original name was Joseph, but who was renamed Barnabas, meaning 'son of consolation' (or 'preaching') by the Apostles. He was one of the original disciples, since he was the alternative choice to Matthias, proposed by Peter (Acts 1: 23) to replace Judas. Though he was not one of the Twelve *Apostles named by Jesus he was, like Paul, later counted as an Apostle, probably because he persuaded the original twelve that Paul's conversion was genuine. His story, told in Acts, is inseparable from that of Paul, but later legends have him as the first Bishop of Milan and as martyred in Cyprus (?in 61). Most representations of him are in scenes from Acts, together with Paul: in Acts 14 it is related that the pagans at Lystra wished to offer sacrifice to them, believing Barnabas to be Jupiter and Paul to be Mercury. In Counter-Reformation treatises it is therefore asserted that Barnabas must have been of majestic appearance, as in the Raphael cartoon (London, V & A) for the Vatican Tapestries of the Acts of the Apostles. His cult was spread by the **Golden Legend* in the Middle Ages, and he was popular in England and especially in Tuscany (the S. Barnaba Altarpiece by Botticelli, now in the Uffizi, was painted for the Florentine church of San Barnaba, and shows him with an olive branch as his attribute). More usually, his attributes are a stone (symbol of his martyrdom), or the Gospel of S. Mark, who, according to some traditions, was the John Mark mentioned in Acts, and who may have been related to him. The *Coronation of the Virgin* by Niccolò Gerini and Jacopo di Cione (1373: Florence, Uffizi) shows S. Barnabas holding open the Gospel of S. Mark. The earliest representation that can be identified is in the apse mosaic in San Paolo fuori le Mura, Rome, of the ? 4th century.

The Barnabites, a small religious Order founded in 1530, are named after his church in Milan.

BAROQUE

As a historical epoch of the 17th and early 18th centuries, Baroque represents a radical cultural transformation, leading to a coherent overcoming of the late 16th-century Mannerism. What Baroque culture tends to overcome is the excessive individualism, fragmentation, formalism, and abstract mode of representation of the post-Renaissance era. One of the main characteristics of the Baroque transformation was the tendency to restore the long-term unity of the fragmented culture manifested as a search for universal values, shared goals in life and faith.

It is therefore not surprising that the possible unity was found in that which is most universal, i.e. in mathematics, closely associated with the ultimate principles of logic, with sufficient reason, and finally with the new principles of theology. All this led to the formation of a possible universal knowledge-science (*mathesis universalis*), seen as a background for communication in a universal language (*clavis universalis*). The traditional tendency to see Baroque knowledge-science as an independent domain obscures the fact that science at that time was an integral part of the general coherence of culture.

Galileo, Huyghens, and Newton are not considered Baroque scientists, whereas the great philosopher and mathematician Leibniz, who was involved in a serious argument about the nature of modern science with Newton, is the Baroque thinker par excellence. We find a similar situation in architecture. So the works of Sir Christopher *Wren, which include astronomy, of Claude Perrault, which include medicine, or of Guarino *Guarini, which include geometry, represent not only different tendencies in Baroque architecture but also different trends in Baroque science. The affinity between science and Baroque culture hints at deeper dimensions of representation, not yet fully appreciated. The new developments in the sphere of knowledge created radically new conditions for the nature of Baroque art. In the atmosphere of the Catholic Reformation, the mathematical nature of universality, identified with the divine order of reality, challenged art to reconcile the abstract, mostly geometrically defined representations with the concrete phenomena of the everyday life. The response of Baroque art to this challenge can be seen in the transformation of the Renaissance receptive into a projective representation, which was to become the foundation of Baroque illusionism. Other responses took place in the formation of Baroque opera, musical polyphony, and in the new integration of painting, sculpture, and architecture in what is conventionally referred to as *Gesamtkunstwerk*. The integration of individual arts became possible owing to a communicative movement between them. In the Baroque way of thinking, the movement, known better as 'Baroque dynamism', is seen as the key to the enigma of creation, the manifestation of the divine order in the terrestrial world, and the continuity of this order. It is characteristic that Leibniz, the most representative thinker of the Baroque era, held firm against Descartes that motion and not extension (*res extensa*) defines physical bodies and the reality of the created world.

It is generally agreed that Baroque has its origins in Rome. The *Council of Trent's brief pronouncements on the function of art in the service of religion (1563), along with an upsurge of confidence in the Roman Church after the Reformation, created the conditions for a new mode of representation sometimes referred to as the 'Jesuit style'. However, this is true only in so far as the Society of *Jesus (established in the 1540s) had similar aims. In architecture, the works of Giacomo della Porta (1532–1602) and Carlo *Maderno (1556–1629) represent the initial steps to the high Baroque architecture of Pietro da Cortona (1596–1669), Giovanni Lorenzo *Bernini (1598–1680), and Francesco *Borromini (1599–1667). Among their most important buildings in Rome are: Cortona's Sta Maria in via Lata (1660), Santi Luca e Martina (1634–69), and Sta Maria della Pace (1667); and Bernini's Cappella Cornaro with the *Ecstasy of Saint Theresa* (1645–52) in the church of Sta Maria della Vittoria, and the church of Sant'Andrea al Quirinale (1661). In St Peter's basilica, there are Bernini's *baldacchino (1633), the *Cathedra Petri (1653), and the great colonnade and piazza outside the basilica (1660–65). Borromini created the most original and imaginative architecture in Rome, but was less concerned with the integration of architecture, painting, and sculpture into a unified result than with the relation of geometry to the meaning of architectural detail and its iconography. Foremost among his buildings are the *monastery of San Carlo alle Quattro Fontane (1634–43), Oratorio dei Filippini (1637–40), and Sant' Ivo della Sapienza (1640–50). Sculpture was represented in Rome mainly by Lorenzo Bernini, but also by his rival Alessandro *Algardi (1598–1654). In painting the critical step towards Baroque proper was the fresco decoration of the gallery in Palazzo Farnese by Annibale *Carracci (1560–1609) assisted by his brother Agostino (1557–1602) and cousin Ludovico (1555–1619), based on the theme *The Loves of the Gods* (1597–1608).

The monumental frescoes in the church interiors, which became a source of inspiration for the rest of Europe, were those of Giovanni Lanfranco (1582–1647), the dome fresco in St Andrea delle Valle and Pietro da Cortona in Sta Maria in Vallicella (1647–51). The most influential of all, and closest to the spirit of the Baroque, was the work of Michelangelo da *Caravaggio (1571–1610).

It was from Rome that Baroque culture radiated out to the Catholic world, even as far as Latin America and Goa in India. Baroque was obviously more successful in Catholic states such as Austria, Bohemia, Spain, and Portugal and, later, in the Catholic parts of Germany, as well as in Hungary and the Low Countries. A good example is the work of Peter Paul *Rubens (1577–1640), whose paintings are often more radical in the Baroque sense than paintings of his Italian contemporaries. Baroque culture also influenced, though mostly indirectly, the Protestant parts of Europe, as can be seen in 17th-century Dutch architecture and painting, and most explicitly in the works of *Rembrant (1606–69).

In European architecture north of Alps, the main influence, apart from Rome, came from Piedmont and particularly from the works of Guarino Guarini (1624–83). His treatment of space as the elaborate interpenetration of vaults, based on the principles of projectivity and spatial continuity, strongly influenced Viennese architects Johann Lukas von Hildebrandt (1668–1745) and Johann Bernhard Fischer von Erlach (1656–1723), as well as the Prague architects Christoph Dientzenhofer (1655–1722), and his son Kilian Ignaz (1689–1751), and Jan Santini-Aichel (1677–1723).

The French architecture of the 17th century illustrates the essential ambiguity of European Baroque, both its radical and its classical tendencies. And yet even in France there is no Baroque and classicism, but only Baroque classicism. This is true not only for the complex of the chateau of Versailles, the inspiration for most of the Baroque residences across Europe during the 17th and 18th centuries, but also for the smaller buildings such as the church of Val-de-Grâce; (1640–49) by François Mansart (1598–1666), or the College des Quatre Nations (now the Institut de France) (1662–70) by Louis Le Vau (1612–70). European Baroque culminates and comes to its end in the middle of the 18th century in such buildings as Kilian Ignaz Dientzenhofer's St Nicholas Church in Lesser Town Square in Prague (1737–51) or the Vierzehnheiligen Church (1743–72) in Franconia by Balthasar Neumann (1687–1753). In retrospect, Baroque can be seen as a culmination of European humanistic culture and also as a foundation of Modernism.

Bartholomew, Saint, Apostle. One of the original *Apostles, the Bartholomew mentioned in Matt., Mark, and Luke is usually identified with the Nathanael in John (1: 45–51; 21: 2), who is best known for asking, 'Can anything good come out of Nazareth?' He is associated with *Philip and may have evangelized India and Arabia. He was eventually martyred, traditionally by being flayed alive, but he is also said to have been crucified and beheaded. An *Apocryphal Gospel is attributed to him. What were said to be his relics were brought to Rome *c.*983 and are still in San Bartolommeo on the Tiber Island, but an arm-reliquary was given to Canterbury Cathedral in the 11th century, and was presumably lost at the Reformation. Because of the nature of his martyrdom he is the patron saint of butchers (cf. St Bartholomew's Hospital, in Smithfield Market, London), tanners, leather-workers, and so on and, from the late 12th century, his attribute is a butcher's knife.

In earlier representations he held a scroll. The first representations are in Rome—San Paolo fuori le Mura (outside the walls), Sta Maria Antiqua, and Ravenna, San Vitale, in the 8th century, and frequently in Byzantine mosaics. By far the best-known representation is the figure in Michelangelo's *Last Judgement*, where he is shown holding his own skin, with the features of Michelangelo himself. Because of the legends associated with him he was not popular during the Counter-Reformation.

*Rembrandt painted two pictures of him, perhaps from a series of Apostles; both are in California (San Diego, Timken Mus. and Malibu, Getty Mus.) and both show him in the traditional way, with black hair and beard, streaked with white, and holding a knife. His gruesome martyrdom was painted and etched by *Ribera more than once (e.g. Florence, Pitti) with vivid realism.

Bartimaeus was the blind beggar seated by the roadside, who was healed by Christ on His last journey to Jerusalem. Although blind, Bartimaeus recognized Him as the Messiah (Mark 10: 46–52): he is one of the few people healed by Jesus to be specifically named in the Gospels. He was not the same blind man as the one who was healed by bathing his eyes in the Pool of Siloam (John 9), who is more frequently represented e.g. in the panel (London, NG) from Duccio's *Maestà*.

Bartolommeo della Porta, Fra (*c.* 1472–1517), was a Florentine painter who became a Dominican monk in 1500, under the influence of *Savonarola. He became head of the San Marco monastery workshop in 1504, a position once filled by Fra *Angelico. Visits to Venice in 1508, and to Rome in 1514 or 1515, brought him into contact with the works of Bellini and Giorgione, and with Raphael. He developed a very marked style, characterized by simplicity in pose, decorum in presentation, gestures and expressions of rapt devotion, with generalized draperies so as to mark the difference between earthly and saintly figures. He thus forms a clear watershed between the tender, charming, often genre quality of 15th-century Florentine religious painting, and the deliberately sober and didactic style of the 16th century. He did not initiate these changes, which were in the air from the 1480s onwards in the work of Perugino and Leonardo, but his powerful and consistent expression of them gave them more force, as did the works of his younger contemporary, Andrea del Sarto. Examples of this graver style are the *Vision of S. Bernard* (1507: Florence, Accad.) and especially the large *Madonna in Glory with Saints and Donor* (1512: Besançon, Cathedral), where the Madonna and Child are floating in the air, rather than realistically sitting on a chair in the 15th-century manner. The *Holy Family* (London, NG) is a good example of his Raphaelesque Madonnas. After his death the San Marco workshop ceased to be of any importance.

basileus *See* BASILICA.

basilica The word may derive from Gk. *basileus* and mean 'house of the king', but the exact origin and meaning are unclear. There is further confusion because the word basilica has an architectural meaning and also a second, ecclesiastical, one. When *Constantine made it possible for Christians to own property and worship openly it became necessary to provide *church buildings large enough to contain hundreds of people. The pagan temples—still in use—had been shrines of a god, and sacrifices were held outside them, so they provided no prototypes, even if they had been acceptable as models. Constantine's architects, however, familiar with large public buildings used as law courts or commercial exchanges, quickly established an easily constructible form that combined reusing redundant building elements and the use of cheap masonry/brickwork; these basilicas were used for the first major Christian churches that were not *martyria. The general shape of these buildings was a large oblong with doors on one short side and an apsidal projection on the opposite one, perhaps for the judge's seat. The main body of the hall had aisles on either side, separated from it by a row of columns. The walls of this central nave rose above the aisles, so that windows in the *clerestory gave light to the nave, as well as the light from lower windows in the aisle walls. Sometimes there were two aisles on either side, instead of only one. This is the genesis of the Christian parish church, established in the 4th century and used for Constantine's great foundations in Rome, the Holy Land, and Constantinople. The Roman (or Latin) type normally has an *apse at the east end for the bishop's throne, a straight entablature over the columns separating nave and *aisles, a covered porch and an *atrium outside, and, sometimes, a *transept.

Variations include the Hellenic type, the Transverse Basilica, and the *hall-church; the first with side chambers flanking the apse (*bema), arches over the columns, a *narthex, and galleries for women over the aisles (*gynaeceum); the second has the nave at right angles to the door/altar axis; the third has the aisles as high as the nave, so that the light in the nave is reduced by there being no clerestory, the windows being only in the aisles.

The second meaning of the word basilica is as a title of honour. The four patriarchal basilicas in Rome are St John Lateran, for the Patriarch of the West (i.e. the pope); St Peter's, for the Patriarch of Constantinople; San Paolo fuori le Mura, for the Patriarch of Alexandria; and Sta Maria Maggiore, for the Patriarch of Antioch. All these have papal altars, i.e. altars at which only the pope may say Mass. San Lorenzo fuori le Mura, for the Patriarch of Jerusalem, is sometimes added. Several other Roman churches are also counted as basilicas, e.g. Sta Croce in Gerusalemme, Sta Sabina, San Sebastiano, Sant'Agnese, and San Clemente. Many other grand churches also claim the honorific, e.g. San Francesco at Assisi and the Santo at Padua, and many others outside Italy.

basilisk A mythical *beast, invented in pre-Christian times, with the body of a dragon or serpent, and the head and wings of a cock. Its looks could kill and its breath was fiery, so it was used as a symbol of lust and of the Devil. In the Vulgate, Ps. 90 'Super aspidem et basiliscum ambulabis...' is translated in NRSV (Ps. 91) as 'you shall tread upon the lion and the adder: the young lion and the serpent you will trample underfoot.' This was interpreted as Christ's victory over the Devil.

Basle, Council of *See* FLORENCE AND FERRARA, COUNCIL OF.

Bassus, Junius *See* JUNIUS.

Bathsheba *See* DAVID.

Batoni, Pompeo (1708–87), was the most fashionable portrait painter in Rome in the 18th century, whose sitters included many of the English *milordi* on the Grand Tour, often posed against the more picturesque bits of ancient Rome. He also painted many conventional altarpieces, including the *Fall of Simon Magus*, intended for St Peter's but now in Sta Maria degli Angeli, Rome; he is notable for having been the first to paint the Sacred *Heart, devotion to which was authorized only in 1765, though probably derived directly from the *Arma Christi. One version is in Rome, Il Gesù, 1765–7, and an *Allegory of the World adoring the Sacred Heart*, of 1781, commissioned by the Queen of Portugal, is in Lisbon, Estrela Basilica.

bays Each opening of an arcade, of any shape of arch, or of a colonnade, with the structure above it, is described as a 'bay'. For instance, the nave of Norwich Cathedral is fourteen bays long; that of Westminster Abbey is eleven bays long; Sta Maria Maggiore in Rome is thirteen bays long.

beads *See* ROSARY.

'beak-head' ornament A form of Romanesque ornament, usually placed around arches, consisting of a row of birds, heads, or sometimes animal heads with their beaks or jaws biting on to a roll moulding. It is often found in Norman Romanesque churches and is common in England.

bear *See* BESTIARY.

Bearden, Romare (1911–88) An African-American abstract expressionist painter who grew up in Harlem in New York City. He expressed the everyday experiences of black people in America, including religious belief and ritual, an inheritance from the *Harlem Renaissance of a generation earlier. An early work was *Golgotha* (1945), and later he produced a series of paintings pertaining to ritual, including *Prevalence of Ritual: Baptism* (1964), and other subjects: *Sermons: The Wall of Jericho* (1964) and *Black Madonna and Child* (1969). In addition to New York/American black heritage, the artist also drew on Caribbean influences. *See also* NORTH AMERICA.

beasts, symbolic Beasts of all kinds—animals, birds, fishes—both real and imaginary, occur in the Bible, often with symbolic meanings: for instance, Christ's words to Peter—'Feed my lambs... Feed my sheep' (John 21: 15–17); or the monsters in the *Apocalypse, such as the beast from the sea with seven heads and ten horns. At the very beginning of Christian art a fish is a symbol for Christ (*see* ICHTHYS), and the whale a symbol of the Resurrection. The use of animal symbolism had been established by e.g. Aesop's *Fables* of the 6th century BC, and was continued in the medieval *Bestiaries. The various beasts in the Apocalypse (see especially Rev. 13) and in the Bestiaries stimulated allegorical interpretations which were often contradictory—e.g. the *ass as a symbol of lust and stupidity, but also of humility and patience. Among the most frequent are *amphisbene, *ape, *basilisk, deer (*see* HART), *dog, *dragon, *goat, *griffin, *hedgehog, hind (*see* HART), *lamb, *lion, *mouse, *ox, *rabbit, *ram, *serpent, stag (*see* HART). (*See also* BIRDS and FISH.)

beatification, beatus Beatification is the final stage before canonization, allowing the use of the title 'The Blessed So-and-So' and permitting a public cult, either in a particular region or in a religious Order (*see* SAINTS AND BEATI). The procedure was formalized in the 18th century by Benedict XIV: in the Middle Ages and later, local cults were often authorized by individual bishops and there are, consequently, many works of art representing people who have never had more than local significance. When such works are removed from their original context the subject-matter may become unintelligible. The Poussin of *Sta Rita of Cascia* (Dulwich Gall.) or the *St Catherine of Bologna*, by the Flemish Master of the Baroncelli Portraits (London, Courtauld Inst.), are both cases where iconographical peculiarities have made it possible to identify the true subjects.

Beatus group of manuscripts Beatus (d. *c.*798), was the Abbot of Liébana in N. Spain. His Commentary on the *Apocalypse (776) was very influential and the illustrations form a distinct group. More than twenty MSS are known, the finest being the one from St-Sever, now in Paris (BN), of 1028/72.

Beatus page The first page of a *psalter, so called from the first words of Ps. 1: 'Beatus vir qui non abiit' (Blessed is the man). The initial B is usually decorated and in some MSS occupies most of the page.

Becket, Saint Thomas *See* THOMAS OF CANTERBURY, S.

Beelzebub *See* DEVIL, THE.

Bel and the Dragon The story of Bel and the Dragon is part of the OT Book of Daniel (Vg. 14: 2–29) which is omitted in Protestant texts of the *Bible, or printed in the *apocrypha. It includes (14: 30–42) the popular story of *Daniel in the lions' den, of which another version (Dan. 6: 10–24) is given in the Hebrew text used by the Reformers.

belfry The part of a bell-tower in which the bells are hung. Often used for the tower itself. *See* CAMPANILE.

Bellini, Giovanni (*c.*1430–1516), was one of the most famous and finest Venetian painters. He was almost certainly trained in the family workshop of his father Jacopo, deriving much, as did his brother Gentile, from his father's two important sketchbooks (London, BM; Paris, Louvre), and even more from his brother-in-law, *Mantegna. Bellini was the truly formative influence of his century in Venice, affecting all the painters of his own and the next generation, since his pupils included Giorgione, *Titian, and Sebastiano del Piombo; no one, even if officially in his brother's studio, or in that of the Vivarini, escaped the influence of his style, colour, and inventiveness.

He was the greatest of that group of Venetian painters called *Madonnieri* (Madonna painters), painting a long series of simple-looking Madonna and Child pictures, sometimes alone, sometimes with attendant saints, of infinite variety and subtlety. Sometimes there is a plain canopy behind the figures with a glimpse of little trees on either side (*Madonna degli Alberetti*, 1487: Venice, Accad.), sometimes a wide landscape (*Madonna of the Meadow*, *c.*1505: London, NG); he achieves a seemingly endless number of variations on the simple theme of the Madonna holding the Child in an upright format ranging from nine inches to 32 inches high, with fewer examples of greater width than height. The type changes little over the years, but certain elements remain constant. The Madonna is always a grave, serious figure, usually with a white coif covering her hair beneath her blue hooded mantle; the Child, either held in her arms, or standing or lying on a parapet across the front of the picture, or—in the larger pictures—held standing on her knee, is almost invariably a robust lively infant, but the group always presents the image consistent with the sacramental character of the group: the Virgin presents to our gaze the Word made Flesh. Whether a private devotional image or an altarpiece, the group is the most significant iteration of the cardinal thesis of the Gospels, and has the hieratic significance of the Sacrament itself, enclosed within the ciborium of the altar. The iconography of these groups is only apparently simple, whether in the plain two-figure examples where the low viewpoint forces the spectator into the classic devotional pose of looking up towards the image, or in the grand altarpieces where the attendant saints remain distinct, not looking towards the Godhead enthroned above them, but meditating on the Mystery enshrined in the vision which they accompany. In this way Bellini conceals the immense skill with which he combines the creation of a work of art with the didactic purpose of the image. Occasionally donors are represented kneeling in overt worship accompanied by their saintly patrons, and thus break this rule of reticence, but even when, as in the votive pictures of doges, men from the historic world appear before the Heavenly throne, the Child may notice, bless, acknowledge them, the Virgin remains impassive and unheeding. She is the corporeal ciborium, the earthly bearer of the Godhead.

Bellini was open to the influence of others, not only of Mantegna, but also of Antonello da Messina, from whom he may have adapted the form of the *Sacra Conversazione (or Antonello from him). Of this type are the grand altarpieces of *S. Giobbe* (1483/5: Venice, Accad.) and *S. Zaccaria* (1505: Venice, in the church) which both develop the theme pioneered in Florence, setting it now so that the architecture within the picture continues the architectural setting outside the picture space, as *Piero della Francesca had done in the *Brera Madonna* of *c.*1475, so drawing the spectator into the spatial arrangement within the picture. The background in all three of his major Madonna and Child altarpieces—the two already mentioned and the triptych of the *Frari Madonna* (1488: Venice, Frari church)—of semi-domes in golden mosaic behind the Madonna, are references to the golden mosaics of St Mark's and are deliberate allusions to the grandeur of Venice as expressed by its major monument.

He created deeply devotional images of the *Pietà* where in the figure of the dead Christ upheld by angels the influence of his father's sketchbooks and of *Donatello's Paduan works is clear, and he was able to take this simple devotional theme a stage further in the poignant *Pietà with the Virgin and S. John* (1460/70: Milan, Brera) and in the marvellous design of the *Pietà* (now in the Vatican Mus.) which once crowned the *Coronation of the Virgin* (1471–4: Pesaro, Mus.) with its pathetic symphony of interlaced hands.

The *S. Francis on Mount Avernus* (*c.*1480–5: New York, Frick Coll.), which is not a stigmatization, despite often being so-called, shows that his observation of nature is the servant of his astonishing ability to convey the most intricate symbolism in terms of the most accurate physical presentation. No detail of this seemingly simple representation of the stigmatized saint in ecstasy outside his desert hermitage is without its deeper meaning, and this power of appearing merely to charm should never deceive one into believing that the picture has no deeper significance. The same argument can be applied as early as the *Agony in the Garden*, apparently painted in competition with Mantegna's similar subject (*c.*1459: both London, NG), continues in the *Transfiguration* (*c.*1487: Naples, Mus.), and is also valid for the *Madonna of the Meadow* (*c.*1505: London, NG). None of these works is as simple as it looks, and Bellini must be counted among the most deeply religious, spiritually informed, and learned artists of the Venetian Renaissance, particularly in Franciscan theological argument and iconography.

bells Soon after the Peace of the Church in 313 it became possible to summon the faithful publicly, and bells (or wooden clappers) were soon used. Bells were certainly known in the West in the 5th/6th centuries, but clappers were normal in the East until the 9th. In the 10th century bells were given names, and the practice of consecrating them—popularly called 'baptism of the bells'—began. Many were decorated with inscriptions or with engraved or moulded ornament, but historically the bellfounder's craft was extremely important since it was probably the means of transmitting the technique of casting sculpture in bronze, which was not fully recovered until the Early Renaissance, despite a few earlier examples.

A Sanctus Bell is a small hand-bell rung at various times during Mass, specifically at the Elevation of the Host, but also at other times in various countries.

Belshazzar, an OT King of Babylon (Dan. 5: 1–30) who gave a great feast for his lords, wives, and concubines where they drank from the golden vessels plundered from the Temple at Jerusalem by his father,

Nebuchadnezzar. A hand appeared and wrote—'the writing on the wall'—*Mene, mene, tekel, parsin*, which nobody could understand. *Daniel interpreted it as meaning Belshazzar's death, which followed that night. The story is told in Dan. 5: 23–31. It is a rare subject in art, but there is a painting by Rembrandt of *c.*1635 in London (NG), and a large and characteristically grandiose *Martin (1820–1) is known from engravings and replicas.

bema (Gk. a tribune or speaker's platform) A dais for clergy in the *apse of an Early Christian church, corresponding to the sanctuary or *chancel. There is a throne (*cathedra) for the bishop in the centre, and a bench (*synthronon) for the clergy at the sides of the throne in the central apse. In Eastern churches it is the space beyond the *iconostasis, and in large churches is in three parts, each with an apse: the altar in the middle, the *prothesis on the north, and the *Diaconicon on the south.

Benedict of Nursia, Saint (*c.* 480–*c.*547/50), founder of the Benedictine Order and 'Patriarch of Western Monasticism', was born in what is now Norcia, near Spoleto in Italy. He studied briefly in Rome before withdrawing to Subiaco, where he lived in a cave, now called the Sacro Speco ('Holy Cave'). He soon attracted disciples, but an attempt on his life *c.*525 led him to go to Monte Cassino, where he settled *c.*529. The monastery there has always been recognized as the mother-house of the Benedictines, but Benedict himself did not actually found any Order. What he did was to write a Rule, *c.*540, which became the foundation of all Western monachism. It is largely drawn from Scripture and from the 'Rule of the Master', written by an unknown Italian contemporary, but it is sensible and avoids fanatical asceticism. He wrote for a community of twelve monks with an abbot, like Christ and the twelve Apostles, and each house was to be autonomous. He divided the day into periods of prayer (the Opus Dei), private study, and manual work for self-sufficiency. From the 6th to the 10th centuries this Rule was gradually adopted in the West, becoming the basic rule for all monastic life outside the E. Orthodox Church. The foundation of *Cluny in the 10th century led to variations on the Rule as formulated by Benedict, but most of the new foundations retained the essentials. The Order of S. Benedict was hugely successful—at the Reformation there were 186 houses in England alone, including the vast foundations at Westminster and St Albans—and in the course of time the monks, by now nearly all priests, did less manual work and turned more to teaching. They ran, and still run, very famous schools, and in Germany in the 17th and 18th centuries their grand houses often had an imperial function, the *Kaisersaal* being a state apartment for imperial receptions, as at Ottobeuren in Bavaria.

Benedict himself is usually represented as a bearded elderly man, often wearing the black tunic, hood, scapular, and cowl of his later Order (except when he is shown in *Olivetan, *Cistercian, or other monasteries, when he usually wears their white habit). An example is the extensive series of scenes from his life, by *Signorelli (1497–9) and Sodoma (1505–8) at Monte Oliveto Maggiore, near Siena. The earliest known representation of him is in the Hermes Catacomb in Rome, of the 8th century, and another, of the 10th century, is in San Crisogono, also in Rome. Among the commonest scenes from his legend are the attempts to poison him, when a beaker broke and spilled the poison in the form of a snake (cf. S. John the Evangelist), and poisoned bread was carried away by a raven (cf. Elijah); when tempted by the flesh he rolled himself naked in a thorn-bush outside his cave, and when visited by Totila, King of the Ostrogoths, in disguise he detected the imposture.

His sister, S. Scholastica, was the first Benedictine nun.

benediction, benedictional Properly speaking, a benediction (Lat. *benedictio*, blessing) is any blessing, but, from the 16th century until the present it was a devotion during which the Blessed Sacrament was exposed for public adoration in a *monstrance. It is rarely represented in art, perhaps because of its relative modernity.

A **benedictional** is a collection of formulas of blessings made for a bishop, according to his personal requirements, e.g. for the feast of the patron saint of his diocese. The blessings are taken from other *liturgical books, such as the missal or pontifical. The *Benedictional of S. Ethelwold* (London, British Library) is a famous illuminated MS of the Winchester School of Anglo-Saxon art, made *c.*971/84 by the scribe Godeman for S. Ethelwold, Bishop of Winchester.

Benjamin *See* JACOB, JOSEPH.

Bentley, John Francis (1839–1902), was, after *Pugin, the leading English Catholic architect, whose only competitor might have been Herbert *Gribble. In 1894 he was commissioned by Cardinal Vaughan to design a new Roman Catholic cathedral in Westminster, and it was politic that it should not conflict in style with the classical Baroque of St Paul's, the High Gothic of Westminster Abbey, or the Tudor Gothic Revival of the Houses of Parliament. Cardinal Vaughan suggested Byzantine, and Bentley, after an Italian journey, was inspired by a combination of San Vitale, Ravenna, the Santo, Padua, and St Mark's, Venice, with the exterior colour-banding in brick and stone of North Italian Gothic. The unusual exterior is marked by an asymmetrically placed *campanile—the tallest church tower in London, 284 ft. high—and is complemented inside by a vast interior space with a sequence of large concrete domes over the nave, choir, and transepts, and smaller ones over aisles and side chapels. He always intended that the interior should be decorated with mosaics and revetments of variegated marbles, although these (slowly being effected) obscure the splendour of his huge brick structures. The pierced marble *transennae of the side chapels (one of which has the finest modern inlaid marble floor in England), and the huge *baldacchino over the High Altar testify to his concern for unity of design and detail. The cathedral and its dependencies were almost complete by the time of the architect's death. The stone *Stations of the Cross* by Eric *Gill (1913–18) are its finest interior sculpture and a noble monument to the artist.

Bernardino of Siena, Saint (1380–1444) Patron saint of Siena. Bernardino joined the *Franciscan order in Siena in 1402 and began preaching in N. Italy in 1417, rapidly becoming famous and attracting huge crowds. He was particularly devoted to the Name of Jesus and was in the habit of holding up a tablet with the sacred monogram *IHS surrounded by flame-like rays. He was Vicar-General of the Observant Franciscans, 1438–42. He was canonized very rapidly, in 1450, and is frequently represented in Italian, especially Tuscan, art. The image is probably based on a death-mask, and he is almost always shown as an elderly man, extremely emaciated, with a pointed nose and chin, generally with his IHS tablet. The picture by Sano di Pietro in Siena, which shows him preaching, was painted in 1427—i.e. in his lifetime. There are reliefs of scenes from his life by Agostino di Duccio on the oratory dedicated to him in Perugia in 1451 (completed 1461), and several frescoes by Pintoricchio in Sta Maria in Aracoeli, Rome, of 1485, in the chapel dedicated to the saint.

Bernard of Clairvaux, Saint (1090/1–1153), founded the *Cistercian Order and was one of the great saints of the 12th century. He was born near Dijon, of a noble family, and entered the Benedictine Abbey at Cîteaux in 1112, moving to a desolate site at Clairvaux, also in Burgundy, in 1115. He became Abbot there and under him the Cistercians developed a more austere form of monasticism in 1118: at his death there were more than 500 houses, including several in Britain. Bernard's attitude to the arts was not favourable, and he strongly criticized some of the Benedictine abbeys, especially *Cluny, for their splendour. In a famous letter he attacked rich decoration in churches, but conceded that it might sometimes be permissible for laymen, though not for monastic houses: 'I say nothing about the vast height of your churches, their immoderate length, their superfluous breadth . . . the curious carvings and paintings . . . '. He goes on to address monks 'in the cloister . . . what profit is there in these ridiculous monsters? . . . To what purpose are those unclean apes, those fierce lions, those monstrous centaurs . . . For God's sake, if men are not ashamed of these follies, why do they not at least shrink from the expense?'

Perhaps because of this, he is not very commonly represented, although he is easily recognized by his white habit, adopted by his Order instead of the black robes, such as the Benedictines originally wore. It is said that Bernard had a vision of the Virgin, in which she instructed him to make this change. Other attributes include a beehive or three mitres—the first because of the eloquence of his preaching (an attribute shared with SS Ambrose and Augustine), and the second because he was offered three bishoprics, but refused them all. There were 100 scenes from his life in stained-glass panels in the Cistercian house at Altenberg, near Cologne, but many have been lost. Among the survivors are several now in St Mary's, Shrewsbury. Of the two most famous scenes in his legend, one is that of the apparition to him of the Virgin, when he was ill and unable to write. There are several Italian altarpieces of this subject, including the one of 1486 by Filippino Lippi, in the Badia,

Florence. At a later date, apparently in Spain, this legend was augmented by the idea that the Virgin inspired him by placing a few drops of milk from her breast on his lips. The most famous representation of this *Lactatio Bernardi* is by Murillo (Madrid, Prado). The second scene shows him praying before a crucifix, when the Crucified Christ bends down and embraces him.

Bernini, Gianlorenzo (1598–1680). His art is the epitome of the *Baroque, which he virtually created in his architecture and sculpture, most of it in Rome. Its repercussions were widespread all over Europe, particularly in Catholic countries, although in its secular forms and tinged with local characteristics, it achieved an almost equal dissemination irrespective of religious conditions.

His first major religious work was the triumphal gilt-bronze *baldacchino over the High Altar of St Peter's (1624–33). It was inspired by the surviving twisted marble columns from Constantine's Old St Peter's, themselves inspired by the columns of the Beautiful Gate of the Temple in Jerusalem. The four columns supporting the corners of the baldacchino are surmounted by a wind-blown canopy, with exuberant angels and putti, and decorative garlands, the whole structure standing over 100 ft. high. His much later *Cathedra Petri* (1657–66) in the apse of the basilica was foreseen from the start as a culmination of the vista through the columns of the baldacchino. The *Cathedra Petri* shows four Fathers of the Church—two Latin, SS Ambrose and Augustine, and two Greek, SS Athanasius and John Chrysostom—upholding the throne of S. Peter, which is illumined by brilliant golden stained glass with the image of the Dove representing the Holy Spirit, the whole surrounded by clouds with jubilant angels and putti. Both works symbolize the continuity of the Church and the supremacy of its doctrinal orthodoxy in a world in which it found itself increasingly under attack from the Reformation. These works also demonstrate the resurgence of Catholicism in the Counter-Reformation period, and its renewal of confidence and energy is shown by the artistic expression of a new upsurge of faith.

Private works, for example the *Ecstasy of S. Theresa of Avila* in the Cornaro Chapel in Sta Maria della Vittoria (1645–52), show him using a similar language of ecstatic devotion expressed in the white marble vision of the saint and the angel, lit by the golden light of the stained glass filtered through gilded bronze rays. The group illustrates S. Theresa's description in her autobiography of her mystical experience: 'God willed that I should see, at my left side, an angel in bodily form . . . He was not very big, but very beautiful; his resplendent face indicated that he belonged to that Order of the celestial hierarchy known as Seraphim, whose faces seem to burn with fire—I have noticed that when angels appeared to me they were not always the same, but it is difficult to express the difference in words. He held a long javelin of gold, with an iron tip which had a flame coming out of it. Suddenly he pierced me to the inmost fibre of my being with it and it seemed to me that, as he drew it out, he dragged me with it; but I felt entirely consumed by the love of God. The pain was so great that it drew moans from me, even though the ecstasy which went with it was so great that I would not have had the pain withdrawn—for this ecstasy was God himself. This suffering was not bodily but spiritual, even though the body was involved in it . . .' The members of the Cornaro family, represented in a more subdued light in the coloured marble 'opera boxes' on either side of the altar, do not see the saint's vision or even look towards the altar, but are engaged in discussion and meditation about the vision. Bernini was trying to render something never before attempted by any sculptor—the expression of a transcendental experience. He achieved a similar expression of emotion and ecstasy in his *Blessed Lodovica Albertoni* (1671–4) in San Francesco a Ripa, where his representation of the dying saint lies above and behind the altar which becomes virtually her catafalque.

His grand papal tombs in St Peter's, of Urban VIII (1628–47) and Alexander VII (1671–8), the latter with the dramatic bronze skeletal Death emerging from the tomb, hourglass in hand, to summon the praying pontiff, are striking examples of his bold use of polychrome marble and gilded bronze; their powerful imagery also reflects the energy and confidence of the Counter-Reformation papacy. From 1633 to 1640, four loggias were cut into the upper part of the piers of the dome of St Peter's, designed for the display of the basilica's major relics. They took the form of balconies surmounted by aedicules framed by the much-restored antique twisted columns (which had inspired the columns of the baldacchino), which were among the only surviving parts of Old St Peter's. Within each frame were white marble reliefs on a dark marble ground, representing the relics, borne by angels. Under the loggias, deep niches were cut into the piers, and these contain gigantic statues of the saints connected with the relics: Bernini's own figure of *S. Longinus*, 14 ft. 6 in. high, representing the centurion who pierced Christ's side with his lance, stands below the loggia of the Lance; Francesco Mochi's *S. Veronica* below the loggia of the Vernicle (*see* VERONICA); Andrea Bolgi's *S. Helena* below the loggia of the fragment of the Holy Cross; François Duquesnoy's *S. Andrew* below the loggia of the relic of the saint (since restored to the Greek Orthodox Church).

His collaborators show the extent to which Bernini's style could not only be communicated to his assistants, but the degree to which they could follow his example.

The equestrian statue (1654–70) of *Constantine the Great is placed on the landing at the junction of the staircase from St Peter's with the Scala Regia of the Vatican palace—the point of intersection between church and palace—and the Scala Regia itself (1663–6), designed with a brilliant use of perspective illusionism to disguise its narrowing site, leads from the remodelled main entrance to the Vatican in the great colonnade of the piazza of St Peter's. The colonnade itself was designed (1656–71) as a massive fourfold file of giant columns curved to enclose the large space in front of the basilica, and described as 'opening its arms to embrace the world'. It is surmounted by statues of saints to give a physical and visual expression to the words 'a cloud of witnesses'. At the same time, it enhances the effect of the façade and minimizes the damage done to the view of Michelangelo's dome by the extension of his central plan into a long nave by *Maderno (1607–12).

Bernini built three churches, all variants on the domed central plan: San Tommaso di Villanova in Castelgandolfo (1658–61) is a *cross-in-square design; the Assunta at Ariccia (1662–4) is circular with a colonnaded portico (i.e. based on the design of the Pantheon, though on a much smaller scale) and with extended porticoes on either side like enveloping arms; and Sant' Andrea al Quirinale in Rome (1658–65), the novitiate church of the Jesuits. This is an oval church with the door and the altar on the short axis, a columned portico with a heavy pediment over it, curved screen walls enclosing the entrance, and a huge dome supported by powerful volute-shaped buttresses. It is of plain stone outside contrasted with rosy red marble pilasters and columns inside, with richly gilded detailing in the dome, and white marble sculpture, with the astonishing imagery of the saint bursting through the broken pediment over the altar to surge upwards towards the angels on the cornice of the dome and the putti on the rim of the lantern. All three churches are brilliant variations on the theme of the *central plan, so important in the development of church design in the Renaissance and Baroque periods. They are also fascinating examples of the reuse of ancient forms, since the first is a cross-in-square, an enlargement of an Early Christian *martyrium, the second is based on the Pantheon, and the third is inspired by the form of the classical Temple of Romula in the forum.

Bernini ran an enormous workshop; his religious works form only a part of his gigantic secular output in sculpture and architecture, and he used a whole tribe of brilliant artists to execute his designs, such as the series of *Angels with the Instruments of the Passion* on Ponte Sant'Angelo in Rome (1669–71). His own original pair which served as models for the rest, are in Sant'Andrea delle Fratte. The gilt-bronze *Sacrament Altar* is in St Peter's, and the galaxy of saints is on the cornice of the great colonnade outside St Peter's. He was a deeply devout man, who practised the Jesuit *Spiritual Exercises*, but was also—as his son Domenico testified in his biography of his father—a man of difficult and stormy character 'terribile nell'ira' (terrible in anger). He predicted his own eclipse, so that within seventy years of his death a reaction towards a placid, unemotional Neoclassicism is not surprising.

Bestiary A collection of moral fables, based on the 4th-century *Physiologus. Bestiaries seem to have originated in England in the 11th century, and contain about 100 tales, mostly illustrated. Animals are a mixture of real and fabulous—the unicorn may be based on a rhinoceros—but their behaviour is not true to life. The pelican, as a symbol of Christ, and the phoenix, as a symbol of the Resurrection, were taken over from the Physiologus. Other moralizings are the unicorn, which could only be captured by a virgin, and was therefore a symbol of the Virgin herself; bear cubs, which are born formless and must be 'licked into shape' by their mother, as a symbol of the Church's mission to reform human nature; or the tigress who, pursuing the hunter who has taken her cub, can be diverted by dropping a mirror. She thinks she sees her cub and is diverted, as the soul is diverted by worldly affairs from pursuing its proper end.

Apart from illustrations in the MSS themselves, subjects taken from the Bestiaries are frequently found on *misericords, and occasionally in sculpture and wall-paintings.

Bethesda A pool near Jerusalem, where an angel (according to legend, the Archangel Raphael) 'troubled the water' at certain times, and the first sick person to bathe was cured (John 5: 2–11). A man who had tried for thirty-eight years to be cured was healed by Jesus, who said 'Take up your mat and walk'. As it was the Sabbath and this was forbidden, the Jews 'sought to kill...' Jesus. Appropriately, this miracle is the subject of a large painting by Hogarth, given by him to St Bartholomew's Hospital in London in 1736, along with its companion, *The Good Samaritan*. *Bethesda* is a comparatively rare subject, but there are earlier Venetian examples by *Tintoretto (1573–81: Scuola di San Rocco), *Veronese (1559–60: San Sebastiano), and Sebastiano Ricci (*c.*1724–30: Royal Coll., London). Hogarth probably knew the picture by Ricci.

Bethlehem The birthplace of King *David and of his descendant, Jesus, lies some five miles south of Jerusalem. The site of the Nativity was known in *c.*150 and *Constantine erected the Basilica of the Nativity over the grotto in 330–9 as a pilgrimage church and *martyrium. This church was rebuilt in the 6th century by *Justinian, but the foundations and some fragments of mosaic survive from the original building. It is preceded by an *atrium and *narthex; the main body consists of a *nave and four *aisles ending at the octagon over the grotto, and the East end consists of a tri-lobed *choir and *transepts.

In paintings of the *Nativity there are sometimes representations of a grand but ruined building adjoining the stable containing the manger. This is King David's palace, symbolizing the Old Dispensation giving way to the New. A good example is the *Portinari Altar* (1475: Uffizi), by Hugo van der *Goes, where the building has David's symbol, a harp, carved over the door.

Betrayal *See* JUDAS.

Betrothal *See* MARY.

Bible (Gk. *biblia*, books) The Bible consists of the Old and New Testaments, the Old being inherited from the sacred writings of the Jews, beginning with the Creation. It consists of a number of books, not generally agreed upon by the Jews themselves until *c.* AD 100, and excluding some books accepted by them. All these books were written in Hebrew, but, in the 3rd century BC, were translated, with variations, into Greek, into what is known as the Septuagint (i.e. the Seventy Books, abbreviated as LXX) for the use of Hellenized Jews. The NT was written in Greek. In all there are 46 books in the OT and 27 in the NT, including the *Deutero-Canonical books of the *Apocrypha. Until the late 4th century there was no generally accepted text of the sacred Scriptures, but, after 382, *S. Jerome produced a Latin version of both Testaments, which became accepted as the *Canon of Scripture. This was called the Vulgate, because it was in Latin, the vulgar tongue, and is still the basic text accepted by the E. Orthodox and W. Catholic Churches. The Reformers of the 16th century rejected the Greek Septuagint text used by S. Jerome and went back to the Hebrew originals. They also used different names for the various OT books, e.g. the Vulgate has Kings (*Regum*) 1–4, where the English Authorized Version has 1 and 2 Samuel and 1 and 2 Kings (see the list of biblical abbreviations on p. xiv).

Various books called *Apocryphal Gospels and Acts are spurious additions to the NT, most of their content being rejected by S. Jerome and all Christian Churches, but widely read in the Middle Ages, and popular with artists and public on account of the picturesque details added to the Gospel narratives.

Illustrations to the Bible may have been inspired by illustrated manuscripts of the Jewish Haggadah (Heb. 'narrative', meaning legends, folk-tales, parables, etc., as distinct from Halachah, Heb. 'the right path', Jewish rules of life, not in Mosaic Law, but part of the Talmud). There are certainly OT scenes in the synagogue at *Dura-Europos (*c.*256) which may be reflected in later illustrations. Early illuminated MSS are mostly of Genesis, the Pentateuch (i.e. the first five books of the OT) and the Gospels, although the Apocalypse was later very popular (*see* BEATUS GROUP). The earliest surviving illustrations are some fragments in Berlin (*c.*400?) and of the Cotton Genesis (London, BL, 5th cent.); the *Vienna Genesis is 6th century and the Codex *Amiatinus, *Rossano Codex, and *Ashburnham Pentateuch are other early examples. The high point of biblical illustration was reached in the great Romanesque Bibles of the 11–12th centuries. *See also* BIBLE MORALISÉE, BIBLIA PAUPERUM, LUTHER, BIBLIOGRAPHY.

b

Bible Moralisée A collection of some 5,000 small illustrations in French MSS, dating from *c.*1240, in Paris, London, and Oxford, with *types and antitypes and explications, often far-fetched. They are 'pictures of pictures' and may therefore go back to much earlier prototypes.

Biblia Pauperum (Lat. Bible of the Poor) The meaning of the phrase is not certain, and may refer to the illiterate or to poor preachers, since the book was popular among poor clergy. It consists of a series of pictures, with explanatory texts, of the main events of the NT with corresponding *typological events from the OT. Unlike the **Speculum Humanae Salvationis* it is fairly strictly biblical. It probably originated in Germany or the Netherlands and many 14th-century MSS exist. In the 15th century it became popular as a *block-book, and, later, as a printed book with woodcut illustrations. The norm is a series of forty full-page illustrations, consisting of a central depiction of an event from the NT flanked by two OT precedents (sometimes one *ante legem*, before the Mosaic Law, and one *sub lege*, under the Law), with two Prophets at the top and two at the bottom, each with an identifying quotation, and further explanatory texts. A fine block-book of the mid-15th century, probably Netherlandish, in Esztergom Cathedral Library, in Hungary, has e.g. the Crucifixion flanked by the Sacrifice of Isaac and the Brazen Serpent, with quotations from Gen. 22: 10, and Num. 21: 8–9. The Prophets are David and Isaiah, and Job and Habakkuk, with short quotations. Many of the subjects in the *Biblia Pauperum* may also be found in paintings, sculpture, tapestries, and stained glass.

birds, symbolic Like animals and fish, birds have been used to carry symbolic meanings, Christian and otherwise. From pre-Christian times birds have symbolized the human soul, and many generalized birds appear in Early Christian art, especially on sarcophagi. Some birds, however, both real and imaginary, have specific connotations (sometimes contradictory) and many derive from the fanciful interpretations in the *Bestiaries.

The **cock** is sometimes a symbol of vigilance, but is usually associated with S. Peter's denial of Christ. The **dove** is perhaps the most frequent, since it was the bearer of good news to Noah when it returned to the Ark with an olive leaf, a sign that the waters of the flood had receded; it was regarded as a suitable sacrifice in the Temple, e.g. at the Presentation of Christ (Luke 2: 24); and, above all, was the interpretation placed on the manifestation of the Holy Spirit at Christ's Baptism (Mark 1: 10; John 1: 32), for which reason there is often a dove in scenes of the Annunciation. It is often considered as an emblem of Peace (despite its being a doughty fighter), because of the connection with Noah, as a sign of God's Peace with mankind, whose wickedness had driven Him to destroy the world. The **eagle** is specifically associated with S. John the Evangelist and the Gospels in general—hence the normal eagle-lectern in churches—but, as the highest flier, may also represent Christ or the human spirit aspiring to God. The **goldfinch**, believed to make its nest in thorn-bushes, and with its patch of red on its head, symbolized the Crown of Thorns. A goldfinch held by the Christ Child in paintings of the Madonna and Child is a premonition of the Passion. A **hen** with her chicks is very rare, but refers directly to Matt. 23: 37—'Jerusalem, Jerusalem, the city that kills the prophets ... How often have I desired to gather your children together as a hen gathers her brood under her wings and you were not willing!' In Monza, Cathedral Treasury, is a silver-gilt dish said to be 6th century with a hen surrounded by chicks; Giulio Romano's *Madonna and Child*, Sta Maria dell'Anima, Rome, also has a hen with chicks. The **owl**, associated with night, is usually a symbol of darkness and evil—owls are often found in the fantasies of *Bosch. In classical mythology it was one of the attributes of Athena/Minerva as a symbol of wisdom, and sometimes survives into Christian images in the same connotation. Michelangelo included an owl in his figure of *Night* in the Medici Chapel tombs. The **partridge** and the **quail** both seem to have a variety of meanings, good and bad, according to the interpretations used by artists, though the quail is often equated with manna, and therefore with the bread of the Eucharist, and appears as a Christian symbol on Early Christian sarcophagi. The **peacock**, **pelican**, and **phoenix** are all unequivocally good. The peacock and phoenix are symbols of immortality, since the ancients believed that the flesh of the peacock was incorruptible. They appear frequently in Early Christian mosaics. The phoenix was well known to renew itself by building its own funeral pyre and rising, three days later, from its own ashes, and is therefore a symbol of the Resurrection. The female pelican fed its young by pecking its own breast and giving the blood to its chicks, as Christians are nourished by the Eucharist. For this reason the pelican 'in her piety' is occasionally represented on the top of Christ's Cross (e.g. Bernardo Daddi's triptych, dated 1334, Cambridge, Mass., Fogg Art Mus.). The **raven**, which fed Elijah in the wilderness (1 Kgs. 17; Vg. 3 Reg. 17 or 3 Kgs. 17) also fed hermit-saints like *Antony Abbot and *Paul the Hermit. In the context of Elijah, it is a symbol of the bringing of the Eucharist for mankind's salvation. On the other hand, its blackness and its raucous croak caused it to be regarded as a bird of ill-omen.

biretta A square cap with three (sometimes four) ridges on the top, not really a *vestment, worn by Western clergy when entering or leaving the sanctuary and also with everyday dress. Priests wear black birettas, bishops purple, cardinals red, and certain monks white, but the Pope does not wear one.

Birgitta *See* BRIDGET, S.

bishop *See* ORDERS.

Blachernitissa A wonder-working *icon of the Virgin (*see* MADONNA TYPES), once in the church of the Blachernae in Constantinople. She was shown standing with hands raised in prayer, as an *orant. A version, known as *Platytera*, shows her with a roundel or *clipeus containing the Christ Child—an allusion to her womb. There is a fine marble relief in Sta Maria Mater Domini, Venice, perhaps of the 11th century, of the Madonna Platytera.

black *See* LITURGICAL COLOURS.

Black Friars *See* DOMINICANS.

black Madonna Several representations of the Madonna, especially *icons, which have become blackened by time and dirt, but are claimed to be venerable.

Black Monks *See* BENEDICT.

Blake, William (1757–1827), the visionary poet and painter, produced conventional biblical illustrations as well as works which are Christian in a Blakean sense. His illustrations to the Book of Job (1820–6), or colour-prints such as *Nebuchadnezzar*, or *Elijah*, are relatively close to traditional iconography, but others, such as *The Elohim creating Adam*, *The Ancient of Days*, or *Albion adoring Christ Crucified* are highly personal. The Tate Gallery, London, has a representative collection.

Blake Prize for Religious Art *See* AUSTRALIA, NEW ZEALAND, AND PACIFIC.

blind An arch is described as 'blind' if it cannot be seen through. For instance, the arcades attached to the walls at Lincoln Cathedral are blind arches. These are frequently used as a decorative motif, for example, under the roof of the Romanesque churches built by Lombard builders in northern Italy and anywhere else they travelled, such as northern Spain; blind arches are found in Ravenna at the top of both the Orthodox and Arian baptisteries. Blind windows and *oculi are often used as decorative features, and are frequently inserted to render a façade symmetrical.

block-book An early printed book, usually of a devotional nature and deriving from earlier illustrated MSS such as the **Biblia Pauperum*, **Ars Moriendi*, or **Speculum Humanae Salvationis*. The name derives from the fact that text and illustrations are cut together from a single woodblock, each block forming one page. The dating is very controversial, but it seems that 'Apocalypse I' (Manchester, Rylands Library) is of 1451/2—i.e. slightly earlier than Gutenberg's invention of movable type—and for some years block-books and books produced by setting type and illustrations separately continued side by side. There are examples of the *Ars Moriendi*, *Biblia Pauperum*, and *Speculum Humanae Salvationis* of *c.*1450 and many of the 1460s: all are Netherlandish or German, and most have hand-coloured illustrations. They were for popular devotional use and were bought by the clergy. Few have survived, and those that have are often well-thumbed.

blue, the colour of heaven, is traditionally associated with the Virgin *Mary, especially as the colour of her mantle. It is not a *liturgical colour in the Roman Church, although it once was—the V & A Museum, London, has several blue *vestments, including a satin chasuble of the late 13th century—and blue is still commonly used in the E. Orthodox and Anglican Churches.

BMV, (Lat. *Beata Maria Virgo*, i.e. the Blessed Virgin Mary) also BVM: *see* MARY.

b

Boaz *See* RUTH.

Bollandists *See* ACTA SANCTORUM.

Bolsena, miracle at Bolsena is a small town near Orvieto in Umbria. The story of the miracle is known in two slightly different forms. In 1263 a German priest, on pilgrimage to Rome, said Mass there, but was plagued by doubts over Transubstantiation, whereupon the *Host bled on the *corporal (in the alternative version he had carelessly spilt some of the consecrated wine and mopped it up with the corporal, which became bloodstained). It is sometimes claimed that it was a factor in the institution (1264) of the Feast of Corpus Christi, but there is no evidence for this: in 1338, however, the relic having been taken to Orvieto Cathedral, an elaborate reliquary was made for it by Ugolino di Vieri, with enamels showing scenes from the legend, and from 1357 a fresco cycle was painted in the chapel devoted to it. Julius II, who visited Orvieto in 1506 and venerated it, must have instructed *Raphael to include it in the Vatican fresco cycle illustrating Divine interventions (Stanza d'Eliodoro, dated 1512).

Bonaventura (Bonaventure), Saint (*c*.1218/21–74), the 'Second Founder' of the *Franciscans, was the contemporary of *S. Thomas Aquinas, and his equal as a theologian. A painting by *Zurbarán, formerly in Berlin (destroyed in 1945), records the legendary meeting between the two in Paris, when both were teaching at the university (i.e. probably in the mid-1250s). When Thomas asked what Bonaventura's sources were, he drew aside a curtain to reveal a crucifix. Bonaventura went to study in Paris *c*.1236/8 and joined the Order of S. Francis there *c*.1243. From 1253 to 1257 he taught in Paris, until he was elected Minister-General of the Order in 1257. He reconciled the various factions then dividing the Order, and, from 1260, wrote the *Legenda Maior*, the official Life of S. Francis, which was accepted in 1263, and in 1266 instructions were given to destroy all previous Lives (fortunately, not fully carried out). The *Legenda* provided the text for the canonical fresco cycle in the mother-church at Assisi, attributed to *Giotto, which forms the principal iconography of S. Francis.

In 1265 Bonaventura refused the offer of the archbishopric of York, but in 1273 the Pope made him a cardinal-bishop, and would not accept a refusal. For this reason, Bonaventura is frequently represented in the grey Franciscan habit, but with a red hat, often hanging on a tree: this was because, when the papal emissaries arrived with this symbol of authority, Bonaventura, who was doing the washing-up, told them to hang it on a nearby tree until he had finished. He was canonized in 1482 and declared a *Doctor of the Church in 1588.

His meditation on the Passion, the *Lignum Vitae*, is illustrated by the tree of the Cross, with its twelve branches bearing medallions of the fruits of the life of Christ (Rev. 22: 2). A large fresco, attributed to Taddeo Gaddi (*c*.1330/40), in the refectory of Sta Croce, the principal Franciscan church in Florence, contains what is probably the earliest image of him, seated at the foot of the Cross composing his book. Iconographically, however, the *Meditationes Vitae Christi* is far more important than the *Lignum Vitae* or even the *Legenda Maior*, but it is by no means certain that Bonaventura actually wrote it. It is likely that he had some part in it, but the actual text may be due to Fra Giovanni de Caulibus, a near contemporary.

Because he was not canonized until 1482 all representations of him tend to be late, but after his elevation as a Doctor of the Church in 1588 there was a revival, including the series by Zurbarán (1629) for the Franciscans in Seville. Since Bonaventura died comparatively young he is usually represented as beardless and not very old (the exception is that some paintings made for Capuchins—who have beards—show him with one too). He may hold a book and may also wear a mitre and bishop's vestments.

bondieuserie This is a pejorative term defined in Robert's French Dictionary as dating from 1861, derived from *bon Dieu* (Good God), and meaning *objet de piété de mauvais goût*—i.e. objects of the kind of sentimental religiosity known in English as 'Repository Art'.

Book of Hours *See* HOURS, BOOK OF.

Book of Kells *See* KELLS.

books, liturgical *See* LITURGICAL.

Borromeo, Saint, Charles, and Cardinal Federigo. Carlo Borromeo (1538–84), who was a member of a rich and powerful Lombard family, was made a cardinal in 1560, although he did not receive Orders until 1563. He took an important part in the final sessions of the Council of *Trent and became a reforming Archbishop of Milan (after 1566), but is chiefly venerated as a hero of the great plague in Milan in 1576. He was a supporter of the *Sacri Monti at Varallo and elsewhere, as part of the campaign against the heretical Waldensian Swiss. In 1577 he published his *Instructionum fabricae et supellectilis ecclesiasticae* (reprinted in 1962: English translation London, 1857), which contains ideas on church building directly derived from Tridentine decrees, and is similar to *Paleotti's ideas on painting. The basic requirement is that churches, and especially cathedrals, must be worthy of God—i.e. the doctrine of *decorum, common to all aesthetic theories of the period. The major church in a city should be elevated and richly decorated, and it should be large enough to accommodate the crowds that come on great feast-days. It should be a Latin cross plan, as, in general, all churches should be: it is commonly said, quite wrongly, that S. Carlo condemned circular churches as pagan, but in fact he admits the use of central plans, saying only that circular temples were more common among the pagans, 'sed minus usitata in populo christiano'. His recognition of the circular form as suitable for memoria (*see* MARTYRIUM) can be demonstrated from San Sebastiano in Milan, founded at his instigation to commemorate the great plague of 1576 and built by his personal architect Pellegrino Tibaldi from 1577.

Carlo Borromeo was canonized as early as 1610, and the series of huge paintings known as the 'Quadroni di San Carlo' (1602–10) in Milan Cathedral were part of the campaign for his canonization: they include works by Cerano (who also designed the colossal bronze statue of S. Carlo, 23 metres high, at Arona) as well as Procaccini and Morazzone. The Karlskirche in Vienna by *Fischer von Erlach is dedicated to him.

His cousin, Cardinal Federigo Borromeo (1564–1631) also succeeded him as Archbishop of Milan and was a hero of the other plague of 1630, described in Manzoni's romantic novel, *I Promessi Sposi* (The Betrothed: 1827 and 1842). Federigo was a great patron of the arts and founded the Ambrosiana Library and Gallery in Milan *c.*1607: it owns many drawings by Leonardo da Vinci, as well as being one of the first free public libraries. His foundation of the Ambrosiana included an Academy of the Arts. Like S. Charles, Cardinal Federigo supported the Sacri Monti (in his case, the one at Varese). His book, *De pictura sacra* (On sacred art: 1625 and 1634) is severely moralistic, like that by his fellow Cardinal Paleotti, but is unusual in apparently denying the presence of Mary at the Tomb.

Borromini, Francesco (1599–1667), Italian sculptor and architect. He was contemporary with *Bernini, and at one time worked for him, but where Bernini's temperament was open and sanguine, Borromini was difficult, envious of the success of his rival, and neurotic to the point of ending his life in suicide. He was a distant relative of *Maderno, who employed him on decorative stone-carving and on alterations at St Peter's, Rome, and after Maderno's death in 1629 he became Bernini's assistant there and elsewhere. He worked in Rome all his life, but sometimes provided designs for others to execute outside Rome. His first independent work was for the poor and austere Spanish religious Order of Discalced Trinitarians, dedicated to the ransoming of Christians enslaved by the Moors. For them he designed their monastery and church, San Carlo alle Quattro Fontane (1638–41), or as it is known from its small size, San Carlino. It is an oval church designed on pure mathematical principles with an oval dome decorated with a pattern of coffering adapted from an Early Christian mosaic in Sta Costanza. The façade, added in 1667, with its undulating line and extraordinary combination of a painted panel (now a wreck) with figure and decorative sculpture, was his last work, finished by others after his death.

Between 1637 and 1650 he built the Oratory of St Philip Neri, using forms inspired by Michelangelo and modifying them with unexpected fantasy. On Bernini's recommendation he was appointed in 1632 architect to the Sapienza (the Canon Law University of Rome), but its amazing star-shaped chapel of St Ivo was not built until 1642–59. He was the architect to the Collegio di Propaganda Fide from 1641 onwards, which afforded him the satisfaction of destroying the small oval chapel by Bernini, and replacing it with one with an unusual oblique vaulting system. The unorthodox undulations of his street façade and his unusual window framings caused him to be accused of 'destroying architecture' and of reverting to Gothic proportions and notions. Though a revival of Gothic ideas is not a wildly inaccurate description—despite its having been intended as bitter criticism—his gift for making constructional elements dominate, his use of geometrical and mathematical formulas as a basis for elaborate and sophisticated designs, the richness and complexity of his detail, enabled him to use forms and decoration to symbolize the meaning of his building.

Where Bernini used polychromed marble and gilded bronze, Borromini's usual materials were the most economical: painted plaster with a very limited use of gilding, but when money permitted, he could rival Bernini in splendour and fantasy. The chapel of the Spada family in San Girolamo della Carità, one of his last works (1660), has walls and altar inlaid with marble and onyx so as to simulate damask hangings, and the entrance to the chapel is closed, not by the usual balustrade, but by a long 'drapery' of red and white striped marble held between two white marble angels, the hinged wing of one of them serving as an entrance gate.

He expressed the function of a building by a subtle use of iconography: the upwards spiral of the lantern of the dome of St Ivo represents the search for wisdom, the torches at the base of the lantern symbolize learning, and the stars, crossed palm leaves and crowns, and the winged cherub heads refer to eternal life.

Other Roman commissions were Sant' Agnese in Piazza Navona, begun in 1652 by the Rainaldis, father and son, who began the circular domed interior; Borromini took over in 1653 when they were sacked, but after building much of the exterior he resigned the commission in 1657 and the Rainaldis were reappointed. His recasting of the interior of the Lateran Basilica (1646–9) may have ensured the stability of this Early Christian church, but at the cost of destroying its original character.

His architecture found few supporters or followers in Italy apart from Guarino *Guarini and Bernardo Vittone in the north; his ideas bore real fruit only in the development of Late Baroque in the 18th-century building campaigns in S. Germany and Austria, with architects such as the *Asam brothers, J. M. *Fischer, Balthasar *Neumann and Lukas von Hildebrandt.

Bosch, Hieronymus (Jerome) (*c.*1450–1516), derives his name from 's-Hertogenbosch in Holland, where his grandfather, Jan van Aken, settled probably from Aachen. Jan is recorded as a painter, as were four of his sons, including Hieronymus's father. Most of the family belonged to the Lieve Vrouwe Broederschap (Brotherhood of Our Lady), a rich and influential society, which shared in the fervent spiritual movement in the Netherlands in the wake of the Brethren of the Common Life, and it is from the records of the Broederschap that most of the information about the artist comes. He may have visited Utrecht, and perhaps the southern Netherlands since a slight influence from Roger van der Weyden is perceptible, but there is no real evidence for his ever having left his native city.

He is a profoundly religious artist, his subjects relating to the dire consequences of vice, folly, and sin, and with the depiction in the most tragic manner of Christ's Passion and Sacrifice. His many layers of meaning reach unequalled levels of fantasy and create an obsessive, haunted world of the imagination, now difficult to interpret, although in their own time their significance must have been more immediate, as they were possibly inspired by contemporary sermons and devotional practices. Modern claims of affinities with Surrealism, Freudian symbolism, or theories that they are the outcome and reflection of mental breakdown may confidently be dismissed.

So too must specious arguments that they are heretical. Many of his pictures were bought by that paradigm of Catholic orthodoxy, Philip II of Spain, and these accusations were refuted by Fray José de Sigüenza in his History of the Order of S. Jerome (1605), who wrote 'his pictures are by no means absurdities but rather ... books of great wisdom and artistic value ... They are a painted satire on the sins and ravings of man ... The difference which, to my mind, exists between the pictures of this man and those of all others, is that the others try to paint man as he appears on the outside, while he alone had the audacity to paint him as he is on the inside ...'

The works attributed to his early period include a simple *Adoration of the Magi* (Philadelphia), a *Marriage at Cana* (Rotterdam) spoilt by later alterations, and an *Ecce Homo* (Frankfurt), in which he first uses grotesque physiognomies for the portrayal of evil, in the crowd howling for Christ's condemnation. A picture such as *The Conjurer* (known from a copy) looks at first sight to represent a charlatan deceiving his audience with a version of the 'Find the Lady' trick, while his accomplice steals the victim's purse; it is, in fact, a tract against gullibility and folly, as is the *Operation for the Stone* (Madrid, Prado) where a man submits to having his head cut open by a quack who claims to be able to remove the stone of folly, which turns out to be a tiny tulip, a pun on a Dutch word for stupid. Two books were published in the late 15th century which were probably known to Bosch: Guillaume de Deguileville's *Pilgrimage of Human Life* appeared in a Dutch translation in 1486, and Sebastian Brant's poem *The Ship of Fools* was published in 1494, though neither was needed to prompt his satiric vein. The late Middle Ages in N. Europe were marked by an agony of soul-searching; the tympana of church portals filled with carvings of the Last Judgement, evoking the terrors of the Dies Irae; Thomas à Kempis's *Imitation of Christ*, which was current from about 1418; the *Vision of* *Tundale, published in Dutch in 's-Hertogenbosch in 1484, contains a horrible description of Purgatory and Hell, and was known to Bosch. Sermons, mystery plays, and books appeared, all dedicated to prophecies of doom and the imminence of the Last Judgement: in fact, in 1499 the end of the world was confidently predicted for 25 February 1524. Deguileville's book uses the metaphor of the ship of religion as the means of salvation, particularly the salvation to be found in the monastic Orders. Brant's *Ship of Fools* is a diatribe against the follies and sins of mankind. Bosch's *Ship of Fools* (Paris, Louvre) could easily be a parody of the ship of salvation, since from the tree serving as a mast floats a pennant with a crescent instead of a cross, and the passengers in the frail overloaded craft exhibit all the most glaring vices—gluttony, drunkenness, lechery, greed. Though clearly a deeply religious man, this did not inhibit him from showing priests, nuns, and monks sharing in all the vices which he pillories, since among the people in the boat are a nun and a monk, and in many other of his works popes and priests, monks and nuns, kings, nobles, and princes, come in for as much castigation as peasants and burghers. In this, he is no different from the didactic literature of his day. Other major works are a series of triptychs—*The Hay Wain* (Madrid, Prado), based on a combination of the text 'All flesh is grass' with a proverb that 'From a hay cart all pluck what they can', *The Last Judgement* (Vienna, Akad.), *The Garden of Earthly Delights* (Madrid, Prado), *The Temptation of S. Anthony* (Lisbon), and the *Adoration of the Magi* (Madrid, Prado). All are vivid moralities. In the *Garden of Earthly Delights*, sin has already invaded Heaven itself; in the left wing as God presents Eve to Adam, the way he looks at her suggests that the Fall has already begun, in the foreground strange birds eat the frogs climbing from the pool, a cat catches a rat, in the background a lion devours a gazelle, and from the heart of the heavenly fountain an owl, which Bosch equates with evil, peers out, though for Sigüenza it is an injunction to look at his pictures with care and perception. In the right wing Hell is a place of bewilderment, terror, and agony, from which a sardonic face (probably a self-portrait) looks out. Even in the *Adoration of the Magi* the portents of the future are already present, with the personifications of evil gazing malevolently from the ruined shelter behind the worshipping kings. In the two versions of the *Crowning with Thorns* (London, NG; Madrid, Prado) Christ's quiet, accusing gaze contrasts vividly with the violent evil of His tormentors. When Bosch died in 1516 Raphael and Michelangelo were at work in Rome, but he would have been more in sympathy with the Gothic world of *Grünewald's Isenheim Altar.

Bosio, Antonio (*c.*1576–1629), began the rediscovery of the *catacombs in Rome after the accidental opening of a subterranean burial-place in 1578. In 1593 he descended into the Catacomb of Domitilla, and nearly failed to find his way out. His *Roma Sotterranea* (written by 1620 and published 1634, but dated 1632) began the archaeological study of the catacombs, and the title was deliberately reused by his great successor, G. B. de' *Rossi, as a mark of homage.

Botticelli, Sandro (*c.*1445–1510). His religious works are of four kinds: (1) his participation in the enterprise in 1481–2 when a group of Florentine painters (some were not Florentines, though all officially worked under the direction of the artistically inferior Cosimo Rosselli) executed the series of frescoes on the walls of the Sistine Chapel in the Vatican; (2) his various quite traditional altarpieces; (3) his Madonna pictures, full of sweetness, charm, and devotion, and with—in autograph examples—a delicacy of handling which belies the hard, steely line of his drawing; and (4) the very late, imaginative works such as the two dramatic *Lamentations* (Munich; Milan, Poldi-Pezzoli), which may be described as revelling in an ecstasy of tormented grief, the *Mystic Nativity* of 1500 (London, NG), his only signed and dated work, and the *Mystic Crucifixion* (Cambridge, Mass., Fogg) in very damaged condition, which is said to be connected with, or an illustration of, one of *Savonarola's apocalyptic sermons describing the fate of Rome under a violent storm of destruction, and a Jerusalem of brilliant salvation, which is represented as Florence.

The *Madonnas*, which are the works most usually thought of in references to his art, are indeed sweet and tender, but they soon became a mainstay of his large workshop and were produced in many versions on his designs. His profoundly neurotic temperament and the ambivalence of his response to the emotionally disturbing sermons and political policies of Savonarola do not fully explain the four pictures which are usually attributed to this period. The two *Lamentations* are harsh in colour and awkward in design and suggest that other hands participated in their creation; the London *Mystic Nativity* is iconographically strange, and the Fogg *Mystic Crucifixion* is strained and awkward in drawing as well as confused in intention. While he did not apparently actually become one of Savonarola's disciples, known as the *Piagnone* or 'snivellers', several members of his family were among them, and it is assumed that he must have suffered some influence from the Friar's sermons and ideas, such as the fanatical asceticism of the 'Bonfire of the Vanities'. He outlived his own art, for by the time he died the High Renaissance, with its rejection of the linear form of his line in favour of a fuller and more subtle treatment of form, such as is found in Leonardo da Vinci, Michelangelo, and Raphael, was already fully developed.

Botticini, Francesco (*c.*1446–97), was a Florentine painter and craftsman who would not merit more than a passing notice were he not the painter of an *Assumption of the Virgin* (London, NG) of *c.*1475/6 which is heretical. It illustrates the *Città di Vita* by a Florentine government official, Matteo Palmieri, which postulates that some angels remained neutral during God's struggle with Lucifer, and these became human souls. Some of them are shown as saints among the crowd of angels surrounding the *Assumption*, setting out the idea that the sanctity and devotion of their lives gained salvation for them and enabled them to regain their place among the angels. Palmieri's work only became known after his death in 1475, and was immediately condemned, but he certainly commissioned the picture and planned it.

Bouts, Dieric (*c.*1415–75), was a Netherlandish painter, born in Haarlem, but working in Leuven, possibly before 1448, and certainly by 1457 until his death. The most striking characteristics of his pictures are the stiff, unemotional, and almost expressionless figures, and the delicate and beautiful landscapes. Iconographically, his most important painting is the altarpiece of the Mystic Meals in St Peter's in Leuven. The central panel is a *Last Supper* which, since Christ is holding a Host above a chalice, is also an *Institution of the Eucharist*; the wings have two, smaller, panels in each, with four other mystic meals from the Old Testament: *Melchisedek bringing Bread and Wine to Abraham* and *The Jewish Passover* in the left wing, and *The Gathering of the Manna* and *Elijah fed by an Angel in the Desert* in the right wing. These are examples of OT *types prefiguring the Eucharist, similar to those in e.g. the **Biblia Pauperum*. Bouts's gift for the unemotional reaches an extreme in two grisly martyrdoms—*S. Hippolytus* tied to four horses which are to drag him limb from limb (Bruges, St Saviour's), and S. Erasmus (*see* ELMO) (Leuven, St Peter's) about to be disembowelled. Both are remarkable for the total impassivity of all concerned. Bouts was also an important influence on German 15th-century painting, as well as on the new art of woodcut illustration in printed books, Holland being an important centre of printing. His son Aelbrecht (*c.*1460–1549) painted an interesting *Assumption* (Brussels, Musées Royaux).

boyhood of Jesus *See* APOCRYPHAL GOSPELS.

Bramante, Donato (probably 1444–1514), was certainly the first great architect of the High Renaissance. He is believed to have been born at Fermignano, near Urbino, which in the 1460s was the most cultured and distinguished court in Italy. He must certainly have been aware of the superb architecture of the new palace at Urbino, begun by Laurana in the late 1460s, and also of the influence of *Piero della Francesca, who was working for Federigo, Duke of Urbino, in the late 1460s and early 1470s, and whose pupil Bramante may well have been. Nevertheless, his early life is obscure until he emerges from the shadows as a fresco painter in Bergamo in 1477 (only ruined fragments survive) and then in Milan, where he probably began the reconstruction of Sta Maria presso S. Satiro in the late 1470s. This church, annexed to a tiny Early Christian church which Bramante rebuilt, has the remarkable feature of a fictive *choir, achieved by a brilliant use of perspective on an almost flat wall, so that from the middle of the nave it appears as a deep three-bay choir. His approach to architecture was thus still strongly influenced by painting, and notably by Piero della Francesca and *Mantegna. In the tribune which he added to Sta Maria delle Grazie, probably from the late 1480s onwards as a choir and also a burial chapel for the Sforza Ducal house, he was clearly influenced by the ideas of mathematical proportion pioneered by *Brunelleschi, and which he probably knew from Leonardo da Vinci, who was working in Milan from 1483 onwards. In 1499, as a result of the invasion by the French, the brilliant Sforza court collapsed. Leonardo went to Mantua and Venice before returning to Florence, and Bramante is next found in Rome, where the *cloister of Sta Maria della Pace was begun about 1500 and, according to the inscription in the frieze, was finished in 1504. The cloister echoes less skilfully the system he had used in the Doric Cloister at Sant' Ambrogio in Milan, where the upper storey consists of two arches separated by a pilaster to each single cloister arch below, while in Sta Maria della Pace a slender column bears on the arch below in a distinctly clumsy fashion. His next work, the tiny Tempietto in the courtyard of San Pietro in Montorio, is dated 1502 in an inscription, but possibly not finished until much later. Here Bramante displays genius in the way he treated the problem of building a tiny temple commemorating the putative site of the martyrdom of S. Peter: a domed *centrally planned building as a *martyrium, the use of the Doric Order as the most suitable for a male saint, in accordance with the principles set out by *Vitruvius for a hero or a god, and the carving of the instruments of the Mass in the metopes of the Order of the colonnade surrounding the *cella* of the chapel itself.

His grasp of the essentials of proportion, and of the iconographic suitability of his designs, led to his appointment as architect for the rebuilding of Old St Peter's which, dating from the time of Constantine in the 320s, was now in a dangerous condition. Bramante's original design was for a centrally planned church, each of its arms being identical. The foundation-stone was laid in 1506 by Pope Julius II, but political troubles interrupted the money supplies, and by the time of Bramante's death very little had been built. What was important in this enterprise was the decision to make the new church, not a *basilican form as previously, but a centrally planned one, expressing thus its role as a martyrium, since it is built over the grave of S. Peter, with a hemispherical dome above the grave of the martyr apostle. It was also in harmony with *Alberti's arguments in favour of the circular or centrally planned church as the noblest architectural expression of the Unity and Eternity of God. No part of Bramante's church is now discernible (and would be unknown, were it not for the *elevation shown on the Foundation Medal of 1506) although he established the size of the crossing, and therefore the scale of the church. It was soon realized that the church he had designed could never be built as he envisaged it, since the slenderness of its supports would have made the dome totally unstable, and all later architects made it their first concern to enlarge the piers and strengthen the supporting walls. Bramante's intention, it is said, was to place the dome of the Pantheon over the vaults of the 'Temple of Peace' (the Basilica of Constantine)—that is, to express a Christian martyrium in terms of ancient Roman grandeur, giving a new meaning to the Renaissance of antiquity.

The concept of New St Peter's as a centrally planned, domed, building inspired *Michelangelo, who declared after various other projects (notably that by Antonio da *Sangallo) had been started on, that 'Whoever departs from Bramante departs from the truth'. It took a genius of Michelangelo's stature to recast the design into manageable proportions and structures of adequate strength, to say nothing of their imaginative power.

brasses, monumental These began, probably in the early 13th century, as a cheap substitute for stone tombs. They consist of a sheet of brass, engraved with a stylized figure of the deceased person, inlaid into a stone slab. The earliest known example is that of Bishop Iso von Wilpe (d. 1231), at Verden in Germany. There are over 7,000 brasses in England, far more than anywhere else, as many are known to have been destroyed in religious wars. The earliest English example is Sir John d'Abernon (d. 1277), in Stoke Dabernon church, Surrey. Brasses are important for giving details of armour, costume, and vestments.

brazen serpent, the When the Israelites were in the wilderness and the Lord sent fiery serpents to punish their disobedience, *Moses was ordered to make a serpent of brass and set it up on a pole (Num. 21: 6–9): those who looked on it were cured, so it is often used as an OT *type of the Crucifixion, because of Christ's saying (John 3: 14): 'as Moses lifted up the serpent in the wilderness, so must the Son of Man be lifted up'.

Brescia Box An ivory casket, also called the Brescia Lipsanoteca (casket for relics), now in the Museum at Brescia, N. Italy. It is an extremely important example of *Early Christian iconography, dating from *c.*350/75, probably of N. Italian (?Milanese) workmanship. There are scenes from the Passion, but not the Crucifixion (still not a subject for art); other scenes include the *Traditio Legis, the Good *Shepherd, the *Woman with an Issue of Blood, *Ananias, and *Apocryphal and OT subjects—*Daniel in the Lions' Den, *Susanna and the Elders, *Jonah and the Whale, and others.

Brethren of the Lord *See* ANNA SELBDRITT, KINSHIP OF CHRIST.

Breughel *See* BRUEGEL.

breviary *See* LITURGICAL BOOKS.

Bridget, Saint (properly, **Birgitta**), patron saint of Sweden (1302/3–73), came of a noble family and married a rich noble, by whom she had eight children, her second daughter being S. Catherine of Sweden. With her husband she made the pilgrimage to the shrine of S. James at Compostela (1341–2), and after his death in 1344 she embraced the religious life. In 1346 she founded a *double monastery for sixty nuns and twenty-five monks living under the Augustinian Rule. She went to Rome in 1349 to secure approval for her Order (granted in 1370) and never returned, spending the rest of her life in Italy and on pilgrimages, especially to the Holy Land in 1371–3. She died in Rome. From about 1344, but especially during her stay in the Holy Land, she received numerous visions which were recorded by two contemporaries. These became known in MSS and were first printed at Lübeck in 1492 (there is also a 15th-century English translation). They were important iconographically, since she claimed to have received accounts of the Nativity and Passion from the Virgin herself, particularly when visiting the Holy Places. Paintings of the Nativity which show the Virgin clad in white, kneeling on the ground, with her mantle and shoes beside her, with the Child lying naked on the ground and emitting light which eclipses the candle held by S. Joseph, are all associated with her visions, although her *Revelations* have much in common with the **Meditationes Vitae Christi* and *Ludolf of Saxony's *Life of Christ*. The panel of the Virgin and Child from *Grünewald's Isenheim Altarpiece is also associated with her, as are various representations of the Passion, including the Flagellation.

She is usually represented in the habit of the Brigittine Order; a black or grey tunic, white veil and wimple, with a black or red band across the forehead. Sometimes she has a pilgrim's scrip and staff, or she may hold a candle, with hot wax falling from it on to her hand as a mortification. She should not be confused with any of the Irish saints named Brigid.

Brigittines *See* BRIDGET, S.

Bruegel (Breugel, Breughel), Pieter (*c.*1524/30–69), was the most famous Netherlandish 16th-century painter. His early association was with Antwerp print publishers. In 1551 he was inscribed in the Antwerp guild of painters, and in 1552 began a long journey through France to Italy, as far south as Sicily. He was in Rome in 1553, and returned north through the Tyrol in 1555, where he made superb drawings of alpine scenery which transformed the treatment of landscape from fantastications of unrealistic rocks into realistic views of nature. For Hieronymus Cock, the most important print publisher in Antwerp, he produced series such as the *Seven Deadly Sins* (1556–7), which established his reputation, and he continued this double activity making drawings for engravers, as well as paintings, until he removed to Brussels in 1563. There he was patronized by Cardinal Granvelle, the Imperial representative in the Netherlands, which belies the story that he was associated in Antwerp with a heretical sect. Had this been so, Brussels, as the seat of a strictly orthodox government and court, would have been no place for him. Though nicknamed 'Peasant Bruegel' and described as a painter of 'drolleries', nothing could have been further from the truth. The greater part of his work is concerned with human folly, continuing the didactic, moralizing vein of *Bosch, using Bosch's language of fantastic horror in many of the drawings he produced for engravers, and in his later paintings a larger, more realistic view of human life. In Antwerp, his friendship with such highly intellectual humanists as the geographer Ortelius and the printer Plantin also disposes of the 'Peasant' label. In 1563 he married the daughter of his earliest print publisher, Pieter Coeck van Aelst, and had two sons, Pieter II and Jan, both of whom became painters, though neither was as eminent as his father.

Those of his series of prints, such as the *Seven Vices* and the *Seven Virtues* (1559–60), that derive from Bosch's imaginative imagery reuse ideas which were still effective, but are unconvincing in an artist who is no longer living in the Middle Ages and is working half a century after Erasmus's *Praise of Folly*. They display an element of humour which would have been alien to Bosch. But in, for instance, the *Virtue of Justice*, he presents such an appalling catalogue of barbarities of execution and torture, unrelieved by any trace of Mercy, that it provides a terrible commentary on the accompanying moralizing text. But in a print such as *Big fish eat little fish* (1557) his shafts of humour strike through, and though a patronizing age may have dubbed them 'drolleries', it is his wry humour that makes his attacks on folly, credulity, vice, and hypocrisy the more telling. *Dulle Griet* (1562: Antwerp, Mus. Mayer van den Bergh), usually translated as Mad Meg, is a vision of the termagant woman charging with her assortment of ill-chosen arms through a world left in turmoil. That it was painted at a time when the Netherlands, England, Scotland, and France were ruled by women, may be a political commentary. The *Triumph of Death* (1562/4: Madrid, Prado), is a grimmer vision of the helplessness of the living against the onslaught of the inevitable; in both these pictures, and in the *Adoration of the Kings* (1564: London, NG), the influence of Bosch still survives. *The Battle between Carnival and Lent* (1559) and *Children's Games* (1560: both Vienna, KHM) show human folly—the children have usurped the city centre; man's business is another form of child's play. There is little moral difference between the ribaldry and licence of the carousing peasants, and the ostentatious religious observance of the pious who leave no alms in the beggar's dish.

In *Christ Carrying the Cross* (1564: Vienna, KHM), his largest picture, he treats the Gospel story as if it happened in his own world. Christ's death is a public execution which the whole town has come out to watch, the two terrified thieves in a tumbril are exhorted by a priest—something he must often have seen—and soldiers grab Simon of Cyrene to force him to help Christ, who has fallen beneath His cross, while Simon's furious wife tries to drag him away, despite the rosary at her belt. *The Census at Bethlehem* (1566: Brussels) and *The Massacre of the Innocents* (1566: Vienna, KHM) also make the events contemporary ones, with the overtones of the bitter strife which now cast its grim shadow over the Netherlands. His most famous pictures are the great series of landscapes, the *Seasons*, in particular the haunting *Hunters in the Snow* (1565: Vienna), which seems not to have any moral overtones, and the *Peasant Wedding Feast* (1567/8: also Vienna) which has been, perhaps wrongly, interpreted as the Marriage at Cana. *The Cripples* (1568: Paris, Louvre) and *The Blind* (1568: Naples, Mus. Naz.) are tracts, the first on the bogus charity collector who battens on the unfortunate, and the second on the folly of trusting to the ignorant—the blind man leads the other blind to disaster. *The Magpie on the Gallows* (1568: Darmstadt) is a parable on the perils of gossip. 'To chatter like a magpie', 'to gossip someone to the gallows', the water of the mill-wheel is 'idle chatter like a mill of words', the rollicking peasants 'dance under the gallows'—all are images of heedlessness ending in disaster. His last picture, *The Storm at Sea* (1568/9: Vienna, KHM), is a presage of the horrors to come, in the image of the storm-tossed ship from which sailors have thrown a barrel in an effort to distract the whale—in 1567 the Duke of Alva had already arrived to suppress, with merciless ferocity, the revolt in the Netherlands.

Brunelleschi, Filippo (1377–1446), was a Florentine sculptor and architect, and the virtual founding father of Renaissance architecture. His first known work is a relief of the *Sacrifice of Abraham* (Florence, Bargello) entered for the 1401 competition for the Baptistery Doors in Florence, which was won by *Ghiberti. He then went to Rome, possibly with the young *Donatello, and studied the ruins of antiquity in order to discover the constructional methods of the Romans, so as to compete for the job of building the dome of Florence Cathedral. He made the first projects for this in 1417, and brought the dome to completion in 1436. He then designed the lantern, for which he made a model (Florence, Mus. dell'Opera) in 1436; the lantern was erected after his death by Michelozzo. Besides this tremendous enterprise, his great religious importance lies in his development of simple mathematical ratios for the two basilicas of San Lorenzo, begun in 1419, but not finished until after his death, and Sto Spirito, planned in 1434 but not finished until 1482, with unfortunate divergencies from his projects. His aim was to re-create the form of the Early Christian *basilicas in terms of the mathematical proportions and the Orders of classical Rome. In Florence he pioneered the concept of the *centrally planned chapel, first in the Old Sacristy of San Lorenzo (1419–28), where there is a strict mathematical relationship (1:1, 1:2, 1:4) between the square ground plan and the walls, the height of the semicircular dome, and the small square *choir. Similarly, in the Pazzi Chapel at Sta Croce, begun after a further visit to Rome *c.*1430, the parts internally and externally are all related mathematically one to another. The same strict adherence to mathematical proportions is to be found in his first work, the loggia of the Innocenti (the Foundling Hospital, built in 1419–24). His unfinished centrally planned Sta Maria degli Angeli (*c.*1434–7) showed him developing this controlling mathematical framework into a more subtle and complicated relationship of the internal central space and the encircling ring of chapels, marked on the exterior by niches in the piers. The building would probably have been domed. He thus provided 'antique' examples of the Early Christian types of church—both basilicas and *martyria—for modern use. He was one of the dedicatees of *Alberti's treatise on painting.

*Vasari, in his Life of Brunelleschi in the *Lives of the Painters*, attributes the discovery of 'central vanishing point' perspective to Brunelleschi, but he also attributes it to Uccello. Apparently Brunelleschi, early in his career, demonstrated his system with a kind of peep-show picture of an architectural scene which appeared, to the single eye with which it had to be viewed, to make everything real and accurate. The discovery, to whichever of the two it was due, had a profound effect on painting from then onwards.

Bruno, Saint (*c.*1032–1101), was the founder of the *Carthusian Order. Bruno was born in Cologne and taught in the famous school of Rheims for some twenty years, where his pupils included the future *S. Hugh of Grenoble and Pope Urban II. About 1080, influenced by Robert of Molesmes (*see* CISTERCIAN ORDER), he went to live as a hermit with six others in a solitary place, later called La Grande Chartreuse, near Grenoble, given to them by his pupil Bishop Hugh. In 1090 he was summoned to Rome by Urban II, where he lived in the ruins of the Baths of Diocletian, subsequently the Carthusian church and monastery of Sta Maria degli Angeli. Later, he went to Squillace in Calabria, where he died. He was never officially canonized, but his cult was authorized for Carthusian houses in 1514, and made universal in 1623. His houses, Charterhouse in English, Certosa in Italian, though never numerous, were greatly influential as schools, following his own scholarly standards. The monks wear white—habit, girdle, scapular, and hood.

The marble statue of him by J.-A. Houdon, of 1766, in Sta Maria degli Angeli, was one of the first pieces of *Neoclassicism in Rome, and shows him as in deep recollection (he is often represented with one finger on his lips, enjoining silence). After 1623 many Carthusian houses commissioned paintings of incidents connected with him (although little is actually known of his life), the most famous being the nineteen by Giovanni Lanfranco (1582–1647) for the Certosa di San Martino, Naples, now dispersed but known from engravings; and especially the twenty-two paintings by Eustace Lesueur (*c.*1648) for the Chartreuse in Paris, now in the Louvre.

Burning Bush *See* BUSH, THE BURNING.

burse (Lat. *bursa*, purse) A *liturgical object. It is a flat wallet, about 12 in. square, used to contain the *corporal, and covered with silk of the appropriate liturgical colour.

Bush, the Burning Exodus 3: 1–3 tells how *Moses came to 'Horeb, the mountain of God. There the angel of the Lord appeared to him in a flame of fire out of a bush; he looked, and the bush was blazing, yet it was not consumed . . . God called to him out of the bush . . .' Moses was commanded to deliver the Israelites out of Egypt. The Burning Bush was often used as an OT *type of the perpetual virginity of *Mary e.g. in the **Biblia Pauperum* and the **Speculum Humanae Salvationis*. There is a painting by Nicolas Froment of 1476 in Aix-en-Provence Cathedral, showing Moses taking off his shoes, as God commanded, with his sheep around him and an angel standing in front of him; but the upper part of the picture shows a burning rose-bush—a symbol of Mary—with the Virgin and Child seated on it. The Child holds a mirror, another symbol of Mary.

Butterfield, William (1814–1900), was a major British church architect of the 19th century. He built nearly 100 churches and related buildings, using a highly personal form of the *Gothic Revival. From 1842 he was involved with the *Cambridge Camden Society (from 1845 the Ecclesiological Society), which reinforced the strong ritualistic element in his church designing. His meticulously planned and scrupulously executed works use a 'Middle Pointed' Gothic, reminiscent of N. German forms, and also of the N. Italian and Sienese use of polychromy which he translated into the combinations of red brick with diapering in black brick and stripes of pale stone. The chapel of Balliol College, Oxford (1862–6), for instance, was described as in the 'streaky-bacon style'. In his masterpiece, All Saints, Margaret Street, London (1849–59), he exploited this type of 'constructional polychromy' all over the outside, combined inside with clustered columns of polished granite, a huge marble *reredos in the chancel inset with paintings by William Dyce, and with every available surface covered with Minton tiles and painted geometrical patterns. His designs for Keble College, Oxford (1867–75) use diapered brickwork and horizontal stone banding in the lower buildings round the quadrangle so as to stress the verticality of the chapel with its contrasts of coloured brick and stone. His architecture has been described as deliberately ugly, exploiting the hardest, harshest reinterpretation of Gothic, and a total rejection of all aspects of historicism, harmony of proportion, and search for expressive beauty. In this he lived in a different world from his major Gothic Revival contemporaries, *Pugin, *Scott, Barry, and *Street.

butterfly The butterfly is a very ancient symbol of the soul, going back to pre-Christian times (cf. the myth of Cupid and Psyche). It was originally a symbol of the Resurrection, the chrysalis being death and the butterfly the new life. The earliest Christian example may be the Antioch *chalice (5th or 6th cent., New York Met. Mus). In 17th-century Dutch painting, however, the butterfly is often a symbol of the transitoriness of human life in *Memento mori pictures and *Vanitas still-life paintings. In the late 18th and early 19th centuries the original symbolism recurred in funerary sculpture.

buttress A section of masonry or brickwork, built against a wall or at the corner of a tower to give it extra support. It may be merely a strip of stonework or brickwork, or it may project to rise in successive stages up the wall. Of such are the buttresses outside the naves of many cathedrals that may project above the level of the aisle roof and be crowned by a *pinnacle. These may be joined by masonry arches reaching across the aisle roof to the outer wall of the *clerestory to join other strip buttresses, which may rise to project above the roof level and themselves be crowned by pinnacles. These strengthening elements are very important since inside the church, they are adjuncts to the *piers or *columns of the main arcades of naves, choirs, and transepts. (Canterbury Cathedral is a good example of how such systems work.)

If the buttresses stand as projections from the aisle wall of the church, or stand clear of the wall, and then provide the support by means of arches reaching across to the wall, they are called *tower* buttresses. They are often used to support tiers of arches that rise to reach across the aisles to abut against the clerestory forming *flying* buttresses. They are essential features of French Gothic architecture, and their use enabled such churches to be built to great heights and to increase the stability of the vaults by providing exterior support. Chartres, Amiens, Reims, and Beauvais cathedrals are examples, and at Le Mans the east end has such an extensive system of flying buttresses that from the open space below the church, the choir appears to have a virtual masonry scaffolding. They are rare in English churches, since English master masons disliked the system and used 'flyers' discreetly, usually concealing these supporting arches under the aisle roof. They were rarely necessary, since English cathedrals tend to length rather than to height. Only at Westminster Abbey do 'flyers' from tower buttresses built in the cloister garth reach over the north range of the cloister to brace the clerestory.

BVM An abbreviation of Beata Maria Virgo or Blessed Virgin Mary. *See* MARY.

b

BYZANTINE ART AND ARCHITECTURE

The art and architecture of the Eastern Roman Empire from 330 to 1453, and its influence in the rest of the Mediterranean world, Russia, and the Balkans.

Constantine the Great achieved sole control of the Roman Empire in 323, and in 330 transferred his capital from Rome to a new city on the site of an ancient Greek city-state on the Bosporus called Byzantium. The new city, named Constantinople after him, became the centre of the Byzantine Empire until its extinction in 1453, when the city fell to its Turkish conquerors and the last Emperor, Constantine XI Palaeologus, died fighting on its walls. For 1,100 years, therefore, Byzantium was a major force in Christian art and architecture, and its influence was strong as far afield as Ravenna, Russia, the former Yugoslavia and the Balkans, Venice, Sicily, and Spain. Manuscripts and portable works of art carried its influence over most of Europe, although Rome, despite its many disasters, remained the spiritual capital until the break between East and West in the 9th century.

After the transfer of the imperial capital to Constantinople in 330, Constantine strove to create a New Rome, with typically Roman monuments and public buildings as in Old Rome, to create the illusion of there being no change from Hadrian (d. 138). Roman symbols were adapted to Byzantine imperial ends; Christ was depicted crowning emperors, endowing them with sacred powers so that the Roman symbol of the delegation of power in the *Traditio Legis became the conferring of semi-divine status upon the holder of the imperial office. In the *Vita Constantini*, Eusebius developed a theology of empire in which the emperor is vice-regent on earth for Christ as Emperor of Heaven. The classical tradition was still alive in the Hellenistic mosaic floors of the new imperial palace; churches such as Constantine's now obliterated original *Hagia Sophia, and St John Studion (*c.*460), despite its ruined state, show the survival of the form created by the Roman *basilica into the 4th and 5th centuries. Constantine and his successors introduced marble from the island of Proconnesus in the Sea of Marmara, as well as importing rarer marbles from Thessaly and Tunisia, and porphyry from Egypt to make their buildings more magnificent. But nothing except archaeological remains survives from earlier than 440, either in the capital or in the provinces.

The dominant policy was to create a unified empire, with the character of a theocratic Christian state, and to achieve this, monarchs from Theodosius I (379–95) to Justinian (527–65) struggled for control of Italy and the Mediterranean lands. One consequence of the enormous size of the empire was the creation of a second capital in the West, first in *Milan and then, when continuance in Milan became impossible because of barbarian invasions, in *Ravenna. It was not originally envisaged that the separation of the empire into two distinct centres of power would be permanent, but local events finally ensured that what began as a convenience became a permanent separation, as it had done at the end of the pagan empire. Barbarian incursions of Visigoths began from across the Danube in the mid-4th century and continued until Theodosius I gained a respite for Italy by making them allies in the Balkans. In 390 in a reprisal for a rebellion in Thessalonica he massacred the population, and penance for this crime was enforced by *Ambrose, Bishop of Milan, under threat of interdict and being refused entry to the church, so establishing the independence of the Church from the State. But the incursions of Visigoths continued and Theodosius used them as mercenaries. When Alaric was in command of a large number of his fellow Goths as mercenaries, the alliance did not work well, and in 410 Alaric the Goth sacked Rome, and his brother Athaulf led the Visigoths into Spain, which was rapidly conquered, to become the first barbarian kingdom. In 455 the Vandals, who had migrated westwards, pressing steadily from barbarian lands beyond the Oder, sacked Rome with a ferocity which has made their name a synonym for pillage and destruction. Justinian's struggle against the various invading northern tribes which had conquered parts of N. Africa (the Vandal kingdom of N. Africa), France, Italy, and Spain, and his wars against the Persians, involved the progressive impoverishment of his enormous empire, which at one time stretched from Armenia to the Red Sea, and from the Danube to N. Africa. The Vandals and the Visigoths were never assimilated into the local population because they had adopted *Arianism, a heresy abhorrent to orthodox Catholics. They were always hated conquerors who lived by exploiting their conquests.

Byzantine art and architecture achieved its distinct form in Constantinople between the 5th century and the death of Justinian, but the size of the empire meant that very varied building systems and artistic styles were developed to serve the same religious and political ends. In the Middle East, where stone was freely available, but wood was scarce, churches were generally stone vaulted, and instead of columns, piers of solid masonry supported the weight of stone vaults, which meant that churches were usually smaller, narrower, and darker. Unfortunately, later Islamic conquest meant that many of these churches have been destroyed, and only ruins remain from such complexes as Binbirkilisse—'the thousand churches'—(near Madensehir in SE Turkey) or Qalb Louzeh (*c.*500, near Antioch).

St Demetrius, Salonika, built in the mid-5th century, is an early example of a basilica with a *nave and four *aisles, a *narthex at the entrance, and a *transept inserted between the *bema, or apsidal east end, to give more room for the clergy. The narthex was originally double, an outer, or exonarthex, giving into an inner esonarthex opening into the inner aisles, with the outer aisles beyond them. A tribelon (a triple arcaded entrance instead of a door) led into the nave, which combines stone piers and groups of columns between them; the columns are reused from earlier, possibly Roman, buildings, and the variety of the capitals is consistent with their having different origins. The nave colonnade supports arcades which bear the galleries over the aisles, and the galleries also have columns bearing arcades which support the beams of the open roof. Arcades, instead of a classical architrave, are themselves a new introduction necessary where brick replaced stone as the common building material. The present church is a replica of the original, burnt in 1917, using much of the original materials.

In Constantinople, Justinian built four important churches, all described by Procopius, the historian of his reign, in *The Buildings of Justinian.* SS Sergius and Bacchus, begun in 526, is roughly square outside, with a narthex in front, and a projecting *apse. The central space inside is octagonal with piers at the angles and columns forming alternate curved and flat sides, and over the aisles round the octagon there is a meandering frieze (emphasizing the spatial complexity) with galleries above, all borne on the columns, the whole being surmounted by a dome. If a classical example is sought for its undulating interior forms it can be found in Hadrian's Villa at Tivoli, itself derived from Near Eastern forms. The centralized plan provided for the congregation in the aisles and galleries, leaving the central area clear for the processions of the Little and Great Entrances and for Justinian and his immediate entourage. It was a complex and sophisticated space for a sophisticated and complex rite. St Irene, begun in 532, is a domed and galleried basilica, repaired after an earthquake in 740 with minor changes, but largely intact in the ground floor including the *synthronon* for the clergy in the apse; the Church of the Apostles, 536–46, was destroyed by the Turks after their conquest of the city in 1453, but it provided the design of St Mark's in Venice; and finally there is Hagia Sophia, 532–7, the greatest of all Byzantine buildings. The last three were all built after the disastrous Nika riots (532) in which most of the city was destroyed. Justinian rebuilt on a scale and with a splendour—and at a speed—which is astonishing. Though the liturgical arrangement was all destroyed when Hagia Sophia was converted to a mosque, the layout of the pavement still indicates the position of the altar, sanctuary, ambo, the placing of the emperor's throne, and probably also *metatorion,* or rooms at the end of the south aisle. Other markings place elements of the ceremonial or social and liturgical zones.

After the Turkish conquest in 1453 Hagia Sophia became the Great Mosque; this ensured that the structure was maintained, though all the mosaics were either destroyed or painted over, though a significant number have now been uncovered. One of the notable aspects of Justinian's churches is that no attempt was now made to keep to Latin church forms; the basilica was increasingly modified to suit changes in the rite which evolved in the 6th century and became ever more marked until by the 8th century not only had the rite changed, but the shape and the symbolism of the church had changed in harmony. Only the *martyrium remained as a fairly consistent form for small 'memoria', usually outside city walls, and these martyria were always *centrally planned, either as Greek cross designs (*see* CHURCH ARCHITECTURE), or small domed buildings. Because of the position of the capital on the Bosporus, many influences from Asia Minor, Syria, and Egypt were absorbed, and Arab and Turkish influence also affected Byzantine art in the 7th and 8th centuries and were carried with it not only through the lands bordering on the Mediterranean, but into Russia, Georgia, the Balkans, the Slav countries, Armenia, and even Spain.

The rapid rise of Arab power after the first defeat of a Byzantine force near Jerusalem in 634, and continual Arab incursions into territories which formed part of the Byzantine empire, led to increasing economic difficulties, particularly marked after the loss of naval supremacy in the Mediterranean by the end of the 7th century. The influence of Islamic thought, leading to a reappraisal of the spiritual aspects of a work of art, eventually resulted in Iconoclasm and a break with Rome, which rejected Iconoclasm. Byzantine artistic development was bound up with these historic, territorial, and above all religious and philosophical changes. The political, dynastic, and internal conflicts provoked by Iconoclasm took their toll, so that by the time the Iconoclastic Controversy was resolved in the 9th century such great changes had taken place in the intervening 100 years that the division of the empire into West and East was almost total, with Byzantium becoming an ever weakening bulwark against Islam, and the separation of the Eastern from the Western Church was virtually certain. Economic difficulties also led to the extensive use of brick instead of stone, the abandonment, or reuse, of the expensive marbles common in more affluent times, and a concentration on a more limited repertory of architectural and decorative forms.

The main development in church building in the 8th and 9th centuries was the increasing use of the *cross-in-square design, with barrel-vaulting over the arms of the cross, and the crossing covered by a dome or a cross vault, or the combination of the central dome with the basilica, with the domed area preceded by a single bay, and flanked by aisles supporting galleries serving as *gynaecea; this form is generally known as the 'compact domed basilica'. The 8th-century Hagia Sophia at Salonika is of this type, but here there were four aisles so that some of the galleries over them were so far back that it was almost impossible to see or hear the service from them. The usual narthex has multiple small domes and the apsidal east end is flanked by domed apsidal chapels. The Church of the Theotokos, also in Salonika, was built in 1028 without the extra aisles, and this compact form became virtually the standard type, particularly because, with the decline of the empire, architecture became progressively a restatement of previously developed themes, with almost no new forms being introduced. Also, the rite itself favoured clusters of small churches rather than the large basilica, or even the compromise between the cross-in-square and the long nave set out by Hagia Sophia. The tendency was increasingly for small highly decorated churches, like jewelled caskets, such as the 11th-century Church of the Chora (the Kariye Camii) in Constantinople, largely rebuilt between 1280 and 1300, and again in the 14th century, the great glory of which is its surviving mosaics and frescoes, or the Holy Apostles at Salonika built between 1312 and 1315, where the domed church itself is quite small, but is surrounded by a U-shaped gallery, with domes at the corners, and preceded by a narthex. The decorative exterior brickwork of the Holy Apostles is an example of Turkish influence.

The main determinant of the changes in the shape of churches lay in the nature of the rite which was performed within them. In the Latin Church, the rite took place at an altar surmounted by a *ciborium, usually on the chord of the apse; the *chancel might be extended into the nave by a *schola cantorum as in San Clemente in Rome, and a transept might provide extra space for the clergy, as in San Paolo fuori in Rome, but the remainder of the nave would be open to the congregation. The rite evolved in Constantinople in the time of Justinian increasingly relegated the congregation to the aisles and the galleries. The nave was a processional way from the *pastophoria which originally adjoined the narthex, and the Gospels and the elements (*see* SPECIES, SACRED) for the sacrifice were carried in state to the altar in the apse, which was veiled by curtains. Later, it became more convenient if the pastophoria were sited on either side of the apse—the *Diaconicon on the south, for the vestments and the Gospels, and the *prothesis, on the north, for the elements. Originally, the elements were prepared from the offerings brought by the faithful and presented at the pastophoria, but when this custom was abandoned, the pastophoria in the narthex became redundant. The procession from the Diaconicon—the Lesser Entrance—now took place from the small chapel flanking the apse on the right, and the Great Entrance with the elements of the Mass was made from the prothesis, the chapel on the left. After showing the Gospels and the elements to the people from the screen or *iconostasis, which closed the apse, or *solea, to view, the celebrant and his attendants retired behind it, and the rite itself took place in the holy of holies, a second screened area within the apse, entered only by the celebrant and his assistant. In the nave, towards the middle, was the *ambo to which the Gospels were carried in procession accompanied by acolytes with lighted candles. Communion was brought to the people outside the iconostasis. The shape of the 'compact domed basilica' or the cross-in-square church suited this rite far better than the long nave of the Latin type, as did the custom of a cluster of small churches rather than one large one. This shape also allowed the mosaic decoration to enhance the symbolism attached to the architectural form.

Mosaic Decoration

For a thousand years, from the 4th to the 14th century, mosaics were the most important aspect of Byzantine art, like sculpture in antiquity, or fresco and panel-painting in the Renaissance. The most important periods of mosaic decoration were the 4th to the 7th centuries, the 9th to the 12th (the gap being filled by the Iconoclastic Controversy), with a resurgence of magnificent quality in the 14th century, before the total extinction of Christian art in Byzantium in 1453.

It has been suggested that the secular mosaic floors in Antioch and in the Great Palace in Constantinople, dating from 330 to 550, which represent hunting scenes and are filled with animals, trees, and flowers, are an evocation of Paradise. Though the repertory consists of entirely secular subject-matter, the imagery and execution is already recognizably Byzantine. This strand of the tradition was also exported to the early Islamic world and is to be found in the Dome of the Rock and the Great Mosque in Cordoba. Church floors were usually executed in Opus Alexandrinum or Opus Sectile: the first consists of geometric designs in various coloured marbles, the second is similar, but more delicate, and sometimes includes small animals or birds. The earliest known wall-mosaics are probably those in Pompeii, but they are small-scale works (e.g. the fountain niche in Oxford, Ashmolean Mus.). It became the custom for rich churches to have mosaics, and for poorer ones to make do with paintings, until the impoverishment of Byzantium and the cost of mosaics limited their use. All mosaic decorations are on the inside of churches, and the shape of Byzantine churches—particularly the domed cross-in-square—is perfect for the art. A very important factor was that under the Byzantine government rigid control was exercised over the content of all religious images. The Second Council of *Nicaea in 787 decided that 'the churches are of the Fathers who build the churches; the art alone is the artist's'; this accounts for the unchanging nature of the content of mosaic decorations, and also of icons. The various subjects—the *Pantocrator, the Virgin, angels, apostles, saints, incidents from the Gospels such as the Annunciation, the Baptism of Christ, the Crucifixion, or scenes from the Life and Miracles of Christ, or from the Life of the Virgin—were assigned fixed positions in the church which were rarely departed from, and which were governed by strict rules. The same Council also defined the spiritual role of the image, in that it affirmed that absolute adoration was for God alone, and that the veneration given to the Virgin and to saints was a relative cult by which the honour (*hyperdulia) offered to the image was passed on to its prototype. To ensure that veneration passed from the faithful to the sacred figures the faces of the venerated ones were always turned toward the worshipper, in full face or at least three-quarter view: those with whom the worshipper desired no contact—Judas, Christ's executioners, or the torturers of martyrs—were in profile or turned away. This convention was followed only in Byzantine mosaics, not in MSS or ivories, and not even in mosaics outside direct Byzantine influence.

Byzantine mosaic decoration had two main aims: to beautify the house of God, and to instruct the illiterate who could then 'read' in them the Gospel story, or follow the great feasts of the Church. There is also a clear, though possibly unconscious, wish to overawe the spectator by making the church a place of majesty and magnificence. It may well have been descriptions of the splendour of the churches of Byzantium and of the drama of their services which, in 988, influenced Vladimir of Kiev to choose the Orthodox rite, rather than the Roman Catholic rite, for his new regime in Russia. The cross-domed Byzantine architectural type was imported along with the rite and appears in the Church of Saint Sophia in Kiev and as far north as Novgorod.

Mosaics are seen at their most effective on undulating surfaces where the slanting rays of the sun and the light of flickering candles illumine them with an almost interior brilliance. This luminosity was enhanced by the deliberately uneven setting of the tesserae to achieve an effect of moving colour and light.

Once established as the chief form of decoration, certain scenes and figures became identified with certain parts of the church, and this became a blend of the liturgical and the artistic, with the shape of the building used to enhance the narrative and the meaning of the subject. The arrangement of the parts was constant: in the dome was the Pantocrator; in the main apse was the Virgin, with or without archangels and angels; below her were Apostles, and saints below them or on the outside of the curve of the apse. Scenes from the Life of Christ which referred to major events—Nativity, Baptism, Crucifixion, and Ascension—were placed on the squinches or the pendentives of the dome. There was an underlying conflict in the sources of inspiration: the Hellenic, with its idealized, 'antique' quality, and the Semitic, with its stress on the idea, the meaning, rather than on beauty, illusion, or perspective. Significance and realism were strangely mingled to produce a hieratic and profoundly Christian art, where Christ was an awesome, majestic presence, with all the figures in a scene represented in sizes which correspond with their importance, rather than in any logic of space or perspective. Another important factor was the non-figurative decoration derived from Near Eastern sources, such as Persia and Mesopotamia, in which humans and animals were merely part of a decorative abstract pattern. This type of mosaic decoration had already appeared in Rome, in the vaulting of the outer ring of the circular church of Sta Costanza (326–37). These mosaics are not only the earliest surviving Christian mosaics, but are entirely Roman in style, though they may also be an instance of an Eastern idea infiltrating into Roman Christian art from a Persian source, and may perhaps lie behind such examples as the Paradise garden in the apse of Sant'Apollinare in Classe (*see* RAVENNA), or the brilliant sunset clouds in SS Cosmas and Damian in Rome (526–30). During the long night of Iconoclasm only non-figurative art was officially permitted in Byzantium, and though Byzantine and Roman mosaics can be considered separately, the impact of Iconoclasm in Byzantium had important repercussions in Rome. Rome, Ravenna, and Salonika are where most of the fine early mosaics survive. The first full sequence of doctrinal mosaics showing scenes from the Gospel narratives, from the Marriage at Cana to the Resurrection, are those in the uppermost register on the walls of Sant'Apollinare Nuovo in Ravenna (520–26), which are earlier than the series (536–46) for Justinian's Holy Apostles in Constantinople, destroyed by the Turks in 1453. San Vitale, Ravenna, is a good example of the mixture of classical and Byzantine styles, in that the Christ in the apse is a youthful, beardless figure, entirely Roman in inspiration, while the two great dedicatory panels of the Emperor Justinian and his Empress Theodora, only twenty years later, are examples of fully Byzantine hieratic art. As a rough guide to date, the early mosaics had a white ground (as at Sta Costanza), later ones had a blue ground (as in the 5th-century porch of the Lateran Baptistery in Rome, and in the Mausoleum of Galla Placidia, in Ravenna), and in the 6th century the ground became almost invariably gold. In Rome, in the apse of Sta Pudenziana (384–9), Christ is flanked by SS Peter and Paul, each with five accompanying Apostles, against a fine architectural background; parallel to it in execution is the fine, almost unrestored, though damaged, apse of St George, Salonika. The apse, *triumphal arch, and the nave walls, have light-coloured grounds, close to antique examples, and may be 4th/5th century.

The scenes in the triumphal arch are of the glory of the Virgin, which would suggest a date after the Councils of Ephesus (431) and Chalcedon (451) when the Nestorian heresy which impugned the Godhead of Christ by maintaining that the Virgin was only the bearer of Christ—Christotokos—was condemned, and she was declared to be the bearer of

God—Theotokos. It is likely that these mosaics were commissioned by Pope Sixtus III (432–40) to commemorate the decision of the Council of Ephesus. They were extensively restored by Torriti in 1295. The apse of SS Cosmas and Damian, notable for its remarkable sunset, is in a fully developed Byzantine style, with a bearded Christ and the elongation of forms characteristic of Byzantine art, while the twelve sheep which represent the Apostles are parallels of the allegorical sheep in Sant'Apollinare in Classe. The basilica at Poreč (Parenzo) in Croatia has fine mosaics dating between 530 and 535, with the Virgin in the centre of the apse, probably the earliest representation of her in this most commanding position. Little but fragments survive in Constantinople, but Salonika shows the development of the art, since the work there is of very high quality. The earliest is probably the late 4th-century dome mosaic in St George, an architectural composition of a distinctly Roman type which had already appeared in Ravenna and Damascus, and similar classical inspiration informs the late 4th-century floral scrolls, with birds and beasts, in the Basilica of the Acheiropoietos. In St Demetrios part of the apse has fine 7th-century figures of saints, flanked by donors who are distinguished from the saints by their square *haloes.

Iconoclasm, which lasted from 726 to 843, was enforced strictly in Constantinople, where such mosaics as were made were of a very severe character. Perhaps some of the finest non-figurative mosaics were those made by Greek craftsmen for the Islamic Dome of the Rock in Jerusalem, built in 688–91, for the Great Mosque in Damascus (715), and the Great Mosque of Cordoba (965–71). Iconoclasm was less powerful in outlying areas, and it is difficult to tell the difference between work done before and after, because figurative art began again where it had left off. Unfortunately, the huge cost of mosaics meant that many churches now made do with wall-paintings. Many Greek craftsmen had migrated to Rome, where lavish patronage expressed Roman disapproval of Iconoclasm. The apse mosaics in the Greek church of Sta Maria in Cosmedin date from 705–7; those in Sta Maria in Domnica, where the role of the Virgin as Theotokos is stressed, and in Sta Cecilia and Sta Prassede, where the apse figures are of the titular saints, whose relics were brought into the churches at this period, all date between 817 and 824, and the choice of subject is designed to stress Roman opposition to events in Byzantium. Many Byzantine features now appear in the iconography, style, and colour, and perhaps the most Byzantine of all are the mosaics in the tiny dark chapel of S. Zeno in Sta Prassede, where the tesserae have been set to catch the glancing light.

In the post-Iconoclastic period the stress was on the transcendental, on awesomeness, on elongated figures, with gold grounds, rich colour, and the use of the shape of the building to increase the impact. In Constantinople, after the lifting of the ban, the *Deësis in a room over the south porch of Hagia Sophia was set, probably *c.*843, with Apostles, saints, and patriarchs such as Methodius and others who had always opposed Iconoclasm. In 869 a new Council endeavoured to re-establish relations with Rome, and the Deësis over the Imperial door of the narthex probably shows the penitent Leo VI kneeling before Christ (880–900). The small church of Christ in Chora, now known as the Kariye Camii, originally 11th century, was rebuilt and endowed by Theodore Metochites between about 1303 and 1320, when he was still an influential court official. The foundation is remarkable both for the quality of the mosaics and the paintings, and for the range and pictorial quality of the subjects surviving in the vaults of the inner and outer narthex. These consist of cycles of the Lives of Christ and of the Virgin. Among them is a tender scene of the Nativity, one of the child Mary helped by an angel to learn to walk towards her mother, an iconographically rare scene of Joseph questioning the Virgin's explanation of her pregnancy, and another, inside the church, of the Dormition of the Virgin, all rendered with a narrative realism and poetry akin to that of Italian 14th-century painting. The burial chapel alongside the main church has superb frescoes of the *Anastasis—the Byzantine form of the Resurrection—Christ's miracles of the Raising of the Widow's Son of Nain, and the Raising of Jairus's Daughter, as well as a Virgin and Child with angels in the dome, and OT scenes in the pendentives.

Outside Constantinople and Rome, the early 11th-century church of Hosios Lukas, near Delphi in Greece, once had a complete NT series, of which only part survives. In colour, technique, and iconography, it is an excellent example of the hieratic, severe style of monastic art, quite different in approach from the more metropolitan style of elegant and subtle classicism to be seen in the church of the Katholikon, Daphni, near Athens, of *c*.1100. Many of the Daphni mosaics have either perished or been over-restored, but the Annunciation to Joachim and Anna, and the moving and reflective Crucifixion are superb, and the Pantocrator in the dome is the most impressive, awe-inspiring of all visions of Christ.

Byzantine loss of control of the Mediterranean at the end of the 7th century resulted in the Muslim conquest of all the islands—Crete, Malta, Sicily, Corsica, Sardinia, and the Balearics. Sicily was occupied from 827 onwards, and Muslim rule lasted for over 200 years.

By the end of the 10th century Byzantine rule in S. Italy had become weak and fragmented. In 1016 Norman adventurers began to arrive in Italy as pilgrims to the shrine of Michael the Archangel on Monte Gargano, and they rapidly infiltrated the country until by 1040 they had conquered most of the south of Italy. In 1059 Pope Nicholas II invested the Norman, Robert Guiscard, with the duchy of Apulia and Calabria, and promised to recognize him as ruler of Sicily, if he could conquer it from the Muslims. By 1072 he had taken Palermo and by 1091 the whole island was under Norman control. During the 12th century Byzantine mosaicists were brought in to decorate some of the most important churches built by the new Christian rulers in and near Palermo. Unlike Byzantine churches of this date, Sicilian ones were generally basilican in shape, so that the artists had to modify the decorative systems. Despite the loss of continuity in development and technical expertise caused by their isolation from their creative centre, and also from Rome, what they created is a clear example of a mid-12th-century Byzantine mosaic decoration adapted to a different shape of church and to the Latin rite. Four sites are particularly important: Cefalù, founded by Roger II in 1131; the Palatine Chapel in the Royal Palace in Palermo, of the 1140s; the Martorana, also in Palermo, of the 1150s; and Monreale, built from *c*.1172/3, and decorated during the next ten years.

Cefalù is a plain Romanesque basilica, with a vaulted presbytery and transepts, and an open timber roof over the nave. The absence of a dome meant that the figure of the Pantocrator was placed in the main apse. Below it are three ranges of figures of unequal height, the upper, taller, row containing the Virgin and four archangels and the two lower rows the Apostles, six in each row. An inscription gives the date 1148. After 1150, the political struggle which had prompted the foundation had been resolved and Roger's interest in the work waned, to be resumed after his death in 1154 by his successor, William I. By 1160 the decoration of the crossing, the transepts, and the two registers of the side walls, was complete. Only the apse is the work of Byzantine mosaicists; the rest of the work was done by their Sicilian workshop. William II completed the church on a reduced plan between 1170 and 1200. Unfortunately, the restorations (1857–68) were very damaging.

Roger's main artistic concern was for the chapel built into his palace in Palermo between 1130 and 1140. Its shape is a synthesis of Greek and Italian forms, with an apsidal end, a square crossing with a dome on squinches with a high drum, short transepts, and a long nave. Each part of the interior is distinct in its roofing system, of which the nave is the most remarkable, as it is covered by a long barrel vault of carved, painted, and gilded wood, with Saracenic stalactites purely Islamic in character and with paintings of Islamic type, not Western or Greek. The conch of the apse has an image of the Pantocrator, with the Virgin below (an 18th-century figure, replacing a window) flanked by saints. The dome contains a second image of the Pantocrator in the centre, with a ring of angels and archangels below. In the drum and squinches are the Evangelists and four prophets. These are the finest unrestored mosaics in the chapel, and are dated 1148. On the west wall is a Christ in Majesty enthroned between SS Peter and Paul; in the nave, transepts, and aisles are narrative scenes from the Old and New Testaments, from the Creation onwards, many fitted into the spandrels of the nave arcades. Despite many alterations and restorations, some perhaps necessary to repair the poor workmanship of hastily trained Sicilian mosaicists, the chapel creates an overwhelming effect of golden splendour.

The Martorana, or Chapel of St Mary, also called after its founder, Admiral George of Antioch, the Cappella dell'Ammiraglio, was built between 1143 and 1151. It was a true Byzantine cross-in-square church, with a dome borne on columns, surrounded by a narrow barrel-vaulted ambulatory with cross vaults at the corners. It originally had three apses—a general plan in Sicily and S. Italy—a narthex and atrium with a porch. Unfortunately it was later converted into a convent and has suffered very damaging reconstruction. The cupola has an enthroned Christ, blessing, with below Him four archangels in poses of proskynesis—a prostration as an act of homage—used probably to fit them into the restricted space. In the high drum are prophets, on the triumphal arch is an Annunciation, with the Visitation opposite, and narrative panels of the Life of the Virgin. There are also two dedication panels: King Roger crowned by Christ, and the Admiral prostrate before the Virgin—both typically Constantinopolitan designs.

The Cathedral and monastery of Monreale was built by William II on the site of the Hagia Kyriaka, the church of an earlier Greek Metropolitan, to house William's own tomb, and those of his dynasty. He imported a Cluniac community from La Cava, near Salerno, but endless difficulties ensued, and it finally fell into decline, with the fortunate result that it has suffered less restoration and has the best preserved 12th-century interior and decoration in Sicily.

It was probably begun *c.*1172/3, but was not finished by the time of William's death in 1189. There are no dated inscriptions, except on the bronze doors by the Pisan sculptor Bonnanus, which have the date 1186, but they were probably made in Pisa. The other pair of bronze doors, by Barisanus of Trani, on the north side were probably made after 1180. The interior is a plain Norman type basilica, with a long nave and aisles, attached to a cross-in-square east end, with three apses, but no dome.

In the semi-dome of the main apse the mosaic is of the Pantocrator, smaller and more stereotyped than that of Cefalù, and in the tier below the Virgin and Child with the Archangels Michael and Gabriel, and six Apostles on either side, with a further tier of saints below. On the triumphal arch is the Annunciation, and the side apses have tiers of saints and prophets. The narrative panels with the Christological sequence continue round the very short transeptal area and in the nave is the OT series beginning with the Creation and continuing after the west end (where there is a Virgin and Child with angels) all round as far as the *presbytery. The aisles have panels of the Miracles of Christ, besides decorative details and figures of saints. The whole decoration is entirely homogenous, and clearly the work of one leading artist, but by many hands working under his strict control. The narratives are not original designs invented by the workshop, but follow time-honoured practices adapted and modernized, in that here the panels are fitted into the spandrel shapes over the arcades of the nave and if necessary the composition is redesigned to fit the shape. It is clear that once the strict Byzantine arrangement of the subjects, designed for a cross-in-square church, had been changed to adapt it to a different shape of church, the rigid control of the decoration—so marked a feature of earlier Byzantine mosaics—broke down.

In the austere post-Iconoclastic period of the 9th and 10th centuries, mosaic decoration consisted mainly of single figures, symbols, and allegories, with a new realism in their treatment. The whole building came to have a symbolic meaning, as the earthly representation of Paradise; the ground level with its marble revetment was this world, and, as the believer's eye travelled upwards, the hierarchies unfolded—holy men and women, donors, prophets, saints, Evangelists, angels and archangels, the Virgin and Child, until the culmination was reached with the Pantocrator in the dome. Symbolism of this type depended on the cross-in-square design of the church. Great care was taken to preserve the frontality which Byzantine imagery demanded, and at the same time to use the angle of the squinch to keep the representation realistic. Daphni is an 11th-century example.

Slowly, richer, and more flexible forms evolved, largely because painting increased in importance as Byzantium became steadily poorer, and mosaics were reserved for the most important sites. The use of marble below and mosaic above gave way when narrative painting took over; the strict optical and iconographical systems were abandoned and the unity of 10th- and 11th-century mosaic decoration was lost. It was so difficult to adapt the strict cross-in-square system to the long-nave church, even where a crossing dome and an apsidal east end existed, that the narratives were arranged to flow either from east to west returning on the opposite side, or they were treated *typologically, with the Old and New Testament facing each other, the Gospel narratives on the right (or south) and the OT

b

parallels on the left (or north). Further extensions of the schemes produced sequences of the Miracles of Christ, the Lives of the Apostles, the legends of saints, placed in the aisles, and the transepts were used for the Life of the Virgin. The west end was the site either of a Christ in Majesty, or a Last Judgement. The main apse becomes the area for the Pantocrator, or one of the other forms of the Christ image—Christ enthroned in Majesty with angels and saints, the Vision of *Ezekiel of Christ with the four Apocalyptic Beings (often found on the E. Mediterranean shores, but which became a common W. Romanesque subject), the Ascension with Christ in a *mandorla borne by angels, the Virgin flanked by angels, or a Deësis with Christ between the Virgin and the Baptist. There was no fixed system for the side apses, which could be used for the Virgin or for saints, but the triumphal arch below the dome—if there was one—and the space over the conch of the apse were used for such subjects as the Transfiguration, Ascension, Pentecost, or Annunciation. In long-nave churches, where the narratives were placed in the arcades, difficulties had to be resolved over the format of the narratives—whether they were to be forced into the spandrels of the arches with inevitable truncations of the figures, as in the Palatine Chapel, or were to be redesigned to fit the new shapes, as at Monreale. The choice of saints to be represented often depended on non-religious reasons—dynastic, political, or based on the preferences of the monastic Order serving the church, as at Monreale.

In Byzantine churches the narrative scenes contain a spiritual or theological meaning besides the incident illustrated; the Sicilian ones do not. The cross-in-square churches offered less space for story-telling, so that economy in the cost of the expensive materials and the laborious technique made for an equal economy in the number of subjects represented, which ensured that these were only those which also exemplified a doctrinal point.

Monreale, in fact, is the best example of a mid-Byzantine biblical cycle, and is not a hybrid Sicilian–Byzantine scheme.

Byzantine art, through its grandeur of conception, its rigorous iconographical systems, and the pervasive influence of Constantinopolitan culture, was the dominant artistic force in the whole area radiating from Constantinople, encompassing territories well outside the empire itself: *Russia and Georgia in the north, the Slav, Bulgarian, and Macedonian areas in the north-west, the Mediterranean lands, such as Sicily, Cyprus, and Crete, reaching as far into Italy as *Ravenna, *Venice, and *Torcello.

It was Venetian trading links with Byzantium that prompted the adoption of Byzantine art, and above all, mosaics, rather than Roman forms, although it was always the Latin rite, not the Orthodox one, which was celebrated. The plan of *St Mark's, with its five domes, triapsidal choir, and enveloping narthex is taken directly from the Church of the Holy Apostles in Constantinople, destroyed by the Turks after 1453, though the strict Byzantine system of mosaic decoration was not followed at St Mark's.

The finest Byzantine work in the Venetian enclave is at *Torcello Cathedral, where the apse mosaics of the early 12th century are of pure Byzantine inspiration, and were probably set by Greek artists since the inscriptions are in Greek.

The only true Byzantine mosaic north of the Alps is in the apse of the little church of Germigny-les-Prés, which was a dependency of the Abbey of St-Benoît-sur-Loire. It is a 9th-century vision of angels surrounding the Ark of the Covenant, an iconographical rarity, set possibly by a mosaicist from Ravenna.

Wall-Paintings and Icons

The great cost of mosaic decorations limited them to imperial foundations, to favoured monasteries, and to places outside the immediate confines of the empire where dynastic or political circumstances justified lavish display. Wall-paintings became a substitute not only for mosaics, but also for the marble revetment in the lower parts of churches. So little survived in Constantinople and Asia Minor after 1453 that it is from churches in the Balkans, the former Yugoslavia, and Russia that some idea of Byzantine wall-painting can be gathered, and of that almost all is 10th to 14th century. From the Iconoclastic period, it is mostly in the rock churches and monasteries of Cappadocia and the remoter areas of Turkey that figure painting continued in the 8th and 9th centuries, but these works were designed to serve isolated religious communities, and the subject-matter was often limited and obscure.

In many of the churches of Macedonia and Serbia, which were then separate countries, but were either part of the Byzantine Empire or had strong dynastic links with Constantinople, artists from the capital were employed. They created an art which was often radically different from that of an earlier age, and which in many ways antedates developments usually attributed to the 14th century in Italy. These new ideas can be seen in examples in the former Yugoslavia, where they do not demonstrate merely local changes, but a general shift in the function of religious art.

The astonishing *Ascension* in the mid-11th-century barrel vault of Sta Sophia in Ochrid (SW Serbia) with Christ in an aureole in the centre and the Virgin, the Apostles, and the usual two angels ranged on either side, and with the surprising vision of a long flight of angels surging towards the altar on the lower parts of the vault, opens a new chapter in the greater freedom with which traditional subjects could be treated. In St Panteleimon at Nerez (near Skopje) the *Deposition* and *Lamentation over the dead Christ*, of *c.*1164, move from the usual static and sober depiction of the Crucifixion alone to a new dramatic and emotional account of the effect of the death of Christ on His mother and His followers. The Church of the Ascension at Mileševa (near Sarajevo) has frescoes of 1234/6 of a touching and tender *Descent from the Cross* but the finest work is a superb *Angel at the Sepulchre* of gravely classical serenity. The Byzantine type of dynastic image is continued in the fresco of *King Vladislav presented by the Virgin to the enthroned Christ*, which was probably a real-life portrait with greater psychological insight than the usual imperial portraits ever achieved. At Sopoćani, between 1256 and 1268, in the Church of the Trinity founded as a cathedral and royal mausoleum, there is not only a series of royal portraits, but, more important, frescoes of a *Dormition of the Virgin* of noble restraint, and an expressive *Harrowing of Hell*.

The growing use of architectural backgrounds is a pointer to the new vision where the artist uses the whole wall as a unit in which to compose, instead of an isolated depiction of an incident or a group of figures. By the end of the century (*c.*1295) at Ochrid, in SW Serbia, in the Church of the Peribleptos, a *Betrayal of Christ* is seen as a violent tumult, and the old rules of representation are treated cavalierly—Christ and the Apostles are full faced or in three-quarter view, Judas is in profile, but the rest of the mob surging round the central, still figure of Christ is treated with vivid realism. Another feature which has become more apparent is the use of continuous representation, where several incidents occurring at different times—and even places—are combined to create a narrative sequence. This feature also appears in late mosaics. Another feature which appears increasingly is the illustration of incidents in the Apocryphal Gospels—notably the Protevangelium of S. James and the Gospel according to Thomas, which are full of picturesque stories—and Lives of Saints, instead of adhering strictly to the canonical Gospels. For instance, in the King's Church at Studenica (N. of Pécs, now in Hungary), a *Nativity of the Virgin*—itself a stranger both to the Gospels and the true Byzantine canon—is set in a wide architectural background and is full of narrative detail without regard to the unity of time or place.

This change to story-telling, instead of the earlier ideals of doctrinal instruction and exemplification, characterizes most of 13th- and 14th-century work. It results from a slackening of the intellectual control formerly exercised by the clergy, but is also a product of the greater ease of execution of fresco and the more immediate effects which could be achieved by painting, as against the grander—and now impossibly expensive—mosaic decoration. The earlier economy in the cost of the materials and the laborious technique of mosaics ensured an equal economy in the number of subjects represented, and care for their deeper significance. These aims are now disregarded. The changes may clearly be seen in three churches at Mistra in the Peloponnese. The Brontocheion has a *Procession of Martyrs* of the mid-14th century of restrained simplicity and rich colour; in the church of the Peribleptos is a *Nativity* of *c.*1400 full of busy incident with many lively story-telling details; in the Pantanassa is a *Raising of Lazarus* probably of *c.*1430, full of fervour, emotion, colour, but the action is diffuse and scattered. The desire to tell a story with the maximum stress on its dramatic quality has diluted the essential meaning and the spiritual significance of this supreme miracle into no more than just another busy scene. It may be that the artist was not equal to the task, but it is also a demonstration that it is the artist, not the 'fathers who build the churches', who is now in control.

The significance of the *icon is, ultimately, linked to classical emperor veneration. What had begun by being, at first, honorific and then symbolic, acquired in the Byzantine environment qualities encouraging mystical veneration when the image became linked with hagiography. This was further stimulated by processions in which images were carried, for instance when invocations were made at times of danger or distress, such as wars, plagues, or other disasters. As a result, the image began to acquire a significance greater than its role as a picture. An encouragement to this attitude is found in the teaching of the 3rd-century Neoplatonic philosopher Porphyry, who taught that images were the visible outward manifestation of invisible mysteries and religious truth. Images, therefore, could become cult objects in the same way as relics, and they were rapidly credited with the power of being wonder-workers. By the 7th century the cult had become dangerously important in religious life, and the veneration of the image could become an end in itself. This attitude was helped by the rules governing the presentation of the subject, which obeyed even more strictly the code laid down for mosaics: the image must show the subject frontally; the sacred figures must be larger than the human figures; the persons, divine or human, must be clearly named in an inscription; the colours used must, as far as possible, obey the rules laid down for the portrayal of the divine, or the miraculous; ideal representation, not a realistic one, was required since the artist may imagine the transcendental but cannot imitate it from nature; if the image were of a saint or martyr, particularly if it were of a priest, then it should be based on a known likeness or description, and vestments, or instruments of martyrdom, and an identifying inscription must be included. There were also certain set forms for the representation of such subjects as the Virgin and Child, where the position of the head and the hands was governed by precept, so that the artist, far from being able to develop the subject, was confined within a set framework. Inevitably, the image became stereotyped.

The believer was encouraged to believe that a concentration on the image could create a current, a direct spiritual contact, between the subject and the believer, and it requires a fairly sophisticated intelligence to perceive where this idea, once firmly rooted, actually stopped short of enduing the image with the same supernatural state and powers as the subject itself. It was an intellectual Rubicon far too often crossed in both East and West. The cult of images reached its zenith in the 8th century, and was accompanied by a movement, parallel but due to quite different causes, towards a huge increase in monasticism. The advance of Islam, with its more austere religion and total rejection of images, created an opposition which became dominant with the rise to the Byzantine throne in 717 of Leo the Isaurian, who found the empire demoralized, a prey to superstition, and decided that the cult of images, encouraged by the Church and above all by monasteries, was largely to blame. The result was Iconoclasm, successful in Constantinople, but far less successful in the provinces, and rejected by monasteries, which, despite violent persecution, endeavoured to preserve their cult objects.

The few surviving early icons, usually executed in the encaustic technique similar to that of the Egyptian Fayyum effigies, are mostly in St Catherine's Monastery, Mount Sinai, and at Bawit in Egypt. Examples at Mt. Sinai are the fine 6th-century *Virgin and Child, with SS Theodore and George, two angels, and the Hand of God,* a large work over two feet high, and the superb 7th-century, almost life-sized half-length *S. Peter,* enthroned in a niche with three medallions at the top with Christ in the centre flanked by the Virgin and S. John. A mid-8th-century *Crucifixion,* with the Virgin and S. John on either side, once had both thieves with their apocryphal names of Demas (also called Dysmas on other examples) and Gestas, though severe damage has left only Gestas, fettered but not nailed to his cross. This may be one of the earliest representations of the two thieves with other forms of crucifixion than that suffered by Christ; it might also be an early rare example where notions of *decorum—that only Christ was actually nailed to the cross, the two thieves being perceived as unworthy to suffer the same fate as Christ—were allowed to modify the

Gospel account. The Crucifixion is depicted according to the Eastern, or Palestinian, form with Christ wearing a long *colobium, an indication that the origin of the image is not Constantinople, since the clothed Christ is the Eastern form, where the Roman or Hellenic form shows Christ nude. Palestine was conquered by the Arabs in 640, and since imperial laws did not operate there, image-making could continue. In fact, S. John of Damascus wrote his three treatises defending images at the monastery of St Saba, near Jerusalem, between 726 and 730.

Two other types of icon were important and popular: the Virgin and Child, and figures of saints, either singly or in rows. The images of saints were probably adapted from mosaics, and used as calendar icons on the saint's name-day. They are usually quite small, but the figures are hieratic, formal, and stiff, and remain virtually unchanging from their early appearance in the Mt. Sinai 10th-century example of SS Zosimus and Nicholas. Icons of the Virgin were the most popular, and follow three forms: the grief-stricken Virgin of the Crucifixion, less common than versions of the Virgin and Child of which the original was said to have been painted by S. Luke. In this image she carries the infant Christ on one arm, while pointing to Him with her other hand—the Hodegetria form, the name being derived from the Hodegon monastery in Constantinople, home of the original, to which wonder-working powers were attributed (*see* MADONNA TYPES). It appears to have been destroyed during the Iconoclastic period, but has survived in countless versions, some painted, and some in the miniature mosaic technique, as for instance in the fine example of *c.*1200 at Mt. Sinai. Another type was the Glycophelousa Virgin, or Virgin of the Loving Embrace, in which she holds the infant Christ close to her cheek. There is a 14th-century miniature mosaic example in the Byzantine Museum, Athens; there is also a rarer variant 13th-century form, known as the Kardiotissa Virgin, after the monastery of that name in Crete, from which it was stolen in 1420, but it has been in Rome since 1498. There is a fine late 16th/early 17th-century example in the Byzantine Museum, Athens signed by the artist Angelos. In this form the Christ Child twists round in his mother's arms and returns her embrace.

On Mt. Athos there are many icons, of which a miniature mosaic icon of the Hodegetria Virgin is dated *c.*1198. A very fine 13th-century *Christ the Redeemer* reflects a more gentle aspect of the Pantocrator; both these works are in the Chilandar Monastery Museum. Another celebrated icon is *Our Lady of Vladimir* (Moscow, Tretyakov Mus.), a Glycophelousa Virgin of the first half of the 12th century, a work of tender, grave beauty, and though only the two heads can claim to be original, they reflect the finest quality of icon-painting in Constantinople. One of the favoured forms in icons was to frame them in gold or silver, often set with gems. Examples of this type are an early 14th-century Hodegetria Virgin, and a double icon of the *Annunciation*, with the panel with the Archangel Gabriel and that with the seated Virgin all framed in elaborately worked silver (National Mus., Ochrid). Old Testament scenes are uncommon, but a very beautiful 14th-century one is the *Hospitality of Abraham* (Athens, Benaki Mus.) showing Abraham and Sarah serving the three angels (Gen. 18).

The iconography of icons follows set precedents; in icons of the Virgin her head is always covered by a veil—the maphorion worn by all women in the East—and the Christ Child is fully clothed. Frontality and immobility are almost invariably maintained, except for images of the Anastasis, where Christ often strides energetically towards the souls in Limbo whom He has come to release, and in icons of the Raising of Lazarus, where though actual movement is absent, there is a latent air of intense drama. From the 11th century onwards the kind of narrative image which had already appeared in mosaic decorations appears also in icons, sometimes following closely on the Gospels, but often illustrating the much freer narratives of the Apocrypha.

The collection of icons has been of fairly recent date, and early examples are scattered from Berlin to New York, some crudely schematic, some of delicate beauty, but only rarely are any datable. Their production in Russia continued into modern times, with many copies of earlier examples. Some of these late examples also have silver or silver-gilt inlays covering all but the face and figure, and these inlays are often diapered in patterns, or encrusted with enamels and jewels.

b

Manuscripts

The purpose of illustrating a text is to clarify it. The original form of a 'book' was a scroll, but by the 4th century the book proper, or codex, came into use made from sheets of vellum stitched together, which enabled pictures and text to be more closely related. The earliest illustrated MSS were secular, not religious, and the earliest known religious illustrated MS of Western Christianity consists of five fragments of an Old Latin version of the Bible, probably written and illuminated in N. Italy in the late 4th century, found inside the bindings of some books in which the pieces of vellum were used as packing. These are the Quedlingburg *Itala* fragments, now in the Berlin State Library. The next in date are 5th-century OT texts, probably adapted from the Alexandrian Septuagint, which itself does not survive. The favourite book was Genesis; for instance the Cotton Genesis (BM), of which only twenty-one damaged illustrations out of 250 survived a fire in 1731, has miniatures of the same width as the text and placed sometimes above, sometimes below, and sometimes two to a page; the *Vienna Genesis (Vienna, Staatsbibliothek), the surviving early 6th-century fragments of a 'de luxe' edition on purple vellum, is illustrated at the bottom of the pages under the text, sometimes in one register, sometimes in two, with vivid story-telling pictures full of movement which form a continuous narrative, much as if the artist were still working from a scroll. The earliest NT MS is the *Rossano Gospels (Rossano, Calabria, Mus. Diocesano), which contains the whole of the first two Gospels; it is a Greek MS, also on purple vellum, probably of *c*.500, and contains fifteen miniatures which include important iconographic innovations. The Codex *Sinopensis (Paris, BN) is of about the same date as the Rossano Gospels; it contains about a third of S. Matthew's Gospel, and is another luxury production written in gold uncials on purple vellum. All these MSS were probably produced for Constantinople, if not in the city; they show very clearly the strong Near Eastern influence—vivid, realistic, dramatic—which overcame the Roman and Hellenic classicism, and the enlargement of religious subject-matter which came from these outside sources.

The *Rabbula Gospels (Florence, Bib. Laurenziana) of 586, also stakes out new ground, and the late 6th-century S. Augustine's Gospels (Cambridge, Corpus Christi Coll., used at the installation of Archbishops of Canterbury) has a full-page Evangelist portrait of S. Luke, with twelve small Gospel scenes round it, and the Evangelist's symbol in an elaborate *tympanum crowning the whole. This MS, almost certainly produced in Italy, is in sharp contrast to the Eastern influenced Byzantine ones, since it reflects Roman forms, although in its introduction of narrative it acknowledges that the purpose of illumination is to enforce the meaning of the text.

One very unusual MS, the origins of which have given rise to much argument, is the *Ashburnham Pentateuch (Paris, BN), which may date from the late 6th or 7th century. Very few MSS have survived from the Iconoclastic period, but one of the most interesting is the 9th-century Khludov Psalter (Moscow, Historical Mus.), in which the psalms are taken from the Septuagint, and several of the illustrations show scenes of Iconoclasm, such as the obliteration of images and the desecration of an image of the crucified Christ depicted as a re-enactment of the crucifixion. These vivid pictures are used to illustrate Psalm 69 (Vg. 68), and other psalms have illustrations portraying the downfall of iconoclasts, and the victory of their opponents. The Psalter was apparently used in Hagia Sophia.

After the end of Iconoclasm, Byzantium enjoyed a second Golden Age during which many MSS were produced. Since it is possible in MS illumination to cover a far wider field than in church decoration, it is not surprising that very varied subjects and influences can be seen in the products, though the most important is a renewed classicism: such examples as the magnificent copy of the *Homilies of S. Gregory of Nazianzus*, written between 880 and 886, with about 200 miniatures, forty-six of them full page, with a fine, though damaged, *Vision of Ezekiel*; one of the pages has portraits of the Emperor Basil I, with his family. The 10th-century Paris Psalter (BN), has fourteen full-page illuminations of which six are of the highest quality, among them the superb *David inspired by Melody* with the unusual detail of animals charmed by his playing of the harp, reminiscent of a secular parallel of Orpheus charming the wild beasts, which may in fact have inspired it, and *Isaiah inspired between Night and Dawn*, and *David between Wisdom and Prophecy*. An outstanding MS is the Psalter of Basil II (976–1025) which has a full-page miniature of the Emperor in Imperial robes, with the Archangels Michael and Gabriel, being crowned by Christ himself (Venice, Marciana Lib.). Basil II also commissioned a *menologion (Vatican)—a form of liturgical calendar with lives of the saints commemorated—of which only five months survive, but which contains 430 miniatures, one on each page, and all on gold backgrounds. All these were either imperial commissions, or produced for the court.

Parallel to this luxury art was a more modest production for monasteries. Monastic psalters use only marginal illustrations. Gospel books are of two kinds; they are either complete texts or are lectionaries—liturgical Gospels in which the sequence is disregarded so as to produce texts to be read in church. Most of the Gospel books have Evangelist portraits at the beginning of each Gospel, the majority based on the type used in the Vienna Genesis—the Evangelist seen writing either a scroll or a book. Lectionaries usually have a decorative headpiece and illuminated initials, though an 11th-century one (New York, Morgan Lib.) has five large illustrations and twenty-one small miniatures in the margins. Perhaps the most unusual of all monastic books is the Klimax, or *Scala Paradisi*, written by S. John *Climacus of St Catherine's Monastery, Mount Sinai. It is an exposition of the qualities and virtues required for a monk to achieve the goal of Paradise, with monks climbing a steep ladder towards Heaven while demons try to pull them off, in some cases dragging them down into the mouth of Hell. The surviving copies are of the 11th and 12th centuries (Vatican Lib. and St Catherine's).

Byzantine book production was disastrously affected first by the Crusader sack of the city in 1204, and the Latin rule which followed, and then came to a total end with the capture of the city by the Turks in 1453. Both sacks brought devastation, as the Crusaders took away books, icons, and treasures from the precious accumulations in churches, monasteries, and the imperial palaces, some of this loot having gone to enrich the West; the Turks destroyed Christian books and icons, and melted down Christian artefacts.

Goldsmiths' work, Ivories, Sculptures, Textiles

The silver *ampullae (pilgrims' reliquary flasks) had images on them probably derived from mosaics and paintings in Constantine's churches in the Holy Places in Palestine, and are virtually the only surviving evidence for these lost works. They include the Crucifixion, with Christ's cross between the two thieves, though Christ is not seen on the cross, but over it; the enthroned Virgin and Child worshipped by the Magi and the shepherds; the Ascension with Christ in a *mandorla borne by four angels, with the Apostles grouped on either side of the Virgin; and the Holy Women at the Tomb, greeted by the angel—all depictions which become almost standard illustrations of the scenes over succeeding centuries, thus suggesting a common source. They appear in MS illuminations from the 6th century onwards, and in, for example, the odd little casket (Vatican, Museo Sacro) in which a pilgrim put his relics of a journey to the Holy Land—earth, stones, scraps of cloth. Its painted lid has crude versions of these scenes, plus the *Nativity* and the *Baptism* of Christ, remarkably close to illustrations in early MSS. The ampullae and the casket were probably made in Jerusalem, despite its not having been a productive centre for art, because the *Crucifixion* on the casket has Christ in a colobium and this is the standard Eastern form, whereas in Constantinople the crucified Christ is nude.

Very little metalwork has survived in E. Byzantine territories. The bronze doors of the S. entrance to Hagia Sophia date from *c.*840, and were made to conform to the Iconoclasm prevailing at the time, with scrolls of leaves and tendrils and ornamental patterns. Other survivors are the pair of 6th-century gold medallions (Istanbul, Archaeological Mus.), some three inches across, with scenes of Christ's life and miracles which were found at Adana (on the south coast of Turkey) and a fine silver paten with gold detail, found at Stuma in Syria, and datable to 565–78 (Istanbul, Arch. Mus.) showing the *Institution of the Eucharist* with two figures of Christ giving bread and, separately, wine to the Apostles.

Outside the Byzantine heartland there are the precious gifts sent by emperors to Popes and legates, as for instance, the silver-gilt cross of Justin II (565–78), presented to Rome.

The great sack of 1204 scattered treasures across Europe; in Venice, enamels from Constantinople were reused in the *Pala d'Oro, and two magnificent enamelled and jewelled 9th- and 12th-century gospel covers are in the Marciana Library. The earlier one has a crucified Christ, in a colobium, indicating a Syrian origin. A magnificent gold and enamel reliquary of the True Cross of *c.*960 is in the Cathedral Treasury, Limburg-an-der-Lahn. None of these precious objects displays any divergence from established iconography. Even the 12th-century silver-gilt reliquary cover (Paris, Louvre) with the *Holy Women at the Sepulchre* shows no change from the scene depicted five centuries earlier. The 12th-century silver-gilt and enamel cross in the Cathedral Treasury at Cosenza (Calabria), presented in 1222 by the Emperor Frederic II Hohenstauffen, clearly emanates from Constantinople: the enthroned Christ on the reverse is surrounded by the Evangelists, each following the traditional design of the scribe at his writing desk; and the *Anastasis* on the 13th-century silver-gilt book-cover (Venice, Marciana Lib.) shows barely any change from the treatment of the subject in the 10th-century Daphni mosaics.

The taste for ivory carvings was inherited from antiquity: they were always luxury objects, prized for the intricate workmanship which the material encouraged, and for the soft delicacy of their colour and polished surface. Imperial consular diptychs were emblems or credentials of a consul's appointment and were current before 384 when an edict of the Emperor Theodosius regularized their issue. They rapidly developed a religious function, becoming memorials inscribed with the names of persons commemorated in church services. Ivory carvings also decorated caskets, reliquaries, book-covers, crosses, figures and carved plaques. *Maximianus' thrones in Ravenna were also decorated with ivory carvings. The principal workshops were in Constantinople, Rome, and Milan; other centres were Alexandria and Antioch, but such workshops spread into many important Mediterranean cities as the material itself was freely available and easily transportable.

On some imperial or consular diptychs or reliefs the imagery is a mixture of the secular and the religious. The very grand *'Barberini' Ivory* (Louvre) is made up of five parts (one is missing) and probably represents Justinian (527–65) riding in triumph, attended by a general holding an emblem of victory, and with Scythian tribute bearers below his horse's hoofs. Over the Emperor's head is a bust of Christ blessing in a roundel held by angels like winged victories—a clear adaptation of a Roman triumphal arch motif—but despite this Christianizing element the Emperor's foot is held by Gaea, the ancient Greek goddess of Earth. Milan must have early reached excellence as a centre, since the leaf in the Castello Sforzesco of the *Holy Women at the Tomb greeted by an angel* is 5th century, and the famous late 4th- or early 5th-century relief of the *Ascension and the Maries at the Tomb* (Munich, Bayerisches Nationalmus.) was probably also made there. The elaborate late 4th-century *Brescia Box with scenes from the Old and New Testaments may have been made in either Milan or Rome since there is a very hazy dividing line between Early Christian works, which may well include those made in Milan, and Byzantine ones which are mainly 5th and 6th century. This category includes the superb ivory throne (Ravenna, Mus. Arcivescovile) probably made in Constantinople (546–56) for Archbishop Maximianus. Its many reliefs include scenes from the Life of Christ, a series of the Life of Joseph as an OT antitype of Christ, and on the front of the throne below the seat are the four Evangelists flanking the Baptist, who holds the Lamb. The extraordinary early 6th-century plaque with the *Empress Ariadne* looking like a bedizened idol (Florence, Bargello) is clearly from Constantinople, as is a group which includes the superb *Archangel Michael* of 519/27 (London, BM). Book-covers were often assembled from diptychs of up to five sections. In Milan (Cath. Treasury) is a 6th-century book-cover with on one side a jewelled cross in a ciborium in the central panel surrounded by scenes from the Life of Christ, on the other side a jewelled Lamb within a ciborium with on either side scenes from the *Annunciation* to the *Entry into Jerusalem*. This book-cover is particularly interesting because some of the small scenes are of rare subjects, drawn from non-canonical sources, and because the *Entry into Jerusalem* follows the form used in the Rabbula Gospels and the Codex *Rossanensis of Christ seated side-saddle on the ass.

The imagery of Christ's Entry into Jerusalem has a long history, since it appears in the Early Christian *Adelphia Sarcophagus* of *c.*340 (Syracuse), and also in the lintel of the Coptic church of al-Mo'allaqa in Old Cairo of the late 4th or early 5th century, but it is not a common subject in Byzantine iconography. A fine late 10th-century ivory plaque of the *Entry* (Berlin) is framed in an intricately pierced canopy borne on slender pierced colonettes, and the same framework is used for a *Nativity* in the Louvre, and also for a *Dormition of the Virgin* (Munich, Staatsbibliothek), of similar date and clearly from the same workshop. This is one of the earliest representations of the Dormition. Some ivory reliefs have imperial connections: the *Emperor Constantine VII Porphyrogenitus crowned by Christ,* of *c.*945 (Moscow), or the *Romanus II and his Empress Eudocia crowned by Christ* (945–9) (Paris, Cab. des Médailles) are examples.

Individual statues do not seem to appear before the 12th century; the *Theotokos Hodegetria* (*see* MADONNA TYPES) in London (V & A) is possibly one of the earliest surviving free-standing statuettes.

Only small numbers of marble carvings have survived; those still in Istanbul (Archaeological Mus.) include the battered pieces of an elaborate carved ambo from Salonika, with arcaded niches containing a *Madonna and Child* and worshippers. The 11th- or 12th-century marble *Deësis,* with Christ, the Virgin, and the Baptist in arcades, now in St Mark's Venice, came from Constantinople, as did both the 13th-century reliefs of the *Madonna Theotokos Aniketos* ('the Invincible') and the *Madonna dello Schioppo,* whose odd name ('of the Explosion') probably derives from an ex-voto given by the naval survivors of the Austrian bombardment of Marghera in 1849. All these works probably came from the 1204 Sack of Constantinople and the following half-century of occupation of the city by Westerners.

Some of the finest sarcophagi are those in Ravenna, which, being made of Proconnesus marble, fairly certainly emanated from the capital. The superb 4th-century example with the Traditio Legis, with Christ and four Apostles in shell-niche arcades (San Francesco) is perhaps the most outstanding, and an unusual one in the Mausoleum of Galla Placidia, believed to be that of Constantius, has the Lamb of God standing on a mound from which flow the four *Rivers of Paradise.

Some fragments of Byzantine textiles have survived, but none is earlier than about the 8th century. Their manufacture was a state monopoly, but the art was derived from Persia, and many of the designs used were Persian ones created over a thousand years earlier. Some magnificent secular silks have designs of confronted eagles, lions, winged gryphons—as for instance on the shrouds of S. Siviard (Sens Cath. Treasury) and of S. Germain l'Auxerrois (Auxerre, St-Eusebius)—but a fragment with an Annunciation and another with a Nativity, both on brilliant scarlet silk twill, are in the Vatican, Museo Sacro. The so-called Dalmatic of Charlemagne, with its scene of the *Calling of the Chosen* (Rome, St Peter's Treasury) is, in fact, a mid-14th-century patriarchal *sakkos of gold and silver silk embroidery on a silk ground. Several splendid sakkoi are in the Museums of Athens, Bucharest, and Moscow (Kremlin Armoury), and a fine *epitaphios of King Milutin (Belgrade, Mus. of Serbian Art) and another from Salonika (Athens, Byz. Mus.) are both of the 14th century. One in London (V&A) can be dated to 1407.

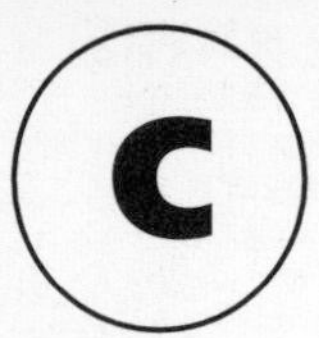

Caiaphas was the High Priest who arranged for the arrest and illegal trial of Jesus before the Sanhedrin, manœuvring *Pilate into responsibility for the actual condemnation and execution. Representations of Christ before Caiaphas are much rarer than those of Christ before Pilate, but extended Passion cycles may include both (Matt. 26: 57–68; similarly Mark and Luke. Only John 11: 49–53 and 18: 12–14, 19–24 tells the story differently). Caiaphas was also responsible for arresting Peter and John, and for the martyrdom of *Stephen (Acts 4: 3–22 and 6: 53–60). *Giotto's fresco in the Arena Chapel, Padua, shows the moment (Matt. 26: 65) when 'The high priest rent his clothes, saying, He has blasphemed . . .'.

Cain *See* ABEL.

calefactory (Lat. *calefaciens*, warming) A room—usually the only one—in a monastery with a fire to warm the old or infirm.

Calendar (Kalendar), Ecclesiastical A list of the major Feasts of the Church, together with the dates of the feast-days of major or local saints. Ecclesiastical calendars agree on most dates, both in East and West, where the Roman Calendar forms the basis, but there are variations for each diocese and also for the various Orders. In Books of *Hours each month is preceded by a calendar, almost always illustrated by the Signs of the *Zodiac or the Labours of the *Month. Major feasts are noted in gold or red letters (hence 'red-letter days'). Because some saints rank as important in one diocese, but not in another Calendars provide important information allowing MSS to be localized (and sometimes dated) with considerable accuracy.

Calf, the Golden *See* GOLDEN CALF.

Calling of the first Apostles At the beginning of His public ministry Christ called twelve *Apostles, the first four of whom were all fishermen, who seem to have been called at about the same time. The accounts given in Matthew and Mark are almost identical, but Luke conflates the Calling with the Miraculous Draught of *Fishes (Luke 5: 2–11). According to Matthew (4: 18–22), 'As he walked by the sea of Galilee, he saw two brothers, Simon who is called *Peter, and *Andrew his brother, casting a net into the sea—for they were fishermen. And he said to them, "Follow me, and I will make you fishers of men." And immediately they left their nets, and followed him. As he went from there, he saw two other brothers, *James son of Zebedee, and his brother *John, in a boat with their father Zebedee, mending their nets, and he called them. Immediately they left the boat and their father, and followed him.' According to John 1: 35–50, the calling of Andrew, Peter, and John took place near Jerusalem, immediately after Jesus's baptism by John the Baptist, and in Galilee only for Philip and Nathaniel (Bartholomew) (James is not mentioned and John does not mention himself, though his inclusion with Andrew and Peter must be assumed).

The scene is rarely represented in the West, and not often in the East, but there is a mosaic of 520–6 in Sant'Apollinare Nuovo, Ravenna, showing the Calling of Peter and Andrew, which is the usual form. What seems to be the first representation of all four is Ghirlandaio's fresco in the *Sistine Chapel (1481/3), where it appears as the counterpart to the fresco of the *Crossing of the Red Sea*, although there is no known *typological connection between them.

Calvary A Latinized form of the Hebrew *Golgotha, meaning '[place of] a skull'. It is recorded as the site of the Crucifixion—as Calvary by Luke and as Golgotha by the other Evangelists. The origin of the name is not clear, but from early times it was regarded as the burial-place of *Adam's skull, so that Christ's blood shed on it would bring redemption to the human race. This is why paintings showing a skull at the foot of the cross often also have drops of blood falling on it.

A Calvary is also a representation—usually sculpture in the round—of Christ on the cross, raised on three steps, and usually with figures of Mary and John (*see* ROOD). It may form part of a Way to Calvary (*see* STATIONS and SACRO MONTE). A special type exists in Brittany, dating from the 15th to the 17th centuries, of very large stone carvings, often with all three crosses and many figures, but most Catholic countries have simpler forms in cemeteries and outside churches. The Church of Scotland commissioned Alberto Morrocco to paint a mural *Procession to Calvary* (1964) for St Columba's, Glenrothes, Fife.

Calvin, Calvinism Jean Calvin (1509–64) was born in France and studied theology in Paris 1523–8, at the time when the influence of *Luther and the first Reformers led to the destruction of images, especially sculpture. He abandoned his studies for the priesthood and began to study law in 1528. He left France and fled to Basle in 1535, publishing the first version of his *Institutio Christianae religionis* in 1536 (final version 1559), in which he propounded the doctrines of Predestination and Justification by Faith alone. In that year he was asked to reform the Church in Geneva, forcing the new doctrines on the citizens by 1538 against strong opposition. He fled to Strasburg for three years, returning to Geneva in 1541, when his party revived. He prohibited all dancing and games and executed several opponents, becoming a total dictator from 1555 to his death. His doctrines went far beyond Luther's and were nearer to *Zwingli's in his opposition to the arts, although he was aware of the danger of fanatical vandalism. Since he taught that good works were entirely useless—all men being predestined to Heaven or Hell from before birth—there was no reason to found churches, hospitals, or other religious charities, and existing churches were stripped of all adornment. In Holland (i.e. the N. Netherlands), where Calvinism was adopted as the official religion in 1618–19, the state of the churches can be seen in paintings by Pieter Saenredam (1597–1665) and others. Where new buildings were needed, as in Huguenot parts of France, they were simply auditoria (*see* CHARENTON). Calvinism was most influential in Switzerland, Holland, and Scotland; but in England, although Calvin's influence was considerable in the 17th century, *Wren evolved an Anglican architectural compromise, combining elements from Dutch churches with others from 17th-century Rome.

Camaldolensians An extremely austere Order of hermits living in separate cells, like the Desert Fathers of the *Thebaid. It was founded by S. Romuald in 1012 at Camaldoli in the mountains between Florence and Arezzo, and based on the Benedictine Rule. *Vasari, who came from Arezzo, was fortunate enough to gain a commission for their church when he was very young, and the hermitage made a deep impression on him. In his autobiography he says: 'I was invited to Camaldoli, the centre of the Camaldolese Congregation, by the fathers of that hermitage, to see what they were proposing to have done for their church . . . I was delighted by the alpine and eternal solitude and peace of that holy place.' He painted his altarpiece and 'I proved how much more one is helped in study by sweet quiet and honest solitude than by the noise of the piazza or of courts, and I recognized my own error in having put my faith too much in men and in the follies and intrigues of this world'. The Order is largely confined to Italy, and white-clad hermits can occasionally be seen in the backgrounds of Italian altarpieces. The *Thebaid* (Uffizi), attributed to Gherardo Starnina, shows scenes from the lives of hermits.

camarín (Sp. small room) A *camarín* is a small chapel above and behind the high altar of a Spanish church, normally visible from the nave. The first known example is in the church of the Desemparados, Valencia, of 1647–67.

Cambridge Camden Society A society founded in 1839, the same year as the Oxford Society for Promoting the Study of Gothic Architecture, both being deeply influenced by *Pugin and the *Oxford Movement. By 1843 it had 700 members, including the Archbishops of Canterbury and Armagh, and in that year it published *Durandus's *On the Symbolism of Churches*. The Society moved to London in 1846, changing its name to the Ecclesiological Society, from its monthly journal, the *Ecclesiologist* (1841–68). Until it was wound up in 1868 both the Society and its journal had a very great influence on the architecture and ritual of the Church of England. It supported *Butterfield, but often dealt harshly with insufficiently Gothic architects.

campanile (Ital. bell-tower) *Campanili* are usually separate from their churches and are square or polygonal in plan, but the earliest surviving examples, in Ravenna, of the 9th century, are circular. They are lightened towards the top by first one opening, then two above it, and so on up to four. 'The Campanile' is usually a reference to the one designed by Giotto and others for Florence Cathedral.

campo santo (Ital. holy field) The usual name for an Italian cemetery. Probably the most famous is that at Pisa, which had many works of art, including 14th- and 15th-century frescoes, largely destroyed in the Second World War. (*See* The TRIUMPH OF DEATH.)

Cana, the Marriage at This was the first of Christ's public miracles, recorded only in John (2: 1–10): 'there was a wedding in Cana of Galilee, and the mother of Jesus was there. Jesus and his disciples had also been invited to the wedding. When the wine gave out, the mother of Jesus said to him, "They have no wine." And Jesus said to her, "Woman, what concern is that to you or to me? My hour has not yet come." His mother said to the servants, "Do whatever he tells you." Now standing there were six stone water jars for the Jewish rites of purification, each holding twenty or thirty gallons. Jesus said to them, "Fill the jars with water." And they filled them up to the brim. He said to them, "Now draw some out and take it to the chief steward." So they took it. When the steward tasted the water that had become wine, and did not know where it came from (though the servants who had drawn the water knew), the steward called the bridegroom and said to him, "Everyone serves the good wine first, and then the inferior wine after the guests have become drunk, but you have kept the good wine until now."'

From at least the 4th century this first miracle was seen as a prefiguration of the Eucharist, and was represented on sarcophagi and in wall-paintings, usually showing Christ pointing with a wand to a set of pots (not always the six specified in the text). Similarly, although Mary is specifically mentioned in the text, she appears first in an ivory carving (the Andrews Diptych, London, V & A) which may be an Early Christian work of *c.*450/60 or a Carolingian copy. The subject was also interpreted as the failure of the Old Dispensation—lack of wine—and its supersession by the New. In later versions the steward is shown tasting the new wine from a goblet; sometimes he is identified as the *architriclinus*—the ruler of the feast—and in later medieval representations this was thought to be his name. Many Byzantine and later medieval examples show Christ at the centre of the table, with the disciples ranged round Him, thus pointing up the parallel with the Last Supper. *Giotto, in his fresco in the Arena Chapel, Padua (*c.*1305/8), has Christ telling the servants to fill the pots, one servant pouring water, and a very fat *architriclinus* tasting with evident enjoyment. Sometime in the Middle Ages a legend developed that the bride and groom were S. Mary *Magdalene and *S. John the Apostle. It is recorded in the **Meditationes Vitae Christi* and in the **Golden Legend* (where it is denied), but it is pure invention and was sharply criticized by Counter-Reformation writers, when the subject returned to popularity, especially among Venetian painters like *Veronese, to whom it offered an opportunity for magnificent architectural settings with crowds of richly dressed contemporary Venetians. Sometimes, indeed, the festal atmosphere makes it difficult to be sure of the subject. Marguerite Huré's window (1925–7) to a design of Maurice Denis depicts the scene at Notre-Dame de Raincy, France.

Canadian art *See* NORTH AMERICA.

cancelli (Lat. grating) An open-work grille or screen of wood, metal, or even stone, separating the nave of a church from the choir or sanctuary, and marking the space reserved for the clergy. The term can also be applied to the railings surrounding a grand tomb.

Candlemas An old name for the Feast (2 Feb.) of the Purification of the Virgin (now called *Presentation in the Temple). It derives from the carrying of lighted candles symbolizing Christ as—in Simeon's words—'a light to lighten the Gentiles' (Luke 2: 32).

candles, candlesticks From the earliest times, lights have symbolized the presence of God, or of Christ as the Light of the World (Luke 2:32). The first mention of candlesticks is in the 5th century, but nothing has survived from such early times. From at least the 12th century candles have been placed on, or near, the altar during the celebration of Mass, and, from the 16th century, it has been the rule in Catholic churches to have two for Low Mass and and six for High Mass, or even seven for a solemn celebration. The Anglican tradition is to have two candles on the altar and two in large standard candlesticks on either side, with six candles along the top of the Rood Screen; some Anglican churches now have six candles on the altar. Candlesticks originated as holders to carry lights in processions, especially during the Easter ceremonies. The Paschal Candlestick (Lat. *Pascha*, derived from 'Pasch', the Hebrew for the Passover, in Christian terms means Easter) holds the large candle which is blessed on Easter Eve or at dawn on Easter Day. The Paschal candle is inscribed with the *Alpha and Omega, a cross, and the number of the year, and has five grains of incense inserted as symbols of the *Arma Christi.

Very large candlesticks, sometimes with seven branches like the Jewish *menorah once in the Temple at Jerusalem, have survived from the time of the Romanesque Cosmati one in Sta Maria in Cosmedin, Rome. They are often major works of art, such as the small gilt-bronze English *Gloucester Candlestick* (1104–13: London, V & A), the seven-branched *Trivulzio Candlestick* of the early 13th century (Milan, Cath.), which is some 15 ft. high (*see* NICHOLAS OF VERDUN), or the one by Andrea Riccio (1515) in the Santo at Padua, which is about 12 ft. high. Seven candlesticks also represent the seven churches of Asia (Rev. 1: 11–12).

canon is an ecclesiastical title which was once universal for all diocesan clergy, but is now limited to those attached to a cathedral or collegiate church. Originally, canons were expected to live a communal life, but in the Middle Ages this was very liberally interpreted, and cathedral clergy often possessed and lived in private property, as well as sharing in the revenues of the cathedral. They were known as 'secular' canons, to distinguish them from 'regular' canons who, as a result of the 11th-century reforms of Pope S. Gregory VII, lived as a community under the Rule instituted by S. Augustine (*see* AUGUSTINIAN CANONS, FRIARS).

After the Reformation, cathedral clergy of the Church of England were reconstituted as 'residentiary' canons, a salaried body responsible for the cathedral, its services, and its maintenance.

Canon of Scripture Those books of the *Bible officially accepted as authentic (*see* APOCRYPHA). All the books of the New Testament are accepted by all Christian bodies: the canon was not fixed until the 4th century (*see* JEROME). The Old Testament canon is not universal, since the Reformers of the 16th century accepted only the Hebrew versions, whereas the Greek versions made for Hellenized Jews were accepted by the Council of *Trent, some being *Deutero-Canonical. Many of the most popular subjects in medieval art are not contained in the canonical books.

Canon tables *See* EUSEBIAN CANON.

cantharus (Lat. bowl, basin) A fountain placed in the atrium of Old St Peter's and used for ritual ablutions by pilgrims. It was a large 2nd-century bronze pine-cone, under a 4th-century canopy supported by porphyry columns; the top of the canopy had bronze arches and grilles, the corners were decorated with dolphins, and bronze peacocks stood in the centre of each side. After the rebuilding of Old St Peter's, Michelangelo moved the pine-cone to the apse at the end of the Cortile del Belvedere in the Vatican, where it still is. It was the origin of the *stoup.

cantoria (Ital. from Latin *cantor*, a singer) A musicians' gallery or tribune in a church for singers or instrumentalists. The most famous ones are the pair made for Florence Cathedral by Luca della *Robbia (1431–8) and *Donatello (1433–9), both now in the Cathedral Museum.

capital (Lat. *caput*, head) A capital and its *abacus are the parts of a column upon which rests either an architrave or an arch. Classical columns usually fall into fixed types: Doric, Ionic, and Corinthian, which are Greek in origin, with the columns varying in proportions of height and thickness, capitals of an increasingly decorative character, and bases ranging from none in the pure Greek Doric form, to decorative mouldings in the other two. When Greek forms were taken over by Roman builders, the forms underwent modifications, and are then known as Roman Doric, etc. with an extra decorative capital—a Composite capital—which is a mixture of Corinthian and Ionic. Columns, capitals, and the entablatures that accompany them are called 'Orders'. When Romanesque developed in western Europe, the classical forms were adapted, so that the Doric became the block-and-cushion capitals of the earliest forms. These were modified with a decorative intent, becoming progressively more ornate—from the simple block, to a scalloped capital, and then through varieties of, at first, rudimentary leaf forms to elaborate leaf capitals adapted from the acanthus of classical Corinthian. In the 12th century they also became fields for narrative sculpture in historiated capitals, as at Autun Cathedral in France, though historiated ones had also been known in Roman orders. The capitals in Byzantine churches were usually intricately carved in a variety of very decorative lacy marble designs.

capitulum (Lat. chapter) The *chapter-house in a monastery.

cappella (ardent, grande, maggiore) *See* CHAPEL.

Capture of Christ *See* JUDAS.

Capuchins *See* FRANCISCANS.

Caravaggio, Michelangelo Merisi da (1571–1610) He began his career as a painter of fancy self-portraits, still-life subjects, and genre scenes, but became a great religious artist. His earliest religious work, the *Flight into Egypt* (*c.*1595/7, Rome, Doria Gall.) is a tender vision of S. Joseph holding the music for an angel violinist playing a lullaby for a weary Madonna nodding over her sleeping Infant. This work introduces one of Caravaggio's dominant characteristics: his creation of a new iconography, the presentation of well-known subjects in an utterly new way, simple, immediate, and appealing more directly to the hearts and minds of those to whom his novel technical methods meant nothing, and those who could see through them to the deeper intentions which lay behind them. The picture was painted for Cardinal del Monte, who obtained for him the commission for his first major public work: the series of three pictures in the French church in Rome, San Luigi dei Francesi, depicting the *Calling of St Matthew*, the *Martyrdom of the Saint*, and an altarpiece of the *Saint inspired by an Angel to write his Gospel.* These works, of 1599–1603, mark the violent contrast between his vivid realism and strong treatment of light and shadow, and the effete Mannerism of his Roman contemporaries such as Zuccaro, or the Cavaliere d'Arpino, in whose studio he had been employed for a while and against whose vapid rhetoric he so passionately reacted. He was less antagonistic to the more elegiac traditionalism of the Carracci, his most notable contemporaries, almost certainly recognizing their artistic genius.

Caravaggio's rejection of the customary grandiloquence of religious art, his often crude, down-to-earth portrayal of his subjects, always in a setting and in the clothes of his own times, is an artistic parallel to the equally evocative sermons and teaching of S. Philip Neri, who in these same years preached the Gospel in the imagery of the everyday world of the poor and humble who followed him around the streets of Rome. Caravaggio was bitterly attacked for his realism: for the dirty feet and sweaty clothes of the poor pilgrims kneeling before the Madonna carrying the heavy burden of the Christ Child in the *Madonna di Loreto* (*c.*1604/5, Rome, Sant'Agostino); for the coarse peasant types of the Madonna and S. Anne and the sturdy Child standing on His mother's foot to crush the serpent's head in the *Madonna dei Palafrenieri* (1605, Rome, Borghese Gall.). The deep pathos of the group of simple peasant-like apostles mourning over the dead body of the mother of their Lord, portrayed in the starkness of the death of the poor and outcast, was rejected by the church for which it was destined, despite its acceptance by its clerical commissioner (the *Death of the Virgin*, 1606, Paris, Louvre). The *Entombment of Christ* painted in 1602–4 for a chapel in S. Philip Neri's own church of Sta Maria Nuova (now in the Vatican Mus.) seems to have escaped virulent criticism, certainly because it does not flout, in its more traditional treatment of the theme, the rigid theories of *decorum which many of his other works strive to overturn.

His brief stay in Malta produced a masterpiece, the *Decollation of St John the Baptist* (1607–8, Valetta, Oratory of St John), expressive of all his ideas. The stark realism of the brutal execution, the phlegmatic indifference of the prison governor, the appalled horror of the old woman onlooker, the passive obedience of the peasant maidservant who has been sent to collect the trophy, the eager curiosity of the prisoners peering from behind their bars, are depicted in the light falling from a high unseen window, echoing the actual lighting of the chapel, falling on to the picture from a small lantern in the vaulting.

His influence was immense, but mainly outside Italy; Rubens, in Rome during his lifetime, admired him, and his effect on Neapolitan painting was felt by Ribera, who transmitted the influence to Spain, where it worked powerfully on Velázquez. The painters of the Utrecht School in Rome soon after his death took his ideas back to Holland, where

Rembrandt's religious painting owes much to the liberating influence of Caravaggio's art.

Angus Trumble (*TLS* 20 May 2011) contrasts two recent books on the artist: Andrew Graham-Dixon's *Caravaggio A Life Sacred and Profane*, and Michael Fried's *The Moment of Caravaggio*, and remembers a third:

> Whereas Graham-Dixon evokes an almost Victorian, and certainly infectious, quest for the biographical subject he obviously loves, immersing himself in what is recoverable of the artist's world—at times clambering down a ladder into a dank cell in Valletta, or up one to get a better view of the truly amazing *Seven Works of Mercy* in Naples—Fried's is a far more abstract, and more distant view from the professorial podium. Graham-Dixon's account of the artist's death at Porto Ercole, alone and in agony, is a tour de force of prose drama, infinitely sad; Fried is concerned with the closest possible reading of certain paintings, and somewhat detached from the accumulating narrative of the artist's life. Both authors follow in the impeccably scholarly footsteps of Helen Langdon, whose *Caravaggio: A Life* appeared in 1998.

cardinal (Lat. *cardo*, hinge) Originally, the word applied to the senior clergy of the Roman parishes—the hinges on which the Church depended—who developed into papal advisers, much later becoming Princes of the Church and the electors of popes. There are three grades of cardinal—Cardinal-Deacon, Cardinal-Priest, and Cardinal-Bishop, but these do not necessarily correspond to the actual rank of the holder, since an Archbishop may be a Cardinal-Deacon. In the early 4th century the Cardinal-Priests were simply the priests of the Roman titular churches (*see* TITULUS), and Cardinal-Deacons had charge of all the hospitals and charitable foundations in Rome, corresponding to the fourteen *regioni* of ancient Rome. Cardinal-Bishops do not appear until the 8th century, when, as bishops of the seven sees surrounding Rome, they became the principal advisers of the pope: the Dean of the College of Cardinals always has the title of Bishop of Ostia, the port of Rome. Since 1179 the cardinals alone elect the new pope: their number was fixed at seventy in 1586, but now has no limit and there are more than twice as many.

Cardinals could, in theory, be laymen and were often the representatives of their native countries: the last English cardinal so appointed was Bainbridge (d. 1514), by Henry VIII; although Cardinal Wolsey was very active politically he never resided in Rome. Cardinals rank with royal princes and are distinguished by their scarlet robes, and especially the curious red *hat, the symbol of the cardinalate. The most frequently represented are *SS Bonaventure, Charles *Borromeo, and *Jerome, although *S. Jerome (the most frequent of all shown with a red hat) died centuries before the rank was formalized.

Cardinal Virtues *See* VIRTUES.

Caribbean art *See* NORTH AMERICA.

Carlo Borromeo, Saint *See* BORROMEO.

Carmelites An Order of Mendicant Friars, originating from Mt. Carmel in the Holy Land. *Elijah triumphed over the priests of Baal there (1 Kgs. 18: Vg. 3 Reg. 8), and there may have been a group of hermits living there later—by *c.*500 there were Greek monks in a community which became the Carmelites, founded by S. Berthold *c.*1154, living under a very strict rule. After the failure of the Crusades the community was re-established in W. Europe and reorganized as an Order of Friars by the Englishman *S. Simon Stock. In England they were known as White Friars, from their habit of a belted brown tunic, brown *scapular, and white mantle. The Order was dedicated to the Blessed Virgin of Mount Carmel, and many paintings show her as a Madonna of Mercy, i.e. protecting Carmelite friars and nuns under her mantle, or as handing the scapular to S. Simon Stock (e.g. the Tiepolo of *c.*1720 in Milan, Brera). The original rule was so strict that it was relaxed by Eugenius IV in 1432, and this event was recorded in a unique fresco by Fra Filippo *Lippi (himself a Carmelite) in Sta Maria del Carmine, Florence. Fragments of this were discovered in 1860 and show the great influence exerted by *Masaccio on Lippi at the beginning of his career (before 1427). The Carmelite nuns were founded under this rule in 1452 and soon became widespread in Europe. In the 17th century the Order was again divided into the Calced ('shod') and Discalced (i.e. wearing sandals) when *S. Theresa of Avila and her helper, S. John of the Cross, returned to the stricter Rule. Carmelites are essentially contemplatives, and their greatest saints include Theresa, John of the Cross, and the Florentine S. Maria Maddalena de' Pazzi.

Caro, Sir Anthony, OM, RA (1924–) An influential British sculptor whose career has stretched over fifty years. He was a part-time assistant to Henry Moore (1951–53), and much influenced by sculptor David Smith during a visit to the USA in 1959. In his characteristic and influential abstract metal sculpture, Caro used standard industrial parts and scrap bolted and welded together, and often painted. By doing away with the pedestal, Caro brought sculpture into the viewers' own space. From the 1980s onwards his semi-abstract and figurative work took up historical and political themes; an example is *The Last Judgement* (1995–99, Germany, Künzelsau, Collection Würth), an enormous environmental assemblage in weighty dark timbers on the massive theme of human cruelty.

A redemptive and hopeful spirit animates the major architectural installation of 2008 in the parish church of St John the Baptist, Beaubourg, Nord-Pas de Calais, France. The origin of this commission was a request from the diocese of Lille to make good the bomb damage suffered during the Second World War, which developed into a project attracting European funding. Called *The Chapel of Light*, it enables Caro to enter into the spaces, the history, and the future of the building, while giving free rein to many of his sculptural motifs and insights. No ecclesiastical commission in his country of birth has yet come his way.

Carolingian art and architecture The art and architecture of those countries of W. Europe influenced by the Emperor *Charlemagne and his successors, *c.*750–900. Charles Martel, 'the Hammer', who defeated the Muslims at Poitiers in 732, ruled France as 'Mayor of the Palace' when the Merovingian dynasty was coming to an end (*see* PRE-ROMANESQUE). His son Pepin the Short consulted the Frankish nobles and the pope before removing the last Merovingian King Childeric II and assuming the title himself. Pepin's son Charles, known as Charlemagne, was crowned as emperor by Leo III in 800. He built churches, was a patron of learning and art, and what he created endured as a goal to be striven for, although his vast empire broke up shortly after his death in 814. Old St Peter's in Rome was the model for several large churches, such as the Abbey of Centula (or St-Riquier), near Abbeville in N. France, built by a close associate of Charlemagne, Abbot Angilbert, and dedicated in 799. A great deal is known about St-Riquier, now destroyed, from the Chronicle of Hariulf, of 1088. It had a second two-storey *transept at the west end, creating a huge *westwork with chapels at an upper level, the chief one being dedicated to the Saviour, to offset the otherwise preponderant emphasis on the saint's *shrine, sited above the *crypt projecting beyond the main *apse. The westwork also contained a double *narthex, the inner one having a stucco relief of the Nativity on a gold *mosaic ground, which was probably the origin of the idea of the later elaborate systems of *portal sculpture. With two axial crossing-*towers smaller staircase towers in the westwork for access, and towers at the two entrances from the large *atrium in front of the church there were nine towers in all. It was the most important church in the north, and became the model for many other major churches, e.g. at Corvey, built 873–85, near Hildesheim, in Germany. The taste for huge westworks, a frequent feature of Carolingian churches, and the long-lasting trend towards magnificence and size which characterize both Romanesque and Gothic in the North probably originated at St-Riquier. The liturgy at Angilbert's St-Riquier followed Roman practice, as was Charlemagne's wish, but he retained much of the colour and elaboration of the Gallican rite in a *laus perennis* or continuous liturgy, marked by frequent and elaborate processions.

The siting of a saint's shrine in a separate chapel beyond the main apse was particularly convenient when it became a centre of pilgrimage. It ran counter, however, to the precedent set by St Peter's, Rome, of the main *altar being over the tomb of a saint, and this older custom became the dominant one, although it caused difficulties over access to the shrine by pilgrims, particularly in monastic churches. The majority of larger churches were founded by bishops whose relics became the object of veneration, and this led to their becoming centres of pilgrimages, as for example at St-Martin at Tours, St-Étienne at Nevers, and St-Hilaire at Poitiers. One of the most important developments in church design came in the early 9th century at St-Philibert de Grandlieu, near Nantes (destroyed by Vikings, which drove the Abbey finally to remove to Tournus in Burgundy). It was originally a typical *basilican church with a central apse at the east end, flanked by two minor apses which did not project as far as the main apse—the so-called 'apse echelon system'. The solution to the press of pilgrims was to raise the *choir apse above the level of the *nave and to extend the *aisles round the apse to make a passage round the shrine so that pilgrims could venerate the relics without causing disruption to the services in the choir. This was the genesis of the *ambulatory system of an east end, and it rapidly became the norm in the North, particularly for pilgrimage churches, which could then have extra chapels radiating from the ambulatory. A later modification with openings in the walls of the apse, so that there was a view of the choir from the ambulatory, became very important in Romanesque and Gothic churches.

Although Angilbert's abbey at St-Riquier is in France, it is as much part of the first stage of Carolingian Romanesque as any built in Germany, where a number of churches followed its lead, particularly in the development of the westwork. However, the best known Carolingian building of this period is Charlemagne's palace chapel at Aachen (Fr. Aix-la-Chapelle), with the foundations laid after 794 and the building largely complete by 798. Basically, it is a simplified version of San Vitale in *Ravenna, with none of the subtleties of its Byzantine original, but with the addition of the now essential westwork. Later rebuilding has altered the original complex by adding a high Gothic choir and side chapels, and by crowning the westwork with a high spire and pinnacles. Inside, the eight massive angled piers surrounding the central open space continue upwards to support a domical vault. In the tribune at first-storey level is Charlemagne's throne, which means that this was probably the model for the long-lasting design of palace chapels on two levels, the upper level for the royals, their family, and members of the court, and the lower level for servants, retainers, and guards.

The famous plan in the library of the monastery of *Sankt Gallen near Lake Constance, made *c.*820, was an ideal design for a monastic foundation with all its dependencies, and though none is now known to have followed it exactly, the design is important because so many monastery builders faced the problems inherent in planning, or rebuilding, premises for large communities. Perhaps the most impressive survivors are the great churches of Reichenau, on Lake Constance, with the remains of their monasteries: the Minster at Mittelzell (724), St Peter at Niederzell (799), and St George at Oberzell (836), all of them enlarged in later years. The Minster summarizes them: an atrium, a huge multi-storey westwork with a first *transept, a nave, and aisles, a second transept with a crossing-tower and a choir beyond. The Reichenau churches were painted inside, particularly St George, where wall-paintings of the second half of the 10th century depict the miracles of Christ, often more than one in the same field, e.g. the *Healing of the Leper* and the *Raising of Jairus's daughter*; in another the *Raising of Lazarus*. The architectural settings of the subjects, and the framing of these paintings with roundels, some with doves, some with crosses, and a wide Greek key ornament in imitation mosaic, suggest a strong influence from the mosaics of Rome and Ravenna. In St Peter, the choir has paintings of *c.*1100, with a *Christ in Majesty* with the symbols of the Evangelists and seraphim in the apse, with two rows of Apostles and Prophets below, also reflecting Byzantine influence. Corvey, near Hildesheim, was founded from the destroyed Corbie of 822, near St-Riquier, and built between 873 and 885. It has a huge two-towered westwork and was important for the choir design, because the chapels flanking the main apse were joined by a corridor outside the apse—another variant of the system begun at St-Philibert de Grandlieu which developed into the virtually universal choir and ambulatory. Fulda (NE of Frankfurt) was first founded by S. Boniface (the English missionary Wynfrith) in 742–4, and after he was martyred in Friesland in 754 a transept and apse were built on the model of Old St Peter's in Rome to house his shrine, a further instance of the continued influence of St Peter's in the design of churches of the early stages of German Romanesque.

Carolingian MS illumination of the late 8th and 9th centuries opens another world, in which the most celebrated MSS are also important as historical, even personal, documents. One of the earliest, which marks the opening of a new era of magnificence, is the *Godescalc Gospels* (Paris, BN), written in gold on purple vellum by the scribe whose name it bears for the palace chapel at Aachen to commemorate the baptism in Rome by the Pope of Charlemagne's son at Easter 781. The frontispiece, with its gold illumination, is of a fountain which both symbolizes the event and the book itself—the Gospels as the fountain of salvation. Upon the fountain stand the peacocks of royal power, which are also the birds of incorruptibility and the symbol of eternity, and there are other charming details all with a meaning—the quails which typify manna, and hence the bread sent by Divine providence, the cocks of spiritual vigilance, the hart which in Ps. 42 (Vg. 41) typifies the soul's thirst for God. Godescalc clearly used as his source an Early Christian MS which Charlemagne probably brought back from Rome. Another feature of this MS was the introduction of a new script; this was the Carolingian minuscule, which was made standard throughout the empire. The court scriptorium at Aachen also owed a great deal to both English and Italian illumination; on his Italian journey in 781 Charlemagne met Alcuin of York and invited him to lead the reforms being undertaken in his domains, and he also brought back an Italian scholar, Paul the Deacon, who may have brought a painter with him. Alcuin settled at Tours, where a great scriptorium was founded, much influenced by British illumination, though other areas show the effects of a variety of elements—late Antique, Byzantine, Roman, and Eastern.

Books were now lavishly embellished. The so-called 'Ada School', named after the *Ada Gospels* (Trier, Civic Library) of the end of the 8th century said to have been written for a sister of Charlemagne, are characterized by fine full-length Evangelist 'portraits' probably inspired by earlier Eastern models, particularly in their strivings for depth in the settings and for a three-dimensional quality. Such manuscripts were often associated with magnificently carved ivory covers, including the Ada group connected with Charlemagne's court, others with the court of Louis the Pious, and importantly the Metz School including the splendid Drogo Sacramentary. The production of luxury books became a main function of the royal scriptorium, now headed by Einhard (*c.*770–840), who became Charlemagne's biographer and Alcuin's successor at Aachen. The *Dagulf Psalter* (Vienna, Nat. Lib.), written between 783 and 795, was presented by Charlemagne to Pope Adrian I; it is written partly in gold and silver, partly in 'minium' (a red colour) and once had a fine ivory binding (now in the Louvre). Another MS on purple vellum written in gold, with full-page Evangelist 'portraits' as well as other illuminations in gold and colours, is the *S. Riquier Gospels* (Abbeville, Municipal Lib.) given *c.*800 to his Abbey by Angilbert, and saved when the Abbey was destroyed.

Probably the most striking feature of Carolingian illumination is the rapidly developed skill in placing figures in rationally designed settings, and the development of a more impressionistic treatment of forms and draperies, which seem filled with new life and energy, clearly inspired by Early Christian examples. The most outstanding example of the lively and impressionistic style of the Reims scriptorium is the *Utrecht Psalter.

One of the results of the arrival in the north of Early Christian MSS was an enlargement of the subjects emanating from Carolingian scriptoria. The *Comedies* of Terence were copied at Corvey between 822 and 826, probably from a 4th-century version with miniatures which recorded the 2nd- and 3rd-century Roman theatre. The 4th-century *Psychomachia* of Prudentius, on the conflict of *Virtues and Vices, became a rich source for portal sculpture and painting. The *Physiologus, a 3rd- or 4th-century Alexandrian moralizing Bestiary, was copied in a 9th-century scriptorium, and Cicero and Boethius were copied in the 9th and 10th centuries. The architectural treatise on the Classical Orders by the 1st-century Roman architect *Vitruvius was also known at Charlemagne's court in an early MS which is now only known from later copies.

Another feature of classical origin was the acanthus leaf, which first appeared in Canon tables and frames, but soon became an important part of the whole page. This can be seen in the *Drogo Sacramentary* (Paris, BN) written for Charlemagne's son who was Archbishop of Metz, *c.*842–50, with small miniatures of the Life of Christ, martyrdoms, and various rites embedded in rich acanthus scrolls. Its beautiful ivory cover shows contemporary liturgical scenes from the mid-9th century. The three grandest Carolingian MSS, exceptional in their incorporation of motifs and scenes from an Early Christian picture cycle into a new work, are the *Grandval Bible* (London, BL) of *c.*840 and the *Vivian Bible* (Paris, BN) of 846, made in Tours for Charles the Bald, and the *Gospel Book of the Emperor Lothair*, commissioned as a peace-offering by Charles the Bald and made 849–51 (Paris, BN), which has a full-page 'portrait' of the enthroned Lothair painted in strong colour and with a well-managed perspective setting. These were the swan-song of the Tours scriptorium, which disappeared tragically in 853 when it was the victim of a Viking raid. Other centres continued to be productive: Metz, Reims, Corbie, and possibly St-Denis, whence may have come the superb Codex Aureus (Munich)—the golden gospels of Charles the Bald—of 870, still with its original cover, a masterpiece of illumination and goldsmith's work by two brothers, Beringar and Liuthard, recorded in the dedication. The wonder is that in the century after Charlemagne's death, which saw so much strife, upheaval, and destruction, so much was produced that was so truly magnificent.

Carracci There were three painters of this name, all from Bologna. Lodovico (1555–1619), the eldest, probably established the workshop and the family style, which by its qualities of seriousness, dignity, draughtsmanship, sobriety of colour, and absence of irrational fantasy, helped to seal the doom of *Mannerism. He was influenced by *Correggio and *Tintoretto whose works he had seen in Parma and Venice before 1578, when he was established in Bologna, where by 1585/6 he founded, with his cousins, a teaching Academy which became the training ground for most of the younger Bolognese painters of the next generation, including Domenichino, Guido Reni, and Guercino. His cousin Agostino (1557–1602) worked mainly as an engraver, executing many plates after works by High Renaissance and Venetian painters which helped also to wean artists and patrons away from the moribund vapidity of late Roman Mannerism.

Annibale (1560–1609) was Agostino's younger brother, and the greatest artist in the family. He travelled widely—to Parma, Venice, Tuscany—shared in the Academy and in family commissions in Bologna, before going to Rome in 1595 to execute the fresco decoration of the Gallery in the palace of Cardinal Farnese, his major secular work and his masterpiece. This work is strongly influenced by Michelangelo's Sistine Ceiling, but its classical mythological subject-matter is treated with a sense of humour and a lightness of fantasy marvellously allied to his solid feeling for form and colour. His assistants were Agostino and the young Domenichino, whose landscapes helped to establish the subject-matter in Rome, and were a major influence on *Poussin.

Carthusians An extremely austere contemplative Order, founded by *S. Bruno in 1084 at the Grande Chartreuse (in English, Charterhouse; Ital. Certosa), a desolate place near Grenoble, snow-covered for much of the year. There was originally no Rule, but each monk had his own cell, meeting the others only for services and, on feast-days, for meals. Silence was observed and much time spent in prayer. A code of rules evolved up to 1581, and, from the 12th century, there were also a few communities of nuns. Carthusian history was uneventful, but they suffered greatly in England under Henry VIII and in France at the Revolution, and again in 1901 (the Grande Chartreuse itself was returned to them only in 1941). The London Charterhouse at Smithfield refused to take the oath by which Henry made himself Supreme Head of the Church in England, and Prior John Houghton (canonized in 1970) and others were hanged, drawn, and quartered in 1535, and ten of his monks were starved to death in Newgate Prison. A series of the Carthusians, including Houghton, was painted by *Zurbarán in 1638 (Cadiz, Mus.).

The Certosa at Pavia is a very grand example of a Carthusian monastery, with small cottages for the monks round a large central court (it is now largely secularized). They wear white habits, with a belt of white leather, and also a long black cloak and hood. The famous liqueurs, green and yellow Chartreuse, once their main source of income, are now made only in Spain, by professional distillers.

Caspar (Gaspar), one of the three *Magi. He is often, but not invariably, represented as the European.

cassock The everyday dress—not a *vestment—of clergy in the East (where it is called a *rason) and West. It is a long, close-fitting coat, reaching to the ankles and buttoned down the front. It is not exclusive to the clergy, but is also worn by servers, choristers, vergers, and others when officiating. For priests it is black (white in the tropics), for bishops purple, for cardinals red, and white for the pope. In the Church of England clerics who wear it often use a leather belt.

Castelseprio is a small town a few miles N. of Milan. In 1944 a cycle of very damaged wall-paintings was discovered in Sta Maria foris Portas ('outside the gates'), of the Infancy of Christ and Life of Mary, partly from *Apocryphal Gospels such as the *Protevangelium of James. The paintings seem to be the work of east Christian artists (?Syrian or Constantinopolitan), or of local men trained in the East, since the iconography is Byzantine and perhaps antedates *iconoclasm. The dating is controversial, but is probably 7th or 8th century, and certainly not later than 945.

catacombs are underground burial-places, the most famous being those in the outskirts of Rome, although others are in Naples, Syracuse, parts of N. Africa, and especially Malta. The origin of the name is thought to be *ad catacumbas*, 'in the hollows', from the nature of the ground about 2 miles outside Rome. They derive from two separate facts; the absolute prohibition under Roman law of burial within the city walls (for all practical purposes, the Aurelian Walls), and the geological nature of the Roman Campagna, which consists of several types of tufa rock, one of which can be cut with comparative ease, but which hardens to form a dry and stable structure. Roman law also maintained the sanctity of dead bodies, even those of executed criminals, which was why Joseph of Arimathaea was able to bury Jesus honourably in a sepulchre 'where no one had ever been laid' (John 20: 41). The early Christian community of Rome, therefore, had to bury their dead outside the city, but were able to do so even in times of persecution. This helps to explain the myth, still not quite extinct, that the catacombs were originally places of refuge during the great persecutions. (Nevertheless, on 6 August 258, during the persecution by the Emperor Valerian, Pope Sixtus II was martyred with four of his deacons in the catacomb of Praetextatus, where he was celebrating Mass.) On the whole, the pagans cremated their dead, but Jewish and even heretical Christian sects, as well as some pagans, seem to have been buried in catacombs.

A catacomb was begun by digging into the slope of a hillside or excavating a flight of steps and then hollowing out a passageway, about 3 ft. wide, with openings at right angles. Some of these openings led into chambers, called *cubicula*, which might belong to a single family or group, while other openings continued for a short distance as links to a new passage parallel to the original one. It has been conservatively estimated that there may be 60–90 miles of such underground passages, originally containing up to three-quarters of a million bodies, in already known catacombs. In 1955 a new one was discovered, quite by chance, in the Via Latina, and there may be many more. The catacombs were dug and maintained by *fossores*, who alone were able to find their way through the dark passages with small oil-lamps, many of which have survived. Once a passage had been dug, small openings were excavated in the sides, called *loculi*, each of which was large enough to contain a body, or several bodies if necessary, lying parallel to the passageway. Once the body was inserted the *loculus* was sealed with a slab (*tegula*), cemented in to prevent the smell of corruption from escaping into the passage. The *tegulae* usually had an inscription or some other means of identification, so that relatives would be able to identify the resting-places of their dead, so that other members of the family could be joined to them. The surviving inscriptions allow us to recognize the Christians who were buried there. Once all the *loculi* were filled, the only way to get more space was by digging downwards, so the earliest graves are at the top, and below them there are sometimes as many as seven layers, each about 10 ft. high, and inaccessible from the ground level. Since the great majority of *loculi* have been broken into, these upper *loculi*, if they have inscriptions on their *tegulae*, may be important for dating the catacomb. In the *cubicula* there are often arched openings above some tombs. The tomb is covered by a slab which served as an altar for the celebration of Mass on anniversaries, particularly if the graves were those of martyrs. These niches are known as *arcosolia*. In the earliest times the slab may also have served as a table for an *agape.

The first catacombs were on the property of rich Christians and the passages always end at the boundaries of the owner's land; but by about 217 the Church itself became the owner and administrator of the catacombs, especially after the Peace of the Church from 313 onwards, when the veneration of the martyrs was at its height. By the 5th century the barbarian raids and invasions had made the whole area unsafe, and the raids of 410, 537, and 756 led to the removal of the relics of the martyrs to safer places within the walls: in 609/10 twenty-eight cartloads of relics were installed in the pagan temple of the *Pantheon in Rome, rededicated to Sta Maria ad Martyres and, over the centuries, the catacombs were forgotten and unvisited, until, almost a thousand years later, the areas were occasionally visited by such Counter-Reformation saints as Philip Neri or Carlo Borromeo. On 31 May 1578 a dramatic rediscovery was made by *Bosio, which led to the beginnings of a scientific investigation of these forgotten cemeteries, which culminated in the 19th century in the explorations and publications of G. B. de' *Rossi.

The catacombs were extensively decorated with frescoes, rather poor in quality, as well as sarcophagi and a multitude of small objects such as seals, gold glasses, lamps, rings, and *ampullae, most of which were stolen long ago, although many have survived in museums (e.g. the British Museum and Vatican) and churches in Rome. In the earliest times the subjects of frescoes and sculpture were very vague, and could easily be interpreted in a pagan sense, doubtless as a measure of self-protection—for example Cupid and Psyche (an allegory of the soul), Orpheus and the Animals, the Good *Shepherd, Vines (which could stand for Bacchus or for Christ's saying 'I am the true vine'). They were followed by such allegorical subjects as Daniel in the Lions' Den, Jonah and the Whale, the Good Shepherd, *orants, and similar figures. In one of the oldest catacombs, that of Priscilla, there is what may be the earliest known painting of the Madonna and Child (early 3rd cent.?), accompanied by a prophet who has been identified as *Isaiah or *Balaam. Later, there are scenes from the Old and New Testaments and Eucharistic allegories (a fish and loaves of bread), as well as pictures of Christ and the Apostles. Many of the scenes represented are very damaged, and their interpretation is therefore often controversial, as is the dating, since there are so few known dates which can be held to apply.

catafalque A sort of staging covered by a black pall, used to support the coffin during a funeral. The term usually includes the candles round the bier. A catafalque is also used to represent the body when there is no actual coffin, as in memorial Requiem Masses on anniversaries. Late 16th- and 17th-century catafalques, especially for royal personages, were often extremely elaborate and included sculpture. A drawing by Inigo *Jones for the catafalque of James I (d. 1625) shows that it was 35 ft. high and included a version of *Bramante's Tempietto as well as mourning figures.

Cataneo, Pietro, was a Sienese architect whose *I Quattro Primi Libri dell'Architettura* was published in 1554. In opposition to contemporary theorists such as Serlio and *Palladio he restates the case for long-nave churches, especially cathedrals: 'Although the Ancients gave the principal Temple in the city a circular, oval, quadrangular or octagonal shape . . . we Christians should have the figure of the Son of God, Christ crucified, to commemorate our Redemption and should always have the principal church in the form of a cross. Also, since the human form of Christ was of perfect proportions, so . . . the main church should be like a well-proportioned human body.' He gives a woodcut showing such a plan, but it involves very long transepts (the arms) in proportion to the nave (the body) and the choir (the head). This theological argument in disregard of aesthetics, and the site itself, was taken up by writers following the decrees of the Council of *Trent, such as S. Carlo *Borromeo.

cathedral A cathedral is simply the church with the bishop's throne (*cathedra*), originally in the apse, as in the 7th-century cathedral at Torcello, Venice, or the rare medieval survival in Norwich Cathedral. It was the custom for bishops to preach from the *cathedra*, hence the expression 'ex cathedra' for an authoritative statement. A cathedral is normally, but not always, the largest church in the diocese, but the Lateran, not St Peter's, is the cathedral of Rome, and the cathedral at Assisi is very small by comparison with the *basilica of S. Francis. In the Middle Ages cathedrals were true community centres, often serving for secular purposes such as meetings, or even as covered markets in bad weather. Many cathedrals, especially in England (e.g. Canterbury), were formerly monastic churches, and therefore have a very large sanctuary in proportion to the nave. They also have numerous chapels to allow for daily celebration by all the monks or cathedral clergy, so the design problems presented to the architect are different from those of a parish church.

CATHEDRALS OF THE UNITED KINGDOM, RECENT WORKS OF ART AND ARCHITECTURE IN

The millennial celebrations of 2000 gave rise to projects worldwide. The following notes list some of the art, sculpture, and architecture projects undertaken in the years immediately preceding and following the year 2000 in the cathedrals of the United Kingdom. This is not to say that other places of worship such as parish churches and college chapels did not undertake commissions of note, but the cathedrals as a group have exhibited a confidence, ambition, and insight where relations with the arts have been concerned. A nationwide encouragement of this development can be seen in the National

Gallery's exhibition *Seeing Salvation* in the year 2000, and its accompanying much-reprinted catalogue, *The Image of Christ*, written by Gabriele Finaldi. This exhibition has benefitted the art and religious connection, albeit coming to it from another direction, as had the commission given to Henry *Moore for his *Madonna and Child* (1943-4).

The projects discussed arose from differing occasions, guided by various office holders, and with varying financial arrangements and ecclesial purposes.

Liturgical furniture

Sculptor William Pye's large *Font* (2000) for Salisbury Cathedral, recalling a 'brimming bowl', was installed prominently in the nave following a decade of experiment. It is three metres wide and its capacity is 1,300 litres. Tim Pomeroy worked on marble procured from Cave Michelangelo, Carrara, Italy, to carve a frieze of some 500 figures for his *Font* (2011), sited centrally in the nave of Glasgow's Roman Catholic St Andrew's.

A number of designers and artists have provided furniture for the Eucharist. Robert Ingham's *Nave Altar* (2011) for St Asaph Cathedral uses glass panels to deliver the see-through feature in the three-sided altar required by the Dean's project group. Another furniture designer, Luke Hughes, provided the long-awaited *Holy Table* (2011) for the centre nave site in St Giles, Church of Scotland, Edinburgh. Materials, lighting, and surface treatment followed the successful search for the single block of brilliant white Carrara; it needed to be of sufficient strength, beauty, and significance to stand in its own right, 'unadorned with cross, cloths or frontals, candles or flowers'. Hughes also assisted in Winchester Cathedral's stone *Altar* (2011) made from Jerusalem limestone, with a central panel made by Rachel Schwalm, from pure pigment, LED lighting, and marble dust. Supreme among the altars is that in Canterbury Cathedral's St Anselm Chapel by Stephen *Cox (2006). The altar's slender cavity hints at an empty tomb and suggests the life to come. The marble used comes from the saint's own region high above the alpine town of Aosta.

Although not a cathedral, Westminster Abbey resolutely commissioned sculpture and carving in its commemorative role in the period 2006–10—and these are noted for their consistent high quality (the individuals and organizations honoured are enclosed in brackets):

- steel lettering and inscription by Tom Phillips RA (UK Armed and Auxiliary Forces post-Second World War Conflicts)
- lettering by Lida Kindersley in John Burton's tablet (Lilian Carpenter) and Peter Foster's gravestone (Peter and Margaret Foster)
- John Maine RA, memorial (Intelligence Services MI5, GCHQ, and SIS)
- Lucy Haugh, gravestone (Burke, Baron Trend and wife Patricia)
- Ken Thompson, gravestones (John Rae) and (Michael Mayne)
- lettering by Heather Newton (Ursula Vaughan Williams).

Sculptured figures

David Wynne's winsome design, placed in the East window of the Ely Cathedral's Lady Chapel, gives a new slant on Madonna types. Below it, and integrating the whole space is blacksmith Chris Topp's lettered cadenza on Maria in collaboration with John Maddison's rendering of John 1:14 as altar façade. Antony Gormley's work has been shown to advantage in choice sites: *Flare II* in the Geometrical Staircase at St Paul's Cathedral and then in Salisbury Cathedral (2011), and *Transport* (2011) in the Crypt at Canterbury Cathedral.

Southwark Cathedral looked further afield, in 2006 inviting Peter Randall Page to make the memorial to the 1736 burial of the Mohegan (Connecticut) Chief Mahomet Weyonomon, and in 2010 welcoming *Help Me*, a Zimbabwean carving in soapstone of a weeping crouched figure by Elvis Mamvura.

A Western *Crucifixion* by an Orthodox sculptor Kirill Sokolov (1930-2004) and donated to Durham Cathedral by his widow is of wood, bone, iron, and stone, cast in bronze. Hereford Cathedral's rolling programme (2007-11) undertaken by several artists has honoured local saints with carvings and canopies, while Claudia Brown's set of six etched *Perspex Sculptures* (2007) at St Albans Cathedral in the Ramryge Chantry Chapel represents stages of bereavement. Students of the City and Guilds of London Art School have been carving new *Grotesques* to replace decayed corbel-table sculptures at St George's Chapel, Windsor. Lincoln Cathedral's 13th-century imp now has a competitor in stonemason Michael Thacker's *Dragon* (2009).

Installations and other interventions, paintings, and glass

St Paul's Cathedral hosted the high-profile *Morning Beams* structure (2006) by Yoko Ono, and went on to devote the two large panels at the nave's east end to Sergei Chepik's oil paintings *I am the Way, the Truth and the Life* (2008); following at the same site was Mark Alexander's *Red Mannheim* silk-screen prints (2010). Martin Firrell's *The Question Mark Inside* (2009) projected on to the cathedral dome texts contributed by artists, by members of the public, and by well-respected thinkers.

Encouragement to icon painters was given by Rochester Cathedral's large mural (2005) by Sergei Fyodorov. Many continue to follow this example of the icon: Aidan Hart's *Theophany of the Lord* (2007) in Carlisle; anonymous icons (2010) and *Crucifixion* (2011) by Helen McDowie-Jenkins in Chelmsford, who also provided Bristol with *Two Icons* (2010); Wakefield received an *Icon Crucifix* (2010) from Christobel Paslaru. Westminster Roman Catholic Cathedral's programme of mosaics benefitted from *The Dream of Gerontius* (2003) and *Cardinal Newman* by Tom Phillips RA; *S. Francis* (2008) by Leonard McComb RA; and Christopher Hobbs contributing *S. Joseph and the Holy Family* (2006).

Other achievements

Of the remaining architectural and structural achievements to be noted, chief are the tower's completion at Bury St Edmunds (2005) and the continuing developments around the entrance approaches, the rotunda, and the Lutyens crypt at Liverpool's Roman Catholic Metropolitan Cathedral. In a similar spirit of accommodating a growing family and its new or rediscovered activities and ministries, several new works (not all visible to tourist or worshipper) stand out. Norwich is not the first to give clever architectural solutions to its age-old need to offer hospitality, with disused spaces finding new purposes. Chester's musicians required proper spaces for rehearsal (sometimes more than one choir at the same time), and for a functional, accessible music library if the proud and ancient choral tradition was to be maintained and developed. Again, a clever structural solution was found (2003) for the musicians' demanding brief.

Technical solutions have been found to another problem faced by many old cathedrals—the danger of fire: addressing this problem in order to secure its roof space (the longest nave roof in Europe and highlight of the 'tower tour'), Winchester Cathedral's series of specially crafted fire doors fit and secure openings of various eras. A more immediately visible outcome can be seen at Leeds in the cleaning and reordering of liturgical fittings and confessionals, which give the interior a kiss of life. The same can be said of St Paul's where Wren's masterpiece concluded its radical cleaning inside and out in 2011, so marking the 400th anniversary of its completion.

The examples mentioned above have proved costly, most have required the assistance of national, commercial, or trust funds, and some have come as gift. Wise and faithful governance according to the historical (often ancient) patterns obtaining in each cathedral increasingly holds the arts consciously in dialogue with the duties of worship, ministry, and care of the fabric. So the Winchester fire doors are more than 'just fabric' and St Albans repristinating a Chantry Chapel for the bereaved is no mere pastoral fad. Alongside the individual projects there is an increasing openness to the arts issues in exhibitions of work by invited and sometimes self-proposed artists; regional Arts Council England Offices like to know what is afoot and are more often glad to get involved than the churches have yet discovered; the same is true of national, regional, and city colleges and universities. At the time of writing, many important projects are in the planning stages, for instance at Chichester and Manchester. *See* STAINED GLASS.

Cathedra Petri (Lat. chair of Peter) What is thought to be the original *cathedra* of S. Peter, a wooden chair, was enclosed by *Bernini in an elaborate bronze sculpture at the back of the choir of St Peter's in Rome. The bronze chair is upheld by two Latin *Fathers of the Church, SS Ambrose and Augustine, and two Greek, SS Athanasius and John Chrysostom. It dates from 1656 to 1666.

Catherine of Alexandria, Saint (?4th cent.). Her cult is not known before the 9th century, at Mt. *Sinai, where her body was 'transported by angels' (i.e. monks?). In the legend she was an Alexandrian lady of royal descent, who became a Christian and resisted the advances of the Emperor (either Maxentius (d. 312) or Maximian (d. 310)), and also disputed with fifty pagan philosophers appointed by the Emperor to persuade her to apostatize. She not only defeated them in argument, but converted them as well; as a result of which they were all instantly martyred. The Emperor then ordered her to be broken on a spiked wheel (or wheels), but the machine flew apart, killing and injuring the executioners. She was then beheaded. All this depends on a Greek *passio* or record of her suffering, not earlier than the 6th/7th century and probably derived from *Eusebius's *Ecclesiastical History*, where an anonymous Alexandrian lady resisted Maxentius/Maximian. In the Middle Ages her cult was widespread, partly due to the Crusaders and partly to the **Golden Legend*—there are mural paintings in Winchester Cathedral of *c.*1225, as well as stained-glass windows in York Minster. Because she referred to herself as 'the bride of Christ', from the 14th century she is usually shown receiving a ring from the Christ Child, seated on His mother's lap, the so-called *Mystic Marriage of S. Catherine* (but *see also* S. CATHERINE OF SIENA). Scenes of her disputing with the philosophers and of her martydom are also common. Her attributes are numerous—a wheel (a 'catherine wheel' firework commemorates the explosion of the intended instrument of her martyrdom), a crown (royal descent), a book (learning), or a sword (beheading). She is also a patron of young girls and students (especially philosophers). She often features in *Virgo inter Virgines pictures, or as one of the *Vierzehnheiligen (the fourteen Holy Helpers). Cycles of her Life include those by Spinello Aretino, of *c.*1387, at Antella, near Florence; Masolino in San Clemente, Rome, 1428–31; and *Tintoretto (Venice, Sta Caterina) of 1590–2.

Catherine of Bologna, Saint (1413–63), was a child maid-of-honour at the court of Ferrara until she became a nun in 1426/8. She was born in Bologna and returned there as abbess of a newly founded convent of Poor Clares (*see* CLARE) in 1456. She wrote several books of devotion, some of which were printed, and she also worked as a calligrapher and illuminator—a breviary still in her convent is said to be her work. There is a curious Flemish painting of *c.*1475 by the Master of the Baroncelli Portraits in London (Courtauld Inst.), which shows her with three donors and also her body, dead but incorrupt, in the background. A contemporary painted terracotta bust of a nun by Niccolò dell'Arca, the Bolognese sculptor, in Modena (Gall. Estense) is thought to represent her.

Catherine of Siena, Saint (1347 (or possibly 1333)–1380), was born Caterina Benincasa, the 24th and last child of a Sienese dyer. Unlike her namesake, S. *Catherine of Alexandria, her life is well documented, partly by the *Life* written in 1393 by her friend and confessor Raimondo of Capua, and partly by the 382 letters she dictated (she herself could not write). Against family opposition, in 1363 she became a *Dominican Tertiary—she is always represented wearing the Dominican habit—and was active in nursing and charitable works, soon gathering a body of faithful disciples. In 1367 she had a vision—like Catherine of Alexandria—of Christ offering her a ring as a 'bride of Christ'. Unlike Catherine of Alexandria, however, representations of this often show Christ as an adult, rather than the small child usual in representations of the *Mystic Marriage of S. Catherine of Alexandria*: there is an unusual picture by Bergognone (*c.*1490: London, NG) of the *Madonna and Child, with SS Catherine of Alexandria and Siena*, but in it the Christ Child hands the ring to Catherine of Alexandria, while the other Catherine holds the Virgin's left hand. In 1375 she had a further vision in Pisa and received the *Stigmata. At that time she became involved in international politics, going to *Avignon to persuade the French Pope Gregory XI to return to Rome, which he did in 1376, on the same day as Catherine returned to Italy. Gregory died in 1378, and the Great Schism began, with a pope in Rome and another in Avignon, but Catherine supported the Roman pope, Urban VI, until her early death in 1380. She was canonized in 1461 by the Sienese Pope *Pius II, and became a patron saint of Siena and also of Italy, and, in

1970, was declared a *Doctor of the Church, at the same time as *S. Theresa of Avila, the first women to be so nominated. In 1471 *Sixtus IV forbade representations of her with the stigmata, but this ban was lifted by *Urban VIII, allowing representations of her with rays of light emitted from the wounds, but no blood. She is also often shown with a crown of thorns (e.g. Carlo Dolci: London, Dulwich Gall.). Other attributes are a lily, a book, and a heart. There is a fresco, much restored, of *c.*1385 by Andrea Vanni, who knew her, which may be the earliest portrait (Siena, San Domenico), and a statue by Neroccio de' Landi (1474: Siena, Sta Caterina), as well as many other Sienese paintings, e.g. by Giovanni di Paolo and Vecchietta, following her canonization in 1461. Marthe Flandrin and Elisabeth Faure painted frescoes of the saint's life in 1932–34 for the Church of Saint-Esprit, Paris.

Cazalet, Mark (1964–) A British artist and teacher in painting, printmaking, and engraved and etched glass, he studied in Falmouth, Chelsea, Paris, and India. He is much interested in lyric landscape and colour.The poetic resonances and confidence with metaphor within his work predispose those with the care of places of worship towards him; Cazalet is at home in the theological and ecclesiastical language used in discussions leading up church commissions. As a consequence, the following have commissioned works from him: Worcester Cathedral (2000); Wesley's Chapel, London (2001 and 2003); Manchester Cathedral (2001); Chelmsford Cathedral (2004); and numerous parish churches including St Alban's, Romford (2006) and St Clement's, Notting Hill, London (2009). He completed the *Epiphany Cross* reredos for the Church of the Epiphany, Doha, Qatar in 2012.

SEE WEB LINKS

- Website of Mark Cazelet.

Cecilia, Saint (?3rd cent.), is the patron saint of music and musicians. There is considerable doubt about the existence of this virgin-martyr, at least in the form given in her *passio, which dates from *c.*500 and mixes in elements from Valerian and Tiburtius, who were real martyrs, whereas there is no early evidence for a martyr named Cecilia. Her legend states that she, a Christian, refused to marry a pagan noble, Valerian, but converted him and his brother Tiburtius: they were martyred, but not before an angel appeared to Valerian and Cecilia and crowned them with roses and lilies. Cecilia was ordered to recant, but refused and was condemned to be suffocated in the steam of her own bathroom. She survived this, and an executioner was ordered to behead her, but failed to do so after three blows and she was left to die, surviving for three days and leaving her house to the Church. A *Titulus Ceciliae* (*see* TITULUS) is known to have existed before 545 and the present Roman basilica of Sta Cecilia in Trastevere is identified with it. A 6th-century mosaic in Sant'Apollinare Nuovo, Ravenna, is the earliest representation of her. In 821 Cecilia's body was discovered by Pope Paschal I in a catacomb (either Calixtus or Praetextatus), together with the bodies of Valerian and others. Paschal had her body enclosed in a cypress coffin in a marble tomb and, with the others, reinterred in Sta Cecilia in Trastevere. In 1599 the church was greatly restored and the coffin was found and opened. The body was incorrupt, but exposure to the air caused it to crumble after a few days: it was seen by many people and full descriptions were written by *Bosio and Cardinal Baronius, the church historian. The sculptor Stefano Maderna (*c.*1576–1636) was commissioned to make a statue of her exactly as she was found, lying on one side as if asleep. This was made in 1599–1600 and is in the church. A copy is in the Catacomb of Calixtus, where her body is thought originally to have been buried.

Since the 16th century she has been adopted as the patron of music and musicians and is often represented with an organ (which she is supposed to have invented), as in Raphael's famous painting of 1516 in Bologna. In fact, the connection with music is due to a misunderstanding of the Latin antiphon in the order of the Office for her feast, but at least we owe Dryden's poem and Handel's music for the *Ode for Saint Cecilia's Day* to it.

There are cycles of her legend on an altarpiece by the Master of S. Cecilia, an unknown Florentine painter sometimes confused with *Giotto. This altarpiece, now in the Uffizi, was painted for Sta Cecilia in Florence before 1304 and has a large central image with narrative scenes on either side. There is also a fresco cycle in Florence, Sta Maria del Carmine, by an unknown early 15th-century Florentine painter, but most representations of her show her as a single figure with an organ or some other musical instrument.

celestial hierarchy *See* ANGELS.

cella memoriae, trichora, coemeterialis A small building in a *cemetery, over a grave, in which Christians, and also some pagans, met for feasts on anniversaries (*see* AGAPE). In the case of martyrs such chapels, whether above or below ground, are usually called *martyria (or confessiones); in *catacombs they are also called *cubiculae* or *memoriae*. A *cella trichora* (or *trichorus*) is a *memoria* with three apses, like a clover-leaf, or, more commonly, a square central plan with three apses and the entrance on the fourth side. *Alberti's San Sebastiano at Mantua (*c.*1460) is a Renaissance revival of the form; fittingly, it is now a memorial to the war dead of Mantua.

cemetery (Gk. *koimeterion*, sleeping-place) Most pagans cremated their dead, but all Christians and a few pagans practised inhumation. A cemetery is therefore a plot of consecrated ground for burials, but is above ground, whereas a *catacomb is excavated below it. The great Roman *basilicas originated as cemetery churches, and it was the custom to build small *celle memorie* as funerary chapels in which an *agape could be held on anniversaries.

cenaculum (Lat., also *coenaculum*, dining-room: in Italian *cenacolo*, Anglicized as cenacle) The 'upper room' in Jerusalem which was the scene of the Last Supper and of Pentecost, and perhaps also the Incredulity of *S. Thomas (Mark 14: 15; Luke 22: 12; Acts 1: 13). A small church seems to have been built on the spot *c.*117/38 and was later enlarged: since 1551 it has been a mosque. The upper storey is the Cenaculum, the lower is traditionally the site of *David's Tomb. The word *Cenacolo* is sometimes used in Italian to denote a painting of the Last Supper, or the room in which it is (e.g. Castagno and Andrea del Sarto in Florence).

The Cenacle is also an Order of nuns, founded in France in 1826.

censer A *liturgical vessel, also called a thurible, in which incense is burned during liturgical ceremonies. The practice of burning incense was originally a means of honouring pagan emperors and was therefore avoided by the earliest Christians: the earliest recorded use of it by Christians is in *Etheria's account of her pilgrimage *c.*381/4. A censer is a pierced metal container into which burning charcoal and grains of incense are put, so that when swung on the three chains securing it clouds of sweet-smelling smoke are produced. The thurifer is usually a deacon or other acolyte. Censers are often made of silver and are of fine craftsmanship.

centrally planned churches have the parts equal, or nearly so, about the centre. They may be square, round, octagonal, or of other geometrical form, and are often a Greek *cross. The earliest type of centrally planned building was the tomb. This might consist of a central space with a niche or *arcosolium for one or more sarcophagi. For a large family or a community the tomb might have a number of such niches, and if one of the bodies interred there was that of a martyr, then from the late 2nd century onwards an altar would be included for memorial services, or the martyr's sarcophagus might itself become the altar. Thus the transition from tomb to *martyrium is simple, and the centrally planned form was particularly convenient for small memorial chapels. Many large churches began as martyria, and were later transformed into long-nave churches for the accommodation of pilgrims. The Constantinian Church of the Holy Sepulchre in Jerusalem was built as a rotunda, with an attached nave, and the rotunda inspired the churches built by the military Order of the Knights *Templar. The round or octagonal building was also the preferred form for *baptisteries, and the central plan also lay at the heart of *Byzantine church building, with the extensive use of the *cross-in-square design. It was also particularly suitable for such monastic buildings as *chapter-houses.

The central plan was revived during the Italian Renaissance, when symmetry and a renewed appreciation of classical forms and proportions stimulated architects such as *Brunelleschi, *Alberti, and *Bramante. The desire to return to the early concept of a martyrium inspired designs for the rebuilding of St *Peter's in Rome, especially the 1506 plan by Bramante. The church finally designed and begun by *Michelangelo was centrally planned with the high altar under the dome, over the *confessio of the tomb of S. Peter. The later addition of extra bays to one arm modified the original central plan into a long-nave design. The circular, octagonal, or cross-in-square design, with a central altar, or with the altar in a projecting apse, was also very popular in Italy for rural pilgrimage churches, and during the early *Baroque period the evolution into an oval form increased its appeal, since this combined the advantages of intimacy with a definite axis and extra space. This was exploited by *Bernini and *Borromini, and also by German and Austrian Baroque architects. In the Protestant North, the central plan proved popular, because it assists in the creation of an *auditory church, and *Wren used this form for many of his City churches. Some modern Roman Catholic churches—Liverpool Cathedral, for instance—have been built on a circular plan with a central altar in an endeavour to combine the example of Early Christian churches with the space needed for a large congregation.

centurion *See* LONGINUS.

ceremoniale *See* LITURGICAL BOOKS.

Certosa *See* CARTHUSIANS.

Chagall, Marc (1889–1985), was a Russian painter who was in Paris 1910–14, and was influenced by Cubism. After the Russian Revolution he was made Commissar for Fine Arts in Vitebsk in 1917. He returned to Paris in 1923, and painted in an imaginative style and rich colour poetic evocations of Russian-Jewish life, increasingly religious in feeling and of a Surrealist character. From 1941 to 1948 he was in America. A visit to Chartres stimulated him to design stained-glass windows for the church at Plateau d'Assy (near Chamonix) in 1957, and for the cathedrals of Metz, 1958–68, and Reims, 1974. For the synagogue in the Hadassah medical centre near Jerusalem his windows represent the *Blessings of Jacob* and of *Moses*, and the *Twelve Tribes of Israel*; and for the Knesset in Jerusalem he designed tapestries of *The Creation*, *Exodus*, and the *Entry into Jerusalem* (1960–9). He also designed memorial windows in Tudely church (1966 and 1978) near Tonbridge in Kent, and windows in Chichester Cathedral (1978). Between 1955 and 1966 he painted a series on religious subjects—*The Bible Message*—now in the Cimiez Museum, Nice, S. France.

chalice *See* LITURGICAL VESSELS.

Chalice, the Antioch A silver and silver-gilt chalice, now in the Metropolitan Museum, New York, found near Antioch in 1910 and originally claimed to be the actual cup used at the Last Supper. It is now thought to date from the 5th, or more probably early 6th century. The iconography is not clear, but there are two figures of Christ, one bearded and one beardless, with ten other figures, perhaps Apostles, a lamb, an eagle, and symbolic vines.

Cham A son of *Noah (Noe), commonly called *Ham.

chancel The terms chancel, choir, and presbytery are sometimes used as if they were interchangeable. Strictly speaking, the chancel, from the Latin *cancellus*, a screen, refers to that part of a church separate from the nave, in which the clergy officiate. The point of division in small churches is usually the arch separating the two parts, hence 'chancel arch', and the area beyond it is the chancel which includes choir, choir stalls, and altar. In major churches the division is beyond the transept crossing and is often marked by a pulpitum, or stone screen with a central door, usually called the choir screen since it is the point at which the chancel begins, the choir being specifically that part of the chancel in which the service, or the Office, is sung. Many cathedrals have the *choir stalls in the chancel inside the choir screen, and the choir immediately beyond as the presbytery or sanctuary, with the high altar preceded by altar rails, though frequently only several steps mark the transition. Some cathedrals, such as Lincoln, have a second choir, later and more splendid than the first, but normally nowadays only the first one contains the sanctuary with the altar, the second choir now being the *retrochoir. Both the choir and the presbytery are flanked by the choir aisles, which lead into the retrochoir behind the choir and the presbytery. In Continental churches the choir and sanctuary are often surrounded by an *ambulatory and this may have chapels off it, creating an ambulatory with radiating chapels. Such an east end is usually called a chevet.

In many churches—even among the grandest—there may now be no pulpitum, the distinction between nave and chancel being marked only by a screen of arches, a simple rail, or by some steps (Salisbury is an example, because of mistaken early modernization; Coventry is a modern example). The existence of a pulpitum is usually because the church had a monastic past.

chantry *See* CHAPEL.

chapel, from late Latin *cappella*, the cloak of S. Martin, a relic venerated by 7th-century Frankish kings, and by extension used for the place in the royal palace where the relic was kept, and later for any place in which relics were preserved. Because the relic was finally kept in a church, a chapel became a subsidiary part of a church. It also acquired other meanings, as varieties of chapels came into being.

One of the reasons prompting the creation of separate chapels within a church was the Early Christian rule that a church should contain only one altar, and that only one Mass per day might be said at it. For monastic houses and pilgrimage churches, chapels containing altars with separate dedications provided a way round this rule, which in Byzantine churches was managed by building an adjoining church on the same site, or by rededicating a chapel as a church.

A chantry chapel was one founded by endowment by a benefactor, which provided for memorial Masses for the souls of the founder and his family. They were a favourite form of medieval piety, were normally built within a cathedral or church, and were distinct from other chapels and altars served by the cathedral clergy in that their foundation usually included provision for a chantry chaplain. Most English cathedrals and major churches have examples from the 13th to the 16th century. On the Continent, many French cathedrals have later chapels built out between the nave buttresses and off the transept, which were endowed as family chapels, and in Italy such chapels often attained great fame. Probably the most famous of all is the Medici chapel in San Lorenzo, Florence, with both architecture and tomb sculpture by Michelangelo. All the English chantry chapels were abolished at the Reformation, and the French ones died out at the Revolution. A yearly Mass is still said in the Medici chapel, a far cry from the original charter, but a pious memorial act.

Lady chapels, dedicated to the Virgin Mary, are generally found as part of the *retrochoir or the *ambulatory. So many cathedrals and major churches on the Continent are dedicated to the Virgin that a separate Lady chapel was often considered unnecessary. Chapels were also dedicated to the patron saints of institutions such as guilds, and served as focal points for their corporate identity. The church of Sant' Eligio in Rome, for example, is still the guild church and seat of the Goldsmiths' and Jewellers' Company. Charitable foundations such as the Venetian *scuole employed major artists to decorate their premises. Unlike families which might die out or become too poor to maintain their chapels, guilds had both wealth and continuity. In major Italian churches the 'Cappella Maggiore' or 'Cappella Grande' is the *choir and the 'Cappella del Sacramento' is the chapel for the reserved Sacrament. Many Continental churches also had baptismal chapels, particularly after S. Charles *Borromeo's injunctions on the setting for fonts. Another Continental custom which, if it existed in England, died out with the Reformation, is the French 'Chapelle Ardente' (in Italy the 'Cappella Ardente')—a funerary chapel where the coffin would be placed on a *catafalque accompanied by a blaze of lighted candles (*see* HEARSE).

'Chapel' is also used to designate Nonconformist places of worship planned like *auditory churches, as well as being the term used in convents, schools, even in monasteries not normally open to outsiders, and for places for prayer in private houses, which because they have no regular services or reserved Sacrament, are more akin to *oratories.

Chaplet *See* ROSARY.

chapter-house A room, or a separate building, in a monastery or in the precincts of a cathedral, set aside for the transaction of secular affairs by the abbot and *choir monks, or the *canons of a cathedral. The name derives from *capitulum*, a chapter from the monastic Rule, which was read before the day's business. They were often built off the eastern arm of the *cloister, with a low vestibule and a double entrance, giving into a large vaulted chamber. Most Continental examples are rectangular, but English ones are more elaborate, and are often polygonal. There are, however, rectangular chapter-houses at Bristol, Durham, and Chester (12th cent.), and Canterbury and Ely (14th cent.), the latter doubling as the Lady Chapel.

There are about thirty polygonal chapter-houses extant, ranging from 18ft. in diameter to 59 ft., the earliest being the decagonal ones at Worcester (12th cent.) and Lincoln (early 13th cent.). One of the grandest is at Westminster Abbey, the first to have the huge traceried windows which become a feature of later chapter-houses, as well as of west fronts. Westminster also has many of its original 13th-century floor-tiles, including some showing the design of the original rose-window in the north transept, and one with the inscription 'Ut rosa flos florum sic est ista domus domorum'—'As the rose among flowers, so is this among buildings'. The striking feature of most of the polygonal examples is the way in which the vaulting ribs, in increasing complexity, all meet on a central column. The simple arched seats of the early monastic examples became elaborated later, as at Ely.

One of the few surviving French examples, at the Abbey of Fontfroide, near Narbonne, is square with four columns supporting the vaulting. In Germany, the *Kapitelsaal* is usually no more than an ordinary vaulted room, although the grand Benedictine abbeys of the Baroque period often have superb decoration. In Italy, the form is normally rectangular, but in Florence, the famous Pazzi Chapel by *Brunelleschi was built as a family chapel which could double as the chapter-house, with a splendid entrance vestibule incorporated in the cloister arm.

Charenton, le Temple Charenton, near Paris, was the site of the most famous French Huguenot church—called 'Temple' to distinguish it from Catholic churches—and an *auditory church which influenced *Wren and many other Protestant architects in N. Europe who had to deal with the problem of audibility of sermons. The first Temple was burned down in 1607, and the Huguenot architect Salomon de Brosse (d. 1626) rebuilt it, from 1623, as a two-storey building with galleries, perhaps based on the ancient Roman basilica at Fano by Vitruvius. The Temple was destroyed in 1685 as a result of the revocation of the Edict of Nantes by Louis XIV, which revoked all the privileges and religious freedom once accorded to Huguenots, but it is known from 17th-century engravings.

Charge to Peter, Christ's *See* TRADITIO CLAVIUM.

Charity *See* VIRTUES.

Charlemagne (Carolus Magnus, Charles the Great), Emperor (*c.*742–814), King of the Franks from 771 and first Emperor of the Holy Roman Empire from 800. He extended his kingdom into N. Italy, Germany, and even Hungary, and then into N. Spain, driving back the Moors. He was crowned in Rome, on Christmas Day 800, by Pope Leo III as the first Emperor of the Holy (i.e. Christian) Roman Empire, but his great achievement was the 'Carolingian Renaissance' (*see* CAROLINGIAN ART). He founded many schools and was personally responsible for patronage of the Seven Liberal *Arts, especially Latin literature, and art and architecture in the ancient Roman style. His Palace Chapel at Aachen, consecrated in 805, derives from the Byzantine San Vitale at *Ravenna, and he reintroduced Greek and Roman formal motifs into Western Christian art. He was never officially canonized, but was often represented as a saint, e.g. in the fragment of an altarpiece attributed to the Master of Moulins (London, NG). Likewise, the equestrian statue by A. Cornacchini (1725), in the portico of St Peter's, is a pendant to the equestrian statue of *Constantine, the first Christian Emperor of the Roman Empire, by Bernini. A small equestrian statue of the 9th century (Louvre), said to represent him, is probably his grandson, but is derived from the equestrian Marcus Aurelius in Rome, then thought to represent Constantine.

According to some versions of the legend of *S. Giles, Charlemagne was absolved from a sin by the saint, who received a message from an angel, but S. Giles died before Charlemagne was born, and the legend probably refers to his grandfather, Charles Martel.

Charles Borromeo, Saint *See* BORROMEO.

Charonton, E *See* QUARTON.

Charterhouse *See* CARTHUSIANS.

Chastity *See* VIRTUES.

chasuble *See* VESTMENTS.

cherubim and seraphim are *angels of the first or second orders. Cherubim are first mentioned in the OT (Gen. 3: 24) as guarding the Tree of Life in the Garden of Eden. Subsequently they are mentioned as guardians of the Mercy-Seat in Solomon's Temple (Exod. 25: 18–22)—'two cherubim of gold . . . at the two ends of the mercy-seat . . . The cherubim shall spread out their wings . . . They shall face one to another . . . ' They are mentioned several times in the OT and in the Apocalypse, and are believed to be referred to in the Vision of *Ezekiel (Ezek. 1: 47 ff.), but the description is unclear. Seraphim, on the other hand, are mentioned only once (Isa. 6: 2–3) 'seraphs . . . each had six wings: with two they covered their faces, and with two they covered their feet, and with two they flew.'

In art, cherubim and seraphim are often represented as chubby children with wings, sometimes only a head and two wings. Because cherubim are referred to as 'burning coals of fire' (Ezek. 1: 13) they are often coloured red, symbolizing burning love, while seraphim may be blue, the colour of Heaven, but it often occurs the other way round. A seraph with six wings appeared to *S. Francis of Assisi when he received the stigmata, and the scene is normally so represented.

C

chevet *See* CHANCEL.

chimere A sleeveless gown of silk or satin, worn by Anglican bishops and doctors on important occasions, but not strictly a *vestment.

China *See* NON-WESTERN CHRISTIAN ART.

Chi-Rho A Sacred Monogram symbolizing Christ (*see also* NOMEN SACRUM). It is composed of two Greek letters, Chi and Rho (X and P), from the Greek name for Christ, combined to form ☧. The Greek letters Chi and Iota, *X* and *I*, are from the Greek for Christ, Jesus, combined as ⁕ and when combined with the Chi-Rho make the symbol ☧. Another form is ☧ sometimes with *Alpha and Omega attached to the cross-bar. These hidden references to Christ, and perhaps also to the Cross, occur before 312, when the Emperor *Constantine had a vision of the Sacred Monogram on the night before the battle in which he defeated Maxentius (*see* LABARUM). The monogram occurs very frequently in Early Christian art and lasted until the clandestine symbolic reference was ousted by representations of the Christ. *See also* IHS and ICHTHYS. During the period of *iconoclasm the only representations of Christ permitted were the monogram, Alpha and Omega, and the Cross.

choir The choir is the part of the church set aside for the sung portion of a service; as the Book of Common Prayer puts it, 'In quires and places where they sing . . .', and the name of the place has become also the name of the body of singers. Choirs derive ultimately from the *schola cantorum, of which the finest surviving example from early times is in the 12th-century reconstruction in San Clemente, Rome, of the one from the Early Christian church, the remains of which lie beneath the present basilica. During the celebration of the Eucharist at the altar in the apse, the *schola cantorum* was where the service was sung, and other offices chanted. Because more space was required for the singers than was afforded by the apsidal area, the *schola cantorum* was extended deep into the nave.

In order to accommodate a choir, two solutions to the problem of space presented themselves. Either extend the apse further eastwards, or allow the choir to encroach further upon the nave. Both solutions were combined, particularly in monastic churches, where not only did the east end tend to become deeper, but the choir, as the part of the *chancel lying between the nave and the presbytery or sanctuary, was extended to the crossing.

In many English medieval churches, particularly in those which were once monastic, a choir screen or pulpitum separated nave from chancel. Many of these ancient abbeys have since become cathedrals, and the stone choir screen, often elaborately carved and with statues on the nave side, has a central door from the nave into the chancel, e.g. Canterbury, Lincoln, and York. Inside the chancel, the *choir stalls are placed in rows and their backs convert the chancel into a closed area, shutting it off from the choir aisles. The enclosure is frequently continued into the sanctuary by screening arcades. Many English churches, even some whose origins were monastic, have lost their choir screens, often through the destructive energies of reformers eager to clear away the last traces of monasticism, or of later restorers advocating an anachronistic open view down the nave as far as the altar.

The pulpitum was also the place for the *rood, and its top was the rood loft. But in major churches during the 17th and 18th centuries the site of the rood on a stone pulpitum was often used for the organ, and the rood loft became the organ loft.

In French churches the choir is now usually open towards the nave, and separated from it by no more than altar rails, or grilles and gates. High choir stalls sometimes shut off the choir from the aisles, and though the altar is now usually visible from the ambulatory, a number of major churches—e.g. Paris, Notre-Dame—have stone screens with fine carved panels. Some panels from the screen in Notre-Dame, Paris, are now in the Louvre, but Chartres still retains part of the enclosure with narrative panels of the life of Christ dating from the 16th century facing the ambulatory. Though no early medieval pulpitum has survived in France, very beautiful fragments of the 13th-century one formerly at Chartres are in the crypt. At Albi, in S. France, the 13th/14th-century cathedral, built as a bastion against the Cathar heresy, is uncompromisingly harsh architecturally, but has a huge enclosed, late Gothic carved wooden choir in the centre of the cathedral, like a church within a church, extremely rich and decorative, with a profusion of ornament and hundreds of small carved figures. Another unusually elaborate late Gothic *jubé* or rood screen is in the early 16th-century funerary chapel built by Margaret of Savoy at Brou, near Bourg-en-Bresse. A number of 16th-century tombs have survived, notably at the Abbey of La-Chaise-Dieu, near Le Puy, and Appoigny, near Auxerre, and the nearby Cistercian Abbey of Pontigny has a splendid 17th-century *jubé*.

The inspiration for such an enclosed choir as Albi almost certainly came from Spain, where the choirs of a number of cathedrals, penetrating deeply into the nave, are often enclosed by high gates and choir stalls, many of them, like Albi, late 15th century in date. Enclosed choirs are rare in Italy, where the sanctuary is usually open to the nave, but the choir stalls ranged on either side of the altar, and sometimes at the back of the altar, are often of great splendour. In the Netherlands, some important choir screens have survived; at St Joseph's, Antwerp; a late 15th/16th-century one at Aarschot, near Leuven; a splendid, elaborate early 16th-century Gothic screen in Notre-Dame, Paris; and Tournai Cathedral has a magnificent Renaissance one, but they are rare, as is the case in Germany.

choir monk A monk who is professed (has taken the vows which mark his separation from the world, and his full entry into the Order of his monastery) takes part in the daily recital of the Office in choir. Novices also take part in the daily offices. In the West, though not the East, they usually now become priests. Lay brothers do not take part in the Office, and therefore the choir monks tended to do less manual work and became teachers, or scribes and illuminators of manuscripts.

choir screen *See* ROOD.

choir stalls By the 6th century, with the spread of the Benedictine Rule, seating in monastic churches must have been provided in order that the Divine Office—the *Opus Dei*—could be properly celebrated. Hence the creation of the *schola cantorum. In most monasteries the Office was recited, or chanted, once during the night and seven times a day. The monks' choir stalls often had hinged seats with small shelves underneath, called *misericords on which they might prop themselves during the long services. Most monastery stalls are simple, but in the choirs of English churches of secular *canons, many of which later became cathedrals, the choir stalls became elaborate constructions, with tall intricately carved pinnacles surmounting each seat, many with misericords. The earliest surviving English choir stalls are parts of those at Rochester Cathedral, of the 1220s, but in general the most magnificent examples are from the 14th to the 16th century. The stalls in the chapels of the Order of the Bath in Henry VII's Chapel, Westminster Abbey, and the Order of the Garter in St George's Chapel, Windsor, have tall carved pinnacles, the Westminster ones dating from *c.*1520 with additions of 1725, and the Windsor ones from 1478–85. Each stall has hanging over it the banner of the knight, and an enamelled plaque with his arms is fixed to the back of the seat. Particularly fine choir stalls are in the cathedrals of Lincoln, Gloucester, Peterborough, and Ely. Those at York are 19th-century replacements for the ones burnt by the mad brother of the painter John Martin.

Spanish choir stalls often have very fine carved panels of biblical subjects and figures of saints, martyrdoms, or patriarchs in their backs, as in the surviving Gothic ones in León Cathedral (now dispersed), and in the series (1537–43) in the monks' choir of San Marcos, also in León. Toledo has two tiers of stalls, the lower tier, carved in 1495, with 54 reliefs depicting the conquest of Granada in 1492, and an upper tier of 1539–43. Barcelona Cathedral has two tiers, one of 1394–9, with intricate canopies of the pinnacle type of 1456–9, and Oviedo has a (restored) series of the 14th century, with fine misericords, and high backs with elaborate canopies. In France, elaborate choir stalls are rare, because of losses during the 16th-century Wars of Religion and the French Revolution. Among the survivors are those at Moutier d'Ahun, near Avallon in the Creuze, with high backs carved with Renaissance ornament, some dated 1679–80. Montréal, near Carcassonne, has a series of 17th-century Baroque carved stalls with misericords, with the top of one tier crowned by a group of the sculptors drinking to celebrate the completion of their work. Other notable ones are at Colmar, where the 18th-century stalls are like secular *boiseries*; Montbenoît has early 16th-century stalls, and misericords with scenes of Aristotle ridden by Phyllis, and Samson and Delilah. Marmoutier has the finest stalls in Alsace, of 1770.

Belgium has some fine mostly 16th- and 17th-century choir stalls, notably at Aarschot, Antwerp (in S. Jacques, and S. Paul); Leuven is particularly rich with stalls from the 1440s to the 1660s in the cathedral, S. Gertrude, and S. Michel; Vilvoorde, near Brussels, has one of the finest two-tier series, of 1663, with Baroque figures in high relief in their backs. In general, these stalls are of carved oak, with high backs crowned by a flat cornice-like element.

In Italy there are fine carved walnut stalls in Sant' Ambrogio, Milan, of 1469, and Cremona Cathedral of the late 1550s. The most striking Italian stalls are those of *intarsia* work, dating from the 1440s to the 1570s. Woods of various colours—walnut, oak, box, ebony—are used to make pictures of towns in *trompe l'oeil* perspective and figures of saints. Among the finest are those in the Frari church in Venice, of 1463, and Siena Cathedral of 1503. Other notable ones are in the Certosa of Pavia of 1487–8, and San Giovanni Evangelista, Parma, where the seat backs have *intarsia* views of Parma, and Sta Maria Maggiore, Bergamo, where the backs have scenes from the OT.

German choir stalls are usually carved in oak, and 15th/16th-century ones often have pinnacles over them, like the ones in Ulm Minster of 1469–74. But their real splendour is to be found in the widespread upsurge of the elaborate and highly decorative Baroque stalls of the 17th and 18th centuries, of which only a few are cited here. Those at Waldsassen, of 1681–1704, are among the richest, with exuberant putti supporting the canopies. The Abbey of Banz has stalls of 1710–19 in the upper choir with panels with the Life of S. Benedict, with inlays of ebony, mother-of-pearl, and silver, and there are inlaid stalls of 1729 at Fürstenfeldbruck. The Abbey of Ottobeuren has a series of carved and inlaid stalls of 1748–67.

Switzerland also is rich in splendid carved oak stalls, and among the finest are those at Lausanne Cathedral, some of the 13th century, and others of 1509, with figures of saints in their backs. Moudon, near Lausanne, has a series with prophets and apostles in their backs, arranged as a concordance of OT and NT figures. Estavayer-le-Lac, near Fribourg, has stalls like the Moudon ones, with figures of saints in the backs, misericords, and crowned by a high cresting. At the Abbey of Einsiedeln, near Schwyz, the late Renaissance stalls of 1675–80 have almost free-standing figures, and at Ittigen, near Fribourg, the elaborate stalls of 1703 have rich high crestings. Beromunster, near Lucerne, has tiers of 17th-century stalls with high backs with scenes in them, and a high superstructure.

chrism A consecrated oil, used e.g. in Baptism and usually kept in an *aumbry.

chrismarion *See* BAPTISTERY.

Chrismon *See* CHI-RHO.

Christ Christos is a translation into Greek of the Hebrew word Messiah, 'The Anointed One', whose coming had been awaited by the Jews for centuries. It is a title of Jesus, not part of His name. When He asks 'Whom do men say that I am?', Peter replies 'You are the Christ, the Son of the living God' (Matt. 16: 16), and this title was an essential part of the case against Him, as when the High Priest said 'I put you under oath before the living God, tell us if you are the Messiah, the Son of God.' Jesus said to him, 'You have said so. But I tell you, from now on you will see the Son of Man seated at the right hand of Power and coming on the clouds of heaven' (Matt. 26: 63–5).

Life and Miracles The sources for the life of Christ are almost exclusively the four Gospels, Acts, and I Corinthians. The few references in contemporary pagan sources have no bearing on Christian art, but a major source for artists from the earliest times was the *Apocryphal Gospels and Acts which were written over several centuries (cf. the Life of *Mary). They provide picturesque details about such things as the Nativity which delighted artists and patrons, irrespective of their objective truth. Usually they give additional details to fill out a bald statement in the Gospels—e.g. the Flight into Egypt—but occasionally they tell wholly imaginary stories with no scriptural backing e.g. that the Christ Child made clay models of birds, blessed them, and they flew away.

Artists depicting events in the life of Christ are sometimes responding to a variety of pressures such as nationalism, commerce, and career advancement. The Hungarian painter Mihály Munkácsy (1844–1900), for example, was encouraged by the Austrian dealer Charles Sedelmeyer to produce a trilogy—*Christ in front of Pilate* 1881, *Golgotha* 1884, and *Ecce Homo* 1896. The immense popularity of these large canvases resulted in extensive tours in Europe and further afield. In the United States they were purchased by the wealthy John Wanamaker, whose religious and entrepreneurial instincts led him to install them at Eastertide in his innovative department store in the city of Philadelphia, USA, for some years. They can now be viewed in the Déri Museum, Debrecen, Hungary.

The following list of events and miracles is concerned with those most frequently represented in art and is not necessarily those most significant theologically.

(1) Life. The *Annunciation; *Nativity, and Adoration of the Shepherds; *Circumcision; *Presentation in the Temple; Adoration of the *Magi (*Epiphany); Massacre of the *Innocents; Flight into *Egypt (Rest on the Flight, Return from); Christ among the *Doctors; *baptism and *Ecce Agnus Dei; *Temptation; *Transfiguration.

(2) Works. *Calling of the first Apostles; Giving of the Keys to Peter (*Traditio Clavium and *Traditio Legis); the *Tribute Money; Mary *Magdalene washes Christ's Feet; Mary and *Martha; the Woman of *Samaria; the *Woman taken in Adultery.

(3) Miracles, other than Healing. The Marriage at *Cana; the *Loaves and Fishes; Miraculous Draught of *Fishes; Christ walks on the *Water, and Stilling of the Tempest; the Gadarene swine.

(4) Miracles of Healing. Many such miracles are recorded in the Gospels and it is not always easy to distinguish them since pictures do not always show what is being cured; but the following occur frequently. The Pool of *Bethesda, the Man with Palsy, the blind man/men born blind, the Healing of the *Demoniac, the Leper/ten Lepers, the Deaf and Dumb Man, the *Woman with an Issue of Blood, *Jairus's Daughter, the Raising of the Widow's Son at Naim, the Raising of *Lazarus.

(5) The Passion. The *Entry into jerusalem; the *Expulsion of the Traders from the Temple; *Judas and the Betrayal; the *Last Supper (*Communion of the Apostles); Christ washes the Apostles' *Feet; the Agony in the Garden of *Gethsemane; Christ before *Caiaphas; *Peter's Denial; Christ before *Pilate; the *Flagellation; the *Crown of Thorns and *Mocking of Christ; *'Ecce homo'; Christ carrying the Cross (*Via Crucis), Road to *Calvary, *Stations of the Cross; *Crucifixion; *Deposition; *Unction and *Lamentation; *Pietà; Entombment. *See also* ARMA CHRISTI, IMAGO PIETATIS, and MAN OF SORROWS.

(6) The Resurrection and Post-Resurrection Appearances. The *Resurrection; the *Maries at the Tomb; *Anastasis; the Appearance to Mary *Magdalene, *'Noli me tangere'; the Way to, and Supper at *Emmaus; the Incredulity of *S. Thomas; Christ walking on Water; the *Ascension. *See also* LIMBO and MAJESTAS DOMINI; the appearances of Christ in the Upper Room after the Resurrection.

Portraits and Representations of Christ There is no evidence at all for the actual appearance of Christ, and even 'descriptions' of His physical characteristics are evidently imaginary as well as being much later than the Ascension. For many years also, the Jewish revulsion from representations of the Divine affected the first Christians (mostly Jews themselves), and He was therefore symbolized by such things as the *Chi-Rho monogram, the fish (*Ichthys), a lamb, or a cross. Not until much later did representations of Christ's person begin to appear, in the *catacombs, on *sarcophagi, and at *Dura-Europos, *c.*232/56. At this time there emerged the two versions of Christ's person which may be called Greek (or Hellenistic) and Oriental. The Greek version is a young man, beardless and with short curly hair, so that Christ as the Good *Shepherd is easily confused with *Hermes Kriophoros or even Orpheus. The mosaic recently discovered under St Peter's shows Christ as the Sun-God Helios, but it was soon argued that these images were too beautiful, since the passage in Isaiah 53—which was always taken to refer to the Messiah—says that 'He was despised and rejected' (though Isaiah surely means His mission, not His person). At about the same time, however, there emerged the figure of Christ as Teacher, based on pagan sarcophagi showing bearded philosophers, seated and teaching from a scroll. This type, bearded and older-looking, developed into the Oriental Christ-type, with an austere face, staring eyes, a full, pointed beard, and long dark hair. This is the type which was standard in Byzantium after the *iconoclastic period, during which the only permitted representations of Christ were the Chi-Rho and the Cross. This overpowering and majestic image was used for the *Pantocrator mosaics in Byzantine churches and ultimately completely displaced the Greek type. The 6th-century mosaics in Ravenna (San Vitale and Sant'Apollinare Nuovo) show both types side by side, with a beardless Christ raising Lazarus but a bearded figure before Caiaphas.

The hieratic Byzantine image was continued in the Romanesque period in the West, but gradually softened into a gentler, more human, image from the Gothic period onwards, when Christ's humanity and sufferings were stressed (compare the agonized figure in *Grünewald's Isenheim Altar with the Pantocrator in Cefalù Cathedral, or the 'Beau Dieu' on the *trumeau* (*see* PORTAL SCULPTURE) of Amiens Cathedral). This milder image has remained constant since the Early Renaissance and was common to both sides during the Reformation—there is little difference between the Christ-types of Rubens and Rembrandt.

One further category remains—the small group which claim to be (or be copies of) authentic images, or even to be miraculous images 'made without hands' (*acheiropoietos). *Eusebius, writing before 323, claimed to have seen a statue of Christ healing the woman with an issue of blood: 'The woman with a haemorrhage, who as we learn from the holy gospels was cured of her trouble by our Saviour, was stated to have come from here [Caesarea Philippi] . . . On a tall stone base at the gates of her house stood a bronze statue of a woman, resting on one knee and resembling a suppliant with arms outstretched. Facing this was another of the same material, an upright figure of a man with a double cloak neatly draped over his shoulders and his hand stretched out to the woman . . . This statue, which was said to resemble the features of Jesus, was still there in my own time, so that I saw it with my own eyes . . . ' The statue probably existed, as it is mentioned by other writers, but it is inherently unlikely that it represented the miracle and it is generally believed that what he saw was a Roman conqueror receiving the surrender of a city or province, personified as a woman. The story of *Abgar and the *Mandylion bears a close resemblance to the story of *Veronica's Veil, impressed with an image of Christ's face. What are said to be copies of these exist in several places and may be the prototypes of the E. Orthodox icon. *S. Luke is also said to have been a painter as well as a physician, and to have painted a picture of the Madonna and Child. This itself became a favourite subject for 15th-century Flemish artists, who produced them for the chapels of their local Guilds. (*See also* ARMA CHRISTI; DEËSIS; DIVINE, REPRESENTATIONS OF; HEART, THE SACRED; IMAGO PIETATIS; LAMB; MAJESTAS DOMINI; SALVATOR MUNDI; SOL INVICTUS; VOLTO SANTO; WINEPRESS.)

Christmas The Feast of the *Nativity of Christ. The actual date of the birth of Christ is unknown, but it is known to have been celebrated on 25 December 336 in Rome, probably as a counter to the pagan midwinter festivals. The Saturnalia fell at this time, and the *Natalis Sol invicti*, the birthday of the Sun, is known to have been celebrated in a Roman temple dedicated on 25 December: Christ was called the Sun of Righteousness. Another possible date was 6 January, the *Epiphany, which is still kept as Christmas in the Armenian Church. *See also* SOL INVICTUS. The choice of a winter date led to Northern painters from the Middle Ages onwards developing an interest in winter landscapes.

Christopher, Saint, is said to have been a martyr during the persecution of Decius (250), but almost nothing is known about him although he was extremely popular from the 13th century onwards because of his picturesque legend, told in the **Golden Legend*. He was said to have been a giant who wished to serve the greatest king in the world and finished by being converted to Christianity by a hermit. The hermit—who often features in pictures of Christopher—told him to live by a deep and powerful river, using his huge stature and strength to carry pilgrims and travellers across it. One night a child asked to be carried across, but as the water got deeper so the child got heavier, and, even with his tree-staff, Christopher could only just manage to get across. The Child (who was the Christ-Child) explained that the burden he had borne was that of the whole world and its creator. He was told to plant his staff in the ground, and next morning it had flowered, and bore dates. Subsequently, Christopher preached successfully in Asia Minor and was martyred. A first attempt to kill him by soldiers shooting arrows not only failed, but one of the arrows was deflected and blinded the king who had ordered his martyrdom. He was later decapitated. One of the few representations of this part of the story was the fresco cycle by Mantegna and others in the Eremitani Church, Padua, of the 1450s. Much of it was destroyed by bombs in 1943, but some parts survived and the others are known from photographs. On the other hand, prints, pictures, and sculptures of him as the Christ-bearer (i.e. Christophoros) were extremely common from the 13th to the 16th centuries because it was believed that if one looked on a representation of him one would not die a sudden death on that day. Consequently, travellers saw an image—often very large—on many church walls. The idea has persisted into the 20th century, with medallions in cars and lorries. Because of his help to travellers and against fatal accidents he is included among the fourteen Holy Helpers (*Vierzehnheiligen). The evidently fabulous nature of his legend led *Erasmus to attack it, and in this he was followed by the Reformers and also the Council of *Trent, so that representations are rare after the 17th century.

Christus Patiens (Triumphans) *See* CRUCIFIX.

church architecture The cardinal difference between a pagan temple and a Christian church is that the temple was believed to be the dwelling of the god or goddess, to whom priests or priestesses of the cult offered sacrifices. No matter how large it might be outside, it was not intended to be entered by devotees of the cult. In a Christian service the presence of the faithful is essential, and the buildings reflect the need to house a congregation. Only rarely, and centuries later, was the revulsion against paganism sufficiently overcome for a pagan temple to be converted into a Christian church (the *Pantheon, the most famous Roman temple, dedicated to 'All the Gods', was re-dedicated in 608 as Sta Maria ad Martyres).

Any building may be a church, since the term 'church' originally meant the body or association of the faithful, and only later came to mean a particular kind of building. The first church (architecturally speaking) was the 'large upper room' (Mark 14: 15; Luke 22: 12) where Christ's celebration of the Passover with His disciples at the Last Supper was the moment of the Institution of the Eucharist (*see* COMMUNION OF THE APOSTLES), and the 'upper room' (probably the same one) where the Apostles met after the Resurrection and 'were constantly devoting themselves to prayer, . . .' (Acts 1: 13–14). In S. Paul's Epistles there are many references to 'churches' in Greece and Asia Minor, both in the sense of a community of the faithful, and houses where they met. All that is required is a place big enough for a gathering of people, and the early churches were *house-churches, as is testified in Acts 3: 46, where the faithful went to the breaking of bread 'from house to house'. The earliest surviving example is the 3rd-century one excavated at *Dura-Europos. In Rome, the churches of Sta Sabina, Sta Prassede, Sta Pudenziana, and Sta Prisca of the 4th and 5th centuries are all believed to have been built on the sites of private houses. Once the great divide from a persecuted sect to a legally recognized church was crossed in 313, with Constantine's Edict of *Milan, specially designed buildings followed. They had existed before the Edict, but during the great Roman persecutions which ended with the severe 4th-century one by the Emperor Diocletian they were confiscated and destroyed as cult centres.

The two basic forms of church were established in the 4th century: the *basilica and the *martyrium. The earliest form of Western church for congregations of any size was adapted from the familiar form of the Roman basilica. The enclosure which once was occupied by the magistrate's seat, and the *apse containing the statue of the emperor, became a *presbytery, with the *altar placed on the chord of the apse, which was made large enough to contain the bishop's throne or cathedra, since all the early churches were originally episcopal. There were also seats for the attendant clergy round the apse. The presbytery in the first church of San Clemente in Rome (4th cent.) was increased in size when it was rebuilt in 1108 and in the 12th century the *schola cantorum, which extends deep into the nave and has an *ambo for the ceremonial reading of the Gospel, was made from parts which survived from the original church. Sacristies were also necessary for the vestments and plate used at the altar, and these were usually placed off the *transept which was introduced between the nave and the *choir to give extra space for the clergy, and for access to subsidiary apses and side chapels. A *baptistery was also necessary and one was usually built adjacent to the church.

At first the *orientation of churches was not important, but by the 5th century it became customary to build churches with the main or high altar at the east end; although many old churches do not conform to this system it became general in the North, and the rule in Byzantium. Many churches were approached through an *atrium, some with a fountain or *cantharus. The entrance to the church itself was, in the earliest times, always through a porch or *narthex, because the unbaptized neophytes were admitted only until the end of the homily and then left the church before the Canon, or Eucharistic sacrifice, and waited in the narthex to be readmitted for the final blessing. A single narthex, or—as in major *Carolingian churches—a double narthex, also served for the ordering of processions and is sometimes, particularly in England, called a Galilee. In the large *Romanesque churches of N. Europe, mostly 8th to 12th centuries, the narthex or narthices formed part of the *westwork. The various functions which churches came to serve inevitably modified the type of building, so that very different forms of church evolved. The earliest clearly differentiated type was the martyrium, from which came the *centrally planned church, out of which the *cross-in-square design was evolved, to become particularly important in *Byzantine church building, where it became the almost universal shape, although the grandest of all Byzantine churches, the Hagia *Sophia, is not a cross-in-square church.

Another highly specialized form was the *abbey or *priory, originally designed not for congregational use, but only for the religious community. Some abbeys became important *pilgrimage churches, which involved radical modification of their original simple basilican form, through the introduction of an *ambulatory from which projecting chapels could be built, creating the ambulatory with radiating chapels.

Many abbeys and priories have dwindled into *parish churches; others have become cathedrals. Those which were once abbeys retain many features which were special for their purpose, and even Canterbury, always a cathedral, was also originally monastic. In France and Italy the great cathedrals were rarely monastic in origin, but were served by secular *canons as were many in England. *chantry chapels are a feature of many English cathedrals and monastic churches. The custom in France and Italy was for family chapels off the aisles, which were often built out between the buttresses of the nave. Some chapels have become major works of art almost distinct from the churches to which they are attached. This is particularly the case in Italy, as in the two Medici Chapels (one by Brunelleschi, doubling as the sacristy, the other by Michelangelo) in San Lorenzo in Florence. One of the indications of a monastic, or a community origin, for English cathedrals is the aggregation of separate areas linked together in the sequence of nave flanked by aisles leading to the first transept, usually crowned by a crossing *tower where the nave and the transepts meet, and with the nave separated from the *chancel by a choir screen (*see* ROOD) which has *choir stalls on either side entirely enclosing the choir. The choir aisles can often be closed off by gates, and behind the *sanctuary is a *retrochoir, usually the original site of a shrine, marked now only by a simple slab or perhaps a tomb. There is invariably a *Lady chapel off the retrochoir or ambulatory. In some English *Gothic cathedrals, a second transept crosses the choir, often between the end of the choir stalls and the sanctuary. Major French churches have usually lost their choir screens, and do not have second transepts; the view down the nave to the altar is now unimpeded. The ambulatory with radiating chapels is uncommon in England and Italy, but it is the norm in France, in French-inspired Spanish Gothic churches, and many German ones. Another striking difference between French and English major churches is that the French chevet (*see* CHANCEL) is usually rounded, whereas in English churches the east end is usually rectangular. Another major difference is that French cathedrals strive for immense height, while the cumulative quality of English ones leads to great length. In Germany, the *hall-church is found more frequently than elsewhere, although there are instances in France and Italy.

Towers are a feature of virtually all great abbey churches and cathedrals in Europe, as are *portals with fine sculpture, ranging from single entrance doors to three or even five doorways. In some cases the sculptured west portals have counterparts on the north and south façades. Few English sculptured portals have survived undamaged. In some parts of France, the whole west façade has become a field for sculpture with often complex iconography, and in Italy some major church façades are decorated with mosaics, marble and bronze sculpture, inlays of coloured marbles, or tiers of marble colonnettes. Many have *aedicules to contain the statues of saints. Inside, the most striking features are the nave *arcades which support the *triforium, which may be an open gallery, a sequence of arcaded openings, or a blind triforium, above which is the *clerestory. In French Gothic cathedrals the vaulting is usually simple in form, whereas English Gothic vaulting is often very elaborate and conceived as part of the decoration. Windows are often filled with *stained glass, and at the ends of the transepts there are often huge *rose windows. Many English Gothic cathedrals have *chapter-houses and *cloisters, reminders of their earlier monastic status.

The very rich 15th-century development of Italian Renaissance church design was the work mainly of three great architects: *Brunelleschi, *Alberti, and *Bramante, whose outstanding contribution was the revival of classical and Early Christian forms, both basilican and centrally planned. The 16th century in Rome was dominated by *Michelangelo's rebuilding of *St Peter's, planned as a new form of martyrium; by new forms of church such as Vignola's *Gesù, and his use of the central plan. There followed the development of the *Baroque by *Bernini, *Borromini, and others. The effect of these radical changes of style, and of the iconographic significance attached to them, soon percolated outside Italy, at first to France, during the mid-16th and 17th centuries, and eventually to England. *Wren's rebuilding of St Paul's, and his development of the *auditory church, of which other important Protestant and Calvinist examples were created in Holland and N. Germany, and in France at *Charenton, demonstrate the extent to which the Counter-Reformation marks the parting of the ways between the Catholic Europe in the South and the Reformed Church in the North, in the design and decoration of churches. Only in Catholic S. Germany and Austria in the 18th century did the most beautiful, tender, joyous, and at the same time sophisticated expression of Baroque reach its highest achievement in the work of Johann Michael *Fischer, the *Asam brothers, *Neumann, and *Fischer von Erlach.

The late 18th century witnessed both a revival of Classicism and a romantic type of Gothic Revival, which resulted in the curious spectacle of architects as eminent as Soane and Barry offering alternate church designs in Classical or Gothic. During the later 19th century no such compromises were possible; a missionary spirit emerged with the *Cambridge Camden Society when deviations from the strict canon of early Gothic became an architectural heresy to be equated virtually with moral turpitude. The chief protagonists of the Gothic Revival were *Pugin, *Scott, and *Butterfield. Eventually, other voices were heard, and in the late 19th century in two Roman Catholic churches in London, *Gribble and *Bentley expressed ideas far removed from the now time-worn Gothic Revival formulas. Because Scotland was mainly Presbyterian and ardently Reformed Church, the Gothic Revival forms of the Anglican Church had a more limited impact. Of far greater importance was an austere Classical Revival, best demonstrated by the magnificent Caledonian Road Church, Glasgow (1856), by Alexander Thomson, appropriately known as 'Greek' Thomson. (The church is now derelict after arson and vandalism.) France also experienced a Neoclassical revival, mainly in decoration, but it became a dominant architectural form with Soufflot's Ste-Geneviève in Paris (begun in 1757), renamed the Panthéon during the French Revolution, and in the church of La Madeleine (1806–42) built at the behest of Napoleon in the style of a Classical Corinthian temple. A Gothic Revival was hardly needed, though some neo-Gothic churches were built; what was needed was supplied by *Viollet-le-duc, who laboured for a lifetime restoring and rehabilitating magnificent Romanesque and Gothic churches which had suffered first the destructive forces of the 18th-century 'Enlightenment' for whom these masterpieces were the tasteless products of ignorance and superstition, and secondly, the anti-religious violence of the French Revolution.

The Gothic Revival had some currency in Germany and Austria, with Scott's successful competition design for St Nicholas, Hamburg (1840), and Heinrich von Ferstel's Votifkirche, Vienna (1858), a traditional 14th-century Gothic design with the typical German high, open-work spires like those of Ulm and Freiburg im Breisgau, though the major enterprise of Gothic Revivalism was the completion of Cologne Cathedral (1842–80) on its original Gothic design. But the power of Neoclassicism was far greater, largely because it had become the dominant secular style, so that the Nikolaikirche, Potsdam, first projected by Gilly in 1797, and finally built by Schinkel in 1843, is uncompromisingly a Roman Pantheon design, with features inspired by the Paris Panthéon and Wren's St Paul's.

Notable late 19th/20th-century designs include the basilica of the Sacré-Cœur in Paris, begun in 1875 in a Romano-Byzantine style, and based on Bramante's early plan for St Peter's, but not finally finished until 1919, and in contrast *Le Corbusier's pilgrimage church at Ronchamp, and his monastery of La Tourette. The really important aspect of church building from about 1750 onwards is that nothing has emerged, either in shape or in iconographic significance, which has not already been built. The history of church design becomes a history of the reuse of old motifs, plans, forms, leavened by a strong influence from contemporary secular building. The only new things are the techniques of building and the use of new materials. Perret's use of concrete for Notre-Dame at Le Raincy, outside Paris (1922–3), and St Joseph at Le Havre (1952) as part of his rebuilding of the city after the Second World War was novel, but the forms are those of the past, and so even are the enormous height of the tower of St-Joseph and its brilliant use of stained glass. Spence's rebuilding of Coventry Cathedral (1952–62) gives a new twist to the use of side chapels—one a Chapel of Industry, the other with an ecumenical theme—both being centrally planned additions to a traditional basilican form. The two Roman Catholic cathedrals of Clifton (Bristol) of 1970–3, and Liverpool (1959–67) reuse the central plan, Clifton as a half-circle, Liverpool as a full circle, both lit from above through a high lantern; both are novel variations on an old theme. The Anglican cathedral of Liverpool, built on the opposite hill to the Catholic cathedral, was begun in 1904 and finished, after much modification, in 1990. Like St Patrick's, and St John the Divine in New York, it is possibly the last grand gasp of the Gothic Revival, unless that honour be reserved for the new cathedral at Washington. Does not Ecclesiastes say (AV 1: 9) 'that which is done is that which shall be done; there is no new thing under the sun'?

Church, symbols of the (*see also* ECCLESIA). The Greek word *ecclesia* is used by S. Paul (1 Cor. 1: 2) to describe the body of believers, in the sense still current in expressions like 'The Church teaches . . .', but it very soon became a name for the actual place of worship, as distinct from a synagogue. In the first sense it was soon personified, usually as a woman—*Mater ecclesia*—and was also represented symbolically, especially in the *catacombs and in Early Christian art generally, sometimes as the Good *Shepherd, or Noah's *Ark, or as an *orant figure. In a mosaic of 422/32 in Sta Sabina, Rome, there are two richly dressed female figures inscribed *Ecclesia ex gentibus* and *Ecclesia ex circumcisione*—i.e. the Gentile and Jewish branches of the Church, also symbolized by SS *Paul and *Peter, and sometimes also by women labelled *Jerusalem* and *Bethlehem* (or *Rome*), with sheep coming from town gates and going towards the figure of Christ (sometimes also represented as a lamb). The Ecclesia Triumphans is usually a woman, crowned and carrying a banner and orb: Mater Ecclesia is also crowned, but with bare breasts—Giovanni *Pisano's figure in Pisa Cathedral could be a representation of Charity except for the crown.

From about the 9th century Crucifixion scenes may show a woman standing beside the Cross, catching Christ's blood in a chalice: from this the contrast between the New and Old Dispensations became symbolized in the figures of *Ecclesia and Synagoga.

ciborium (Lat. from Gk., a cup) This word applies to two quite separate things: (1) A domical canopy supported on four columns, covering the altar in Roman basilicas and certain other churches. It was derived from the canopy carried over Byzantine emperors. This canopy is now usually referred to in the West as a *baldacchino. Originally, the ciborium was provided with curtains.

(2) The second, now usual, meaning is a chalice-shaped receptacle with a cover, used to contain the consecrated Hosts (bread) at the Eucharist or Mass and when reserved in the *tabernacle or *aumbry. It developed in the West about the 12th century from a *pyx, mounted on a stem and foot. It is always gilded on the inside and is usually covered with a silk or linen veil when in the tabernacle or aumbry. Ciboria are not used in the E. Orthodox Church.

Cimabue (*c.*1240–1302/3?), Florentine painter. The name by which he is commonly known is a nickname—'Oxhead'. Attributions to him are difficult, and mostly based on tradition, because his only certain work is a mosaic of *S. John* in the apse of Pisa Cathedral, datable 1302. Nevertheless, he is placed at the head of the founders of modern art and credited with the responsibility for a more naturalistic style than the Byzantine formulas which served until then, largely because of the strong tradition which ascribes to him such large and impressive works as the *Sta Trinità Madonna* (Florence, Uffizi: perhaps *c.*1285/6), which is held to be the precursor of *Giotto's *Ognissanti Madonna* (Florence, Uffizi). Giotto himself is generally believed to have been his pupil, mainly because their names were coupled by *Dante, in his *Purgatorio*, as an example of one man's fame being obscured by his successor's. But the softening of Byzantine rigidity and formality in composition and presentation, the more human qualities of the relationship between the Virgin and the Infant Christ, certainly become more observable in Cimabue's great altarpiece, and a new approach to naturalism is just perceptible in the very damaged frescoes in the Upper and Lower churches of St Francis at Assisi, especially in the portrait of S. Francis himself. Though it is likely to have been much restored, it is an attempt at a real portrait, unlike earlier and contemporary icons of the saint. His great *Crucifix* in Sta Croce is an example of the Christus Patiens type of *crucifix, but it was almost entirely destroyed in the 1966 flood in Florence.

cincture *See* GIRDLE.

Circumcision of Christ Under the Law of Moses, every Jewish boy must be circumcised on the eighth day after birth (Gen. 17: 12 and elsewhere), as a sign of the Covenant between God and Israel. At the same time the child is named; in addition, the first-born male child must be redeemed (*see* PRESENTATION IN THE TEMPLE), and on the 40th day the mother must be purified—the latter two often being done together. Luke (2: 21–2) records: 'And when eight days were accomplished for the circumcising of the child, his name was called Jesus . . . And when the days of her purification according to the Law of Moses were accomplished, they brought him to Jerusalem, to present him to the Lord . . . '. Luke does not say where the circumcision took place, but at that time it was usually performed by the parents, so presumably it was in Bethlehem (as stated in the *Pseudo-Matthew).

The similarity between this initiation rite and Baptism was a reason for not requiring Gentile converts to the early Church to be circumcised (cf. Acts 15), and it probably also misled many later artists into assuming that, like baptism, the rite was performed by a priest in the Temple, causing iconographical confusion between representations of the Circumcision and the Presentation, as is the case with *Mantegna's triptych (*c.*1464: Florence, Uffizi), where the priest (perhaps confused with *Simeon, quite incorrectly) holds a knife and is accompanied by a boy with a bandage on a tray—but Joseph carries the two turtle-doves required for the Presentation ceremony.

Christ Himself declared that He had not come to destroy the Law, but to fulfil it, and He therefore had been circumcised. It was also seen by Christians as the first shedding of His blood and was therefore not only one of the Seven *Sorrows of Mary, but also the first act of the Passion. Some medieval representations of the Instruments of the Passion include the knife.

Representations of the Circumcision are rare compared with the Presentation. The Feast of the Circumcision would have to fall on the Octave of Christmas, 1 January (whereas that of the Presentation/Purification is on 2 February), and 1 January was a day of pagan revelry, strongly condemned by the early Church. Probably for this reason there is no definite record of a Feast of the Circumcision before 567, and although representations of it date from the 6th/7th century in the West, it was not observed in the East or, significantly, in Rome itself until the 11th century.

Cistercian Order Two monks from the Benedictine Abbey of Molesmes in Burgundy, Alberic and Stephen Harding, believed that they were not following the Benedictine Rule as strictly as they should, and convinced their abbot, Robert, so that in 1098 all three left Molesmes with eighteen of their companions to found a new, more austere, house at Cîteaux (Lat. Cistercium), near Dijon. They suffered great hardship, and when Robert was ordered to return to Molesmes they struggled on, led first by Alberic and then by Abbot Stephen Harding, working the soil, harnessing the waters of their swampy and deserted site. The abbot of *Cluny believed that they could not survive, much less prosper, but they were to become a new force in agriculture; they used the rivers to power cornmills, sawmills, and oil presses, built dams to create fish ponds, reclaimed the marshes, built brick kilns, and planted vineyards (the famous Clos de Vougeot was originally a Cîteaux vineyard).

In 1112 they were joined by *Bernard of Clairvaux with about thirty companions, including his five brothers. Where Cluny and its dependent abbeys were centres of learning and art, Cistercian houses were dedicated to agricultural labour, and were always in remote riverside sites, where land was reclaimed from abandoned swamps to become productive farms and orchards. The Order spread widely over W. Europe, with about 700 houses by the end of the 13th century, following the same patterns of enterprise and similar architectural forms; even the same type of name prevailed, almost always expressive of their sites near rivers, valleys, or springs, e.g. Chiaravalle in Italy, Marienthal and Heilsbronn in Germany.

Many houses were founded in England, where huge sheep runs were established (Fountains, Rievaulx, Byland, Kirkstall, all in

Yorkshire, and Tintern in Wales); at all these abbeys large numbers of *lay brothers worked, and the Cistercians became the most important producers of wool in the country. The lay brothers' quarters were often of vast extent.

The constitutions of the Order made each abbey independent, but all were subject to an annual Chapter held at Cîteaux. Similar annual Chapters soon became obligatory for all religious Orders. Cistercian monasteries followed an almost uniform building plan, of which Fontenay, near Montbard, is the finest example of the original type, and almost the only intact survivor. Their churches normally had square-ended chevets (*see* CHANCEL); each arm of the transept usually had two chapels on the east side; they were stone built with fine masonry, and were usually barrel-vaulted (which increased the sonority of their sung offices) with slightly pointed transverse arches (*see* CHURCH ARCHITECTURE). They deliberately rejected all that Cluny stood for. Only later abbeys such as Pontigny, near Auxerre, founded in 1140, but partly rebuilt 1170–1210, sometimes had apsidal choirs with ambulatories and radiating chapels, which, however, were not allowed to break the simple lines of the outside walls of the church. In general, they were lit by windows in the aisles and in the west and east ends, but the later churches, being slightly higher, admitted clerestory windows. Many of the English houses built fine towers (as at Fountains); though these were always late additions, since Bernard had forbidden anything more than a low belfry, which should not break the roof-line. Unlike Cluniac monasteries, around which towns grew up, Cistercian houses remained isolated and self-contained, and their extensive agricultural enterprises were run from granges often at a distance from the mother-house. Guest-houses and hospices were separated from the monastery enclave, to which women and children were not admitted.

The Cistercian habit is white, unlike the black of the Benedictines.

civil religion A term for the religious dimension of public life, first expounded in Rousseau's *The Social Contract* (1762), and more recently by Robert Bellah in an essay entitled 'Civil Religion in America' (in the journal *Daedalus*, winter 1967). This concept draws upon the beliefs, symbols, and rituals that illustrate the ordering of the collective identity, chiefly: the existence and providential nature of God; reward of virtue and punishment of vice; and the exclusion of religious intolerance. While no one religious tradition need be exclusively privileged, the expression of American civil religion in terms of the visual arts, as well as literature and music, resonates with such biblical archetypes as Exodus, Chosen People, Promised Land, New Jerusalem, and Sacrificial Death and Rebirth. Civil religion and the use of Christian symbols and subjects also figure large in the history of the visual arts of Mexico. *See* also NORTH AMERICA.

Clairvaux *See* BERNARD, S.

Clare of Assisi, Saint (Ital. *Sta Chiara*) (1193/4–1253). Founder of the Poor Clares, or Second Order of *S. Francis. She was born in Assisi and joined San Francis in his work there. In 1212 she received the habit from Francis and settled with some companions at San Damiano, the church restored by him, becoming Abbess of the small community in 1215. Like the Franciscans themselves, her Order spread very rapidly, closely following the Franciscan ideals of poverty, chastity, and obedience. Clare was supposed to have defeated an attack on Assisi by Saracen mercenaries in the pay of Frederick II by appearing on the city walls with a pyx (or monstrance) containing the Blessed Sacrament. Hence she is sometimes represented with a pyx or monstrance, dressed in a grey or brown habit, with a white coif and black veil. Like other Franciscans, she has a rope girdle round her waist, with three knots representing poverty, chastity, and obedience, and sometimes she has a crosier, as an Abbess. She was canonized in 1255, two years after her death. The church of Sta Chiara in Assisi was begun in 1257 and her body was translated there in 1260. The large *dossal there with her image and eight scenes from her life, probably dating from the 1280s, is an example of the type of cult image begun by Bonaventura Berlinghieri's *S. Francis* dossal (1235: Pescia, San Francesco).

clausura The part of a religious house normally inaccessible to laymen or people of the opposite sex. *See* CLOISTER.

clavus (pl. *clavi*) In ancient Rome a purple stripe on the toga was a mark of distinction worn by high officials, senators, and the emperor. In Early Christian and Byzantine paintings and mosaics figures often wear *clavi*, usually two, one on each side, from the shoulder to the hem. The greater the width, the more important the person, and Christ Himself is often shown with *clavi*. Good examples exist in Ravenna, e.g. San Vitale.

Clement, Saint (d. *c.*100). Pope Clement I was probably the third Bishop of Rome after S. Peter and author of an important Epistle (1 Clement) on church government. His *acta* are not earlier than the 4th century: they claim that he was exiled to the Crimea and martyred by being tied to an anchor and thrown into the sea. SS Cyril and Methodius, 'the Apostles of the Slavs', claimed to have discovered his remains and the anchor and translated them to Rome *c.*868, where they are buried in San Clemente (probably a church named for a different Clement). The church has 11th(?)-century frescoes of his life. His usual attribute is an anchor and, anachronistically, a papal tiara, since they had not then been invented.

Clement of Alexandria, Saint (*c.*150–*c.*215), records some of the earliest Christian *symbols—the dove, the fish (i.e. *Ichthys), or the lyre, as being acceptable for Christians to use on *seals and rings.

Clement VII, Pope (1478–1534). Giulio de' Medici was the illegitimate son of Giuliano de' Medici, born soon after his father was murdered in 1478. He became a cardinal in 1513 and pope in 1523, succeeding the unpopular Dutch Pope Hadrian VI. He had been an efficient assistant to his cousin, Leo X, and to Hadrian, but was a political failure as pope, partly because he was too concerned with Medicean affairs in Florence and partly because he was unable to take firm decisions: he switched support between Francis I of France and the Emperor Charles V, antagonizing both, and wavered over the problem of Henry VIII's divorce. Nor did he face the problem of Protestantism in Germany and the results included the catastrophe of the Sack of Rome in 1527 by Protestant mercenaries in the service of the Holy Roman Emperor, Charles V. Nevertheless, like his forebears he was a highly cultivated man and a patron of the arts. He was involved in Leo X's scheme for *Michelangelo's work at the family church in Florence, San Lorenzo, and, just before he died, he himself commissioned the painting of the altar wall of the Sistine Chapel from Michelangelo, which his successor Paul III decided should be a *Last Judgement*. Sebastiano del Piombo, Michelangelo's friend, painted Clement several times (e.g. Vienna, KHM; Doria Gall., Rome); he also employed Benvenuto Cellini.

clerestory (clearstory) The uppermost range of windows in a church. In English and French Romanesque churches there is a passageway inside at this level and invariably this passage is set within an arcade which conforms to the storey below. The clerestory passage enables the windows to be repaired without the need to erect a scaffolding. In English Gothic churches the clerestory passage frequently survives, whereas in French Gothic churches the service passage is on the exterior. The elimination of the internal passage in French Gothic is a result of the designers' use of a thin-wall system of construction, enabling very large windows (often with magnificent stained glass) to be used at clerestory level, the thrust of the vaulting and roof being borne by flying buttresses, rather than the structure of the wall. In many German, Spanish, and Italian Romanesque churches there is no clerestory arcade at all, but merely windows in a flat wall above the *triforium.

clergy portraits *See* NORTH AMERICA.

Climacus (Klimakos, Klimax), Saint John (d. *c.*650), was the Abbot of St Catherine's Monastery on Mt. Sinai and author of the *Scala Paradisi* or *Ladder of Paradise*, which sets out the qualities needed by a monk to achieve Heaven. It was illustrated by a ladder, like Jacob's, reaching from Earth to Heaven, up which monks are painfully climbing, with a fair number falling off or being pulled off by hovering devils. It is a fairly common subject on icons, but does not occur in the West. Often the ladder has thirty rungs, one for each year of Christ's life. His nickname derives from *climacus* (Lat. ladder).

clipeus A round shield. *See* IMAGO CLIPEATA.

cloister (Lat. *claustrum*), was originally the wall or enclosure surrounding a monastery, from which arose the term *clausura* for that part of a monastery or convent to which lay people were not normally admitted. By extension, cloister is used for the central quadrangle of a monastic house, surrounded by a covered walk which, in English medieval examples, has traceried windows on the inside of the walk with a green lawn or garth in the centre, often used as a burial ground for monks or nuns. In secular cathedrals the same Latin word was also used to refer to the close—the extent of the land surrounding the cathedral controlled by the chapter; in both cases the word became synonymous with the spaces that most symbolized the life of the monk or cleric.

Cloisters were essential passages of communication between various parts of the buildings which gave off it, such as the *chapter-house, the fountain or cistern for ablutions, the *refectory, the *calefactory or warming-room, and it led to the internal doorway into the church. It was also used for processions, for exercise, for reading and study, and—in appropriate weather conditions—as the scriptorium for the writing and illuminating of manuscripts. In this way, all the significant aspects of religious life were seen as attached to this garden representing the quartered universe and the source of the four rivers of paradise, decussating the world from the Tree of Life at the centre. For the monks it was seen as a vision of paradise as well as the symbol of the soul's true home and, according to Durandus writing in the 13th century, symbolized heavenly paradise.

The two oldest cloisters in Rome are those of San Paolo fuori le Mura, of the 12th/13th century, and San Giovanni Laterano, of 1215–32. Both have arcades round the central cloister green of double twisted columns inlaid with mosaic of *Cosmati work. Later Italian cloisters, such as that of Sta Croce, Florence, have simple colonnades, and at the Badia in Florence and elsewhere the cloister is two-storeyed, with colonnades on each floor. The most remarkable French cloisters are the early 12th-century ones of Moissac, near Montauban, alternating double and single columns, the double ones with elaborate historiated capitals with biblical narratives, and corner piers with reliefs of saints.

Sto Domingo de Silos, near Burgos, in N. Spain, has a 12th-century two-storeyed cloister similar to Moissac, with important historiated capitals on the lower floor.

Cluny, Cluniac Order The reformed *Benedictine Abbey at Cluny, near Mâcon in Burgundy, was founded in 909 and became one of the greatest Benedictine foundations, whose influence was felt all over Europe, especially on *Romanesque architecture and sculpture. By the mid-12th century more than 1,000 houses were associated with it, and its great religious importance was reflected in the splendour of the three churches on the site. It was an 'exempt' house; that is, the community elected its own abbot, and was subject only to the pope. Its freedom from lay and episcopal interference, and the social position of its six earliest abbots, all of whom were later canonized, gave the Order its power and prestige. Over the next 300 years it spread all over France, England, Germany, Spain, and Italy. Decline came in the late 12th century; by the 16th century Cluny itself had lost its independence. It was finally destroyed by the French Revolution and the buildings were sold off.

Three churches succeeded one another at Cluny: of the first modest church, dedicated in 927, little is known. Cluny II, built between 955 and 1000, was more ambitious; perhaps about 200 ft. long, including the narthex, and nearly 100 ft. across at the transepts, from which there extended a deep choir ending in an apse echelon. Cluny III, begun in 1086 by Abbot S. Hugh, who ruled the Order for sixty years, was huge, with a nave of eleven bays nearly 120 ft. wide, a double transept (the only example in France), a total length of about 600 ft., and vaulted throughout. It was the largest church in Christendom until the rebuilding of St Peter's in Rome in the 16th–17th centuries, and was able at one grand ceremony to house over 1,200 members of the Order. The portal sculpture was executed mainly between 1109 and 1122, and the church was finally completed in the mid-1130s.

All the churches inspired by Cluny II and III were vaulted, partly because two Hungarian invasions in the 10th century made fireproof building essential, and partly because vaulting aided the acoustical effect of the Gregorian chant which was a feature of Cluniac services. At one time chanted services continued day and night. In the apse was a gigantic painting of *Christ in Majesty*, some idea of which may be gained from the same subject in the chapel at Berzé-la-Ville, near Cluny. So impressive was Cluny III that the great Benedictine scholar Mabillon described it in 1682: 'Even when one sees its majesty a hundred times, each time one is overwhelmed.'

The Congregation of Cluny achieved cultural and artistic pre-eminence, first because it revived the strict monastic Rule after the collapse caused by the wars of the 10th century; and, secondly, because it gave impetus to the re-establishment of learning, and the development of fine building and its corollaries: sculpture, painting, manuscript illumination, music, and the arts in general. The few surviving sculptures testify to the skill of the carvers, and to the careful programming of the arts dedicated to the church. Despite the conformity in their services, music, customs, and rule, Cluniac architecture was less uniform, though all their churches were of the long nave, Latin cross form with an east end originally of the apse echelon type—a kind of chevet (*see* CHANCEL) developed from the 9th century to accommodate secondary altars.

Cluny II became the model for many houses of the Order, and for the rebuilding of earlier churches. Though many have been destroyed, churches inspired by Cluny II include St-Étienne at Nevers (west of Bourges), built 1083–97, which follows the scale and style of Cluny II with the new arrangement of the choir derived from Cluny III, with an apse ambulatory and radiating chapels; as well as La Charité-sur-Loire (N. of Nevers), of which only part survives, and Paray-le-Monial (N. of Roanne), of *c.*1100, the finest surviving daughter-house of Cluny. This arrangement of the east end is closely connected with the development of the *pilgrimage churches.

Little survives of Cluny III. At the French Revolution the buildings were sold off to a builder who used them as a quarry until 1823 (to facilitate his depredations he blew up the church). Of the church, only a part of the SW transept, one large tower, and a smaller turret survive, but the fragments of the transept, 100 ft. high to the crown of the vault, give some idea of its size. The surviving buildings house a museum with models of what the abbey once was, and a collection of eight remarkable figured capitals. Nothing survives of the influential sculptured portal.

Although the building of Cluny III was the work of Abbot Hugh, the construction was planned by Gunzo, a former abbot of Beaune, who was known as a musician, and who planned the new church on a module of five Roman feet (one Roman foot = 11 5/8 in., or 29.5 cm.), with subsidiary formulas of perfect numbers derived from *Isidore of Seville, Pythagorean musical numbers, and Platonic sequences of squares.

Among the works of art which derive from Cluny are the *Transfiguration* portal of La Charité-sur-Loire (*c.*1100) and the great portal at Vézelay (*c.*1120–32) which, although only briefly a Cluniac house, owes much to its example. At Beaulieu-sur-Dordogne in the Corrèze, an ancient Benedictine house which became Cluniac in 1072, there is a fine *Last Judgement* portal, as well as a statue of the Virgin and Child (*c.*1100) nearly two feet high, of wood covered with silver. Other important centres which were either directly controlled by Cluny or strongly influenced by it were St-Martin-des-Champs in Paris, Cluniac from 1079 onwards; St-Gilles-du-Gard in Provence, where the 12th-century portal reflects influence from Cluny; the cloister capitals (from 1110) and the great portal at Moissac of 1135; and sculpture from both Ste-Marie-la-Daurade of *c.*1170 and St-Étienne at Toulouse of *c.*1120–40 (now in the Musée des Augustins, Toulouse). Others include what survives of Payerne and Romainmoûtier in Switzerland, and the only survivor in Spain, San Salvador de Leyre, founded in 1085. All the English houses have been destroyed.

In illuminated manuscripts, the Bible of S. Martial, Limoges, of the end of the 11th century, the Cluny Antiphonal of *c.*1000, other MSS such as the Hrabanus Maurus written for Cluny between 954 and 994, and the Cluny Lectionary of *c.*1110–20 (all in Paris, Bib. Nat.) show the progression from the formalism and pattern-making of the 10th century to the more vivid and lively style of the 12th century.

An important development from Cluny was the religious movement which succeeded it—the *Cistercian order, dedicated to greater austerity, and determinedly opposed to the art which had flourished at Cluny.

Coat, the Holy The narrative of the Crucifixion describes how Christ's clothes were divided: 'When the soldiers had crucified Jesus, they took his clothes and divided them into four parts, one for each soldier. They also took his tunic (AV has 'coat'); now the tunic was seamless, woven in one piece from the top. So they said to one another, "Let us not tear it, but cast lots for it to see who will get it." This was to fulfil what the scripture says, "They divided my clothes among themselves, and for my clothing they cast lots"...' (John 19: 23–4; Ps. 22: 18; Vg. 21: 19). The soldiers casting lots at the foot of the Cross is a common detail in scenes of the Crucifixion, but the coat itself is rare—it is usually confined to the *Stations of the Cross, as the tenth Station—but the great *Espolio* by El *Greco (1577–9: Toledo, Cath.) is designed around the glowing red robe. Relics of the Holy Coat itself are claimed by the cathedral at Trier and the church at Argenteuil, near Paris, but both traditions go back only to the 12th century. The relic at Trier is claimed to have been found by S. Helena in the Holy Land and given by her to the cathedral, largely on the basis of an ivory depicting a seated woman outside a church greeting a reliquary-chariot and a procession of clergy. It was the cause of considerable controversy in the 19th century. The relic at Argenteuil is recorded in 1156 as 'the garment of the Child Jesus', so it cannot be the one recorded in John.

cock The cock as a symbolic *bird was known in antiquity as a symbol of vigilance, since it crows for the dawn, but it is most often associated with Peter denying Christ (Luke 22: 61–2; John 13: 38). This scene occurs frequently in Early Christian art, e.g. the 4th-century Lateran Sarcophagus 174, where the cock is perched on a column with Peter and Christ on either side. It is also a symbol of the Resurrection, since Christ rose 'very early in the morning'. It can also represent repentant sinners, since after denying Christ, Peter 'wept bitterly'. The first weathercock on a church tower is recorded in 820, seemingly as an encouragement and comfort to the faithful, as well as a warning to malefactors to repent.

Codex Amiatinus *See* AMIATINUS.

Codex Rossanensis *See* ROSSANO.

coenobium (Lat. from Gk. *koinobion*) a *monastery.

coffering A useful form of architectural decoration, used on ceilings, vaulting, domes, semi-domes over apses, and arches, consisting of sunken squares, or rectangles, or other shapes, often stepped, derived from Roman classical architecture, and revived during the *Renaissance by *Alberti. Classical coffering is usually in rectangular squares, though lozenge-shaped coffers are found in Rome (i.e. the semi-domed apses of the Temple of Venus and Rome, where the lozenge shapes diminish in size as the semi-dome rises), and complex forms occur in Baroque architecture (Borromini: Church of San Carlo alle Quattro Fontane, where the oval dome is coffered in an intricate pattern of diminishing crosses, octagons, and hexagonal lozenges). George Dance used the lozenge-shaped form in All Hallows by the Tower, London, in 1765–7. Coffering is useful in construction in that the hollowed-out shapes lighten the load to be supported.

Cole, Thomas (1801–48) An American landscape painter of the Hudson Valley School, who was born in England but emigrated to the United States in 1818. He was inspired by the dramatic vistas of the Hudson River Valley to produce grand intimations of the natural religious spirit (the series entitled *The Voyage of Life*), and to use epic landscape as a stage for biblical stories, for example, *Angels Ministering to Christ in the Wilderness* (1843); or essentially Christian theological expositions, as in the series entitled *The Cross and the World: The Pilgrim of the World on his Journey* (1846–48). *See also* NORTH AMERICA.

collegiate church (Ital. *collegiata*) From 816 canons living in community in large towns where there was no bishop began to serve what were often cathedral-like churches. There are no longer any in England, but Westminster Abbey and Beverley and Southwell Minsters were originally collegiate. *Collegiate* are common in Italy, usually as the largest and most splendid church in a fair-sized town which does not have a bishop.

Collins, Cecil (1908–89) An English painter of visionary works, illustrator, and tapestry designer, whose spiritual insights came from the ascetic tradition of the early Christian centuries. His publication *The Vision of the Fool* (1947), with its angelic figures (often wounded, and with their feet not touching the ground) was not easily comprehended by a readership only recently concerned with the practicalities of munitions, rationing, and prefabs. His images—*Fool picking his nose in front of a Bishop* was one—gained him few understanding friends, but their witness to an inviolate eternal innocence, making a bid for Original Righteousness, ran deep in his work, as also in that of his painter wife *Elizabeth Collins* (1904–2000). The latter's bequest results in many UK galleries possessing works by Cecil Collins. His *Icon of Divine Light* (1973) is an altarpiece in Chichester Cathedral.

In *Cecil Collins Painter of Paradise* (1979) Kathleen Raine identifies the artist as 'a symbolist painter but not a 'literary painter', and explores similarities to Blake and other artists. Collins had felt drawn to the surrealists and their sense of civilization's ending, even exhibiting with them in 1936, but pulled clear of them to pursue his own vision of newness and resurrection. All this is beautifully explored in the Tate 1989 *Cecil Collins* exhibition catalogue following curator Judith Collins's sensitive attention both to the artist's life and also to the drawings and their craft. Collins may be one of those prophetic artists whose day may come round again according to need.

colobium A long tunic, sleeveless or with short sleeves, similar to that worn by the Jewish High Priest. *Crucifixes of the *Triumphans* type often show Christ wearing a colobium, often with long sleeves. *See also* VOLTO SANTO.

colonial art of New England, New France, and New Spain *See* NORTH AMERICA.

colonnade A row of columns. In a church these may bear arches or a straight entablature, which in turn, like the arches, is the support for the upper storeys of the building. Early Christian churches, such as Sta Maria Maggiore in Rome and San Paolo fuori le Mura outside Rome, are churches in which the nave has columns bearing a straight entablature derived from classical precedents. Technically, these are called 'trabeated' from Lat. *trabs* or *trabis*, 'beam'.

colonnette A small column, often a tall thin one attached to a large column or to a pier. Often, in Gothic churches, a large column may have clusters of colonnettes arranged in batches and varying in thickness to make its profile more decorative; in many major English churches these colonnettes may be of *Purbeck marble in contrast with the stone of the larger element. In wall arcades the columns may have decorative, usually leaf capitals, and here the capital may be of Purbeck while the stone colonnettes also have Purbeck capitals. The practice is distinctively English.

colours *See* LITURGICAL COLOURS.

colours, papal *See* HERALDRY.

columbine *See* FLOWERS AND FRUIT.

column A vertical structure, usually cylindrical but sometimes rectangular or polygonal, supporting a lintel or arch, or standing alone as a monument, sometimes supporting a statue. In the classical orders, despite their variations in height and thickness, columns never have attached *colonnettes. In Romanesque and Gothic churches, columns do not obey any fixed rules of proportion as in classical forms, but depend entirely on the master mason's geometrical framework to decide the relationships of the parts of his building—the arcade, the triforium, and the clerestory. There are no fixed patterns or rules, but the master mason's system will depend on his individual application of mathematical principles largely based on Pythagoras and/or the Golden Section, or on musical relationships.

Commandments, the Ten The commandments given by God to *Moses on Mt. Sinai (Exod. 31 and 34), and tablets engraved with them were kept in the *Ark of the Covenant. They are set out in Exod. 20: 1–17, and Deut. 5: 6–21, but the enumeration varies slightly between the Churches. In some Anglican Post-Reformation churches they are inscribed on wooden or stone tablets and hung over the altar or communion-table, apparently as a substitute for an altarpiece or reredos, in a manner reminiscent of the Ark which contains the scrolls of the Law in a synagogue.

Communion of the Apostles This is also called The Institution of the *Eucharist, which took place at the *Last Supper. Representations of the Last Supper usually show Christ seated at table with the Apostles on either side of Him, sharing a meal. An early 6th-century mosaic in Sant'Apollinare Nuovo, *Ravenna, shows Christ and the Apostles with a fish on a table (*see* ICHTHYS), but earlier *catacomb paintings probably represent an *agape rather than the Last Supper. From very early times, especially in the E. Orthodox Church, a more sacramental interpretation is given by showing Christ standing, with a chalice and sometimes a Host (*see* ELEMENTS), giving Communion to the kneeling Apostles. The form was invented in the East and occurs much later in the West; its non-historical character is shown by the fact that *Paul is sometimes included among the Apostles at the Last Supper, excluding *Judas. Occasionally, the figure of Christ is repeated, once giving the wine and once the bread, as in the silver patens of 565–78 (Istanbul, Mus., and Washington, Dumbarton Oaks). The 6th-century *Rossano Codex has two separate scenes, the Last Supper and the Institution of the Eucharist, and 900 years later this was repeated by Fra *Angelico in a series of panels decorating a cupboard in which eucharistic vessels were kept (*c.*1450: Museo di San Marco, Florence). At about the same time *Bouts painted his *Mystic Meals* (1464–8) and the Flemish painter Joos van Gent painted a *Communion of the*

Apostles (1474) for the Confraternity of the Holy Sacrament in Urbino.

During the Reformation period the sacramental aspect was stressed in Catholic countries, e.g. Tintoretto's *Last Supper*, in San Giorgio Maggiore, Venice, where it is opposite the *Gathering of the Manna*, its OT *type, but in countries influenced by the Reformers the Last Supper is shown as a simple meal (Dürer's woodcut of 1523).

C

Communion, Last, of Saint Jerome *See* JEROME.

Communion, Last, of Saint Mary Magdalene *See* MAGDALENE.

Compostela, Santiago de A city in NW Spain which, since 865, has claimed to have the body of the Apostle *James (Sant'Iago), and which therefore became one of the four great centres of pilgrimage in the Middle Ages (the others were Rome, Jerusalem, and Canterbury); but the *pilgrimage churches were built on the route to Compostela and thus played a great part in the development of *Romanesque. The cathedral of Santiago is 11th–12th century, with later additions, and has two important *portals: the *Puerta de las Platerías*, the silversmiths door, mostly *c.*1104, and the huge *Pórtico de la Gloria* on the inner façade, of 1168–1217.

Conception, the Immaculate *See* IMMACULATE *CONCEPTION.

confessio Strictly speaking, the place where a martyr suffered—'confessed' for Christ—and usually died. By extension, the place, normally beneath the altar, where the saint's remains are enshrined. Often, as in some Early Christian churches in Rome, the tomb would be visible through an opening in the floor, but it became usual for a grille to be placed over it, to prevent either accidental damage or deliberate desecration (*see* ANTEPENDIUM). The most famous *confessio* is that of S. Peter in Rome, and under the high altar of Sta Maria in Trastevere is the 'fenestella confessionis', the window opening over the site of the tomb, probably of Pope S. Callixtus (217–22), who had a 'house-church' on the site recorded in 222. *See also* MARTYRIUM.

confession *See* SACRAMENTS.

confessional Until the 16th century confessions were heard by a priest seated in the church, with the penitent kneeling or sitting near him, as is still the custom in the E. Orthodox Church. By the time of the Counter-Reformation greater privacy was desired and the Council of *Trent laid down rules, echoed by S. Charles *Borromeo in his *Instructiones* (1577) for box-like structures, usually set against the outer walls. In 17th- and 18th-century Baroque churches these are often grandiose examples of woodwork with columns and figures. Since the 19th century they have become less prominent features. In many modern Catholic churches they have become like cupboards in the wall, one each for priest and penitent with a grille in the wall between.

confirmation *See* SACRAMENTS.

confraternity (Lat. *confraternitas*, brotherhood) A pious association of the laity, devoted to the care of the poor and sick or the burial of the dead. They began in the 9th century, but were especially important in Italy and the Netherlands in the 13th–15th centuries. They had banners, insignia, and often chapels of their own, and, like *guilds, were useful for making business contacts. In Italy especially they commissioned many major works of art and even buildings; and, since many contracts have survived in their archives, they are of primary importance in the history of art. Many charitable confraternities still exist, e.g. the Society of S. Vincent de Paul.

consecration crosses Consecration is the dedication of a person or thing to God, and the consecration of an altar or a church involves an elaborate ceremony performed by a bishop. It is not undertaken until the church is complete enough to be used (and nowadays free of debt), so many churches were not consecrated until many years after they were begun—Sta Croce in Florence, the great Franciscan church, was begun *c.*1252, worked on seriously from 1294/5, and consecrated with great pomp by the Greek Cardinal Bessarion in the presence of Pope Eugenius IV in 1442.

By the 8th/9th century relics were deposited in a small recess in the altar-slab, called a sepulchre, and sealed with a slab and marked with incised crosses. If the church itself was being consecrated twelve crosses were incised into, or attached to, the walls (normally inside the church) and a candle bracket attached beneath them. They marked the spot were the walls were anointed with *chrism, and are proof that the church has been consecrated. They may never be removed without desecration.

consignatorium (*locus chrismatis*) Also called chrismarion, this was the place near the *baptistery, where the newly baptized were 'signed' with chrism. There are some very early examples among ruins in N. Africa.

console An ornate bracket, projecting from a building, sometimes used to support a pediment or a cornice, or to support a heavy masonry window frame. Normally, a console has a curved or double-curved S-shape. The first use of a large pedimented window frame borne on massive consoles was devised by Michelangelo for the Medici Palace in Florence in 1517. These were often called 'kneeling windows'. *See also* SCROLL.

Constance, Council of In 1414 there were three 'popes', so the Emperor Sigismund persuaded John XXIII to call a Council to settle the Great Schism. John and both his rivals were deposed and a new Pope, Martin V, was elected in 1417. The Council closed in 1418 and Martin returned to Rome in 1420, which he found in a ruinous and abandoned state. He began by clearing the accumulated filth in the streets and set about repairing the damage to the Vatican, St Peter's, and the Lateran, as well as many churches. He employed the leading artists of the time, including Gentile da Fabriano and Pisanello, while *Masaccio and Masolino also worked in Rome: according to Vasari, the altarpiece, now given to Masolino, of Pope Liberius founding the *Liberian Basilica (Naples, Capodimonte) shows Liberius with the features of Martin. A side effect of the Council was that it attracted artists and patrons from Italy and N. Europe to Switzerland and gave rise to the interchange of ideas, but it is impossible to be more specific.

Constantine the Great, Emperor (d. 337), was the son of Constantius, Augustus of the West, and *Helena (later canonized). Constantine was in York in 306 when his father died, and he was proclaimed Augustus by the army. After a power-struggle for some years he invaded Italy in 312 and defeated his rival Maxentius at the Milvian Bridge, outside Rome. His biographer, *Eusebius, claimed that many years later Constantine told him he had had two visions, the first of a cross of light in the sky, with the words *In hoc signo vinces*—'In this sign conquer'—and the second instructed him to put the *Chi-Rho on the *labarum and the shields of his soldiers (*see* TRUE CROSS, LEGEND OF THE). It is certain that Constantine became favourably disposed to Christianity from then on, and in 313, together with his rival in the East, Licinius, he issued the Edict of *Milan, arguably one of the most important events in European history. Later, Licinius began persecuting Christians in the East and was defeated and executed by Constantine in 324, who thus became sole Emperor. He determined to leave Rome and found 'New Rome' on the site of the ancient city of Byzantium. This was probably partly due to the strategic advantages of the site on the Bosporus, at the point where Europe and Asia meet, and partly perhaps because the old senatorial families in Rome were obstinately pagan. The new capital was named *Constantinople, and he began a huge programme of building, secular and religious, as well as founding churches in the Holy Land.

In 325 he presided over the First Council of *Nicaea, though he was then probably still unbaptized—he seems to have been baptized only on his death-bed, but this was not uncommon at the time. He is venerated in the East as a saint, and even as 'the thirteenth Apostle'. By the 5th century there was a legend that he had been baptized by Pope Sylvester in Rome, at the Lateran Baptistery. The so-called 'Donation of Constantine', by which he was supposed to have conferred dominion over all Italy to the Pope, as well as primacy over the Eastern Patriarchates, probably dates from the 8th/9th century. It was discredited by Cardinal Nicolas of Cusa (1401–64) and proved a forgery by Lorenzo Valla (1406–57), priest and humanist. There is a huge 4th-century bronze portrait-head of Constantine in Belgrade (Nat. Mus.), but until comparatively recent times the only surviving ancient bronze equestrian statue, which actually represents Marcus Aurelius, was believed to represent him. It stood outside the Lateran throughout the Middle Ages as a symbol and memorial of the first Christian Emperor, until it was moved by Michelangelo to the Capitol in the 1530s, by which time its true identity was known.

Constantinople, formerly Byzantium and now Istanbul, was founded by *Constantine in 330 as the New Rome and capital of the empire. Constantine's original building programme probably included only three churches, but he provided secular buildings appropriate to the capital, such as fora, senates, a palace, a hippodrome, and triumphal arches and columns. The Nika riots of 532 burned down about half the city, but *Justinian's rebuilding included Hagia *Sophia, SS Sergius and Bacchus, and St Irene. In the 7th and 8th centuries the Arabs and natural disasters destroyed much of the city, and the Latin occupation of 1204–61 still further reduced its importance, and the empire finally collapsed with the Turkish conquest in 1453. Its surviving art includes some superb ivories, MSS, and icons, most of which were looted during the Latin occupation and the sack of the city in 1204 by the Crusaders.

consular diptych *See* DIPTYCH.

Continuous Representation The ancestor of the strip-cartoon: a method of telling a story by means of scenes from e.g. the life of a saint, shown as a sequence. Thus, a central *icon of a saint may be framed by scenes from his/her life (*see* CLARE, FRANCIS) and scenes of posthumous miracles. It is also used of paintings which show several phases of the action in different parts of the same picture. The method was common in the Middle Ages and up to the mid-15th century in Italy, and was revived in the 16th century, e.g. in the *Life of Joseph* panels by Bacchiacca and Pontormo (London, NG), or El Greco's *Martyrdom of S. Maurice* (1580–2: Escorial).

convent, conventual A convent is a community of men, women, or both—monks, friars, and/or nuns—living in a religious house. If the term is applied to the house itself, it usually means a nunnery, a community of women. The term 'conventual' is most often applied to Franciscans of the Reformed Order (Ordo Minorum Conventualium).

conversi (Lat. changed) Lay brothers in a monastery, or the accommodation for them. In *Cistercian houses they were often very numerous. The exact status of these laymen is a matter of debate.

Conversion of Saint Paul *See* PAUL.

cope Originally a Roman outdoor cloak, it is a semicircle of heavy cloth, about 11 ft. in diameter, draped over the shoulders and reaching almost to the ground. It differed from the chasuble only by being open at the front. Copes as *vestments may go back as far as the 6th century, when they had a hood, but by the 12th century this became a mere decoration, usually triangular and with a tassel attached. From the 13th century the cope was closed at chest level by a morse, an embroidered band sewn on at one side and closed with a clasp at the other. Copes and morses were often extremely rich—the *Syon Cope is a celebrated example of *opus anglicanum, and *Ghiberti records in his autobiography making an elaborate morse for Martin V (now lost), 'with the figure of Our Lord blessing' on the clasp. Though not strictly a Eucharistic vestment, copes are worn by Western clergy for several liturgical functions. In the East they are simply elaborate cloaks, not confined to priests or bishops.

Copley, John Singleton *See* NORTH AMERICA.

Coptic art and architecture The Copts were native Egyptian Christians, who, after the Council of Chalcedon in 451, became a separate Church embracing the Monophysite heresy (that Christ had only a divine, and not a human nature as well). They were mostly peasants, opposed to the merchants in the towns and to the Byzantine government. The great period of their art was between the 5th and 8th centuries, and again after 1169. Their early churches are derived from Early Christian and Byzantine examples, often with triconch ends, but in the 11th/12th centuries 'broad churches' were built with multiple altars and many separate domed spaces. Their art is simple, with bright, flat colours and very intricate surface patterning in reliefs and MSS, surprisingly like *Irish MSS of the 9th century, and sometimes using ancient Egyptian motives—e.g. the *Madonna Lactans derived from Horus and Isis. The Islamic conquest of Egypt in 640–2 caused changes, and from the 9th century there was some influence from Islamic abstract art. After Saladin's conquest in 1169 the art of the Copts grew formalized and was, from the 16th century, influenced by the E. Orthodox Church. It may have influenced the development of *Romanesque in the West, but too little is known to be sure.

Corah *See* KORAH.

coral It was an ancient Roman superstition that a branch of coral would avert the evil eye and evil spirits generally. The idea persisted for many centuries, and medieval paintings of the Madonna and Child often show the Child with a piece of coral hung round His neck—

as a talisman against the Devil! Piero della Francesca's *Senigallia Madonna* (Urbino, Gall.) is a good example.

corbel, corbel table A bracket but less decorative than a *console. It may also be one of a series of small blocks of progressively projecting masonry that helps to bridge the gap across an opening so that a dome may be built over a crossing. This is known as 'corbelling out'. A corbel table is a row of corbels usually under the eaves of a building that forms the outer row of supports for the roof beams. In Romanesque churches these are often carved with human or animal heads.

cornice The topmost part of the architrave of any classical order. It also describes the decorative element frequently found on the edge of a roof overhanging a building.

corona lucis (Lat. crown of light) In early times, even pre-Christian, rulers sometimes dedicated their crowns to temples or churches. In churches the crowns were usually hung above an altar, often with lamps suspended from them. From this arose the custom of hanging a large circle or wheel horizontally, with spikes around the upper rim to take candles or lamps, to make a crown of light. A celebrated example, given by Frederick Barbarossa in 1165, hangs in Aachen Cathedral.

Coronati, Quattro Santi (Lat. *Sancti Quattuor Coronatorum*, i.e. Four Crowned Saints) There were certainly four martyrs venerated in Rome by the 4th century in the church of the Santi Quattro Coronati, and even in England, at Canterbury, by 619. Unfortunately, there is no clear legend, but two—or even a third, which is clearly an incompetent fiction. The first tells of four Roman soldiers martyred by the Emperor Diocletian in 306 for refusing to sacrifice to Aesculapius; the second, more probable, one is of five stone-cutters in Sirmium (in modern Hungary), named Simpronian, Claudius, Nicostratus, Castorius, and Simplicius, who seems to have been forgotten. They refused to make an image of Aesculapius at the command of Diocletian and were martyred accordingly, also in 306. The legend gives details of the imperial quarries at Sirmium which lend verisimilitude to this version. In the Middle Ages they were very popular as patrons of the *guilds of masons, carpenters, and builders generally, especially in Italy and the Netherlands. The best-known example is the group in a niche on the outside of Orsanmichele in Florence, by Nanni di Banco. Orsanmichele was a Guild church and the group was commissioned in 1413 for the Guild of Masons and Carpenters. The four figures wear togas and are not crowned, but reliefs below them have scenes of sculptors at work. The series of paintings in SS Quattro Coronati in Rome by Giovanni da S. Giovanni, of 1623, plays safe by including elements from both versions of the legend.

Coronation of the Virgin This is really a part of the iconography of the *Assumption, which is often subdivided into four parts—the *Dormition, Burial, the Assumption proper, and the final Coronation as Queen of Heaven. The Coronation is not a biblical subject, or even a prominent one in the **Golden Legend*, but is based on Ps. 44: 11–12, 14 (Vg. version only) and the Song of Songs (4: 8), paraphrased as 'Veni electa mea ... in thronum meum' (Come chosen one to my throne), words often inscribed on a book held by Christ, as in Torriti's mosaic in Sta Maria Maggiore in Rome (*c.*1290). The Byzantine Dormition iconography was adapted and expanded for *portal sculpture, and the two figures of the Coronation fitted into the pointed arch shape of Gothic tympana, so the broader base was often filled with reliefs of the Dormition and Burial. The first such portal seems to be at Senlis Cathedral, in NW France, *c.*1180, and was soon followed by other Gothic cathedrals such as Bourges, Strasburg, Paris.

In Italy Torriti's apse mosaic is one of the first large examples, but the first known panel painting is by Guido da Siena (*c.*1280: London, Courtauld Gall.). The usual arrangememnt is for Christ and Mary to be seated side by side, or with Mary kneeling as Christ holds the crown over her, but there are several variations. In some cases the coronation is performed by God the Father, with or without Christ being present; in others both hold the crown, as in Dürer's *Life of the Virgin* woodcut of 1510, with the Holy Ghost as a dove. *Quarton's celebrated painting in Villeneuve-lès-Avignon shows Father and Son as identical bearded figures, and again has the dove of the Holy Spirit. A very strange contemporary version, again probably French, is the panel in Basle, inscribed 'I.M.' and dated 1457. God the Father is shown in the centre as a bearded old man crowned with an imperial crown, and, on His right hand, a figure of Christ holding the crown and a sceptre, while opposite Him is an identical figure, but beardless, also holding the crown and a sceptre, which must be an unconventional representation of the Holy Spirit. Later artists—Titian, Tintoretto, Rubens—tended to concentrate on the Assumption, rather than the physical crowning. The Coronation also features as one of the Seven *Joys of Mary and as the fifth Glorious Mystery of the *rosary.

corporal (Lat. *corpus*, body [of Christ]) A square of linen, on which the consecrated Host is laid. A second one, now called a pall, is used to cover the chalice. It is similar in function to the *antiminsion in the E. Orthodox Church.

Corporal Works of Mercy *See* MERCY.

corpus (Lat. body) (1) The body of the crucified Christ when separated from the cross on a crucifix—e.g. an ivory *corpus* which has become separated from its original wooden cross; (2) a body of writings, such as Canon Law—the *Corpus juris canonici*; and (3) the Feast of Corpus Christi (Corpus Domini). This Catholic Feast, commemorating the Institution of the Eucharist (*see* COMMUNION OF THE APOSTLES), ought to be celebrated on Maundy Thursday, but because of the Passion liturgy no separate Feast was allotted to it until the 13th century. It is now celebrated on the Thursday after Trinity Sunday throughout the Western Church, but not in the East. It was instituted, following a series of visions by S. Juliana of Liège (d. 1258), by Urban IV, who ordered it to be observed from 1264. S. Thomas Aquinas is said to have composed the service (including the hymn *Pange lingua*), and it was universal in the West by the 14th century. Urban is said to have been influenced in his decision by reports of a miracle at *Bolsena, and this was also responsible for the only major work of art directly associated with the Feast, Raphael's fresco in the Vatican. However, a number of confraternities of the Holy Sacrament commissioned related works from at least the 14th century: a famous example is the altarpiece commissioned from Joos van Gent by the confraternity at Urbino, representing the *Communion of the Apostles*, with a *predella* by Uccello depicting an anti-Semitic legend of the *Profanation of the Host* (*c.*1465–74: Urbino). From the earliest times it was the custom to carry the consecrated Host in procession, a practice which gave rise to the development of the *monstrance.

Corregio, Antonio (probably 1489–1534), was born in Correggio, near Parma, and is by date a painter of the High Renaissance, but by style far closer to the Baroque; there are even aspects of his art which antedate French 18th-century painting. He was probably a pupil of *Mantegna, but was influenced by *Leonardo—as were most early 16th-century N. Italian artists—which led him to develop a soft and tender manner of painting, admirably suited to the rather emotional character of his art. He must have visited Rome before 1520, since influences from such disparate sources as Raphael and Michelangelo appear in his work after that date. His early very Mantegnesque work, *The Madonna of S. Francis* (1514–15: Dresden), was followed by his first fresco decoration—the ceiling of the Camera di San Paolo in Parma painted about 1518. This, though painted in an abbess's reception room in a convent, was a totally secular decoration, owing much to Mantegna's use of *di sotto in sù*—figures seen from below in sharp perspective—and to Leonardo's softness of handling. His major works are the frescoes in domes in two churches in Parma, *S. Giovanni Evangelista* (St John the Evangelist: 1520–1) and the *Assumption of the Virgin* (1526–8: Cathedral), in concentric circles of ascending figures, both stunning in their use of powerful *di sotto in sù* perspective, and both using the device of placing large figures on the lower edge of the dome to throw those above into stronger effects of recession. The pendentives also have large powerfully receding figures which increase the effect, devices later important in Baroque painting. His many altarpieces include the emotional and ecstatic pair of the *Lamentation over the Dead Christ* and the *Martyrdom of Four Saints* (both 1524–6: Parma), the tender *Madonna of S. Jerome* (1527–8: Parma), and the *Nativity* (1529–30: Dresden), pictures known as *Il Giorno* and *La Notte* (Day and Night) because of the radiant light in 'Day', and the Christ Child as the source of light in the 'Night'—an effective artistic device, but also an iconographically significant one. His even larger *Madonna and Child with SS George and John the Baptist* (1531–2: Dresden) achieves in a religious work a voluptuous sensibility akin to that in his secular works.

Cosmas and Damian, Saints, are the two best-known of a group called the *Anargyroi—healing saints—who would not accept payment. The Anargyroi are popular in the East, but the cult of Cosmas and Damian spread rapidly to the West. Little is known about them, but they are supposed to have been twins, martyred in Syria, perhaps under the Emperor Diocletian. They are mentioned in the Roman Canon (4th/5th cent.?), had a church in Constantinople dedicated to them by the 5th century, and the present church in Rome before 530. It is the first example of the conversion of a pagan Roman temple into a Christian church, and the mosaics in the apse show Cosmas and Damian and also the founder, Pope Felix IV (526–30), whose portrait there is the earliest known papal portrait. Their most famous miracle was the first recorded transplant operation, when they grafted the leg of a dead negro on to a white man whose own leg was severed (or gangrenous). They are naturally the patron saints of doctors, along with S. Luke, as well as of the Medici family (*medici* means physicians). In Florence, the Medici commissioned Fra *Angelico's altarpiece for San Marco (1438–40: still there), which shows them prominent in the foreground, dressed in the red robes and tall hats of physicians. The nine scenes in the *predella* are now in several museums, but the one with the transplant miracle is still in San Marco. Cosmas and Damian also flank the *Madonna and Child* in the Medici chapel of San Lorenzo, but these statues, although designed by *Michelangelo, were executed by Montorsoli and Raffaello da Montelupo (1533–4). They are also prominent in the so-called *Medici Madonna* by Roger van der *Weyden (*c.*1450: Frankfurt, Städel).

Cosmati A conventional name for several families of marble-workers active in Rome and its neighbourhood between *c.*1100 and *c.*1300. 'Cosmati work' is a kind of mosaic, made from *tesserae of white and coloured marble, porphyry, serpentine, *giallo antico*, and, later, glass and gilded glass, the decorative designs being separated by plain white marble. It was probably an ancient Roman tradition, but was greatly influenced by *Byzantine mosaics, although Cosmati work is always decorative and non-figurative. It was used for pavements and as decoration on ciboria, bishops' thrones, chancel screens, and sometimes on façades. The first recorded worker was Paolo, who signed his work in Ferentino Cathedral, 1108–10. Many later names are known, including Petrus Romanus and Odericus, who came to London *c.*1268 and made a pavement for Westminster Abbey, and also the tombs of Edward the Confessor and Henry III. He/they are probably identical with Pietro d'Oderisio. The pavement of Trinity (St Thomas's) Chapel in Canterbury Cathedral is also attributed to him. These are the only known works outside Italy, but most of the older Roman churches have examples. The absence of the papacy in *Avignon (1309–77) meant that the tradition died out during the 14th century.

cotta A simple linen tunic like an *alb, but worn without a girdle. It is not a Eucharistic *vestment, but rather a short surplice.

Councils, Ecumenical The Ecumenical or General Councils are assemblies of bishops and other senior prelates, representing the whole inhabited world (*oikoumene*). The first was probably the meeting described in Acts 15, but they are usually numbered from Nicaea I, called by the Emperor *Constantine in 325, up to the 21st, Council of the Roman Catholic Church, Vatican II, 1962–5. Only the first seven, up to Nicaea II, in 787, are regarded by all churches in East and West as Ecumenical. For those which dealt with matters concerning the arts *see* *NICAEA; *EPHESUS; *CONSTANCE; *FLORENCE and FERRARA; and *TRENT.

Counter-Reformation Sometimes also called Catholic Reform, this was the reaction of the Roman Church to the late 15th-century demands for reform which culminated in the Lutheran and Calvinist movements from 1517 onwards. In 1512–17 the Fifth Lateran Council had made some attempt at internal reform, and, from the 1520s, new religious Orders also combated Lutheran ideas, but the real impetus came from the *Jesuits after 1540, and from the Council of *Trent, which held 25 sessions between 1545 and 1563, introducing far-reaching reforms, most of which endured until the 1960s. The Jesuits and the Tridentine Reformers were both deeply convinced of the importance of the visual arts and music, and from the mid-16th to the mid-17th century they revitalized religious art, encouraging the formation of the *Baroque style. *See also* IGNATIUS, S.; BORROMEO, S. CHARLES AND FEDERIGO; DECORUM, and REFORMATION.

Covenants, the Old and New Also called Old and New Dispensations. A covenant is a binding agreement. The Old Covenant is the bond recorded in the OT between God and His Chosen People by the establishment of the Law given by God to Moses which is recorded in Exod. 19: 5–6 and elsewhere. The *Ark of the Covenant was the evidence of God's promise, of which the essential obligation for the Jewish people was obedience to the Ten Commandments and the other enactments of Mosaic Law embodied in the Old Covenant. Jeremiah (31: 31–4) foretells a new, less legalistic, Covenant in the hearts of men. For Christians the New Covenant was created by the life and death of Christ, specifically by the Institution of the Eucharist (cf. Matt. 26: 28; Mark 14: 24; Luke 22: 20 and 1 Cor. 11: 23–5), the celebration of which is the evidence of the New Covenant, as the existence of the Ark was of the Old. The history of the world is thus seen as three stages—*ante legem*, before the Law, i.e. from the Creation to Moses; *sub lege*, from the giving of the Law to Moses until the coming of Christ, and *sub gratia*, the Grace given by Christ. This is the theme of the frescoes in the *Sistine Chapel.

cowl Properly speaking, a long sleeveless garment with a pointed hood hanging down the back, characteristic of monks. Usually it refers solely to the hood, as in 'to take the cowl', to become a monk or friar. When the monastic tonsure meant that the whole of the top of the head was shaven some covering was necessary during winter night services.

Cox, Stephen, RA (1946–) A British sculptor much influenced by the writings of Adrian Stokes (1902–72) with his feel for the art, culture, and geology of the Mediterranean. Cox is also influenced by the ancient dignity of porphyry, and by the art of India where he has won awards and gained commissions. These three factors have come together in a number of works that have proved of special interest to the Church in Britain, especially with its growing awareness of other world religions: see for example, *Tondo: Ascension* (1983, South Bank Centre); *Reredos* and *Altar* (1993, Haringey, London, St Paul's); *Eucharist* (1996, Newcastle upon Tyne, St Nicholas Cathedral); *Saint Anselm Altar* (2006, Canterbury Cathedral).

Cranach, Lucas (1472–1553), appeared in Vienna *c.*1500, painting portraits and religious works with German landscape settings of a Romantic intensity which became typical of the so-called Danube School of landscape painters: examples are the *Crucifixions* in Vienna (KHM of *c.*1500) and Munich, of 1503, or the *Rest on the Flight*, of 1504 (Berlin). In 1505 he moved to Wittenberg as Court painter and there met *Luther, by whom he was deeply influenced. He established a large studio, assisted later by his two sons, and his work suffered in quality, but the shop produced numerous woodcut illustrations to the Bible, Luther's works, and Reformation tracts. Cranach himself also painted Luther (Leipzig) and made a woodcut (1520), probably both from the same drawing, as well as *Luther* and *Melanchthon* (1532: Dresden). At the same time he was producing a very popular series of erotic nudes—*Eve*, *Venus*, *Lucretia*, and similar themes. In 1550 he moved to Augsburg, and then to Weimar, where he died.

Creation, the The first book of the Bible is called Genesis, and the first words of the first chapter are: 'In the beginning God created the heaven and the earth.' The following thirty-one verses recount the creation of day and night, the division of the sky from the waters, the separation of earth and water into land and sea, the creation of grass and trees, stars, sun, and moon to mark time and the seasons, fish, birds, beasts, cattle, insects, and finally on the sixth day God created man from the dust of the earth, and breathed life into him. On the seventh day He surveyed what He had done, and 'saw that it was good', and then He blessed that day, and rested. He set the man in a fruitful garden amid rivers, which was Paradise, and then He made woman from a rib taken from his side, to be a companion for him, and *Adam later named her Eve.

Many artists have depicted the Creation, but the two outstanding visions of it are by *Bosch and *Michelangelo. Bosch excels at the serene beauty of the Paradise garden, but into it creeps the tiny images of the sins which will come to dominate the world, and the portents of the Fall of *Man, the temptations of desire and the rapid corruption of Eve's innocence into disobedience and shame. Michelangelo's vision is truly cosmic; he begins with God creating order from the primeval chaos, separating night from day, land from the waters in a vast sweep of His arm. His image is of God Almighty, borne up by angels and with Wisdom sheltering beneath His arm (Prov. 8: 22–30) giving life to the inert body of Adam who holds out to Him his flaccid arm to receive the vital spark of life, summoning the timorous Eve from the side of the sleeping man, followed by the subtle vengefulness of the Serpent who tempts Eve into the sin of disobedience and destroys the peace of Paradise, so that together they are driven forth, stumbling in grief and remorse into the harsh inhospitable wilderness of the world, to fulfil God's curse: 'By the sweat of your face you shall eat bread until you return to the ground, for out of it you were taken; you are dust and to dust you shall return.' The Michelangelo precedent has not deterred artists from attempting powerful treatments of the Creation narrative: Rico Lebrun's 1960 mural *Genesis* is organized around the figure of Noah (in Frary Hall, Pomona College, Claremont, CA).

The story of the Creation is often dismissed as a myth, particularly when it is confronted by the discoveries of anthropologists, palaeontologists, astronomers, and astro-physicists. But what matter? The myth—if myth it is—itself makes order out of chaos. It expresses in vividly simple terms the sequences which the labours of later scientific learning have not greatly affected. Whether one believes in an act of Divine creation, or in the 'Big Bang' theory, or accepts some other less dramatic slow creative process, through which mankind eventually emerged into a flawed existence, is not the point here. The point is how the artist, faced with no more than the first thirty-one verses of Genesis, and the following forty-nine verses which tell of the Fall and its consequences, provided a visual counterpart of explanations of phenomena which scientific theories have not yet fully explained, and created through images which live in the mind, and match by the force of his creativity the poetry and expressiveness of the eighty verses which were the vital spark for his imagination.

credenza A small table or shelf in a niche near an altar where the water and wine and other things needed are placed before Mass is celebrated.

Crib, the Christmas According to Luke (2: 7), at the *Nativity Mary laid the Christ Child 'in a manger'. Some wooden fragments, which purport to be from this manger, have been venerated in Sta Maria Maggiore in Rome at least since the 8th century, and possibly much earlier. In 1223 *S. Francis of Assisi celebrated Christmas by having a crib, with hay and an ox and *ass at Midnight Mass. John of Greccio, who was present, claimed to have seen a vision of the Christ Child in the crib. This is the subject of a fresco from the official series of the Life of S. Francis in the Upper Church at Assisi, and from this derives the practice of erecting a crib, with figures of the Holy Family, angels, ox and ass, and three shepherds during the Christmas season; for *Epiphany the three *Magi are substituted for the shepherds. The ox and ass, though always associated with the Nativity, are not mentioned in the NT, but derive from the *Apocryphal Gospel known as the Pseudo-Matthew. Over the centuries these groups became a distinct sculptural type (Ital. *presepe* or *presepio*) and, from the 17th to 19th centuries, a Neapolitan speciality, with whole families such as the Sammartino, producing elaborate groups with scores, or even hundreds, of figures (examples in Naples, Mus. di San Martino). In France the village of Santon in Provence also specialized in making small clay figures for cribs, but they are far cruder than the Neapolitan works.

croce dipinta (Ital. painted cross) A painted *crucifix (i.e. not three-dimensional) produced in Italy between the early 12th century (the first dated one is of 1138: Master Guglielmo: Sarzana) and the late 14th. It is a cruciform wooden shape, varying in size between a foot or so for an altar cross up to some ten feet for the huge ones intended to hang above the altar or stand on a *rood. They have a painted representation of the Crucified Christ, usually accompanied by side scenes from the Passion or of mourning figures. Most of the large ones have been cut down, but apart from the actual cross they often had extensions at the ends of the arms, with half-length figures of the Virgin and S. John; an *Ascension* at the top and/or a roundel with a bust of Christ; and sometimes an extension at the foot of the cross has a weeping Magdalene or *Adam's skull.

crosier, crozier (probably from medieval Latin *crocia:* crook) A long staff with a spiral head, like an elaborate shepherd's crook, symbolic of a bishop's authority. A pastoral staff is recorded in the 7th century as belonging to bishops and, later, also to abbots and abbesses. In the East such a staff is topped by a cross between two serpents, the Western crook being a later symbol of the shepherd. The actual crook is often a very elaborate piece of sculpture. The pope is the only bishop who does not have a crosier.

cross (1) types of; (2) standing crosses; (3) Legend of the True Cross: *see* TRUE CROSS.

(1) Types of cross. The cross is by far the most common symbol of Christianity, but it was not used in the earliest centuries, because of its shameful association with *Crucifixion, the death penalty for the worst malefactors. Early symbols include the *Chi-Rho and the *Anchor of Hope, both of which include crosses, but unobtrusively. From *Constantine onwards the cross was universally adopted, the principal forms being (i) the Latin cross (*crux immissa*), with a long vertical intersected by a shorter horizontal at about two-thirds of the way up; (ii) the X shape, Saltire, or *S. Andrew's cross (*crux decussata*); and (iii) the Greek cross, **+**, where the arms are of equal length. The Tau cross, T, like a Latin cross with the top cut off, may be Egyptian in origin (*ankh*) and older than Christianity—for this reason it is often associated with the OT, as in the *brazen serpent, a *type of the Crucifixion. It is also commonly used for the crosses of the two thieves, *Dismas and Gestas. A Y-shaped ('forked') cross occurs occasionally, as in the Siena Cathedral pulpit (1265–8), by N. and G. *Pisano, or more obviously in the cross in St Maria im Kapitol, Cologne, of *c.*1300.

Variants of the Latin cross have additional horizontal bars, with a shorter bar or bars above the normal one—one with three bars of diminishing width upwards is a papal cross; with only one short bar it is a patriarchal cross ('cross of Lorraine'), the short bar being regarded as the *titulus. In the E. Orthodox Church (Russian and Byzantine) a form is used consisting of a patriarchal cross with an oblique bar below the longer arm: this symbolizes the body of Christ or the *suppedaneum*, the piece of wood to which His feet were nailed. Other common forms are the Celtic or Irish cross, with a circle round the arms of a Latin (or Greek) cross, and the Maltese, which is said to show four arrowheads with their points meeting in the centre, like a Greek cross. It is well known as the emblem of the Knights of *Malta, and, through them, the St John Ambulance Brigade.

By the 13th century a cross or crucifix was kept permanently on the altar, perhaps first in the East. A processional cross is a crucifix on the end of a long pole, carried in processions and accompanied by two acolytes carrying candles.

(2) Standing crosses. It is not until the 8th to the 12th centuries that the great standing crosses appear, and then not only in Ireland but in all the British Isles. The earliest in Ireland are probably two at Ahenny (Co. Tipperary), one over 11 ft. high and the other over 12 ft. Both have scenes carved on their bases, not dissimilar to those found on Pictish stones in Scotland, and the ornamentation of the cross itself is a translation into stone of metal ornament—spirals, interlacings, and bosses. The arms of the crosses are joined by similarly decorated circles (the so-called Celtic cross). Some crosses are carved from fine limestone, which allows for more detailed working, some—like the Moone cross (Kildare)—are of granite, so that the carving is cruder, though the Moone cross has many figure scenes, on all four sides, which must be read as a sequence: Adam and Eve, the Sacrifice of Abraham, Daniel in the Lion's Den, on the east side; the Fiery Furnace, the Flight into Egypt, the Loaves and Fishes, on the south side, to represent God's providence in the Old and New Testaments; the Crucifixion, with Christ in Glory at the top of the cross on the west side, for Salvation; and on the north side, scenes from the Life of S. Anthony to represent the life of contemplation. On the base are the twelve Apostles, in rows like so many little gingerbread men. The symbolic and didactic purpose of the images is of paramount importance, and where these crosses have sculptured scenes they must be read as texts, or rather as sermons in stone. Among other important crosses are those at Monasterboice (Louth), particularly the cross of Muiredach, datable to the early 10th century. It is notable how often a cemetery—possibly once the precinct of a monastery—will contain two or more of these great monuments. Muiredach's cross is covered, front and back, with narrative scenes in small panels, with the Crucifixion on one side and Christ in Glory on the other, and the sides have rich interlacings and panels of spirals. In the iconography of the Crucifixion it is remarkable that while European forms so often have the Virgin and S. John flanking the cross, in the Irish ones it is invariably the men with the lance and the reed and sponge, imagery of Byzantine origin (*see* LONGINUS, STEPHATON), even if the figures are rudimentary in form.

With standing crosses in Great Britain, it is simpler to begin with the major work—the Ruthwell cross now preserved in the parish church of Ruthwell in Dumfriesshire. It stands 17 ft. high. Two faces have figure sculpture: on the front is Christ in Judgement, crushing beneath His feet the lion and serpent of evil, framed by a runic inscription connected with the poem of 'The Dream of the Rood'. On the same face is a figure of S. John the Baptist with the Lamb, the hermit saints Paul and Anthony, the Flight into Egypt, and what may be a Nativity. On the opposite face is Christ with the Magdalene at His feet, as the symbol of forgiveness, in contrast to the Christ of Judgement. There are also representations of the manifestations of the Godhead: the Annunciation, a pair of figures which may be either the Visitation or Martha and Mary, with their unseen reference to the Raising of Lazarus, the Healing of the Blind Man, and the Crucifixion at the base. All these subjects are fairly high reliefs carved within the stone, and framed by the inscription. On the other two sides are inhabited scrolls, birds and beasts climbing through flowering and fruiting vines. The Bewcastle cross, in the churchyard on a bleak hillside in Cumbria, only a few miles away, is simpler. There are scenes on only one face: a Christ in Judgement in the centre, S. John the Baptist above, and a S. John the Evangelist below Him. The other sides have a mixture of inhabited scrolls and intricate panels of knot ornament. The difference between the two crosses is increased by the better state of preservation of the Ruthwell cross, which still has its original cross at the top, although repaired after being damaged during the Reformation; only the shaft survives of the Bewcastle cross. It would seem reasonable to believe that Bewcastle follows Ruthwell, and that both are datable *c.*800. The date originally given to the Bewcastle cross of before 700 was based on an inscription which has now been discredited as evidence. In both, the imagery is partly, but not wholly, Mediterranean in origin. Similar scenes from the Life of Christ appeared on ivories in Ravenna and in MSS from Italy, although strong currents from Northumbrian MSS and metal-work are also present. Many other standing crosses existed; Huneberc, a 9th-century Anglo-Saxon nun at Heidenheim, in her account of S. Willibald, says that it was the custom of landowners to erect a cross sometimes as a boundary marker, and also as an object of devotion for the pious. Few other crosses survive as more than fragments—the Aberlemno Slab, Forfarshire, carved with abstract interlace ornament and sparsely inhabited scrolls, the huge cross at Kildalton, on the island of Islay, so close to the Irish types as to confuse the origin of the forms, the Gosforth cross (Cumbria), tall and thin—15ft. high—like a trimmed tree-trunk. Here the imagery is very strange: a Christ with outstretched arms, probably intended for a Crucifixion, but with no cross, and two men below, one with a lance, and the other with what may have been intended for a reed and sponge. The rest of the figure sculpture illustrates a Norse myth—the destruction of the gods from the Ragnarok cycle—which may be the adaptation of an Icelandic cycle to Christian purposes. Between the figure scenes are panels of ornament. Of the many fragments of cross shafts the important ones are the Easby cross (London, V & A) with its mixture of rows of Apostle heads and its rich inhabited scrolls, the remains of the three shafts at All Saints, Ilkley (Yorks.), Acca's cross at Hexham Abbey, or the Lowther cross from Westmorland (now BM). Aycliffe, Co. Durham, has two fragments of a shaft, preserved in the parish church, with a Crucifixion flanked by the men with lance and reed, and the other, which does not seem to belong to the first, has a Crucifixion of S. Peter with crude panels of interlaced beasts. The very fine fragments of the small (*c.*3 ft.) shaft at St Andrew's Auckland (Co. Durham) of *c.*800, has unusual features. The Annunciation and the inhabited scrolls have appeared at Ruthwell, but these fragments have a Crucifixion with Christ tied to the cross (an image of Syrian origin), a bearded Christ with two Apostles, and another group of figures which may be Abraham and the Angels, or a second group of a beardless Christ with two Apostles, the image being one already known in Ravenna in Sant'Apollinare Nuovo, where the bearded Christ of the Passion is contrasted with the post-Resurrection beardless Christ.

crossing The point at which the nave and transepts meet.

cross-in-square describes the shape of a church in which a centrally planned cross form is enclosed within a rectangle. Where the arms of the cross are vaulted, the central crossing may be either a simple cross-vault or a dome. The corners between the arms of the cross and the rectangle may be open to the central cross form, or closed off as side chapels or sacristies. Since their ceiling level is lower than the height of the vaulted arms of the cross, these corner spaces can also be made into galleries with a view into the cross. The shape is most suitable for small churches, and was much used in

*Byzantine architecture. It was revived during the Renaissance and was used for small pilgrimage churches, convent chapels, and shrines. It became, however, one of the main shapes of the *auditory church, particularly in the Netherlands and in *Wren's City churches.

Crown of Thorns One of the Instruments of the *Passion, recorded by three of the Evangelists (Matt. 27: 29; Mark 15: 17; and John 19: 2). There is a record of a relic of it in the 5th century, and it was said to be in Jerusalem in the 6th: S. Louis, King of France, had a part, and built the Ste-Chapelle in Paris (1248) to receive it. He gave away fragments in golden reliquaries, one of which is said to be in the British Museum. The one in the Ste-Chapelle was destroyed in the French Revolution, but fragments are still in Notre-Dame, Paris. In the 16th/17th centuries there was a controversy over whether *Crucifixions* should show Christ as still wearing the Crown of Thorns, but, as there was no clear guidance from Scripture, it was left to the artist to decide—Rubens, for example, used both forms.

crozier *See* CROSIER.

crucifix, crucifixion Together with the Madonna and Child, representations of the Crucifixion are by far the commonest subjects of Christian art. The actual crucifixion is described by all four Evangelists (Matt. 27; Mark 15; Luke 23; John 19), but it was never represented in Christian art until some 400 years after the event. There is, however, the so-called 'blasphemous graffito', probably of the 3rd century, from the Palace of the Caesars in Rome, which represents a man with arms outstretched in the attitude of crucifixion, but with the head of an ass. Another man stands near by, apparently praying, and a Greek inscription reads 'Alexamenos worships his god'.

This helps to explain the lack of Christian representations of so important a subject—crucifixion was a horrible and degrading punishment inflicted only upon slaves or at least non-Roman citizens (which is why S. Peter was crucified, but S. Paul was beheaded). It was officially abolished by *Constantine as part of his pro-Christian policy, but seems to have continued for some time and it was probably not until the early 5th century that people were prepared to accept representations. The two earliest known are both of around 430—the panel from the wooden doors of Sta Sabina in Rome, and a small ivory relief, one of four now in the British Museum. Before this time there had been symbolic representations, such as the sarcophagus (Rome, Lateran Mus.) where a cross carries a garland of victory and a *Chi-Rho. The Sta Sabina panel shows Christ between the two thieves, with a background symbolizing Jerusalem; and the BM ivory shows Christ alone, with the inscription 'REX IVD', flanked by *Longinus the centurion, and two figures on His right, probably Mary and S. John. Both reliefs depict the scene and are therefore best described as *Crucifixions*, not crucifixes. A crucifix is essentially a cross with a fully modelled figure (technically a corpus) attached to it, but such three-dimensional objects were open to criticism as idolatrous and breaking the Commandment about graven images. They are rare in Byzantine art, as is free-standing sculpture in general, and the development of crucifixes in this sense comes much later. Another important point about the two early representations is that the figure of Christ is standing against, rather than hanging from, the cross. He wears only a loin-cloth and is fastened by four nails, but is triumphing over death rather than dying. This emphasis on victory, not on an agonizing death, is characteristic of all the earliest representations, as *Christus Triumphans*.

From the 6th century Christ usually wears a long robe, called a *colobium, as in the *Rabbula Gospels of 586. In all these He continues to stand with feet separate, and with one nail in each. By the 9th century a Byzantine type emerges, in which He is shown as dead and wearing a larger loin-cloth (*perizoma*). In this type His eyes are closed, the head is bowed, and the body sags markedly. Because of the arching of the body there is no longer space for narrative scenes in the side panel and it is now filled with a decorative pattern. These two types evolve in East and West into the painted crucifixes known as *Christus Triumphans* and *Christus Patiens*. They are best seen in the Italian form of painted crucifix called *croce dipinta, the earliest datable example of which is of 1138. Before then, however, the fully modelled crucifix had established itself, one of the greatest early examples being the *Gero Cross* (before 976: Cologne Cath.), which emphasizes the torments of death found in the *Patiens* type. This form was greatly developed in the West from *c.*1230, in consequence of the emotionalism of Franciscan preaching, and evolved through the mystical piety of crucifixion imagery into the theme of the Virtues actually crucifying Christ so that Salvation and the gift of eternal life should flow freely into the world. The Cardinal Virtues of Fortitude, Temperance, and Prudence are joined by Justice, Love (*Caritas*), Faith, Hope, Perseverence, Wisdom, Reason, and Free Will (the power to opt for good or evil), and some of them nail Christ to the cross, while the crowned Love, as the major virtue, spears his side, Ecclesia, also crowned, collects the blood which spurts from the wound, and Synagoga, dejected and blindfolded, stands with broken staff and with the tablets of the Law hanging from her limp hand. Such images (with individual variations) appear in MSS such as a psalter from the Upper Rhineland of *c.*1275 (Besançon) and in another late 13th-century psalter from Strasbourg (now Donaueschingen) where the tree-cross is surmounted by a 'pelican in piety' (*see* BIRDS). The ecstatic piety which inspired such imagery was frequently found in nunneries, and appears to have lasted until the mid-14th century. It is perhaps relevant that it was a Northern rather than an Italian development. The pathetic aspect of post-Franciscan crucifixes was partly due to the twisting of the body and the crossing of the legs which occur when only one nail is used to secure both feet. The development of the tree-cross is another form of crucifixion imagery, also more Northern than Southern in extent. The Y-shaped cross, with Christ's hands fixed to the rising arms of the Y, as in crucifixes of *c.*1300 (Cologne and Friesach), is a form of the tree-cross which combines the crucified Christ with the Tree of *Jesse, as in a MS illustration of the **Speculum Humanae Salvationis* of *c.*1340–50 from Lake Constance (Kremsmünster) and a similar image in an Italian portable altarpiece of *c.*1400 (Hanover). The idea is also present in a *rood-cross and shrine (1360–70: Doberan monastery) where the cross sprouts flowers, and with the crucifix in the chancel arch of St Lorenz, Nuremberg of *c.*1450, which is a rood-cross made of the *Tree of Life, with the phoenix and the pelican, a lion (*see* BEASTS), and the Symbols of the Evangelists. In *Grünewald's Isenheim Altar this concentration on the suffering of Christ reaches an emotional intensity which perhaps overemphasizes the humanity of Christ, and it is notable that contemporary Italian works are far more restrained. In Spain, on the other hand, during the 16th and 17th centuries a type of polychromed crucifix was developed in accord with Counter-Reformation piety. There was considerable argument over whether three or four nails should be shown—the theologian Suarez said it was impossible to answer, *Molanus left it to the artist's discretion, but the painter and theorist *Pacheco recommended four. An interesting example is the *Christ of Clemency* (Seville Cath.), by the sculptor Montañés under the influence of Pacheco, who was also responsible for the polychromy. The document of commission (1603) has survived, stipulating that Christ should be shown 'alive, before his death... looking down at any who might be praying at His feet... and the eyes wide open'. For this reason, Christ is shown without a wound in His side, since the Gospels make it clear that the centurion's spear-thrust was inflicted to make certain that Christ was already dead.

At this time too, Counter-Reformation feeling was against the earlier crowd scenes, where scores of figures tended to obscure the central action, as with Tintoretto or with the *Sacri Monti. The great Baroque artists, whether Protestants like Rembrandt (*Raising of the Cross*: 1638, Munich, with Christ isolated by a blaze of light from other figures) or Catholics like Velázquez (1631: Prado) and Van Dyck (*c.*1621–5: Naples) concentrate on the figure of Christ, often silhouetted against a dark sky. More contemporary interpretations include *Picasso's depiction of the same subject (1930, Musée Picasso, Paris); *Chagall's *White Crucifixion* (1938, Art Institute, Chicago); Josef Beuys *Montage* of wood, newspaper, nails, telegram, thread, and bottles (1962/65, State Gallery, Stuttgart, Germany); and a painting by Duncan Grant (1942–43, St Michael and All Angels, Berwick, Sussex).

cruet Two small jugs made of glass or precious metal, containing the wine and water to be used for the Eucharist, together with a small bowl of water for the celebrant to rinse his fingers. *See* LITURGICAL VESSELS.

crypt (undercroft) A subterranean chamber, usually vaulted for strength, below the main floor of a church. It is usually below the choir and often housed relics (*see* CONFESSIO). From *Romanesque times, when the level of the choir was raised above that of the nave, especially in *pilgrimage churches, it became possible to build large crypts partly above ground and partly below, which could be lit by windows just above ground level.

cubiculum *See* CATACOMBS.

cupola (Ital.) A dome.

Cuthbert, Saint (*c.*634–87). For centuries the most popular saint in N. England and S. Scotland, he became a monk at Melrose in 651, and, after a short stay in Ripon, became Prior of Melrose *c.*661. Later he was Prior of Lindisfarne and was made Bishop of Hexham, but was allowed to exchange it for Lindisfarne, where he died. Eleven years later his body was found to be incorrupt, but the Danes destroyed Lindisfarne and his shrine was moved about in N. England and Scotland until it was enshrined in Durham in 999. After Durham Cathedral was built it was moved again in 1104, and his body was found to be still incorrupt. This famous shrine was destroyed by the Reformers, but his body was reburied and was re-examined yet again in 1828, when some relics—vestments, a pectoral cross, and an early example of a portable altar—were removed and are now preserved in Durham Cathedral. His Life (Oxford, University College, of the 11th/12th cent.) is the first fully illustrated Life of a saint produced in England. The text is by a monk of Lindisfarne *c.*700, and there is a second Life by Bede, *c.*720, both of which made Cuthbert famous in Europe. The earliest representation of him is a sculpture in Carlisle Cathedral, of the 10th/11th century, and there is a 15th-century window devoted to him in York Minster.

The *Lindisfarne Gospels, by far the most famous work of art associated with Lindisfarne, were written about twenty years after Cuthbert's death.

cypress A pre-Christian symbol of death, since it was believed that once it was cut it would never grow again, and it is often found round churchyards. It was said that coffins were made from cypress wood—'In sad cypress let me be laid . . . ' (Shakespeare, *Twelfth Night*, Act 2, sc. 4). In Early Christian art a palm branch crossed with a cypress branch is a symbol of victory over death or of Christ's Resurrection.

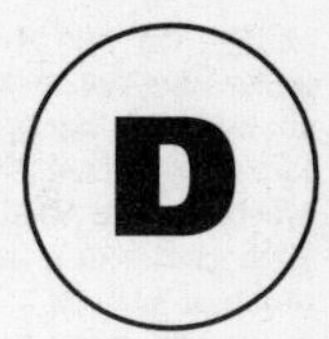

Dalila (Delilah) *See* SAMSON.

dalmatic and tunicle are *vestments. The tunic worn by Roman patricians in the 3rd century reached to below the knee and had wide sleeves, decorated with bands and *clavi. Originally white, it became the distinctive vestment of a deacon (and the smaller tunicle of a subdeacon), and by the 12th century was coloured according to the season. It was stabilized as a short, square-cut tunic, open at the sides, and with *apparels on the front, back, and sleeves.

Damascus, the Road to *See* PAUL, SAINT.

Damian, Saint *See* COSMAS.

Dance of Death (Fr. *Danse macabre*; Ger. *Totentanz*) A late medieval subject, often painted on cemetery walls, showing skeletons forcing living men and women to dance with them—a skeleton pope with a live one, down to pairs of beggars. Usually there are also skeleton musicians and explanatory verses. The earliest known example was in the cemetery of the Holy Innocents in Paris, of 1424/5, later destroyed, but partly known from copies. By far the most famous *Dance* is the series of woodcuts by *Holbein, designed in 1523/6, but not published until 1538, when it was immediately successful. In Italy an earlier form of the same idea—the Three Quick and the Three Dead, probably derived from Petrarch's *Trionfo della Morte*—can be found in the mid-14th century, at the time of the Black Death (*c.*1348). In the Campo Santo at Pisa there are the remains of a fresco attributed to Francesco Traini with the Three Living Kings confronted by three corpses. Where a single skeleton appears with one living person the subject is usually called a *Memento mori.

Daniel One of the five Major Prophets in the OT, with *Elijah, *Ezekiel, *Isaiah, and *Jeremiah. His OT book consists of two parts, a narrative of Daniel and his companions and the miracles worked on their behalf, and some apocalyptic visions containing references to 'the Son of Man', the Archangel Gabriel, and the resurrection of the dead. Apart from the canonical Book of Daniel there are three short accounts in the *Apocrypha—The Song of the Three Holy Children, The Story of *Susanna, and *Bel and the Dragon, all of which are in the Greek OT, but not in the Hebrew version. Daniel was one of four Jewish boys chosen during the Babylonian Captivity to be trained as officials at the court of King *Nebuchadnezzar, the other three being named Shadrach, Meshach, and Abednego. The king had a dream which none of his astrologers could interpret, but which was explained by Daniel: the king saw a great image and '... its appearance was frightening. The head of that statue was of fine gold, its chest and arms of silver, its middle and thighs of brass, its legs of iron, its feet partly of iron and partly of clay. As you looked on a stone was cut out, not by human hands, which struck the statue on its feet of iron and clay and broke them in pieces' (Dan. 2: 31–4). The interpretation was that the golden head was the kingdom of Nebuchadnezzar, which would be succeeded by three others, each inferior to its predecessor, until the kingdom of God 'shall crush all these kingdoms and bring them to an end, and it shall stand for ever'. The king then made Daniel ruler of the province of Babylon and also promoted his three companions. Later, however, Nebuchadnezzar set up a great golden image and commanded all his people to worship it. Daniel's companions, as Jews, refused to do so and were delated to the king, who commanded them to be bound and thrown into a burning fiery furnace, which was so hot that the heat from it killed the executioners who threw them in. 'Then King Nebuchadnezzar was astonished, and rose up quickly. He said to his counsellors, "Was it not three men that we threw bound into the fire?" They answered the king, "True, O king." He replied, "But I see four men unbound, walking in the middle of the fire, and they are not hurt; and the fourth has the appearance of a god." Nebuchadnezzar then approached the door of the furnace of blazing fire, and said, "Shadrach, Meshach, and Abednego, servants of the Most High God, come out! Come here!" So Shadrach, Meshach, and Abednego, came out from the fire' (3: 2–6). Nebuchadnezzar then had another dream, of a huge tree reaching up to heaven, and visible to the ends of the earth, but a holy one came down from heaven and ordered it to be cut down, leaving only a stump. Daniel again interpreted this as a warning to the king—who was the tree—that unless he mended his ways, 'You shall be driven from human society, and your dwelling shall be with the wild animals. You shall be made to eat grass like oxen.' This happened, but Nebuchadnezzar's reason was restored to him (ch. 4). He was succeeded by his son, *Belshazzar, who gave a great feast at which an unknown hand wrote on the wall *Mene, mene, tekel,* and *parsin,* which only Daniel could understand and interpret as a warning, and 'that very night Belshazzar the Chaldean king was killed. And Darius the Mede took the kingdom' (ch. 5). Men jealous of Daniel's position prevailed upon Darius to issue a decree 'according to the law of the Medes and Persians, which cannot be revoked', forbidding prayer to anyone except Darius for thirty days, on pain of being thrown into a den of lions, but Daniel was seen to pray to God three times a day. Darius regretted his order but could not alter it, so Daniel was cast into a den of lions. Darius sealed the mouth of the den and passed a sleepless night. Then at daybreak he hurried to the den of lions and found Daniel unharmed. He said, 'My God sent his angel and shut the lion's mouths . . . because I was found blameless before him; . . . O king, I have done no wrong.' He was taken out of the den, and Darius commanded that those who had accused Daniel, should be thrown into the den of lions, with their children, and their wives (ch. 6). Additional details are given in the apocryphal books known as the Song of the Three Holy Children, Bel and the Dragon, which has the story of the lions' den and also another relating Daniel's exposure of fraud by the priests of Bel. The Story of Susanna is perhaps the best-known and most frequently painted incident in the history of Daniel, in spite of its absence from the Book of Daniel itself.

Representations of Daniel with lions occur in the earliest Christian catacombs and as late as 1849, by Delacroix (Montpellier); but that may have been an opportunity to paint lions, as Susanna certainly was an opportunity to paint a female nude. With three other Major Prophets he occurs on the Sistine Ceiling by Michelangelo, and often in groups of statuary, sometimes identified simply by a scroll with his name. There is a large and beautiful painting in Glasgow, which may be by Giorgione or Titian, and may represent *Christ and the Adulteress* or *Daniel proving Susanna's innocence,* but there is also a representation of Daniel in a stone relief from Ein Samsam Synagogue Archaeological Museum of the 4th or 5th century AD in Golan, Katzrin, Israel.

Dante Alighieri (1265–1321), the greatest of Italian poets, was a Florentine, exiled in 1301, who died in Ravenna after completing his *Divine Comedy* (the title is not his). The poem, in three parts and 100 Cantos, is intended as a guide to salvation and describes (*Inferno*) Hell as an abyss of nine descending circles, beginning with *Limbo and ending in the frozen lake reserved for traitors. The second and third Books (*Purgatorio* and *Paradiso*) describe the Earthly Paradise, concluding in the Beatific Vision. Dante's vision of Hell, far more sympathetic than the disgusting lingered-over horrors of a *Tundal or *S. Bridget, exercised great influence over Italian, and indeed European, art: major examples are *Botticelli's drawings to illustrate the *Divine Comedy* (Berlin and the Vatican) and *Blake's illustrations.

Dathan *See* KORAH.

David, Gerard (d. 1523), was born in Holland, but was active in Bruges from 1484, continuing the tradition of gently pietistic *Madonnas* established there by Hans *Memlinc. In 1498 he painted two large pictures for the Justice Hall in Bruges, representing the grisly legend of Sisamnes, a corrupt judge who was flayed alive and his skin used to cover the seat occupied by his son, also a judge. David's only fully documented work is that of the *Virgo inter Virgines (1509: Rouen, Mus.), which he gave to the Carmelite convent in Bruges, where his daughter was a nun. The Justice scenes are also interesting because they include Renaissance ornament of garlands held by 'putti' over the Judge's throne.

David, the second OT King of Israel (d. *c.*970 BC). With *Moses a *type of Christ, and an ancestor of the Messiah who was 'of the house and lineage of David'. He is also venerated as the author of the Psalms, or at least of the seventy-three which are specified as 'of David'. His story, full of violence, deceit, lust, and murder, is told at length in four books of the OT: in the NRSV 1 Sam. 16 to the end, the whole of 2 Samuel, and 1 Kgs. 1 and 2. There is a variant version in 1 Chron. from ch. 10 to the end. (In the Vulgate the Books are 1, 2, and 3 Kgs. and 1 Paralip.). A portrait of the king is seen in the Syriac translation of the Book of Kings (Syria, 7th century, ink and gold on parchment, the Holy Monastery of St Catherine, Sinai, Egypt).

David was the youngest son of *Jesse, to whom the Lord sent the Prophet *Samuel after King *Saul had lost God's favour and been rejected by Samuel. Samuel was told to anoint a son of Jesse as the future king of Israel, the actual son to be pointed out to Samuel by God. He sent for seven sons in turn, but rejected them all. He was then told that the youngest, David, was in the fields herding his father's sheep and he demanded that he should be sent for at once. This was the Lord's anointed. Some time later Saul's unstable temperament cast him into depression and music was recommended as a cure. David was a skilled musician (traditionally a harpist) and he was brought to the court and succeeded in soothing the king. He became Saul's armour-bearer, and, when Saul was at war with the Philistines, the Philistine champion Goliath challenged any of Saul's warriors to single combat. No one was anxious to take up the challenge, since Goliath was a fearsome warrior 'whose height was six cubits and a span'—i.e. more than nine feet. David asked to be allowed to fight him and told how, while keeping his father's sheep, he had killed both a lion and a bear. He was offered armour and a sword but refused both and took only his sling and five carefully chosen stones. After exchanging insults 'David put his hand in his bag, and took out a stone, and slung it, and struck the Philistine on his forehead; the stone sank into his forehead, and he fell face down on the ground.' David, not being weighed down by armour, rushed up, seized Goliath's own sword, and cut off his head. The Philistines were so overcome that they fled in a rout, pursued by David and the Israelite army, and David returned in triumph. Unfortunately, 'the women came out of all the towns of Israel, singing and dancing, to meet King Saul, with tambourines, with joy, and with musical instruments'. They sang 'Saul has killed his thousands, and David his ten thousands. Saul was very angry, for this saying displeased him.' Jonathan, Saul's son, and Michal, his daughter, helped David when Saul tried to kill him by throwing a javelin at him. Jonathan tried to reconcile his father to David, whom 'he loved as his own soul', but after another attempt to transfix him with a javelin David realized he must flee and Michal, to whom he was now married, let him out of a window by night and put a dummy in his bed to conceal his absence. After another attempt at reconciliation Saul threw a javelin at his own son, and Jonathan realized that they must part. David took refuge in the cave at Adullam and soon gathered about 400 men. Saul was still pursuing him, and on one occasion was sleeping in a cave in which David and his men were also hidden, but David steadfastly refused to kill Saul, the Lord's anointed, and did no more than cut off the hem of his robe to show that he had had him in his power. Saul confessed 'You are more righteous than I' and then went home.

David and his men lived more or less by exacting tribute, but his request to Nabal, a rich farmer, was contemptuously refused. His wife Abigail was warned that David would use force, so she hurried, and took two hundred loaves, two skins of wine, and five sheep ready dressed, and five measures of parched grain, one hundred clusters of raisins, and two hundred cakes of figs, and sent them to David, without telling Nabal. David met her and was placated by her. Nabal himself was very drunk that night, and when Abigail told him next morning what she had done he had a stroke and died about ten days later. David then married her, his first wife Michal having been given by Saul to another.

Once again, Saul pursued David to destroy him, and once again David and a companion crept into Saul's camp by night, taking away Saul's own spear and the pitcher of water by his head. Finally, Saul was at war with the Philistines and was so afraid of their army that he consulted a witch at Endor, who brought up the spirit of Samuel. Samuel told Saul that the kingdom had been given to David, and that on the next day 'you and your sons will be with me'. David, who was then serving with the Philistines, was not trusted by all of them and was sent away, only to find that his camp had been burned and all the wives and children taken away by Amalekites. With 400 men David pursued and routed them, recovering his own two wives and all the others. Meanwhile the Philistines defeated the Israelites and pursued Saul and his sons. They killed Jonathan, and his two brothers, and the archers hit Saul and wounded him severely. He ordered his armour-bearer to kill him, so that he should not fall alive into the hands of the Philistines, but his armour-bearer refused so Saul took a sword and fell upon it. 'So Saul died, and his three sons, and his armour-bearer, and all his men, that same day together.'

The second Book of Samuel (Vg. 2 Kgs.) tells the story of David, King of Israel, and his sons Amnon and Absalom, as well as David's adultery with Bathsheba. David reigned as King of Israel for 40 years, 33 of them in Jerusalem, which he captured, as his capital city, and to which he brought back the *Ark of the Covenant. On its return he danced before it, clad only in a linen ephod, incurring the scorn of his first wife Michal. He hoped to rebuild the Temple, but this was in fact done by his son *Solomon.

'Late one afternoon, when David ... was walking about on the roof of the king's house, ... he saw from the roof a woman bathing; the woman was very beautiful': she was Bathsheba, the wife of Uriah the Hittite, one of David's generals, and David 'lay with her ... and the woman conceived'. David recalled Uriah from the war and told him to go home and rest, but Uriah would not sleep with his wife as David had hoped, so he was sent back to the battlefield with a letter to the commander saying, 'Set Uriah in the forefront of the hottest fighting, and draw back from him, so that he may be struck down and die.' This murderous plot succeeded, Uriah was killed, and David married Bathsheba, but the Lord sent Nathan to reprove David and prophesy that the child Bathsheba was carrying would die and 'the sword shall never depart from your house'. Later, however, Bathsheba conceived again and that child was Solomon, David's successor.

David had two older sons, Absalom and Amnon. Absalom's sister was Tamar, and Amnon fell passionately in love with her, so he pretended to be ill and asked her to make him some cakes and feed him, whereupon he raped her and immediately he loathed her and had her put out of the house. Two years later Absalom gave a feast, and when Amnon was drunk he had him killed. Later, Absalom rebelled against David, but was defeated and the mule he was riding 'went under the thick branches of a great oak. His head caught fast in the oak, and he was left hanging between heaven and earth, while the mule that was under him went on.' He was found and killed by Joab, David's general. David died soon afterwards, nominating his son Solomon as his successor.

From the earliest times David was a favourite subject for artists, possibly because of his Messianic importance to Jews and Christians alike. The earliest known representations of him are in the Catacomb of Calixtus (3rd cent.) and on the wooden doors of Sant'Ambrogio, Milan (4th cent., very damaged). He was a favourite subject for Byzantine artists as well as in the West, where *psalters, mainly in the Beatus of the first page of the Psalms, almost always have a frontispiece of him crowned and playing his harp: many have illustrations from his story throughout the text (e.g. a MS in the Pierpont Morgan Library, New York). Another favourite subject was the Jesse Tree, showing the genealogy of Christ from the 'house and lineage of David'. The most popular subject, however, was David killing Goliath, from the Calixtus Catacomb onwards, and especially among sculptors. One panel of the Baptistery Doors by *Ghiberti (before 1447) is devoted to the defeat of the Philistines, with David killing Goliath in the foreground. Ghiberti's contemporary *Donatello created the first free-standing bronze nude since antiquity as his enigmatic *David*. The similar bronze by Verrocchio dates from the late 15th century, but the most famous of all single figures is the huge marble *David* by *Michelangelo (1504: Florence, Accad.), which is the epitome of High Renaissance classicism. The contrast with the tempestuous Baroque energy of *Bernini's *David* (1623: Rome, Borghese) could hardly be greater. In the 17th century the beheading of Goliath was an extremely popular subject, often deriving from Caravaggio's painting of 1605 (Rome, Borghese), which shows David holding up the severed head. Versions of this were produced by Caravaggio's followers all over Europe. (In many cases the severed head is a self-portrait—it certainly is in the case of the Caravaggio.) An unusual variant is the *Triumph of David* by Poussin (London, Dulwich), which represents the head of Goliath carried on a pole into Jerusalem, with musicians and the women singing, which so enraged Saul.

The story of David is so full of incidents that more than 60 have been recorded as subjects for painting, sculpture, and MS illumination, but, next to Goliath, probably the most popular is Bathsheba bathing. In the biblical text she is described merely as washing herself (*mulierem se lavantem*), and the earliest representations mostly show no more than bare feet, but, like *Susanna, the subject offered a chance to paint the nude and this was soon exploited e.g. by Memlinc (Stuttgart), in a painting which may have had a *Susanna* as a pendant. The subject was again popular in the 17th century, and there is a great Rembrandt (1654: Paris, Louvre) of Bathsheba pensively considering David's letter of invitation.

DD (dd), DDD (ddd) The first is Latin for 'he gave as a gift' (*donum dedit*); the second 'gives, devotes, and dedicates' (*dat, dicat, dedicat*). These are common in classical pagan inscriptions and were taken over by the Christians, in which case the first D usually stands for *Deo*—'he gave to God', or 'he gave as a gift consecrated to God'.

deacon *See* ORDERS, HOLY.

Deadly Sins, the Seven These are Pride, Avarice, Lust, Envy, Gluttony, Anger, and Sloth (*accidie*). They are rarely represented individually, but often in conjunction with the *virtues. There is, however, a painted table-top by *Bosch (Madrid, Prado) which represents the Deadly Sins alone. Some of them were included by *Giotto in the Arena Chapel frescoes.

deambulatoria (deambulacra) A covered walkway, of classical origin, surrounding the body of a church, like the one built by Constantine round the Holy Sepulchre in Jerusalem. It is very similar to an *ambulatory, and, like it, may have altars. Sometimes used as a synonym for a cloister. The French is 'déambulatoire'.

Death, Dance of *See* DANCE.

Death of the Virgin *See* DORMITION.

decade *See* ROSARY.

Decalogue The Ten *Commandments.

Decollation of the Baptist The beheading (Lat. *decollare*) of *S. John, by order of *Herod, to please his wife, Herodias, the head being brought to the feast by *Salome (Matt. 14: 3–12; Mark 6: 17–29), who asked for it, at her mother's instigation, as a reward for her dancing. The feast of the Baptist's martyrdom is celebrated on 29 August; he is one of the few saints to have two feasts, the other being for his birth on 24 June. The word 'decollation' is usually associated with the Baptist, but may also be applied to other saints martyred in this way, e.g. *SS James of Compostela, *Denis, and *Catherine of Alexandria.

decorum The idea that the figures, gestures, dress, and surroundings should be appropriate to the subject-matter, especially in religious art. In the Counter-Reformation period this was extended to cover the proposition that what might be appropriate in an allegorical ceiling for a palace (e.g. female nudes) would not be proper in an altarpiece. At its final session in 1563 the Council of *Trent passed a decree on music and images, stating that musical settings were not to be so elaborate that the words could not be clearly heard and understood, and reaffirming the decree of the Second Council of *Nicaea on the legitimacy of the veneration of images as 'through the saints the miracles of God and salutary examples are set before the eyes of the faithful' but, nevertheless, all superstition should be removed and all lasciviousness avoided, and all works of art intended for churches had to be executed either under the supervision of the bishop, or passed by him as suitable. The controversy over what was acceptable had been a matter of aesthetic debate for many years, most notably in the 1540s, after the unveiling of *Michelangelo's *Last Judgement* in the Sistine Chapel. The nudity of the figures was severely criticized, because it was in the Pope's own domestic chapel, although it was accepted that few people will be fully dressed when the Last Trump sounds. The classic defence of the artist was offered by *Veronese in 1573, when he was summoned before the Venetian Inquisition to explain his huge painting for SS Giovanni e Paolo in Venice (now in the Accademia). The record has survived, and it seems to show that the painting was originally intended as a *Last Supper*. Veronese refers to it as 'the Last Supper of Jesus Christ with His Apostles in the House of Simon' and says it is about 40 feet wide. The Inquisitor asked why he had included a man with a nose-bleed, soldiers dressed in the German fashion, and a buffoon with a parrot, and he replied that he claimed the same licence as poets, to add such things as he felt necessary, and in this case he had a large space to fill. He admitted that at the Last Supper only Christ and the Apostles were present, but he quoted Michelangelo's *Last Judgement* as a precedent for artistic licence. In the end he was told to 'correct and amend' his picture, and it seems that he did so by simply re-titling it *The Feast in the House of Levi*.

Among the writers concerned with decorum in the visual arts, including architecture, were *Amannati, Carlo and Federigo *Borromeo, *Cataneo, *Gilio, *Molanus, and *Paleotti. The desire not to offend against propriety led to the vapid inanity and over-blown theatricality of much 17th- to 19th-century religious art, including that known as *bondieuserie*. In the early 17th century *Caravaggio was attacked for the 'low' realism of his sacred subjects, specifically the awkwardness of the Evangelist *Matthew, unaccustomed to writing, and having his hand guided by an angel; the dirty feet and sweaty headcloths of the peasants adoring the Child in the *Madonna of Loreto*; and the treatment of the *Death of the Virgin*. Nevertheless, it is this sense of actuality which informs much of the best religious art of the period.

dedication crosses *See* CONSECRATION.

deer *See* HART.

Deësis, Deisis (Gk. humble petition) A representation of Christ seated, with the Madonna on His right and the Baptist on His left, with their hands outstretched, interceding for the human race. The earliest known example is in Sta Maria Antiqua, Rome, of the 7th century, but from the 10th century it was a common subject in the East, as in the 12th-century mosaic in Sta *Sophia. On an *iconostasis it is normally placed immediately above the Royal Doors. In the West it gradually became the central part of a *Last Judgement*, as in the *portal sculpture at Amiens or Mainz cathedrals, or as part of an Apocalyptic subject, as in Jan van *Eyck's Ghent Altar. Strictly speaking, a Deësis consists of these three figures only—other saints alter the subject, although in Russia S. Nicholas is often substituted for the Baptist.

Delilah (Dalila) *See* SAMSON.

Delivery of the Law *See* TRADITIO LEGIS.

Deluge *See* NOAH.

De Mille, Cecil B. and early pioneers *See* FILM.

Demoniac, Healing of the There are many references in both OT and NT to demonic possession, but three of Christ's miracles of healing are usually considered under this heading. First, He gave power to the Apostles, which they exercised in His name (cf. Acts). See Matt. 10: 1; Mark 3: 10; Luke 9: 1. Second, the Gadarene Swine: Matt. 8: 28 ff.; Mark 5: 1 ff.; Luke 8: 26 ff. Third, the boy healed immediately after the *Transfiguration: Matt. 17: 14 ff.; Mark 9: 17 ff.; Luke 9: 38 ff. *Raphael's last work, the *Transfiguration* (Vatican Mus.) shows this immediately below the scene of the Transfiguration itself.

demons Belief in evil, as well as good, spirits is very ancient. In classical Greece the souls in Hades (*see* UNDERWORLD) were represented as small winged figures (*eidola) and these were transmuted into demons in the Middle Ages. Representations of such evil spirits are rare in Early Christian art, where the *Devil is usually shown as a serpent (as in the Garden of Eden), often with a human head, but the idea of demons as assistants to the Devil—the fallen angels under Lucifer—was very popular in the Middle Ages, especially in Last Judgement scenes on cathedral *portals. Such demons take numerous, highly imaginative, forms, usually half-human, half-animal, grinning ferociously as they herd the damned into Hell. Other forms of demons are asps, basilisks, dragons, Harpies, and Sirens (often with a tail in each hand). The legend of the Temptation of *S. Antony gave occasion for inventive fantasy, especially in the work of Northern artists such as *Bosch and *Bruegel.

Denis (Denys, Dionysius), Saint (d. *c*.250). A patron saint of France, whose cult was widespread there, and in the Low Countries, Spain, and Germany, especially after the 9th century, when he was disingenuously confused with the Dionysius converted by S. Paul in Athens, thus giving a spurious antiquity to the Church in France. This story was given wide circulation from the 13th century by the account in the **Golden Legend*. Denis was in fact an Italian missionary in Gaul, who settled with two companions on an island in the Seine and became Bishop of Paris, but was martyred by the pagans on what is now Montmartre. After he was beheaded he carried his own head some two miles to the spot on which the Abbey of *Saint-Denis was later founded, and which became the burial church of the kings of France. He is represented as a bishop, sometimes with a mitre on his head and carrying a second head, sometimes beheaded but carrying his head. Many French and Belgian churches have paintings, sculpture, or stained-glass windows representing him, as well as St-Denis itself. An altarpiece commissioned in 1416 by the Duke of Burgundy for his own abbey at Champmol, near Dijon, is now in the Louvre.

Denis, Maurice (1870–1943) A French painter and creator of cartoons for frescoes, stained glass, and mosaic. He was a member of the Institut français and of the Nabi group of (mainly French) painters. He became an important theoretician of fine art. Haunted by the mawkishness and archaizing tendency of so-called Sulpician religious art, in contrast he sought sincerity, luminosity, and joy using an iconography of restrained realism. He became the great master of religious art after founding with Georges Desvallières the *Ateliers d'art sacré* ('studios of sacred art') in 1919. Important commissions followed, both public (the ceiling of the Théâtre des Champs Elysées, 1912), and religious (eight windows for Le Raincy, 1924). He was particularly talented at directing teams of artists who worked on the decoration of buildings in construction (Holy Spirit, Paris, 1933–34). A tireless visitor to salons and exhibitions, he was responsible for the opening of a religious art section at the Salon d'automne.

Deposition from the Cross, the The account in the Gospels of the taking down of the body of Jesus from the Cross (also called Descent from the Cross) is in all four Gospels. Mark (15: 42–7) says: 'When evening had come, and since it was the day of Preparation, that is, the day before the sabbath, Joseph of Arimathaea, a respected member of the council, who was also himself waiting expectantly for the kingdom of God, went boldly to Pilate, and asked for the body of Jesus. Then Pilate wondered if he were already dead; and summoning the centurion, he asked him whether he had been dead for some time. When he learned from the centurion that he was dead, he granted the body to Joseph. Then Joseph bought a fine linen cloth, and taking down the body, wrapped it in the linen cloth, and laid it in a tomb that had been hewn out of the rock. He then rolled a stone against the door of the tomb. Mary Magdalene and Mary the mother of Joses saw where the body was laid.' Matthew (27: 57–66) and Luke (23: 50–5) have similar accounts, but John (19: 39–42) adds: 'Nicodemus . . . also came bringing a mixture of myrrh and aloes, weighing about a hundred pounds. They took the body of Jesus and wrapped it with the spices in linen cloths, according to the burial custom of the Jews. Now there was a garden in the place where he was crucified, and in the garden there was a new tomb in which no one had ever been laid. And so, because it was the Jewish day of Preparation, and the tomb was nearby, they laid Jesus there.' Because the next day was a great feast the body had to be buried before sunset to avoid defilement, but the stages between the death of Christ on the Cross and His actual burial came to be extended in works like the *Apocryphal Acts of Pilate or Gospel of Nicodemus (which is much the same thing) and in medieval works of devotion, such as the **Meditationes Vitae Christi*. From the 9th century in Byzantium and the 10th/11th in the West this subject became very popular, ending up as the 13th *Station of the Cross. In the development from the Crucifixion to the Entombment various stages were made—Deposition, Lamentation (and later *Pietà*), Bearing of the Body, *Unction (EPITAPHIOS), Setting of the Guard on the Sepulchre. Originally there were Joseph and the two Maries, but later many other figures were added—the Blessed Virgin, Nicodemus, John, and various servants of Joseph. By the 13th/14th century the emotional aspects were heavily stressed, both in the *Meditationes* (in Italy) and in works like the **Golden Legend* (in the North). The *Meditationes* has: 'Attend diligently and carefully to the manner of the Deposition. Two ladders are placed on opposite sides of the cross. Joseph ascends the ladder placed on the right side and tries to extract the nail from His hand. But this is difficult, because the long, heavy nail is fixed firmly into the wood; and it does not seem possible to do it without great pressure on the hand of the Lord. Yet it is not brutal, because he acts faithfully; and the Lord accepts everything. The nail pulled out, John makes a sign to Joseph to extend the said nail to him, that the Lady [i.e. Mary] might not see it. Afterwards Nicodemus extracts the other nail from the left hand and similarly gives it to John. Nicodemus descends and comes to the nail in the feet. Joseph supported the body of the Lord: happy indeed is this Joseph, who deserves thus to embrace the body of the Lord! Then the Lady reverently receives the hanging right hand and places it against her cheek, gazes upon it and kisses it with heavy tears and sorrowful sighs. The nail in the feet pulled out, Joseph descends part way, and all receive the body of the Lord and place it on the ground. The Lady supports the head and shoulders in her lap, the Magdalene the feet, at which she had formerly found so much grace. The others stand about, all making a great bewailing over Him . . .' This description is closely followed in contemporary paintings, such as *Duccio's *Maestà* or the version of it by Ugolino di Nerio (London, NG). By the 15th century the scene becomes a theme for meditation rather than a record of an event, as in the altarpiece by Fra Angelico (Florence, San Marco) and the contemporary *Escorial Deposition* by Roger van der *Weyden (Prado). The theme was popular again in the early 17th century, as in the great Rubens altarpiece in Antwerp Cathedral of 1611–14. It is also seen in Max Beckmann's etching (1918), and a telling rendering by Ceri Richards (1960) hangs in St Mary's, Swansea, Wales.

De' Rossi *See* ROSSI.

Descent from the Cross *See* DEPOSITION.

Descent into Hell (Limbo) *See* LIMBO.

Descent of the Holy Spirit *See* PENTECOST.

Desert Fathers *See* THEBAID.

Deutero-Canonical books of the Bible These are books of the OT which are called *Apocrypha in Protestant Bibles (e.g. the Authorized and Revised Versions), but which are included in the *Vulgate. They are 1 and 2 Esdras, Tobias, Judith, Wisdom, Ecclesiasticus, Baruch, Prayer of Manasses, 1 and 2 Maccabees, part of Esther, and part of Daniel. They contain many stories, e.g. Susanna and the Elders, Tobias and the Angel, Judith and Holofernes, which have been represented by generations of painters and sculptors and are universally regarded as part of Christian subject-matter. *See also* APOCRYPHAL GOSPELS.

Devil, the (Satan, Beelzebub, Lucifer) The ancient world had evil spirits or *demons (*see also* EIDOLON), so the idea of a Prince of Devils was easily accepted. At the very beginning of the OT (Gen. 3: 1 ff.) the serpent, 'more crafty than any other wild animal', tempted Eve; although not explicitly stated this was understood as the work of the Devil. In Job (1: 6 and elsewhere) the tempter is called Satan, a name also found in Jewish non-biblical writings. In the NT (Matt. 4: 1–11) Christ is 'tempted by the devil', whom He addressed as Satan. Lucifer as the leader of the fallen angels is derived from Isaiah (14: 12) and Rev. (12: 7–9)—'there was war in heaven: Michael and his angels fought against the dragon . . . and the great dragon was cast out, that old serpent called the Devil, and Satan, which deceiveth the whole world'. During the Middle Ages there was considerable speculation, especially among the Franciscans and Dominicans, as to whether minor devils were the children of fallen angels and human women. The earliest representations show devils as basically human, but with wings and usually dark blue or purplish in colour—the earliest example of a blue angel is in the 6th-century mosaic of *Christ separating the Sheep from the Goats* (Ravenna, Sant'Apollinare Nuovo), where the angel appears with the goats. Later, devils are common in *Last Judgement* scenes, especially from the 11th century onwards, in Romanesque and Gothic *portals. These are usually horrid monsters, often presided over by a semi-human creature with an animal head. Later, they may also be represented as monks or women, but with give-away little horns and cloven hooves peeping out from their skirts. Medieval fantasy reached a climax in the 15th and 16th centuries with *Bosch, *Bruegel, and *Grünewald, when the Devil was also portrayed as black. Dürer's engraving of 1513, *The Knight, Death, and the Devil*, and Grünewald's *Temptation of S. Antony* are perhaps the end of this series. On the whole, Italian 16th-century artists avoided such Gothic fantasies, and *Signorelli's devils in his Orvieto frescoes are the more frightening for being all too human. Jacob *Epstein's rendering (1958) outside Coventry Cathedral continues in this tradition.

The Devil is also represented symbolically by various animals—the serpent, often with a human head, as in Hugo van der *Goes's *Temptation of Eve* (Vienna KHM); a dragon, or a lion (1 Pet. 5: 8): 'Like a roaring lion, your adversary the devil prowls around, seeking someone to devour.'

Dextera Domini (Dei) Latin for the right hand of the Lord (or God). An early way of symbolizing God the Father, e.g. in Creation scenes, was by a hand appearing in the sky. It was also used in Baptism and Annunciation scenes: a good example is the ivory relief in Munich of the *Ascension*, *c*.400, in which Christ reaches upwards to clasp the extended hand appearing from a cloud. In Annunciation scenes it survived into the 15th century.

Diaconicon (diakonikon) In the E. Orthodox Church the equivalent of a *sacristy. It is usually a small apse or chamber to the right of the altar, the *prothesis being to the left.

diastyla A **cancello* or partition, separating the *bema from the nave in an E. Orthodox church.

dikerion (dicerion) A two-light candlestick, symbolizing the Two Natures of Christ, used by Greek Orthodox bishops to bless the people. *See also* TRIKERION.

Diocesan Advisory Committee for the care of churches (DAC). *See* FACULTY CONSENT.

Diocletian Roman Emperor from 284 to 305, when he retired to his native Dalmatia. He was a great administrator but an implacable enemy of Christianity. He began the last, and worst, of the persecutions in 303, especially in Palestine and Egypt, which *Eusebius witnessed. The persecution stopped in the West in 306, but dragged on in the East until 311, and ended only with the Edict of *Milan in 313. Probably much Early Christian art was destroyed in the persecutions, but one important effect was the development and use of 'neutral' subject-matter, which could have a non-Christian sense if necessary.

Dionysius of Furna 'The Painter's Manual of Mount Athos' (*Hermeneia*) was thought to be a Byzantine treatise on the painting of *icons and frescoes when it was first published in the mid-19th century. It is actually by Dionysius of Furna, who was active in the mid-18th century, but it may well reflect much earlier practices—some of it derives from a similar manual of 1556. Nevertheless, it has misled many into thinking it characteristic of the best period of Byzantine art. Book I describes technical procedures; II, biblical subjects; III, Saints; and IV, the arrangement of paintings in churches.

diptych (from Gk. *diptyches*, two tablets) A pair of tablets hinged together to open like a book. Originally the two inner leaves were covered with wax and used to write on. **Consular diptychs** are panels of ivory elaborately carved and given by newly appointed consuls to friends: they usually have a portrait of the consul and his name, so they can be closely dated up to 541, when the office was abolished. Some surviving examples may be late 4th century and have pagan subject-matter, others are Christian, and some have been converted to Christian purposes. The meaning of the word changed in the early Church, when the custom grew up of reading the names of benefactors, living and dead, during the Mass. These names were inscribed on diptychs, but very soon the list of names grew too long and the practice was abandoned. Many diptychs were made into book-covers, especially fine ivory ones, which could be adapted and sometimes made up from several pieces. Painted diptychs occur very early as icons and became common in Italy from the 13th century. Probably the most familiar examples are small panel paintings by 15th-century Flemish artists such as *Memlinc, where the right-hand panel shows a Madonna and Child and the left has a portrait of the owner in prayer, often accompanied by his or her patron saint. On the back of the portrait panel there is often a coat of arms which may help to locate and date the diptych.

discalced (Lat. *discalceatus*, unshod) Literally, bare-footed; but usually meaning wearing sandals. Certain austere Orders, particularly the Observant *Franciscans and the Reformed *Carmelites, have practised this since the 16th century.

Disciples of Christ Not the same as *Apostles or *Evangelists, although both Apostles and Evangelists were disciples. According to Luke (10: 1), 'After this the Lord appointed seventy others [i.e. as well as the Apostles] and sent them on ahead of him in pairs to every town and place . . .'. Luke 9: 1 also has 'Then Jesus called the twelve together and gave them power and authority over all demons and to cure diseases', but in the Vulgate there is a distinction: this passage reads 'Convocatis autem duodecim apostolis' whereas the other passage has only 'et alios septuaginta duos et misit illos binos ante faciem suam' ('He then called the twelve apostles' and 'and another seventy-two and sent them in pairs before him'. This number is repeated in Luke 10: 17, which says 'Reversi sunt autem septuaginta duo' ('When the seventy-two returned'). NRSV notes the discrepancy in a footnote.

discus (diskos) In the E. Orthodox Church a large metal dish with a rim, sometimes mounted on a foot, which is the equivalent of the paten in the West, though considerably larger. It frequently has a *Last Supper* engraved on it. *See* LITURGICAL VESSELS.

Dismas is named in the *Apocryphal Gospel of Nicodemus (or Acts of Pilate) as the Good Thief, who was crucified on the right side of Christ: the Bad Thief was Gestas. The same Apocryphal Gospel names the centurion as *Longinus.

Dispensation, the Old and New The *Covenant given by God to Israel corresponds to the Old Testament, which is shared by Synagogue and Church, whereas under Christ the New Dispensation is set forth in the New Testament.

Dives and Lazarus This is one of the few *parables represented fairly frequently in art; Dives (Lat. a rich man) is recorded in Luke 16: 19–31 as *Homo erat dives*, i.e. a rich man, not necessarily named Dives, who lived luxuriously, while Lazarus, the beggar covered in sores, lay at his gate hoping for crumbs. After both were dead, Dives, in Hell, saw Lazarus 'afar off in Abraham's bosom': he pleaded with Abraham to send Lazarus to warn his living brothers of the fate awaiting the selfish and uncharitable, but Abraham said that they had Moses and the Prophets, and if they would not listen to them, neither would they listen even though 'one rose from the dead' to warn them. This is regarded as referring to the other *Lazarus, raised from the dead by Christ, who also prefigures the Resurrection. Dives is also taken as a *type of Gluttony (*Gula*), one of the Seven *Deadly Sins. The words 'in Abraham's bosom' are often represented quite literally in medieval *portal sculpture, for instance at Moissac.

Divine, representations of the Early Christian art was influenced by the Jewish prohibition in the First Commandment—which was not always observed by Hellenized Jews (cf. *Dura-Europos). The commandment, however, forbids the worship of 'an idol' (Vg. has 'a graven thing') rather than the making of images as such (*see* ICONOCLASM). Nevertheless, the earliest Christians were wary of representing Divinity, although Christ as Man was obviously permissible, and the symbolizing of the Holy Spirit as a dove or as tongues of fire has explicit biblical sanction (John 1: 32 and Acts 2: 3–4). As early as the 3rd century, at Dura-Europos, there is a hand appearing in the sky as the Hand of God (*Dextera Domini), and this symbol also occurs in a mosaic in Sta Maria Maggiore, Rome, and in several sarcophagi, as well as at San Vitale, Ravenna (Ezek. 2: 9 'a hand was stretched out to me and a written scroll was in it'). In NT scenes, the Baptism of Christ, the Ascension, and Pentecost may contain examples of the Hand of God as well as the dove of the Holy Spirit. In OT scenes, e.g. the Creation, there is a hand in the 6th-century *Vienna Genesis. The condemnation of Arianism (325) meant that an image of the Son is a 'translated image' of the Father, based on a conflation of John 14: 9 and 10: 30—'whoever has seen me has seen the Father' and 'The Father and I are one', as in the 6th-century Ravenna mosaic in San Michele in Africisco. A 9th-century Psalter (Stuttgart) shows two identical figures, one with a plain halo and one with a cross on it, but this type was condemned, e.g. by S. Augustine. From about the 7th century the image of God the Father as the Ancient of Days, an old man with a beard, gradually becomes general and is often assimilated to the antique Olympian Jove in Renaissance art.

DNJC (Lat.) abbreviation for *Dominus noster Jesus Christus* (Our Lord Jesus Christ) or, more commonly, *Domini nostri Jesu Christi* (of Our Lord . . .).

Doctors, Christ among the This is the only incident from the childhood of Christ recorded in the Gospels (not counting some highly coloured stories in various *Apocryphal Gospels). S. Luke (2: 41–51) alone tells how He went with Joseph and Mary to Jerusalem for the Passover when He was 12 years old. On the return journey they thought He was among the travellers, and went a day's journey before they looked for Him among the others. When they did not find Him, they returned to Jerusalem . . . and found Him 'in the temple, sitting among the teachers, listening to them and asking them questions. And all who heard him were amazed at his understanding and his answers. And when they saw him they were astonished; and his mother said to him, "Child, why have you treated us like this? . . . your father and I have been searching for you in great anxiety." He said to them, "Why were you searching for me? Did you not know that I must be in my Father's house?"' The scene is rarely represented, and only three early examples are known—two ivories, in Milan and the British Museum, and an illustration in the *Gospels of S. Augustine*, c.600, in Cambridge (Corpus Christi Coll.). In the 14th/15th centuries *Giotto, *Duccio, and Fra *Angelico all show Christ seated 'among the teachers' but in the later Middle Ages there tended to be more emphasis on Joseph and Mary's anxiety and subsequent relief, so the scene came to be counted as one of the Seven *Joys of Mary. This is very explicit in the **Meditationes Vitae Christi*. The small panel of 1342 by Simone *Martini (Liverpool, Walker Gall.), which shows the boy Christ returning with His parents—'Then he went down with them, and came to Nazareth, and was obedient to them'—seems to be the only rendering of the subject. The same theme is also seen in William Holman Hunt's *The Finding of the Saviour in the Temple* (1854–60, Birmingham Museum and Art Gallery).

Doctors of the Church Usually this means the great theologians of the early Church, four Greek and four Latin. The Fathers of the Church are easily confused with them, since some are to be found under both names, but the Fathers are a mixed group of writers, never formally defined as the Doctors have been. The four Greeks are SS Basil (d. 379), Gregory Nazianzen (d. 389), John Chrysostom (d. 407), and, added later, Athanasius (d. 373); the Latin are SS *Ambrose (d. 397), *Augustine (d. 430), *Gregory the Great (d. 604), and *Jerome (d. 420). They are usually represented as a group, wearing pontifical vestments and mitres, although Jerome is often shown, anachronistically, as a cardinal. The Greeks all wear the *omophorion with its black crosses: both groups are usually identifiable from books or scrolls with their names. The Greek Doctors occur frequently in mosaics, as in Sicily at Cefalù, Monreale, and Palermo (Cappella Palatina), and with the Latins in a 14th-century mosaic in St Mark's, Venice. They are also shown in Raphael's *Disputa* in the Vatican, and Bernini's *Cathedra Petri (1656–66) in St Peter's shows the Chair upheld by two Greek, SS Athanasius and John Chrysostom, and two Latin, SS Ambrose and Augustine.

Since 1568 many more Doctors of the Western Church have been named, including SS *Thomas Aquinas, *Antony of Padua, *Bonaventure, and (in 1970) two women, SS *Catherine of Siena and *Theresa of Avila. There are now about thirty in all.

dodecaorton In the E. Orthodox Church a series of twelve representations of the Great Feasts of the Byzantine Church, usually displayed on an *iconostasis. The Feasts vary, but the usual series is Annunciation, Nativity, Presentation in the Temple, Baptism, Transfiguration, Raising of Lazarus, Entry into Jerusalem, Crucifixion, Harrowing of Hell (*Anastasis), Ascension, Pentecost, and Koimesis (*Dormition of the Virgin). There are also miniature versions for private devotion as triptychs, single panels, and so on.

dog As a symbolic *beast the dog is somewhat ambiguous. In antiquity dogs seem to have been regarded as the friends of man, but in the OT they are often destroyers, as in Ps. 22 (Vg. 21) or in the fate of Jezebel, or the Devil as a Hound of Hell. Nevertheless, their reputation for fidelity and watchfulness was recognized in Early Christian sarcophagi of the Good Shepherd, or in the story of *Tobit. These are rather rare, however, and in the Middle Ages the dog seems to be a symbol of fidelity in the tomb-effigies of knights and ladies, although this is a controversial interpretation. In Jan van *Eyck's *Arnolfini Marriage* (London, NG) the little dog is generally accepted as a symbol of marital fidelity. The coincidence that the Latin name for the *Dominican Order—the Order of Preachers—is *Dominicanes* led to the pun *Domini canes*, the watch-dogs of the Lord, and they are then shown as black and white hounds guarding the flock. An attribute of S. Dominic himself is a black and white dog with a lighted torch in its mouth. Black and white are the colours of the Dominican habit.

Dolours *See* MATER DOLOROSA (under *MADONNA TYPES) and *SORROWS OF MARY.

DOM (Lat. *Deo optimo [et] maximo*, to God, most good, most great), a dedicatory inscription often found on temples dedicated to Jupiter and taken over by the Christians.

dom (duomo) Probably derived from *domus Dei* (the house of God), it became *Dom* (Ger.) or *duomo* (Ital.) and a name for a cathedral.

dome A structure that can be either circular in plan, or oval, hexagonal, octagonal, or a combination of these forms. It may have a high profile, or be hemispherical, or flattened. The most important domes in the world are those of the Pantheon in Rome (AD 100–25), Hagia Sophia in Constantinople (532–7),

Florence Cathedral (1417–25), St Peter's, Rome (1545–64, finished 1590), St Paul's Cathedral, London (1686–1719), and the Capitol, Washington DC (1857–63). The normal construction of a dome involves a transition from its interior supports, usually arches rising from powerful piers, to a drum, which is the supporting element of the dome proper. The drum may be an exiguous ring of masonry corbelled out from the walls, or a high element that raises the dome in height, decorative on the inside of the church and usually given either some decoration or a colonnade on the outside. Of such types are the domes of Florence Cathedral, St Peter's, St Paul's, and the Capitol, which has two drums, contributing greatly to its height and impressiveness. In many Byzantine cross-in-square churches, and in many French Romanesque ones, the drum is missing and the dome rests directly upon a transition from the square of the crossing to a circular or octagonal form by means of squinches or pendentives or by the already mentioned corbelling out from the walls.

Domine quo vadis? *See* QUO VADIS?

Dominic, Saint (*c.*1170/5–1221), was canonized in 1234 after an exceptionally short interval, like his contemporary and fellow founder of an Order, *S. Francis. The Order of Preachers, or Black Friars, usually known as *Dominicans, was one of the new *mendicant orders of friars working in towns, like the Franciscans. Dominic was born in Spain and became a priest *c.*1194. In 1204, accompanying his bishop in S. France, he first encountered the Albigensians, or Cathars, whose heretical doctrines (e.g. marriage is wholly evil) constituted a major threat to the Church. He decided to combat the heresy and went to Rome in 1205 to get permission to do so, first by establishing communities of women to reconvert those who had lapsed. In 1208 the murder of the papal legate caused a civil war, fought with extreme savagery on both sides. Dominic founded his Order to act as centres of learning and preaching in the cities, on the model of the Franciscans. The first General Chapter was held in Bologna in 1220, where Dominic died in the following year. Following his canonization a large church there was re-dedicated to him and in 1264 a grand tomb—the Arca di San Domenico—was commissioned from Nicola *Pisano, and Dominic's relics were moved there in 1267. The Arca was largely executed by Nicola's assistants and was almost completed by Niccolò dell'Arca, who died in 1494. The three figures still lacking, of an angel holding a candlestick, and of SS Petronius and Patroclus, were carved by *Michelangelo in 1494/5, while he was living in Bologna. The Arca has a series of reliefs with scenes from the saint's life, which helped to establish his iconography. The commonest incidents represented are (1) the raising from the dead of Napoleone Orsini after falling from his horse, (2) the occasion when, in controversy with the Albigensians, Dominic challenged them to throw a book of their writings into a fire and he would throw one of his (or, in some versions, a Bible): theirs were burnt, but his bounced out unharmed, (3) his meeting with S. Francis, and (4) Reginald, who joined the Order after seeing a vision of the Virgin herself giving him the black and white habit. These and other scenes were painted by Fra *Angelico and Fra *Bartolommeo, both of whom were Dominicans.

The earliest known representation of the saint himself is thought to be the icon-like half-length from the School of Guido da Siena, of the first half of the 13th century (Cambridge, Mass., Fogg Mus.). There is a Florentine painting of *c.*1270, of the *Madonna with SS Francis and Dominic*, and a terracotta bust by Niccolò dell'Arca, but that is datable as late as 1474/5 (Bologna, San Domenico). Dominic is always shown in the white habit and black cloak of his Order, and may be holding a lily or have a star on his breast or above his head; he is sometimes accompanied by a black and white dog holding a lighted torch in its mouth. He is often wrongly associated with the invention of the *rosary, but in spite of such famous paintings as *Dürer's *Madonna of the Rose Garlands* (1506: Prague, Nat. Mus.), or *Caravaggio's *Madonna of the Rosary* (1605–7: Vienna, KHM), or *Tiepolo's ceiling fresco in the church of the Gesuati, Venice, of 1737–9, the earliest connection between Dominic and the rosary seems to be late 15th century; nevertheless, devotion to the rosary is characteristic of the Dominicans.

Dominican Order Officially, the Order of Preachers, *Ordo Praedicatorum*, also called the Black Friars, or, in France, Jacobins. Like the *Franciscans, they are not a monastic order but *mendicant friars and, again like the Franciscans, they are based in towns and cities and work in the world. S. Dominic's efforts against the Albigensians began with training communities of women from *c.*1206, so that the

Second Order, of nuns, in fact preceded the First although it was not officially established until 1218. In 1215, in Toulouse, Dominic had gathered sixteen men around him and it was decided to apply to Rome for permission to found a new Order devoted to setting up centres of learning and preaching to maintain orthodoxy and combat heresy. After considerable hesitation Innocent III gave permission to use a modified form of the *Premonstratension Rule and the first house was founded in Toulouse. Within a very few years there were sixty, several in university towns: in England the houses at Blackfriars in London and in Oxford were especially famous. Because of their reputation as theologians the Dominicans were employed, after Dominic's death, as Inquisitors when the Inquisition was established in 1227. In later years this association did them considerable harm, so that they never became as popular as the Franciscans. Their Latin name, *Dominicanes,* was easily made into *Domini canes*—the watch-dogs of the Lord, and they were portrayed as black and white dogs driving away the wolf of heresy, particularly in the fresco by Andrea da Firenze of 1366–8 in the chapter-house of their great *auditory church in Florence, Sta Maria Novella. The Dominican habit is white with a black mantle and hood, hence the black and white dogs.

Among the most famous members of the Order are S. *Thomas Aquinas, S. *Catherine of Siena, S. *Antoninus, S. *Peter Martyr, Jacobus de Voragine, author of the **Golden Legend,* Vincent of Beauvais, author of the **Speculum Majus,* and several painters, notably Fra *Angelico (recently beatified) and Fra *Bartolommeo.

Dominions (Dominations) *See* ANGELS.

domus ecclesiae (Lat. house of the church) *See* DURA-EUROPOS.

Donatello (*c.*1385/6–1466) was the greatest Florentine sculptor before Michelangelo, and the inventor of a dramatic style based on Christian pathos and classical Roman forms. He was apprenticed to *Ghiberti and worked on the first Baptistery doors (1403–6), but later began to work for Florence Cathedral, at first in a Gothic style quite close to Ghiberti's (the *David,* 1408/9, reworked 1416: Florence, Bargello). He may have gone to Rome 1409/11, and he was certainly there in 1431–3. His heroic style, based on a close study of Imperial Roman and Early Christian art, is first seen in his *S. Mark* (1411–12: Florence, Orsanmichele) and *S. John the Evangelist* (1413–15: Cathedral). The relief of *S. George and the Dragon* (*c.*1417: Orsanmichele, below the statue of S. George) is one of the first examples of the new science of perspective applied to low-relief sculpture, and it is further developed in his highly dramatic relief of *Herod presented with the Head of the Baptist,* made for Siena Baptistery in 1427, which shows Herod recoiling in horror at the realization of what he has done. From 1443 to 1453 Donatello was in Padua, where he made the High Altar of the Santo (now reconstructed) and the first major bronze equestrian monument since antiquity. This is the statue of the *condottiere* Gattamelata, which is patently based on the only surviving classical example, the *Marcus Aurelius* of AD *c.*176 (then thought to represent Constantine, the first Christian emperor). Donatello's greatness as a religious artist is due to his rejection of superficial prettiness and his realization that expressive distortion, and even downright ugliness, convey more powerful emotions. His *Baptist* (1438: Venice, Frari), and, above all, his *Magdalene* (*c.*1455: Florence, Baptistery) are outstanding examples of this.

donor portraits From the earliest times important people have associated themselves with major projects, as Roman emperors' names are often found on temples built by them. Their successors, the Byzantine emperors, felt themselves to be God's secular representatives and therefore encouraged a visual association between themselves and Christ. Justinian and his empress, Theodora, are shown as heading processions in the 6th-century mosaics in San Vitale, Ravenna, and in a mosaic in Hagia Sophia in Constantinople Basil I (867–86) or Leo VI (886–912) is shown prostrate before Christ (*proskynesis), as his subjects would prostrate themselves before him. Popes building churches had portraits of themselves offering the building to its patron saint or to Christ, in addition to the normal inscriptions. The earliest known such papal portrait is of Felix IV (526–30) shown offering a model of SS Cosmas and Damian, Rome, converted by him from a pagan temple, to Christ in the presence of S. Peter. Another Roman mosaic, in Sant'Agnese fuori le Mura, shows Pope Honorius presenting a model of the church to S. Agnes (*c.*625), and the first papal portrait of this type to be shown with a square halo, indicating a living man, is of John VII, *c.*707, in the Vatican Grottoes. Throughout the Middle Ages there was a custom of showing the donor on a smaller scale than the sacred figures, but by the early 14th century in Italy they began to appear on the same scale, though usually kneeling. Giotto painted a real portrait of Enrico Scrovegni presenting a model of the Arena Chapel in Padua to the Virgin *c.*1306/9, and in 1317 Simone Martini was commissioned by Robert of Anjou to paint a large altarpiece of the newly canonized S. Louis of Toulouse, with himself kneeling beside him. This was a piece of political propaganda, because Louis was Robert's elder brother and heir to the kingdom of Naples, but in 1296 he had entered the Franciscan Order and renounced his claim to the throne. He is shown as being crowned by two angels with a celestial crown, while holding an earthly one over his brother's head. Robert's claim was not universally recognized, and the influence of a newly canonized saint must have been considerable. It is noticeable that the kneeling Robert is clearly a portrait, but the saint has an impassive icon-like appearance.

Throughout the 14th and 15th centuries this tendency to diminish the difference between sacred and profane became more marked: Jan van *Eyck's donor figures in the Ghent Altar are completely realistic, but confined to the outside of the wings. His *Madonna of Canon van der Paele* (1436: Bruges, Mus.) shows the canon kneeling and presented by S. George, but is a real portrait on the same scale as the figures of Mary and the Christ Child or SS George and Donatien. By the mid-15th century Fouquet's *Étienne Chevalier with his patron S. Stephen* (Berlin) shows them not only equal, but actually with the same features. In Ghirlandaio's frescoes in the Sassetti Chapel (*c.*1483: Florence, Sta Trinità) Francesco Sasseti and his wife take no part in the story of S. Francis, but are flanked by their patrons in this world, the Medici family and their humanist protégés. The tradition of representing the donor, his wife, and all their children on a much smaller scale persisted in Germany, and it is interesting that even Dürer used it in his Paumgartner Altar of *c.*1503 (Munich), but abandoned it in his *Madonna of the Rose Garlands*, painted in 1506 in Venice (Prague, NG). By 1526/30 Holbein, in his *Madonna of the Burgomaster Meyer* (Darmstadt), represented the Burgomaster himself, his first, dead, wife and second wife with all the children on exactly the same scale as the Madonna and Child, as a sort of bourgeois family group. Gradually the element of protection and reverence died out, but two special cases must be mentioned. One is the type where the donor is not an individual but representative of a religious confraternity, a *guild, or even the citizens of a town. The *Madonna della Misericordia* type, with several figures sheltering beneath the Madonna's outstretched cloak, as in the *Piero della Francesca in San Sepolcro of *c.*1460, is one example, and later ones include the Annibale Carracci of the 1590s (Oxford, Christ Church), showing the Madonna and Child hovering above the city of Bologna, and the enormous altarpiece in Este Cathedral by *Tiepolo, of 1758–9, of *Sta Tecla saving the city of Este from Plague*, which was unkindly but acutely described by Roberto Longhi as 'Dio Padre basso, Santa Tecla soprano'.

The other special category is that of illuminated MSS, where the scribe/illuminator is shown presenting the Gospels he has illuminated to the Evangelist, or a finished book to the patron who commissioned it, or paid for it, as in the miniature of Jean Wauquelin presenting his *Chroniques du Hainault* to his patron, Duke Philip the Good of Burgundy.

Doom An Old English word for the Last Judgement, from Dóm, sentence.

door, church A door is an obvious symbol of the way to salvation through the church, and for this reason the main door is usually directly opposite the altar. In Byzantine churches the sanctuary is separated from the congregation by an *iconostasis, which itself has three doors, the central one (the Holy or Royal door), being closed and opened as part of the liturgy. Among the earliest surviving doors are wooden fragments with reliefs from Sant'Ambrogio in Milan (*c.*386) and Sta Sabina in Rome (*c.*432), which has one of the earliest representations of the Crucifixion. From the 11th century onwards, doors with bronze reliefs began to be made, and among the survivors from the 11th/12th centuries are Hildesheim in Germany, *c.*1015, San Zeno in Verona and Pisa Cathedral in N. and central Italy, and a group in S. Italy and Sicily including Benevento, Monreale Cathedral with two doors, one by Barisanus of 1179 and the other by Bonanus of Pisa, of 1185; Trani of *c.*1175, and Troja by Oderisius, of 1127. During the Gothic period *portal sculpture was concentrated on the stone sculpture surrounding the doors, which were themselves usually plain. The Baptistery at Florence is the principal work of the early Renaissance, beginning with the bronze doors made by Andrea Pisano (1330–6) and followed by the two pairs which are *Ghiberti's masterpieces; the first of 1403–24, and the second of 1425–52. One of the few survivals from Old St Peter's in Rome is the bronze door by *Filarete (1445). St Peter's now also has a 20th-century bronze door by Giacomo Manzù (1908–1991), who also made doors for Salzburg Cathedral.

Dorcas *See* TABITHA.

Dormition of the Virgin (Lat. *dormitio*, sleep; also called Death of the Virgin, Transito, and Koimesis) The account of the Death and Assumption of the Blessed Virgin depends on various *Apocryphal books of the 2nd to 5th centuries, e.g. the *Transitus Mariae* of the 4th/5th century, popularized in the West by the **Golden Legend*. The Dormition is the first in a series of events often grouped together as a single scene under the title of the *Assumption. The first scene is the Annunciation of her impending death, usually by the Archangel Gabriel, as a mirror-image of the *Annunciation, but with Gabriel holding a palm branch, not a lily, as in Duccio's *Maestà* (1308–11), which has a series of panels telling the story in detail. In another version of the story the palm is brought by S. John the Evangelist, whom Christ had made responsible for the care of His mother; in any case, the palm was carried by John at the funeral. Next, John is joined by the other Apostles, miraculously assembled from all over the world. Sometimes they include S. Paul and sometimes they omit *Thomas (who arrives later), then in their presence Mary 'falls asleep' (*dormitio*). In the next episode, also represented by Duccio, her body is carried on a bier to the Valley of *Jehoshaphat, where the Apostles had been instructed by Christ to wait three days (in an obvious reference to the Resurrection). The bier was carried by SS Peter and Paul, preceded by John with the palm and surrounded by the other Apostles. However, a crowd had gathered and a man named Jephonias attempted to overturn the bier, whereupon his hands were withered and stuck to the bier. In some accounts he was freed only when he confessed to belief in Christ, in others, an angel appeared and chopped off his hands, which remained stuck to the bier. Usually this scene is preceded by one showing Christ receiving His mother's soul as a tiny child wrapped in swaddling-clothes, but this may be inserted between the carrying of the bier and the burial scene. In later representations the tomb is usually shown as filled with roses and lilies as Mary ascends to Heaven. The Assumption itself is often made the central focus of the picture, and here the absence of Thomas from the death-bed is explained by his mission in India. True to his original doubting nature, he at first would not believe in the miracle, so the ascending Virgin dropped her girdle from Heaven to convince him (this was the relic preserved in Prato Cathedral). This subsidiary scene is often shown in the background, on a small scale, as in the altarpiece by Aelbrecht Bouts (Brussels, Mus.).

At the top, particularly in French *portal sculpture, the *Coronation of the Virgin completes the cycle.

There are no surviving Byzantine representations of the subject from pre-Iconoclastic times, but an icon in St Catherine's Monastery, Mount Sinai, of *c.*1250 and perhaps of Venetian origin, is very similar to the Duccio panels, which probably have a common source in Byzantium.

From the late 15th century the Dormition is often treated as an independent subject, though with internal references to other parts of the story. The paintings by Mantegna (Madrid, Prado) and Hugo van der Goes (Bruges, Mus.) are focused on the grieving Apostles, although the van der Goes has (and the Mantegna originally had) an apparition of Christ receiving her soul. This tendency to concentrate on the death-bed reached a climax in *Caravaggio's altarpiece of 1605–6 for Sta Maria della Scala in Rome. Although accepted by the commissioner it was rejected by the clergy as lacking in *decorum and a painting by Saraceni was substituted. In 1607, on the advice of Rubens, it was bought by the Duke of Mantua and from him by Charles I of England. It is now in the Louvre.

Dorothy, Saint (d. *c.*313?), virgin and martyr, is said to have been one of the last victims of the Emperor Diocletian's persecution, but her *acta* are legendary and her cult is unknown in the East and hardly occurs in the West before the 14th century. She is not mentioned in the original **Golden Legend*, but was added to it. The cult was widespread in Italy and Germany up to the 16th century.

She was supposed to come from Caesarea in Cappadocia and to have refused to marry or to worship idols and was therefore condemned to death. On her way to execution a lawyer called Theophilus called mockingly to her to send him some fruits from the garden of paradise to which she claimed to be going (it was then February). Before she was beheaded she prayed, and an angel (or in some versions, the Christ Child) appeared with a small basket containing three roses and three apples. Dorothy asked him to take them to Theophilus, who was instantly converted and was himself martyred. This is the only part of her legend that is ever represented, but she can be confused with *S. Elizabeth of Hungary, whose attribute is also roses. Dorothy also appears among the *Virgo inter Virgines and sometimes as one of the Holy Helpers (*see* VIERZEHNHEILIGEN). She is the patron saint of gardeners.

dorsal *See* DOSSAL.

dorter An obsolete name for the dormitory of a monastery.

dossal (dorsal) A dorsal (Lat. *dorsum*, back) is a cloth hanging behind an altar. A dossal (Ital. *dossale*) is derived from it, but is a painting or relief, usually the width of an altar but relatively low, which stands on or hangs above the altar slab. An *antependium or altar-frontal hangs in front of, and below, the altar slab. Antependia are easily damaged and dossals are probably the result of trying to avoid this: some antependia may have been converted into dossals by shifting their position, and also perhaps by remaking them. Italian dossals date from the early 13th century until well into the 14th, after which they were superseded by altarpieces and **predelle*. A good 13th-century example is the one by Margarito of Arezzo in London (NG). *See also* PALA D'ORO and REREDOS.

double church The usual meaning of a double church is one in two tiers, one above the other, like the Upper and Lower churches of S. Francis at *Assisi, or the Ste-Chapelle in Paris. A variant of this occurs in palace chapels, where the ruler and his court occupy the upper levels and the space below is occupied by the servants and public. *Charlemagne's Palatine Chapel at Aachen was of this type and was followed by others, culminating in the splendid early 18th-century chapel at Versailles. A double-ended church is one with an apsidal projection at both east and west ends. The form was probably invented for Early Christian churches in N. Africa, but later medieval examples are mostly German, although there are also Carolingian and *Romanesque examples in France.

double monastery A double monastery is a foundation for both men and women, with separate living quarters sharing a single church with separate choirs for each community. Most of these monasteries were ruled by the abbess. They were known in the East in the late Roman Empire and spread to the West, but most had died out by the 10th century on account of the barbarian incursions, but a few were re-established, such as the Abbey of Fontevrault, near Saumur, which was a favourite place of retirement for royal widows, who often became their abbesses. It was the burial place of several English kings and queens. They were, however, favoured by *S. Bridget of Sweden, whose Brigittines preserved them in N. Europe, especially Poland, where they survived into the 19th century.

dove The dove is perhaps the most important symbolic *bird, since it is mentioned in the Bible with several meanings. In the OT it is the symbol of reconciliation and peace after the Flood, when a dove returned to *Noah bearing an olive leaf (Gen. 8: 8–11). Doves were also acceptable sacrifices, since they were offered at the *Presentation of the Christ Child (Luke 2: 24). Above all, the Holy Spirit appeared and descended 'like a dove' at the *Baptism of Christ (Mark 1: 10; Luke 3: 22; and John 1: 32); this does not mean that the Holy Spirit actually looked like a dove, but that It manifested Itself and descended as a dove might do (the Vulgate has *tanquam*, as if). For this reason the Holy Spirit is usually shown in *Annunciation scenes as a dove, since no artist has been able to represent a spirit except corporeally. In a more general sense, doves can represent the Church, the Christian soul, the Seven *Gifts of the Holy Spirit, or the Twelve Apostles. They are very common in catacombs and on Early Christian sarcophagi.

In representations of certain saints—e.g. *Gregory the Great, *Dominic, *Thomas Aquinas, and *Theresa of Avila—doves symbolize the inspiration of the Holy Spirit.

Sculptured doves made of gold or silver were hung above altars or fonts from at least the 6th century, and in the Middle Ages from *c.*1000 such doves were also used as *pyxes to contain the Blessed Sacrament. A few Western examples still exist, e.g. in Amiens Cathedral, but they were and are common in the E. Orthodox Church (ARTOPHORION).

dragon (Lat. *draco*) A fabulous monster, apparently universal, since it appears in classical antiquity as well as in Far Eastern art. Dragons appear to be based on crocodiles or lizards and are always evil in Christian art, although during the medieval period they were also used to symbolize untamed nature. *Serpents, with which they are often confused, may be evil (the Fall of *Man) or beneficent (Moses and the *brazen serpent). In *Bestiaries dragons usually figure as very large crocodiles, breathing fire, with spiky wings and a long serpentine tail, often with a barb. Occasionally, they have a wolf's head rather than a crocodile's. There are several biblical references to them, including Ps. 91 in AV (Vg. 90): 13 'Thou shalt tread upon the lion and adder: the young lion and the dragon shalt thou trample under feet'. NRSV has 'serpent' instead of 'dragon'. Christ or a saint treading on a dragon is a frequent figure on standing *crosses and *portals, often used to symbolize the taming of nature in the foundation of a city or building. The identification with Satan is specifically made in Rev. 12: 3–4 and 7–9; the first recounts how the 'great red dragon' tried to kill the new-born child (*see* APOCALYPTIC WOMAN), the second says 'And war broke out in heaven; Michael and his angels fought against the dragon. The dragon and his angels fought back, but they were defeated, and there was no longer any place for them in heaven. The great dragon was thrown down, that ancient serpent, who is called the Devil, and Satan . . . was thrown down to the earth, and his angels were thrown down with him'. In the Apocryphal part of the Book of Daniel (Vg. ch. 14) the story of *Bel is told, in which Daniel unmasked a non-existent dragon, fed large quantities of food which was actually eaten by the priests of the cult. Dragons also appear as victorious effigies during Rogation processions but later emerge defeated on the feast of the Ascension—re-enacting the triumph of the Resurrection over nature.

Many saints are associated with dragons, notably Michael the Archangel, *George, *Margaret of Antioch, St Marcellus (Paris), St Sylvester (Rome), and *Philip the Apostle.

Draught of Fishes *See* FISHES.

dress, clerical The everyday dress of clerics, as distinct from *vestments. In Early Christian times clerics wore the ordinary dress of laymen, but avoiding display and garish colours. They also retained the ankle-length gown from the 6th century, when most laymen had adopted trousers. In the West this tradition persisted in many countries, especially Protestant ones, until the 19th century. The *cassock, which is partly a vestment, was perhaps the chief distinguishing feature of a priest in Catholic countries, although monks and nuns wore the *habit of their Order. In the East priests wear the *rason, their version of a cassock.

Clerical dress is not a matter of importance for Christian art, except that it may serve to identify the sitters in portraits.

drum *See* DOME.

Drunkenness of Noah *See* NOAH.

Drusiana *See* JOHN THE EVANGELIST, S.

Duccio di Buoninsegna (*c.*1255/60–in or before 1318, probably 1315/18) was the earliest great painter of Siena, and is to Sienese painting what *Giotto is to Florentine. Duccio's style is still *Byzantine yet in him Byzantine austerity and gravity is infused with the humanity, the drama, and the pathos of the Passion which stems from the influence of the Franciscan and Dominican religious revival. The *Rucellai Madonna* (Uffizi) was probably commissioned from him in 1285 for the Florentine church of Sta Maria Novella. This huge altarpiece (over 14 ft. high), while less adventurous and innovative than either of the comparable pictures by *Cimabue and Giotto, still reflects the new feeling of the late 13th century. His masterpiece is the even larger altarpiece of the *Maestà* (Siena, Mus. dell' Opera) painted between 1308 and 1311, when the completed work was carried in triumphant procession to the cathedral, where it was installed as the altarpiece of the high altar. It was removed and partially dismembered in 1771. The work presented two faces: the altar was surmounted by the *Maestà* itself—that is, the Madonna and Child enthroned in majesty surrounded by saints—and the back of the huge panel (roughly 12 ft. high and 14 ft. wide) is composed of a number of small panels with the story of the Passion, incidents from the Life of Christ before the Crucifixion, and His appearances after the Resurrection. Originally there were representations of saints and apostles in the small pinnacles which normally crown a work of this kind, but some of these have disappeared, and others have been dispersed (e.g. three in London, NG). The *Maestà* on the front is a fairly traditional work of grave beauty and hierarchical organization, the most touching figures being those of the four angels behind the throne, their chins propped on their hands as they gaze with puzzled tenderness at the Madonna and Child. But in other respects the panel is traditional: the saints stand in a row with four kneeling in front, and there is a row of angels standing behind them, each row clearly distinct from the one below. It is only on the back of the altarpiece, which was probably visible to the faithful from the ambulatory, that the didactic nature of the work is both clear and outstanding. No other sequence of paintings illustrating the Passion is as full as this one, for fourteen panels are devoted to the story of the Passion, of which twelve are divided into two, making twenty-six narratives in all. The story begins with Christ's entry into Jerusalem (a double panel) continuing through His arrest and trial to the Crucifixion (again a double panel), and then through the Deposition to the Resurrection. The last panel shows Christ appearing to the Magdalene—the *Noli me tangere*. In the panels showing incidents after the Resurrection, Duccio employs the Byzantine device of differentiating between Christ when in the world, and the Risen Christ by using gold in the folds of His garments, so that He appears irradiated. The crowning panels on the front of the *Maestà* illustrate the Life of the Virgin from the Annunciation to the Dormition and Entombment, and the *predella* tells the story of Christ's Nativity to His being found in the Temple. The work is outstanding both for the detailed content and for the subtle treatment of the figures and their facial expressions, which in such scenes as the Apparition of Christ to the Apostles behind closed doors, and the Incredulity of Thomas, display a range from incredulity and hesitancy of belief to astonishment and faith. Duccio also painted a number of *Madonnas*, more or less Byzantine in type.

duomo (Ital. for cathedral) *See* DOM.

Dura-Europos, now called Qalat es Salihiye, a town on the Euphrates between Aleppo and Baghdad, was held by the Romans until 257. Their fortifications destroyed houses at the town's edge, including a synagogue and the earliest known Christian church, the remains of which were discovered in 1921. Both were typical Middle Eastern houses. The synagogue dated from *c.*200 and was enlarged in 245, and despite the commandment against images was decorated with wall-paintings which are the earliest surviving OT cycle (now in the National Museum, Damascus). In the Christian church, a small courtyard was surrounded by a room for the instruction of neophytes; a room with a place for an altar and a bishop's throne, and large enough for fifty to sixty people; a baptistery with a canopy over the baptismal tank; and rooms which were probably sacristies and store-rooms. The remains of the baptistery contained the best of the surviving wall-paintings (now in Yale University Art Gallery), mostly of subjects centred on redemption from sin, salvation, and resurrection. This example of a modest *domus ecclesiae* probably dates from the early 3rd century, and is the sort of *house-church which served many early Christian communities.

Durandus, Gulielmus (*c.*1230/7–96), was born in Provence and spent most of his life at the papal court as a canon lawyer. He was made Bishop of Mende, in S. France, in 1285, but lived mostly in Rome, where he died. He is best known for his *Rationale divinorum officiorum* (*c.*1286), and a pontifical, which was the ancestor of the *Pontificale Romanum*. The *Rationale* is an elaborate treatise on liturgy and the appointments of churches, with a very medieval mystical interpretation of their symbolism. It was first printed in 1459 and had many later editions; surprise is sometimes expressed by modern writers at his insensitivity to the Gothic architecture of his own day, but in fact, coming from the South of France and living in Italy it is probable that he never saw any of the major monuments. In any case, he was more concerned with allegorical exegesis than with actual buildings. Book I (of eight), on the symbolism of church buildings and appointments, was translated in 1843, by two Anglican clergymen, Neale and Webb, founders of the *Cambridge Camden Society, who took the text at its face value. It was very influential on the *Oxford Movement in the Church of England.

Dürer, Albrecht (1471–1528), painter and engraver, was born and died in Nuremberg. Despite the brilliance of his paintings, it is in his graphic work that his great importance lies. He is the greatest master of woodcut and copper-engraving, achieving a technical mastery and a range of expression never seen before or excelled since. Only Rembrandt, in etching, comes anywhere near him. Many of his graphic works were produced in series, beginning in 1498 with the woodcuts of the *Apocalypse, where he not only made the blocks for the illustrations (which include the memorable *Four Horsemen of the Apocalypse*) but also cut the text, so that it is the first whole book produced and published by an artist himself. It became the definitive iconography of the visions of S. John, and was copied throughout the 16th century. Other series are the *Great Passion* (1498–1510), the *Little Passion* (1509–11), the *Life of the Virgin* (1501–11), and the *Engraved Passion* (1507–12). He produced a continuous stream of single prints of ever mounting technical virtuosity, such as the *Prodigal Son* (1497), *S. Eustace* (*c*.1501), the *Adam and Eve* (1504), the *Knight, Death, and the Devil* (1513), illustrating unflinching faith in the face of peril and temptation—very much a tract for the times—*S. Jerome* and the enigmatic *Melencolia* (1514). The influence of his prints was enormous; not only were they immediate and memorably dramatic in their narrative power, so that they astonish by their vivid imagery and layers of iconographic meaning; they were easily transported, cheap, and therefore readily available. They spread all over Europe, and their influence can be seen even in Italy, where *Pontormo, for instance, borrowed from him despite the general disdain of Italian artists for any art produced outside their own country.

He visited Venice, certainly in 1505–7, and possibly also in 1494–5, and knew and admired Bellini. In Venice, he painted the *Madonna of the Rose Garlands* (1505–6, now Prague, NG, but very damaged) to prove his skill to sceptical Italians, and a *Christ among the Doctors* which strongly suggests a knowledge of Leonardo da Vinci. He also travelled to the Netherlands in 1520–1, and the illustrated diary of his journey provides a fascinating record of what he saw and whom he met: practically everything and everyone of note, but the fever he contracted in Zeeland probably hastened his death. In this diary he records meetings with *Erasmus, and he also records his own admiration for *Luther (whom he never met). In one passage he urges Erasmus to abandon his moderate position: 'Oh Erasmus of Rotterdam, where wilt thou stop? Behold how the wicked tyranny of worldly power . . . prevails. Hear, thou knight of Christ! . . . Guard the truth. Attain the martyr's crown . . . make thyself heard.'

Dürer was much affected by the Reformation, and the spiritual conflicts in which it enmeshed him are reflected in the fate of the altarpiece which he intended to present to his city as a memorial of himself; only the wings, representing the *Four Apostles* (1526; Munich), which also double as the four 'humours', were finished, the projected *Sacra Conversazione* being abandoned as no longer acceptable in a Lutheran society.

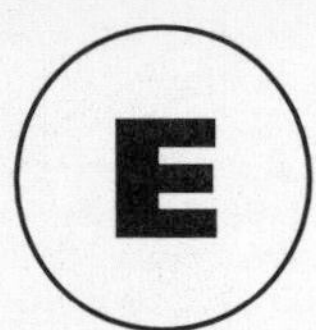

eagle One of the most important symbolic *birds, as it has several allegorical meanings, sometimes contradictory. In pre-Christian times the eagle was the symbol of Jove (Jupiter, Zeus), and was therefore already associated with divinity. From this it became an ancient symbol of power, for the wings of the great figure of the Victory of Samothrace (*c.*186 BC: Louvre) are those of an eagle. Later it became a symbol of Roman power, and eagles crowned the standards of the legions from the 1st century BC, and an eagle is below the throne of the Emperor Augustus in the *Gemma Augustea* (1st cent.: Vienna, KHM). The eagle came to be associated both with Christ Himself and with His Ascension; the eagle was believed to be able to look at the sun without blinking, as Christ could contemplate the Godhead, and the eagle was able to fly higher than any other bird, hence the connection with the Ascension.

The vision of *Ezekiel led to it being an *Evangelist symbol of S. John, because it soars into the heavens; his Gospel opens with the words 'In the beginning . . . ', and he also reflects the soaring nature of the Apocalypse with its vision of heaven. Lecterns, from which the Lessons and the Gospel are read, are commonly in the shape of an eagle with outspread wings to support the Bible, and an eagle is often used on pulpits to support the preacher's desk. In *Bestiaries are other interpretations—it could renew its youth, as in Ps. 103 (Vg. 102): 5, 'thy youth is renewed like the eagle's', and this it did by flying near the sun and dipping itself three times in a pool of water, symbolizing Baptism in the names of the Father, Son, and Holy Ghost. An eagle trampling on a snake symbolized Christ's triumph over sin, and as in Greek mythology Ganymede was carried off by Jove's eagle, so the eagle of Christ could snatch up a human soul and bear it up to heaven. But since the eagle is a bird of prey, it might also typify the Devil for, as Job said, 'The earth is given into the hand of the wicked . . . like an eagle swooping on prey' (9: 24–6).

EARLY CHRISTIAN ART AND ARCHITECTURE

This is the art and architecture of the first five centuries of the Christian era, up to the rise of the *Byzantine style of the Eastern Roman Empire, and the collapse of the Roman Empire in the West. Knowledge of this period, and of the life, growth, and development of the faith and the Church has increased largely through the study devoted since the 16th century to Christian *archaeology. From the first three centuries little has survived, partly because of persecution and consequent destruction, partly because of the subsequent success of Christian congregations, the redevelopment of their buildings and sites, and the consequent destruction of early mural paintings in particular. On the other hand, burial sites were protected in Roman law, even those of executed criminals, so most of the extant early Christian art, such as the paintings in the catacombs and carved sarcophagi, is associated with burial,.

The earliest surviving examples of Christian art pre-date by many years the official recognition of Christianity as a permitted religion in 313. They were certainly current by the middle of the 2nd century, and some may be even earlier. They are almost entirely Roman—little has survived in the East, though the baptistery in *Dura-Europos is a significant exception—and the artistic forms and conventions in use in classical or pagan art were a natural starting-point, only the subjects being different, and only gradually did their meaning become explicitly Christian. The development of a new kind of art was greatly helped by the emergence of a popular art in the late 2nd century which developed in parallel with the expiring forms of Hellenistic art, partly through the need for an art able to express movement and emotion, and with a concentration on narrative, of which the Columns of Trajan and Marcus Aurelius are typical, but also because the late Roman world of the Tetrarchy—the four co-emperors who shared power in the late 3rd and early 4th century—was less interested in the beauty of classical form than in an expressive naturalism. In the time of Constantine narrative subjects, such as those carved for the Arch of Constantine, developed the convention of showing the important characters, such as the emperor, as larger than the figures of those surrounding him, in order to stress his rank by contrast with the earlier reused roundels on the same arch. This convention was very long-lasting, and accounts for the discrepancies of scale which persisted as far into the future as the 14th century.

Probably the earliest examples of Christian art are practical things like rings and *seals, engraved with innocuous emblems such as a *dove, an *anchor, a *lighthouse, or a *ship with a cross-shaped mast. To these neutral symbols were added the Good *Shepherd, *Ichthys, *Loaves and Fishes, *Sol Invictus (i.e. Christ as Helios, the Sun God or Light of the World), all of which are found in paintings from the 3rd century onwards in the *catacombs outside the city walls (Roman law forbade burials within them).

Almost all Early Christian painting has been found in the catacombs, although some is to be found in places such as the apartments that became part of the *Titulus Byzantis* (SS Giovanni e Paolo). It is simpler, cruder even, in technique and conception than contemporary examples of pagan art and is often deliberately ambiguous in its imagery: vintage scenes, or a shepherd carrying a sheep over his shoulders, carved on a sarcophagus, or painted on the wall or ceiling in a catacomb could be either pagan or Christian, though the very ambiguity suggests the true meaning. The symbol *Chi-Rho often appears in such contexts, since it is one which would be understood only by a Christian. Sometimes it is difficult to tell if an image is Christian or not, an example being the early 3rd-century wall-painting of a woman nursing a child in the Catacomb of Priscilla, which may be a very early *Virgin and Child*, or may be the Egyptian goddess Isis and her son Horus, whose cult was well established in Rome. In view of the links between the new religion and Judaism, and the Jewish hostility towards images, as a result of the Second Commandment, it may seem surprising that art found favour at all, but this rule was not so strictly followed among the Hellenized Jews of the Diaspora. The walls of the 3rd-century synagogue at Dura-Europos on the Euphrates show an extensive use of biblical illustration, as does the Jewish cemetery on the Appian Way outside Rome. The Christian use of images is therefore not surprising, particularly as many—if not most—of the Christian converts in Rome, where the majority of catacomb images survive, had never been Jews.

Even when Christianity was a proscribed faith there was no interference with Christian *cemeteries, which were protected by the Roman law which regarded as sacrosanct the bodies and the burials even of those whom the State had executed. Burial places were either privately owned, or belonged to corporations founded for the purpose; Christians could thus be buried together, and parts of many catacombs centre round the graves of those who had died for their faith. On the earlier graves, OT subjects predominated: *Jonah and the Whale, Moses striking the Rock, Daniel in the Lions' Den, Daniel judging Susanna, Noah receiving the Dove with the Olive Branch*, all symbols of the Resurrection or of Salvation. Allusions to the Eucharist were common: loaves and fishes, a standing cup and loaves, sometimes a representation of the rite itself, as in the 3rd-century Cappella Greca in the Catacomb of Priscilla. Not until the 4th century did overt references to Christ become common, possibly because of a reluctance to make an image of the Deity. A fine bust of Christ, flanked by the signs of *Alpha and Omega, in the 4th-century Catacomb of Comidilla, must be one of the earliest attempts at a 'portrait', a 4th-century figure of a youthful Christ in the *confessio* of SS Giovanni e Paolo, and a 4th-century half-figure with the gesture of an Orant, believed to represent the Virgin, is in the Coemeterium Maius on the Via Nomentana. The Orant, a figure of a woman standing with her arms upraised in the old gesture of prayer, and thought to represent the soul, or faith, or the triumph of the Church, is ubiquitous in catacomb paintings from the 3rd century onwards. In the 4th century scenes of Christ's mission and miracles become common: the *Raising of Lazarus*, the *Samaritan Woman at the Well*, the *Marriage at Cana*, *Christ blessing the Loaves* at the feeding of the five thousand, and even such scenes as *Hercules conquering the Hydra*, *Orpheus taming the wild beasts* or mosaic floors showing *Bellerophon* at Hinton St Mary and Lullingstone in England, are assimilated from pagan to Christian belief by being equated with the conquest of evil.

During the persecutions, which began in the short reign of the Emperor Decius (249–51), and continued at intervals in various parts of the empire and rose sporadically to hideous violence, private religious meetings were forbidden, and the only permitted clubs, or guilds, were for funeral societies. Property owned by the Church was confiscated, and books and furnishings destroyed, but once the fury of persecution passed property was often recovered by the community. The accusations could be brought on several grounds, one of the commonest being the Christian's refusal to sacrifice to the deified emperor or to the Genius of Rome because it was idolatrous; to refuse was treason. But they were sustained by their faith that persecution would be followed by Christ's Second Coming which would overthrow pagan power. As the empire weakened, the act of emperor-worship became more important, since it signified a bond uniting Roman citizens to the Roman civic power personified by the emperor. A note of caution should be sounded concerning the comprehensiveness of persecution, since the Christian congregation appears to have been thriving in the garrison town of Dura during the Decian persecution, with the burial of the church in the reinforcement of the fortifications in 256/57 before the town was overrun by the Sassanids.

Eventually, the size of the empire compelled division of control, and forced further divisions into smaller units, always with the military independent of the civil administration. At the end of the 3rd century, in 293, power was divided between four men—two Emperors, *Diocletian in the East, Maximian in the West, and two Caesars chosen by them as their destined successors—Galerius by Diocletian, and Constantius by Maximian (portrayed in amity in the *Tetrarchs*, the commemorative porphyry group made probably in Egypt, now on the NW corner of St Mark's, Venice). The Western capital was moved from Rome to Milan, where it remained until barbarian invasions forced it to move to Ravenna. The Eastern capital was at Nicodemia, in what is now N. Turkey. In 303 Galerius persuaded Diocletian to launch the fiercest and longest persecution of Christians, which continued with varying intensity in different parts of the empire of the East until 313, but only lasted from 303 to 306 in the West. In 305 both Diocletian and Maximian abdicated, and were succeeded as emperors by Galerius and Constantius, but internecine struggles for power between the rulers lasted until Constantius died in York in 306, and his son *Constantine was elected by a Roman army as co-emperor with Maxentius, son of Maximian, who had been elected in Rome. A six-year struggle for precedence—and survival—followed during which the futility of persecuting Christians was realized, since it did nothing to diminish the appeal of their beliefs, and alienated otherwise uncaring citizens, disgusted by the spectacle of barbarity towards willing victims. The dying Galerius finally issued in 311 a lukewarm decree which gave a large measure of freedom of conscience. His successor was Maxentius, but in 312 Constantine invaded Italy and defeated and killed his rival at the Battle of the Milvian Bridge over the Tiber north of Rome. During the night before the battle (or, according to Eusebius, during the day) Constantine is said to have seen a vision of a cross in the sky and heard the words '*In hoc signo vinces'. Victory made him Emperor of the West, but he had to share the purple with the anti-Christian Licinius, who had seized the Balkans, until he defeated and killed him in battle in 323, becoming sole ruler.

After Constantine's victory in 312, the Edict of *Milan was issued in 313 giving equal rights to all religions and restoring property confiscated during the persecutions. Although the Edict did no more than free Christians from persecution, Constantine's policy displayed a distinct bias in favour of Christianity. He grasped the political advantage of using the Church and its organization as an extension of imperial power, so that as Christianity spread its prelates, priests, and sees increased in number and importance in parallel with the imperial administration (the word diocese originally meant province of government). The Church also adopted certain imperial symbols and practices for Christian purposes, such as the *Traditio Legis—the giving of the Law by Christ to Peter—which was derived from Roman tradition in delegating authority. Despite the division of the empire into East and West and the removal of the centre of Western government to Milan, Rome had retained its primacy, and remained the capital of the ancient world, and the seat of the papacy. By 326 Constantine was building a new capital for his empire nearer to his eastern frontier and in 330 dedicated his new city on the Bosporus, creating Constantinople.

Architecture

In contrast with pagan temples, which were small in size, because their rites did not require many celebrants, nor a congregation, the growing size of Christian communities required first the adaptation of existing often domestic buildings, then the building of large churches, able to hold many hundreds of the faithful and a numerous clergy. Because of a natural revulsion against them, very few pagan temples were converted for Christian use until at least the end of the 4th century; examples are the Parthenon, the Pantheon, and the Temple of Apollo at Daphne. Christianity was also largely an urban religion, spreading more slowly in rural areas, where pagan beliefs and customs were deeply ingrained. The Communion developed as a relatively free liturgy within accepted local conventions, but increased in more uniform formality and solemnity in parallel with court ceremonial, to match the role of the emperor as the earthly representative of Christ the King. There is, therefore, a fundamental change from the modest *house-church which had been the earliest meeting-places of Christians—'they broke bread at home' (Acts 2: 46, NRSV) or 'breaking bread from house to house' (AV and Vg.)—to adapted structures, and finally to a large *basilica, and these new buildings, developed from established Roman civic structures, mark the transition from the first sites of private Christian worship to the second stage of Early Christian architecture.

Despite Constantine's establishment of his capital—the New Rome—in what was the already ancient city of Byzantium, soon known as Constantinople, Early Christian art and architecture in Italy is markedly different from the forms which developed in Byzantium in the 5th, and particularly in the 6th centuries, by which time the cleavage between Eastern and Western Churches was significant. Although the West—mostly Italy, and especially *Ravenna, *Milan, and *Venice—was affected by Byzantine art, the development of Western Early Christian art pursued a different course from that of Byzantine art proper.

Constantine's own church-building programme in Rome and the Holy Land was concentrated on especially venerated sites. He may have given the old imperial palace of the *Lateran to the Pope as early as 312–13, perhaps within weeks of the Battle of the Milvian Bridge, as an official residence for him as Bishop of Rome, and a majestic church was built alongside to become the cathedral (which it still is), originally dedicated to Christ the King, and only much later rededicated to both SS John. The church has a huge nave with double aisles on either side, and an *apse in the west end (the adoption of an orientation to the east came later from Byzantine custom). The *titular churches within the walls of Rome were built on the sites of private buildings, including houses, or *insulae* with shops and flats as at SS Giovanni e Paolo, or a warehouse (or mint?) as at S Clemente, or baths as at Sta Pudenziana. The Pauline Epistles describe the origin of house-churches as belonging to a small number of Christian converts who had opened them to the faithful (Rom. 16.3–5 and 23). In Rome, these properties later became basilicas such as Sta Prisca, Sta Prassede, and Sta Pudenziana (Prisca and Pudens are mentioned in Tim. 4: 19, 21). The veneration of martyrs' graves or the places where they had suffered, often led to the building, usually on a *central plan, of a *martyrium or *cella memoriae over the spot, and the many martyrs and faithful buried in the Roman catacombs led quickly to the building of large halls nearby where funeral feasts and *agape were held. These then became burial sites, as the faithful sought to be buried near a martyr's tomb, as at the Church of the Apostles (San Sebastiano) on the Via Appia, one of the earliest, San Lorenzo on the Via Tiburtina, SS Marcellino e Pietro on the Via Labicana, and Sant'Agnese on the Via Nomentana. The precise dating of these is difficult but all may be Constantinian, though it is possible that the Church of the Apostles was begun by Maxentius (*c.*278–312). All, of course, adjoined catacombs and were outside the city walls, and for these structures the most suitable model was used: the traditional Roman civic basilica.

A feature of most Christian basilicas was the *confessio either under or in front of the high altar. *Baptisteries were always built separately from the church, preferably in front of the main door, and either a round or octagonal central plan was used for them. Until the 6th century, only cathedrals had baptisteries. St Peter's Basilica, begun probably between 319 and 322, on the site of the tomb of S. Peter, and San Paolo fuori le Mura, not begun until 384 (replacing a modest memorial church built over the grave of *S. Paul, who was beheaded nearby, outside the city walls—hence the church's name) were both huge basilicas with four aisles flanking the central nave, an apsidal end, and were approached through an *atrium and a *narthex. San Paolo fuori was the first to have the apse in the east, but it was burned down in 1823, and the present church is a pious effort at reconstruction. It retains the basic shape of the original, with the transepts which were a medieval addition, but with the tragic loss of most of its original mosaics. When the rebuilding of St Peter's was begun in 1506, thousands of graves were found inside, and two chapels in the Grotto under St Peter's have ossuaries under them for the remains removed at the rebuilding.

Mosaics

The decoration of the early churches, and particularly of the basilicas, was mostly with *mosaics. One of the most elaborate series of mosaics is in Sta Costanza, a domed circular building of disputed date reputed to have been used as the burial chapel of Constantine's daughter. A huge mid-4th-century prophyry sarcophagus (now Vatican Mus.) once in the chapel, is said to have been her sarcophagus. The mosaics are ambivalent in their imagery, causing some to associate them with Constantine's nephew Julian the Apostate; the possibly late Antique ones in the vaulting of the ambulatory use originally pagan motifs, such as birds pecking grapes, luxuriant foliage and birds in a garden amid vases, the grape harvest, with putti pressing the grapes; such motifs were later invested with Christian meanings. The late 4th-century mosaics in the apses of chapels off the *ambulatory represent the Christian subjects of the *Traditio Clavium—Christ giving the keys to S. Peter—and the Traditio Legis—Christ giving the Law to S. Paul, though usually S. Peter is the recipient of the scroll of the Law, since it was S. Peter that Christ had named as the rock upon whom His Church was to be built. The late 4th-century apse mosaic of Sta Pudenziana (converted from a large *thermae* bath around 390), named in the text held in Christ's hand as 'ecclesia sancta pudentiana'—Pudens's church—is the most hieratically explicit, and clearly didactic. Christ, depicted as teacher and lawgiver, though also enthroned in majesty as judge, is seated in front of a hill, representing Golgotha, with a jewelled cross rising from it. On either side of the cross are the four symbols of the Evangelists—the *Tetramorph—possibly their earliest representation, and on either side of Christ are the Apostles, with S. Paul on His right, the position of honour, and S. Peter on His left. Behind them are two female figures, a woman in Roman dress behind S. Paul, representing the *Ecclesia ex gentibus*, because despite the precedence Christ gave to S. Peter, S. Paul's whole mission was to the Gentiles, and Rome was Gentile hence the precedence usually given in Rome to S. Paul. The woman behind S. Peter represents the *Ecclesia ex circumcisione*, since this was the Jewish people taught by Christ Himself, and the first mission field of the Apostles, except S. Paul. Behind the two groups of figures are depicted the churches relevant to the two *Ecclesiae*, the Rotunda of the Anastasis or Resurrection in Jerusalem behind S. Paul, and the Church of the Nativity in Bethlehem behind S. Peter. These are valuable pointers to the forms of two of Constantine's major churches in the Holy Land, of which only fragments have survived. Unfortunately, the mosaic was barbarously damaged in 1588, and some of the figures lost or mutilated, when a misguided cardinal tried to modernize the church according to the tastes of the time. It has also been very heavily restored. The placing of S. Paul and S. Peter occurs in other Roman apse mosaics—in the original mid-4th-century apse mosaic of St Peter's, later destroyed, but known from a fresco copy of the design which has similar positions for Jerusalem and Bethlehem, and also includes the four rivers of Paradise issuing below Christ's throne. This arrangement of Apostles and cities is also found in later Roman works such as the *c.*530 apse of SS Cosmas and Damian; in the early 7th-century Chapel of St Venantius in the Lateran Baptistery; in the early 9th-century group of *Christ with Saints* in the apse of Sta Prassede; and in the remaining fragment of the mosaic once in the atrium of St Peter's, of *c.*970–90 (now in the Vatican Grotto). In San Lorenzo fuori, the late 6th-century apse mosaic has S. Peter on Christ's right, but the two cities are in their traditional positions.

The largest series of early mosaic decorations in Rome are the panels on the *Triumphal Arch and the nave walls of Sta Maria Maggiore of *c.*432–40. The ones on the arch include a version of the Flight into *Egypt, and in the nave are OT subjects, mainly from the Books of Exodus and Joshua, and despite extensive restoration and some losses they are the most important Early Christian narrative series extant. Among the other major decorations are those in the Chapel of St Venantius in the Lateran Baptistery, of *c.*640. The chapel has a *Pantocrator flanked by angels in the crown of the apse, and below is a Virgin *orans* flanked by the figures of three saints and an ecclesiastic on either side, and the figures of saints continue outside the arch of the apse. The similarity between the Virgin and the figure of the Virgin in the *Ascension* in the *Rabbula Gospels of *c.*586 suggests that the mosaic may also represent an *Ascension*, while the treatment of the figures of the saints is very close to that in mosaics in San Vitale, Ravenna. The Oratory of Pope John VII in St Peter's of *c.*705 was destroyed when the rebuilding began after 1506. Fragments from its decoration—a *Nativity*, a *Virgin and Child*, *Pope John holding a model of his chapel*—have survived in the Vatican Grottoes, and among other fragments is a half-length, over-life size *Virgin*, now an altarpiece in Florence, San Marco.

Sculpture

*Sarcophagi carved with emblems or with figures are often ambiguous in their imagery, but this may partly be because the sculptors, in the early years of Christianity, were working within a strong pagan tradition, and many sarcophagi were part-carved in provincial workshops and exported to Rome to be finished according to the purchaser's wishes. Some were clearly made specially for Christian clients, and that they adapt the forms which had long been used for pagan clients is no more surprising than the use of pre-Christian building forms, or traditional mosaic designs. It was the most expensive form of burial, and presupposes that the occupant of the tomb came from a higher, or more opulent, position in society than those buried in the *cubicula* of the catacombs. A definite line of development can, however, be seen in the way the imagery changes, though it is worth noting that few sarcophagi are dated and only very occasionally are they datable. Among the ambiguous forms are those where the main body of the casket is decorated with the graceful SSS of strigil ornament, with perhaps a figure of a Genius with an upturned torch at either end—a traditional antique form of mourning figure—and a single figure in a central relief, perhaps of a shepherd with a sheep on his shoulders, the classical *Hermes Kriophoros here doubling as the Good Shepherd, or an Orant, again quite unspecific in meaning. Sarcophagi of this type are in the Terme Museum, Rome.

One of the traditional forms of tomb sculpture was in the form of a row of arches enclosing figures, the central figure clearly of more importance than the flanking ones—a philosopher or lawgiver, for instance. This too was adapted to the new faith, and the central figure was readily transformed into Christ, as lawgiver or judge, with the flanking figures as the Apostles. This could be done with complete anonymity, as is seen in examples in Ravenna, San Francesco, and Arles Museum, though by the time these were made the necessity for discretion or secrecy was long past. Sometimes the impersonal character of the imagery in the main reliefs is incompatible with the incidents from Christ's infancy carved on the lid, suggesting that the two parts were made separately.

This is perhaps the case with the sarcophagus of Titus Julius Gorgonius in Ancona Cathedral. Sometimes the approach is by symbols: no central figure, but a Chi-Rho flanked by men clearly intended as the Apostles, as in a sarcophagus in the Lateran Museum, Rome, and another in Notre-Dame, Manosque, Basse-Alpes, in S. France, though in both cases the guards set over the Holy Sepulchre are represented, making clear the identity of the Chi-Rho with Christ. There are many in which incidents from the OT are mixed with ones from the NT, or there are two parallel NT incidents, usually paired as types and antitypes: the *Sacrifice of Abraham* paired with *Christ before Pilate*, or *Judas betraying Christ* paired with *S. Paul arrested*, each incident in its own niche enclosed by columns, as in a sarcophagus now in Algiers Museum. But the grandest of all is the large 'double-decker' sarcophagus made in 359 for *Junius Bassus, Prefect of Rome, now in the Museum of St Peter's, Rome. There are ten 'scenes' in all, with a *Traditio Legis* of Christ entrusting SS Peter and Paul with their missions in the centre of the top register, flanked by the *Sacrifice of Abraham* and the *Arrest of S. Paul* on one side, and with *Christ before Pilate* on the other, and in the lower register the central *Entry into Jerusalem* is flanked on the left by *Job and his Comforters*, and *Adam and Eve*, while on the right side are *Daniel in the Lions' Den* and *S. Paul led to Execution*; Job and S. Paul as examples of supreme patience under suffering, and the Fall of Man which made Salvation necessary paired with Daniel as one of the great examples of deliverance and salvation. What appears at first sight to be a curious mixture becomes, upon analysis, a recondite sequence of the historical, the symbolic, and the typological, which is added to by the tiny figures of lambs, in the spandrels of the arches of the lower register. By an analogy with the frequent metaphorical identification of Christ with the Lamb, they portray incidents—the *Miracle at Cana*, the *Washing of the Feet*, and the *Raising of Lazarus, Abraham entertaining the Angels*, the *Manger of the Nativity*—all of which can be interpreted on several levels, historical, metaphorical, and symbolic. The programme for this complex work shows that by the 4th century the basic outward facts of the biblical stories had been invested with multiple layers of inward significance.

Almost no sculpture in the round has survived, and perhaps was never made, because of the fear of making images like the statues of pagan gods. Among the few survivors are statuettes of the Good Shepherd, who might double as Hermes Kriophorus, and philosophers who may be discreet images of Christ giving the Law (the Traditio Legis). In these cases, Christ is always depicted *as* the Good Shepherd, or *as* a lawgiver, never as Himself. Other notable works of sculpture are ivory reliefs, used as the covers of Gospel books, such as the 6th-century one with scenes from the *Life of Christ* (Milan), and *diptychs. Among the most notable of these are the two leaves depicting the *Archangel Michael*, one 4th century (London, BM), and the other of 470, part of the diptych of the Consul Severus (Leipzig); the late 5th-century double-leaf diptych with six *Miracles of Christ* (London, V & A); and the single leaves, one with the *Maries approaching the Angel at the Sepulchre* (late 4th cent.: Milan) the other with the *Maries at the Sepulchre* and the *Ascension* (late 4th/early 5th cent.: Munich). Two ivory caskets have survived, the *Brescia Box and a casket in London (BM), of *c.*430, consisting of four small panels portraying scenes from Christ's Passion in *Continuous Representation. *Christ condemned by Pilate*, and striding away with a symbolic cross as if towards *S. Peter with the accusing maidservant and the crowing cock*, is followed by *Judas hanging from a tree* next to what is probably the earliest clear representation of the *Crucifixion*, more explicit than the one in the doors of Sta *Sabina, with the Virgin and either S. John or Joseph of Arimathea on the left of the cross and Longinus on the right. The third panel shows the *Resurrection*, with soldiers sleeping beside a domed tomb with an open door, approached by the Holy Women, and the last is of *Christ appearing to the Disciples* with doubting Thomas reaching for the wound in Christ's side. Most carved ivory panels were made for the embellishment of useful objects, among which perhaps the most important is the throne of *Maximian in Ravenna. The *Projecta Casket (London, BM) is an example of the deliberate mixing of Christian and pagan imagery.

Among other survivals is a small number of remarkable silver objects: the Antioch *chalice (New York, Met. Mus.); and a silver-gilt reliquary with four reliefs sent by Pope

Damasus to S. Ambrose (*c.*382: Milan Cath. Treasury). A large silver dish, the *Missorium of Theodosius I, Valentinian II, and Arcadius,* made probably in Italy to commemorate the decennial of 383, for use as a table centre, was found at Badajos, W. Spain, suggesting that it probably was Visigothic loot (now Madrid, Acad. de la Historia). A hoard of Christian silver of the second half of the 4th century was found in 1975 at Water Newton in Cambridgeshire at the site of the Roman town of *Durobrivae* (now British Museum, London). It includes votive plaques similar to pagan examples, and what may be the earliest surviving vessels for use in the liturgy. Engraved texts give tantalizing clues to the social and liturgical contexts.

Manuscripts surviving from Early Christian times are very few: the *Vienna Genesis, the *Rossano Gospels, the *Rabbula Gospels, and the *S. Augustine Gospels* (Corpus Christi Coll., Cambridge), which may have been those sent by Pope Gregory the Great to S. Augustine at Canterbury. The *Ashburnham Pentateuch is probably also late 6th or 7th century.

Earthly Paradise *See* PARADISE and EDEN, GARDEN OF.

Easter The principal feast of the Liturgical Year is Easter Sunday, the culmination of Holy Week and of the services connected with the Passion and *Crucifixion, and *Resurrection of *Christ. Easter Sunday is the celebration of the Resurrection. The date of Easter varies every year because it has to fit in with the Jewish Passover, since historically it occurred at that season. The calculation of the date of both feasts depends on the phases of the moon, since they must fall at the time of the Paschal full moon, which varies yearly between 21 March and 25 April. This agreement about the date was not finally reached until 669 in England, following the Synod of Whitby in 664, the problem of divergent dates having arisen through differences of calculation between Rome, Jerusalem, Alexandria, Gaul, and the Celtic Church in Ireland. This had led to the confusion of Easter being celebrated in one centre perhaps as much as a week or a fortnight after another centre.

Easter candlestick *See* CANDLESTICK.

Eastern Orthodox Churches Originally the Church in the Byzantine Empire, headed by the Patriarch of Constantinople, the Orthodox Church now consists of the four ancient patriarchates of Constantinople, Antioch, Alexandria, and Jerusalem, together with several other self-governing churches, of which the most important are the Greek and the Russian. All of them celebrate the Byzantine liturgy, but in various more or less archaic forms of the vernacular languages—neither modern Greek nor Russian is the tongue in use. From the 9th century there was a gradual separation from Rome, and the schism of 1054 is often thought to mark a parting, but the Turkish conquest of Constantinople in 1453 was more decisive in determining isolation from the Western Church. The Eastern Church is intensely conservative. *Icons and devotion to the saints are marked features, as is the importance of monasteries, especially the ancient ones on Mt. *Athos.

Theologically, there are few differences between the E. Orthodox and W. Catholic churches, and attempts have been made to reconcile them, notably at the Council of *Florence (1434–7) and in recent years. In liturgy and the arts the rigid conservatism of the Orthodox has inhibited all new ideas and formal experiment, and centuries-old artistic and musical traditions remain unchanged.

Eastern Orthodox Fathers *See* FATHERS.

Easter Sepulchre On Maundy Thursday in Holy Week, the Western rite concludes with the removal of the Blessed Sacrament to an *Altar of Repose. In the Sarum and other medieval rites, it was often removed to a recess in the north wall, considered as Christ's tomb, until the vigil of Easter. Of such is the one in the North choir aisle of Lincoln Cathedral, *c.*1290–1300, with the figures of sleeping soldiers carved on the base. A rare survival of an old form of Easter Sepulchre is in the Christian Museum of Estergom, Hungary, where a wooden shrine like a miniature chapel, which was wheeled into the church on Maundy Thursday, has a high pinnacled roof and polychrome figures of the Apostles on pedestals round the gilded traceried exterior. There are carved, polychromed panels all round the base, the long sides with sleeping guards, the short sides with the three Maries and the Angel at the tomb at one end, and at the other end, the Resurrection. It was the custom to place a wooden figure of the dead Christ inside the shrine, to remain there until Easter Sunday morning. It is datable *c.*1480. None of these types of Easter Sepulchre has anything to do with the chapels containing a representation of the Entombment or the *Lamentation over the Dead Christ, which are found over much of Europe, particularly in France. The sculptural figures of which these consist combine several themes, which in manuscripts are often treated separately: the carrying of Christ's body to the tomb; the anointing of the body on the stone of *Unction; the Lamentation, with the dead Christ either outstretched on the ground on a shroud, or held in her arms by His grieving mother. The carrying of Christ's body appears in 9th-century manuscripts; the anointing (*see* EPITAPHIOS) appears in 12th-century manuscripts, and in sculpture in the long frieze of capitals on the west front of Chartres Cathedral, 1150–5; the Lamentation is frequent from the 10th century onwards, mainly in manuscripts, and its most notable representation in fresco is the one by Giotto in the Arena Chapel, Padua, *c.*1306. The sculptural groups which combine the Lamentation with Christ's body laid on the flat top of a sarcophagus, with or without a shroud, appear in Germany as early as the 14th century (Freiburg im Breisgau, *c.*1330 in stone; Oberwesel, Rhineland, in a wood carving with separate figures grouped around the dead Christ, *c.*1330–40). One of the stimuli to the development and popularity of the theme is Franciscan piety, e.g. the **Meditationes Vitae Christi*, in which the anguished state of the Virgin on meeting her son carrying His cross is recounted, and in general they reflect an increased devotion to Christ's agony in the Passion, and to the suffering of the Virgin; but the most powerful impetus came from the widespread development of *mystery and Passion Plays with their vivid evocations of events in the Bible, particularly the Gospels, represented in costumes of the time, as if they were current events. In Italy, the emphasis was on the Lamentation, often deeply emotional, as in the groups by Niccolò dell'Arca in Sta Maria della Vita, Bologna, 1463, and Guido Mazzoni in San Giovanni della Buona Morte, Modena, 1477–80. Though not strictly relevant to the theme of the Easter Sepulchre, yet part of a popular Easter devotion to images which evoke the sufferings of the dead Christ and his Holy Mother, is the series of forty-six small chapels forming the pilgrimage route of the *Sacro Monte at Varallo in N. Italy. Their sequence of incidents from the Life of the Virgin, from the Annunciation to the Assumption; and of Christ from the Nativity to the Resurrection, all executed in life-sized polychrome sculpture and painting by Tanzio da Varallo and others from 1517 onwards, testify to the influence of religious drama on devotional works of art.

In France, the subject of the Entombment became very popular, and there are many splendid groups in churches and hospital chapels all over the country with life-size figures of the Virgin, S. John, the Holy Women, Nicodemus, and Joseph of Arimathaea mourning the dead Christ laid upon the tomb or being borne to it, dating from the 15th to the 17th centuries, sometimes combined with the tomb of a donor in the same chapel, sometimes as an independent place for devotional meditation. It does not appear that any particular rite was ever connected with these chapels, despite their suitability for the liturgy of Easter.

The earliest carved group, with seven figures, made in 1419/20 in Langres, has now disappeared, and the earliest surviving painted group, with Christ laid upon a tomb-slab with no shroud beneath Him, combined with an anointing, is in a *predella* panel of an altarpiece of a *Virgin of Pity*, of *c.*1425 (Nice, Musée Masséna). The earliest surviving group with full-sized carved figures is in Tonnerre, in Burgundy, dated 1453. This sets the iconographical type for other Burgundian examples, such as those at Sémur-en-Auxois, near Auxerre, dated 1490, and at Chaource, near Troyes in Burgundy, of *c.*1515, where the polychromed group is set in a deep tomb-like area under the high altar, with—unusually—the soldiers set to guard the tomb standing at the entrance to the chapel. This is perhaps the most beautiful and moving of all these monuments. Other notable ones are in Solesmes, near Le Mans, attributed to Michel Colombe, *c.*1496, and, grandest of all, Pontoise near Paris, where the 16th-century *Entombment* is preceded by the *Three Maries coming to the Sepulchre*, and surmounted by the *Resurrection*, in carved wood, added in the 17th century. With few exceptions the most telling characteristic of the French examples is the restraint with which the deep grief of the Virgin and the other figures is expressed. It is a reflective and meditative grief, designed to inspire the faithful with an understanding of the acceptance of the sacrifice made for mankind's salvation, and where a more emotional expression appears, the effect of the work in inspiring a deep meditative response is weakened.

'Ecce Agnus Dei' (Lat. 'Behold the Lamb of God', AV John 1: 36; NRSV: Here is the Lamb of God) These words were spoken by *John the Baptist immediately before he baptized Christ. The word Lamb was a reference to Christ as the *Agnus Dei, the sacrificial lamb of the Passover. Representations of the Baptist often have *Ecce Agnus Dei* on a scroll, and they are also sometimes found on paintings of the Baptism of Christ.

'Ecce Ancilla Domini' (Lat. 'Behold the handmaid of the Lord', AV and Vg. Luke 1: 38) In S. Luke's Gospel, 1: 38, these words were Mary's reply to the Archangel Gabriel at the *Annunciation. It is also the title of a painting by *Rossetti (1849/50: London, Tate), which was one of the first Pre-Raphaelite (*see* PRB) works. NRSV (Luke 1: 38) gives the words as 'Here am I, the servant of the Lord'.

'Ecce Homo' (Lat. 'Behold the man', AV and Vg. John 19: 5; NRSV has 'Here is the man') According to S. John, these were the words used by *Pilate when he showed Christ to the people, to which their response was 'Crucify him!' In pictures of this subject Christ is shown wearing the Crown of Thorns and dressed in a purple robe, usually holding a reed (Matt. 27: 29). Representations of Christ alone, sometimes of His head only, crowned with thorns, are called *Man of Sorrows. *See also* STATIONS OF THE CROSS.

'Ecce Virgo Concipiet' (Lat. 'Behold, a virgin shall conceive', AV and Vg. Isa. 7: 14; NRSV 'Look, the young woman is with child') These words are those of *Isaiah's prophecy of the birth of Christ, and may appear on a scroll held by him, when he is represented as an OT *type, e.g. in the **Biblia Pauperum*, referring to the *Annunciation. The words may also appear occasionally on representations of the Annunciation.

Ecclesia and Synagoga (Lat. church and synagogue) are two female figures symbolizing the Old and New Dispensations (*see* COVENANTS). They are frequently found on medieval *portals as sculpture in the round. Ecclesia is crowned and holds a sceptre or cross and has a chalice or a model of a church, Synagoga is blindfolded, her crown is awry (NRSV and AV Lam. 5: 16–17, 'The crown has fallen from our head ... our eyes have grown dim'; the Vg. is almost identical), and she holds a broken sceptre or spear or the Tablets of the Law. Occasionally, Ecclesia rides on a *Tetramorph. From Carolingian times they occur in MS illuminations of the Crucifixion, and ivories such as the 9th-century one in London (V & A), but they were particularly popular in portal sculpture.

Sta Sabina in Rome (422–32) has a mosaic of two female figures, but they represent *Ecclesia ex circumcisione*, i.e. the Jewish Christian Church, and *Ecclesia ex gentibus*, the Church of the Gentiles, and are therefore not in opposition as are Ecclesia and Synagoga. Similar figures are the Wise and Foolish Virgins, Rachel and Leah (Gen. 29: *Jacob preferring Rachel), and it has been suggested that Jacob struggling with the Angel is an OT *type of the Triumph of the Church over the Synagogue.

Ecclesiological Society *See* CAMBRIDGE CAMDEN.

Eden, Garden of In the OT, after God had created the world and man, He 'planted a garden in Eden, in the east; and there he put the man whom he had formed. Out of the ground the Lord God made to grow every tree that is pleasant to the sight and good for food, the tree of life also in the midst of the garden, and the tree of the knowledge of good and evil' (NRSV Gen. 2: 8–9; AV is virtually identical; Vg. has 'And the Lord God had planted a paradise of pleasure from the beginning: wherein he placed man whom he had formed').

In art, the Garden of Eden is virtually inseparable from the events which took place there: the Creation of Man and Woman, the Temptation, and the Fall. It has been suggested that part of the 4th-century mosaics in the ceiling of Sta Costanza in Rome, where trees, birds, and animals are depicted, represents Paradise. The 5th-century mosaic of the Good Shepherd in the Mausoleum of Galla Placidia in Ravenna, where Christ is seated in a garden with the sheep around Him, the grape harvest of the 6th- or 7th-century Antioch Cup (New York, Met. Mus.), and the background of the 6th-century apse of Sant'Apollinare in Classe,

Ravenna, with trees, plants, birds, and animals, may all be among the early visions of Paradise. Certainly some of the most striking such visions are those by Hieronymous *Bosch in the left wings of both the *Garden of Delights* and the *Haywain* (both Madrid, Prado), where the fantastic garden and the main events are all depicted. *See also* MAN, FALL OF.

e

Edessa Portrait of Christ, the One of the images of *Christ, allegedly sent to King *Abgar in Edessa, during Christ's lifetime. The original was lost centuries ago, but there are a number of copies—one, in the Metropolitan Museum, New York, is Russian, probably 16th/17th century, and is inscribed in Russian: 'The image of the Lord which was sent by the Lord himself to King Abgar of Edessa for healing and this image was placed in the monastery of St Silvester [in Rome] with great honour to the glory of God's great miracle.'

Edict of Milan *See* MILAN, THE EDICT OF.

Education of the Virgin *See* MARY.

Egeria the Pilgrim *See* ETHERIA.

Egypt, Flight into, and Return from Egypt Two incidents in the Life of Christ, related in the Gospel, Matt. 2: 13–25 (all versions). After the *Magi had worshipped the Infant Jesus in Bethlehem, an angel warned them not to return to Jerusalem. After they had left, an angel appeared to *Joseph in a dream, and told him to take Jesus and His mother, and flee to Egypt, and to stay there until he was told to return to Israel, because *Herod would search for the child to kill Him. Joseph then took Jesus and His mother by night, and fled to Egypt, and stayed there until the death of Herod: 'This was to fulfil what had been spoken by the Lord through the prophet, Out of Egypt I have called my son.' Later, the Gospel continues telling how an angel appeared in a dream to Joseph and told him to take Jesus and His mother, and return to Israel, 'for those who were seeking the child's life are dead'. Joseph then returned with them to Israel, but when he heard that Archelaus was ruling over Judaea in place of his father Herod, he was afraid to go there. After being warned in a dream, he went to the district of Galilee and settled in a town called Nazareth, so that what had been spoken through the prophets might be fulfilled, 'He will be called a Nazorean.'

The Herod against whom the angel warned the Magi and Joseph was Herod the Great, who reigned from 37 BC to 4 BC. The Archelaus whom Joseph feared on the return from Egypt was the eldest son of Herod, who inherited part of the kingdom; the Romans deposed him in AD 6. The prophecy the Evangelist refers to is in Hosea (Vg. Osee) 11: 1, a mysterious statement reading, 'When Israel was a child, then I loved him, and called my son out of Egypt'. The second prophecy, in Matt. 2: 23, is one for which no prophet has been identified; the term Nazorean (AV and Vg. Nazarene) refers not only to a man from Nazareth, but was also a Jewish name given to followers of Christ, as in Acts 24: 5.

From the bare account in Matt. 2: 13–15 a complex iconography has emerged, increased by picturesque details from the *Apocryphal Gospels. The earliest representation of the story is a partial one in the mosaics on the *Triumphal Arch of Sta Maria Maggiore, Rome, of 432–40, which pad out the Gospel with incidents from the Latin version of the so-called Gospel of Thomas, such as the story of Joseph's doubts about Mary's explanation of her pregnancy, while from the Pseudo-Matthew comes the story of the arrival of the Holy Family in Sotinen, and the homage of the Governor Affrodosius. The next earliest representations appear to be an 8th-century fresco in Sta Maria Antiqua, Rome, and two dating from the 9th century, a Carolingian wall-painting with a boy carrying a bundle walking behind the ass, which Joseph leads (*c.*800, Müstair, SW Switzerland), and one of the reliefs on the Ruthwell cross of *c.*800. (*see* CROSSES, STANDING.) The subject did not become popular until after the 10th century, when various other elaborations were added. The Virgin seated on the ass usually holds the Christ Child, as in one of the scenes in the 12th-century bronze doors at San Zeno, Verona, but sometimes Joseph does, as in the wing of an altarpiece of *c.*1280–90 (Perugia), where Joseph carries Him on his shoulders. Other details inspired by the Pseudo-Matthew are the idols which fall from their columns as the Holy Child passes (1115–30: relief in main portal, Moissac), and the story of the palm-tree which bowed its branches when the Christ Child told it to, so that the Virgin might reach its fruits (Hans Baldung Grien: 1512–16, Freiburg Cath.), after which He bade an angel take a palm branch to Heaven, so that it might be the reward of martyrs. A spring also appeared at His command.

Other additions to the story are that they were accompanied by S. Joseph's three sons, Salome the midwife, and the ox and ass from the stable. From an Arabic Gospel of the Infancy comes a story of an encounter with robbers, when one of their leaders ransomed them himself (14th cent.: tympanum, Thann, St-Thiébaut); they later become the two thieves, Gestas and Dismas, crucified on either side of Christ. The story is repeated by *Ludolph of Saxony. The **Meditationes Vitae Christi* tells the story about the idols falling as the Holy Family passed, and that on their return seven years later they met S. John the Baptist at the edge of the desert and went to the house of S. Elizabeth, where S. Joseph was warned to go to Nazareth. The **Golden Legend* also says that the Holy Family spent seven years in Egypt. Eventually the more picturesque accretions were abandoned, and the usual rendering is the Virgin holding the Infant Christ, seated sideways on the ass led either by a boy or S. Joseph in front, as in the Giotto (*c.*1306: Arena Chapel, Padua), where two young men and a woman follow, or are sometimes accompanied, as in the Gentile da Fabriano *predella* (1423: Uffizi), by two maidservants behind the group. In the Michael Pacher (1471–81: St Wolfgang am Abersee, church) there is still an idol tumbling in the background. The only way to tell if the scene is of the Flight or the Return, is by the age of the Christ Child, but a MS illumination from a Flemish Psalter (early 13th cent., Berlin Printroom) has both S. Joseph's Dream, and Jesus led by S. Joseph, with His mother walking behind Him, and a panel by the Master of the Aachen Altar, *c.*1510, has Jesus leading the Virgin with S. Joseph and the laden ass walking behind them.

A variant of the subject, the *Rest on the Flight into Egypt,* first appeared by the mid-14th century (Master Bertram: 1380, Grabow Altar, Hamburg), and in the 16th and 17th centuries became popular as a pastoral version of the story (Titian: *c.*1512, Longleat, Warminster; Tintoretto: 1583/7, Venice, Scuola di San Rocco); often with effects of moonlight, torchlight, and firelight (Elsheimer: 1609, Munich; Rubens: 1614, Kassel; Rembrandt: 1647, Dublin). Other charming additions to the story have been made, such as playful angels (Poussin: 1636/7, Winterthur), or a musician angel to lull the travellers to sleep (Caravaggio: 1595/6, Rome, Doria Gall.). There is also a rare variant of *The Return from Egypt* by Poussin (1628/9: London, Dulwich Gall.) where, as the Holy Family are about to embark on a boat to cross the river, the Christ Child looks up and is the only one to see and understand the meaning of the cross upheld in the sky by little putti.

Writers of such works as the *Meditationes Vitae Christi* and the *Golden Legend* based their accounts of Christ's infancy largely on the Apocryphal Gospels, despite their rejection by S. Jerome in his work of emendation, but their picturesque quality made them popular with artists and patrons alike. *See also* CHRIST.

Egypt, Plagues of *See* MOSES.

eidolon (Gk. pl. *eidola*) A small winged figure symbolizing for the ancient world the human soul in Hades. It was also used for a spectre or phantom. In the Christian Middle Ages these winged figures were often transmuted into *demons. *See also* EROS.

Elders, the twenty-four, of the Apocalypse In S. John's vision of the end of the world, the elders are those who are seated nearest to the throne of God. They are mentioned several times in Rev. 4: 4, 10; 5: 8–10; 7: 11 ff. and elsewhere: 'And round about the throne were four and twenty seats: and upon the seats I saw four and twenty elders sitting, clothed in white raiment; and they had on their heads crowns of gold... The four and twenty elders fell down before him that sat on the throne, and cast their crowns before the throne'. Iconographically, there are connections with the *Allerheiligenbild, the *Adoration of the Lamb, and the *Majestas Domini, but the illustrations to the *Beatus MSS and *Dürer's *Apocalypse* are straightforward illustrations to the text. The earliest representations are probably in the 15th-century mosaic in San Paolo fuori le Mura, Rome, and other early Roman churches. The subject also occurs in medieval tympana of the *Majestas Domini*—Moissac, *c.*1115, Chartres, 1145, and other French and Spanish churches. The Ghent Altar, by the van *Eyck brothers (1432) is closely connected with the theme, though not an illustration of it.

Elements, the Sacred *See* SPECIES, THE SACRED.

elevation (in architecture) This term describes the appearance of the vertical aspect of a building from outside—i.e. the front elevation, or the side or rear elevation. It is also used to describe a church vertically inside, i.e. the nave elevation, and is very useful when the nave, or the choir or transept, are composed of different parts, such as an arcade and triforium. In elevation drawings, the rules of perspective are ignored, so that the parts may be measured to the same scale, and each part is seen individually.

Elevation of the Host/Chalice At the celebration of the Catholic rite of the *Eucharist, when the central point of the Mass is reached at the words of consecration, the celebrant raises the consecrated Host above his head so that it is visible to all the congregation. This is repeated after the wine is consecrated and the chalice is raised (though this was not usual until the 16th cent.). The practice is thought to have begun *c.*1200 in the Paris region, since the people in the nave were becoming ever more separated from the clergy in the chancel and needed to know what was happening. It is not used in the E. Orthodox Church, since the consecration takes place behind the closed doors of the *iconostasis, neither does it take place in the Anglican rite. The Elevation is usually shown in representations of the celebration of Mass, as its most symbolic moment: e.g. in the picture by the Master of *S. Giles (*c.*1500: London, NG), although in another picture of the *Mass of S. Hubert*, from the Studio of the Master of the Life of the Virgin (*c.*1485/90: also London, NG), the specific circumstances of that Mass, when an angel appeared bearing a stole for the celebrant, are shown, as also in the case of the Mass of *S. Gregory. The Elevation also appears in the background of the Roger van der *Weyden altarpiece of the *Seven Sacraments* (before 1445: Antwerp Mus.) since all the Sacraments are represented surrounding the Crucifixion.

Eleven Thousand Virgins *See* URSULA, S.

Elias *See* ELIJAH.

Eliezer *See* ISAAC.

Eligius (Fr. **Eloi**), **Saint** (*c.*588–659/60), was a goldsmith who became the trusted adviser of the Merovingian kings Clotaire II and Dagobert. After 639 he became a priest and in 641 was made bishop of Noyon in N. France and Tournai (now in modern Belgium), where he was active in founding monasteries. His cult was widespread in France and especially in Flanders, but his connection with the goldsmiths' guild spread it all over Europe, and he is often represented in guild chapels: he is the patron of all metal-workers, including garage mechanics, and farriers. This is because he is supposed to have had trouble with a horse he was shoeing, so he cut off its hoof, shoed it, and replaced the hoof on the stump. He is also said to have been disturbed in his work by the Devil in the form of a young woman, so he took his hot tongs from the forge and seized the Devil by the nose. Both these legends are shown on the relief by Nanni di Banco below the statue of Eligius on Orsanmichele, the guild church in Florence (*c.*1413). A *predella* by Botticelli (1490: Florence, Uffizi) is based on the relief. He is also represented as a bishop holding a horseshoe, and sometimes as a working goldsmith, as in the painting by Petrus Christus (1449: New York, Met. Mus.), which may have come from the Antwerp Guild. In Rome, the church of Sant'Eligio degli Orefici, claimed to have been designed by Raphael, is still the guild church of the goldsmiths.

Elijah (Gk. and Vg. **Elias**) was one of the five Major OT Prophets, with *Isaiah, *Ezekiel, *Jeremiah, and *Daniel; he was believed to have lived in the 9th century BC. He preached relentlessly against the apostasy of the kings of Israel, who had adopted the worship of the idol Baal and other false gods, prophesying disasters which came to pass as a great drought. No separate book of his prophecies is included in the OT, the account of his life and work being within the books of 1 and 2 Kings (in both NRSV and AV; Vg. 3 and 4 Ks.). Elijah first appears in Kgs. 1: 17, before Ahab, King of Israel, who, incited by his wife Jezebel, had built an altar to Baal. Elijah prophesied that there would be neither dew nor rain for three years. God then told him to live beside the Wadi Cherith (AV and Vg. 'brook Kerith'), where he was fed by ravens. When the brook dried up, he was told to go to Zarephath, near Sidon, where he was fed by a widow who believed his prophecy that her barrel of meal and cruse of oil would not fail until the day God sent rain on the earth. When the woman's son died, Elijah took the dead child from her, and stretching himself three times upon his body, prayed that God should return the boy's soul to his body. He then restored the resuscitated child to his mother, who exclaimed that she now knew that 'the word of the Lord in thy mouth is truth'. This scene is among those depicted in the 3rd-century Jewish synagogue in *Dura-Europos.

Elijah challenged the priests of Baal to the contest of a fiery sacrifice, which should prove to all present the supremacy of God over the false god Baal. Each should prepare a sacrifice of a bull, and call on his deity to send fire to consume it. After many hours of invocation, while Elijah mocked them 'Cry louder! ... either he has wandered away, ... or he is asleep ...', the priests were unable to persuade Baal to consume their sacrifice. When Elijah prayed, God sent fire which consumed his sacrifice, and after Baal's priests had been killed by their disillusioned followers, he went to the top of Mt. Carmel, bade his servant look out to sea, until eventually the man saw 'a cloud no bigger than a man's hand' (NRSV 'person's hand') which had risen from the sea. It became a great storm, which ended the drought. Ahab's wife Jezebel, furious at the death of her priests, sought to kill Elijah; he fled to the wilderness, where he was fed by an angel with food which gave him strength to journey for forty days and nights to a cave on Mt. Horeb (Sinai), the mountain of God. There occurred the mysterious event of the storm, the earthquake, and the great fire, but only after that came the still, small voice of God telling him to anoint new kings for Syria and Israel to replace the idolaters, and to summon *Elisha to be his successor. King Ahab, who persistently apostatized, repeatedly repented and was forgiven, even after he condoned the wanton murder, on Jezebel's order, of Naboth, whose vineyard he coveted. Elijah's dire prophecies of the shameful deaths of Ahab and Jezebel were eventually fulfilled, but meanwhile God took Elijah into Heaven. A chariot and horses of fire parted Elijah from Elisha, and carried him into Heaven, and as he rose his mantle fell on Elisha's shoulders.

In Matt. 17: 1–8, at the *Transfiguration, Elijah and Moses appeared on either side of Christ. Some believed that Elijah had returned in the person of S. John the Baptist, and the evidence for this in the answers to Christ's question to the disciples: '"Who do men say that the Son of Man is?" And they said: "Some say John the Baptist, but others Elijah, and still others Jeremiah, or one of the prophets"' (Matt. 16: 13–14). Elijah's ascension (like *Enoch's translation) is a prototype of both the Ascension of Christ and the Assumption of the Virgin.

The story of Elijah has provided many symbolic NT prefigurations. His meeting with the widow, and his promise of unfailing meal and oil (1565: J. Massys, Karlsruhe) symbolizes God's inexhaustible grace. The raising of the widow's son prefigures Christ's three miracles of the raising of the son of the widow of Naim, Jairus's daughter, and Lazarus, as well as His own Resurrection. Elijah in the wilderness fed by the angel is a symbol of the Eucharist, and so appears in *Bouts's altarpiece of the *Mystic Meals* (1464–8: S. Pieter, Leuven); it also prefigures Christ's fast in the desert. The ascension of Elijah, with his cloak falling on Elisha (symbol of the Charge to the Apostles) is the most frequently represented scene, particularly in Early Christian art (Rome, cemetery of Domitilla, 1st cent.; Catacomb of Via Latina, mid-4th cent., with the chariot and quadriga derived from classical representations of Helios or Apollo). A double Bible illustration (Vatican, *c.*9th cent.) shows Elijah before Ahab, and his ascension in a chariot with his cloak caught by Elisha. Carmelites were especially devoted to Elijah, whom they considered as 'patron and father' because he had lived in a cave on Mt. Carmel; fresco cycles of his life are a frequent decoration in Carmelite churches and refectories, notably on Mt. Athos. The massacre of the priests of Baal was a popular subject in Byzantine and Russian art. The right aisle walls of the Early Christian church of San Martino ai Monti, Rome, has frescoes by Gaspar Dughet (17th cent.) of incidents from the life of Elijah set in landscapes of the Roman Campagna. An English 19th-century 'history' picture by Thomas Matthews Rooke represents *Elijah reproving Ahab*, who is accompanied by his furious wife Jezebel, after the murder of Naboth (1878: S. London Gallery).

Elisha (Gk. and Vg. **Eliseus**) was the disciple of *Elijah whom the prophet called from the plough to be his successor. His life and work is told in the OT: 2 Kgs. 2 and 4 (Vg. 4 Kgs. 2 & 4). When Elijah was taken up to heaven, Elisha caught his mantle as it fell from the fiery chariot (a prefiguration of Christ's Calling of the Apostles); to prove that Elijah's powers had been given to him, he struck the Jordan with the mantle, the waters parted, and he crossed dry foot (depicted in a sarcophagus relief in Arles). He cursed a crowd of urchins who mocked him as 'baldpate'; two bears came out of the forest and killed them (depicted in a sarcophagus relief in Vienne; Giandomenico Tiepolo: 1759, Udine, fresco in the Chiesa della Purità, a church for the instruction of the young). The mantle and his bald head are constant features of his iconography. He repeated some of Elijah's miracles, and multiplied twenty loaves and some corn-cobs to feed a hundred men, a scene depicted in Italian art as an OT antitype for Christ's multiplication of the loaves and fishes, and as a parallel to the gathering of the manna (Tintoretto, Venice: ceiling, Upper Hall, Scuola di San Rocco). He healed Naaman, captain of the army of the king of Syria, of leprosy by telling him to wash seven times in the Jordan (12th-cent. enamel plaque attributed to Godefroi of Huy, London, BM) and transferred the leprosy to his own servant Gehazi, as a punishment for secretly asking Naaman for a reward. He rendered eatable a poisoned mess of potage (Vasari, 1566: Uffizi) and made the bitter spring drinkable at Jericho, where his acclamation is treated as an antitype of Christ's entry into Jerusalem. His last acts were to anoint Jehu as King of Israel, replacing Ahab and his line, and to order him to kill all Ahab's family, his wife Jezebel, his captains, and all the priests of Baal; and when he was dying (2 Kgs. 13: 14–20) he bade Joash, now King of Israel, shoot the arrow which began the war to liberate Israel from Syria (W. Dyce, 1844: Hamburg). Even Elisha's dead body was miraculous, since a dead man thrown into his tomb years later when his funeral bearers fled from bandits, was restored to life by contact with the prophet's bones. Incidents from Elisha's life are also illustrated in Spanish Bibles (e.g. León, Sto Isidoro, of 940–1162, and the Bible of S. Millán de Cogolla, 12th–13th cent., Madrid Acad.).

Elizabeth, Saint She was the mother of *S. John the Baptist. In the NT, Luke 1 describes her as a descendant of Aaron, and tells how her husband *Zacharias was told by the Angel Gabriel that a son would be born to them. Six months later, Gabriel announced to *Mary that she would conceive her son, Jesus, telling her that her cousin Elizabeth, who had been called barren, was now in her sixth month 'for nothing will be impossible with God'. Mary then travelled to the hill town of Judaea where Zacharias and Elizabeth lived, and at the *Visitation Elizabeth greeted her as 'the mother of my Lord'. Three months later Elizabeth bore a son. She is not again mentioned in the Gospels. Some apocryphal writings, used by the Byzantine historian Nicephorus Callistus (*c.*1256–1355) in his *Church History*, claim to establish the degree of relationship between Elizabeth and Mary by stating that Zacharias's father had married a sister of Mary's mother Anne.

The vagueness of the location of Elizabeth's house has led to many conjectural sites, but tradition has settled on ʿAín Karím, now a western suburb of Jerusalem. Elizabeth has no specific iconography, but is invariably depicted as an elderly woman. An early version of the *Birth of S. John* and the *Visitation* is in a Byzantinizing Sienese painting of *c.*1250 (Siena). Ghirlandaio's fresco cycle of the *Life of the Baptist* (1486–90: Florence, choir of Sta Maria Novella) has scenes of the *Angel appearing to Zacharias*, the *Birth of the Baptist*, and the *Naming of the Baptist*. The *Visitation* is part of the Marian cycle on the opposite wall. Elizabeth also appears in two groups of the *Holy Family* by Raphael, the 'Canigiani' (*c.*1505–7: Munich), and the 'Francis I' group (1518: Paris, Louvre). The *Visitation* figures in one of the panels of the bronze doors by Bonanno (late 12th cent.) in the Porta di San Raineri, Pisa Cathedral, and in a panel by Nicholas of Verdun of 1205 in the *Shrine of the Virgin*, Tournai Cathedral. It is also in Giotto's Arena Chapel frescoes, *c.*1306, Padua, in the *Life of the Virgin* series, and similarly in Taddeo Gaddi's Baroncelli Chapel, 1332–8: Florence, Sta Croce. Other notable versions of the subject are by Pontormo (*c.*1528–9: Carmignano, San Michele) and Sebastiano del Piombo (1521: Paris, Louvre; and 1522: Lendinara, San Biagio). The rare scene of the *Flight of S. Elizabeth with the Infant S. John* to escape the Massacre of the *Innocents, a subject usually found only in the East, is in a 6th-century codex in Bobbio, near Piacenza, and in a fresco in an early rock church at Toqale Kilisse in Cappadocia.

Elizabeth of Hungary, Saint (1207–31), Queen. In 1221 she married Louis IV of Thuringia, and spent a fortune on almsgiving, hospitals, and orphanages. Louis joined the Third Crusade and died of plague in 1227, and his brother then drove her from court. In 1228 she became a Franciscan Tertiary at Marburg, devoting herself to charity, working at spinning and menial tasks for the poor, and died as a result of her austerities. She was canonized in 1235, and her relics were at St Elizabeth, Marburg (finished in 1231), where they were the object of a popular pilgrimage until 1539, when they were removed by the Lutheran ruler, Philip of Hesse. She is depicted as young and beautiful, either crowned or carrying one or more crowns, typifying her virtues.

In the Murillo, *S. Elizabeth ministering to the Sick*, after 1661: Seville, Hospitál de la Cáridad, she bathes the head of a sick man while wearing a crown over her veil, and similarly in the right wing of Hans Holbein the Elder's 1516: *Martyrdom of S. Sebastian* (Munich). In Simone Martini's fresco (early 1330s: Chapel of St Martin, Assisi, San Francesco, Lower Church) she wears royal robes, and in the statue in the choir of St Elizabeth, Marburg, she carries a model of the church dedicated to her when she was canonized. Her great-niece, Mary of Hungary, Queen of Naples, commissioned a painting of her from Pietro Cavalini, *c.*1308, in Sta Maria Donna Regina, Naples, and she figures among the saints in the side panels of Piero della Francesca's Perugia Polyptych, 1460, where she is dressed as a Franciscan Tertiary holding a fold of her robes filled with roses, a frequent device for alluding to her charity. She is more depicted by Northern artists than Southern ones.

Elmo, Saint There is much confusion between two saints both known as S. Elmo. The first is S. Erasmus, who was martyred during the Emperor Diocletian's persecution (i.e. between 303 and 312), who is also known as S. Ermo, or Elmo, and is one of the fourteen Auxiliary Saints (*see* VIERZEHNHEILIGEN). He was the Bishop of Formia, and his cult became popular south of Rome. After the destruction of Formia by the Saracens his relics were transfered to Gaeta, where in 1106 the cathedral was dedicated to the Virgin and S. Erasmus. He is represented in *Grünewald's S. Erasmus and S. Maurice* (1517–23; Munich). The other is S. Peter Gonzales (*c.*1190–1246), a Dominican preacher who worked extensively among the seafaring people of the N. Spanish coasts. He was called Sant'Elmo, or by elision San Telmo by them, and became the patron saint of sailors. St Elmo's fire, the electrical discharge often seen playing around the masts and rigging of ships, was believed to be a sign of his protection.

Elohim (Heb. gods) The term is used in early Pentateuchal sources to describe heathen gods, and also for supernatural beings, but it later became a frequent name for the one God of Israel. Its plural form is used to express the sense of 'majesty'. In the singular, Eloi, it appears only once in the NT in Christ's last words on the cross (Mark 15: 34). There is a picture by *Blake with the title (London, Tate). *See* NOMEN SACRUM.

Emblem is not quite identical with *attribute or *symbol. An emblem is an image illustrating a motto or epigram (usually in Latin), accompanied by an explanatory text—i.e. it is a visual support to a fundamentally literary concept. Emblems may be associated with persons or things, or even ideas; e.g. a dragon may be an emblem of SS George, Margaret, or Michael; a crown may represent kingship, or a palm a martyr. This is very much the same as a triangle as a symbol of the Holy Trinity. Emblem-books began with Andrea Alciati's *Emblematum Liber* (Augsburg, 1531), which ran to 150 editions, and was translated into Italian, French, German, and Spanish by 1549. The most famous English example of an emblem-book is Francis Quarles, *Emblemes*, 1635, but for the visual arts the most important was Cesare *Ripa's *Iconologia* (1593), which provided engravings to serve as models for generations of painters and sculptors. In art-historical usage 'attribute' is a commoner term for objects connected with saints or other personages than 'emblem', but the purpose is the same: to characterize the idea or to make the person immediately recognizable. For instance, the attribute of S. Catherine is the wheel on which unsuccessful attempts were made to martyr her; the palm she holds is her emblem as a martyr.

Emmaus, Way to, Supper at, and Return from. This was the occasion of the first appearance of Christ to two disciples after His Resurrection. On the same day that the Holy Women and the disciples who found Christ's tomb empty realized in grief and wonder the truth of His prediction of His Resurrection, two disciples, according to Luke 24: 13–36, were walking to Emmaus, about seven miles from Jerusalem, talking about all that had happened. Jesus himself drew near and walked with them, but they did not recognize Him, and when He asked what they were talking about that made them so sad, Cleopas asked Him if he were the only stranger in Jerusalem who did not know about the things that had happened there in these last days. He asked them, 'What things?' They told Him about Jesus and how He had been crucified, and about the events at the tomb and their bewilderment. 'Then He said to them, "Oh, how foolish you are and how slow . . . to believe all that the prophets have declared . . . "' and

He then explained all the things in the scriptures which related to Himself. When they reached the village, they persuaded Him to stay with them, and when He was at table with them, 'he took bread, blessed and broke it, and and gave it to them. Then their eyes were opened, and they recognized him and he vanished from their sight.' They remembered what had happened at the Last Supper, and how Jesus had broken the bread, and the words He had said as He gave it to them, 'This is my body . . .'. They immediately returned to Jerusalem, and found the disciples gathered together, 'saying, "The Lord has risen indeed, and he has appeared to Simon".' Then they told what had happened on the road, 'And while they were talking about this, Jesus himself stood among them.'

Only S. Luke tells this story of the dramatic re-enactment of the central event of the Last Supper, the Institution of the Eucharist at the *Communion of the Apostles. It is possible that Cleopas was the husband of one of the Holy Women, Mary (AV and Vg. Cleophas), who was the Virgin's sister (John 19: 25) or cousin. Simon Peter (S. Peter) was not the only Simon among the disciples; a Simon is mentioned in both the Gospels of SS Matthew and Mark among Christ's brethren, and would have been a relative of Mary of Cleophas, were he the Simon in question.

The earliest representation of the Emmaus story is in the first series of mosaics in Sant' Apollinare Nuovo in Ravenna made before 540, where the meeting of Christ and the disciples is followed by another panel showing the disciples gathered together with Christ appearing in their midst. The mosaic in Monreale of 1182–92 shows four scenes: the meeting on the road, the supper at which Christ breaks the bread, the moment after the disappearance, with the empty place where Christ had sat, and the disciples arriving to tell the assembled group what had happened. A relief of the subject is in the cloister of Sto Domingo de Silos, of 1085–1100, in N. Spain, and a capital on the Portail Royal at Chartres shows Christ and the disciples on the road. Most of the illuminated MSS with the Life of Christ include the Emmaus story, such as the Egbert Codex of 980 at Trier, and the Ste-Chapelle Evangeliary of 1280 (London, BL). Dürer's *Small Passion*, 1511, is his only Passion to have the *Walk to Emmaus*. Altobello Melone's *Walk to Emmaus* (?1516–18: London, NG) has Christ as a pilgrim, with staff, and a shell in his hat. Caravaggio painted two versions of the *Supper at Emmaus*, one (1598: London, NG) with two disciples with gestures of total astonishment on either side of a beardless Christ, perhaps to illustrate the original non-recognition, and also because it is a post-Resurrection appearance; and a second version (1606: Milan, Brera), with a traditional bearded Christ, is less dramatic, but has a man and an old serving woman as witnesses. There is a *Walk to Emmaus* by the 16th-century central Italian painter Lelio Orsi (London, NG), with the pilgrims under a stormy sky; and a *Supper at Emmaus* by Rembrandt of 1648 (Paris, Louvre) seen at the moment of recognition, with even the serving man caught up in the drama of the event. The same theme can be seen in a Karl Schmidt Rottluff (1918) woodcut and the reredos (1958) by Ceri Richards in St Edmund Hall Chapel, Oxford.

Enclosed Garden *See* HORTUS CONCLUSUS.

enclosure *See* CLAUSURA, CLOISTER.

encolpion or **enkolpion** (Gk. worn on chest). An oval medallion of Christ or the Virgin Mary, suspended from a chain, worn round the neck of Eastern bishops. It may contain relics, and Eastern bishops sometimes wear two enkolpia and a pectoral cross. It is also called a Panagia. An encolpion may also commemorate a marriage, or other state or family event.

end of the world *See* SIGNS OF . . . WORLD, JUDGEMENT, and FOUR LAST THINGS.

Enoch (Vg. **Henoch**) Two Enochs are recorded in the OT. The first, in Gen. 4: 17–18, was the son of Cain, born after the murder of *Abel; Cain built a city which he named after his son. Gen. 5: 18 records a second Enoch, descended from *Seth as the seventh generation after *Adam, and in Gen. 5: 21–4 he is recorded as the father of Methuselah and it is also said that 'Enoch walked with God; and then he was no more, because God took him'. S. Paul's Epistle to the Hebrews (11: 5) says 'By faith Enoch was translated that he should not see death'. It had long been part of Jewish tradition that Enoch, like *Elijah, was assumed into Heaven without dying. S. Jude, Epistle 14–15, refers to Enoch as a scourge of the ungodly. The second Enoch is revered as a patriarch and as the subject of one of the most important Jewish pseudepigrapha, a collection of books in which Enoch is credited with receiving revelations on evil, angels, Gehenna, and

Paradise. The full text is known only in Ethiopic, but there are segments in Greek, Hebrew, Aramaic, and Latin, parts of which have been found among the Qumran fragments. These so-called 'Books of Enoch' are thought to date from the 2nd century BC. Enoch's translation into heaven, like Elijah's, is a prototype of both the *Ascension and the *Assumption.

entablature The part of the classical order that rests on the abacus at the top of a capital.

Entombment *See* DEPOSITION.

Entry into Jerusalem This event, narrated in all four Gospels, marks the beginning of *Christ's Passion, when he entered Jerusalem to popular acclamation, riding on an ass, with palm branches strewn before him. It is commemorated on the Sunday preceding Holy Week (the Sunday before Easter) called Palm Sunday in the Anglican rite, and Passion Sunday in the Roman Catholic rite, with the distribution of palms to the congregation. In many illustrations of the event boys are depicted as climbing trees for a better view (particularly in Byzantine art), though this picturesque detail also occurs in Western art, e.g. in Duccio's *Maestà* (1308–11: Siena), and James Ensor's *Entry of Christ* (1989, Getty Museum, CA, USA).

Envy (*Invidia*) *See* DEADLY SINS.

Ephesus, Council of, was the 3rd General Council of the Church, held in 431. It was called by the Emperor Theodosius II, who was anxious to settle the controversy caused by the Nestorian heresy—the doctrine denying the Orthodox belief that Christ was a single Person, true God and true Man, but was instead two separate Persons, one Divine, one Human. At the Council, Nestorius, whom Theodosius had made Bishop of Constantinople, was deposed and his heresy condemned, and eventually Theodosius agreed to accept this. The real importance of the Council of Ephesus, and of the subsequent Council of Chalcedon in 451, was the firm establishment of the Virgin as the *Theotokos, the Mother of God, whereas for the Nestorians she was no more than the Christotokos—the bearer of Christ. (*See* COUNCILS, ECUMENICAL.)

ephod A Jewish ecclesiastical vestment worn by High Priests, and described in detail in Exod. 28: 6–12 and 39: 2–5. It was shaped like a waist cloth, made of linen with gold, blue, purple, and scarlet decoration, supported by shoulder pieces and with a girdle. The shoulder pieces had onyx stones set in gold, engraved with the names of the Children of Israel. A plain white one was worn by Samuel serving the Tabernacle (1 Sam. 2: 18) and by David (2 Sam. 6: 14–16) when dancing and leaping before the Ark, exposing himself and thus incurring the contempt of Michal his wife, Saul's daughter.

epigonation (Gk. thigh) A Eucharistic vestment worn by all Eastern bishops and other dignatories, but in the West only by the pope (subcinctorium) when celebrating. It consists of a stiff piece of material embroidered with a cross or other image, suspended from the girdle to hang at about knee level on the right. It is a symbol of the spiritual sword of justice.

epimanikion Epimanikia are embroidered cuffs worn by clergy of the E. Orthodox Church over the sleeves of the *sticharion (or alb). There is no Western equivalent to this *vestment.

Epiphany (Gk. *epiphaneia*, manifestation) Epiphany and Theophany both mean a manifestation of a god; in ancient Greece, for instance, the term was used by the Delphians for the day on which Apollo manifested himself to them. In Christian usage, it refers to any manifestation of Christ as the revelation of God to the world.

The Feast of the Epiphany originated in the 3rd century in the Eastern Church as a celebration of Christ's birth, His recognition by the *Magi, and His *Baptism, and it remains one of the major Eastern festivals, held on the 6 January, ranking with Easter and Pentecost in solemnity. *Christmas was first celebrated in the 4th century and became, particularly in the West, the major feast celebrating the Incarnation as the manifestation of God to the world. The celebration of the Epiphany was introduced into the West in the 4th century, and by the 5th was associated only with the Adoration of the *Magi, which became the manifestation of Christ to the Gentiles since the Magi were the first non-Jews to whom God had manifested Himself. This is in contrast to the *Nativity, which was the manifestation to the Jews, God's Chosen People, in the persons of the shepherds. As the feast of the Adoration of the Magi, it is now specifically called the Epiphany in the West, is limited to the Magi, and as in the East, celebrated on the 6 January.

All the manifestations of the divinity of Christ are, in fact, epiphanies. In the Eastern Church, the feast of the Epiphany combines the Nativity and the Baptism of Christ as the manifestation to the Jews, the Adoration of the Magi as the manifestation to the Gentiles, and the miracle at Cana as the first manifestation of His divine powers. The Baptism of Christ is narrated in all the Gospels in virtually the same terms, and is the first of the manifestations in which the Voice of God is heard by those present. The *Transfiguration is another such manifestation. Christ's many miracles, and particularly the raising of the widow's son at Nain, of Jairus's daughter, and, supremely, of Lazarus, as well as His many cures of the sick and possessed, are major manifestations of His divine power as much as they are of His mercy and goodness. The *Resurrection is the supreme manifestation, and is followed closely by the appearances of Christ to the disciples. The *Ascension completes the Christological series of manifestations of His power and divinity. The *Assumption is another manifestation of divine power and love.

Two ivory plaques, probably made in Milan, show the Emperor Otto II and the Empress Theophanu before Christ. In one (*c*.980/3: Milan, Castello Sforzesco) He is adored by the monarchs, who hold their little son (later Otto III) before them; in the other (*c*.982/3: Paris, Cluny Mus.) He crowns them. Both can be termed epiphanies—the manifestation of Christ as the protector of His votaries and His anointed, and their epiphany as recipients of His favour. The model found favour with a number of Byzantine emperors, as mosaics in Hagia Sophia testify, and was also adopted in mosaics of Christ crowning monarchs such as the Norman kings of Sicily, Roger in the Martorana in Palermo, and William II in Monreale, for whom claims to legitimacy could be enhanced by images manifesting divine approval.

Epistle side *See* GOSPEL SIDE.

epitaphios (Gk. tomb) is a large veil or cloth simulating a shroud, with a representation of the Crucified Christ, which is carried in procession in Byzantine rite services on Good Friday. It can also be an ornamental bier on which is laid a figure of the Crucified Christ, and carried in procession to simulate the Deposition, before being placed on the altar. There is one of the veil type in London, V & A, dated 1407.

epitrachelion A *vestment in the E. Orthodox Church worn by bishops and priests, similar to the W. stole. It is a long strip of material, about five in. wide, with an opening for the head, and decorated with crosses and a fringe. Deacons wear a corresponding vestment called an *orarion.

Epstein, Sir Jacob (1889–1959) An American-born sculptor who received British citizenship in 1911. Along with Chagall and Feibusch, he brought life and new strengths to the British Church and art scene, especially during his last twelve years. His *Jacob and the Angel* (1940–41 Tate Britain) showed his vehement capacities applied to the biblical narrative. His work had attracted fierce criticism from Church authorities before this, but the customarily slow ecclesiastical confidence leading to commissions began to grow. The Warden of New College, Oxford found working with the sculptor in connection with the *Lazarus* (1951) for the College Ante-Chapel a pleasing experience, and the feeling was mutual. The *Madonna and Child* (1957) unveiled in Cavendish Square, London for the Convent of the Holy Child Jesus was much admired; *Christ in Majesty* (1956) matches for inspiration the architectural solution of Llandaff Cathedral's interior reordering by George Pace; Coventry Cathedral places his *St Michael and the Devil* (1960) at its main entrance; the poet and sculptor are well paired in the William Blake Memorial, Westminster Abbey (1957).

Erasmus *See* ELMO, S.

Erasmus, Desiderius (*c*.1469–1536), was born in Rotterdam, the illegitimate son probably of a priest of Gouda. He and his elder brother were at school at Deventer, where except for one teacher, who belonged to the 'Bretheren of the Common Life', teaching was based on antiquated medieval textbooks. Only at the end of their stay were modern textbooks introduced, including the classics. At their father's death, their guardians forced them into the monastic school at Bois-le-Duc ('sHertogenbosch), and both unwillingly entered Augustinian monasteries, Erasmus at Steyn, near Gouda, *c*.1488, where in 1492 he was ordained. In the monastery, study of the classics enabled him so to perfect his Latin that in 1493 he became secretary to the Bishop of Cambrai. He was allowed to study in Paris, probably in 1495, and in 1499 travelled to England with a pupil, Lord Mountjoy, and met Thomas More and John Colet, who turned him against scholasticism to the study of the NT. In Paris, he published *Adagiorum Collectanea*, a book of classical sayings from Latin authors, and about this time he gave himself the name Desiderius. He learned Greek between 1500 and 1503, so as to edit the works of S. Jerome and translate the NT, and wrote a Greek translation of the NT with a Latin retranslation. In 1506–9 he was in Italy, with a year in Venice at the press of Aldus Manutius, who published his *Adagia*, and went to Rome and Naples. He was disappointed by Italy, claiming that it provided no intellectual stimulus. In London, in More's house, he wrote *Moriae Encomium* ('In Praise of Folly') staying there until 1514, with intervals teaching Greek and Divinity in Cambridge.

On leaving England, he was recalled to his monastery, and refused to go. He visited Leuven before settling in Basle to work in Froben's printing office in 1514, to edit four volumes of S. Jerome's letters and the NT, the Greek text and notes of which were published in 1516 with the new Latin form. The Chancellor of Brabant obtained him a sinecure and a useful prebend, but he returned to England in 1516 to stay with More. The attempt to recall him to his monastery terrified him, and he appealed for release from his Order, a plea granted in 1517. He was in Leuven for the next four years, with forays to Basle, but the storm over the *Reformation blew ever harder. Finally in 1521 he moved to Basle for eight years, publishing his *Colloquies* on disparate subjects which ran to twenty-five editions by 1522, though they provoked bitter attacks from both the Catholic and the Reformed parties; there was no place in this conflict for wit and sharp humour. He was forced to take sides, and in 1524 he attacked Luther in a pamphlet on free will. By now, Basle City Council had sided with the Reformers, banned Catholic services in 1529, and closed the University. Erasmus fled to Freiburg im Breisgau. There he worked on editions of the Fathers, and in June 1535, he returned to Basle, now quiet, to see his edition of the Early Christian theologian Origen through the press, together with the last of the *Adagia*. He died there in July 1536.

His most important works are landmarks of learning and intellect. His new edition of the Greek NT from early MSS, and his translation into classical Latin, remained in use from 1516 until the 19th century. His reliable texts opened up the study of the Church Fathers, including SS Jerome, John Chrysostom, Irenaeus, Basil, Ambrose, and Augustine. In the bitter troubles of the Reformation his fate was to fall between the two camps: his attacks on the privileges and corruptions of the Church made him powerful enemies among Catholics, while his tenacity in adhering to the old faith led him to be denounced by the Lutherans. Ultimately it was his own who treated him worst: his writings were censured by the University of Paris, and in 1558 Pope Paul IV prohibited his works. The Council of Trent mitigated this harsh inquisitor's verdict, but the ban was reimposed in 1590 by another implacable pope, Sixtus V, and lasted until modern times against many unexpurgated works.

The iconography of Erasmus is complicated by the many versions by assistants and copyists, but the best autograph portraits are those by Quentin Massys, Dürer, and Holbein. The Massys of 1517 is in Rome (Barberini Gall.); the Dürers are a charcoal drawing (1520: Paris, Louvre) and an engraving made in 1526 from a medal. In the margin of a 1515 copy of *In Praise of Folly* Holbein drew a little portrait of Erasmus writing at a desk (Basle, Print Room). The other Holbeins are paintings, one of 1523 portraying him with his hands resting on a closed book (Longford Castle) of which the most important versions, by various artists, are in the Royal Coll. (Hampton Court), Louvre, Oxford (Bodleian), and with an open book at Turin, Besançon, and elsewhere. A drawing of hands for the Longford Castle portrait is in the Cabinet des Dessins, Louvre. Profile portraits of Erasmus writing of 1523 are in the Louvre and Basle. There is a half-length portrait (*c.*1531/2: NY, Met. Mus.), and a roundel of his head only (1531/2: Basle Mus.). There is also an anonymous woodcut of 1530, in a book published by Joh. Opirinus, Basle, showing him dictating to his secretary, Gilbertus Cognatus, in Freiburg University. Most are perfect portraits of a scholar, and integrate a modern scholar's portrait into a pictorial tradition which began with Evangelist pages in medieval MSS, and continued in such works as those by Antonello da Messina (1450/60: *S. Jerome*, London, NG), and in frescoes by Ghirlandaio and Botticelli (1480: *S. Jerome* and *S. Augustine*, Florence, Ognissanti), and others, including Dürer.

eremite (Gk. *eremites*, a hermit) *See* HERMITS.

Eros (Gk. love) In classical Greek times Eros was the god of sexual love, which could invade and possess a man, and could range from the most noble and self-sacrificing kind, to crude attraction, infatuation, and blind passion. In Hellenistic times, with changes in literature, poetry, and art, the dangerous Eros was transformed into a winged child, or even a baby, or into Cupid (Lat. *cupido*, desire) and given a toy bow and arrows, and was frequently multiplied into many children, as Erotes. *Agape (Gk. brotherly love) described the feeling which inspired the commemorative feasts held, as expressions of love, in pagan times, and later in Early Christian ones, at the graves of relatives and friends, and particularly at those of martyrs. The Greek word *eros* was never used in the NT—only *agape*.

The *Renaissance took over the Hellenistic approach to the theme of Eros. The powerful and unpredictable god was emasculated and survived only as a winged child, becoming the little *putto of so many altarpieces and mythologies, sometimes singly but often in galaxies of playful children. One of their earliest appearances in the Renaissance is in the base of the tomb of Ilaria del Carretto (*c*.1406: Lucca Cath.) where a chain of little winged putti uphold a funerary garland. In several of Mantegna's pictures of the Madonna and Child, and even in his *Risen Christ* (1460: Uffizi), the figures are surrounded by a skein of disembodied children's heads each with only a pair of wings. In Michelangelo's *Sistine ceiling each of the prophets is accompanied by figures of children, not playful enough to be putti, but which are perhaps to be considered as the Genii or messengers of Divine Inspiration accompanying the prophet, and often partaking of the mood of the prophet and his prophecy. No such figures accompany the sibyls; but forming part of the thrones of all the prophets and sibyls are pairs of putti in varied poses, struggling, playing, or supporting part of the cornice of the throne, and others uphold the tablets with the name of the prophet or sibyl. Raphael, in his *Sistine Madonna* (1512–13: Dresden) placed two little winged putti at the base of his altarpiece, and the idea becomes a useful means of filling an awkward space, or diversifying or enlivening a traditional theme, as in Poussin's *Adoration of the Shepherds* (1637: London, NG). In the same artist's unusual representation of the *Return from the Flight into Egypt* (1628/9: London, Dulwich), however, the grim significance for the Christ Child of the vision of the cross held by the little winged putti which He alone sees, is softened by the playfulness with which the quartet of plump infants tumble their dreadful burden. *See also* EIDOLON, ANGELS, GENIUS.

Esau *See* JACOB.

Escorial, el, was built by Philip II of Spain, some 30 miles from Madrid; the huge, austere complex includes a monastery, palace, library, and infirmary, centred on a large church with a high dome, with a royal mausoleum under the high altar. The building, designed on a grid plan derived from *Filarete's Hospital in Milan, was laid out by Juan Bautista of Toledo in 1563, and continued by Juan de Herrera, whose major work it was until its completion in 1584, although Philip controlled every detail of the building in which he lived for fourteen years until his death in 1598. The church (1578–82) is on several levels: a double choir precedes the nave, and the high altar is flanked by the tombs of the Emperor Charles V, Philip's father, surrounded by his family, and of Philip and three of his four wives (his second wife, Queen Mary Tudor of England, is not included). The gilt-bronze effigies of the dead are by Pompeo Leoni. Behind the upper choir is a marble crucifix by Benvenuto Cellini. The Escorial is important as the main means for the introduction of Italian *Mannerist art into Spain, since most of the artists employed in its decoration were Italians, principally Federigo Zuccaro and Tibaldi.

Philip II was a notable collector of pictures, and acquired works from his domains in the Netherlands by *Bosch, and Roger van der *Weyden, commissioned from *Titian the *Martyrdom of S. Lawrence* as an altarpiece, and from El *Greco the *Martyrdom of S. Maurice* (which he disliked) and the *Exaltation of the Name of Jesus*. Philip IV kept part of his huge collection in the Escorial, part in Madrid. It included works by Velázquez, *Rubens, *Tintoretto, Giorgione, and *Correggio, many of which were bought by Velázquez on his Italian journeys (1629–31 and 1648–51) and which greatly influenced Spanish painters of the 17th century.

Espolio, el (Sp. disrobing), is the title of a painting by El *Greco, of 1577–9, in Toledo Cathedral. It represents Christ about to be stripped of His garments before the

Crucifixion. One of the executioners grips His robe to pull it from Him. The incident is not specifically mentioned in the Gospels, though it is implied in the fact that the soldiers diced for His garments. It is, however, described graphically in the **Meditationes Vitae Christi.* The subject became well known as the 10th of the 14 *Stations of the Cross, but is comparatively rare on its own. The earliest representations are a late 13th-century Umbrian painting in Perugia, and a Byzantine 14th-century painting in Bologna, but the subject is closely related to the Mocking of Christ, and it undoubtedly influenced pictures and sculpture of Christ in Distress (Fr. *Christ aux Outrages*), which show Him before the Crucifixion, or the German *Schmerzensmann*, which usually show Him as dead (Lübeck Master, early 15th cent., Lübeck Cath; H. Holbein the Elder, 1502: Hanover, both showing Christ seated on the Cross, and sculptures in St-Nizier, Troyes and Chaource, nr. Troyes). The subject is easily confused with the many versions of the *Mocking of Christ.*

Espousal of the Virgin Mary The story is told in the *Apocryphal Gospel of the Protevangelium of James. After Mary's Presentation in the Temple, where she was placed when she was 3 by her parents, Joachim and *Anne, as a thank-offering for her birth, she lived in the Temple until she was 12 (in some texts 14). A decision then had to be made about her future. The High Priest prayed for guidance, and an angel appeared and told him to assemble the widowers. Each should bring a rod which was to be laid on the altar. Among those assembled was Joseph, and when the High Priest returned the rods to them, a dove flew from Joseph's rod and settled on his head. The High Priest told him that he was to marry Mary, but Joseph protested that he was an old man, with sons, and to marry so young a woman would make him a laughing-stock in Israel. The High Priest warned him of the dangers of refusing to obey God's will, and Joseph then accepted her, but left her in his house and went away from her. A similar tale, with minor variations, is in the Pseudo-Matthew. The term 'Espousal' (Lat. *desponsatio*) is often used because this can also signify 'betrothal', since the Virgin was not married to Joseph in the normal sense of the word.

The *Marriage of the Virgin* was painted in MSS, such as the opulent *Bedford Book of Hours* (1423–30: London, BM), and in an altarpiece attributed to the Master of Flémalle, where it forms half of a double panel with the High Priest at prayer, while Joseph tries to escape (early 15th cent.: Prado). The most striking representations of the scene are those by Perugino (*c.*1500–4: Caen, Mus.) and the similar, but far superior, example by *Raphael (Milan, Brera). Both make a feature of the ring, which Perugia Cathedral claims to own, the Perugino now in Caen having been painted for the chapel in which the relic is kept. Most Italian versions of the subject show Joseph placing a ring on Mary's finger; most Northern ones show them joining hands.

Two interesting details may be noted: in all the versions of the subject cited here a disappointed suitor breaks his useless rod across his knee. This incident is not in the Apocryphal narratives, and must therefore be drawn from an unknown common source, since it occurs in both Northern and Southern versions of the subject. The other point is that the scene of the *Marriage* is in the church porch in the two Northern pictures, and in a piazza in the two Italian ones, with a church in the background. This is because marriages were normally celebrated *ad portas*—that is, in the porch of a church, rather than inside, since it was a civil contract in which the parties are themselves the ministers of the sacrament, and the presence of a priest was to bless the parties, who held a candle to signify that they made their vows before God. The two Italian examples dispense with the candle. *See also* MARRIAGE.

Esther (5th cent. BC), like *Judith, is a Jewish heroine. Her story is told in the OT Book of Esther, with Apocryphal additions: the reason for its inclusion in the Jewish canon is probably because it records the Feast of Purim, celebrating the deliverance of the Jews from extermination. King Ahasuerus (Assuerus), perhaps to be identified with Xerxes I of Persia (reigned 486–465 BC), gave a great feast, and, after seven days drinking, decided to show off his wife Vashti to the assembled nobles. When sent for, Vashti refused to come, and the King and his advisers decided that 'just as she has defied the King Artaxerxes, so now the other ladies . . . will likewise dare to insult their husbands . . .' (Esther 1: 17), so Vashti was banished and the King decided to take a new wife. The new queen was Esther, a surpassingly beautiful Jewess, the adopted daughter of Mordecai (Mardochaeus), a Jewish palace official. Haman (Aman), the chief minister, ordered all palace officials to prostrate themselves before him, but Mordecai refused to do so and Haman was so enraged that he plotted to kill, not only Mordecai, but all the Jews in the Persian Empire, and he prevailed upon the King to allow this. But the King discovered that Mordecai had saved him from being assassinated, and he ordered that Mordecai should be honoured, which increased Haman's rage against the Jews. Esther pleaded with the King for her people when she gave a feast for him and for Haman, at which she denounced Haman. He was hanged on a gallows which he had himself erected for Mordecai. But it was impossible to rescind the order for the murder of the Jews, so Esther obtained a decree allowing the Jews to arm themselves against their enemies and they slew thousands. This salvation of the Chosen People is celebrated by the institution of the feast of Purim, and became a Christian *type of Salvation, as in Michelangelo's Sistine Chapel fresco (which is unusual in showing Haman as crucified). Esther also became an OT type of *Mary, with Esther's coronation as a parallel to the Coronation of the Virgin, and her intercession for her people becoming a type for Mary interceding for humanity. There is an Esther series by Filippino Lippi (*c.*1480), divided between Ottawa (NG), Chantilly, Florence (Horne Mus.), and the Louvre. The subject was very popular during the Baroque period as it provided a pretext for Oriental sumptuousness. Many Dutch painters, including Rembrandt, exploited this aspect.

Etheria, called variously Egeria, Aetheria, and Silvia, was a 4th-century nun, probably a Spanish abbess, who made a pilgrimage to the Holy Land. She wrote an account of her travels, which survives in a MS found in 1884 by J. F. Gamurrini, called 'Peregrinatio Silviae'. He believed that the pilgrim was S. Silvia. In 1903 she was correctly identified from a 7th-century eulogy written by Valerius, a Galician monk. His précis of her journey accords so well with her own account as to make the identification certain, and supplies part of the missing portions of her own narrative. The missing pages at the beginning of her account, in a Latin dialect, which may be Galician, might have indicated where she came from, but this may be surmised from two of her comments: that the Euphrates in the speed of its flow recalled the Rhône, and that a bishop whom she met remarked on her having come 'from the ends of the earth'—which to him would have been the far west of Europe.

Her pilgrimage was made between 381 and 384, though these dates only cover the surviving portions of her record—perhaps a third of what she wrote. The first part of her text describes her pilgrimage from her journey to Mt. *Sinai as far as her arrival in Constantinople on her way home. After this she gives an account of the liturgy in the Holy Places in Jerusalem—the great church on *Golgotha, the *Imbomon on the Mt. of Olives, Sion, and others in the neighbourhood. She climbed Mt. Nebo, to the spot where Moses was allowed to see the land of Canaan, and later she went to the land of Uz, to the tomb of Job, and on the way passed the places where she was told that Abraham met Melchisedek, and the Baptist baptized, and she was given apples from his garden. On her return to Jerusalem she decided to return home as it had now been three full years since her arrival, but on her way she visited Edessa in Mesopotamia, to see the tomb of the Apostle *Thomas, and to see the city of King *Abgar. She was delighted to be given a better version of the letter to Abgar than the one in her convent. From there she went to Charra, where God bade Abraham go (Gen. 12: 4), and saw what purported to be his house, and was shown *Jacob's well. From Antioch she went to Tarsus, to Seleucia, and then to Chalcedon and Constantinople. Then she planned to go to Ephesus, but that part of her MS is missing. She visited all the churches of Constantinople, and on all her journeys she was given hospitality by monks and bishops.

Etheria's first-hand account was used by Peter the Deacon, Librarian of Monte Cassino, for his compilation (1137) on the Holy Places, in which he adds that it was collated from 'I might say, all the books'. Peter used the Venerable Bede's work on the Holy Places, which provided the core of his information, but included material from Etheria, proving that a copy of her MS was in Monte Cassino, probably the one found in Arezzo in 1884. Peter did not repeat Etheria verbatim, but condensed her words, providing information probably derived from the lost parts of the MS, often conflated with later sources.

Etimasia *See* HETOIMASIA.

Eucharist (Gk. *eucharistia,* thanksgiving) The principal act of Christian worship, and the greatest *sacrament; also called the Mass, Holy Communion, or the Lord's Supper. It is the commemoration of Christ's sacrifice of Himself for the Redemption of mankind from its sins. The presence at, or the receiving of, the Eucharist by the faithful at Communion, is to participate in the supreme act of worship. *See* SPECIES.

For the Institution of the Eucharist *see* COMMUNION OF THE APOSTLES. The actual representation of the celebration of the Eucharist is rare, except in the case of miracles such as the Mass of *S. Giles. Common Eucharistic symbols of the sacred elements are vines and grapes for the wine, and wheat-ears or sheaves of corn for the bread. A sculpture entitled *Eucharist* (1996) by Stephen Cox in St Nicholas Cathedral, Newcastle upon Tyne, shows the (circular) fractured host and the (elliptical) brimming contents of the chalice.

EUROPE: 20TH- AND 21ST-CENTURY PAINTING, SCULPTURE, STAINED GLASS

Introduction

If Christian art, like all art, is partly the product of historical circumstance, then its European expression in the previous and present century has been more complex and multifaceted than at any period since the Renaissance. In retrospect, three underlying preconditions for this complexity are now discernible—political, economic, and sociological.

Politically, these include two global conflicts (the First and Second World Wars) between major European nations, the transformation of Russian society between 1917 and the death of Stalin, the Spanish Civil War, the Holocaust, Hiroshima, the Cold War, and the reunification of Germany, and the emergence of the European Community.

Economically, one might identify oscillating cycles of poverty and affluence, the primacy of market economies, and of modes of consumption (what Marx called 'commodity fetishism') over those of production.

Sociologically, these embrace globalization, urbanization (both physical and mental), mass migration across many relatively open borders, the weakening of traditional family and community structures, Freud, the emergence of feminism, ethnic consciousness, and the rise of HIV/AIDS.

All three of the above have provided discrete yet interlocking contexts for *all* artistic production and consumption. Yet even before 1900, Christian art had been subject to a further trio of cultural pressures that have proved critical for its style, content, and reception.

One, further advanced in Europe than elsewhere, is secularization, whose consequences may have led over time to the declining power and efficacy of 'traditional' Christian iconography, and increasing evidence that with a few honourable exceptions (all cited below) most European artists were increasingly unlikely to be keyed into religious culture, because there was no identifiable religious culture for them to be keyed into. This poses both a challenge and a problem for Christian art.

A second negative constraint on Christian art has been that, historically, the 'modern', 'modernity', and now increasingly 'post-modernity', have been placed in a negative cultural juxtaposition to 'traditional' Christian narrative, symbol, and image.

A third not unconnected mutation has been the critical role of the modern museum and its fashionable bedfellow, the artefact-driven 'material religion' approach to religious art, in accelerating what might be called the cultural desacralization of Christian art, whereby such art is stripped of its affective power and simply becomes a mere art object.

Confronted with such powerful, even destructive forces as these, can Christian art confidently recalibrate the historical relationship of art to faith and faith to art for what remains of the 21st century? Clearly, Christian art, like Christian theology and institutions, has often responded powerfully and creatively to the advent of two World Wars. Clearly, too, such art has reflected and even assimilated secular art movements, from Expressionism to Surrealism, from Abstraction to Installation Art. Equally discernible are two more deep-seated transformations.

One is an identifiable movement away from a narrowly and exclusively Christian art towards works that are only implicitly religious in their inspiration and hence without identifiable religious themes or traditional symbols. This is, in short, a mutation from religion to *spirituality, and itself a major shift in cultural history.

A second transformation is that from about 1900, many major European artists increasingly sought to find meaning within themselves rather than from supernatural stories or the rituals of institutional churches. Today, as one critic describes it, 'modern artists now have the singular opportunity of *presencing* the spiritual significance of the totality of human experience in their recognition of the foundational necessity of the religious imagination'. Such an invitation is in no sense antithetical to Christian art. Indeed, it has been integral to European art and artists from the Catacombs to the present day, and it continues to offer a daunting visual and cognitive challenge to artists and religious institutions alike.

The response of both, throughout Europe, has never been uniform in terms of quantity or quality, due to widely differing national histories, confessional cultures, and traditions of ecclesiastical patronage. In addition, the inherent Christian dialectic between Word and Image persists, if less sharply focused than hitherto, as does the debate about the communicative efficacy of 'traditional' Christian symbolism in a nominally Christian but normatively post-Christian Europe. An additional newly emergent issue is the role and relevance of the visual arts in fostering or inhibiting interfaith understanding in an increasingly multicultural subcontinent.

Meanwhile readers may wish to carry two thoughts with them as they read. One is that, as Burch Brown wrote over twenty years ago, 'the art that has the greatest significance is not necessarily the art of institutional religion but rather the art which happens to discern what religion in its institutional focus needs most to see'. The other is that perhaps *all* religious forms and symbols need to be interpreted in the light of each new generation's experience: only then can the truths they point to be rediscovered and so once more communicated.

France

Two major schools dominated French Christian art up to the Second World War: the Society of St John, founded the previous century by Fr Lacordaire, comprising artists influenced by Thomist, Benedictine, or mystical theology who openly acknowledged their Christian faith; and the *Ateliers d'art sacré* ('Studios of Sacred Art'), founded in 1919 by Maurice *Denis and Georges Desvallières on the model of a medieval workshop and informed by theology and liturgy, as well as by different artistic disciplines. In parallel, *Les Catholiques des Beaux-Arts,* ('Catholics in the Fine Arts') was founded in 1909, a 'collective, moral, and religious grouping whose goal is beauty', but with no particular artistic direction. Among smaller groups, there was also *L'Arche* (1917), and in 1919 *Les artisans de l'autel* ('The Altar Craftsmen') and *La Rosace.*

These movements, all centred on strong personalities, were involved in great decorative schemes for new churches such as Holy Spirit, Epinay-sur-Seine; Le Raincy; Saint-Louis de Vincennes, etc. They comprised painters Maurice Denis, Georges Desvallières, V. Reyre, M. Flandrin, P. Peugniez, and sculptors H. Charlier, M. Froidevaux-Flandrin, Lambert-Rucki, Sarrabezolles, Fernand Py (who was also a jeweller), as well as glass craftsmen L. Barillet, J. Hébert-Stevens, M. Huré, Gruber, Max Ingrand, and the blacksmith Subes.

In 1925, 1930, and 1937 large international exhibitions of decorative and industrial art and technology had a section for religious works. Two reviews appeared, *L'Artisan liturgique* ('the Liturgical Craftsman'), edited in Belgium, and *l'Art Sacré* ('Sacred Art') founded in 1935 by J. Pichard and taken over in 1936 by two Dominican priests, Fr Regamey and Fr Couturier. This last would have a major influence on the Church by encouraging it to commission important international artists regardless of whether they were Roman Catholic (Rouault, Braque, Bonnard, Chagall, and Richier in Assy; Matisse at Vence; Leger at Assy and Audincourt). Their followers, Manessier and Bazaine, as well as others such as le Moal, Bertholle, and Elvire Jan would invent a non-figurative art of light, particularly appropriate for their numerous windows. Furniture and liturgical objects were treated with powerful simplicity by sculptors such as L. Zack, Adam-Tessier, Szekely, and Ph. Kaeppelin. The first exhibition of sacred art (*Salon d'art sacré)* opened in 1951, and the review *Art Chrétien* ('Christian Art') appeared in 1955.

After a period in the doldrums, a new burst of energy came in 1980, with commissions (independent or in partnership) from the national Committee for Sacred Art (a subcommittee of the episcopal council for liturgy), the editor of the *Chroniques d'art sacré* ('Chronicles of Sacred Art'), and the Directorate of Plastic Art (part of the Ministry of Culture). They awarded commissions to well-known artists for liturgical furniture (Rabinowitch at Digne) and, especially, for windows (R. Morris at Maguelone; Dibbets at Blois; A. Nemours at Sallagon; Sarkis at Saint-Jean du Grais; Garouste at Talant; Ubac, Viallat, Alberola, Honegger, and Rouan at Nevers). Most recently Sir Anthony *Caro completed an important ensemble of sculptures in the choir of the parish church at Bourbourg (near Calais) in October 2008, and in October 2011, six windows by the German artist Imi Knoebel, executed by the Marcq-Simon and Duchemin studios, were dedicated at Reims Cathedral.

e

Germany

In late 19th-century Germany, initiatives for the promotion of art in Protestant churches took the form of associations for Christian art, of which parishes were generally obligatory members. While church architecture of the time largely imitated medieval styles (neo-Romanesque or Gothic Revival and culminating in 'neo-Baroque' in Berlin Cathedral), religious painting was generally in the Nazarene style, while Roman Catholic churches tended more to the 'neo-Byzantine' style pioneered at Beuron Abbey. After a brief decorative art nouveau period, the Bauhaus movement, reacting against these historicist styles, promoted material-oriented practicality in architecture and church interiors, while the Liturgical Movement (Romano Guardini) emphasized emptiness of space and simplicity of liturgy.

In Dresden in 1928, Protestants active in both Church and art worlds founded the independent association *Kunstdienst* to foster the encounter between contemporary art (notably *neue Sachlichkeit* 'New Realism' and Expressionism) and architecture, particularly the Roman Catholic Dominikus Böhm and Protestant Otto Bartning. They promoted stripped-down, kitsch-free design for sacred spaces and liturgical objects, inspired by the theology of Paul Tillich. With the Nazi persecution of modern art, works by sculptors such as Ernst Barlach (Güstrow and Magdeburg Cathedrals), Ludwig Gies (Lubeck Cathedral), and Käthe Kollwitz were removed.

During the post-Second World War years, in a number of newly established Protestant church buildings (particularly in the GDR) *Kunstdienst* facilitated cooperation between the Church and mostly non-Christian artists such as Johann Peter Hinz, Halberstadt, Wieland Förster (now at the Kaiser Wilhelm Gedächtniskirche, Berlin), Siegfried Krepp (south doorway, Berlin Cathedral), Karl Biedermann (Zion Church, Berlin and S. Elsbiety, Wroclaw, Poland), mostly in opposition to ecclesiastical traditionalism and state repression. Siegfried Press gave shape to the interiors of 43 churches of both confessions, mostly, but not exclusively in the GDR, in a minimalist style. The construction and reconstruction of church buildings necessitated by war damage and urban expansion was largely characterized by simple concrete architecture (often symbolizing a tent or arch), and brought about a revival of stained glass, for example, by Paul Corazolla, Inge Pape, Georg Meistermann, Hans Gottfried Stockhausen, Gabriel Loire, Alfred Manessier, Achim Freyer, Jochem Poensgen, Wilhelm Buschulte, Johannes Schreiter, Markus Lüpertz, Sigmar Polke, Hella Santarossa, Georg Ettl, Xenia Hausner, and many others.

In the 1960s and 1970s, explicitly secular 'all-purpose spaces' came into fashion, the result of debates between theologians and architects at conferences such as the *Kirchbautage*, which were supported by the Evangelical Church in Germany (EKD)-sponsored *Institute for Church Construction and Contemporary Religious Art* at the University of Marburg, which had been cofounded by the EKD (former directors Rainer Volp, Horst Schwebel, and currently Thomas Erne), who also coedited the ecumenical journal *Kunst und Kirche*. The institute also organizes exhibitions to parallel the *Documenta* exhibitions in Kassel. Since the early 1990s, *Artheon* has promoted the relationship between contemporary art and churches, helping artists and churches to make contact, organizing symposia, and editing a bulletin.

In the same period, for the first time the EKD held a consultation on Protestantism and Culture, the outcome of which was the installation of a liaison bureau (led by Petra Bahr) and the provision of increased support for the arts, with, for example, exhibitions in city churches such as the Hospitalhof, Stuttgart, organized by Helmut A. Müller; St Matthew's, Berlin Kulturform, curated by Chisthard G. Neubert; and also the Roman Catholic St Peter's, Köln, and its priest Fr Friedhelm Mennekes SJ.

These various endeavours have led to greater open-mindedness to and contact with modern art over the last 25 years. Modern art can now be found in the design of interiors including the principal liturgical furniture (altar, font, and pulpit) by artists such as Ingrid Hartlieb, Franz Bernhard, Klaus Simon, Walter Pokorny, Ulrich Rückriem, Stefan Balkenhol, Achim Kühn, Rudolf Bott, Anish Kapoor (whose multifaith peace chapel can be found in the crypt of the totally reconstructed Frauenkirche in Dresden), Günter Ücker (the same in the Reichstag), Heinz Maack, Thierry Boissel, and Madeleine Dietz.

For sculpture one should mention work by Ewald Mataré (teacher of Joseph Beuys) at Köln, and Otto Hajek and Fritz Koenig, both in the (Roman Catholic) Maria Regina Martyrum Chapel, Berlin (which also houses Georg Meistermann's famous apocalyptic altar painting), while nearby the Protestant Plötzensee Chapel has modern Stations of the Cross by Alfred Hrdlicka. Both churches work together as an ecumenical place of remembrance of Nazi victims.

Outstanding examples of painting in churches include Richard Seewald (Norderney), Antoni Tapies (Worms), Alfred Rainer (St. Eberhard, Stuttgart), Emil Wachter, Werner Tübke, Georg Baselitz, Johannes Heisig, Ben Willekens (in St. Theresia Münster, together with the altarpiece by Erwin Heerich and Stations of the Cross by Silke Rehberg), Hermann Buß, Winfried Muthesius, Volker Stelzmann, Thomas Gatzemeier, and Michael Triegel. Finally, an extraordinary curiosity in the Dorfkirche, Staaken (Berlin-Spandau) is Gabriele Mucchi's ecumenical fresco *Reformers of the 16th century* (from the beginning of the new millennium). From Martin Luther to Ignatius de Loyola, they are assembled under the Cross of Christ. The painting is hung exactly on the line where the Berlin Wall once ran dividing Europe and this church.

Ireland

In the early decades of the twentieth century, Irish art was largely influenced by the Arts and Crafts ethos, particularly through the rise of stained-glass workshops like that of the artist Harry Clarke (b. Dublin 1889). His distinctive vision added a palette of vivid jewel-like colour to French Symbolist imagery in important church commissions throughout Ireland.

Stained glass also provided Irish churches with some of the most significant examples of Modernism through the work of Evie *Hone, who achieved an international reputation. Hone, like her companion the equally influential Modernist painter Mainie Jellett, had studied Cubism in Paris in the 1920s. Both were devout Christians who created significant religious work that pushed a new language of form into the prevailing conservative cultural nationalism that characterized much of early 20th-century Irish art, especially after independence and throughout the mid-century. This nationalism was more generally expressed through a kind of Celtic revivalism and a neo-Hiberno-Romanesque style that typified the work of Irish artists in the substantial number of large churches and religious buildings commissioned on into the 1950s, best seen in the figurative work of stone-carvers such as Albert Power and Seamus Murphy.

Throughout the latter half of the 20th century, a generation of Irish painters such as Tony O'Malley, Patrick Collins, and Patrick Graham, and northern painters such as Colin Middleton and Gerard Dillon, worked from a context of faith, but employing a highly personal and poetic symbolism usually without a specific or figurative Christian language. Others included Patrick Scott, who produced many commissioned works for churches using large compositions of gold leaf and pigment in contemplative iconic abstraction but espoused no belief.

Recent decades have been marked by works from artists such as Dorothy Cross that reference Christianity and the Catholic Church in an increasingly disillusioned and critical view. A few recent artists using Christian imagery from a sincere faith have received recognition: for example, the painters Patrick Pye or Hughie O'Donoghue. O'Donoghue, although born in Manchester, achieved wide prominence in Ireland in the 1990s with his major *Passion* cycle of public-scale paintings.

Italy

The most significant developments in modern Italian Christian art occurred between 1920 and 1975. In 1923 Gino Severini formed a friendship with Jacques Maritain, who encouraged him to rekindle his faith. Between 1924 and 1935 Severini executed a series of vibrant frescoes and mosaics in various Swiss churches. In the early 1920s the Futurist painter Gerardo Dottori also began to explore the possibility of a modern religious art. While his imagery remained fundamentally traditional in character, it differed from the consciously archaizing style adopted by Carlo Carrà in works such as *Lot's Daughters* (1919) through its incorporation of abstract elements and geometric forms.

Both Severini and Dottori were referenced in the 'Manifesto of Futurist Sacred Art' (1931), in which F. T. Marinetti stressed the need for Christian imagery to engage with the formal innovations of Modernism and embrace his movement's machine aesthetic. This was a surprising development given Futurism's Nietzschean roots and the radical anticlericalism of its early political statements. Considering the papacy an 'enemy in the house' for its bitter opposition to the *Risorgimento* (Italy's 19th-century struggle for unification) the Futurists had urged 'de-Vaticanization'. This idea found support within the nascent Fascist movement although Mussolini quickly discarded it, desiring to transform the Church into a pillar of his regime. It is partly in the context of this ideological evolution—which culminated in the Lateran Pacts of 1929—that one can account for the existence of Marinetti's manifesto, for Futurism's official line was one of support for the regime throughout the inter-war years.

Despite the fact that such attempts to 'update' religious art were strongly censured by Pope Pius XI in a discourse of 1932, Marinetti's recommendations inspired the creation of numerous bizarre works in which the soaring imagery of Futurist 'aeropainters' acquired an explicitly celestial dimension. Altogether more serious was the austere yet lyrical work of Fillia (Luigi Colombo)—the leading exponent of Futurist sacred art—who also executed a mural for the church of Notre Dame du Bon-Secours in Lourtier, Switzerland (1932), designed by the Rationalist architect Alberto Sartoris.

During Second World War, Christian iconography was employed in an allegorical manner to convey the suffering of the Italian people under Fascism, as in Renato Guttuso's expressionist *Crucifixion* (1941). In 1939 Italy's greatest modern religious sculptor Giacomo *Manzu began a series of bronze bas-reliefs addressing the same theme. In one image a bloated soldier wearing an unmistakably German *pickelhaube* impassively regards the limp figure of Christ, hanging by his wrist from the Cross.

In the post-war period, works of note include Lucio Fontana's extraordinary *Via Crucis* (1947), with its agonized forms in glazed ceramic, the three elegant bronze doors of Orvieto Cathedral by Emilio Greco (1962–64) depicting angelic figures and Works of Mercy, and Pericle Fazzini's monumental sculpture *The Resurrection* (1970–75), in the Vatican's Paul VI Audience Hall. Mimmo Paladino has also drawn on early Christian iconography in the context of his wider fascination with mythology and ritualistic imagery.

The Netherlands and Belgium

Although there has been some interaction between artists from the Netherlands and Belgium in the field of Christian art in the period from 1900 onwards, it is appropriate to treat each country separately.

In the Netherlands, despite the fact that restrictions on the Roman Catholic Church were lifted in the middle of the 19th century, the Reformed Church has still been the dominant Christian denomination in the country since that time. This denomination is often associated with whitewashed walls and little or no art in its churches, but a number of significant works of art have been commissioned for its places of worship during the 20th century.

Of particular note are stained-glass windows, such as the *Baptism of Christ* (1936, Haarlem, New Church); the *Creation* window (1957, Haarlem, St. Bavo Church); and the *Creation* windows in the Jerusalem Church in West Amsterdam. In fine art, a Dutch artist who expressed his faith explicitly in his work was Jan Toorop (1858–1928). In 1905, Toorop converted to Roman Catholicism and thereafter concentrated on religious art, producing many figurative works depicting Christ and the saints.

In Belgium, the main denomination during this period has been Roman Catholicism. A number of artists have expressed their faith in their work, while others have reacted against it. Amongst the former are Gustave van de Woestijne (1881–1947) and Georges Minne (1866–1941). Both were heavily influenced by Symbolism and the Flemish Primitives, and were members of the First Group of Latem, a small group of artists with a faith commitment who settled and worked in the small village of Sint-Martens-Latem outside Ghent.

Notable examples of Van de Woestijne's work are *Sunday Afternoon* (1914, Museum of Fine Art, Brussels), which evinces the influence of the pale colours of Italian frescoes, the atmospheric *Last Supper* (1927, Groeninge Museum, Bruges), and *Christ in the Wilderness* (1939, Museum of Fine Art, Ghent).

Minne was primarily a sculptor. He produced evocative sculptures such as *John the Baptist* (Ghent) and *The Prodigal Son* (Ghent), and also produced the statue of the Sacred Heart in the National Basilica of the Sacred Heart, Brussels.

An altogether different response to Christian faith can be seen in the work of James Ensor (1860–1949). His *Entry of Christ into Brussels* (1888, Malibu, Getty Museum), often seen as presaging Expressionism, was thought as blasphemous by some, but it also points to the identification of the artist with Christ, who felt himself (Ensor) to be an outcast.

Russia

The cultural-historical trajectory of Christian art in *Russia since 1900 is a varied and complex one. Between 1900 and 1910, for example, many artists, scholars, and laymen joined Tsar Nicholas II in seeing the revitalization of icon painting as crucial to social cohesion and political stability. They were overtaken by the 1917 October Revolution, subsequent persecution of the Orthdodox church, and official disapproval of the artistic depiction of Christian themes. Yet the same two decades also saw an extraordinary subtext of religious themes present in many paintings of the Russian avantgarde, who, in one art-historian's phrase, 'far from renouncing the methods of icon painting, church frescoes, and ceremonies ... reprocessed and transmuted them'.

As both painter and stage designer, Natalia Goncharova (1881–1962) clearly believed in the divine presence as well as the intrinsic beauty of the holy image. Her lithograph series *Mystical Images of War* (1914) was essentially a *galère* (the Virgin and Child, the Archangel Michael, etc.) vested with magical powers to save Holy Russia, while her costume designs for the ballet *Liturgie* (1915) have been described as 'perhaps the most spectacular exploration of Orthodoxy by an avantgarde artist'.

Kasimir Malevich (1878–1935) reconfigured traditional iconography more in a context of spirituality and self-transcendence. He used single forms that were congruent with infinity rather than abstract or representative within reality, and each had no object other than itself. For Malevich these *were* icons, living things, not representations, and he presented them as such, famously displaying *Black Square* (1915), 'the true, real conception of eternity', over the corner of a room, which was the traditional domestic location for icons, and putting the painting above his own deathbed in 1935.

Vassily Kandinsky (1866–1944) was a Russian Orthodox Christian with a strong belief in the need for a spiritual revival in the materialistic West, and who in *Concerning the Spiritual in Art* (1912) saw abstraction as the most powerful way of maximizing the psychological and spiritual impact of a painting. To break away from representation would lead to a new kind of religious art of far greater significance than anything hitherto, with the artist himself as a kind of prophetic visionary, offering through his work, glimpses of a reality more profound than the material world. Much of his work achieves precisely this.

Marc *Chagall (1887–1985), although a Russian-born Jew, and always on the margins of the Russian avantgarde, clearly responded to the poetics of Orthodox iconography rather than to its specifically Christian significance. In doing so, whether in *The White Crucifixion* (with its manifestly Jewish Christ, and images of anti-Semitic pogroms in Chagall's native Vitebsk), or in his protracted Rembrandt-like Old Testament etchings for Vollard, he invariably transforms the ingrained images of the characters and events in question.

Subsequent developments in Russian Christian art between the 1930s and 1970s were characterized by the death or diaspora of many of its leading players, the hegemony of Socialist Realism (which appropriated many Christian motifs into its own iconongraphy), State persecution of Orthodoxy, and the ideological vicissitudes of successive brands of cultural politics.

Latterly, however, following *glasnost,* the political and cultural re-emergence of the Orthodox Church, and the reintroduction of icon-painting (both mass-produced, and as a monastic specialism), the creative relationship between Russian art and religion that flourished at the outset of the 20th century may well be reactivated in the 21st century.

Spain and Portugal

While the Christian art of the Iberian peninsular remains primarily representational and realist, whether in church settings, at pilgrimage sites, or in folk art and popular culture, political upheavals, regional identities (especially Catalan), and cultural movements such as Modernism, Surrealism, and Dada have also left their mark.

Pablo *Picasso (1881–1973), born Catholic, but vociferously agnostic and anticlerical, not only echoes the apocalyptic strain deeply embedded in Spanish art, but often implies a theological subtext beneath his playful recycling of Christian symbols. In *La Crucifixion* (1930), for example, he utilizes the medieval tradition of simultaneity, showing the deposition of the thieves, nailing to the Cross, piercing of Christ's side, and even his triumph over death within a single frame, while his *Weeping Woman* (1937, Tate, Liverpool) draws deeply from the same iconographic tradition. It is perhaps only in *Guernica* (1937) that Picasso goes beyond the appropriation of Christian symbolism, and creates his own 'religious' vocabulary to express both misery and loss, and ultimate issues of meaning and reality.

Salvador Dalí (1904–89), despite his somewhat ambiguous and self-proclaimed Catholic identity, clearly drew upon the Spanish mystical tradition for his now iconic *Christ of St John of the Cross* (1951, Kelvingrove Art Gallery and Museum, Glasgow, Scotland). Here Dali wanted to create the image of a Christ who transcends and transforms suffering, emphasizing his beauty rather than his suffering, and his role as a mediator between God and the Earth. The visual outcome is a bewildering mixture of physical absence and spiritual presence.

Equally iconic is the 'Sagrada Familia' of Antoni Gaudí (1852–1926) in Barcelona. Commenced in 1883 it is less a church than a symbolically supercharged artwork. With its four spires, and vast coloured mosaic interior behind three open portals (Faith, Hope, and Charity) decorated with nativity scenes, it merits Henry-Russell Hitchcock's verdict on it as 'possibly the greatest ecclesiastical monument of the last hundred years'. In 1893, Gaudí was among the founders of Barcelona's still extant 'Cercle Artistic de Sant Luc', a guild of young Catholic artists (modelled on the German Nazarenes), of which Joan Miró was also a member.

Elsewhere, high-quality contemporary Christian art is relatively scarce. One exception is Jose Gutierrez Soloma whose *Procession of Death* (1930, Reina Sofia Museum in Madrid) is a powerful and widely reproduced fusion of Goya and Max Beckmann, while another is the combination of Pablo Serrano's hyper-attenuated crucifix and Francisco Ferrano's indented stained glass cubes in Fisac's Church of the Coronation, Vitoria, 48 km south of Bilbao.

More problematic as 'Christian' art is the work of Catalan Antoni Tàpies (1923–2012), although his recurrent cruciform emblems and emphasis (especially in *Homage to Matter,*

2006) on the spirituality of the material world, place him firmly within the Spanish mystical tradition.

Of Portuguese birth, although now resident in Britain, is Paula Rego (1935–), whose work sometimes reframes, both literally and metaphorically, 'traditional' Christian visual narrative. The Visitation, the Annunciation, Martha, Mary Magdalene are depicted as family dysfunction, sexual oppression, and pubescent angst. Powerful and unnerving, her imagery does not so much reduce its Christian prototypes to archaic fable but paradoxically relocates them firmly in the present. Rego's *Crivelli's Garden* (National Gallery, London) is an outstanding example of such work.

e

Eucharistic vestments *See* VESTMENTS and also LITURGICAL BOOKS, OBJECTS AND VESSELS, TABERNACLE, and ARTOPHORION.

Eusebian Canon This was a system of notation devised by *Eusebius of Caesarea to enable the reader of one Gospel to refer to parallel passages in other Gospels. While the early MSS of the Gospels were divided into chapters, or *kephalaia*, often arbitrarily according to where they were written, the present chapter divisions were devised by Stephen Langton, Archbishop of Canterbury, who died in 1228. The modern division of the texts into verses was devised by Robert Estienne, generally known as Stephanus, printer to King Francis I of France, who used his new system in a Greek and Latin edition of the Bible printed in 1551.

Medieval MSS of the Gospels were prefaced by the Eusebian Canons arranged in columns listing the parallels with the references noted, usually in red, in the margins of the texts. The Eusebian Canons were first used in the *Rabbula Codex (586: Florence, Bib. Laurenziana) and became common practice. The Canon tables are usually very decorative and sometimes the only embellishment in the MS.

Eusebius of Caesarea (*c.*260–*c.*340) was trained in theology by S. Pamphilus (*c.*240–309), a scholar martyred in Caesarea, an important theological centre (near Haifa) during the Emperor Diocletian's persecution. Eusebius followed the teaching of his master in his vigorous opposition to the arguments of Sabellius, who promoted a 2nd- and 3rd-century heresy which denied the Trinity, arguing that God was a single, supreme being, and that Christ and the Holy Spirit were lesser creations. After the martyrdom of S. Pamphilus, Eusebius fled to Tyre and thence to Egypt, where he was imprisoned. He became Bishop of Caesarea, in 315. His fame rests on the *Eusebian Canons, and on his *Ecclesiastical History*, a primary source for the history of Christianity (mainly in the East) from its Apostolic beginnings to his own times. He quotes extensively from earlier writers, and his work has caused him to be called 'the Father of Church History'. He also wrote an account of the Diocletian persecution through which he lived, an important work on biblical topography, a eulogistic life of Constantine, whom he advised, and who, he claims, told him of the vision preceding the battle of the Milvian Bridge. He also wrote books paralleling OT prophecies with the Life of Christ.

In his *History* Eusebius records the following: the woman with the haemorrhage who was cured by touching Christ's robe came from Caesarea, and a memorial of the event existed at the gates of her house. This was a bronze figure of a woman kneeling at the feet of a man, said to resemble Jesus. Eusebius says that he saw the monument, but later archaeologists have maintained that the group, which is not an unknown type of monument, represents a city or state, personified by the kneeling woman, paying homage either to a ruler or to a conqueror. He also claims that images of Jesus, Peter, and Paul were 'preserved in coloured portraits which I have examined'. He is also the source of the story of the *Edessa portrait of Christ.

Eustace, Saint, probably never existed, although a church in Rome dedicated to him dates from the 8th century. He was of unknown date, but was popular in the Middle Ages as patron of huntsmen, and is usually included among the fourteen Helpers (*see* VIERZEHNHEILIGEN). He is said to have seen a stag with a crucifix between its antlers, which is also the attribute of *S. Hubert, so the two are probably conflated. His legend also claims that he was a Roman general and was later martyred with his wife and family. There is a splendid engraving by Dürer of *c*.1501, which is identified by Dürer as Eustace, and a painting by Pisanello (London, NG) probably represents him rather than S. Hubert.

evangeliary, an, is a liturgical book which contains either (1) the texts of all four Gospels, or (2) the extracts which are to be read from the Gospel during Mass on any particular day.

Evangelists, the Four; Evangelist Symbols The four Evangelists, *Matthew, *Mark, *Luke, and *John, are traditionally regarded as the authors of the *Gospels, but only Matthew and John were among the original Twelve *Apostles. Nevertheless, Mark and Luke were occasionally included among the Apostles, displacing less well-known figures. The great Byzantine church of the Holy Apostles in Constantinople was a case in point. The earliest representation of the Evangelists as four men with Christ in their midst, is probably the one in the Catacomb of Marcus and Marcellianus in Rome, *c*.340. The Hellenistic tradition of putting a 'portrait' of the author at the beginning of the MS of his works is probably the source of the 'portraits' of the Evangelists at the beginning of codices of their Gospels. The earliest example known is that of Mark in the 6th-century *Rossano Codex (the other 'portraits' are presumed lost). Before then, the Evangelists were associated with the *Tetramorphs and winged animals, based on the interpretation by *S. Jerome of texts in Ezekiel (1: 5–10; 10: 14) and Rev. (4: 6–7). Matthew was symbolized by an angel, because his Gospel begins with the human ancestry of Christ; Mark by a lion, because the lion is a creature of the desert, and his Gospel begins with John the Baptist 'the voice of one crying in the wilderness'; Luke by an ox, a sacrificial animal, because his Gospel begins with the story of Zachariah entering the Holy of Holies to sacrifice; and John by an eagle, a bird that soars high into the heavens, because his Gospel begins with the words, 'In the beginning was the Word, and the Word was with God', words which carry the reader into the heavens. The earliest representation is probably that in the mosaic in Sta Pudenziana, Rome, of about 400, and in the wooden doors of Sta Sabina, Rome, of *c*.430. This symbolism was not general in the East until the early 14th century, but the *Rabbula Gospels of 586 have symbolic Evangelist figures. The symbols were popular on tympana in the West, usually as part of a *Majestas Domini, as at Chartres (West façade). From the 15th century the Evangelists were normally represented as men, sometimes with realistic representations of their symbols—e.g. the original altarpiece by *Caravaggio for San Luigi dei Francesi in Rome, where the angel was shown as a handsome boy, guiding Matthew's hand as he wrote his Gospel. This version was refused and the existing one shows the angel hovering in the sky, but the first version was characteristic of Caravaggio's literal rendering of scriptural subjects, and though it was typical of aspects of Counter-Reformation art, it was held to breach the rule of Decorum, in that the bare-legged Matthew with his hand guided as he wrote made him look like an illiterate peasant. The symbols are normally used only when all four Evangelists are represented. When only one or two of them is represented they may have different attributes—e.g. S. John is often shown with a serpent emerging from a chalice.

Eve *See* ADAM.

Exaltation of the Holy Cross A feast of the Catholic Church, which, since Vatican II, has been renamed the Triumph of the Cross. The feast is still held on its original date of 14 September, and commemorates the return of the Cross to Jerusalem. The Cross had been taken to Ctesiphon after the Persians took Jerusalem in 614, but in 627 the Emperor Heraclitus defeated the Persian conqueror Chosroes (Khusrau) in the decisive battle of Nineveh, and then took Ctesiphon; he recovered the Cross, and brought it back to Jerusalem. In the Byzantine rite the feast is linked with the finding of the True Cross by the Empress Helena in 326, and the dedication of the Church of the Holy Sepulchre in Jerusalem on 13 September. The story of the True Cross is the subject of *Piero della Francesca's fresco cycle, begun in 1452, in the church of San Francesco in Arezzo in Tuscany.

Exarch In the Byzantine Empire, an Exarch was a governor acting for the Emperor in a distant province. *Ravenna was an Exarchate from the mid-6th century to 750, which is why it is such an important centre of *Byzantine art. In the E. Orthodox Church, the term may apply to a bishop deputizing for a patriarch or other prelate.

exedra A niche or semicircular recess. It was a feature of ancient Roman buildings, such as the Baths of Diocletian in Rome. In *Early

Christian churches it became an apsidal area behind the altar, with the bishop's throne (*cathedra*) in the centre and seats for the clergy (*synthronon*) on either side. The apsidal ends of Torcello Cathedral, or San Clemente in Rome, are examples.

exegesis is a Greek word meaning guiding and, interpreting, and normally refers to biblical exegesis, the interpretation and elucidation of a difficult, complex, or obscure text. It is directly opposed to *eisegesis*, which is to read a meaning into a text instead of trying to discover the true meaning of the text itself.

Though few—if any—art historians would claim to be exegetes, yet the practice of art history often requires the methods used by an exegete: an examination of the work of art in a literal sense, to define its materials, form, and condition, its origins and dating, its purpose and if possible, its creator and the auspices under which it came to be created, its significance in its own time, and for later periods. To these enquiries must be added an elucidation of content and iconography—that is, the identification of its subject and meaning; whether it has an anagogical aspect—that is a spiritual, mystical, or allegorical intention; and whether it has a tropological meaning—that is, in the case of a religious subject, whether, for example, the representation of a NT event includes, and intends, a deliberate parallel with an OT event. S. Thomas Aquinas in the *Summa* and Dante in the *Convivio* both added allegory and moral significance to the literal and anagogical levels of meaning. One of the most important things, when dealing with religious art, is to avoid the danger of *eisegesis*, which would be to interpret the work of art from a narrow or partisan standpoint, or one influenced by fashion or ideological conformity or controversy. *See also* ALLEGORY.

Exercises, The Spiritual A system for meditation on the Life and Passion of Christ devised by *S. Ignatius Loyola at *Manresa, the mother-house of the Jesuits. They were enlarged, revised, and refined by him during the greater part of his life, and are designed to lead the mind and heart—since they are planned to make their appeal to both—to victory in a continued struggle for perfection. The meditations are arranged to last for four weeks: the first week is given to the consideration of sin and its results, and to meditation on the four last things—Death, Judgement, Heaven, and Hell; the second week to the Life and mission of Christ as an example for imitation; the third week to Christ's Passion as the price paid for the soul's redemption; the fourth week to the glory of the Resurrection, the joys of Paradise, and the progress of the soul towards salvation. The normal four week's course can, however, be shortened to last only ten days or, for instance, for the duration of a short retreat. They owe their power to their brilliant combination of intellectual and emotional appeal, their vivid imaginative gift, their psychological insight, and not least to the ordered progress of the meditations. They were first published in Rome in 1548, having been translated into Latin from their original Spanish, and they have since been translated into most languages.

The *Spiritual Exercises* have been used by artists—Bernini, for instance, was known to practise them—because their evocative visual power is a stimulus to the imagination in the depiction of the dramatic episodes in religious art.

Exodus (Lat. going out) is the name in Latin and Greek of the second OT book of the Bible, and relates the story of *Moses, and the liberation of the Jews from their captivity in Egypt. It recounts the story of the oppression of the Jews by their Egyptian taskmasters, the birth and preservation of Moses, the fruitless attempts by Moses to persuade the Pharaoh to release his people, culminating in the terrible plagues by which the Pharaoh was finally brought to concede their liberty, the institution of the *Passover, their escape to safety across the *Red Sea, and their long journey through the desert to Mt. *Sinai. The Book of Exodus is continued by those of Leviticus and Numbers, with the story of the journeys of the Israelites towards the Promised Land. Though traditionally the Book of Exodus is ascribed to Moses, modern biblical scholarship believes it to be a composite work, written probably over many centuries, with the date of the Exodus itself probably between 1260 and 1200 BC, and compiled in a written account between 900 and 500 BC.

Their deliverance from the Egyptian yoke was the decisive event of Jewish history, as the paramount example of God's favour towards his Chosen People, and the Passover remains the distinctive major celebration in the Jewish calendar. It is celebrated at the same time as the Christian Easter, because Christ was condemned to death immediately before the Passover, and therefore the dates must concur. The imagery of the Passover has often been evoked by Christian writers, with reference to Calvary and the sacrifice of the Eucharist.

There are innumerable works of art connected with the story of Exodus. A small sample is appended:

The earliest in a Christian church (some scenes from Exodus have survived from the 3rd-century synagogue in *Dura-Europos) are of 432–40: Rome, Sta Maria Maggiore, mosaics in the NE side of the nave (the orientation of the church is with the apse in the NW) are of the *Life of Moses* from his childhood, and continue as far as *Joshua's victory over the Amorites*. The series must at one time have been complete, but now there are serious gaps in the narrative. The *Brescia Box includes five scenes from the *Life of Moses*, including his finding, his marriage, and his stay in the house of his father-in-law Jethro, and his receiving the Tables of the Law. The 5th-century doors of Sta Sabina, Rome, contain, in the OT scenes, four miracles of Moses, and the Gathering of Manna. *Bouts included the Passover in his altarpiece of the *Mystic Meals (1464–8: Leuven, St-Pierre). The *Life and Mission of Moses* was painted on the wall of the *Sistine Chapel (1481–3) as a typological parallel to the *Life of Christ* on the opposite wall. *The finding of the Infant Moses* was painted by Veronese (*c.*1570: Prado), and Tiepolo (1755–60: Edinburgh, NG of Scotland). Tintoretto painted *The Gathering of the Manna* as an OT type of the *Last Supper* on opposite walls of the choir of San Giorgio Maggiore, Venice (1592–4). Poussin painted a number of incidents from the Book of Exodus: *The exposition of Moses* (1627/9: Dresden, and 1654: Oxford, Ashmolean); *The Finding of Moses* (1638 and 1647: Louvre); *Moses and the Burning Bush* (1641: Copenhagen); *Moses changing Aaron's rod into a serpent* (1644–5: Louvre); *The Crossing of the Red Sea* (*c.*1637: Melbourne); *The Gathering of the Manna* (1637–9: Louvre); *The Adoration of the Golden Calf* (1626: San Francisco, and 1635–7: London, NG). A *Moses with the Tables of the Law* is ascribed to Rembrandt (1659: Berlin). The theme continues to the present day: *Os Retirantes* 'The Migrants' (1944, Sao Paulo Museum of Art) by Brazilian of Italian descent Candido Portinari (1903–62), imbued with the Catholic culture, draws the plight of displaced persons of his own day into connection with the Biblical Exodus narrative.

exonarthex *See* NARTHEX.

Exposition of the Blessed Sacrament This is a normal part of the Roman Catholic service of Benediction, when the Host of the Blessed Sacrament is exposed in a *monstrance for the veneration of the faithful. It is also exposed in a similar manner during the service of *Quarant'ore. In a very few churches there is a continuous exposition, by special dispensation. Among these are the Tyburn Chapel in London, and Sto Isidoro in León, N. Spain. The privilege has also been granted to a few churches in Rome. The feast of *Corpus Christi is another occasion when the Blessed Sacrament is exposed in a monstrance, and sometimes carried in processions.

The first instance recorded by an illustration is in a Roman missal of 1373, which represents a procession in which a bishop carries a monstrance with the Blessed Sacrament. The devotion of the Exposition of the Blessed Sacrament did not become common until the 16th century, but wherever, and for whatever reason, the devotion has to be authorized by the bishop, or by an Apostolic indult.

Expulsion from Paradise *See* ADAM.

Expulsion of the Traders from the Temple This is recorded by all four Evangelists, but John gives the most detail: 'Jesus went up to Jerusalem. In the temple he found people selling cattle, sheep, and doves, and the money changers sitting at their tables. Making a whip of cords, he drove all of them out of the temple, both the sheep and the cattle. He also poured out the coins of the money changers and overturned their tables. He told those that were selling the doves, "Take these things out of here! Stop making my Father's house a marketplace!"' (John 2: 13–16). Eric Gill was commissioned to carve this subject (1922–23) for Leeds University War Memorial.

The subject may be seen as a NT antitype of the OT Expulsion from Paradise, and in El Greco's painting (1597–1603: London, NG, and other versions) reliefs are depicted on the Temple walls of the Expulsion from Paradise and Abraham sacrificing Isaac.

Exsultet (Exultet) rolls The rolls are long strips of parchment or vellum with the prayers, canticles, and lessons of the liturgy of the Midnight Mass of Easter Eve, accompanying the blessing and lighting of the Paschal *candle, which symbolizes the pillar of fire guiding the Israelites in the desert, and also the Resurrection of Christ. The ceremony goes back to the 7th century; the thirty-odd surviving manuscript examples of the rolls were strongly influenced by the Byzantine rite, and were produced from the 11th to the 13th century chiefly in S. Italy, many of the finest coming from the Benedictine monastery of *Monte Cassino.

On Easter Eve the deacon carried the roll in procession to the *ambo or pulpit, or to the *rood screen, and began the chant with the words *Exsultet iam Angelica turba coelorum* (Now let the angelic heavenly host exult). As he chanted the story of the Creation, the crossing of the Red Sea, the arrival of the Jews in the Promised Land, and the fate of Jerusalem, he allowed the roll to unwind over the edge of the pulpit or rood. The MSS are illustrated with pictures of the events he recited, the pictures being upside down to his text, to help the congregation to follow his narrative. One of the finest examples is in London (BL), probably made in Monte Cassino in the 11th or early 12th century.

Extreme Unction *See* SACRAMENTS.

Exultet *See* EXSULTET.

ex-voto (Lat. from a vow) *See* VOTIVE.

Eyck, van Two painters, brothers, worked in the Netherlands between 1422 and 1441. Hubert, the elder, was established in Ghent; in the five references to him in the archives between 1424 and 1426, although the name is differently spelt each time, it seems fairly certain that the same person is intended. The name that matters is the one which appears in a quatrain on the frame of the *Adoration of the Lamb*, commonly known as the Ghent Altar, which roughly translated says that Hubert began the work, and his brother Jan 'second in art' completed it at the request of Joos Vijd. The last line of the verse is a chronogram containing the date 6 May 1432. 'Arte secundus' does not mean that Jan was considered inferior to Hubert, but merely that he was second chronologically—i.e. younger. The date establishes when the altarpiece was set up in the chapel founded by the donors, Joos Vijd and his wife Elizabeth Borluut in what was then the church of St John the Baptist in Ghent, rededicated to S. Bavo in 1540. An inscription recorded as having been on Hubert's tomb (destr. 1578) in the Vijd chapel gives the date of his death as 18 September 1426. The Ghent Altar was completed by Jan by 1432. No other work by Hubert has been positively identified—there are several plausible ascriptions—and nothing by Jan can be positively dated before 1432. Jan, however, figures in the records of two princes: from 1422 to 1424 he was working in The Hague for John of Bavaria, Count of Holland, and he then worked for Philip the Good, Duke of Burgundy, as his court painter, and he also served his master as a confidential envoy. He was in Bruges and Lille in 1425; for over a year, 1426–7, he was on a mission for the Duke; in 1427 he was in Tournai. He returned from travelling in February 1428, and was then away on another journey to Portugal (almost certainly connected with the Duke's marriage to Isabella of Portugal) from which he returned in 1429. Only after January 1430 did he settle in Bruges, where he married, and where he died in July 1441. This busy and peripatetic career suggests two things: that a great deal of the Ghent Altar must have been carried either to an entirely finished state, or to approximate completion, before Hubert died, and that Jan's hand in the work can be restricted to those parts which accord best with his later works. The characteristics of Jan's art are his realism, the directness of his vision, and his technique.

It is obvious that the Ghent Altar is an amalgamation of disparate elements—even of disparate types of vision. The altarpiece consists of three parts: a large central area, and two wings which close over it, each wing painted on both sides. In all, there are twenty panels, of which four on the outside of the wings are again divided into an upper and a lower section. Inside, the altarpiece is divided into two registers. In the upper one the following are represented: Christ the King, portrayed enthroned and crowned with the papal triple crown as King of Heaven, with an elaborate crown of temporality at His feet; he is flanked by the Virgin Mary on His right, robed and crowned as Queen, and on the left by S. John the Baptist wearing an opulent jewelled robe over his traditional animal-skin clothing. This is, therefore, a representation of the Heavenly Throne as it is described in the Book of Revelation, and in S. Augustine's *De Civitate Dei* (the City of God) as the 'Eternal Beatitude of the City of God and the Perpetual Sabbath'. In the wings, the *Angel Musicians* on the right and the *Angel Singers* on the left are appropriate to this vision; *Adam* and *Eve*, flanking them on either side, are not. The lower part of the altarpiece consists of a large panel, as wide as the three panels of the Heavenly figures above, representing the *Adoration of the Lamb* by groups of the Elect, and this single large panel is flanked by two panels in each of the wings, representing further groups of worshippers—*Pilgrims, Hermits,* the *Knights of Christ,* and the *Just Judges* (the last is a copy of a panel stolen in 1934 and never recovered).

On the exterior of the wings, the upper part contains the *Annunciation,* with two prophets (Micah and Zechariah) and two sibyls (Erithrea and Cumae) with their identifying texts in niches over the Virgin and the Angel, and over the little view of the room in which the scene is set. Below are grisaille paintings of fictive statues in niches of the two SS John—the Baptist as the then patron saint of the church, and the Evangelist, as the saint on one of whose feast-days the chapel and altarpiece were dedicated—and the two donors who not only pray before their patron saints but also before the celestial vision inside.

The central scene of the *Adoration of the Lamb* takes place in Paradise—a meadow full of flowers and flowering shrubs, palm-trees and rivers, with views of fantastic cities representing the Heavenly Jerusalem. On the altar stands the Lamb, blood spurting from His breast into a chalice, with on the altar frontal the communion words 'Behold the Lamb of God who takes away the sins of the world', and at the bottom of the picture the fountain of water is shown as if flowing down towards the real altar where Mass was said. Many of the figures among the pilgrims coming to adore the Lamb of the Eucharist are intended to be identified, through attributes, emblems, and details in their robes, but though the iconography is sometimes deducible from the 13th-century **Golden Legend* the very large number of figures—more than 300 have been counted—makes this both difficult and otiose, since they in fact represent humanity, portrayed as the Elect, worshipping the Eternal Godhead and the Trinity, for at the top of the Adoration panel is an aureole in which hovers the Dove, emblem of the Holy Spirit. Seen horizontally, God is flanked by the Virgin through whom the Incarnate Godhead entered the world as Man, and the Baptist who preached the coming of Salvation, while seen vertically, the Trinity appears as God the Father, the Holy Spirit, and God the Son in the Sacrifice of the Eucharist.

The division of the work between the brothers suggests not just a development of the original project but a change, and this is borne out by the *Annunciation* on the outside of the wings. The two small panels with the view through the window with the central Romanesque column (an emblem often used to portray the Old Dispensation which ends with the Incarnation) and the niche with the water vessel and basin and the hanging towel, always attributes of the Virgin Annunciate, are backed by the figures of *Adam* and *Eve* who are seen in a totally different order of reality from the Heavenly vision which they frame. They are truly human, Adam even with one foot protruding from his niche into the world of the spectator. Such an illogical arrangement of the Annunciation, which in any case takes place in a space far too small to contain the figures, suggests that these two central panels are late insertions into the scheme. Likewise, the portraits of the donors also seem to belong to the real world of Adam and Eve rather than to the visionary scene of the Adoration of the Lamb. But it must be assumed that Hubert at his death left some of the panels partly finished as well as some fairly far advanced; also it seems likely that the first project for the altarpiece was different in character. Hubert had a workshop in Ghent, since a visit of the city aldermen to his workshop, and a payment from city funds as gratuities to his assistants, are recorded in 1425–6; this is probably in connection with the original project for the work. His assistants must have been of considerable competence if, in view of Jan's frequent lengthy absences, the completion of such a work—its measurements when open are over 12 ft. high by over 18 ft. wide, plus the outside of the wings, over 12 ft. high by over 9 ft. wide—was achieved by 1432, only six years after Hubert's death. From the religious standpoint, the importance of the Ghent Altar does not lie in the iconographic novelty of its elements, taken separately. It is their conjunction in a single work which is novel. The compilation of the iconographic programme is the work of a learned cleric (such programmes were not within the competence of a layman), who drew on Revelation, on S. Augustine, on the various Masses for such feasts as All Saints, Christmas, Easter, and Pentecost, and on the liturgical cycle of the year—Advent and Lent—and on some of the prophecies and passages from Isaiah and Ezekiel. The most likely source which brings all these texts—and the inscriptions are many and were clearly of great importance to the altarpiece—into conjunction is the work by a 12th-century commentator called Rupert of Deutz whose book, *De Victoria Verbi Dei* (Concerning the Victory of the Word of God), had considerable influence on Eyckian iconography. It supplied the texts which figure so largely on the various panels. The other important aspect of the work is the standard of execution which it set. The rest of Jan's work never falls below the quality of the Ghent Altar; its most impressive feature is the piercing naturalism of his treatment of his subjects, by demonstrating how it can be done, and meeting the challenge *Aac ixh xan* (Als ich kan: As I can) which he inscribed on his presumed portrait of a *Man in a Turban* (London, NG; probably a self-portrait), signed and dated 1433. It required an artist of quite another temperament to introduce into the chilly brilliance of van Eyck the feeling, emotion, and drama which is to be found in Roger van der *Weyden.

Jan's other works include unusual treatments of the theme of the Virgin and Child, such as the curious *Virgin in the Church* (Berlin) where the setting is a splendid but extraordinarily miniaturized Gothic church, no flight of fancy, but an exposition of the role of the Virgin as the embodiment of the Church and illumined by the Wisdom of God, in that no other explanation but a supernatural one can be found for the brilliance of the sunlight which streams in from the North. The *Annunciation* (Washington, NG) is in a similar church, through which the Holy Spirit descends upon the Virgin, and in which the Romanesque architecture of the lower part, changing to Gothic in the upper parts, symbolizes the transition from the Old Dispensation to the New. The elaborate inlaid floor depicting various OT scenes (Delilah cutting Samson's hair, Samson slaying the Philistines, David and Goliath) are well-known parallels between the Old Testament and the New. Another *Virgin enthroned in a church* (the Dresden triptych) with donors and their patron saints in the wings and a grisaille *Annunciation* on the outside of the wings, is to be understood as having the enthroned Virgin in the place of, and personifying, the altar, with the Holy Child held by the Virgin becoming the Sacrament present in the tabernacle on the altar. *The Madonna of the Fountain* (Antwerp) is a variant on two themes: the *Hortus Conclusus and also the Fountain of the Water of Life, as in Jeremiah's words 'the Lord, the fountain of living waters' and Christ's words to the woman of Samaria at the well, when he said 'the water that I will give will become in them a spring of water gushing up to eternal life'. In all van Eyck's work there are hundreds of tiny details—a scene carved on the arm of a chair, in the capital of a column, in an inlay in the floor—which look at first sight like mere decoration, as if the artist could not bear to leave any surface plain, but when the subjects are examined carefully they will be found to contribute to the meaning of the whole. These pictures are not just to be looked at; they are to be 'read' and studied; they serve a didactic religious function and the significance of the iconography is the sole reason why these details are present.

Eye of God An equilateral triangle with a single eye inside it, and with rays emanating from it (rarely without them) is a symbol of the all-seeing Eye of God. Such a triangle is itself a symbol of the Holy *Trinity, and usually also has rays emanating from it, for example in the lantern of the dome of San Carlo alle Quattro Fontane in Rome, or in Federico Zuccaro's *Angels adoring the Trinity* in the Gesù, Rome, where the triangle encloses an *Alpha and Omega. There are several biblical references to the all-seeing Eye of God; in the Psalms (34: 15 (Vg. 33: 16)): 'The eyes of the Lord are on the righteous'; and similarly Prov. 15: 3: 'The eyes of the Lord are in every place'.

Usually, representations of an eye tended to be avoided, since they were often equated with the Evil Eye. No medieval example has yet been found, but the symbol has been connected with Masonic ritual, since medieval masons' guilds were often dedicated to the Holy Trinity. A rare example of the radiant triangle with a single eye is in Pontormo's altarpiece of the *Supper at Emmaus*, painted in 1525 for the Carthusians of Galuzzo (Florence, Uffizi), where it dominates the top of the picture over Christ's head. In the Palazzo del Tè at Mantua it is used as a secular symbol of vigilance. In the 18th and 19th centuries it was used in Courts of Justice to remind judges of their responsibilities, but in St Aloysius, near St Pancras station in London, built by French Catholic refugees *c.*1808 (destroyed 1939/45), it was still, above the altar, a symbol of God's omnipresence.

Ezekiel, the Visions of Ezekiel, a priest and the son of a priest, was the third Major OT *Prophet in succession to *Isaiah and

*Jeremiah. When the armies of Nebuchadnezzar conquered Judah (597 BC) he was taken captive to Babylon and lived in a refugee settlement between the Euphrates and Babylon. After thirty years in captivity he experienced a vision (he had four in all) in which he described the *Tetramorph, the extraordinary winged creature with four faces—those of a man, a lion, an ox, and an eagle. These are generally accepted as the symbols of the four *Evangelists, respectively Matthew, Mark, Luke, and John. The Word of God came to him often, bidding him denounce the sins of the Jews. If he failed to do so then their guilt would lie upon him, but if he obeyed, then they would be responsible (Ezek. 3: 18–21). God also ordered that they should be told that their sins were the cause of their present captivity and the destruction of the Temple in Jerusalem, which the prophet records as having taken place eleven years after the captivity began (586 BC). The fall of Jerusalem is the occasion of the mention of the only personal detail of the prophet: he records the death of his wife as happening at that time (24: 16–18).

He also proclaimed man's personal responsibility by God's condemnation of the exculpatory proverb 'The fathers have eaten sour grapes, and the children's teeth are set on edge', in that God had said 'All lives are mine ... it is only the person who sins that shall die, ... A child shall not suffer for the iniquity of a parent, nor a parent suffer for the iniquity of a child; the righteousness of the righteous shall be his own, and the wickedness of the wicked shall be his own.' But later God says 'But if the wicked turn away from all their sins ... and keep all my statutes ... they shall surely live' (18: 2–5, 20, 28; Vg. 18: 2–9, 20, 28). Ezekiel also had a vision of being carried by God into a valley of dry bones, and God saying to him 'Can these dry bones live?' and then 'Prophesy ... and say to them: O dry bones, hear the word of the Lord ... you shall live ... and know that I am the Lord.' This was not only a promise of the restoration of Jerusalem, but is also a promise of the Resurrection (37: 1–5). From ch. 40 onwards, Ezekiel is mainly concerned with the planning of the new Temple and the ordering of its services, confident of the restoration to come. In 44: 1–2 he describes the Temple gate which God decreed should not be opened; this is construed as a prediction of the *Porta Clausa. There is a shadowy legend, however, that like Jeremiah, he suffered martyrdom at the hands of his own embittered people.

There are few representations of his Visions. One is a mid-5th-century mosaic in Hosios David in Salonika of the four symbolic beasts; another, by Fra Angelico, is a wheel within a wheel (1: 15 ff.), the spaces between the spokes of the outer wheel containing figures of prophets, with their names on the spokes, and in the inner wheel SS Peter, Paul, James, and Jude, and the four Evangelists, each with his symbolic head and their names on the spokes. At the bottom of the picture are the figures of Ezekiel and Pope S. Gregory the Great (author of a commentary on this obscure passage).

Probably the best-known representation is a small picture by Raphael (*c.*1517: Florence, Pitti) in which God is borne up on the Tetramorph, and a ray of light shoots down upon Ezekiel on the earth below. Ezekiel is one of the seven prophets painted by Michelangelo in the *Sistine Chapel ceiling; he represents him as a vigorous, vehement man engaged in fierce disputation.

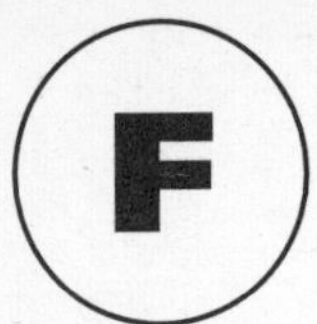

F or **FF** *See* FECIT.

fabbrica, fabrica The Italian and Latin words for the fabric of a building, but often applied—as in Veneranda Fabbrica di San Pietro—to the office charged with the upkeep of major churches and the supervision of the funds for maintenance. In Italy the members of the Fabbrica, or Operai, were often responsible for the selection of architects, e.g. *Brunelleschi for the building of the dome of Florence Cathedral.

façade The front of a building, which faces the spectator. The front of a transept is also its façade, and the rear of a building may also be said to have a façade, if it is viewed in its own right. The façade may be of the same date as the rest of the building or may well be later, as for instance, the 19th-century façades of the 13th-century cathedral and Sta Croce in Florence. However, it may be very close to the same date as the rest of the building, but be the work of a different architect succeeding to the job, and preferring his ideas to those of his predecessor, as for instance, the work of Giacomo della Porta at the Gesù in Rome after Vignola's death. Nor does the façade need to fit the church, as for instance at San Michele, Lucca, where the façade towers over the level of the nave, or at Orvieto Cathedral where the size of the façade in relation to the building is governed not by the height of the nave but by the amount of sculpture the commissioners wished to be incorporated, so that it is not so much a façade as a screen in front of the building.

FACULTY CONSENT

The installation of a permanent (though not necessarily a 'fixed') work of art into a Christian place of worship in the UK will almost always require the procurement of some kind of formal consent. The Faculty system in force in the 16,000 Anglican places of worship in England is well known, if not perhaps well understood. The churches, chapels, and meeting houses that make up the rest of the estimated 45,000 Christian places of worship in the UK usually operate their own, generally more centralized consent system.

Therefore, before committing time, funds, or emotional energy, both artist and patron should be careful to establish what consents and other consultations will be required. The consent process may also have an impact on aspects of the artwork itself, such as size, materials, subject, and location; it is important that artists are prepared to work within a process involving a degree of collaboration.

What follows is a very brief précis of the system in force in the Church of England at present, as described more fully in the Faculty Jurisdiction Rules 2000. The precise process followed varies slightly between the 43 dioceses of the Church of England. Advice on the systems in force in other denominations is readily available on the Internet or from the respective regional offices.

Most art currently being installed in church buildings is either commemorative or votive, or both. In these cases there is normally a fairly traditional artist/patron relationship. When the patron is not either the minister or the parochial church council (PCC), it is important that they should be brought in on the proposal at an early stage. A formal resolution of the PCC will be required before a Faculty petition can be submitted.

Once there is general agreement that the proposal is something that will be welcomed within the parish, it is time to bring in the other consultative bodies. First amongst these is the relevant *Diocesan Advisory Committee for the Care of Churches (DAC), which is the statutory adviser to the Chancellor of the Diocese in determining the faculty petition. Early engagement with the insurers brings benefits, and may well hold down premiums in some cases. (In the Church of England the diocesan chancellor is the chief representative of the bishop in the adjudication of the temporal affairs of his diocese.) The DAC will need to see sufficient information to make a judgement on the suitability of the proposal. This would normally include a sketch or model of the proposal, details of materials, location, fixings, size, and some statement explaining the iconography and general concept of the artwork. In cases involving prominent art installations in listed church buildings, formal Statements of Significance and Needs may also be required, giving details of the building and how the art installation will impact upon it, and why that impact is justified. Successful cases suggest that such Statements benefit all proposals.

At this initial stage, a balance needs to be found in the amount of information supplied. There is no point in paying for detailed mock-ups if the DAC is going to turn down the proposal, but equally it is important that there is enough information for the DAC to form a clear understanding of what is proposed. The application very much needs to be fitted to the proposal. The DAC's initial reaction to a proposal may not be particularly positive, but this should not be perceived as external interference by the DAC in the creative process. The DAC's comments are aimed wholly at making the finished piece a stronger, more telling player in the liturgical and architectural setting of the church, something that in the future will reflect well on both patron and artist. That is not to say that the artist must agree with what the DAC says. Indeed, the most enjoyable and fruitful cases involving artworks are those that result in a lively debate between artist and committee, and as often as not result in the artist being allowed to proceed as originally intended.

Depending on the scale of the artwork, its location, and the significance of the building into which it is to be put, it may also be necessary to consult with one or more of the five National Amenity Societies, the local authority, English Heritage, and the Church Buildings Council. The rules governing these consultations are complex and subjective, and it is best to take the advice of the diocese concerned on this matter. In some cases these consultations are carried out by the diocese on behalf of the applicant, while in others it is left to the applicant. Responsibility for this should be ascertained at an early stage. The importance of early stage consultations cannot be over-emphasized.

In addition to the DAC, which is obliged to give its advice on the matter, any or all of these other consultees may wish to become involved in the discussion about a new artwork, and have a statutory right to do so. All will have opinions to express on matters the artist may consider wholly to be within his or her purview. This is inevitable and must be met graciously. The interests of these external bodies often have less to do with art or liturgy than conservation of the historic character of the church building. The DAC may prove to be an ally to the artist in communicating the worthiness of his or her proposal in that context.

The process of DAC and other consultations can take as little as four weeks or very much longer, depending on the complexities of the case and, to no little degree, the determination of the applicant. Correspondence can become protracted and it is important not to underestimate the potential administrative burden involved in bringing more complex cases to a conclusion. It will be to the advantage of the project if a single, effective point of contact can oversee the project—perhaps the artist or the patron or the minister.

After the DAC has been able to give its formal recommendation for the works, the second part of the Faculty process comes into play: the petition to the Chancellor of the Diocese. The DAC's recommendation, the comments of any other consultees, the comments of any parishioners who have seen notice of the proposal, as well as all the documents illustrating the proposal and correspondence discussing it, are sent to the Chancellor to enable him or her to make a judgement on the case. The Chancellor will study the case to ensure that all procedures have been properly followed. Provided there have been no objections received, or at least no objections the Chancellor considers should be upheld, the Faculty can be granted.

In cases where there have been objections and the Chancellor considers they are valid and should be heard, a hearing of the Consistory Court may be convened. The Chancellor presides over the court, which may be held in private by written representations or in public, often in the church concerned. Consistory Court hearings of this type are rare, and when the objections raised have come from one of the formal consultees, they are usually better dealt with by an informal dialogue before the case reaches the Chancellor, which would avoid the need for a court hearing.

There are two more important things to know about Faculties in the Church of England:

No contractual obligation can be entered into until Faculty consent is in place. Any contractual disputes within a church will be heard in the Consistory Court and the Chancellor may take a dim view when obligations have been entered into in advance of a Faculty being granted.

In cases where works are carried out in an Anglican church building without Faculty consent (including the installation of artworks), this is viewed as contempt of the Consistory Court, which, being an extension of the High Court, could carry a severe sanction.

Faith, hope, and charity *See* VIRTUES.

Fall of Man *See* MAN, THE FALL OF.

Fall of the Damned *See* JUDGEMENT.

Fall of the Rebel Angels *See* ANGELS and DEVIL.

Falling asleep of the BVM *See* DORMITION.

Family, the Holy *See* HOLY FAMILY.

Fathers of the Church Unlike the *Doctors, who are strictly defined, the Early Fathers are a large group of writers, some as late as the 12th century, but they are more narrowly defined as writing not later than the 6th century, orthodox and personally holy—the looser definition even includes some doctrinally controversial figures as Origen or Tertullian, who nevertheless can be used to show that a particular doctrine was current in the Church at that date. In art the figures represented are usually the Greek and Latin Doctors, who are automatically included among the Fathers. The commonest are SS Athanasius, Basil, Gregory Nazianzen, Ambrose, John Chrysostom, Jerome, Augustine, and Gregory the Great (d. 604), one of the latest.

Fathers, Desert *See* THEBAID.

fecit or **fieri fecit** (Lat. he made/caused to be made) The word *fecit* (often abbreviated to F), preceded by a name, is an assertion of authorship of a work of art. FF, or *fieri fecit,* associated with a name, means that the person named was the donor of the work, not the artist. An imaginary inscription on a work of art might run: AMDG IO. SMITH FF. A.D.N.J. C. MDIV, meaning *Ad maiorem Dei gloriam Johannes Smith fieri fecit anno Domini Nostri Jesu Christi MDIV,* or, To the greater glory of God John Smith caused this work to be made in the year of Our Lord Jesus Christ 1504. *See also* OPUS.

Feeding of the Multitude *See* LOAVES AND FISHES.

Feet, Washing of the Disciples' On Holy Thursday, after the Last Supper, Jesus took a towel and washed the feet of His disciples, in spite of the objections of Peter, as an example to them (John 13: 4–16). The subject is often represented in cycles of the *Passion, but more rarely as a single scene, for instance *Jesus washing Peter's feet* (1882–86 Ford Madox Brown, Tate). The act of humility prefigures the Crucifixion, and washing is a cleansing of the disciples, similar to Baptism.

Feibusch, Hans (1898–1998) A German painter, sculptor, lithographer, and writer.

Feibusch was one of the artists whose works were undoubtedly branded as degenerate and publicly burned at the time of Hitler's *Entartete Kunst* exhibition (Munich 1937). Fleeing to England, he brought muralist and architectural knowledge and skills which the Church of England took up fully (with encouragement from Dr George Bell, then Bishop of Chichester) in the post-war repairs and reconstruction to places of worship. He produced over 30 murals including those in St Wilfred's, Brighton (1949); St Elizabeth's, Eastbourne (1944); Chichester Cathedral (1951); Preston (1956); St Ethelburga, Bishopsgate, London (1962); St Alban's, Holborn, London (1965–6). His text *Mural Painting* (1946) is a European, historical, and technical account, and pleads for the churches to take the artist seriously. Failing sight in his seventies led him into sculpture. Examples are found in Ely Cathedral (1981); St John's Wood (1979); St Alban's, Holborn, London (1985).

fenestella *See* CONFESSIO.

feretory There are two separate meanings to the term which can be either a fixed shrine-chapel containing a *reliquary, or a movable reliquary-shrine, both of which are usually placed behind an altar. The shrine of S. Edward the Confessor, behind the high altar of Westminster Abbey, is an example of the first. The reliquary containing the body of *S. Cuthbert which, after it was saved from the destruction of Lindisfarne, was carried all over Northumbria before coming to rest in Durham Cathedral, is an example of the second, and one closer to the derivation of 'feretory' from the Latin for 'bier'. Relics which attracted great popular devotion were often carried in procession over considerable distances as, for instance, during fund-raising campaigns for the rebuilding of Chartres Cathedral after the fire of 1194.

Examples of processions with a reliquary are in Gentile Bellini's two pictures in the Accademia, Venice: one is the *Procession in Piazza S. Marco*, where the splendid reliquary of the *True Cross, which belonged to the *Scuola di San Giovanni, is carried under a canopy accompanied by all the members of the Scuola. Such processions were not always uneventful, as is recorded in his painting of the *Miracle at the bridge of S. Lorenzo*, when the jostling of the crowds had toppled the reliquary into the canal, where it eluded those who plunged in to rescue it, this honour being reserved to the Grand Guardian of the Scuola, Giovanni Vendramin, who jumped into the canal and retrieved the reliquary.

fieri fecit *See* FECIT.

Filarete (Antonio Averlino, called **Filarete)** (1400–69). He adopted the name Filarete late in life, deriving it from the Greek 'lover of virtue'. His earliest known work is a bronze door for *St Peter's Rome (1445) which Vasari qualifies as 'disastrous'. This was made for Old St Peter's and is one of the few surviving pieces from the old building incorporated in the doors of the new building. It has two large figures of SS Peter and Paul with, above them, the Salvator Mundi and the Virgin, and below them scenes from the martyrdoms of the two Apostles. There are also interesting scenes from the life of Pope Eugenius IV (1431–47), relating to his unsuccessful attempt to reunite the Eastern and Western Churches in 1439, with proposals which the Byzantines rejected. In 1451 Filarete was commissioned by Francesco Sforza, Duke of Milan, to build a large hospital, the Ospedale Maggiore, so big that he did not live to finish it. His design was not only grandiose, but novel, in that the main block enclosed a central arcaded courtyard, while on either side was a further complex of buildings on a grid system, each having four small arcaded courts. One side was for men, the other for women and abandoned children. This was a major influence on later hospital design, but Filarete's building now has other uses. During the years he was working on the Ospedale Maggiore he completed his architectural treatise, the *Trattato d'architettura,* which Vasari, unkindly but understandably, described as the most ridiculous book ever written. It circulated widely in MS (not printed until the 19th cent.) and perhaps its most interesting features are his designs for an ideal city to be called Sforzinda. The treatise contains designs for centrally planned churches and for a building ten storeys high, to exemplify man's rise from Vice to Virtue, from a brothel on the ground floor rising to an observatory at the top, representing philosophical aspirations.

FILM

In 1893, at the Chicago World's Fair, Eadweard Muybridge showed his moving pictures of animals to the paying public making the purpose-built Zoopraxographical Hall the first commercial film theatre. From those early beginnings film began to dominate cultural life in Europe, USA, and throughout the world. It is now a global industry embracing not only Hollywood, Europe, and Indian 'Bollywood' films but all continents; for instance, one of the most vibrant film festivals is in Burkina Faso.

Films provide us with our contemporary texts. The heyday of cinema-going was in the 1940s, reaching a peak in 1946 (UK average weekly attendance of 31.5 million).The high level of attendance was somewhat eroded in 1950s (UK weekly attendance 21.1 million). The decline in cinema-going continued so that by the 1980s in the UK it was at just over one million weekly admissions. In recent years, the downward spiral has been halted, and there is something of a revival (UK weekly admissions in 2010 were 3.3 million). Nevertheless, today film is even more pervasive than in the heyday of cinema-going. Statistics show that the total size of the film audience in UK in 2010 was estimated to be 4.6 billion, calculated from all sources—cinema, DVD/Video, View on Demand, and film on television. Cinema comprises only 4 per cent of that audience. It is estimated that there were 81 film-viewing occasions per person in 2010—an average of seven films per month per person. Screens dominate the lives of our contemporaries.

The popular success of cinema in the 20th century led to its being labelled an entertainment rather than an art. It is often considered a product for consumption rather than something to be admired. Film-making is an industry; films are extremely expensive products with Hollywood films costing up to £188 million to make. The average cost of making a Hollywood film is £41 million, while Bollywood films cost up to £12 million. Clearly those investing such sums in a product are not doing so for philanthropic purposes but to achieve a good rate of return—artistic merit is not always uppermost in the mind of a production company. The producers, in an attempt to leave nothing to chance, spend on average a further £23 million on marketing for a Hollywood film. The potential returns for a good 'property' are immense. For instance, a successful film such as *Spiderman 2* (Sam Rami, 2004) was made for about £126 million, and the world-wide box-office takings were £495 million. Television and DVD sales can add a further £65 million to the profits of an individual film.

Film-making is a complex and skilful art utilizing the techniques of Modernism with its mix of shots, the ability to cross-cut between characters and narratives—flashbacks and flash forwards. Film can employ a variety of paces and camera angles, imaginative use of sound, and different colour palettes. Such is the spectacular smorgasbord of cinematic techniques that each film could almost be a Cubist painting. Add to that mix all the influences and elements from literature and drama, skills of sound, camera, music, and acting from artists all over the world, and it is possible to see a most eclectic and Modernist mix that transcends conventional pigeon-holing as high or low culture. The techniques of film-making suggest Modernism but the nature of watching narratives on screen suggests Realism. We believe (if only fleetingly) what we see—there is an illusion that the camera cannot lie. Film is a mix of these traits of Modernism and Realism.

The Judaeo-Christian tradition was mined for stories to be filmed in this new medium. And the French pioneers of cinema all filmed Christian subjects. The Lumière brothers filmed *The Passion Play* at Horwitz in Bohemia. Georges Méliès in 1897 made a short film, *Le Christ Marchant sur les Flots*. A great innovator, Méliès was the first to use stop-motion photography to produce trick cinematic effects. This short film, now lost, showed the rolling sea upon which a mist appears and from the midst of the mist Christ is seen walking on the water. The illusion that the camera cannot lie implied that miracles can happen (on screen at least). Ferdinand Zecca followed his short film *L'Enfant Prodique* (1901), with what is quite possibly the first feature-length film (44 minutes), *La Vie et La Passion de Jesus Christ* (1903).

The work of the French pioneers demonstrates some of the recurring problems of filming the Bible. Zecca's life of Christ is little more than a series of *tableaux vivants*. Early biblical films were frequently used to illustrate lectures and the segmented nature of the film's screenplay suited this purpose. This method relied heavily on the works of Gustave Doré, James Tissot, and the Pre-Raphaelites to provide the artistic template. The canon of tableaux employed in the films based on the gospels is almost identical to the 50 tableaux that have dominated Western Christian art. Most films about Jesus offer a walk through these 50 tableaux. This is partly because that compendium of gospel stories is the film that people already have in their heads. The screenplay is usually based on all four gospels spliced together.

With the increasing commercial success of cinema, the focus of film-making began to move from France to the United States. The same artistic influences were apparent in Sidney Olcott's *From the Manger to the Cross* (1913), the Christ segment in D. W. Griffith's epic *Intolerance* (1916), and Cecil B. DeMille's film *King of Kings* (1927). Griffith and DeMille belong to a more confident era of film-making and audiences grew rapidly. The production values grew in tandem with burgeoning budgets and dramatic sets. The artistic template from which these increasingly confident directors worked remained that suggested by art. For instance, the British artist John Martin (1787–1854) was a strong influence on Griffith as can be seen in the Babylonian segment of *Intolerance* and the crucifixion scene in the Christ segment. There is nothing intimate or pastoral about Martin's art—these are epic canvases engulfing huge themes, and they inspired Griffith and others to create films of similarly epic proportions.

The Hebrew Bible also provided source material for many movies. As with the gospels, these were the stories everyone knew and had embedded in their mind and they had formed the canon of Western art. In the first decade of film-making, numerous films based on the Hebrew Bible had been made including: *Moses in the Bulrushes* (Gaumont, 1903), *Samson and Delilah* (Ferdinand Zecca, 1903), *David and Goliath* (Sidney Olcott, 1908), *Noah's Ark* (Arthur M. Cooper, 1909).

The movie pioneers were sincere in thinking that their product would deliver a spiritual experience to the audience. Such 'lazy awe' is not possible—audiences would marvel at the wonders on screen but increasingly they had to be enticed into cinemas with a hint of sex and spectacle. DeMille was the master at combining the two: his *King of Kings* creates a back story for the courtesan Mary Magdalene, and *Sign of The Cross* (1932) has Claudette Colbert bathing in asses' milk, with a lesbian dance scene, as well as uneasy sexual moments during the martyrdom of early Christians. Fred Niblo's *Ben-Hur* (1925) boasts not only a magnificent chariot race but nudity.

The era of sound movies coincided with the more austere period of the 1930s and 1940s. Different films were being made and although great epics such as *Gone With The Wind* (Victor Fleming, 1939) were made, these were the exceptions. Film-going was popular but as an antidote to economic depression. With the advent of the Second World War, explicitly religious films offered comfort and solace and were often little more than morality tales. In *Destination Unknown* (Tay Garnett, 1933), a stowaway miraculously helps a drifting boat in danger of sinking. A similar plot was employed in *Strange Cargo* (Frank Borsage, 1940). Putting faith in the Christ-like figure is salvific in both dramas, a comforting message in times of depression and war. A mixture of comfort and morality were evident in the two Father Malone films directed by Leo McCarey and starring Bing Crosby, *Going My Way* (1944) and *The Bells of St Mary's* (1945). The same was true of Spencer Tracy's portrayal of a priest in *Boys Town* (Norman Taurog, 1938) and its sequel *Men of Boys Town* (1941). Other notable religious films in this period included the uplifting *The Song of Bernadette* (Henry King, 1943) and the amusing Faustian comedies *The Devil and Daniel Webster* (William Dieterle, 1941) and *It's a Wonderful Life* (Frank Capra, 1946). The British film *Black Narcissus* (Michael Powell and Emeric Pressburger, 1947), had a religious setting—a convent in the foothills of the Himalayas—but focused on the psychological complexity of the characters and the serious theme of colonialism. It was a forerunner of the more adult and complex films of the late 1950s and 1960s.

The success of DeMille's Technicolor epic *Samson and Delilah* (1949) paved the way for the era of the wide-screen epic. This not only marked the end of post-war poverty, but was an attempt to present something bigger and more colourful to counter the attractions of television, the new medium that was shrinking cinema audiences.

DeMille's remake of *The Ten Commandments* (1956) was the model for these spectacular epics in Technicolor, Cinemascope, Todd-AO, and Cinerama. Religious subjects were well suited to the medium. Often a few lines of Biblical narrative would be expanded to a full two-and-half hours as was the case with *Solomon and Sheba* (King Vidor, 1959), *The Story of Ruth* (Henry Koster, 1960), and *Sodom and Gomorrah* (Robert Aldrich, 1962). There was a reluctance to show the person of Jesus on the screen in the epics of the 1950s, however. Christ was glimpsed only at a distance and fleetingly, or only his hands and a back view: *The Robe* (Henry Koster, 1953), *Ben-Hur* (William Wyler, 1959), *The Big Fisherman* (Frank Borsage, 1959), *and Barabbas* (Richard Fleischer, 1961). These films concentrated on the effect of Jesus rather than on his person. Films about early Church history—especially Roman persecution—became popular for the same reason: *Demetrius and the Gladiator* (Delmer Daves, 1954), *Quo Vadis* (Mervyn LeRoy, 1951). The epics of 1950s and 1960s were breaking away from the templates provided by Western art and being led instead by the spectacle that was now technically possible. To this were added the whiff of sex and violence, as well as the political, moral, and social anxieties of the day that were made to parallel the screen stories. *The Ten Commandments* becomes an epic struggle between totalitarian Communism and God-fearing freedom—explicitly in a prologue, spoken by DeMille himself, and implicitly in the narrative. *The Ten Commandments* ticked all the prerequisites and did extremely well at the box office.

In the midst of this era of spectacle, there was a small-budget French film that paralleled the story of a village Passion play with the story of villagers in Turkish-occupied Greece. In the film the Passion story becomes a reality. The film, *Celui Qui Doit Mourir* (Jules Dassin, 1957), was a critical success, winning a prize at the Cannes film festival. The critical success of this Christ film was one of the factors that led Hollywood to turn once again to the gospel stories and to dare to portray the person of Christ.

Nicholas Ray helmed *King of Kings* (1961) giving a political reading of the gospel story. It is sensitive in its interpretation of miracles and the resurrection—all of which are reported rather than shown. It is in tune with Biblical scholarship, especially as it parallels the story of Jesus of Nazareth with Jesus Barabbas. The film is memorable for its expressionistic use of colour and its wonderfully constructed sets that indicate Ray's artistic inclinations and his interest in architecture. The film exemplifies Ray's gift for presenting the psychological complexity of his characters, but it is let down by a ponderous script. It was unfairly dismissed by critics at the time who had had their fill of Biblical epics. Much the same criticism could be levelled at George Stevens' *The Greatest Story Ever Told* (1965). It is the most expensive gospel story film ever made and was a labour of love by the director, who had been changed by his Second World War experiences, particularly the liberation of the Jews from extermination camps, which he witnessed and filmed. His intention was to make a film that showed the Jews were not to blame for the death of Christ. The personal importance of this led to an obsession with perfection—the composition of each shot is meticulously framed and beautifully filmed on location in Arizona and Utah. The film originally ran for four hours and twenty minutes. As with Ray's *King of Kings,* it is careful to take account of mainstream Biblical scholarship. Dominated by an austere but powerful performance by Max Von Sydow, the film is somewhat spoilt by an array of cameos by star Hollywood names, most famously John Wayne as the centurion at the cross. This is disorienting but was done to bolster box-office appeal. It is a worthy and respectful film, which, like *King of Kings* before it, failed to excite the critics and the public who were weary of a surfeit of great epics. Like the rest of George Stevens' oeuvre, this film deserves re-examination.

If *King of Kings* and *The Greatest Story Ever Told* fell foul of the critics, it was John Huston's *The Bible* (1966) that finally put paid to expensive, spectacular biblical epics. This is a curiously uninvolving and passionless film based on the first 22 chapters of Genesis. Some 'awe' is aroused by the scenes of creation, the construction of Noah's Ark, the tower of Babel, and the city of Sodom—all these images were influenced by Western art. The only performance of any note and depth is Huston's own as Noah.

Epics had become too expensive and audiences' taste for this sort of spectacular event had diminished. This was the era of British kitchen-sink dramas, French *auteurs*, and the existential angst of Ingmar Bergman. It was not until the arrival of computer-generated imagery (CGI) that spectacular epic films would reappear. As if to emphasize the cultural difference between the 1950s and 1960s, the Italian film director Pier Paolo Pasolini made three religious films. The first, *La Ricotta* (1961), a spoof on the making of a religious epic got him into trouble with Church and State in Italy. In 1964 he made *Il Vangelo Secondo Matteo*, a film based exclusively on the text of Matthew's gospel but which focused on Jesus' social teachings. The film was dedicated to Pope John XXIII and the Second Vatican Council. Using non-professional actors, minimal props, and little money on sets, the film manages to seem more authentic and to capture the spirit of the gospel more successfully than those gospel stories on which Ray and Stevens lavished their millions in their desperate striving for authenticity. Two years later, Pasolini made *Teorema* (1968), in which a mysterious stranger brings (economic and sexual) salvation to a bourgeois family, which is often seen as Pasolini's modern take on the Christ event.

The 1950s and 1960s saw religious themes emerging in mainstream cinema. For instance, there are two thrillers: Alfred Hitchcock's *I Confess* (1953) played with the priest's duty not to break the seal of the confessional even in the face of murder; the second, the menacing and melodramatic *Night of the Hunter* (Charles Laughton, 1955), was a classic and rare example of a Hollywood Expressionist film. Other notable religious films of the 1950s included *The Nun's Story* (Fred Zinnemann, 1959), set in a convent where sexual tensions and hard decisions about life choices for the nun mirror her decision not to remain neutral in the struggle against Hitler. These brief descriptions demonstrate that religious dilemmas were far more likely to be found in thrillers and love stories than in the average American or Italian biblical epic. Religion also provided content for serious dramas such as Bryan Forbes' film *Whistle Down the Wind* (1962), in which schoolchildren mistake an escaped convict for Jesus. Other films dramatized historical events: *Inherit the Wind* (Stanley Kramer, 1960) explored the creationist versus evolution debate in the USA; Otto Preminger's film *The Cardinal* (1963) heralded the changes about to happen in the Roman Catholic Church as well as the role of the Church during the rise of fascism in Europe. The consultant on the film was Joseph Ratzinger (later Pope Benedict XVI). Stories of conscience and religious principle were filmed in two critical and box-office successes that had started life as theatre plays—*Becket* (Peter Glenville, 1964) about the martyrdom of Thomas Becket and *A Man for All Seasons* (Fred Zinnemann, 1966) about Thomas More's struggle with his conscience leading to his martyrdom during the reign of Henry VIII.

With the development of cinema, there emerged directors whose work, while never making huge amounts of money, used their skills to make films that had great depth—socially, politically, and spiritually. These *auteurs* are the great artists of cinema. The late 1950s and 1960s saw a remarkable group of films by the Swedish director Ingmar Bergman, dealing with religious themes of death, of the absence of God, and loss of faith. The son of a Lutheran pastor, Bergman was, in this period of his life, obsessed with existential questions of faith and doubt, and particularly the question of suffering. His oeuvre of films, beginning with *Crisis* (1945) and ending over 50 films later with *Saraband* (2002), frequently reference religious questions and none more so than five films he made between 1957 and 1963: *The Seventh Seal* (1957), *The Virgin Spring* (1960), *Through a Glass Darkly* (1961), *Winter Light* (1962), and *The Silence* (1963).

Bergman is the most prominent of a number of directors who explicitly and implicitly address Christian theological themes. The earliest of this group is Carl Theodor Dreyer, the Danish film-maker whose sparse style suited and supported his spiritual themes. His two most successful films are the silent *The Passion of Joan of Arc* (1928) and the film that depicts a miracle of resurrection, *Ordet* (1955). The Scandinavian landscapes provide a perfect backdrop to the sparse style of Bergman and Dreyer.

The same sparse, spiritual style while also confronting religious themes is a hallmark of the work of the French director Robert Bresson and the Russian director Andrei Tarkovsky. This is implicit in all their work and explicit in Bresson's *Diary of a Country Priest* (1958) and *The Trial of Joan of Arc* (1962), and in Tarkovsky's *Andrei Rublev* (1966) and *The Sacrifice* (1986). Among these theological directors is the Italian Roberto Rossellini. His neo-Realism was of immense significance in the development of world cinema and a counter to glitzy, star-strewn Hollywood films. Although an atheist, he made *The Flowers of St Francis* (1950), *Agostino d' Ippona* (1972), and a gospel film *Il Messia* (1975) that focused on the ordinary life of Jesus as a carpenter.

The Spanish director Luis Buñuel whose films were full of surreal imagery, was, like Rossellini, an atheist. He once famously said 'Thank God I'm an atheist!'. His films are full of religious imagery, usually mocking the Roman Catholic Church and organized religion. His earliest films such as *Un Chien Andalou* (1929) and *L'Age d'Or* (1930) start the process of pinpointing the hypocrisy of organized religion. Two films, however, stand out as not only being critical but offering a glimpse of two characters, a priest in *Nazarin* (1959) and a nun in *Viridiana* (1961), who actually try to live as Jesus lived, and who are subsequently vilified by church and bourgeois society. Incidentally, the plot of *Nazarin* was 'borrowed' for the commercially successful British film *Heavens Above!* (John and Roy Boulting, 1963). Three further films in the 1960s return to Buñuel's sharp and surreal criticism of the church: *El angel exterminador* (1962), *Simon del desierto* (1965), and *La Voie Lactee* (1969). Other than Bergman, Buñuel is the most prolific of the theological film-making auteurs.

In the 1970s there was a spate of filmed versions of Jesus' life. There were two musicals, the rock opera *Jesus Christ Superstar* (Norman Jewison, 1973) and the hippy *Godspell* (David Greene, 1973). *Jesus Christ Superstar* offers a reading of the gospels that presents a very human Christ, and *Godspell,* although it was not a successful film, portrays Christ as a 'clown' challenging society's values in a gentle, hippy way. The Campus Crusade for Christ got behind what is known as *The Jesus Film* (Peter Sykes, John Kirsh, 1979), Campus Crusade state that it may be the most watched film of all time, having been seen by six thousand million people and converting 200 million people to Christ. The film itself is unremarkable—a very straight filming of the gospel of Luke. A year before, an Indian film was made in Hindi about the life of Christ called *Daya Sagar* (A. Bhimsingh, Christopher Coelho, 1978). It boasts 19 million viewers and 7 million conversions on the Indian subcontinent. The film is simplistic in its retelling but is enlivened by a few Bollywood-style dance routines. The other notable 'Jesus' films of the 1970s were Franco Zeffirelli's *Jesus of Nazareth* (1977), which was a very inclusive TV film carefully causing no offence to any denomination and playing the story very straight but with high production values and good performances. The other was the antithesis of this, *Monty Python's Life of Brian* (Terry Jones, 1979), a wonderful spoof not only of the life of Christ but particularly on biblical films like those of Zeffirelli.

More controversy was to follow in the 1980s when Jean-Luc Godard made a contemporary film about the Virgin Mary, *Je Vous Salue Marie* (1985). This film by the most intellectual of film-makers is an intensely personal attempt to express his philosophy using a new cinematic language. It illumines and brings new insight to the story of the Virgin Birth. The film caused a scandal on account of its sexual content and made very little money, but it remains a genuine attempt at a spiritual film. The other notable 'Jesus' films were *The Last Temptation of Christ* (Martin Scorcese, 1988) and *Jesus of Montreal* (Denys Arcand, 1989). Scorcese's film, based on Kazantzakis' novel *The Last Temptation of Christ* (1955), poses a theological debate about the struggle in Jesus' psyche, and for all of us, between flesh and spirit, the human urges and spirituality. One dream sequence shows Jesus making love to Mary Magdalene and this gave some notoriety to what is undoubtedly a serious theological film. Arcand's film *Jesus of Montreal* translates the gospel events to Montreal with clever parallel stories that merge, and at the same time mounts a sharp attack on the greed of capitalism and the complacency of the Church.

What is clear about religious and theological films is that they reflect the social, political, and moral context in which they were made. A film about Jesus in any particular era tells us more about that context than it does about the life of Christ. The same is true of stories from Church history. The life of Joan of Arc has been filmed numerous times in the history of cinema, and each version places contemporary concerns on the story.

Aside from films about Christ, the 1970s and 1980s spawned some interesting films based on Church history. Michael Reeves made *Witchfinder General* (1968) dealing with witchcraft hysteria and superstition during the English Civil War. A similar theme but set in the French town of Loudon was explored in Ken Russell's typically exuberant style in *The Devils* (1971). Three historical films focusing on the theological debate about liberation theology were *The Mission* (Roland Joffé, 1986), *Black Robe* (Bruce Beresford, 1991), and *Romero* (John Duigan, 1991). Other historical films include: an exploration of the life of *Thérèse* (Alain Cavalier, 1986), which was made using a very sparse style to highlight the spirituality of the subject; *Babettes Gaestebud* (Gabriel Axel, 1987) set amid the stark unadorned Scandinavian landscape, which depicted the healing and transforming power of the Eucharist in 19th-century Denmark. Two prize-winning religious films appeared in the 1990s: Antonia Bird's *Priest* (1994) about a homosexual priest and an incident of incest within his parish, and the Oscar-winning *Dead Man Walking* (Tim Robbins, 1995) exploring the relationship between a prisoner on death row and the nun Sister Helen Prejean.

At the beginning of the new millennium, apart from *The Miracle Maker* (Derek W. Hayes and Stanislav Sokolov, 2000), which was a simple retelling of the gospel story using claymation for the main story and animation for the parables, there were no significant Biblical films. The controversies of the 1980 Jesus films, increasing secularism, and the mockery of the Monty Python team seemed to bring a halt to biblical films until the emergence of Mel Gibson's *The Passion of the Christ* (2004). This was a personal project of Gibson's and had the specific theological aim of putting the cross at the centre, and virtually to ignore the social teaching of Christ. Here was Gibson's attempt to take the Church back to the days before the Second Vatican Council. The antithesis of Pasolini's *Gospel According to Matthew*, it was nevertheless filmed in the same location at Matera in southern Italy. In striving for authenticity of language (Greek, Latin, and Aramaic), like the gospels it laid itself open to accusations of being anti-semitic. It was explicit in its attempt to adequately show Christ's sacrifice. It became the highest-grossing Biblical film of all time.

The street-wise American director Abel Ferrara also revisited Matera to make a film, *Mary* (2005), that was theologically up to date and based on the Apocryphal Gospel of Mary interlaced with crises of faith of an actress, a journalist, and a film director bearing a striking resemblance to Gibson. It is a counter to Gibson's film. In 2006, a hurriedly-made film of *The Nativity Story* (Catherine Hardwicke, 2006) was filmed in a traditional way with carefully composed tableaux. By contrast, Mark Dornford-May made *Son of Man* (2006) with the action transferred to an African township at a time of political repression. This political and liberationist reading countered Gibson's traditionalist theology, but demonstrated that religion could be profitable for film-makers. The film was followed by *The Chronicles of Narnia; The Lion, the Witch and the Wardrobe* (Andrew Adamson, 2005) and *The Da Vinci Code* (Ron Howard, 2006) both of which made more money than Gibson's film.

Following the destruction of the Twin Towers in New York city, there has been an increased interest in religion and spirituality, not only in films but also on the part of secondary and tertiary education. Part of that response is a desire to understand Islam and how to integrate other religious cultures into British culture—this has been a recurring theme of British films: *Monsoon Wedding* (Mira Nair, 2001), *Bend it like Beckham* (Gurinder Chadha, 2002), *Ae Fond Kiss* (Ken Loach, 2004). Similarly, Ridley Scott's epic *Kingdom of Heaven* (2005) revisited the Crusades from a perspective that was sympathetic to Islam, and its message is one of harmony and integration.

In consecutive years, 2009–11, three religious films won major prizes at European film festivals, *Lourdes* (Jessica Hausner, 2009), *Des Hommes et Des Dieux* (Xavier Beauvois, 2010), and *Tree of Life* (Terence Malik, 2011). Hausner's film is a beautiful observation of a possible miracle on a pilgrimage to Lourdes. Beauvois' film is about the faithful and costly commitment of a group of monks to the local people during the Algerian war. Malik's film is a complex meditation on Job and thus on grief, suffering, and humanity's place in the divine purpose.

There are also contemporary directors who frequently reference religion and the theological. The most prominent are American Martin Scorsese and Danish Lars von Trier. Scorsese started to train as a priest when a young man and has never lost his fascination with religion and Catholicism, especially in his streets of New York canon from *Taxi Driver* (1976) to *Gangs of New York* (2002) with their offers of redemption. He made explicit some of these underlying themes in *The Last Temptation of Christ* (1988). Lars von Trier is influenced by his fellow countryman Dreyer and by the Russian director Tarkovsky, whose films are shockingly intense and starkly pose and play with theological concepts. *Breaking the Waves* (Lars von Trier, 1996) and *Dancer in the Dark* (Lars von Trier, 2000) are heartrending tales of sacrificial atonement. *Dogville* (Lars von Trier, 2003) and *Manderlay* (Lars von Trier, 2005) are films about grace both literally—it is the main character's name—and theologically. Two of his recent films contain explicitly religious and theological themes: *Antichrist* (2009) is about grief, pain, and despair, and *Melancholia* (2011) is about depression and the end of the world.

This brief overview of explicitly religious films offers only a partial sketch. This has ignored the many film-makers playing with Christian iconography and offering small religious tropes within avowedly secular films. The text has also ignored the whole horror genre and the fascination with exorcism. Superheroes of science fiction, comic books, and Westerns have also found their way onto the cutting room floor—not every saviour figure is a Christ figure. The text does not touch on religious documentaries, although there are many fine examples.

One of the problems with Judaeo-Christian comment on film is that the focus is often exclusively on narrative. This is hardly surprising as the tradition is itself based on founding narratives. Films are more than story; they should be viewed not only for their texts but for their contexts and reception. Adulation should be given not only to star directors and actors but also to cinematographers, editors, screen writers, all of whom demonstrate the complex skills that make a film a work of art.

Film is increasingly used by clergy, teachers, and others as illustration. In churches it is by no means unusual to show a clip of a film in much the same way that some will quote from poetry and literature. These clips are unlikely to be from religious films but are likely to be arbitrarily selected to make a point—this, in effect, imposes a religious reading on a work of art. Not every rescue by a hero battling against evil makes the hero a Christ figure. Viewing with overtly Christian glasses can do injustice to the source material. A less contentious use of film is the film group. Christians will attend film groups in much the same way as book groups. These film clubs do not have to be limited to religious films, for all movies have values, worldviews, and a morality that it is possible to engage with in much the same way as one engages with other religious viewpoints and traditions. Both the use of clips in worship or religious instruction, as well as the communal watching of films underline the fact that films are now our modern texts. They are the culture we share. The watching of contemporary films bridges the gap between the specifically religious Christian world and the contemporary world. It becomes an aid to contextualizing the Christian message and learning the concerns and enthusiasms of a wider group.

Another growing use of film within Christian communities is the making and editing of films to enhance worship. Digital technology has brought the ability to make films to most communities. Short segments as aids to meditation and to illustrate points can easily be filmed. This democratization of film-making is most often seen in alternative worship groups but its use is likely to increase. Just as artists will exhibit video installations, so preachers and Christian communicators will begin to utilize this accessible medium. The screen dominates many aspects of our contemporary lives and the religious sphere is no exception.

SEE WEB LINKS

- Website of the British Film Institute.
- International Movie Database

Finding of the Holy Cross (*Inventio Crucis*) *See* CROSS and HELENA, S.

Fioretti di San Francesco *The Little Flowers of S. Francis* is a collection of stories, legends, and sayings of the saint, compiled mainly from accounts by those of his original companions who still lived in Assisi. Some of them—among them Brothers Leo and Ruffino—were disregarded, when not actively persecuted, because they strove to adhere to the way of life set out by the saint, while under *S. Bonaventura the Order had become more formal and more organized. *The Life of S. Francis* which Bonaventura wrote in 1263 was a more traditional type of hagiographic account, which eliminated much of the vivid personality of the founder, whom he had never known, and forced him into a more conventional mould. Friars who had shared the saint's poverty and humility told stories of him to the young men who came to the Portiuncola, who wanted to know the 'real' S. Francis, as against the more orthodox version of him being propagated by the Life of the saint written by S. Bonaventura. These stories formed the basis of the *Fioretti*, which were written in Tuscan Italian *c.*1322 (not the saint's native Umbrian dialect) and are probably based on the Latin *Actus Beati Francisci et Sociorum ejus* (Deeds of the Blessed Francis and his Associates) and other accounts. The earliest known MS of the Italian version is 1390 and is in Berlin, and the first printed edition of 1476 was published in Vicenza. Many editions and translations have followed ever since. The *Fioretti* reveal the simplicity, humility, and insistence on absolute poverty and obedience which inspired the life of the saint and the community he gathered around him, as well as the lyrical and poetic qualities of his life and work, but they are rarely used by artists, since the stories capable of visual realization are those which occur in the official Life, which would also be more acceptable to most commissioners.

fire *See* SACRAMENTALS.

Fire, Tongues of *See* PENTECOST.

Fischer, Johann Michael (1692–1766), was a leading German *Baroque architect who built 32 churches and 22 abbeys, as well as secular works. He was born near Regensburg, and settled in Munich in 1718/19. His first major commission was the abbey church at Osterhofen, near Passau, built 1726–8, and decorated by the *Asam brothers from 1729 to 1735. Fischer was essentially an architect with a Baroque concern for structure which remains solid and noble under the exuberant *Rococo decoration which is a feature of all his churches. He favoured the wall-pillar system, which eliminated exterior buttressing by providing piers to support vaulting and domes within the structure, and also allowed him to insert side chapels between the piers with balconies over the chapels, sometimes with projecting balustrades. His syncopated rhythms of void and solid, salient and re-entrant forms are always held together by a massive cornice which dominates the decoration.

The small church of St Anna am Lehel, Munich, built in 1727–9, and decorated by the Asam brothers in the 1730s, was destroyed in 1944, but has since been rebuilt. In it Fischer explored the rich field of the centrally planned church, from which he developed extended central plans, with curved transepts projecting from a central circular, domed area, and apsidal-ended choirs. His many commissions include the great abbeys of Fürstenzell (1741–8) near Passau, Zwiefalten (from 1742) near Ulm, and Ottobeuren, west of Munich, as well as the much smaller abbey of Rott-am-Inn, south of Munich, almost his last work (1759–63), and arguably his finest church. Though long-naved, it has the compact quality of a centrally planned church, with a sequence of three domical vaults, the largest over the central, dominant, octagon where there are balconies over the short sides. The dome, frescoed by Matthias Günther, is a bravura piece of illusionism, derived, like most of the ceilings and domes painted for these churches, from examples by Roman Baroque painters, such as Baciccio in the Gesù or Pozzo in Sant' Ignazio. They all express the triumphalist Catholicism of the Counter-Reformation, which appears later in Germany than in Italy, because of the devastating wars of the 17th/18th centuries. The Rococo decoration is French by origin, although in Germany it develops as strongly in religious buildings as in secular ones. Much of the sculpture at Rott-am-Inn, notably the high altar with the *Trinity*, is by Ignaz Günther (1725–75), the greatest German sculptor of the period, and is of matchless beauty and expressiveness.

Fischer von Erlach, Johann Bernhard (1656–1723), was the most learned Austrian *Baroque architect of the 18th century. He was born at Graz, and studied in Italy for over ten years the architecture of antiquity, the Renaissance, and his Baroque predecessors—*Bernini, *Borromini, and Pietro da Cortona. By means of engravings he also studied French Baroque architecture, visited England and probably met Wren, whose St *Paul's was still being built. In 1705 he obtained an important court position in Vienna. Most of his works are secular, but he built three major churches, two in Salzburg. The Dreifaltigkeitskirche (the Trinity church, unfortunately much altered) was begun in 1694. It was inspired by Borromini's Sant' Agnese in Piazza Navona, Rome, on an oval plan with a two-towered front and a dome over the central oval. The Kollegienkirche (University church) was built from 1696 to 1707 on a plan adapted from Lemercier's Sorbonne church in Paris, but with a salient curved front between flanking towers, and a high dome. Even more unusual is the Karlskirche in Vienna, dedicated to S. Carlo *Borromeo, and built from 1715 to commemorate a plague. It is a brilliant amalgam of historical examples: the oval plan of Borromini's Sant' Agnese, the rich interior decoration of coloured marble from Bernini's Sant' Andrea al Quirinale, the colonnaded portico from the Pantheon, the twin towers of St Peter's—or perhaps even Wren's St Paul's—and, most unusual of all, huge twin columns flanking the portico derived from the ancient Roman Trajan and Antonine Columns, with spiralling reliefs commemorating the plague, and with curious minaret-like tops. He was knighted in 1696, and in 1721 published his history of architecture, *Entwurff einer historischen Architectur*, which he had been compiling since 1705, perhaps inspired by Wren, on comparative principles and including not only the Temple of Solomon and Hagia Sophia, but also a pagoda. It was translated into English in 1730. James *Gibbs owned a copy.

fish Like the *dove and the *lamb, one of the commonest Early Christian symbols with a concealed meaning. It was a pre-Christian symbol of good fortune and health and had the added advantage that the Greek word *ichthys, a fish, is an acrostic meaning Jesus Christ, Son of God, Saviour (it is not known who discovered this double meaning). Fishes are associated with the miracles of the *Loaves and the Miraculous Draught, as well as Christ's calling the Apostles 'Fishers of men', but in the NT there is never any connection with Christ Himself. The fish was common on seals from the earliest times and may have referred to the Christian soul living in the waters of Baptism as the fish lives in water. In the *catacombs a group of people with fishes and bread loaves may be read as a pagan *agape, the miracle of the loaves and fishes, or what it prefigured, namely the Eucharist.

Similarly, the 'great fish' symbolized *Jonah and in turn, the Resurrection. In later art a young man carrying a fish represents Tobias (*see* TOBIT).

Fishes, Miraculous Draught of There appear to be two miraculous catches of fish—the first connected with the Calling of the Apostles (Luke 5: 1–10): 'He got into one of the boats, the one belonging to Simon, and asked him to put out a little way from the shore. Then he sat down and taught the crowds from the boat ... When he had finished speaking, he said to Simon, "Put out into the deep water and let down your nets for a catch." Simon answered, "Master, we have worked all night long but have caught nothing. Yet if you say so I will let down the nets." When they had done this, they caught so many fish that their nets were beginning to break. So they signalled to their partners in the other boat to come and help them. And they came and filled both boats, so that they began to sink. But when Simon Peter saw it, he fell down at Jesus' knees, saying, "Go away from me, Lord, for I am a sinful man!"'

The second account, recorded only by John, is a post-Resurrection appearance of Christ (21: 3–7). 'Simon Peter said to them, "I am going fishing." They said to him, "We will go with you." They went out ... but that night they caught nothing. Just after daybreak Jesus stood on the beach; but the disciples did not know that it was Jesus ... He said to them, "Cast the net to the right side of the boat, and you will find some." So they cast it, and now they were not able to haul it in because there were so many fish. That disciple whom Jesus loved said to Peter, "It is the Lord!" When Simon Peter heard that it was the Lord, he put on some clothes, for he was naked, and jumped into the sea ...'. Immediately following this is the account of Jesus giving the Keys to Peter and His saying, "Feed my sheep". In the best-known work of art illustrating this incident, *Raphael's tapestry in the Vatican (cartoon in the Royal Coll. on loan to the V & A), the account in Luke is followed, but the Keys and Sheep are added, so that the two versions are shown together. The separate incident of Christ walking on the *Water to rescue Peter is conflated with the Draught of Fishes in Konrad Witz's picture of 1444 (Geneva), where the Sea of Gennasaret is clearly Lake Constance.

Five Wounds of Christ *See* ARMA CHRISTI and STIGMATA.

flagellants In Early Christian times hermits, following the example of S. Jerome, were accustomed to scourge themselves as a penitential exercise. In 1260 a popular movement in Perugia resulted in large crowds flagellating themselves (or each other) as a devotional practice (*disciplinati, battuti*) which spread rapidly. In 1261 the Church repressed such hysteria, but the Black Death (1348–9) revived the idea of extreme mortification as a penance, and the practice spread widely, especially in Germany, where it soon deviated into heresy. Further measures against such fanaticism in 1349, and again by the Council of *Constance in 1417, had some effect. In Italy the movement was regulated and lasted, more or less, into the 19th century, being similar to the *confraternities. Flagellants wore long white garments with a pointed hood, but with an opening at the back, exposing back and shoulders. They are occasionally recorded in 14th/15th-century paintings such as the *Madonna with Battuti*, by Antonio Veneziano of 1388 (Palermo, Mus. Diocesano).

Flagellation of Christ After Pilate's condemnation of Christ, and before He was crowned with Thorns, He was scourged (Matt. 27: 26, and Mark 15: 15, John 19: 1). This was normal practice under Roman law for those condemned to crucifixion, which may explain the brevity of the biblical mention. The Flagellation is virtually unknown in Byzantine art, and even in the West does not occur before the 9th century, e.g. in the *Utrecht Psalter. The subject probably originated in Psalter illustrations. By the 12th/13th century it occurs on Italian processional crosses—which are strongly Byzantine in style, though not in iconography. It became popular in the West under the influence of Franciscan piety in the 13th/14th centuries, although it does not form one of the *Stations of the Cross, but both the **Meditationes Vitae Christi* and the *Revelations* of S. *Bridget describe it. The type was soon established as Christ in the centre, bound to a tall column, with an executioner on either side; often only these three figures are represented, but other versions, more correctly, have Pilate seated as a witness, since Roman law required the magistrate who had passed sentence to see it carried out. In this case there are usually spectators as well, as in the panel from Duccio's *Maestà* (1308–11: Siena, Cath. Mus.). The increasing realism of 15th-century art, especially in the North, led to more stress on the brutality of the scene (cf. *imago pietatis). The column and scourge alone also occur frequently in the *Arma Christi.

An entirely new theme is found in the Counter-Reformation period, emanating from Rome. In 1223 Cardinal Colonna had returned from Jerusalem with a small granite column, which he believed to be the actual column of the Flagellation in spite of its small size. He placed it in Sta Prassede in Rome, where it still is, and a new iconography developed in the 17th century which had been foreshadowed in S. Bridget's account: Christ is shown on hands and knees tied to the column or crawling painfully to retrieve His garments. The most explicit picture of this is by *Murillo (Boston, Mus.), which clearly shows the colonnette, but the picture by Velázquez (London, NG) is clearly related. There are also paintings by Rubens and others, and several Spanish polychrome sculptures, as well as the *Angel of the Column* by the Bernini school, on the Ponte Sant'Angelo across the Tiber in Rome. Further examples of this theme are *Christ at the Column* (1910) by Georges Desvallières (Maurice Denis Museum, Saint-Germain-en-Laye, France).

flagon *See* LITURGICAL VESSELS.

flèche (Fr. arrow) A tall, very ornate thin spire, often made of wood, which rises above the choir or above the nave crossing instead of a tower. The cathedral of Notre Dame, Paris, is an example of a *flèche* over a crossing, and while Reims is an example of one over the choir. There is no English equivalent, since they were not used.

Flight into Egypt *See* EGYPT.

Flood, the *See* NOAH.

Florence and Ferrara, Council of (1431–5). This Council, which began in Basle and was transferred to Ferrara (1438–9) and Florence (1439–43), and ended in Rome, was mainly concerned with the reunion of the Greek and Latin Churches, under the threat of the Turkish invasion which ended in the Fall of Constantinople in 1453. Although agreement was reached under Pope Eugenius IV, the populace of Constantinople rejected the terms, and East and West have been separated ever since. Although inconclusive in ecclesiastical affairs the Council in Florence and Ferrara had important consequences for the arts in Italy. Cardinal Bessarion, one of the Greek leaders, remained there and promoted the study of Greek, leaving his famous library to the Republic of Venice. It was housed—much later—in the splendid Biblioteca Marciana built by Sansovino from 1537. The presence of the Greeks, including the Emperor John VIII Palaeologus, in Italy is also reflected in many works of art, e.g. Pisanello's medals, the *Baptism* by Piero della Francesca (London, NG), which can be approximately dated from the fact that Greek prelates are shown in it, and, in particular, the bronze doors of Old St Peter's in Rome, made by *Filarete *c.*1433–45, to record the pontificate of Eugenius IV (1431–47). These doors were transferred to New St Peter's and still exist.

flowers and fruit Large numbers of flowers and fruit have been associated, often for no obvious reason, with symbolic meanings and sometimes with several at once. Some of the commoner are listed here. **Almond.** This is a symbol of divine favour, as *Aaron's rod blossomed (Num. 17: 1–8). In Italian it is *mandorla, an almond-shaped glory. **Apple.** Eve is usually shown as offering an apple to Adam, but the fruit is not specified in Genesis, and it is thought to derive from the similarity of the Latin *malum*, apple, to *male*, wickedly. In pictures of the Madonna and Child an apple refers to Christ as the Second Adam and Mary as the Second Eve. **Carnation** (pink). A symbol of marital fidelity which is common in 15th-century Netherlandish and German marriage portraits. **Clover.** The three leaves of the clover symbolize the Holy Trinity. **Columbine.** The similarity of columbine to *columba* (Lat. dove) leads to the columbine as symbol of the Holy Spirit, and further, if there are seven blooms on the stalk, to the Seven *Gifts of the Holy Spirit. They may also represent the Seven *Sorrows of Mary. **Gourd.** This is an attribute of *Jonah and thus a symbol of the Resurrection, especially if combined with an apple, as in Crivelli's *Madonna* in Washington (NG). **Grapes** or **Vine.** Grapes and ears of wheat are very common Eucharistic symbols, as well as representing the True Vine. In Early Christian art they may be combined with cherubs in what can be interpreted as symbols of Bacchus. Two men carrying an enormous bunch of grapes on a pole refer to Num. 13: 23, the spies sent by Moses to the Promised Land. **Iris**, like the lily, is a symbol of purity, but it was also thought to have sword-shaped leaves and therefore to refer to the sword which should pierce Mary's soul (Luke 2: 35). **Lily.** The principal symbol of purity and particularly connected with the Annunciation, when it is usually carried by Gabriel. It is an attribute of several virgin saints, e.g. *S. Clare, as well as male saints such as SS Joseph, Dominic, or Antony of Padua. **Pomegranate** is a symbol of Resurrection, especially when it is cut open to show the seeds inside. It is often held by the Christ Child in Madonna pictures. **Rose.** Like the lily, one of the principal symbols of the Virgin, the 'rose without a thorn', but also of SS Dorothy and Elizabeth of Hungary. The rosary derived from rose-garlands of red and white—red for martyrdom and white for purity. Sometimes yellow roses are used.

The symbolic use of flowers and fruit in *genre scenes and *Vanitas still-lifes, especially in Dutch and Netherlandish 16th/17th-century paintings, can be clearly established in such obvious Eucharistic symbols as a roll of bread and a glass of wine, or in the case of a painter like Daniel Seghers (1590–1661), who was a Jesuit working in Antwerp and collaborating with Rubens, in pictures of the Virgin and Child surrounded by wreaths of flowers. In other cases, especially with Dutch painters, it is impossible to be sure that symbolism was intended.

Flowers, Little, of Saint Francis *See* FIORETTI.

Fons Vitae (Lat. Fountain of Life) The practical reasons for placing fountains outside churches and in cloisters are matched by their powerful symbolic meanings. These derive from many passages in the OT and NT, and have been illustrated by artists from the times of the *catacombs onwards. The earliest biblical reference is in Gen. 2: 10–14, where the four *Rivers of Paradise are named. They appear in mosaics, such as the apse of San Vitale, *Ravenna, where the rivers issue from under the celestial globe on which Christ is enthroned, and in one of the mosaics in the Mausoleum of Galla Placidia, Ravenna, where deer drink from the fountain, as in Ps. 42: 1 (Vg. 41: 2) 'As the deer longs for flowing streams, so my soul longs for you, O God', and the same image appears in the apse mosaic of San Clemente in Rome where the deer drink from the rivers which pour from the rock beneath the acanthus from which rises the cross of the Crucifixion.

The image of the Fountain of Life appears in Ps. 36: 9 (Vg. 35: 10) 'For with you is the fountain of life' and in Prov. 14: 27, 'The fear of the Lord is a fountain of life' and these texts inspired an illumination in a MS written in the Rhineland *c.*781–3 (Paris, Bib. Nat.) where a fountain enclosed in a colonnade is approached by deer and birds, including peacocks, quails, cocks, ducks, pheasants, storks, and doves. The MS was written for the baptism of *Charlemagne's son Pepin in Rome. It is also expressed in the vases with doves coming to drink, for instance, in mosaics in the Mausoleum of Galla Placidia, one of them shown with a jet of water spouting from it, an idea originating in Roman pre-Christian mosaics.

The words in Isa. 12: 3 'With joy you will draw water from the wells of salvation' are illustrated by the *Well of Moses*, in the Abbey of Champmol in Dijon, which once had a Crucifixion at the top, but now consists of the figures of the prophets, including Isaiah and Moses, who is himself an example in that he struck the rock from which the water of salvation flowed for the Israelites in the desert (Num. 20: 10–11).

The text in Rev. 7: 17 (Vg. Apoc.) 'For the Lamb will . . . guide them to springs of the water of life' is illustrated in the van *Eyck *Adoration of the Lamb* in the Ghent Altar (Ghent, St Bavo), where the streams of pilgrims approach the altar of the Lamb, with the fountain below, and even more vividly in the *Fountain of Life* by a van Eyck follower (Prado) where a huge Gothic edifice enthroning God the Father, with the Lamb at His feet, flanked by the Virgin and S. John the Evangelist and musician angels, has an elaborate fountain with on one side true believers, and on the other blindfolded non-believers. *The Blessed entering Paradise* by Dieric Bouts (Lille) shows an angel guiding the saved into Paradise, dominated by an elaborate fountain, and similar fountains appear in most of the representations of Paradise by Bosch, notably in the Paradise wing of the *Garden of Delights* (Madrid, Prado).

More vital than these texts are the words of Christ to the woman of Samaria at the well, recorded in John 4: 14: 'The water that I will give will become in them a spring of water, gushing up to eternal life.' This subject found its greatest favour in the late 16th and 17th centuries, and one of the finest illustrations of it is by Annibale Carracci (Vienna, KHM).

Another important subject, relating to the Virgin, is in the Song of Solomon (AV Song of Songs, Vg. Canticle) 4: 12: 'A garden locked is my sister, my bride, a garden locked, a fountain sealed'; and in 4: 15: 'A garden fountain, a well of living water'. Both are treated as prophecies of the Virgin Birth (*see* HORTUS CONCLUSUS). In the Eastern Church, the tradition (derived from the *Apocryphal Protevangelium of James) was that the Annunciation took place when Mary was drawing water at the well, and there was also a tradition that an angel announced to Anna that she was to bear a child. In the Church of Chora (the Kariye Camii) in Constantinople both these events are shown in the mosaics, with Mary approaching the well, and Elizabeth standing beside a flowing fountain—taken to be the symbol of the *Immaculate Conception, Mary's birth free of original sin.

font (Lat. *fons*, fountain) A basin containing water used in *baptism, not to be confused with *stoup. Once baptism became a general rite, instead of being performed only occasionally, and after infant baptism became general in the West, the provisions made for it were modified. The rite was no longer reserved to the bishop, and the font which replaced the separate *baptistery was given a specially designated place in the church. Because the original symbolism of a baptistery was a tomb, in that the neophyte's progress from pagan to Christian was symbolized by a 'descent' into the tomb with Christ, and a 'resurrection' in a sinless state, so the font often followed the older baptismal shapes. By about the 10th century, it became a circular or rectangular bowl, raised for convenience on a pedestal or base. Even the older type of deep basin or tank, such as those in the free-standing baptisteries (e.g. Rome, Ravenna, Florence, Parma), were modified to allow for baptism by affusion (the pouring of water over the forehead) by fixing a smaller basin inside at a higher level. For instance, the huge octagonal tank at Parma has a small quatrefoil basin within it; Parma also has a separate smaller font supported by a red marble lion.

In most medieval churches the font was placed near the main door, symbolizing baptism as the entry into the Christian community. In 1559 the Archbishop of Milan, S. Carlo *Borromeo, issued instructions for the building of baptisteries as separate chapels within the church, enclosed by railings or gates, with the font sunk into the floor and with adequate space for those present to stand round it. Practical difficulties often prevented these returns to the older forms being introduced, but their purpose was to make the rite more solemn.

Fonts are of two basic types: the huge tank, like those in the separate Early Christian baptisteries, or like the circular red marble one in Verona, nearly 10 ft. across; and the type with the bowl or basin, which might be circular or rectangular, sometimes barely raised above the floor, but more often at waist height. Often, there was a second basin, drained separately so that the water used did not return to the font; this was essential for the baptism by immersion of infants, for hygenic reasons, though the practice was eventually abandoned for reasons of health.

Fonts were not placed in every church; in towns, it was usually only in the main parish churches, occasionally in the cathedral, if this also served as a parish church. Abbeys often had fonts, especially when appropriation became common (that is, when an abbey owned property through which it acquired the rights of presentation to a living in the town) or if part of the abbey church served as a parish church. An abbey or priory could thus control a large number of parishes from which tithes, rents, fees, and dues were obtained. Baptism was supposed to be free, but some abbeys required a fee or, more discreetly, a donation, and control of the font became a source of deep grievance, since infant mortality was high and often sudden, and a child who died unbaptized could be denied Christian burial, and was also believed to be unable to enter Paradise. The Abbot of Sherborne impeded access to the font, and anger over the monks' dilatoriness in the speedy baptism of sickly infants finally erupted in 1437 into a riot in which the abbey church was burned down. The townsmen had to pay for a new abbey, but the Abbot was forced to relinquish control of the parish church and the font.

The decoration of fonts is very varied. Some early ones are no more than crude stone bowls; many have elaborate figurative carving. Romanesque fonts are remarkable for the variety of their ornament: extraordinary and fantastic beasts—dragons, griffins, winged lions—though usually these are references to the power of the Devil which is defeated by the sacrament. The battle between Good and Evil is given vivid life by scenes of S. Michael Archangel thrusting the Devil into Hell; of fighting warriors personifying the struggle been Good and Evil; of Christ rescuing a soul in danger; of rampant lions recalling the words in AV 1 Pet. 5: 8, describing the Devil as a 'roaring lion, seeking whom he may devour' and the prayer to be preserved from the lion's mouth. The source of much of this imagery is the *Speculum Majus by Vincent of Beauvais of *c.*1250. Calendars, such as appear at the beginning of Books of *Hours, also provided models. The use of calendars suggested the passage of time, and therefore the span of life; the rite of baptism brings the promise of eternal life. Signs of the Zodiac and the Labours of the Months taught the same lesson. Twelfth-century fonts of black Tournai marble are found in Belgium, France, and Germany, some being imported into England after the Norman Conquest (eight are still in use). Typical, but also the most elaborate in England, is the one in East Meon in Hampshire; the rectangular block, made *c.*1130–40, is supported on a massive central pier with four short columns at the corners, and is carved on all its faces; among the scenes is the unusual one of an angel showing Adam how to dig. Twelfth-century lead fonts are also found in English churches, as a cheaper and more available metal than bronze. The grandest and most beautiful bronze fonts are those in Liège and Hildesheim. The first, made by Rainer, or Renier, of Huy in 1111–18, now in St-Barthélemy, Liège, was removed with the loss of two of its supporting oxen and its cover from Ste-Marie-aux-Fonts (destroyed 1793). The reliefs include S. John the Baptist preaching, and baptizing penitents, the Baptism of Christ, the Baptism of the centurion Cornelius by S. Peter, and the Baptism of the philosopher Craton by S. John the Evangelist, all identified by inscriptions. The oxen supporting the font refer to the altar of Solomon's Temple (2 Chron. 4: 3–4, Vg. 2 Paralip. 4: 3–4) borne by twelve oxen. The splendour of the imagery and workmanship owes much to the example of Ottonian and Byzantine illumination. The font in Hildesheim Cathedral, made in 1220, is a cauldron-shaped vessel borne by four kneeling men symbolizing the four *Rivers of Paradise; it has high-relief groups all round it, with a Baptism of Christ as the central motive. It has retained its conical cover, also with high-relief figures and a finial ending in leaves and a crown.

From the 13th century onwards, the imagery becomes more conventional, and rarely has the vivid quality of the earlier period. The preferred shape is now more frequently octagonal, giving fields for scenes from the Gospels, but many now have abstract patterns or foliage, or even armorial bearings. Fonts had covers, secured by a strong padlock in order to prevent the theft of holy water for use in witchcraft, and many of these heavy covers were supplemented by a feature which became a striking element of design in the late 14th and 15th centuries, in the form of elaborate and often towering structures of carved wood. At Ufford (Norfolk) the pinnacled cover, surmounted by a 'pelican in piety' (*see* BIRDS, SYMBOLIC) is as tall as the nave itself, and the lower panels slide upwards over part of the upper tiers when the font is used. In Canterbury Cathedral, the octagonal black and white marble font of classical design was crowned by a splendid cover with many carved figures, made in 1639. It was destroyed by the Puritans, but was rebuilt in 1662 in two tiers, with extra sculpture, the whole being raised by a pulley.

Sometimes these elaborate covers were built like shrines or *ciboria, as in the two-tiered one at Trunch (Norfolk; 14th/15th cent.), and the 16th and 17th centuries saw the development of a type of font cover and setting which closely resembled a ciborium. They were free-standing edifices intended to enhance the importance of the rite by making its setting more impressive. Outstanding French examples are the hexagonal one at Magny-en-Vexin, north of Gisors, datable 1534, and the octagonal one at Guimiliau, near Morlaix in Brittany, made in 1675. The finest English example is the octagonal one in Durham Cathedral, erected in 1663, which is 40 ft. high and 9 ft. across at the base.

The most magnificent Renaissance font is the one in the Baptistery of Siena Cathedral, which was made between 1417 and 1430. The hexagonal marble basin has bronze reliefs and six gilt-bronze statuettes of Virtues round it, by sculptors including Ghiberti, Jacopo della Quercia, and Donatello, whose relief is of the *Feast of Herod* showing the king as horrified by the Baptist's head on the charger, presented to him by Salome. A high central element supports a marble tabernacle with five reliefs of prophets in niches by della Quercia (the sixth side is a door), and the whole is crowned by a finial with a figure of the Baptist, also by della Quercia.

In England, the Reformation did not deal quite so harshly with fonts as it did with stained glass and rood screens. In many churches the font was replaced by a basin placed near the pulpit, but during the Commonwealth there was a wholesale destruction of fonts. After the Restoration in 1660 they were returned to their original position and function. The Wren parish churches, built after the Great Fire of London in 1666, though they followed the Reformed Church design of the auditory church, placed the font in its traditional position near the door. The Reformed Church, however, favours baptism either at the altar table or in front of the pulpit. During the 18th and 19th centuries private baptism became widespread with a consequent decline in the ritual significance of the font, and a revival in its use often coincided with its removal to the east end, so that public baptism was performed in view of the congregation. The combination of the Gothic Revival and the Tractarian Movement resulted in a determined effort to return to the old placing of the font in the west, or at the entrance to the church. This has now been almost abandoned in the Catholic Church, where baptism now usually takes place at the altar, or, in modern churches, where the font is built close to the main altar. Anglican churches normally baptize in fonts in the original place—e.g. the new cathedral at Coventry.

Fortitude One of the four Cardinal *Virtues, the others being Justice, Prudence, and Temperance. Fortitude is often symbolized by a woman in armour and carrying a shield, but an interesting exception is the figure by Nicola *Pisano on his Pisa Pulpit (1259), which is clearly taken from an antique statue of Hercules with the lion's skin and is thus one of the earliest borrowings from antiquity preceding the Renaissance.

Fortune, Wheel of 'Fortuna' has a long classical history. In Roman mythology, Fortuna, in full Fors Fortuna, rather than being unlucky, was venerated as a bringer of fertility and increase, and was introduced into the galaxy of deities, probably in the 9th century BC, from outside Rome, where her cult was centred on the huge temple complex of Fortuna Primigenia at Praeneste (now Palestrina) as early as 700 BC. Praeneste also had an important oracle. Her main temple in Rome, of *c*.100 BC, is in the Forum Boarium, and is wrongly called 'Fortuna Virilis'. Her entry into Christian iconography is through Boethius's *De consolatione philosophiae*, written in prison while awaiting execution in 524, where Fortuna explains to him that he should not complain about the reversal of fortune, since it is her nature to change. The first illustrations were probably in a MS of Boethius *c*.1100 and are common from the late 12th century, as in the Ratisbon MS of 1165 (Munich), where Vices and Virtues are contrasted and Fortuna is a woman with two faces standing on a wheel. There are two illustrations in the *Hortus Deliciarum* of Abbess Herrad of Landsberg (1167–95); in one the figure of Fortune, enthroned on mountains, cranks a wheel, on which aspirants on the left rise towards the king seated at the top, and fall on the right side with crowns awry, finally tumbling to destruction. The other shows the Wheel of Avarice with beasts personifying greed, rapacity, argument, swinishness, within the spokes. A late 12th-century MS in Schwäbisch-Gmünd, near Stuttgart, shows the two wheels of False and True Religion. In the first the greedy prior achieves his ambition of becoming abbot, but as the wheel turns he falls into disgrace, and in the other the virtuous prior rises to become abbot, and gives up his position through humility to devote himself to learning and piety.

The wheel imagery appears also in rose windows, where the shape and the tracery suggesting the spokes of a huge wheel are found in several churches, for instance the cathedrals of Basle and Trent, and on the façade of San Zeno, Verona (11th/12th cent.); St-Étienne, Beauvais (12th cent.), where tiny figures rise on one side to fall on the other; and the south front of Amiens Cathedral (13th cent.). Dürer made two images of *Fortune*, the first a small wood engraving of *c*.1496 (Berlin), and a large, far more elaborate engraving of *c*.1501–3 (London, BM), also known as Nemesis, or Fate, showing a nude, winged woman riding on a globe holding in one hand an elaborate standing cup, in the other a bridle. She rides on clouds with an extensive landscape below, representing her triumph over the world.

Forty Hours Devotion *See* QUARANT'ORE.

fountains at the entrance to churches. The custom of placing a fountain or cistern in the *atrium of churches, for the washing of hands, and sometimes also of faces and feet, was established in Early Christian times. It follows from the tenet that purity was required of the believer externally as a symbol of cleanliness of heart necessary for an approach to God and the sacraments. Besides its practical purpose, there were also powerful symbolic meanings (*see* FONS VITAE). The earliest reference is to a fountain in the atrium at Tyre, and at St Felix, Nola, were brazen basins and a row of marble basins. These fountains were also held to represent the four *Rivers of Paradise, and were symbols of the four Evangelists as 'living waters'. The *cantharus (now in the courtyard of the Belvedere of the Vatican) stood in the atrium of Old St Peter's, and by *c*.500 a further external fountain below the steps of the atrium was placed there for the 'convenience of the throngs of people'. Natural springs were preferred, but if none was available rain-water cisterns supplied the water.

S. Paulinus of Nola (353/4–431) describes the cantharus in the atrium of St Peter's; and apparently fountains with lions' mouths spouting water were in the atrium of Hagia *Sophia in Constantinople. The modern holy water *stoup at the entrance to all Catholic churches is the surviving form of this custom of ablutions before entering a church.

Four Holy Crowned Ones *See* CORONATI, QUATTRO SANTI.

Four Horsemen of the Apocalypse This is part of the vision of S. John, in which he describes the end of the world in Rev. 6: 1–8 (Vg. Apoc. 6: 1–8). 'Then I saw the Lamb open one of the seals, and I heard one of the... creatures call out... "Come!" I looked, and there was a white horse! Its rider had a bow; a crown was given to him and he came... to conquer. When he opened the second seal, I heard the second creature call out, "Come!" And out came another horse, bright red; its rider was permitted to take peace from the earth, so that people would slaughter one another; and he was given a great sword. When he opened the third seal, I heard the third living creature call out, "Come!" I looked, and there was a black horse! Its rider held a pair of scales in his hand, and I heard what seemed to be a voice in the midst of the... creatures saying, "A quart of wheat for a day's pay, and three quarts of barley for a day's pay ...!" When he opened the fourth seal, I heard the voice of the fourth... creature call out, "Come!" I looked and there was a pale green horse! Its rider's name was Death, and Hades followed with him; they were given authority over a fourth of the earth, to kill with sword, famine, and pestilence, and by the wild animals of the earth.' This terrifying vision of the end of the world was popular in the Reformation period, and the classic representation of it is the woodcut in *Dürer's *Apocalypse* (1498). The Four Horsemen are sometimes interpreted as Christ conquering the world, War, Famine, and Plague, and Death.

Four Last Things, the Death, Judgement, Heaven, and Hell. *See also* SIGNS OF THE END OF THE WORLD.

fourteen Holy Helpers (the Auxiliary Saints) *See* VIERZEHNHEILIGEN.

France *See* EUROPE.

Francis of Assisi, Saint (1181/2–1226). The founder of the *Franciscan order, S. Francis is certainly the most popular saint in the West, after the Apostolic period, and the influence of his Order is equally great. He was the first major poet to write in Italian, and his feeling for humanity and for nature is usually regarded as a formative influence on the new, realistic, art of *Giotto and his followers, and hence on the whole course of Western art. Compared to most medieval saints, his life is well documented. He was born in Assisi, the son of a well-off draper, and led a carefree wordly life until he was taken prisoner in a minor war between Assisi and Perugia; after about a year of captivity and illness he returned to Assisi a changed man. While praying in the derelict church of San Damiano, near Assisi, he heard a voice telling him to repair the church. This he did, *c.*1208, by selling cloth belonging to his father, which led to a breach between them. Francis became an itinerant preacher under the protection of the Bishop of Assisi, attracting seven disciples. This was the beginning of the Order, which received approval from Pope Innocent III in 1210. In 1212 Francis made his first attempt to go to the Middle East to convert the Saracens: in 1219 he actually succeeded in meeting the Sultan, who seems to have been impressed by him, but who did not convert. In 1220 Francis resigned as Minister-General of his own Order, which was growing enormously, and a new Rule was approved by Honorius III in 1223, although it became the cause of many difficulties later. In his last years many of the most famous events of his life occurred—he wrote the *Canticle of Brother Sun*, invented the Christmas *crib, and in 1224 he received the *Stigmata. Two years later, worn out at the age of 45, he died. He was canonized in 1228, probably the shortest interval between death and canonization ever known. His relics were transferred in 1230 to the huge new basilica and monastery dedicated to him in Assisi, where they still rest below the Lower Church.

Iconographically S. Francis is unique. At least four *Lives* were written, mostly by contemporaries, in the forty years after his death. The *Vita prima*, by his friend Thomas of Celano, describes his physical appearance, though rather vaguely, so that two different visual traditions start in the 13th century. Celano's *Vita prima* was written in 1228 and was followed by a revised *Vita secunda* in 1246, and a further book on his miracles in 1250/3. These and other writings were all subsumed in the *Legenda Maior* (or *Vita Maior*), commissioned by the Order from *S. Bonaventura in 1260 and finished in 1262/3. This was accepted as the definitive *Life*, and the General Chapter of the Order decreed in 1266 that all others should be destroyed (fortunately, this was not always done). It is, however, the *Legenda Maior* which is the source for the twenty-eight scenes from the life of S. Francis, painted in the most conspicuous position along the walls of the nave of the Upper Church at Assisi, probably under the direction of the young Giotto in the 1290s. These narrative scenes are among the earliest in Italian art to be filled with the new realism, and consequently are of the greatest importance in the history of Italian art. They are also important as a deliberate attempt to create an official visual biography, dependent on, and strictly conforming to, the official written biography. Indeed, the scenes have titles written below them (now much damaged) so that a literate person could explain the meaning of the scenes to illiterate pilgrims. This pictorial biography fixed Franciscan iconography for centuries and is followed, notably, by Giotto in his shorter cycle of frescoes in the Bardi Chapel in Sta Croce, the great Franciscan church in Florence. The twenty-eight scenes at Assisi are (1) *Francis honoured by the Simpleton*, (2) *Francis gives his Cloak to a poor Knight*, (3) *His Vision of a heavenly Palace*, (4) *Francis praying in San Damiano*, (5) *He renounces his Father*, (6) *The Dream of Pope Innocent III*, (7) *Innocent approves the First Rule*, (8) *The Vision of the fiery Chariot*, (9) *The Vision of the Thrones* *in Heaven*, (10) *Francis expels the Devils from Arezzo*, (11) *The Ordeal by Fire before the Sultan*, (12) *Francis transfigured*, (13) *The Crib at Greccio*, (14) *The Miracle of the Spring*, (15) *Francis preaching to the Birds*, (16) *The Death of the Knight of Celano*, (17) *Francis preaching before Honorius III*, (18) *The Apparition at Arles*, (19) *Francis receives the Stigmata*, (20) *His Death*, (21) *Visions of Fra Agostino and the Bishop of Arezzo*, (22) *Funeral of Francis and Discovery of the Stigmata*, (23) **S. Clare grieving over the Body of Francis*, (24) *The Canonization of S. Francis*, (25) *Pope Gregory's Vision*, (26) *The Healing of the Man from Ilerda*, (27) *The Woman raised to Life*, (28) *S. Francis liberates the Heretic.*

Images of the saint, as distinct from narrative cycles, go back to the 1220s, but there can be no question of a portrait in the modern sense. What seems to be the earliest image is the fresco in the Sacro Speco at Subiaco, near Rome, which must be earlier than 1228, since it is inscribed Fr Franciscus (not Sanctus) and has no halo. Nor does it show the stigmata, so it may be earlier than 1224. The first certainly datable altarpiece is in San Francesco, Pescia, and is signed and dated 1235 by Bonaventura Berlinghieri. This is a gaunt and formal cult-image, accompanied by six scenes from the saint's life on a smaller scale. Other similar images are in San Francesco, Pisa, attributed to Giunta Pisano, and the important altarpiece in the Bardi Chapel of Sta Croce, Florence (the chief Franciscan church in Tuscany), by a Florentine master of the mid-13th century.

The most familiar image is that by Cimabue in his fresco of the *Madonna and Child with S. Francis* in the Lower Church at Assisi, but this must have been painted at least half a century after Francis's death. It does, however, resemble the more human type shown in the Giotto cycle and may represent some tradition preserved in Assisi itself. It is said to be much restored.

From the Counter-Reformation period, when the Franciscans were very active, there occur changes in the iconography, which is no longer closely tied to the *Legenda Maior*. Francis is often shown in ecstatic prayer, holding or contemplating a skull (El Greco, Zurbarán). He is always bearded, clad in a brown or grey habit girdled with a rope with three knots symbolizing the vows of Poverty, Chastity, and Obedience, and he always bears the stigmata. The actual colour of the habit may correspond to that worn by the branch of the Order commissioning the painting.

Franciscan Order One of the two great *Mendicant Orders of *friars founded in the early 13th century (the other is the *Dominican). *S. Francis of Assisi was joined by three companions *c.*1209, and he soon realized that, if others were to join him, they would need a Rule to live by. As he was extremely anxious for ecclesiastical approval he sought papal recognition from Pope Innocent III, which was granted in 1210 after the Pope dreamed that the Lateran Basilica was falling down but was supported by an insignificant little man—Francis himself. This first Rule enjoined absolute poverty, but the phenomenal success of the Franciscan ideal was such that it became obvious that so large an organization needed to own property and have settled bases in towns if it were to carry out its mission to townspeople—the old monastic Orders were all based in the remote countryside and did little for the newly important cities. The Franciscans spread all over Europe in Francis's lifetime, reaching England in 1224. They became guardians of the Holy Places in Jerusalem in 1324 (and still are), and in 1493 they built the first Christian church in the New World, in Haiti.

Francis himself resigned as Minister-General in 1221 and a new Rule was drawn up, confirmed by Honorius III in 1223. Elias became the new Vicar-General, and later Minister-General. He was a competent manager, but later lapsed into schism. He was responsible for the huge Basilica at Assisi, dedicated to S. Francis, but against all the saint's principles. The bitter dissension over the interpretation of absolute poverty caused great trouble over almost three centuries, although efforts to heal it were made by *S. Bonaventura, Minister-General 1257–74, and again in 1517, and, finally, in 1897. The original friars, including many of those who had known Francis himself, were divided into 'Spirituals' and 'Conventuals', but the Conventuals soon became the majority, since they were an organized and successful body, building huge Mendicant churches, where their preaching and charitable activities flourished. They also became an important force in the universities in the towns. The Spirituals eventually dwindled into a schism called the *Fraticelli*, which was ruthlessly repressed in the 15th century, although their ideal of absolute poverty was a constant spur to the Conventuals. The Fraticelli were followed by the Observants, who wished to observe the Rule more strictly, in the 14th/15th century and in 1517 a formal separation was made between them and the Conventuals. The Capuchins were an offshoot of the Observants (1529–1617). The Minims, Recollects, and others were also variations of the Order. They can sometimes be distinguished by the colour of their habits—the original grey, worn by the Capuchins, the usual dark brown, and the black of the Conventuals. All wear the rope girdle with three knots.

After Francis himself the principal saints of the Order were *Antony of Padua and Bonaventura, but there were many others, as well as popes and prelates. The main devotions associated with them are the Christmas *crib and the *Stations of the Cross, both of which are characteristic of their emphasis on emotion, which so profoundly affected the arts in the 13th/14th centuries. During the Middle Ages they also actively propagated the doctrine of the *Immaculate Conception.

The Second and Third Orders are the Poor Clares, a contemplative Order for women, founded by *S. Clare, the friend of S. Francis, and the Tertiaries, both men and women, who live in the world and take no vows, but live by the Franciscan ideals. Abbreviations for the various bodies are: OSF, Order of S. Francis, Ordo Sancti Francisci; OFM, Order of Friars Minor, Ordo Fratrum Minorum; OFMC, Order of Conventual Friars Minor, Ordo Fratrum Minorum Conventualium; OFM Cap., Order of Capuchin Friars Minor, Ordo Fratrum Minorum Capuccinorum.

Francis Xavier, Saint (1506–52), was one of the founders of the *Jesuits and, like *S. Ignatius Loyola himself, a Spaniard. He is also called the Apostle of the Indies, on account of his enormously successful missions in India, Japan, and China. He studied in Paris and met S. Ignatius there in 1529, taking vows with him in 1534. By 1542 he had arrived in Goa, the Portuguese colony in India, going on from there to Ceylon, Japan, and China, where he died. His body was brought back to Goa, where it still is, and a series of silver reliefs in the Cathedral was made to commemorate his missions. He was canonized in 1622, at the same time as S. Ignatius himself, and there are paintings by both Rubens and van Dyck from about that time. In the 1670s two altarpieces of the *Death of S. Francis Xavier* were being painted by Baciccia (Rome, Sant'Andrea al Quirinale, the Jesuit Novitiate) and Maratta (Rome, Il Gesù, the Jesuit mother-church): in the Maratta there is an 'Indian' in the background, but he is a Red Indian, with a feathered head-dress. Francis is usually represented in the black gown of a Jesuit, holding a crucifix, or, sometimes, a flaming heart. A legend tells how he dropped a crucifix overboard on one of his journeys—he was always seasick—and it was returned to him by a crab (or lobster).

frater Part of a monastery used for meals or recreation. An obsolete word for a refectory.

fraticelli (Ital. little friars) Loosely used of all Mendicant friars, but properly of the ultra-rigorist and heterodox Spiritual Franciscans, brutally suppressed in the 15th century.

fresco (Ital. fresh) A method of painting on walls, practised mainly in Italy from the 14th to 19th centuries. It is wonderfully flexible, very permanent, and relatively cheap. Fresco was known in antiquity, but it is not certain from the examples recovered from Pompeii and other Roman excavations if the same technique was used then as the Italian method described by Cennino Cennini in the early 15th century. He sets out the method of 'buon fresco', or 'true fresco', as distinct from 'fresco secco', or 'dry fresco', often used with it for additional details or for corrections. The crucial difference is that true fresco is permanent, where dry fresco is only painting in distemper which will brush off or perish with time.

True fresco requires the preparation of a wall with one or more layers of coarse plaster. This fairly rough coating, called an *arricciato*, is the surface on which the artist first works, drawing in a reddish pigment called *sinopia* (hence the term for such drawings, recovered when frescoes are removed from their original walls, as in Sta Apollonia, in Florence, revealing the astonishing draughtsmanship of Andrea del Castagno). In later years, cartoons were also used, and the design punched in charcoal dust through lines pricked in the cartoon, which could then be reused if necessary. Once the *arricciato* with its *sinopia* had been established, a layer of fine lime plaster, called the *intonaco*, was then applied over the area to be worked, but this coating had to be fresh and wet; the painting, executed with pigments diluted with lime water and applied to the wet *intonaco*, sank into the plaster and became an integral part of it. When the *intonaco* dried work had to stop, and any left-over dry plaster was cut away. Usually, the artist prepared only the area he felt confident of completing in the day, hence the term *giornate*—day's work—used to describe the various joined-up patches of a large fresco. The artist also had to have a very clear idea of the drawing underneath, since the *intonaco* obscured the *sinopia*. In the 13th-century use of fresco, the drawing was often repeated on the wet *intonaco* and the flesh tones were underpainted with *terra verde*, a greenish earth colour, and then re-done with varied tones of red earth, ochre, and white lime, so that the lower layers of shading shone through and created modelled forms. The normal size of a portion would be a head or head and shoulders, allowing the artist time for a surprising amount of detail. In the late 14th and 15th centuries these preliminary under-paintings were abandoned in favour of free working, and the great fresco painters of the 16th century prided themselves on the promptness and accuracy of their tonal judgements, always making allowance for the fact that fresco dries out paler than its wet colour, and is in any case not a technique permitting great depth of tone. The fresco painter's palette was very restricted. White was the white lime of the original plaster, the colours were predominantly the natural earth colours, so that brilliant blues, greens, and reds were often extras, applied separately and thus vulnerable to damage. A great master, such as *Michelangelo, worked in very large *giornate*, particularly on the *Sistine Chapel ceiling, where the primal scene of *God separating Light from Darkness* appears to have been painted in one vast sweep, and the brilliance and variety of his colour are the result of careful contrast and juxtaposition.

Fresco, probably *secco*, was used in mosaic decoration, since the design could be followed closely in the placing of the *tesserae* of coloured or gilded glass, which did not involve the obliteration of the under-drawing as was the case with the *intonaco*.

The great advantage of fresco over other forms of wall-painting is that it combines permanence with cheapness. Mosaics are even more permanent, but very costly. Fresco was also rapid in execution, and allowed very large surfaces to be decorated with pictures that enhanced the beauty of a church and contributed vividly to religious teaching. The great limitation of fresco is that it requires an absolutely dry wall, and preferably a dry atmosphere, since damp from below or through the wall is totally destructive. Hence it was not much favoured in Venice until the advent of *Tiepolo, who used fresco for ceilings as well as for walls. Obviously, fresco-painting was not practised in the damper months of the Italian winter, nor has it proved successful north of the Alps, despite 19th-century efforts to revive it in Germany and England.

The techniques of wall-painting described by *Theophilus are not true fresco.

friar (Lat. *frater*; Fr. *frère*; Ital. *fra*, all meaning brother) A friar is not a monk, although both are Regulars, i.e. live under a Rule. The old monastic Orders lived in seclusion, apart from the world, but in the 13th century the main *Mendicant Orders were founded, with the intention of evangelizing the towns. Their members were to beg their bread and preach, whereas the monastic Orders tried to be self-sufficient in their remote locations. The two major Mendicant Orders of Friars are the *Franciscans and *Dominicans, both founded in the early 13th century. The Carmelites were re-founded in 1245, the Augustinian hermits in 1256, and the *Servites in 1424.

Friars Minor *See* FRANCISCANS.

Friars Preachers *See* DOMINICANS.

Friedrich, Caspar David (1774–1840), was born in the Baltic port of Greifswald, and worked for most of his life in Dresden, where he died. He was a German Romantic painter who, like Wordsworth, had a quasi-religious feeling for Nature, enhanced by his melancholy cast of mind. In 1808 he painted the *Cross in the Mountains* (Dresden) as an altarpiece for a private chapel, although it is a *Landscape with a Crucifix* rather than a *Crucifixion*. It started a debate on the propriety of such pantheistic implications. Ruins of Gothic abbeys in woodlands or in the snow, ghostly Gothic cathedrals emerging from mists, the enigmatic *Winter landscape* (1811: London, NG) with a cripple who has discarded his crutches lying in front of a crucifix in a snowy landscape; or glowing sunsets with figures on the shore silhouetted against the light, all have religious overtones which can be sensed but are only occasionally obvious.

Friends, Society of ('Quakers') A dissenting Protestant body founded by George

Fox in the mid-17th century in England and taken to America by emigrants, where William Penn founded the State of Pennsylvania. The Friends are opposed to any clerical body and meet in ordinary meeting-houses, referring to churches as 'steeple-houses'. In general they oppose the visual arts and the only well-known work of art associated with them is *The Peaceable Kingdom* by the American Primitive Edward Hicks (1780–1849), himself a Quaker preacher. Almost a hundred versions of the *Peaceable Kingdom* are known, and it is enormously popular as a Christmas card (a purpose of which Hicks would certainly have disapproved): it illustrates Isa. 11: 6–8—'The wolf shall live with the lamb, and the leopard shall lie down with the kid; and the calf and the lion and the fatling together; and a little child shall lead them. And the cow and the bear shall graze, their young shall lie down together: and the lion shall eat straw like the ox. The nursing child shall play over the hole of the asp, and the weaned child shall put its hand on the adder's den.' In the background there is usually a group of Red Indians concluding a Treaty with Penn, which is also represented separately in other paintings. Ironically, Hicks was himself a distant cousin of Elias Hicks whose secession in the 1820s caused bitter dissensions among American Friends. Edward himself said that painting 'appears to me to be one of those trifling, insignificant arts which has never been of any substantial benefit to mankind'.

Frink, Dame Elisabeth, RA (1930–93) A British sculptor and graphic artist formed by her Catholic upbringing and schooling, like many in her post-Second World War generation she was readied for Christ narratives to be near to much of her work. Bragging strength and empty weakness inform her *Judas* (1963), and her *Goggle Heads* (1969 onwards) hint at weakness of mind garlanded with imperial dignities. Then in the Christ figures she strives to imbue the divine and the human: she achieved this in the *Crucifixion* (1966) for the central altar of the Metropolitan Cathedral, Liverpool, the *Risen Christ* (an image of exceptional joy and buoyancy) outside the Solihull Church of Our Lady of the Wayside, and a suspended *Crucifixion* figure for St Bernadette's, Belfast, Northern Ireland. Another fine outdoor piece is the St Edmund (1976) commissioned by West Suffolk County Council for the grounds of Bury St Edmunds Cathedral. Close to death, she finished the *Christ* for the outside of Liverpool Cathedral's West portal, a welcoming figure with a gentle yet commanding presence. Her most satisfactory ecclesiastical commission is often thought to be the *Head of Christ* (1983) in All Saints, Basingstoke, Hampshire, sited with architectural and liturgical aptness at the springing of two arches where the Baptismal liturgy is done.

frontal *See* ANTEPENDIUM.

fruit *See* FLOWERS.

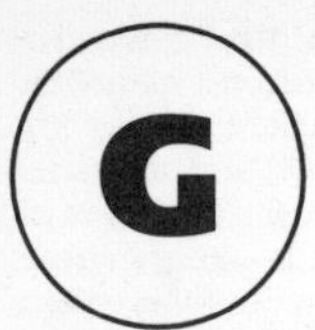

Gabbatha (Heb.), in Greek *Lithostratos* (John 19: 13). The place where Pilate condemned Jesus to death—'at a place called the Stone Pavement, or in Hebrew Gabbatha': the pavement in Pilate's palace. *Piero della Francesca's *Flagellation* (Urbino) marks the place where Christ stands as an elaborate stone pavement.

Gabriel *See* ANGELS.

Galaktotrophousa *See* MADONNA TYPES (Madonna Lactans).

Galilee *See* NARTHEX.

Gall, Saint, Abbey of *See* SANKT GALLEN.

Galla Placidia, 'Mausoleum' of *See* RAVENNA.

galleries in churches *See* AUDITORY CHURCH, TRIFORIUM.

Garden of Eden *See* EDEN.

Garden Enclosed *See* HORTUS CONCLUSUS.

Garden of Gethsemane *See* GETHSEMANE.

Gaspar (**Caspar**) is one of the *Magi. He is often, but not invariably, represented as the European.

Gate of Heaven *See* PORTA COELI.

Genealogies of Christ The accounts of Christ's human ancestry, given in the Gospels of Matt. 1: 1–17 and Luke 3: 23–38, vary greatly, both in numbers and names, though descent from Abraham to David is common to both. S. Luke begins with Adam, and S. Matthew with Abraham, but after David they diverge. Both end with Joseph, Christ's earthly father who is assumed to have married, in Mary, a woman also of the House of David.

Figures of the ancestors of Christ occasionally appear in 12th-century French portal sculpture, though identifications are difficult. David and Solomon are frequently found, but the learned Benedictines Mabillon and Montfaucon believed the twenty-two kings and queens and other OT figures on the portal of *Saint-Denis to be monarchs of the Merovingian dynasty, which ensured their destruction during the Revolution. There are seventeen such figures on the Portail Royal at Chartres and at Le Mans and Bourges some survived, though damaged. No key to their identity has been found, and doubts always exist because some of the groups include Moses, which suggests that the figures may be typological. Interest in Christ's ancestry resulted in a new development—the Tree of *Jesse, which first appears in book-illumination and stained glass (notably at Chartres) before becoming part of portal sculpture. After the late 12th century, OT figures are rare in portal sculpture, but a new form appears in the row of kings placed in a gallery high on the façade, as at Notre-Dame, Paris (restored), Chartres (the south transept portal), and Reims. No solution has yet been found to the problem whether these are kings of France or Christ's ancestors, though the latter is more probable: in medieval times local people always identified them by the names of kings (which is natural, even if wrong). In the north transept portal of Chartres is a sequence of figures of the descendants of Adam and Eve, as in Gen. 4, identified by the names on their bases.

The only other major sequence of ancestors is the series by *Michelangelo in the lunettes and spandrels of the ceiling of the Sistine Chapel in the Vatican. These figures follow the genealogy according to S. Matthew.

Genesis, the Book of The Book of Genesis is part of the Pentateuch, the five books of the OT attributed to Moses, but probably written between the 9th and 4th centuries BC. The books are Genesis, *Exodus, Leviticus, Numbers, and Deuteronomy. Genesis is the first book of both Jewish and Christian scripture, and is concerned with the history of the world, beginning with the Creation, the Fall of Man and his expulsion from Paradise, the Flood, the history of the Patriarchs, and, in particular, the Covenant God made with Abraham that the Jews should be His Chosen People. Exodus is the story of the flight of the Jews from Egypt. The remaining three books, Leviticus, Numbers, and Deuteronomy, codify the laws which govern the conduct of all aspects of Jewish life. This comprehensive legislation, set out in a written text, earned the Jews the title of 'People of the Book', a title later also extended to Christians, who were recognized as deriving from Judaism.

Genesis and Exodus have provided, more than any other books of the OT, themes for the visual arts. Some of the grandest examples of *portal sculpture, such as the Portail Royal at Chartres and the Virgin portal of Notre-Dame, Paris, have column figures inspired by the OT, and particularly by the Patriarchs and Prophets. *Adam and Eve is a constant theme in painting. The Life of Moses forms one half of the Early Renaissance fresco cycle on the walls of the *Sistine Chapel as part of the *type and antitype sequence with the Life of Christ on the opposite wall, and *Michelangelo's Sistine Ceiling decoration is almost entirely on themes taken from Genesis. In N. Europe, after the Reformation, Genesis provided, more than any other OT book, subjects to replace the pictures of saints, which, with a few exceptions, such as the Evangelists, SS Peter and Paul, and the other Apostles, vanished from the artists' repertories. At least a third of *Rembrandt's religious subjects are taken from the OT, the remainder being from the Gospels and Acts of the Apostles, but the OT subjects include such unusual ones as *Belshazzar's Feast* (London, NG), *Uzziah* (Chatsworth, Duke of Devonshire), and *Manoah's Sacrifice* (Dresden). Many 17th-century Dutch artists, especially those close to Rembrandt, painted OT subjects which were rarely, if ever, attempted earlier, e.g. Aert de Gelder's *Jacob's Dream* (London, Dulwich Gall.) or the very rare *Levite and his Concubine* (Judges 19: 10–30) by Eeckhout (Budapest). Pre-Reformation subjects from the OT tended to be chosen with reference to NT passages, but, since Dutch painters were not painting altarpieces, they (or their patrons) had a wider choice of subject-matter.

Genius (pl. *genii*, Lat. a tutelary spirit) In ancient Rome a spiritual guide, very similar to the later Christian idea of a guardian angel. During the persecutions Christians were required to swear by the Genius of the Emperor as a test of loyalty, and in consequence many were martyred for refusing what they saw as an idolatrous oath. Later, however, the classical Genius as a nude youth, sometimes winged, and holding a reversed, extinguished, torch as a sign of mourning became a commonplace of Christian funerary sculpture, especially in 18th/19th-century monuments. *See also* ANGELS, EIDOLON, EROS.

genre Genre painting and Christian art seem at first sight to be contradictory terms, and certainly in the 18th century they would have been, since history painting—Christian or pagan mythologies—was regarded as the highest branch of art, while genre was ranked below portraiture and only just above still-life.

Nevertheless, there are several ways in which genre/narrative subjects from everyday life connect with Christian art. In the beginning, there were the Early Christian arcane subjects, where some people round a table with a few loaves and fish on it were not just eating an *agape but were symbolic of the Eucharist, the fish being *Ichthys. In the Middle Ages, when Christianity was established, we find incidental scenes such as the *misericords or the scenes at the bottom of pages in MSS (e.g. the Luttrell Psalter in the British Library) taken from everyday life, sometimes none too edifying, but always subordinate to the main subject. Later there are scenes like the Early Christian ones, apparently of purely incidental interest, but which are—or may be—symbolical in intention, e.g. the ewer and towel in the *Annunciation* panel in the *Eyck Ghent Altar, or the numerous *Madonna and Child* pictures with the Child holding a bird, or as in the Gerard David of the *Virgin feeding the Christ Child*, not breast-feeding him—a well-known religious subject—but with a spoon from a bowl of milk. Here the difficulty is not to fall into the trap of over-interpretation, but in the Reformation period it became necessary once again to use ambiguous imagery and much Dutch and Flemish still-life painting of the 17th century is now regarded as symbolic in intent (*see* FLOWERS AND FRUIT). For instance, the *Vanitas pictures produced in Calvinist Holland were loaded with symbols such as a guttering candle, a skull, a moth or butterfly, which are transparent references to the short span of human life. There are also still-life pictures with only a loaf, sometimes with a few slices cut from it, a goblet and a glass flask of red wine, and perhaps a few grapes, clear references to the Eucharist. Another subject, not popular but not uncommon, outwardly genre but in fact religious, is the *Seven works of Mercy*, like the one from the studio of Teniers the Younger (Dulwich) which is treated as if it were a series of events in a market-place.

A different use of genre is seen in Lutheran and other propaganda pictures during the Reformation period. This is savagely satirical, often obscene, and was intended to combat the supernatural claims of the Roman Catholic Church. Lucas *Cranach was responsible for many such woodcuts. Finally, in the 19th century there developed a new form of art, religious in intention, but not treating the usual themes of Christian iconography. It was a sort of 'holy genre', perhaps developed from such 17th-century (and earlier) scenes as *Caravaggio's *Rest on the Flight into Egypt*, with Joseph holding the music for an angel to play a lullaby on a violin, or scenes of *S. Anne teaching the Virgin to read or sew. A notable example of this form is *Millais's *Christ in the Carpenter's Shop* (1849–50: London, Tate), which was intemperately attacked by Charles Dickens, or the melodramatic *Shadow of the Cross* by Holman *Hunt (1869–70: Manchester).

George, Saint Almost nothing is known of his life, but he is presumed to have been a soldier who was martyred at Lydda (now Diospoli, in Palestine) during the Emperor Diocletian's persecution of 303–12. His cult became widespread and popular from the 6th century onwards in Byzantium, Syria, Egypt, Armenia, and Ethiopia, where he was venerated as a warrior-saint and is often associated with others such as S. Demetrios or S. Theodore. His cult spread to Gaul, Ireland, and eventually to England, where he was venerated in Anglo-Saxon times.

His historical existence is usually accepted, and fortunately he is now no longer identified with George of Cappadocia, a 4th-century *Arian cleric who appears to have combined his heretical beliefs with near brigandage and who seized the see of Alexandria in 357, but was murdered by a mob in 361.

S. George was very popular during the Crusades, as an example of the Christian Knight, and many churches were dedicated to him in Syria, Lebanon, and what is now Iraq. The famous story of his fight against the dragon and the rescue of the princess appears to be a conflation of his exploits with the classical legend of Perseus who, at either Arsuf or Joppa, near Lydda, killed a sea-monster and rescued Andromeda; George's legend was popular with the Crusaders and gained further popularity from the **Golden Legend*. He became a patron saint of England, without displacing either S. Edward the Confessor or S. Edmund of Bury, and the patron of the Order of the Garter, founded by Edward III in 1347. He is also the patron saint of Genoa, Barcelona, Portugal, the Spanish Order of Calatrava, the Teutonic Knights, and was held in great veneration in Venice.

A long series by Carpaccio was devoted to him in the Scuola di San Giorgio (now in San Giorgio degli Schiavoni) in Venice. He is one of the dedicatees of the pilgrimage church of the *Vierzehnheiligen by *Neumann and he also appears in the amazing 'altarpiece' in the Abbey church of Weltenburg by the *Asam brothers, as well as the monumental statue by Bernt Notke, of 1489, in St Nicolas, Stockholm, intended as a memorial to a Swedish victory over the Danes. Two paintings in the National Gallery, London, by Uccello and Tintoretto, illustrate the story in the *Golden Legend*: the dragon terrorized a town and had to have two sheep sacrificed to him daily. Soon the supply was exhausted and a young man or woman had to be sacrificed. 'The name of a youth or maiden was drawn in a lottery, and no family was exempt'; on the day S. George arrived the King's only daughter was to be the victim. This accounts for the dead body of a young man in the Tintoretto, behind the fleeing princess who occupies the foreground. 'But George . . . set bravely upon the dragon as he came towards him; and with a prayer to God he brandished his sword, and dealt the monster a hurt that threw him to the ground. And the saint said to the damsel: "Fear naught, my child, and throw thy girdle about the dragon's neck!" Thus she did, and the dragon, setting himself erect, followed her like a little dog on a leash'—which is what is shown in the Uccello. Other examples of this theme include Albrecht Altdorfer's painting *St George in the Forest* (1510, Pinakothek, Munich), and D. G. Rossetti's *Wedding of S George and the Princess Sabra* (1857, Tate Britain, London).

Germany *See* EUROPE.

Gesamtkunstwerk The German word was first used in the 19th century but refers to art and architecture of previous eras. A *Gesamtkunstwerk* exists when painting, sculpture, ornament, and architecture combine together to create a 'total work of art' such as in a Gothic cathedral or a Renaissance or Baroque palace; and where the final result is more than the sum of its parts.

Gestas *See* DISMAS.

Gesù, il As the mother-church of the *Jesuit Order in Rome, the Gesù is part of the large complex forming the Order's mother-house. The church was begun in 1568 by *Vignola, and became an influential design for churches of the Order in Europe from Como to Lisbon, from Perugia to Cracow, and in the New World, and also for many non-Jesuit churches. Several Jesuit churches in Germany, however, are far more Gothic in design than the Gesù, and it is clear that the Order never imposed the Roman design. In plan it is similar to Sant' Andrea, Mantua, by *Alberti, in that it is an aisleless nave with side chapels opening off the nave. The dome over the crossing throws a strong light on the choir, on the high altar, and on the shallow transepts, which are no deeper than the nave chapels.

The design was determined by Cardinal Farnese, who had undertaken to pay for the church, and in a letter to Vignola he set out the brief which the architect was to follow: 'Father Polanco has been . . . sent by the General of the Jesuits, and has been discussing with me . . . the building of the church . . . You are to keep a watchful eye on the cost, which is not to exceed 25,000 ducats, and, within that limit, the church is to be well proportioned in length, breadth, and height, according to the rules of architecture . . . to consist of one single nave, with chapels down each side . . . The nave is to be vaulted, and is not to be roofed in any other way, in spite of any objections they may raise, saying that the voice of the preacher will be lost because of the echo. They think that this vault will cause the echo to resound, more than is the case with an open timber roof, but I do not believe this, since there are plenty of churches with vaults, of even bigger capacity, which are well adapted to the voice. In any case, you are to observe the points I have raised—namely, cost, proportion, site, and vaulted roof: as for the form itself, I depend on your judgement, and on your return you can give me an account, when you have agreed with all the other people concerned, after which I will make up my own mind, to which opinion you will all conform. Farewell.'

Perhaps the most interesting feature of these instructions is that a vaulted roof was insisted upon; it is also a feature of Sant'Andrea. Vignola's church was of white stone inside and austere in its decoration. A painting of 1639, on the occasion of a visit by Pope Urban VIII, shows the plain vaults and apse (surprisingly the papal coach and horses, and those of members of his entourage are shown inside the church), and the only decoration is by tapestries and hangings. Later, the interior was covered with elaborate coloured marbles, and Baciccio painted (1672–83) an exuberant Baroque decoration on the ceiling, in which plaster figures merge into the painting with spectacular illusionist and perspective effects. *Pugin, on his brief and unhappy visit to Rome, said afterwards: 'I attempted to say my prayers in the Gesù; I looked up, hoping to see something which would stimulate my devotion. But I saw only *legs* sprawling over me. I expected them to begin to kick me next, and rushed out.'

Vignola died when the cornice level had been reached, and the dome was built by Giacomo della Porta. Instead of Vignola's restrained façade a more showy and complicated one by della Porta was substituted, with large volutes to obscure the buttresses of the vaults; these were derived from Alberti's Sta Maria Novella in Florence.

Gesuati A religious order, not to be confused with the *Jesuits (in Italian *Gesuiti*). It was a congregation of laymen, founded *c.*1360 by the Sienese Bl. Giovanni Colombini, and was largely confined to Italy. The order was dissolved in 1668, but their church in Venice, Sta Maria del Rosario, was taken over by the Dominicans and contains works by Tintoretto, Sebastiano Ricci, Piazzetta, and, especially, Tiepolo.

Gethsemane (Heb. oil-press) The scene of the Agony in the Garden was a garden at the foot of the Mt. of Olives, just beyond the brook Kidron, where Christ and His disciples went after the Last Supper and where He was captured. The story is told in Matt. 26: 36–56 and Mark 14: 32–52, where Gethsemane is named, and in Luke 22: 39–53. In John 18: 1 it is mentioned only as 'across the Kidron valley to a place where there was a garden'. On arrival, Christ told the disciples to wait while He prayed; then, taking Peter, James, and

John, He told them to watch and pray, while He prayed further away, asking 'Father, if you are willing, remove this cup from me'. At this point Luke says that an angel appeared to Him and He began to sweat 'like great drops of blood'. Returning to the three disciples He found them asleep, and said to Peter, 'Simon, are you asleep? Could you not keep awake one hour?' Again He prayed, and again He found them asleep 'for their eyes were very heavy'. Finally, He woke them and the soldiers arrived to arrest Him.

Early representations, such as the *Brescia Box or the mosaic in Sant'Apollinare Nuovo, Ravenna, show no trace of the Agony, only a mild disturbance among the Apostles, but the 6th-century *Rossano Codex first shows some of the drama of Christ's agony. Two different interpretations can be found in the versions of the subject by *Mantegna and Giovanni *Bellini, and that by El *Greco (all three in London, NG), and the *Capture of Christ*, by *Caravaggio (on loan to Dublin, NG). In the earlier versions by Mantegna and Bellini it is still light and the three sleeping figures are prominent in the foreground: in the Greco there is a stormy moonlight, with the soldiers arriving on the right, and an angel holding a chalice above a small scene with a vision of the sleeping Apostles, to the left of Christ.

Ghent Altar *See* EYCK.

Ghiberti, Lorenzo (1378–1455), was a Florentine sculptor who made the second and third pairs of bronze doors for the Baptistery in Florence (the first pair was by Andrea Pisano, 1330–6). Ghiberti won a competition held in 1401, against six others, including *Brunelleschi, with a relief of the *Sacrifice of Isaac*. His and Brunelleschi's reliefs have survived (Florence, Bargello). He was formally commissioned in 1403 to make twenty-eight scenes from the OT, matching the Pisano reliefs of John the Baptist, but the scheme was changed to NT subjects. These panels, finished in 1424, closely resemble Andrea Pisano's in consisting of stylized Gothic figures in high relief against a neutral background, set in a Gothic quatrefoil frame. They were so successful that he received the commission for the third doors in 1425 and was allowed to treat the OT scenes as he thought best. This door was finished in 1452, so most of Ghiberti's working life was devoted to these two tasks. The new doors are entirely different from his first and mark a crucial point in Early Renaissance art, since Ghiberti shows in them a new awareness of classical antiquity and of the new science of perspective, pioneered by Masaccio, Brunelleschi, and *Donatello. The OT panels are reduced in number to ten, each in large rectangular frames and shown in perspective, with figures of varied depths of relief, to obtain a realistic effect like looking through a window. By using the medieval device of Continuous Representation—representing various episodes from the story in different parts of the relief—Ghiberti managed to include far more than ten scenes, and to give much greater narrative force to each scene. The *Isaac* relief, for example, shows five separate stories. Partial gilding (rediscovered only during the Second World War) added to the pictorial effect. These doors were planned by 1437, so they are among the earliest works of the Florentine Renaissance and break decisively with Ghiberti's earlier Gothic style. He became an avid collector of antiquities, and wrote, *c.*1452, an autobiography, the earliest known by an artist, as part of his *Commentarii*, an attempt at a humanistic treatise on ancient art, optics and perspective, and on the history of art in Tuscany in the previous two centuries. This, the *Third Commentary*, is a precious source for the history of Tuscan art. Ghiberti also made other religious works in sculpture, such as three statues for Orsanmichele, two shrines, and he designed stained-glass windows for Florence Cathedral.

Ghost, the Holy *See* TRINITY, THE HOLY.

Gibbs, James (1682–1754), was born in Aberdeen, and went to Rome *c.*1703 to study for the priesthood. He soon abandoned this, briefly studied painting, then entered the architectural studio of Carlo Fontana, the most influential teacher of the day. He returned to Britain in 1708. In 1714 he joined *Hawksmoor as one of the surveyors appointed under the 1711 Act for the Building of Fifty New Churches, but was forced out in 1715 because of his political connections, his rival Colen Campbell having denounced him as a Catholic and a Jacobite. Nevertheless, between 1714 and 1719 he built St Mary-le-Strand, in the middle of one of London's busiest streets; here he combined strong influences from *Wren, whom he greatly admired, with Roman Baroque forms.

In 1722–6 he built his masterpiece, St Martin-in-the-Fields, which combines a Classical hexastyle portico with a Wren type of tower and steeple, thus developing the Wren type of parish church with galleries, which became virtually traditional for large Anglican churches. His *Book of Architecture* (1728) became the most influential source for the design of churches in the New World. He was also a prolific designer of grand funerary monuments, several of which are in Westminster Abbey.

Gideon (Vg. **Gedeon**) (*c.*12th cent. BC) His story is told in Judges 6–8 of the OT. He led the Israelites to victory over the Midianites after a visit from an angel who told him of his destiny and instructed him to put meat, broth, and unleavened cakes on a stone: the angel touched them with his staff and they were consumed by fire, and the angel vanished. Gideon obeyed the angel's command to destroy an altar of Baal on his father's land. Later, when the Midianites threatened to destroy Israel, Gideon asked God for a sign, putting a fleece on the earth of his threshing-floor. Next morning the fleece was wringing wet and the earth dry; next day, the ground was wet and the fleece dry. Gideon therefore raised an army of 32,000 men, but was told by the Lord to reduce the number. He finally brought ten thousand to the waterside to drink—those who knelt to drink were dismissed, those who scooped the water in their hands were retained, only three hundred in all. Gideon armed them with a sword, trumpet, and a pitcher with a lighted torch inside, and during the night they fell upon the Midianites, blowing their trumpets, breaking the pitchers, and waving the torches so that in the confusion the enemy was utterly routed.

The story of Gideon was principally used in Byzantine and early medieval art as an OT *type of the Annunciation, the fleece untouched by the dew being seen as a symbol of Mary's perpetual virginity, and it is sometimes shown together with the Annunciation. The battle is hardly ever represented, but there is a painting of it by Poussin (Vatican Mus.), and Gideon himself is sometimes represented in French Gothic cathedrals (a roundel in the west portal at Amiens, and stained glass at Laon and Saint-Quentin) as a knight in armour with a pitcher.

Gifts of the Holy Spirit, the Seven These are listed in Isa. 11: 2 (Vg.) as Sapientia, Intellectus, Consilium, Fortitudo, Scientia, Pietas, and Timor Domini. These are translated as 'Wisdom and understanding, the spirit of counsel and might, the spirit of knowledge and of the fear of the Lord', i.e. Pietas (Piety) is omitted from the Protestant versions, as not being in the Hebrew. The Seven Gifts are sometimes symbolized by seven doves (of the Holy Spirit), but an altarpiece by Luini of 1526 (London, CI) has the dove of the Holy Spirit with seven rays emanating from it, each labelled with the name of the gift.

gild *See* GUILD.

Giles, Saint (d. *c.*710/740?), was a hermit who founded a monastery at Saint-Gilles in Provence, which became a medieval *pilgrimage centre on the routes to the Holy Land and to Santiago de Compostela. His legend (10th cent.) contains incidents which can be dated between the 6th and 9th centuries. The most popular scenes from his life are when the King of the Goths hunted a hind which fed Giles on her milk, but the King's arrow struck Giles instead. The remorseful King founded a monastery for him. The other subject is that of the Emperor *Charlemagne (d. 814), who could not bring himself to confess a grave sin. An angel appeared to Giles while he was saying Mass (*The Mass of S. Giles*) with the name of the sin on a paper and a promise of absolution. Both scenes are represented on two panels by the Master of S. Giles (London, NG), but a third legend tells how Giles went to Rome and was granted papal privileges for his monastery, as well as two stone tablets (or cypress doors) which floated from the Tiber to the Rhône near his monastery. This extremely rare subject is shown in Master Bertram's *Apocalypse* (London, V & A). Giles is the patron saint of cripples (hence St Giles, Cripplegate, in the City of London), blacksmiths, and nursing mothers. His hind should not be confused with *S. Hubert's stag.

Gilio da Fabriano was a theologian whose *Dialogo . . . degli errori e degli abusi de' pittori . . . il Giudizio di Michelangelo . . .*, Camerino, 1564 (Dialogue . . . concerning the errors and abuses of painters . . . the Last Judgement by Michelangelo), is a characteristic product of the Council of *Trent. Gilio recognized Michelangelo's genius as an artist, but objected to apparently trivial features in his *Last Judgement* in the *Sistine Chapel of the Vatican—angels without wings, the presence of the non-biblical Charon, and similar irrelevancies. He protested especially against mere virtuosity and insisted on the importance of the subject and *decorum. *See also* BORROMEO, and PALEOTTI.

Gill, Eric (1882–1940), was an English stonecarver, engraver, and typographer. His early training included lettering under Edward Johnson, and he began earning his living as a letter-cutter in 1903. He carved the *Stations of the Cross* for Westminster Cathedral (1914–18), the *Prospero and Ariel* on Broadcasting House, London, ten panels for the New Museum, Jerusalem (1934–7), and bas-reliefs of the *Re-creation of Adam* (1935–8) for the League of Nations, Geneva. He became a Dominican Tertiary, and founded a short-lived Guild of Craftsmen to promote a religious attitude to art and craftsmanship, in an effort to counteract the material and social trends of the time. In 1924 he was connected with the Golden Cockerell Press, and illustrated a number of books. His influence has been strongest on modern typography, through his creation of Perpetua and Gill Sanserif types.

Giotto di Bondone (1266/7 or, less plausibly, 1276–1337) Giotto, rather than *Cimabue, is accepted as the starting-point for an art that is naturalistic, full of dramatic narrative, and psychological insight. He broke free from the rigid formality and the stereotyped formulas characteristic of late Byzantine art in Italy, from which Cimabue had begun to move away, which is why they are always considered to be the first among Florentine artists. This is confirmed by the mention of them both in Dante's *Purgatorio* (XI. 94–6), an unheard-of honour for an artist, though less complimentary to Cimabue, in that the verse, roughly translated, runs: 'Cimabue thought to have the mastery, but now the cry is for Giotto, so that the fame of the other is dimmed'.

Whether or not Giotto executed the cycle of frescoes of the *Life of S. Francis* in the Upper Church at Assisi, where the saint is buried, is still—and will probably remain—a subject of argument; what cannot be denied is that this work, which may plausibly be dated to between the late 1290s and the early 1300s shows a new feeling for drama and a typically Franciscan humanity and psychological insight not found in his contemporaries. A painting by Giuliano da Rimini in Boston (Gardner Mus.), dated 1307, is clearly a copy of one scene from the series and provides the only reliable terminal date. The series of the *Life of S. Francis* consists of 28 frescoes, 26 grouped on either side of the nave in four bays with three frescoes in each bay, an extra bay with one fresco on either side near the entrance, and one fresco on either side of the door. The narrative is based on the *Legenda Maior* by S. Bonaventura, the official life of Francis, written between 1260 and 1263 and also based on oral tradition and on earlier Lives of the saint. The frescoes are the first official pictorial biography, and the first derived from S. Bonaventura, with inscriptions (recently recovered) referring to the *Legenda Maior*. The narratives are very direct in the way they tell their story, almost no recourse being had to *Continuous Representation, and they have an altogether new quality of expression and drama. The obvious differences in the handling of various scenes points to the fact that several painters worked on the cycle, but the important point is that it shows one controlling mind.

In its dramatic expressiveness it bears a close resemblance to many aspects of the great cycle of frescoes, certainly by Giotto, although undocumented, in the Arena Chapel in Padua, datable after 1303 and before 1309, or perhaps 1313. This is devoted to the *Life of Christ*, prefaced by a *Life of the Virgin* and the *Lives of Joachim and Anna*, the Virgin's parents. These frescoes are arranged in three tiers, divided on one side by six windows, with two frescoes between each window, and on the other side in continuous banks, separated only by vertical strips of ornamental painting—floral designs with small quatrefoils with various biblical scenes in them.

On the entrance wall is a *Last Judgement* with the usual groups of the Elect being welcomed into Paradise while the Damned are consigned to a particularly nasty Hell. At the bottom of the fresco is a group of the Virgin and two angels before whom kneels the donor, Enrico Scrovegni, offering a model of the chapel, which was a gift made in expiation of his father's notorious sin of usury. Below the frescoes on the walls is a series of *Virtues and Vices*, and above the arch of the choir is a *Paradise* with God the Father enthroned and surrounded by angels, and on either side of the arch are the Angel and the Virgin of the *Annunciation*.

In this series Giotto does not use the method of condensing his narrative by using Continuous Representation; every scene stands on its own, so that great dramatic power is achieved in such scenes as the *Betrayal*, with the look passing between Christ and Judas, as the betrayer is about to give the kiss by which he designated his victim, or the *Lamentation over the Dead Christ* where the agony of distress of the little angels fluttering in the sky and the grief of the holy women and S. John is so intense as almost to be audible. Several of the Vices are memorable descriptive images—Envy with a viper for her tongue, Anger tearing her dress, Despair hanging by the neck with clenched hands.

In the scene of the *Crucifixion* in the Arena cycle, the depiction of Christ on the Cross differs radically from the form used up to then. No longer is the body of Christ disposed in a swaying curve with purely schematic rendering of the muscles, as had been usual in 13th-century crucifixes; Giotto's Christ hangs with straight torso and knees slightly bent as if to take His weight, and the anatomy of His torso is far more naturalistic. The same characteristics are also found in the large *Crucifix* in Sta Maria Novella in Florence, which is attested as by Giotto by evidence going back as early as 1312. The *Crucifix* in the Arena Chapel, usually attributed to his workshop, has the same features, in marked contrast to the great Cimabue *Crucifix*, once in Sta Croce in Florence (destroyed in the great flood of 1966), in which the older, less naturalistic form prevailed.

Two other fresco cycles survive in Sta Croce, Florence: the *Lives of the two SS John* in the Peruzzi Chapel, and the *Life of S. Francis* in the Bardi Chapel, plus a fresco of *S. Francis receiving the Stigmata* on the outside of the chapel. Both cycles were badly damaged by 18th-century whitewashing, and over-enthusiastic restoration in the 19th: they have recently been stripped of this restoration, and, although badly damaged, now show much more force and character. The S. Francis cycle follows the main lines of the Assisi cycle, though with fewer scenes, and both series display the new 14th-century interest in naturalism, straightforward composition, and Giotto's genius for narrative and characterization. They are undated, but clearly much later than the Paduan frescoes.

The *Ognissanti Madonna* (Florence, Uffizi), though neither signed nor documented, is universally attributed to him, while other easel pictures, even signed ones, are generally believed to be productions of his large and important workshop. The celebrated mosaic of the *Navicella* (the Ship of the Church, with Christ walking on the Waters), dating from soon after 1300, in the atrium of St Peter's in Rome, was totally reworked in the 17th century, when it was transferred from Old St Peter's to the newly rebuilt basilica. Two fragments of the original survive, but the present mosaic preserves only the vestiges of Giotto's design.

A *Stigmatization of S. Francis* (Paris, Louvre) is inscribed with Giotto's name, and the Stefaneschi Altarpiece in the Vatican is recorded as his in a document of 1342, but neither is accepted as his by many critics; the *Dormition of the Virgin* (Berlin), however, is usually accepted though it is neither signed nor fully documented.

In 1334 Giotto was made supervisor of the cathedral building works in Florence, 'on account of his great fame', and although there is little evidence that he had any architectural experience, he is commonly, but probably wrongly, credited with the campanile of the cathedral.

girdle also called a cincture (Lat. *cingulum*, a belt). A cord, usually of white linen, symbolizing continence and used to gird an *alb. During the Middle Ages girdles were occasionally of silk and embroidered or set with gems. In the E. Orthodox Church there is no exact equivalent, but a *zone is not dissimilar. Franciscan friars wear a rope girdle over their habit, with three knots on the free end, symbolizing the vows of poverty, chastity, and obedience.

Girdle of the Virgin *See* THOMAS THE APOSTLE, S.

gisant (Fr. Recumbent) A recumbent effigy on a tomb, represented as alive and praying, or dead. They are often lifelike portraits, being frequently made from death-masks. A gruesome variant, known in French as a *transi* (a desiccated corpse), consists of a *gisant* in the panoply of his earthly glory as a prince or prelate, with a *transi* below, visible through the arcade supporting the upper slab with the effigy, but representing the same man in an advanced stage of decomposition, often with worms and toads. An early example is the tomb of Bishop Fleming (d. 1431) in Lincoln Cathedral, but *transis* were particularly favoured in France in the 15th and 16th centuries, a very famous example being the tomb of Valentina Balbiani (d. 1572) by Germain Pilon, now in the Louvre. *See also* MEMENTO MORI.

glass *See* STAINED GLASS, GOLD GLASSES.

globe A globe, like an *orb, was a symbol of power in the ancient world and was an attribute of both emperors and divinities, especially Jupiter. Christ may be shown holding a globe or orb and a sceptre as a symbol of kingship, as in the paintings by Roger van der *Weyden (Louvre) or the globe may be at His feet, as in Early Christian sarcophagi, in representations of the *Majestas Domini, or Roger's Beaune Altarpiece or Hugo van der *Goes's *Trinity* (Edinburgh). In Byzantine art archangels usually carry an orb as a symbol of their status, e.g. the ivory *Archangel Michael* (London, BM).

Later, the cult of the *Immaculate Conception led to representations of Mary standing on a globe (or full moon), surrounded by other symbols, as in the Velázquez of *c.*1618 (London, NG).

g

Glorious Mysteries *See* ROSARY.

glory *See* HALO, MANDORLA.

Glory, Christ in *See* MAJESTAS DOMINI.

Gluttony *See* DEADLY SINS.

Glycophilousa *See* MADONNA TYPES (Madonna Affetuosa).

Gnadenstuhl (Ger. Seat of Grace) *See* SEAT OF MERCY.

goat Primarily a *beast symbolic of evil, but also a symbol of Christ. In Lev. 16: 5–22 there is a description of the sacrifice of a goat as a sacrifice for sin, while a second goat was driven into the wilderness—a scapegoat—to atone for the sins of Israel: this became an OT *type of Christ, who carries the sins of the world. Usually, however, the goat symbolizes sin, as in Matt. 25: 32–4 on the Last Judgement: 'as a shepherd separates the sheep from the goats: and he will put the sheep at his right hand, and the goats at the left... Then he will say to those at his left hand, "You that are accursed, depart from me, into the eternal fire."'

The goat was believed to be insatiably lustful, and was therefore associated with the *Devil, and there are medieval carvings of witches' covens, with naked women riding on goats. The earliest representations of goats as sinners go back to 4th-century sarcophagi or the 6th-century mosaic of the *Separation of the Sheep from the Goats* in Sant'Apollinare Nuovo, Ravenna.

Capricorn, the Goat, is also a Sign of the *Zodiac and connected with the Labours of the *Months.

God *See* TRINITY, THE HOLY, and also DIVINE.

God's Eye *See* EYE.

Goes, Hugo van der, (d. 1482) became a Master in the Ghent Guild of Artists in 1467. In his early years he was much employed on commissions for civic ceremonies, mostly in Bruges. In 1475 he entered the monastery of Rode Klooster, near Brussels, as a *lay brother and benefactor, but continued to paint, receiving visitors and patrons, and even travelling. During the return from a visit to Cologne in 1481 his persistent bouts of severe depression suddenly overbalanced into madness and attempted suicide, but he recovered some peace of mind before his death the following year. Despite his short active life he created a considerable body of work. Only Roger van der *Weyden equalled him in intensity of feeling, and in technique he was the equal of all his contemporaries and predecessors. There are no signed works, but one huge painting is recorded by *Vasari and serves as the touchstone for all others. This is the *Portinari Altarpiece* (Florence, Uffizi), a triptych 8½ ft. high by nearly 20 ft. wide when open. It was commissioned by Tommaso Portinari, an agent of the Medici bank in Bruges, and sent by him to the family chapel in Sta Maria Nuova in Florence. It created a sensation among Florentine artists, accustomed only to small Northern works, by its size, the splendour of its cool colour, and its technical brilliance. The central panel is an *Adoration of the Shepherds*: the Virgin kneels in adoration of the Infant lying on the ground surrounded by diminutive angels, behind her are the traditional attentive ox and the unconcerned ass; S. Joseph stands next to a massive column of a ruined palace with David's harp carved over the door, and beside him lies his wooden patten, recalling God's injunction to Moses: 'Remove the sandals from your feet, for the place on which you are standing is holy ground' (Exod. 3: 5). Shepherds crowd in and kneel in wonder, the youngest peering over the heads of those in front, while another comes running. The wings have, on the outside, an *Annunciation* as grisaille simulations of statues, and on the inside of the left wing Tommaso Portinari and his two sons with their patrons, SS Thomas and Anthony

Abbot, and in the right wing his wife, Maria Baroncelli with her daughter, and their patrons, SS Mary Magdalene and Margaret. Behind the donors stretches a wide landscape with tiny figures of the pregnant Virgin supported by S. Joseph, followed by the ass she had been riding, and under bare leafless trees the Magi's servant enquires the way. The adventurous colour, ranging from the red of S. Joseph's robe, the deep blue of the Virgin's dress, the iridescence of the angels' wings and their robes, some white, some pale blue and the cluster of foremost ones in dazzling brocades, is matched by the daring contrasts of scale: the donors are far smaller than their patrons, and the angels smaller still. In the foreground the vases with the flowers also have a symbolic role: the *albarello* (a shape of jar used by medieval Italian pharmacists) painted with the grapes of the Passion holding the red lily of the Passion, the white irises of the virginity of Mary, the blue iris of the sword which would pierce her heart, the glass of water with its reference to S. Augustine's comment on the *Virgin birth—that it was like light which passes through a glass without altering it—and its significance as the water of Salvation and the symbol of Mary's purity. Even the wheatsheaf has its meaning: Bethlehem means the 'House of Bread', as well as Christ's words 'I am the bread that came down from Heaven' (John 6: 41), 'Man does not live by bread alone' (Matt. 4: 4), and the words of the Lord's prayer, 'Give us this day our daily bread'.

All Hugo's other works depend on this one, which must have been painted by 1476, by which time he was already a lay brother. The Monforte *Adoration of the Kings* (Berlin), so called from the religious house in Spain from which it came, has lost its wings and its top, and lacks the tense and elaborate symbolism of the Portinari, though there are the meaningful details of the irises, columbines, and ruined building, and through the doorway are seen two stolidly indifferent men, while two young pages have doffed their hats. The *Adoration of the Shepherds* (also Berlin) has two prophets drawing back veils (of prophecy?) one on either side, the eager shepherds running in to a scene crowded not just with the Virgin and S. Joseph but by all the angels clustered round the crude wooden crib in which lies the tiny Child. In the foreground are the usual flowers and the wheatsheaf, and in the far distance a shepherd recoils in terror from the brilliant angel in the sky. The small diptych of the *Lamentation* (Vienna, KHM) is probably one of his earliest works. The left wing has the *Fall*, with Eve reaching up to pluck a second apple from the tree to give to Adam who extends his hand for it. The serpent watching her is like a lizard, but with a human head. The right wing is a *Lamentation*. The First Adam is confronted by the Second Adam, who has paid the price of the first one's disobedience; the Fall faces the Redemption; the lush beauty of Eden contrasts with the bare hillside and the stark cross against the stormy sky where ravens circle. The **Seat of Mercy*, one wing of a diptych (Edinburgh, NG, on loan from the Royal Coll.), is borrowed from the same subject by the Master of Flémalle (Hermitage) (*see* ROGER VAN DER WEYDEN) but follows the recognized iconography. Probably his last work was the *Dormition of the Virgin* (Bruges, Mus.), a confused, troubled composition with a large part of the scene occupied by the apparition of Christ amid a crowd of angels coming to receive the soul of His mother, dying with the twelve Apostles tightly clustered about her bed. For once, Hugo's gifts as a narrator and designer fail to convince. His influence was considerable, not only through the impact of the *Portinari Altarpiece* in Florence, but by the effect of his work on 15th-century French artists.

gold, myrrh, and frankincense were the gifts brought by the *Magi at the *Epiphany. The story of the Magi appears only in Matt. 2: 1–12, and although the Evangelist never says how many there were, the number of gifts suggests three—gold for kingship, frankincense for homage, and myrrh for suffering. Both frankincense and myrrh are aromatic gum resins, the first used in the preparation of incense, and the second from the tree *Commifera myrrha*, used to delay the decay of dead bodies, and probably included in the spices used in funeral rites, as Luke 23: 56 suggests and John 19: 39–40 affirms for the Entombment of Christ.

Golden Altar *See* PALA D'ORO.

Golden Calf, the Worship of the The story of the Israelites' backsliding into idolatry is told in Exod. 32: 1–20. In the absence of *Moses, who was communing with God on Mt. Sinai, his brother *Aaron was persuaded by the people to make a golden calf and build an altar. 'The Lord said to Moses, "Go down at once! Your people . . . have acted perversely;

they have been quick to turn aside from the way that I had commanded them; they have made for themselves an image of a calf, and have worshipped it, and sacrificed to it."' Moses pleaded with God, who relented. 'Then Moses turned and went down from the mountain... as soon as he came near the camp and saw the calf and the dancing, Moses' anger burned hot, and he threw the tablets [of the Law] from his hands, and broke them... He took the calf that they had made, burned it with fire, ground it to powder, scattered it on the water, and made the Israelites drink it.'

g

There is a reflection of this event in 1 Kgs. 12: 26–33 (Vg. 3 Reg. 12: 26–33): Solomon's son Rehoboam was a harsh ruler, and Jeroboam led a revolt and he made 'two calves of gold... He set one in Bethel, and the other he put in Dan.' While he was sacrificing to them an unnamed prophet appeared and predicted the disaster which later overtook him.

In the *Bible Moralisée the ashes of the Golden Calf, mixed with water, symbolize Baptism. The scene of idolatry was represented as early as the *Brescia Box, *c.*370, and it also appears in the *Utrecht Psalter, illustrating Ps. 81: 9–10 (Vg. Ps. 80: 9–11), in a 14th-century relief in Ratisbon Cathedral, in *Raphael's Loggie in the Vatican, and in a Tintoretto in Venice, Sta Maria dell'Orto. Moses is often shown breaking the Tablets of the Law, as in Rosselli's fresco (1481) in the *Sistine Chapel. Moses destroying the Golden Calf appears in Romanesque capitals at Autun and Vézelay, but is rare in MSS after the Middle Ages (for instance, in psalters). Perhaps the most striking later painting of the subject is *Poussin's *Worship of the Golden Calf* (*c.*1635: London, NG), and there are two by Claude, of 1653 and 1660 (Manchester), after which the subject virtually disappears.

Golden Gate In the Protevangelium of James, one of the *Apocryphal Gospels which furnished so many of the picturesque stories used by artists before they were abandoned in the 16th century, is the story of Joachim and *Anna. Anna is grieving because Joachim has been away for forty days, and because she is childless. An angel appeared to her and told her that she was to have a child. Joachim had a similar vision, and returned to Jerusalem with a thank-offering from his flocks, and 'Anna stood at the gate and saw Joachim coming and ran and hung upon his neck saying "Now I know the Lord God has blessed me... and she that was childless shall conceive".' The child that was born to her was *Mary, who was to become the mother of Jesus. In another Apocryphal Gospel, the Pseudo-Matthew, largely taken from the Protevangelium, the angel who appeared to Anna bade her meet Joachim 'at the Golden Gate of the Temple'. This is the story as told in the **Golden Legend*, where, in the account of the Nativity of the Virgin, the angel tells both Joachim and Anna to meet at the Golden Gate.

The scene was very popular, and appears in the fresco cycle by *Giotto in the Arena Chapel, Padua, and in the fresco by Agnolo Gaddi in Sta Croce, Florence, as well as in many other works.

In Acts 3: 2, 10, the Apostles Peter and John healed a cripple begging for alms at 'the gate of the temple called the Beautiful Gate', but this does not seem to be identifiable with the Golden Gate. Among the many works of art portraying the incident of the healing of the cripple is the cartoon by *Raphael (London, V & A) for the tapestry designed for the *Sistine Chapel of the Vatican.

Golden Legend, the Also called *Lombardica Historia*, it is a compilation of the legends of the saints, and a treatise on the Church's liturgical year, written by Jacobus de Voragine (or Voraigne). He was born about 1228/30 at Varaggio, or Varazze, on the Gulf of Genoa. He became a Dominican in 1244, and ruled the Dominican province of Lombardy from 1267, until he was persuaded to become Archbishop of Genoa in 1292. He strove to bring peace to a city in which internecine strife was endemic, and won such a reputation for his simple life and charity that at his death in 1298 he was venerated as a saint, and was beatified in 1816. His books include a commentary on S. Augustine, a Chronicle of Genoa, and, between 1255 and 1266, one of the most famous books of the Middle Ages. He called it the *Legenda Sanctorum*, the legends of the saints. More than five hundred MSS still exist; a French translation was made in the 14th century, and in the first century of printing over 150 editions and translations appeared. Its popularity ended with the Renaissance when, in Erasmus's damning words, 'its feigned miracles and strange lies... which the farther they are from the truth, the more readily they are believed' brought it into disrepute. However, from its first appearance to its unhappy eclipse, it was an undisputed iconographical source, like the *Apocryphal Gospels to which it owed so much, second only to Holy Writ itself.

The book is divided into four parts—the four seasons of the Church's year—corresponding to the four phases of mankind's spiritual history: the Fall, equated with Lent; Repentance and Renewal, from Advent to Christmas, with the Prophets from Moses to the birth of Christ; Reconciliation from Easter to Pentecost, with the life of Christ; and Pilgrimage, from Pentecost to Advent, or life in the world of temptation. Some of the longer chapters are about Christ's life and mission, and their reflection in the liturgy. Jacobus was not a historian, much less an etymologist, though the book is full of weird examples: he was a moralist. He wrote as much to preach as to inform. His purpose was not to present history, nor was he deliberately writing fiction; his aim in the *Legenda* was moral teaching, and an exhortation to, and exaltation of, Christian faith, virtue, and steadfastness. His stories of the fortitude and sufferings endured by the saints are to show their endurance as examples of indomitable faith; the wonders they performed (and even he at times says that the story of a miracle may not be true) are designed to encourage the faithful. His saints are heroes, invincible even in their deaths; his villains, particularly the Devil, are conquered by the virtues of their victims and are avenged by the angels. The *Legenda* is popular history, a compendium of popular beliefs, garnered from other hagiographers, from folk-tales, and local legends. These stories were the life and soul of medieval imagery, so that Emile Mâle, the learned French writer on medieval iconography, could say that the *Legenda* was one of the books which gives a clear picture of medieval thought and belief. It is to Jacobus that one first turns when faced with a strange carving on a capital, or an obscure incident in a MS or a portal.

The book was first translated into English as the *Golden Legend* about 1450. Caxton redid the translation and printed it in 1483. Wynkyn de Worde reprinted Caxton's version several times, but it then lost its popularity, until in 1892 William Morris reprinted it in the afterglow of the Romantic Movement's reappraisal of the Middle Ages.

goldfinch *See* BIRDS, SYMBOLIC.

gold glasses, known in Italy as *fondi d'oro* (gilded bases) are usually the bottoms of bowls or drinking glasses from which the upper parts are now missing. They were made from two layers of glass, to the first of which a layer of gold-leaf was fixed. The design was etched into the gold, and the second layer was either laid over it and fired on, or a layer of molten glass was blown on to it. They date mostly from the 3rd to the 5th century; many have been found in the catacombs, where they were used as grave-markers, stuck into the mortar sealing the niches at the funeral so as to make later recognition easier. They appear to have been made also as wedding or celebratory gifts, and although some may have been used for the Eucharist, there is no evidence for it. Sometimes a saint is represented, the most popular being SS Peter and Paul, but the commonest inscription is *vivas* (may you live), suggesting their drinking-glass origin. The craft was almost certainly Egyptian, as some examples found in Egypt pre-date the catacombs, and the tradition—if nothing else—survived into the Middle Ages. Possibly, gilded glass may have suggested the use of gold grounds in mosaics, and even have influenced the painting of icons and pictures on a *gold ground, a practice which lasted from Byzantine times to the 14th century in Italy. Gold is precious, timeless, and untarnishable, and thus suitable for the representation of devotional subjects.

The British Museum has a fine collection of gold glasses, including a bowl found in Cologne with eight biblical subjects round the rim. The Vatican also has a large collection from the Roman catacombs.

gold-ground paintings This is a recent name for what used to be called 'Primitive' paintings, i.e. Italian and Netherlandish paintings earlier than the 15th century. From very early Christian images up to the beginning of the 15th century, the use of a gold ground as the background to the figures was almost universal. The practice derived from *mosaic decoration where, by the 5th century, gold *tesserae formed the normal background. This transferred very naturally to panel paintings, and gold was also used in luxurious MSS such as the 10th-century *Gospels of Otto III* (Munich) or, as a very late example, the *Hours of Engelbert of Nassau* by the Master of Mary of Burgundy, *c.*1490 (Oxford: Bodleian). Since the gold ground consisted of a sheet of gold beaten out into an extremely thin film and then glued to the panel or vellum before the rest of the picture was painted, it could never be used in fresco painting (except for minor details) for reasons of cost. Gold grounds were the rule in panel paintings from the late 11th century; the ground might be either plain or with an embossed pattern, made by punching a design into the gesso ground of the panel, to which the gold film was then applied. The object was to express a celestial and eternal ambience, and the diaper patterns could suggest to some extent the flickering light effects characteristic of mosaic gold grounds.

The end of gold grounds came with the developing realism of *International Gothic, and it died out in the Early *Renaissance with the interest in naturalistic backgrounds of landscape and interiors.

Golgotha (Heb. [place of] a skull) (*See also* ANASTASIS, CALVARY, HOLY SEPULCHRE) According to Matthew, Mark, and John, Christ was crucified at a place just outside the city-walls of Jerusalem called Golgotha (in Latin Calvaria, as in Luke). The origin of the name is unknown, but a later tradition identifies it with the burial-place of *Adam's skull, thus forming a satisfying OT/NT *type and antitype. Because Christ was buried nearby, the site is also that of the *Holy Sepulchre and the *Anastasis. About 325/6 *Constantine began building a great basilica on the spot (fragments of which still survive), to commemorate both the Crucifixion and the Resurrection. This first church was consecrated in 336 and is attributed to Eustathios, a priest from Constantinople, and Zenobius, a Syrian. It has been much rebuilt, but still consists essentially of a basilica linked to a centrally planned *martyrium, similar to the Church of the Nativity in Bethlehem.

Goliath *See* DAVID.

Good Samaritan *See* SAMARITAN.

Good Shepherd *See* SHEPHERD.

Good Thief *See* DISMAS.

Gospel side Western churches, particularly urban ones, are not always orientated east-west, so it is convenient to describe what should be the north or south side as the Gospel and Epistle sides, because for centuries until very recently the Gospel was read from one side of the altar and the Epistle from the other. The Gospel side was that on the left of the worshipper, and on the left of the celebrant as he faced the altar with his back to the congregation.

Gospels, Apocryphal *See* APOCRYPHAL.

Gospels, the four (Gk. *Evangelion*, Old Eng. *Godspel*, i.e. good news) The four Gospels of SS Matthew, Mark, Luke, and John embody the core of Christian revelation, and bring the 'good news' of mankind's redemption. The four versions are uniform in intention, but differ in detail, which is why they are distinguished as 'the Gospel according to Matthew' or 'John' . . . The three Gospels of SS Matthew, Mark, and Luke are called the Synoptic Gospels, because although they vary in detail they often correspond in what they relate; their similarities show their interdependence, in that they are based on their common experience. They all knew Jesus, although two of the Evangelists, Mark and Luke, were not Apostles. S. Luke appears to have sought out the Virgin and from her he obtained the story of the Annunciation, and his account of the Nativity is a more personal and intimate one than either of the other two. One reason for their diversity is that each begins at a different point: S. Matthew with a genealogy tracing Christ's lineage back through David to Abraham. He alone tells the story of the Magi before Herod, the massacre of the Innocents, and the Flight into Egypt. S. Mark begins with John the Baptist as the forerunner, and the baptism of Christ. S. Luke begins with the parents of the Baptist and his birth, then tells of the Annunciation, the Nativity, the Presentation in the Temple with the prophecies of Simeon and Anna, and the story of Christ disputing with the Doctors in the Temple. S. John plunges straight into the fundamentals with the momentous opening words 'In the beginning was the Word, and the Word was with God, and the Word was God.'

The main difference between the three Synoptic Gospels and S. John's is his greater emphasis on a detailed account of Christ's teaching, particularly in ch. 6, where the Institution of the Eucharist is presaged, that only actually took place during the Last Supper. Some incidents appear only in one Gospel, for instance only Matthew has the Sermon on the Mount, and only he and Luke record the Lord's Prayer. They all recount different miracles and parables, probably because they were not witnesses to all of them. The major events are given by all four—the Baptism, with its recognition of Christ's divinity, the Calling of

Andrew, Peter, James, and John, and later of Matthew, the Transfiguration, the Entry into Jerusalem, the Passion and the Crucifixion, the Resurrection and the injunction to the disciples assembled in the upper room to go out and preach the good news. The Ascension is recorded in Luke's Acts of the Apostles. John's account of Jesus's trial and Crucifixion is the fullest, since he alone was there, and was the only disciple to stand with Mary beneath the Cross.

The unique status of these four narratives, the more convincing because they vary and are therefore not stereotypes, was recognized by the 2nd century. There are also a number of *Apocryphal Gospels which are often heretical, and never challenged the authority of the four. They were effectively weeded out by the scholarship of *S. Jerome, who translated the Greek MSS into Latin to create the Vulgate, the standard Latin text, by 386. The picturesque, and sometimes absurd, stories in the Apocryphal Gospels were the source of many works of art, but their use ceased by the 16th century.

In Early Christian times the Gospels are often represented as the four *Rivers flowing from the enthroned Christ (as in the apse mosaic in San Vitale, Ravenna) or as books or scrolls (as in the mosaic in the Mausoleum of Galla Placidia, Ravenna, where the names of the Gospels may be distinguished on the scrolls). The earliest illustrated Gospel book is a 6th-century one (Corpus Christi, Cambridge) and the 6th-century *Rossano Codex is a fully illustrated Gospels. For selections from the Gospels to be read during the liturgical year *see* LITURGICAL BOOKS.

g

Gothic, International *See* INTERNATIONAL GOTHIC.

GOTHIC ART AND ARCHITECTURE

The use of the word 'Gothic' (championed by Raphael and *Vasari) to describe a style of architecture was originally coined as a synonym for 'barbaric', relating to the uncultured northern tribes of Europe. Vasari in the 'Introduction to the arts of design' in his *Lives of the Artists* (1550 and 1568) abuses what he calls *maniera tedesca*—the 'German manner'—as forms to be avoided. Critical discussion of the style came first from Italy: Petrarch, who died in 1374, gloried in the perfection of classical antiquity, and described the architecture of his own age as ugly; yet during his travels across Europe he had seen Cologne Cathedral (then unfinished) and called it a 'beautiful temple, and magnificent'. The French architect Philibert de l'Orme in his treatise *Nouvelles inventions* of 1561, describes vaults that master masons make for churches as *voûtes modernes* (modern vaulting) and mentions ribs by name as liernes and tiercerons which he calls 'French fashion'—*mode Françoise.* Wren refers to Gothic, but calls it 'Saracen', believing it to have been brought into Europe as a result of the Crusades; but he insists that to deviate from Gothic in restoring a Gothic building would be wrong. He prefers classical, but is tolerant of Gothic.

Although most of the architecture and art of southern Europe built at the same time as the 'Gothic' appears distinct from the style, it was subject to many of the same influences and can still be considered 'medieval'. However, even the word 'medieval' (first used by Leonardo Bruni in 1452) was used pejoratively along with the term 'the Dark Ages', both originating from the humanist tradition of the 15th century, which tended to separate history into three periods—the classical, middle, and modern periods —with the latter, the Renaissance, bypassing the 'middle time' and restoring direct links with the classical world. Although each country defines its own medieval timeline, it broadly spans from the sack of Rome in AD 410 until around the middle of the 15th century. The Early Middle Ages (*c.*400–1000) in art history is covered by the *Early Christian period and the *Romanesque up to around the middle of the 11th century. In England much of this period is covered by *Anglo-Saxon and Norman art and architecture. The High Middle Ages (*c.*1000–1300) in Britain begins with Early English Gothic from 1180 to 1275 (Rickman) or 1307 (Pevsner), and is followed in the Late Middle Ages (*c.*1300–1500) by Decorated Gothic (1275–1380) and Perpendicular (1380–1520) which continues until the beginning of the Renaissance. By extension, though less accurately, the other arts produced within the same time-span came to be given the same names.

The ease with which this period could be consigned to lesser status was clearly due to its utilization of 'un-classical' proportions and representations, but also because it was a period when both art and architecture were not the subject of treatises. At the time of their making the works were considered to be self-explanatory and their creators were seen more as conduits for God's will rather than implementers of particular systems or theories. This lack of written confirmation of artistic intent has led to much speculation as to the real meaning, value, and mediative qualities of medieval artistic endeavour and has often resulted in the conclusion that the change in style was brought about by advances in technology. However, it is more likely that any technical innovations arose from the desire to develop new spatial characteristics rather than the other way around. In this environment, short on original textual explanations of artistic and architectural method but rich in artefacts, the international nature of the period has often been coloured by historians intent on emphasizing national characteristics over a broader understanding of the status of the work of art at the time. This situation may have mirrored similar trends during the medieval period, but it is more likely to have come about as the result of contemporary political and social issues. One such development saw attempts by many revisionists to raise the profile of the commoner with respect to the making of and the influence on the medieval period, trying to wrestle the representational nexus from the aristocracy, and place it closer to the life of the peasant and the changing spatial relationships manifested in the countryside. However, it was the townsfolk—comprising merchants, tradesmen, and artisans—who were more influential in these changes within society, often assisting in the construction and use of art and architecture, particularly in festivals and performances, even if these were still commissioned predominantly by the aristocracy. This resurgence in the articulation of popular faith that characterized much of the artistic production of the High Middle Ages also had a negative aspect, leading to the witch-hunts and heresies of the Late medieval period and encouraged the widening reach and increasing brutality of the Inquisition amidst the destructive wake of the Black Death that swept through Europe in the 14th century. Although it is this later, and apparently dark, period that resonates as 'Gothic' in the popular imagination, it was in the creative endeavour of the period as a whole that the foundations for the Renaissance were laid. The rediscovery of Aristotle and the birth of Scholasticism; the beginnings of Natural Science; the development of the first mechanical clock (12th century); advances in optics resulting in the first eyeglasses (13th century) as well as a new understanding of the relationship between perspective, time, and space; and, perhaps most significantly, the development of the first printing press (15th century) are but a few advances of the period. Although the Humanists of the Renaissance built on many of these developments while claiming a closer link with the past glories of Greece and Rome, it would be fairer to see the whole of the Gothic period as the last unselfconscious flowering of the classical world (albeit within a Christian milieu), and as an essential part of the foundations for Renaissance innovation.

Amidst the historiography of Gothic art and architecture three main trends can be discerned. The first, prevalent in the work of many French medievalists, rests on the interpretation of the works iconographically; understanding the works in terms of their pictorial and representational narratives. This is evident in the art historical writings of Émile Mâle and Henri Focillon. A different understanding of the period is evident in many of the German writers of the 20th century such as Richard Krautheimer, Otto von Simson, Joseph Sauer, Günther Bandmann, and Hans Sedlmayr, where the concentration is more on the meaning of the work as a whole, understanding the works, particularly those associated with cathedrals, as a *Gesamtkunstwerk*, a total work of art in which all aspects contribute to a whole that is more than the sum of its parts. Many critics of this type of understanding cite the apparent 'Catholicism' of the method and its insistence on ascribing representational meaning as a significant factor in the reality of the work as its primary flaw. They argue that the analysis undertaken through this method runs too close to mystical ideas and leads to uncorroborated constructions rather than observed truths. In contrast with this method, most British medieval historians of art (particularly at the Courtauld Institute) have concentrated on the evidence embodied in the works themselves (Harvey, Pevsner, Kidson, Crossley, Ayers), preferring to speculate on stylistic matters and developments in technical and geometrical innovation rather than on potential lost relationships. In reality, Gothic art and architecture is partly realized in all three methods.

More recently, commentators are beginning to be more holistic in their approach to understanding the cultural iconography of the period, attempting to describe medieval mentalities (Le Goff, Duby) as well as the use of Gothic art and architecture in the liturgical calendar (Binski, Draper, Frost). This attitude to the works is beginning to reveal new characteristics of the pieces of art and their setting, as well as the relationships between medieval buildings and their locations, suggesting there was a much greater integration of the artistic culture with the lives of the people. It is not that the commoner 'read' the works, or that they were tutored through them, but rather that they experienced them in an imminent way through participation in festivals and in many other rituals undertaken by their community. They were not spectators but witnesses, and even if they were unaware of the depth of meaning available, they were as essential to the revelation of order established within the event as any cleric or performer. This aspect of medieval mediation inherent in festivals was also a critical factor in the meaning of the art and architecture of the period; reality was not present only in the heavenly world or in the earthly world, but in a hierarchy that extended between the two; light, matter, and movement mediated and made present this hierarchy. Architecture and art were opportunities to reveal this continuity. This aspect of Gothic art and architecture became partially obscured during the following centuries until the *Baroque when the dynamics of light and movement and their representation—as well as the combined use of all the arts—returned.

The rehabilitation of the Gothic style of architecture came only in the mid-18th century and was felt by many to be evidence of a cultural eccentricity, as for instance in Horace Walpole's Strawberry Hill, begun in 1747. It was not until the 19th century that revivalism, particularly in England, made it not just respectable, but earnestly to be cultivated and studied, though this eventually resulted in attitudes as violently polemical as those of any Italian Renaissance writer. For *Pugin, and other contemporary proponents of the *Gothic Revival, such as *Scott or *Butterfield, Gothic in church building became an article of faith, and deviation from it almost as bad as heresy. But even these examples were more linked to social ideas than notions of light metaphysics and symbolic mediation.

The original developments that brought about the transition from *Romanesque architecture, occurred largely in churches built in the area round Paris—the Île de France—amidst the theological speculations of Hugh of St Victor, the School of Chartres, and the University of Paris. The feebleness and poverty of 10th-and 11th-century French monarchs meant that there was no royal patronage for large Romanesque abbeys in the small part of France which they controlled; all the important foundations were built in the richer territories of their major vassals—Burgundy, Normandy, Aquitaine, Provence. In the early 12th century, when prosperity and royal authority revived, the restoration of dilapidated abbeys and the building of new churches became possible and necessary. The new speculations emerging from the theologians of the 'Twelfth-Century Renaissance', influenced by the rediscovery of many Greek texts from the Arabic lands to the south, demanded new spatial arrangements not possible using the massive 11th-century barrel vaults of the *pilgrimage churches. The first changes are visible in the lighter pointed groin vaults of *Cluny and its dependent abbeys, which still needed heavy walls to support their weight, then the use of rib vaults at Durham in 1093, and their first use in France at Lessay in Normandy in 1100. Their rapid spread in France from *c.*1130 came when the transformation of church interiors into large, high, and well-lit spaces was perceived and the advantages of this new means of distributing the weight of vaulting had been worked out, probably independently of Durham. With pointed ribs built as a framework to support a thinner, lighter infilling, the weight of the vault could be directed down the shafts which united the ribs physically and visually to the columns or piers of the nave arcade, and by means of flying buttresses be largely transferred to a bearing point outside the building. Once the walls no longer had to carry all the weight of the vaulting they could be made thinner, to the point of becoming no more than panels with large windows in them, to admit light or be filled with stained glass. Eventually there developed the elaborate system of flying buttresses, supported by massive tower buttresses, which were in turn crowned with pinnacles that exert a powerful stabilizing downward pressure on the tower buttress.

The significance of Gothic lies above all in the increase in light and often colour through the use of *stained glass. Abbot Suger of *Saint-Denis, who rebuilt parts of his abbey between 1137 and 1144, in particular the choir, using rib vaults and stained-glass windows, created the first example of what becomes distinctively Gothic architecture. He was determined that his abbey should express his belief that light, colour, richness, and beauty are reflections of the Celestial Hierarchy (after Pseudo Dionysius), and that the awe they inspired would open people's minds to the majesty of God.

The first wave of great churches in the Île de France, all begun between the 1140s and 1170s, include Sens, Noyon, Laon, Senlis, Notre-Dame in Paris, and Mantes, all rib-vaulted with an apsidal choir and ambulatory (Laon alone later changed to a flat choir), and a towered west front. Of these, the largest was Notre-Dame in Paris, begun in 1163, with a nave 110 ft high. It was the largest church in Christendom after St Peter's in Rome, compact in design, with a fine regularity and symmetry in the west front. All these churches stressed clarity and light, and simplicity in ornament, for the capitals of the columns and piers supporting their nave arcades are based on stylized leaf forms, and even the Last Judgement portals have lost the grim menace of Autun, Conques, and Moissac.

The next wave of churches are of the 13th century and later, and close in date. The rebuilding of Chartres after the disastrous fire of 1194 was with a nave higher than Paris, and with double aisles in the apsidal choir surrounded by an ambulatory and radiating chapels. The west front, which survived from the earlier church, and the transepts are the most complex and grandest examples of *portal sculpture. Bourges was rebuilt from 1192, and is unusual in having no transepts and continuous double aisles designed to accommodate large numbers of pilgrims visiting the relics. Reims was begun in 1211, and Amiens in 1220, both following to a large extent the form established at Chartres. Both also have important portal sculpture, particularly Reims. Beauvais, begun in 1227, was designed as the culmination of the striving for height, light, and structural lightness, but ended in disaster. The choir vaults collapsed, were not rebuilt until the next century, and the further collapse of an over-ambitious crossing tower to the 16th-century transepts ended the project; only the choir and transepts remain.

The rebuilding from 1231 to 1281 of the choir and nave of Saint-Denis introduced more decorative forms, known as Rayonnant, in the tracery of its huge clerestory windows, and in windows behind the arcades of the gallery which increased the amount of light. Other late 13th-century features were greater complexity in the west towers, as at Amiens, where the logic of the interior is at variance with the elaboration of the façade. In the next century more complicated rose windows and the proliferation of ornament added to traditional designs overwhelms Rayonnant to become the 'Flamboyant'. Most of the later major churches follow the established models; only in some minor churches of the 13th and 14th centuries is more innovation found. The Ste-Chapelle in Paris, built as a palace chapel *c.*1244 on the two-storey model of Charlemagne's chapel at Aachen, has windows in its upper chapel nearly four times the height of the supporting wall below them; St-Urbain at Troyes was begun in 1262 by an Englishman who followed the column design of Salisbury Cathedral inside. Even the Ste-Chapelle was later modified to meet the taste for the Flamboyant when the west front was rebuilt with a larger, more florid rose window.

By 1507, when the *Tour-au-Beurre* of Rouen Cathedral was finished, or the church of Caudebec-en-Caux, near Rouen in 1539, or 1545 when the apse of St-Pierre in Caen was finished with Renaissance balustrading outside and Flamboyant vaulting with pendant drops—stone adaptations of timber roofs—the structural simplicity of Gothic had become part of a greater ornamental programme. St-Eustache in Paris was begun in 1532; it is still a grand Gothic church, but the arcades are round-headed, and the piers have classical capitals.

Gothic did not take a firm hold in England until the rebuilding of Canterbury Cathedral choir in 1174, with an extra area for the shrine of the archbishop, S. *Thomas Becket, murdered in the cathedral in 1170. The important features introduced by the new choir and shrine area (now called Trinity Chapel) are pointed arches, rib vaulting, and the lavish use of polished *Purbeck marble (a typically English phenomenon) for details in arcading and for the attached columns and capitals of the very tall piers of the arcade. Other notable features are the greater length of the east arm finished in 1184, compared with the Norman nave, and two pairs of transepts, one pair at the end of the nave, the other crossing the choir, a system taken from Cluny. The rebuilt Canterbury prompted the rebuilding of many Norman churches, and certain features become common: great length, with nave, choir, retrochoir, Lady Chapel, like an enfilade of rooms; a square east end; no striving for height—York at 102 ft. is an exception; the retention of the Romanesque 'thick wall' construction, with the outer walls and the main arcade piers strong enough to bear most of the weight of the vaulting, and also provide a passageway at triforium and clerestory level; the dislike of flying buttresses seems general, and where they exist they usually hug the aisle roofs, or are even concealed under them; rib vaulting ranges from the simplest type, with no ridge rib, as at Wells and Salisbury, to multiple ribs from seven at Lincoln to eleven at Exeter, meeting on a ridge rib running from one end of the vault to the other, with bosses at the intersections which are often, as at Exeter, major pieces of sculpture; a large crossing tower and towers at the west front; a stone screen between nave and choir; polished Purbeck to contrast with paler stone. Where W. front sculpture exists, it is usually statues of saints, now mostly 19th-century restorations. Owing to the pillaging of many churches and monasteries in Britain during the Reformation, surviving iconographical programmes are rare, which makes the west front of Wells, begun in 1220, unusual and important, as is also the survival of the Romanesque sculpture at the west front of Lincoln despite its total rebuilding from 1192. In Salisbury, the cathedral chapter used the opportunity presented by the relocation of the whole city, including the cathedral, around 1220 to forge a plan that united the whole area during the Rogation processions, and York, Worcester, Ely, and Durham all had major rebuilding campaigns.

Westminster Abbey, the church most influenced by French precedents, was begun in 1245 with apse, ambulatory, and five radiating chapels. Henry III built it to combine the functions of Reims for coronations, St-Denis as a royal mausoleum and shrine for a royal saint, and the Ste-Chapelle as a palace chapel, and it includes one of the most complete examples of a Cosmatesque decorated pavement in northern Europe. Progress was rapid at first but stopped in 1284, and was not resumed until *c.*1375 when the nave was built, though not fully completed until 1500, and the west towers are mostly 18th century. The 14th century brought great changes in the treatment of space and vaulting: at Ely the Octagon and the Lady Chapel, with its development of the ogee arch and the 'nodding' arches of the projecting canopies; at Gloucester, the rebuilding of the choir within the shell of the old Romanesque choir, to house the tomb of Edward II, murdered in 1327, with the tracery descending in long mouldings from the all-over lierne ribs of the vault to form a screen over the arches and walls of the old choir; and above all the introduction in 1351 of fan vaulting in the cloisters of Gloucester, which was used rather tentatively in St George's Chapel, Windsor, begun in 1474, and reached its apogee in King's College Chapel, Cambridge, completed by 1515. Henry VII's Chapel at Westminster Abbey, which replaced the founder's Lady Chapel, was completed by 1512, with an unusual variant of fan vaulting, and houses the tomb of the king and his queen with gilt-bronze effigies by the Italian sculptor Pietro Torrigiani. Though Gothic in England lingered on into the next century, the end marked by the beginning of the Tudor dynasty, its driving force was as exhausted here as it was in France by the 1530s.

In the 13th century Germany looked towards France as the source from which their Gothic derived. Cologne Cathedral, begun in 1248, is a clear example of the spread of the St-Denis type of Rayonnant, and of Amiens as a model for its height—151 feet. Strasbourg was a German city until the 17th century, and the cathedral combines a deep Romanesque crypt in the choir, with a nave, built 1250–75, also derived from the nave of St-Denis. The west front was built from 1277, and is inspired by St-Urbain in Troyes, and has layers of tracery called the 'harp effect', because long 'strings' of stone hang like an open-work screen over the windows above the porch. The single tower and open-work spire—an entirely German feature—rises to 466 ft., and was finished in 1439. Freiburg im Breisgau has the earliest of these great towers and open-work spires, of 1275–*c.*1340, and there are similar ones at Ulm, Vienna, Antwerp, Utrecht, Malines (Mechelen), and Leuven. The churches themselves follow French forms.

The finest example of French Rayonnant outside France is Prague Cathedral, built by the Bohemian kings to serve the same purposes as Westminster Abbey. It was begun by a French architect, but its major creator was Peter Parler from 1356. He used vaulting derived from St-Urbain, and also from Bristol Cathedral, where the first flying ribs were built from *c.*1300. Prague remained only a choir, but his father's work at Schwäbisch-Gmünd in 1361–79 is a *hall-church on the design of the Ste-Chapelle, and the work of his sons at Kutná Hora, near Prague, of 1388, has a web of lierne vaulting with flying ribs and main ribs running down to melt into the piers, a feature not only increasingly common but one which the whole Parler family exploited.

The popularity in Germany of the hall-church design, and influences from St-Urbain, English lierne network in vaulting patterns, and the Ste-Chapelle dominate 14th- and 15th-century German churches, as in the north choir aisle of Brunswick Cathedral in 1469, where the round piers have small columns twined round them.

Gothic in Spain is also almost entirely derived from France, with the major influence stemming from Bourges. The cathedrals of Burgos and Toledo were both begun by 1221–4; Burgos is single aisled and less high than Bourges, Toledo double aisled. Both have ambulatories and radiating chapels, and Burgos is a grand example of French High Gothic growing on foreign soil. The east end has an octagonal funerary chapel, the Capilla del Condestable, built by a German architect between 1482 and 1494, an example of the rivalry between royalty and grandees in that it competes with royal chapels in splendour and fashion. The vault has an open-work tracery star, the windows have Flamboyant tracery, and the walls are covered with details and figures with armorial bearings. By the late 14th century, the Spanish custom of placing the choir to reach far down the nave and enclosing it within gates was a general feature. León is another French Rayonnant church; the only totally un-French churches are Barcelona and Palma cathedrals. Barcelona was built from 1298 to 1450, and has the peculiarity that the aisle chapels are placed one above the other, and since the windows in the upper chapels are very small the church is very dark. The slender nave piers are so tall that the small oculi of the clerestory are pushed up against the vault, and even the large choir windows fail to admit much light. Palma de Majorca was captured from the Moors in 1229, and the cathedral, begun in 1360, has a nave 145 ft. high and aisles 95 ft. high. The slender nave piers are wide apart, and the east wall of the nave rising above the choir has a huge round window. The exterior buttresses have been described as a palisade above which tower buttresses with double flyers uphold the vault.

Seville was the first Christian church to be built in an area which had been Muslim for over seven centuries. It is the largest of all medieval churches, built from 1402 until the 16th century, with a nave, and four aisles of equal height, making it very dark, since the only light comes from the clerestory and the outer aisle windows. The great free-standing tower—La Giralda—is that of the mosque it replaced. Granada Cathedral, built from 1528, following the reconquest in 1492, merges Gothic and Renaissance forms. The same characteristics appear at Salamanca and Segovia, both 16th-century churches.

In Italy Gothic presents a totally different character, for it shows little influence from France except that several Cistercian houses had introduced Burgundian architectural forms between 1172 and 1219—Chiaravalle, near Milan, Fossanova, south of Rome, Casamari, SE of Rome, San Galgano, now a ruin near Siena, and Vercelli, near Turin, which combines characteristic Cistercian form with a Romanesque crossing having a tower borne on squinches, and four angle towers. Italian builders appear to have adapted existing characteristics rather than adopting French models. The large number of small dioceses lacked the resources to embark on ambitious building campaigns, so that where cathedrals existed they were usually civic enterprises.

The cathedral of *Milan is undeniably northern Gothic, but is a special case and had no imitators. Pointed arches are used in both the large 13th-century *Mendicant Order preaching churches in Florence, the Dominican Sta Maria Novella, and the Franciscan Sta Croce, and both have the widely spaced arcades and the spaciousness of Bourges in their ancestry, though Sta Croce is timber-roofed not vaulted. Sta Maria sopra Minerva, begun in 1281 for the Dominicans, is the only Gothic church in Rome, and it follows in the same mould. The Florentine Baptistery has a long history but it appears that much of the revetment and mosaic work was completed during the 12th and early 13th centuries. Its form appears Romanesque but it too manifests a complex relationship of iconography and movement similar to many of the churches of northern Europe. Florence Cathedral, begun in 1294 by Arnolfo di Cambio, the architect of Sta Croce, has the same concern for simplicity and space. This was a civic enterprise *par excellence*, enlarged still further in the 14th century, so that an enormous void remained over the crossing as a problem which it took *Brunelleschi to solve. The campanile, said to have been begun by *Giotto, was built from 1334, and has some of the most famous 14th- and 15th-century sculpture. The huge complex at Assisi was begun in 1228, with the Upper Church of San Francesco as a simple nave and choir with the Lower Church under it, both providing large areas for fresco decoration; and still further below is the crypt in which S. Francis is buried. San Domenico in Bologna was partly a monastic and partly a preaching church. Later additions have enriched and complicated it with, for instance, the chapel housing the saint's shrine. The cathedral, San Petronio, was a civic enterprise begun in 1390 on an enormous scale, which continued building until the mid-17th century. The huge square bays are 63 ft. across and 145 ft. high, and are flanked by aisles half the width of the nave bay, with two side chapels to each aisle bay, making it one of the largest medieval churches in Italy. Its main work of art is the portal sculpture by Jacopo della *Quercia. Orvieto Cathedral, planned in 1264 as a result of the miracle of *Bolsena, was begun in 1290. It looks like a Romanesque church, but the pointed arches and the richly decorative façade, which stands like a high screen over the nave roof, are evidence of its mainly 14th-century date. The cathedral of Siena has a nave and transepts of 1220–60, a dome over the crossing of 1260, and a west front begun by Giovanni *Pisano between 1284 and 1297, which in the 14th century was modelled on the front of Orvieto; building continued well into the 14th century. The huge campanile was begun in the late 12th century, as part of the first church on the site. Among the few outstandingly Gothic churches is a tiny, 14th-century, very ornate gem, Sta Maria della Spina, in Pisa, which originally stood on the river bank, before being rebuilt higher up in 1871.

Gothic architecture—particularly the 13th-century High Gothic from Chartres to Beauvais, or Westminster Abbey, Prague, or Strasbourg cathedrals, or the major Italian Gothic churches, such as Milan, Florence, and Siena—was enormously expensive; the work extended over more than one architect's lifetime. Most, like Paris, Amiens, and Prague, had two successive architects, Reims had no fewer than four, Florence had at least three; not many kings, bishops, or inaugurating civic authorities who began the enterprise lived to see it completed. The imagery of the sculpture in the portals and the stained-glass windows combined with the overall architectural framework to articulate the mediative possibilities of the liturgy and so called for complex programmes to be devised by clerics. Wars, plagues, famines, and civil strife came and went; eventually money and courage were found to continue and usually to complete the work, although sometimes, as at Prague, work stopped for good because of religious strife. Throughout the 12th and well into the 14th century in France there was an unremitting drive for height, from the 100 ft of Paris to the 157 ft of Beauvais, and this ambition affected patrons and architects all over N. Europe. The building of all these churches required imagination, effort, faith, and dedication of an unusual order, both by the patrons who promoted them, by the laity who supported them, and a perpetual search for knowledge and experience by the masons who created them. As Abbot Suger comments: 'Through the beauty and splendour of the church the dull mind would be awakened to the majesty of God'.

What about the other arts in the same period? There is no change in the subject-matter and some, such as images of the Virgin, became less hieratic, less formal, and more tender. A greater degree of realism appears in both sculpture and painting, an interest in the naturalistic, as for instance, in the work of Jan van *Eyck. The portal sculpture by Claus Sluter at the remains of the Abbey of Champmol at Dijon, of *c.*1402, shows the Duke and Duchess of Burgundy kneeling before the Virgin, and it is obvious that they are real portraits, not stylized effigies as is, for instance, the head of Edward III on his tomb in Westminster Abbey of about twenty-five years earlier.

The sculpture of Giovanni *Pisano is more emotional, more poignant than that of his father Nicola. But emotion and drama were evident earlier, for example in the Cologne *Gero Crucifix* of 970 or Gislebertus's *Eve* of 1125–30 at Autun. Yet it is undeniable that there is a change of feeling which can be recognized as specifically Gothic. The *Christ* in the centre of the Chartres west front has moved a long way from the *Christ* of Moissac, and the *Christ* on the trumeau at Amiens, known as *Le Beau Dieu*, has gone a long way further in the transition from a God of Justice to a God of Mercy. The hieratic Virgin of the Chartres portal who is the epitome of the Theotokos, the God-bearer, becomes in the fragment of the choir screen of Chartres of a century later, the tender mother of a new-born Babe leaning over His cradle with an infinitely caring gesture. At Reims the rate of change accelerates. From the grave and thoughtful Virgin of the Annunciation of *c.*1230, she becomes the assured, poised Virgin of the Visitation of *c.*1240, and the Angel of the Annunciation of *c.*1245–50 stands in total contrast and looks at Mary with a smile that proved irresistible to lesser sculptors such as the creator of the trumeau of the south front of Amiens, known as the *Vierge Dorée*, of 1260–70, whose smile has become a smirk, and the Angel of the Annunciation at Regensburg of *c.*1280 is a caricature of the over-popular 'Reims smile'.

Statues of the Virgin and Child were made in a variety of materials—painted wood, ivory, marble, metal, and inlaid with enamels and jewels with gilded crowns. Those of the 14th century often have the slender form and swaying pose which derived from ivory statuettes, where the curve of the tusk dictated the pose of the figure. These statues became as traditional as the Madonna pictures of the Venetian 'Madonnieri'—no two exactly alike. In the late 14th and 15th centuries a more vivid realism appears; voluminous draperies give the figure weight, often contrasting sharply with small delicate features, and Mary carries the Christ Child on one hip with a strong shift of balance. In a *Visitation* at Troyes of the early 16th century, realism has converted the two figures of Mary and Elizabeth into burghers' wives greeting each other on a grand feast-day. But realism of a more profound kind created the groups known as the *Pietà*, popular in northern France, Flanders, and Germany, where the distraught Virgin holds her dead Son on her knees. Other vividly realistic creations are the *Easter Sepulchre groups of the Entombment of Christ, of which there are a large number spread across France, and into Germany and N. Italy.

Tombs were one of the major concerns of both patrons and sculptors, ranging from simple stylized effigies to intensely realistic figures carved from death-masks. In St-Denis, a number of very fine tomb figures ranging from the 13th to the 17th century survive, and in Fontevrault Abbey the tombs of the Angevin kings and queens of England—Henry II and Eleanor of Aquitaine, Richard Lionheart and his second queen Eleanor of Guyenne—though they are stylized effigies. The tombs of Henry III and Eleanor of Castile of 1291, and the grim Edward III (d. 1377) with his six children as mourners in the niches of the tomb base round the choir of Westminster Abbey are magnificent examples of English metal-casting. The double tomb of Richard II and Anne of Bohemia of 1394–5 has an effigy of the King which is remarkably like the large portrait of the King in the Abbey and his image in the Wilton Diptych (London, NG) and is evidence of the mounting interest in naturalism. The tombs of the Dukes of Burgundy—Philip the Bold by Sluter of *c.*1410 and John the Fearless of 1469 (Dijon, Mus.)—follow in this style of regal magnificence, with winged angels at their head, and rows of weepers in the niches round the base of the tomb. The monument to the Emperor Otto II of 1240–50 in Magdeburg, riding victoriously under a columned canopy, is the forerunner of the Scaliger tombs by the Campione family in Verona of the 14th century where, fully armed, the Veronese rulers ride beneath canopies like ornate ciboria. The Bamberg Rider can be matched with the Bassenheim Rider of S. Martin and the beggar of *c.*1240, both as vividly realistic in the horsemen and their mounts as the Emperor monument, yet not portraits—if anything, the horses are more lifelike than the men. Early 13th-century sculpture in Germany shows a certain dependence on French portal sculpture; in Bamberg, the figures of the Virgin and S. Elizabeth have the massed draperies which appear at Reims and in some of the figures of the south transept portal at Chartres.

Among the grandest examples of German sculpture of the mid-to-late 13th century are the figures of the rulers of the house of Wettin in the choir of Naumburg Cathedral. They appear to be real portraits, but are in fact brilliantly stylized figures, which seem to be expressive not of physical reality but of idealized character. By the 14th century the portrait makes a real appearance in Germany and France and is further shown in the heads by Peter Parler at Prague Cathedral and in the work of Tilman Riemenschneider at Rottenberg ob der Tauber in the early 16th century (although this already indicates a change in style). One of the major types of altarpiece popular in Germany is the 'Schnitzaltar', a complex of carved wood among which one of the largest is at Blaubeuren Abbey of 1483–4 by M. and G. Erhart, and the most memorable is the Isenheim Altar by *Grünewald with the sculpture by Nikolaus von Hagenau.

By the time Gothic finally established itself in Italy, the artist, thanks to Vasari, is rarely anonymous. Arnolfo di Cambio is probably more famous as the architect of Sta Croce and Florence Cathedral than as a sculptor, but his *Monument to Cardinal de Braye* in San Domenico, Orvieto, of *c.*1282, is a totally new form of tomb, and one which continued for about two centuries. At Orvieto, the panels outside the cathedral attributed to Lorenzo Maitani have a thin, febrile quality, quite different from the more energetic quality of Romanesque sculptors such as Antelami in Parma. The works of Giovanni Pisano in Pisa and Siena mark a change in style from that of his father. In Florence, Orcagna's Tabernacle in Or San Michele with the *Death and Assumption of the Virgin* was begun in 1355; the first resurgence of art after the Black Death of 1347–8 stresses the hieratic, symbolic, and emotional, and it is to this end that vivid facial expressions and gestures are used. Andrea Pisano's first pair of doors for the Baptistery of 1330 were the models set for the 1401 competition which *Ghiberti won. Andrea's son Nino worked in both Florence and Pisa, where he made the tender and softly modelled *Madonna and Child* (Pisa, Mus.), once in Sta Maria della Spina. Among the important forms of monument are the various large shrines commemorating, for instance, S. Peter Martyr in Sant'Eustorgio, Milan, of 1339, and S. Augustine in San Pietro in Ciel d'Oro in Pavia of *c.*1342–60, both by Giovanni di Balduccio, and the similar grand shrine of S. Dominic in San Domenico, Bologna, of *c.*1267, the work of many hands from Nicola Pisano and his school, and Niccolò dell'Arca up to the final figures by *Michelangelo in 1494/5. Among the important works are those by Jacopo della *Quercia in the early 15th century, including the tomb of Ilaria del Carretto in Lucca Cathedral of 1405–8, the Fonte Gaia in Siena of 1414–19, and the panels round the door of San Petronio, Bologna, begun in 1425 and which only stopped with the artist's death in 1438.

Painting all over Europe followed the same trends as those characterizing the sculpture of the age: the forms are more slender, there is more emphasis on grace and charm, and above all more interest in, and stress on, the naturalistic in setting and in the treatment of figures, in the rendering of animals, and the management of perspective space within the picture. In 14th-century panel paintings, the gold ground remains the norm, and in big polyptychs in Italy the elaborate frames become more complicated and spiky. In Italy also fresco cycles become very important.

Very little medieval painting has survived in England because of the depredations of the Reformation and later of the Puritans: the battered wreckage of the superb Westminster retable survives to illustrate the quality of much of what is lost. Manuscripts fared better; once their jewelled or precious metal covers had been pulled off, the book itself was of no further interest. Fortunately, a large amount of stained glass has survived; the windows of Canterbury and York, of Merton College, Oxford, of Tewkesbury Abbey, as well as individual windows in many parish churches. Another great art of which examples have survived in Italy, as well as in England, is *opus anglicanum, a highly valued form of embroidery for vestments and altar frontals popular for royal gifts to popes and prelates. Books of *Hours became an important aspect of MSS painting all over Europe from the 13th century onwards. No great noble or lady could be without one.

The *Parement de Narbonne* (Louvre), an altar frontal with the *Crucifixion* and scenes of the Passion, in grisaille on silk for Lenten use, painted *c.*1370, is a fine example of French 14th-century painting, and at this time artists also began to paint private devotional pictures on such themes as the *Pietà*.

Fourteenth- and early 15th-century painting in the Empire is strongly influenced by Italian art—*Giotto and Simone *Martini lie behind the flowering of Bohemian *International Gothic painting in Prague and the style spread to Nuremberg and to Cologne and was the main stimulus in the creation of the 'soft style' 'Beautiful Madonnas'—tender, swaying Madonnas, serene and noble ladies, in delicate colour and charming settings such as the *Garden of Paradise* of *c.*1420 (Frankfurt, Städelisches Mus.), or of Konrad von Soest, in his altarpiece of the *Crucifixion* in Nieder-Wildungen, of 1404, where the stark tragedy of the event is mitigated by the grieving Holy Women, the rich clothes of the officials, and playful dogs.

Italian art of the 13th century is still Romanesque; how rational is it to try to push 14th-century painting into the strait-jacket of a style in which it does not belong? The art of *Cimabue, Giotto, *Duccio, or Simone Martini is better described as medieval rather than Gothic, although there is a case for that description in Orcagna's Strozzi Altar (Florence, Sta Croce), and in the irrational, spiky world of Stefano da Zevio or Giovanni di Paolo.

Gothic Revival The notion that Gothic architecture was peculiarly appropriate for ecclesiastical buildings dates back to the Renaissance. Tellingly, when Archbishop William Laud (1573–1645) sought to symbolize religion in his classically inspired Canterbury Quadrangle at St John's College, Oxford (1631–6), he did so with the carving of a Gothic church. The term 'Gothic' (*dei Gotthi*) itself is also a product of the Renaissance, coined by Giorgio *Vasari (1511–74) to describe the architecture of the proceeding centuries. It was brought into common use in English as an architectural description by John Evelyn (1620–1706), who referred to 'a certain Fantastical and Licentious Manner of building, which we have since call'd *Modern* (or *Gothic* rather)', in his translation of Fréart de Chambray's *Parallèle* (1707).

As this suggests, although early-modern architects and writers accepted that medieval models might be contextually appropriate for certain buildings, they tended to see Gothic architecture as inherently inferior to a more classical approach. Thus, in some of his London churches, Sir Christopher *Wren found himself 'oblig'd to deviate from a better style', adopting a revived Gothic architecture to suit the site. Similarly, his pupil, Nicholas *Hawksmoor, was willing to use forms derived from medieval architecture in his additions to All Souls College, Oxford (1708–30) and Westminster Abbey (1734–45), and was even content to describe Gothic as a product of 'ye purest times of Christianity'. Nonetheless, given a free hand, he invariably chose classical architecture, seeing Gothic as sometimes suitable but also second-best.

The idea that Gothic architecture might be superior to the classical styles that succeeded it is a product of the 18th century. As early as 1716, the Gothic Temple at Shotover Park, Oxfordshire was set up to symbolize the tradition of English Liberty—a liberty that was believed to owe its origins to the Goths. This appropriation of Gothic as a national style was to prove enormously important, both in popularizing it as a secular architecture and also in influencing church building. By the 1770s, *The Builder's Magazine* was claiming that the 'Grecian taste certainly best suits ... publick buildings ... but for religious structures, Gothic, undoubtedly, ought to be preferred'.

The attractions of the Gothic as a national architecture and as a Christian style were enhanced by parallel developments in art, literature, and antiquarianism. The appeal of medieval building as an exemplification of the Romantic ideal of the sublime was made plain in the paintings of Caspar David *Friedrich and J. M. W. Turner (1775–1851). The rise of the Gothic novel in English and the growth of the German *Sturm und Drang* (storm and stress) movement both contributed to a renewed interest in medieval forms. Finally, a still more scholarly approach to the architecture itself enabled designers and commentators to articulate a clearer sense of what Gothic actually amounted to. The research of the antiquary Thomas Rickman (1776–1841) proved particularly important in this respect, not least by categorizing the development of medieval styles into Norman, Early-English, Decorated, and Perpendicular, and helping to distinguish between the Romanesque and the Gothic.

This Gothic Revival was a genuinely pan-European movement, with Johann Wolfgang von Goethe (1749–1842) wanting to substitute the term 'German' for 'Gothic' and the French politician François-René de Chateaubriand (1768–1848) celebrating the contributions of his own nation to the style in his *Génie du Christianisme* (1802). Much of the early 19th century would be dominated by debates over the real origin of Gothic architecture, with French, German, and British writers all claiming the credit for their respective countrymen.

In England, this patriotic emphasis would prove especially attractive to the beleaguered Church of England, which turned with increasing commitment to Gothic architecture in the 1820s, partly because of its presumed cheapness in comparison with the ornamentation required by classical designs, but mainly because these neomedieval forms stressed the continuity of the Church as an English institution, its long-standing place within the national community. From the 1840s, too, the writings of the Roman Catholic architect Augustus *Pugin and the agitation of the High-Church *Cambridge Camden Society further entrenched these attitudes by deliberately eliding the distinction between faith and style. For them—and for an increasing number of Anglicans—only Gothic architecture was Christian architecture. Classicism, the product of ancient Greece and Rome, was now seen as pagan.

Not everyone accepted such an analysis, it must be said. Many English non-conformists and some evangelical Anglicans instinctively rejected this medieval turn. The pious Protestant parson Francis Close (1797–1882) spoke for them in arguing that *The 'Restoration of Churches' is the Restoration of Popery* (1845). Some Roman Catholics, too, argued that Gothic was inappropriate for the Tridentine Rite (*see* TRENT), preferring to adopt *Baroque styles more closely associated with the modern papacy. But the general belief that Gothic was the English ecclesiastical architectural style *sans-pareil* is hard to deny. Certainly, the extent to which other denominations eventually adopted neomedievalism is striking, with the Congregationalist architect James Cubitt (1836–1912) and the Wesleyan Minister F. J. Jobson (1812–82) each arguing that for their chapels only Gothic would do. Even the Society of Friends acquired a number of Gothic Meeting Houses.

As a result, the mid-19th century witnessed a remarkable revival of Gothic architecture. Much of this was secular—from Charles Barry (1795–1860) and Augustus Pugin's new Palace of Westminster (1840–52) to George Edmund *Street's Royal Courts of Justice (1873–82). Still more was religious, with hundreds of new churches erected and thousands restored. In a generation, architects moved from the sort of English Perpendicular initially praised by Pugin to the early French adopted by William Burges (1827–81), and back again. Amongst the most prolific Gothic architects of the day was George Gilbert *Scott, who favoured 13th-century English work. One of the most original was William *Butterfield, whose church of All Saints, Margaret Street (1849–59) was an elaborate polychromatic confection of themes derived from England, Italy, and beyond. All these architects also built abroad, especially in Britain's colonial dependencies, taking the Gothic Revival and planting it in Canada, Australia, India, and elsewhere.

Beyond the British Empire, the Gothic Revival had a certain following in Germany, and Scott's winning the competition for the Nikolaikirche in Hamburg in 1844 placed him in the forefront of revivalists. Cologne Cathedral, left unfinished by its original Gothic builders, was brought, between 1824 and 1880, to a conclusion in an imitation of the original. In Austria, Ferstel's Votivkirche in Vienna, 1856–79, is a recreation of the true Gothic of Ulm and Freiburg, crossed with the two-towered silhouette of Cologne. In France, the main Gothic Revival architects were Gau, at Ste-Clothilde in Paris, 1846–57, Lassus at St-Jean-de-Belleville, Paris, and *Viollet-le-duc, at St-Denis-de-l'Estrée in St-Denis outside Paris in 1864–7. In Italy, little Gothic Revival was necessary; its most notable examples are the façade of Milan Cathedral, a project revived under Napoleon in 1805 and completed by C. Amati in 1813, and in Florence the façades of the cathedral by Emilio de Fabris in 1866–87, and of Sta Croce from 1857 to 1863 by Niccolò Matas. Another extraordinary manifestation of the interest in Gothic is Gaudi's eccentric Sagrada Familia in Barcelona, begun in 1881 and still unfinished; and there was an interest in the style in America: for instance, Renwick's St Patrick's Roman Catholic Cathedral in New York, 1859–79, with a later spire.

By the third quarter of the 19th century and well into the 20th century, the unquestioned form in English church building was the Gothic Revival style, as may be seen in the Anglican Cathedral, Liverpool (1904–78), by Giles Gilbert Scott (1880–1960). In the United States, too, G. F. Bodley's (1827–1907) National Cathedral, Washington DC (1907–90) effectively illustrates the continued appeal of the Gothic, not least for Episcopalians. The Gothic Revival tower erected at St Edmundsbury Cathedral between 2000 and 2005 to designs by Stephen Dykes Bower (1903–94), is evidence not only of the perennial attractiveness of the style but also of a return to Wren's argument for its use when contextually appropriate. *See also* NEO-CLASSICISM.

Gothic vestments *See* VESTMENTS.

graffiti (Ital.) Everyone knows what modern graffiti are: scrawls defacing any surface offering scope for this form of destructive exhibitionism. The urge to do this is not only a modern craze; examples can be found throughout history from classical times onwards. One form has yielded valuable information. These are the *graffiti* made by Early Christians, pilgrims, mourners, and visitors, mainly in the Roman *catacombs and under *St Peter's. They are found in Latin and Greek, literate and illiterate, sometimes scratched into the surface, sometimes written in chalk or charcoal with names and dates. Many include invocations and prayers, accompanied even by crude drawings; they were studied and recorded in detail by G. B. de' *Rossi. They range from a list of names in the Catacomb of S. Calixtus, probably a record of those buried in the *cubicula*, to inscriptions such as, in the Catacomb of Priscilla, *Paule vives* (Paul, may you live), or in the Catacomb of SS Peter and Marcellinus, *Marciane dormi in pace* (Marcian, sleep in peace), or another in the same catacomb marking a family grave, *Locus severi* under a crude *Chi-Rho. In the papal crypt of the Catacomb of S. Calixtus many *graffiti* are scratched one over the other, some of the upper layers being by barbarians: *Ildebran*, and *Etele(d)i ep.*, presumably a northern bishop called Ethelred. Many *graffiti* are invocations, a frequent one being forms of *petite pro me Eustachi* (pray for me, Eustace) and *Sante Suste in mente habeas in horationes Aureliu repentinu* (Saint Sixtus, remember in your prayers penitent Aurelius). In the Catacomb of Priscilla an inscription records three pilgrims from Gaul dated 24 March 375. Some *graffiti* are plainly pagan, for instance ones ending in injunctions to come with a flask of wine for a libation, indicating that the same catacomb served both for Christian and pagan dead. Efforts to stamp out the bringing of wine and food into the catacombs were made by S. Ambrose in Milan in 384, and in Rome the practice died out when the great basilicas were built over the catacombs, as at San Sebastiano, and Sant'Agnese fuori le Mura. These became burial chuches, as did St Peter's which, when it was rebuilt in the 16th and 17th centuries, yielded hundreds of graves in the nave, the bones from which were placed in two crypts under the later building.

Grail, the Holy A complex legend involving *Joseph of Arimathaea and King Arthur, deriving from Celtic mixed with Middle Eastern legends. According to the original story, the Grail was the cup used at the Last Supper, which came into the possession of Joseph, who used it to contain the blood and water when he washed Christ's body for burial. Another version is that it was used to catch the blood and water issuing from Christ's side after it was pierced by *Longinus with the *Holy Lance.

Around 1200 this legend was conflated with the legend of King Arthur and his Knights, the Grail being a symbol of perfection: according to this, Joseph came to Britain, to Glastonbury, from where the Grail was eventually taken up into Heaven (or was buried and lost). None of this ever received any ecclesiastical recognition, but it developed into a poem, *Parzifal*, written *c.*1205 by Wolfram von Eschenbach, a Bavarian knight and epic poet and 'Minnesinger' (troubadour is the closest equivalent) who wrote *c.*1200–20 and whose poem later influenced literature and music—Malory, Tennyson, Wagner—but not the visual arts, except as illustrations to the poems. Visual representations of the theme can be seen in the *Quest for the Holy Grail* and *The Attainment: the Vision of the Holy Grail to Sir Galahad* (1890–94), tapestries by Edward Burne-Jones, William Morris, and John Henry Dearle (Private Collection, London).

grapes *See* FLOWERS AND FRUIT.

graven images In Puritan North America for much of the colonial period (specifically in the US) the attitude towards Christian art was iconoclastic, and for the most part, the only art identifiable as Christian was the work of limners and carvers who made funeral and memorial tablets and gravestones, in addition to the painted portraits of Christian clergy. Much later, as a result of the Civil War and in the spirit of the American Renaissance and Civil Religion, sculptors such as Daniel Chester French and Augustus Saint-Gaudens produced memorial reliefs and statuary that helped establish their international reputations. *See also* NORTH AMERICA.

Grayfriars *See* FRANCISCANS.

Greco (Domenikos Theotokopulos), (1541–1614), known as El Greco, was Cretan by origin. He received some training in Crete (a signed icon of the *Dormition* exists in Syros) before he moved to Venice, where he is said to have been a pupil in Titian's workshop; certainly his main training was in Venice, where the principal influence on him seems to have been *Tintoretto. He moved to Rome *c.*1570, where he is said to have played an inglorious role in the controversy over Michelangelo's *Last Judgement*, being reported to have said that if it were destroyed he would repaint it and that he 'would have made it with honesty and decorum suitable for good quality in painting'. Pacheco, in his *Arte de la Pintura* records that in 1611, when comparing Titian and Michelangelo, El Greco said that 'Michelangelo was a good man, but he did not know how to paint'.

By 1577 he was in Toledo; why, and when, he went to Spain is unknown, though it may well have been because of his attacks on Michelangelo's nudes in the Sistine Chapel. There is some evidence that he had friends, if not family, in Toledo.

His first work in Toledo was the high altar and two side altars in Sto Domingo el Antiguo, painted between 1577 and 1579, which was the time limit specified for eight of the pictures involved. The *Assumption* (now in Chicago) is over 16 ft. high, and the *Trinity* (now Prado), nearly 10 ft. high, was placed above it. The *Assumption* was flanked by the figures of the two Saints John—the *Baptist* on the left and the *Evangelist* on the right (both these are still *in situ*, whereas the original large works have been replaced by copies). Above them were half-length figures of *S. Bernard* (private coll.) and *S. Benedict* (Prado), and crowning the *Assumption* was an image of the *Holy Face* imprinted on *Veronica's napkin, which probably replaced the donor's arms. The side altars contained an *Adoration of the Shepherds* (private coll.) and a *Resurrection* (still *in situ*) both 7 ft. high. This huge complex shows that El Greco's art was fully developed at the very start of his Spanish career. It also shows how much he was influenced by Venetian example, since the scale of these works is on a par with Titian's *Assumption* in Sta Maria de' Frari.

He tried, but failed, to obtain court patronage from Philip II, whose preferences lay with the serene, controlled art of Titian; the Mannerism of El Greco's *Martyrdom of the Theban Legion* was so alien to the king's tastes that he rejected the picture. El Greco remained in Toledo for the rest of his life, and continued to produce huge altarpieces of passionate and ecstatic feeling, violent in changes of scale, sharp and acid in colour, with a quivering emotionalism which reaches perhaps the highest peaks of religious expression. He was conditioned by his Venetian training, by his own religious devotion, and also by the strong influence of the **Spiritual Exercises* of *S. Ignatius, the Spanish founder of the Jesuit Order. The practice of the *Exercises* encourages an immediacy of experience, a mental participation in the events and details of the sufferings of Christ's Passion, which clearly heightened his artistic imagination and imparted to his works great emotional intensity. Artistically, he carried to Spain with him the influences of what he had seen in Venice and on his way to, and in, Rome, and these stem from such diverse sources as Dürer's engravings, Titian, Tintoretto (in particular), Bassano, Pontormo, Parmigianino, Raphael, and even the disliked Michelangelo. But these influences were so thoroughly assimilated that they are entirely submerged in his own artistic personality. He also introduced into Spanish art the influence of his native Byzantine experience, almost certainly reinforced by Byzantine survivals in Venice.

One of the many remarkable characteristics of his pictures is his predilection for the vertical; even his many individual heads of saints and of Christ (a very important part of his œuvre) tend to be uprights, and of his four known landscapes only one is a horizontal canvas, and there is only a rare roundel or square one.

The format facilitates and probably also encouraged the internal verticality of his treatment of his subject; saints and incidents from the NT (no OT subjects are known) are often surmounted by ecstatic visions of angels, and placed high in the picture space with groups of worshippers clustered below. His vision did not always meet with approval.

The *Espolio* (the Disrobing of Christ), which he painted in the same years as the Sto Domingo el Antiguo commission, was rejected by the Toledo Cathedral Chapter, who complained that Christ was represented disrespectfully by being surrounded by his executioners in such a way that some of them stood higher in the picture than He did. El Greco sued them for his fee, and the assessors unanimously praised the picture and supported his claim; the popularity of the picture is attested by many copies. But the objection to it is very revealing of the attitude of clerical commissioners to any novel treatment of such a subject, and the experience made the artist very wary of any similar exercise of artistic licence. For instance, in his most celebrated work, the *Burial of the Conde de Orgaz* (Toledo, San Tomé) painted in nine months despite its huge size of 15 ft. by nearly 12 ft., the celestial vision occupies well over half the picture and the miracle of the intervention of the two saints dominates—as it should—the foreground, leaving the ranks of the spectators crammed into serried rows between them.

The dead man was Gonzalo Ruiz, Lord of Orgaz, who died in 1323. He was a benefactor of the church of San Tomé and in his will he left a charge on the town as a bequest to the priest of San Tomé, and the legend of his funeral is that because of his charitable life he was borne to his tomb in the church by S. Stephen and S. Augustine. After many years the townsfolk of Orgaz, which is part of Toledo, refused to continue to pay the money. The parish priest sued them, and in 1570 won his case. It was to commemorate this that the Archbishop of Toledo authorized in 1580 the painting of the picture for which the town of Orgaz had to pay. El Greco had difficulty in obtaining his fee, for the value of the work was assessed so highly, but the surprising thing is that so grand a picture should have been painted to commemorate so obscure, so local, and so singular a miracle.

His son Jorge Manuel, born in 1578, worked in his father's workshop, but was very slenderly endowed with talent. The only really capable artist who was in the workshop and whose independent work was strongly influenced by El Greco was Luis Tristán (1585/6–1624). The workshop itself was very well organized and played a large part in the production of series of half-length figures of Saints, Evangelists, Apostles, Christ crowned with thorns or blessing, the Holy Face with or without S. Veronica holding the cloth, and large numbers of Adorations of the Shepherds (always Shepherds, never Kings), Assumptions, Immaculate Conceptions, Baptisms of Christ, and Resurrections, many produced on almost identical designs with variations only in such details as the angels or ancillary figures, or in the colours.

Greek Church, Fathers of the *See* EASTERN ORTHODOX CHURCHES, FATHERS.

Greek cross *See* CROSS and CHURCH ARCHITECTURE.

green *See* LITURGICAL COLOURS.

Gregory, Mass of Saint, was a legend, first found in the 15th century, which is not mentioned in any of the Lives of the saint, or even in the **Golden Legend*, to the effect that a vision of Christ as the Man of Sorrows, often accompanied by the Instruments of the *Passion, the *Arma Christi, appeared to the saint while celebrating Mass, but was not seen by the other people present. It seems to have originated in a Byzantine mosaic in Sta Croce, Florence, which was engraved by I. van Meckenen (*c.*1450–*c.*1503), with an inscription saying that S. Gregory had caused it to be made following his vision. It became immensely popular because of the indulgences attached to it, and cheap woodcuts were sold at fairs. Its popularity was concentrated in Germany and the North, not in Italy, and was killed by the Reformation. Three miracles are sometimes represented together, as in the three-part reredos relief by Luigi Capponi (late 15th cent., Rome, San Gregorio Magno), two showing the saint saying Mass while souls released from Purgatory by his intercession appear behind the altar, and in the third the bleeding Christ appears from the chalice, one version of the legend saying that this was to convince a woman who doubted the transubstantiation. Among the many other representations of this subject and variants on it is its appearance on the left side of *Quarton's *Coronation of the Virgin*, a woodcut by Dürer (1511), with Christ emerging from the altar with the Instruments of the Passion, and paintings of the same subject by Bernt Notke (1504: Lübeck, Marienkirche) and by Hans

Baldung Grien (1511: Cleveland). Guercino painted the *Soul of the monk Justus released from Purgatory* for San Paolo, Bologna, in 1647, and variants on this subject include the release of the soul of the Emperor Trajan. *See also* ELEVATION OF THE HOST.

Gregory the Great, Saint (Pope Gregory I), (*c.*540–604), was the son of a senator and became prefect of Rome in 573. He founded a Benedictine monastery in his own house, and became a monk there in 574. He used his great wealth in Sicily to found monasteries there, and his Roman wealth to relieve poverty, and to endow his Roman monastery, later rebuilt and rededicated to him as San Gregorio Magno. In *c.*578 he was sent to Constantinople as the pope's diplomatic representative. He became the spiritual guide of members of the imperial family, but came to have a low opinion of the court, and a distaste for Byzantine politics which influenced him when he became pope. He returned to Rome *c.*585, and Bede's famous story of his seeing fair-haired Anglo-Saxon children in the Roman slave-market and describing them as 'Not Angles but Angels' has the ring of truth, since Gregory sent a mission to England in 596, led by monks from his own monastery, headed by *S. Augustine of Canterbury.

He became pope in 590, when Italy was devastated by floods which swept away the granaries holding Rome's grain store, followed by famine and plague. Invasions by Goths and Lombards ravaged the North, and cities were abandoned as people fled to the lagoons. He had to contend with Byzantine attempts to supersede Rome as the spiritual head of the Christian Church, and in 593, in opposition to Byzantine policy, he made a separate peace with the Lombard invaders. Despite his worsening relations with Byzantium, he tried to improve relations with the *Exarch of Ravenna, and with the Lombards, through Queen Theodolinda, to whom he sent the *ampullae now in the Treasury of Monza Cathedral. He strove to remedy the deplorable state of the Church in Gaul, caused by bad rulers, civil war, and poor quality churchmen, and in Visigothic Spain he obtained the rejection of the Arian heresy in favour of orthodox Catholicism.

His major books were the *Liber Regulae Pastoralis* of *c.*591, on the duties of bishops—translated into English by Alfred the Great—and the *Dialogues* of *c.*593, on the life and miracles of S. Benedict and other saints, which served, despite some indiscriminate acceptance of wonders, as a model for later hagiographers, such as the author of the **Golden Legend*. His sermons and his letters show his extensive pastoral and political activity.

He is one of the four Latin *Doctors of the Church, and the first to describe the pope as 'the servant of the servants of God'. He prepared the original Gregorian Sacramentary, one of the early forms of the Mass, and established Gregorian Chant by reorganizing the *scholae cantorum*. He was canonized by popular acclaim immediately after his death, and is portrayed as early as the 9th century, in a MS of his sermons (Trier), with the dove of the Holy Ghost on his shoulder, inspiring his words, and this imagery became fixed in e.g. a 10th-century MS showing him dictating his instructions to bishops (Paris, BN), and in a column figure in the south porch of Chartres Cathedral. Other images are a Zurbarán in Seville, the Veronese *Feast in the House of Levi* in the pilgrimage church of Monte Berico, Vicenza, and in the Rubens altarpiece in Sta Maria in Vallicella, Rome. Many miracles were associated with him, such as the release of souls (e.g. the monk Justus and the Emperor Trajan) from Purgatory at his intercession, the ending of a plague in Rome after a vision of the Archangel Michael sheathing his sword over the Castel Sant'Angelo (commemorated in the gilded figure over the castle), and the miracle of the dalmatic (or shroud) of the Baptist which he gave to the Empress Constantia and she rejected as unauthentic: he cut it with a knife and it bled. A painting of this by Andrea Sacchi of 1625, which includes the dove of the Holy Ghost, is in the Vatican Gallery. By far the most famous of the miracles attributed to him, but not mentioned until almost a thousand years after his death, is the 'Mass of S. Gregory' (see below).

Grey Friars *See* FRANCISCANS.

Gribble, Herbert (1847–94), was the architect of the Brompton Oratory in London, the first Italianate Catholic church in England to challenge the prevailing Gothic Revival of *Pugin. A competition was held in 1878 for which the specified style was Italian Renaissance, because John Henry Newman (later Cardinal) pointed out that Gothic would not be a sensible choice for the Congregation of the *Oratory, founded in 1564. Gribble's winning design, built 1880–4, was a combination of *Alberti's Sant'Andrea, Mantua, *Vignola's

Gesù, and the Oratorians' own Chiesa Nuova (Sta Maria in Vallicella) in Rome, and far closer to Roman Baroque than to Renaissance. This effect is heightened by the wide aisleless domed nave, by the rich marble revetment of the piers, and by the twelve marble statues of the Apostles by the Baroque sculptor Giuseppe Mazzuoli, carved between 1679 and 1695, which were bought for the Oratory in 1895 when they were removed from Siena Cathedral, which was 're-Gothicized' in 1890. The Baroque inlaid marble altar of the Lady Chapel, together with its statues, originally erected in 1693 in San Domenico, Brescia, was re-erected in the Oratory in 1883. Gribble died while he was working on the revised 1891 design of the colonnaded portico.

griffin, gryphon, a mythical beast, described in a mid-13th-century *Bestiary (Bodley MS 764) as follows: 'the Gryphon is at once feathered and four-footed ... The hinder part of its body is like a lion: its wings and face are like an eagle. It hates the horse bitterly, and if it comes face to face with a man, it will attack him.'

Because it had four feet, but also had wings, it was classed—without being specifically named—among the unclean creatures (Lev. 11: 13–20) because it combined two separate types of creature, a bird and a beast. It was also credited with the power of discovering and hoarding gold and, as a guardian of treasure, it was placed on portals and gates, which caused it to become one of the symbols of knowledge (*Scientia*), but ambivalently also of usury. Its supposed combination of the courage of the lion and the acuity of the eagle suggested to Dante that it could be used as a symbol of Christ. It also frequently appears in heraldry.

Grünewald (*c.*1470/80–1528). Mathis Neithardt-Gothardt was first mentioned by the Reformer Melancthon, who probably knew him, in 1531. He called him a lesser artist than *Dürer, but infinitely superior to Cranach. Mathis was first called Grünewald by Sandrart, his earliest biographer, in 1675–9, about 150 years after the artist's death. He is presumed to have been born in Würzburg *c.*1470/80, and a Master Mathis held an appointment as court painter at the Prince-Bishop's court in Mainz between 1508 and 1526. As a result of his extreme Protestant sympathies he was in Frankfurt in 1526 and in 1527 he moved to Halle, where he died in 1528. There are no fully signed works, but two paintings have the initials MGN and two drawings also have rudimentary initials. The group of works ascribed to him has an unarguable homogeneity, however, which marks them as the products of an artistic intelligence which stands at the opposite pole to Dürer, to whom, astonishingly, they were once attributed. Grünewald's characteristics are his use of emotional distortion and his brilliant—fantastic even—use of colour. His major work, the Isenheim Altar (Colmar, Mus.), was painted between 1512 and 1516 for the chapel of a lazar-house and is a complex work on three separate layers, of which the central panels of the first two layers divide so that they close over the one below. The lowest layer is a carved altarpiece by Nikolaus Hagenauer, finished *c.*1505, of S. Antony Abbot enthroned between S. Augustine and S. Jerome, with a *predella* with five niches in which is a Christ blessing flanked by the Apostles. The *predella* was carved by Desiderius Berchel, and this form of carved wooden altarpiece is a common German form.

When closed, the *Crucifixion* is visible—a stunning vision of agony, grief, and horror. Christ hangs from the cross at the moment of death, His hands distorted by the agony of the nails, His feet twisted and distorted by the huge nail that transfixes them. His body is spattered with bloodstains and His head, sagging to one side, streams with the blood flowing from the crown of vicious thorns. No other Crucified Christ in all Western art exceeds this one as an expression of the full ghastly horror of Christ's terrible death. On one side the distraught Virgin is upheld by S. John, and at their feet the grief-stricken Magdalene kneels, weeps, wails in despair. On the other side stands the Baptist, book in hand, and with an outstretched finger points to the Christ of whom he was the forerunner. At his feet is the Lamb holding a reed cross, with blood gushing from its heart into the chalice of the Eucharist in front of it.

This, therefore, is not a simple image, though a terrible one, of the Crucifixion. On one plane it is the most terrifying exposition of the agony endured by the Redeemer, and the grief of the onlookers; on another plane it is a vision embodying the words said every day on the altar above which it stands: 'Behold the Lamb of God who takes away the sins of the world', and in front of S. John the Baptist is inscribed the text from S. John the Evangelist (3: 30): 'He must increase but I must decrease.' On yet another plane, the altarpiece expresses the function of the place where it stood; the chapel of a lazar-house, a place where the inmates were separated from the world, cast out because of the skin and nervous diseases with which they were afflicted. They were invited to see in Christ's body a reflection of themselves and their sufferings, to realize that outward disfigurement does not imply inward lack of grace, and as Christ though blameless suffered the ultimate in degradation and death and yet rose again to the splendour of eternal life, so they too might aspire through their sufferings and their penitence—for unlike Christ, no man is sinless—to a rebirth in a regenerated state. For this reason, the pointing Baptist stresses mankind's way to salvation, and the Lamb and the chalice with the blood of the sacrifice flowing into it are reminders that the way to renewal lies through the sacraments.

On either side of the *Crucifixion* are panels with, on the left, *S. Sebastian*, one of the 'plague saints', and on the right, *S. Antony Abbot*, patron saint of the Antonines, the Order running lazar-houses, because he was invoked against 'S. Anthony's fire', or erysipelas. Below in the *predella* is a *Lamentation over the dead Christ*.

When the wings are opened—for the *Crucifixion* splits down the middle—on the left wing is the *Annunciation*, which takes place in a curtained-off part of a chapel. The kneeling Virgin casts a bashful sidelong glance at her heavenly visitant, who is propelled by a swirling wind, while in the spandrel of the arch above her the prophet Isaiah holds an open book inscribed with the prophecy beginning 'Behold a Virgin shall conceive and bear a son'. The central part is an *Allegory of the Nativity* where, in a rocky landscape, the Virgin nurses the Holy Child while an orchestra of musician angels and little *amoretti* in a fantastic Gothic shrine serenade her and the Infant Christ, and accompany with their music a vision of the pregnant Virgin aureoled in golden and flaming light. In front of her, on the step, is the glass vase of clear water which is one of the symbols of her virginity. In the sky above the Virgin and Child is a vision of Heaven with God the Father in a glory of golden light, and below on the mountain top scintillating angels bring the message to the shepherds.

The right-hand wing has a *Resurrection*, with Christ rising from the tomb in an aureole of brilliant light, with His arms outstretched to show his pierced hands. The stricken guards fall away from the empty tomb in terror, blinded by the miracle. The *Allegory of the Nativity* opens in the middle to reveal the carved saints in their niches, and the *predella* of the *Lamentation* splits to reveal the carved *predella* of *Christ and the Apostles*. The carved centrepiece is flanked on either side by visions of the two hermits *SS Antony Abbot and Paul the Hermit* conversing quietly while the natural world around them is wildly tormented. On the other side is a *Temptation of S. Antony*, where the saint is the helpless victim of a nightmare of terrifying devils with, in the foreground, a devil suffering the ghastly torments of an inmate of the hospital. The background is a serene vision of icy mountains with the celestial conflict of Good and Evil.

This huge work is nearly 9 ft. high by 16 ft. wide when closed, and the total painted surface of all ten panels is over 50 ft. in width, plus the painted *predella* which measures over 2 ft. high by 11 ft. wide. The work is unusual and impressive, not only for its iconography but also for its outstanding colour. Although Grünewald's vision is essentially German in character, this does not mean that he was oblivious of, or rejected, the rapidly percolating influence of Italian Renaissance art; it is that the use he makes of it is quite different from Dürer, and in fact many of Dürer's engravings have a visionary quality of which his own paintings do not partake. Where Dürer used the Renaissance to achieve balance and control, Grünewald uses its lessons in perspective and in an almost Leonardesque creation of a naturalistic world to further his intensely dramatic poetic vision.

There are several other versions of the *Crucifixion*, notably in Washington (NG), and Basle, and one at Karlsrühe combined with a *Christ falling on the road to Calvary*, in which the brutality of the executioners is depicted with vivid realism. It is the only one of his works to have a biblical quotation in German.

gryphon *See* GRIFFIN.

guardian angel *See* ANGEL.

Guarini, Guarino (1624–83), was perhaps the most innovative Italian Baroque architect of the late 17th century. He was born in Modena, joined the *Theatine Order, and during his novitiate in Rome studied the architecture of *Bernini and *Borromini, who were then working. After ordination in 1648, he wrote treatises on mathematics, geometry, fortification, philosophy, and theology, which he taught in Modena until 1655. In 1660 he was in Messina, where he built his first church, destroyed in the 1908 earthquake. In 1662 he was in Paris, where he built Ste-Anne-la-Royale; it was praised by Bernini in 1665, and its remarkable double dome must also have impressed Wren, who was then in Paris. The building was partly finished in 1720, but demolished in 1823.

He may have been in Lisbon, where Sta Maria da Divina Providencia was built to his design, but it was destroyed in the earthquake of 1755. He was in Turin from 1666, where he took over the partly built church of his Order, San Lorenzo, transforming the design into a remarkable central plan with deep alternating concave and convex chapels. Over the central space, an open dome of superimposed interlaced arches supports the lantern, similarly built up from interlaced arches, so that a flood of light enters through the windows inserted in the web of arches. There is a similar dome over the altar, and an oval choir beyond. The body of the church has a rich decoration of dark-coloured marble, in contrast with the brilliant light above. The mystery of the design is heightened when it is realized that none of the elements, such as arches, pendentives, and piers, which normally would be the supporting members, supports anything, all the weight-bearing elements being concealed within the outer shell. Soon after his arrival in Turin he was asked to complete the chapel of the SS Sindone, the Holy *Shroud, believed to be Christ's shroud. This major relic of the House of Savoy was in a shrine built behind the apse of the cathedral, and visible from it. Work had stopped in 1667 when the black marble interior had reached the entablature. Guarini modified the interior by raising three large arches, one to span the opening to the choir, and the others to unify the entrances from the cathedral and from the royal palace. On these arches he raised a high drum with large windows within vaulted openings, crowned by arches which support a sequence of arches of decreasing span. These culminate in the lantern like an openwork star within which hovers the dove of the Holy Ghost, each row of arches having windows below them, so that the dome is flooded with light in contrast to the darkness of the chapel below. His architecture is deeply symbolic: the triple motive of the Trinity; the darkness of the tomb rising into the Resurrection; and, in San Lorenzo, the structural mystery of a building apparently upheld by invisible forces.

He recorded his works in his *Architettura Civile* and *Architettura Ecclesiastica*, conflated into a single volume in 1737 by his most inspired follower, Bernardo Vittone (1704/5–70), whose own churches are in remote country areas of Piedmont. Guarini's major influence was on the German Baroque architects of the 18th century. One remarkable feature of his writings is his understanding and appreciation of Gothic architecture, which—compared with Classical—he found to have qualities of mystery, surprise, and almost of the miraculous.

guild (Old Eng. *gi(e)ld*, payment) Throughout the Middle Ages a guild was an association of men, established for commercial, religious, and social purposes. The connection with 'payment' is that membership involved a fee. In general, particularly from the 13th to the 15th centuries, besides its charitable enterprises, the religious activity of a guild, in processions, ceremonies, and celebrations, in the founding of guild chapels, and the commissioning of guild altarpieces, such as the one by Piero della Francesca for the guild of the Misericordia in San Sepolcro, was an important part of its social presence. In the North, altarpieces showing S. Luke painting the Virgin and Child from life seem to have been a favoured subject for the chapels of the painters' guilds. An example by Roger van der *Weyden (Boston) was probably painted in the mid-15th century for the guild chapel in Brussels and many versions of it are known.

In craft guilds, entrants to the art or craft had to serve an apprenticeship, and in Germany had to complete a year (*Wanderjahr*) as a journeyman—literally, to travel to a master in another city and be employed in his workshop. Only then could he apply to become a master, which enabled him to have apprentices and his own workshop. The quality of his work, usually visible from public commissions, was an important factor in his position in the guild system, and most guilds also controlled materials, such as, in the Netherlands, the quality of the wood used for panel paintings.

Each art or trade had its own guild in the city where its members worked, which limited the mobility of artists. In Florence, for instance, the *Arte della Lana*, the wool guild, was the major guild because Florentine trade in woollen cloth was the city's largest industry, but only merchants and manufacturers belonged to the guild, not the workforce. The *Arte della Lana* was a major patron of art and architecture and was responsible for the competition for the Baptistery doors in 1401, paying for them until *Ghiberti completed his second pair in 1452. Painters belonged to the guild of *Medici e Speziali*—Doctors and spice dealers—because artists' colours were included among the spices imported from abroad, and S. Luke, S. Paul's 'beloved physician', was believed to have been a painter. Sculptors, masons, and builders were lumped together, and masons' guilds were among the most competitive and exclusive of all, as the building history of any great Gothic cathedral will attest. Orsanmichele, again in Florence, was turned into a church in 1366–80 and the guilds were made responsible for it: as a result, there are fourteen statues on the outside including three by Nanni di Banco—the *SS Quattro Coronati* (*see* CORONATI) for the Carpenters and Stonemasons, the *S. Philip* for the Stocking-makers, and the *S. Eligius* for the Smiths. *Donatello carved the *S. Peter* for the Butchers, *S. Mark* for the Weavers, and the *S. George* for the Armourers. Ghiberti made the *Baptist* for the Cloth Merchants, the *S. Matthew* for the Bankers, and the *S. Stephen* for the great Guild of Wool Merchants. Altogether, these commissions lasted from the late 14th century until the 16th.

The guild system could only be escaped by an artist holding a court appointment. He could then have assistants and apprentices. The system collapsed partly through the court artist's exemption being successfully exploited, but even more by the claims made by artists to be free of petty regulations through the God-given nature of their genius. Leonardo da Vinci was admitted to the Florentine guild in 1472 after being trained in Verrocchio's workshop, but was then a court artist in Milan. Michelangelo barely completed half of his four-year apprenticeship with Ghirlandaio, became a member of the Medici household, and never belonged to any guild. Through his faith in his own genius, and his continuous employment by the papacy, the system received a major set-back. In Venice, the guild system was made unnecessary by the *Scuole, which provided the prestige, patronage, social and charitable functions exercised by guilds elsewhere. Apprenticeship lasted longest because there was nowhere else to learn the art or craft, but it suffered an abrupt decline once Academies of art were founded in the 16th century, though they in turn came to exercise many of the functions of a guild.

The other form of guild is a purely religious association, like the Roman Catholic Guild of the Blessed Sacrament. Some modern craft guilds have been founded, such as Eric *Gill's Guild of SS Joseph and Dominic for the revival of religious art, but they are usually dependent on one man and are short-lived.

gynaeceum (Gk. pl. *gynaecea*) In Byzantine churches, the gynaecea were the galleries reserved for women. Usually, they were reached by staircases rising directly from the *narthex. In some Western churches separate areas, usually in the galleries or tribunes, were reserved for women; these were called matronea.

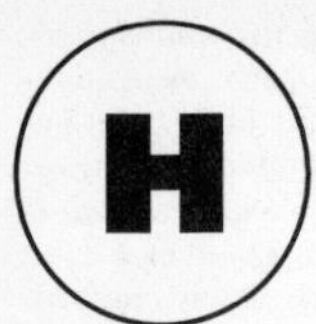

Habakkuk (Habacuc) *See* PROPHETS.

habits, monastic and religious Among the older religious Orders (e.g. Benedictines) it became usual to wear distinctive dress, marking them as members of a particular Order, and distinguishing them from laymen. The usual form was a long tunic with a belt or girdle, a cape (scapular) over the shoulders, a hood (veil for nuns), with a mantle for outdoors. The colours are usually dull—black for Benedictines, grey or brown for Franciscans, black and white for Dominicans. Secular priests wear more or less the same as laymen, usually black or grey, and Jesuits also wear secular-type *dress outside their houses. Most Orders of nuns always wear their habits, some variations to this rule being introduced for certain types of charitable or nursing work, and in America such exemptions are common. Anglicans and ministers of the Reformed Churches do not have any hard and fast rule, except that of decorum. *Vestments are worn only during liturgical functions. It is often possible to localize and identify works of art from the habits worn by the saints or donors portrayed.

Hades *See* LIMBO, UNDERWORLD.

Hagar was the Egyptian slave of Sarah, *Abraham's wife. Her story is told in the OT in Gen. 16 and 21, 25: 12. Sarah was barren and she proposed that Hagar should bear a child to Abraham, but became jealous when Hagar was pregnant. Hagar fled into the desert, but an angel persuaded her to return and Ishmael was born. Later, by a miracle, Sarah herself became pregnant at the age of 90, and *Isaac was born, after which Sarah persuaded Abraham to send Hagar and Ishmael away. Hagar placed Ishmael under a bush to die, but an angel appeared and showed her a well in the desert, which saved their lives.

Haggai (Vg. **Aggeus**) *See* PROPHETS.

Hagia Sophia *See* SOPHIA.

hagiography (Gk. *hagiographa*, holy writing) Writing about the lives and acts of saints. Such writings range between a farrago of credulous nonsense (much of the **Golden Legend*) and the strictest historical scholarship (*see* ACTA SANCTORUM). It is an unfortunate fact that the most improbable legends often make the best works of art.

hagioscope *See* SQUINT.

Hagiosoritissa A Byzantine iconographical theme of the Virgin in prayer, turned towards a bust of Christ or the Hand of God (DEXTERA DEI) in the upper corner.

Haidt, John Valentine (1700–1780), A Moravian church painter born in Danzig who trained as a goldsmith and studied drawing at the Royal Academy of Arts in Berlin. In 1745 he joined the Moravian community of Herrnhaag and became a lay preacher. By 1746 he was determined to paint rather than preach, and as a critique of developments in the Moravian church, declared that, 'if they will not preach the martyrdom of God anymore, I will paint it all the more vigorously'. In 1754 he left Europe for Bethlehem in Pennsylvania where he became an official church painter whose paintings were, according to Walter Peters, 'literally visual aids in expounding the Scriptures not only in Moravian churches but also in Moravian mission chapels among the Indian nations and other mission fields'. His paintings were primarily on Passion subjects: *Christ before Herod* (1762), *Christ Scourged* (1758), and *Lamentation over the Body of Christ* (1758). *See also* NORTH AMERICA.

hall-church A church in which the nave and the aisles are approximately the same height, and therefore lit from side windows. Churches of this type are mainly found in Germany (*Hallenkirchen*) from the 13th century onwards, although the earliest is 11th century.

The advantages of the form are the increased spaciousness and unity of the interior, with no transepts and the choir more closely related to the nave. It was an alternative to the Late Gothic drive for height. The form was also used in some German Baroque churches.

halo (Gk. disc of the sun) A circular glory of light round the head of a holy personage, a nimbus. Such discs were used in Hellenistic times, and for Roman emperors, to mark them off from ordinary mortals. Haloes were not used by the first Christians, and the earliest known use of a halo, with a cross inscribed on it to denote Christ, is of *c.*400 (ivory in Dijon, Mus.). Originally haloes were reserved for divine persons, but by the mid-5th century they were used to denote saints, especially the Virgin. The *S. Laurence* in the Mausoleum of Galla Placidia, *Ravenna, is probably the earliest known example. By the 6th century haloes were usual for *saints and beati, and square ones were used for living people, e.g. Pope John VII (before 707) in a mosaic now in the Grotte Vaticane under St Peter's, Rome. A *mandorla or aureole is much larger than a halo and envelops the whole body, perhaps signifying a greater degree of sanctity, as in representations of the Transfiguration, Ascension, or the Assumption of the Virgin. Beati were denoted by rays rather than a halo proper, as may be seen in a *predella* by Fra *Angelico in London (NG), which may have been intended to speed the process of canonization—it shows both S. Vincent Ferrer (canonized 1458) and *S. Catherine of Siena (canonized 1461). There are examples of saints shown with haloes before their official recognition.

By *c.*1300 the growing desire for realism led to problems with the flat gold disc behind the head. In *Giotto's Fresco of the *Last Supper* in the Arena Chapel, Padua (*c.*1306), the Apostles with their backs to the spectator have their haloes suspended in front of their faces. In *Masaccio's *Madonna and Child* (1426: London, NG) the Christ Child's halo is seen in perspective, above His head rather than behind it, but that of the Madonna is still the old-fashioned upright disc. The plate-like halo was superseded during the 15th century by a thin golden ring in perspective and it was gradually dropped altogether. During the Counter-Reformation period, however, it was reintroduced, but in the form of a glory of flickering light-rays, as in the work of El *Greco and *Tintoretto.

Ham (Cham) was *Noah's second son. In the OT, Gen. 9: 23–7, Ham mocked his father's nakedness when he found him drunk and Noah cursed him: 'a servant of servants shall he be unto his brethren'. His sons were thought to be the founders of Canaan, Egypt, Cush, and Put.

Haman *See* ESTHER.

Hand of God *See* DEXTERA DOMINI.

Harlem Renaissance A movement of artists, musicians, and writers who made Harlem, New York City the centre of African-American cultural life in the 1920s and 1930s, following the Great Migration of 1914–18 from the southern United States. The concentration of creative energy in a relatively free social context was to bring new life and expression to all the arts in New York and well beyond in following decades. Painters influenced by the Harlem Renaissance include Romare Bearden, William H. Johnson, and Jacob Lawrence. *See also* NORTH AMERICA.

Harrowing of Hell *See* ANASTASIS, HELL, LIMBO.

hart A male deer, a stag. Ps. 42 (Vg. 41): 2, 'As a deer longs for flowing streams, so my soul longs for you, O my God' has always been a symbol of a Gentile convert, preparing for the waters of baptism. According to the *Bestiaries, deer could find and kill snakes and therefore stood for Christ, who kills the Serpent/Devil. The deer then needed water to wash away the poison, as baptism cleanses original sin. A mosaic in San Clemente, Rome, of *c.*1125, shows this. A stag is also the attribute of *S. Hubert and *S. Eustace. A hind is a female deer and is the attribute of *S. Giles. AV and Vg. use the old word 'hart'.

hat, the red A popular phrase for the cardinalate. It was a very broad-brimmed, flat-topped hat with fifteen tassels on either side. It was never actually worn after the cardinal was invested with it, and after his death it was hung over his grave until it perished, when it was swept up and thrown away—*sic transit gloria mundi*. Archbishops often use a version, green and with fewer tassels, on their letterheads, but do not actually have them. Neither kind is now used.

Hawksmoor (Hawksmore), Nicholas (1661–1736), was *Wren's assistant from c.1679, first as a clerk, and after c.1682 on architectural projects, notably the rebuilding of the City churches destroyed in the Fire of London in 1666. From 1691 he was Wren's assistant on the rebuilding of St Paul's Cathedral. The 1711 Act for the Building of Fifty New Churches, which was to provide churches for new areas of London, appointed Hawksmoor as one of the surveyors (he was later joined briefly by *Gibbs). For this project he designed six large churches, all free-standing and notable for their robust and imaginative style. They are St Alphege, Greenwich (1712–14), St Anne's, Limehouse (1712–24), the grandest of them all, St George-in-the-East (1714–34; gutted 1941 but surviving as a shell), St George's, Bloomsbury (1716–27), Christ Church, Spitalfields (1714–29), and St Mary Woolnoth (1716–27), a City church which survived the Great Fire but was rebuilt because of delapidation. Although he was naturally much influenced by Wren, Hawksmoor's churches are more vigorous, less urbane, and more heavily ancient Roman than those of any of his contemporaries, with towers of massive strength, and detailing which often verges on the eccentric. Because most of them were built on unencumbered sites he was able to develop further the *auditory type of church used by Wren.

His last work, just before his death, was the design for the towers of Westminster Abbey, where he combines an obligatory but very personal interpretation of Gothic with the characteristic weight—dourness even—of his other churches. In 1729 he designed the towers, quadrangle, and hall of All Souls College, Oxford, in a personal interpretation of Gothic, and in the same year the mausoleum at Castle Howard, Yorkshire, in his most austere Roman Classical.

hearse Nowadays the name for a carriage carrying a coffin, but originally a triangular candle-stand with one candle at the top and seven down each side, used in Holy Week. It became the name of a candle-stand on or near a catafalque (cf. herse-cloth), and the funerary association led to the name being given to the carriage.

Heart, the Sacred In the later Middle Ages there were devotions to the Five Wounds of Christ, as in the *imago pietatis or *Arma Christi, and to the wound in His side (cf. *Longinus). The later devotion to the Sacred Heart was developed by S. John Eudes in the 17th century and given impetus by the visions (1673 and later) of S. Margaret Mary Alacoque (d. 1690), and finally authorized in 1765. *Batoni painted one of the first pictures of the new form of the devotion, and set in train an unfortunate proliferation of sentimental oleographs and plaster statuettes.

S. John Eudes also encouraged a parallel devotion to the **Immaculate Heart of Mary**, which can be traced back to the prophecy of Simeon (Luke 2: 35) 'a sword will pierce your own soul too', and to the Seven *Sorrows of Mary: a heart pierced by a single sword or surrounded by seven swords being its principal symbol. Pietro Annigoni's reredos *The Immaculate Heart of Mary* (1961) is in the Church of the Immaculate Heart, Hayes, Middlesex.

Heaven The state of beatitude attained by the righteous after death. For artists this is impossible to represent—unlike the pains of *Hell, which give ample opportunities for a variety of contorted poses. Even such devout men as Fra *Angelico could not manage to represent Heaven except as a sedate dance in a flowery meadow (*Last Judgement*, Florence, Mus. di San Marco). The theological concept is simply not realizable in concrete images: *Paradise may be more or less adequately represented in terms of earthly bliss (*Bosch in his visions of the Garden of Eden (left wing of the *Haywain*, for example), and Giovanni di Paolo, *Expulsion from Paradise* (New York, Met. Mus.); *Bouts, in *The Blessed entering Paradise* (c.1470: Lille)), but eternity is beyond the representative arts.

hedgehog According to the *Bestiaries, the hedgehog lies on its back to impale grapes or other fruits on its spines. It then takes them home to feed its young. Two morals can be drawn: the first, that it exemplifies the virtue of Prudence; and the second, that it symbolizes the Devil, picking off half-hearted souls and making away with them.

heilige Sippe, die *See* KINSHIP OF CHRIST.

Helena, Saint (c.250–c.330), Roman Empress and mother of the Emperor *Constantine. In spite of the attractive legend that she was an Englishwoman, daughter of Old King Cole, she was probably born in Bithynia, the daughter of an innkeeper. She seems to have become a Christian c.312, after the cessation of the great persecution under the Emperor Diocletian, and she had great influence on her son, perhaps encouraging him to issue the Edict of *Milan in 313. She founded several churches, including Sta Croce in Gerusalemme in Rome, the Basilica of the Nativity in Bethlehem and the Basilica on the Mt. of Olives, but she is best known for her journey to the Holy Land *c.*326, and the discovery there of the *True Cross, together with three of the Holy Nails and the superscription. The discovery was certainly made before 346, during excavations for Constantine's Basilica of the *Holy Sepulchre, and the 4th-century pilgrim *Etheria records venerating the objects at Easter. The story of the Invention (i.e. discovery) and Exaltation of the True Cross is at its most elaborate in the **Golden Legend*, and by far the best-known cycle is the one by *Piero della Francesca in San Francesco, Arezzo, which is based on it. Helena is usually represented in this context, but when she appears alone she is recognizable by a large cross and the crown she wears, as well as suitably rich clothing. One of the four great piers under the dome of St Peter's in Rome is dedicated to her and contains a fragment of the Cross. Her statue there is by Bolgi (1629–49). (*See also* LONGINUS.)

Heliodorus A very rare subject, known from *Raphael's Fresco in the Vatican (Stanza d'Eliodoro: 1511–14), as part of a cycle of miraculous interventions on behalf of the Church. Heliodorus was a 2nd-century BC official sent by his king to confiscate the gold and silver treasure in the Temple at Jerusalem. The High Priest explained that the money was in trust for widows and orphans, and the Temple was sacrosanct. Nevertheless, Heliodorus attempted to seize the treasure, but a horseman in golden armour appeared miraculously with two youths like angels, who scourged him and drove him off. Representations of this scene are usually paired with similar subjects—in the huge painting by Solimena (1725: Naples, Gesù Nuovo) it becomes the Old Testament *type of *Christ driving the Traders from the Temple*. A painting by *Tiepolo of *c.*1725–30 (Verona, Mus.) was probably part of a similar cycle. Outside Italy the subject is virtually unknown.

Helios *See* SOL.

Hell In pre-Christian times belief in some sort of afterlife led to the ideas of the *Underworld and Hades, with Charon as a kind of judge. Nevertheless, it was not until the 8th or 9th century that Christian ideas, linked with the Last *Judgement, began to crystallize in terms of representation. Since *Heaven is so difficult to express in formal terms, artists found the representation of Hell in terms of fantastic demons and contorted sinners much easier to realize. The subject of Christ's Descent into *Limbo, sometimes called the Harrowing of Hell, was very popular, especially in the East, where the *Anastasis was even more popular as a subject than the Western form of the Resurrection. In the West some imaginative torments appear among the Damned in the mosaics at *Torcello (12th/13th cent.), on the tympana of French and other Gothic cathedrals, and the mosaics in the Baptistery of Florence (13th cent.). Dante's *Inferno* (after 1300) gave considerable direct impetus through the illustrations to MSS of the poem (e.g. *Botticelli, *Blake). *Bosch and *Bruegel in the Netherlands developed the fantastic elements of the theme, while *Signorelli and, above all, *Michelangelo in his *Last Judgement*, remained closer to the spirit of Dante. The Mouth of Hell is sometimes represented as the jaws of a whale ('*Leviathan, the great sea-monster') in which Jonah spent three days and three nights, being regarded as a *type of Christ's Descent into Limbo. El *Greco's *Adoration of the Name of Jesus* (the Escorial and London, NG) is an example.

hen and chickens *See* BIRDS, SYMBOLIC.

Hepworth, Dame Barbara (1903–1975) A British sculptor of stylized, and later, of purely formal and abstract figures in stone, wood, and bronze. She became lifelong friends with fellow student Henry *Moore (at Leeds (1919–24) then at the Royal College of Art, London), obtaining a travel scholarship to Italy 1924–5. Her first one-woman show (1949) was in the United States, at Durlacher Bros. New York. By mid-century she achieved a world-wide reputation, and made *Construction (Crucifixion)* for the interior of Salisbury Cathedral in 1966. Found to be too large to be admitted through any of the building's doors, it stood outside for a season before being moved to the curtilage of St Thomas Cathedral, Portsmouth, Hampshire. Here, too, the site proved unsatisfactory. Now sited at Winchester Cathedral, Hampshire, it is fully appreciated. She wrote:

> I much wanted to make a Crucifixion which enabled one to recognize the figure of Christ on the Cross and the rudimentary forms to the left and the right, to make spaces where one could enter, and bring one to one's knees. But to do it in a way which entirely fitted the development of my own

calligraphy, and to be at home on a hillside, or in an old cathedral or in a new, and to be valid in all respects two thousand years hence.

And of this work's circlet for the head she said: 'in envisaging a faceless Christ I seek only to portray eternity, and the mood in which to accept Christinity'.

The best collections of her work are at St Ives, Cornwall, where she settled to spend the second half of her life, at the Tate, and at Wakefield.

heraldry In the Middle Ages heraldry was so much a part of life that the employment of heraldic symbols as an identifying shorthand soon spread from military and court circles to the Church, especially the grander prelates, who, in any case, usually came from noble armigerous families. The idea of the *Arma Christi shows how deeply heraldry had penetrated, and armorial bearings served to identify popes and other prelates, Orders, and even specific sees. The unique nature of the papacy was recognized by allowing the use of gold and silver together, in spite of a general rule that 'metals' should only be used on 'colours' or 'furs'. The papal arms are, therefore, gold and silver, with crossed keys, one gold and the other silver, with the tiara and other symbols of the papacy. Individual popes used their own family arms in conjunction with these, so that from the late 13th century, at least, individual popes can be identified, for instance, on tombs which have lost their inscriptions, but on which a coat of arms has survived. Bishops and their sees had arms of their own, especially on seals, so that arms on a building, a tomb, a painting, or a manuscript can often be dated and localized with some precision—even parts of a building may be dated in sequence if one part has the arms of a cardinal and another has the same man's arms as pope. Pictures and MSS, which are easily divorced from their original setting, can thus be given back their context.

heresy, heretical subjects Heresy is a formal denial and rejection of defined doctrine, and is therefore rare. For obvious reasons, it is difficult to know how many works of art have been destroyed because of heresy, but very few survive, and most are dubiously heretical. In the early period, from the 3rd century onwards, doctrine was still being defined, so that a variety of interpretations was legitimate—the *catacombs or the *Hypogeum of the Aurelii present problems of interpretation, many of which were deliberate, in order to mislead possible persecutors. These are, properly speaking, heterodox rather than heretical. Later, the *Arians (Arius d. 336) did present deliberately unorthodox images, most of which have been destroyed, but *Ravenna has the Baptistery of the Arians and Sant' Apollinare Nuovo had some apparently heretical subjects. Among the few later works it seems that in the 15th century *Botticini's *Assumption of the Virgin* (London, NG) may be unique. *Bosch later came under suspicion of heresy, but his orthodoxy was defended by a priest, and his works were collected by Philip II, a champion of orthodoxy. The situation in the Reformation period is confused, but it seems that few truly heretical works have survived, in spite of accusation and counter-accusation.

Hermes Kriophoros (Gk. Hermes the Ram-bearer) Hermes (Mercury in Roman mythology) was the messenger of Zeus and god of fertility in flocks and herds, spending much of his time seducing nymphs. He was also the patron of street-wise tricksters and thieves, so he may seem out of place in a Christian context. There are, however, statues of him carrying a lamb (or calf) on his shoulders in his capacity as patron of flocks, centuries before Christ. He was therefore used as the iconographical model for the Good *Shepherd, since in times of persecution the Christian motive could be interpreted as pagan—i.e. it was a 'neutral' image. The statuette in Rome (Lateran Mus., probably late 3rd cent. AD) is a good example, and many more can be found on *sarcophagi and in the *catacombs. After the triumph of Christianity it was no longer necessary to have recourse to such ambiguity and the Good Shepherd mosaic (*c.*450) in the so-called Mausoleum of Galla Placidia in *Ravenna is one of the last examples in the West, although many later mosaics show Christ with lambs, sometimes symbolizing the Twelve Apostles (e.g. Rome, Sta Prassede) and sometimes the faithful in general.

hermits (Gk. *eremites*, desert-dwellers), also called eremites, and anchorites. From the 3rd century, partly to escape persecution, many men began to withdraw into the Egyptian desert to live austerely as solitaries, mainly in the upper Nile valley near Thebes (*see* THEBAID). After a time they came to have a loose organization in small communities. This was the origin of Egyptian monasticism, and was partly due to *S. Antony Abbot. In the East they still exist, e.g. on Mt. *Athos, but in the West they soon became monastic orders, and only the *Carthusians and *Camaldolensians represent something of the original idea.

Herod, Herodias A confusing number of rulers named Herod are mentioned in the NT, and tend to be amalgamated into one tyrant. Herod the Great (d. 4 BC) is nevertheless the Herod, called 'King of the Jews' by the Romans who kept him in power. He asked the *Magi to return to Jerusalem, so as to discover where the Infant Jesus was, because he feared the 'King of the Jews' who was to be born, and when this stratagem failed, he ordered the Massacre of the *Innocents. His son, Herod Antipas, had *John the Baptist imprisoned and executed. John had accused him of adulterously marrying his niece, Herodias, who was the wife of another member of his own family. She was already the mother of *Salome, whose dancing so excited Herod that he was induced to give her the severed head of the Baptist. It was this Herod before whom Jesus appeared, sent by Pilate for trial. Herod Agrippa I was responsible for the execution of *S. James the Apostle, and Herod Agrippa II was the 'King Agrippa' before whom *S. Paul was brought (*c.*60), before being sent to Rome.

heroön A shrine dedicated to the memory of a dead hero, usually pagan, or a sacred place; the Christian equivalent is a *martyrium. The mausoleum of the Comnenian Emperors (11th/12th cent.) in Byzantium was specifically called a heroön.

Hetoimasia (Hetimasia, Etimasia) (Gk. for preparation [of the Throne]) A Byzantine motif showing the preparation of the Throne for the Last Judgement, as a substitute for the representation of the Judgement itself. Many representations of the 'empty throne' with e.g. Gospel books on it are thought to be references to the presence of the Divine, rather than directly connected with the Second Coming (e.g. several 5th-cent. mosaics in Ravenna), but they can also be included in the definition. There are many references to thrones and kingship in the Bible, but Ps. 9: 7–8: 'But the Lord sits enthroned for ever, he has established his throne for judgement. He judges the world with righteousness'; and Rev. 4: 2 and 5: 1 are perhaps the clearest references. The subject is very rare in the West, and unknown after the early Middle Ages.

Hierarchy, the Celestial *See* ANGELS.

hierarchy, the ecclesiastical Only the papacy and the episcopate can claim Divine institution, but the phrase 'The Hierarchy' usually means the governors of the Church—i.e. deacons, priests, bishops (especially diocesan bishops), superiors of religious orders, archbishops, patriarchs and primates, cardinals (who, in theory, need not be priests at all), and the pope.

Hieronymus *See* JEROME, S.

High Altar *See* ALTAR.

High Priest The first High Priest of the Israelites was *Aaron, who was chosen by God. His vestments are described in great detail in Exod. 28, especially v. 4: 'These are the vestments which they shall make: a breastpiece, an *ephod, a robe, a chequered tunic, a turban (AV *mitre), and a sash.' These are often represented in pictures of the Circumcision, sometimes rather fancifully. By the time of Christ the High Priest had been installed by the Romans as a puppet head of state, as well as religious leader of the Jews, which was why Christ was taken before him and was then passed on to Pilate. The High Priest was the only person allowed, once a year, to enter the Holy of Holies, where the *Ark of the Covenant was kept. For Christians, Christ Himself is the unique eternal High Priest.

hind *See* HART.

historiated initial In illuminated MSS it was usual to begin a new chapter or book with a large decorated initial letter (cf. BEATUS PAGE). If it contains figures or scenes, e.g. a 'portrait' of the author, it is described as historiated.

Hodegetria (Hodigitria) *See* MADONNA TYPES.

Holbein, Hans (1497/8–1543), was a painter and designer, born in Augsburg, S. Germany. He was trained in the workshop of his father, Hans the Elder, and by 1515 was in Basle working first for a painter and then designing prints for publishers, including Froben, for whom in 1515 he made the title-page for S. Thomas More's *Utopia*. It was probably through Froben that he met *Erasmus, of whom he made several portraits. His early religious paintings in Basle include the Oberreid Altarpiece—a pair of wings with a *Nativity* and the *Adoration of the Kings* (Freiburg im Breisgau, Cathedral). The *Nativity* is notable because the whole scene is lit by the light emanating from the Infant Christ lying on the straw in front of the Virgin, following the Northern tradition derived from the vision of *S. Bridget. The *Passion Altar* (Basle, Mus.), a series of eight scenes from the Agony in the Garden to the Entombment, was probably painted for Basle Town Hall *c.*1520. The *Solothurn Madonna* (1522: Solothurn, Mus.) is more traditional, but the stark realism of the *Dead Christ in the Tomb* (1521/2: Basle, Mus.) is astonishingly novel (*see* UNCTION, STONE OF). Both these works were probably painted after Holbein had visited N. Italy. He remained in Basle until 1526, working on decorations (lost) for the Town Council, and designing for printers, notably the title-page for *Luther's Bible (1522), and making the drawings for the forty-one woodcuts for the original edition of the *Dance of Death, which was not published for political reasons connected with the Reformation, and which eventually appeared with extra plates in 1538 in Lyons. It was an enormous success, running through many editions. Possibly because of unrest caused by the Reformation, which destroyed patronage for religious works, Holbein went to France *c.*1524, and the *Noli me tangere* (Royal Coll.) and the Leonardesque *Last Supper* (Basle, Mus.) were probably painted either during or after this visit, possibly made in the hope of obtaining French royal patronage. He may have seen the original of Leonardo's *Last Supper* during his N. Italian journey, or he may have known an engraving. In 1526 he was commissioned to paint the *Meyer Madonna* (Darmstadt) which he designed as a Madonna of Mercy, protecting Meyer and his family (Meyer was the leader of the Catholic party in Basle). Holbein left for England in 1526, because increasing religious strife in Basle had destroyed his prospects. He was encouraged by Erasmus's accounts of England under Henry VIII and he came with an introduction to More. When he arrived, Henry was still nominally a Catholic monarch and anti-Luther, though in 1527 he began his efforts to divorce Catherine of Aragon.

During this visit, Holbein turned to portraiture; his work as a religious painter had almost ended, since when he returned to Basle in 1528 he was faced with a climate in which religious art was now impossible. On Shrove Tuesday 1529 an iconoclastic riot resulted in the destruction of religious images in churches. By 1529 he had accepted Luther totally, although he was still troubled over dogmatic matters, since in 1530 he is recorded as saying that 'he needed a better explanation of Holy Communion before he would go', and a little later, that 'he was among those who do not object, but want to conform to other Christians'. As early as 1526, Erasmus had said that 'Basle was a place where the arts are freezing', and by the time that Holbein returned the climate was even more chilly. He finished the *Meyer Madonna* for Meyer's private chapel, and painted the sad portrait of his own wife and children (Basle, Mus.), and travelled to Freiburg im Breisgau to make the drawing for his last portrait of Erasmus, who had gone there to escape the religious turmoils in Basle. He made some polemical prints against the papacy and the Church, painted decorations on classical themes for the Town Hall, and in 1532 returned to England for good, where he painted the portraits by which he is now chiefly known.

He became court portraitist to Henry VIII, whose own break with Rome left no scope for religious works, except the elaborate woodcut for the frontispiece of Coverdale's Bible (1535) where Henry is shown as the head of the Church, and a miniature of *Solomon receiving the Queen of Sheba* (Royal Coll.) with Henry as Solomon, seated on an imperial throne. For Henry, Holbein was merely one of the means for his own glorification, and an advertisement for his wealth and power, as in the dynastic portrait group destroyed in the fire of Whitehall Palace, 1698, of which only the cartoon with Henry survives (London, NPG). Little wonder that the miniature portrait of Holbein (probably by a follower: London, Wallace Coll.) shows him as a grimly disillusioned man.

Hollywood Biblical epics *See* FILM.

Holofernes *See* JUDITH.

Holy Blood (Saint-Sang) The Chapelle du Saint-Sang in Bruges claims to possess drops of Christ's blood, collected by *Joseph of Arimathaea; the relic was given to Thierry, Count of Flanders, in 1149 by the Patriarch of Jerusalem. Other places claiming similar relics are Weingarten Abbey, in Germany, and the cathedrals of Sarzana, Mantua, and Menton in France.

The chapel in Bruges is one of the earliest examples of Italian Renaissance influence (1529–34) in the Low Countries. A *Lamentation* of *c.*1520 in the chapel is by a Bruges master, greatly influenced by Quentin Massys; the anonymous Bruges master is known as the Maître du Saint-Sang, or Master of the Holy Blood.

Holy Coat *See* COAT.

Holy Door 1. The *Porta Sancta.* A door in the entrance porch of St Peter's, Rome, which is sealed by brickwork except in *Holy Years, when it is opened by the Pope on Christmas Eve of the year preceding the Holy Year and closed by him on the following Christmas Eve. Other similar doors in the basilicas of the Lateran, Sta Maria Maggiore, and San Paolo fuori are opened and closed by cardinals. The earliest record of the ceremony, in 1450, is the fresco by Fra *Angelico in the Chapel of St Nicholas in the Vatican. A papal medal was usually struck in commemoration.

2. In the E. Orthodox Church the *iconostasis has three doors, the central one being the 'Royal Door' or Greater Entrance. The side doors carry *icons of Christ and the Virgin, as well as of the patron Saint.

Holy Face *See* MANDYLION, VERNICLE (VERONICA), VOLTO SANTO.

Holy Family Strictly, a representation of Jesus, Mary, and Joseph in a more or less domestic setting, e.g. with Mary feeding the Child, or Joseph working as a carpenter, distinct from the traditional scenes of the Nativity, Adoration of the Magi, or Flight into Egypt. Such representations were unknown in the earliest periods, but were popular in the Middle Ages, when the group was extended to include the infant Baptist playing with the Christ Child, sometimes including *S. Elizabeth or *S. Anne, and gradually evolving into the *Kinship of Christ, with a dozen or more figures. During the Counter-Reformation there was a reaction against this informal domesticity, and a new subject was created—*The Two Trinities*—i.e. the earthly one of Jesus, Mary, and Joseph, and the heavenly one of God the Father, Son, and Holy Ghost, with Jesus common to both (cf. the *Murillo, London, NG).

Holy Ghost (Holy Spirit) The Third Person of the Holy *Trinity, usually represented as a dove (*see* BAPTISM) or as tongues of fire (Acts 2: 3–4): *see* PENTECOST.

Holy Grail *See* GRAIL.

Holy Helpers, the fourteen *See* VIERZEHNHEILIGEN.

Holy House *See* LORETO.

Holy Innocents *See* INNOCENTS.

Holy Kinship *See* KINSHIP.

Holy Lance 1. According to the Gospel (John 19: 34), after Christ died on the cross 'one of the soldiers pierced his side with a spear, and at once blood and water came out'. This was elaborated, especially in the **Golden Legend*, into the story of *Longinus, supposedly the soldier's name (from the Greek for lance), who was also identified with the centurion who believed. What was claimed to be this lance was in Jerusalem in the 6th century and was broken in the capture of Jerusalem by the Persians in 615: the point was saved and was sent to Constantinople. In 1241 it was given to S. Louis, King of France, together with the alleged *Crown of Thorns, and kept by him in the Ste-Chapelle, Paris, until they disappeared in the French Revolution. The other part was also said to have reappeared in Constantinople before the 10th century and was later taken by the Turks, who gave it to Pope Innocent VIII in 1492. It is now in St Peter's, in one of the piers of the crossing, with *Bernini's sculpture of Longinus.

2. A small knife shaped like a lance, with a cross-shaped handle. In the E. Orthodox Church it is used to cut the Eucharistic bread before consecration, and commemorates the piercing of Christ's side.

Holy Name *See* NOMEN SACRUM.

holy oils *See* SACRAMENTALS.

Holy Places, the A generic term for all the places in the Holy Land associated with Christ's life and mission, but usually confined to such important sites as the Church of the Nativity in *Bethlehem, the Temple in Jerusalem, the Garden of *Gethsemane and the Mt. of *Olives, the *Via Dolorosa, *Calvary, and the *Holy Sepulchre, both these last being now in the Basilica of the Holy Sepulchre. Pilgrims are known to have visited these sites at least since the 3rd century, and the visit of the Empress *Helena in 326 led to the discovery of the *True Cross and the building of several great churches by the Empress and her son, the Emperor *Constantine. These churches still exist, but have been destroyed and rebuilt many times. The accounts of *Etheria in the late 4th century and of *Theoderich in the 12th are therefore peculiarly valuable.

Holy Rood (Holyrood) *See* ROOD.

Holy Sepulchre Perhaps the most important of the *Holy Places, the Church of the Holy Sepulchre—properly, the Church of the Resurrection or *Anastasis—covers the site of *Calvary and the Sepulchre itself; 'in the garden there was a new tomb in which no one had ever been laid' (John 19: 41). It is generally agreed that *S. Helena discovered the site (which had been destroyed by earlier Romans) *c.*326, and her son, the Emperor *Constantine, built a *martyrium to commemorate the Crucifixion and Resurrection. It was consecrated in 336, and was referred to by the pilgrim *Etheria at the end of the 4th century. It was destroyed by the Persians in 614, and again destroyed in 1009. The rotunda alone was rebuilt *c.*1048 and enlarged by the Crusaders to cover the whole site: the state of the church is described in the 12th century by *Theoderich. The circular (?polygonal) shape of Constantine's building was widely imitated in the Middle Ages, especially in Germany and England, and the churches of the *Templars were free imitations of the general form, as in the existing church in Cambridge or the church in the Temple gardens, London, of which the circular portal is the original door of the Holy Sepulchre church. Another example is the one at Tomar, in Portugal.

Holy Shroud *See* SHROUD.

Holy Souls *See* PURGATORY.

Holy Spirit *See* TRINITY, THE HOLY; HOLY GHOST.

holy water *See* SACRAMENTALS.

Holy Week The week before Easter Sunday, usually reckoned as beginning on Palm Sunday. Each day has its own rite, deriving from the events of the Passion as re-enacted in Jerusalem on the actual sites. They are recorded in detail by *Etheria in the late 4th century, and may go back to Apostolic times. It is the custom to cover all crucifixes, sculpture, and paintings in Catholic churches during Holy Week and the week preceding it. The events of Holy Week are the narrative subject matter of John Ward's chancel arch mural (1970, St Mary's, Chesham, Buckinghamshire).

Holy Year In 1300 Boniface VIII declared a Jubilee (cf. Lev. 25) offering an indulgence to any pilgrim who came to Rome, confessed and received communion, and visited the four major basilicas, St Peter's, St John Lateran, San Paolo fuori le Mura (St Paul's outside the Walls), and Sta Maria Maggiore. The response was so great that the only bridge then over the Tiber, the Ponte Sant'Angelo, was so congested that several pilgrims were crushed to death and the first rule of the road—keep to the left—was thereafter enforced. Boniface had intended the Holy Year to be kept only once a century, but in 1343 Clement VI changed it to every fifty years. Urban VI reduced it to thirty-three, thought to be the length of Christ's earthly life, and, in 1470, Paul II reduced it to twenty-five years, thus giving each new generation a once-in-a-lifetime opportunity to make the pilgrimage. The last Holy Year was 2000.

The pilgrimages rapidly became organized like modern package tours and it is highly probable that many artists took the opportunity to see ancient and modern works of art in Rome, but there is little direct evidence of this. It is said that Roger van der *Weyden's apparent knowledge of Fra *Angelico's art may have come from an Italian journey in 1450, and Angelico's own fresco in the Vatican has a clear reference to that year, since it shows the ceremony of the opening of the *Holy Door.

Hone, Evie (1894–1955) A devout Irish painter and stained-glass artist, who was born in Dublin, then studied in London under Sickert and then Meninsky, before moving to Paris where Albert Gleizes was her formative teacher from 1921 to 1931. With her friend and fellow-student Mainie Jellett's influence, her painting became abstract, but encountering the vehement spirituality of Rouault's work she turned to stained-glass design and a more figurative idiom. Her glass can be seen in St Michael's, Highgate, London and the National Cathedral, Washington, DC, and in churches in Ireland. War damage to the chapel of Eton College, Berkshire, brought her a high-profile commission to replace the nine lights of the large East Window, completed in 1952. The upper register depicts the *Crucifixion*, and the lower the *Last Supper*, flanked by **Melchisedek* and the *Sacrifice of Isaac*. Hone's vibrant and strong colours were to prove a taxing context for John *Piper when invited to complement them with adjacent windows to North and South (1957) representing the *Parables*.

Honorius Augustodunensis, called Honorius 'of Autun', was an early 12th-century monk, who worked in Canterbury and Germany but probably had no connection with Autun. He wrote several theological treatises, but his *Speculum Ecclesiae* (*c.*1090/1120) was the source for many works of art: it was a series of sermons on the great Feasts of the Church, in which a NT subject was contrasted with its OT *types, and even with the *Bestiaries, which were used to provide examples—however incredible—from the animal world of the fulfilment of the OT in the NT. The arrangement of biblical subjects *ante legem*, *sub lege*, and *sub gratia*—i.e. before Moses gave the Law, under the Law, and under the New Dispensation, goes back far beyond Honorius, but he was one of the first to reduce it to a system. It is exemplified in the 1481 Sistine Chapel fresco cycle. Several French cathedrals, notably Lyons and Chartres, have stained-glass windows based on Honorius.

Hope *See* VIRTUES.

horae (Lat. hours) A Book of *Hours.

Horns of the Altar Projections on the altar of the Temple at Jerusalem (Exod. 27: 2), which became transferred to the Christian altar as corners—corner and horn both deriving from Lat. *cornu*, a projection.

Horns of Moses *See* MOSES.

Hortus Conclusus (Lat. enclosed garden) A popular subject in the later Middle Ages, representing the Madonna and Child in a walled garden with a well or fountain, and usually with several female saints (cf. *Virgo inter Virgines). The subject derives from the Song of Solomon (AV Song of Songs; Vg. Cantic.) 4: 12: 'A garden locked is my sister, my bride, a garden locked, a fountain sealed'; and 4: 15: 'A garden fountain, a well of living water . . .'. All these were interpreted to refer to Mary's virginity, and to the Fons Vitae, the water of life ('well of living water'), or the 'fountain sealed', another reference to Mary's virginity. A very similar subject is *Maria im Rosenhag*, the Madonna and Child against a background of roses, also popular in the early 15th century. Perhaps the most charming example is the *Paradise Garden* of 1410/15 (Frankfurt, Städel), by an anonymous German master. *See also* PORTA CLAUSA.

Hosea (Osee) *See* PROPHETS.

Hospitallers, Knights *See* MALTA, KNIGHTS OF.

Host, the Angelic (Heavenly) *See* ANGELS.

Host, the Sacred *See* SPECIES.

Hours, Books of The name comes from Lat. *horae*, Fr. *heures*, the appointed times of prayer (Ps. 119, Vg. 118): 164, 'Seven times a day do I praise thee'. The hours are properly eight, but are usually reduced to seven by taking Matins and Lauds together at first light. They are followed by Prime, Tierce, Sext, and None (i.e. One, Three, Six, and Nine), nominally at three-hourly intervals, followed by the evening services of Vespers and Compline. These hours were observed by religious houses, but at varying times according to the season. Devout lay people who wished to follow the sequence also said much shorter versions of these prayers. They used the *psalter, which is a *liturgical book, and also Books of Hours, which were not. From the 13th to the 15th centuries huge numbers of such books were produced, many hundreds of which have survived. No two are the same, since most were made for a particular patron in a particular diocese. Most were produced by specialist workshops in Paris and the Low Countries employing lay artists and calligraphers, unlike the monastic scriptoria which produced liturgical books. By the 15th century many wealthy burghers and nobles commissioned their own books, sometimes more than one, and the choice of saints in the Calendar or of consecrations for churches allows many to be localized with precision, and coats of arms in the margins often identify their owners. The grander examples were very expensive and ordered by wealthy and noble families, but many more were produced and sold to pious middle-class patrons, especially from *c.*1480, after the invention of printing. The contents vary, but all have a Calendar, usually at the beginning, which indicates special, local, Feasts as well as the major ones such as Christmas and Easter. There are various Gospel sequences and invariably the 'Little Hours of the Blessed Virgin', with psalms and the Office of the Dead. Calendars also included the popular Signs of the *Zodiac and the Occupations of the *Months, as in one of the grandest of all Books of Hours, the *Très Riches Heures* of the Duke of Berri, illuminated by the Limbourg brothers (before 1416: Chantilly, Musée Condé). They are also extremely important in showing parallel developments with panel-painting—the *Très Riches Heures* is a major work of the *International Gothic style; the *'Milan–Turin' Hours*, associated with the van *Eyck brothers, is an early example of realistic detail, as are the *Boucicaut Hours* (Paris, Mus. Jacquemart-André). The *Hours of Étienne Chevalier* (Chantilly) are by Jean Fouquet, who is equally famous as a panel-painter, but neither the Master of the *Rohan Hours* (*c.*1419: Paris, BN), nor the Master of Mary of Burgundy is known to have painted in oils, although the *Rohan Hours* have a tragic intensity hardly found in contemporary French painting, and the *Hours of Mary of Burgundy* (Vienna, National Library) explore a combination of minute detail and illusionistic perspective. In the 16th century cheaper printed versions were produced, but the Reformation greatly reduced demand.

house-church The earliest Christian meeting-places were in private houses (Acts 20: 7–8) and, for 'fear of the Jews', were inconspicuous. The earliest known example is the one excavated at *Dura-Europos, which was clearly a church and not just a house: it dates from *c.*250 and has a *baptistery, which makes it recognizable as a church, apart from the paintings of OT and NT scenes. The earliest one known in England is in the Roman villa at Lullingstone, Kent, dating from the 4th century (i.e. after the Edict of *Milan). The early Roman basilicas seem to have been built on sites which were once house-churches, which may have varied between individual houses, parts of an *insula* (a block of flats), or private baths, shops, or warehouses converted to a new use. Acts 2: 46 says, '. . . breaking bread at home' (AV 'breaking bread from house to house').

Hubert, Saint (d. 727), was so worldly that he hunted a stag on Good Friday, but he had a vision of a crucifix between the stag's antlers and was converted. He became Bishop of Tongres-Maastricht (703/5), and, later, first Bishop of Liège. He was known as the Apostle of the Ardennes region of Belgium, but is more famous as patron of hunters, a patronage he shares with *S. Eustace (who may never have existed, but had an identical vision). It is sometimes possible to discover which saint is intended only from external evidence—e.g. Dürer's engraving of *c.*1501 is referred to by Dürer himself as *Eustachius*; the altarpiece from the studio of the 15th-century German Master of the Life of the Virgin (London, NG 252 and 253) has another scene which can only refer to Hubert; but yet another picture in the NG, by Pisanello, is thought to represent Eustace, simply because Hubert is rarely, if ever, represented in early Italian painting. S. Giles also has a hind (not stag) as his attribute.

Hugh of Grenoble, Saint (1053–1132), was a pupil of *S. Bruno at Reims and became Bishop of Grenoble in 1180. His vision of seven stars (which are his attribute) referred to the arrival of S. Bruno with six companions to found a hermitage at La Grande Chartreuse, a remote spot given to them by Hugh. It became the mother-house of the *Carthusians. The best-known legend told of S. Hugh is that he visited the Chartreuse one feast-day and found the monks in a trance with plates of meat on the table before them. Their rule forbade meat, even on feasts, but they had been accidentally served with it. Hugh blessed it, the meat became turtle (which counted as fish), and the monks revived. It is the subject of a picture by *Zurbarán (Seville, Mus.).

Hugh of Lincoln, Saint (*c.*1135/40–1200) was a French Carthusian monk, trained at the Grande Chartreuse, who was sent to England *c.*1178 and became Bishop of Lincoln in 1186. He rebuilt the cathedral, which had been badly damaged by an earthquake, and was an adviser to one Scottish king and three English ones. He died in London, but his tomb in Lincoln Cathedral was second only to Becket's at Canterbury as a place of pilgrimage (both were destroyed by Henry VIII). He was canonized in 1220 and his relics were translated to the Angel Choir of Lincoln in 1280. He is rarely represented in art, but his usual attribute is a white swan, which he kept as a pet, and sometimes a chalice with the Christ Child, deriving from a vision seen by one of his clergy: the painting by *Zurbarán

(1638: Cadiz, Mus.), one of a series of Carthusian saints, shows him with both attributes.

The so-called 'Little S. Hugh' was not a saint, but a 9-year-old boy who was found murdered in 1255 and was the excuse for an anti-Semitic pogrom in which nineteen Jews were hanged, accused of ritual murder. S. Hugh, the bishop, himself had protected the Jewish community in Lincoln, even at the risk of his own life.

Hugo van der Goes *See* GOES.

humeral (veil) (Lat. *humerus*, shoulder) A scarf, some 8 by 3 ft., usually matching the material and colour of the *vestments, or of white silk, formerly worn (from the 8th/9th cent.) by the subdeacon or deacon at High Mass, and also by the celebrant at Benediction or processions of the Blessed Sacrament. The practice derives from an ancient gesture of respect, covering the hands when touching sacred things. A humeral is worn over the shoulders and covers the hands, but not the *monstrance.

Humility, Madonna of *See* MADONNA TYPES.

Hunt, William Holman (1827–1910) was in the Royal Academy Schools in London in 1844, where he was a fellow pupil of *Millais. In 1848 they met *Rossetti, and their friendship led to the foundation of the *PRB. From the first, Hunt expressed the group's original aims: to concentrate on powerfully moralizing and edifying subjects, such as *The Hireling Shepherd* (1851: Manchester), perhaps his finest PRB picture. His most famous work, *The Light of the World* (1853–6: Oxford, Keble Coll. Chapel, and 1904, London, St Paul's Cath.), was ill-received at first; it was defended by Ruskin, who explained in a letter to *The Times* the symbolism of the overgrown door and the words 'Behold, I stand at the door and knock ...' and described it as '... one of the very noblest works of sacred art ever produced in this or any other age'. Its secular counterpart was *The Awakening Conscience* (1852: London, Tate), which sets out in the most painstaking and elaborate detail of the kind which is intended to be read as a text, the circumstances of sin (a man is visiting his mistress) and the girl's impulse to repentance, though the harshness of the actual painting itself is repellent.

In 1854 he made his first journey to the Middle East, convinced that by painting biblical subjects in Egypt and Palestine he could achieve true fidelity to the Gospels. His first example of this new departure was *The Scapegoat* (1854: Port Sunlight near Liverpool), where he depicts the OT sin-sacrifice driven into the Dead Sea, with obsessive detail and in harsh, almost crude colour. He made two further journeys in 1869 and 1873; the resulting pictures are always accurate in his rendering of local settings and types, as in the distressingly anecdotal *The Shadow of Death* (1869–70: Manchester) which shows Christ stretching Himself after labouring at the carpenter's bench. His Middle Eastern subjects rarely amount, however, to more than biblical genre of the type also painted by his French contemporary Tissot between 1882 and 1892.

In 1905 he published *Pre-Raphaelitism and the Pre-Raphaelite Brotherhood*, the best-documented memoir of the movement, of which he was convinced he was the leading light.

hyperdulia (Gk. more than veneration) Adoration (*latria*) is due to God alone, but veneration (*dulia*) may be given to the saints and angels: because of her status as *Theotokos, Mary the Mother of God, though a creature, is entitled to special veneration: *hyperdulia*. The question was particularly important in the *Iconoclastic Controversy, and the Eastern and Western Churches still hold differing views on images (*see* ICON). The controversy was revived by the 16th-century Reformers, who again differed among themselves.

Hypogeum of the Aurelii A hypogeum is an underground chamber. The Hypogeum of the Aurelii is not quite a *catacomb, since it is a series of underground vaults inside the Aurelian Walls of Rome, and therefore of very early date. The chambers are richly decorated, some of the motifs being pagan and some Christian, while others present great problems of interpretation. It seems certain that a shepherd with his flock is an early example of Christ as the Good *Shepherd.

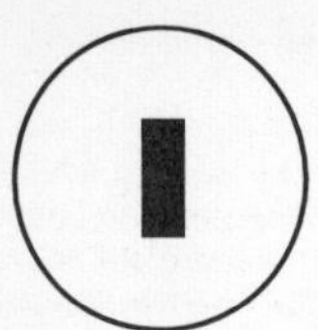

IC, IC XC, IC XC NIKA One of the oldest forms of the *Nomen Sacrum. It stands for the Greek letters meaning Jesus Christ Victor (or Conqueror). It is sometimes arranged in the form

IC XC Jesus Christ
NIKA Victor (or Conqueror)

Ichthys (Gk. fish) From very early times a fish was a symbol of Christ, of the newly baptized (swimming in the Water of Life), and later of the Eucharist. It often appears on seal-rings and in the catacombs. In Greek, however, the letters ICHTHYS are the first letters of words meaning Jesus Christ, Son of God, Saviour, and this is thought to derive from the earlier use of a fish as a symbol of Christ (*see also* CHI-RHO and NOMEN SACRUM).

icon, iconoclasm Icons (Gk. images) are small panel-paintings of Christ, the Virgin, or saints, which are the most obvious expression of Orthodox piety. There is at least one in every home and the churches have *iconostases filled with them. They are known to have existed in the time of *Eusebius, before 340, since he records icons of Peter and Paul (and *compare* ABGAR). A few survive from the 6th to 9th centuries, nearly all in St Catherine's Monastery on Mt. Sinai, in spite of the enormous destruction of icons during the 8th/9th centuries in the Iconoclastic Controversy. An icon is not the same as a Western devotional *image, since they are regarded as holy in themselves and veneration is paid to them as prototypes of the saints they represent. This veneration could obviously become idolatry, and the fear of this led the Emperor Leo to ban them in 726. The Iconoclastic Controversy continued, with the prohibition of any representation of Christ except the *Chi-Rho and the *Alpha and Omega symbols, until 843 and the 'Triumph of Orthodoxy'. The Second Council of *Nicaea had already decided in 787 that *latria* is the worship which is paid to God alone, but *hyperdulia*, the veneration paid to Mary or the saints, is permissible and that the veneration paid to icons is referred to the prototype represented. The victory of the Iconodules over the Iconoclasts led to an enormous production of icons from the 9th century up to 1453, after which they were produced in Crete and Russia. Because of the veneration surrounding them there were few stylistic changes over the centuries, unlike the West, where images of e.g. the Madonna and Child became increasingly realistic. (*See also* BYZANTINE ART.)

In modern literary criticism and in computer language *icon* has different, and misleading, meanings.

iconography, iconology The original meaning of iconography was a collection of portraits, as in the series of etchings by van Dyck of his contemporaries in the early 17th century. It came to mean the identification of symbolic figures or saints—a woman with an anchor was Hope, a man with an X-shaped cross was *S. Andrew. This study, greatly developed in the 19th century, has led to the elucidation of many works of Christian art, such as the sculptural programmes of the Gothic cathedrals. The word *Iconologia* first occurs as the title of *Ripa's book (1593), which deals with personifications, such as the woman with the anchor meaning Hope; but it has been extended in the present century to mean the study of the way in which symbols are transmitted and may change their meaning, or, in particular, meaning in the visual arts; iconography is descriptive, iconology is explanatory, but is often pushed too far in the search for recondite meanings in simple things.

iconostasis (Gk. a stand for icons) Originally an open screen of columns (*templon*) separating the sanctuary from the rest of the church, as in older Roman churches such as Sta Maria in Cosmedin. It is now a distinguishing feature of an E. Orthodox church, and is a screen often holding tiers of icons. From the 14th/15th centuries it became ever larger and, especially in Russia, made of wood, entirely separating the sanctuary from the body of the church, and pierced by three doors, the smaller lateral ones leading to the *Diaconicon and the *prothesis, and the large central Royal (or Holy) Doors, two half-doors behind which the Eucharist is celebrated. There is invariably an icon of Christ on the right of the Royal Doors and one of the Virgin on the left. Other icons are arranged in strict order, always including the Baptist, the patron of the church, a *Deësis, and some scenes commemorating the Feasts of the Church. In the Greek Orthodox Church the iconostasis is comparatively low and there may be no more than three tiers of icons, but in the Russian-Slav Church, since the time of *Theophanes and *Rublev in the early 15th century, the iconostasis may be the full height of the building and carry as many as seven rows of icons. The largest surviving example, from the Cathedral of the Dormition in Vladimir, now partly in museums in Leningrad and Moscow, had a *Deësis* attributed to Rublev, which alone was over 10 ft. high.

icthus *See* ICHTHYS.

idolatry Worshipping as divine any person or thing other than God. *See* IMAGE, ICON. For Solomon's idolatry, *see* SOLOMON.

Ignatius Loyola, Saint (1491–1556), was the founder of the *Jesuits (Societas Jesu). He was the son of a minor Spanish nobleman, destined for a secular career, but he was wounded in the siege of Pamplona in 1521, when his leg was broken and badly set, leaving him with a limp. A long convalescence was spent reading the *Life of Christ* by *Ludolph of Saxony, lives of the saints, and the **Golden Legend*. He spent a year (1522–3) in retreat at Manresa, near the great monastery of Montserrat, and there began to write the *Spiritual Exercises*, which became one of the most important books of the *Counter-Reformation. Because of its insistence on visualizing as intensely as possible the subject of contemplation—the imminence of death, the Passion, a meditation on Hell—it exerted enormous influence on the religious art of the late 16th and 17th centuries.

Ignatius began to study and went to several universities, ending up in Paris in 1528, where he became Master of Arts in 1534. In that year, with six companions including *S. Francis Xavier, he took a vow to form the Company of Jesus, later the Jesuits. The new Order was approved by Paul III in Rome in 1540 and was intended to meet the Protestant threat by concentrating on foreign missions and, especially, educational work among the educated classes. Their colleges became the best in Europe and a powerful influence for many years. Ignatius himself was elected Superior-General and spent the rest of his life in Rome directing their world-wide activities.

There are no contemporary portraits, but a death-mask exists in several casts and is the best evidence for his appearance. Paintings by Jacopino del Conte, made on the day of his death, and by Alonso Sanchez Coello, made from the masks, provided models. The Coello was destroyed in 1931, but there are many copies. S. Ignatius is usually represented in the black Jesuit gown, with the motto AMDG (*ad maiorem Dei gloriam*—to the greater glory of God) or the monogram *IHS, and sometimes with a volume of the Jesuit Constitutions or the *Spiritual Exercises*. There is an elaborate altar dedicated to him, with a statue by Legros, in the Gesù in Rome, the mother-church of the Society, and a huge allegorical ceiling (1691–4) by Pozzo in Sant'Ignazio, the Roman church dedicated to him.

IHS also called the Sacred Monogram (*see also* NOMEN SACRUM). It is now generally agreed that the letters IHS or a monogram of them (sometimes also IHC) are an abbreviation of the Greek letters forming the name of Jesus. Such contractions are recorded as early as the 4th and 5th centuries, but the monogrammatic form was popularized by *S. Bernardino of Siena, and even more by the *Jesuits, who use it and the initials AMDG (*see* IGNATIUS LOYOLA) as their motto. Various fanciful interpretations include the popular Iesus Hominum Salvator (Jesus, Saviour of Mankind) and *In hoc signo [vinces].

ikon *See* ICON.

'image not made with hands' *See* ACHEIROPOIETOS.

images Under Mosaic Law the Second *Commandment forbade the making of 'an idol, whether in the form of any thing that is in heaven above, or that is on the earth beneath, or that is in the water under the earth. You shall not bow down to them, nor worship them'. This was to prevent idolatry, but in the OT itself there are examples of images made by Divine command: *Moses and the Brazen Serpent (Num. 21: 8–9), the *cherubim on the *Ark of the Covenant (Exod. 25: 18–20), and *Solomon's Temple (1 Kgs. (Vg. 3 Reg.) 6: 23–35). Nevertheless, a certain fear of images was inherited by the first Christians, especially the Jewish converts, so that the use of symbols was widespread in the early centuries—a fish for Christ, a dove for the Holy Ghost, an anchor for the virtue of Hope, and many others. In the early 4th century the Council of Elvira, in Spain, was opposed to images, but the idea gained ground that an image was not to be worshipped in itself, but was a legitimate 'prototype' of the person or subject represented. In the E. Orthodox world this led to the *Iconoclastic Controversy of the 8th and 9th centuries and the ultimate 'Triumph of Orthodoxy' in 843. The Second Council of *Nicaea in 787 had already decided in favour of *icons (not the same thing as images) and in the West a more realistic type of art emerged (it is notable that in the East almost all sculpture is in relief and free-standing figures are very rare). For the West the matter was finally decided by the Council of *Trent, in opposition to the extreme destruction wrought in the 16th century by the followers of *Calvin and *Zwingli or the Puritans in Britain. In the early 16th century the contrast between Eastern and Western attitudes can be seen in *Vasari's account of the friar Fra Bartolommeo, who wanted to show his abilities as a painter of the nude: 'He painted a S. Sebastian, nude, very realistic in the colouring of his flesh, with an air of great charm, and whose body was likewise executed with corresponding beauty. This won him endless praise among artists. It is said that when this picture was exhibited in the church, after the friars had found women in confession who on looking at it had sinned through the captivating and sensuous likeness to a real figure, given by Fra Bartolommeo's skill, they had it removed from the church . . . it was bought by Giovan Battista della Palla and sent to the King of France.' Such a story would have been inconceivable in the Eastern Church.

imago clipeata (pl. *imagines clipeatae*) Ancient Roman patrician families kept death-masks (*imagines*) of their ancestors in shrines in their houses. They were often of wax, painted in naturalistic colours, and were carried at family funerals. Sometimes they were painted on a round shield (*clipeus*) and hung in a temple. The early Christians often used the form to contain a bust of Christ or the Good Shepherd, supported by angels, within a shell niche, painted or on an ivory diptych. There are many sarcophagi with a central shell niche containing a bust of the deceased (sometimes man and wife): a particularly fine example is in Syracuse Museum, of Adelphia and her husband (*c.*340), with scenes from the OT and NT.

imago pietatis (Lat. image of pity; also Gk. *akra tapeinosis*, Ger. *Schmerzensmann*, and occasionally in Italian, misleadingly, *pietà*) A devotional image of Christ showing His wounds, very similar to the *Arma Christi or the *Trinity (as a '*Seat of Mercy'), and not intended to represent any actual incident in the Passion. The usual form is a half-length figure, upright in the tomb, with eyes open or closed, and arms folded to show the wounds. It is a purely symbolic image, not an Entombment, and originated in the East, probably before the 12th century. It was based on an icon in Sta Croce in Rome, now lost but known from copies. It was greatly developed in the West in the 13th and 14th centuries in keeping with late medieval piety, especially Franciscan. The earliest known Western example is by a 13th-century Florentine painter, in the Horne Museum, Florence. Such images were common in Germany, especially in sculpture, and survived the Reformation but became rare after the mid-16th century, being replaced to some extent by the Sacred *Heart. Apart from the single figure there are variants showing Christ supported by Mary, or Mary and John, or angels. Similarly, representations of the Holy Trinity often show Christ as dead (Baldung Grien, London, NG; Hugo van der *Goes, Edinburgh, NG) or crucified and upheld by God the Father, a form usually called *Seat of Mercy*, or in German *Gnadenstuhl*. The Giovanni Bellini in Milan (Brera), which shows the dead Christ supported by Mary and John in a realistic landscape setting, is an *imago pietatis* although it looks at first sight like an Entombment.

Imbomon (Gk. summit) The circular chapel on the Mt. of *Olives, which is the traditional site of the *Ascension. The first chapel was built before 378, but the present one was built by the Crusaders, with additions by the Muslims (who venerate Christ as a prophet). A depression in the rock is said to be Christ's footprint.

Immaculate Conception, the The dogma that *Mary, 'in the first instant of her conception, was . . . preserved exempt from all stain of original sin'. It is commonly confused with the *Virgin Birth of Christ, or even with a virginal birth of Mary herself. The belief itself is of great antiquity, but the first official Feast was proclaimed by *Sixtus IV in 1476 and it was not until 1854 that it was formally defined (cf. *Assumption). The earliest known dated representation of the subject—inherently difficult to symbolize—is a painting by Carlo Crivelli, dated 1492 (London, NG), which has a scroll inscribed with words from Ecclesiasticus (Vg. 24: 14), 'Ab initio et ante saecula creata sum' (in the NRSV it is v. 9: 'Before the ages, in the beginning he created me, and I shall not cease to be').

In the 15th and 16th centuries it was not a frequent subject, but there is an altarpiece at Cortona by *Signorelli of 1521 which, though stylistically crude and old-fashioned, is iconographically innovative, with Mary standing on a column with Adam and Eve below—Mary being the Second Eve as Christ is the Second Adam—and with six prophets surrounding her.

In Spain in the 17th century great interest was taken in the subject, which was painted by Murillo, Velázquez, and Zurbarán among others. Francisco *Pacheco was a painter and father-in-law of Velázquez, but is best known for his book *El arte de la pintura* of 1649, which contains a description of the correct way to represent the Immaculate Conception: 'The version that I follow is the one that is closest to the holy revelation of the Evangelist and approved by the Catholic Church on the authority of the sacred and holy interpreters . . . In this loveliest of mysteries Our Lady should be painted as a beautiful young girl, 12 or 13 years old, in the flower of her youth . . . And thus is she praised by the Husband: *tota pulchra es amica mea*, a text that is always written in this painting. [See Song of Solomon 1: 16, 'Ah, you are beautiful, my love . . .'.] She should be painted wearing a white tunic and a blue mantle . . . She is surrounded by the sun, an oval sun of white and ochre, which sweetly blends into the sky. Rays of light emanate from her head, around which is a ring of twelve stars. An imperial crown adorns her head, without, however, hiding the stars. Under her feet is the moon. Although it is a solid globe, I take the liberty of making it transparent, so that the landscape shows through . . .'. The Zurbarán in Edinburgh (NG) has a temple, palm, cypress, tower, and the City of God in the background. Rev. 12: 1, 'A woman clothed with the sun, with the moon under her feet, and on her head a crown of twelve stars' is normally associated with the subject, as in the picture by Velázquez (*c.*1618: London, NG).

impluvium In ancient Roman houses the *atrium, or central court, had a shallow depression to collect rainwater. Early Christian churches had a similar arrangement, with the water used for ritual ablutions before entering the church. The most famous example—a fountain rather than a pool—was the *cantharus of Old St Peter's.

Incarnation The Incarnation, i.e. God becoming man in the person of Christ, is a basic Christian dogma, but is hardly susceptible of representation in art. It is therefore symbolized, either as the *Annunciation (at Mary's words 'let it be with me according to your word', or as the *Nativity.

incense *See* SACRAMENTALS and THURIBLE.

Incredulity of Saint Thomas *See* THOMAS, S.

India *See* NON-WESTERN CHRISTIAN ART.

Infancy Gospels *See* APOCRYPHAL GOSPELS.

'In hoc signo vinces' (Lat. 'In this sign shalt thou conquer') *See* CONSTANTINE and CHI RHO.

Innocents, Massacre of the Chapter 2 of S. Matthew's Gospel tells how, after the birth of Christ, the *Magi came to Bethlehem to adore the 'King of the Jews'. But as they did not know where He had been born, they stopped in Jerusalem and asked where they should go. King Herod, puzzled and anxious, enquired from the chief priests and scribes, and was told that it must be Bethlehem. He sent them there, telling them to return to him when they had found the Child. They were warned in a dream not to do so, and Herod was 'infuriated and he sent and killed all the children in and around Bethlehem, who were two years old or under' (Matt. 2: 16–18). *Joseph, however, had already been warned in a dream to take Mary and the Child to *Egypt, where they remained until Herod's death, when an angel again appeared in a dream and told Joseph to return.

There are representations of this dramatic subject from the 5th century, including a mosaic in Sta Maria Maggiore, Rome, an ivory in Milan Cathedral, and a sarcophagus in St-Maximin in Provence. Later examples include works by Giotto (Padua, Arena Chapel), an engraving after Raphael, and Bruegel, in what is perhaps a political allegory (provoked by the Spanish occupation of the Netherlands), as well as Rubens and Poussin. The Hospital of the Holy Innocents (Spedale degli Innocenti) in Florence was the first Foundling Hospital in the world, and is a major work of Early Renaissance architecture by *Brunelleschi (1419–24), but is also famous for the Della Robbia blue and white terracotta plaques of the foundlings in swaddling bands on the façade—innocents saved.

i

INRI An abbreviation of the Latin *Iesus Nazarenus Rex Iudaeorum* (Jesus of Nazareth, King of the Jews), on the *titulus written by Pilate (John 19: 19–22; 'It read, Jesus of Nazareth the King of the Jews... and it was written in Hebrew, in Latin, and in Greek. Then the chief priests of the Jews said to Pilate, "Do not write 'The King of the Jews', but 'This man said I am King of the Jews'". Pilate answered, "What I have written I have written."' (*Quod scripsi scripsi*). On crucifixes there is usually just INRI, but sometimes it is written in full in all three languages.

Institution of the Eucharist *See* COMMUNION OF THE APOSTLES.

instruments, liturgical *See* LITURGICAL OBJECTS.

Instruments of the Passion *See* ARMA CHRISTI, PASSION.

intarsia A term describing inlays of marble or of wood, which are often skilfully used to make pictures in panelling, the backs of choir stalls, or bookcases. The most elaborate examples of wood intarsia are Italian (Urbino and Mantua), and marble examples are found in the elaborate 17th- to 19th-century Neapolitan *pietre dure* antependia. The term is also sometimes used to describe patterned marble floors, which are more accurately described as *opus cectile or opus Alexandrinum.

intercession Prayer on behalf of all people, or some, or oneself, especially in times of famine, plague, or other trouble, is common to most religions. *Votive images or churches are, so to speak, acknowledgements of intercession by one's patron saint, or of a city by its patron, or—in the case of plague—*S. Roch, *S. Sebastian, or the Virgin Mary (cf. *Sta Tecla protecting the city of Este from plague* by *Tiepolo, 1759, Este, Chiesa delle Grazie, or *Palladio's Redentore church in Venice, built after the plague of 1570). There are, however, a few examples surviving of a special subject, the Madonna interceding with Christ for humanity, and His intercession with God the Father (*Intercessio Christi et Mariae*). This shows Christ displaying His wounds and Mary pointing to her breast. In the 12th century Mary was seen as 'mediatrix of graces', second only to Christ Himself, the Mediator between God and man, as described in a book of 1156, ascribed to *S. Bernard. The subject was very popular in the late Middle Ages, especially in Germany and the Netherlands, but was condemned by Luther, *Zwingli, and other Reformers, so that few examples survive. An early altarpiece (*c.*1402: New York, Met. Mus. at The Cloisters) from Florence Cathedral has an explicit inscription with Mary saying 'Dearest Son, because of the milk I gave you have mercy on them', referring to a group of figures kneeling at the bottom of the painting. Christ says 'My Father, let those be saved for whom you wished me to suffer the Passion'. Undoubtedly the finest work of art representing this rare subject is the altarpiece by Filippino *Lippi of *c.*1495 for San Francesco del Palco, Prato (now in Munich). It has an *Annunciation* in roundels at the top and an *imago pietatis in the *predella* below. Other versions of the subject are combined with the Last Judgement and some are related to the *Madonna Misericordiae type.

intercolumniation The spaces between columns.

International Gothic This is the name given (in the 1890s by Louis Courajod) to a form of Gothic painting, MS illumination, and sculpture, and is also reflected in the architecture of the period, especially in the Cathedral of Cologne, St Vitus Cathedral in Prague, and the Decorated Style in England. It arose in connection with the 'Court Style' of Paris *c.*1350, and is linked with Simone *Martini and the School of *Avignon. Figures are elegant and draperies cast in flowing curves and the subjects tend to be courtly. International Gothic art is largely secular and aristocratic, as in the hunting scenes in both the mid-14th-century *Chambre du Cerf* in the Palais des Papes in Avignon and in one of its greatest monuments, the *Très Riches Heures* (nominally a Book of *Hours), made for the Duc de Berri, brother of the King of France, by the Limbourg brothers before 1416. The novelty of the style in painting lay principally in the realistic depiction of details, especially of costume and animals—the sketchbooks of Giovanni de' Grassi and Pisanello show this new interest—rather than in naturalism in the wider sense. From France and the Duchy of Burgundy the style rapidly spread to E. Europe and to Lombardy, and, from there, to the rest of Italy. Naples, where both Giotto and Simone Martini were employed, and Prague, where Simone's influence was also felt, were two of the more surprising centres. Gentile da Fabriano and Pisanello took it to Florence and Rome, and Gentile's *Adoration of the Kings* for the Strozzi family of Florentine bankers (1425: Uffizi) is one of the masterpieces of the style. Florentine painters like Lorenzo Monaco were profoundly affected by the new realism of detail, as was the sculptor *Ghiberti, but in Florence the style of *Masaccio and *Donatello was ultimately the foundation of Renaissance art.

In Germany and Bohemia the style was linked to the *Weiche Stil*, or Soft Style, which was less realistic and represented gentle, rather sentimental figures, as in the *Schöne Madonna* types. In the West, religious art in the early 15th century thus came to be more naturalistic and at the same time more sentimental and subjective than its counterpart in Orthodox lands, where the austerely theological forms of the Byzantine tradition remained in force for centuries. This is perhaps the point of separation between the Theotokos, the God-Bearer, and the Mother and Child representations of Western art.

Invention of the Holy Cross (Lat. *invenire*, to discover) The finding of the *True Cross by *S. Helena.

Ionic *See* ORDER.

Ireland *See* EUROPE.

Irene, Saint *See* SEBASTIAN, S.

Irish art Christianity came to Ireland about the end of the 5th century as a result of S. Patrick's preaching. By the 6th century notable monasteries had been founded at Clonard and Clonmacnoise, and by the mid-6th century S. Columba had founded Derry in the north, Durrow in the centre, Iona on the west coast of Scotland, *c.*563/5, and had begun to evangelize that part of Scotland which was then Irish. 'White martyrdom' was much sought after—that is, ascetic conditions in hermitages inspired by the Desert Fathers, crude stone huts in barren bogs or wild crags, such as Skellig Michael off the coast of Kerry. In more settled places learning flourished, and by the mid-6th century the Canon tables and historical charts of *Eusebius of Caesarea had been introduced, as were S. Jerome's translations of the Gospels. In the 7th century, such was the reputation of Irish piety and learning that many English monks joined them, and Irish missionaries spread into Friesland and Germany.

S. Columbanus from Bangor *c.*590 founded a monastery at Luxeuil in France, and later was at Jouarre, and other places in central France, before going with Irish companions, among whom was Gall, to Italy; Gall became a hermit in Switzerland, and the monastery of *Sankt Gallen was eventually founded over his tomb. S. Columbanus went on to found Bobbio, near Piacenza, where he died in 615, leaving there not only Irish monks, but also MSS typical of Irish art, some of which are now in the Ambrosiana Library, Milan. Irish influence waned after the Synod of Whitby, 663/4, and fewer English tended to go to Ireland after SS Theodore and Hadrian established Canterbury, where Theodore (d. 690) was Archbishop, as a flourishing centre. In the north, links with Ireland continued. S. Willibrord, a Northumbrian who had spent twelve years in Ireland, went to Friesland as a missionary in 690, founded Utrecht in Holland and Echternach in Luxemburg; S. Kilian, another Irish missionary, was martyred in Würzburg in 698; Alcuin of York, who had had an Irish teacher, went to Aachen at the invitation of *Charlemagne and then settled at Tours, in France, with Irish students, who carried northern English and Irish styles into *Carolingian MS painting at the famous Tours scriptorium.

The earliest Irish MS to survive is the Cathach of S. Columba of the 6th century (Dublin, R. Irish Acad.). The curious name of this MS means 'champion' or 'warrior', and refers to its use as a talisman carried into battle before the O'Donnells, to whose family S. Columba belonged. It consists of part of a damaged psalter, written in an early Irish script which probably dates from the time of S. Columba; the text is that by S. Jerome, and the decoration of the capitals makes very sparing use of the dots which later become such a feature of Irish MSS. The Book of Durrow (Trinity Coll., Dublin) was made probably in the 2nd half of the 7th century, and may be a copy of a MS brought back to Northumbria from Italy by Benedict Biscop (d. 690), founder of the twin monasteries of Wearmouth and Jarrow. The text was probably written and painted by Irish scribes and painters in the north, since it has the regularity usual in Northumbrian MSS. It displays a feature of these MSS by having an introductory page—a 'carpet-page' of abstract ornament and rhythmic decorative animal interlacing of a type derived from Anglo-Saxon metalwork.

The most splendid piece of Irish church plate is the 8th-century Ardagh Chalice (Dublin, Nat. Mus.), the silver bowl of which has rich ornaments of gold, bronze, and enamels. In monastery ruins at Derrynaflan, a 9th-century silver chalice (now also Dublin, Nat. Mus.) with ornaments similar to those of the Ardagh Chalice was found together with a superb paten and stand, and other objects; these all show the very high level of Irish metalwork in the 8th and 9th centuries, well meriting the description of the scholar Giraldus Cambrensis in the 12th century, that it was 'the work of angels'.

The Irish monasteries mingled their devotion, their learning in theology, hagiography, and symbolism, and also their great artistic creativity and patronage, with a vigorous pursuit of worldly power, particularly in their struggles against the encroaching privileges demanded by Armagh, as the custodian of the right to claim the 'tribute of S. Patrick'. Against this increasing pursuit of the worldly, a reaction in the mid-8th century centred on the two monasteries of Tallaght and Finglas, near Dublin, which flourished in the last years of the 8th century until disaster struck.

The Norsemen had already raided England and destroyed Lindisfarne in 793; the first raid on Dublin was in 795, Iona was attacked in 801/2, forcing the Columban community to seek refuge at Kells, near Dublin. Bangor was destroyed in 822 or 824, and by 830 the Norsemen, under their chief, Turgeis, had set up profitable trading centres at Dublin, Limerick, Waterford, and Wexford, where good harbours were able to shelter 100 to 200 Viking longships. These ports were frequented by ships from the Mediterranean, Byzantium, Russia, and the Baltic, one of the chief 'commodities' being Irish slaves taken on Viking forays. Although the raids on Irish settlements continued unabated, so did the internecine warfare among the Irish chieftains. By the mid-10th century all Ireland was under tribute to the Norsemen, but they were slowly Christianized, chiefly by intermarriage. The striking thing is the speed of regeneration of the Irish communities—as soon as a town or settlement was destroyed, it was rebuilt. But the devastation means that the architecture of the 6th to the 10th centuries has survived only fragmentarily. The Skellig Michael hermitages may have been no more than beehive-shaped dry-stone huts, but some of them, like the remains of the earliest known monasteries, which were often built as clusters of similar hermitages, show that these could be as much as 30 ft. in diameter and 18 ft. high. Most churches were tiny, with walls of huge stones, usually unbonded, and often roofed with stone flags with strainer arches to help bear the enormous weight, creating an attic space underneath. The doorways are rarely more than gaps in the stone walls, with a lintel. Only about nine or ten of these stone-roofed churches have survived; most fell in under their own weight.

Glendalough is more informative: it was founded at the end of the 6th century as a collection of hermitages by S. Kevin, but by the end of the 7th or early 8th century a monastery and a cathedral, 48 ft. long by 30 ft. wide, was built, but it fell victim, like so many others, to Viking raids. Probably the best remains of the 10th to the 12th centuries are the round towers, which were built adjoining churches to serve as belfries, look-outs, and uncertain places of refuge. They range from about 50 ft. to about 95 ft. high, and some 18 ft. in diameter, with conical tops and four windows at the top from which bells were rung (their old Irish name means 'bell-house'). They had as many as four or five timber floors, reached by ladders, and the doors were usually 8 to 10 ft. up, so that they should have been defensible, though many were burnt out. Glendalough, Monasterboice, Cashel, and many others are of the same type, built with carefully cut and shaped stone, so that it must be assumed that the small, rather insignificant stone churches, or the continued use of wooden ones, was by design and not because of lack of ability.

The stone monuments of the end of the 7th century are blocks some 6 ft. or more high, carved with Greek crosses in circles, the ends of the crosses often being twisted into spiral decorations. Some have a schematic representation of the Crucifixion, with the lance and sponge thrust upwards by rudimentary figures, a motive of Byzantine origin (the *North Inishea* and *Duvillaum Slabs*, Mayo), or with crosses ornamented with spirals and interlacings, as the *Fahan Mura Slab* (Donegal); these were erected in the 7th century possibly as gravestones. It is not until the 8th–12th century that the great standing *crosses appear, and then not only in Ireland, but also in all the British Isles.

During the 8th century, manuscripts had a wide European development between Ireland, Northumbria, Utrecht, Bobbio, England, and Sankt Gallen, one feature of which is the increasing size and richness of the *Chi-Rho symbol, and the 'carpet-page'. The Book of *Kells has the power and splendour of the Ardagh Chalice.

All this prodigious development stopped with the Viking raids. Later the Danes joined in, and regrettably the Irish continued their own family feuds, sometimes even enlisting the Norsemen as allies. One result of these devastations was wholesale emigration and in the later 9th century Irish scholars were welcomed in Europe for learning and holiness, settling in Liège, and in Laon. Another result was the emergence for the first time of a king of all Ireland—in 967 the Norsemen were defeated in battle by Mathghamhain and his brother Brian, who after his brother's murder became sole king by 1002. He was known as Brian Boru, from the tribute which he exacted from those he subjugated, and his victory over the Vikings at the Battle of Clontarf in 1014 ended their total control of the country. He died immediately afterwards, and anarchy returned; the Vikings, however, remained in their ports as settlers as well as traders.

Major changes came in the 12th century stemming from the control of the Church lying entirely with the monasteries. The Christianized and urbanized Norse population refused to accept the authority of the abbots and sent bishops to be consecrated by the Archbishop S. Anselm in Canterbury, and between 1093 and 1103 he persuaded the King of Munster to reform the Church in Ireland. By 1110 two archbishops and twenty-four bishops were appointed, and the King gave Cashel of the Kings to the Church. In 1134 Cormac's Chapel was consecrated at Cashel, built by masons brought from Europe and England who introduced European *Romanesque forms such as rib vaulting and portals with engaged columns. Irish masons, however, quickly treated the new forms merely as a surface decoration, their 'beak-head' ornament incorporating human was well as cat's heads. Benedictines had arrived in 1109, and the Augustinian canons in the early 12th century. In 1142 the *Cistercians arrived, and by 1157 Mellifont was built, and they were soon followed by the Premonstratensians, and all the other major orders, including eventually the Franciscans and the Dominicans. The Cistercian churches were, for Ireland, of unparalleled size. The ruins of Mellifont (Louth), Jerpoint (Kilkenny), and Duiske (Co. Cork) show that the churches range from 100 to 175 ft. in length, with transepts, and all the usual features of a Cistercian monastery. They all had affinities with Burgundian, or more usually, English Cistercian houses such as Fountains, Rievaulx, or with Tintern in Wales, and strove for the same rigorous architectural standards as their Continental counterparts.

Politically, Ireland was divided into five kingdoms: Munster in the south, Connacht in the west, Leinster and Meath in the centre, and Ulster in the north, itself subdivided into several kingdoms. There had been a High Kingship, but the system broke down though internal warfare, during which a dispossessed king, Dermot Mac Murrough, took refuge in Bristol and there gathered a crowd of Norman and Welsh adventurers. Dermot got the backing of Henry II of England, who approved but would take no part. Unfortunately Ireland has always been a temptation to marauding invaders. There were successive landings in 1169/70, in which Norman mailed knights proved invincible, and in 1171 Henry came to inspect his new province. The barons divided the country into feudal estates, and sacked it, plundering Armagh, devastating Clonmacnoise, and by the early 13th century most of the Irish except for Ulster, had submitted, including the churchmen.

There had long been a church of St Patrick's outside the walls of Dublin. When the saintly archbishop, Laurence O'Toole, died in 1181, Henry II appointed a layman, John Comyn, and sent him to Rome to a compliant pope to be ordained and made a bishop. He began rebuilding St Patrick's, and in 1220 his successor made it a cathedral, with building continuing until 1270. Although Christ Church Cathedral in Dublin was originally built by

Vikings in 1038, the present Anglican church is a 13th-century Gothic one, with a Norman crypt, and it was thoroughly, but well, restored in the 19th century by Street. These buildings are without any Irish tradition, and are no more than English and European Gothic transposed into another land. From the time the Augustinians and Cistercians arrived in the 12th century Irish art was totally submerged in the styles and forms which were brought in from overseas. The Norman onslaught on the monasteries was as pitilessly destructive as that of their Viking ancestors; the production of MSS and metalwork stopped, since all was now imported. Henceforward, there is no true Irish art, only art in Ireland as the counterpart of what was created in Britain and in Europe. The final devastation came with the onslaught of Cromwell. His legacy was not only occupation and colonization: it brought also the banning of the Catholic religion, the proscription of its priests, and the domination of Anglo-Saxon and Scottish colonists as rulers and in religion. Between the Battle of the Boyne in 1690 and the great famine of 1847, the majority of parishes had churches in the proportions of one or more Anglican to four Catholic and other Nonconformist denominations such as Quaker, Methodist, Moravian, Presbyterian. Very often there is little architectural distinction between the Catholic and the Nonconformist churches: most are small, single-storey, modest buildings, of no particular quality, and interesting more because they existed in so hostile a religious climate than for any architectural reason. Among the most interesting features of the small country churches built by all the non-conforming churches was the use of the T-plan—a nave with a transeptal east end. This design enabled the largest number of people to see the altar or the pulpit. Another curious feature was the provision, in Presbyterian and Moravian churches, of two doors, one for each sex, and this feature was often copied in Catholic churches, which also separated men from women in church. Most of these humble country churches had nothing to do with architecture in the grander sense; they were built by the poor, for the poor, with the simplest materials, and sometimes great poetry is to be found in the circumstances of their creation, like the little church at Spink, near Abbeyleix, Co. Leix, which bears the moving inscription 'Anno famis et pestis' (i.e. 1847, 'Year of famine and plague'). Yet another unusual feature is the provision of a house for the priest or minister, under an extension of the roof, with only a separate doorway and a change in fenestration to mark an upper storey.

The 18th century saw the creation of a Palladianism which is not entirely a copy of the English form, and marvellous plaster-work which is distinctively Irish, but it is an almost totally secular art. In the mid-18th century two cathedrals were built in Waterford, both by John Roberts: the Catholic St Patrick's of 1764, designed for a large congregation, since it has galleries on three sides of the nave as well as a second gallery at the west end, and the Anglican Cathedral for the Church of Ireland in 1774, in a style reminiscent of Gibbs. The churches built by the Anglican Board of First Fruits are of an almost standard design—a plain hall, with a tower at the west front, usually with a spire.

The Catholic Emancipation Act of 1829 marked a milestone. Not until then was the Catholic Church legally free to build churches again and to establish seminaries, though the terrible legacy of the intervening centuries still haunts the land. Very splendid Anglican and Catholic churches have been built, virtually all in either a Gothic Revival or pseudo-Romanesque style, irrespective of confession. The few Catholic cathedrals built before 1829 were, with the exception of Waterford, modest affairs. Dublin, Belfast, and Cork still only have Catholic pro-cathedrals. Dublin, unusually, is a Greek Revival design with Doric porticoes and a low octagonal dome. Dublin's St Mary's Metropolitan chapel, so like the late 18th-century St-Philippe-du-Roule in Paris that it was probably based on it, was a more characteristic type. Many Catholic churches now imitated Roman forms, as for example St Mary's Dominican church in Cork, 1832–61, with a rich Roman-type interior of 1875–88. Some of the Gothic Revival churches were distinctly 'Gothick', such as the Anglican cathedral at Tuam, Co. Galway, of 1827, based on English Decorated Gothic, or the almost gimcrack Gothick of the Anglican church at Monkstown of *c.*1830, and the splendid Catholic church of St Malachy, Belfast, of 1844, with an exuberant interior with a fine fake Perpendicular tracery ceiling with pendant drops.

Many Catholic churches are by *Pugin and his son. Typical of the grander, serious type of Gothic Revival churches are the magnificent pair in Cork. The Catholic one is by the younger Pugin, of 1868–79, in a style reminiscent of

Coutances in Normandy, and the Anglican one is by Burges, 1865–79, with three towers and spires, the central one 240 ft. high; it is probably the most splendid church in Ireland. But nothing of the ancient artistic quality has surfaced over the imported styles, nor been able to rise above the temptations of facile religiosity in Catholic church art—*bondieuserie is rarely resisted. The greatest danger many of these historic Catholic churches—both town and village ones—face is the pointless 'modernization' of their period interiors according to ill-considered interpretations of Vatican II. *See also* EUROPE.

Isaac was the son of *Abraham and was himself an OT *patriarch. He was born miraculously when his mother, Sarah, was 90, and, because of his birth, *Hagar and her son Ishmael were sent away (Gen. 17 and 18). When he was still a boy, God commanded Abraham to sacrifice him as a burnt offering, but an angel appeared at the last moment and stopped him (Gen. 22: 1–18). This obedience was seen as a *type of Christ's sacrifice, Isaac carrying the wood for the fire prefiguring the carrying of the Cross. When Isaac was 40 his parents sent to kinsmen to find him a wife (Gen. 24: 12–61), and their envoy, Eliezer, found Rebekah, the daughter of Bethuel and sister of Laban. The meeting of Eliezer and Rebekah at the well was also seen as prefiguring Christ and the Woman of Samaria. Rebekah returned with Eliezer and married Isaac, but was barren for twenty years before bearing twins, *Jacob and Esau. Jacob cheated his brother of the paternal blessing, since Isaac was then almost blind (Gen. 27).

Earlier, Isaac had passed Rebekah off as his sister, since they lived among the Philistines and he feared that they might kill him in order to take Rebekah (Gen. 26: 6–11). The king, Abimelech, saw 'Isaac fondling his wife Rebekah', and realized that he had been deceived, but he nevertheless ordered that they should not be harmed. This scene is extremely rare, but it is one of four Isaac scenes in 'Raphael's Bible', the frescoes in the Vatican Loggie executed by Raphael's pupils and assistants (1518–19). Isaac died at 180 and was buried by Jacob and Esau, who were by then reconciled (Gen. 21–8 and 35: 29).

Isaiah The Prophet was the author of the OT book bearing his name (although modern scholarship has divided him into two, if not three). His book contains several Messianic prophecies frequently quoted as OT prefigurations, the best-known being 'Behold a virgin shall conceive, and bear a son' (Isa. 7: 14, AV; Vg. has 'Ecce virgo concipiet et pariet filium'; NRSV has 'Look, the young woman is with child'); 'Unto us a child is born ...' (AV 9: 6; Vg. 'For a Child is born to us'; NRSV has '... has been born'); and 'A shoot shall come out from the stump of *Jesse, and a branch shall grow out of his roots' (11: 1). In addition, the passage (6: 1 ff.) recounts a vision of the Lord and of seraphim (*see* CHERUBIM), and (40: 3) 'A voice cries out "In the wilderness prepare the way of the Lord" (Vox clamantis in deserto ...), which became associated with *John the Baptist.

An *Apocryphal Ascension of Isaiah, dating from the 1st century AD, may have been known to *S. Paul (Heb. 11: 37): the first five chapters describe Isaiah's martyrdom by being sawn asunder and the rest of the book (chs. 6–11) describes his vision, being taken by an angel to the seventh Heaven, where he saw God. The first Heaven is above the firmament, and much like the Earth, but the second to the sixth hardly differ from one another.

The earliest representation of Isaiah may be in the *Catacomb of Priscilla (3rd cent.), where a man pointing to a star near a woman and child may symbolize Isaiah's prophecy concerning the Virgin and Child, but this is very controversial, and the painting is badly damaged. There are, however, many early representations—a 4th-century *gold glass, Byzantine mosaics as well as those in Ravenna and Rome, and medieval MS illuminations, many of which show Isaiah's lips cleansed by a burning coal (6: 5–7). Portal sculptures include Moissac and the cathedrals of Chartres and Amiens, as well as single figures for Florence Cathedral (Nanni di Banco, 1408), and the *Well of Moses*, Dijon, *c.*1402. He is almost invariably shown as an old man with a long beard, holding a scroll with *Ecce virgo concipiet* or *Virga de radice Jesse* on it, or with a branch (for Jesse), or with a saw, the instrument of his supposed martyrdom. An interesting exception is the figure by Michelangelo in the *Sistine Chapel, where he is beardless and comparatively young, like the statue by Nanni di Banco for Florence Cathedral, which Michelangelo must certainly have known. Raphael's figure in Sant'Agostino, Rome, of 1511–12, is stylistically almost a plagiary of Michelangelo, but iconographically returns to the traditional bearded figure.

The memorable quality of Isaiah's prophecies in AV is often because his words so inspired Handel's *Messiah* that the music rings in one's ears on hearing them. Who has not been stirred by the ringing cry of 'Comfort ye, Comfort ye, my people!', or moved by 'A man of sorrows, and acquainted with grief'?

Isenheim Altar *See* GRÜNEWALD.

Ishmael *See* HAGAR.

Isidore of Miletus *See* ANTHEMIOS.

Isidore of Seville, Saint (*c*.560–636), was born in Seville and became its archbishop. He converted the Visigoths from *Arianism and presided over the Councils of Seville (619) and Toledo (633). He was canonized in 1598 and made a *Doctor of the Church in 1722, but is best known as the 'Schoolmaster of the Middle Ages', on account of his many books, especially the *Etymologies*, an encyclopaedia ranging from fabulous animals to medicine to theology, which served as a guide to many artists, in particular sculptors working on cathedrals.

ISLAMIC AND CHRISTIAN INTERACTIONS IN ART

Contacts between Christian art and Islamic art can be detected with varying degrees of certainty, sporadically over centuries, and in different countries and media. The Islamic era begins with the *hijrah*, the exodus from Mecca to Medina in AH 1/AD 622, of the followers of the Prophet Muhammad, who had turned away from idolatry. Islamic art is conditioned by Islam, but not all its productions are acceptable to all Muslims, and there is some participation of non-Muslim groups: hence it is best defined as the art produced for rulers or populations of Islamic culture. It is less strictly aniconic than is sometimes supposed. The Qur'an V. 91 lists idols among various abominations; nevertheless, a tradition relates that, following the return from Medina in 630, when the Prophet Muhammad was cleansing the Ka'bah at Mecca from idols, he covered a portrayal of the Virgin and Child with his hand to prevent their being effaced.

Architecture and its decoration

At the early expansion of Islam (AD 630 onwards) contacts are typically the acquisition of buildings or the adaptation to new purposes of architectural forms and modes of decoration. The Dome of the Rock (AH 72/AD 691–92), Jerusalem, resembles a Byzantine martyrium in structure, but bears an anti-trinitarian inscription in mosaic, conveyed in the right angles and circles of a plain 'kufic' script. The Umayyad mosque at Damascus (AH 96/AD 714-15), takes over a site that was previously a temple, then a church; today it retains the shrine of the head of Saint John the Baptist. The late antique and Byzantine scroll-work is at the origin of the Islamic arabesque and the same is true of geometric patterning.

In Spain, the Great Mosque of Cordoba (AH 377/AD 987 onwards) was built on the site of a church; in the 14th century, following the Reconquista, a cathedral was built within the mosque using Islamic forms. The use of the *squinch arch spread from Spain to church builders in southern France. The visual resemblance is clear regarding the use of conical domes on drums in East Christian churches and in Muslim tombs of eastern Anatolia, the Caucasus, and northern Iran about the 10th and 11th centuries, but questions of influence or reciprocal influence are less so. Some degree of influence is to be admitted from Byzantine architecture to Ottoman. In the period of the Crusades, Islamic inventions in castle-building, such as the bent entrance, were adopted in the Crusader states of Outremer and brought back to Europe.

The decorative and portable arts

The Copts of Egypt had a strong textile tradition in wool and linen that would have fed into Islamic production. During the Fatimid period (AD 909–1171), some degree of Coptic patronage may be inferred from the lustre decoration on some pottery vessels of the 10th or 11th century: examples include an emphatic cross (British Museum), and a Coptic priest with a censer (Victoria and Albert Museum, London). Lustre technique was practised in Spain, at first in Malaga under Arab rule, then from the mid-14th century under Christian rule at Valencia. Large dishes from the latter sometimes bear the IHS monogram. The earliest phase of the great Ottoman pottery production is marked by two dated pieces with Armenian inscriptions: a Mass cruet of 1510 in memory of one Abraham of Kütahya, and a flask made in that centre in 1529 (British Museum).

Close contact in Spain or Sicily in the 11th or 12th century is demonstrated by an *aquamanile in base metal alloy in the form of a peacock, inscribed in Arabic and Latin by a Christian artist using alternative names (Musée du Louvre). In Sicily in the 1140s, artists presumed to be Muslim and working in Fatimid style constructed and painted the wooden ceiling of the Cappella Palatina, Palermo, for Roger II. Attributable to Syria in the 13th century, a few pieces of inlaid metalwork (silver into brass) include Christian scenes or figures (notably, a basin and a canteen, Freer Gallery of Art, Washington, DC).

Whether by trade or crusade, various valuable items entered cathedral treasuries. Patterned silks were used in religious contexts as wrappings. Notable among silks is the 'Shroud of St Josse' (Musée du Louvre)—a compound twill decorated with elephants and camels, and a kufic inscription shows that this was woven in eastern Iran for a personage who died in 961. It was acquired during the First Crusade, and presented to the Abbey of St Josse, Normandy. Fatimid rock crystal vessels were highly prized: small containers, probably originally intended for cosmetics, may have been used for relics; a fine rock crystal ewer was used as a cruet (formerly in Abbey de Gramont, then in the Church of Milhaguet until stolen in 1980). A rare type of glass beaker that may have been made in Syria, Egypt, or even Byzantium has traditionally been associated with St Hedwig of Silesia (d. 1243).

Already in the 8th century, the decorative effect of kufic script on a coin of 774 struck for the 'Abbasid caliph al-Mansur was imitated on coins minted in England for King Offa (r. 757–96). In the later 12th century pseudo-kufic was used as ornament on the Cathedral of Le Puy, Auvergne, and also on ciboria in Limoges enamel. By the time of Giotto (d. 1337) pseudo-kufic was used in Christian paintings as a dignified ornamentation on haloes and drapery; the script is sometimes softened into a pseudo-cursive script. Also in Christian painting from about 1500 onwards, carpets are shown beneath the feet of holy persons; design and probability suggest that they are of Ottoman manufacture. This mode continues with secular subjects.

Arts of the book

The codex form of book, which seems to have been used in the Islamic world since the 7th century, may have been adopted from Coptic prototypes. When Arab book illustration flourished in the 13th century in Syria, the style—palette, figure drawing, concentration of composition in a shallow plane—are features shared with some Syrian Jacobite work, suggesting a shared culture. The format for author portraits may have passed from classical prototypes, by way of East Christian books.

In Iran, under Mongol rule in the early 14th century, the *'Jami' al-Tawarikh* ('World History'), composed by Rashid al-Din in Tabriz, contained *inter alia* Jewish and Christian material. The surviving fragments of the great copy made in 1314 have illustrations in a style strongly influenced by Chinese painting. They portray: Old Testament figures such as Abraham, Moses, and Jonah, under their arabized names (the Khalili Collection); and the *Annunciation at the well* derived from the Proto-evangelium of Saint James, and the *Birth of the Prophet Muhammad*, which follows the type for a Christian Nativity (Edinburgh University Library).

Also presumably assembled in Tabriz are the celebrated albums of mainly later 14th- and 15th-century material (Topkapi Saray, Istanbul, and Staatsbibliotek Preussischer Kulturbesizt, Berlin). These contain a small number of Western prints, of which a few are explicitly Christian. There are also some coloured studies in Islamic style, loosely datable *c.*1400, that follow East Christian or Byzantine iconography (Christ in majesty; Head of the Virgin). The studies were occasionally used as a basis for individual paintings or manuscript illustrations: preserved in albums, a Virgin and Child adored in a church (Staatsbibliothek, Berlin), a Head of the Virgin (Topkapi Library, Istanbul), the latter being reproduced in the 1440s to convey the Christian maiden addressed by Shaykh Sanan in a *Mantiq al-Tayr* of 'Attar (David Collection, Copenhagen).

In Iran, from the 15th century onwards, figures from the shared Abrahamic tradition are occasionally illustrated. In the second half of the 17th century, under Safavid rule, the painter Muhammad Zaman produced single-album pictures in which various European traits are evident. Though some of his subjects are biblical, scholarly opinion has turned against the view that he was trained in Italy and converted to Catholicism. In the Qajar 19th century, Christian subjects were occasionally used, together with other European motifs, as decoration on lacquered penboxes.

In India under the Mughal Emperor Akbar (1556–1605), borrowing from Christian art may first have occurred in the 1570s in a *Hamzahnamah* illustration of a sun-worshipper that seems to reflect an Agony in the Garden (Museum für angewandter Kunst, Vienna). The influence of Christian art was reinforced by the visits of three Jesuit missions: 1580, 1591, 1595. Invited by Akbar, these missions brought books and paintings to explain their beliefs. At this period and subsequently under Jahangir (1605–27), painters, who were often of Hindu extraction, made reference to this material, producing both close copies and variations. Subjects include: the Nativity, Holy Family, Deposition, Last Judgment with Resurrection of the Dead (Royal Library, Windsor Castle), saints. Under Akbar, the Nativity scene type was adapted for portrayals of royal births. In 1602 the Jesuit Father Jerome Xavier completed for Akbar a life of Christ in Persian (*Dastan-i Masih,* also known as *Mirat al-Quds The Mirror of Holiness*). Forthwith Akbar's son Salim (later to reign as Jahangir) ordered a more fully illustrated copy. Under Jahangir and Shah Jahan (1628–66), royal iconography adopted halos and cherubs, motifs that spoke to counterparts in previous Indian iconography. The Holy Family continued to be a subject in the painting of Lucknow in the late 18th century.

Italy *See* EUROPE.

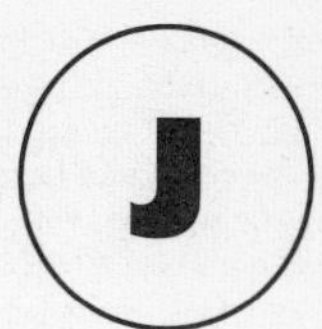

Jacob was an OT *patriarch (later called Israel). Very late in life *Isaac's wife Rebekah had twins. The first was 'red, all his body like a hairy mantle; so they named him Esau', and the second was Jacob. Esau was his father's favourite and Jacob his mother's. Esau, who was a hunter, was once very hungry and sold his birthright to his younger brother for 'a mess of pottage' (NRSV: bread and lentil stew) (Gen. 25: 24–34).

The aged Isaac was then almost blind, and he asked Esau to go hunting and get him a dish of venison (NRSV: savoury food), when he would bestow his paternal blessing on Esau. Rebekah persuaded Jacob to kill two kids, which she would cook as venison, and he could use the goatskins on his hands and neck to imitate Esau's hairiness and deceive Isaac into taking him for Esau. Isaac was suspicious—'the voice is Jacob's voice, but the hands are the hands of Esau'—but he nevertheless gave his blessing. Esau was furious when he discovered that he had been cheated of his birthright (Gen. 27: 1–38). Rebekah persuaded Isaac to send Jacob to her brother Laban to find himself a bride: this is sometimes regarded as a *type for the *Flight into Egypt. On the way, Jacob lay down to sleep on a stone as a pillow and dreamed that he saw a *ladder ('Jacob's Ladder', Gen. 28: 10–22) with 'the angels of God ascending and descending on it. And the Lord stood beside him' and promised him that the land on which he lay would be his and his children's, and they would be as numerous as the dust on the earth. When Jacob awoke he made the stone into an altar. (The stone he used as a pillow is allegedly the Stone of Scone, since 1996 in Edinburgh Castle, on which the kings of Scotland were crowned.) This was at Bethel, the place of *Abraham's sacrifice, about 12 miles from Jerusalem. Later, Jacob stopped at a well and enquired for Laban. Rachel, Laban's younger daughter, was pointed out to him and he fell in love with her at once. Laban said he must serve him for seven years before he could marry her 'and they seemed unto him but a few days', but then Laban cheated by substituting his older (and plainer) daughter, Leah, on the marriage night, claiming that it was the custom of the country that the elder daughter should be married first. In reply to Jacob's furious reproaches he agreed that Jacob could marry Rachel as well, but would have to serve another seven years (Gen. 28 and 29: 1–30).

After this Jacob agreed to continue serving Laban if he got all the speckled and streaked goats and dark sheep ('Jacob's Sheep') for himself from Laban's flocks. Again Laban cheated by telling his sons to take all such animals from the flock, so Jacob cut twigs of poplar, hazel, and chestnut, partly peeled them, and put them in the troughs. The result was that all the goats and sheep which drank from the troughs bore speckled offspring and Jacob's selective breeding meant that he soon had all the best animals. After twenty years he decided to return to his homeland and, when Laban was away, departed with his two wives, two concubines, children, servants, camels, and flocks. By then he had eleven sons and a daughter, Dinah. Rachel herself had a son, *Joseph, after many barren years (Gen. 30: 1–24 to 31: 1–34).

Laban caught up with them and accused Jacob of stealing his household gods, as well as his daughters. Jacob denied this (he did not know that Rachel had actually stolen her father's gods because she and Leah felt that he had cheated them of their dowries), and allowed Laban to search their tents. Rachel had put the idols in camel-bags and then sat on them in her tent, refusing to rise, pleading that 'the way of women is upon me', i.e. that she was ritually unclean. Jacob and Laban then agreed to part in peace. Jacob sent messengers on ahead to Esau, but when they returned with the news that Esau was coming with four hundred men Jacob 'was greatly afraid and distressed', so he sent a large present of camels and cattle to Esau. He remained alone and that night 'a man wrestled with him until daybreak. When the man saw that he did not prevail against Jacob, he struck him on the hip socket; and Jacob's hip was put out of joint as he wrestled with him.' The stranger blessed him and renamed him Israel, and Jacob realized that he had had a supernatural experience: 'I have seen God face to face, and yet my life is preserved' (Gen. 32: 24–32). For this reason, the stranger is always represented as an angel although he is not so referred to in Genesis. After this he met Esau, who embraced him and declined his gift, but Jacob insisted on it as a peace-offering. Esau invited him to Seir, where he lived, but Jacob continued his journey to Canaan. Here his daughter Dinah (Gen. 34) was raped by the son of the local chieftain, Hamor. Anxious to make amends, Hamor proposed to marry Dinah to his son and for the two tribes to intermarry. Jacob's sons pretended to agree, provided that all Hamor's men agreed to be circumcised. When this was done 'when they were still in pain' two of Jacob's sons killed them all and despoiled the city. Jacob reproached them and, fearing vengeance, moved on again, back to Bethel, where he made all his people purify themselves and hand over their idols, which he buried beneath an oak. Again God appeared to him, confirming His promises and his new name Israel (this is why the modern state is so named). Rachel died after giving birth to Benjamin and was buried at Bethlehem. Finally, Jacob returned to his father Isaac, who then died at 180 and was buried by Jacob and Esau (Gen. 35: 29).

Joseph, Rachel's first child, was hated by his brothers because he was his father's favourite and was given a 'coat of many colours' (NRSV has 'a long robe with sleeves'), and more so on account of his dreams, which indicated that they were to be ruled over by him. They plotted to kill him and made Jacob believe he was dead, although he had actually been sold into Egypt (*see* JOSEPH for this part of the story). Eventually Jacob and all his family went to Egypt, where Jacob died at 147. His body was embalmed by Egyptian physicians and buried at Machpelah, with *Abraham, Sarah, Isaac and Rebecca, and Jacob's own first wife, Leah. From Jacob's sons sprang the Twelve Tribes of Israel listed in Gen. 49. One of the very rare pictorial series of the Twelve Tribes (sometimes regarded as the *type of the Twelve Apostles) is by *Zurbarán, eleven being in the Bishop's Palace, Bishop Auckland, Durham, together with a copy of the twelfth, *Benjamin*, the original of which belongs to the Earl of Ancaster. Jacob and the Angel is the subject of sculptures by Jacques Lipchitz (1932, bronze) and Jacob *Epstein (1941, alabaster).

The story of Jacob is mainly in Gen. chs. 25; 27–37; 42; 45–50. The migration of Israel into Egypt ended in the Israelites' captivity, and finally to their liberation by Moses.

Jacobus de Voragine *See* GOLDEN LEGEND.

Jael (Vg. **Jahel**) **and Sisera**. Sisera was a general whose army was routed by the Israelites. He escaped and took refuge in Jael's tent. She gave him a drink of milk, and, when he fell asleep, she took a hammer and drove a tent-peg into his head. She then showed his body to Barak, the Israelite general. There seems to have been no reason for this murder, since Jael was not an Israelite, but she is reckoned as a Jewish heroine, like *Judith and *Esther. The story is told in Judges, chs. 4 and 5. Representations of it tend to be melodramatic, and can be confused with the equally bloody decapitation of Holofernes by Judith.

Jahweh *See* NOMEN SACRUM and TETRAGRAMMATON.

Jairus was the chief administrator of the synagogue at Capernaum. Mark (ch. 5) tells how his 12-year-old daughter was dying and he appealed to Jesus, who was then in Capernaum, to come and cure her. On the way, the *Woman with Haemorrhages touched His garment and was cured—(AV 'her faith made her whole'). While this was happening Jairus was told that his daughter had died, but Jesus said to him, 'Do not fear, only believe.' He then went to Jairus's house and said that the girl was not dead, only sleeping, and they 'laughed at him'. Jesus, however, took the parents with Peter, James, and John and sent everyone else away. He then restored the child to life. These two miracles of healing were both due to faith, but representations of the Woman with the Haemorrhages are more common than the raising of the child, since it was not a public miracle.

James the Great, Saint An *Apostle, also called 'of *Compostela', and patron of Spain. He was the son of Zebedee and brother of *John the Evangelist, and was called to be an Apostle with him (Matt. 10: 2). He was the first Apostle to be martyred, *c.*44, by Herod

Agrippa, who had him beheaded by the sword (Acts 12: 1–2). Centuries later, *c.*825, his body was 'discovered' in Spain and was taken to what is now Santiago (i.e. S. James) de Compostela, where a huge *pilgrimage industry developed, as well as a proliferation of improbable legends. Santiago became one of the great centres of pilgrimage, along with Rome, the Holy Land, and Canterbury—Chaucer's Wife of Bath had been to all of them—and there were at least four routes through France using monasteries as staging points.

Before the 13th century he was usually represented as a dark-bearded man holding a book or scroll, or a sword (the instrument of his martyrdom), but from then onwards he was distinguished from the other Apostles by a floppy hat, a long pilgrim's staff, a scrip or a water-bottle, and a scallop shell—this last to show that he had 'been to Compostela', rather like the stickers in the rear windows of cars nowadays. Later, but only in Spain, he was shown as mounted on a white horse and trampling a Moor underfoot. This was because he was believed to have appeared and fought beside the Spaniards at one of the battles against the Moors (1749: Tiepolo, Budapest).

Between AD 44 and the 9th century various legends, mostly nonsensical, were related of him: the most important, and those usually depicted, are the arrival of his body in Spain, Hermogenes, and the hanged boy.

The first of these alleges that his body, after his martyrdom in Jerusalem, was taken on a rudderless boat which eventually landed in Spain. His disciples laid the body on a stone 'which softened as if it were wax' and formed a sarcophagus. The heathen queen, Lupa, was asked to provide a suitable burial-place, but offered to provide oxen to take the stone sarcophagus wherever they wished, knowing that her oxen were in fact wild bulls who would kill the disciples. In fact, the bulls at once became tame and dragged the stone into the queen's palace, instantly converting her. The second, which seems to owe something to the story of *Simon Magus, relates that a magician, Hermogenes, was instructed to send his pupil Philetus to James (who was then still in Judaea) in order to confront him. Philetus was converted and returned to Hermogenes to convert him also, only to have a spell cast on him by Hermogenes. In the end, after loosing demons which returned to torment him, Hermogenes also was converted. This was the cause of James's being dragged before Herod. After his condemnation, James had a rope round his neck, pulled by a man named Josias, and was led to execution. On the way James cured a paralytic. Josias was converted on the spot and was martyred along with James. The great fresco cycle by *Mantegna, formerly in Padua, included the scenes of the Baptism of Hermogenes, James before Herod, James led to execution and curing the paralysed man, all as related in the **Golden Legend*. The final scene, the Martyrdom, is not that of James the Great, but, for an unknown reason, that of James the Less. Yet another legend tells of a German family on pilgrimage to Compostela. They stopped at an inn, where the wicked innkeeper (or his lustful daughter, whose advances had been spurned by the son) hid a silver cup in their luggage and then had them arrested (cf. the story of *Joseph). The boy was hanged, but thirty-six days later, on their return from Compostela, his parents found him still hanging but alive, having been supported by S. James himself. Saint James is the subject of a picture by Jusepe *Ribera (*c.*1600, in the Wellington Museum, Apsley House, London).

James the Less, Saint, was an *Apostle, called 'Less' to distinguish him from James the Great, the son of Zebedee (Matt. 10: 2–4). James the son of Alphaeus, the 'brother of the Lord', the writer of the Epistle, and the first Bishop of Jerusalem may all be the same man, but the Eastern Orthodox believe that the 'brother of the Lord' who was Bishop of Jerusalem was not the Apostle, son of Alphaeus: in any case, very little is known about him. He was martyred in Jerusalem in AD 62, after being sentenced by the Sanhedrin to stoning (or was thrown from the top of the Temple) and, according to the **Golden Legend*, was finally killed by a fuller's mallet. There is some confusion between the two Jameses, and the fresco cycle by *Mantegna, destroyed in 1944, represents scenes from the life of James the Great, except his martyrdom, which is that of James the Less. Single figures often show him as a bishop, and he frequently appears with his fellow-Apostle *Philip. He is always shown in groups of the Apostles, especially on 12th/13th century cathedrals—e.g. Chartres—and there are frescoes in the Santo at Padua and mosaics in St Mark's, Venice. For the 'Protevangelium of James' see below.

James, the Protevangelium of An *Apocryphal Gospel, probably of the mid-2nd century, attributed to 'James, the brother of the Lord' (*see* JAMES THE LESS). It is one of the so-called Infancy Gospels, and called Protevangelium (first Gospel) because it purports to record events earlier than those recorded in Luke. It gives the names of Joachim and Anna (*S. Anne), the parents of the Virgin *Mary, and contains many details used by medieval and later artists. The **Golden Legend* contains a great deal of material derived from it.

Jansen, Jansenism Cornelius Jansen (1585–1638) was Bishop of Ypres in Flanders. His *Augustinus*, published posthumously in 1640, was strongly anti-Jesuit and theologically pessimistic, almost Calvinist. It was condemned in 1649 and again in 1653 (partly for opinions Jansen did not hold), but it had great influence in France, especially at Port-Royal, near Paris, a convent of Cistercian nuns founded in 1626 and suppressed in 1713. The painter Philippe de Champaigne (1602–74), a Fleming like Jansen, had a daughter who was a nun at Port-Royal, who was paralysed and miraculously cured by the prayers of the community. This event was celebrated in his painting of 1662 (Louvre). Like his friend *Poussin, Philippe de Champaigne represented the classical, austere, anti-Baroque trend in French art of the 17th century, opposed to the exuberance of the Baroque, which was equated with Jesuit permissiveness in moral questions.

Japhet (Japheth) was the third son of *Noah (*see* SHEM). His sons were the legendary founders of the Northern races, from the Caspian Sea westwards (Gen. chs. 5–9).

Jehoshaphat, (Vg. **Josaphat**) **Valley of** Traditionally, the valley of the Kidron, near Jerusalem and the future site of the Last *Judgement (Joel 3: 12: 'Let the nations rouse themselves, and come up to the valley of Jehoshaphat; for there I will sit to judge all the neighbouring nations.'). The Kidron valley was in fact a burial-place. According to the **Golden Legend* the body of the Virgin Mary was laid in a new tomb in the valley before her *Assumption.

Jehovah *See* NOMEN SACRUM and TETRAGRAMMATON.

Jeremiah (Vg. **Jeremias**) was an OT *prophet who foretold the destruction in 587 BC of Jerusalem and the Temple. Hence in English a 'jeremiad' is a prophecy of doom. Jeremiah lamenting the fate of Jerusalem was seen as an OT *type for Christ weeping over the city (Luke 19: 41–4), and his prophecies also included the New *Dispensation (Jer. 31: 31–4, *see also* COVENANT) under a *Messiah from the House of *David (Jer. 23: 5–8; 33: 15–16). With *Moses and *Isaiah he was an important prophet, but is not often represented—the earliest examples are in Ravenna (Baptistery of the Orthodox, 5th cent.; San Vitale, 6th cent.), but by far the most famous is the huge brooding figure by Michelangelo in the Ceiling of the *Sistine Chapel of the Vatican.

Jerome (Hieronymus, Girolamo), Saint, and *Doctor of the Latin Church (*c*.345/7–420), was responsible for the Latin version of the Scriptures (the *Vulgate). He was educated in Rome in Rhetoric—i.e. the study of ancient pagan literature—and subsequently mastered Greek and Hebrew, as well as Latin. Like many classical scholars he was cantankerous, polemical, and generally awkward, making his own life unnecessarily difficult. He was baptized by 366 and went to Antioch in 374, retiring into the desert 375–6 to live a life of penitence and austerity, until he went to Constantinople, 380/1, where he began to work on the translation of the Psalms from Greek into Latin. From 382 he worked in Rome as secretary to Pope S. Damasus, until the Pope's death in 385. After some difficulties he left Rome and went to Bethlehem, where he spent the rest of his life working on his translation of the Bible, excluding many of the *Apocryphal writings from the *Canon of Scripture. He was buried in the Basilica of the Nativity in Bethlehem, but his remains were later taken to Sta Maria Maggiore in Rome.

The earliest representation of him is probably a painting on the ivory diptych of Boethius (7th cent.: Brescia, Mus.), but his cult dates mainly from the 13th century. There are four main iconographical types: (1) as a hermit in the desert, very emaciated and usually shown kneeling before a crucifix and beating his breast with a stone. A lion is often shown beside him, since he is supposed to have extracted a thorn from a lion's paw (as in the 2nd-cent. legend of Androcles), and the beast became his companion. There is often also a skull as a *Memento mori. An Antonello da Messina (1460–5: Reggio di Calabria) has cardinal's robes as well as a hat, a lion, and a skull; so has the Cima da Conegliano (1504/10: London, NG). (2) Jerome is tempted by visions of Roman maidens, like *S. Antony, or dreams that he is before the Judgement Seat and is accused of being 'not a Christian, but a

Ciceronian', on account of his delight in classical literature and contempt for the Latinity of most Christian writers. He may also be shown as being awakened from his dream by an angel blowing a trumpet. There is a *Bosch of S. Jerome praying in a half-circle of classical sculpture, possibly referring to the temptation of his pride in his learning (*c.*1505: Venice, Doge's Pal.), and Parmagianino painted a unknown subject, a *Vision of S. Jerome* (1527: London, NG). (3) The commonest representation is that of the scholar in his study, surrounded by books, and with the lion asleep. In these paintings and engravings (Antonello da Messina, 1474: London, NG; Dürer engr. 1514) he is often shown as a cardinal with the red hat beside him. Cardinals were not created until many centuries after Jerome's death, but it is likely that his activity as assistant to Pope Damasus was responsible for this anachronism. (4) *The Last Communion of S. Jerome*. This is the subject of a famous painting by Domenichino (1614: Vatican Gall.). There is also a series by Zurbarán for the *Jeronymite Monastery at Guadalupe in Spain, including a singularly innocuous *Temptation*.

Jeronymites (Hieronymitae) An order of hermits, founded in the 14th century in Spain, who modelled themselves on *S. Jerome's life in the desert. At first they lived singly, but later came together in communities. They were particularly devoted to the care of the sick and dying, consequently receiving legacies and gifts which enabled them to build large houses and to fill them with fine paintings. There were houses in Italy, but far the most important were in Spain and Portugal. Near Lisbon, at Belem, they were in charge of the Portuguese royal mausoleum, and in Spain they had a great house at Guadalupe, which still has the important series painted for it by Zurbarán, of the life of S. Jerome *c.*1639; their house at Yuste was where the Emperor Charles V retired in 1556, and the *Escorial, the huge monastery-palace near Madrid, built by Charles's son, King Philip II, was entrusted to them.

Jesse, Tree of Jesse was the father of King *David. Isaiah prophesied (11: 1–3) 'A shoot shall come out from the stump of Jesse, and a branch shall grow out of his roots. The spirit of the Lord shall rest on him'; and that the *Messiah would come from the House of David. The genealogy of Christ (Matt. 1: 1–17) shows that Jesus was indeed descended from David, and that his descent was consonant with His being the Messiah. In psalters and stained-glass windows from the 11th century onwards Jesse is shown reclining, with a tree growing out of his loins: the branches are labelled with the names of the ancestors, and sometimes also with the Seven *Gifts of the Holy Spirit (or seven doves). The earliest illustration is probably an 11th-century MS in Prague University, and there are 12th-century windows in *Saint-Denis and Chartres Cathedral. There is a famous medieval Jesse Window in Dorchester Abbey, near Oxford, where the stone tracery of the window is formed from the branches of the Tree.

Jesuits, the The usual name for the Society of Jesus (Societas Jesu, abbreviated to SJ). The original Company of Jesus was founded by *S. Ignatius loyola in Paris in 1534, and consisted of five Spaniards, including Ignatius himself and *S. Francis Xavier, one Portuguese and one Savoyard. Pope Paul III recognized their discipline and their potential as agents of the *Counter-Reformation, and formally established them in 1540: by 1580 they had 5,000 members, many of whom were martyred and later canonized. Unlike monks or friars they lived in the world and had no distinctive habit, but were prepared to go anywhere and do whatever was necessary. They were well-educated and underwent many years of training, so that one of their most important activities was teaching. They founded schools and universities, especially in Germany and E. Europe, which were very important in winning back large areas from Protestantism. They were also very active in the missions, from China and Japan to Latin America. Their third major activity was preaching, and their use of Ignatius's *Spiritual Exercises*, with its intensely visual approach, made them important patrons of the arts. Their mother-church in Rome, *Vignola's *gesù, was widely used as a model—many Jesuits were, or became, architects, and built churches from Goa in India to Peru based on the Roman model, but they also adapted to local forms and tastes. *Bernini was himself much influenced by Jesuit ideals, and his art expressed them perfectly, but it is not true to say that *Baroque is the 'Jesuit style'.

Their phenomenal success, especially during the 17th century, made them many enemies (not all outside the Catholic Church), and for political reasons they were suppressed in 1773, although they continued in Russia and Austria, and in Germany under Frederick the Great, as well as in America. They were finally re-established in 1814.

Jesus is a form of Joshua (Heb. Saviour). For His life and miracles *see* CHRIST, and under individual subjects.

Jesus, Society of *See* JESUITS.

JEWISH AND CHRISTIAN INTERACTIONS IN ART

The Christian character of much Western art raises important questions about the interactions between Jews and Christians in visual art. How have Jews been represented in Christian art? How have Jewish artists engaged with Christian themes and symbols? Do Jews and Christians place a similar value on art and beauty?

Engaging with these questions is best done by surveying some key examples of Jewish-Christian interactions in the history of art, from antiquity to the present. First, however, to be confronted is the prevalent myth that Jews do not produce representational art or that Judaism assigns only a negative value to the visual arts. This notion is based on a misunderstanding of the Second Commandment, which ignores both its scriptural context and its subsequent application. The Second Commandment appears first in Exodus 20:4 and again in Deuteronomy 5:8. While there is a slight variation in the Hebrew, the wording of both verses is close enough that they can be translated identically: 'You shall not make for yourself an idol, whether in the form of anything that is in heaven above, or that is on the earth beneath, or that is in the water under the earth.' The broader treatment of images in the Hebrew Bible emphasizes that this injunction is aimed at idolatry, and is not rooted in any deep-seated iconoclasm. For instance, the Bible describes Bezalel, creator of the Ark of the Covenant and the tent of meeting, as filled 'with divine spirit, with ability, intelligence, and knowledge in every kind of craft' (Exod. 31:3), and the sumptuous imagery of Solomon's Temple is recorded in loving detail (1 Kings 6). Building upon such examples, Jewish tradition emphasizes the principle of *hiddur mitzvah*, which encourages Jews to enhance the performance of a *mitzvah* (commandment), through beautiful means, such as elegant ritual items. Jewish law also makes clear that art should not be the object of undue trepidation. The Mishnah, a collection of Jewish law compiled in the 3rd century AD, even relates the story of a rabbi who enters a bath decorated with a statue of Aphrodite, since 'that which one treats not as a god is permitted' (Abodah Zarah 3:4). Altogether, there is little support in either Jewish texts or material practice for the notion of the 'artless Jew', which as Kalman Bland and Margaret Olin have demonstrated is a modern invention, generated by 19th-century philosophers and art historians.

The notion of Jewish aniconism was still prevalent in 1932, when Clark Hopkins led the discovery of a 3rd-century AD synagogue at Dura-Europos, in what is now eastern Syria. Stunned by the figurative murals he encountered on its walls, including depictions of the binding of Isaac and Moses parting the Red Sea, Hopkins declared that 'there was absolutely no precedent, nor could there be any' for this kind of illustration by Jews. Other early interpreters, such as Erwin Goodenough, could comprehend the synagogue only as the product of some hypothetical brand of mystic Judaism, with close parallels to early Christianity. For Kurt Weitzmann, the images at Dura constituted a key stepping stone for later Christian art. These interpretations have been largely dismissed by later scholars, who have tended to emphasize Dura's connections with the rabbinic Jewish culture of the period rather than its deviation from 'normative' Judaism, or its relation to Christianity. However, the frescoes at Dura demonstrate that Jews and Christians in antiquity did possess a comparably rich visual heritage. Moreover, the creations of Jews and early Christians in this period both belong to a wider, shared artistic climate, from which artists of each faith drew freely, with little fear of religious syncretism, a fact vividly demonstrated in the zodiac mosaics discovered in late antique synagogues at Sepphoris and Beth Alpha in present-day Israel.

In the medieval period, illuminated manuscripts reveal various influences and exchanges between Jews and Christians. Christian conventions for representing Jews, including a distinguishing pointed hat, were frequently adopted by Jews when representing themselves, as in the late 13th-century *Birds' Head Haggadah* from Germany. Christian artists were also commissioned by Jews to illuminate religious texts, although it is often difficult to determine the religious affiliations of anonymous artists. The late 15th-century Florentine *Rothschild Mahzor*, for instance, was illustrated by no fewer than three workshops, with varying knowledge of Judaism. In medieval Spain, Jews and Christians were not only in dialogue with one another but often with Muslims as well. Several synagogues bear clear affinities with Islamic art, including the 14th-century synagogue of El Tránsito in Toledo, which is decorated with Arabic quotations from the Qur'an. Such close identification with Islamic culture—even after falling under Christian control—may reflect a Jewish nostalgia for Muslim hegemony. The complicated inter-religious dynamics of the Iberian peninsula are further demonstrated by the transformations of Santa Maria la Blanca in Toledo, an Islamic-inspired synagogue from the 13th century, which was later rededicated as a church.

From the medieval period to the early modern period, Jews appeared in various guises in Christian art. One frequent motif—typified by a pair of 13th-century female figures from Strasbourg Cathedral in France—was the downcast, blindfolded *synagoga* (synagogue), standing in contradistinction to a triumphal *ecclesia* (church). In addition to such allegorical depictions, Jews were sometimes targeted directly, as in Paolo Uccello's *Miracle of the Profaned Host* (1468) for the altarpiece of Corpus Domini in Urbino, Italy. In Uccello's six-part painting, a Jewish usurer procures the Eucharist, which he boils and stabs until it miraculously bleeds. Ultimately, the Host is rescued and the offending Jew and his wife and children are burned at the stake. While such imagery had a variety of intentions and implications, its primary effect, as Dana Katz argues, was to reinforce the prevailing Christian social order. At times, Jews did feature sympathetically in early modern art, as in the works of Rembrandt, who used his Amsterdam Jewish neighbours as models, especially when treating the Old Testament. While historians such as Steven Nadler refrain from exaggerating Rembrandt's philo-Semitism based on images such as *The Jewish Bride* (1666), Rembrandt did demonstrate a keen interest in Judaism; probably encouraged by Rabbi Menasseh ben Israel, whose writings he illustrated and whose portrait he executed.

When social and political restrictions on European Jews were gradually lifted in the 18th and 19th centuries and they were able to avail themselves of similar opportunities as their Christian peers, they entered a field with few positive images of Jews, and even fewer created by Jews themselves. These first generations of modern Jewish artists understood that they were entering a Christian domain. Some, such as the Russian sculptor Mark Antokolsky and the German painter Max Liebermann, faced this challenge head-on by creating images of Jesus. Marc *Chagall followed their example, famously painting the *White Crucifixion* in 1938, in which he used the figure of a Jewish Jesus to call Christian attention to the suffering of European Jewry. While Chagall turned the Crucifixion into a signature of sorts, which appears in hundreds of his works, various Jewish artists have imagined their own Jewish Jesus, including Jacob *Epstein, Adolph Gottlieb, Philip Guston, Emmanuel Levy, Adi Nes, Louise Nevelson, Barnett Newman, Abraham Rattner, Mark Rothko, and Max Weber. Some Jewish artists have taken the further step of producing works of art for Christian spaces, including: Jacques Lipchitz and Chagall's works for the Church of Notre Dame in Assy, France; Jacob Epstein's monumental *Christ in Majesty* (1954–5) at Llandaff Cathedral in Cardiff, Wales; the Rothko Chapel in Houston, Texas (ded. 1971); and Louise Nevelson's Chapel of the Good Shepherd in St Peter's Lutheran Church in New York City (ded. 1977). Recently, the Jewish artist Tobi Kahn has created spaces intended to facilitate Jewish *and* Christian worship. This may represent a new frontier, in which Jewish-Christian relations can not only be studied through art, but practised also.

Jezebel *See* ELIJAH (ELIAS).

JHVH *See* NOMEN SACRUM, TETRAGRAMMATON.

Joachim and Anna *See* ANNE, S.

Job (also called S. Giobbe [Job] in Venice and elsewhere in Italy) was the supreme OT example of long-suffering *Fortitude and a *type of Christ. He was very rich and contented and an example of uprightness. Satan argued with God that anyone in his position could be righteous, but in affliction he would curse God. God allowed him to be tried, and Satan caused him to lose all his herds and flocks, and the men who tended them, and, as a crowning disaster, a house collapsed, killing his seven sons and three daughters at one blow. Job bore these afflictions patiently, so Satan struck him with sores (AV boils, but sores in the Vg.), so that he sat in ashes (on a dunghill in the Vg.), scraping himself with a potsherd. Three friends came to console him, but in fact made matters worse by saying it must have been his fault in some way (hence the expression 'Job's comforters'). Even his wife tried to get him to curse God, but he rebuked her foolishness: in the Book of Job (2: 9) she only speaks to him, but she is often represented as throwing a bucket of water over him, beating or even whipping him. As well as the legendary accretion of his wife's activities, there are also musicians who try to soothe the pain of his sores and are paid with his scabs, which turn into gold pieces. He was therefore often chosen as a patron of hospitals. These additions are probably due to an apocryphal Jewish 'Testament of Job' (?2nd cent. AD), and in the Middle Ages the beating was seen as a type of the *Flagellation, as his declaration (19: 25–6): 'I know that my Redeemer lives... in my flesh shall I see God' is a prophecy of the Resurrection. Finally, God spoke from a whirlwind and Job acknowledged that he could not grasp His ways, or understand His purposes. Satan was defeated and Job was restored to his former state, with another seven sons and three daughters, and twice as much material wealth.

The story was taken over by the early Christians, and is represented at *Dura-Europos (*c.*240), as well as in the catacombs and on the sarcophagus of *Junius Bassus. *Blake made twenty-one large watercolour illustrations to the Book of Job *c.*1818/20, and a second set, engraved in 1823–5. Giuliano Vangi's *Job*, carved in the Funeral Chapel (2001–2), Azzano di Serravezza, Tuscany, deserves note.

Joel was an OT Minor *prophet, *c.*400 BC, whose very brief Book contains prophecies of *Pentecost and the Last *Judgement. Joel (2: 28–32) is quoted verbally in Acts (2: 17–21), describing Pentecost, and Joel (2: 31) 'The sun shall be turned to darkness, and the moon to blood, before the great and terrible day of the Lord comes' and (3: 2) 'I will gather all the nations, and bring them down to the valley of *Jehoshaphat' may be *Signs of the end of the world, preceding the Last Judgement. Joel is one of the prophets painted by Michelangelo in the *Sistine Chapel.

John, Saint, Apostle and Evangelist John the Apostle, the Evangelist, and 'the Divine' are traditionally the same person, although attempts have been made to split him into two, or even three. John 'the beloved disciple' was the son of Zebedee and the brother of *James the Great. He was originally a follower of *John the Baptist, and witnessed the *Baptism of Christ, in whom, at the Baptist's words 'Behold the Lamb of God', he recognized the Messiah (John 1: 35–9). He was the only one of the Apostles to be present at Jesus's trial before Caiaphas, and to stand with *Mary by the Cross (*see* ROOD) and the account in his Gospel is therefore that of an eyewitness. Traditionally, he died as a very old man in Ephesus, perhaps *c.*96–104. He wrote three short Epistles before writing the Fourth Gospel, which presupposes the existence of the other three, the so-called Synoptics (though some modern theologians believe, on internal evidence, that it was written earlier). He was banished to the Greek island of Patmos during the persecution under the Emperor Domitian (81–96), and there he wrote his Book of Revelation (the *Apocalypse), which is very different in style from his Gospel (hence the argument that it is by a different John). The so-called 'Acts of John' are *Apocryphal, but were used in the **Golden Legend* and elsewhere to provide some of the commonest scenes from his legend, including the raising from the dead of Drusiana, with whom he had lodged in Ephesus, and the occasion when, challenged by the High Priest of Diana of the Ephesians, he drank from a poisoned chalice. He made the sign of the Cross over it and the poison emerged in the form of a serpent or snake. The attempt to martyr him in boiling oil is said to have taken place in Rome, near the Latin Gate, and the spot is now marked by the small church of San Giovanni in Olio. The Lateran Basilica in Rome is also dedicated to him (and to S. John the Baptist).

The iconography of John is twofold, first as a young, beardless, man in Gospel scenes such as the raising of *Jairus's daughter, the *Transfiguration, and the Agony in the garden of *Gethsemane; and especially at the *Last Supper and *Crucifixion. In scenes of the Last Supper he is often shown as 'leaning on Jesus' bosom' (AV John 13: 23), which presented problems to artists (*see* LEONARDO DA VINCI). (NRSV says 'reclining next to Jesus', suggesting the use of classical dining couches). As his *Evangelist Symbol he has an eagle, and often a book as well. He is the patron saint of writers, printers, and theologians.

He is often closely associated with *S. Peter, especially in scenes from the Acts of the Apostles, such as the healing of the cripple (3: 2). Secondly, he appears as a very old man with a long white or grey beard, often shown on Patmos writing his Revelation. Cycles of his life are sometimes paired with the Baptist's, as in Giotto's frescoes in Sta Croce, Florence, where he is shown, following the Apocryphal account, on Patmos, raising Drusiana, with the rare scene of his death—he caused a grave to be dug and was raised from it by Christ Himself, to be assumed into Heaven. *Bosch painted a memorable image of S. John on Patmos, young and beardless, wrapt in his vision of an angel and the Virgin and Child (*c.*1500: Berlin, where there is also a Geertgen of *S. John meditating* seated in a superb landscape, beside a tiny lamb emitting rays).

John the Baptist, Saint, is an OT Prophet and a NT martyr. He was six months older than Christ and related to Him (*see* VISITATION), as their mothers were cousins. John is also called the Forerunner, or Precursor, since he predicted the coming of the *Messiah, whom he recognized in Jesus. All that is known about him is contained in the Gospels, all four Evangelists giving the same main facts, but some apocryphal stories were added to his legend later. His birth was itself miraculous, since his parents, *Zacharias and *Elizabeth, were old and childless, when the Archangel Gabriel appeared to Zacharias in the Temple, told him that his wife would bear a son who was to be called John, and struck him dumb. There are many representations of the birth of John, with Zacharias seated in a corner, writing his name on a tablet. Later, John retired to the desert, living on wild honey and locusts and wearing a garment of camel-hair with a leather girdle. He is sometimes shown as quite a small boy, determinedly setting out from home (Giovanni di Paolo, after 1426: London NG), but single figures show him as an emaciated man with wild hair and beard, clad in skins. According to Luke (3: 1), in the 15th year of the Emperor Tiberius (i.e. *c.* AD 28), he left the desert and began to preach and baptize. This culminated in the major event of his life, the *Baptism of Christ in the *Jordan, when the Holy Ghost, 'like a dove', descended upon Christ and John recognized the Messiah, whom he later pointed out to *Andrew and *John, later the Apostles, who brought *Peter to Jesus (John 1: 35–44). Most *baptisteries are dedicated to him, and many have narrative cycles of his life. Soon afterwards he denounced *Herod for his incestuous marriage with his niece Herodias, who was his brother's wife. Herodias was furious, and, when Herod gave a great banquet at which her daughter Salome danced and Herod was so entranced that he foolishly promised her anything she wanted, she told Salome to ask for John's head on a dish. Herod had to keep his promise and John was decapitated without trial (the 'Decollation of the Baptist'), thus becoming the first martyr of the New Dispensation, even earlier than *S. Stephen. The severed head 'on a charger' was a popular subject both in painting and sculpture such as the Nottingham *alabasters in the late Middle Ages. The NT narrative of the Baptist ends here, but later apocryphal writings such as the Protevangelium of *James and the **Golden Legend* tell how, during Herod's massacre of the Innocents, a mountain opened to receive the infant John and his mother Elizabeth until the persecution ended (or until they were rescued by the Holy Family on the return from Egypt). After his death, John descended into *Limbo and announced the coming of the Messiah, a subject more common in the East than the West, but represented in the mosaics at Torcello, in Venice. John's headless body was buried by his disciples, but the Emperor Julian the Apostate, about 361/2, had his bones dug up and burned, although some members of the Order of St John of Jerusalem—the Knights of Malta—saved some relics. (The Order did not exist in the 4th century.) This very rare subject was painted by the Dutchman Geertgen tot Sint Jans at the end of the 15th century (Vienna, KHM). The artist was called after the picture.

Other images of the Baptist show him with wings, since he was a messenger, like an angel: this image is virtually always Eastern. In the West he usually holds a reed cross, which sometimes has a scroll attached reading *Ecce Agnus Dei* (Behold the Lamb of God), which is what he said to John and Andrew (John 1: 35–6), or *Ego vox clamantis in deserto* (I am a voice crying in the wilderness), recalling the prophecy of Isaiah (40: 3; John 1: 23). Together with the *Ecce Agnus* there are some representations of him pointing to an actual lamb, sometimes with blood pouring from it into a chalice, and sometimes shown as a lamb—even, rarely, a child—on a dish held by him. This never occurs in the East after the 7th century, when a Council, held in Constantinople in 692, specifically forbade the representation of Christ as a lamb. This ruling was effective in the E. Orthodox Church, but mostly ignored in the West, where the commonest form is that of a lamb with a halo, holding a flag with a red cross on it (hence the number of inns called the Lamb and Flag). On the other hand, the *Deësis—figures, usually half-length, of Christ in the centre with the Virgin Mary on His right and the Baptist on His left—are normal on the *iconostasis of an Orthodox church, but rare in the West. The Ghent Altar (*see* EYCK) is the best-known Western example.

Another subject, especially popular in Italy in the 15th and 16th centuries, shows the infant Christ playing with His infant cousin, usually with Mary and Elizabeth or Anne present—famous examples are Leonardo da Vinci's *Madonna of the Rocks* (Louvre and London, NG) and his cartoon also in the NG. There is no biblical authority for this, but the Baptist (often depicted as S. Giovannino, Italian for 'little S. John') is the patron saint of Florence, and the subject, common by the 15th century, seems to have originated in the 14th from an Italian adaptation of the Protevangelium of James. One of the odd features of Byzantine representations of the Baptism of Christ (i.e. in the Arian Baptistery in Ravenna) is to make Christ almost a child and the Baptist a grown man, although there was only some six months between them.

John Climacus, Saint *See* CLIMACUS.

John of Jerusalem, Saint, Knights of *See* MALTA, KNIGHTS OF.

John Nepomuk, Saint (*c.*1340/50–93), was born in Nepomuk in Bohemia and became Vicar-General of Prague when Wenceslaus IV, a violent despot, was in conflict with the Church. The King is said to have tried to force John to betray the Queen's confession: when he refused the King had him thrown into the Moldau from the Charles Bridge in Prague. By the 17th century he was widely venerated throughout E. Europe as a patron of bridges and protector against floods and there are still hundreds of bridges carrying a statue of him, including one on the Ponte Milvio in Rome. He was officially canonized in 1729. In the series of *Seven Sacraments* by G. M. Crespi Confession is symbolized by him (Turin, Pinacoteca).

Jonah (Vg. **Jonas**) was an OT *prophet. The Book of Jonah is only four chapters long, but was popular among the Early Christians, since it was seen as foretelling the Resurrection. Jonah was a *type of Christ, as well as being quoted by Him in this context (Luke 11: 29–30; 'For just as Jonah became a sign to the people of Nineveh, so the Son of Man will be to this generation'). Jonah was called by God to go to Nineveh and preach repentance, but he tried to evade this difficult task by embarking on a ship leaving Joppa. A great storm arose and the crew tried to find the cause of God's wrath, so Jonah confessed that he was trying to escape from God's command and told them to throw him overboard. Reluctantly, they did so, and the storm ceased: Jonah meanwhile was swallowed by a 'great fish' (usually called a whale in English), which vomited him up again after three days and three nights (Jonah 1: 17). This was held to be Christ's prophecy of His Resurrection (Matt. 12: 40; 'for just as Jonah was three days and three nights in the belly of the sea monster, so for three days and three nights the Son of Man will be in the heart of the earth'). Jonah then went to Nineveh and preached repentance, prophesying the destruction of the city in forty days' time. This was so effective that the King ordered fasting and penance and God spared the city. Jonah felt let down and 'it was very displeasing to Jonah and he became angry' (Jonah 4: 1) so he lay down outside the city and prayed for death. He fell asleep under a tree ('gourd') which sheltered him from the sun and which grew enormously during the night, but on the next day it was eaten by a worm and Jonah was scorched by the sun and an east wind. This was interpreted as a lesson in compassion which he had conspicuously failed to show.

These two subjects, Jonah being swallowed by the great fish (or being regurgitated), and asleep under the tree, were very common in Early Christian art, especially in the *catacombs and on *sarcophagi. This was partly because the symbolism was not obvious—the connection between a great fish (sometimes not even looking much like a fish) and the Resurrection is clear only to those who have been instructed—and in the case of Jonah sleeping it could, if necessary, be passed off as the pagan myth of the handsome Endymion put to sleep by the Moon Goddess Selene. Jonah is normally represented as a nude young man in this case. The earliest known example is a sarcophagus in Arles of the 3rd century, and they continued until about the 6th. In the Middle Ages, the **Biblia Pauperum* has Jonah thrown overboard and *Joseph in the well as types for the Entombment. Perhaps the best-known example is the figure by *Michelangelo, immediately above the altar of the Sistine Chapel, which occasioned awe among artists of the early 16th century on account of its virtuoso foreshortening. *Vasari describes it: 'Then who is not filled with admiration and amazement at the awesome sight of Jonah, the last figure in the chapel? The vaulting naturally springs forward, following the curve of the masonry; but through the force of art it is apparently straightened out by the figure of Jonah, which bends in the opposite direction; and thus vanquished by the art of design, with its lights and shades, the ceiling even appears to recede. What a happy age we live in! And how fortunate are our craftsmen, who have been given light and vision by Michelangelo'. The figure of Jonah is also important because he looks upwards to where, on the ceiling above his head, God is creating the world, and down to where, before the *Last Judgement* was painted, there was a figure of Christ, and towards the altar beneath that.

Jonathan *See* DAVID.

Jones, David (1895–1974) A British painter and draughtsman, mainly in watercolours, of landscape, still life, portraits, animals, and literary and imaginative subjects; engraver, essayist, and poet.

If his studies before and after his First World War army service in France left him 'completely muddle-headed as to the function of art in general', no more had the intervening war experience itself, vivid though it was and tenaciously remembered, left him with a philosophy of life and a scheme for his art. Friendship with Eric *Gill led to Jones being received into the Roman Catholic Church in 1921. Here he was challenged and inspired by Jacques Maritain and thus by the philosophy of Thomas *Aquinas.

Peter Levi wrote, 'in his severest engravings he was warm, in painting of solemn beauty lyrical and humorous' (*DNB Supplement* 1986). Jones' art seems content to stand aside from any 20th-century strong identity; desirous to service as handmaid—to use an earlier period's term—to the liturgy of the church and to the Arthurian and Celtic themes he espoused. His art, like Gill's, was appreciated and taken up in the American Quarterly *Liturgical Arts*. Latterly his Roman calligraphic work has been popular. The Tate and the National Museum of Wales have strong representation of the artist's work. The conflict of war, Arthurian legend, and other themes treated in verse and prose, inform his *In Parenthesis* (1937) acclaimed by T. S. Eliot, and *The Anathemata* (1952).

Jones, Inigo (1573–1652), was the first British classical architect. He was born in London, of Welsh origin, and his earliest years are obscure, but he was certainly in Italy around 1600 and also in Denmark, *c.*1603, in which year he was in England and referred to as a 'picture maker'. He seems to have been well informed on Italian art and was employed for many years on designs for the Royal masques. His annotated copy of *Palladio's *I Quattro Libri* (1570) is in Worcester College, Oxford, and has the date 1601 on the title-page. This seems to indicate an interest in architecture as well as his presence in Venice at that date (the book was published there), but it is also significant that this book, which determined the whole course of Jones's career, and, through him, the course of British architecture in the early 18th century, was based on Italian practice in the mid-16th century rather than that of Jones's own time when he was in Italy. Later, in 1613–14, Jones spent some 15 months in Italy with Lord Arundel, the great collector, and he is known to have studied Palladio's works in Vicenza, as well as staying in Padua and Rome. Before then, a drawing of *c.*1608 (London, RIBA) shows an early attempt at church design, in a rather gauche drawing for a façade for Old St Paul's, which is a pastiche based on *Vignola's Gesù in Rome—but the Gesù as executed, not as Vignola designed it, and for which a better design had by that date been engraved. In 1608 it seems unlikely that the mother-church of the *Jesuits would be regarded as a suitable model for the first major church to be built or restored in England since the Reformation. In fact, Jones's introduction of Italian classical architecture into England occurred with two secular buildings, the Banqueting House in Whitehall (1619–22), and the Queen's House at Greenwich, begun earlier, in 1616, but not completed until 1635 and greatly altered at the end of the century. In 1615 he became Royal Surveyor.

As a church designer he introduced classical forms in three buildings—the Queen's Chapel at St James's Palace, for Charles I's Catholic Queen Henrietta Maria, 1623–7; St Paul's, Covent Garden, for the Earl of Bedford's new development, 1631; and the great portico for the façade of St Paul's Cathedral, 1634–42. The exterior of the Queen's Chapel is very plain, almost domestic in appearance, but the interior is richly decorated and has a shallow coffered barrel vault. By contrast, the church for the Earl of Bedford, whose religious views were somewhat Puritan, is of extreme austerity and rigorous classicism—it is an ancient Roman temple with a portico of four Tuscan columns. The Earl is said to have demanded something cheap—'in short, not much better than a barn'. Jones replied, 'You shall have the handsomest barn in England'. This design was the first to be made for a specifically Protestant church in England, and its austerity and classicism are no doubt intentional. The ancient temple-front motif recurs in the design for the huge portico of ten Corinthian columns 56 ft. high on the west front of Old St Paul's. It was destroyed in the Great Fire of 1666 and mourned by John Evelyn, who was one of the few competent to judge, as 'That beautifull Portico (for structure comparable to any in Europ) ... now rent in pieces'.

Among the many dubious or false attributions to Jones is the porch of St Mary the Virgin, Oxford. It was actually built by a mason named Jackson, almost certainly to a design by Nicholas Stone, in 1637. Its twisted columns make it far closer to contemporary Baroque and, in fact, reminiscent of Bernini, than anything by Jones.

Jones's own religious position has been a matter of discussion. His name, Inigo, perhaps from Ignatius, and his evident Italian sympathies, have suggested that he might have been a Catholic, but no less a person than the papal agent accredited to the Queen called him 'puritanissimo fiero', which is difficult to interpret, but seems to be dismissive of the idea.

Jordan, the River The Jordan is mentioned several times in the Bible, especially as the place where *John the Baptist baptized Christ. The Jordan valley is a long, fertile tract, running N–S through Palestine, between the Sea of Galilee and the Dead Sea, dividing the farmers from the nomads. The west side is the Promised Land, seen by Moses and entered by *Joshua, when the waters receded to let the Israelites cross into the Promised Land (Josh. 3: 16). It was also the place where *Elijah ascended into Heaven and *Elisha walked across the river after smiting the water with Elijah's cloak (2 Kgs. 1: 8 (Vg. 4 Reg.) 2: 11–14). Naaman the leper was cleansed in its waters (2 Kgs. 5 (Vg. 4 Reg.) 5: 10–14).

It is frequently symbolized in scenes of the Baptism of Christ, as in Ravenna (Baptisteries of the Orthodox and of the Arians: 5th/6th centuries) as a pagan River God, sometimes inscribed *Jordann*, as an indicator. Early Christian sarcophagi and catacomb paintings (e.g. Lucina, 2nd cent.; the earliest Christian representation) also have personifications of the Jordan. *Giotto was probably the first artist to drop the symbolism in favour of a more naturalistic treatment of the scene.

Josaphat *See* JEHOSHAPHAT.

Joseph The OT *Patriarch was the eleventh son of *Jacob, and became Pharaoh's chief minister. His story is told in Gen. 37, and 39–50. He was the first-born of Rachel, who died after giving birth to her second son, Benjamin, Jacob's twelfth. He soon became resented by his ten elder brothers, the children of Leah and Jacob's concubines, on account of his tale-bearing, his dreams foretelling that he would rule over them, and his 'coat of many colours' (also described as a 'long robe with sleeves') given to him by his doting father. An example of this theme is Ford Madox Brown's *Coat of Many Colours* (1864–6 Walker Art Gallery, Liverpool). When he was 17 he was sent to check on his brothers, who were tending the family flocks, and they conspired to kill him. Reuben, the eldest, advised them not to kill him, but to put him in a dry well, intending to rescue him later, but a passing caravan of merchants found him and took him with them to Egypt to sell him there. Reuben returned and was distressed to find him gone, so they decided to soak his coat in the blood of a goat and tell their father that he had been eaten by a wild beast. Meanwhile, he was sold for '20 pieces of silver' (cf. Judas betraying Christ) to Potiphar, the captain of Pharaoh's guard. His abilities soon became evident, and he was made the ruler of Potiphar's household, but he was a handsome young man and Potiphar's wife tried to seduce him. He refused, saying that Potiphar had promoted him and he could not betray his trust. She was so angry at being spurned that she seized his cloak as he rushed from the bedroom and showed it to Potiphar as proof that Joseph had attempted to rape her while no one was in the house. Joseph was thrown into prison, where he again became the governor's right-hand man, and there he met Pharaoh's butler and baker, who had displeased Pharaoh. They both dreamed on the same night, and, as the Egyptians attached great importance to dreams, they wanted interpretations of their dreams, which Joseph supplied. The butler would be restored to favour, but the baker would be hanged; both of these predictions came true, but the butler, who had promised to help, forgot all about Joseph when he returned to favour, until two years later when Pharaoh himself had dreams which disturbed him and which none of his priests could interpret. The butler then remembered Joseph, who told Pharaoh that his seven fat kine eaten by seven lean ones, and his seven good ears of wheat and seven poor ones were a prediction of seven years of plenty, followed by seven of famine. He suggested that one fifth of each year's crops should be set aside against the lean years to come, and he was appointed to oversee this. He was so favoured by Pharaoh that he held the royal signet-ring, rode in a chariot immediately behind Pharaoh's own, and was married to the daughter of the Egyptian Priest of On.

When the famine came it was so severe that it was felt even in Canaan, and Jacob sent his ten sons, but not Benjamin, to Egypt to buy food. When they arrived, Joseph immediately recognized them, but they did not recognize him. He spoke sharply to them, accusing them of spying, and locked them up for three days before allowing them to buy corn, on condition that they left Simeon as a hostage and returned with Benjamin. On the way home they found some of the money they had paid in one of the sacks and they greatly feared they would be accused of stealing it. However, they got safely home, but Jacob refused to allow Benjamin to go back with them, until all the corn was eaten and he realized they would have to go again, taking Benjamin with them. They went, taking back all the money originally paid as well as gifts. They were astonished at being invited to a meal with Joseph, where they were seated in the exact order of their age and fed with dishes from Joseph's own table—but Benjamin got much more than his elders. When they left for home Joseph had his silver cup hidden in Benjamin's sack and sent men after them to bring them back. They were terrified, but Joseph finally revealed his identity and forgave them. He then told them that there were still five more years of famine to come, instructing them to bring the aged Jacob and all seventy members of his household back to Goschen in Egypt. After an emotional reunion, Pharaoh appointed them to manage his flocks, since they were skilled shepherds and 'all shepherds are abhorrent to the Egyptians' (Gen. 46: 34). Jacob blessed Pharaoh and remained in Egypt until his death, seventeen years later, at 147. On his death-bed Jacob blessed Joseph's two sons, Ephraim and Manasseh, in the wrong order, but this was prophetic. Jacob's body was embalmed and returned to Hebron. Joseph, who was 110 when he died, was also embalmed but his body was taken, centuries later, by *Moses to the Promised Land.

Joseph is sometimes seen as a *type of Christ and his coat, which was in one piece, may prefigure the Holy *Coat. His chastity is also seen as prefiguring his NT namesake, *S. Joseph.

An elaborate pictorial series was painted for the bedroom of the Borgherini Palace in Florence about 1515. Panels by Andrea del Sarto, Pontormo, Bacchiacca, and Granacci are now divided between the National Gallery, London, the Uffizi and Pitti Galleries in Florence, and the Borghese Gallery in Rome. They are difficult to read and there are several incidents shown on the same panel, a return to the medieval method of *Continuous Representation. Horace Vernet painted a *Joseph's Coat* (1853: London, Wallace Coll.) titled in French as *Joseph sold by his brothers*.

Joseph, Saint, the spouse of *Mary and foster-father of Jesus. All that is known of him is contained in Matt. 1 and 2 and Luke 2, the former probably based on his own testimony and the latter on Mary's. In Matt. 13: 55 he is referred to as 'the carpenter', which indicates a fairly humble position, confirmed by the fact that, at the *Presentation in the Temple of the infant Jesus, his offering was two turtle-doves, whereas well-off people were expected to provide a lamb. On the other hand, he was descended from King *David, a pre-condition of the family origin of the *Messiah. Traditionally, he was much older than Mary, and certainly he is not mentioned in the Bible after the finding of the 12-year-old Jesus among the *Doctors (Luke 2: 48–51), so it is supposed that he died before the Passion and probably before the beginning of Christ's mission. *Apocryphal books, especially the Protevangelium of *James and a much later *History of Joseph* (5th/6th cent.?) provide missing details which were largely incorporated into the **Golden Legend*, and from it became normal in representations of his life. His status as protector of Mary and the infant Christ meant that he appears in a subordinate role in NT scenes such as the *Nativity and Adoration of the Shepherds, or of the *Magi, the Presentation in the Temple, and, especially, in the Flight into and Return from *Egypt. He does not appear in scenes of the Annunciation, but in this case has his own leading part in the angelic reassurance (Matt. 1: 18–20): 'When his mother Mary had been engaged to Joseph, but before they lived together, she was found with child from the Holy Spirit. Her husband Joseph . . . planned to dismiss her quietly. But just when he had resolved to do this, an angel of the Lord appeared to him in a dream, and said "Joseph, son of David, do not be afraid to take Mary as your wife, for the child conceived in her is from the Holy Spirit."' The *Golden Legend* precedes this with an account of the *Espousal, whereby Joseph, somewhat reluctantly, found that the Holy Ghost had chosen him. From this it was assumed that he was a widower with a family, who would therefore be the 'brethren of the Lord' (*see* KINSHIP OF CHRIST). Single figures of him often have him holding the flowering rod as his attribute, while others show him with a lily, the symbol of his chastity, and some have the lily growing from the rod. In many medieval representations he seems to be rather a bumbling old man, crouched miserably on the ground in a corner of Nativity scenes (Giotto, Arena Chapel, Padua; pulpits by Nicola and Giovanni Pisano), or blowing on a fire to heat soup (K. von Soest, Nieder-Wildungen, Westphalia) and even, in some mystery plays, as almost a cuckold. In the 14th and 15th centuries the popularity of the Holy Family as a subject for small devotional paintings helped to raise him in public esteem, since such subjects were extremely popular in the West, taking the place of icons in the East. During the 17th century his cult was greatly forwarded by the Jesuits and, especially in Spain, by *S. Theresa of Avila. He is represented most sympathetically in Murillo's *The Two Trinities*, *c.*1640: Stockholm, an early version of the same subject in London, National Gallery, painted towards the end of his life. A statue of S. Joseph may be found in most Catholic churches, and a great number of them are dedicated to him. He appears in J. E. Millais's *Christ in the House of his Parents* (1849–50, Tate).

Another legend from the *History of Joseph* purports to record his death in the presence of both Jesus and Mary, and he became the patron saint of a holy death.

Joseph of Arimathaea, sometimes called Saint, was, with *Nicodemus, a secret disciple of Jesus, and took His body down from the cross and buried it. Joseph was rich and a respected member of the Sanhedrin, but did not agree with the condemnation of Jesus. He asked Pilate's permission to bury the body of Jesus, and, with Nicodemus, wrapped it in a linen *Shroud and put it in a new rock-cut tomb which he had intended for himself. All this is in the four Gospels (Matt. 27: 57–9; Mark 15: 43–6; Luke 23: 50–3; John 19: 38–41), but a much later legend (12th cent.) makes him bring the Holy *Grail to Glastonbury in England. In representations of the Entombment (*see* CHRIST) he is usually richly dressed and holding Christ's head and shoulders, while Nicodemus holds His feet.

Joshua (**Josue**) was the OT *Patriarch who succeeded *Moses as the leader of the Israelites and established them in the Promised Land. Joshua is a variant form of Jesus, and this similarity of name led to Joshua being considered to be a *type of Christ, although his bloodthirsty career seems to militate against it. He was born probably about twenty years before the Exodus from Egypt and spent forty years in the wilderness before bringing the Israelites into Canaan. His story is told mainly in the Book of Joshua, together with long passages in Exodus, Numbers, and Deuteronomy.

Moses chose twelve men, one from each of the Tribes of Israel, including Joshua and Caleb. Their mission was to spy out the land of Canaan, and they returned with a huge bunch of grapes carried on a pole by two men, signifying the land 'flowing with milk and honey'. Caleb and Joshua recommended an immediate assault, but the other ten demurred, saying that the cities were large and strongly fortified. There were popular mutterings against Moses, and the Israelites were condemned to forty years of wandering in the desert. Moses died after seeing the Promised Land, in the knowledge that he would not enter it. Joshua, who had been consecrated as his successor, reached the banks of Jordan and determined to attack Jericho. In his turn, he sent two men as spies to Jericho, where they lodged with Rahab the harlot, whose house was part of the city wall. She let them down on a rope in return for a promise that she and her household would be spared if the Israelites sacked the city. She was told to bind a red cord in her window and the promise was duly kept. The campaign began with a miraculous crossing of the swollen Jordan, when the priests carrying the *Ark stood in the middle of the river and 'the waters flowing from above stood still, rising up in a single heap', so that the whole of the people of Israel crossed dryshod, as at the Crossing of the Red Sea under Moses. Again Joshua chose one man from each tribe to carry a large stone from the bed of the river, 'and those twelve stones ... Joshua set up in Gilgal' as a memorial. Near Jericho, Joshua saw a man with a drawn sword, who said: 'As commander of the army of the Lord I have now come.' This *angel was later identified by Christians as the Archangel Michael, Prince of Hosts. Joshua then besieged Jericho, and was instructed by the Lord: '"You shall march round the city, all the warriors circling the city once. Thus you shall do for six days, with seven priests bearing seven trumpets of ram's horns before the ark. On the seventh day you shall march round the city seven times, the priests blowing on the trumpets. When they make a long blast with the ram's horn ... then all the people shall shout with a great shout; and the wall of the city shall fall down flat, and all the people shall charge straight ahead" ... Then they devoted to destruction ... all in the city, both man and woman, young and old, and oxen, sheep, and donkeys' (Josh. ch. 6). But Rahab and her household were spared. Other cities were sacked in this way, and five kings were defeated when Joshua called upon the Lord and the sun stood still 'about a whole day' until 'the Israelites had inflicted a very great slaughter on them until they were wiped out ... '.

Joshua divided all these conquests between the tribes of Israel, excluding the Levites, who, as hereditary priests, were maintained by the other eleven. He died at 110, after a solemn assembly at which, like Moses, he delivered his testament (Josh. ch. 24).

Joshua is hardly ever represented as a single figure, although he became one of the medieval Nine Worthies—the three Jewish heroes being Joshua, David, and Judas Maccabeus. There are, however, many cycles of his deeds, from the mosaics in Sta Maria Maggiore, Rome, of the early 5th century, through the *Joshua Rotulus and the *Bible Moralisée to the panel of *Ghiberti's Baptistery Door in Florence. The most frequent scenes represented are the passage of the Jordan, the walls of Jericho, and the sun standing still. The Fall of Jericho is sometimes shown as a type of the Last Judgement, and Joshua leading his people into the Promised Land as Christ opening Heaven to all people, not only the Jews.

Joshua Rotulus, the (Joshua Roll) An illuminated MS in the Vatican Library of OT scenes, in the form of a scroll (*rotulus*), not a codex. It has many vivid pen and wash drawings, reflecting the Alexandrian style of the 5th century (cf. VIENNA GENESIS), but it was itself written and illustrated in Constantinople at some date between the 7th and 10th centuries—the dating is very controversial, but the 8th century is probable.

Joys of Mary, the Often called the Seven Joys (cf. *Sorrows), the number can vary from five to twelve or more, but they are usually the *Annunciation, *Visitation, *Nativity, *Epiphany, Finding in the Temple (i.e. Christ among the *Doctors), the *Resurrection, and *Ascension. (*See also* ROSARY.)

jubé *See* ROOD.

Judah and Tamar (Gen. 38). Judah was the fourth son of *Jacob and conspired with his brothers to put *Joseph in a dry well, before selling him into slavery (Gen. 37: 26–7). He had three sons, Er, Onan, and Shelah. Er was married to Tamar, but died childless. According to Mosaic Law, Onan had to marry Tamar and raise up children to his brother, but he refused to do so and spilled his seed upon the ground (38: 8–10). He also died, and Tamar was told she would marry Shelah when he was old enough. This did not happen, so she laid aside her widow's clothes, veiled her face, and seduced Judah, taking his signet, staff, and bracelets as a token (14–15). When she was three months pregnant Judah said she should be burnt as a harlot, but she produced his tokens and he had to admit his guilt. This story is said to be a *type of Christ and the *Woman taken in Adultery. It is very rare, but the earliest example is the 5th-century mosaic in San Lorenzo, Milan. For some reason it seems, like other obscure OT subjects, to have had a brief popularity in Holland in the 17th century—Bol (1644: Boston), Eeckhout (1645: Berlin and Moscow), B. Fabritius (Leningrad), A. de Gelder (The Hague and Vienna, Akad.) and Lastman. Horace Vernet painted a *Judah and Tamar* (1840: London, Wallace Coll.) during the craze for semi-Eastern subjects in France after the Napoleonic wars.

Judah was the one who negotiated with Joseph in his role as Pharaoh's minister, when he required his brothers to bring him Benjamin, and was the one who volunteered to be a hostage instead of Benjamin, but Joseph refused, insisting that they should not return without Benjamin. They were forced to comply, but despite Jacob's fears, the interview ended in a family reconciliation (Gen. 42 and 43).

David, was of the House, or Tribe, of Judah, and they supported him when he was made king (2 Sam. 2: 4; Vg. 2 Kgs. 2: 4).

Judas Iscariot, one of the Disciples, always referred to in the Gospels as 'the Betrayer', was the treasurer of the group, and is often shown clutching a money-bag. Apart from the Betrayal he is hardly mentioned in the NT; but in John 12: 4–6 he objects to the waste of 300 *denarii*, the value of the ointment used to anoint Christ, which could have been sold and 'the money given to the poor'. In his Gospel John implies that Judas would have kept some of it, since it was avarice that led him to betray Christ. This, however, is unlikely since the 30 pieces of silver he actually received (Matt. 26: 15) was a small sum, and, in any case, he returned it when he realized what he had done. According to Matthew (27: 3–5) he returned the money and hanged himself; but Acts (1: 18) says that he fell, and 'his bowels gushed out'—which was not necessarily suicide. Naturally enough, Judas is rarely represented, and then only in those scenes where he played an essential part—the Last Supper, the Betrayal and the Kiss of Judas (sometimes both, as in *Giotto's Arena Chapel frescoes in Padua). The Kiss was a frequent subject in Byzantine art, often standing for the Passion in general. There is a mosaic in Sant' Apollinare Nuovo, *Ravenna (early 6th cent.), and these mosaics often include subsidiary scenes of Peter cutting off the ear of Malchus (John 18: 10), and occasionally also the young man who fled, leaving his cloak behind (Mark 14: 51–2). Judas returning the pieces of silver can also be found in Byzantine examples—another mosaic in Sant'Apollinare Nuovo, or the *Rossano Codex, *c.*550, and was taken up again by Dutch painters in the 17th century, including Rembrandt himself. A very rare representation of Judas's suicide is an ivory (London, BM, *c.*450) which also has one of the earliest representations of the Crucifixion. The portal of Sta Maria la Real, Sangüesa, near Pamplona in N. Spain, has another of the very rare representations of the suicide of Judas in a column figure, but one much smaller than the other column figures. The problem of depicting the traitor caused many artists to make him hatefully ugly, even simian, as in Giotto's famous contrast between him and Christ in the Arena Chapel *Kiss*. In the 15th century the Last Supper was usually shown with a long table parallel to the picture-plane, with Christ in the centre, *John next to Him, and the others ranged along the far side, with Judas alone on the side nearer the spectator, often clutching the money-bag. An example of this arrangement is the fresco by Andrea del Castagno, *c.*1450, in Sta Apollonia, Florence. Fra *Angelico, on the other hand, avoided the problem by depicting the *communion of the Apostles—i.e. after Judas had gone out, rather than the Last Supper (cf. a fresco and a panel from the Silver Cupboard, both in San Marco, Florence). It was *Leonardo da Vinci who showed greater insight into the psychological drama by putting Judas on the same side as Christ, but with his head in shadow. The novelty of this is illustrated by *Vasari's *Life* of Leonardo, concerning the *Last Supper* in Sta Maria delle Grazie, Milan, which Leonardo left unfinished: 'It is said that the Prior used to keep pressing Leonardo, in the most importunate way, to hurry up and finish the work, because he was puzzled by Leonardo's habit of sometimes spending half a day contemplating what he had done so far; if the Prior had had his way, Leonardo would have toiled like one of the labourers hoeing in the garden, and never put his brush down for a moment. He complained to the Duke . . .'. Leonardo explained that men of genius sometimes work hardest when they seem to do nothing, but are in fact thinking deeply. He then said that he still had two heads to do: the head of Christ was one, and Judas was the other. He found it difficult to visualize the majesty of divinity on the one hand, and the depravity of the traitor on the other: 'However, said Leonardo, he would try to find a model for Judas, and if he did not succeed then there was always the head of the tactless and importunate Prior.'

The OT *types of Judas may be the brothers of *Joseph, Delilah and *Samson, or Abner killed treacherously by Joab (2 Sam. 3: 27 (Vg. 2 Reg. or 2 Kgs.)). An example of this theme can be seen in the print of *The Kiss of Judas*, Oskar Kokoschka (1916).

Jude, Saint An *Apostle, usually identified with Thaddaeus, perhaps the brother of 'James' and one of the 'brethren of the Lord'. He was the author of the Epistle of Jude, and seems to have been martyred in Persia together with his fellow-Apostle *Simon Zelotes. They almost always go together—many churches are dedicated to them jointly—but according to legend Jude was sent to *Abgar. He is said to have been martyred by being beaten with a club, or killed by a halberd, and either may serve as his attribute. He is the patron of lost causes, and it is well known that *The Times* occasionally has a Public Notice of thanks to S. Jude 'for favours received'.

Judgement, the Last In pre-Christian times the idea of blessedness for the good and punishment for the evil after death was widespread, so the Christian dogma of the ending of the world with everyone judged according to their actions was easily accepted, but it took a considerable time to evolve an iconographical programme. At first, on sarcophagi and in the catacombs, it was symbolized by Christ and the Apostles seated as judges, or as Christ with sheep on His right and goats on His left (Matt. 25: 31–46) as in the 6th-century mosaics in Sant'Apollinare Nuovo, Ravenna. Christ has six sheep on either side, representing the Apostles as blessed, on the Triumphal Arch mosaic in Sant'Apollinare in Classe. Not until about the 9th century did the theme develop, and in Byzantium it was still referred to indirectly by the *Hetoimasia, or preparation of the Throne of Judgement, or a *Deësis, with the Virgin and S. John acting as intercessors for humanity, or an enthroned Christ as the Ancient of Days: 'I beheld till the thrones were cast down, and the Ancient of days did sit... his throne was like the fiery flame, and his wheels as burning fire. A fiery stream issued and came forth from before him: thousand thousands ministered unto him, and ten thousand times ten thousand stood before him: the judgement was set and the books were opened' (AV: Dan. 7: 9–10; NRSV: 'As I watched thrones were set in place, and an Ancient one took his throne...').

The earliest Western example is probably an ivory plaque (9th cent.?), in London (V & A Mus.). The earliest known Italian example is a wall-painting in Sant'Angelo in Formis, near Capua, of the 11th century. These may be influenced by the *Apocryphal Apocalypse of Paul (4th cent.) and the much later Apocalypse of the Virgin derived from it: these are full of descriptions of the torments of the damned which are so dwelt upon by Western artists in the Middle Ages. Basically, the composition consists of three tiers of figures ranged round a very large figure of Christ enthroned in judgement and surrounded by angels, some with trumpets—'he shall send his angels with a great sound of a trumpet, and they shall gather together his elect from the four winds, from one end of heaven to the other' (Matt. 24: 31). Below these are figures of Apostles, Prophets, or Patriarchs and the lowest tier is usually devoted to the Resurrection with the Damned on the right (i.e. Christ's left) and the Blessed on the other side. It was a favourite subject for *tympana in the great cathedrals, especially French and German (Autun, Chartres, Reims, Bamberg, etc.), as well as on internal west walls (*Torcello mosaic, Giotto's fresco at Padua). The Torcello mosaic (12th/13th cent.) contains many features from Eastern Orthodox iconography—the *Anastasis, or 'Harrowing of Hell', the *Parousia, or Second Coming, the Deësis, Hetoimasia, and Resurrection.

*Giotto's Fresco (*c.*1305) shares some of the ideas of *Dante, who was a major influence on Italian artists, in the arrangement of the Damned in Hell in tiers of figures in a mounting crescendo of horror. The representation of Hell was changed radically by *Signorelli, in his Orvieto fresco, by his abandoning grotesque semi-animal tormentors for even more terrifying humans with flesh the colour of rotting meat. The rendering of the Last Judgement and Hell culminated in the vision of *Michelangelo, whose huge fresco in the *Sistine Chapel (1536–41) broke with all tradition in representing Christ as a Jupiter Tonans figure, as if launching thunderbolts, rather than an impartial Judge. He also made the Blessed into figures streaming upwards at His right hand, while the Damned fall headlong to the earth in a swirl of figures rather than the traditional tier arrangement. Although it was universally admired as a work of art, it met with violent opposition from several *Counter-Reformation writers, not only because of the nudity of all the figures (most had the sense to realize the occasion demanded it).

From the 13th century the subject was also used for altarpieces, as in the one painted for the Hospice de Beaune *c.*1450 by Roger van der *Weyden, which has a central figure of the Archangel Michael weighing souls, another frequent element of the subject, sometimes including a devil attempting to pull the scales his way. Later versions of the subject, such as this, sometimes have a sword and a lily issuing from Christ's mouth above the Damned and Blessed respectively, symbolizing spiritual and earthly power. Christ may also be seated on a rainbow, and there may be attendant angels carrying the Instruments of the *Passion. Rarer variations include angels rolling back the heavens and the Good Thief *Dismas carrying his cross. The 'sign of the Son of man in heaven' (Matt. 24: 30) is sometimes symbolized as a cross, as in the apse mosaic of Sant'Apollinare in Classe, Ravenna, but it may also be regarded as a separate subject, like the *Signs of the end of the world, which immediately precede the Last Judgement. Other biblical references which are cited include Ps. 9: 7; Isa. 49: 2; Mark 13: 24–37; John 5: 28–9; and Rev. 20: 11–15.

According to an old tradition, the site of the Judgement will be the Valley of *Jehoshaphat.

Judgement of Solomon *See* SOLOMON.

Judith Her story is told in the Book of Judith, one of the OT *Apocrypha. Like *Jael and *Esther she was a Jewish heroine, 'the glory of Israel' (Judith 15: 9), a saviour of her people. She was a beautiful young widow when the Assyrian army, under its general Holofernes, arrived in Bethulia (probably an imaginary city), where she lived, and besieged it. When the water-supply ran out the elders were on the point of surrender, but she persuaded them to allow her to try to deliver the city. She 'took off her widow's garments, bathed her body with water and anointed herself with precious ointment. She combed her hair, and put on a tiara, and dressed herself in the festive attire she used to wear while her husband Manasseh was living. She put sandals on her feet, and put on her anklets, bracelets, rings, earrings, and all her other jewellery. Thus she made herself very beautiful, to entice the eyes of all the men who might see her' (10: 3–4). Taking her maid with her, she went to the enemy camp and pretended to be fleeing from the city, offering to show the Assyrians ways into the city. Holofernes was smitten with her beauty and she stayed in the camp, eating her own kosher food, which her maid had in a bag. She was allowed to go through the lines to pray. On the fourth day Holofernes gave a great feast, 'to his own servants only'. 'Holofernes was greatly pleased with her, and drank a great quantity of wine, much more than he had ever drunk in any one day since he was born' (12: 20). His servants discreetly withdrew, but he was stupefied by the wine, and Judith took his own sword, held him by the hair, and cut off his head with two blows. She then put the head in the bag carried by her maid, and together they passed the sentries. She returned to Bethulia and 'took the head out of the bag, and showed it to them, and said, "See here, the head of Holofernes. The Lord has struck him down by the hand of a woman. As the Lord lives, who has protected me in the way I went, I swear that it was my face that seduced him to his destruction and that he committed no sin with me to defile me and shame me."' She told the elders to hang the head on the highest point of the walls and to send out a raiding party to attract attention. When the Assyrians discovered the headless body they were totally unnerved and fled, most of them being killed by the children of Israel. The book concludes with Judith's song of victory (cf. Jael, and Deborah's song).

Judith was sometimes regarded as a *type of the Virgin Mary, the means of salvation of her people (13: 18—'you are blessed by the Most High God above all other women on earth'). Michelangelo in the *Sistine Chapel painted four scenes of miraculous intervention, pairing Judith and Holofernes with Esther and Haman. In 1495, following the expulsion of the Medici from Florence, the bronze *Judith* by Donatello, which had stood in the garden of the Medici Palace, was set up outside the Palazzo della Signoria and provided with an inscription describing it as a symbol of civic liberty.

Julius II, Pope Giuliano della Rovere was the nephew of Sixtus IV and was made a cardinal in 1471. He was Legate in France 1480–2 and fled there in 1494 in fear of his enemy Alexander VI Borgia. He was elected pope in 1503 and died in 1513. He was a violent man, devoted to restoring papal power in Italy and to the recovery of the papal territories alienated by Alexander VI in favour of his son Cesare Borgia—in 1506 he appeared in armour at the head of his troops at the recovery of Perugia and Bologna. When *Michelangelo was commissioned to make a statue of him to overawe the Bolognese he suggested putting a book in the pope's hand, but Julius said 'Put a sword there—I know nothing about reading'. In fact, Julius's greatest claim to fame was his patronage of the great artists of the High Renaissance, Michelangelo, *Raphael, and *Bramante, alternately bullying and encouraging them to give of their utmost. In temperament—his *terribilità* was legendary—he was remarkably like Michelangelo himself and they admired each other deeply in spite of volcanic quarrels. His great dream of rebuilding St Peter's never got beyond the laying of the foundation-stone on the 18 April 1506 and Bramante's original design was completely changed by his successors, but it was Julius who had the force of character to realize that the old church was collapsing and something had to be done. Unfortunately, his fund-raising activities were a proximate cause of the Reformation movement in N. Europe. His tomb, in San Pietro in Vincoli in Rome, erected in 1545, is composed of the miserable surviving bits of the grandiose project which Michelangelo planned in 1506, and which he later described as 'the tragedy of the tomb'. Its finest element is the gigantic figure of Moses.

Junius Bassus (d. 359) was Prefect of Rome, and one of the first members of a Roman patrician family to become a Christian. His sarcophagus (St Peter's Mus.) is a major work of *Early Christian sculpture and worthy of his rank. It has ten very high-relief carvings, representing the Sacrifice of Isaac, S. Peter arrested, the *Traditio Legis, Christ arrested, Christ before Pilate, Job, Adam and Eve, Christ's Entry into Jerusalem, Daniel in the Lions' Den, and S. Paul on the way to martyrdom. The choice of these subjects and their interrelationship is not clear at first sight, but was certainly deliberate and very carefully worked out as a series of *types and antitypes. The actual forms are those of Late Antique Roman art, and the figure of Eve is famous as a direct copy of the classical *Venus pudica* type (e.g. the *Medici Venus*).

Justice One of the four Cardinal *Virtues. The others are Prudence, Temperance, and Fortitude. It is symbolized by a woman, crowned and blindfolded, and holding scales and/or a sword. The scales are a pre-Christian symbol, but the sword may be that of the *Sol Justitiae*, namely Christ with sword and scales, as in an engraving by Dürer (*c.*1498/9). A well-known statue of a blindfolded woman, with scales in one hand and a sword in the other, stands on top of the dome of the Old Bailey (Royal Courts of Justice) in London.

Justinian (482/3–565) was Emperor in Constantinople 527–65. He was the nephew of the Emperor Justin, and married the harlot Theodora in 522: her strength of will enabled him to survive the Nika riots in Constantinople in 532. When he talked of flight she refused to go and said, 'Imperial purple makes a very fine shroud.' They are portrayed as co-rulers in the mosaics of San Vitale, *Ravenna. Justinian's main achievements were the codification of Roman law and his huge building programme of churches and public works, by far the most famous being Hagia *Sophia, although he built some twenty-five other churches in Constantinople and restored others, e.g. the Church of the Nativity in *Bethlehem. Procopius wrote, in the 550s, a history of his building works, including a description of Hagia Sophia as it was before the partial collapse of the dome in 558.

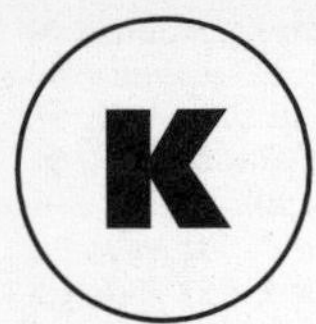

Kahlo, Frida *See* NORTH AMERICA; RETABLE; VOTIVE.

kamelauchion The cyclindrical black hat worn by E. Orthodox clergy. Monks and bishops have a veil at the back in addition.

kamision *See* STICHARION.

Katherine *See* CATHERINE.

katsi A *censer.

Kells, the book of An illuminated manuscript of the Gospels written *c.*800, and now in Trinity College, Dublin. It may have been begun by Irish Columban monks on the Scottish island of Iona and brought to Kells (Co. Meath) when Iona was abandoned after the first Viking raid, 801/2, and finished *c.*806. It is very richly decorated with interlaced patterns in a style similar to that of the *Lindisfarne Gospels, produced in Northumbria in the previous century. The Book of Kells is one of the masterpieces of *Irish art, perhaps the richest of all illuminated manuscripts. The concordance tables are set within arcaded frames, each Gospel has a 'portrait' of the *Evangelist and his symbol; the *Chi-Rho at the beginning of the genealogy of Christ in S. Matthew's Gospel, and the 'carpet-page'—a page of decorative ornament—are exceptionally fine. There are also full-page illuminations of the Virgin and Child, the Temptation, and the Arrest of Christ—possibly the first time these have appeared in a Western manuscript. The initials and borders have rich spirals and interlacings, with ribbon-like animals intertwined, and a wealth of colour. There is influence from *Carolingian MSS in the use of arcades, of Merovingian in the letters made up from animals, and from Northumbria in the vine-scrolls, which have already appeared in northern stone *crosses, and in the Lindisfarne Gospels.

Keys of Saint Peter *See* TRADITIO CLAVIUM.

Kings, the Three *See* MAGI.

Kings, Three Quick and Three Dead *See* TRIUMPH OF DEATH, and MEMENTO MORI.

Kinship of Christ (Ger. *die heilige Sippe*) In the NT there are several references to 'the brethren of the Lord' (Matt. 12: 46, also Mark 6: 3; John 7: 3; Acts 1: 14; and 1 Cor. 9: 5), who may have been children of *S. Joseph by a previous marriage, or descendants of *S. Anne. In the Middle Ages the legend grew up (e.g. in the **Golden Legend*) that S. Anne had married three times; first, to Joachim, by whom she had Mary, the Blessed Virgin; second, to Cleophas, by whom she had a daughter, Mary Cleophas, who married Alphaeus and bore him four sons—SS *James the Less, *Simon, and *Jude, all *Apostles, as well as S. Joseph the Just (called Barsabbas), who was not an Apostle because 'the lot fell upon *Matthias' (Acts 1: 26); third, to Salomas, by whom she had Mary Salome, who married Zebedee, and her sons were *S. James the Great, and *S. John the Evangelist. In all, including S. Joseph and Jesus Himself, this gives a total of seventeen people, but sometimes others with doubtful claims, such as S. Servatius of Tongres (d. 384), are included for local reasons, so that as many as twenty-three figures may be shown (e.g. in a painting by the Master of Frankfurt (Frankfurt). Quentin Massys painted the *S. Anne* altar, a triptych (1509: the centre in Brussels) with eight adults, including the Virgin and S. Anne, and six children, including the infant Christ. The wings, now in Vaduz, have scenes from the Life of the Virgin. The subject was popular in N. Europe during the 15th and early 16th centuries, particularly on account of a vision (1408) seen by a French nun, Ste Colette Boilot. In the 16th century, following attacks by the Reformers, and because of its dubious theological implications, the subject was abandoned. An example, unusual because Italian and early 16th century, is recorded in the will of Angelo Conti (8 Dec. 1500), commissioning 'images of S. Anne and her daughters, to wit the glorious Virgin Mary with her Son Jesus Christ, S. Mary Cleophas, S. Mary Salome with her sons, and SS Joseph and Joachim'. The painting, by *Perugino (*c.*1502), is now in Marseilles (Mus. Longchamps) and has six adults and seven children, most of them named.

Kiss of Judas *See* JUDAS.

knapped flint Flint stones cut ('knapped') in half and used showing the dark inner part. These flints may be set at random, or carefully arranged in even rows, and are a feature of many old buildings in East Anglia.

Knights of Malta *See* MALTA.

Knights Templar *See* TEMPLARS.

knop The bulbous part of the stem of a chalice (*see* LITURGICAL VESSELS), usually in the centre, which allows the priest to get a better grip. It seems to have been in use by the Jews in pre-Christian times.

Koimesis (Gk. falling asleep) *See* DORMITION OF THE VIRGIN.

Korah, Punishment of Numbers 16 tells how Korah (Corah), together with Dathan and Abiram and 250 of their followers, rebelled against the authority of *Moses and *Aaron. The earth opened and swallowed Korah, Dathan, and Abiram, and their followers were consumed by fire. This subject is extremely rare in Christian art, but there is a significant example of it in the Sistine Chapel of the Vatican, by *Botticelli, *c.*1481, where it was intended to demonstrate the divine nature of the vocation to the priesthood. The Vulgate names them as Core, Dathan, and Abiron, and adds another, Hon.

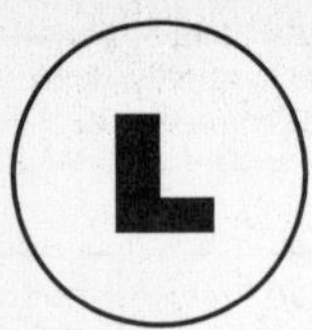

Laban *See* JACOB.

labarum According to *Eusebius, the Emperor *Constantine had a vision of a cross in the sky, with the words *In hoc signo vinces* (In this sign you will conquer), and that night he dreamed that he was to put the *Chi-Rho symbol of Christ on the banner (*labarum*) of his army. The next day, he defeated Maxentius in the battle of the Milvian Bridge (312). From then on, the *labarum* was used by the Roman army.

Labours of the Months *See* MONTHS.

labyrinth In the three great Gothic cathedrals of Chartres, Reims, and Amiens, a labyrinth or maze was inlaid into the floor of the nave and was used also to record the names of the architects in a central plaque. Only the one at Chartres has survived, although the central plaque is missing. The maze is circular, over 42 ft. wide, and the 'path' is nearly 1,000 ft. long. The custom existed of using the maze as a substitute for a pilgrimage, by following its winding 'path' on one's knees with suitable prayers. The Reims labyrinth survived until 1778, when one of the canons, irritated by children and beggars playing on the twisting route, paid for it to be replaced by plain paving-stones. The inscriptions on the plaque were recorded and list the architects as Jean d'Orbais, master until 1231, 'who began the choir' and must therefore have made the first design, Jean le Loup (1231–47), who finished the choir and laid the foundations of the west front, Gaucher de Reims (1247–55), who worked on the portals, and may therefore have been a sculptor, and Bernard de Soissons (1255–90), who built five vaulted bays (the nave has nine bays as far as the beginning of the huge transeptal area) and 'made the O' or rose window. A fifth master who may have once been included in the inscription was Robert de Coucy (1290–1311), who continued the west front and built the towers. Bernard de Soissons is usually credited with being the sculptor who created the famous 'Reims smile'.

The maze at Amiens has also been destroyed, but the plaque survived until 1828 and recorded the date the church was begun as 1220, and the architects as Robert de Luzarches, Thomas de Cormont, and his son Renard, who made the inscription in 1288. The sketchbook of *Villard de Honnecourt illustrates a circular maze of the Chartres type.

Lactans *See* MADONNA TYPES.

ladder A ladder is one of the Instruments of the *Passion, referring to the ladders placed against the cross during the *Deposition. In *Jacob's dream he saw a ladder 'set up on the earth, the top of it reaching to heaven; and the angels of God were ascending and descending on it. And the Lord stood beside him' (Gen. 28: 12–13). This was the inspiration of the ladder symbolism in the visions of S. John *Climacus and *S. Romuald, both of whom saw monks ascending a ladder to Heaven.

Lady altar An altar dedicated to the Virgin Mary, usually in a *Lady chapel.

Lady chapel Most pre-Reformation cathedrals and major churches have a chapel dedicated to the Virgin Mary. It is usually part of the *retrochoir or *ambulatory; occasionally it is a separate but contiguous chapel, as at Amiens.

Lady Day 25 March, the Feast of the *Annunciation.

La Farge, John (1835–1910) An American artist and writer who, after an early career painting landscapes and figures, was given a commission (1876) to decorate Trinity Church, Boston (Massachusetts), including mural painting and the design and manufacture of stained glass, a project that significantly elevated the quality of ecclesiastical art in the United States. His work for churches in

New York City included the Church of the Ascension, Church of the Incarnation, the Church of St Paul the Apostle, Judson Memorial Church, and the chapel of Columbia University. Public commissions included four great lunettes entitled *History of Religion* for the State Capitol in St Paul, Minnesota, and a similar installation in the Supreme Court Building in Baltimore, Maryland, with Justice as its theme. Among his writings are *The High Life in Art* (1908), *The American Art of Glass* (a pamphlet), *The Christian Story in Art* (date uncertain), and *Considerations on Painting* (1895). He was the father of Christopher La Farge, a partner in Heins & La Farge, the original architects of the Cathedral Church of St John the Divine, New York City. *See also* NORTH AMERICA.

lamb Like the *dove or the *fish the lamb is a symbol of several different things. The lamb includes sacrifice, innocence, purity, S. John the Baptist, the Church, the Apostles, and, above all, Christ. In Gen. 4: 4, Abel's sacrifice of the lamb is accepted by God, and Cain's anger at the refusal of his offering ends in his killing his brother. In Gen. 22: 7–8, Isaac asks his father the question: 'The fire and the wood are here, but where is the lamb for a burnt offering?' and when Abraham answers him, 'My son, God will provide for himself a lamb for a burnt offering', he discovers the terrifying truth, that he is the lamb. The sacrifice of Isaac has always been seen as a *type of the Crucifixion, since Isaac bearing the wood for the sacrifice is equated with Christ bearing the Cross. In Exod. 12: 3–5, 21, Moses gives instructions for the preparation of the Paschal lamb for the Passover meal, which again becomes a type of Christ's sacrifice and the salvation which flowed from it. The first prophecy of Christ's sacrifice is Isa. 53: 7, repeated in Jer. 11: 19, as the 'lamb brought to the slaughter', a reference to the lamb sacrificed daily in the Temple at Jerusalem.

In the NT the vital words are those of the Baptist (John 1: 29, 36), when he recognizes Jesus as the Christ: 'Behold the lamb of God, who takes away the sin of the world.' These are the words of the *Agnus Dei, said daily in the Mass, always with the invocation 'have mercy on us, give us peace'. In Rev. (Apoc.) 5: 6, 12; 12: 11; and 22: 1, the stress is on Salvation emanating from the Lamb, since amid the Beasts and the Elders 'stood the Lamb as if it had been slaughtered' and 'the river of the water of life flowing from the throne of God and the Lamb'. This is the theme of van *Eyck's *Adoration of the Lamb*, where the pilgrims approach the altar on which stands the Lamb with blood flowing from his breast into a chalice.

Another symbol of salvation is the figure of the Good Shepherd who bears home the lamb that was lost. This was a favourite subject in the paintings in the *catacombs, and it also appears in the Mausoleum of Galla Placidia in Ravenna of *c*.440. The Lamb as the symbol of the Apostles appears in the three lambs which gaze up at the huge Cross in the mid-6th-century apse of Sant'Apollinare in Classe, Ravenna, and which represent the three Apostles present at the Transfiguration symbolized by the Cross. The Apostles and the Christian community appear in the file of twelve lambs which approach Christ on the arch of the apse in Sant'Apollinare in Classe, and in San Vitale in the main apse and also in the ones which issue at the top of the mosaic from the towered gateways representing Bethlehem and Jerusalem. The same imagery appears in the mosaics in the apses of the Roman Early Christian churches of SS Cosmas and Damian (early 6th cent.), Sta Prassede (*c*.827/44), and Sta Cecilia in Trastevere (817/24). After this the file of lambs as the image of the people of God dies out.

*S. Agnes, martyred in early girlhood, is also usually accompanied by a lamb, which may partly be due to a pun on her name, but which may also express her youth, innocence, and sacrifice. In Leonardo da Vinci's *Madonna and Child with SS Anne and John the Baptist* (Paris, Louvre) the Virgin tries to thwart Jesus as the Child struggles to embrace the lamb and to enter, in fact, into his vocation as Christ.

The Lamb is one of the attributes ('Behold the Lamb of God') of S. John the Baptist, who is often represented either with one close to him, or in his arms, as in Memlinc's pictures in Munich, where he points to the lamb beside him, or in the wing of an altarpiece in Vienna (KHM), where he points to the lamb he holds in his arms. The Codex Aureus of S. Emmeran of 870 (Munich), at the opening of S. Luke's Gospel, has an *Agnus Dei* with a halo with a cross within it round the lamb's head, and the same image appears in many other MSS, as well as the copper-gilt book cover of *c*.1160 (Paris, Bib. Nat.) where the lamb with a nimbus is in the centre, with a banner flowing from a rod ending in a cross. Another good example is the glazed terracotta roundel from the Andrea della Robbia workshop (Florence, Museo dell'Opera), where the nimbused lamb stands supporting a banner with a red cross on it—this is the image which eventually became an inn sign as the 'Lamb and Flag'. In a Council held in Constantinople in 692 the representation of Christ as a lamb was forbidden, but this Council was largely disregarded in the West.

The banner with the red cross, held by Christ, is part of the iconography of the Resurrection, since it is the symbol of Victory, as in Piero della Francesca's *Resurrection* (Sansepolcro). In Byzantine mosaics of the *Anastasis or Harrowing of Hell, Christ also holds a long staff ending in a cross, as in the huge *Last Judgement* mosaic in Torcello Cathedral.

Lamentation over the Dead Christ This is not recorded in any of the Gospels, but the subject evolved from the 11th century as a devotional image rather than an illustration of a historical event. It is sometimes combined with the Anointing on the stone of *Unction, which has biblical authority (John 19: 39–40) and may stand by itself. In the East the *epitaphios is a version of the Anointing rather than Lamentation, but in the West medieval piety came to lay more stress on the grief of Mary and the disciples, so that Lamentation scenes often include Mary, John, the Holy Women, Joseph of Arimathaea, and Nicodemus, and even mourning angels. In Italy, from about the 13th century, the stone of Unction was gradually superseded by a stone sarcophagus, in spite of the rock-cut tomb mentioned in the texts, and thus the subject merged with the Entombment (*see* CHRIST), becoming a pause between *Deposition and Entombment, while the *Pietà became a separate devotional image on its own.

Giotto's Arena Chapel in Padua (*c.*1306) is an excellent example of the Lamentation, with Christ's body laid on the ground after the Deposition and before being entombed. The atmosphere of passionate grief is that found in the *Meditationes Vitae Christi* or the *Life of Christ* by *Ludolph of Saxony. In the North the subject was especially popular in the 14th–15th centuries and is often shown at the foot of the Cross. The *Villeneuve Pietà* (Paris, Louvre) is a particularly fine example and others include those by Botticelli (Munich), Annibale Carracci (London, NG), and Rubens (1614: Vienna, KHM).

According to the *Speculum Humanae Salvationis*, the OT *types include Jacob weeping over Joseph's coat and Adam and Eve mourning Abel.

Lampridius A 4th-century (?) writer who is the first to record a 'portrait' of Christ (*see* ABGAR). He says that the Emperor Alexander Severus (222–35) had several portraits in his *lares* (i.e. household gods), including those of Moses and Christ, but the *Historia Augusta*, which has preserved his text, is virtually worthless as history.

Lance, the Holy *See* HOLY LANCE.

lancet window A tall pointed Gothic window.

LANDSCAPE

A genre of painting that is not normally reckoned to fall within the category of 'Christian art'. But as long as artists possess Christian sensibilities and seek to create works that have full artistic integrity, it is likely that the works they produce will, at some level, bear a degree of Christian interpretation. In the Judaeo-Christian tradition the physical world is the theatre for God's engagement with humanity. Real or imagined places with specific topographical characteristics feature in some of the most famous episodes from biblical literature: the *Paradise of Eden, the Wilderness of Sinai, the Jordan Valley, the Sea of *Galilee, and the *Mount of Olives. These and other named locations are contexts within which God's great acts as creator, sovereign, and redeemer occur.

In Western Christian art, tracts of imaginary or real landscape may form backdrops to depictions of biblical episodes and scenes from later Christian history and tradition, most notably those associated with the incarnation. The landscape elements are often anachronistic in character, reflecting the region and period of a painting's origins (as well as time-bound concepts of 'place' and 'landscape') rather than being an accurate representation of the scenery of the Bible lands in ancient times. Landscape elements may be visually nuanced to strengthen the emotional and theological message of an image: examples include Giovanni *Bellini's *Agony in the Garden* (1460s); and the *Adoration of the Lamb* panel in the *Ghent Altarpiece* (completed 1432) by Hubert van *Eyck (d. 1426) and Jan van *Eyck (d. 1441). In traditions of *icon painting, landscape elements are deployed more sparingly, often appearing only when specifically called for by the relevant biblical narrative (even these motifs have been susceptible to omission as the tradition has developed): examples include the Oaks of *Mamre, the wilderness of *Elijah or Saint *John the Baptist, and the mountain of the *Transfiguration.

In post-Reformation Europe, and increasingly in the context of the creativity associated with the Romantic movement, artists began to move beyond inherited conventions associated with the painting of landscape in its own right (these had tended to serve political or dynastic aspirations). Reflecting the consciously subjective engagements of the artists, it became more common for paintings of the landscape and nature *as such* to be invested with religious feeling, sometimes resulting in a blurring of the boundaries between 'landscape painting' on the one hand and 'religious art' on the other. John *Martin's (1789–1854) dramatic representations of biblical cataclysms are essentially imaginary landscapes; other painters depicted actual mountain scenery with 'sublime' qualities with the intention of triggering feelings of awe and reverence towards a transcendent creator God, which, according to the writer Joseph Addison (1672–1719) and others, were inspired by an experience of the scenery itself.

In Germany Caspar David *Friedrich (1774–1840) took this 'Christian sublime' to new intellectual levels, painting far-reaching and thrilling imaginary landscapes, some of which contained symbolic elements such as crucifixes or evergreen trees. One of these, the *Tetschen Altar* (1807) was produced specifically as an altarpiece, thereby giving a landscape a focal place in a particular sacred context. In the USA Protestant painters associated with the Hudson River School, including Thomas *Cole (1801–48) and Frederic *Church (1826–1900) were, to an extent, inheritors of this tradition: beautiful unspoiled landscapes, again as subjects in their own right, could create a sense of awe and inspire faith while offering revelations of the character of a creator God—Cole saw himself as a prophet and teacher as well as a painter.

In common with most of his contemporaries the devout Anglican John Constable (1776–1837) accepted without hesitation that the natural world bore the imprint of its divine creator. It is notable that he also viewed rural scenery (including churches, farms, and dwellings) in the places with which he was most familiar as evidence of a divinely ordained structuring and regulation of English society as a whole. This 'Christian Georgic' outlook is reflected in Constable's most famous paintings of scenes in the Stour Valley near Dedham, 60 miles from London. These classic landscape paintings—which often include carefully placed church towers—are, to an extent, 'religious' works. Another English painter, Samuel *Palmer (1805–81), also a devout Anglican, produced landscapes in the 1820s with a strong visionary quality, containing symbolic elements and occasionally captioned with biblical quotations. In the early part of his career Palmer, influenced by William *Blake, and striving to apprehend his subject-matter with the 'inner eye', made a series of almost mystical images in which the rural scenery is visually transformed in order to show the extent to which God's providence is active and acknowledged within it. But with England's population substantially urbanized by the 1820s, and rural poverty widespread, the ideals of country life presented by both Constable and Palmer obscure what were harsher realities. Palmer's most visionary landscapes have been compared with the later works of Vincent van Gogh (1853–90) who was deeply involved with Protestant Christianity and is often said to have projected a distinct and personal religious sensibility into some of his most famous landscape paintings, including *Starry Night* (1889).

Until the mid-19th century the scientific study and interpretation of natural phenomena (through disciplines such as botany, geology, and meteorology) were viewed, to a considerable extent, as branches of theology: the sharper the scrutiny and understanding of the creation, the deeper the understanding of God, its creator. John *Ruskin (1819–1900), a Protestant Christian who was a critic and naturalist as well as an artist, observed and described features and rhythms in the landscape and nature in which he found 'moral meaning' or 'types' of divine attributes. This habit of mind was shared, at least initially, by his contemporaries, the Pre-Raphaelite painters. Like Ruskin, they made detailed depictions of landscape and nature, consciously seeking to reveal 'divine truths' found in and beyond natural phenomena. Some of their works are landscapes in their own right, others feature landscape as the highly detailed backdrop in narrative paintings which refer to biblical episodes or other moments from Christian history: in Holman *Hunt's (1827–1910) *The Scapegoat* (1856) landscape elements work hand-in-hand with the narrative and symbolic aims of the work. The Pre-Raphaelite artists also produced many pictures depicting Holy Land scenes.

Movements in 20th-century landscape painting owe more to their 19th-century counterparts than is often acknowledged. Some of the most important 20th-century painters in England possessed well-documented Christian sensibilities, and in many cases this, at least from time to time, informed their work. Stanley *Spencer's (1891–1959) localized vision of events from the life of Christ coupled with a Realist style seems to follow in the tradition of the Pre-Raphaelite painters. A different kind of affinity exists between the work of John Constable and John *Piper (1903–92), the latter's sensibility ascribing great value to the Christian heritage of rural communities, with a visual focus on places of worship (although stylistically John Piper is often most indebted to Samuel Palmer). Piper, conversant with John Ruskin's quasi-theological writings on landscape and nature, also designed several church stained-glass windows which were based on his own painterly abstractions of landscape motifs, resulting in a radical and confident placing of pure landscape imagery within sacred contexts. Graham *Sutherland (1903–80) a Catholic whose early (1920s) works were in the tradition of Samuel Palmer in both style and spirit, was soon to develop a habit of close and visionary apprehension of detailed forms of nature reminiscent of Ruskin's approach, although Sutherland's more poetic vision was more directly nurtured by an engagement with the work of Catholic critic and philosopher Jacques Maritain (1882–1973).

In the post-war period the St Ives artist Peter Lanyon (1918–64) was keen to invest his paintings with references to the full range of lived experiences in the landscape, including the sense of tragedy and social decay found in a former mining community. Lanyon, like many of his Modernist contemporaries, was also ready to tap into the 'universal' language of myth, and produced a notable work *St Just* (1953), which in conception and appearance is simultaneously a landscape and a Crucifixion: using new artistic freedoms Lanyon seamlessly combined Christian redemption mythology with personal expression and place-specific references.

Kenneth Clark's classic volume *Landscape into Art* (1949) alerts the reader to the habit of Western landscape painting to mirror the changes in the theological climate which have taken place over history. More recent writers who have explored aspects of the theme of 'religion and landscape' in Western art include Robert Rosenblum in his *Modern Painting and the Northern Romantic Tradition: Friedrich to Rothko* (1975) and the 'neo-Ruskinian' Peter Fuller in *Theoria: Art, and the Absence of Grace* (1988). Almost two hundred years of the 'visionary' tradition in English landscape painting is charted in Jerrold Northrop Moore's *The Green Fuse* (2007). The ways in which the religious, social, and intellectual contexts for landscape painting evolved in 19th-century Britain are revealed by Christiana Payne in *Where the Sea Meets the Land: Artists on the Coast in Nineteenth Century Britain* (2007).

lantern The topmost element of a dome.

Last Judgement *See* JUDGEMENT.

Last Supper The last meal, probably Passover, eaten by Christ with His disciples, before the betrayal by *Judas. It may be represented either factually, as a simple meal, or symbolically, as the Institution of the *Eucharist or *Communion of the Apostles, but from very early times the fish (ICHTHYS), symbolic of Christ, appears on the table, as in the

6th-century mosaic in Sant'Apollinare Nuovo, Ravenna. In the biblical description there is a distinction between the meal and the sacrament (Matt. 26: 21–5 and 26–8; Mark 14: 18–20 and 22–4; Luke 22: 15–16 and 17–20; cf. also John 13: 2 and 1 Cor. 11: 23–7). In paintings where Christ is shown with a chalice and even a Host, and where the Apostles are kneeling rather than seated at table, the subject is properly called the Communion of the Apostles rather than the Last Supper. *Leonardo da Vinci was the first to concentrate on the psychological drama of the moment when Christ announced that one of the Apostles would betray Him (Milan, Sta Maria delle Grazie, *c.*1496), but this is perhaps a representation of the Betrayal as much as a Last Supper. Further examples of this subject are Emil Nolde (1909 State Art Museum, Copenhagen, Denmark) and Evie Hone's windows of the 1940s in Eton College Chapel, Berkshire, and St Michael's, Highgate, London.

Last Things, the Four *See* FOUR LAST THINGS.

Lateran Basilica, the San Giovanni Laterano (St John Lateran) is the cathedral of Rome, and one of the four Major *Basilicas. It derives its name from the Roman family of the Laterani who originally owned the site, on which stood the barracks of the imperial guard. The site and buildings were given by Constantine, after he defeated Maxentius at the Milvian Bridge, establishing himself as Emperor of the West and ending the persecution which had begun under the Emperor Diocletian (although it had stopped in the West before that date), to be the residence of the Bishops of Rome. The first church, built over the remains of the barracks in the very early 4th century, probably by Miltiades, Pope from 311 to 314, was dedicated to the Saviour, but the dedication was later changed to the two saints John—the Baptist and the Evangelist. From the beginning it has always been a church with a nave and four aisles, with a deep choir and an apsidal end. It has suffered many disasters: looted by the Vandals in 455, restored by Leo the Great, Pope from 440 to 461, and many times since after damage by earthquakes, fires, and further sackings.

Eventually, Pope Innocent X, in preparation for the impending Jubilee Year of 1650, employed *Borromini to rebuild the interior. His work, in which he coupled together the ancient columns of the nave, stabilized the structure at the cost of the surviving Early Christian appearance of the interior, and the addition in 1735 of Galilei's grandiose façade eliminated the early façade and its modest towers in favour of a disproportionately inflated late Baroque structure. The central bronze doors were the original antique doors of the Roman Senate, which Borromini removed and adapted by enlarging them with a new framework for the entrance to his reconstructed nave. Fortunately, he preserved most of the Early Christian and medieval monuments, displacing them from their original sites into the cloisters and dependencies.

The transept had already been redone by Giacomo della Porta for Clement XIII from 1597 to 1601, and was decorated by the Cavaliere d'Arpino, to make it one of the major examples of Mannerist art in Rome at the end of the 16th century, and more interesting than admirable. The choir and apse were rebuilt in the late 19th century, and the 13th-century mosaic by Torriti and Camerino was reinstated from the original apse, though heavily restored. The cloister, one of the finest in Rome, was built in 1215–32 and is one of the outstanding examples of Cosmatesque work by the Vassaletti, father and son, who also built parts of the even finer cloister of San Paolo fuori le Mura. Adjoining the basilica is the Baptistery, built in the time of Constantine and reconstructed in the mid-5th century by Sixtus III and extensively restored by Urban VIII in 1637. The centre now consists of a circle of eight porphyry columns joined by an architrave above which is a second order of smaller columns of white marble. In the middle is a green basalt basin once used for baptism by immersion, with a 17th-century bronze cover. The huge buildings flanking the basilica were once the patriarchate and papal residence until the exile in Avignon from 1305 to 1375. They were severely damaged in the great fire of 1308 and when the papacy returned to Rome in 1377, the residence was moved to the Vatican. Sixtus V demolished the remains of the old palace and the new one by Domenico Fontana was built from 1586 onwards as a proposed summer palace, but the Quirinal palace was used instead. The Lateran palace now contains three museums—for Classical art, Christian art and epigraphy, and an Ethnological Museum of Missionary work.

Opposite the Lateran is the Scala Santa, or Sancta Sanctorum, the ancient chapel of the popes, once in the patriarchate, until the old buildings were demolished. It was then moved to the new building by Fontana. The ancient chapel was approached by the great staircase of the old palace, identified by a tradition going back to the 8th or 9th centuries, with the staircase of the Praetorium of Pilate's palace, climbed by Jesus during His trial, and brought to Rome from Jerusalem by the Empress Helena, Constantine's mother. Its twenty-eight marble steps are enclosed in a wooden casing, which the faithful climb on their knees.

LATIN AMERICAN CHRISTIAN ART AND ARCHITECTURE

The 16th-century westward expansion of the kingdoms of Spain and of Portugal took to South America the art and architecture as well as the religion of the colonizing powers. The influence of Spanish, Portuguese, and French Baroque, all following the lead of the Italian Masters, prevailed into the 20th century until with growing self-consciousness, the countries of the new continent began to break free from European influence, or to explore more freely its movements and forms. The following snapshots of four prominent cathedrals introduce the varied cityscape impact, past and present, of the pervasive and dominant Roman Catholic factor on the countries' indigenous cultural forms. Next a selection of these countries' artists and their contribution further explores the nexus between visual art and Christianity within the Latin American cultures.

Brazil's capital city Brasilia boasts its concrete-framed hyperboloid Metropolitan Cathedral of Our Lady Aparecida (1970) by the Brazilian architect Oscar Niemeyer (1907–2012), with its four exterior sculptures of the *Evangelists* by Alfredo Ceschiatti, and its three mobile *Angels* by Marianne Peretti suspended by steel cables in the nave. Sixteen fibreglass windows give a light-filled nave to this structure, on which the design of Liverpool Metropolitan Cathedral (1962–7) has some influence. The building is situated in the Federal Government Offices quarter, but with visitors being chiefly tourists, this cathedral as yet lacks context. By contrast, Colombia's capital, Bogotá, has in the Catedral Primada (1823) an outstanding example of Iberian Classicism, which names its plaza after the national hero Simón Bolívar (1783–1830), whose leadership successfully coordinated opposition to the ruling colonial powers, and whose statue occupies the defining place of honour in the plaza. The present cathedral, successor to many lesser structures, contains wood carvings whose design originated in imported European copper engravings. A third example of a capital city centre cathedral is Lima. This vast Baroque structure contains the body of the Spanish soldier Francisco Pizarro, conqueror of Peru and founder of Lima, which was to displace the previous regional Inca capital city of Cuzco. In the course of its early design history, the building (with its frequent earthquake destructions) lacked cohesion, but in 1565 it began to assume its present shape, and today is famed for its choir stalls, for the Chapel of the Immaculate Conception, and for the carved ivory figure of Christ, gift of Charles V 'on whose Spanish empire the sun never set'. The region's Aztec architecture (which influenced the Art Deco style) is invoked for the fourth example—Brazil's Catedral Metropolitana in Rio de Janeiro, completed in 1976. It was dedicated to St Sebastian, and designed by Joaquim Corrèa who used concrete and plastic glass. Corrèa's truncated cone motif provides distinctive Mayan architecture allusions, whether simply to give local colour or perhaps more likely, as a reparative gesture towards the objects of the Christian conquistadors' bloodthirsty campaigns. The altar is at the centre of the structure's truncated cone, which itself echoes the city's Sugar Loaf Mountain. Four giant windows feature the defining creedal characteristics of the Church: its Unity, its Holiness, its Catholicity, and its Apostolicity.

The 16th-century expansion of the Iberian empires introduced first Portuguese and then Spanish religious art into South America, Pope Alexander VI having effectively partitioned the new territory in 1493 and 1494. The exploits of Cortés and Pizarro, together with the forced administration of Baptism, laid the foundations for the vehement anticlericalism of later centuries, and, as will be seen, to the energies of Liberation theology.

Beneath the political and economic events of the colonial period a strong current of devotion (particularly in rural areas) can be detected in the many reinterpretations of European Christian art forms: originals from Flanders and Spain were shipped out, but a distinctive South American Baroque treatment of *St Sebastian's Carriage* by a follower of 17th-century Diego Quispe Tito, for instance, for a church in Peru shows Inca nobles in the procession of the Eucharist, seen as displacing the Inca sun festival of Inti Raymi. Jesuit missions in Paraguay, Brazil, and Argentina trained sculptors to represent the Virgin Mary as an indigenous woman, long, straight hair framing her face. The Andean Virgin, drawing on the region's agricultural Earth Mother imagery, appears as or within the mountain's apex in a Bolivian painting in Potosí by an unknown artist of the late-17th or early-18th century. A recent volume edited by Alejandro R. Garcia-Rivera and Mia M. Mochizuki and entitled *Encounters of Faith: Art and Devotion in Latin America,* successfully explores the art of this colonial period, seeking to answer the twin queries: What is the life of theology in art? And what is the life of art in theology?

Famous objects of pilgrimage enshrine the indigenous peoples in devotional Christian art, for example, the black *Christ of Esquipulas* (1595) by the Guatamalan sculptor Quinto Cataño and the 'Indian' *Virgen de la Candelaria* (1576) at Copacabana, by an indigenous Bolivian artist Tito Yupanqui.

Such appropriation of existing imagery was to be transferred into the violent and urgent political sphere once the campaigns for independence began to gain strength in country after country. The Church quickly began to lose its hold over such traditionally powerful means of teaching and stirring devotion as sculpture and the mural painting of church buildings' interiors and exteriors. Instead, such internationally known proponents as José Clemente Orozco, David Alfaro Siqueiros, and Diego Rivera were adorning governmental and educational buildings' wall spaces with the same narrative compositions, this time of revolutionary progress, as their predecessors would have been commissioned to produce for ecclesiastical purposes. There was small amount of overlap, but depicting Miguel Hidalgo the 19th-century revolutionary priest leader's charisma as *Troubled Priest* (1957) gave Orozco but a fleeting historical subject matter when seen against the sweeping and near-total anticlericalism set in train by political upheavals.

More subtly, Rivera's geometrical and architectural *Flower Day* (1925) smuggles a Christ reference (as well as a shaman one) into his composition, and *Creation* (1922–3) picks up on the biblical Creation story. Frida Kahlo, who married Rivera, would freely revert to the popular *retablo or *ex-voto tradition of appeal to the saints. Fernando Botero invoked ecclesiastical imagery in the second half of the 20th century but usually only sardonically, commenting on cardinals' robes and governmental grandeur as modelled by his pumped-up subjects.

Liberation theology was the response beginning in South America at the end of the 1960s made by some parts of the Christian community that refused to claim neutrality or political indifference. The urgency of its programmes and interventions on behalf of the poor led to few lasting works of visual art; on the other hand vehement political movements and prophetic insights freely annexed the biblical and Christian imagery to their own cause in a vernacular and ephemeral urban mural style. Two such artists from different parts of the continent were the Argentinian Leon Ferrari (1920–) who set forth his view of the religion and power nexus with regard to the Vietnam war in his popular 1966 image of Christ crucified upon a diving fighter plane, and Brazilian Nelson Leirner whose non-political image of the pop singer Roberto Carlos (1941–) felt free to associate his cult status in 2006 with devotion to Christ. The Cuban-born Ana Mendieta (1948–85) sounded echoes of the Virgin and the Saints in her 1973–80 *silueta* series of feminist 'earth-body' sculpture; the Brazilian Cildo Meireles (1948–), with his radically political family background in Brazil, projected his view of the material and spiritual, and potentially tragic capacities of the Church in his 'Cathedral Building' installation of 1987. The violence of dictatorships is condemned in Christian-related iconography of artists such as Gonzalo Diaz in Chile, Roberto Valcarcel in Bolivia, and Luis Caballero in Colombia.

The ongoing ambiguity of the Church's outlook on new art commissions for its buildings can be seen in the continuing reluctance to consecrate the Franciscan church at one of Brazil's *fiat* townships at Pampulha (a suburb of Belo Horizonte, Brazil). The artist Candido Portinari (1903–62) provided a cycle of the patron saint's life in ceramic tile (1944) for the building's architect Oscar Niemeyer. This fashionable work attracted American commissions for the United Nations building and for the Library of Congress.

This Portinari trajectory raises the question of the contribution of Latin American artists in other continents and cultures. An instructive example is that of the Brazilian sculptor, painter, and printmaker Ana Maria Pacheco (1943–). The work of this artist academic has now been shown widely in the UK and elsewhere, her installations mixing genres conventionally kept distinct, so as to be at home in gallery, theatre, and liturgy. In her *Shadows of the Wanderer* (2004), the component figures' physiognomies are strongly individualized but their tragedic power (the story is that of Virgil's Aeneas and Anchises) engages with the contemporary viewer's anxieties and concerns.

Maximino Cerezo Barredo (1932–) is a painter whose works are to be found in many places of worship in Christian Latin America, e.g. the murals *The Passion and Resurrection of the Latin American people liberated by Christ* (1980, in Chagres, Costa Abajo, Panama), and *The Conquest of the Beloved Land* (1979, in the cathedral of St Felix of Araguaia, Mato Grosso, Brazil).

Latin cross plan *See* CROSS, CHURCH ARCHITECTURE.

latria *See* ICONOCLASM.

Laurence (Lawrence), Saint (d. 258). Laurence was a Roman deacon associated with Pope S. Sixtus II and was martyred a few days after him. Sixtus entrusted him with the treasures of the Church, including the sacred books, which is why Laurence is the patron saint of librarians. The other treasures he sold and gave to the poor, so that when he was questioned he could point to the poor of Rome as 'the treasures of the Church'. This seems to be an obvious allusion to the story of the Roman matron, who, asked about her jewels, pointed to her children, saying: 'These are my jewels'. Laurence is often represented as a deacon, young and beardless, wearing a dalmatic, the deacon's *vestment, and holding a purse. Usually, however, his attribute is a gridiron, supposed to be the instrument of his martyrdom: in fact, as a Roman citizen, he would have been beheaded with a sword, like S. Paul, and the gridiron seems to have been a gruesome later invention. One ingenious suggestion is that an early scribe wrote *assus est* (he was roasted) instead of *passus est* (he died). Nevertheless, the earliest surviving representation of him, in a mosaic in the Mausoleum of Galla Placidia, Ravenna, of *c.*450 shows him with a gridiron. He was buried outside the walls of Rome and the basilica of San Lorenzo fuori le Mura, built over his tomb, was begun *c.*330. There are at least five other major churches dedicated to him in Rome, as well as in Milan, Ravenna, and many other places, and, as he was a Spaniard by birth, the great monastery-palace of the *Escorial was dedicated to him and has a gridiron plan.

He is often represented in company with *S. Stephen, since both are patron saints of deacons and the body of S. Stephen, after it was translated to Rome, was buried in Laurence's tomb. The most famous cycle of his life is in the Chapel of Nicholas V, in the Vatican, of 1447–50, where Fra *Angelico painted a series of frescoes showing his *Consecration as a Deacon, Receiving the Treasures of the Church* and *Giving them away*, and his *Condemnation and Martyrdom.* In the same chapel Fra Angelico painted a parallel cycle of the life of S. Stephen. Other cycles are in San Lorenzo fuori le Mura (12th cent. wall-paintings), stained glass in Bourges and Poitiers, and frescoes attributed to *Masolino or his follower Paolo Schiavo in Castiglione d'Olona (*c.*1435?), also of SS Laurence and Stephen. Single scenes usually show Laurence's martyrdom, one of the best-known being the very late altarpiece by Titian for the Escorial itself (1554–67).

lavabo (Lat. I will wash) Before the Canon of the Tridentine Mass, the priest recites the words 'Lavabo inter innocentes manus meas', words taken from Ps. 25: 6, in the Vulgate; 'I will wash my hands among the innocent' (NRSV Ps. 26: 6 'I will wash my hands in innocence'). This indicates the origin of the name of the wash-basin, and also the rule that sacristies must have a basin for the priest to wash his hands before saying Mass. Many old churches have very fine lavabos, e.g. the marble one made in Donatello's workshop for Brunelleschi's Old Sacristy in San Lorenzo, Florence. On either side of both the Old Sacristy and Michelangelo's New Sacristy (the Medici Chapel) are two small chambers called, from their function, *lavamani* (Ital. hand-washing). During the post-Vatican II Mass, the priest now prays: 'Lord, wash away my iniquity, cleanse me from my sin', while washing his fingers.

Lawrence *See* LAURENCE.

Lawrence, Jacob (1917–2000) Throughout his lengthy artistic career, Lawrence concentrated on depicting the history and struggles of African Americans. Lawrence's work often portrayed important periods in African-American history, including a series of paintings of the lives of Frederick Douglass and Harriet Tubman, as well as a series of pieces about the abolitionist John Brown. Lawrence was only 23 when he completed the 60-panel set of narrative paintings entitled *Migration of the Negro*, now called *The Migration Series* (1940–41). *See also* NORTH AMERICA, HARLEM RENAISSANCE.

lay brothers, sisters (in Latin *conversi*) By the 11th century most monks were also priests or deacons, but many lay people wished to live in a religious community, under vows, but were illiterate or did not wish to become priests or professed nuns. It became the practice for them to join an Order but without engaging in the full liturgy or learning Latin. They undertook the domestic duties of a convent—growing vegetables and herbs, running the infirmary, guest-house, and kitchens. They usually remained in the convent for the rest of their lives. When the Cistercians began to be sheep-farmers on a huge scale they had hundreds of lay brothers to tend the flocks, not all of whom had a true vocation.

Lazarus *See* DIVES.

Lazarus, the Raising of In the Parable of *Dives and Lazarus (Luke 16: 19–31) Abraham says that 'If they hear not Moses and the prophets, neither will they be persuaded, though one rose from the dead.' This is the prologue to the account of Christ's raising of another Lazarus from the dead, and is given only in John 11: 1–45. It records how Lazarus's sisters, *Martha and Mary, sent to tell Christ that their brother was sick. 'When Jesus heard it He said, "This sickness does not lead to death; rather it is for God's glory, so that the Son of God may be glorified by it."' Yet despite His love for the sisters and their brother He lingered for another two days before making any move to return to Judaea, at which His disciples protested, reminding Him that the Jews there had recently tried to stone Him. When He reached Bethany, 'he found that Lazarus had already been in the tomb four days'. There were many mourners with the sisters, but when Martha heard that Jesus was coming she went to meet Him: but Mary stayed in the house. Martha said to Jesus, '"Lord, if you had been here, my brother would not have died. But even now I know that God will give you whatever you ask of him." Jesus said to her, "Your brother will rise again." Martha said to him, "I know that he will rise again in the resurrection on the last day." Jesus said to her, "I am the resurrection and the life. Those that believe in me, even though they die, will live. Do you believe this?" She said to him, "Yes, Lord, I believe that you are the Messiah, the Son of God, the one coming into the world."'

When Mary heard that Jesus had come, she went in tears with some of the mourners 'and knelt at his feet and said to him, "Lord, if you had been here, my brother would not have died."' Jesus was then taken to the tomb, while some around them wondered 'Could not he who opened the eyes of the blind man have kept this man from dying?' Jesus then told them to take away the stone that sealed the cave which was the tomb. Martha, for all that she believed that Jesus could have prevented Lazarus's death, did not realize that He could do far more than merely prevent it. She exclaimed in horror, '"Lord, already there is a stench because he has been dead four days." Jesus said to her, "Did I not tell you that if you believed, you would see the glory of God?"' The mourners did as He ordered, the stone was removed, Jesus thanked God for hearing His prayer, and 'cried out with a loud voice, "Lazarus, come out!" And the dead man came out, bound hand and foot in his shroud, with his face wrapped in a cloth. Jesus said to them, "Unbind him and let him go."' The effect on the onlookers was predictable; some believed, like Martha, that Jesus was 'the Messiah, the Son of God'; others, to whom such an idea was unthinkable, went to the Pharisees, to warn them that what they had seen portended division and trouble.

It was after this greatest, most public miracle, an incontrovertible manifestation of His identity, that the chief priests and Pharisees determined to kill Him. At the feast that John (12: 1–9) says was held in the house of Martha and Mary, to which many had come, as much to see Lazarus as Jesus, Mary poured perfume on Christ's feet. Judas's angry protest at the waste of money, which S. John attributes to his greed and dishonesty, rather than his care for the poor, finally determined Judas to betray Christ.

In art, the Raising of Lazarus has been represented from the catacombs onwards—in the Catacomb of S. Calixtus, by 240–50, and in the Catacombs of Domitilla in the 4th century. In the Great Frieze Sarcophagus (320–5: Rome, Mus. Naz.) Martha, or Mary, kneels at Christ's feet while He gestures with a wand—the wonder-worker's attribute—and Lazarus in his cerements stands in the open tomb. In a 5th/6th-century Syrian ivory pyx (Paris, Cluny Mus.) Martha holds a cloth to her face in front of the open tomb in which Lazarus still stands, making the gesture which fills out the words, 'Lord, already there is a stench', a gesture which reappears vividly in many images, such as the *Gospels of Otto III* (10th cent.: Munich) where a man holds his nose. The two large carved panels of *c.*1125–40 in Chichester Cathedral show Christ arriving in Bethany with Martha and Mary at his feet, and Lazarus coming out of his tomb with a disciple obeying Christ's order, 'Unbind him and let him go.' The telling gesture indicating the expected foul smell is rarely omitted, but often it is used to indicate non-believers, as in paintings by Albert van Ouwater (*c.*1445–50: formerly Berlin), Geertgen (*c.*1480–90: Louvre), and Jan Joest (1505–8: High Altar, Kalkar, nr. Wesel), where richly dressed onlookers cover their faces in expectation of the stench. Among the most dramatic interpretations of the story is the huge one by Sebastiano del Piombo (1517–19: London, NG), strongly influenced by Michelangelo, and a painting by Jan Lievens (1631: Brighton) in which Lazarus rises from the tomb like a wraith.

The Raising of Lazarus is a *type of the Resurrection which it so positively promises. In many early representations the tomb is a cave which the Gospel says it was, but in later images the tomb is of the kind which would be familiar to a Western spectator. In some, Lazarus sits on the tomb slab as he regains consciousness, like a Man of Sorrows in an *imago pietatis, or discarding his grave-clothes steps forward out of the tomb like the Christ of the Resurrection in the frescoes by Piero della Francesca (*c.*1459/60: Sansepolcro) and Castagno (*c.*1447: Florence, Sant'Apollonia).

Leah *See* JACOB.

Le Corbusier (1887–1965) was born at La Chaux-de-Fonds in Switzerland; his real name was Charles-Édouard Jeanneret-Gris; he adopted his pseudonym in 1920, to separate his work as an artist from his architecture. He was influenced by the Arts and Crafts movement, and towards Nietzsche's and Ruskin's ideas about the social obligations of the artist. He travelled widely in Europe, and later to America and Russia. In Paris in 1908–9 he worked in the architectural office of Auguste Perret, a specialist in reinforced concrete and modular design. In Berlin in 1910–11 he was briefly in the office of Peter Behrens, another master of concrete and steel building. The theories expressed in his large literary output from 1912 onwards have contributed, as much as his buildings, to make him the most controversial architect of this century. He built only two churches: the pilgrimage chapel of Notre-Dame-du-Haut at Ronchamp, near Belfort, and the Dominican monastery of La Tourette, at Éveux-sur-l'Arbresle, near Lyons. Ronchamp (1951–5) is a total contrast to his usual use of rectangular forms, being a series of curved forms with abrupt towering elements. The remarkable roof appears to float over the building like a huge cowl, and is joined to the structure by virtually invisible metal struts, with the space between wall and roof filled with stained glass. The walls appear to be immensely thick and are pierced by irregularly placed small stained-glass windows. La Tourette (1953–63) is a rectangular complex, with an open central space; it marks a return to the rectangular forms in shuttered concrete and modular design usually associated with him. Two rows of monks' cells are above the communal rooms over an internal cloister, and the church has unusual features such as an underground side chapel lit by light-catching funnels projecting from the roof.

lectern, lectionary A lectern is a sloping desk supporting a liturgical book at a convenient height. It was developed from an *ambo and is also called a *pulpitum*. It is usually made of wood or metal, often gilt-bronze, in the form of an eagle with outspread wings mounted on a column and supporting the book, perhaps from the symbol of S. John the Evangelist. The pelican, another symbolic *bird, is also used, but is much less common. In cathedrals the lectern may support the choir-books and is therefore very large, so that it may be read by several people. A **lectionary** (Lat. *lectiones*, readings) is a book containing all the necessary extracts from Scripture to be read during services.

legenda (Lat. things to be read) The word 'legend' now tends to have a derogatory implication—something not true, or at least dubious. Originally it meant literally those things which were to be read in books (which might, or might not, be true), such as the *Acta Martyrum* read in church and compiled from at least the 2nd century. Thus, the 'Legends of the Saints' means the things written about them, whether true or not, and not necessarily implying that anyone believed them. *See* GOLDEN LEGEND. In modern usage, it often refers to the text accompanying an illustration.

Legenda Aurea *See* GOLDEN LEGEND.

Lenten Veil *See* HOLY WEEK.

Leo the Isaurian *See* ICONOCLASM.

Leo X, Pope (1513–21). He was born in 1475, the second son of Lorenzo the Magnificent, and as a Medici, was closely involved in Florentine politics, being made a cardinal at the scandalous age of 13. He continued the Fifth Lateran Council, summoned by his predecessor Julius II in 1512, but it failed to deal with the problems of reform and Leo utterly failed to grasp the significance of *Luther, whom he excommunicated in 1521. As a patron of the arts he was a worthy successor to Julius II, whose plan to rebuild St Peter's he continued, appointing his favourite artist, *Raphael, to succeed *Bramante (d. 1514). To raise money for this huge project he permitted the sale of indulgences in Germany, causing Luther to nail his ninety-five Theses to the church door in Wittenberg in 1517 and effectively beginning the German Reformation. His other acts of patronage were less damaging—Raphael's continuation of the Vatican Stanze, his cartoons for tapestries of the Acts of the Apostles in the Sistine Chapel, and the Vatican Loggie ('Raphael's Bible') with forty-eight OT scenes and four NT, along with stucco grotesque decoration in the newly discovered ancient manner. *Michelangelo he employed only in Florence, on the façade of the family church of San Lorenzo (which never got further than the model) and the Medici Chapel (1516 onwards, but never completed).

Leonard of Porto Maurizio, Saint *See* STATIONS OF THE CROSS.

Leonardo da Vinci (1452–1519). His influence was fundamental despite the small number of his pictures. An unfinished *Adoration of the Kings* (Uffizi) was begun in 1481; two versions of the *Virgin of the Rocks* (Louvre; London, NG) were probably begun soon after his arrival in Milan *c.*1482/3. Both versions are notable for the new and powerful dramatic current between the figures, and for the mysterious quality of the group, enhanced by the unrealistic grotto in which they are set. His most famous work, the *Last Supper* (Milan, Sta Maria delle Grazie, begun probably well before 1497), is the supreme image of the subject. He created a vision of Christ which, in beauty, serenity, sensitiveness, meaning in gesture, strikes through its damaged surface to become the unforgettable image. The psychological understanding with which he groups around this calm centre the confusion, distress, incomprehension, revulsion, disbelief, of the twelve Apostles; the skill with which he isolates Judas as the only one whose face is entirely shadowed, makes all earlier versions of the *Last Supper* into no more than factual illustrations. No one had previously grouped the Apostles with such skill in breaking them up into groups of three, and yet uniting them through their varied reactions to Christ's prophecy. There are no trivial details; the food on the table is limited to some small bread rolls, a few fruits, and some mostly empty platters. For once, John does not lie with his head on Christ's shoulder; he forms part of the same group as Judas, so that within these three figures there is the trusting, grieving, acceptance of John, the vigorous protests of Peter, and the shadowed face of Judas clutching the money-bag. No previous artist had thought out the iconography of the scene with such insight, and in fact Leonardo is alone in having chosen the exact moment of Christ's announcement 'One among you will betray me', since these shattering words can be seen as the motive force of the various reactions of the Apostles.

Two examples of the *Madonna and Child* have also survived: the cartoon in chalk and charcoal (London, NG; probably *c.*1500) of the Virgin with her mother, S. Anne, and the Infant Christ reclining across her lap (a motive later used by both Michelangelo and Raphael) and the little S. John the Baptist leaning towards Him; and the painted cartoon of S. Anne with the Virgin sitting on her lap and leaning forward to restrain the Christ Child who endeavours to bestride the lamb (Louvre). Both pictures are full of psychological insight: S. Anne, in the London version, with her finger pointing upwards and her shadowed seriousness contrasts with the Virgin's tender delight in the two children; in the Louvre version, the anxious Virgin seeking to restrain her Son from His tragic destiny, symbolized by the Lamb, is contrasted with the serene yet enigmatic smile of S. Anne. Possibly the secret of these two pictures lies in Leonardo's exploitation of the device of the half-smile, the tender expression full of love and joy and inward meaning. Yet this can rebound terribly in an image such as the presumably fairly late *S. John the Baptist* (Louvre) where the enigmatic smile and the pointing finger are combined in what is almost a caricature of the expression, which had become strained and, possibly, soiled by its use in such secular images as *Leda and the Swan*, and of course in such famous secular pictures as the *Mona Lisa*.

The other field in which Leonardo's influence was wholly creative was, surprisingly, architecture. No building can definitely be ascribed to him, although it is known that he planned at least one. But in the 1480s and 1490s *Bramante was also working in Milan. Leonardo's interest in architecture which occurs in these years was almost certainly influenced by contact with the most creative architectural intellect of the end of the 15th and the early years of the 16th century, particularly in the field of the centrally planned church.

It may be questioned whether, in his religious works, he was ever motivated by a sentiment of faith. Yet his intellectual power was such that the images of the Virgin and the Last Supper which he created have had more and deeper religious impact than other artists of the time, except perhaps for his great contemporaries, Michelangelo and Raphael.

Leonine City The Vatican area, including St Peter's and the Castel Sant'Angelo, was originally outside the walls of Rome. It was enclosed in the Leonine Wall on the right bank of the Tiber by Pope Leo IV in 848–52 as a defence against the Saracens.

leper's squint *See* SQUINT.

Leviathan In the Book of Job, at the climax of his suffering in ch. 40: 15–24, God finally speaks to him from the whirlwind, telling him to look at Behemoth, and He describes a terrifying creature, which only He can approach. 'Under the lotus plant it lies, in the covert of the reeds and the marsh, . . . Can anyone take it with hooks, or pierce its nose with a snare?', and He continues in 41: 1–34, 'Can you draw out Leviathan with a fish hook, . . . can you put a rope in its nose, or pierce its jaws with a hook? . . . From its mouth go flaming torches . . . Out of its nostrils comes smoke . . . its breath kindles coals and a flame comes out of its mouth . . . It is king over all that are proud.' Job answers in humility, confesses his ignorance and folly, 'therefore I despise myself, and repent in dust and ashes'. He is forgiven and restored.

God's description of Behemoth and Leviathan are those of a crocodile and a whale, and in Ps. 104: 25–6 are the words, 'Yonder is the sea, great and wide, There go the ships, and Leviathan that you made to sport in it.' Again clearly, it is a whale. Isaiah 27: 1 begins, 'On that day the Lord with his . . . strong sword will punish Leviathan the fiery serpent, Leviathan the twisting serpent, and he will kill the dragon that is in the sea.' These vivid words lie virtually dormant in religious imagery, since the only occasion for the depiction of sinners or Hell in Byzantine art is in the Resurrection—the *Anastasis—where Christ descends into Hell to rescue the souls of the just who were awaiting His coming. In the mosaic of the Anastasis in the Katholikon in Daphni, of *c.*1100, Christ pins down Satan under His feet with His cross which He uses like a lance, but Satan is no figure of horror, but a man not unlike a river-god. In the 12th-century mosaic in *Torcello, the Anastasis has a huge figure of Christ treading the gates of Hell underfoot and grasping Adam by the wrist while other souls, enclosed within caverns, acclaim the Saviour; there is no Devil. In the West the Resurrection does not include any equivalent to the Anastasis; instead it is normally followed by the Ascension. The Last Judgement is rarely a

Byzantine subject, but an important Western one and in its imagery Job, the Psalms, and Isaiah merge in, for instance, 12th-century French MSS and *portal sculpture. In the affecting story of the clerk Theophilus, who repented of his bargain with Satan and appealed to the Virgin to save him (1130–40: Souillac, 40 miles N. of Cahors), the Devil is a horrific creature, and in the Last Judgement tympanum of the Abbey of Beaulieu (1130–40: *c.*25 miles further east) the souls of the damned are swallowed by serpents and horrible beasts, which is not altogether new, since as early as in a Carolingian Psalter of 820–30 (Stuttgart) sinners are dragged away by devils. At Conques, *c.*1135–40, in the Last Judgement on the main portal of a celebrated pilgrimage church on the road to Compostela, Leviathan swallows the damned and the long procession of horrific punishments flows from S. Michael, who drives the condemned sinners to perdition. After this the imagery remains constant; the damned enter the quite literal mouth of Hell. Gothic sensibility in no way diminished this taste for the terrifying; the Last Judgement portal at Reims, of *c.*1240, adds a further line from God's description of Leviathan in Job 41; the smoke of its nostrils is like a boiling pot. The cauldron becomes another element in the imagery of Hell, and at Bourges about forty years later, a huge fire with bellows-wielding devils burns beneath the cauldron in which the damned stew. As the 14th century advanced, it was not because manners softened, or the taste for horrors diminished; there were merely fewer opportunities for their grand sculptural display. But the imagery of Leviathan did not die out. The Italians had never cared for such things, but in the North it survived with a new lease of life in *Bosch's and *Bruegel's fires and cauldrons in *Last Judgements* and the *Fall of the Rebel Angels* and even in El *Greco's *Adoration of the Name of Jesus* (1576–9: sketch London, NG; finished work Escorial) the gigantic mouth of Leviathan seethes with the bodies of the heretic damned. *See also* JONAH.

Liberal Arts *See* ARTS.

Liberian Basilica The Roman *Basilica of Sta Maria Maggiore founded by Pope Liberius (352–66). It is also called Sta Maria ad Neves on account of the 'Miracle of the *Snow', or Sta Maria ad Praesepe, because of the alleged relic of the *crib preserved there. It has a splendid series of Early Christian mosaics. The church was very badly damaged in riots after the election of Pope Damasus in 366, and was rebuilt for the first of many times by Pope Sixtus III in 432–40.

lighthouse The great lighthouse on the island of Pharos at Alexandria was about 370 ft. high and was one of the Seven Wonders of the Ancient World. In Early Christian iconography the ship was a symbol of the Church, bearing the soul through life to the haven of Heaven, so in the earliest years the lighthouse was used in *catacombs and cemeteries to indicate the safe passage of a soul.

lily The best-known symbolic *flower. It is the principal symbol of purity and thus associated with the Virgin *Mary, especially in scenes of the *Annunciation, where one is often carried by Gabriel. *S. Joseph also frequently carries a lily, and by extension many other saints renowned for their chastity, e.g. *S. Antony of Padua, *S. Clare, or *S. Francis of Assisi.

Limbo (Lat. hem, edge) The outskirts of *Hell. According to the *Apocryphal Gospels, Christ descended into Limbo, where the souls of the righteous were waiting for Him to release them and lead them into Heaven. He is often shown taking Adam by the hand after breaking down the Gates of Hell (*see* ANASTASIS). This *Limbo Patrum* was often associated with biblical references to Abraham's Bosom and Paradise (Luke 16: 22; 23: 43; Ephesians 4: 9; and 1 Pet. 3: 19–20). The so-called *Limbo Infantium*, much debated in the Middle Ages, was believed to be a place of joy for unbaptized children, who could not enter Heaven, but were sinless. Limbo should not be confused with *Purgatory, since it is not a place of punishment or expiation, but a place of waiting.

Lindisfarne Gospels (London, BL) One of the most splendid of all manuscripts, it was written between 698 and 721 by Eadfrith, Bishop of Lindisfarne, in the island monastery, also called Holy Isle, off the coast of Northumbria. The scheme of the MS is similar to that of the Book of Durrow (*see* IRISH ART), though differing in detail. The Lindisfarne MS has features adapted from the Codex *Amiatinus and from Italian MSS, such as arcaded Canon tables and naturalistic Evangelist 'portraits'. The S. Matthew 'portrait' is a simplified version of the Ezra 'portrait' in the Amiatinus. This MS was probably derived from a copy of the Codex Grandior, or Pandects of the Old Testament, which Ceolfrith, Abbot of the twin monasteries of Jarrow and Wearmouth, had brought back from Italy from the library of the 6th-century historian Cassiodorus. Other features of the Lindisfarne MS are the very fine 'carpet-pages'—purely ornamental pages of abstract ornament composed of intricate spirals and interlacings, clearly influenced by Anglo-Saxon metalwork and jewellery—and a magnificent *Chi-Rho at the beginning of S. Matthew's Gospel. Many of the capital letters are outlined in dot contouring, a simple device which enriches the text, and which probably ultimately derives from E. Mediterranean MSS. Its only competitor in magnificence is the later Book of *Kells.

lintel A straight beam of stone or wood over a door or a window. Because the weight of the superstructure bears down upon it, it is often provided with a relieving *arch to deflect weight from it.

lion Since the greatest antiquity—in Egypt, Assyria, early biblical times—the lion has been a symbol of strength, fortitude, courage, and, having been given the role of King of Beasts, has been synonymous with majesty, authority, and nobility. Epithets such as Lion of Judah, William the Lion, Lionheart, testify to the equation between the lion and the character assigned to it. The Middle Ages added more qualities, such as magnanimity, watchfulness, vigilance (because it was believed that lions sleep with their eyes open). Lions were also considered as a bulwark against sin and evil, and were widely used to bear the columns supporting the porches of many Italian churches. Under their paws, small creatures, sometimes even a man, intended to personify evil and sin, were crushed. Porches at San Zeno, Verona, and of cathedrals at Bergamo, Parma, Modena, in the north, and of Bari, Bitonto, Troia (where they even support columns framing windows), are fine examples.

Yet with disconcerting ambivalence, lions were also equated with sin and evil, since 1 Pet. 5: 7 refers to 'your adversary, the Devil, like a roaring lion, prowls around seeking whom he may devour'. In a mosaic of *c.*500 in the antechamber to the chapel of the Archbishop's palace in Ravenna, Christ, representing the triumphant Church Militant, treads on a serpent and a lion as symbols of evil and sin, an imagery frequently repeated in the Middle Ages. Ps. 10: 5, referring to the wicked, says: 'they lurk in secret like a lion in its covert, they lurk that they may seize the poor . . . and drag them off . . . they crouch and the helpless fall by their might.' The lion is frequently represented winged, as the symbol of S. Mark the Evangelist, and appears as one of the figures of the *Tetramorph in the late 4th-century apse mosaic in Sta Pudenziana, Rome. The Winged Lion of S. Mark is also found in the 4th-century Mausoleum of Galla Placidia, Ravenna, and in 6th-century mosaics in San Vitale, Ravenna. It is probably familiar as the arms of the City and State of Venice of which S. Mark was the patron saint.

Daniel in the lions' den is found in 3rd-century *Early Christian painting in catacombs as a symbol of Salvation, and as such is part of the sarcophagus of Junius Bassus (359: Rome, Mus. of St Peter's), and the spread of the imagery is shown by its appearance in an early 4th-century mosaic in a mausoleum at Centelles, north of Barcelona. The late 12th-century Bestiary (Oxford, Bodleian Lib.)—a good example of its kind—credits the lion with extraordinary qualities, but always to make them an example of Christ. The hunted beast obscuring its tracks with its tail becomes the image of Christ hiding his love of mankind in Heaven until sent by God to redeem the world; sleeping with its eyes open is an image of Christ dying on the cross and buried as a man, but watching in Heaven; and the lion cubs, born dead, but after three days given life by the male lion breathing on them, or by the lioness licking them, is an image of the Resurrection. Fantastic as the interpretations of nature are in Bestiaries, they were treated as truth, such was the power of the 'authority' on which they were based—the *Physiologus. *See also* EVANGELIST SYMBOLS.

Lippi, Fra Filippo (*c.* 1406–69), was probably *Masaccio's only pupil, since he was a monk in the Carmelite convent in Florence when Masaccio was painting in the Brancacci Chapel there. Lippi is first recorded as a painter in 1430, and his earliest works are totally dependent on Masaccio. By 1437 he had absorbed the influence of both *Donatello and Flemish painting, the first for its dramatic effect and the second for its detailed naturalism. In 1437 he began painting the *Madonna and Child with Saints and Angels* (the Barbadori Altarpiece, Louvre), using the *Sacra Conversazione form of unified design newly developed by Fra *Angelico, instead of the picture being divided into separate panels as was the common form until then. By the 1440s the older form was almost totally superseded, except for old-fashioned painters, or, more likely, for old-fashioned patrons. He also adopted the motif of the kneeling Madonna adoring the Christ Child, who is lying on the ground, in a series of *Mystic Nativities* (Berlin and Florence), an idea also exploited by Flemish 15th-century painters, and derived from the visions of *S. Bridget. He was also interested in borrowing from classical antiquity and especially in the expression of movement, as may be seen in his principal fresco cycle, begun in 1452 (Prato Cathedral), of scenes from the lives of SS John Baptist and Stephen.

Fra Filippo's son, **Filippino** (1457/8–1504), cleared up his father's estate when he died at Spoleto, leaving the cathedral frescoes unfinished. Filippino, then aged about 12, went to Florence and worked with *Botticelli. Filippino's early *Madonnas* are an amalgam of those by his father and Botticelli, but he introduced some new motifs, e.g. the *Madonna Lactans* (London, NG), a comparatively rare subject, as well as the very rare subject (from the **Speculum Humanae Salvationis*) known as the Intercession of Christ and the Virgin (1495: Munich), in which she bares her breast and He points to His wounds as they intercede with God the Father for humanity. His frescoes in Sta Maria sopra Minerva, Rome (1488–93), also include *sibyls as well as genuine Roman antiquities in the scenes from the lives of SS Thomas Aquinas and Philip.

Lipsanoteca *See* BRESCIA BOX, THE.

Lithostratos *See* GABBATHA.

Little Flowers of Saint Francis *See* FIORETTI.

liturgical books are those used for religious services and also for daily use by the clergy and laity. Apart from the *Bible, which is used in the liturgy of every branch of the Christian Church, those which are most likely to be produced with decorative bindings and text and with illustrations are the *Books of Hours. In the Roman Rite the **Missal** (*Missale Romanum*) contains the text of the Mass. This consists of the Ordinary, the unchanging framework (Kyrie, Gloria, Creed, offertory prayers, Preface, Sanctus, Canon, the Lord's Prayer, Agnus Dei, Communion, the ablutions, and the final prayers and blessing). The Canon is the core of the Mass and includes the Consecration and the rest of the Mass to the end prayers. The changeable parts of the Mass are called the 'Propers', that is, the parts which vary (i.e. are proper to the season or the day: the opening prayers before the Kyrie, the Epistles and Gospels which change every day and precede the Creed, and the Preface which changes according to the season, or a special feast-day, or a votive Mass). Altar editions of the Roman Missal, and of the English Missal and Anglican Missal which were produced as part of the Catholic Revival in the Church of England, may be richly decorated and illustrated.

Roman Catholic and Anglican deacons, priests, and bishops, and members of religious orders, are required to recite the Divine Office every day, and members of the laity may choose to do this too, either 'in choir' (corporately in church) or privately. The **Breviary** (*Breviarum Romanum*) contains the Roman Catholic Divine Office, and Anglican clergy use the traditional Office of Morning and Evening Prayer (Matins and Evensong) from the **Book of Common Prayer** or the modern one from **Common Worship.**

The **Roman Ritual** (*Rituale Romanum*) is a manual on the performance of certain functions, such as the administration of the sacraments—e.g. baptism, matrimony, burials. The **Roman Pontifical** (*Pontificale Romanum*) contains the order of ceremonies and prayers usually reserved to a bishop, such as confirmation, ordination, the consecration of a church or an altar.

For the Anglican Church these rites are contained in the **Book of Common Prayer** (BCP), which was first produced in 1549 as a comprehensive replacement, in English, for the Latin Missal and other liturgical books. It was substantially revised in 1662, with minor revisions later, and remains normative for the Church of England. An Alternative Service Book in modern language was published in 1980; this was replaced in 2000 by Common Worship, which contains both traditional and modern texts. Other churches in the Anglican Communion have their own prayer books based on the Book of Common Prayer and modern revisions of these.

The **Roman Martyrology** lists for every day of the year the martyrs and saints commemorated on that day. It is limited to the Western Church, but a similar *Menologion* is used in the East.

The Anglican Church has its own Calendar of festivals, holy days, and commemorations, based on the Pre-Reformation Calendar with some later revisions and additions.

The ***antiphonal** contains all the chants of the Sung High Mass, also the psalms and hymns. Its counterparts are the **Gradual**, so called because the verses of the psalms were originally sung on the lowest step (*gradus*) of the *ambo before the Epistles and Gospel. It contains the sung portions of the Mass used throughout the year in the Roman Catholic Church. *See also* EVANGELIARY, LECTIONARY, and PSALTER.

Books of Hours are not true liturgical books, but are versions of the Divine Office arranged for lay devotion. They are often sumptuously decorated, as for instance in the *Très Riches Heures* of the Duke of Berri by the Limbourg Brothers.

liturgical colours In the 6th-century mosaic in San Vitale, Ravenna, of the Emperor Justinian accompanied by his court, the attendant priests wear white robes with a fine dark, or red, stripe (*see* CLAVUS) running from shoulder to hem on either side. S. Apollinare, and Bishop Ursinius, in Sant'Apollinare in Classe, wear the same dress, but with splendid coloured or gold overmantles. Up to the 9th century there does not seem to have been any special system; the robes worn by priests were usually white, like those of the Roman upper classes, though more special ones may have been used in church by the higher clergy. By the 10th century a deacon's distinctive vestment—the dalmatic—was white with a red stripe. As late as the 12th century, when coloured vestments first appeared, they had no special significance, and were often just the best ones available for a grand feast-day. Pope Innocent III (1198–1216) was the first to order that white was to be worn for feasts, red for martyrs, black for the penitential seasons (Advent and Lent), and green for all other times. Advent is treated as a penitential season because it is intended to be a period of reflection and penitence in preparation for the joyful coming of Christ into this world.

In paintings from the 13th to the 15th century bishops were depicted in white *albs with richly coloured, gold-bordered tunicles, dalmatics, and chasubles (*see* VESTMENTS). For the Roman Catholic Church the system was formalized in 1570 as follows: Advent: violet, blue, or black except for the third Sunday of Advent, *Gaudete* Sunday ('Rejoice'), when rose garments may be worn; Christmas and Epiphany: white and gold; Ash Wednesday: violet, blue, and black lasting through Lent until relieved at the fourth Sunday of Lent, mid-Lent Sunday, or *Laetare* ('Be glad'), when rose-coloured vestments may be worn. Passion Sunday: red; the rest of Lent violet as far as Easter Day, when white and gold are worn; Pentecost: red; Trinity Sunday: white and gold; the rest of the year: green. Feasts of the Virgin: white; Apostles, Evangelists, and martyrs: red; non-martyr saints: white or yellow.

In England before the Reformation there were several local Colour Sequences, of which that used at Salisbury (the Use of Sarum) is the best known, and this became predominant: the colours are similar to the Roman ones, except that violet for Advent is interpreted as blue, not purple; yellow is used instead of white for some non-martyr saints ('holy women, not virgins'); the ferial ('ordinary') colour is red, not green; and in Lent violet is not used, but unbleached linen, often decorated with symbols of the Passion forms the Lenten Array. Since the 19th century the colours of *vestments have been strictly regulated in the Roman Catholic Church: black is not now allowed, and blue and yellow are no longer liturgical colours in the Catholic Church. The rest of the 1570 rules are followed. In the Church of England there are still variations, with some cathedrals and churches following the Sarum tradition (especially in the use of Lenten Array), though most now use the same colours as the Roman Catholic Church.

These colours obtain for the priest's vestments, and also for fabric altar furnishings—veil, pall, frontal, and any others such as falls on the lectern or the pulpit. Obviously, these rules do not apply where an altar has a permanent frontal of marble inlays, or a painted or precious metal *antependium such as the *Golden Altar* of Sant'Ambrogio, Milan, or where the *ciborium is an elaborate structure, as at St Peter's, Rome.

In the Orthodox Church coloured vestments are worn, and in many of the grander churches cloth of gold enriched by jewels is frequently seen. Since the altar is always behind the *iconostasis, it is not visible to the people. In most Anglican churches Eucharistic vestments are now worn, though some clergy wear *cassock and *surplice (or cassock alb) and stole. These are also worn for baptisms, weddings, and funerals. For the choir offices of Matins and Evensong cassock, surplice, scarf, and academic hood are the correct dress. A cope in the appropriate liturgical colour may be worn at any of these services, especially at festivals. In the Reformed and Lutheran

Churches no coloured dress is permitted; a black preaching gown with white 'Geneva' bands is the most usual.

liturgical objects and vessels **Liturgical objects** may be divided into two classes: the immovable and the movable.

The principal immovable ones are the *altar and its adjuncts, the *tabernacle, and the *baldacchino. These are followed in importance by the *ambo or other *lectern, the *font, the *pulpit, the *pulpitum, and the *confessional. The *reredos is usually immovable; where one exists it is normally fixed either to the altar or to the wall behind it. An *altarpiece is a painting which hangs over an altar. *Altar-rails are fixtures, but their liturgical use in Catholic churches is tending to be superseded by the giving of Communion to a standing instead of a kneeling congregation; it does not change the function of the rails where they exist as a separation between the nave and the presbytery. Most Anglican churches retain them and their liturgical use. *Aumbries are normally fixtures, and are often found in older parish churches built into the choir wall.

The movable objects include the *cross which, in Catholic churches, usually stands above the tabernacle, hangs above the altar, or is fixed to the wall behind it. It may not stand in front of the tablernacle. In Anglican churches, since there is no tabernacle, it stands in the centre of the altar. The sanctuary lamp is a red oil-lamp, or a red candle in a deep glass holder, which in all Catholic churches burns before the tabernacle, or either hangs or stands near it, often—if the altar is of the old type against the rear wall of the presbytery—on one of the steps, or gradines, originally called a **predella*, at the back of the altar. Some High Anglican churches also place a light before the reserved Sacrament. The *candlesticks are also usually placed on the gradines. On basilical altars in Catholic churches, where the priest faces the congregation, low candle-holders are used on the altar itself, though in cathedrals and very large churches they may either stand separately or be held by acolytes. This—like the use of a basilical altar—is a return to Early Christian usage when nothing was placed on the altar but the chalice and paten and the Missal. Where the Catholic church is an old one, brought up to date with the introduction of a basilical altar, it almost certainly still has its original high altar, in which case the six candles for High Mass will still stand on the high altar at the back of the church. The seven-branched candlestick of Jewish origin, called a menorah, is often found, having been introduced from the Holy Land after the Crusades. The Paschal candlestick is normally placed on the Gospel side of the altar in Catholic churches, and is lit from before the midnight Mass of Easter Saturday until Ascension Day. A *monstrance is used for the Exposition of the Blessed Sacrament, and for the carrying of the Sacrament in processions.

Altars usually have an *antependium or frontal. Sometimes these are richly decorative and precious works of art (as in Sant'Ambrogio, Milan), or are part of the very elaborate, Italian 18th- and 19th-century inlaid marble *pietra dura* altars (examples in the Oratory Church, London). More usually, they are of fabric, and changed to conform to the *liturgical colour of the season. A credence table, or *credenza, is placed adjacent to the altar for the cruet containing the water and wine for the consecration, and for the other vessels, such as a ewer or water-jug and a flagon or jug for the wine used by the celebrant. Some older Anglican Communion plate includes magnificent silver ewers and flagons. A small reading stand may be provided for the Missal (*see* LITURGICAL BOOKS) or the Service Book; sometimes a small cushion may be used (as in the *Mass of S. Giles*, *c.*1495, London, NG). *Altar-cloths are of linen; once three were required on Catholic altars, but now a single under-cloth is used. The top cloth must hang to the ground on either side. The other pieces of altar linen are the *corporal, the purificator with which the chalice is wiped, and the small towel with which the priest dries his fingers after rinsing them before the consecration. Altar cards are now a thing of the past, but once they stood on the altar propped against the tabernacle (and may be seen in old pictures of religious ceremonies) so that the priest could use them as a reminder of the rubric at moments when it would be inconvenient to turn to the Missal. He removed them when he opened the tabernacle to reach for the *ciborium, but with the passing of the Tridentine Mass they are no longer needed.

The remaining movable objects are the *dossal, which strictly should follow the liturgical colour of the season, but is often a semi-permanent hanging behind the altar, and riddels, or side curtains, once an obligatory part of a ciborium altar, but now disused. In some Anglican churches (e.g. Tring, Herts.) the altar still retains its riddel posts. The pall is either a large, decorative cloth which covers the altar entirely, or is the small linen cover over the chalice. It was originally the Early Christian form of cover for an altar, and was often richly embroidered and bejewelled. S. John Chrysostom, in the 4th century, warned against too much attention being paid to such adjuncts. An example may be seen in the 6th-century mosaic in San Vitale, Ravenna, of Abel and Melchisedek making their offerings on either side of an altar thus covered. It was revived as an altar-cloth in the Anglican Church in the 17th century. Where there is no antependium or frontal, such a cloth may be laid over the altar. It is rarely used in the Catholic Church. A third form of pall is the large cloth covering a coffin. A fall is a small decorative cloth which hangs over the reading stand, or over the edge of the pulpit, in which case it follows the seasonal liturgical colour, and the term is also used for the long strip of material which covers the gap between the altar-cloth and the frontal, in which case it is a permanent hanging.

Liturgical vessels The principal one is the chalice (Lat. *calyx*, cup) in which the wine is consecrated for Communion. In Early Christian times it was often made of glass (which was then a valuable material) or earthenware, and as late as the 8th century S. Boniface on his German missions used a wooden chalice. By the 4th century gold or silver had become general, and SS John Chrysostom and Augustine both mention chalices set with gemstones. While the size, shape, and decoration of chalices have, over the centuries, been influenced by fashion, the basic shape is a cup on a stem with a *knop, on a foot large enough to make it stable. Until the 12th century Communion in both kinds was normal, and a larger two-handled chalice was used for the faithful. After the 12th century the custom began to die out, and in 1415 the Council of Constance withdrew the chalice from the laity. It was apparently common for a small tube or pipette called a *calamus* to be used, instead of the communicant actually drinking from the chalice. Communion in both kinds has recently been restored to Catholics, but it was restored immediately after the Reformation in the Church of England. Anglican chalices then became much larger. Communion in both kinds now required more wine than was used in the Catholic service; for this reason flagons became necessary. During the 17th and 18th centuries, these extra liturgical vessels developed into magnificent pieces of ecclesiastical silver plate, and most large churches, particularly cathedrals, often have splendid and costly examples, all post-Reformation. In small or less grand churches, a glass flagon or decanter is often used. As late as the 8th century, chalices might still be made of common materials, but these were slowly replaced by gold or silver vessels, the latter gilt inside the bowl; silver-gilt is now their normal material, although since 1969 the use of common materials has been permitted.

The paten, which holds the larger Host used by the celebrant, normally has a slight well in the centre which fits the top of the chalice. In the first millennium, the paten was much larger, since leavened bread was used, but after the slow adoption of wafer-bread in the 9th century it became the present saucer-sized vessel. In the Anglican Church, the reintroduction of leavened bread after the Reformation caused the paten to become much larger, and in the 18th century it frequently became a large 'tazza' on a raised foot, of a type still used in the E. Orthodox Church. In the 19th century the Oxford Movement revived the use of wafer-bread, though both forms coexist. *See also* PYX. The server or an acolyte also has a small, brass or bronze Sanctus Bell which he rings at various stages in the Mass, notably before the Consecration and to summon the communicants.

A ciborium is always, in the Catholic Church, provided with a veil, usually of white silk, to show that it is the one containing consecrated wafers. In the Anglican Church a ciborium is used if many communicants are expected, as at the watch-night service at Christmas. Incense is presented to the celebrant or the deacon by the *acolyte or server in the incense boat together with the *censer (or thurible). At the *asperges which precede High Mass in a Catholic church, or when an object is to be blessed, the holy water is contained in a *situla, or in a basin, and is sprinkled by an *aspergillum. A chrismatory is a small casket sometimes of silver, but often of brass, which is made to contain phials of the three holy oils which have been used since the earliest times, possibly as early as the 2nd century. They are (1) the oil used at baptisms, (2) the oil used at the anointing of the sick (both these are olive oil), and (3) chrism, which is a salve made of olive oil and balm, used in confirmation and at the sacring of a monarch at coronation, and a bishop or priest at ordination. The chrismatory is normally kept in an aumbry sometimes near the altar, sometimes near the font. Fans were once in common use in the Western Church, but are now no longer used. They were carried before bishops, prelates, and popes on ceremonial occasions, to ward off insects both in processions and during Mass. The manner of their use is recorded as early as the 5th century, when they are described as being made of thin tissues, or peacock feathers, and large peacock feather fans on tall poles were until Vatican II carried behind the pope on state occasions. Fans are still in use in the Eastern Church, and are made of thin metal plates on long handles. An acolyte will use a fan of this type, called a rhipidion, to keep flies from the bread and wine. Another object in use in the Eastern Church is an *Asteriskos, a star-shaped metal grid which is placed over the paten to ensure that the pall does not touch the consecrated Host or bread. The E. Orthodox method of giving Communion in two kinds is to dip the host in the wine, and to place the intinctured Host in the communicant's mouth. When leavened bread is used, the bread is sprinkled with the wine with a small gold or silver spoon which is used to put it in the communicant's mouth.

Loaves and Fishes, Miracle of the The account of this miracle is in all four Gospels (Matt. 14: 16–21; Mark 6: 35–44; Luke 9: 12–17; John 6: 5–13) in virtually identical form, and is the only one to be so recorded.

Jesus had been teaching a large crowd which had followed him from the town, and when evening came the disciples asked him to send the people away to buy food in nearby villages. As Matt. 14 tells the story: 'Jesus said to them, "They need not go away. You give them something to eat." And they replied, "We have nothing here but five loaves and two fish." And he said, "Bring them here to me." Then he ordered the crowds to sit down on the grass. Taking the five loaves and the two fish, he looked up to heaven, and blessed and broke the loaves, and gave them to the disciples, and the disciples gave them to the crowds. And all ate and were filled; and they took up what was left over of the broken pieces, twelve baskets full. And those who ate were about five thousand men, besides women and children.'

This astonishing miracle is a prophecy as well as a wonder, in that it foretells the Institution of the Eucharist at the Last Supper (*see* COMMUNION OF THE APOSTLES), as well as having OT antitypes in the miraculous Manna in the Desert (Exod. 16: 4–12), and the inexaustible jar of meal and jug of oil (1 Kgs. 17: 14) from which the widow fed Elijah. Like them, the miracle is a prototype of Salvation, referring directly to Christ's own words, 'I am the bread of Life' (John 6: 35), and again, 'I am the living bread which came down from heaven. Whoever eats of this bread will live forever . . . ' (John 6: 51).

In early religious art it is one of the most frequently represented events. Loaves and fishes appear in paintings in the *catacombs as symbols of the Christian faith of those buried near by, and in the Catacomb of Domitilla is a wall-painting of *c.*375–80 of Christ blessing the loaves. The imagery of the miracle of the loaves and fishes remains constant for centuries: Christ stands between two disciples and lays His hands on the two offerings. The earliest representation of the miracle is on the 'Trinity' sarcophagus (*c.*315: Rome, Lateran Mus.) where Christ performing the miracle of the loaves and fishes is flanked on the left by the first miracle of His ministry, changing the water into wine at the Marriage at Cana, and on the right by the last, the Raising of Lazarus. This points to the process of thought that the first two events symbolizing the Eucharist lead to the third, the Resurrection. Sometimes a more condensed rendering of the theme appears in Roman sarcophagi where the miracles are depicted as taking place in columned niches, with Christ blessing the fish offered to Him by a disciple, while touching the bread in a basket at His feet with His staff (sarcophagus, *c.*350, Rome, Lateran Mus.). The same rendering appears in the 5th-century doors of Sta Sabina, Rome. In Sant'Apollinare Nuovo, Ravenna, a mosaic of *c.*500 follows the frontal form of the image, and in the Codex Aureus of Echternach of 1020–30 (Nuremberg) the same arrangement of the figures is followed. However many incidents may be grouped together, or how many disciples may be grouped around Christ, or how large a crowd may be depicted, the arrangement of the scene remains basically the same.

By the 12th and 13th centuries the subject was becoming rarer; it appears in some carved capitals in French medieval churches, in the 12th-century mosaics in Monreale, Sicily, and in Mt. Athos and some Serbian fresco cycles. It is rare in the Renaissance. The scene appears in Michael Pacher's St Wolfgang altarpiece, of *c.*1481, and there is a large painting of the subject by Tintoretto in the Great Hall of the

Scuola di San Rocco, Venice, of 1579–81, but the iconography does not use the older formula. The subject reappears, however, in a different guise in e.g. the Master of Alkmaar, *The Feeding of the Hungry* (*c.*1504, Amsterdam, Rijksm.) in a series of the Seven Works of Mercy, where Christ Himself distributes the bread to the poor.

An emblem panel of *The Loaves and Fishes* (1986–7) by sculptor John Skelton appears as a pierced relief in the outside wall of the Community Centre (on the site of the former Brighthelm Church), North Road, Brighton, Sussex. *See also* CHRIST, LIFE AND MIRACLES.

loculus (Lat. small place) In the *catacombs a *loculus* is a recess large enough to receive one or more bodies. *Loculi* were cut horizontally out of the soft rock one above the other, sometimes reaching five to seven deep on either side of the corridors. They were closed by a stone or marble slab, or a large tile, bearing the names of those buried within, sometimes with an inscription or epitaph, sometimes with a painting or symbol to make it more easily recognized by the families of the dead.

In Catholic churches, the term is also used for the small recess (or 'Sepulchre') cut in a fixed *altar to hold the relic or relics sealed into it.

Lombardica Historia *See* GOLDEN LEGEND.

Longinus, Saint, (prob. from Gk. for lance) is by tradition the soldier who pierced Christ's side with his spear, but the name is also attached to two other men: the centurion present at the Crucifixion, and the centurion who commanded the posse of soldiers sent to guard Christ's sepulchre. According to the *Bibliotheca Sanctorum*, S. Longinus is a conflation of all three.

The first—the man who pierced Christ's side—is only in John 19: 34–5, where the description of the deed is strikingly explicit, 'one of the soldiers pierced his side with a spear, and at once blood and water came out. (He who saw this has testified so that you also may believe. His testimony is true and he knows that he tells the truth)', and S. John was the only disciple who was there. This soldier is also mentioned in the early 5th-century apocryphal 'Acts of Pilate', and is named Longhinos in a miniature in the Syriac Evangeliary (Florence, Bib. Laurenziana) of before 580. He is frequently the figure shown about to pierce Christ's side, and labelled Longinus, in paintings of the Crucifixion, such as the 8th-century fresco in Sta Maria Antiqua, Rome. The first Greek Father to call 'the soldier with the lance' a saint was S. Germanus, patriarch of Constantinople from 715 to 729, in the *Historia mystica ecclesiae catholicae* of which he is the presumed author. The second Longinus is the centurion present at Christ's death, who confessed his belief in Christ's divinity in the words 'Truly this man was the Son of God' (Matt. 27: 54). He figures in Bede's commentary on S. Luke's Gospel, although in Luke 23: 47 the centurion says only 'Certainly this man was innocent.' The third Longinus is the centurion who commanded the posse of soldiers sent to guard Christ's sepulchre, although these, according to Matt. 27: 65, were the same men who were present at the Crucifixion (the apocryphal Gospel according to S. Peter calls their officer Petronio).

In Eastern and Greek Orthodox tradition, despite the statements by S. Germanus, only the centurion who declared Jesus to be the Son of God is the one revered under the name of Longinus, and he is believed to be the same man who afterwards commanded the guard over the sepulchre. Western tradition, however, says that either Longinus was the soldier who pierced Christ's side, or that he was the believing centurion. In both traditions, he abandoned his military life and settled in Caesarea in Cappadocia, where he led a saintly life until he was martyred. Greek tradition maintains that he originally came from Caesarea and returned there to become a missionary and the first bishop of the area. The story of Longinus shows how difficult it is to identify a person so imprecisely defined. According to the story in the **Golden Legend*, the soldier who pierced Christ's side and the centurion present at the Crucifixion are one and the same, but the account of his later career is highly fantastic.

Longinus figures in what is probably the earliest explicit representation of the Crucifixion, in a small ivory plaque on a casket of *c.*430 (London, BM). The man raises his arm in a thrusting movement indicative of the missing lance, although he stands on the left side, whereas it is generally accepted that the wound in Christ's side was on the right side, and was so as early as 586 in a miniature in the *Rabbula Gospels. The man usually on the left side with the sponge on a reed is *Stephaton, though in Irish reliefs on crosses and in MSS the position of the two is often reversed as late as the 10th century. Longinus is only represented in Crucifixion scenes, except for the huge statue by Bernini in one of the niches in the piers of St Peter's, Rome, where he commemorates the relic of the lance, held in the reliquary balcony above him. In this statue, Bernini used the legend that Longinus suffered with his sight, which was cured when he rubbed his eyes with the hand stained by Christ's blood, hence his gesture of astonishment and delight. *See also* HOLY LANCE.

Loreto, Holy House of (Ital. *Santa Casa*) Loreto, south of Ancona, on the east coast of Italy, became a place of pilgrimage in the late 12th century because of cures of the sick attributed to prayers offered before an image of the Virgin and Child said to have been brought by angels from Palestine. Angels are also said to have transported, in 1291, the Virgin's house in Nazareth, the site of the Annunciation and where she had lived with S. Joseph and the Christ Child, first to Tersatz, near Rijeka, then to two sites near Recanati, twenty miles south of Ancona. In a fourth and final move, the house was moved to Loreto, where the present shrine is. A hermit at Recanati claimed to have had a vision of the Virgin in which she told him the identity of the structure. No contemporary records substantiate any part of the story, which was merely a local legend until 1460, when an account was written by the Guardian of the Shrine, which he had inscribed on a tablet placed within the Santa Casa. The authenticity of the relic of the 'Domus et Imago' of the Virgin at Loreto was accepted in bulls of 1464 and 1471 by Pope Paul II and by many later popes. The only earlier evidence of Loreto as a celebrated pilgrimage centre is in a reference by Flavius Blondus, in his *Italia Illustrata*, written between 1430 and 1440, to a famous shrine of the Virgin at Loreto, with many valuable ex-votos (*see* VOTIVE) in the church.

A Greek writer, Phocas, who visited the Holy Land in 1185, says that there were two churches in Nazareth, one containing, on the left of the altar, the entrance to a cave in which was Joseph's house, where the Annunciation had taken place, and on the right of the altar was a small structure which had contained the Virgin's chamber. In 1253 S. Louis, King of France, on his way back from captivity after the defeat of his ill-starred Crusade to Egypt, apparently saw the church and Joseph's house, but in 1262 it was destroyed by the Sultan of Babylon. Sir John Maundevile, who was in Palestine in 1350, says that it was 'all downe'. In the 17th century, the foundations of 'Joseph's house' were explored by the Franciscan guardians of the shrine at Nazareth, and declared by them to be the same size as the Santa Casa. Later geological investigations have supported the source of the Santa Casa since it is made of a limestone which is local to Nazareth, but not to Loreto. The improbability of the means of the transportation of the Santa Casa to Loreto does not invalidate the claim that it was once part of a structure in Nazareth, brought to Loreto to join the image, at some date before 1291.

The original pilgrimage church containing the Santa Casa was a simple rectangular building, which was replaced with a new church begun in 1468. It had a succession of architects, including Giuliano da Maiano in 1476, and Giuliano da Sangallo who began the dome in 1498–1500. *Bramante strengthened the piers of the dome and built the twelve apsidal and circular side chapels surrounding the crossing and the *transepts, which are attached to the seven-bay *nave and the *aisles with their twelve shallow side chapels. He also designed the façade, though this was modified during later construction. Antonio da *Sangallo the Younger completed what Bramante had begun in removing all trace of its Gothic beginnings in favour of Renaissance forms, such as semicircular arches instead of the earlier pointed ones (which survived in the nave) and he also increased the size of the piers of the dome, but his modifications made seeing the Santa Casa from all parts of the church, and circulating round it, more difficult. Later restoration in 1886 has restored much of the original internal arrangement. The Santa Casa itself is inside a rectangular marble structure in the centre under the dome, and was designed by Bramante and executed by most of the major sculptors of the 16th century. The four entrances have fine bronze doors (1568–76), and the original house, some 31 ft. by 14 ft., now has a later roof. At one end was a Renaissance altar, with over it a niche containing a cedarwood image of the Virgin and Child which with the *iconostasis was destroyed by a fire in 1921. There are now modern copies.

Part of the devotion paid to the Virgin at Loreto is the so-called Litany of Loreto, consisting of forty-nine invocations addressing her as Mother and Virgin with a number of epithets, such as Mother most loving, and Virgin most pure, followed by others symbolic of her office, virtues, and powers, such as Mirror of Justice, Tower of David, Gate of Heaven, Refuge of Sinners, Queen of Angels, . . . of Peace, . . . of Apostles, all titles which were applied to her in the writings of the Fathers during the first six centuries. The Litany is normally said at *benediction.

Lot The story is told in Gen. 19: 11–38. Lot first appears in the Bible when he is named as Abraham's nephew. After the great migration towards Canaan, Abraham and Lot separated, Abraham going on to Canaan, and Lot choosing the fertile valley of the Jordan and settling in Sodom. When the sins of the 'Cities of the Plain' so angered God that He decided to destroy them, Abraham interceded so effectively that Lot and his family were spared. The angels who had come as harbingers of the doom of Sodom and Gomorrah forbade anyone to look back as they fled. Lot's wife did so, and was turned into a pillar of salt. Lot took refuge with his two daughters in the small city of Zoar, and because he was afraid to stay there, he went up into the hills with his daughters and lived in a cave.

Both Lot's daughters had prospective husbands, but they refused to believe his warnings, and must have died in the destruction of the cities. The two girls were so certain that they would never now have husbands or children, that they conspired together to make him drunk and to commit incest with him. Both became pregnant, both bore a son, the elder called hers Moab, and he became the ancestor of the Moabites, the younger called hers Benammi, and he became the ancestor of the Ammonites. The *Flight of Lot and his Family* was depicted on an Early Christian sarcophagus of *c.*340 from the San Sebastiano cemetery (Rome, San Sebastiano), in the 5th-century Cotton Genesis (London, BM), the 6th-century Vienna Genesis, the 7th-century *Ashburnham Pentateuch (Paris, Bib. Nat.), and fairly regularly thereafter in most of the major biblical cycles, most of which also depict the destruction of the cities. Lot's flight with his family was painted by Giusto de' Menabuoi in a fresco in the Padua Baptistery (1348–53), by Benozzo Gozzoli in one of the Campo Santo frescoes (1468–84) in Pisa, by the Raphael School in the Vatican Loggie (1518–19), and by Rubens (1625: Paris, Louvre). The drunkenness of Lot and his incest with his daughters appears in the Vienna Genesis. It is also a scene carved on an ivory *pyx of 1400, together with *Aristotle and Phyllis* and *Samson and Delilah*, as examples of the folly of man (Münster Cath. treasury). There is an etching by Lucas van Leyden, of 1560, and a painting by Simon Vouet (1633: Strasburg). It was never a popular subject because of its scabrous nature, but it was one of the occasions on which artists could legitimately paint the female nude, or semi-nude.

Lot's wife turned to a pillar of salt is considered to be an example of the penalty for backsliding, or for hankering after forbidden fleshpots. This is often depicted by making her a wraithlike figure in the background, silhouetted against the flames. The fruit of the sins of Lot's daughters was that their offspring, the Moabites and the Ammonites, as loathed neighbours of Israel, were continually at strife and were eventually destroyed by Israel.

Louis of Toulouse, Saint (1274–97). He was born in Provence, the second son of Charles of Anjou, King of Naples, and the grand-nephew of Louis IX of France, himself a canonized saint. From 1288 to 1295 Louis was a hostage in Spain at the court of the King of Aragon, and while there he was greatly influenced by two Franciscans. When back in France in 1296 he renounced his claim to the throne of Naples (his elder brother having died), in favour of his younger brother Robert, and he entered the Franciscan Order, being appointed Bishop of Toulouse by Boniface VIII soon afterwards. He died in 1297 and a process of canonization was begun by King Robert in 1300, which was successful in 1317. This was commemorated by a large altarpiece, commissioned from Simone *Martini by King Robert and dated 1317. It shows S. Louis crowned by two angels, and simultaneously holding a crown over Robert's head. The profile of Robert is an early example of portraiture in Italian 14th-century painting, and the scenes from the saint's life below are also probably the earliest example of a **predella*. Most representations of Louis occur in Franciscan churches, e.g. a fresco in Assisi, also by Simone Martini, and one by Giotto in Sta Croce, Florence. There is also a bronze statue by Donatello on Orsanmichele, Florence. Louis is the patron saint of Toulouse, Marseilles, Naples, Perugia, and Valencia, where his relics were transferred by the King of Aragon in 1423. He is usually shown as a youthful bishop wearing his Franciscan habit under a cope decorated with the French fleur-de-lis, as in the Simone *pala*. An example of this theme is Christopher Whall's window (1920) in

Gray's Inn Chapel, Gray's Inn Road, London. The *Glorification of Saint Louis* is the subject of the apsidal fresco (1927) by Maurice Denis in Saint-Louis de Vincennes, France.

Low Countries, The *See* EUROPE.

Loyola, Saint Ignatius *See* IGNATIUS.

Lucifer *See* DEVIL.

Lucy (Lucia), Saint She was martyred during the persecution of the Emperor Diocletian, probably *c.*304, in Syracuse in Sicily, where an inscription referring to her is datable *c.*400. Her name was included from the earliest times in the Roman and Ambrosian rites. She is one of the saints in the great frieze of virgin-martyrs in Sant'Apollinare Nuovo, Ravenna, dating from the early 6th century. The first dedication of a church to her in Rome was by Pope Honorius I (627–38): this is probably Sta Lucia in Selci on the Esquiline Hill, heavily restored in the 16th century. Her feast on 13 December is kept in Scandinavia as a Feast of Light, probably because her name suggests a pun on the Latin for light. Her largely fantastic legend contains a horrific story of her blinding, and she is seen carrying her attribute of two eyes on a dish in Domenico Veneziano's *S. Lucy Altarpiece* (Florence, Uffizi) painted in the mid-15th century, and one of the most important examples of the *Sacra Conversazione. The *Burial of S. Lucy* (Syracuse) is one of *Caravaggio's last pictures.

She is also frequently represented with other virgins in *Virgo inter Virgines pictures.

Ludolf of Saxony (Ludolph the Carthusian) (*c.*1300–78), was the author of a *Vita Christi* (first printed in 1474), which was very popular in N. Europe, but was little more than a version of the **Meditationes Vitae Christi*; he is also thought to be the author of the **Speculum Humanae Salvationis* (*c.*1324?), both of which deeply influenced 14th- and 15th- century painters.

Luke, Saint, the Evangelist was accepted from the 2nd century onwards as the author of the Third Gospel and of the Acts of the Apostles. He was probably born into the pagan society of Antioch in Syria, and many details about him can be gleaned from the Acts and from the Pauline Epistles. He appears to have been converted to Christianity by the missionaries from Cyprus and Cyrene (Acts 10: 20), or by Barnabas (Acts 11: 22), and was thus a member of the earliest Christian community; followers of Christ were first called Christians at Antioch (Acts 11: 26). Traditionally, he was unmarried and a doctor—S. Paul refers to him as 'the beloved physician' (Col. 4: 14), and he appears to have written his Gospel and the Acts when living in Greece, possibly at Thebes, and his relics were transferred from there to Constantinople by Constantius II (337–61), and placed in the Church of the Holy Apostles, rebuilt by Justinian in 536–46 (destroyed by the Turks after 1453). S. Luke writes idiomatic Greek, and was careful to translate Hebrew and Aramaic terms, and both the Gospel and the Acts were written for educated Gentiles, for whom he is recording the history of Jesus and striving to explain His personality, His mission, and His divine origin and power. After the end of the Gospel, the Acts carry the story of the Christian movement forward to a point where S. Paul is awaiting trial (there is no mention of the result) during the persecution of the Emperor Nero (*c.*65–7). Because S. Luke gives a much fuller account of Jesus's predictions of the disasters which would fall on Jerusalem during the seige of the city (Luke 19: 41–4; 20: 20; 23: 27–31) it is thought that it must have been completed after 70, when he knew what had happened.

S. Luke lays particular stress on Christ's human understanding (the parable of the Prodigal Son, Luke 15: 11–32), on His immediate reaction to suffering and grief (the widow of Nain, Luke 7: 11–17; the peninent woman, Luke 7: 37–50), on His love of prayer, His austerity, and on the power of the Holy Spirit. He also records the role women played in Christ's mission. As a Gentile, writing for Gentiles, S. Luke is particular to stress that Christ's message is for *all* mankind, not just for Jews.

He was very close to S. Paul, and from references in the Epistles, and the sudden change in the Acts from a record to a personal narrative marked by the use of 'we' (Acts 20: 5), makes it clear that he travelled with S. Paul on his second journey, meeting him and his companions at Troas (on the western tip of Turkey), whence they came eventually to Jerusalem, where S. Paul met S. James. He accompanied S. Paul on his third journey, was in Malta with him on his way to Rome, and stayed with him during the two years he was under house arrest, and also after he was in prison; in 2 Tim. 4: 9–11, S. Paul says 'Only Luke is with me.' In Rome, S. Luke must have met S. Peter, and S. Mark (whom he already knew).

It has been claimed that S. Luke was one of the seventy (or 72?) disciples (only S. Luke mentions the number in Luke 10: 1–12) and that he was the unnamed disciple with Cleopas on the road to *Emmaus—a story which he alone tells (Luke 24: 13–35). His martyrdom is also considered legendary; it is mentioned only in Coptic and Ethiopian sources, where he is said to have been hanged from an olive-tree. He is the obvious choice as patron saint of doctors, and in Florence, where, in the Guild of 'Medici e Speziali' (doctors and spice dealers), drugs and artists' colours were included, he also became the patron saint of painters, hence the name of their official body was the Accademia di San Luca. The association of artists with S. Luke stemmed from the early Eastern tradition that he had painted the Virgin and Child, and was the author of the so-called *acheiropoietos image.

Images of S. Luke are obviously the work of the artist's imagination. The earliest are in icons, miniatures in MSS, and sarcophagi—the latter as early as the 4th century in Apt Cathedral and Arles, both S. France. He is one of the four Evangelists flanking S. John the Baptist in the ivories on *Maximian's throne, and is represented in a 6th-century mosaic in San Vitale, Ravenna, holding his Gospel, with his writing table before him and his symbol of the ox above him. Similar imagery is in the full-page 'portraits' which preface the relevant Gospel in Gospels and Evangeliaries, such as the *Coronation Gospels* of Charlemagne (*c.*800: Vienna), the Irish/ Northumbrian Gospel Book of S. Chad (early 8th cent.: Lichfield Cath.), and the *Gospels of Otto III* (980–1002: Munich). Later images include *The Inspiration of S. Luke* by Herman Rode in the S. Luke Altarpiece (1484: Lübeck), *S. Luke painting the Virgin* by Roger van der *Weyden (*c.*1440: Boston and Munich), and Mabuse (1515: Prague, and 1520: Vienna), a fine life-size bronze by Giambologna (1597–1602: Florence, Orsanmichele), and the paintings on the side walls and the altarpiece in the Contarelli Chapel by *Caravaggio (1597–1602: Rome, San Luigi dei Francesi). The ox as the symbol of S. Luke derives from the *Tetramorph, and is more extensively used than any image of the saint himself, and in many MSS miniatures is the main means of identifying the particular Gospel. The earliest use of the symbol is probably that in the 4th-century apse mosaic in Sta Pudenziana, Rome. *See also* EVANGELIST SYMBOLS.

lunette The semicircular area or opening, usually over a window or doorway. *See* TYMPANUM.

lunette, lunula *See* MONSTRANCE.

Lurçat, Jean (1892–1966) A French artist born in Bruyères, Vosges, who studied in Paris and met Matisse, Cézanne, and Renoir. War service in 1914–16 was followed in 1917 by his first tapestries, the art form which he famously revived. Much travelling in Europe was followed by eventual residence (in 1933) in New York. He worked with Balanchine for ballet designs, extending his range to Russia in 1934, where he exhibited, aligning himself with revolutionary authors and artists. The influence of medieval tapestries led him to stay in Aubusson and work for a revival of tapestry, using a simplified palette and robust weaving. His political sympathies led him to associate with the fighters of the Communist resistance in the Second World War. His talent, meanwhile, and his career had attracted the attention of Fr. M.-A. Couturier, whose Dominican studies and knowledge of art led him on the eve of Second World War to discuss with the artist sacred themes as a subject for Lurçat's art. Religion provided a 'collective' iconography, and a church was just the architectural setting for such as tapestry, urged Couturier. The eventual resulting commission—the 56 square metres of *The Apocalypse* (1948)—commands the apse of Notre-Dame-de-Toute-Grâce at Assy, Haute-Savoie, France. Among Lurçat's other numerous tapestries are Chichester University Chapel's East Wall *Creation* (1962) and *Bethlehem* (1962) in the Vatican Collection of Modern Religious Art.

Luther, Martin (1483–1546) was the founder of the Reformation. He came of peasant stock in Saxony, received a good education, and went to Erfurt University in 1501. In 1505, he entered a Reformed Augustinian monastery in Erfurt, was ordained in 1507, and in 1508 went to Wittenberg University to lecture on moral philosophy. In 1510 he was sent to Rome by his Order, and though deeply impressed by Rome as the hub of the Christian world and a place sanctified by the blood of many martyrs, he was scandalized by the luxury and licence of the court of Pope Leo X. He returned to his University, became a doctor of theology in 1512, but began increasingly to question traditional Catholic beliefs. He slowly abandoned normal religious obligations—the daily Mass and the recital of the Divine Office—and had a revelation that the essence of the Gospels lay in believing that justification was by faith alone, and unaffected by man's actions and works. Soon after this, Leo X decided to raise money for building the new St Peter's by a campaign for the sale of indulgences. Previous similar campaigns in Germany had caused great unrest, people feeling that the money raised kept the papacy in luxury at the expense of local religious enterprises. Luther, a man of passionate nature, bitterly attacked the sale of indulgences, and in 1517 nailed his famous ninety-five Theses, or arguments against them, to the door of the castle church at Wittenberg. Their rapid spread through Germany brought instant support from all who advocated the reform of the Church and equally instant denunciation by the ecclesiastical authorities.

The bitter struggle that ensued resulted in Luther's excommunication in 1521, and became as much a civil battle as a religious one. The disruption provoked destructive attacks on churches and religious houses (violence which Luther condemned), led to a dangerous relaxation of moral behaviour, and culminated in the brutally suppressed Peasants' Revolt of 1524–6. Finally in 1529 the Diet of Speyer decreed that each state should govern its own religious affairs. The Reformation spread rapidly over N. Europe, splitting into various sects of which that formed by *Calvin in Geneva was the most severe. Luther, who in 1525 had married an ex-nun, Katharina von Bora, waged his bitter war against Catholicism by means of pamphlets, which often, when his opponents' arguments seemed to be dangerously convincing, degenerated from considered, if passionate language, into vulgar abuse. After a lifetime of struggle, in 1545 he retired to Eisleben, though often recalled to Wittenberg, and died in Eisleben, contemplating the success of his life's work with less than total satisfaction. Probably his finest literary achievement, far exceeding his large output of pamphlets, was his translation of the Bible into German, beginning with the NT in 1522 (though it was by no means the first such translation) and his fine hymns which gave the congregation a share in the service.

Portraits of Luther include two by *Cranach the Elder, court painter at Wittenberg: a pair of roundels of him and his wife, therefore 1525 or later (Basle), and one of Luther in 1532 (Dresden). Satirical prints exist, such as the one by Hans Baldung Grien of 1521, depicting him as a visionary monk with a halo and the dove of the Holy Ghost, and another, anonymous, shows him trundling a wheelbarrow with Melanchthon and other reformers with, on his back, a crate containing the Catholic preachers he had expelled, followed by Katharina carrying a baby. One by Cranach the Younger, shows him preaching with, on the left, his followers receiving Communion, while on the right the pope, cardinals, and priests are in the mouth of Hell. To Luther, images were neither good nor bad, and only idolatrous ones were condemned. He encouraged didactic illustration of the Bible and religious paintings, provided that the pictures were faithful to the narrative, but in the works of the younger Cranach and his studio only cold, dogmatic allegories resulted. Luther always favoured illustrating the OT rather than the NT, and the 1534 edition of his Bible had 84 OT to seven NT illustrations, and none of the Crucifixion. *Dürer's woodcuts and engravings of the *Passion* and the *Crucifixion* found no echo in Luther, although in an early edition of the Bible he used Dürer's *Apocalypse* to attack the papacy by crowning the Whore of Babylon with the papal tiara. The only chapel he consecrated was that at Schloss Hartenfels in Torgau, planned in the traditional royal chapel design on two floors, with the upper balcony for the court and the lower floor for retainers. The emphasis was on *altar, *pulpit, *font, and organ, but later church designs allowed of no hierarchical divisions of the space, which could be rectangular or elliptical, like a lecture hall (*see* CHARENTON), with the pulpit more important than the altar.

Luther's seal, used from 1516 and explained in a letter of 1530, was a complex piece of symbolism. In the centre was a heart surmounted by a black cross, representing faith in the Crucified, because the true believer is justified; the cross is black to signify mortification, but leaves the colour of the heart unchanged, since the just man lives by his faith. The cross is set against a white rose, because faith brings joy and peace, and white is the colour of spirits and angels. All is set against a blue sky to signify Heaven and round all is a gold ring as a sign that the bliss of Heaven is eternal, gold being the loveliest and most precious of metals.

Luxuria is a word that has come down in the world. In Latin it began by meaning luxuriance, rankness of growth, or profusion in crops, but soon came to mean extravagance, licentiousness, dissoluteness. As early as the 5th century, the epic poem *Psychomachia* by

Prudentius (348–*c.*410) personifies Virtues and Vices as women fighting for man's soul. It was very popular in the Middle Ages, and sixteen illustrated MSS survive from the 9th century to 1289. The personifications also provided material for *portal sculpture, *fonts, and carved book-covers. The most horrific versions of Luxuria, interpreted as lust, are the 12th-century portal sculptures in Moissac and Charlieu, where a woman is being devoured by snakes, and in a capital at Vézelay, the lustful man, tempted by vice, does not realize until Satan grabs him that the woman-Vice is also a devil.

Four paintings by *Bosch depict a gamut of sins and contain telling and haunting nightmare visions of their outcome, made more disturbing by the subtlety of their portrayal; in *The Seven Deadly Sins* (1475–80: Madrid, Prado) Lust is depicted only obliquely, yet the scene is labelled Luxuria; in *The Garden of Earthly Delights* (1503–4: Madrid, Prado) all appears to be innocent, but the implications are clear; in *The Prodigal Son* (1510: Rotterdam), the terms for the gratification of Lust are still being negotiated; and in *The Last Judgement* (Vienna, Akad.), its results are hideously depicted. *See also* VIRTUES AND VICES.

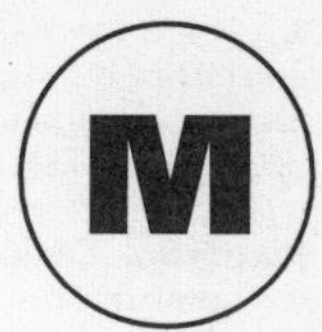

Maccabees, the After the death of Alexander the Great in 323 BC, his empire was divided between his generals. The Seleucid rulers of Syria controlled most of what is now Turkey, Syria, and Palestine. In an effort to Hellenize his entire kingdom, Antiochus IV Epiphanes ('God manifest') in 175 BC set up pagan altars in the Temple in Jerusalem. A man attempting to sacrifice on a pagan altar was killed in 168 BC by an aged priest, Mattathias. Antiochus then declared the Jewish religion illegal and its practices punishable by death. The Jews rebelled under the leadership of Judas Machabeus ('hammerer') and his brothers, and by 164 BC they controlled Judaea. In 161 BC Judas was succeeded by his brother Jonathan who was appointed High Priest by the conciliatory Seleucid king Demetrius, and was in turn succeeded as leader and High Priest in 143 BC by his brother Simon. The accession in 135 BC of John Hyrcanus, Simon's son, was followed at his death in 104 BC by strife between his sons, which resulted in Judaea becoming a Roman province under Pompey in 63 BC. Hyrcanus II left the running of the kingdom to his minister Antipater, who made his sons *Herod and Phasael governors, and Herod, later the Great, became king (37 BC to 4 BC).

The four Books of the Maccabees are named after Judas Machabeus. Books 1 and 2 were declared canonical by the Councils of Florence (1438–45) and Trent (1545–63); they are included in the Apocrypha in the Anglican Authorized Version. All the Books were written in Greek (no Hebrew version survives), probably in Alexandria. Book 1, probably of *c.*100 BC, provides the best historical record of the period. Book 2 is usually dated after Book 1, but before AD 70. Of poor historical value, it is more devotional, emphasizing God's continuing care for his people. Book 3 was probably written by an Alexandrian Jew between 100 BC and AD 70 and recounts the vain efforts of Ptolemy IV to enter the Temple in Jerusalem (217 BC), and his subsequent persecution of Egyptian Jews. On an analogy with Book 1, the Syriac Church admits Book 3 to the canon. Book 4, probably also written later than Book 3, but before AD 70, is a devout treatise using the history of the Maccabees as examples. All four Books are important for their teaching on immortality, on suffering as expiation, and on the worth of prayers for the dead, the last providing valuable arguments for the doctrine of *Purgatory.

The Holy Maccabees were a Jewish mother and her seven sons who died horribly for refusing to transgress Jewish law by eating pork, as is recounted in 2 Macc. 7. Their courage impressed the Early Christians deeply; it is referred to obliquely by S. Paul in Heb. 11: 35–6, and was praised by SS Gregory Nazianzus, John Chrysostom, Ambrose, and Augustine. Antioch is accepted as their place of martyrdom, and their relics were transferred in 551 to Constantinople, and in part to San Pietro in Vincoli, Rome, by 590. Their feast was displaced by one in honour of S. Peter in chains and by Lammas Day (1 Aug.). In 1876 a 9th-century sarcophagus with seven compartments containing bones and ashes was found, and two lead leaves with inscriptions relating to the seven brothers.

The story of the warrior Maccabees gives little scope for imagery. Their valour failed even to stir the Crusaders. The seven brothers and their heroic mother, however, moved the Middle Ages, and despite their being Jewish, they were venerated for their courage and steadfastness in suffering. Some very damaged 7th-century frescoes in Sta Maria Antiqua in Rome are thought to represent the seven, their mother, and the aged Eleazar who was also martyred. The martyrdom of the Maccabees appears in miniatures in a 9th-century MS of the Homilies of S. Gregory Nazianzus (Paris, BN) and in the Bible of S. Stephen Harding (12th cent.: Dijon). In the 13th century, in the left portal of the south porch at Chartres, the martyrdom of S. Stephen is accompanied by figures believed to be the Holy Maccabees, as OT types of the first NT martyr. The Master of

S. Giles, active *c.*1500, painted the seven as decapitated (Amiens), and in the 19th century Antonio Ciseri painted a dramatic rendering (Florence, Sta Felicità).

Maderno, Carlo (1556–1629), came from the northern lake district of Lombardy, and was the most important Baroque architect working in Rome at the end of the 16th and beginning of the 17th century. He was in Rome by 1588, and became the architect of St Peter's in 1603, being responsible for converting *Michelangelo's centrally planned design into a long-nave church. His solution to this problem was as successful as the brief permitted, given that it was a major alteration to a masterpiece; he added three bays, two large side chapels, and an atrium which provided the church with the façade which Michelangelo had not built, and for which he had left neither plans nor drawings. Unfortunately, the extra length had the visual effect of pushing the dome back and, since the approach to St Peter's is up a slight slope, this tends to dwarf the dome and spoils its soaring quality for those approaching the front. Work lasted from 1607 to 1612, and on it he employed his nephew *Borromini as his assistant. He also constructed the *confessio in front of the high altar, for which *Bernini later made the *baldacchino. Maderno also completed the façade of Sta Susanna in 1603, creating the first truly Baroque façade in Rome, which in its skilful management of carefully graduated forward movement, from flat pilasters to free-standing columns, is the antithesis of the flat repetitiveness of Mannerist façades such as that of the *Gesù.

MADONNA TYPES

Images of the Virgin Mary vary in type according to the function of the image, its location—catacomb, church, private devotion—and the qualities attributed to it. The earliest images of the Madonna are found in Roman catacombs from the 3rd century onwards, and they influenced the development of art in Byzantium, where variants on the types were created, but then tended to remain rigid formulas.

Constantinople was created from the transformation of the older city of Byzantium from 324 onwards, but it is difficult to envisage any serious production there of works of art much before the mid-4th century. Those created in the 4th and 5th centuries were often destroyed or perished through age, but they had been much copied and the new icon acquired the name and attributes of the original. If the copy were venerated also in a different place, it often acquired a new name and possibly new attributes as well. The result is consistency in the image, but inconsistency in definition. The perpetuation of old forms in later versions is partly because the artist had little creative freedom and might not deviate from formulas and models established perhaps centuries before, and also because of a belief that repetitions of a sanctified image were as holy as the originals. It is necessary to remember that in Byzantium adherence to an established model was of prime importance, as also were the words—the title—inscribed on the image. This attitude towards images is exemplified by Symeon, Archbishop of Thessalonika (d. 1429), who wrote about the difference in Eastern and Western treatments of subjects, saying that 'the Latins introduced innovations contrary to church tradition, in that icons established in honour of their divine prototypes were confected and adorned in an irreverent spirit opposed to the holy icons'. Silvester Syropoulos, a Greek dignatory who came to the Council of Ferrara in 1438, was blunt about Western imagery, and said he could not revere any of the images of saints in a Latin church because he could not recognize them, and even if he did recognize Christ he did not revere Him either, because he did not know in what terms He was inscribed; in other words, for him to venerate the image it had to have the correct inscription on it, which is why Byzantine, and later Greek, images have inscriptions or titles on them. The Western artist was never bound by such rigid controls as would inhibit his creative freedom. The Western Church controlled what was created, but never forbade technical or stylistic variations if they were doctrinally acceptable. It seems reasonable to assume, therefore, that anything created in the 3rd century, or up to the mid-4th, particularly if it is in a catacomb, establishes a type which, if it appears in E. Church art, is in all probability derived and perpetuated, however distantly, from the example in Roman Early Christian art.

The most influential image of the Virgin is the **Panagia Nikopoia** (All-Holy bringer of Victory) in which the Madonna is seated on a throne holding the Christ Child in front of her, as if enthroned on her knees. It has a resemblance to much earlier pre-Christian images of the Egyptian goddess Isis with her son Horus on her lap. This image stresses her role as the **Theotokos** (God-Bearer) and was important in the struggle against the Arian heresy (*c*.319–81), which maintained that Christ was not the Son of God, but was created by Him as a God-inspired prophet, which reduced His mother to the role of Christotokos (Christ-Bearer). In the Latin Church of the West, Arianism was rejected, but it was the form of Christianity adopted by the Visigothic barbarian invaders of the 5th and 6th centuries. The apse mosaic of the cathedral in Parenzo (now Poreč) on the Dalmatian coast, of the mid-6th century, contains a Theotokos Nikopoia with saints and ecclesiastics which is the earliest example of the Virgin in the major position in an apse.

In scenes of the *Adoration of the Magi*, she appears as the Theotokos, usually facing frontally in a hieratic pose, but the frieze format of sarcophagus sculpture required a side view, as in the early 4th-century sarcophagus in San Lorenzo fuori, Rome, where the Magi advance with their gifts towards the Virgin seated facing them, holding the Christ Child on her knees. In the Cathedral Treasury, Milan, is a silver-gilt reliquary of the late 4th century with, on the front, an *Adoration of the Magi* with the enthroned Madonna holding the Child in the formal hieratic position with two of the Magi, one on either side of her. In the mosaic frieze in Sant'Apollinare Nuovo, Ravenna, of the early 6th century, despite this part of the frieze having been made—by Greeks—under the Arian rulers, the Virgin of the *Adoration of the Magi* faces frontally in a hieratic pose with the three Magi approaching her from the left. This remains a standard image over centuries, as in the 6th-century ivory diptych (Berlin), the icon in St Catherine's Monastery, Sinai, of the 6th/7th century, both made in Constantinople, the 8th-century Franks Casket where the carved whalebone panel of the *Adoration* is accompanied by panels with the legends of Wayland the Smith, Romulus and Remus, and other pagan scenes (London, BM), and in most Virgin portals in French Romanesque cathedrals. It is also the form used by Henry Moore for the *Madonna and Child* carved in 1943/4 for St Matthew's, Northampton. Eventually, as a result of the more human and tender Franciscan influence, the image became less formal in 13th-century Italy, and blended with the more tender **Theotokos Hodegetria** (or Odegetria) in which the Virgin points to the Child, sometimes still seated on her lap, sometimes held on her left arm. This gentler image tends to supersede the Nicopoia type, which is rare after the 13th century. The blending of the two types is seen in grand Italian altarpieces (or civic works) of the *Maestà type such as those by *Cimabue, *Giotto, *Duccio, and Simone *Martini. A version familiar in the United Kingdom is *Our Lady of Walsingham* (Norfolk), seated on a throne crowned and holding a sceptre in the form of a lily, with the Christ Child seated on her lap, clothed and with his hand raised in blessing. The images in the Holy House of the (Anglican) Shrine and the (Roman Catholic) Slipper Chapel at Walsingham, much copied elsewhere, are 20th-century versions of the original, said to have been burned at Smithfield with other sacred images during the Reformation. A similar image, but standing instead of seated, is known as *Our Lady Help of Christians* and is found in some UK churches of the 19th and early 20th centuries.

The Theotokos Hodegetria (her pointing gesture means that Christ is 'the Way') is the type of the 'portrait of the Virgin' traditionally believed to have been painted by S. Luke, and to have been sent from Jerusalem to Constantinople in the 5th century, possibly by the Empress Eudoxia. It is named after the Hodegon Monastery in Constantinople, where the original was kept at least from the 12th century onwards (a name often means that the cult image was usually kept there), and was the *palladium of the city, carried in processions weekly, and always when danger threatened. It is believed to have been destroyed after the fall of Constantinople in 1453, though it is also claimed that it, or most probably a copy, is in St Mark's, Venice, as part of the loot from the Venetian sack of the city in 1204. As probably the most influential of all the devotional images of the Madonna, it gave rise to variations each portraying a gesture of increasing tenderness. It is also the most popular image of the Madonna in the West, where it is found from *c*.600 in the Pantheon, Rome, and as far afield as the Book of *Kells. A variant with the Christ Child held on the

Madonna's right arm is known as the **Dexiotrophousa**, and both forms may be found in the same church, as in the mosaics at Hosios Lukas, in Greece.

There are many other variants on the Hodegetria, based on the response between the figures. If the gesture between mother and Son is tender and affectionate, she is the Theotokos **Eleousa** (compassionate); if the Christ Child embraces her, or twines His arm round her neck, she is the **Glycophilousa** (loving). The Eleousa was popular from the 8th century onwards, and is the type used in the *Vladimir Madonna* (1130: Moscow, Tretyakov). A further extension is the Virgin suckling the Christ Child, which is known as the Theotokos **Galaktotrophousa** (milk-giving). This is the oldest of all images of the Madonna and Child, since it appears twice in Early Christian wall-paintings in the Catacomb of Priscilla, Rome, of the early 3rd century, and is therefore a type existing long before the foundation of Constantinople, and is itself a Christianized version of the Egyptian goddess Isis, suckling Horus.

These gentler, less formal treatments of the theme of the Madonna and Child were the ones that dominated the subject in Italy and France from the 14th century onwards, and account for its popularity in painting, sculpture, MSS, and all forms of decorative art, and among the great galaxy of artists working from the 14th century onwards in Italy and in the North. One notable difference is that in Early Christian, Byzantine, Romanesque, and Gothic painting, sculpture, and MSS, and in the 14th century generally, the Christ Child wears a robe and rarely has more than a shoulder bare. In the 15th century, He is usually shown either nude or with only an exiguous loincloth. This is a late result of the Monophysite heresy, which dominated much of the East from the 8th century, and claimed that Christ had only a Divine nature, not a dual Divine and Human nature. The representation of the nude Child was to stress that He was indeed True God and True Man, and to make evident in His likeness to a normal human man-child that He shared His Humanity.

Four other formal types of Madonna image are the **Virgin Orans**, where she stands without the Christ Child, her arms raised in the gesture of prayer. Assuming that it does represent the Virgin, and not just an Orant (haloes are not found until the 4th century), this image first appears in the Catacomb of the Coemeterium Majus, Rome, in the 3rd century, and although less common than the Nikopoia, it is found in Constantinople, where it was called the Theotokos *Blachernitissa, from the Blachernai church where it was kept. Two marble reliefs, both made in Constantinople, one 13th century (Berlin) and a second late 13th/early 14th century (Athens), demonstrate by their similarity the continuity of an established Byzantine image. The Blachernitissa is allied to two variants, the **Platytera**, where the Virgin Orans, with arms widespread, has an image of the Christ Child enclosed within a *clipeus, either round or oval, on her chest, alluding to her having borne Him in her womb, but stressing His divine independence of His human mother.

In this form she appears in the mosaic in the conch of the apse in the narthex of the Church of Christ in Chora of 1315–20 (later the Kariye Camii mosque) in Constantinople. Another variant is a Virgin praying, half-length or standing with her hands raised in front of her, palms outwards, facing the spectator—a good 12th-century example with a Greek inscription is in the conch of the apse of SS Maria e Donato, Murano, outside Venice. The Madonna with a clipeus enclosing only the head of the Christ Child appears in two wall-paintings of the 6th or 7th century in Sta Maria Antiqua, Rome, one a half-length Madonna holding the Christ Child in a clipeus on her left shoulder, and the other of the *Three Holy Women*, SS Elizabeth and Anne standing with infants in their arms on either side of the Madonna with the Christ Child in an oval clipeus.

Another figure, either half-length or standing, is the **Maria Deomene** (intercessor), also called the **Hagiasotorissa** (Holy Sorrow). She always stands on the right of Christ as Judge, her hands raised towards Him, pleading for mercy for sinners. A marble relief of the Maria Deomene of the 12th century is in Washington, and a damaged mosaic is in the Church of Christ in Chora. If the group also includes S. John the Baptist on the left of Christ, then this is a *Deësis (Intercession), the Virgin and the Baptist as the first who recognized the Divinity of Christ having the right to stand beside Him and plead for the human race.

Other images of the Madonna were created in response to new needs, to the attribution of new qualities, or develop from varying aspects of the Life of the Virgin, as it assumed a more important role in popular religious life. While celebrations and feasts connected with such events as the Annunciation, the Nativity, the Purification, and the Assumption are part of the Church's calendar, and have images relating to the events, a concept such as the *Holy Family originally did not, yet the subject became a popular one, and was recognized in the post-Tridentine Roman Missal and the present post-Vatican II one (*see* MURILLO). Other charming images of the Virgin are of the Madonna in a garden—the *Hortus Conclusus—such as the Stefano da Zevio (early 15th cent.: Worcester, Mass.), and the allied subjects of the *Madonna in the Rose Bower* by Stefan Lochner (1438/40: Cologne, Wallraf-Richartz Mus.), the *Madonna of the Rosehedge* by Schongauer (1473: Colmar, St-Martin), and the group of virgin saints seated round the Madonna and Child—the *Virgo inter Virgines. There is also *Mary in the Burning Bush*, the best example of which is the altarpiece by Nicholas Froment (1476: Aix-en-Provence Cath.), since Moses's vision of the burning bush not consumed or damaged by the fire is an image of the Virgin's perpetual virginity.

The **Mater Dolorosa**—the Virgin of Sorrows—describes four different images: the first, a rare half-length of the Madonna weeping (early 15th cent.: Konrad von Einbeck, St Moritzkirche, Halle a.d.S.); the second is part of the *Stations of the Cross, the moment when the sorrowing mother meets her Son on His way to Calvary; the third is the *Stabat Mater*, the Virgin standing beneath Christ's cross, usually as part of a *rood, and as such more properly considered as part of her supreme sorrow, the Crucifixion, than as a Madonna type; and the fourth, the pathetic grief-stricken mother supporting her Son's dead body. Examples of the last subject—the *Pietà*—are legion: enough, perhaps to cite Giovanni *Bellini, *The Pietà* (1460: Brera, Milan), and *Michelangelo, *The Pietà* (1501: St Peter's, Rome). The word itself is Italian for 'pity' (or sometimes for 'mercy'). A Spanish form is the *Virgen de los Dolores* (Virgin of Sorrows), which is linked to the Seven Sorrows of Mary and the *Rosary.

The **Madonna of Misericord** is a devotional image expressing her votaries' faith in her as intercessor. This was a favourite subject for charitable bodies from the late 14th century onwards in Italy and Germany, whose guilds also exercised a corporate function, much as a modern Friendly Society, but with a religious commitment for their members. Typical examples are the sculpture over the south sacristy door of Milan Cathedral, by Giovanni di Fernach (1380s), the large marble by Bartolommeo Buon where her votaries crowd beneath her outspread mantle (*c*.1451: London, V & A), and perhaps the best known, by *Piero della Francesca, where the central panel of the large polyptych of the *Misericordia* (*c*.1460: Sansepolcro) follows the traditional form of the votaries (or the commissioners of the work, who were guild-members) sheltering beneath her cloak.

The **Madonna del Latte** (the Madonna feeding the infant Jesus) is a 'modern' version—in fact 14th century—of the catacomb image which also prompted the Theotokos Galactotrophousa, although it is highly improbable that any artist of the 14th century knew of its Early Christian antecedents, though Byzantine ones would probably have been familiar. It is another of the images of the Christ Child which stress His human nature, in that He required sustenance like any other human baby. There are many instances in Italian 14th- and 15th-century art, but perhaps the two most famous are the marble half-length *Madonna and Child* by Nino Pisano (1367/8: Cappella della Spina, Pisa, now Mus.), and the *Litta Madonna* by Leonardo da Vinci (1485/90: Hermitage). Allied to this type is the rare, very pregnant **Madonna Expectans**, which is known in an example in Washington National Gallery (?15th-cent. French) and of which the most famous is by Piero della Francesca (*c*.1460: the cemetery chapel, Monterchi, near Arezzo, Tuscany).

The **Madonna of Humility** is a variation of the Nativity scene, in which the Virgin, and S. Joseph if he is also included, worship the Christ Child, who lies on the ground before her. The Portinari Altar by Hugo van der *Goes (*c*.1475: Florence, Uffizi) and several versions of the *Virgin adoring the Christ Child* by Fra Filippo *Lippi (notably *c*.1459: Berlin) are perfect examples.

The **Madonna of the Rosary** is a celebration of a devotional practice universal among Catholics. *Dürer painted a large picture (*c.*1507: Prague), now very damaged, of *The Feast of the Rose Garlands* which shows rosaries being distributed, and *Caravaggio painted a large picture of the *Madonna del Rosario* (1604/7: Vienna, KHM) in which a rosary hangs from the fingers of a Dominican on the left.

The **Dalit Madonna** (2002) by Jyoti Sahi from the Church in India has been acquired by the Methodist Church Collection of Modern Religious Art, London. *See also* MARY and IMMACULATE CONCEPTION.

m

Madonnieri is a Venetian word, usually applied to painters who specialized in devotional pictures of the Madonna. The works of great artists, such as Giovanni Bellini, were often imitated to produce cheap, but popular, images.

Maestà (Ital. majesty) is a type of Italian picture of the Virgin and Child, always of impressive size, which was usually painted as an altarpiece, though few of any age still remain in churches. They date from the 2nd half of the 13th century, and fall into two groups. The first is a large painting of the enthroned Madonna, holding the Christ Child on her arm or on her lap, often with the gesture of the Hodegetria (*see* MADONNA TYPES). She is usually surrounded by angels, who support the throne. Examples of this type are by Guido da Siena (Siena, Palazzo Pubblico, dated 1221, but probably more correctly 1271), *Cimabue (the *Sta Trinità Madonna*), *Giotto (the *Ognissanti Madonna*), and *Duccio (the *Rucellai Madonna*; all Uffizi). The second form is a work on an even larger scale, with a Madonna and Child closely surrounded by saints and angels, portraying her as the Queen of Heaven by virtue of her role as the *Theotokos. The grandest examples of this type are the Duccio in Siena (1308–11: Cath. Mus.) painted with scenes of the Passion on the back, which were originally visible from the ambulatory of the choir (and thus served a didactic purpose for those who stopped to 'read' them), the fresco by Simone *Martini (1315 and 1321: Siena, Palazzo Pubblico), and the Ambrogio Lorenzetti (1331: Massa Marittima, Palazzo Pubblico), which was then already considered as an 'old theme'. The last two examples were specifically commissioned as civic works, as distinct from the essentially religious purpose of the Duccio *Maestà*. The *Maestà* type derives ultimately from apse mosaics, where Virgin and Child with saints was often under a dome with the *Pantocrator. (*See also* MAJESTAS.)

Magdalene, Mary, Saint, was one of the most devoted followers of Christ. She was possibly, but improbably, the sister of *Martha and *Lazarus, since they were established in Bethany. 'Magdala' or 'Magadan', or Migdal, is one of the towns near Tiberias on the Sea of Galilee (and now called Teverya), and her name indicates that she came from there. In Luke 7: 36–50, Christ had gone to eat in the house of a Pharisee, 'And a woman in the city, who was a sinner, having learned that he was eating in the Pharisee's house, brought an alabaster box of ointment. She stood behind him at His feet, weeping, and began to bathe his feet with her tears, and to dry them with her hair. Then she continued kissing his feet and anointing them with the ointment. Now when the Pharisee who had invited him saw it, he said to himself, "If this man were a prophet, he would have known who and what kind of woman this is who is touching him—that she is a sinner."' But Jesus read his thoughts and told the parable of the two debtors, and when the Pharisee is compelled by logic to agree that it must be the greater debtor who loved the most, Christ administers the magisterial rebuke, '"Simon, do you see this woman? I entered your house; you gave me no water for my feet, but she has bathed my feet with her tears, and dried them with her hair. You gave me no kiss, but from the time I came in she has not stopped kissing my feet. You did not anoint my head with oil, but she has anointed my feet with ointment."' Finally he turns to the woman and says to her '"Your sins are forgiven. Your faith has saved you; go in peace."' Traditionally the woman is Mary Magdalene, but her name is not given. But in the next chapter, Luke 8: 2, comes the verse, 'As well as certain women, who had been cured of evil spirits and infirmities: Mary called Magdalene, from whom seven devils had gone out', has rightly or wrongly been associated with the 'woman who was a sinner'.

In the accounts of the Crucifixion, in Matt. 27: 56, Mary Magdalene is named among the women who followed Jesus from Galilee, and who were witnesses of the Crucifixion 'looking on from a distance' and after the Entombment 'Mary Magdalene and the other Mary [presumably Mary the mother of James and John, mentioned in the previous verse] were there sitting opposite the tomb.' The final moment comes in Matt. 28: 1–10: 'After the sabbath, as the first day of the week was dawning, Mary Magdalene and the other Mary went to see the tomb' and there follows the earthquake, the angel that rolls back the stone and speaks to the women, 'Do not be afraid; I know that you are looking for Jesus who was crucified. He is not here; for he has been raised, as he said. Come, see the place where he lay. Then go quickly and tell his disciples, "He has been raised from the dead."' In Mark 15: 40–1 the account is similar, but in v. 47 'Mary Magdalene and Mary the mother of Joses saw where the body was laid.' S. Mark's account carries S. Matthew's further, for in ch. 16 he names the other Mary as Mary the mother of James and Salome, who had brought spices, so that they might anoint him. There follows their finding the stone rolled back from the tomb; as they entered the tomb, they saw a young man in a white robe, who confirmed that Christ had risen and bade them '"tell His disciples and Peter that he goes before you into Galilee . . ." and they fled from the place, for terror and amazement had seized them, and they said nothing to anyone, for they were afraid.' They undoubtedly believed that they had seen ghosts, or 'devils'. In Luke 23: 55, 'women also, which came with him from Galilee, followed after, and beheld the sepulchre' and they prepared spices and ointments for the next day. The most precise account is in John 19: 25: 'Now there stood by the cross of Jesus his mother, and his mother's sister, Mary the wife of Cleophas, and Mary Magdalene'. In John 20: 1–2: 'Early on the first day of the week, when it was still dark, Mary Magdalene came to the tomb and saw that the stone had been removed from the tomb. So she ran and went to Simon Peter and the other disciple, the one whom Jesus loved, and said to them, "They have taken the Lord out of the tomb, and we do not know where they have laid him."' And later, when the others discovered that she spoke truly, and they then had gone home, Mary Magdalene lingered, and the most touching moment comes in vv. 11–18: 'But Mary stood weeping outside the tomb. As she wept, she bent over to look into the tomb; and she saw two angels in white, where the body of Jesus had been lying, one at the head and the other at the feet. They said to her "Woman, why are you weeping?" She said to them, "They have taken away my Lord, and I do not know where they have laid him." When she had said this, she turned around and saw Jesus standing there, but she did not know that it was Jesus. Jesus said to her, "Woman, why are you weeping? Whom are you looking for?" Supposing him to be the gardener, she said to him, "Sir, if you have carried him away, tell me where you have laid him, and I will take him away." Jesus said to her, "Mary!" She turned and said to him in Hebrew, "Rabbouni!" (which means Teacher). Jesus said to her, "Do not hold on to me, because I have not yet ascended to the Father. But go to my brothers and say to them, 'I am ascending to my Father and your Father, to my God and your God.'" Mary Magdalene went and announced to the disciples, "I have seen the Lord"; and she told them that he had said these things to her.' (S. Mark says that they would not believe her.) These are the last times that she is mentioned in the Gospels.

The conflation of the three women into one, and that one Mary Magdalene, is rejected by the Orthodox Church, which believes the three women to be distinct persons. In the West, Gregory the Great (540–604) declared them to be one woman, Mary Magdalene, and this was accepted until the 12th century, when it was refuted by Bernard of Clairvaux, and other Cistercians. Since then the position has been unclear, no ruling on it having been made by Church Fathers and other authorities, though more recently there has been a move to treat them as three persons. In logic, there seems very little reason to merge Mary of Bethany, Martha's sister, with Mary of Magdala, whom both Matthew and Luke place among 'the women who followed him from Galilee', and with the unnamed woman who bathed Jesus's feet at the banquet, unless one also concedes that 'she was a sinner', which is not totally improbable, without, however, being necessarily identical with Mary Magdalene.

During the Middle Ages many legends sprang up about the later life of the Magdalene, all without any foundation. One current in the East by the 8th century claimed that Lazarus and his sisters were put in a rudderless boat and sent to sea, landing miraculously in Cyprus, where Lazarus became a bishop. About 890/900 his relics were translated to Constantinople. Centuries later, an elaborated version of the legend recounts that *c.*40, the three Maries, Mary the wife of Cleophas, Mary the wife of Zebedee and mother of James and John, and Mary Magdalene, with their maidservant Sarah, together with Lazarus, Martha, Maximinus, and Sidonius, being persecuted in Jerusalem, fled in a boat which grounded on the shores of Provence at what is now Les Saintes-Maries-de-la-Mer. Mary Cleophas and Mary the wife of Zebedee, and Sarah, who was an Ethiopian, were buried there, and their bodies were enshrined by King René of Provence in 1448 in the fortress-church. Mary Magdalene is said to have retired to a hermitage in a grotto at Ste-Baume, at St-Maximin (near Aix-en-Provence) where the monastery established by S. Cassian was rediscovered at the end of the 13th century, when it became a pilgrimage site. The Magdalene is said to have died at St-Maximin, and Charles of Anjou, later King of Naples, claimed to have found her relics in 1279, creating a pilgrimage. The relics of Mary Magdalene were also said to have been transferred to Vézelay in the mid-11th century, generating an extremely popular pilgrimage, particularly since Vézelay was a staging post on the Pilgrimage Road to Santiago de Compostela. Sarah is considered by gypsies to be their ancestress and patroness, so that there is a twice-yearly gypsy pilgrimage to Les Saintes-Maries-de-la-Mer. The tradition of the Magdalene's death in France was certainly confused at a very early date with that of the death of *S. Mary of Egypt (see below).

The Magdalene has been the subject of innumerable works of art. If the tradition is accepted that the 'woman who was a sinner' and the Mary Magdalene from whom Christ cast out seven devils is the same person, then she may well be the woman weeping at Christ's feet in Giovanni da Milano's fresco cycle (*c.*1365: Florence, Sta Croce). The subject was popular in the 16th and 17th centuries, as in Veronese's *Feast in the House of Simon* (Louvre: before 1573). She is one of the figures near the cross at the Crucifixion: sometimes kneeling at the foot of the cross, as in Giotto's *Crucifixion* in the Arena Chapel, Padua, of *c.*1305, or clinging to the foot of the cross, as in the Simone Martini *Crucifixion* (*c.*1340: Antwerp), or kneeling grief-stricken as in Grünewald's Isenheim Altar (*c.*1515/16: Colmar); and always at the Deposition, either supporting the Virgin or bewailing the dead Christ as in Fra Angelico's *Deposition* (1436–40: Florence, San Marco), where she kisses the feet of the dead Christ. Almost always she is distinguished by her often splendid clothes, particularly in Venetian and Netherlandish painting, for instance, in Joos van Cleve's *Deposition* (*c.*1518: Edinburgh), and even in many of the Lamentation groups which became such a feature of French churches in the 16th century (*see* EASTER SEPULCHRE). This was because of the common acceptance that if she were the 'woman who was a sinner', then rich clothes were normal among such women. The last scene which has biblical authority is that in the Garden, when she mistook the risen Christ for the gardener as in the *Noli me tangere* by Titian (London, NG), and one of the most evocative renderings is that by Rembrandt (1638: Royal Coll.).

Another iconography, without biblical sanction, depends upon the later legends. These include the popular subject of the *Penitent Magdalene*, varying from the erotic semi-nude, scarcely covered by her long (usually blonde or auburn) hair, popular in Italian 16th- and 17th-century paintings such as the Titian (*c.*1533: Pitti) or the Veronese of fifty years later (1583: Prado), spanning the years of the Council of *Trent. Another treatment of this theme is found as early as *c.*1280, based on the **Golden Legend*, by the anonymous Florentine painter known as the Magdalene Master (Florence, Accademia). This consists of a large central image of the saint, with four scenes from her legend on either side, partly biblical and partly from the *Golden Legend* and other late sources. This story tells how she retired to a mountain and lived in solitude for thirty years without food, but borne up by angels seven times a day at the canonical hours. At this point the story is crossed with that of S. Mary of Egypt, a penitent prostitute who went to Jerusalem and was unable to enter the Church of the Holy Cross until she repented and vowed to renounce the world. She retired to the desert and there her clothes fell to pieces, but her hair grew so thickly that she was covered by it. After forty-seven years she received communion from a monk in the desert and died. In the Magdalene Altarpiece the saint is shown covered with hair, and this became a constant feature of representations of her. The scenes at the sides are thus composed of three biblical incidents and five made up from the two legends—the Feast in the

House of the Pharisee, the Raising of Lazarus, and the Risen Christ in the Garden, followed by the Magdalene preaching in Marseilles, Borne up in the Desert by Angels, Fed by an Angel, her Last Communion, and her Funeral. The scene of her being borne aloft is often wrongly called her Assumption. Perhaps the most powerful image of her as a gaunt and haggard creature, moving in her very ugliness, is the wooden statue by Donatello (Florence, Baptistery) which is echoed in a painting by Pollaiuolo (Colle Val d'Elsa, formerly Staggia, near Siena).

Magi, the (Gk. *Magos*, from Old Persian *Magus*) In Matt. 2: 1–23, the story of the Magi opens with their arrival in Jerusalem from the east in the days of Herod the Great. They are described simply as 'wise men', and as a result of their question, 'Where is the child who has been born King of the Jews? For we observed his star at its rising and have come to pay him homage', Herod had the books of prophecies examined, and it was discovered in Mic. 5: 2 that the Christ, the Messiah, would be born in Bethlehem. He sent the wise men there, saying that they should return when they had found Him so that he might also come to worship the Child. '... ahead of them went the star they had seen at its rising, until it stopped over the place where the child was. When they saw that the star had stopped they were overwhelmed with joy. On entering the house, they saw the child with Mary his mother, and they knelt down, and paid him homage. Then opening their treasure chests, they offered him gifts of gold, and frankincense and myrrh. And having been warned in a dream not return to Herod, they left for their own country by another road.' An angel appeared to Joseph in a dream and warned him to fly with the Child and His mother into Egypt. When Herod realized that the wise men had tricked him by not returning, he had all the children in Bethlehem up to 2 years old massacred. Only Matthew tells this story, and his only description of the seekers is as 'wise men', and in the Greek Testament they are called 'sages'. They were probably members of the Mazdean, a Zoroastrian priestly caste of Persians. No number is mentioned, and the tradition that there were three is merely inferred from the three gifts, nor are they given names. It was not until about 200 that Tertullian, a Carthaginian who was converted in Rome in 195/6 and returned to Africa to become eventually one of the African Fathers of the Church, called them Kings, and this became common only from the 6th century. The first to say that there were three and to name them as Caspar (or Gaspar), Melchior, and Balthasar was Origen (d. 254), and these names also became current from the 6th century. While the shepherds were the first Jews to venerate Christ, arriving immediately after His birth, the first Gentiles to recognize and worship Christ were the Magi, hence the Feast of the *Epiphany, held on 6 January, marks the beginning of the mission to the Gentiles. The Magi came to be venerated as saints, and 'relics' were said to have come from Constantinople to Milan, whence they were taken to Germany by the Emperor Frederick I Barbarossa in 1162, and are now in Cologne Cathedral, in one of the grandest reliquaries made by *Nicholas of Verdun.

The prophecies which underlie Matthew's story are in Num. 24: 17, 'A Star shall come out of Jacob, and a Sceptre shall rise out of Israel'; in Ps. 72 (Vg. 71): 10–11, 'May the kings of Tarshish and of the isles render him tribute, may the kings of Sheba and Seba bring gifts. May all kings fall down before him: all nations give him service'; Isa. 60: 3 and 6, 'Nations shall come to your light, and kings to the brightness of your dawn' and 'all those from Sheba shall come: they shall bring gold and frankincense'.

The earliest representations of the *Adoration of the Magi* are in the Roman catacombs: that of Priscilla, 2nd century; of Petrus and Marcellinus in the 3rd; of Domitilla in the 4th. The Magi following the star and worshipping the Christ Child in the cradle combines the Nativity and the Adoration in a 4th-century Lateran sarcophagus, and this combination also appears in the 12th-century mosaics of the Cappella Palatina in Palermo. The Virgin enthroned with the Child and with the three Magi wearing Phrygian caps and short tunics, as a sign of their eastern origin, as in the fresco in the Catacomb of Priscilla, also appears in the mosaics in Sta Maria Maggiore, Rome, of *c.*435 (with only two Magi) and in Sant'Apollinare Nuovo in Ravenna, of *c.*550, and here the names appear for the first time in art (though they are probably later insertions). Basically, the theme of three Magi approaching the Virgin and Child is based on the classical image of barbarians offering homage to Roman Victory. In the Ravenna *Adoration* none is shown as a king: Balthasar is middle-aged, with a black beard, Gaspar is white-bearded, Melchior is young and beardless, and all are white. By the 9th century the tradition arose that they represented the three races: Melchior was an African, and therefore black, Balthasar was an Asian, and Gaspar European, and there was also a tradition that they represented the three ages of man, but in art a good deal of confusion occurs. They do not change from Magi to Kings before the 10th century (in e.g. the Benedictional of S. Aethelwold: London, BL), but Johannes of Hildesheim (d. 1375) wrote a *Historia* of the relics then in Cologne, in which Melchior is made a Nubian and therefore black. A great deal of the imagery of the various incidents was not invented in the West, but taken over from Eastern MSS, and from such objects as the 6th-century *ampullae in the cathedral treasury at Monza, near Milan, and Carolingian ivories. The **Golden Legend* disseminated the story, and dramatic representations made it popular, with inevitable influence on painters, so that in pictures such as the *Adoration of the Kings* by Gentile da Fabriano (1423: Uffizi) the Magi acquire armies of retainers and are very splendidly accoutred, with elaborate crowns and gorgeous clothes.

The subject was very popular in the 17th century, with fine examples by Rubens, in which the ages and races of the Kings tend to be treated with great artistic freedom. Other versions of the story in art include the Magi following the Star, the meeting with Herod, and in a delightful 12th-century capital from St-Lazare, Autun (Mus. Rolin), the three crowned Kings lie three in a bed sleeping under the star with the warning angel hovering over them.

Magus, Simon *See* SIMON.

Majestas Domini (Lat. the Majesty of the Lord) This, the grandest, noblest of the images of Christ, stems from the visions of the OT prophets and from the Book of Revelations (Vg. Apocalypse). Isaiah, in 6: 1–3, describes the Lord sitting on a throne, surrounded by seraphim (*see* CHERUBIM); Ezekiel, in exile in Babylon, says (1: 1, 26–8, and 10: 1–19) that the heavens opened and 'I saw visions of God', and he describes the *Tetramorph and the cherubim who surround the splendour of God. Daniel had a vision during a dream (7: 9, 13–14) in which he saw an awe-inspiring figure of God, and he awoke terrified. S. John, in Rev. 4: 2–10, had a vision of God seated on a throne and surrounded by the tetramorph and the twenty-four Elders, robed and crowned on their thrones. In the last chapter of Revelations (21: 1–3) he saw the new Jerusalem, the holy city, which is another vision of the Godhead. Other prophets have had glimpses of the majesty of God—Job (37 and 38), and David and the Psalmist in many of the psalms, notably in Pss. 29, 91, 93, 104, and 145.

These visions inspired the creation of images which should express visually the words of the prophets. They began very simply; in 4th-century carved sarcophagi—for instance, in the sarcophagus of Junius Bassus (359: Rome, St Peter's)—Christ is depicted seated between Apostles with His feet resting on an image of the heavens as His footstool. From this plain, almost ordinary beginning, the images begin to assume greater grandeur in, for instance, the late 4th-century painting in the *Catacomb of SS Peter and Marcellinus, where Christ is depicted enthroned between SS Peter and Paul above an image of the Lamb standing on a mound from which issue the four rivers of Paradise, and with the tutelary saints of the crypt on either side. The enthroned Christ, seated within a globe of the universe, appears in the apse of one of the side chapels of Sta Costanza, Rome, of the early 4th century, made as a *Traditio Clavis. In the panel with the Ascension in the doors of Sta Sabina, Rome, of 432, Christ has risen to glory and stands holding a scroll, flanked by the A and Ω, within a roundel, and surrounded by the symbols of the Evangelists, above the Virgin and Apostles gazing upwards. The subject was also fully developed at Bawit, in Egypt, in the 5th-century apse of the monastery of St Apollo (now in the Coptic Mus., Old Cairo), where Christ in Majesty is surrounded by the symbols of the Evangelists, while below are the Virgin and Child enthroned flanked by the Apostles.

An image of Christ in Majesty, as a subject on its own, is at the head of the long mosaic frieze in Sant'Apollinare Nuovo, Ravenna, with the enthroned Christ raising His right hand in blessing. The group of Christ and the angels was part of the Arian decoration done (520–6) under Theodoric, before the frieze of saints was made after the church had returned to Catholic orthodoxy. The clumsy restoration of the left hand holding the sceptre replaces the presumed (and later normal) book with the inscription 'Ego sum rex gloriae' (I am the King of Glory). After this, the subject became more frequent—the apse of San Vitale, Ravenna, of 597, shows Christ in Majesty, seated on the globe of the universe, giving the crown of martyrdom to the saint on His right, and holding a closed book in His left hand. In the apse of Sant'Angelo in Formis, near Capua, the apse painting of *c.*1050 is of Christ in Majesty with the Dove of the Holy Ghost above Him, and the Tetramorph surrounding His throne. By the time some of the grand *Pantocrator images were created in Daphni, Greece (1100), and in Cefalù, Sicily (*c.*1145), the awe-inspiring image of Christ holding the open book with its double inscription in Greek and Latin, 'I am the light of the world. Who follows me will not walk in darkness but will have the light of life', the importance of the subject had begun to wane in the South, but not in the North.

In the North the subject was very important in illustrated Bibles and Gospels. One of the most impressive is in the Vivian Bible, made in Tours in 846 (Paris, BN), where Christ is seated on the globe of the universe, within a diamond-shaped frame which includes the Evangelist symbols, while in the four corners of the page they are shown preparing the Gospels, and the roundels at the four corners of the frame enclosing Christ have images of the prophets: Isaiah, Ezekiel, Jeremiah, and Daniel. The same system was used in the Golden Codex of S. Emmeram of 870 (Munich), the only difference being that Christ is enclosed in a *mandorla, which now becomes the norm. The apse of the Cluniac priory at Berzé-la-Ville (1100–40) near Cluny is one of the few surviving painted examples in the North and here Christ is flanked by SS Peter and Paul, the titular saints of the Monastery of Cluny, of which the priory was a summer residence. The tympanum of the great portal at Moissac (1120) of Christ in Majesty, with the Evangelist symbols and angels and the twenty-four Elders, is a combination of the Majestas Domini with the Christ of the Last Judgement. With the tympanum carvings of the Prior's Door of Ely Cathedral (1140), and the portals at St-Trophime, Arles (mid-12th cent.), and the Portail Royal at Chartres (1145–51), Sta Maria del Camino, Carrión de los Condes in N. Spain (1165), and the Pórtico de la Gloria, Santiago de Compostela, and in painted examples in, for instance, the Panteón de los Reyes in León and the apse of San Clemente de Tahúll, now in Barcelona (Mus. de Arte de Cataluña), all late 12th century, the scheme reaches its zenith.

In the mid-12th century came the development of the Virgin Portal, and the change to portals portraying the Last Judgement, with Christ as Judge, showing his wounds, often with the Virgin and S. John the Baptist in their traditional roles as mediators, and including all the picturesque details of the saved and the damned. In the 15th century the theme was revived in painting in the North in, for instance, the *Ghent Altar, and in the Memlinc *Christ as King and Priest* (1490: Antwerp), and then virtually vanished, until it was revived spectacularly in the giant tapestry designed by Graham Sutherland for Coventry Cathedral in 1962. Another example of the theme can be see in a window by Edward Nuttgens (1952) in St Etheldreda, Ely Place, London. Another 20th-century *Majestas*, by Jacob *Epstein (1955), an aluminum sculpture, hangs in Llandaff Cathedral, Wales. It is a rare subject in Italy after the mosaics in Roman Early Christian churches, and in the 14th century the best example is the façade mosaic of Sta Maria Maggiore, Rome, by Rusuti. Later, almost invariably Christ in Majesty appears in scenes of the Last Judgement.

Majesty, Christ in *See* MAJESTAS.

m

Malchus, who was one of the crowd that came to arrest Jesus in the Garden of Olives, was the servant—or slave—of the High Priest. Three Gospels agree that one of Jesus's followers drew a sword and cut off Malchus's ear. S. John (18: 10–11) is the most explicit: 'Then Simon Peter, who had a sword, drew it and struck the high priest's slave, and cut off his right ear. The slave's name was Malchus. Jesus said to Peter "Put your sword back into its sheath. Am I not to drink the cup that the Father has given me?"' Only S. Luke (22: 51–2) says that Christ healed Malchus's ear.

The incident is frequently represented in scenes of the capture of Christ, and in many early ones Malchus is hardly more than a boy. It is interesting to trace the course of this treatment of the incident, which must stem from Byzantine tradition, since an early Byzantine Gospel Book in the Vatican Library (Cod. Grec. 1156) has an illustration depicting exactly this. In the *Betrayal* scene in the Egbert Codex (*c.*980–90: Trier) S. Peter brandishing a sword pushes Malchus to the ground, and Christ, as Judas kisses him, extends His hand to heal the boy's ear, and in a Byzantine Evangeliary (end of the 11th cent.: Parma) S. Peter with a knife slashes at the ear of a beardless Malchus while he is actually grabbing Christ—

another Byzantine tradition, which appears in the Winchester Cotton Psalter, of *c.*1050 (London, BL), where the boy Malchus grasps Christ's wrist. In one of the side panels of a *croce dipinta by a painter called Guglielmo (1138: Sarzana Cath.), and in a 12th-century wall-painting in the Church of Nohan-Vicq, near Châteauroux, in central France, S. Peter attacks a child-sized Malchus. The late 12th-century mosaics in the western vault of St Mark's, Venice, also have S. Peter in the *Betrayal* holding a boy Malchus to the ground while cutting off his ear with a knife. The tradition was still active into the 1290s in the Upper Church of St Francis, Assisi, where in a very damaged fresco of the *Betrayal*, now attributed tentatively to Jacopo Torriti, S. Peter holds Malchus to the ground during his attack, while Christ extends a hand to heal the boy's ear. The Byzantine tradition, probably through the influence of the Egbert Codex, still survived as late as the Passion Altar at Hofgeismar, near Kassel, of *c.*1320, where S. Peter sheathes his sword, and a boy Malchus points to his ear, which Christ extends His hand to heal. But by the 13th century generally the old tradition was either forgotten or disregarded, because in the rood-screen at Naumberg of 1220 a stone relief shows S. Peter with a huge sword slicing off the ear of a fully grown and violently resisting Malchus. The Giovanni Pisano pulpit relief of the *Betrayal* (1302–10: Pisa Cath.) has a fully grown Malchus, and the incident with a man, not a boy, also appears in the 12th-century portal friezes in St-Gilles-du-Gard and Chartres. In the fresco of the *Betrayal* by Giotto (*c.*1306: Arena Chapel, Padua), as in all three of the Dürer Passion series (all between 1498 and 1512), Malchus is a fully grown man. The reason for the change in iconography is unknown, but could stem from depictions of the scene in Passion plays.

Malevich, Kasimir *See* EUROPE and RUSSIAN ART AND ARCHITECTURE.

Malta, Knights of, also called **Knights Hospitallers,** or **of S. John of Jerusalem.** They were founded in the 11th century originally as a religious order in Jerusalem to care for pilgrims who fell sick, possibly with the merchants of Amalfi who founded a hospital between 1023 and 1048, as a Congregation of Hospitallers under the patronage of S. John the Baptist. When Jerusalem was captured in 1099 in the First Crusade the hospital was found to be in full operation, despite Turkish rule. During the period of the Christian Kingdom of Jerusalem the Order changed, and by 1125 they had become an Order of Knights building castles and hospitals on the pilgrimage routes and dedicated to the struggle against the Turks. When Jerusalem was lost in 1187, Richard Cœur de Lion, King of England, established them in Acre and they held the city and port for nearly 100 years. After Acre was lost, they settled in Cyprus in 1291, and in 1310 they took Rhodes. They built a large fleet, becoming a naval power, and held Rhodes until 1523, when after a long siege the surviving 180 knights left their citadel with the honours of war. After a short time in Crete, the Emperor Charles V in 1530 gave the Order the island of Malta. During the occupation of Rhodes the Order developed its final form. It was divided into seven (later eight) 'Langues' or Tongues. Each Langue was divided into Knights of Justice who had to be of noble birth and take vows of celibacy, poverty, and obedience; lesser ranks were Knights of Obedience, and Chaplains; and the lowest ranks were Sergeants-at-Arms and Servitors. There were also the Knights of Grace, nominated by the Grand Master and Council because of services to the Order and under this rule the painters *Caravaggio and Mattia Preti were admitted. The original uniform was a black habit with a plain white cross, which later became an eight-point cross on the left breast, known thereafter as a Maltese cross. It is based on four arrow-heads with the points meeting in the centre. Each Langue had its own convent or auberge, where its Knights lived. The Order had many convents all over Europe, graded by size as priories, commanderies, and baillies. In 1540 Henry VIII confiscated the 43 commanderies of the Order in England. In 1565 the sporadic attacks of the Turkish forces against Malta and Gozo became a grand assault by 180 ships and 30,000 men. The defenders numbered 600 to 700 knights, and about 8,000/9,000 men-at-arms. The ferocious siege of the fortified harbour lasted all through the summer until a relief force from Sicily finally arrived. Valletta, which was then built, became the capital with vast new fortifications, but the Turks, after their naval defeat at Lepanto in 1571, never again attacked Malta. The importance of the Knights lasted until the early 17th century; after this a slow, sad decline set in. The French Revolution cost the Order its properties and revenues in France, and when Napoleon in 1798 took Malta, because the Knights were unwilling to defend it, he gave them three days to leave, taking only their relics and personal possessions with them. The Order eventually settled in Rome in 1874 and still functions largely in charitable works from the Priorato di Malta on the Aventine, where a fine church had been built for it by Piranesi in 1764–6.

The Priory in Clerkenwell which was the Order's headquarters in England is still there, but now functions mainly as headquarters of the St John Ambulance Brigade and is quite separate from the Sovereign Order in Rome.

The finest of the Order's works of art are three by Caravaggio all painted on the artist's arrival in Malta in 1608: the portrait of the Grand Master, Alof de Vignacourt (now in the Louvre), a *S. Jerome in meditation* (Valletta, St John's Cathedral), and his masterpiece, the *Decollation of the Baptist* (Oratory of St John), his only signed picture. St John's was covered in paintings by Mattia Preti in 1662–7. The fortifications are the grandest survivals of this major branch of architecture.

Mamre, the Oaks of (Heb. strength), in the OT was one of the dwelling-places of Abram (as he then was) after he had separated from his nephew Lot because of quarrels between their herdsmen over grazing (Gen. 13: 1–13). Gen. 13: 18 says 'So Abram moved his tent and came and settled by the oaks of Mamre, which are at Hebron, and there he built an altar to the Lord.' At Mamre (Gen. 14: 18–19) Melchisekek, King of Salem and priest of God Most High, brought bread and wine to Abram, and blessed him. Gen. 18 tells how, at the oaks of Mamre, three angels appeared to Abraham (as God had now renamed him) and he made a feast for them. One of them—who was God—prophesied that when they next passed that way Sarah would have a son. She was listening at the entrance to the tent, and laughed to herself, saying how was this possible for one as old as she was? God heard her laughing and asked 'Is anything too wonderful for the Lord?... I shall return to you in due season, and Sarah shall have a son.' It was then, as the Lord and the angels were on their way, that God disclosed to Abraham His intention to destroy Sodom and Gomorrah, and Abraham pleaded with God for the cities and He relented so far as to promise that if ten righteous men could be found, He would spare the cities. The two angels went to Sodom, but in the event no good men could be found, and after warning Lot to leave with all his family, the cities were destroyed (*see* LOT).

Later, Abraham moved to Beersheba in the Negeb, and there Sarah bore a son whom Abraham called Isaac, and later he must have returned to Hebron, because when Sarah died (Gen. 23) Abraham went to the Hittites, in whose land Hebron lay, and asked to be allowed to buy the cave of Machpelah, to the east of Mamre, as a burial place for Sarah and for his family, and in due course he, Isaac with Rebekah his wife, and Jacob and his wife Leah, were buried there.

In the *catacomb of the Via Latina, is a 4th-century scene of Abraham and the three angels. The rare scene of the meeting of Abraham and Melchisedek appears in a mosaic of *c.*430 in the nave of Sta Maria Maggiore, Rome, and Melchisedek appears with Abel in one of the presbytery mosaics in San Vitale, Ravenna, sacrificing to God as prototypes of the Eucharist. *Abraham feasting the angels* under the oak at Mamre is in the facing mosaic in San Vitale, with Sarah standing listening in the door of the tent. The scene of Melchisedek offering the sacrifice appears in the 12th-century mosaics in the Abraham cupola in the atrium of St Mark's, Venice, and also in the altarpiece by Nicholas of Verdun at Klosterneuberg (1181: outside Vienna), and in the altarpiece of the *Mystic Meals* by Dieric Bouts (1464–8: St Pieter, Leuven) Melchisedek offers the chalice of wine to Abraham in one of the four symbolic prototypes of the Eucharist surrounding the scene of the *Last Supper*. A fresco of the *Angels visiting Abraham* in the Upper Church of St Francis, Assisi, is attributed to Jacopo Torriti or to the circle of Cimabue, of the early 1290s, and *Abraham prostrating himself before the Angels, and feasting them under the tree* is one of the mid-12th-century nave mosaics in the Cappella Palatina, Palermo. The 12th-century mosaics in the Abraham cupola, in the atrium of St Mark's, Venice, contain all the main incidents of Abraham's life, including *Abraham feasting the Three Angels*, which is also the subject of an icon (14th cent.: Athens, Benaki Mus.), and the scene of Abraham and the three angels is included in one of the panels of Ghiberti's second pair of doors for the Florence Baptistery (1425–52), the so-called Gates of Paradise. One of the finest treatments of the story is in the frescoes painted by Tiepolo for the Archbishop's palace in Udine, N. Italy (1725–8), where the aged Sarah kneeling at the tent door is rebuked for her incredulity by a resplendent angel, while in another scene Abraham abases himself before his heavenly visitors.

Man, the Fall of

> Of Man's First Disobedience, and the Fruit
> Of that Forbidden Tree, whose mortald Taste
> Brought Death into the World, and all our woe,
> With loss of Eden, till one greater Man
> Restore us, and regain the blissful Seat,
> Sing, Heav'nly Muse, . . .

The opening words of Milton's epic poem of *Paradise Lost* are a fitting introduction of the story of Man's first disobedience, his fall from Grace, and its consequences. Gen. 3: 1–24 tells the tragic story very simply, and it is with the treatment of the account by artists that this article is concerned.

In Gen. 3: 1, the serpent, which God had made with the other animals in Gen. 1: 24–5, asked Eve, whom God had created in Gen. 2: 18–24, from which of the trees in the garden of Eden she might eat the fruit. In all innocence, she replied that she might eat the fruit of any tree, but not that of the tree in the middle of the garden on pain of death. The serpent then suggested that God had deceived her, by concealing the benefits which would come from eating the fruit of that tree. Eve was tempted into eating the forbidden fruit, and gave some to Adam. 'Then the eyes of both were opened, and they knew that they were naked; and they sewed fig-leaves together and made loincloths for themselves.' That evening, when God was walking in the garden, they hid themselves. He called them, and when Adam told Him why they had hidden themselves, He accused them of having eaten the forbidden fruit; Eve immediately blamed the serpent for having tricked her into it, for which God cursed the serpent, and then told them that their punishment for disobedience would be pain in childbirth for her, and hard labour for him. 'Therefore the Lord God sent him forth from the garden of Eden to till the ground from which he was taken . . . and placed the cherubim, and a sword flaming and turning to guard the way to the tree of life.'

The first representations of Adam and Eve are in the *catacombs, sixteen in all, of which those in the 3rd-century Catacombs of SS Pietro e Marcellino, and Priscilla, are typical: the pair stand beneath the tree trying to conceal their nakedness by holding fig-leaves to themselves. It is a staple scene in illustrated books of the Bible, often in narrative sequences such as that in the 6th-century *Vienna Genesis and in the 9th-century Bible in San Paolo fuori in Rome. The 12th-century mosaics in Monreale, Sicily, include a long sequence from the Creation, including simple, but lively narratives of the Fall and Expulsion from Paradise, and the Creation cupola of the atrium of St Mark's, Venice, with an elaborate 12th-century mosaic decoration competing with that of Monreale, also has very vivid scenes of the Fall and Expulsion; both have telling images of Eve's sorrow and Adam digging.

In the *Très Riches Heures* (*c.*1411–16: Chantilly) painted for Jean, Duke of Berri by the Limbourg Brothers, who created in this masterwork the most sumptuous manuscript ever made, there is an illustration of the Garden of Eden where Eve is tempted by a serpent with a woman's head and body who offers her the fatal fruit. This is one of the earliest images of the serpent with a human head and body.

The Brancacci Chapel in the Carmine church, Florence, painted between 1425 and 1428, has a fresco by Masolino of the *Fall of Man*, also with a serpent with a woman's head, and on the opposite wall is Masaccio's powerful rendering of *The Expulsion*, in which Eve's cry of lamentation is so vivid as almost to be audible. Ghiberti's second pair of doors (1425–52) for the Baptistery, Florence, has a panel of the Creation, which includes, in the background, the Fall, where again the serpent has a woman's head. In striking contrast, the Expulsion on the right of the panel with a sorrowing Eve provides the greatest contrast to her resplendent figure surging from Adam's side in the centre of the panel. Jacopo della Quercia's carved panels for the door of San Petronio, Bologna, executed between 1425 and his death in 1438, form a strong stylistic contrast, in their low relief and their more rugged technique, with the highly worked images of Ghiberti; by now, the human-headed serpent seems to be the standard rendering. Hugo van der Goes in the Netherlands strikes a new note, in his *Fall of Man*, by painting the serpent as a giant lizard-like creature with a human head. Eve has obviously just eaten part of the apple and she reaches up to take another from the tree for Adam, who stands expectantly before her, while the seductress lizard gazes at her victims. The picture, of *c.*1481, is the left side of a diptych, the other half being a *Deposition* (both Vienna, KHM) with the body of Christ outstretched before the distraught

Holy Women—the first sin, and the price paid for its redemption. Hieronymous *Bosch uses the story of the Creation, the Fall, and the Expulsion, as pointers to the deadly significance of his main themes. In three of his major works, *The Haywain* (Prado), *The Last Judgement* (Vienna, Akad.), and *The Garden of Earthly Delights* (Prado), all painted in the middle period of his career, 1480–1510, the left wings of the triptychs contain scenes of the creation of Adam and Eve, the Fall, with the serpent leaning from the tree, with a human head and arms, and in the wing of the *Haywain* offering Eve the apple, followed by the Expulsion. In the wing of the *Garden of Earthly Delights* the expression of astonishment and awakening desire in Adam's face as God presents Eve to him presages the events to come.

The Sistine Ceiling frescoes by Michelangelo, painted between 1508 and 1512, start with God creating the world and continue with the *Creation of Man*, and of *Eve*, and have one of the most powerful images of the *Fall and the Expulsion*. In the *Fall*, the serpent has a long sinuous tail wound round the tree, but its entire body and head is that of a young woman; Adam leans forward, a big-bodied, muscular man, who reaches into the tree to find a fruit for himself, Eve is curious and takes the apple from the persuasive serpent. Both are equally guilty. In Raphael's first work in the Vatican, the Stanza della Segnatura (1508), the ceiling contains eight small paintings, including a *Fall of Man*, which may have been painted by his assistant, Sodoma. It also has the now traditional human-headed serpent, but here Adam and Eve seem both to be genuine innocents. This *Fall of Man* must have been painted well before Michelanglo reached the subject. But the long gallery of the Loggie in the Vatican is decorated with a series of small panels, frequently called 'Raphael's Bible', painted by members of Raphael's workshop between 1515 and 1519, depicting events in the Book of Genesis, including the Fall and the Expulsion. These panels had little to do with Raphael and depend heavily on Michelangelo's Sistine Ceiling, but are totally conventional in their imagery.

The major exception to this rendering of the Fall is in Rembrandt's etching of 1638, where Eve is an unkempt, dumpy young woman, and Adam an unglamorous man with a worried expression who raises an admonitory finger and tries to interpose his hand between Eve's mouth and the apple. Far from the Devil being a beguiling young woman, a large lizard-cum-dragon winds itself with a menacing claw round the tree and, overshadowed by a huge bat's wing, its gargoyle-like head holding in its mouth another apple still on the bough, glares down at the all-too-willing victim. Adam's exculpatory 'The woman tempted me' is a foregone conclusion. *See also* ADAM AND EVE, EDEN.

Mander, Noel Percy (1912–2005) An English organ builder born in Crouch, Kent to journalist Percy Mander and his wife Constance Emmie Mander, formerly Pike. With the onset of the First World War, the family moved to to Brockley in South London, where Mander was introduced to the stimulus of music (he sang in the choir at St Peter's Church) and to organ-playing. His mother received lessons from Frederick Bridge, organist at Westminster Abbey. In 1925 the family moved to East Sheen and Mander attended Haberdasher's Aske's school in Hatcham, but found the classroom constricting and left as soon as he could.

His first employment was with the publishing firm A & C Black, where he delighted in the books; but office life was not to his taste and he quickly looked elsewhere and found his life's devotion—organs, especially organs in Anglican churches. After a period working with a self-employed organ restorer (Ivor R. Davies), Mander set up his own business in 1936 by renting a nave at Christ Church, Jamaica Street, Stepney, from where he carried out repair work, notably at St Peter's, Bethnal Green and, because of closure or upgrading, also oversaw the relocation of several organs for use elsewhere. But the first bombing raids of the Second World War on London destroyed the church and his workshop, and in October 1940 he joined the Royal Artillery—to see duty across North Africa (during which he repaired an organ in Algiers), and on into southern Italy. An injury and some later illness took him out of active service, but during recuperation at Naples he wrote to every clergyman in the London diocese to solicit work on his return to England. It was an initiative that was to be richly rewarded in both employment opportunities and professional standing.

When Mander returned to London (having been regularly consulted throughout his absence by officials of the diocese about the worth of organs in many war-damaged churches), he was appointed official organ-builder to the Reorganization Committee with authority to requisition closed churches as stores to house organs from churches across the diocese, the organs themselves awaiting repair, reconditioning and, it was hoped, later use in fresh venues. This commitment provided Mander with an unrivalled knowledge of needs and opportunities, and from a works that he established in 1946 in the former St Peter's School at Bethnal Green, he was soon ruffling feathers at several firms of considerable standing. In part, this can be attributed to establishing new methods of working for his staff—by, for instance, providing tuners with vans that enabled them to move from job to job much more easily and efficiently than if restricted to public transport; but there was also a certain resentment that Mander was unwilling to adhere to the 'rules of the trade'. A good example of this arose in connection with a historic 17th-century organ at Adlington Hall in Cheshire. Defunct for a century and more, it had been inspected and judged as beyond repair, but for Mander, influenced in part by knowing that a maternal ancestor, George Pyke England (1765?–1815) was an organ builder, the task was a challenge not to be ducked. Although many of the pipes were crushed and soundboards split, Mander was able to restore them (1958–59), and an instrument, for its size, rated as the earliest unaltered organ in Britain and one on which Handel played, was rescued for later generations.

This success was accompanied by restorations of other historic instruments—at St Mary, Rotherhithe; at St John's, Upper Norwood; at St Mary, Finedon; and at St Philip, Salford; and by major reconstructions, as well as the creation of entirely new instruments. Especially notable was the work done at: St Pancras, Euston Road; St Michael, Croydon; St Lawrence Jewry; St Vedast, Foster Lane; Peterhouse, Cambridge; Livery Hall of Worshipful Company of Merchant Taylors; St Giles, Cripplegate; Corpus Christi, Cambridge; Jesus College, Cambridge; Sheffield Cathedral; St Paul's School; Canterbury Cathedral; Usher Hall, Belfast; and an instrument for a bombed Wren church, St Mary Aldermanbury, which was transported stone by stone from London to Westminster College, Fulton, Missouri, to form part of a memorial (1969) to Winston Churchill, his 'Iron Curtain' speech having been delivered there in 1946.

But if a single instrument had to be chosen to demonstrate the pinnacle of Mander's career, it has to be that at St Paul's Cathedral. He was approached in 1970 to rebuild and provide a new case for an 1881 organ known as the 'Willis-on-wheels' and his success ensured he was a natural candidate to modernize Willis' 1872 chancel organ. The instrument, originally of 52 stops, had grown over the years to a 'ninety-sixer', and owing to somewhat piecemeal repairs and additions had lost its musical integrity. Much debate ensued, but Mander was able to begin work in 1972. The work was immensely complicated and the finished instrument sported 107 stops, grouped in a Chancel Section (Great, North Choir, Pedal, Swell, South Choir, and Solo organs), a Dome Section (Fifth Manual, and a Pedal organ) and, on Mander's initiative, an entirely new West Section incorporating a diapason chorus (to lead congregational singing) and three reed trumpets for ceremonial use. Work was completed in time for the Queen's Jubilee *Service of Thanksgiving* on 7 June 1977, Mander himself being recognized later by the award of an MBE.

Within a few years of this triumph, Mander judged his professional contribution was complete and in 1983 he passed the firm to his eldest son, John Pike Mander, and retired with his wife Enid (whom he had married at St Peter's, Bethnal Green in June 1948 and with whom he was to have five children), to Earl Soham, near Woodbridge in Suffolk. There, as well as maintaining friendships at Westminster, Fulton, from whom he was to receive an Honorary Doctorate, and pursuing much neglected reading (except about organs), he became sensitive to the needs of the rural community and relished the opportunity to help elderly villagers with the mundane tasks of life—carrying coal buckets, helping with shopping and such like, much in the spirit of his wife who, as well as being the resident nurse at the family firm, had extended her firm gaiety and compassion to children in Bethnal Green by taking them on educational trips across the city.

In a volume of essays published to mark his achievements, *Fanfare for an Organ-builder* (1996), Mander's principal contributions are given as his initiative in saving and restoring many historic British organs, his insistence on high-quality materials and workmanship, and his promotion (where possible) of a tracker action—that is, a mechanical, rather than electronic or pneumatic, linkage between organ key and organ pipe. But his interests were wider than that summary suggests: active in the Council of Christians and Jews (in several churches he worked happily alongside the muralist, Hans *Feibush (1898–1998)); sometime Master of the Worshipful Company of Parish Clerks (1970); fellow of the Society of Antiquaries (1974); and a loyal supporter of many causes in the East End of London. He remained active into his nineties and on his death in 2005 was accorded a full set of obituary notices in the national press, as well as a fulsome notice in *The New York Times,* which was the first to be published.

mandorla (Ital. almond) is an oval, shaped like an almond, and used to enclose a figure in glory. Among examples are its frequent use in the *Majestas Domini, for Christ in the *Ascension or the Last *Judgement, and in many instances of *portal sculpture. It is also a means by which an artist may give particular emphasis to one of the figures in his composition, as for instance Orcagna to the Virgin in the *Assumption in his carved altarpiece in Orsanmichele (1359: Florence). On the north side of Florence Cathedral is a door known as the Porta della Mandorla, after the almond-shaped mandorla framing the *Virgin in Glory,* above the prophets; this is a joint work by Antonio di Banco and his son Nanni, and Donatello. A mandorla of an unusual type is that by Mantegna in an *Ascension* (1463/4: Uffizi, Florence), where the mandorla surrounding Christ is entirely composed of winged *putti. In some images of the Virgin the Holy Child is shown in a *clipeus which may be shaped like a mandorla (*see* MADONNA TYPES, under Virgin Platytera). A mandorla is never used to enclose a living person, but is reserved to souls in glory.

Mandylion (Mandeylion, Sudarion) A cloth said to have been imprinted with the features of Christ, and sent to King *Abgar the Black of Edessa (now Urfa, N. Syria). According to an Armenian tradition, it was miraculously imprinted with the image; according to a Syrian tradition, it was a painting made by Abgar's emissary, Hannan. The image was said to have been accompanied by a letter from Christ, the text of which became a charm throughout Christendom during the Middle Ages. No credence is now attached to any of these stories, but there certainly was a picture, or icon, in Edessa in 544, and its removal to Constantinople in 944 was commemorated by a special feast-day. It was placed in a special chapel in the palace, and copies of it were legion, since one was thought essential in every church. In Byzantium, the name Mandylion was preferred to the earlier Sudarion. The image shows Christ full face, with long hair and beard, and heavy eyebrows, not at all like a Roman god, but very close to what later becomes the *Pantocrator image.

During the occupation of the city after the sack of 1204, it is thought to have been stolen in 1207 by French Crusaders. It was either lost at sea, or was in the Ste-Chapelle in Paris, and was destroyed during the French Revolution. A number of the copies have survived: the one in San Silvestro in Capite, Rome, is considered to be either the original or an early copy. There are also copies in the Vatican; in San Bartolomeo, Genoa; in the Armenian church on the Isola di San Lazzaro, Venice; and in Cyprus. In the monastery of St Catherine, Sinai, is an icon of *c.*945 of Abgar holding the Mandylion, accompanied by five saints. Unsuccessful attempts have been made to conflate the Mandylion with the Holy *shroud in Turin. *See also* ACHEIROPOIETOS, and CHRIST, PORTRAITS OF.

Manessier, Alfred (1911–93) A painter, engraver, and designer of stained-glass windows, tapestries, and liturgical vestments. A member of the School of Paris, in 1943 his conversion at the Trappist monastery at Soligny was the beginning of his essentially spiritual journey. His non-figurative art, with its lively colours, was witness, however, to his attachment to Christian symbolism, gaining him numerous commissions, particularly religious ones, in France, Germany, and Switzerland. He was the first artist to envisage the possibility of placing abstract windows in an ancient church, at Les Brésaux (1946–9). He completed window/walls at Hem (1957), Moutier (1965–9), Albi sur Chéran (1978); and some major ensembles: Brême (14 windows 1966–71), Abbeville (29 windows in 1993, the year of his death).

manger *See* CRIB.

maniple *See* VESTMENTS.

Manna, Gathering of Manna was the 'bread' which God, in the OT, provided in the wilderness of Sin (Exod. 16: 13–28; Num. 11: 7–9) for the people of Israel after their escape from Egypt. Though the various places where the Israelites went are mentioned in Exodus their exact location is now difficult to establish. Even Mt. Sinai (or Horeb) is not fixed with absolute certainty, and the wilderness of Sin may be either near the present location of Mt. Sinai at the southern end of the Sinai peninsula, or in the 'Arabian' desert east of the Gulf of Aqaba. Exod. 16 recounts how the people complained against Moses for the hardships they suffered, lamenting the loss of the flesh-pots of Egypt and their 'fill of bread, for you have brought us out into this wilderness to kill this whole assembly with hunger'. God then told Moses that every day He would rain down bread from heaven, that the people should each day collect enough for that day and no more; some tried to keep it overnight, but found that it had gone bad and bred maggots. On the day before the Sabbath, they should gather two days' supply, and it would not go bad, but on the Sabbath some went out to gather, but found none. Exod. 16: 13–14 says 'in the morning . . . when the layer of dew lifted, there on the surface of the wilderness was a fine flaky substance, as fine as frost on the ground'. Num. 11: 7–9 is more explicit about manna, which looked like coriander seed, and it was ground in mills or mortars, boiled, and then made into cakes, and 'the taste of it was like the taste of cakes baked with oil'. The manna was accompanied by coveys of quails, so that the people also had meat to eat.

m

Manna was rich in symbolism, for it is the bread of life that God provides (John 6: 31–5, 48–51). The crowd that had followed Jesus after the feeding of the five thousand, 'said to Him . . . "Our ancestors had the manna in the wilderness; as it is written, 'He gave them bread from heaven'." Jesus said " . . . it was not Moses who gave you the bread from heaven, but . . . my Father who gives you the true bread from heaven. For the bread of God is that which comes down from heaven and gives life to the world." They said to him, "Sir, give us this bread always."' Later, in 48–51, Jesus says, 'Your ancestors ate the manna . . . and they are dead . . . I am the living bread that came down from heaven . . . '.

The 12th-century atrium mosaics of St Mark's, Venice, include a dome with scenes from the story of Moses, containing in the lunette over the north door the *Gathering of the Manna and the Quails*. Scenes with the *Gathering of the Manna* are frequent in conjunction with scenes of the *Institution of the Eucharist*, on tabernacles, antependia, and in chapels of the Holy Sacrament. The altarpiece of the *Mystic Meals by Bouts (1464–8: St Pieter, Leuven) is an example of the association of the two subjects. A picture of *The Israelites gathering Manna* by Ercole de' Roberti (active 1470–96: London, NG) is thought to have been one of a group in which the centre was a *Last Supper*, with Christ holding a Host, between SS Peter and John, with other Apostles, ascribed to Roberti (London: NG), and a further panel of *Melchisedek blessing Abraham*, known from a copy (whereabouts unknown), is thought to have been a third picture in the group, which may have been a **predella* or part of a piece of church furniture. The two large pictures either side of the choir of San Giorgio Maggiore, Venice, are the *Gathering of the Manna* and the *Last Supper*, both by Tintoretto (1591–4), and the huge paintings by Tiepolo of *c.*1735–40 for the church at Verolanuova, near Brescia, are of the *Gathering of the Manna* and the *Sacrifice of Melchisedek*, another prototype of the Eucharist. In some early images of the *Gathering of the Manna* it is represented quite literally, with the ground covered with small bread rolls (13th-cent. Bible, Smyrna), and in a stained-glass window in the Jacobskirche, Regensburg, of 1400, a fountain sprays the Israelites with small loaves.

Mannerism Broadly, the term defines an artistic phase between the High Renaissance and Baroque periods that is characterized by significant deviations from the principles of the classical tradition, signalling the end of the Renaissance. First developed in Italy, the style associated with Mannerism also influenced artistic developments further afield, in France, Spain, and Northern Europe. The precise dating of Mannerism has been disputed by historians, but generally it is considered to have emerged around 1520 (the year of Raphael's death) and declined at the end of the 16th century. Until the early 20th century the existence of such a recognizable intermediate period (between the Renaissance and the Baroque) was not even considered. This can be seen, for example, in the seminal work *Renaissance und Barock* (1888), by the German art historian Heinrich Wölfflin, in which (as the title implies) the author considers only a direct transition between the two major periods. This is not to say, however, that art historians of the time did not identify certain unclassical traits in the 16th century that demonstrably departed from the principles of the Renaissance, such as order, harmony, symmetry, and proportion. On the contrary, these 'traits' were generally viewed as 'perverse and decadent' (Shearman), or what Wölfflin called an 'art in decay', but these were broadly dismissed during the 19th century as falling outside the mainstream artistic developments of the time.

Mannerism was first applied in France in the mid-17th century to denote a style that was in decline and out of fashion. By the late 18th century Mannerism (or *manierismo*) was largely a derogatory term describing an art of extreme artificiality. Its origins, however, can probably be traced to the Italian *maniera,* whose meanings highlight an internal conflict, even contradiction. On the one hand, *maniera* was originally applied to the 'literature of manners', indicating certain exemplary or desired human qualities associated with 'courtly grace' (Shearman). This was more or less equated with the classical notion of 'decorum', which constituted one of the key aspects of Renaissance Humanism and underpinned the role of rhetoric in the visual arts. On the other hand, when subject to individual licence, these desirable qualities of *maniera* can lead to a certain contrivance, artifice, or even conceit. Such a tendency could be said to underlie Mannerism as both a reaction to Renaissance conventions and as an attempt to develop a new artistic sensibility. By relaxing the 'rules' of the classical tradition, artistic virtuosity takes on a new level of importance.

Early evidence of the application of *maniera* to art can be seen in Giorgio *Vasari's *Vite* (1550), where the author uses the word to describe the work of Michelangelo. While clearly intended to convey Michelangelo's extraordinary virtuosity and ingenuity, Vasari's choice of terminology may also imply the potential dangers of individual artistic licence, especially for artists like himself endowed with lesser talents.

The question of the unclassical nature of Mannerist art is closely allied to its apparent 'unnaturalness', given that the application of the principles of classicism in the Renaissance assumed an imitation of nature itself (Bialostocki). For some historians, the work of Mannerist artists and architects signalled for the first time (in the history of art) a divergence from nature (Shearman). But such a shift required a reinterpretation of the traditional relationship between *natura naturata* ('constituted nature') and *natura naturans* ('constituting nature') in the visual arts (Bialostocki). In the former, nature is treated as a complete and finite entity, while in the latter it is incomplete and in a state of becoming. We can see this relationship at work in the design and iconography of Mannerist gardens and villas, which variously invoke the concept of a 'perennial spring', where nature is presented in allegorical terms as permanently fertile and therefore abundant. Hence, rather than merely imitating nature, in the classical sense, Mannerism transforms it for its own ends.

This development, however, was not motivated by exclusively aesthetic concerns. Distorted or 'out-of-scale' treatment of elements, evidenced in painting, architecture, and sculpture, served other symbolic purposes, which relate to the Mannerist preoccupation with abundance and fertility; artists attempted to retrieve, in some way, the original (primitive) source of divine creation—in its 'embryonic' form—which had been lost or simply concealed by the fruitless search for an ideal (mathematically ordered) model of the world. This was often expressed through the agency of sophisticated mythological narratives, communicated by means of complex juxtapositions of architectural and figurative relief, painting, and landscape, much of which consciously drew upon recent archeological finds (from numismatics to sculpted reliefs). In these, the priority given to the conventions of pictorial (perspective) representation in the Renaissance, to spatially structure sacred or secular events, is replaced by a new interest in the material and colouristic qualities of surface.

At the same time, we see the restraint of Renaissance pictorial or proportioned space, where each figure or element is allotted a place within the overall hierarchy of the scene or setting, being transgressed by a new expressiveness. In painting and sculpture this expressiveness tends to exploit the manipulative possibilities of the human form, with exaggerated muscular poses and sometimes bizarrely elongated limbs. It opens the way to greater ambiguity of meaning, placing more demands on the viewer to make sense of the representation.

In architecture, the assumed conventions of the classical architectural vocabulary are transcribed into an unorthodox, sometimes ironic deployment of juxtaposed elements. Accordingly, the proportional relationships of Renaissance art and architecture, which ensured continuity between the whole and its constituent parts, gives way to a more vivid demonstration of the transformational potential of individual elements.

Notwithstanding this move away from the 'constraints' of Renaissance ideals, what was ultimately at stake in Mannerist art and architecture was the expectation of some form of coherence, or synthesis of symbolic meaning, at a time when the age of Humanism was gradually being eroded and replaced by the new priorities of the emerging scientific age, which began in earnest at the early 17th century. This transition, moreover, brought with it a profound and irreversible change in the perception and understanding of the world, from a predominantly ontological to an essentially epistemological perspective. Evidence, furthermore, of this search for synthesis in Mannerist art can be found in the highly sophisticated allegorical treatments of pagan mythology, which served as analogues to Christian moral and redemptive themes.

The combination of sometimes-complex allegorical/symbolic structures in Mannerist art and architecture, and the proclivity to distort or radically transform the established classical conventions of the Renaissance, required from the artist/architect a prior knowledge of the 'rules' of classicism, in order to knowingly disturb or even dismantle its edifice. Similarly, this 'burden' was also placed upon the spectator fully to appreciate how the persuasive elegance of Mannerism took the ideal models of the High Renaissance as its starting point. Mannerism therefore is in every sense a reaction to its predecessor, but it quickly establishes its own distinctive sensibility and outlook—hence the justification for treating it as a 'free-standing' artistic phase.

Unlike the Baroque, whose emergence can be dated fairly safely to the beginning of the 17th century (allowing for anticipations in the earlier work of Michelangelo), the beginning of Mannerism is more difficult to date confidently, being much more closely interwoven with its preceding age. This explains why many of the greatest artists of the High Renaissance, such as Raphael and Michelangelo, are also recognized as having Mannerist traits.

The impact of social, political, and cultural change on the emergence of Mannerism has been disputed. For some the shift from Renaissance to Mannerism was 'ideally easy and attended by no crisis' (Shearman). For others, however, Mannerism was the result of a crisis in the Renaissance, which more broadly pointed to changes between the 'Christian Middle Ages and the Scientific New Age' (Hauser).

One distinctive feature of the religious, political, and cultural 'crisis' of the Roman Catholic Church during the tumultuous changes of the 16th century, was the growing importance of the villa as a retreat from urban life, with its role in the pursuit of *vita contemplativa* (Coffin) as opposed to the dominance of *vita activa* in Renaissance treatments of the ideal city (Mazzotta). This shift reflects in part a 'loss of faith' in the city as a context for moral, religious, and political instruction for the citizen, as was the case in the Renaissance. As exemplified in Villa d'Este, where variety and complexity of themes replace economy of means prevalent in the earlier Renaissance palace, the Mannerist villa provided a fertile setting in which to envisage the notion of a synthesis of religious, political, philosophical, and cultural outlooks, through the salvaging and reappropriating of decaying or fragmented elements of the classical past.

The most productive field of creativity in Mannerism was painting, indicated by the significant number of examples in Italy by such artists as *Pontormo, Bronzino, *Rosso, Salviati, *Parmigianino, Primaticcio, Beccafumi, Giulio Romano, and *Vasari. Early traces, however, of Mannerism can be found in Raphael's *Transfiguration* (1516) and in his frescoes in the Stanza dell'Incendio del Borgo (1514–17) in the Vatican. These latter works had a particular influence on Giulio Romano, assistant to Raphael, who was subsequently to become one of the most celebrated of Mannerist artists and architects. His frescoes in the Sala dei Giganti, in the Palazzo del Te in Mantua (1532–5), with the cataclysmic scenes of destruction wrought by muscular giants, serve equally as an evocation of dramatic, political, religious, and cultural change as an expression of the 'dismantling' of the edifice of the High Renaissance.

Mannerist tendencies in sculpture generally come later than in painting, although anticipations can clearly be traced in some of Michelangelo's early work, such as his *Bacchus* (1497). Here, the evident sensual treatment of the body, with its almost languid *contrapposto* pose, is a precocious expression of Mannerist art. It is, however, in Michelangelo's later design for the Medici Chapel in Florence (1519–34) that the contorted poses of the famous reclining figures—Dawn, Dusk, Day, and Night on the tombs of Lorenzo de' Medici and Giuliano de' Medici—convey most forcefully a departure from the equipoise, refinement, and harmony characteristic of Renaissance figurative sculpture. These Mannerist traits in Michelangelo's sculpture provide the context for the work of Alessandro Vittoria, *Ammannati, and Giambologna, who trained in Flanders, where a new virtuosity in the treatment of large free-standing figures with exaggerated poses and enhanced features can be discerned. This is seen, in particular, in the design of elaborate public fountains, such as that of Neptune by Ammannati in Florence. Here the artist was able to exploit the visual opportunities of sculptures in the round, situated in an elaborate theatrical setting of cascading water and supporting sculpted elements. At the same time, abundance and richness of detail abound in brass and other metal works such as candlesticks and tableware by Mannerist sculptors such as Benevenuto Cellini and Antonio Gentili. These works anticipate the asymmetrical and 'encrusted' treatments of *Rococo art.

In architecture signs of Mannerist sensibilities and techniques can be found quite early in the 16th century. These are evident, for example, in the wall articulation of façades and gateways, where 'Albertian' restraint is replaced by a new preoccupation with monumentality. Bramante's use of exaggerated rustication (*bugnato*), in his design for the Porta Giulia at the Vatican and his unfinished Palazzo dei Tribunali along via Giulia (1511), are cases in point. Influenced by ancient Roman practice, this distinctive wall treatment, with its over-scaled projecting stone blocks, would later become a hallmark of many Mannerist buildings, serving as the framework for sometimes playful or ironic transformations of classical architectural features. Also, familiar classical motifs become the target for reinvention or radical appropriation, as in Michelangelo's Vestibule for the Laurentian Library in Florence (begun in 1525) and his later Porta Pia (1561–5). Among the many examples of Italian Mannerist architects should be highlighted in particular Ammannati, Giulio Romano, Giambologna, who returned to Italy *c.*1555, Bernardo Buontalenti, together with the antiquarian Pirro Ligorio, whose designs for the Villa d'Este and Casino of Pius IV reflect the influence of archaeology on architecture in the mid-16th century.

The reception of Mannerism in Northern Europe was mixed. For some artists the understanding of Mannerism was more a result of observation and recording of Italian works rather than the actual production of art and architecture of any significance in their own countries or regions. Given that the Renaissance arrived late in the Netherlands and in the German states, and that many artists lacked knowledge of its historic background, Mannerism was either considered an isolated phenomenon or merely a continuation of the High Renaissance. However, artists such as Heemskerck, Mabuse, Floris, Spranger, and Golzius witnessed first-hand, or through correspondence, the dramatic artistic changes taking place in Italy in the 16th century. Through these artists' experience and knowledge, elements of Mannerism were disseminated to Northern Europe and contributed to the development of such styles as 'Antwerp Mannerism'. At the same time, this dissemination saw the beginnings of an outsider's academic perspective of the classicism that anticipated the Grand Tour of the 17th and 18th centuries. It was in France, however, that Mannerism would establish a firmer foothold outside mainland Italy, initially in the court of François I in Fontainebleau, which attracted a number of important Italian artists and architects such as *Rosso, Primaticcio, and Sebastiano Serlio.

With the full-blown influence of the Counter-Reformation on art, towards the end of the 16th century there occurs a return to a more direct form of artistic expression, departing from the compositional complexity characteristic of Mannerism. This is demonstrated in the paintings of *Caravaggio in Rome and the *Carraci in Bologna (and later in Rome) presaging the *Baroque period, even ushering in its arrival. In architecture and sculpture, however, the period of the late 16th century was unremarkable, highlighted by the numerous projects by Carlo Maderno, Domenico Fontana, and Giacomo della Porta.

Manoah, in the OT, was the father of *Samson, whose birth was announced by an angel. Manoah offered a sacrifice to God, and the angel disappeared in the flame from the altar (Judg. 13: 2–24). This very rare subject was painted by *Rembrandt (1641: Dresden), one of several by him on the subject of Samson.

Man of Sorrows, the This is a name given to Christ which epitomizes the Passion. The words come from Isa. 53: 3, in the Authorized Version: 'He was despised and rejected of men, a man of sorrows and acquainted with grief...' (NRSV has 'He was despised and rejected by others; a man of suffering and acquainted with infirmity...'). The whole chapter is one of Isaiah's most poignant prophecies of Christ's sufferings during the Passion, and in the preceding chapter, Isa.

52: 13–14, he makes an indirect prophecy of the Crucifixion.

Visual images of the words, Man of Sorrows, do not begin to appear in general use until the theme of the Mocking of Christ became a part of the imagery of the Passion. This is because of the great reluctance during the Early Christian period to illustrate, describe, or even name the manner of Christ's death. Crucifixion was a shameful death, and as S. Paul says (1 Cor. 1: 22–3) 'For Jews demand signs and Greeks desire wisdom, but we proclaim Christ crucified, a stumbling-block to Jews and foolishness to Greeks . . .'. Even S. Peter (Acts 5: 30) says, confronting the High Priest and Council, 'The God of our ancestors raised up Jesus, whom you had killed by hanging him on a tree . . .'.

The earliest truthful representation of the Crucifixion is in an ivory plaque, one of three on a casket (*c.*430: London, BM), but Christ's trial, on the preceding plaque, shows Pilate washing his hands, and Christ striding away carrying a purely symbolic cross. These are, however, by their size and function, private images. Even so graphic a series of images as the story of Christ's miracles and His Life in the early 6th-century mosaics in Sant'Apollinare Nuovo, Ravenna, has a gap—not accidental, but deliberate—between Christ led to execution, with a symbolic cross carried by an assistant, and the Women at the Sepulchre. Images of the Mocking of Christ or the Crowning with Thorns do not occur before the 9th/10th centuries, and then in Gospel books, not murals or mosaics, and do not become a normal part of the representation of the Passion in public works of art before the late 10th and early 11th century. The *Crowning with Thorns* is implied but not made explicit in some Early Christian sarcophagi (one in the Lateran has a soldier holding a laurel crown over Christ's head), but the references are all recondite. Precise details do not appear openly until the 11th century, in the gold *antependium in Aachen Cathedral with a vivid *Crowning with Thorns*, and in the 12th century in Sant'Angelo in Formis, near Capua, in a wall-painting with the *Mocking of Christ*, and the similar scene in the mosaic of the *Betrayal* in St Mark's, Venice. It does not become a frequent (could one say popular?) theme until the 14th century; the *Mocking of Christ and His crowning with thorns* is one of the subjects on the back of the Duccio *Maestà* (1308–11: Siena, Cath. Mus.) and it appears in a fresco by Barna da Siena (1381: Collegiata, San Gimignano). The more reflective version, the *Man of Sorrows*, is in one of the pages of the *Très Riches Heures*, finished, after the death of the Limbourg brothers in 1416, by Jean Colombe (Chantilly), and a deeply meditative quality is achieved in the fresco by Fra Angelico (1437–45: San Marco, Florence) of *Christ crowned with thorns*, enthroned, but surrounded by the symbols of the insults to which He was subjected—a head spitting, a stick striking His ghastly crown, the hands which struck Him—a work designed for private prayer in one of the cells, with a nun and a monk sitting on the ground on either side, not physically contemplating Christ, but meditating on His agony. Another, a Northern image by Geertgen tot Sint Jans of the late 15th century, combines the theme of the Man of Sorrows, the German 'Schmerzensmann' (Suffering Man), and the *Arma Christi, with the Instruments of the Passion held by sorrowing angels, and with the grieving Virgin, Mary Magdalene, and S. John reflecting on the horror of Christ's blood-spattered body.

The Arma Christi often became part of the theme of the Man of Sorrows, and also appear in the Mass of *S. Gregory. Yet another poignant variation on the Man of Sorrows is the late 15th- and early 16th-century sculptures of *Christ on Golgotha*, a form particularly developed in France. Christ, hands and feet bound, stripped except for an exiguous loincloth, and still crowned with thorns, waits sitting exhausted on a knoll of ground while the cross of His ghastly death is made ready. An early datable example of *c.*1475 is in Guerbigny, near Roye, N. France; Troyes, in Champagne, has three, one in St-Nizier, another in St-Urbain, both early 16th century, and a third probably of 1540 in the heroic Michelangelesque mode in St-Nicholas. There is a strikingly tragic one in Chaource, near Troyes, of *c.*1500, in a church which has a fine *Entombment* of the *Easter Sepulchre type. Another Netherlandish one (*c.*1495: Utrecht) testifies to the popularity of these themes of the Suffering Christ in the North, as did the subject of the Mocking of Christ, which also appealed to Northern taste, perhaps because it lent itself to faces close to caricatures, such as those in the Altdorfer (1509–18: St Florian), Bosch (1490–1500: London, NG), and Grünewald (1508: Munich).

Almost certainly one of the factors that have made the phrase, the Man of Sorrows, so memorable is Handel's great aria in the *Messiah*.

Manresa, a town about forty miles north of Barcelona, is where *S. Ignatius Loyola spent a year (1522–3) in prayer and meditation after a pilgrimage to the Marian shrine at Monserrat, and where, in a cave which became his place of retreat, he wrote the first draft of the **Spiritual Exercises*. The cave at Manresa is now itself a place of pilgrimage; the name is often given to Jesuit retreat-houses.

Mantegna, Andrea (*c.*1431–1506). His first major work, the fresco cycle of the *Life of S. James and S. Christopher* in the Ovetari Chapel of the church of the Eremitani in Padua, completed in 1459, was one of the great losses of the Second World War when it was destroyed by a bomb in 1944. Three of the scenes of the Life of S. James were remarkable for the painter's use of very strong effects of perspective, for his introduction of classical architecture as a setting, and for the vigour of his drawing. The only surviving parts are an *Assumption* and a *Martyrdom of S. Christopher. The Assumption* was critized because only eight of the Apostles were shown, there being no room for any more. The *S. Christopher* has little of the drama and interest of the lost works (known now only from photographs). His most important surviving religious works are the *Madonna and Saints* (*c.*1456–9: Verona, San Zeno), three pictures of the *Martyrdom of S. Sebastian*, the *Madonna della Vittoria* (1495–6: Paris, Louvre), and a number of versions of the Madonna and Child theme. The San Zeno altar is outstanding for Mantegna's bold variant of the *Sacra Conversazione form, for he places his subject within a space defined by the actual columns of the frame in such a way that he achieves the best of both worlds—a unified composition which still has the compartmented quality of the older form of polyptych. Of the three *S. Sebastian* pictures (1459: Vienna, KHM; *c.*1475: Louvre; and *c.*1490: Venice, Ca' d'Oro), the last has the inscription *Nihil nisi divinum stabile est, coetera fumus* (Only the divine is firm, the rest is smoke), and is usually considered to be a late work. This subject was usually commissioned because of an outbreak of plague, S. Sebastian being one of the saints to whom intercession was always made. All three are characterized by the hard marble-like quality of the flesh, by the extraordinary concentration of pieces of antique sculpture and architectural fragments in the Paris and Vienna pictures, and are remarkable examples of the combination of antique forms and Christian sentiment. In contrast, the saint endures martyrdom with patient stoicism, while in the Venice picture the saint's agonized expression matches the deeply resigned pessimism of the inscription. Mantegna's love of strong perspective effects is shown in his *Dead Christ* (*c.*1480: Milan, Brera), where Christ bewailed by Mary and another of the Holy Women is seen lying as if on a stone altar, from the unusual viewpoint of his feet. His many small *Madonna and Child* pictures follow traditional lines, though in some of the *Adoration* or *Circumcision* versions he uses an extraordinarily compressed composition and his treatment of what for most painters is a joyous subject often has a darkly foreboding quality.

Manzù, Giacomo (1908–1991) Although apprenticed to various craftsmen and carpenters from an early age, Manzù was largely self-taught as an artist. Religious imagery occupied an important position in his oeuvre. Settling in Milan in 1930 he received his first important commission when he was asked by the architect Giovanni Muzio to decorate the chapel of the Catholic University (1931–2). In the late 1930s, Manzù began his famous series of *Cardinals*, sculpting his sitters enveloped in their liturgical vestments. The simplicity of their conical forms imbues these figures with a profound sense of monumentality and serenity. He exhibited with the *Corrente* group in 1939, being attracted to its critical stance *vis-a-vis* Fascism. That year he also began a series of bas-reliefs on the theme of the Crucifixion which, despite being characterized by a delicacy of line recalling the work of *Donatello, were also passionate and unflinching indictments of Nazi-Fascist violence that were roundly condemned by both Church and State when first shown in 1942. Awarded a professorship at Milan's Brera Academy in 1940, Manzù established himself in Clusone near Bergamo throughout the war, after which he became Italy's pre-eminent sculptor of religious subjects.

During the 1950s and 1960s Manzù worked on three monumental sets of bronze *doors—the first being the so-called *Doors of Love* created for Salzburg Cathedral. In 1952 Manzù received what was undoubtedly the most important commission of his entire career when he won the competition to design a set of doors for St Peter's in Rome depicting the 'Triumph of the Saints and Martyrs of the Church'. In 1961 the theme of the work was changed, and the resulting *Doors of Death* were finally completed in 1964. His vigorous bas-reliefs depict the *Assumption of the Virgin and the *Crucifixion of Christ, as well as acts of martyrdom and other moving meditations on mortality, such as the final panel, in which an infant witnesses the death of his mother. In 1963 Manzù cast the death-mask of Pope John XXIII, who had become a close personal friend of the artist during the years of his engagement with this project. Finally, between 1965 and 1968 Manzù worked on the *Peace and War* doors for the Church of St Laurenz, Rotterdam.

A museum dedicated to the art of Manzù is located in Ardea, near Rome, where he lived and worked from 1964 until his death.

maphorion (Gk. veil) A large veil, called a *maphorion*, was the traditional head-covering of a Greek noblewoman, and therefore traditional also in images of the Virgin Mary and other Holy Women. Even Eve, represented clothed in scenes of the *Anastasis, or Christ in Limbo, as in the fresco in the Church of Christ in Chora (now Kariye Camii), Constantinople, wears an all-enveloping *maphorion* in red, the colour traditionally assigned to her. The colour of the veil worn by the Virgin in images representing her may be blue, brown, or purple, but whatever the colour she is almost always, in Byzantine and Italian art, but not always in Northern art, shown wearing one.

The Emperor Leo I added, in the 5th century, a circular chapel to the church of the Blachernai in Constantinople to house a relic, believed to be the Virgin's *maphorion*, which had been transferred from a church in Jerusalem. In some early chronicles the relic is said to be a shroud, preserved together with her veil and girdle; in a 10th-century chronicle it is confused with an *omophorion. In the 14th century the Blachernai relic is also called a shroud. The Blachernai church was destroyed by fire in 1434, and the relic perished with it.

Three artists during the Early Renaissance, who may be deemed typical painters of the Madonna and Child subject—Fra Angelico, Botticelli, and Bellini—usually enveloped the Virgin in a blue garment which also covered her head, so that the tradition was clearly preserved from Byzantine art. In one painting of the *Pietà* by Bellini, however (Milan, Brera), the Virgin wears a red *maphorion*, perhaps to exemplify her role as the Second Eve, holding the body of Christ, the Second Adam.

Margaret, Saint (also called **Marina**), was martyred at Antioch of Pisidia (now Yalvaç, Turkey) during the persecution by the Emperor *Diocletian (other sources say the Emperor Decius). The account of her martyrdom was translated from Greek into Latin at an early date, and it was then that her name was changed from Marina to Margaret. The narrative of her torments is extremely fantastic, and includes a dragon which swallowed her, and from whose belly she escaped by attacking it with a cross which she held. From this popular legend arose her patronage of women in childbirth. In the East she was venerated in her original name.

In the West she is first mentioned in the 9th century. Her cult was spread by the translation of her relics from the East to San Pietro della Valle on the Lake of Bolsena, then in 1145 to the cathedral of Montefiascone, with some relics acquired by Venice. She is also claimed by Spain, where she is possibly confused with Margarita of Orense. A mystery play, based on her ordeal, and the **Golden Legend*, which includes her dying promise to help women in labour, made her one of the most popular saints of the Middle Ages.

In art she is invariably shown with her dragon at her feet, sometimes on a lead (like the princess in Uccello's *S. George and the Dragon*, London, NG). There is a 14th-century picture of her, surrounded by ten scenes from her life and death (Vatican Mus.); a 14th-century carved relief of her, with S. Catherine of Siena, is in Antwerp (Mus. Meyer van den Bergh); she is included in the Book of Hours of Anne of Brittany (16th cent.: Paris, BN); a figure of the saint is carved on a finial of the bed in Jan van Eyck's *Arnolfini Marriage Group* (1434: London NG); and a large painting by Titian of *S. Margaret and the Dragon* (*c.*1565: Prado) all attest to the wide spread of her cult.

Margaret of Scotland (Scotland's patron saint, 1046–93) is depicted in Paula Rego's painting of *St Margaret* (2002) in Durham Cathedral.

Margaret Mary Alacoque, Saint *See* HEART, THE SACRED.

Maria Maggiore, Santa, Rome *See* LIBERIAN BASILICA and SNOW, MIRACLE OF THE.

Maries at the Sepulchre The four Gospels all differ in their accounts of the events after the Entombment of Christ, but a careful reading of the four texts suggests that either two or three Holy Women (but not necessarily all the same ones) came to the tomb on the early morning of the day after the Sabbath, bearing spices with which to prepare Christ's body. All the Gospels agree that Mary Magdalene was one of the women. Matthew says two women (Matt. 18: 1–10), Mark says three women (Mark 16: 1–13), Luke says three women, but his account suggests that other, unnamed, women also came (Luke 24: 1–12, 33–5). John says that the Magdalene came to the tomb before it was light, and only he tells of the pathetic meeting between the grief-stricken Magdalene and the Risen Christ (John 20: 1–18). Accounts also differ about what happened after the encounter at the tomb. Matthew says that the women returned to the city and told the eleven what they had seen. Mark, in one version, says that they were so terrified that they told no one, but in another version that when they told the Apostles what they had seen, no one would believe them. Mark also says that when Christ appeared to 'two . . . as they were walking into the country' (a clear reference to the *Emmaus incident) they went back and told the others, who would not believe them. Luke also says that when Mary Magdalene and the other women told the Apostles 'it seemed to them an idle tale', and only Peter went to see, found the empty tomb and the linen cloths lying by themselves, but then went home amazed, inferring that he told no one either. John says that Mary Magdalene came and told the disciples 'I have seen the Lord', but he does not say how her story was received.

The imagery of the Maries at the Sepulchre has always included two and sometimes three women. The ivory plaque, one of the three on the British Museum Casket (*c.*430), shows only two, but the number of women seems dependent on the amount of space available to the artist. In two early ivories, possibly carved in Milan, one has two women (late 4th cent.: Milan, Castello Sforzesca), the other, three women (early 5th cent.: Munich), but both these ivories and the British Museum one have the same type of tomb: a small temple—a *martyrium—usually with an open door, despite all the Gospels describing it as a rock tomb which S. Peter stooped to enter, closed by a stone rolled across the entrance. This martyrium type of tomb continued in Byzantine art and was only slowly superseded—though with exceptions such as the doors of Sta Sabina (*c.*432: Rome)—to the type with a canopied sarcophagus. The earliest change is perhaps found in the Egbert Evangeliary (980: Trier), where the Holy Women approach under a pedimented canopy borne on columns towards an angel seated on the lid of a tomb under a similar canopy, and in a Sacramentary of 1100 (Paris, BN) from Limoges, the angel is seated on the lid of a sarcophagus with a canopy. The canopied sarcophagus is portrayed in scenes on the sides of 12th-century Italian crucifixes (*see* CROCE DIPINTA). In the 13th century, the 'altar' tomb, with a flat top, sometimes with a canopy over it, becomes the form usual in Italy, and in the 14th century the angel is usually depicted seated on the displaced lid of the tomb, as in the *Maries at the Sepulchre* in the Duccio *Maestà* (1308–11: Siena, Cath. Mus.). Also some representations of the scene show two, or three, soldiers sleeping near by, but many omit them, and some ivories also have Christ ascending above the scene with the Maries. In the sculpture groups of the *Entombment*, which are one of the features of 16th-century sculpture in France (*see* EASTER SEPULCHRE), three Maries coming to the sepulchre figure only in the impressive one in St-Maclou at Pontoise, where they approach, from one side, the burial group in the cave-like construction in which the large group of the Entombment is placed—an example of *Continuous Representation in an age when it had largely been abandoned as old-fashioned, but surviving with vigour, in that above the Entombment is a 17th-century wooden group of the *Resurrection*, making a complete narrative of the last stage of the Passion.

Two rarely depicted scenes, the first of three Holy Women buying spices, appears on a 12th-century holy water stoup in Modena Cathedral, and the second, of Mary Magdalene telling the Apostles what had happened at the tomb, to their obvious disbelief, is on one of the capitals from the old cloister of Pamplona Cathedral (*c.*1145: Pamplona, Mus. de Navarra).

Mark, Saint (Lat. *Marcus*), (d. *c.*74?), was an *Evangelist, but not an *Apostle. He is usually identified with John Mark, son of the Mary to whose house S. Peter went after his miraculous liberation from prison (Acts 12: 6–19). He was a cousin of S. Barnabas, and accompanied him and Saul (later S. Paul) on a missionary journey, but left them part of the way along, with the result that his relations with S. Paul were strained (Acts 15: 37–40). Mark and

Barnabas later went to Cyprus leaving S. Paul to continue his missionary journeys with Silas. Later still they were in Rome with *S. Peter, and during S. Paul's Roman imprisonment he and Mark were reconciled (2 Tim. 4: 11 and Phil. 1: 23). It was probably in Rome, where Mark was S. Peter's interpreter, that he wrote his Gospel which, traditionally, records S. Peter's recollections and is known as the Marcan tradition. Very little is known of Mark's life after he was in Rome with S. Peter, but he is said to have been the first Bishop of Alexandria, where he was martyred. Legend has it that during this event a violent thunderstorm scattered the pagans, and the local Christians were able to take his body, bury it, and later build a *martyrium. The body was found and smuggled out of Alexandria, by then in Muslim hands, by some Venetians *c.*828. These episodes are the subject of two paintings by Tintoretto, for the Scuola di San Marco in Venice (1562–6: Venice, Accad. and Milan, Brera).

S. Mark's relics were taken to St Mark's, Venice, in 828/9, and he has been associated with the Venetian state ever since. His Evangelist symbol—the winged lion—is everywhere the symbol of Venetian rule, and indicates the close ties between the Church in Venice and the Republic, becoming the symbol of the State even more than of the Church. Many legends are recorded in the **Golden Legend*, and illustrated by generations of Venetian artists, from the unique series of mosaics in St Mark's (12th/13th centuries) to the Bellini brothers and Tintoretto, who made his name with the *Miracle of the Slave* (1548: Venice, Accad.), showing the saint rescuing a Christian slave from torture at the hands of pagans.

S. Mark is usually represented as a bearded man, not unlike S. Peter, holding the book of his Gospel, and often accompanied by his lion. The earliest known image of S. Mark is the 6th-century mosaic in San Vitale, Ravenna, where he is portrayed with his symbol of the lion. His 'portrait', shown writing his Gospel, often appears at the beginning of his Gospel in early medieval Gospel books, such as the 6th-century *Rossano Codex, the 7th-century Book of Durrow, and the *Lindisfarne Gospels (both the latter in Trinity Coll. Dublin), and S. Chad's Gospels (early 8th cent.: Ltchfield Cath.). *See also* VENICE AND SAINT MARK'S.

Marriage is a double ceremony, in that the Church, in the East as well as the West, established strict rules concerning its purpose, its validity, its duration, and the circumstances in which it was contracted. Its sacramental character lay—and still lies—in its being conferred only by the contracting parties on each other. The function of the Church is to ensure that it is a legal contract, for which from earliest times the following conditions were attached, based on laws of Theodosius II of 438 in the East and his co-emperor Valentinian III in the West. The four conditions distinguished between the essentials and the non-essentials, which were matters of custom. The essentials were (*a*) that the man and the woman were of equal status (i.e. that neither was a slave, since slaves might not marry), (*b*) that they broke no law by marrying (i.e. that neither was already married, or betrothed to another), (*c*) that they consented freely, and (*d*) that there were witnesses. A marriage which fulfilled these conditions could not be broken, even if none of the local customary ceremonials were included.

The function of the Church now is to endeavour to fulfil the last three essentials (the first is no longer held to apply, but it still did where serfdom survived because a serf might not marry without his or her master's consent), and the religious aspect of the ceremony is the blessing given by the priest. Two witnesses now suffice, but once as many as ten were required (at Ruth's wedding to Boaz (Ruth 4: 2) ten witnesses were present when Boaz undertook to marry her). It was customary for marriages to consist of two separate ceremonies: a betrothal, and a nuptial, and the betrothal ceremony was a formal contract. In it, an *arrha* or 'earnest-money' of a single coin was given to the bride, and also a ring as part of the *arrhae* as an indication of her betrothed's willingness to endow her with his worldly goods, although the *arrhae* was also a survival of the barbarian form of 'bride-purchase'. In Greek and Roman practice a dowry should be promised, or even paid, by the bride's father or family at the betrothal ceremony, and this contract was always a written one and formed a settlement on the bride, for which witnesses were necessary. A veil was put on the bride, the vows were exchanged with a 'hand-fast'—the man and woman holding each other's right hand—a solemn kiss exchanged, and she wore the veil until her nuptials. This formal betrothal was called, in the West, an *ordo in nuptiarum subarrhatione* (rite for a nuptial by giving of an earnest). A betrothal ceremony had to be public, and was often held in a public place, such as the church porch. This practice is illustrated in scenes of the *Espousal of the Virgin, where the nuptial ceremony takes place either at the church door, in the church porch, or in the piazza outside. Chaucer's *Wife of Bath*, in the *Prologue* to her tale, says:

My Lords, since when I was but twelve years old,
Thanks be to God Eternal evermore,
Five husbands have I had at the church door.

(Twelve was the lowest age for a legal marriage, and she was indeed lucky to be in England in the late 14th century, and not in the 3rd or 4th centuries in either the East or West, where two marriages were permissible but incurred a year's penance, three were forbidden, a fourth was disallowed and annulled, treated as fornication, and punished with excommunication.)

Almost every successive Council which dealt with the problems of disputed marriages insisted that more than one witness was necessary. Hence the insistence on the essential public nature of the ceremony, and the presence of several witnesses as the strictest conditions for the legality of a marriage, for which the priest was made responsible in order to prevent the evils of forced, secret, or improperly conducted marriages. The Lateran Council of 1215 first instituted the publication of banns to ensure that a valid objection could be made against the proposed marriage. Because of widespread evasions of these rules, the Council of *Trent laid down that banns should be published (usually in front of the congregation in a parish church, not a private chapel), on three separate occasions, and the marriage was to be solemnized before a priest and the witnesses. A record had to be made of it in the church registers and signed by the contracting parties and the witnesses (or their marks attested by the priest), for it to be a valid marriage. The new rules were one of the many attempts to put an end to the evils of clandestine marriages.

Representations of marriages exist from Early Christian times, often in the form of engraved or gilded glass receptacles in some of which the pair clasp each other's right hands, or are depicted side by side being crowned by Christ (the crowning of the married pair is a feature of an Orthodox wedding). This scene also appears on some medallions or *encolpia, usually made of gold and dating from the 4th to the 6th centuries. The *Projecta Casket (*c.*380: London, BM) includes portraits of the couple on their marriage casket. The *Espousal of the Virgin is often part of a representation of the Life of the Virgin, in MSS and fresco cycles such as those by *Giotto in the Arena Chapel, Padua, and by Taddeo Gaddi (Sta Croce, Florence). A marriage scene in cycles of the Life of Christ is that of the *Marriage at Cana*, but this usually concentrates on the changing of the water into wine, rather than on the bridal pair who are hardly more than an excuse for depiction of Christ's first miracle. Another marriage scene is represented in a panel painting of the *Life of S. Etheldreda*, in which she is shown making a royal marriage before a bishop, who blesses the couple while they clasp their right hands together (*c.*1425: London, Soc. of Antiquaries). One of the most unusual marriage pictures is the *Arnolfini Marriage* (van *Eyck, 1434: London, NG), where a Florentine merchant in Bruges is shown marrying Giovanna Cenami, daughter of a Lucchese merchant in Paris. The scene is set in a bedroom with, on the wall behind them, a mirror in which figures are reflected, including perhaps that of the artist, who signed the picture with the words *Johannes de eyck fuit hic* (Jan van Eyck was here) with the date 1434. The solemnity of the pair, his right hand raised in affirmation of the vows he makes, her right hand in his left, the lighted candle over their heads, symbolizing the presence of God, the pair of discarded pattens, recalling God's order to Moses, 'Remove the sandals from your feet, for the place on which you stand is holy ground', the little dog at their feet, a symbol of fidelity, all contribute to make this the most unusual certificate of marriage (or perhaps betrothal). *Bruegel's *Marriage Feast* (*c.*1567: Vienna KHM) may be a covert *Marriage at Cana*, rather than the peasant banquet it depicts, itself perhaps an allegory of gluttony, in that far to one side a woman earnestly entreats a young bearded man, while servants pour water into pitchers.

Marriage of the Virgin *See* MARY and ESPOUSAL.

Martha and Mary of Bethany, sisters of *Lazarus. The first mention of the two sisters is in Luke 10: 38–42, where a woman named Martha welcomed him into her house. 'She had a sister named Mary, who sat at the Lord's feet, and listened to what he was saying. But Martha was distracted by her many tasks; so she came to him and asked, "Lord, do you not care that my sister has left me to do all the work by myself? Tell her then to help me." But the Lord answered her, "Martha, Martha, you are worried and distracted by many things; there is need of only one thing. Mary has chosen the better part which will not be taken away from her."' From the manner in which Christ spoke to Martha it may be assumed that this was not the first time he had been her guest, and from the place that this event has in S. Luke's Gospel, it is clearly well before the account of the raising of Lazarus in Bethany. The story of this last, most public and striking of Christ's miracles is recounted only in John 11: 1–45. In its sequel (John 12: 1–9), when Jesus is having supper with Lazarus and his sisters, Mary anointed his feet with ointment of spikenard, and wiped them with her hair. This aroused the cupidity of Judas, who protested at the waste, saying that this costly perfume could have been sold and the money given to the poor. (But, as S. John remarked, it was not that he cared about the poor; but because he was a thief; he kept the common purse and used to steal what was put into it.) Then Jesus said, 'Leave her alone. She bought it so that she might keep it for the day of my burial. You always have the poor with you, but you do not always have me.' This was followed on the next day by the entry into Jerusalem and the beginning of the events which culminate in the Passion.

The anointing of Christ's feet appears also in Matt. 26: 6–13, Mark 14: 3–9, and Luke 7: 37–8, but it is said to have taken place at a supper given in the house of Simon the Leper in Bethany. In both Matthew and Mark this event is immediately followed by the preparations for the Passover, so that it is probably another version of the story in John. John specifically states that it was Mary, Martha's sister, who 'anointed the feet of Jesus, and wiped his feet with her hair', but in the versions given by Matthew and Mark an unidentified woman poured ointment on His head, while in Luke the action took place in the house of a Pharisee called Simon, and a 'woman who was a sinner' wiped His feet with her hair. In the East these three women were separate, but a long-lasting tradition in the West conflated them, so that Mary *Magdalene became Martha's sister.

Luke's account (10: 38–42) of the difference between Martha and Mary has led to their becoming *types of the Active and Contemplative Lives, and NT parallels of the OT types of Leah and Rachel. The subject of Christ in the House of Martha and Mary is rare in medieval art; it appears in a Gospels written at Trier for Otto III (late 10th cent.: Aachen) and was copied in a Book of Pericopes (biblical extracts) of Henry II (1007/12: Munich), and is also one of the scenes in Giovanni da Milano's fresco cycle of the *Life of the Magdalene* (*c.*1365: Florence, Sta Croce). It became popular in late 16th-century Dutch painting, where it was treated as an adjunct to a profuse still-life and kitchen scene, as in Pieter Aertsen's *Christ in the House of Martha and Mary* (1553: Rotterdam, Boymans Mus.) and Joachim Bueckelaer's version (1566: Amsterdam, Rijks.), where the biblical event is pushed into a room in the background, with piles of vegetables, fruit, and game in the foreground. It may thus have become a way of 'ennobling' the humble genre of still-life painting by incorporating a Gospel subject, or it may be that Protestant feeling was opposed to a straightforward religious subject. The contemporary picture by Tintoretto (*c.*1567: Munich) has the domestic details, but relegated to the background. One of the finest treatments of the subject (Edinburgh, NG of S) is by the mid-17th-century painter Vermeer, which is a large-scale picture by a Catholic painter working in a Protestant milieu: it has no genre element at all, depicting only Christ and the two sisters. Earlier Spanish versions of the subject are by Velázquez (both 1618: London, NG, and Edinburgh, NG of S), where the scene seems to be represented in a picture on the wall of the kitchen where an elderly woman appears to be advising a rather sulky maid making *aioli* to consider the example.

Martin, John (1789–1854), was an English painter of huge melodramatic pictures, mostly illustrating such scenes as *Joshua commanding the Sun to stand still* (1816), his first sensational success. He preferred OT subjects, since in them he could indulge his taste for vast scenes of catastrophe, such as *Belshazzar's Feast* (1826), *The Deluge* (1834), and *The Destruction of Sodom and Gomorrah* (1852). Some of his works enjoyed great esteem in Paris, where they fitted in with the French tradition of 'history' painting, but this favour was more among writers and poets than artists; they were, in fact, the kind of Romantic art that was hardly more than the fag-end of 'grand manner' Baroque. After 1826 he began to issue his works as mezzotints; illustrations to the Bible, such as *The Last*

Judgement and *The Great Day of His Wrath*, and to Milton's *Paradise Lost* enjoyed great success. Virtually all his paintings have darkened into near-oblivion. Charles Lamb, in 1827, described his *Joshua*... as 'confused... frittered into 1000 fragments' and John Constable dismissed his works as 'pantomimes'. He was called 'Mad' Martin, but this epithet can with greater justice be applied to his brother Jonathan, a religious fanatic, who in 1818 tried to shoot the Bishop of Oxford and was consigned to an asylum from which he escaped; in 1829 he set fire to York Minster destroying the 14th-century wooden roof and interior of the choir, was tried for arson but found 'Not guilty because insane', and spent the rest of his life in the asylum of Bedlam.

Martini, Simone (*c*.1284–1344), was a Sienese painter who was a pupil of *Duccio. His earliest dated work is the large fresco in the Town Hall of Siena of the *Maestà* (1315, and 1321)—a Madonna and Child enthroned amid saints—which was painted as a civic counterpart to the *Maestà* by Duccio in the cathedral. In 1317 he was paid for an unusual altarpiece of *S. Louis of Toulouse* (Naples, Gall. Naz.), shown in the act of resigning the crown of Naples to his brother Robert of Anjou. This event took place in 1296, and Louis became a Franciscan four months later. He was made bishop of Toulouse by the pope, died in 1297, and was canonized in 1317. The picture was clearly commissioned by King Robert as 'evidence' of his quasi-divine right of succession, since his right to the throne of Naples had been contested since his accession in 1309 because of suspicions of undue pressure on Louis. The altarpiece displays two characteristics of Simone's art: his use of sinuous fluid line in the fall of draperies, and his vivid naturalism in the unusually strongly characterized portrait of Robert, and in the narrative sequence of the five small *predella* panels—one of the earliest examples of a *predella*—with events from the saint's story. This use of rich colour and naturalistic detail stems from Duccio's example; it also shows an awareness of the naturalism of Giovanni Pisano's pulpits in Pisa and Siena, and of French Gothic.

When Simone went to *Assisi is not known; there he painted a chapel in the Lower Church with scenes of the life of S. Martin, for a Franciscan cardinal who died in 1312 leaving money to the basilica, probably to pay for the decoration, and whose earlier contacts with Naples and the court of King Robert may have suggested the employment of Simone. The frescoes show the same interest in sinuous line, and the same gifts of vivid naturalism in gestures, facial expressions, and dramatic narrative as was found in the *S. Louis* altarpiece, but on a more extended scale. Such telling details as the group of musicians and singers in the scene of S. Martin's investiture as a knight show a gift for naturalistic drama infused with an unexpected sense of humour.

In 1324 Simone married the sister of the painter Lippo Memmi, who became his partner. Both signed the *Annunciation* (Uffizi), dated 1333. In this masterpiece of craftsmanship in painting and gilding, it is felt that Lippo Memmi's part was probably confined to the two side panels with their more mundane figures of saints on the grounds that only an artist of Simone's imaginative powers could have executed the superb central group of the angel and the Virgin, recoiling in alarm from her heavenly visitant. The picture is documented as an altarpiece, making it one of the earliest—if not the earliest—appearances of the Annunciation as the main subject of an altarpiece—understandable, perhaps, in Siena, since the city was dedicated to the Virgin. What would seem to be—on stylistic grounds—a later polyptych, now largely dispersed, consisted of an *Annunciation* on separate panels, very similar in design to the Uffizi one, though much smaller, with panels representing the *Crucifixion* and the *Deposition* (these four are in Antwerp, Mus.), the *Entry into Jerusalem* (Louvre), and the *Entombment* (Berlin, Staatliche Mus.), showing an even stronger dramatic feeling, with highly emotional treatment of the figures and gestures reminiscent of Duccio's Passion scenes in the Siena *Maestà*, but even more vehement in expression. The *Crucifixion* and *Entombment* bear the signature of Simone alone—*Pinxit Symon*—and the work may have been painted in *Avignon, where he went in 1340/1, originally on a business matter with the papal curia, remaining there until his death.

At Avignon he painted the small and iconographically unusual *Christ returning to His Parents after disputing in the Temple* (Liverpool, Walker Gall.), dated 1342, a work showing astonishing psychological insight in the way the dramatic narrative is treated. It is probable that Simone (or the commissioner) derived the subject from ch. XIV of the **Meditationes Vitae Christi*, where there is a vivid account of the way in which the young Jesus became separated from Joseph and Mary, and of their anxious search for Him, their finding Him in the Temple three days later, Mary's sorrowful reproaches, and His less than apologetic response. Another unusual work was a manuscript illumination of an *Allegory of Virgil* (Milan, Ambrosiana) as a frontispiece for the manuscript of Virgil belonging to his friend the poet Petrarch (who described him in a letter as 'ill-favoured', but who praised him in two sonnets for his skill as a painter). Two frescoes in the cathedral of Ste-Marie-des-Doms, Avignon, now surviving only as *sinopie* (underpainting in a reddish pigment), of a *Christ in Majesty with Angels*, and a *Virgin and Child with Angels*, must have been commissions from the papal court. The *sinopie* have been transferred to the Palais des Papes, the paintings themselves having perished, although early 19th-century engravings provide a fuller record of what these magnificent works once looked like. Simone's residence in Avignon was one of the ways in which the influence of Italian 14th-century art spread into N. Europe, and his courtly style was an important element in the development of *International Gothic.

m

Martin of Tours, Saint (316/17–397), was born in Pannonia (now Hungary), where his father was stationed with the Roman army. Martin's first contact with Christians was in Pavia, but his wish to become a catechumen (to seek instruction as a Christian convert) was violently resisted by his pagan father, who forced him to enter the army when he was 15.

When he was stationed in Amiens in 338 a half-naked beggar asked him for alms, he cut his fur-lined cloak in two, and gave half to the man. The following night he had a vision of Christ, wearing his half-cloak, saying to the angels, 'Martin, who is only a catechumen, covered me with his cloak.' This became the most famous subject in his iconography. He became a member of the imperial guard, from which it was almost impossible to resign, but in 354 he finally gained his freedom, and immediately joined S. Hilary, Bishop of Poitiers. Popular opposition to soldiers becoming clerics at first prevented his being made a deacon, so he lived in a villa outside Poitiers where he founded, at Ligugé, the first community in Gaul to live as monks. He dedicated himself to evangelizing the peasants and farm slaves, who were still pagan; Christianity was purely an urban faith. In 371, on a visit to Tours, he was forcibly enthroned as bishop by the people, but he insisted on living outside the city so as to continue his missionary work among the peasantry, founded the first seminary for the training of priests at Marmoutiers, and established a rudimentary parish system in the countryside.

In 384 he opposed bitterly, but fruitlessly, in the imperial court at Trier, the trial and execution of a Spanish heretical preacher called Priscillian because he rejected the right of a secular civil court to try a religious offence. Although he lost, the right was eventually conceded. The great basilica, dating from 1008, which became one of the main pilgrimage churches on the road to Santiago de Compostela, was the fourth built to house his shrine—earlier ones were either burnt accidentally or by Norsemen raiders who came up the Loire. This huge church was totally destroyed during the French Revolution, and a street driven through where the transepts had been.

A 6th-century mosaic figure of S. Martin offering a crown is in Sant'Apollinare Nuovo, Ravenna. A fresco cycle of ten scenes from his life by Simone Martini is in the Chapel of St Martin in the Lower Church of Assisi, painted in the 2nd quarter of the 14th century. Images of S. Martin, particularly of the incident of the cloak, range across the whole of European art in painting, sculpture, MSS, and stained-glass windows, from the 10th century onwards, and among the most striking examples is a bronze plaque attributed to the Paduan Andrea Brizio (Il Riccio) (early 16th cent.: Venice, Ca' d'Oro); and a large painting by Van Dyck (1621: Royal Coll., Windsor Castle). A Jordaens of *S. Martin curing a possessed man*, of 1630, is in Brussels Museum.

Martyr, Saint Peter *See* PETER.

martyrium A martyrium is a small chapel or church built to commemorate the place where the martyr was buried, or where the martyrdom took place, though these were usually *memoria*—memorial chapels. The continuity between such commemorative buildings and the *heroön* of ancient Greece is clear. *Heroa* were small, often circular, temples containing an altar for sacrifices or libations, built either in honour of a hero or over his tomb. The earliest martyria were built by the first Christians to commemorate those who had died heroically in the various persecutions. The principal ones were S. Peter's shrine in Rome, under the present church, and a 'Chapel of the Popes' in the Catacomb of Calixtus outside Rome, which is defined as a burial-place of martyrs by inscriptions on the walls. Most early martyria, in Italy and in other parts of W. Europe, are tombs with a courtyard or covered area where commemorative meals (*see* AGAPE) and services were held on the martyr's anniversary, and which also became Christian burial-places. Among Roman ones built after the Peace of the Church in 313, and outside the walls as was the rule for burial-places, were Old St Peter's (begun by 324), St Paul's (begun 384, on the Ostian Way, near his place of execution), San Sebastiano (*c.*312/13?), San Lorenzo (*c.*330), and Sant'Agnese (*c.*350), the latter having as one of its dependencies Sta Costanza, the tomb of Constantine's daughter, not a martyrium, but built as a rotunda (it may have been a pre-Christian building); this became a favourite shape for *memoria*. Other forms of martyria were the *cross-in-square, Greek cross (*see* CROSS and CHURCH ARCHITECTURE), and the octagon.

The most important memorial churches built by Constantine in the Holy Land include the Church of the Nativity at Bethlehem, by 333, and the Church of the Holy Sepulchre, dedicated in 336 on the site of Golgotha. Both these churches—later destroyed—consisted of a rotunda with a nave and atrium attached, so that by the early 4th century the forms used for such major memorials were defined. Many Christian martyria were later transformed into *pilgrimage churches, to which relics have often been transferred far from their original resting-place. Two of the most interesting later ones in Rome are the circular *Tempietto in the courtyard of San Pietro in Montorio, built by Bramante in 1506–12 over a wrongly identified place of S. Peter's crucifixion, and the octagonal San Giovanni in Oleo, near the Porta Latina, built in 1509 and attributed to Bramante, but later reconstructed by Borromini, on the presumed site of the unsuccessful attempt to martyr S. John the Evangelist in boiling oil, after which the saint was exiled to Patmos.

Mary, the Blessed Virgin The name is derived from the Aramaic and Greek Maryam form of the Hebrew Miriam, and becomes Maria in Latin.

Mary is not often mentioned—with one exception—in the NT, either as Mary or as the mother of Jesus. There are five mentions in Matthew's Gospel, only one in Mark, duplicating one of Matthew's statements, two in John: eight in all. The exception is Luke who devotes his first two chapters to an account of the birth of S. John the Baptist and the events of the birth and childhood of Jesus. After this Luke only mentions Mary once, repeating Matthew and Mark. In the Acts of the Apostles, which Luke also wrote, he only once mentions the mother of Jesus.

Meagre as this documentation may seem, if the events in the Gospels and the Acts are arranged as a narrative a coherent biography emerges. There are, however, other sources, though they were rejected by *S. Jerome. These are the *Apocryphal Gospels, in particular the so-called 'Infancy Gospels', the Protevangelium of S. James, the Gospel of Thomas, and the Pseudo-Matthew. The Protevangelium was current possibly as early as the late 1st century, and if not as early as that then certainly from the 2nd to the late 3rd century and was largely accepted in the East as canonical. It provided a wealth of picturesque stories which, up to the end of the 15th century in the West, appeared in narrative cycles in MS illumination and church decoration, and also provided subjects for pictures of single incidents in the life of the Virgin and of her Son alongside the incidents vouched for by the Gospels. In some instances, the details provided by the Apocrypha were accepted without demur. For example, the parentage of S. John the Baptist is part of Luke's Gospel (1: 5–24), but the Virgin's parents appear as Joachim and Anne only in the Protevangelium of S. James and the Pseudo-Matthew, where the accounts continue to be similar as far as the story of the flight into Egypt. The relationship of Mary to S. Elizabeth (which the Angel Gabriel cites to Mary as an example of God's omniscience) is explained by S. Elizabeth being S. Anne's niece and therefore Mary's cousin. So firmly accredited is S. Anne as the Virgin's mother that the identification has never been questioned in the West, even though its source is, strictly speaking, uncanonical.

Representations of the Virgin Mary fall into two distinct classes—narrative scenes in which she plays a part, e.g. the *Annunciation, *Nativity, *Crucifixion, as well as scenes from the Apocryphal Gospels, which are included—for instance, the *Dormition—because the NT says so tantalizingly little about her. This encouraged the use of incidents which supported the cult of the Virgin, from the standpoint of devotion and reverence in her roles as protectress, mediator, Queen of Heaven, all of which (and many others) were assigned to her as the mother of God—the *Theotokos. Many of these attributes are the subject of works in the larger category that consists of icon-type paintings and sculpture of her, sometimes as a single figure, but usually with the Christ Child. For many of these, *see also* MADONNA TYPES.

In the East, now largely Turkey, narrative cycles of the *Life of the Virgin* survive in the rock-churches of Cappadocia, where their isolation has been their main protection against destruction. At Göreme, there are two churches at the Toqale Kilisse, an Old Church of *c.*913–20 and a New Church of *c.*950, both with wall-paintings illustrating scenes from the Protevangelium. The ones in the Old Church are fairly crude, but those in the New Church, which was under the direct patronage of the Patriarchate of Constantinople, are clearly by artists with a metropolitan background. They are vivid in their imagery and technically fluent, and are virtually the only surviving evidence of the quality of painting in metropolitan Byzantium. The 11th-century mosaics in the Katholikon, Daphni, where the incidents represented—Mary's parents praying for a child, her birth, her presentation in the Temple, and her death—are fully representative of Byzantine art, and in Constantinople itself there are the surviving parts of the exceptionally beautiful mosaic and fresco cycles in the Church of Christ in Chora (the Kariye Camii) of the early 14th century. There may have been others—there probably were in view of Byzantine devotion to the Theotokos—but nothing else of consequence has survived.

Interest clearly centres on the iconography of the subjects, its source, and its transmission across time and territory. The earliest examples of the scenes described in the Protevangelium occur in the carved plaques of the ivory throne of *Maximian, made probably in Constantinople and sent to Ravenna (now in the Archbishop's Palace Mus.), where he was bishop from 546 until his death in 553. The same scenes occur in the small 'keepsake' box painted for a pilgrim to the Holy Land in the late 6th or early 7th century (now in Rome, Lateran Mus.). It has images of the *Nativity*, the *Baptism of Christ*, the *Crucifixion* with Christ in a *colobium and between two thieves, the *Maries approaching the Sepulchre*, and the *Ascension*, where the design of the scenes is also very close to those in the *Rabbula Gospels of 586. The earliest surviving MSS which illustrate the Protevangelium fully are two copies of the *Homilies of the Monk James of Kokinobaphos* (Vatican, Lib., and Paris, BN), both of the early 12th century, yet the MS known as the *Menologium of Basil II*, which is in fact a 10th-century collection of Gospel readings, contains many of the same subjects. The inference must be that there once existed a fully illustrated MS of the Protevangelium, which provided a source not just for the narrative, but was also a model for the design of the scenes.

The dependence of the Norman rulers of Sicily on mosaicists from Greece, Byzantium, or Monte Cassino explains why the art and the imagery in their churches follow the systems of Byzantium, although these had to be modified to fit a different form of church design. For instance, in the Cappella Palatina, Palermo, the abbreviated 12th-century mosaic cycle on three sides of a deep niche has an *Annunciation*, a *Nativity* with worshipping shepherds, the *Adoration of the Magi*, *Joseph's dream*, and the *Flight into Egypt*, and then continues with the *Life of Christ*. This can be explained by the importance of the feasts which commemorate the events, but it also stresses the Annunciation to the Shepherds and the visit of the Magi as defining Christ's mission as the Messiah both to the Jews and the Gentiles. The cathedral at Monreale, Sicily, has a mosaic narrative cycle of *c.*1185 which begins with the *Angel appearing to Zechariah*, continues with the *Annunciation* to Mary, the *Visitation*, the *Nativity of Christ* with the arrival of the shepherds, the *Presentation of Christ in the Temple*, and *Christ among the Doctors*, the *Magi*, and the *Marriage at Cana*, following the Gospels of SS Luke and John, and then continues with the *Life of Christ*, until the Virgin returns to stand beneath the cross, to receive her Son's body when He is lowered from the cross, and to assist at His entombment. She stands centrally in the scene of the *Ascension*, although she is not mentioned in the Gospels as being present, and she is not named among the group of Apostles at the scene of *Pentecost*, although the probability of her presence is suggested by Luke's statement in the Acts, that she prayed with the others in the Upper Room. The importance of the Apocrypha to the narrative, and the belief that they complement the canonical narrative, is shown by the adherence to the Gospels in the first nine incidents, and the divergence from them in those after the Crucifixion.

Narrative cycles first appeared in Italy in the mid-5th century in the mosaics in the Triumphal Arch of Sta Maria Maggiore, Rome, which include incidents from S. Luke and from the Apocrypha, and in the 7th/8th century at *Castelseprio. They became a feature of *portal sculpture in France, since most major cathedrals included a Virgin Portal, which contained the standard scenes of her Life, and often contained some of the more popular legends, such as that of the repentant deacon Theophilus whom she saved from his pact with the Devil. Scenes from the *Life of the Virgin* were also a constant feature of MS illuminations, particularly in Books of *Hours, ivories, and small gold or silver reliefs in Gospel covers. Once Franciscan influence began to play a prominent role in Marian devotion, the *Life of the Virgin* became an even more popular subject, an early example being the mid-13th-century scenes in Cimabue's frescoes in the choir of the Upper Church at Assisi. A major influence came also from the **Golden Legend*, which included so many of the legends which had grown up around the Virgin. The major narrative cycle in the West is *Giotto's long fresco sequence in the Arena Chapel, Padua, of *c.*1306, which tells the story in three rows of frescoes, starting with the story of the Virgin's parents, Joachim and Anne, continues with the *Life of the Virgin* until it merges into the *Life of Christ*, and ends with the *Last Judgement*. It is the definitive cycle in which the narrative is composed from NT and Apocryphal sources with absolute freedom, and set out with absolute clarity pictorially and with unsurpassed mastery of gesture and expression. Other major Italian cycles include those in the choir of Orvieto Cathedral by Ugolino d'Ilario, 1357–64, and the double cycle in the choir of Sta Maria Novella, Florence, by Ghirlandaio, of 1486–90, with the *Life of the Virgin* on one side and the *Life of S. John the Baptist* on the other. A later cycle is Dürer's series of woodcuts (1509–11) of the *Life of the Virgin*.

Much the largest class of images of the Virgin consists of icon-type paintings and sculpture, sometimes as a single figure, but usually with the Christ Child, the *Madonna and Child* probably being the most frequent subject in Christian art. The image of the Christ Child held by His mother, either in her arms or enthroned on her knees, is not intended as an image of tender motherhood, but is the symbol of the Incarnation, the central doctrine of Christianity, that Christ is True God and True Man. Hence in Byzantine and then in Italian art the unfailing seriousness of the Virgin's demeanour, her head covered by her *maphorion, her face grave and usually unsmiling, either looking down, or gazing at the worshipper who comes to adore the Saviour. It is only in the North, in Germany and the Netherlands in particular, that the veil became rare, often being replaced by her long golden hair held by a diadem, or by an elaborate jewelled crown. After the mid-15th century the Madonna and Child groups lost their hieratic quality, and became pious, if not actually secular, images of a loving mother cuddling her baby.

In Italy the transition to the *Madonna and Child with Saints* is an adaptation of the large-scale apsidal mosaics and paintings of church decoration to the smaller format of the *altarpiece. At first, the saints stood each in a framed compartment on either side of the main panel of the Madonna and Child, as in the complex altarpiece by Simone *Martini (1319: Pisa) where the central Madonna is accompanied by forty-three compartments of varying size each containing a half-length image of a saint. The form was slowly modified to bring the flanking saints closer, and by 1437–40, in the *Annalena altarpiece* (Florence, San Marco), Fra *Angelico abandoned divisions in the parts of the altarpiece, and placed all his saints around the central group of the *Madonna and Child*, creating the type of work known as a *Sacra Conversazione, with the figures as a single group.

Yet another class of images of the Virgin pertains to events which are distinct from her part in the narratives, and are marked by major feasts, all of which have generated works of art. The calendars of Byzantine festivals, most of which became feasts in the West, were the *Purification of the Virgin*, known in the West as *Candlemas on 2 February, which merged with the *Presentation of Christ in the Temple*, the first occasion on which He was recognized as the Messiah by Simeon and Anna; the *Annunciation on 25 March; the *dormition on 15 August, which became in the West the *Assumption and Coronation of the Virgin; the *Nativity of the Virgin* on 8 September, established in the West probably in 695, and in the East in the mid-12th century; the *Presentation of the Virgin in the Temple*, on 21 November, established in the East possibly as early as 730, certainly by 1150, and in the West by the late 14th century, but which had already been included in the *Life of the Virgin* cycle by Taddeo Gaddi in the Baroncelli Chapel in Sta Croce, Florence, as early as 1332–8; all become a normal part of cycles

m

of the *Life of the Virgin*. The *Immaculate Conception on 8 December, celebrated in England in the early 11th century, was established in the East in the 12th and made official in the West in the 14th century. This feast stressed the importance of her mother, S. Anne, and is the subject of such images as *Masaccio's *Madonna and Child with S. Anne*, and *Leonardo da Vinci's *Madonna and Child* cartoons.

Other images have been created to stress particular aspects of her cult, such as that by Nicolas Froment of *Mary in the Burning Bush* (1476: Aix-en-Provence Cath.)—the vision of Moses from Exod. 3: 2–6—in which the Virgin and Child replace God in the centre of the fire. This is a celebration of Mary's perpetual virginity, in which the burning bush left unchanged by the fire symbolizes her virginity, unaffected by the conception and birth of Christ. Other instances are the *Hortus Conclusus, and the *Holy Family in, for example, Michelangelo's *Doni Tondo* (*c.*1504: Florence, Pitti) and Raphael's *Canigiani Madonna* (*c.*1505/7: Munich). Certain devotions have also inspired works, for instance, the *Pietà, where the Virgin supports the body of her dead Son, and the *Rosary, as in *Dürer's *Madonna of the Rose Garland*, which portrays the probable origin of the devotion as a festivity originally of a confraternity in Piacenza in 1250, and which became popular also in Germany and among Catholics generally. Caravaggio's *Madonna of the Rosary* (*c.*1605: Vienna, KHM) stresses the role of the Dominicans in its spread and popularity. The feast was made official in 1571, as a commemoration of the victory over the Turkish fleet at the Battle of Lepanto. The feast of Sta Maria ad Nives was established as a commemoration of the founding of Sta Maria Maggiore (the *Liberian Basilica) in Rome, because of the Miracle of the *Snow. There are, in fact, as many images of the Madonna as her role in the Gospels, and as devotion and faith can devise. *See also* MADONNA TYPES and IMMACULATE CONCEPTION.

Mary of Egypt, Saint (d. *c.*270, or 5th cent.?), was an anchorite in the desert near the Jordan, but her story is so close to that of the *Magdalene that it may be an imitation. Her *Life* is a 7th-century narrative, popular in the East and in the West, where it was made widely known by the **Golden Legend*. She was supposed to have been an Egyptian prostitute who worked in Alexandria for seventeen years, until, at the age of 29, she decided out of curiosity to join a pilgrimage to Jerusalem, paying her passage in kind to the sailors. When she tried to enter the Basilica of the Holy Cross she found herself unable to do so, until she vowed to live chastely in the desert. On her way there she was given three pieces of silver, with which she bought three loaves, and on these she lived for forty-seven years. Her clothes fell off with age and her hair grew so that she was entirely covered by it, which can lead to a confusion with the Magdalene. In the desert she met the monk Zosimus and she walked over the Jordan to receive communion from him at Easter. He promised to return next Easter, but found her dead. She had died immediately after he left and had written a message asking him to bury her, which he did with the help of a passing lion, as also in the account of the hermit S. Paul.

It is only when she carries three loaves that she can be certainly identified, as in the wing of an altarpiece by *Memlinc (1480: Bruges, Hospital); otherwise she is easily confused with the Penitent Magdalene. Scenes from her life are fairly common, such as her receiving communion, or her burial, both in the East and in the West from the 9th century (Sta Maria Antiqua, Rome), as well as the stained glass in Chartres, Bourges, and Auxerre. A 12th-century carved capital in Toulouse, Musée des Augustins, has a series of scenes from her legend.

Mary Magdalene *See* MAGDALENE.

Masaccio (1401–28) was the greatest painter of the Florentine Early Renaissance. He was born in San Giovanni Valdarno, and moved to Florence in 1417. Nothing is known of his artistic training, but he entered the Guild in 1422. The name he is always called by is a pejorative of Maso (Tom), meaning awkward (or even bad-tempered). His fame rests on five surviving works. The first is a triptych, dated 1422, of the *Madonna and Child with Saints*, painted for the country church of San Giovenale in Cascia, and the *Madonna and Child with S. Anne*, *c.*1424/5 (both Uffizi), representing the sequence of generations, S. Anne, the Virgin's mother, the Madonna's hieratic quality as the *Theotokos, and, in the nude Child, the affirmation of His human nature.

The polyptych painted for the Carmelite church in Pisa in 1424–6 was broken up in the 16th century, and the surviving parts widely dispersed. In the central *Madonna and Child* (London, NG) the majestic Theotokos holds a very human Child, munching grapes—an allusion to the Passion—and the strong natural lighting marks the gulf between it and the charming *International Gothic of contemporary Madonnas by Gentile da Fabriano or *Masolino. It is also an example of the new interest in perspective (*see* BRUNELLESCHI), in that the halo of the Madonna is of the old-fashioned plate-like type vertically behind her head, but that of the Child hovers above His head in perspective.

The fresco of the *Trinity* (Florence, Sta Maria Novella) is recorded in early sources as 'A Crucifixion with Death below' (an allusion to the legend that Adam was buried on Golgotha, below the Cross, a conjunction of the Fall with the Redemption). It is in the traditional form of the *Seat of Mercy, but here, unusually, it is flanked by the Virgin and S. John, and the donors kneel outside the *trompe-l'œil* 'chapel', described by Vasari as 'seeming to be tunnelled into the wall', since above the group of the *Trinity* is a deep coffered ceiling. Below is a fictive altar slab and a painted sarcophagus with the skeleton lying on the top. The brilliance of the architectural setting probably also stems from Masaccio's contact with Brunelleschi, and perhaps even with *Alberti, before the latter's official return to Florence *c.*1428.

The fresco cycle in the Brancacci Chapel (Florence, Sta Maria del Carmine) was commissioned by Filippo Brancacci, who was prominent in anti-Medicean politics, and was exiled in 1436. The cycle occupies both side walls of the chapel, and the altar wall, on two levels. Some of the scenes were destroyed by a fire in the 18th century. Both Masaccio and Masolino were involved 1424–7/8. The scenes by Masaccio are the *Expulsion from Paradise*, where the naturalism of the figures is matched by the psychological insight of Adam's shamed sorrow and Eve's howl of grief, in sharp contrast with Masolino's anodyne version of the *Fall of Man*. The rest of the cycle is devoted to the history of S. Peter. The *Tribute Money* in the upper-left register established Masaccio's mastery in the construction of the narrative from Matt. 17: 24, with the figures set in a landscape in scale and in harmony with the group, and in the nobility of the figures of Christ and the Apostles. It is so natural that it is not at first realized that it is a perfect example of *Continuous Representation in that the fish with the money is being taken from the lake on the left, and the coin is being paid to the tax-collector on the right. Below the *Tribute Money* is the *Raising of the Prefect's son*, together with *S. Peter enthroned*. The story comes from the **Golden Legend*, and tells how S. Peter raised the dead child. The scene was originally surrounded by members of the Brancacci family, and only the architecture, the imposing group of S. Peter and monks of the Carmine on the right, and the group of the Prefect, S. Peter in the centre, and a few background heads are by Masaccio. The rest is by Filippino *Lippi, who repainted, *c.*1484–5, the Brancacci family portraits which the Medici had defaced. On the upper right of the altar is the *Baptism of the Neophytes*, illustrating Acts 2: 41, and lower sections on either side of the altar by Masaccio are *The Distribution of Goods*, the *Death of Ananias*, and *S. Peter's shadow healing the sick*. These scenes are from Acts 4: 32–7, and 5: 1–16. In the *Raising of Tabitha* (Acts 9: 36–41), opposite the *Tribute Money*, the work is mostly by Masolino.

In 1428 Masaccio left for Rome, possibly attracted by a commission to paint a chapel for Cardinal Branda Castiglione in San Clemente. He appears to have begun a *Crucifixion*, and some parts of it and other frescoes have been attributed to him, but not very convincingly. Masolino inherited the commission, since the Cardinal remained his patron. Masaccio is said to have died 'of poison', but this was a common verdict on anyone who died young and mysteriously. His reputation never diminished, and he is rightly considered the fountain-head of the new and vital art which developed in Florence during the next two centuries. One lost work is also important: he painted a ceremony in the courtyard of the Carmine, with the architecture of the buildings and a large crowd of men in procession. This was probably before the Brancacci Chapel, and the commission may in fact have stemmed from its success. One of the boys then being educated as an orphan by the Carmelites was Filippo *Lippi, who may even have been a 'garzone'—a studio helper—during the time that Masaccio was working there. His early work was strongly influenced by Masaccio.

Masolino (*c.*1383/4–1447?) was a Florentine painter whose career is inseparably linked with that of *Masaccio. He was not Masaccio's teacher, although he was older and outlived Masaccio. He was an *International Gothic artist and may have helped *Ghiberti with the Florentine Baptistery Doors, but he came under the influence of Masaccio while they both worked on the Brancacci Chapel frescoes. He was in Hungary in 1427, and in Rome *c.*1430, after Masaccio's death, decorating a chapel for Cardinal Branda Castiglione, for whom he also painted a series of frescoes (1435) in Castiglione Olona, near Como. By then he had reverted to the International Gothic style more congenial to him. There are two panels in London (NG) from an altarpiece for Sta Maria Maggiore in Rome, which are generally thought to show both Masaccio and Masolino working together, and which illustrate the difference in their styles.

Mass *See* EUCHARIST, SACRAMENTS.

Massacre of the Innocents *See* INNOCENTS.

Mass of Saint Giles *See* GILES.

Mater Dolorosa *See* MADONNA TYPES.

Mater Misericordiae *See* MADONNA TYPES.

m

matroneum The *matronea* were the areas of the church reserved for women. They were usually in galleries reached by staircases from the *narthex, and in Western churches are part of the *triforia. They are now rarely used. *See also* GYNAECEUM.

Matthew, Saint, *Apostle and *Evangelist (Heb. *Mathaniah*, God-given; Gk. *Matthaios*, Lat. *Matteo*). The calling of S. Matthew is narrated in his own Gospel (Matt. 9: 9–13): 'As Jesus was walking along, He saw a man called Matthew sitting at the tax-booth; and He said to him "Follow me". And he got up and followed Him.' In Mark 2: 14, and Luke 5: 27, he is named as Levi, son of Alphaeus, and in all three accounts Jesus was present at the banquet which Matthew gave, 'And as He sat at dinner in the house, many tax-collectors and sinners came and were sitting with Him and His disciples. When the Pharisees saw this they said to His disciples "Why does your teacher eat with tax-collectors and sinners?" But when He heard this He said "Those who are well have no need of a physician, but those who are sick... For I have come to call not the righteous but sinners."' The Pharisees despised tax-collectors as agents of the occupying Romans, and classed them with public sinners. S. Matthew himself was probably no more than an employee of a farmer of taxes, and in this he resembled Zacchaeus, who is mentioned in Luke 19: 1–10 as a 'sinner' with whom Christ also dined, saying to the ever critical Pharisees, 'The Son of Man came to seek out and save the lost.' S. Matthew was named by Christ as an Apostle in Mark 3: 17–18 and Luke 6: 14–16, and when he himself listed the Apostles, he describes himself (10: 2–4) as the 'tax-collector'.

S. Matthew's Apostolic mission is said to have taken him to Pontus, Syria, Macedonia, and Ethiopia where, according to a tradition recounted in the **Golden Legend*, he was killed while saying Mass. His relics are said to have been brought back to Paestum in S. Italy in 954 and taken to Salerno where, because of local strife and Saracen raids, they were so well hidden that they were not rediscovered until 1050, since when they have been enshrined in the Cathedral crypt.

S. Matthew is usually pictured as a mature bearded man and only rarely as youthful. As an Evangelist he is usually accompanied by his symbolic angel, his representative in the *Tetramorph. The earliest representation of him writing the Gospel inspired by his angel is the 6th-century mosaic in San Vitale, Ravenna, and many illustrated Gospel books from the 7th century onwards with picture pages of the Evangelists at the start of the texts include S. Matthew—notably the Book of Durrow (7th cent.: Trinity Coll., Dublin), where all the Evangelist emblems are highly stylized, the 8th-century St-Gall Gospels (Sankt Gallen), where he is writing accompanied by his angel, and the 8th-century *Lindisfarne Gospels. The vaulting of the crossing of the Upper Church of St Francis, Assisi, painted by Cimabue between 1277 and 1280, has figures of all four Evangelists (now very damaged). The large bronze statue of him on the outside of the Guild church of Orsanmichele, Florence, made by Ghiberti in 1419–22, was commissioned by the Arte del Cambio, the bankers' guild. The finest representation of S. Matthew is in the Contarelli Chapel, in San Luigi dei Francesi, Rome, where the pictures by *Caravaggio on the walls are of the *Calling of S. Matthew* and the *Martyrdom of the saint* and the altarpiece is of the *Saint inspired by an Angel to write his Gospel.* An earlier altarpiece of the same subject by the artist was rejected by the church as lacking in decorum. It was eventually in Berlin, where it is said to have been destroyed in 1945 in the Second World War.

Matthias, Saint (Gk. *Matthias*), *Apostle. After the suicide of *Judas Iscariot it was necessary to choose another Apostle in his place. 'Peter stood up among the believers and said, "... For it is written in the book of Psalms 'Let another take his position'... So one of the men who have accompanied us during all the time that the Lord Jesus went... among us until the day he was taken up from us—one of these must become a witness with us to his Resurrection." So they proposed two, Joseph called Barsabbas, who was also known as Justus, and Matthias... And they cast lots for them, and the lot fell on Matthias and he was added to the eleven Apostles' (Acts 1: 15–26). S. Peter's quotation from the Psalms is not in the modern text (Ps. 69: 25) which only says 'May their camp be a desolation, and let no one live in their tents.' His election to the mission which Judas had betrayed is the only mention of S. Matthias in the NT; nothing more is known of him. He is often confused with S. Matthew and given the same attributes as the Evangelist. He is presumed to have been martyred, but confusion with S. Matthew results in the place being named as Ethiopia, though Jerusalem is more likely. Legend says that he was stoned for his rejection of Jewish Law, and killed finally by having his head cut off. His relics are said to be in Sta Maria Maggiore, Rome, and in Trier, Germany. Although rarely represented, he appears in two 13th-century Roman mosaics, in Sta Maria Maggiore and San Paolo fuori, and in a 10th-century fresco in the crypt (once the 5th-cent. church) of San Chrysogano, Rome. He also figures in a panel attributed to *Masolino (London, NG) which came from Sta Maria Maggiore. One of the few works with scenes from his life is the 16th-century polyptych by Barend van Orley which shows a ray of light shining on him during his election, as recorded in his legend, and also his martyrdom (Vienna, KHM, and Brussels).

Maurice, Saint, and the Theban Legion. The martyrdom of S. Maurice and his companions is first mentioned *c*.450–5 by Eucherio, Bishop of Lyons, and amended in a 9th-century version. According to Eucherio, Maurice and his companions were soldiers in the Theban Legion sent by the Emperor Maximian to subdue a revolt by the Bagaudi tribe in Gaul and also to kill any Christians in the area. When Maurice, who was the principal officer of the Legion, and his men, who were Christians, discovered that they were to kill Christians, they refused to obey. The Emperor, infuriated by their mutiny, ordered a decimation which proved useless, as did a second one, whereupon he ordered the decapitation of the entire Legion, which Eucherio said was 6,600 men. Their bodies were recovered by Bishop Theodore of Octodurum (now Martigny) and reburied in a basilica at Agauno (now St-Maurice-en-Valais; both places are in Switzerland). It is historically correct that Maximian gathered an army in Italy in 286 to subdue the Bagaudi, which crossed the St Bernard pass and was stationed at Agauno about sixty miles from Geneva. A Theban Legion is a known part of the Roman army and in the 4th century was in Egypt, where it was probably recruited. What most probably happened was that a number of men in the Theban Legion (and perhaps others also) who were Christians refused to take part in a pagan sacrifice and that Maximian made an example of them, first by two decimations, and when they proved futile, executed them all. No Legion ever numbered 6,600—many were not even half that—and the executed men were probably a cohort perhaps of 500, though the number of men to a cohort varied considerably. There was a Gallo-Roman burial ground near Martigny, and Theodore was Bishop of Octodurum in 380, already a century after the event, and it is possible that he transferred remains from there to Agauno, giving the Theban Legion a new life as mass martyrs.

The saint was very popular in Germany, and because the Theban Legion came from Egypt, he generally appears as black. There are two statues of S. Maurice in Magdeburg cathedral. Hans Baldung Grien, in his *Adoration of the Magi* (1507: Berlin) depicts him as black, and in attendance on a black Melchior, and in a Grünewald altarpiece (1521–5: Munich) he is also painted as a black saint. A woodcut by Dürer (1497), known as the *Martyrdom of the Ten Thousand*, is particularly horrific and gruesome, but the best known and finest treatment of the story is the El Greco (1582: Escorial), commissioned by Philip II. El Greco painted S. Maurice and his companions as white, and shows them in discussion, nobly indifferent to their fate, while the martyrdoms proceed behind them. Philip disliked the picture.

Maximian, the throne of, is a large high-backed wooden chair covered with elaborately carved ivory plaques with narrative reliefs, framed in deep borders of reliefs with vine trellises inhabited by animals. In the centre of the upper front border is a monogram, interpreted as that of Maximian, bishop and viceroy of *Ravenna, 546–56. The throne was probably made in 547 as a gift by the Emperor Justinian for the dedication of the church of San Vitale, Ravenna, in that year. The carved panels on the front of the chair represent S. John the Baptist between the four Evangelists. The other subjects are the story of Joseph, and the Life of Christ, one of the most complete narratives beginning with the Annunciation and making extensive use of the picturesque details provided by the *Apochryphal Gospel of the Protevangelium of James.

Of the original thirty-nine reliefs of the Life of Christ only twenty-seven have survived, and these do not now carry the narrative further than the *Entry into Jerusalem*. The arguments over the origin of the throne have been fuelled by the variations between the reliefs, which display marked difference in their approach to late Hellenistic style crossed with a new Christian directness. It may have been made in either Constantinople or Alexandria, more logically in the former. It is the only surviving Early Christian throne of its kind, restored badly in 1884, again in 1919 when reliefs recovered from other collections were restored to it, and the restoration finally completed in 1956.

The throne is said to have been given by the Doge of Venice in 1001 to the Emperor Otto III, who restored it to Ravenna. It now stands in the Chapel of St Peter Chrysologus (also called the Oratory of St Andrew) in the archiepiscopal palace.

Meditationes Vitae Christi (Lat. Meditations on the Life of Christ) This book was, with the **Golden Legend*, one of the most important sources of Western Christian iconography in the later Middle Ages. Traditionally, its author was *S. Bonaventura, but from the 19th century it was ascribed to the 'Pseudo-Bonaventura' and then to Johannes de Caulibus, an Italian *Franciscan friar. The author was certainly a Franciscan, writing for a Franciscan nun—probably called Cecilia—as the whole book is inspired by the simple, rather sentimental, piety of the early Franciscans. Recently it has been suggested that Johannes de Caulibus died *c.*1270 and the *Meditationes* were not written until about 1300/20; but the new Franciscan approach is undeniable and was the cause of its immense popularity and influence on the arts. *Ludolf of Saxony's *Vita Christi* derives directly from it, and the *Revelations* of *S. Bridget of Sweden are similar and had almost equal influence in N. Europe.

There are 100 meditations arranged in chronological order from the decision in Heaven to send a Redeemer, through the Annunciation and Life of Christ to the Ascension and Pentecost. Most of the material is derived from the NT, but greatly expanded with details from earlier *Apocryphal literature and from the author's imagination. Some meditations are invented, as in the story of Christ's appearance to His mother on the morning of the Resurrection, which became a popular subject for paintings, though entirely without scriptural authority. Many details were designed to arouse pity, and others to interest the woman for whom the book was written—hence much concerning the life and feelings of Mary, especially in descriptions of the Passion (cf. *Stations of the Cross, a Franciscan devotion). Much of the text is derived from sermons by *S. Bernard of Clairvaux, and in turn was taken over by Ludolf, but the author's own visual imagination is seen in details such as the description of the Deposition (Meditation 81): 'Two ladders are placed on opposite sides of the cross. Joseph (of Arimathaea) ascends the ladder on the right and tries to extract the nail from His right hand . . . The nail pulled out, John makes a sign to Joseph . . . Nicodemus extracts the other nail from the left hand and similarly gives it to John. Nicodemus descends and comes to the nail in the feet. Joseph supported the body of the Lord: happy indeed is this Joseph, who deserves thus to embrace the body of the Lord! Then the Lady reverently receives the hanging right hand and places it against her cheek . . . The nail in the feet pulled out, Joseph descends part way, and all receive the body of the Lord and place it on the ground. The Lady supports the head and shoulders in her lap, the Magdalene the feet . . . '

This sense of immediacy appealed to painters, many of whom followed his descriptions closely. In N. Europe Ludolf's version was more popular, the *Meditationes* being more favoured in Italy.

Melchior is one of the *Magi.

Melchisedek (Melchisedech) The OT says little about him, but that little is important. After the Battle of the Valley of Sidim (now the Dead Sea) between rival kings of the area, King Chedorlaomer of Elam and his allies sacked Sodom and captured Lot,

Abram's nephew. When Abram, living by the Oaks of Mamre, heard about Lot's fate, he summoned all his men, pursued Chedorlaomer and defeated him, liberating Lot, his family, and all his goods. After the battle, he was met in the Valley of Shaveh (the King's Valley) by King Melchisedek of Salem, the ancient Canaanite priest-king of Jerusalem. He blessed Abram and said 'Blessed be Abram by God Most High, maker of Heaven and earth . . .'. And Abram gave him a tenth of all the spoils (Gen. 14: 8–20). The Valley of Shaveh lies probably west of the Dead Sea, where ran the ancient trade route of the King's Highway.

In Ps. 110: 4 (Vg. 109), are the lines: 'The Lord has sworn and will not change His mind, "You are a priest forever according to the order of Melchisedek."' These passages were used by S. Paul in the Epistle to the Hebrews (5: 5–10; 6: 20; 7: 1, 15–17, 20–5) as evidence that Christ, who offered the sacraments of bread and wine, was a priest of the order of Melchisedek, and thus superseded the priesthood of Aaron and the Levites. To this day, the words are part of the Ordination to the Priesthood in the Catholic Church.

The earliest representation of the sacrifice of Melchisedek is in the 5th-century Moses cycle in Sta Maria Maggiore, Rome, and the next in date is in one of the 6th-century lunette mosaics in San Vitale, Ravenna, where two sacrifices pleasing to God, those of Abel and Melchisedek, are shown beneath the Hand of God. The Klosterneuberg Altar of 1181 by Nicholas of Verdun contains a scene of the crowned Melchisedek making his offering beneath the blessing Hand of God. The scene also appears in the 13th-century sculptured scenes on the inner west front of Reims Cathedral, and in Dieric Bouts's sacrament altar of the *Mystic Meals (1468: Leuven, St Pieter).

Memento mori (Lat.) is an imperative injunction to 'Remember that you must die'. Its main emblem is a skull, hence its frequent appearance in pictures of saints, particularly penitent ones, such as SS Jerome and Mary Magdalene. It often figures in pictures of saints meditating, such as S. Francis. During the 18th and 19th centuries, the custom arose of wearing mourning rings, commemorating a dead relative or friend. These usually had a picture of a tomb, or an urn, and though a less urgent reminder, recalling a dead person to mind was a reminder to the wearer of the same inevitable end.

Pictures of *S. Jerome* often have extra attributes, as in the engraving by Dürer (1514), where he sits at his desk writing, with his lion near by, and about the room are a skull, an hour-glass, a candle, all traditional emblems of mortality. In two pictures by Zurbarán of *S. Francis meditating*, the saint holds a skull (1639 and undated: London, NG). A Titian (*c.*1552: Milan, Brera) depicts *S. Francis* with an hour-glass and a skull, and another Titian (*c.*1565: St Petersburg) of *The penitent Magdalene* shows her holding a skull. The grim fresco of *The Triumph of Death* by ?Traini (*c.*1360: Pisa, Campo Santo) depicts a noble cavalcade passing three decomposing corpses in open coffins, with one horrified rider holding his nose. The corpses 'speak', with labels saying 'As you are, so once were we. Thus you will be', 'Rich must die as well as poor', and 'None escapes death'. The damaged wall-paintings of *Doom* (The Last Judgement) so frequently found in English medieval churches, over the choir arch or on the west wall, were intended as reminders of the transience of human life. (*See also* VANITAS, and DANCE OF DEATH.)

Memlinc, Hans (*c.*1430/40–94), came from Seligenstadt, near Frankfurt, and may have received his early training in Cologne before entering Roger van der *Weyden's workshop, *c.*1459/60. He settled in Bruges after Roger's death and by the time he died there he had had a very successful career painting placid, devotional pictures and diptych portraits. One of his earliest works, painted *c.*1470, is a triptych of the *Adoration of the Magi* in which the central panel and the wing with the *Presentation* (Prado) are clearly adapted from the Roger *Adoration* (Munich) which was originally in St Columba's church in Cologne, where he probably saw it. He has nothing of Roger's imaginative power, neither was he averse to repeating himself, since virtually the same composition is used in the *Adoration of the Magi* altarpiece (Bruges, Hospital Mus.) of 1479. In his *Crucifixion* altarpiece with double wings (Lübeck, Mus.) the fainting Virgin and the grief-stricken Magdalene are lost in the crowd of onlookers and 'extras' and his keen eye for detailed portrayal of the incidental figures swamps the central tragic event. For Roger, the Crucifixion was a meditative subject, concentrating on the Sacrifice and never including the two thieves; Memlinc takes up the older, Byzantine, tradition of van *Eyck and the Master of Flémalle where the thieves do not suffer the same form of crucifixion as

Christ, but are tied to their crosses. The enlargement of the subject decreases its impact.

Other major works include the *Last Judgement* (Gdańsk, Mus. Pomorskie) which was commissioned by Jacopo Tani, the Medici agent in Bruges, and was on its way to Italy in 1473 in a ship belonging to Tommaso Portinari when it was captured by pirates from Danzig (now called Gdańsk) and given by them to hang in St Mary's, Danzig. In many details it follows the pattern of Roger's Beaune *Last Judgement*, except that Memlinc returns to the older system of S. Michael weighing souls: the soul of the damned rises—'is found wanting' in the words of Daniel (5: 27)—and the soul of the just man sinks. In this case, he is a portrait of Portinari, of whom Memlinc also painted a separate portrait. The outside wings have grisaille simulations of statues of the Virgin and Child and S. Michael defeating Devils, with superb donor portraits of Tani and his wife.

The *Lamentation* triptych (Bruges, Hospital Mus.) of *c*.1480, also depends on models set by Roger, but does not rise above quiet piety; it has wings containing one of the rare images of 'Saint' *Wilgefortis. He also produced a large number of *Virgin enthroned with Saints* with or without donors (London, NG; Vienna, KHM; Bruges, Hospital), all with the same stereotyped design and brilliant handling of detail. He also followed Roger in devotional diptychs, combining the sitter in prayer in one wing with a Virgin and Child in the other. The finest of these is the diptych of *Martin van Nieuwenhove* (1484: Bruges, Hospital). The *Shrine of S. Ursula* (*see* URSULA) (Bruges, Hospital), dedicated in 1489, is a reliquary in the form of a small church, made of very delicately carved and gilded wood. The front has a panel of the *Virgin and Child* with the donors, two nuns from the Hospital; the rear panel is of *S. Ursula* sheltering a group of diminutive figures of her eleven thousand virgins beneath her cloak. Each side has three small pictures depicting the affecting legend of the pilgrim saint and her companions. The panels depicting the pilgrims in Cologne have views of the city, complete with the choir of the cathedral and the beginning of one of the towers with the famous crane which remained perched on it for the next four centuries, and a large church clearly intended for Gross St Martin.

memoria *See* MARTYRIUM.

Mendicant Orders, churches The Mendicant Orders (Lat. *mendicans*, begging) arose in the early 13th century, the two most famous being the *Franciscans and the *Dominicans. Unlike monks, mendicant *friars lived by begging their bread in towns, instead of living in settled communities in the countryside. Friars took vows of poverty, chastity, and obedience; and the vow of poverty meant that they could own nothing, either individually or—originally—as a community. Again unlike the monastic Orders, they were not bound to live in one place, but could move from town to town on preaching missions. At first this caused considerable hostility from the bishops and parish clergy, but in 1256 Pope Alexander IV allowed the friars to continue. They were so successful that the original Franciscans and Dominicans were soon followed by the Carmelites (1245) and the Augustinian hermits (1256). Later Orders were the Servites (1424) and several other smaller ones.

Preaching formed an important part of their mission to the towns and they attracted much support, so that they began to build 'mendicant churches'—large open halls in the new Gothic style, with particular attention to acoustics. They were mainly responsible for the introduction of Gothic forms into Italy, late in the 13th century and early in the 14th. By a curious quirk, they were much patronized by rich families, such as the Bardi and Peruzzi bankers in Florence, and the chapels of these families were decorated by the greatest artists of the day—Giotto, in the case of the Bardi and Peruzzi. Among the most famous of their churches are Sta Croce (Franciscan) and Sta Maria Novella (Dominican), both in Florence; San Domenico and San Francesco in Bologna; SS Giovanni e Paolo (Dominican) and the Frari (Franciscan) in Venice, and Sta Maria sopra Minerva (Dominican), the only genuine Gothic church in Rome.

'Mene, mene . . .' *See* BELSHAZZAR.

menologion (Gk. from 'month' and 'word') A *menologion* is a liturgical book used in the Eastern Church. It contains the lives of the saints, arranged as a monthly sequence beginning from the start of the ecclesiastical year in September. Several types of books are grouped under this umbrella heading. They include a *menaion*, one of the twelve liturgical books containing parts of the Divine Office, varying from month to month, and corresponding to the 'Proper' of the Mass in the

Western Church; a *synaxarion*, containing an account of the saint or the feast being commemorated on that day; and a book listing the feasts of the day and their appropriate biblical readings. The most famous *menologion* is that made for the Emperor Basil II sometime after 979 (now Vatican Lib.). It is in fact a *synaxarion* following the usage in Constantinople, and the surviving parts run from September to the end of February. It is a lavish book with 430 illustrations on gold grounds, and seventeen miniatures without texts, two of them without titles. The book has been designed so that each illustration occupies half a page and the text is limited to only sixteen lines. The miniatures illustrate, with great artistic skill and with backgrounds of elaborate architecture and beautiful landscapes, such subjects as prophets, the translation of relics, and saints whose horrific martyrdoms are graphically depicted.

The importance of the illustrations in this MS is that they represent an early version of a Christian cycle, which was extensively revised during the Macedonian Renaissance of the 12th to 14th centuries, as exemplified in Daphni (*c.*1100), and in the Church of Christ in Chora (Kariye Camii), Constantinople, of 1310.

menorah (Heb.) A *menorah* is a seven-branched lamp used in the Sanctuary in the wilderness during the Jewish exodus from Egypt. Detailed instructions for its manufacture, its material (pure gold), and its form, for the snuffers and trays, for the olive oil which it burnt, the daily attendance on it, are all laid down in Exod. 25: 31–6; 27: 20; 30: 21; Lev. 24: 2; and Num. 8: 2–4. S. John saw a vision of seven golden lampstands, which Christ said represented the seven Churches (of Asia) (Rev. 1: 12, 20; 2: 5). The *menorah*, which remained alight all night in the Sanctuary, is the ancestor of the sanctuary lamp which burns all the time before the tabernacle containing the Blessed Sacrament in all Catholic churches and in some very High-Church Anglican ones. The word is also used to describe any seven-branched candlestick.

The most celebrated representation of the *menorah* is in a relief inside the Arch of Titus, in the Roman Forum, commemorating the Emperor's triumph after the fall of Jerusalem in 70. Among the treasures being carried by the soldiers are the *menorah*, the Table for the Shewbread, and the silver trumpets from the Temple.

The *menorah* is the most common symbol of Judaism.

mensa *See* ALTAR.

Mercedarians are a Spanish mendicant religious Order dedicated to the care of the sick; it was originally founded to help in the redemption of Christian prisoners of the Moors. Besides the usual religious vows of chastity, poverty, and obedience, the friars took a fourth vow—that of offering themselves as hostages for those whom they redeemed from captivity. They are said to have been founded by S. Peter Nolasco *c.*1220/5, and their Rule was written by the jurist S. Raymond de Penafort. They spread rapidly through Europe, and some Mercedarian friars accompanied Columbus on his voyages of discovery, and stayed to found houses in Latin America. An Order of Mercedarian nuns was founded in Seville in 1568, but both Orders have declined in modern times, and though the fourth vow is still taken, the Order is now devoted to the care of the sick.

Little is known of S. Peter Nolasco's life (1189–1256), but a late tradition states that he was a Crusader against the Moors in Spain, and that he redeemed many Christians captured by Moors in Valencia and Granada, which were then part of Moorish Spain. They wear a white habit and a hooded cloak, and a *scapular on their chests.

Many Mercedarians were martyred, perhaps the most striking being S. Serapion, an English Crusader with King Richard I, Lionheart, who was imprisoned with him in Austria in 1192–4. He became a Mercedarian in 1222 and ransomed many Christians until, when he was a hostage in Algeria, he was martyred with appalling barbarity in 1240. *Zurbarán painted many portraits of Mercedarians, including a haunting *S. Serapion martyred* (1628: Hartford, Conn.) which with great art conceals the full horror of his death.

Mercy, Madonna of (Mater Misericordiae) *See* MADONNA TYPES.

Mercy, Works of There are seven corporal works of mercy: to feed the hungry, to give drink to the thirsty, to clothe the naked, to visit the sick, to visit prisoners, to harbour strangers, and to bury the dead. In Matt. 25: 34–45, Christ lists all these works except burying the dead, and ends His parable with the words, 'just as you did it to one of the least of these who are members of my family, you did it to me'. In Tobit 12: 13, when the Archangel Raphael reveals his identity to Tobit, he says 'when you did not hesitate to get up and leave your dinner to go and bury the dead', this reference to the seventh work of mercy being the OT completion of Christ's NT list.

An ivory relief in the Psalter of Queen Melisande (1131/4: Basle Lib.) and the reliefs by Antelami on the west portal of Parma Baptistery (1196) are among the early representations of the subjects. A cross-shaped *Last Judgement* (1235/40: Vatican) has six of the works of mercy below a Last Judgement, and this conjunction of the two subjects is frequent. A painting of all seven works by the workshop of Teniers II (*c.*1630/40: Dulwich) shows them performed in an everyday setting in the Netherlands by townspeople, and in an altarpiece (1490/1500: anon., Antwerp) each of the works is performed by specific persons, with Christ Himself as a witness: Isaiah feeding the hungry, S. Willibrod giving drink to the thirsty, Abraham sheltering strangers, S. Elizabeth of Hungary clothing the naked, S. Catherine of Siena tending the sick, S. Martin visiting prisoners, and S. Louis burying the dead. The same system was used by H. R. Hoffman in the chancel reliefs (1570: Trier Cath.). In the Church of the Misericordia, Naples, is a Caravaggio of 1607, of all seven works of mercy, with the rare classical subject of *Roman Charity*—the daughter breast-feeding her imprisoned father, sentenced to starve to death—for feeding the hungry. In the chapel of the Hospitál de la Caridád, Seville, the marble altarpiece by Pedro Roldàn of the *Entombment of Christ* depicts burying the dead, and the six other works (1668) are by Murillo, with instances from the OT and NT: *The Miracle of the Loaves and Fishes*, for feeding the hungry, *Moses striking the Rock*, for drink for the thirsty, *S. Elizabeth of Hungary tending the sick* (all in the Hospital), *Abraham and the Angels*, for hospitality to strangers (Ottawa), *Liberation of S. Peter*, for visiting prisoners (Hermitage), *Christ healing the Paralytic at the Pool of Bethesda* (London, NG), and *The return of the Prodigal Son*, for clothing the naked (Washington, NG).

Mercy-Seat *See* SEAT OF MERCY.

Messiah (Messias) is the Hebrew for 'the Anointed One', translated into Greek as *Christ (Christos). For centuries the Jews had awaited the coming of the Messiah, hence the importance of Peter's recognition of Jesus—'You are the Messiah, the Son of the living God' (Matt. 16: 16) and the High Priest's question to Jesus: 'tell us if you are the Messiah, the Son of God'. Jesus said to him 'You have said so...' (Matt. 26: 63–4). In Mark 14: 61–2, Jesus's answer is forthright, 'I am', and He continues with the words which provoked the High Priest to condemn Him for blasphemy.

mestizo A term related to indigenousness, but referring more specifically to a creative mix of races and classes in Mexican culture, more pronounced there than in the United States or Canada. It is also helpful in describing the art produced by the dynamics of class and by the mixing of high and popular art, secular and religious, that is a significant part of the history of all of North America. *See also* NORTH AMERICA.

metatorium *See* DIACONICON.

Mexican art *See* NORTH AMERICA.

Mexican muralists A significant movement in the 20th-century painters who helped to establish a public aesthetic of social progress and defining nationalism while drawing on the history, religious life, and folk traditions of Mexico. Towering figures in the movement included Diego Rivera, Jose Clemente Orozco, and David Alfaro Siqueiros. *See also* LATIN AMERICA, NORTH AMERICA.

MHP.ΘY is a Gk. abbreviation of *Meter Theou, Mother of God* (*see* THEOTOKOS) and, as a symbol, is found on most *icons of the Virgin and Child. Sometimes other words are added, defining the type of the Virgin. *See also* MADONNA TYPES.

Michael, the Archangel *See* ANGELS.

Michelangelo Buonarroti (1475–1564). His reputation as the most brilliant sculptor of his day was established at the age of 25 by the *Pietà* in St Peter's, in which he solved the aesthetic problem of placing the body of the crucified Christ across the knees of His grieving mother by converting her voluminous draperies into a podium to support His body and disguise the clumsiness of placing a full-grown man across the knees of a woman. The group combines the Germanic iconography of the *Pietà* (stipulated by the French cardinal who commissioned it) with a Hellenistic treatment of form. He was then variously employed in his native Florence in carving the gigantic *David* (1501–4) and the roughly blocked-in *S. Matthew* (begun 1504 as the first of a series of Apostles for the cathedral, but never finished; both now in Florence, Accademia), and on a cartoon (later destroyed) for a battle piece for the Palazzo della Signoria. He was summoned to Rome by Pope Julius II, who in 1506 commissioned from him a tomb which proved to be the burden and tragedy of his life. Its truncated remains were finally erected in 1545–6 (Rome, San Pietro in Vincoli), incorporating the grandiose *Moses* of 1516, the only part entirely by his hand (the two figures of *Leah* and *Rachel*, personifying the Active and the Contemplative Life, were designed by him; assistants executed most of the work, and he finished them).

The most outstanding painting of the first part of his life, from 1508 to 1512, is the vault of the *Sistine Chapel in the Vatican. In it are set out in images of unforgettable imaginative power the history of the world from the Creation to the Sacrifice of Noah after the Flood, in a sequence of four large and five smaller panels, together with the vividly characterized figures of seven Prophets and five Sibyls who prophesied the coming and the fate of the Messiah. Around the frame of each of the five smaller histories are the four figures of the *Ignudi*, or nude athletes (of the original twenty, one is almost totally lost, though known from engravings). The function of these figures, which serve both to separate the histories from one another and from the Prophets and Sibyls below, has always been argued about and variously interpreted. They appear to have the practical role of serving as a transitional stage from the far larger figures below them to the smaller scale of the histories, and the aesthetic function of expressing through their celebration of ideal male beauty the splendour of God's creative power.

Below the Ceiling proper, in the spandrels and lunettes over the windows, are represented the Ancestors of Christ—those who 'walk in darkness' and are the ancestors of those who will eventually 'see a great light' (Isa. 9: 2). The corner elements, composed of double spandrels, contain scenes of God's miraculous saving interventions: *David and Goliath, Moses and the Brazen Serpent, Esther's plea for her people against the conspiracy of Haman*, and *Judith victorious over Holofernes*. The Sistine Ceiling is the iconographic culmination of the existing decoration on the walls below: the opposition of the Lives of Moses and Christ, the Old Dispensation and the New, painted in 1481–2 by a team of painters including Botticelli, Ghirlandaio, and Perugino, and eventually the tapestries designed by *Raphael (1516 onwards) to hang on the walls of the lowest area of the Chapel. Seen as a whole, they completed the religious sequence from the Creation to the mission of the Apostles for the conversion of the world, the decoration of the Chapel forming a coherent and carefully planned exposition of Genesis, Exodus, the Gospels, and the Acts of the Apostles, together with the authors of the relevant prophecies.

Recent cleaning of the Ceiling reveals that the colours are close to those of the 1481–2 series immediately below—that is, they have the same limpidity and brightness that one normally finds in 15th-century frescoes, while the forms of the figures and the conception have the amplitude and grandeur which are Michelangelo's special contribution to 16th-century art. Many years later, Michelangelo was given the task of painting the altar wall with a huge representation of the *Last Judgement*. While the Ceiling is the natural transition stylistically from the early *Pietà* and the *David* to the style he developed in the Medici Chapel (Florence, San Lorenzo, 1520–34), the *Last Judgement* (1536–41) shows that his art had undergone a complete change. He is no longer concerned with pure beauty of form, but uses the human nude to express the most profound spiritual experience. The trumpeting angels summon the dead to resurrection from their graves on the left side of the wall, and they swirl upwards to judgement before the majestic but minatory Christ, surrounded by the martyred saints, whose cry for justice is expressed by the display of the instruments of their terrible deaths. The just are welcomed among the elect, the unjust are driven in descending spirals on the right side towards the devils who drag them to Hell. In a vivid image, taken from Dante, Charon, with eyes glowing like fire, swings his oar to drive the damned from his frail bark into the pit, and—perhaps the most telling detail of all—the mouth of Hell glimmers darkly at the bottom immediately over the altar, on which stands the traditional crucifix, the emblem of Faith and Salvation standing between Mankind and perdition.

Michelangelo was now in his sixties, and had abandoned Florence for Rome for good in 1534; age and the aftermath of the horrors which had befallen Rome in the Sack of 1527, and Florence in the siege and capitulation of

1529–31, which he had personally experienced, had changed for good the character of his art, which now reflects deep pessimism and disillusion, a state of mind reinforced by the unending troubles over the Julius Tomb. The *Last Judgement* was not only acclaimed as a masterpiece by the artists of Rome; it was also bitterly criticized, vilified, by powerful and influential religious reformers—which, even more painful, included many of his friends—because of the number and character of the nudes it contained. The open religious climate which had enabled him to do virtually the same thing on the Ceiling, had now narrowed down to a carping prudery, so that successive popes were urged to destroy it, or to 'clothe' the offending nudities. It was, however, felt to be inexpedient, if not actually ungrateful, to mutilate his masterpiece while still depending upon him for the building of St Peter's, so that the repainting of parts of the *Last Judgement* was left until after his death. Most of the offending loincloths have now been removed.

Further instances of this change in the character of his art are offered by the contrasts between his early and later treatment of the theme of the Madonna and Child: in the difference between the *Bruges Madonna* of *c.*1503/5 (Bruges, Notre-Dame), the *Medici Madonna* of *c.*1525, and the cartoon of the *Virgin and Child with S. Joseph and other figures* (London, BM) made for Condivi to use for his picture of the same subject in 1553; and also the extreme contrast between the St Peter's *Pietà* and the late one which he intended for his own tomb (1550–5; Florence, Mus. dell'Opera).

His last works in painting were two frescoes in the Cappella Paolina, Pope Paul III's private chapel in the Vatican (1545–50), of the *Crucifixion of S. Peter* and the *Conversion of S. Paul*. Both contain groups of massive figures in circulatory movement, such as he had used in the *Last Judgement*, but with increased emphasis on the elements of horror and dread, particularly in the figure of S. Peter, who rears himself from his cross to glare out at the spectator with menacing force, while in both pictures the onlookers are characterized by attitudes and expressions of oppressive dread.

Michelangelo's work in architecture, which began with the abortive project for a façade for San Lorenzo, in Florence, continued with the Medici funerary chapel in San Lorenzo, Florence (the 'New Sacristy', 1519–34), with the tombs of two insignificant Medici dukes, with their splendid sculpture, and an abandoned project for a double tomb for 'the two *Magnifici*'—Lorenzo and his brother, Giuliano, murdered in the Pazzi conspiracy of 1478. It culminated in his achievements at St Peter's on which he worked from 1547 until his death seventeen years later. He was adamant in his refusal to entertain any other form than the central plan as the only one truly expressive of the Oneness and Perfection of God. The parallel theme of the burial-place of S. Peter as a martyrium was first set out by *Bramante in 1506, but jeopardized by proposals for the more traditional long-nave basilica put forward by Raphael, and then again by Antonio da *Sangallo's misguided amalgam of the two forms by his addition of a second smaller central space tacked on to the larger one. Though Michelangelo and Bramante cordially detested each other, Michelangelo never wavered in his declaration that 'who departs from Bramante departs from the truth'. The portions which were built under his control are the three huge apses which constitute the north, south, and west parts (St Peter's has a reverse orientation), and he also designed a dome which he wished to build as a pure hemisphere, despite the increased stress this would have imposed on the supporting structure. A hemispherical dome, though of entirely differing design, was planned by Bramante as an expression of the idea that the major church of Christendom should be crowned by the purest architectural form. Michelangelo also felt strongly the idea of the 'restoration' of Early Christian Rome absorbing the grandeur of classical Roman antiquity. In the event, the dome built after his death has an elliptical, and therefore higher, and more stable form—perhaps fortunately so, in that the later extension of the eastern arm to form a long nave (1607–12, by *Maderno) enables it in some measure to override the disadvantage of being too low when seen from the piazza in front of the basilica.

Michelangelo's architectural triumph lies in his being the only man of his time who was able to grasp that the translation of the huge spaces of the ground-plan demanded a construction with equally bold and massive structural elements. He worked for nothing, giving his services until extreme old age and increasing frailty prevented his visiting the site, but continuing to advise and oversee the work until his death. He was also fortunate that successive popes recognized his ability, his honesty, his single-minded devotion to the task, and supported him in his vision.

Milan became a Roman city called Mediolanum in 222 BC, but it remained obscure until the reign of the Emperor Diocletian in the 3rd century AD, when it became an imperial residence until 404. Its history is closely linked with the early years of the Church, and it is famous for the Edict of Milan (see below) of 313. The episcopate of *S. Ambrose (374–97) saw the building of many Early Christian churches, including Sant'Ambrogio, San Lorenzo Maggiore, San Simpliciano, and the first church on the site of the later Sant'Eustorgio. There were also three 5th-century churches, but, with one exception, these churches preserve no trace of their early origin, except in the survival of their plans, which were basilical with nave, aisles, and an apsidal east end. San Lorenzo is the exception, in that it was a domed centrally planned church, with an imposing forecourt constructed with reused Roman Corinthian columns, of which sixteen are still *in situ*. It has three small attached centrally planned chapels, all differently shaped; Sant'Aquilino (where S. Ambrose baptized *S. Augustine in 387), Sant'Ippolito, also of the 4th century, and San Sisto of the 5th century, and only in these is there visible evidence of their original construction, particularly in Sant'Aquilino, where the font has been excavated. The chapel also has important mosaics of the 4th/5th century, including one of Christ as *Sol Invictus. San Lorenzo was rebuilt in the 12th century, and again in 1573, and it is difficult at first sight to perceive its great antiquity under its 16th-century reconstruction.

In the 5th century, barbarian incursions forced the removal of the court of the Empire of the West to a new site in the Adriatic marshlands, and *Ravenna became the new imperial capital. Milan became the prey of successive waves of barbarian invaders, who reduced it to ruin, though some revival came with the Lombards who conquered most of Italy from 568 onwards, except for Rome and areas still held by the Byzantines in the extreme south. In the 8th century the Lombards occupied Ravenna briefly, but an alliance between the papacy and the newly established power of the Franks led to the eventual destruction of Lombard power achieved by Charlemagne in 773. The 10th-century Ottonian emperors concentrated civic and religious power in the archbishops, but in the mid-12th century a movement towards the establishment of a Commune in Milan led to continual strife between nobles and populace. Although there was nominal acceptance of the imperial overlordship, Frederick Barbarossa determined to reassert his dominion, and besieged Milan in 1158 and 1162, rendering it uninhabitable. Eventually, most of the N. Italian cities combined under the leadership of Pope Alexander III, and the first defeat of imperial troops by a citizen army was at Legnano in 1176. The Peace of Constance in 1183 gave Milan its autonomy. The most notable work undertaken after the defeat of Barbarossa was the system of canals, the Naviglio Grande, which used the river Ticino and other smaller watercourses to create a network of waterways, linking the city with Pavia, Abbiategrasso, and other towns, enabling the city to be provisioned by barge.

Most, if not all, the Early Christian churches lay in ruins. A few churches had been built in the 8th to the 11th centuries, notably San Satiro in 846, of which only one chapel survives, now annexed to Sta Maria presso San Satiro, by *Bramante, and in the 11th and 12th century the rebuilding of Sant'Ambrogio had been undertaken in a characteristic Lombard *Romanesque form. The 12th century saw a great effort of rebuilding and restoration, including that of Sant'Eustorgio, which became a Dominican church in 1227, and was vaulted by the late 13th century. The chapels on the right of the nave were all 15th-century additions, built by important local families, and at the far end of the church is the Portinari Chapel, built in 1462 for Pigello Portinari, head of the Medici Bank in Milan, by the Florentine Michelozzo, who followed the architectural precedents established in Florence by *Brunelleschi. The Chapel was designed to hold the family tombs, and also to be a better site for the Shrine, or *Arca* of *S. Peter Martyr, a huge monument with sculpture by Giovanni di Balduccio, made in 1336–9, which in scale and richness probably inspired the *Arca* of S. Dominic in Bologna.

During the 13th century the city prospered, but the appointment by Pope Urban IV (1261–4) of Ottone Visconti as archbishop in 1262 led to the city's domination by the Visconti until 1447. As rulers, they varied over the years from worthy to bloodthirsty tyrants, but under their rule the city grew and on the whole prospered, being made a dukedom by its imperial overlord.

Milan Cathedral was begun in 1386 as a joint enterprise of Duke Giangaleazzo Visconti, the diocese, and the civic authorities, who were the most active in furthering the work. Since it was built next to his palace, the

Duke envisaged it as playing the same regal and political role as Paris or Prague cathedrals, and this probably determined its Northern *Gothic design. The building history is long and chequered; no single architect was responsible, and even when one man had been appointed, others continued to submit designs. A succession of eminent architects from France and Germany were called in at various times to offer advice, but their proposals evoked bitter controversy. They disliked all they saw, and said so, thus raising the hackles of the Italians; and there were also fundamental differences about the mathematical systems used in Italy and the North. All the successive foreigners were speedily sacked, but the most interesting record is that of the disputation between the Italians and the Frenchman Jean Mignot. They countered his accusation that the rules of geometry (*scientia*) were being flouted by retorting that *scientia sine arte nihil est* (science is nothing without art), which earned the obvious rebuke that *ars sine scientia nihil est* (art is nothing without science); in other words, the Italians insisted that their experience and practice (*ars*) which included their own contested geometrical theory, would suffice. It did, although some aspects of the building are almost anti-Gothic. Despite all the predictions that it would fall down, the Milanese had a grasp of structural limits which rarely let them down, and they were building in marble, a much stronger material than the limestone of the North.

The design follows the Bourges model, though Milan has aisled transepts. The finest part of the first campaign is the choir with its three huge Rayonnant tracery windows. The great height of the nave (155 ft.) and the aisles, and the inadequacy of the clerestory and aisle windows make the church very dark, despite the late 15th-century dome, which takes the interior to 220 ft., and the tower above it to 360 ft. The outside has more than 2,000 statues, and 98 pinnacles; the west front is a 19th-century adaptation of the style of the building.

The last Visconti was followed by his son-in-law, the condottiere warrior Francesco Sforza, whose court became one of the most brilliant and cultured in Italy, particularly during the reign of Lodovico, nicknamed 'Il Moro', when both Bramante and *Leonardo da Vinci worked in Milan. Lodovico's devious policies led in 1499 to the first of the successive invasions by the French, to his own downfall, to Italy becoming a battleground between France and Spain, and to the eventual domination of the whole peninsula first by Spain and then by Austria.

The main monuments of the Sforza period were the hospital—the Ospedale Maggiore—begun by *Filarete in 1456; the Castello; Bramante's Sta Maria presso San Satiro, and his huge choir of Sta Maria delle Grazie, where Leonardo painted the *Last Supper* in the convent refectory. The gloom of the long years of Spanish and Austrian domination, beset by plague, famine, and misgovernment, were relieved temporarily by the archiepiscopates of S. Carlo *Borromeo and his nephew Cardinal Federico. These were marked by the reform of the clergy, the building of San Fedele (1569), and San Sebastiano (1577) by the city, inspired by S. Carlo, as a thank-offering after the terrible plague of 1575–6, and the creation of the Ambrosiana Library and Museum (1603–9) by Cardinal Federico. Napoleon's conquest of N. Italy, from 1796 until his final eclipse in 1814, was followed by renewed Austrian occupation, lasting until the War of Independence (1848–9), and the unification of Italy.

Milan, the Edict of ('The Peace of the Church') Sporadic persecution of the Christians from Nero onwards was mainly provoked by their refusal to sacrifice to the statue of the Genius of the Emperor, which they considered to be idolatry: martyrdom usually followed. The longest, and most severe, persecution was that of Diocletian and his co-Emperor Galerius, which lasted from 303 to 306 in the West and until 313 in the East. The text of this Edict—which does not seem to have been an Edict, and may not have been promulgated at Milan—is found in *Eusebius and Lactantius: both record that in 311 the dying Galerius issued an ordinance granting toleration to Christians 'who might again rebuild the houses in which they used to meet'.

After defeating Maxentius, *Constantine and his then co-Emperor Licinius renewed the ordinance, probably in March 313: 'When we, Constantine and Licinius, Emperors, met at Milan . . . we decided . . . that it was right that Christians and others should have freedom to follow the religion they favoured . . . We therefore announce that . . . all who choose that religion . . . are not to be in any way troubled or molested . . . Moreover, concerning the Christians, we before gave orders with respect to the places set apart for their worship . . . all who have bought such places should restore them to the Christians, without any demand for payment'. Eusebius adds: 'those who restore without seeking compensation may expect to recoup from our generosity'.

Permission to own property allowed the development of Early Christian church architecture, and the iconography of paintings in *catacombs and on carved sarcophagi became more explicitly Christian. Apart from a few years under the Emperor Julian the Apostate (361–3), there were no further persecutions.

Millais, Sir John Everett (1829–96), was a child prodigy who entered the RA Schools in 1840. There he became friendly with Holman *Hunt, and through him he met *Rossetti in 1848, as a result of which the Pre-Raphaelite Brotherhood (*see* PRB) was formed. In 1850 he exhibited *Christ in the House of his Parents* (1849; London, Tate), better known as *The Carpenter's Shop*, but by this time Rossetti had blurted out the meaning of the enigmatic letters PRB after the signature, and the disclosure provoked misunderstanding, culminating in a virulent piece of totally unjustified invective and accusation of blasphemy from, astonishingly, Dickens in his weekly paper *Household Words*. The position was saved by Ruskin, whom they did not then know; he defended and praised them in a letter to *The Times*. This turned the tide; though criticism still continued, the group of young painters found patrons.

In 1853 Millais was elected an ARA, and this marked the virtual break-up of the Brotherhood. In 1854 he married Effie Grey, whose marriage to Ruskin had been annulled in 1853, and settled into being a painter of fashionable portraits and skilfully executed but often trivial genre subjects. He never again attempted serious religious art.

Minims are an Order of Mendicant Friars, and later of nuns, founded by S. Francesco di Paola (1416–1507) in 1444, near Cosenza in Calabria. The Rule was of great austerity; they lived on a perpetual Lenten fare, with total abstinence from meat, fish, eggs, butter, cheese, and milk. They practised extreme humility, considering themselves the least of all religious Orders, hence their title Ordo Fratrum Minimorum, where the Franciscans were only Minorum. Despite the rigours of their Rule, by the early 16th century the Order flourished in Italy, France, Germany, and Spain, where the first house for enclosed nuns was founded in Seville in 1495. There was also a Third Order for the laity (active mainly in S. America), who led a slightly less austere life. The Order never penetrated into N. Europe.

Their founder was the confessor of King Louis XI of France, and his successor Charles VIII also favoured him, and S. Francesco di Paola eventually died in France. The Order suffered badly during the French Revolution when religious Orders were disbanded and expelled, and their houses confiscated during waves of anticlericalism between 1791 and 1870. It survives in Italy and Spain, where it continues its mission to the poor. Their habit is of undyed woollen cloth, with a hood and cowl, and a girdle of unbleached woollen rope.

Pictures of S. Francesco di Paola were very popular in Italy, Spain, and France, where Jean Bourdichon, who knew him, made his death-mask. Ribera (Naples, church of San Francesco); Rubens (1630–2: Dresden); Piazzetta (Rovigo); Tiepolo (Venice, Accad.); Murillo (Madrid, Prado) all painted scenes of his miracles, or showing him meditating or invoked as a thaumaturge by the sick.

A major church of the Order was built by François Mansart in Paris between 1611 and 1672, perhaps his finest church, but it was later demolished.

minster (Lat. *monasterium*, via Ger. *Münster*) was originally the name given to the church of a large monastery or house of Secular Canons (cf. COLLEGIATE). Some cathedrals still use the name, e.g. York, and Southwell, and Ulm in Germany. It is also applied to former monastic churches, now parish churches, such as Beverley and Wimborne, or in place-names such as Minster Lovell or Minster in Thanet.

Mirabilia Urbis Romae is the earliest known guide to Rome. It was written probably by a canon of St Peter's about 1130/50 to give an account of the surviving ancient monuments and the major churches of Rome, together with legends of Early Christian martyrs mixed with stories of Roman emperors. The earliest known copy in the Vatican Library is attributed to the late 12th century, because the list of popes ends with Celestine II, pope from 1191 to 1198. The title by which the book is now known was only applied to it in the 14th or 15th century. A second version, known as the *Graphia*, contains most of the original text, with the parts differently arranged; its date appears to be close to the original. Later writers used the *Mirabilia* and the *Graphia* very freely, and it was as the *Graphia* that the work entered English literature in the *Polychronicon* by Ranulf Higden, a 14th-century monk of Chester who used parts in his section on Rome. Higden's book was later printed by Caxton, who added to it to bring it up to date from 1357 to 1460. In 1450 an English Augustinian, John Capgrave, visited Rome for the Jubilee and must have had a copy of the *Mirabilia*, for after his return he wrote his *Solace of Pilgrims* in 1452, borrowing freely from the *Mirabilia*, and adding comments of his own, often less than laudatory.

The *Mirabilia* reflects the 12th-century revival of interest in the historical importance of Rome, once the capital of the known world with the surviving evidence of her past greatness, as well as her contemporary position as the seat of the papacy. As the place of martyrdom of SS Peter and Paul, Rome was also a major *pilgrimage site. So terrible had been her fate with the sacks by the Vandals in 410 and 455, continuous war, famine and plague, that the city had shrunk so that it only occupied a tiny area within the original Roman walls, the rest being given up to vineyards, pasture for cattle and goats, market gardens, and uninhabited waterless wastes. Earlier visitors recorded their dismay and grief at what Rome had become, as did Alcuin who accompanied Charlemagne in 800: 'Roma caput mundi, mundi decus, aurea Roma, Nunc remanet tantum saeva ruina tibi' (Rome capital of the world, pride of the world, golden Rome, Now of so much there only remain your savage ruins), and Hildebert Archbishop of Tours, in Rome in 1100, in even sadder words so often quoted: 'Roma quanta fuit ipsa ruina docet' (Rome, what once you were, only your ruins teach us).

When the *Mirabilia* was written, the Vatican and St Peter's was in an enclave within walls built by Leo IV between 847 and 853, bounded on the side facing the city by the Tiber. The city itself was huddled into the area within the great bend of the river and extended on the landward side no further south than the ancient Roman bridge (which after one of the great floods became the Ponte Rotto, its broken piers still visible from the new Ponte Palatino), eastwards to the Capitol, and thence northwards to the old port of the Ripetta near the mausoleum of Augustus. Very few of the great pilgrimage sites were within this tiny area: St Peter's within its own city across the Ponte Sant'Angelo, the Pantheon renamed Sta Maria ad Martyres when the bones dug up from the Colosseum were placed there in 609, Sta Maria in Aracoeli on the Capitoline Hill, which appears in the *Mirabilia* as the site of the earliest Western version of the legend of *Augustus and the Sibyl (Aracoeli means Altar of Heaven). On this eminence stands the Palazzo dei Conservatori and the Senate—Rome's town hall and civic centre—and below it is the Mamertine Prison, where SS Peter and Paul were imprisoned, and on the hillside opposite is San Pietro in Vincoli, which owned the chains said to be those of S. Peter in Jerusalem when he was liberated by the Angel (Acts 12: 6–11). The great basilicas of the Lateran, Rome's cathedral, Sta Maria Maggiore, and Sta Croce in Gerusalemme were islands in the vast expanses within the old city walls, while Sant'Agnese, San Sebastiano, San Lorenzo, and San Paolo were all *fuori le mura*, outside the old walls, so that to visit them pilgrims went in large parties for safety from the brigands that infested the ruins.

The first Jubilee proclaimed by Boniface VIII in 1300 was so successful in the huge numbers of people who came to gain the indulgences granted to those completing the pilgrimage to the seven major basilicas, that another was called for 1350, and later popes shortened the intervals to twenty-five years. The *Mirabilia* remained a popular guide to what to see and what to know about it, despite its inaccuracies and its flights of fancy. 1420 marks a turning-point in the history of Rome and the papacy, for Martin V ended the schism and the 'Babylonian exile' in *Avignon and returned to Rome. New guides began to appear: *Alberti's *Descriptio urbis Romae* of *c.*1432/4, hardly more advanced than Giovanni Dondi's *Iter Romanum* of 1375, and also at the same time as Alberti, Niccolo Signorini's *Descriptio*, while Poggio Bracciolini included a famous description of ancient Rome compared with its fallen state in his *Historia de varietate Fortuna* (History of the diversity of fortune) in the early 1430s. Flavio Biondo's *Roma instaurata* (Rome restored) of *c.*1445, dedicated to Pope Eugenius IV, was a far more learned work, the fruit of his study of coins, inscriptions, and ancient authors, so that his book as a guide to the ancient city is almost archaeological in its efforts at historical accuracy. Francesco Albertini was a new type of author. He was a Florentine priest, a canon of San Lorenzo who had studied music, poetry, and art. He was in Rome by 1502, and in 1510 published two valuable books, saying in the preface to the first, *Opusculum de mirabilibus novae et veteris urbis Romae* (Pamphlet about the new and ancient marvels of the city of Rome), that Cardinal della Rovere, nephew of Julius II, had urged him to refute the fables in the *Mirabilia*. The second book, written in Italian, is the *Memoriale di molte Statue et Picture sono nella inclyta Cipta de Florentia* (Memoir on the many statues and pictures in the illustrious city of Florence). In his *Opusculum* he rewrote the parts about ancient Rome, adding a new section on the Rome which was being reborn under Julius II and *Bramante.

By the mid-16th century guidebooks were being supplemented by engravings and the interest they evoked and the standard of their scholarship was raised by the two principal purveyors, the Frenchmen Lafreri and Dupérac. In turn, the need to provide for scholars and students, as well as visitors who were tourists, resulted in *Palladio using his extensive researches into Roman architecture in two guides produced in 1554, *Le Antichità di Roma* (The antiquities of Rome) on the topography of Rome based on contemporary scholarship and ancient authors, and *Descritione de le Chiese* (Descriptions of the churches), a companion volume in which he comments that many of the older books contain descriptions of destroyed buildings, while he has added ones newly built. Palladio's pocket-book guides in Italian remained current for 200 years, and were the standard guides until the mid-18th century. From 1557 Palladio's main competitor was the *Le Cose maravigliose dell'alma città di Roma* (The marvels of the noble city of Rome) by Valerio Dorico with all kinds of padding with lists of popes etc., plus a large amount of Palladio treated as a useful quarry of information. In 1565 a version of the *Alma città* published in Venice is specifically designed for foreigners visiting the city. Foreign travel was no longer only for pilgrims, and guides were now big business.

miracle plays *See* MYSTERY PLAYS.

Miracles of Christ *See* CHRIST.

Miriam was the sister of *Moses.

'Mirror of Nature, Learning, Morals, History' *See* SPECULUM MAJUS.

misericord (Lat. *misericordia*, compassion) A small bracket on the under-side of a hinged choir-stall. During long services elderly and infirm clerics could prop themselves on it, while technically standing. They do not seem to be earlier than the 12th century and lasted in England until the Reformation. Medieval ones are often carved with distinctly secular subjects from the *Bestiaries, the *Labours of the Months, and miscellaneous domestic scenes, as well as subjects from the **Biblia Pauperum*, **Speculum Humanae Salvationis*, and the Psychomachia (*see* VIRTUES).

Misericordia, Madonna della (Mater Misericordiae) *See* MADONNA TYPES.

missal *See* LITURGICAL BOOKS.

mitre *See* VESTMENTS.

Mocking of Christ All four Gospels relate the event, the account in Matt. 27: 27–31 being the longest. After Pilate ordered Christ to be scourged He was brought back into the palace: 'Then the soldiers of the governor took Jesus into the governor's headquarters, and they gathered the whole cohort around him. They stripped him and put a scarlet robe on him, and after twisting some thorns into a crown, they put it on his head. They put a reed in his right hand and knelt before him and mocked him, saying, "Hail, King of the Jews!" They spat on him, and took the reed and struck him on the head. After mocking him, they stripped him of the robe and put his own clothes on him. Then they led him away to crucify him.' Matthew does not mention Christ's being shown to the people by Pilate.

Mark 15: 16–20 is virtually the same, only the robe is described as purple. Luke 23: 11 is very brief, but varies the place where the mocking happened; he says it was in Herod's palace, whereas all the others, including S. John (19: 1–3) make it clear that it took place in the governor's—that is, Pilate's—palace. S. John continues (4–6) enlarging on S. Matthew's account by relating how Pilate was so unwilling to condemn Christ that he brought him out, still wearing the purple robe and the crown of thorns, and showed him to the crowd, saying, 'Here is the man', and even after they howled 'Crucify him', he still hesitated, tried to release him, but he was so afraid of the riot the priests and their partisans would foment, that he then washed his hands. This is the moment known in Latin as *Ecce homo* (Here is the man). The mocking of Christ, and its sequel, are usually represented separately.

Because in the Early Christian world there was such a resistance to the representation of Christ's Passion, crucifixion being a criminal death, in the earliest images this dramatic moment was usually glossed over, as was the Crucifixion itself. It occurs in a few early Bibles, Gospels, and books of pericopes, such as the one prepared for the Emperor Henry III at Echternach (1043–5: Bremen). *Giotto in the Arena Chapel, Padua, frescoes (*c.*1306) adds a rarity, a negro in the crowd, but no one is in military dress, although the Gospels specifically say that it was Roman soldiers who mocked Christ. Clearly, the intention is to lay the blame on mankind generally, not on a particular people. *Duccio in the Siena *Maestà* (1308–11: Siena, Mus. dell'Opera) also has the Mocking of Christ at the hands of civilians, though there are soldiers in the background. Fra *Angelico included the *Mocking* in his series of frescoes in San Marco, Florence (1437–45), but conceived it as a subject for meditation, with Christ enthroned with a crown of thorns on His head, surrounded by the symbols of the insults offered to Him—a head spitting, a reed held above Him, an open hand to slap Him—and below the step on which the scene is set are the seated figures of a nun and a monk who meditate on the subject. It is notable that the Northern representations of the scene are more violent and horrific than the Italian ones. Two scenes by *Bosch (1508–10: London, NG, and Escorial) also show the mockers as citizens as well as soldiers. *Grünewald's treatment of the scene (1503: Munich) is also violent. Christ is blindfolded, and set upon by men wearing the costumes of *landsknechten* (mercenary troopers) while a complacent Pilate looks on, and in Dürer's two *Passions* (1509: the Small Passion, and 1512: the Engraved Passion) the crowd is mostly of civilians. In Altdorfer's very violent scene (1518: altar in St Florian's, near Linz) there is only one soldier, and he is an onlooker. One of the most comprehensive illustrations to the story of the Passion is the *Calvary* at Playben, Brittany, France, of 1632–40. This is a large free-standing monument surmounted by a Crucifixion, with the Resurrection to one side, and with all the incidents of the Passion in high-relief figures in the frieze underneath. (*See also* ECCE HOMO, and PASSION.)

Molanus, Johannes (Jan Vermeulen) (1533–85), was a Professor of Theology at Leuven whose *De picturis et imaginibus sacris* (Concerning holy pictures and images: Leuven, 1570) was revised and reprinted in 1594 as *De historia sanctarum imaginum* (Concerning the history of holy images). They are strongly in the spirit of the Council of *Trent and insist on rejecting the apocryphal details beloved of artists—he condemns the **Golden Legend*, points out that there is no real authority for the representation of the Death of the Virgin and specifically condemns the *Swoon of the Virgin. His outlook is non-practical, but gives an idea of what influenced patrons (*compare* BORROMEO, PALEOTTI). His stern rationalism was intended to counter Protestant iconoclasm. He also wrote a history of Leuven which contains some references to earlier Flemish artists, the most important being to Roger van der *Weyden.

monastery (Gk. *monasterion*, from *monos*, alone) Originally, those who wished to retire from the world, to pray and contemplate, became hermits, or anchorites. They lived alone, in lonely, even desolate, places, and survived by cultivating a piece of land, if possible, or on food given them by villagers in the hope of the Divine protection invoked by the anchorite whom they supported. Such were the Desert Fathers—S. Paul the Hermit (d. *c.*340), S. Antony of Egypt (d. 356), and others who retired to the Egyptian desert to live lives of extreme asceticism in caves or crude huts. The fame of S. Antony's piety brought him disciples, and in 305 he organized them into a community of hermits (hence his other name of S. Antony Abbot), or *lavra* (Gk. street), consisting of separate huts, but subject to an abbot. They also flourished in Palestine in the 4th century. S. Pachomius (d. 346) was the founder of the Christian coenobitic tradition, for men living not in separate huts but in communal buildings at Tabennisi, near Thebes in Upper Egypt, known from the area as the Thebaid. He eventually founded communities for men, and women, where they lived according to a Rule established by their founder, which influenced those of, among others, S. Basil and *S. Benedict of Nursia.

S. Benedict's life first as a hermit in the *Sacro Speco (Holy cave) at Subiaco, and then in the community which eventually grew up round him, ended in 525 when he and a small group of monks moved to Monte Cassino in S. Italy, where he lived until he died, and where he planned the Rule which was to become the norm of Western monasticism. Slowly, with time and less devoted followers, the vision weakened and in 787 S. Benedict of Aniane, a vigorous reformer, instituted considerable changes which included a loss of autonomy for individual monasteries, changing them into a more centralized congregation. Most other Orders, of monks and nuns alike, follow a Rule based ultimately on S. Benedict's, with additional vows for specific purposes, such as the *Mercedarians.

The design of monasteries is largely dependent on the aims of the Order, and the size of a community. In general, monastic buildings are enclosed within a wall with a gatehouse and porter's lodge, and with the various parts disposed around the church: the *cloister, usually on the south side of the church, the *chapter house, the refectory and kitchens, the dormitory, the abbot's separate quarters, the parlour (for receiving visitors), the library, the infirmary, the lay brothers' accommodation, and buildings such as storerooms, bakehouses, workrooms, and stables. Some monasteries also had a guest house, a school, a hospice for the old and sick, or provided a home within the enclave for male pensioners, who gave land, property, or money and in return lived in accommodation provided by the monastery—a primitive form of annuity. The dormitory might also have a night stair giving directly into the church for the Offices of Prime and Matins, which were said during the night (Hexham Abbey has an example). Monastery churches were sometimes open to the people, and although most monasteries preferred to have a separate church for the laity, often part of the church might be allotted to them, as at Sherbourne Abbey, where the choir was for the monks and the nave for the laity. Many monasteries became *pilgrimage centres, which involved considerable difficulties for the normal monastic observance of the Offices, which had to be maintained despite the disturbance caused by huge crowds. All monasteries had a *clausura. Many Benedictine abbeys still have famous schools—such as Ottobeuren in S. Germany, San Giorgio Maggiore in Venice, Ampleforth in N. England.

The control of the monastery was in the hands of its abbot, who was (or should be) elected by the monks to rule them. This self-government was often reinforced by prescient founders who obtained from the pope a guarantee of their liberties, creating a form of monastery known as 'exempt'—that is, exempt from the jurisdiction of the local bishop, who could become jealous of the autonomy enjoyed by a powerful monastic house. To counter this, bishops often interfered with elections, and only too frequently their pressure was exerted to compel a monastery to accept the bishop's designated abbot, who might then turn out to be a child or a layman, and who then became an office holder 'in commendam'. Often this type of abbot, who never set foot in the house, but drew—and spent—its revenues on his own private life, brought the house to the brink of disaster. Many great abbeys, such as Canterbury or Westminster were forced to sue the crown for a 'congé d'élire' and to pay heavily for the permission to elect their own abbot.

Individual monasteries were designed, or grew, as circumstances, terrain, and resources dictated. The most famous plan is the one at *Sankt Gallen, a design on parchment for an ideal layout of a large monastery. Most Orders built their monasteries according to a plan especially designed for their particular needs; those of the *Carthusians (Charterhouses in English, but with their name deriving from the Grande Chartreuse, their mother-house in the high Alps) and the *Camaldolensians (from Camaldoli, in the Apennines *c.*30 miles from Florence) were built with cells disposed round a central space, each cell having a small plot of garden which the monk cultivated. Food, water, firewood, books, and other necessities were brought to each cell daily, so that the monk's prayers and contemplation were only interrupted by attendance at the Offices, for which he went to the church. There was a refectory for meals on Sundays, the only time, other than church, when they were all together. The monks of the Grande Chartreuse had one other obligation—that of succouring travellers on the dangerous, but much used, route through the Alps. The only Order which had no obligation to manual work was the Vallombrosans (from Lat. *vallis umbrosa*, shady valley, from their site in the hills near Florence). They were founded *c.*1020, and are a strictly enclosed contemplative Order, following the Benedictine Rule. They popularized the system of *lay brothers, which became general in the 11th century.

Monasteries were usually built of stone, and churches were almost always vaulted, which greatly enhanced the singing of the Offices. Some monasteries, such as *Cluny in Burgundy (and Cluniac houses generally) had churches with intricately carved capitals and elaborate portals with sculpture, rich furnishings, stained-glass windows, finely decorated and illuminated antiphonals and Gospels, paintings and statues. The Abbey church at Cluny was, at one time, the largest vaulted church in Europe, and probably the wealthiest and the most magnificent.

The *Cistercians also imposed a strict plan on all their houses so that a monk, sent from one monastery to another, always knew his way among buildings arranged in the same order. The Order rejected all decoration; austerity reigned in their churches as in all their houses. Capitals were plain, glass was white with only abstract designs in the leading, crucifixes were of wood, books were undecorated, altar furnishings and candlesticks were of iron, even chalices were only silver-gilt, only plain undecorated linen was used on the altar, and in their dress no decoration was allowed. The masonry of their buildings was very plain, but the craftsmanship of their builders was outstanding. Even towers to their churches were forbidden, until their lands became so extensive that a means of making their bells more audible required them to be hung at greater height than the original low belfries. The first Cistercians were not so austere in such things as they later became and this change was effected by *S. Bernard of Clairvaux, who was appalled at the lavish arrangements of Cluny and its dependencies. Cistercian houses had no hospices or schools, and guest houses were outside the monastery. One consequence of the disciplined arrangements of monasteries, the essential provision of fresh water, and the careful arrangements made for the disposal of sewage, meant that their cleanliness was a powerful protection against the pestilences that afflicted towns and cities where crowded humanity lived in unhygienic conditions.

A few monasteries were double—that is, monks and nuns sharing a site, and a church, with separate houses for each community, and sharing also some of the practical work and buildings, such as storerooms, etc., and even kitchens. Such was Fontevrault, near Tours, which was founded in the early 12th century, and though the monastery was ruled by the abbess, the monks provided the chaplains and were responsible for the management of the house. Many of the abbesses were royal princesses, English and French alike at the beginning of the foundation, and a number of Plantagenet kings and queens were buried there, including Richard I, Lionheart; their tombs now stand in the deserted and disused church.

The work undertaken in monasteries varied according to the Order. Some, like Cluny, Winchester, St Albans, Bury St Edmunds, were producers of fine manuscripts, the work of the *scriptorium being divided between the scribes and the illuminators. Others, like the Cistercians, were farmers, turning the desolate sites wherever they settled into productive farmlands and vineyards, as in Burgundy where they were first established, or into vast sheep runs, as in N. England, though they also produced fine MSS, as undecorated as the rest of their surroundings. Some monasteries had workshops for the production of goldsmiths' work, or bronze casting, often producing artists who were great craftsmen, like Roger of Helmarshausen, near Göttingen, in the early 12th century; Roger is believed to be *Theophilus. The painter Fra *Angelico became Prior of San Marco in Florence, where Fra *Bartolommeo later also became head of the important workshop producing many works of art. Stanbrook, near Gloucester, is a Benedictine nunnery of enclosed and contemplative nuns, refounded in 1838 after being driven out of France in 1793, which specializes in printing.

Convents are essentially the same as monasteries. They are not specifically the province of nuns; Franciscan houses are called convents, as in the mother-house of the Order, the Sacro Convento in Assisi. Neither is the Rule the same, in that the male members of Mendicant Orders are Friars—Carmelites, Franciscans, Dominicans, Mercedarians, Capucines, Minims—and the nature of their work takes them out into the world. The nuns of those Orders were usually enclosed, Carmelites particularly so. Most monastic Orders have suffered greatly from persecution. In England, they were destroyed at the Reformation, their communities expelled, and their monasteries expropriated to become stone quarries for their new secular owners; in France they were dispossessed during the French Revolution and they suffered from anticlerical legislation until well into the 20th century; in Germany, in the Netherlands, and in E. Europe, they suffered terribly during the Wars of Religion, and from later ideological antagonists. Many have now revived, and a number of new Anglican communities were founded as part of the Catholic Revival in the Church of England, and spread to other parts of the Anglican Communion. The oldest surviving religious house in the UK is the (Roman Catholic) Bar Convent in York, founded in 1686 and still in operation today. *See also*

ABBEY, AUGUSTINIAN CANONS, MONKS, NUNS, ORDERS.

monastic orders *See* ORDERS.

Monica, Saint, was the mother of *S. Augustine of Hippo. She died at Ostia, near Rome, in 387, soon after Augustine's baptism, and is known only from the mentions of her in his writings. She is very rarely represented in art, but the once-famous picture of mother and son by Ary Scheffer (1855: Louvre) is a prime example of *bondieuserie.

monk (Lat. *monachus,* from Gk. *monos,* alone) A monk is a member of a monastic community. They derived originally from the coenobitic communities (*see* MONASTERY) which rejected the total solitude of hermit life in favour of a community life separate from the world and given to prayer, asceticism, contemplation, and work. S. Athanasius's praise in Rome of the life of S. Antony in Egypt led many men, and women, to become monks and nuns. Most monasteries followed the Rule formulated in the 6th century by *S. Benedict of Nursia, but with the passage of time the discipline became relaxed. S. Bendict of Aniane, near Montpellier in S. France, began a strict reform in the late 8th century, and varieties of Benedictines emerged over time, such as the Cluniacs, the Cistercians, the Carthusians, the Camaldolensians, mostly in the 10th century, and the impetus of the founder was restored. In the 13th century emerged the Orders of Friars—who are not the same as monks—and in the 16th century other religious Orders were founded for men who live according to a Rule, but are not monks, such as Jesuits, Oratorians, and Theatines (*See also* ORDERS).

Monks first pass through a period when they are postulants—they have expressed a desire to enter the community and the Order, and pass about six months living in the community without any commitment on either side. If the postulant continues, he becomes a novice, wears the habit and follows most of the rules of the Order without, however, being totally committed to the life, or the Order to him. A novitiate lasts at least a year, often longer, during which the novice receives instruction and training. The next step is when he makes his profession, the ceremony at which he takes his vows (chastity, poverty, and obedience are the main ones, though some Orders have extra vows peculiar to themselves). The vow of obedience involves stability: he may not leave the monastery except with the permission of his superior. He is then vested with the habit which he will wear until his death. Should he wish to leave the monastery, he may do so freely during his novitiate, and no stigma attaches to him for doing so, and any property which he may have brought into the community is restored to him. After his profession, his vow of poverty means that he gives up all personal property, and anything which he may inherit after his profession he must assign to the community. He may only be deprived of his habit, and ejected from his monastery, for very grave matters, such as heresy, for which he will have been excommunicated, or for conduct which is incompatible with his continuance in the Order. A monk is not a priest, and may not perform the functions of a priest, such as hearing confessions, or saying Mass. He may, however, become one if his superiors consent.

*Zurbarán painted many monks and friars, particularly martyred Mercedarians, notably *S. Serapion* (Hartford, Conn., Wadsworth), Carthusians (*S. Bruno and Pope Urban II*: Seville), *S. Francis* (London, NG), a series of *Hieronymite Friars* (1638–40: Guadalupe), the Carthusian *S. Hugo in the refectory* (1641–58: Seville); Giovanni Bellini painted *The murder of S. Peter Martyr* in his Dominican habit (London, NG, and Courtauld Inst.); El Greco painted the Trinitarian *Fra Hortensio Paravicino* (*c.*1610: Boston, Mass.). (*See also* NUN and CONVENT.)

monkey *See* APE.

monogram, the Sacred *See* CHI-RHO and NOMEN SACRUM.

monstrance (Lat. *monstrare,* to show) or **ostensorium** (Lat. *ostendere,* to show or reveal) A monstrance is a vessel used in the Catholic Church; it is usually made of silver-gilt, with a base like a chalice for stability, and with a stem supporting a large flat disc, usually designed like a sun-burst with rays emanating from the small windowed compartment in the centre into which a host is inserted. A monstrance is used for the exposition of the Blessed Sacrament during the service of Benediction, and if the Sacrament is to be carried in procession, as at *Corpus Christi. It is also used for ceremonies of solemn blessing. Some churches have a perpetual exposition of the Blessed Sacrament—examples are Tyburn Chapel, near Marble Arch in London, and Sant'Isidoro, León.

Monte Cassino is a mountain some 60 miles north of Naples and 80 miles south of Rome. On it stands the famous Benedictine monastery of Montecassino, the mother-house of the Order. *S. Benedict, after his unhappy experience at Subiaco, moved to the mountain top above the town of Cassino, built a refuge for himself and his small band of followers, and remained there until his death in 547. Other religious who came after him founded the Order which bears his name. His foundation was the Rule which he wrote for his community, which was soon adopted as the ideal one for Western monasticism: humane, moderate, but strict, rejecting excessive asceticism, and adapatable to conditions and climates in most western and north-western lands. The simple refuge of the saint and his followers grew rapidly into a large monastery, which became famous as the great light of civilization in a barbarous age and area, and as a result, became a target for invaders. First came the Longobards *c.*581. The community took refuge in Rome and only returned in 717, when it flourished until in 888 the monastery was sacked and burnt by the Saracens, as was a nearby abbey where the abbot and his flock were killed. The survivors went to Teano, near Capua, but this also was burnt in 896 and only in 950 did the community return from Capua, their last refuge, led by Abbot Aligerno, who rebuilt the monastery and restored the Rule. His successor was Desiderio, the son of the Prince of Benevento, and their most illustrious abbot. He built a grandiose church, with bronze doors made in Constantinople, and imported Byzantine mosaicists to decorate the church; they remained to found a workshop which supplied artists and inspiration for the works undertaken in Palermo, Cefalù, and Monreale for the Norman kings of Sicily.

A great earthquake destroyed the whole complex in 1349; it was rebuilt between 1357 and 1366, and the monastery now entered a long and difficult period, trying to remain neutral between first the Angevins and Aragonese in Naples, and then the Aragonese and the papacy. It dwindled in power and dedication so that in 1454 it sank into being an abbey 'in commendam'—a benefice given by an uncaring pope as a lucrative sinecure. Its last commendatory abbot was Cardinal Giovanni de' Medici, later Pope Leo X, and in 1504 it was joined to the community of Sta Giustina of Padua. It then enjoyed peace and quiet, the buildings were slowly restored, its studies revived, and the community flourished. It again suffered under the French in 1798, and was secularized by Joseph Bonaparte in 1806, but was restored in 1815, and flourished again until it was totally destroyed in 1944 during the Second World War. It has been rebuilt in its previous form, and its most precious possessions—its library, its founder's relics, and its furnishings, which were removed by the Germans to Rome when they fortified it against the Allied advance in Italy—have now been restored to it.

Montfaucon, Bernard de (1655–1741), was one of the great Benedictine scholars especially in Greek palaeography, who also published *L'Antiquité expliqué* (Antiquity explained: 15 vols., 1719–24: in French and Latin) and *Monuments de la monarchie françoise* (Monuments of French monarchy: 5 vols., 1729–33: also French and Latin). Both were later translated into English. The first was a very early attempt to explain ancient pagan iconography by reference to works of art, but the second is extremely important in containing good engravings of many works of art destroyed in the Revolution and otherwise lost—e.g. much of *Saint-Denis.

Months, Labours (Occupations) of the Images of common, usually agricultural, occupations appear in *portal sculpture, in MS illuminations (especially Books of *Hours), and on reliefs. In portal sculpture, there is a complete set of the twelve months at St-Denis in roundels. They probably escaped the destructive attentions of both the clergy of the Enlightenment and the vandals of the French Revolution by their virtual insignificance. Other sets are at Amiens, Autun, Chartres, Sens, and Vézelay. In many series, e.g. at Amiens, the Labour is accompanied by the appropriate Sign of the Zodiac for the month. The quite sudden appearance of these symbolic representations on grand church portals from the 12th century onwards may perhaps be connected with the increasing importance given to agricultural improvements made by some of the monastic orders, notably the Cistercians, as well as cathedral chapters dependent on their lands for a large part of their revenues. Though the representations are never stereotyped and often show local variations, certain scenes are almost universal.

Changes are usually because of climate: English examples are a month behind French, and Italian are a month ahead of French. In England, the survivors are usually found on *misericords, for instance at Gloucester and Worcester in the 14th century, and at Malvern and Ripple (Worcs.) in the 15th century. In Italy, Antelami carved a complete set of reliefs, some almost free-standing groups, each Labour with the corresponding Sign of the Zodiac, in the Baptistery at Parma, where he was working in 1078, which makes them one of the earliest examples.

Probably the most famous French series is in the superb MS of the *Très Riches Heures* made for the Duc de Berri by 1416/17, where full-page miniatures have many scenes of agricultural work mixed with splendid courtly amusements. A similarly grand series is in the Palazzo Schifanoia ('begone dull care') in Ferrara, painted by Francesco del Cossa and Cosmè Tura in 1456–70. In almost no series does any work appear to be done in January, which is given up to feasting; February, too, in France usually has people warming themselves at a fire, although a woodcutter may be bringing in timber. In Italy peasants prune vines or dig. March in France is for ploughing, in Italy for pruning vines, April is for gathering herbs and flowers, but, for the courtly, for dalliance and getting engaged, while in Ferrara the preparations for the *palio*—a horse race—occupy men's minds. May is for hawking and hunting in France; in Italy the hay harvest has begun, which in France is not before June. Men scythe and women rake up the hay into haycocks; while in Italy, reaping the corn harvest has begun, with threshing in July. Some special labours occur: in July in Ferrara, the flax is crushed to make linen, and only in Italy in August is coopering for the forthcoming vintage represented, together with threshing. September everywhere is the vintage month, and in October all plough and prepare for sowing spring wheat, and in November everyone drives the pigs out into the oak woods, and the swineherd thrashes the trees to bring down acorns for the pigs to eat. In December the pig is slaughtered and its flesh salted down for the winter, while the huntsmen hunt the boar, and bread is made for the forthcoming festivities. The Labours of the Months are invariably connected with agriculture, or sport, rarely with urban trades or work, since these were continuous occupations, independent of locality, climate, and the seasons, and with no ostensible connection with monastic or other religious foundations, much less with court life. Sport is among the subjects in a series of four fused glass windows by Nicholas Mynheer (2012) for the Chapel of the Holy Trinity in Abingdon School, Abingdon, Oxfordshire. These draw liturgical and scholastic themes together across the school year and the community's culture.

Moore, Henry, OM, CH (1898–1986) A British sculptor born in Castleford, Yorkshire, who mastered traditional methods at Leeds and the Royal College of Art, but studied alternative approaches and cultures in the British Museum. Mother and Child and the single female figure were his two main themes. Of these the first was given expression at St Matthew's Northampton in *Madonna and Child* (1943–4), a commission from Canon Walter Hussey at a time of war when materials and transport facilities were difficult to come by. The piece marked Moore's return to sculpture following a period where drawing alone had of necessity been his chief means of expression. The work, much noticed in Continental Europe and the USA, came to symbolize a serious a step forwards for art and the Church, the work itself with its upper, more 'human' detailing and the 'rockier', ancient character of the lower can be seen as the sculptor's response to theology's requirement for such a work to exhibit the two natures (divinity and humanity) of Christ. Another such meditation resulted in the same subject but a different idiom (1983, St Paul's Cathedral). International status came with his unflagging professional commitment.

Morales, Luis de (1509/19–85/6), called 'El Divino', was a Spanish painter who worked in an emotional *Mannerist style, highly personal and of exalted religious feeling. He was probably trained in Seville, and seems to have been influenced by currents from the N. Italian works of *Leonardo da Vinci and his Milanese followers, and perhaps also by the Sienese Beccafumi, which he can only have known from engravings or copies. He is documented from 1539 until the end of his life in Badajoz, on the Portuguese frontier. His paintings are entirely representative of the first wave of the Counter-Reformation, and reflect the powerful influence of the *Spiritual Exercises* of *S. Ignatius Loyola. Examples of his devotional style are the *Pietà* (1560/70: Madrid, Acad.) and variants, or his versions of the

Madonna and Child theme (e.g. London, NG; New York, Hispanic Soc.).

Mordecai *See* ESTHER.

More, Sir Thomas (1478–1535) The son of a judge Sir John More, Thomas More was placed, *c.*1491, in the household of John Morton, Archbishop of Canterbury, who was Lord Chancellor under King Henry VII in 1487 and was made a cardinal in 1493. Thomas More began to study law in 1494, was called to the Bar in 1501, and became a lecturer in law until he thought of becoming a priest, but decided that he was not called to celibacy. He entered Parliament in 1504, married in 1505, and the advancement of his public career accelerated after Henry VIII became king in 1509. He held various appointments from 1510, became a Privy Counsellor in 1518, accompanied Henry to the Field of the Cloth of Gold in 1520, was knighted in 1521, became Speaker of the House of Commons in 1523, and succeeded Cardinal Wolsey as Lord Chancellor in 1529. His glittering career was accompanied by continued royal favour, the king treating him with every sign of warm friendship until in 1532 when his career and favour ended with his opposition to the king's divorce from Catherine of Aragon. He resigned as chancellor and lived as a private person; he was willing to sign the Act of Succession which legitimized the king's daughter by Anne Boleyn (Elizabeth, later Queen Elizabeth I) and Jane Seymour's son, later Edward VI, although they threatened the rights of Catherine of Aragon's daughter, Mary (later Queen). But he refused to sign the Act of Supremacy, which made Henry the head of the Church in England instead of the pope. He was imprisoned in the Tower of London for fifteen months, with John Fisher, Bishop of Rochester, who was also imprisoned on the same charge of treason. Bishop Fisher was beheaded on 22 June 1535, More was tried for high treason on 1 July and sentenced to be hanged at Tyburn, but the sentence was commuted to decapitation and he was beheaded on Tower Hill on 5 July 1535, his body buried in St Peter's *ad vincula* in the Tower, and his head exhibited on London Bridge. His daughter Margaret Roper bought it a month later, and preserved it in spices until it was buried in the Roper tomb in Canterbury. He was canonized in 1935.

His household in Chelsea was famous as a resort of scholars: John Colet, Dean of St Paul's, William Grocyn, the foremost teacher of Greek and Latin in the University of Oxford, and above all Desiderius *Erasmus, who was one of his major correspondents and a resident in his house on his visits to England. More's literary works are in Latin and English. His most famous is *Utopia* (1515/16), which he began during his mission to Flanders, and which was published in England in 1516 in Latin. It describes an ideal island, where the inhabitants live according to natural laws, and where there is freedom of conscience in religion, and where men and women are educated equally by the state. The text contains numerous barbed shafts against contemporary follies, injustices, and abuses. It was not translated into English until 1551, but was published in German by 1524, French by 1530, Italian by 1548, and Spanish as late as 1790. He wrote extensively on Lucian, on various subjects in divinity such as the *Supplication of Souls* (1529), and on epigrams; an *Apology of Sir Thomas More* (1533) is an explanation of his reasons for disagreeing with the king; when he was in prison he wrote the *Dialogue of Comfort against Tribulation*, and treatises on the Passion.

He was also a friend of *Holbein, whom he helped to royal patronage on the painter's first visit to England (1526–8), though when Holbein returned in 1532, More was already out of favour. During his first visit in 1527 Holbein painted the portrait of More as Chancellor (1527: NY, Frick Coll.), and made the drawing of the More family (Basel), which was a study for the large group portrait (Kremsier Castle, burnt 1752). Copies of the group portrait by Rowland Lockey painted *c.*1593 are at Nostell Priory (National Trust: W. Yorkshire) and, with variations, National Portrait Gallery, London.

morse *See* COPE.

Mortal Sins *See* DEADLY.

mosaic The art of mosaic began with pavements made of different coloured pebbles, but it became a wall-decoration, e.g. at Pompeii, long before its development as a major art form by *Early Christian, and especially *Byzantine, artists. A wall-mosaic is made by laying a rough coat of cement on the bare wall and then laying a second, finer, layer to it with large-headed nails embedded in it as an extra means of fixing to ensure that the layers did not separate. On this second layer an artist (*pictor imaginarius*, image painter) drew the outlines of the design and indicated the colours. A third, thin, layer of fine cement was then laid, a small patch at a time, in which the *tesserae* were embedded. Tesserae (Lat. dice) are small cubes cut from slabs of marble, tile, alabaster, and coloured glass or plain glass with gold or silver foil sandwiched inside it. Sometimes semiprecious stones like onyx or cornelian were also used. For a large mosaic many thousands of tesserae were needed, all graded by size and colour, with small cubes for details of faces or hands and larger ones for drapery and backgrounds. Great care was taken not to lay them evenly, so that rays of sunlight or the moving light of processional candles would catch the undulating surface, giving a richly flickering effect, heightening the other-worldliness of the original design. This always had the hieratic figures ranged in order of majesty, from the *Pantocrator in the golden dome down to the saints on the walls below. The figures were, as far as possible, arranged frontally, and where narratives were essential, as in such subjects as the Annunciation or the Nativity, use was made wherever possible of the corner shape of the squinch at the base of a dome to place the figures in opposition without breaking the rule of frontality. Where a narrative was made on a flat wall surface the formal system was used as far as possible, and in such a scene as Abraham serving the Three Angels who sit at table, or Abraham about to sacrifice Isaac, the figures remain as frontal as possible, and although their bodies and heads may be turned in slightly three-quarter view, they never present a profile unless the character is so bad that any 'communication' with it is out of the question. By 'communication' another aspect of Byzantine art is revealed: the belief that the spectator was able to enter into communion with the original of the painted or mosaic figure meant that a person such as Judas would always be presented in absolute profile, so that communication through eye-contact was impossible. Where the image is of Christ, the Virgin, or a saint, the believer might offer praise, worship, supplication, thanks, to the image, which as the *representative* of the holy one would enable the suppliant to reach and communicate with the holy one. This very sophisticated view of the image must never be confused with idolatry, which would be the worship of the image *itself*: nothing would be further from the Byzantine mind, the image being a doorway through which the believer could enter spiritually the world of the holy one. Any other interpretation would involve either idolatry or witchcraft. Perhaps the eye-contact aspect could be expressed as the 'eye as the window of the soul', so long as the eye itself is regarded metaphysically.

The process of mosaic decoration was necessarily slow and very expensive, both on account of the actual materials and the months of skilled labour, which is why it reached its apogee in the Eastern Roman Empire. Byzantium was not only very rich, but was also a theocracy, where the emperor was God's vice-regent on Earth and the resources of the state were devoted to the glory of God in church building and decoration. Even the Byzantines, however, could afford this only in major, usually metropolitan, churches. During periods of economic crisis, or in small village churches, the much less expensive technique of *fresco painting was developed, which in turn led to the rise of a more naturalistic art in the West, particularly in Italy.

The first example of an Early Christian mosaic is the *Sol Invictus or *Christ as Sun-God*, discovered in the 1940s below St Peter's in Rome, dating from *c*.300, soon followed by the semi-pagan decorations in Sta Costanza, Rome, of *c*.325. Other splendid early cycles in Rome (Sta Maria Maggiore, Sta Pudenziana, etc.), Milan (San Lorenzo), and *Ravenna followed. Here again certain trends exist. The earliest mosaics had white backgrounds (Sta Costanza is a good example), then blue backgrounds were used (as in the Mausoleum of Galla Placidia in Ravenna), and finally gold grounds came into use in the 6th century, and superseded all others. Byzantium itself has relatively few surviving mosaics because of the havoc wrought after the Turkish conquest in 1453, though many survive in Greece, and others, often, if not mainly, by Greek artists, are in Sicily and Venice in the West, or Russia in the East.

The essence of mosaic decoration lies in its formal and hieratic qualities, and these demand adherence to its own very stringent conventions. The 16th-century Venetian campaigns to continue the decoration of St Mark's with mosaic pictures which introduce perspective and naturalism merely used unsuitable and expensive materials to create anachronistic wall-paintings which clash painfully with the earlier work, where the formal characteristics of the medium had been understood and respected. Most later mosaic decorations, such as the 19th-century ones in St Paul's Cathedral and the 20th-century ones in

Westminster Cathedral, fail for these reasons. They are merely more permanent forms of painting, rather like the altarpieces in St Peter's where the pictures have been 're-made' in mosaic, and the originals removed to the Vatican Gallery.

Mosaic Law begins with the Ten Commandments, which prohibit idolatry or pantheism, demand the honouring of one omnipotent, omniscient Creator God alone, require man's obedience to Him, and elevate his conduct towards his fellow man into a moral code. He should honour his parents, he must not kill, steal, lie, commit adultery, nor covet his neighbour's wife nor his goods. The Law also established rules which governed the relation between religion and state, and the duties and obligations of one to the other, and to the people. God also established a moral code involving the impartiality of justice, the relationship of master, servant, and slave, the treatment of women and other dependants, minorities and refugees, the punishment of transgressors, and honesty in commercial undertakings. Man being fallible and prone to seeking his own advantage, has broken many or even all these Laws, but for an honest man they remain, in greater part, a permanent obligation not only among Jews, but on all mankind, since the influence of Judaism on Christianity (and also on other faiths) is such that the moral code established by Mosaic Law has transferred in great part to Christians and become in time a social obligation. The religious observances and the dietary rules may differ, individual legal frameworks may have changed, but the Commandments have remained valid throughout the ages, and the rules they laid down still govern the larger part of the law in countries claiming to be civilized, Christian or not, and have the power of a universal and acknowledged moral code.

Moses (Heb. *Moshe*, draw out) was the greatest leader of the Jews and their major lawgiver. The laws he laid down, which are recorded in the OT books of Exodus, Leviticus, Numbers, and Deuteronomy, are the foundation of Jewish law, and have had a deep effect on Christianity through their extension into the NT. The mission God thrust upon an unwilling Moses, to free the Jews from slavery in Egypt, and to lead them into the Promised Land, 'flowing with milk and honey', is recounted in the Book of Exodus.

The Jews had entered Egypt about the 18th or 17th century BC, because of a famine, but Jacob's sons were recognized by *Joseph, who settled them in Goshen, in the Nile Delta (Gen. 35–50). They flourished there as herdsmen and shepherds and multiplied, until 'a new king arose over Egypt, who did not know Joseph' (Exod. 1: 8). This was probably Seti I (1308–1290 BC). He was alarmed at the size of this alien community and drove them into slavery, ordering their midwives to kill boy babies, or to throw them into the Nile. When Moses was born his mother hid him for three months and then put him in a basket which she placed among the reeds on the river bank, where Pharaoh's daughter used to bathe. She found him and saved him, and his sister Miriam, who was watching, arranged for a nurse, who was, of course, his mother. Later Pharaoh's daughter adopted him and named him Moses because, she said, 'I drew him out of the water' (Exod. 2: 10). He grew up in the palace, but aware of his Jewish origins, and legend says that he was accused of trying to usurp Pharaoh's crown. He had to choose between two cups, one with a ruby ring, which meant death, the other a burning coal. An angel prompted him to choose the coal, which burnt his tongue so that he stammered. When he saw a Jewish slave being beaten by an Egyptian overseer, he intervened and killed the man, hiding his body in the sand. The deed became known, and Pharaoh sought him to punish him. He fled to Midian, on the western side of Arabia, settled there, married the daughter of the High Priest, Jethro, and tended his father-in-law's flocks.

One day God spoke to him from a blazing bush which burnt without being consumed and ordered him to free His people from their slavery in Egypt, for under the new king, Ramases II (1290–1224 BC), their position had worsened. '"Moses, Moses," he said, "Come no closer! Remove the sandals from your feet, for the place on which you stand is holy ground" . . . and Moses hid his face, for he was afraid to look at God' (Exod. 3: 1–6). God told Moses to obtain the liberation of the Jews from Pharaoh. Moses protested his incapacity because of his stammer; God overrode him, and told him to take Aaron as his helper. First, however, he had to persuade the Jews that freedom was possible. They had been in Egypt so long that any other place was alien to them. The first meetings with Pharaoh went badly; the Jewish slaves, who had been forced to work in the brickfields, were now told to make bricks without straw being provided, and when they protested they were told they had to find their own straw. For their new troubles they blamed Moses and Aaron, whom God sent back to Pharaoh to renew the demand, and to convince him Aaron threw his rod on the ground and it turned into a serpent. The court magicians did likewise, but Aaron's snake swallowed theirs, but still Pharaoh refused. God sent the first plague: the Nile turned to blood so that there was no water to drink, but the magicians did the same, and Pharaoh still refused. The second plague was of swarming frogs, but the magicians did the same; Pharaoh asked Moses to rid the land of them, but when Moses did so, he still refused. The third plague was of gnats, which covered everything (the AV says 'fleas'); the same thing happened, and was followed by a fourth plague of flies, with the same result. The fifth plague was a pestilence which struck the livestock—cattle, horses, sheep, donkeys, camels—and all died, but none of the plagues touched the land where the Jews lived. The infuriated Pharaoh again refused. The sixth plague was of festering boils which afflicted humans as well as animals, but with the same result. The seventh plague was of thunderstorms with violent hail and rain, which stripped vegetation, felled trees, and killed everything in the fields. After three days, Pharaoh promised to let them go, but unmindful of past disasters, again 'hardened his heart'. The eighth plague was of locusts, which devoured all that the storms had left. Pharaoh's ministers besought him to let the Jews go; the country, they said, was ruined. For some time, Moses had been increasing his demands. At first he had asked for the people to go three days into the desert to sacrifice, now he wanted them to go with all their families, their cattle, and their belongings. Pharaoh offered only that the people should go, and everything else be left behind. Moses refused. The ninth plague was of darkness—such darkness that no one could move. Moses and Aaron insisted on full liberation; Pharaoh drove them out in fury, and threatened to kill them if they returned. The tenth and last plague was the most terrible. Instructed by God, Moses told the Jews each family was to take an unblemished lamb and kill it, smear the blood on the lintel and both doorposts of their houses, roast the lamb with bitter herbs and unleavened bread, and eat it, girded for travel, their sandals on their feet and staff in hand. That night, He would send the Destroyer to kill the first-born in every house, child and beast alike, and only the houses with the blood on their lintels and doorposts would be spared—the blood of the lamb would be their salvation. That night, a terrible cry went up in Egypt. Pharaoh sent for Moses and Aaron during the night and said, 'Rise up, go away from my people . . . Go, worship the Lord as you said. Take your flocks and your herds . . . and be gone. And bring a blessing on me too!'

Then started the great trek, first to the sea where they camped, and where Pharaoh, who had already regretted letting them go, decided to overtake them with an army and force them back. The Jews, who had lived for so long in Egypt where only recently had life become harsh, but where it had once been safe and soft, clamoured to go back even to slavery rather than die in the wilderness. Moses told them to be firm, and the pillar of cloud which had gone before them to show them the way, and the column of fire which had given them light from behind both moved behind them. He struck the waters with his staff and they parted, so that the people passed through dryshod, and the Egyptians followed. When the Jews were all safely across, Moses again struck the waters and they returned and overwhelmed the Egyptian host.

The wanderings of the Jews in the wilderness of Arabia lasted for forty years. They suffered thirst because the water they found at Marah was bitter, until Moses threw a miraculous piece of wood in it, and the bitter water became the water of salvation. Again, in the wilderness of Sin, they murmured against Moses, remembering 'when we sat beside the flesh-pots, and ate our fill of bread, for you have brought us out into this wilderness to kill this whole assembly with hunger'. God then send *manna for bread and quails for meat. Again they complained about lack of water at Rephidim in the south of the Sinai desert, and God told Moses to gather all the elders together, and in their presence he struck the rock and water gushed out, though Moses had doubted that this could happen, for which God told him that though he would see the Promised Land, he would not enter it himself. Their next trial was an attack from the Amalekites, desert brigands who fell on them seeking plunder, for when the Jews left Egypt they took with them all the gold and jewellery they had borrowed from the Egyptians. In the battle, the Jews were winning when Moses held up his arms, and losing when he lowered them, so

Aaron and Hur, traditionally Miriam's husband, sat him on a stone and held up his arms on either side. The Amalekites were defeated. When the Jews camped below Mt. Sinai, Moses was in the land where he had guarded his father-in-law's flocks, and Jethro visited him bringing his wife and two sons with him. On Jethro's advice, Moses instituted a judicial system, with judges and an ultimate appeal to himself. God then summoned Moses from the mountain, ordered that the Jews should purify themselves, and on the third day should gather at the foot of the mountain. Then He descended in fire, smoke, and earthquake and proclaimed the Ten Commandments (Exod. 19 and 20), as well as many other laws. Moses was commanded to come up the mountain, where he remained for six weeks, and He instructed him about building the tabernacle and the sanctuary, established the Sabbath, and gave him the stone tablets engraved with the Law.

Meanwhile (Exod. 32) the discontented people lost faith in Moses and, quickly reverting to their pagan past, asked Aaron to make them an idol which should go before them, saying, 'as for this Moses, the man who brought us out of Egypt, we do not know what has become of him'. Clearly fearful, Aaron collected their gold ornaments and made a golden calf, set it on an altar, and called for a festival 'to the Lord' the next day. God told Moses to go down at once, threatening dire punishment on the idolaters. When Moses saw what they had done, he smashed the tablets of the Law, destroyed the idol, crushed it, and threw its dust in the water, which he made them drink. He bitterly reproached Aaron for his part in the affair, and it eventually led to armed strife in the camp, between the idol worshippers and Moses's supporters and many of the idolaters were killed.

Moses once more climbed the mountain, and again stayed six weeks, and when he returned his face shone with such light that men 'were afraid to come near him' (Exod. 34: 30), the origin of the images of Moses with small horns on his forehead. He then reformed the camp by establishing a marching order, and made a census of men of military age, so that their caravan should be more orderly and defensible. When they reached the centre of the Sinai peninsula there was more trouble; the people were sick of manna, they longed for the fish, fresh vegetables, and fruit of Egypt, and Moses was discouraged because they regretted freedom and would have given it up for the longed-for delights of Egypt. God sent a huge flock of quails to punish them for their selfish cravings, and they gorged on the birds so that they were ill and some even died of their greed. Even Aaron and Miriam spoke out against Moses, for which Miriam—though not Aaron—was stricken for a week with leprosy.

From the oasis south of Beersheba, near the edge of Canaan, Moses sent out twelve scouts to spy out the land, to see if there were fortified towns, and if the soil were fertile. They returned after forty days and reported that the land was indeed flowing with milk and honey, but that the Canaanites were well armed and lived in large well-fortified cities. They brought back pomegranates, figs, and a bunch of grapes so large that it took two men to carry it. Caleb, one of the spies, and Joshua, were keen to go on; the other tribe leaders hesitated, even saying that they should perhaps go back to Egypt. An angry God declared that none from the original tribes, except Caleb and Joshua, should enter the Promised Land; only a new generation should inherit it. The next set-back was the revolt of *Korah, Dathan, and Abiram, all members of the tribe of Levi, but God's response was swift; the ground opened up and swallowed them and all their households. While they were encamped at Kadesh, Miriam died and was buried there.

They remained at Kadesh so long that forty years had passed since they left Egypt. They started to move once more, but fearing to attack Canaan from the south, they moved up the east side of the Jordan on the ancient caravan route called the 'King's Highway'. Though they promised not to plunder, or eat their way across the land, the petty kings refused them passage, forcing them into the wilderness. During this journey Aaron died, and was succeeded as High Priest by his son Eleazer. Again, the people complained, because they had been promised milk and honey and still only had manna to eat in a waterless wilderness, and they wanted meat. This rebellion was punished by a plague of poisonous snakes, until Moses set up a brazen serpent on a pole, and only those who looked at it were cured. Their journey continued through the land of the Moabites (*see* LOT), where many of the Jewish men cohabited with the Moabite women and were, through them, seduced into the worship of Baal. Another plague ensued and finally Moses conquered the lands of the Moabites and the Midianites and took the land of Moab. By now, a census showed that the only men left from the Exodus were Moses, Joshua, and Caleb. The Jews had become a large, highly organized tribe, hardened by forty years of desert life, and living according to the discipline imposed by Mosaic Law.

Moses's mission was now complete; he had transformed his people from abject submissive slaves, always looking back, like Lot's unfortunate wife, to the flesh-pots of Egypt and hankering for the easier life to be had by exchanging freedom and responsibility for subservience. They were now a hardened, purposive nation, determined to live as free men even if it meant conquering the land Moses said that God had promised to them. Moses laid his hands on Joshua and inducted him as the new leader of his people. He then climbed to the top of Mt. Pisgah which juts out of the range of the Mountains of Moab and looked out towards the west. Below him was the Jordan, twisting and turning in the chasm of the deepest valley on earth, to be lost in the Dead Sea. Jericho, the other side of the river, lay below him, Jerusalem on its heights above it, and behind stretched the wilderness of Judaea and the land of Canaan. God had promised that Moses should see the Promised Land, but also that he should not enter it. He died and was buried somewhere on Mt. Nebo, and his grave has never been found. Legend tells that this was to prevent him from being worshipped by the Jews, and also that the Devil tried to seize his body, but was prevented by the Archangel Michael. He was also said to have been assumed into Heaven, in an early 1st-century text (now lost) in Hebrew or Aramaic, but this account of Moses's assumption appears to have been written by a Pharisee who wished to recall the Jews to the older tradition of the Law and its ideals.

Moses is the towering figure of the OT: leader, lawgiver, teacher, prophet, healer, to whom God spoke face to face as a friend and counsellor. Without Moses the Jews in their long Egyptian bondage would have melted into one of the lesser tribes of the Mediterranean shores, and might well have merged into the barely differentiated populations of the area. He is the OT parallel of Christ, Who fulfilled all Moses's roles, but Who added the extra dimension of widening his mission, so that it was extended from the Jews to the whole human race. There are many incidents which correspond: salvation through the blood of the lamb on lintel and doorposts parallels salvation through the blood of Christ; the piece of miraculous wood which sweetened the bitter water of Marah parallels the wood of the cross as redemption for sin; salvation through Moses's arms being held up during the battle with the Amalekites is a forerunner of salvation through the Crucifixion; the water struck from the rock at Rephidim prefigures the water of Baptism, and is therefore often represented on fonts, e.g. at Hildesheim, and water containing the dust from the Golden Calf is also thought to symbolize the water of Baptism; the brazen serpent which saved those who looked upon it parallels the cross as the means of salvation; manna is the parallel of communion bread, and Aaron's Rod is a parallel of Joseph's rod which flowered, designating him as the spouse of the Virgin Mary.

Many of these events have appeared in works of art. Parts of a Moses cycle have survived in the synagogue in *Dura-Europos, notably the Finding in the Basket, the Burning Bush, and scenes from Exodus. Usually Moses is represented as an elderly, bearded man, staff in hand, and he thus appears in several catacomb paintings, for instance SS Pietro e Marcellino (3rd cent.), and the Cappella Greca, Catacomb of Priscilla (3rd cent.). Moses as a young man, beardless, appears in *The Crossing of the Red Sea* in the New Catacomb of the Via Latina (4th cent.), and also in some of the mosaics in Sta Maria Maggiore, Rome (5th cent.). Most of the major French cathedral portals include a figure of Moses among OT prophets, notably Chartres west front, middle door (12th cent.), and the west portals of Amiens, Reims, and Laon (13th cent.). The *Moses* by Claus Sluter in the *Puits de Moïse*, Champmol, Dijon (1395–1403) shows Moses with the 'horns' on his head which resulted from a 12th-century mistranslation of Exod. 34: 30 ('quod cornuta esset facies sua'—'horned' instead of 'beaming'), and he also appears thus in Perugino's fresco in the Cambio, Perugia (1500–4), and in Michelangelo's great statue of *Moses* on the Tomb of Julius II, San Pietro in Vincoli, Rome (1513–16). There are important cycles which directly compare the Life of Christ with the Life of Moses, such as the series of frescoes on either side of the *Sistine Chapel, painted in 1481–2, which once included the parallel between the Ascension and the legendary assumption of Moses (these two frescoes were destroyed by the collapse of the door into the Scala Regia). They were also subtly designed to insist on papal authority, since the Chapel was—and still is—the main site for Conclaves for papal elections. In the Sistine Ceiling, Michelangelo included *The Brazen Serpent* in one of the double corner spandrels as one of the major deliverances of the Jews. Other examples are the pair facing each other in the choir of San Giorgio Maggiore, Venice, by Tintoretto: the *Gathering of the Manna* and *The Last Supper*, both of 1594. The *Worship of the Golden Calf* by Poussin, *c.*1635 (London, NG), is an infrequently represented subject, but paintings of the *Finding of Moses* are legion, one of the most beautiful being by Tiepolo (*c.*1730: Edinburgh, NG). Tiepolo also painted the *Gathering of the Manna* in the pair of pictures he painted for Verolanuova, near Brescia, N. Italy (1735–40), its pendent being the *Sacrifice of Melchisedek.* Further examples on this theme are Henri Rousseau's *The Finding of Moses* (1892–95, Beyeler Gallery, Basel, Switzerland) and *Chagall's *Moses at the Burning Bush* (1960-66, Message Biblique, Musée Nationale, Nice, France).

Mount Athos *See* ATHOS.

Mount of Olives *See* OLIVES.

m

mouse A dirty and destructive nocturnal animal which was sometimes a symbol of the Devil. One wing of the Merode Altarpiece by the Master of Flémalle (New York, Met. Mus.) shows S. Joseph working as a carpenter, making mousetraps as a symbol of Christ's victory over the Devil. In Bestiaries, the mouse is equated with greedy and destructive men who covet the goods of others.

Mozarabic architecture, art *See* PRE-ROMANESQUE.

Murillo, Bartolomé Estebán (1618–82). Although Murillo painted a few genre subjects—ragged urchins or a gypsy girl flower-seller—and a handful of splendid portraits, he is rightly considered as a purely religious painter, although his choice of subjects was naturally circumscribed by the commissions he received, which were virtually always either from or on behalf of religious institutions, churches, or hospitals. His favourite subjects are the Virgin and Child—in glory, in the visions of saints, in Holy Family groups, and above all, the *Immaculate Conception, a very popular 17th-century subject and one which he made particularly his own. He avoids gory and violent martyrdoms—the closest to this is the *Martyrdom of S. Andrew* (*c.*1675–82: Prado)—his Crucified Christ is not shown on Calvary, but rather as part of the vision of a saint, his closest to suffering is in the distress of the *Prodigal Son* (1668: Washington, NG). His is, none the less, an art of great psychological insight and characterization, but always gentle, even tender.

The many versions of the *Immaculate Conception* necessarily use the traditional iconography of the subject; the Virgin with clasped hands and flowing robes stands on the globe, or on the crescent moon and stars, and is surrounded by little cherubs, as in the splendid example of *c.*1678 (Prado) which was once in the Hospitál de los Venerables in Seville, or the one of *c.*1660–5, also in the Prado. These, and many others like them, follow reasonably closely *Pacheco's instructions on the correct way in which the subject should be represented. He also painted an unusual subject, the *Two Trinities*, one in 1640 (Stockholm, Nat. Mus.) and for the second time at the end of his life, *c.*1670–2 (London, NG) showing the Virgin and S. Joseph with the Christ Child, and above them God the Father and the Dove of the Holy Ghost, the Holy Child being common to both groups.

Mysteries, Glorious, Joyful, Sorrowful *See* ROSARY.

mystery (or miracle) plays These have their origin in liturgical drama, which in the 7th/8th centuries began as dramatic homilies or sermons in dialogue. By the mid-Byzantine period a fully developed liturgical drama had evolved in Byzantium, which probably included a cave for the Nativity, the house of Mary for the Annunciation, the Raising of Lazarus, and similar scenes capable of dramatic realization. Liturgical drama also developed in the West and was presented in church, inserted into the Mass, and of this many Latin texts have survived. After the 12th century, with increasing intrusions of similar material, the representations became incompatible with the Mass and developed into separate functions arranged by guilds and confraternities, usually held in the church or in its immediate confines. In the 13th century the Umbrian *Laudi*, developed by confraternities of the *Laudesi* originally centred on Perugia, spread across Italy and the performances took place either in the church or chapel, or in the square outside. The *Laudesi* were primarily a penitential movement with the members forming a chorus, but by the end of the 13th century

Laudi in dialogue were enacted on a platform in order to be seen by the people, with a few fixed 'sites' such as Paradise and Hell, or a shed for the Nativity, and an artificial mound for the Transfiguration or the Agony in the Garden. Slowly the participants became actors with costumes, and scenery began to appear.

By the 14th and 15th centuries, permanent stages and settings evolved with the need for greater exposition. In Italy, for scenes such as the Annunciation or the House of Martha and Mary, several booths would be on the stage, but there was always a Paradise, raised above the rest, and if a Hell were needed it would have a demon or Leviathan with open jaws. In the German form, each of the incidents had a separate stage, but this required a large open space, where the booths began with Paradise and ended with the Ascension. Another form was the religious procession, where the stages were on carts which served as the 'mansions' for the various events depicted. Often these representations were part of Holy Week, or the festivals of Corpus Christi, Ascension, and Pentecost, and they are recorded as taking place all over Europe. The dramatic representations often lasted for several days according to what the narrative suggested.

Another major form of civic drama derived from the importance of processions. Often they began like the *Laudi*, and were in honour of the patron saint of the city, or of the guild or confraternity, but the spirit of competition in splendour, ostensibly in honour of the patron, soon took over. In Florence in the 15th century, and probably earlier, the guilds organized a procession every year in honour of the patron saint of Florence, S. John the Baptist, bearing candles for use in the Baptistery. Each guild was accompanied by little boys dressed as angels and all carried lighted torches. But the candle slowly evolved into large wooden edifices with images from the Life of the Baptist, borne on their shoulders by the members, the candles themselves being relegated to a very minor role. The yearly Mysteries in Florence sometimes were organized in the churches, but often spilled out into the big squares, such as the Feast of S. Ignatius in the piazza in front of Sta Maria Novella, or that of S. Bartholomew in Piazza Sta Croce. In the 15th century they were such elaborate affairs that architects like Brunelleschi designed the stage settings, which for the Feasts of the Ascension and Assumption in the Carmelite church involved 'angels' revolving in 'domes' high above the spectators' heads, to receive the ascending Christ and Virgin into Heaven, and for the Annunciation in the Church of the Annunziata he devised an elaborate setting in which the Angel Gabriel came down on a wire to the Virgin below, while God the Father appeared in a Paradise high above. The machinery which Francesco d'Angelo devised for a *Sacra Rappresentazione in the Carmine in 1439 was so heavy that it eventually brought the church roof down.

Liturgical dramas The Mass, in symbolic form, reproduces Calvary. On Palm Sunday the Gospel was read by three voices (it still is in major churches), to heighten the realism of the narrative. During Holy Week at Tenebrae on Good Friday, all the candles were extinguished so that the world without Christ should be experienced as darkness. Only one candle was left under the altar to symbolize Christ laid in the tomb, and brought out again to symbolize the conquest of Death.

In 970 Dunstan, Archbishop of Canterbury, described the 10th-century 'Resurrection Play' he had seen in Flanders. It was spread over several days: on Good Friday after the Veneration of the Cross, the cross was carried in a linen wrapping to the 'tomb' which had been prepared on an altar. During the night it was secretly removed, and only the cloth was left. During the first Mass of Easter morning a monk in a white alb came and sat beside the 'tomb'. Then other monks in long cloaks to look like the Holy Women came hesitantly to the 'tomb', thuribles in hand. The 'angel' asked, 'Whom seekest thou?' 'Jesus of Nazareth,' the 'women' answered. 'He is not here,' said the 'angel', 'He is risen. Come and see the place where he lay.' The 'angel' showed the place, the 'women' held the cloth before the congregation, and sang out 'The Lord is risen' and the congregation chanted in triumph and all the bells rang out. Dunstan did not invent this drama, but took over Continental practices, particularly those which spread from the Abbey of Fleury (later St-Benoît-sur-Loire), and during the Middle Ages these dramatic forms were common in churches.

Much of the vividness of medieval sculpture, in capitals and *portals, is derived from this type of dramatic treatment of the Gospel during the services of the various great feasts. Scenes which can only be inferred from the actual Gospel narrative, such as the Holy Women buying spices, in the Portal of St-Gilles-du-Gard, certainly occur, and in some cases the portal sculpture follows a mystery play very closely—an example is the *Mystère d'Adam* on the front of Notre-Dame-la-Grande, Poitiers, which begins on the left with the Fall of Adam and Eve and continues with the figures of the Prophets who in their prophecies of the coming of a Saviour and Redeemer renew the hope of a return to the lost Paradise. The *Play of the Prophets* from this part of the *Mystère* derives from a sermon by the pseudo-Augustine, often read by several different preachers, to render the prophetic texts more vivid. But in general, however vivid the imagery, the real inspiration comes from the Bible.

In England, the earliest mystery play was the Harrowing of Hell, of the late 13th century, and cycles of plays were organized by city corporations which divided the various incidents between the guilds. They were yearly features at Christmas, Easter, Corpus Christi, and Whitsun, held in York, Chester, Coventry, and Wakefield. They were staged on carts which could be moved round the city, and mixed the Gospel narrative or the legend which was being presented with comic by-play. The only surviving records are of the *Play of Mary Magdalene,* based on the legend of her conversion and her life later in Provence, and from Wakefield the *Second Shepherd's Play,* which contains comic interludes of a sheep stealer and the discovery of his trickery, followed immediately by the angel telling the shepherds to go to Bethlehem. These illustrate the difficulty of accounting for genre-type details in religious works as coming from the stage, when the contrary may well be true. There are, however, sufficient carved roof-bosses, paintings, and popular engravings to make it likely that the painters were often inspired by the plays.

The Reformation in N. Europe put an end to the staging both of mystery plays and dramatic interludes during the Mass, even in countries where the Mass itself survived. In France, for instance, they were prohibited in 1548, but lingered on here and there for a few more years. The Oberammergau Passion Play, first given in 1634 and repeated every ten years in thanksgiving for the cessation of plague, is probably ultimately descended from the medieval examples.

mystic marriage *See* CATHERINE OF ALEXANDRIA, S.

Mystic Meals The title of an altarpiece by Dieric *Bouts, of 1464–8, in St Pieter, Leuven (St-Pierre, Louvain), commissioned by the Confraternity of the Holy Sacrament, which has a large square central panel of the *Communion of the Apostles—i.e. the Institution of the Eucharist rather than the Last Supper. Four smaller panels, two on each side, represent the *Meeting of Abraham and Melchisedech* and the *Israelites gathering Manna,* on the left side, and *Elijah fed by an Angel* and the *Passover,* on the right. These four are OT *types of the Eucharist, suitable for the Confraternity.

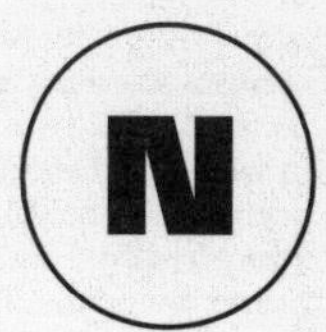

Nails, the Holy The nails used to fasten Christ to the Cross became relics, which were said to have been found by S. Helen with the *True Cross: the Iron Crown of Lombardy, in the cathedral treasury, Monza, so called because it was said to enclose inside the gold and jewelled circlet one or part of one of the nails used in the Crucifixion, and Sta Croce in Rome claim fragments, and others were claimed for the Ste-Chapelle in Paris and elsewhere. From the earliest representations of the Crucifixion in the 5th century there are always four nails, but, from the 13th in Italy at least, only three are shown, probably because this involves crossing the legs and giving a more twisted outline consonant with the Christus Patiens type of *crucifix. The author of the **Meditationes Vitae Christi* speaks of three nails and Nicola *Pisano's pulpit of 1259/60 in the Baptistery at Pisa has three, as have several 13th-century painted crucifixes. Three were normal for many years, but during the Counter-Reformation period the question was revived: *Molanus thought it insoluble, but *Pacheco recommended three, although in his paintings he showed both forms. The Instruments of the Passion—the *Arma Christi—usually have three nails.

Name, the Holy *See* NOMEN SACRUM.

Naomi *See* RUTH.

naos (Gk. temple) The sanctuary or inner cell of a pagan Greek temple. The word was taken over to describe the core of a centrally planned Byzantine church, where the liturgy takes place.

narthex (Gk. casket) The porch in front of the entrance to a church, where in Early Christian and Byzantine churches neophytes and penitents were assembled during the celebration of the Eucharist, to which they were not admitted until after baptism, or in the case of sinners, absolution. Sometimes the narthex was doubled, and an exonarthex for the outer part, and an esonarthex for the inner part, formed an introduction to the nave and aisles in Byzantine churches, and also in *Pre-Romanesque churches in W. Europe. In Byzantine churches stairs led from the narthex to the galleries of the *gynaeceum; in Pre-Romanesque ones they were often elaborated with towers and chapels to become a *westwork, with service staircases leading to the upper chapels, and also to the tribunes of the nave. One of the functions of the narthex was for the organization of processions, for which reason they became known in English churches as galilees, since the procession from the narthex to the altar symbolized Christ's journey from Galilee to Jerusalem for the Crucifixion. The south porch attached to the south transept at Lincoln, and the large chapel at the west end of Durham are both known as a 'galilee'.

Nathanael *See* BARTHOLOMEW, S.

Nativity of Christ (Christmas) The actual date of Christ's birth is unknown, but by 336 it was being celebrated in Rome on 25 December rather than on 6 January, the Feast of the *Epiphany. Nevertheless, it was many years before 25 December became universal (even now some Eastern churches keep the Old Christmas on 6 January). The Adoration of the *Magi, which is specifically associated with Epiphany, was therefore originally a more popular subject for representation, especially in the East. The biblical texts are scanty, even though Luke is supposed to have had his information from the Virgin herself. Matthew (2: 1) says 'In the time of King Herod, when Jesus was born in Bethlehem of Judaea, wise men from the East came to Jerusalem, asking, "Where is the child who has been born king of the Jews? For we observed his star at its rising, and have come to pay him homage."' Luke (ch. 2) gives more detail: Joseph went to Bethlehem, the city of David, for the census and there Mary 'gave birth to her first-born son, and wrapped him in swaddling clothes, and laid him in a manger; because there was no room for them in the inn. In that region there were shepherds living in the fields, keeping watch over their flock by night. Then an angel of the Lord stood before them, and the glory of the Lord shone around them, and they were terrified.' The angel told them that Christ the Lord had been born in Bethlehem and '"this will be a sign for you: you will find a child . . . lying in a manger . . . ". And suddenly there was with the angel a multitude of the heavenly host, praising God . . . The shepherds said one to another, Let us go now to Bethlehem, and see this thing which has taken place . . . So they went with haste and found Mary and Joseph, and the child lying in the manger.'

From a very early date this account was fleshed out with details by the writers of the *Apocryphal Infancy Gospels, especially the Protevangelium of *James and the *Pseudo-Matthew. 'James' tells how Mary was seized with labour pains on the way to Bethlehem, so Joseph found a cave and went in search of a midwife, who witnessed the birth in a great light which shone in the cave. She told *Salome, another midwife, who refused to believe that a virgin had given birth. Salome's hand withered, but was cured when she touched the Child. The Pseudo-Matthew adds to this the first mention of the ox and the ass, indispensable in all representations of the scene and based on Isa. 1: 3, 'The ox knows his master, and the ass his master's crib: but Israel does not know . . .'. The earliest representation of the beasts is on a sarcophagus of 320/5. Since Luke's account of the Nativity is immediately followed by the Annunciation to the Shepherds, naturally the two scenes were amalgamated, either as a background scene with the angel appearing to the shepherds, or as three shepherds (to match the three Magi) arriving 'with haste' to adore the Holy Child. This was a very popular theme in the West from the 15th to the 17th century, and the Annunciation and the Adoration were often coupled in altarpieces or in *predella* panels.

In the East, though rarely in the West, there was also a subsidiary scene of the midwives washing the new-born child. This is thought to be derived from pagan models of the Birth of Bacchus. It occurs in Giovanni *Pisano's two pulpits at Pistoia (1301) and Pisa Cathedral (1310), which have two figures of the Christ Child, one being washed, and the other lying in the manger in swaddling clothes. They also show the figure of Joseph, crouching on the ground with his head supported on his hand, a motive which became extremely popular. These reliefs also show a cave, rather than a stable, and are probably influenced by Byzantine prototypes such as the mid-12th-century mosaic in the Martorana at Palermo. The stable is, in any case, not recorded in the Gospels, only the manger (*praesepio*), which may well have been in a cave, such as still exist in the Holy Land. In the Middle Ages the stable was often shown as part of a ruined building, representing the Old Dispensation (see COVENANTS) or even a ruined palace, that of David, Christ's ancestor, as a *type of Christ's Kingdom. The Portinari Altarpiece by Hugo van der *Goes (Uffizi) shows a ruined palatial building with a carved stone shield over the door bearing a harp, the symbol of David. By the 15th century further accretions had been made. *S. Francis invented the Christmas Crib at Greccio in the 1220s, and in 1372 *S. Bridget of Sweden had seen a vision of the Nativity while actually in the Church of the Nativity at Bethlehem. Her *Revelations* were widely known in Europe by *c.*1400. The **Golden Legend* and the **Meditationes Vitae Christi* also added picturesque details, and in the 15th century they become not only David's palace, but a stable with an incongruous column of marble or porphyry—the *Meditationes* says: 'At midnight on Sunday, when the hour of birth came, the Virgin rose and stood erect against a column that was there. But Joseph remained seated, downcast perhaps because he could not prepare what was necessary. Then he rose and, taking some hay from the manger, placed it at the Lady's feet and turned away. Then the Son of the Eternal God came out of the womb of the mother without a murmur or lesion, in a moment; as He had been in the womb so He was now outside, on the hay at His mother's feet . . .'. This is often shown in Netherlandish altarpieces, e.g. Roger van der *Weyden's Bladelin Altar (Berlin). S. Bridget's description of her vision was also extremely popular and is easily recognized, since Mary is described as taking off her blue mantle and her shoes and kneeling on the ground, dressed in a white tunic, and adoring the naked Child, who lies on a bundle of hay on the ground. A brilliant light emanates from the Child, outshining the candle (or lantern) which is always held by Joseph. The eminently pictorial idea of the luminous Child was used by Northern painters from Geertgen tot Sint Jans (*c.*1490: London, NG) to Gerrit van Honthorst in the 1640s, and there is a lovely Italian example in Guido Reni's huge *Adoration of the Shepherds* of 1640–2 (London, NG).

Nativity of the Baptist *See* JOHN THE BAPTIST.

Nativity of the Virgin *See* MARY.

nature During the Middle Ages nature had two senses: *natura naturata* and *natura naturans*. *Natura naturata* literally means 'nature natured' or 'nature which is already created', and relates to the idea of the creative power of God as evidenced in creation. The latter, *natura naturans*, means 'nature naturing' or 'creative nature', and relates to the creative power of nature itself. In the Renaissance this was developed further and for Baruch Spinoza (1632—77) God and nature, in these created and creative forms, were the same.

nave (Lat. *navis*, a ship) The main space occupied by the congregation in a church, from the entrance to the choir, usually flanked on either side by aisles. The derivation from *navis* is partly because the nave is not unlike an upside-down ship, but also because it is the *Ark of Salvation. The *Apostolic Constitutions* of the 4th century say: 'Let the building be long, with its head to the East... and so it will be like a ship'. Sometimes the nave was reserved, and the laity herded into the aisles, as in the early Byzantine Church, but it is normally the congregational space. Whether the church has only a nave or whether it has aisles depends on the size of the congregation it served. Many single-vessel churches ended up, over the centuries, by having a succession of building campaigns so as to provide more aisles to allow space for side altars and larger congregations. Hundreds of English parish churches are evidence of this.

navicula (Lat. little ship) An incense-boat. *See* LITURGICAL VESSELS.

Nazarener, the Two students at the Vienna Academy, Johann Friedrich *Overbeck (1789–1869) and Franz Pforr (1788–1812), frustrated by the stultifying nature of the teaching, formed in 1809 an association which they called the Lukasbrüderschaft (Brotherhood of *S. Luke). In 1810 they and some others went to Rome, determined to revive religious art by basing their works on *Dürer, *Perugino, and early (i.e. pre-Roman) *Raphael. In Rome they were joined by Peter Cornelius (1783–1867), and others with similar ideas. They worked together on joint commissions—the Casa Bartholdi with the Life of Joseph in Egypt, and the Casino Massimo with illustrations from Dante. Their work and their ideas were received with almost equal praise and blame. Their dress, of wide flowing capes and long hair, marked them out, and was the origin of the at first mocking nickname of 'Nazarener' (an allusion to the description of the Nazarites, in Num. 6). In their aims and in their rejection of the artistic fashions of their day, they were the forerunners of the Pre-Raphaelite Brotherhood (*see* PRB) in England. Their aims were not to overturn the ideals of the Carracci or the Baroque, but to set up a different standard which returned to older models. Pforr died in 1812, and Cornelius and others returned to Germany where they had very successful careers and were seen as 're-creators' of German art. Overbeck, who had become a Catholic, remained in Italy. Many of their adherents believed that by imitating, say, Fra Angelico, they could create works like his, but, as usual in such cases, the imitation of externals blinds the copyist to the true quality of the object of his emulation. The belief that they could revive religion by reviving the artistic forms of earlier times may have been a noble aspiration, but it condemned their works to an empty conventionality.

Nazirite (Heb. separated, consecrated) A Nazirite is dedicated to God, according to Num. 6: 1–21, and may be a man or a woman. A Nazirite must never shave the head nor cut his or her hair, no wine or other product of the vine may be eaten or drunk, and approaching a dead body, even that of the closest members of the family, is a defilement which involves undergoing a rite of purification by shaving the head and retaking the vows, and the previous period of consecration no longer counts. Even if someone dies near a Nazirite the same penalties are incurred. Originally, a Nazirite's vow was for life, but later it could be dispensed by further ceremonies of release. Usually, the decision to be a Nazirite was made by adults, but some have been Nazirites from birth, such as *Samson and *Samuel. The reason for the ban on vine products was because originally the Jews were a nomadic people and vine-growing requires a settled life, like that of the Canaanites and Philistines. It is difficult to see how the Nazirite obligation to avoid dead bodies could be reconciled with Samson's slaughter of Philistines, unless that of enemies does not count.

ND An abbreviation for Notre Dame (Fr.) or occasionally Nostra Donna (Ital.), both meaning Our Lady.

Nebuchadnezzar (Vg. **Nabuchodonosor)** The OT records him as King of Babylon (d. 561/2 BC), the greatest potentate of his age, and the creator of the Hanging Gardens of Babylon, one of the Seven Wonders of the Ancient World. He destroyed Jerusalem in 588–586 BC and carried off most of the Temple treasure and many citizens, including *Daniel. The Book of Daniel tells how Shadrach, Meschach, and Abednego, Daniel's companions, refused to worship an image of Nebuchadnezzar and were thrown into the Fiery Furnace but were rescued by an angel and emerged unharmed. Daniel himself interpreted two of Nebuchadnezzar's dreams (Dan. 2: 31–45 and 4: 10ff.). The first was of a colossal statue of a man, made of gold, silver, bronze, and iron, but with feet of clay, which was utterly destroyed by a stone rolling down a hillside. This predicted the world empires that would follow Nebuchadnezzar's own and that they would all be destroyed by the everlasting Kingdom of God. The second was of a huge tree, reaching up to Heaven, but cut down to a stump by an angel. This was a warning against Nebuchadnezzar's own overweening pride: he took no notice and was driven mad, wandering like a beast and 'ate grass like oxen, and his body bathed with the dew of heaven, until his hair grew as long as eagles' feathers, and his nails became like bird's claws'. In the **Speculum Humanae Salvationis* the destruction of the statue is seen as a *type of the legendary fall of the idols as the Holy Family passed on the Flight into *Egypt, but the best-known image of Nebuchadnezzar is probably the colour-print heightened with watercolour, by William Blake (1795: London, Tate).

Neoclassicism is a form of Classically inspired art encouraged by a revival of interest in ancient art in reaction against the pompous theatricality of Late Baroque and the 'frivolity' of *Rococo. Although it was already a factor in England and France fairly early in the 18th century, a powerful influence came from Rome about 1750, partly because the German J. J. Winckelmann, one of its first apologists, insisted on the 'noble simplicity and calm grandeur' of ancient Greek art (which he knew almost entirely from Roman copies), and partly because, from 1748, the publication of discoveries at Herculaneum and Pompeii were revealing what ancient Roman paintings actually looked like. At much the same time, architectural theorists, like the Jesuit M.-A. Laugier in his *Essai sur l'architecture* of 1753, were promoting a theory of a rational, austere architecture founded on 'first principles', such as he believed were behind Greek architecture. These theories were encouraged by the rediscovery of the Greek temples in Sicily and even those in Greece itself, then still a virtually inaccessible country. Early publications of Greek ruined temples include those by the Frenchman Le Roy in his *Les Ruines des plus beaux Monuments de la Grèce*, 1758, followed by the Britons Stuart and Revett's *Antiquities of Athens*, 1762–1818; they had been in Greece in 1751 but were very dilatory in publication. In France, Roman Classical forms remained popular, and Joseph Peyre advocated adherence to Roman forms and studied Piranesi's prints of Roman ruins and views of the city published from 1745 onwards, and Vasi's prints of views of ancient and modern Rome produced for tourists from 1747 to 1761, as well as the etchings by Bellicard, Duflos, and Barbault from 1748 to 1761. Peyre's manual on architectural teaching of 1765 was heavily Roman orientated. But the most influential architectural theorists of the time were E.-L. Boullée and the Abbé Laugier, though Boullée's megalomaniac projects meant that he built little, and his treatise remained unpublished until 1953. Laugier's *Essai sur l'architecture* set out a theory of Neoclassicism which rejected all Renaissance forms and advocated classical as the perfect embodiment of simple economic needs. Boullée's pupil J.-N.-L. Durand was the most influential teacher of the day, particularly through his books, *Recueil et paralléle des Édifices*, 1800, and *Précis des Leçons*, 1801–5, in which his teaching was very classical. Another Boullée pupil was J.-F. Chalgrin, whose now much altered Paris church of St-Philippe-du-Roule, 1768–74, was built on a basilican plan which largely re-established that design in Europe, and has an imposing Doric portico. Chalgrin also finished Servandoni's St-Sulpice in 1776, and was the architect of the Arc de Triomphe, 1806–35, though its originally more austere appearance was modified to greater flamboyance by the great sculptural groups, particularly that by Rude. Few churches were built during the Age of Reason, but J. G. Soufflot's Ste-Geneviève in

Paris, begun in 1757, was called 'the first example of a perfect architecture' by Laugier. It was still unfinished at Soufflot's death in 1780, was secularized during the Revolution, altered, and renamed the Panthéon in an obvious reference to the Roman temple, and used for the tombs of Revolutionary heroes, whose interment there did not survive for long, and then became the burial-place of Napoleon's marshals. P.-A. Vignon's La Madeleine, on its imposing site at the head of the Rue de la Paix, was ordered by Napoleon in 1806 as a 'Temple of Glory' and only became a church after his defeat in the Peninsular War and the loss of Spain in 1813. It is a heavily designed Corinthian temple, on a high podium, dark inside, with the showy opulence which became almost a hallmark of Napoleon's commissions. The first monument built after the end of the First Empire in 1815 was the Chapelle Expiatoire, 1816–24, by P.-F. Fontaine, an austerely simple chapel of chilly grandeur commemorating Louis XVI and Marie Antoinette, as well as other members of the Royal family who were executed during the Terror. But Neoclassicism slowly modified as the years of the Restoration proceeded, from L.-H. Lebas's very simple basilica of Notre-Dame-de-Lorette, 1823–36, with its rigid trabeated Ionic colonnade, and coffered ceiling as its only ornament, to Lepère and Hittorff's St-Vincent-de-Paul, of 1824–44, on its magnificent site with almost Baroque staircase and carriage-drive approach. Though the massive Ionic portico looks uncompromisingly Greek-intentioned, the two large square towers and the Corinthian pilasters on the corners of the façade and the towers show a renewed interest in historicism in architecture (as if Greek and Roman Romantic Classicism did not also fall within that category).

In Germany, the chill of Neoclassicism proved fatal to the joyous exuberance of Late Baroque. Until the end of the Napoleonic wars in the early 19th century, Germany was either occupied or was a battleground; it continued to consist of a number of independent kingdoms each with a capital where a high quality of architectural design and execution was achieved, largely based on Durand's *Précis des Leçons*, reinforced by the number of young German architects trained in France. The importance of the Greek element in Classical Revival emerged with Karl Gotthard Langhans's Brandenburg Gate in Berlin, 1788–94, his most famous work, which became the first of the monumental gateways which had a Europe-wide popularity in the early 19th century. Though built in Greek Doric, its proportions were more elegant than those of true Doric, but it marked the entry of Greek rather than Roman into European architectural style. David Gilly, a member of a Huguenot family established in North Germany, was employed by King Friedrich Wilhelm to work in Berlin, but his son Friedrich would have far outshone his father had he lived beyond 1800. He had travelled in England and France, knew the work of Soane, and had absorbed much of the ethos of the 'glory architecture' sponsored by Napoleon, and the designs—almost all unexecuted—by Ledoux and Boullée which he had seen in Paris. At his death he left designs for a projected monument to Frederick the Great; these were for a Greek Doric 'Parthenon' raised on a high podium approached by austere Piranesi-inspired triumphal arches and monumental stairways, and an avenue of obelisks. It remained a project, but it inspired a Greek Revival and was particularly formative on Karl Friedrich Schinkel, his fellow pupil in David Gilly's studio. Schinkel became the most important architect working in Berlin and Potsdam. He only built two major churches: a modest and unattractive Berlin cathedral, which was replaced in 1894, and the splendid Nikolaikirche in Potsdam built in 1830–7 to the base of the dome, and finished by Persius, 1842–5, and completed finally in 1850. The main block of the lower part of the structure was designed as a high podium to be dominated by a high dome, and its centrally planned internal space was organized on the system evolved by Wren at St Paul's Cathedral, which was the main inspiration for the dome. Unfortunately, the purity of the design was spoilt by the addition of corner towers, made necessary as stabilizers when the dome was completed by Persius. Schinkel's main contribution lay in his grand civic works, notably the Altes Museum, Berlin, 1824–8.

Heinrich Hübsch, who became state architect in Baden in 1826, when the Greek ideals were beginning to fade, published a telling treatise in 1828 which sums up the dilemma facing architects at the time: 'In what Style should we build?', to which the answer in many areas was unsympathetic to Classical. In Munich, however, no such doubts prevailed. Leo von Klenze had been a pupil of Gilly in Berlin, and in Paris of Durand, and Percier and Fontaine. He became architect to Ludwig I in Munich in 1816, and he was principally a civic architect concerned with public monuments such as the Sculpture Gallery, town-planning systems, the royal palace, and adjacent state buildings. While he began as a severe 'Grecian', his style modified over the long years he worked in Munich—his last building was in 1863, the year before his death—from his early Classicism to an acceptance of Italian 16th-century Renaissance, and even to the Roman-cum-Romanesque of the *rundbogenstil* (round arch style), a term proposed by Hübsch in his 1828 treatise for such medieval revivals. Klenze's recreation of Gilly's design for the Frederick the Great memorial was built to commemorate German heroes and worthies; it was a Greek 'Parthenon' built outside Regensburg on a hill overlooking the landscape, and like Gilly's project, it had a grand substructure of monumental approaches and stairways. It was originally designed in 1816–21, but was not built until 1830–42, by which time such a powerfully Classical style was being superseded by the simple, more domestic Biedermeyer. Klenze's only church was the palace chapel of All Saints, 1826–37, partly Classical in the mode of Vignon's La Madeleine, but with a sequence of domes inspired partly from Byzantine via St Mark's, Venice. The end of the Grecian-inspired Classical Revival is clearly marked by the design by Persius of the Friedenskirche (Peace church) in Potsdam, built 1845–8 after his death, but which is an Early Christian basilica, even to the point of having in the apse a mosaic brought from Murano, outside Venice. Historicism in architecture now ranges freely but this freedom was short-lived, in that the *Gothic Revival which was to become so important had already begun to point in new directions.

A very fine example of Classical, blending Greek and Roman, was built in Copenhagen: the cathedral of Vor Frue Kirke (Our Lady) by Christian Hansen, in 1810–29. This has a Doric portico with, over it, a plain tower; inside, the long nave has on either side square piers with round-headed arches, supporting a heavy, but slightly more decorative Roman Doric colonnade, which in turn supports a massive Roman coffered barrel vault, pierced by a few small openings which are square in the nave, and circular in the diagonally coffered dome so as to provide lanterns. The church is magnificent, but of chilly grandeur, its main decoration being Thorwaldsen's classicizing statues of Christ in the apse, and the Apostles against each of the nave piers. He also built the chapel of the Royal palace of Christiansborg, which alone survived the fire of 1884, with an exterior based on Vignola's Sant'Andrea in Via Flaminia, Rome.

In England, the major architect of the age, Sir John Soane, created a style of Classical simplicity, but with great sophistication; he was unsurpassed in his use of sequences of spatial relationships and austere decoration. To his great rival, Nash, whose architecture he despised, all was grist to the mill, and he moved easily from Classical of a Roman rather than Grecian type, to an often gimcrack crocketty Gothic. The true architecture of the 19th century was the new iron, brick, and glass of utilitarian buildings—railways, factories, mills—but these functional expressions of the age were dismissed as too vulgar and commonplace to be considered as suitable for public buildings whether civic or religious. For these, some form of decorative fantasy was needed, hence noble porticoes and grandiose elevations, fine towers and grand arcades. Even an architect as great as Soane could be drawn into the charade of offering alternative Classical or Gothic designs for a church—a practice which became common as the century progressed. The need to provide more churches for an increasing urban population eventually brought about the Act for the Building of New Churches, 1818, but work proceeded slowly since the aftermath of the Napoleonic wars was not a propitious moment financially. The forms dictated by Romantic Classicism involved a more sophisticated visual and educational background than did Gothic, ever present in Westminster and Southwark, and in so many cathedrals and parish churches nationwide; the fact was that though the Commissioners for the Act eventually built many churches, most of them were in 'Gothic', because it was much cheaper; it eliminated expensive columned porticoes. After about 1830 'Commissioners' Gothic' became a term, if not of contempt, certainly of disillusionment with what could be expected even of the best talent if working on such stony ground.

The best Classical churches were built privately in the more affluent parts of London, and include Thomas Hardwick's St Marylebone, begun as a small chapel in 1813, but soon increased in size and importance; the Inwoods, father and son, at St Pancras church from 1818 excelled themselves in Greek Revival, with a tower combining the Choragic Monument and the Tower of the Winds in

Athens, and vestries on either side of the choir which project well beyond the building and are crowned by copies of the Atlantes of the Erechtheum. One of the most striking examples was Nash's All Souls, Langham Place, at the junction of Upper Regent Street with the already developed Portland Place, so placed that it forms an eye-catching pivot from Nash's own development of Regent Street via Portland Place to his Park Crescent, which leads to his development of Regent's Park itself. The circular columned portico of the church encloses the cylinder providing the main entrance, which then rises to project above the portico to be crowned by a sharp spire, creating a strong if anachronistic contrast to the Classical portico below. But the preference for Gothic was confirmed by such excellent examples as John Pinch of Bath's St Mary, Bathwick, of 1814–20 and by Barry's charming St Peter's, Brighton, of 1823. These were private, not Commissioners' churches; in fact, of the 214 churches built by them only 40 were Classical.

Perhaps the finest Neoclassical was produced north of the Border. The New Town of Edinburgh was developed from 1770 onwards, beginning with Charlotte Square in the west, which was designed by Robert Adam, and reached along the wide George Street to Dundas House at its eastern end, designed by William Chambers. Charlotte Square had a church on its west side, forming a striking focal point at the end of George Street. Now that most of the area is given up to offices rather than to the residential purposes for which it was built, the redundant and empty St George's has gained a new life as the West Register House—an extension to the main Register House built by Robert Adam in Princes Street. It is a centrally planned building, with a block-like projecting pavilion on either side, so that the tetrastyle Ionic portico is embedded between them, crowned by a high entablature and parapet, with above it a tall drum with columns round it and a further drum section supporting a dome and lantern. The interior is now filled with five floors housing documents. In building the church in 1811, Robert Reid used Adam's original designs, but modified them extensively. The whole area of the New Town continued to be developed with further squares, crescents, and circles built from 1815, after the Napoleonic wars ended, all lined with massive, severe, even dour stone houses, and fine churches, such as St Andrew and St George on George Street, by the engineer Major Andrew Frazer, 1782–7, an oval, or rather elliptical, building, which was the first use in the UK of this form, earlier than the Neoclassical oval All Saints, Newcastle, built in 1786. It has a fine tetrastyle portico of Corinthian columns, and a tower and steeple over 160 ft. high, and a galleried interior like most Nonconformist preaching churches. The further development of the New Town was a 19th-century version of the 18th-century development of Bath by the Woods, and further churches were built, such as St Mary's, Belleview Crescent, by Thomas Brown, 1824, with a projecting hexastyle Corinthian portico with over it a high tower built in stages with a progression of Orders from Doric at the clock stage through Ionic to Corinthian below the pointed dome and lantern. The final grand buildings in the whole complex were the Royal Institution (now the Scottish Royal Academy), 1822 and 1831, and the National Gallery, 1850, immediately adjoining Princes Street on the Mound, both by W. H. Playfair, and both in uncompromising Grecian form. Edinburgh was not the only Scottish city to develop very grand Grecian Revival churches, and the finest were by an architect who bore the sobriquet of 'Greek' Thomson. Alexander Thomson built three churches in Glasgow, of which the finest was the Caledonian Road Free Church, 1856–7, on a high podium, surmounted by a deep hexastyle portico flanked by a huge, tall square tower crowned by a small square lantern. This magnificent building in one of the poorest quarters of the city has now been vandalized probably beyond saving, but his St Vincent Street church, 1859, and his Queen's Park church of 1857 mark a talent as original and as inventive as Soane, and are well preserved. Thomson's churches were all built for strict Nonconformist congregations, and his austere designs reflect that uncompromising faith. The Romantic Classical trend in Scottish architecture was not only manifested in its religious buildings, but also for such utilitarian structures as the Water Works in Perth, and much of the architecture of Aberdeen by Archibald Simpson reflected, and still does despite so much disastrous demolition, a love of the regularity and authority of the Classical.

It is not surprising that most New World architecture followed the fashions of the Old World, the difference now being that instead of local builders relying on Campbell's *Vitruvius Britannicus*, of 1715 onwards, or Gibbs's

Rules for Drawing the Several Parts of Architecture, of 1732, or any of the other important books on ancient and modern architecture which poured from the European presses in the 18th century, the architects themselves were now in America, though they were new arrivals there and European trained. Romantic Classicism therefore was as important in the Eastern states of America as it was in Europe. Benjamin Latrobe was born in England, the son of a Moravian pastor, spent part of his childhood in Germany, and then returned to England where he became a pupil of Samuel Pepys Cockerell in architecture, and of John Smeaton in engineering, so that he acquired not only a solid training in his first choice, but also an important training in hydraulics, canals, harbours, and bridge-building. He arrived in Richmond, Va., in 1795, where his first patron was Jefferson, and he moved to Philadelphia in 1798, where his first works were civic ones, a bank and the city's new Water Works, both in an uncompromising Greek Revival style (both now destroyed). He had a long and busy career, but probably his finest work was the Roman Catholic cathedral of Baltimore, 1804–14, which demonstrates his understanding of, and admiration for, Soane. The church is an elongated central plan, with a low central dome borne on Soane's type of depressed arches, with galleries over the aisles borne on Ionic columns, with a repetition of the low dome on segmental arches over the high altar, which is backed by a screen of four Ionic columns with shallow niches between them. His decoration is restricted to shallow square coffers in the arches over the aisle galleries, and to circular ones in the main and subsidiary domes, with a typically Soane type of rosette in them. The building is a masterpiece of majestic restraint. Grecian Classicism in America was not derived either from first-hand knowledge or from such important secondary material as Le Roy or Stuart and Revett. What were in general use were manuals of the 'How to do it' type, prepared by men like Asher Benjamin, who wrote seven books, at first spreading Robert Adam's designs which he knew through their publication by Wm. Pain. He designed various buildings in the Connecticut Valley, and to supplement his income began publishing manuals such as *The Country Builder's Assistant*, 1797, and was influenced by Pain's *Practical House Carpenter* of 1789. When he moved to Boston in 1802, he called himself a 'housewright'. In 1806 he published *The American Builder's Companion*, and its 2nd edition of 1811 draws heavily on Wm. Chambers's 1759 *Treatise on Civil Architecture*, but after this Benjamin's books are more handbooks on architectural theory and practice, plus technical knowledge, than mere pattern-books. His fifth and sixth books, *The Practice of Architecture*, 1833, his *Builder's Guide*, of 1838, and his last, *The Elements of Architecture*, 1843, go a long way further than his earlier pattern- or style-book approach in treating of the use of cast iron, and tests for stress and strength in American timber. He was a competent teacher, particularly for rural builders. He died in 1845.

John Haviland, of English birth and training, was in Russia in 1815, but in Philadelphia by 1816. His *Builder's Assistant*, in three volumes, 1818–21, was the first to detail Greek Orders, but despite his early Greek Revival interest he abandoned it for the Gothic Revival, in which he had a long career. The third important writer was Minard Lafever, who was American born, began as a carpenter and was a self-taught architect. In 1829 he wrote *The Young Builder's General Instructor*, was a Greek Revivalist in *The Modern Builder's Guide*, of 1833, and in *The Beauties of Modern Architecture* revealed himself in a sensitive and sophisticated light. He made much use of English guides such as Peter Nicholson on technical matters, as in Lafever's *Modern practice of staircase and handrail construction*, 1838. Lafever reacted strongly against the romantic and fanciful Gothic of Batty Langley and Horace Walpole, but despite his earnestness he was never among the followers of Pugin. He was a very eclectic architect, whose best Gothic building was the fine Holy Trinity, Brooklyn Heights, 1844–7, but whose civil works were often in Renaissance and Palladian styles. Above all, the 'How to do it' books were written to help rural builders to cope with the development in the West, where generally wood was the only available material in communities which needed civic and religious buildings in their creation of new towns as they pushed out the frontiers of the West. This was much the same that had occurred in the earlier 18th century when adaptations of James Gibbs's church designs became common in New England towns.

St Paul's, which became the Anglican cathedral of Boston, was built by Alexander Parris in 1819–21, in Ionic, and his Unitarian church known as the Stone Temple was built in Quincy, Mass., in 1828, in a style similar to the Greek Revival churches then being built in England. By the mid-century fashion in building style was moving away from Grecian in the direction of a more eclectic Classicism, which included Renaissance forms, and also toward the *rundbogenstil* (round arch style, adapted from Romanesque), particularly with the influx of German or German-trained architects such as Leopold Eidlitz from Prague, and Paul Schulze, who had already provided designs for the Appleton Chapel at Harvard before settling in America. The Harvard Chapel was a version of the frankly Romanesque Revival Ludwigskirche in Munich, omitting one of its towers, but Thomas Tefft, who made his first mark when still a student with a brilliant design for the railway station in Providence of 1848, went on to build churches in New England in brick with tall spires in a *rundbogenstil*, which he later abandoned for a style closer to Barry.

The Gothic Revival seemed to impose rather more discipline on architectural fantasy, once the stricter forms of Romantic Classical had become old-fashioned, but it was fairly short-lived, lasting hardly more than a couple of decades, from 1855 to 1875, and its vogue was largely due to the popularity of Ruskin's *Seven Lamps of Architecture* (1840) and *The Stones of Venice* (1851–3). But the Civil War from 1861 to 1865 ended any building enterprise, so that the most notable High Gothic in America, the Memorial Hall at Harvard, projected in the 1860s, was not built until 1870–8, but it has to be admitted that any form of Gothic in America is rootless as it never is in Europe, where it is vividly present in its original creation. *Rundbogenstil* succeeds because it is more adaptable to secular building, and H. H. Richardson, after a couple of High Gothic churches, the Unitarian Church, Springfield, Mass., which he built after the Civil War when he returned to America from the École des Beaux-Arts in Paris, and his Grace Episcopal Church in Medford, Mass., of 1867–8, made his first true mark with his Brattle Street church in Boston of 1870–2 in a powerful Romanesque which suited his feeling for mass and stone, and he created a formidable impact with his Trinity Church, Boston, of 1873–7, where Old and New World meet in the French of the central Auvergne and a Butterfield type of apse, transepts, and tower of massive solidity. Though he said that the massive central tower owed its inspiration to the Old Cathedral of Salamanca, there would also appear to be a hint of Tournai Cathedral and the Grossintmartin of Cologne. His various civic works—the Hampden County Courthouse, Springfield, Mass., of 1872, and the Allegheny County Jail in Pittsburgh, of 1884–8, are demonstrably penitential works in their rough-hewn stone, and his seminal Marshall Field Store, Chicago, 1885–7, in *rundbogenstil* (now destroyed), demonstrates his assimilation of Romanesque and its successful translation to new uses and modern life.

In sculpture the imitation of simple Greek forms often led to insipidity and few overtly religious subjects were undertaken, although allegorical figures continued to be popular, especially on funerary monuments, which provided many commissions for sculptors. Flaxman, Canova, and Thorwaldsen were all major Neoclassical sculptors who provided large allegorical monuments, but Flaxman's claim to have Christianized monumental sculpture probably means no more than that he used piously generalized figures instead of the Baroque rhetoric of his predecessors. In Thorwaldsen's grandiose figures of *Christ* and the twelve *Apostles* in Copenhagen Cathedral, Vor Frue Kirke, the giant figure of Christ stands in the apse, and the Apostles each stand against one of the square piers of the nave. They do not, however, give any impression of religious feeling, but more the sensation of an effort to reconcile Christian with Classical heroes. Neither was there any movement towards religious sculpture in France, where religious expression had been out of the question during the Revolution, and where artistic endeavour afterwards had tended to concentrate on Napoleonic rather than on divine glory.

History painting was almost entirely concerned with Greek and Roman history and the few religious subjects, sometimes set as subjects for competitions such as the French Prix de Rome, were often treated in a late Baroque style rather than a truly Neoclassical manner. Ingres painted a few religious pictures, such as the *S. Symphorian* (1834: Autun Cath.), provoking him to self-exile in Italy, so angry was he at its public reception. His main art was his portrait-painting. His pupil Hippolyte Flandrin specialized in religious wall-painting, mainly in Paris churches, but remained a marginal figure. Neoclassical painting did, however, merge into an early Romantic feeling in the works of the *Nazarener and the Pre-Raphaelites (*PRB), creating a new form of religious art, which, however, too readily lent itself to the production of sentimental pictures leading to *bondieuserie and its counterpart, *repository art, of which even so fine a painter as Ingres could be guilty. In England, there was no call for paintings in churches, and William Dyce was more an administrator than artist. His religious pictures, close to the Nazarene in type, are always sincerely felt, though verging sometimes on religious genre-painting.

Nepomuk, Saint John *See* JOHN.

Neri, Saint Philip *See* PHILIP.

Neumann, Johann Balthasar (1687–1752), was an inventive German Baroque architect, contemporary with the *Asam brothers, and J. M. *Fischer in Germany, and the Austrians *Fischer von Erlach and Hildebrandt. He was born in Cheb, in Bohemia, but moved to Würzburg in 1711 and studied architecture and surveying, becoming a military engineer. By 1717 he had travelled widely and he must have seen works by famous contemporaries, including *Guarini and Juvarra. In 1719 Johann Philipp, Graf Schönborn, became Prince-Bishop of Würzburg, and immediately began planning a new palace, of which Neumann was the architect. In 1729 he was made director of all building in Würzburg and Bamberg, and in 1733 Trier as well. Johann Philipp also introduced him to other Schönborns, notably Friedrich Karl, also a Prince-Bishop, for whom he built churches as well as continuing the Residenz.

Neumann's first church was the Schönborn family chapel attached to the cathedral, and the chapel in the Residenz in the 1720s/30s, a brilliant design of interlocked ovals in a rectangular shell. He pursued this system of creating a series of oval spaces one merging into the next, almost dissolving the walls by flooding the interior with light, and crowning the whole with a shallow dome which seems to float over the space below. His masterpiece is *Vierzehnheiligen, closely followed by the Abbey of Neresheim, 1747–53, composed from a series of interlocked ovals on different axes, with a circular choir. His brilliant mixture of painting and exuberant white and gilded sculpture, combined with the effulgence of light, create effects expressive of the popular devotional enthusiasm of the time.

Newman, Barnett *See* NORTH AMERICA.

New Zealand *See* AUSTRALIA, NEW ZEALAND, AND PACIFIC.

Nicaea, First and Second Councils of The first General (Ecumenical) *Council was called by the Emperor Constantine himself in 325, in an effort to end the Arian heresy. Little about it is known with certainty and it had no effect on the arts. The Second (7th Ecumenical) Council, originally called by the Empress Irene at Constantinople in 786 to settle the *Iconoclastic Controversy, was broken up by Iconoclastic soldiers. It reconvened at Nicaea in 787 and condemned Iconoclasm, asserting that *hyperdulia*, the veneration given to *icons, is not *latria*, the worship which is due to God alone. Nevertheless, the spirit of Iconoclasm lingered on. Another ruling made by the Council, forbidding *double monasteries, was observed in the East, but largely disregarded in the West.

niche A recess in a wall, usually upright and sometimes framed with mouldings and surmounted by a pediment, and sometimes left unadorned. It is normally made to contain a statue or an ornamental vase. Examples of the unadorned type are found in neoclassical buildings, such as the wall behind the altar of the Catholic cathedral in Baltimore. An example of the more decorative type is the niche in the façade of Orsanmichele in Florence made by Donatello and Michelozzo for Donatello's bronze *S. Louis of Toulouse* and now containing the group of *The Incredulity of S. Thomas* by Verrocchio.

Nicholas of Bari (Myra), Saint, is one of the most popular of all saints, both in East and West, especially under his nickname Santa Claus (from Dutch Sint Niklaas). Almost nothing is known of his life, but he is said to have been born *c.*270 and to have died on 6 December *c.*345/52. The custom of giving presents to good children on 6 December led to its association with Christmas since Nicholas is also the patron saint of children. His cult was popular by the 6th century, but the earliest Life dates from the 9th century, and in the West the cult was forwarded by the **Golden Legend*. He was Bishop of Myra (now called Dembre, in Turkey) and is always represented as an elderly bearded man in episcopal vestments, Orthodox in Eastern representations, Latin in Western ones. He rarely has any attribute in Eastern icons, but usually has three golden balls or discs in Western paintings. His relics were in his cathedral in Myra, but by 1087 it had fallen under Turkish rule and the relics were stolen ('rescued') by sailors from Bari in S. Italy, probably pre-empting a similar raid by Venetians. Among the many miracles attributed to him are several in aid of seamen, and he is often shown flying down to rescue storm-tossed mariners. Many improbable stories can be found in the *Golden Legend* and elsewhere, but the most frequently represented include those of the impoverished nobleman who was contemplating selling his three daughters into prostitution, since he could no longer support them. They were rescued by Nicholas, who threw a bag of gold through the window on three successive nights—hence the golden balls as his attribute. He discovered once that, in a time of famine, an innkeeper had killed three boys, cut them up, and salted them in tubs to provide food for his table. Nicholas invoked them and they arose from the brine-tubs. A similar miracle occurred when, during a famine in his own diocese, Nicholas asked a ship's captain to unload part of his cargo of grain. When the captain objected that he would be unable to deliver the full load he was carrying, angels came down from Heaven and poured sacks of corn into the hold to make up the loss. A *predella* by Fra Angelico (Vatican Mus.) shows this and also Nicholas coming to the rescue of a ship in a storm. The three boys and the three girls are part of an altarpiece by Gerard David (Edinburgh, NG).

Nicholas of Tolentino, Saint (1245–1305), was an Augustinian friar, born near Ancona in the Marches of Italy and active from 1275 in Tolentino, where he is buried. He is said to have worked 300 miracles. In the 16th to 18th centuries his cult spread from Antwerp to Lima in Peru: he is a patron saint of both cities. In art he is shown as an Augustinian friar in a black habit with a leather girdle, with a star on his breast or above his head, and holding a lily and/or a book. The chapel in his church at Tolentino has a series of paintings of his life (*c.*1340), but he is otherwise rarely represented. The young Raphael painted an altarpiece of him in glory (1501), but it was destroyed in 1789 and is known only from two fragments and a bad copy. He was canonized only in 1446, and the panel by Piero della Francesca (Milan, Poldi-Pezzoli Mus.), once thought to represent S. Thomas Aquinas, has been shown to be part of a lost altarpiece of the *Madonna and Child with Augustinian Saints*, other parts of which are in London (NG), Lisbon, and New York (Frick Coll.).

Nicholas of Verdun (documented 1181–1205) was the leading sculptor, metal-worker, and enameller in the Maas (Meuse) area. His masterpiece, the most important surviving 12th-century enamel work, is the *ambo he made for Klosterneuburg Abbey, near Vienna, signed and dated 1181, and still there. In the 1330s it was converted into a *retable in the form of a triptych, and six new enamels were added to his original forty-five. The theme is the *typological one of the parallels between the Old and New Testaments, used from the earliest times, but here more elaborately set out than in any other surviving contemporary work. The inscription—*ante legem—sub gratia—sub lege* is illustrated by scenes from before and after the Giving of the Law to *Moses, with parallels from the Life of Christ and concluding with the Last Judgement. Nicholas's only other documented work is a shrine in Tournai Cathedral, signed and dated 1205, but in poor condition.

The most important attribution to him is the Shrine of the Three Kings in Cologne Cathedral, one of the largest of all *reliquaries, although he cannot have been responsible for all of it. He may also have been the leading master on the huge bronze *Trivulzio Candlestick* (Milan Cath.), some 15 ft. high and dating from the early 13th century. The seven-branched top rises from a *Jesse Tree, on the knop is a Virgin and Child with the Magi, and the base is composed of interlaced branches inhabited by symbolic figures of the Liberal *Arts, the *Rivers of Paradise, the Signs of the *Zodiac, *Virtues overcoming Vices, and other allegories. Other attributions include a shrine (1183) in Siegburg, near Cologne, and four *Prophets* in Oxford (Ashmolean Mus.).

Nicholas V, Pope Tommaso Parentucelli (1397–1455) was the first humanist pope and the founder of the Vatican Library. He was in Florence in the 1420s before going to Rome in 1426. He became a cardinal in 1446 and pope in 1447, when he began an enormous campaign of reconstruction in Rome, which had been almost ruined by the long absence of the papacy during the Great Schism: he rebuilt the walls, cleared the papal states of mercenary soldiers, repaired the forty *Station churches and the seven Basilicas (see ROME), especially St Peter's, by then in a dangerous state. His architectural adviser was *Alberti and they planned to rebuild the choir of St Peter's, and perhaps the whole basilica, but work ceased on Nicholas's death. He brought the disastrous Schism to an end by persuading the rump Council of Basle to dissolve itself, and in 1449 he persuaded the rival pope Felix V to abdicate. In the Vatican itself he employed Fra *Angelico, whom he knew from his time in Florence, to paint frescoes in two chapels. Only one survives, with scenes from the lives of SS Stephen and Laurence. In thanksgiving for renewed unity in the Church, he proclaimed 1450 as a Jubilee Year, which brought large numbers of pilgrims to Rome, but the Fall of Constantinople in 1453, and the failure of the European princes to do anything, clouded his last years.

His greatest legacy was the huge number of MSS he acquired for the Vatican Library, including many translations from Greek into Latin.

Nicodemus A learned member of the Sanhedrin, who, like *Joseph of Arimathaea, dissented from the condemnation of Jesus without His having been heard. He had earlier visited Jesus secretly, at night, but had been puzzled at being told that he must be 'born again'. Nicodemus—unlike Joseph of Arimathaea—is mentioned only in S. John's Gospel. After Christ's death on the cross Joseph asked Pilate's permission to bury Him decently. This was granted (under Roman law, all bodies, even those of executed criminals, were sacrosanct), and Joseph and Nicodemus took down the body, wrapped it 'after the manner of the Jews' in a shroud with myrrh and aloes of about a hundred pounds weight brought by Nicodemus. They then put the body in a new rock-cut tomb, which Joseph had intended for himself, and rolled a stone in front of it. All this comes from the Gospels, but the story was elaborated in the *Apocryphal Gospel of Nicodemus (also called 'Acts of Pilate'), and in the much later **Meditationes Vitae Christi* (13th cent.). This describes the *Deposition: 'Two ladders are placed on opposite sides of the cross. Joseph ascends the ladder placed on the right side and tries to extract the nail from His hand. But this is difficult, because the long, heavy nail is fixed firmly into the wood; and it does not seem possible to do it without great pressure on the hand of the Lord ... Afterwards Nicodemus extracts the other nail from the left hand and similarly gives it to John. Nicodemus descends and comes to the nail in the feet. Joseph supported the body of the Lord ... The nail in the feet pulled out, Joseph descends part way, and all receive the body of the Lord ... ' (this account mentions only three nails).

In paintings of the Entombment it is not always clear which is Joseph and which Nicodemus, but as a rule Joseph is more richly dressed, and Nicodemus is at Christ's feet, while Joseph supports His head and shoulders, as in the passage from the *Meditationes*.

Nicopoia (Panagia Nikopoia) *See* PANAGIA.

nimbus *See* HALO.

Noah (Noe) The OT Patriarch was told by God to build an ark to preserve life during the Flood, described in Gen. 6–9. He was commanded to take into the ark two of every living creature, male and female, and all the food necessary for them and for himself and his family—his wife, his three sons, Shem, Ham, and Japhet (Vg. Sem, Cham, Japheth), and their wives. The ark floated on the waters for a year and 11 days (Gen. 7 and 8: 4, 13), and when Noah thought the waters had receded he sent out a raven, which failed to return, a dove which returned because it found no place to rest, and later the dove again, which returned with an olive leaf so that Noah knew that the waters had receded from the earth.

After the retreat of the waters, Noah sacrificed to God, and God promised never again to destroy the world with a flood. The sign of this Covenant is the rainbow (Gen. 9: 13–14). Later Noah drank new wine, pressed from the grapes of the new vineyard, and was drunk and lay naked in his tent. His son Ham mocked his father's nakedness and Noah cursed him for it; Japhet and Shem respectfully covered their father (Gen. 9: 8ff.).

Noah's Ark is as rich in symbolism as the *Ark of the Covenant. It is a symbol of the Church as the vessel of salvation, sheltering good and evil alike in beneficent animals and harmful predators, and despite the dangers which beset it, overcoming them as the means by which the faithful are saved to enjoy the fruits of God's Covenant. The First Epistle of Peter (3: 20–1) compares this salvation by water with baptism. The dove bearing the olive branch is so common a symbol as to need no elaboration; the story of Noah's drunkenness and his sons' reaction to it becomes an allegory of temptation, folly, sin, and retribution. It was in this sense that *Michelangelo treated the account in Genesis in his ceiling of the Sistine Chapel, a very rare example of the depiction of the three scenes of the Flood itself, and of Noah's Sacrifice, and Drunkenness. There is a very early

(6th century) illustration of the Flood in the *Vienna Genesis, and in the *Ashburnham Pentateuch (6th or 7th cent.). The ruined fresco by Uccello of the *Flood* (Florence, Sta Maria Novella) is a famous example of 15th-century experiments in perspective. *Noah's Sacrifice* (1847) painted by Daniel Maclise is in the City Art Gallery, Leeds, Yorkshire.

'Noli me tangere' (Lat. Touch me not) Words spoken by the Risen Christ to the Magdalene at the Tomb, when she mistook Him for the gardener and then recognized Him (AV John 20: 14–18)—'Touch me not for I am not yet ascended to my Father' (NRSV 'Do not hold on to me, because I have not yet ascended to the Father.'). This is a way of representing the *Resurrection indirectly.

The finest of the many representations of the scene is the early Titian (London, NG) and the Rembrandt (Royal Coll.). The version by Graham *Sutherland (1961) is well positioned in Chichester Cathedral.

Nomen Sacrum (Lat. holy name, pl. *nomina sacra*) From at least 300 BC pious Jews were reluctant to write the name of God, for fear of profanation—cf. Exod. 3: 13–14; 'But Moses said to God, "If I come to the Israelites and say to them, 'The God of your ancestors has sent me to you', and they ask me 'What is his name?' what shall I say to them?" God said to Moses, "I AM WHO I AM." He said further, "Thus you shall say to the Israelites, I AM has sent me to you."' For this reason the word *Adonai* (the Lord) was used, or the Hebrew consonants *JHVH (or *YHWH), omitting the vowel signs. This was misread by Christians, and in the 16th century these letters (called the Tetragrammaton) were transliterated, especially by Protestants, as 'Jehovah', a meaningless word. Modern writers use Jahveh or Yahweh. Such a *nomen sacrum* is not always the same as a Sacred Monogram like the *Chi-Rho or *IHS (IHC); nor is it a simple abbreviation such as DNJC (*Dominus noster Jesus Christus*) or DOM (*Deo optimo et maximo*). Other references to Christ include XPC, XPS, and XC—all derived from the letters of Greek *Christos*. 'The Almighty', 'The Ancient of Days', 'Elohim' are other *nomina sacra* for God.

NON-WESTERN CHRISTIAN ART

This discussion focuses on Christian art in China, Africa, and India along with their immediate neighbours. It begins with a general observation about missionaries and closes with a note about museums.

The missionary's pressing task is translation, whether of language or imagery. From the early centuries onwards and its initial expansion enabled by trade and technology, there has been transmission of Christian text and imagery. Missionaries bring with them what is familiar, are confronted with what may be unfamiliar, and to varying degrees engage with the encountered culture. They strive to root the Gospel in what is distinctive in each culture. The resulting art, sculpture, and architecture have received little of the steady scholarship accorded to much European and Western art; instead these are the subjects of sporadic attention, from, as yet, an uncoordinated variety of disciplines and sources.

China

This vast country is the initial focus of an article in *The Church and the Arts* (1992, edited by Diana Wood). In *The Western Discovery of Non-Western Art* (pp. 571–85) A. F. Walls introduces Cardinal Celso Costantini (1877–1958), who was Apostolic Delegate in China during a politically disturbed period (1922–33), that saw the missions converting to church-building norms which took note of Chinese traditions in style and materials. Reflecting on his experience, Costantini found that Confucius and other Chinese sages had prepared for the Gospel in the same way as had Greek philosophers in the Mediterranean world. 'Evangelize, not colonize; respect the country's art and culture; purge foreign forms from sacred art'—these and similar principles emerge from his memoirs, published in Italian and abridged as *Réforme des Missions au XXe siècle* (Paris, 1960). As secretary of the Sacred Congregation of the Faith, he gained a hearing and a following for his insights.

With all the sensitive international and tourist implications, the architecture of cathedrals in reviving and now thriving Christianity in China, shows varying art options that are being adopted in the city of Shanghai. Holy Trinity, formerly the Anglican cathedral, has been restored, with a jade font and platform, affirming its 1896 design by Sir George Gilbert *Scott. In the Roman Catholic St Ignatius Cathedral (to a 1905–10 design by English architect William Doyle) the American-trained stained-glass artist Fr Thomas Lucas, SJ is project consultant for installing windows (40 per cent complete at the time of writing) with Chinese-Christian images, thus modifying and uniting the building's interior. And all this after the cathedral was redesignated as a state-owned grain warehouse for a decade following the Cultural Revolution's vandalizing of the interior and smashing some 300 square metres of stained glass.

Accounts of the Paiwan Catholics in Taiwan take an optimistic view of an artist becoming Christian and of a theologian seeing something in a new light. So, for instance, the chieftain ancestors depicted in the central post of a traditional ritual house provided a robust, straight figure with victoriously upraised arms, ready for redesignation into a Christ figure. Analysis from another standpoint is undertaken by Chang-Kwo Tan in *Journal of Material Culture* 7 (2) 2002. Here the 'Paiwan Cross', mixing traditional and Christian imagery, is considered as a syncretic object in mediating and reconciling traditional religions and Catholicism.

Meanwhile, in the United States Daniel Johnson Fleming (1877–1969) of Union Theological College, New York City, included plentiful images in the well-produced *Heritage of Beauty: Pictorial Studies of Modern Christian Architecture in Asia and Africa, illustrating the influence of Indigenous Cultures* (1937). Similar illustrated volumes of his were to follow: *Each with his own Brush: Contemporary Christian Art in Asia and Africa* (1938), and *Christian Symbols in a World Community* (1940). Emphasis is laid on illustrations because of the need to see artworks in their context if some feel for them is to be gained—not always easy when faced with a book of reproductions of an artist's paintings or even an exhibition giving little context, either to the artwork or to the artist's art education background, or place in the community of artists, or standing in the surrounding visual culture's development. This is a particular difficulty for the study of such works from a missiological perspective such as that of the well-funded and energetic Overseas Ministries Study Centre, New Haven, Connecticut. Successive artists-in-residence at the centre were given exhibitions and publications in New Haven, these being the eponymous Five Asian Artists invited to show in 2007 at the Museum of Biblical Art (MOBIA) in New York: Nalini Jayasuriya (Sri Lanka), Sawai Chinnawong (Thailand), Nyoman Darsane (Bali), He Qi (China), and Wisnu Sasongko (Indonesia). Scholarly publications about art and architecture developments within the fast-developing Christianities of Asia are much needed. The artists-in-residence programme has continued, however, and its 2011–12 holder, Emanuel Garibay (Philippines), is the subject of the OMSC publication *Where God Is*, a well-illustrated account of the artist's paintings introduced by Rod Pattenden, who has been editing the ACAA journal *IMAGE*.

Africa

African non-Western art, together with art works from other parts of the world, were gathered in 1950 for Rome's *Art of the Missions* exhibition held in the Vatican celebrations of the *Anno Santo*. Ecclesiastics and theologians invited scholars in other walks of life to join in their studies, the eloquent title of Fr Kevin Carroll's *Yoruba Religious Carving: Pagan and Christian Sculpture in Nigeria and Dahomey* (1967) benefitting from W. B. Fagg's foreword. An ethnographer at the British Museum, Fagg ventured as follows:

> This book should inspire many who are devoted to the Christian purpose in Africa to experiment without paternalism in the Africanization of Christian Art. . . . many affinities can be found between Christianity and the 'pagan' religions and none is more striking to my mind than the similarity between their fundamental philosophical concept of 'force' and the Christian concept of grace.

Carroll enumerates some factors encountered by a hardwood religious carving if it is to survive for up to a century in a tropical village: fire, termite, wet and dry rot, warfare, neglect, and destruction by Christian or by Moslem converts, or by witch-hunting cults, or by government officials. His own collection of rescued Yoruba sculpture is housed in the United States, some in Washington, New York, and in the African Art Museum of the SMA Fathers in Tenafly, NJ. An uncommon model of Christian presence is the introduction of Christian art education. The graduates of Margaret Trowell's art school initiative in Makerere in Uganda of the 1930s benefitted from Trowell's own studies at the Slade School of Art. These stood her in good stead when she later progressed her teaching initiative towards validation by London University. African outlook, forms, and technique characterize examples of the Christian subject matter produced by her first students: for the Fort Hall Memorial Cathedral, Kenya, inaugurated by the Archbishop of Canterbury, Elimo Njau painted his *Life of Christ in Pictures* murals (1959), and the preparatory sketches were contributed for display in the Kibo Art Gallery on the slopes of Mount Kilimanjaro, Marangu, Mochi, Tanzania. A selection of the Makerere Christian art works are deposited in the Library of SOAS, London. Uganda's subsequent turbulent history has resulted in decades of constant change in the country's education aims and leadership.

Another example, in the Roman Catholic tradition, comes from 1950s Rhodesia (now Zimbabwe), where the Swiss-born Fr John Groeber (1903–72) brought his architectural studies to bear on the design and building of the Uganda Martyrs Chapel (completed 1960) in the Serima Reserve in Central Mashonoland, and named after the area's dominant chieftancy. Albert B. Plangger's *Serima: Towards an African Expression of Belief* (1974: Mambo) recounts the mission schoolboys' training in drawing, carving, and ceramics. Taught 'to express, not to picture', the young artists, steered away from 'any apeing of tradition or pandering to Western pattern', produced a profusion of spirited imagery setting out Gospel narratives and lives of martyr saints on all available wood surfaces of the building's exterior and interior. Evelyn Waugh, British novelist and Africa travel writer, found Groeber had been able:

> to make Africans do what none but Africans could have done, and what no Africans in this huge region ever did before; to leave a church where they and their descendants can worship and which their descendants will cherish with the pride and awe with which we in Europe survey the edifices of our Middle Ages. (Evelyn Waugh, *A Tourist in Africa* 1960).

Circular structures in Africa have yielded a useful model for missions, distancing themselves from European originals. And so the Carmelite White Fathers in Rhodesia (later Zimbabwe) met their need for a church at Avila in the north of Manicaland with a round, thatched church in the Hwesa style, thus setting the scene for Zimbabwe's confidence in building and decorating its churches according to its own traditions. Local forms were for borrowing, snatching, assimilating.

Once launched into the stock of church art, works commissioned by such experienced bodies as the Society of African Missions are no more exempt from market processes than their Western counterparts. So the *Stations of the Cross*, linocuts by Bruce Onobrakpeya (1969) made at the encouragement of Fr Kevin Carroll MFA (1930–93) for a suburban church in Ebote Metta, Lagos, appeared in a London sale of African Modern and Contemporary Art in 2011.

India

India continues to attract students of its non-Western Christian art, especially from the German and the English-speaking worlds.

John F. Butler (1909–82) was one of Methodism's art scholars with extensive, first-hand knowledge of the subject of his book containing much helpful information—*Christian Art in India* (Madras, 1986). Here, discussed and illustrated (with good bibliography and annotations), are the early Mughal and 19th-century phases of his subject. In the latter category there is an account of All Saints Memorial Church, Peshawar (in the Punjab, close to the Afghanistan border), built in 1884 by the Church Missionary Society to a design that boldly incorporates Islamic architecture features. Slender minarets adorn the building's four corners, a gilt cross surmounting the central dome. The interior arrangements accommodated Muslim sensitivities, locally crafted screens permitting women to observe the purdah rule (*Church Missionary Gleaner* Nov 1884). Butler succeeds in his aim of locating his subject in the mainstream of art and architecture: the Portuguese, French, and

English contributions are treated on their own terms and as engaging with the country's prevailing artistic traditions. Reflecting on modern Christian art in Madras city, he asks himself 'is this picture aimed at making an Indian Christian believer more at peace in his cosy Zion?' Or perhaps it is meant rather to challenge him, or to speak to his Hindu neighbour? (p. 150).

There were many other centres of scholarship working to record, analyse, and promote Christian art in the non-Western world. In Germany Arno Lehmann's *Die Kunst der Jungen Kirchen* (1957) is translated as *Christian Art in Africa and Asia* (1969), while F. zu Löwen's *Christliche Bilder in altindischer Malerei* (1958) with its many illustrations has not yet been translated. The Asian Christian Art Association (ACAA, founded in Bali 1978) actively encourages the visual arts in Asian Churches and published a quarterly magazine entitled *IMAGE*. A brief history of the association by Alison O'Grady mentioning its publications, exhibitions, and consultations can be found in *IMAGE* 123–124 and at http://www.asianchristianart.org

There have been institutions which by their very terms of reference inclined towards some of the factors involved in non-Western Christian Art: the Schweich Lectures for 1928 were given by Sir Thomas Arnold, Companion of the Order of the Indian Empire, and a former Dean of the Oriental Faculty, Punjab University. His death prevented him from preparing his notes for publication—a task devotedly carried out by another noted Orientalist of the next generation, Oxford's Laudian Professor of Arabic, Sir Hamilton A. R. Gibb (1895–1971), who edited Arnold's *The Old and New Testaments in Muslim Religious Art* (1932). (Arnold had previously collaborated with Laurence Binyon in *The Court Painters of the Grand Moghuls* 1921.)

German, English, and American scholarship have come together happily in *Christian Themes in Indian Art* (New Delhi, Manohar Publishing, 2012). This volume, ecumenically coauthored by Anand Amaladossan SJ and Gudrun Löwner, with substantial American chapters invited from Naomi Wray, ensure that Roman Catholic, Lutheran, and Methodist approaches and insights are given full play in this profusely illustrated volume. Its layout is historical, and its maps indicate the country's regions of religious affiliation (overall 2–3 per cent of the population is Christian).

The strong tradition of Saint Thomas reaching Kerala in the year 52, before his martyrdom 20 years later, is set in the context of the known sea-trading links of Syria with Persia and Kerala, and of the ancient shrine of the Good Saviour (*Bom Jesus*) in Goa. Francis Xavier (1506–52) landed there in 1542, and in 1560 the first Christian posters were printed. Ivory statuettes of *Jesus and John and Mary* and of the *Good Shepherd* were to follow, as also were statues of Jesus, assimilated to those of the young Krishna, sucking his thumb after stealing butter from his mother. It was important to have *darshan* (eye-to-eye contact) with the god/dess, so churches placed their cribs outside their buildings to attract the attention of passers-by.

Portable images and conversations drew Christians and Muslims together in the courts of the Moghul emperors who ruled from 1526 to 1764. A more European custom was invoked when Johann Zoffany came to paint a *Last Supper* in the 1780s for St John's Cathedral, Calcutta, modelling the apostles on local worthies. The book's narrative proceeds to the early 20th-century Bengali artists Angelo da Fonseca, Jamini Roy, and Arup Das among many others. Krishna Hawalaji Ara, of Hindu–Dalit background, was a self-taught artist whose life and work point to the shift from the ruling East India Company membership of the Church, towards its current more nationalist composition. Thus, among many styles and strands are the Goan painter Francis N. Souza, who came to Britain and took his work into the 'Modern British' auction catalogues; Alfred D. Thomas, whose style has been likened to that of Edmund Dulac; and Jyoti Sahi 'the theologian with the brush', with his *Dancing Christ on the Cross* and his urge to Sanskritize the Hindu symbols. The 'Warli' paintings, often of Christian subjects, are done by anonymous artists on the red mud walls of houses, using a white wash of ground rice flour. The book's authors lament that the clergy of today are neither in touch with India's modern architectural and artistic scene, nor at home with the traditional rural arts.

Museums

Museums such as the Guimet (Paris) and Metropolitan (New York) include their share of historic and contemporary non-Western Christian art. The enormous international collections of the British Museum yield plentiful examples in Rowena Loverance's *Christian Art* (2007): Sadao Watanabe (mid-20th century) renders *Christ Washing the feet of a Disciple* in the traditional Japanese *katazome* stencilling technique; the Ethiopian Adamu Tesfau's large narrative painting of *Solomon and the Queen of Sheba* (*c.*2003) collapses the time differences of the old and new dispensations and present time, freely to include anticipation of the Magi; Mozambique's recent history leads the TAE Collective to create a *Tree of Life* (2005) from a cache of decommissioned firearms; a quieter, even tranquil 19th-century Chinese domestic scene shows *Dives and Lazarus*, in ink and watercolour in the folk tradition; from the 18th-century a Mughal-style baptismal scene is an unmistakable Indian image; Romauld Hazoumé *La Bouche du Roi* (1999–2004) from Nigeria is an installation of this artist's characteristic jerry cans redolent of political and environmental insights gained from Christianity and African spirituality.

In the examples touched on, the local history of Christianity and its present situation as well as climate, the availability of materials, and of art education are some of the relevant factors. This creative impulse of artists and architects continues to produce work relating to Christianity.

Distant from any of the centres of religion mentioned above is the replacement St Jude's Cathedral, Iqamit (its predecessor destroyed by fire in 2005), begun in 2008 for the diocese of the Arctic. The old building contained an altar cross worked from walrus tusks, and traditional Inuit sleds provided altar rail and pulpit, the font of soapstone being in the shape of a blubber lamp. *See also* AUSTRALIA, NEW ZEALAND, AND PACIFIC; LATIN AMERICA; NORTH AMERICA; EUROPE.

Norbert, Saint (*c.*1080–1134), Archbishop of Magdeburg in Germany and founder of the *Premonstratensian Canons ('Norbertines', White Canons). He was active in N. France as an itinerant preacher, and founded his Order *c.*1120 at Premontré, near Laon, in N. France before being appointed to the see of Magdeburg in 1126. He was associated with *S. Bernard of Clairvaux and his austere *Cistercian Order.

Norman architecture *See* ROMANESQUE.

NORTH AMERICA

A general account of Christian art in North America emerges in relation to the following broad historical contexts: European colonization and the importation of a continuing tradition; creative exchange between indigenous people and the colonists in New Spain; independence and the establishment of new nations—Canada, Mexico, and the United States—with emerging cultural and religious identities; privatization of religion; secularization of art, and the subsequent renaissance of association between art, the religious spirit, and Christian forms and subjects.

In the early 16th century, art that is clearly definable as Christian in form and subject arrived in North America with the first colonizers of New Spain—royal administrators, the military, and mendicant missionaries. Catholic Spain transported to the New World the art of the Renaissance for private devotion, public worship, and education for the conversion of indigenous people to Christian faith.

In *Converging Cultures: Art & Identity in Spanish America* (1996), edited by Diana Fane, Edward J. Sullivan suggests in his essay, 'European Painting and the Art of the New World', that the passage of religious art and culture from Spain to the New World is exemplified by the painting *Virgin of the Navigators* by Alejo Fernández (1475–1545), originally for the chapel in the House of Trade in Seville. The Virgin commands the sky above the harbour and spreads her cloak of protection over ships and the adventurers who sail in them, including Christopher Columbus.

Beginning in 1524 with the arrival of *Franciscan Order missionaries and the political establishment of the Viceroyalty of New Spain in 1535, the influence of European culture and religion radiated from Mexico City into much of Mesoamerica. By the end of the century, more than 400 *conventos* (convents, conventuals) were established to convert the indigenous people by means of visual arts and *church architecture. The *conventos* are described by Samuel Y. Edgerton in his book *Theaters of Conversion* (2001), which provides particular insight into the creative relationship between the missionary friars and indigenous artisans. Contributing significantly to that ambitious initiative was **Pedro de Gante** (*c.*1490–1572), a lay friar born in Flanders and educated in Renaissance arts and sciences. Fray Pedro founded a school of art at San José de Los Naturales, where indigenous people were taught the principles of European art, significantly perspective and chiaroscuro.

Diego Valadés (1533–82), thought to be Fray Pedro's first native and most prominent pupil, distinguished himself in art and literature in New Spain and in Europe. A ***mestizo*** of mixed European and indigenous lineage, Valadés embodied the convergence of colonial and native cultural sensibilities that marked the development of Christian art in Mexico. Mexican artists and artisans applied newly acquired skills and knowledge to produce murals, paintings, and elaborate **retablos* (altarpieces) that were inspired by newly acquired faith but also influenced by indigenous traditions.

Some exemplary work of this period is preserved at San Andrés Epazoyucán, Hidalgo, and in San Nicolás de Tolentino, Actopan, Hidalgo. Throughout Mexico, the subjects of murals, paintings, and *retablos* were for the most part related to the life of Christ, though the Virgin Mary appeared in her many iconographic aspects. **Our Lady of Guadalupe** came to predominate and in time became a national symbol. Individual saints were not widely represented, except for Saint Christopher, who was portrayed as the bearer of Christ onto New World shores, as in *St Christopher Carrying Christ across the Sea* in the *convento* Santo Domingo, Yanhuitlán, Oaxaca.

In addition to the Christian art encouraged by Franciscans, Augustinians (*see* AUGUSTINIAN CANONS, FRIARS), and Dominicans (*see* DOMINICAN ORDER), European art was also promoted by the viceregal establishment, which imported artists as well as art. Among the Spanish and Flemish painters working in Mexico in the 16th century were the master *retablo*-maker **Simón Pereyns** (*c.*1530–1600), who painted *Virgin of Pardon* (*c.*1568) for the Cathedral in Mexico City, and the *retablo* at San Miguel Huejotzingo in Puebla (1586). Examples of the work of **Alonso Vázquez** (*c.*1565–1608) include *The Last Supper* (1580, Museo de Bellas Artes, Seville, Spain) and *Virgin of the Immaculate Conception, (c.*1604, Patronato del Hospital de Jesu, Mexico City). The prominent and prolific painter **Baltásar de Echave Orio** (1558–1623) founded an artistic dynasty that first passed to his son **Baltásar de Echave Ibia** (*c.*1585–1644). The first formal organization of painters in Mexico, *Ordenanzas de pintores y doradores*, was established in 1557.

Spanish colonial expansion continued to advance from Central Mexico north along the Camino Real, the principal trade route to the Rio Grande Valley and the Pueblo culture of New Mexico. Studies of the history and culture into which Christian art was introduced to Mexico and then flourished under the influence of indigenous artists can be found in *Latin America: an interdisciplinary approach* (1999), edited by Julio López-Arias and Gladys Varona-Lacey, which includes an essay on 'Mexican colonial art and architecture from the conquest to independence' by Carol Callaway; also Justino Fernandez's *A Guide to Mexican Art: from its Beginnings to the Present* (1969).

In the following century, as colonization drew more Europeans to North America, innumerable paintings arrived in the New World from Spain. At the same time indigenous artists increasingly influenced new work, especially as it appeared along the northern frontier in Pueblo communities where large-scale *retablos* were produced in reference to European Mannerist and Baroque styles but using new materials and techniques, which included water-based paints in place of oils; pine and tin as well as canvas.

Indigenous artists also asserted themselves, notably **Juan Correa** (1645/50–1716), a *mestizo* who contributed more paintings than any other artist to the decoration of the cathedral in Mexico City. The altar of the Chapel of Kings in the cathedral (1718 and after) designed in the ornate Churrigueresque (*see* CHURCH ARCHITECTURE) style by **Jerónimo de Balbás** (1680–1748), introduced vertical projections, which departed from the usual horizontal design arrangement. Other innovations included the use of the Solomonic and *estipite* columns. The first was influenced by Bernini's *baldacchino in St Peter's, Rome and was used by the anonymous Laguna Santero and his studio from the 1790s. The *estipite* column featured a bowed shaft with truncated pyramids top and bottom, and was prominent in the stone *retablo* in the military chapel dedicated to Our Lady of Light on the Plaza in Santa Fe (completed 1761, now installed in Cristo Rey Church, Santa Fe).

The Spanish missions spread from New Mexico into present-day Texas, the future plains states, and as far north as Idaho. Between 1769 and 1823, twenty-one mission churches were established along the length of California. A history of the California missions is provided by Edna E. Kimbro and Julia G. Costello in *The California Missions: history, art and preservation* (2009).

Local artists in the territories of the New Mexican expansion began carving and painting wooden altar screens and images. Sculpted figures of saints were called *bultos;* small paintings on wood or tin panels were referred to as *retablos,* not to be confused with altarpieces of the same name; and artists who produced them were termed *santeros* (saint-makers). They developed a distinctive New Mexican style by the end of the 18th century. The evolution of colonial Spanish art is recounted in detail by Donna Pierce in her essay in *Converging Cultures,* and in *Painting a New World: Mexican Art and Life, 1521–1821,* edited by Pierce, Rogelio Ruiz Gomer, and Clara Bargellini (2004).

As the pictorial and decorative tradition of Christian art flourished in New Spain, early colonizers from Protestant countries, notably the English in New England, showed little interest in public or private piety through the visual arts. As John Dillenberger points out in his comprehensive and indispensable survey of *The Visual Arts and Christianity in America from the Colonial Period to the Present* (1989), English colonial piety was inspired more by literary sources than visual ones. Consequently, there was little significant Christian visual art in New England until well into the 18th century. Confirming the importance of word over image, portraits of clergy, seen primarily as preachers, were an oblique visual reference to the influence of Reformation Christianity in the English colonial period. A more direct visual prompt to Puritan piety was the aesthetic expression of religion in funerary art, especially carved tomb stones and memorials. Sources in this specialized area include *Graven Images: New England Stonecarving and its Images, 1650–1815* (1999) by Allan I. Ludwig, and *Memorials for Children of Change: The Art of Early New England Stonecarving* (1974) by Dickran and Ann Tashjian.

In 1759 when Québec became an English colony, the Catholic influence of France nevertheless persisted, primarily in ecclesiastical arts and crafts. In both Quebec and in the eastern coastal colonies of America portraits of preachers and other religious figures continued to be a mainstay of religious art until the second half of the 18th century. Even beyond the colonial period in the United States, the art of clergy portraiture was carried on by master painters **Gilbert Stuart** (1755–1828), **John Singleton Copley** (1738–1815), and **Charles Willson Peale** (1741–1827). Peale was among those who established the Pennsylvania Academy of Fine Arts in Philadelphia (1805), the associated art school being the oldest in the United States.

In Quebec, two significant painters of religious portraits and biblical subjects were **Antoine Plamondon** (1804–1895) and **Jean-Baptiste Roy-Audy** (1778–1848). Roy-Audy was a pupil of the architect, wood sculptor, and painter **François Baillairgé**, who, like Roy-Audy after him, also contributed to the fabric of the cathedral in Montreal as well as other churches throughout Quebec.

As the colonization of New Spain and New Mexico expanded northward throughout the western territories of the future United States, the colonies of New France took hold in Lower Canada, first in Quebec City from 1608 and later in Montreal, and in New Orleans in the Louisiana Territory from 1718. Among the first painters in New France were **Abbé**

Hughes Pommier (*c.*1637–86) and Claude François, known as **Frère Luc** (1614–85), whose *Assumption of the Virgin* (1671) for L'Hôpital Général in Quebec is a rarely attributed ex-voto. A comprehensive survey of Canadian art is provided by J. Russell Harper's *Painting in Canada: A History* (1981) and by Dennis R. Reid's *A Concise History of Canadian Painting* (1988).

In addition to paintings of religious subjects in the Renaissance style and clergy portraits, the custom of *ex-votos also played a prominent part in the early French settlements in Canada. One of the most highly regarded votive paintings is *Ex-voto des trois naufragés de Lévis* (1754, for the Church of Sainte-Anne de Beaupré, now in the Musée de Sainte-Anne), which depicts the saint saving three youths from drowning in the Saint Lawrence River. Another is the portrait of Ste. Marguerite Bourgeoys (1700, Musée de Marguerite Bourgeoys, Montreal) by **Pierre Le Ber** (d. 1707). Plamondon painted a portrait of Ste. Marguerite in the 1840s (Maison Saint-Gabriel, Montréal), and a comparison with Le Ber illustrates an essential difference between the simple suggestive expression of an ex-voto and the finished studied likeness of portraiture.

In the ex-voto tradition, the centre of attention at the Marian shrine at the Basilica of Our Lady of Guadalupe in Mexico City is the image of *tilma* (cloak) icon, the legend of which maintains that when the Virgin appeared to Juan Diego in December 1531, she directed him to a hilltop where roses had miraculously bloomed. Diego gathered the roses in his cloak and took them to the archbishop, in whose presence an image of the Virgin appeared on the cloak. The artist **Miguel Cabrera** (1695–1768) produced three copies of the icon and in 1756 wrote an influential essay speculating on the significance of the icon and on how it was produced. It is generally known in English by the first two words of its title: *American Marvel and ensemble of rare wonders observed with the direction of the rules of the art of painting*. Cabrera, an indigenous Zapotec, in 1753 founded the second Academy of Painting in Mexico City, received many commissions from the Jesuits, and painted, among other dignitaries, the archbishop of Mexico.

The culture of New Spain fostered painters in the Caribbean as well, especially in the strategic administrative and trade centre of San Juan on Puerto Rico. **José Campeche** (1751–1809), whose father was a freed slave who restored and painted religious statues, was known for his secular portraits as well as paintings of religious themes, including such subjects as *The Holy Family* (*c.*1778), *The Virgin of the Rosary* (1771–79), and *Our Lady of Mercy* (1795–9), all in the collection of the Instituto de Cultura Puertorriqueña, San Juan, and *Saint Sebastian* (1791, Colección Anteneo Puertorriqueño).

While the tradition of European painting had been thriving and developing in New Spain for more than two centuries, among the first prominent artists to emerge in the English colonies, and among the first to paint biblical subjects, was **John Valentine Haidt** (1700–1780), who trained at the Royal Academy in Berlin before working as a goldsmith in London. Following a religious conversion he emigrated to the Moravian community in Bethlehem, Pennsylvania, in 1754, where he painted portraits and was commissioned to paint nine canvases depicting the life and passion of Christ (1758–79), which are now installed in the Moravian Historical Society in Nazareth, Pennsylvania.

Benjamin West (1738–1820) was born in Pennsylvania but lived and worked in London, where he enjoyed the patronage of George III and was a founder member of the Royal Academy. He painted historic and religious subjects on canvases of heroic scale, including the apocalyptic *Death on a Pale Horse* (1817, Pennsylvania Academy of Fine Arts) and *The Last Supper* (1786, Detroit Institute of Arts). On a much smaller scale is West's *Resurrection* (1808, Philadelphia Museum of Art). West also taught and assisted young American painters, including Copley, Peale, Stuart and Washington *Allston (1779–1843).

Allston, also a poet and composer, lived in London and travelled extensively in Europe from 1810 to 1817. He became a life-long friend of Samuel Taylor Coleridge, whose portrait he painted (1814, NPG London, in Dove Cottage and Wordsworth Museum, Grasmere, Cumbria). Allston worked on such biblical subjects as *The Prophet Jeremiah Dictating to the Scribe Baruch* (1820, Yale University), *Christ Healing the Sick* (1813, Detroit Institute of Arts), and *The Angel Releasing St. Peter from Prison* (1812, Museum of Fine Arts, Boston). He laboured over the problematic *Belshazzar's Feast* from 1817 to 1843

(Detroit Institute of Arts). Allston, who carried traditional European subjects, forms, and style to North America, was a leading figure in the emerging American Romanticism and continued to influence American art through his many students. An account of his life and work is *A Man of Genius: The Art of Washignton Allston*, by William H. Gerdts and Theodore E. Stebbens, Jr. (1979).

In the early 19th century, the new Republic in the United States claimed its intellectual and artistic identity with vigour and confidence. Painting turned from portraiture and epic historic and biblical subjects to embrace the sublime majesty of the natural world. The wonder of the North American wilderness was portrayed as a transcendent reality that also revealed divine immanence in the landscape of the new nation, a concept that later would be expressed as America's 'manifest destiny' to be the new Promised Land from the Atlantic to the Pacific.

While an art establishment emerged in coastal cities, artists also moved with the new country's expansion inland along rivers, into the mountains, and to far parts of the continent. The **Hudson River School** of painters, influenced by the Romantic movement in Europe and related to transcendentalist writers and philosophers in America, were among the first to portray the grandeur of the American landscape on an epic scale. Some painters, notably **Thomas Cole** (1801–48), set biblical scenes and subjects against a mythic wilderness to great dramatic effect, as in *Angels Ministering to Christ in the Wilderness* (1843, Worcester, Massachusetts, Museum of Art) and *The Cross in the Wilderness* (1845, The Louvre).

As a key figure in the Hudson River School, along with **Albert Bierstadt** (1830–1902), **Frederick Edwin Church** (1826–1900), and **Asher Brown Durand** (1796–1886), Cole was inspired by the valley's dramatic vistas to produce grand intimations of a natural religious spirit, in which human beings are inextricably part of a dynamic universe that can seem either threatening or providential, sometimes both at the same time. His impressive religious allegories include two sets of *The Voyage of Life* (1838–1840, first set in Munson-Williams-Proctor Museum of Art, Utica, New York, and the second in the National Gallery, Washington, DC) and a series *The Cross and the World,* which remained unfinished at Cole's death. One completed canvas in that set is *The Pilgrim of the World at the end of his Journey* (1846–48, Smithsonian American Art Museum, Washington, DC).

The Hudson River School, painting nature as an icon of the Creator and a symbol of the divine foundation of the new country, dominated American art until the final quarter of the 19th century, and found some complementary expression in the art of emerging transcontinental Canada, such as *Sunrise on the Saguenay* (1880, National Gallery of Canada, Ottawa) by **Lucius Richard O'Brien** (1832–99) and *Giant Falls* (1872, Montreal Museum of Fine Arts) by **Allan Edson** (1846–88). Canadian artists, however, concerned themselves with the First Nations peoples they encountered and with pioneer life on the prairie rather than with endowing the landscape with overtones of divine providence.

In the course of the 19th century, the many colonies and territories of North America were consolidated into three new nations, beginning with American independence from 1783, Mexican independence from 1810, and the formal emergence of the Confederation of Canada in 1867. In the following decades in the art of those countries and cultures, Christian symbols and biblical narratives were appropriated, reinterpreted, and represented not so much as ends in themselves, but as resonant with the transcendent spirit blessing and legitimizing a new period of civilization.

In the United States, the last quarter of the 19th century became known as the **American Renaissance** as painters and sculptors drew from established themes and forms, including biblical resources, to establish a national art appropriate to the country's appreciation of itself as an emerging power of great influence in the world. The spirit of religion, though not necessarily a specific religion, was recognized as core to the national identity.

This expression of nationhood expressed itself in the public arena as visual representations of *civil religion, appropriating Judaeo-Christian heritage, symbolism, and iconography as moral references that signified the virtues of a new nation, at once continuous in the history of great nations, but at the same time dissociated from the established religion of the Old World, against which the American people had rebelled.

John La Farge (1835–1910), a leading figure in public and church art, designed several stained-glass installations: *History of Law,* installed 1904–1905 in the State Capital in St. Paul, Minnesota, and an installation on the theme of *Justice,* installed 1906–1907 in the Supreme Court Building in Baltimore, Maryland.

The epitome of public art with clearly religious subject matter was **John Singer Sargent**'s series of murals in the Boston Public Library entitled *The Triumph of Religion* (1890–1919). Sargent's work is a history of religion from pagan gods through the history of Israel and the Prophets to the teachings of Jesus. The final panel, and key to the entire work, was to be a painting of the Sermon on the Mount. Owing to controversy over the negative depiction of Temple Judaism, and in light of the increasing shift away from overt public testaments of sectarian religion in public spaces, the final piece was delayed and remained unpainted when Sargent died. The unfinished project marked a transition in the early 20th century from obviously sectarian elements of civil religion toward the privatization of religious sentiment and expression. Sally M. Promey provides a comprehensive and compelling account of Sargent's project and of the nature of religion and the arts in late 19th-century America in *Painting Religion in Public* (1999).

In a more subtle way, but still in the public domain, memorials continued to be a medium by which Christianity, or at least its spirit and legacy, was implied. At least in the northern states, Civil War memorials and statues testified to some degree to the religious cause inherent in the conflict and embodied by the victors. **Augustus Saint-Gaudens** (1848–1907) produced portrait tablets and plaques as well as statues of Admiral Farragut and General Sherman in New York and a bronze commemoration of *The Puritan* (1887, Springfield, Massachusetts), icon of American civil religion. The statue was so popular that more than 20 copies were made for cities and institutions across the country. One of Saint-Gaudens' best-known works is the Clover Adams Memorial in Washington, DC, with its shrouded angel in mourning.

Daniel Chester French (1850–1931) created an enduring image of American ideals with his colossal statue of Abraham Lincoln in the Lincoln Memorial in Washington (dedicated 1922). Within the memorial are two murals, *Emancipation* and *Reunion,* by **Jules Guerin** (1866–1946), each with a central figure of the Angel of Truth respectively breaking the bonds of slavery and rejoining North and South. The murals accompany texts from Lincoln's Second Inaugural Address and the Gettysburg Address with their Judaeo-Christian sentiment and biblical references.

As American civil religion was finding public expression, and as sectarian religion became even more privatized, churches themselves became galleries for art that was pointedly Christian but which also transcended purely devotional or denominational interest. This inspired a religious response and contributed to a worshipful atmosphere, but also invited private or personal aesthetic contemplation regardless of belief. Along with John LaFarge, a leading proponent and practitioner of the arts in churches was **Louis Comfort Tiffany** (1848–1933), whose work predominates in Trinity Church, Boston, directly across Copley Square from Sargent's work in the Boston Public Library. Specializing in stained glass, mosaics, lamps, enamels, and metalwork, Tiffany produced windows, murals, and spaces that captured the imagination and spirit of ritual revival as it advanced into the 20th century. Working for the most part in the Art Nouveau style, Tiffany created chapels and other church environments that included a chapel at the 1893 World's Columbian Exhibition in Chicago, which was moved for a time to the crypt of the new Cathedral of St John the Divine in New York, and subsequently found a home at the Morse Museum in Winter Park, Florida. One of the largest installations of Tiffany glass and decor includes seven lancets of St Michael and All Angels in the apse wall of St Michael's Church, New York City. From the beginning Tiffany collaborated with other artists, first with Tiffany and the Associated Artists, then in 1885 with Tiffany Glass Company, and finally in 1902 with **Tiffany Studios**. Besides comprehensive design schemes in urban churches, innumerable churches of various denominations across the country purchased windows from the prestigious Tiffany Studio. The catalogue to *Masterworks of Louis Comfort*

Tiffany, a 1989–90 exhibition in Washington and New York, edited by Alistair Duncan, is a starting point for further exploration. Joan Elliot Price's *Louis Comfort Tiffany: the painting career of a colourist* (1996) offers a consideration of Tiffany's colour psychology and his painterly approach to work in various materials.

La Farge, after an early career painting landscapes, also completed commissions for significant churches in New York City: Church of the Ascension, Church of the Incarnation, Church of St Paul the Apostle, Judson Memorial Church, and the chapel at Columbia University. His work in murals, design, and the manufacture of glass elevated the quality of ecclesiastical art throughout the United States.

Among the artists prominent in the American Renaissance, one stands out for his almost exclusive treatment of Christian biblical subjects. **Henry Ossawa Tanner** (1859–1937), an African-American who lived and worked in France most of his adult life, produced a prolific body of work based on Gospel accounts of Jesus. Tanner captured the inner drama of scriptural encounters with Jesus, such as *The Visit of Nicodemus* (1888, Pennsylvania Academy of Fine Arts, Philadelphia), *Christ at the Home of Mary and Martha* (1905, Carnegie Museum of Art, Pittsburgh), and *The Resurrection of Lazarus* (1896, Musée d'Orsay, Paris). He also manifested in more impressionistic rendering the mystical quality of Gospel episodes in such scenes as *Angels Appearing before the Shepherds* (1910, Smithsonian American Art Museum), *And He Disappeared out of Their Sight* (1898, Smithsonian American Art Museum), and *The Annunciation* (1898, Philadelphia Museum of Art). The catalogue to *Henry Ossawa Tanner: Modern Spirit* (2012, Pennsylvania Academy of Fine Arts), edited by Anna O. Marley, is a comprehensive guide to the painter's work.

Artists better known for their secular subjects also painted biblical Christian scenes. **Albert Pinkham Ryder** painted dreamlike visions of the natural world and brought a primitive, mystical quality to his biblical subjects, which meant that they could be appreciated as artistic, spiritual experiences apart from and beyond the literal subject matter. Ryder's striking treatment of religious subjects includes *Christ Appearing to Mary* (1885, Smithsonian American Art Museum), *The Resurrection* (1885, The Phillips Collection, Washington, DC), and versions of *The Way of the Cross* (1847, Smithsonian American Art Museum). Other artists of the American Renaissance period who treated Christian subjects include: **Abbott Handerson Thayer** (1849–1921), **Thomas Eakins** (1844–1916), **Hiram Powers** (1805–1873), **Elihu Vedder** (1836–1923), **Sarah Paxton Ball Dodson** (1847–1906), **William Rimmer** (1816–79), **J. William Fosdick** (1858–1937), **William Merritt Chase** (1849–1916), and **Ethel Isadore Brown** (1871–?). Robert Henkes' *The Crucifixion in American Art* (2003), an illustrated survey of artists' treatment of the subject throughout American art history, includes the work of many of these painters and is useful as a comparative approach to the history of art in North America.

The mural tradition that began in the religious establishments of colonial Mexico took a more provocative turn at the time of the country's populist uprising for social and agrarian reform beginning in 1910 with the founding of the *Centro Artistico* by Gerardo Murillo, who signed his works **Dr. Alt**, the model for and teacher of a generation of muralists. After 1920, with the formation of a new government, painters were enlisted to provide large-scale wall paintings for existing as well as new buildings in the capital, including the National Preparatory School, the new building of the Secretariat of Public Education, and redundant churches. Their work was often boldly politicized with the motivating portrayal of peasants and of native traditions, including religious ones, even when the artist's stance was anticlerical or critical of the Church.

The leading muralists of the 20th century in Mexico were **Diego Rivera** (1886–1957), **José Clemente Orozco** (1883–1949), and **David Alfaro Siqueiros** (1896–1974). Octavio Paz provides essays on the muralists, their work, and the influence they had on Mexican culture in his wide-ranging collection of *Essays on Mexican Art* (English translation 1993).

Emblematic of the artist's vision of a new society eclipsing but also enveloping its Indo-European heritage, with secular civil religion replacing the Church, is the Chapel of Chapingo outside Mexico City, which was appropriated for public use. Rivera painted murals there that had reference to Michelangelo and his religious works (*The Adoration of* *the Virgin*, 1913, private collection), but which now also featured the newly empowered peasantry, especially the *Mestizo, in place of biblical figures. Orozco consciously appropriated Christian nomenclature in a series of revolutionary murals in the National Preparatory School that included such titles as *Christ Destroys His Cross* and *The Trench and the Trinity* (1922–24). Siqueiros also drew on Renaissance masters, and, as Paz records, the primitive ideal of a collective Christianity informed his vision of the coming Renaissance in the nascent revolutionary spirit of Mexico. As the Mexican muralists painted in public spaces, drawing on the nation's range of historical influences, so they and others appropriated that heritage in easel painting and other media. The influence of the **ex-voto** or *retablo* tradition and the use of derived devotional symbols, such as the bleeding heart of Jesus, can be read in portraits by **Frida Kahlo**, in whose work autobiographical inspirations are psychologically and emotionally and spiritually charged. **Maria Izquierdo** (1902–55) referenced images of the Virgin Mary, Catholic saints, *alcenas* (cupboards) that served as domestic altars, and *offrendas* (offerings), tables dedicated to commemoration on the Day of the Dead.

In the 20th century, art in American churches began to reach back to the medieval for aesthetic and devotional inspiration, while the art world outside religious institutions claimed the independence of art from cultural determination in a new wave of modernism. With the **Park Avenue Armory Show** of 1913, a course was set in which Impressionism and Abstraction came to dominate art in America, and until the decades following the Second World War, references to traditional Christian visual elements were very few.

An exception to the trend in the United States, and coincidental with the new artistic energy released by the muralists in Mexico, were the artists of the **Harlem Renaissance**. Between 1910 and the Second World War there occurred in America a great migration of southern and rural blacks to northern cities, and Harlem in New York City became its intellectual and artistic centre. As with earlier eras in American history, the thrust of the Harlem Renaissance was literary, represented by writers Countee Cullen, Langston Hughes, and Richard Wright, but visual artists were also drawn to depict the new urban black culture.

The work of **William H. Johnson** (1901–70) chronicled black church piety with such canvasses as *I Baptize Thee* (1940), *Going to Church* (1940-41), and *Swing Low, Sweet Chariot* (1944), all in the collection of the Smithsonian American Art Museum. **Jacob Lawrence** (1917–2000) completed *The Migration Series*, a set of 60 panels, by 1940. A year later the panels proved so popular that they were divided into two sets of alternating numbers, the odd numbers to the Phillips Collection in Washington, and the even to the Museum of Modern Art in New York. Throughout his long career Lawrence painted the history and struggle of African-Americans.

Working with the legacy of the Harlem Renaissance, the abstract expressionist painter **Romare Bearden** (1911–88) continued to express the everyday experience of life in Harlem, including the presence of church and the ambience of faith. Drawing on Caribbean influences as well as African-American sources, he painted a number of religious subjects, including a series on the *Passion of Christ* taken from the Gospels of Mark and Matthew, of which *Golgotha* (1945, Metropolitan Museum of Art) especially achieved notice; another series *The Prevalence of Ritual*, included *Baptism* (1964, Hirshhorn Museum and Scupture Gallery, Washington, DC); *Palm Sunday Procession* (1967–68, Hood Museum of Art at Dartmouth College, NH); *Sermons: The Wall of Jericho* (1964, Romare Bearden Foundation, New York), and *Black Madonna and Child* (1969, Hirshhorn).

Georgia O'Keeffe (1887–1986), with her mentor and colleague Alfred Stieglitz, and other artists including Charles Demuth, Marsden Hartley, Arthur Dove, John Marin, Charles Sheeler, Abram Walkowitz, and Max Weber, were influenced by the avant-garde character of the 1913 Armory Show. O'Keeffe, long resident in New Mexico, evoked in her paintings the serenity, mystery, and power of nature in subtle abstraction. Among her most intriguing paintings is a series of the cross set against the background of the New Mexico hills and sky, among them *Black Cross, New Mexico* (1929, Art Institute of Chicago) and another series of the cross set against the sea, as in *Cross by the Sea, Canada* (1932, Currier Museum of Art, Manchester, New Hampshire). In *Cow's Skull: Red, White and Blue* (1931, Metropolitan Museum of Art), one of her many treatments of relics of nature, the form of a cross can be discerned.

In the second half of the 20th century, many abstract artists understood painting as a metaphysical, even religiously generative act dissociated from any representational function or reference. In that sense, all paintings are sacred, and the artist, liberated from the conventions of meaning can assign his or her own meaning through conceptual titles and forms. A prime example is *Stations of the Cross: Lema Sabachthani* (1958–66, National Gallery, Washington, DC) by **Barnett Newman** (1905–70). Though the panels are completely abstract, their numbers conform to the traditional fourteen devotional *Stations of the Cross (plus one, *BII*, that Newman added), and there is a visual progression, indicated by colour and the position of the artist's signature 'zip', suggesting both movement and mood.

In 1964, **Mark Rothko** (1903–70) was commissioned to create a self-contained devotional space in Houston, Texas. Dedicated in 1971 and known as the **Rothko Chapel**, it functions as a chapel and a museum as well as an educational centre. Rothko created fourteen panels of subtle variation in tonality that surround the viewer and create, together with the architecture, a space inviting spiritual contemplation whether the reference to traditional stations of the cross is comprehended or not. Opposite the chapel stands Barnett Newman's sculpture *Broken Obelisk* (1963–67), which is dedicated to Martin Luther King Jr. It is imbued with the religious associations of King's battle for civil rights, not unlike the Civil War memorials of the previous century.

Another space for which prominent artists were commissioned to provide work is St Peter's Lutheran Church in New York City. Its Chapel of the Good Shepherd is a complete sculptural environment by **Louise Nevelson** (1899–1988). **Kiki Smith** (b. 1954) designed a processional cross, and a *Triptych* by **Willem de Kooning** (1904–97) was installed for a time as a *reredos*, but subsequently removed.

Influenced by but breaking away from strict abstract expression, **George Segal** (1924–2000) created a series of figurative groupings that connect biblical stories to contemporary events and issues. *The Holocaust* (1984, Legion of Honor, San Francisco) is a web of white-painted bronze bodies that invokes Ezekiel's question, 'Can these dry bones live?' In *Abraham's Farewell to Ishmael* (1987, Miami Art Museum), figures in modern dress project complex and timeless human emotions, and the artist's later treatment of the sacrifice of Isaac, *In Memory of May 4, 1970, Kent State: Abraham and Isaac* (1978, Princeton University), makes a powerfully charged connection between the threat of biblical sacrifice and the actual sacrifice of life in the shooting of university students.

The pop artist and celebrity Andy Warhol (1928–87), known for his silkscreen series of portraits and objects, also produced paintings of religious subjects consistent with his Byzantine Catholic background. Jane Daggett Dillenberger in *The Religious Art of Andy Warhol* (1998) has accounted for at least twenty large-scale treatments of The Last Supper, which rival Sargent's Boston Library murals in size. Other silkscreen series, canvases, drawings, and installations include his *Christ 112 Times* (1986 Andy Warhol Foundation for the Visual Arts, New York), and in the collection of the Andy Warhol Museum, Pittsburgh: a riff on Raphael's Sistine Madonna entitled *Raphael 1-6.99* (1985); a series of cross paintings, a striking example of which is *Cross (Red)* from 1992; and, with Jean-Michel Basquiat, *Ten Punching Bags* (1986), each having the face of Christ from his Last Supper series.

In the spirit of Newman and Rothko, Warhol in effect created a 'chapel', albeit temporary, in a New York gallery in 1979. Eighty-three abstract paintings, entitled *Shadows* and hung edge-to-edge at eye level around four walls, surrounded the viewer and suggested a visual pilgrimage in contemplation of the rhythmic progression of variations on the original photograph of a shadow in Warhol's studio. The series is now installed in the Andy Warhol Museum, Pittsburgh.

Akin to the Rothko, Newman, and Warhol contemplative rooms are fourteen immense (20 by 20 ft) abstract panels by Cleve Gray (1918–2004) entitled *Threnody*, completed in 1973 and installed in a gallery at the State University of New York at Purchase. The memorial 'chapel' was dedicated to the dead on both sides of the Vietnam War. Gray also produced series of resurrection triptychs, among other paintings with religious references, and was commissioned to design vestments for churches in Washington, DC and Connecticut.

In addition to abstraction, artists working in various styles and media consciously engaged the interplay of religion and the visual arts. An exhibition, *The Spiritual in Art: Abstract Painting, 1890–1985*, was mounted in the Los Angeles County Museum of Art in 1986. Interdisciplinary engagement prompted a number of significant exhibitions beginning with *The Hand and the Spirit: Religious Art in America 1700–1900*, organized and with a catalogue by Jane Dillenberger and Joshua Taylor in 1972 (University Art Museum, Berkeley, California, and Smithsonian Institution, Washington, DC, among others on tour), followed by *Perceptions of the Spirit in Twentieth-Century American Art* by Jane Dillenberger and John Dillenberger (1977, Indianapolis Museum of Art, and on tour). The catalogues to those comprehensive exhibitions are a good introduction to the early foundations upon which the contemporary mix of art and religion emerged with vigour and bold investigation. Continuing in the new millennium, a commitment to spiritual and religious investigation was captured in the 2005 exhibition *The Next Generation: Contemporary Expressions of Faith*, with a catalogue by Particia C. Pongracz and Wayne Roosa, who curated the show at the Museum of Biblical Art in New York.

Art and artefacts reflecting Canada's Christian heritage were collected for a millennial exhibition entitled *Under the Sign of the Cross: Creative Expressions of Christianity in Canada* in 1999 at the Canadian Museum of Civilization in Hull, Ontario. Many strands of Canadian culture, including the First Nations and emigré communities, were represented, including Serbian artist Slavko Protic whose icon *Mother of God of Canada* (1992) has gold fleur-de-lis and maple leaf patterning. Ukrainian Catholic iconographer Heiko Schlieper (1931–2008) painted a large wall icon of *Christ's Entry into Jerusalem* in the course of the exhibition, and is known for work in churches in Toronto and Edmonton as well as his twenty images of *The Passion of Our Lord* in St Matthew's Anglican Church, Ottawa. Sylvia Daoust (1902–2004), Canada's first established woman sculptor, dealt with many traditional religious subjects, and her 1987 *Madonna and Child* was included in the show.

The relationship between art and Christianity continues to evolve within cultural and historical contexts. In the 21st century, throughout North America, as artists and theologians find common ground for creative exploration, visual artists will no doubt continue to reinterpret received tradition as well as perform the prophetic role of producing new visions. *See* ALLSTON, BEARDEN.

SEE WEB LINKS

- The *Art in the Christian Tradition* (ACT) database is a freely available, regularly updated visual-image internet resource. Designed for scholars, students, pastors, and religious educators, all of the images may be used for educational and/or religious non-profit purposes. Images are added regularly. There are currently 3415 images in the collection.

  The ACT is linked to another Vanderbilt Divinity Library Internet resource, the Revised Common Lectionary. This linking allows leaders of worship and teachers to find visual-art resources related to the scripture readings for each Sunday in the church calendar.

  The visual images in the ACT database represent the continuum of the practice of Christianity from the 1st century AD to the present. Many of the images are interpretations of Christian scripture: the Old Testament/Hebrew Bible, the New Testament, and the Apocrypha. Sarcophagi, mosaics, frescoes, manuscripts, sculpture, architecture, and paintings are searchable by keyword, scripture reference, iconographic content, personal name, time period, and geographic location. ©Jean and Alexander Heard Library and the Vanderbilt Divinity Library, a division of the Heard Library, 2007.

n

Nottingham alabasters *See* ALABASTERS.

NS In French, an abbreviation for Notre Seigneur, Our Lord, but, confusingly, in Spanish an abbreviation for Nuestra Senora, Our Lady.

nun A woman living under religious vows, a female monk. Most Orders of nuns are based on similar Rules to those of monks—e.g. the Poor Clares are Franciscans and the Second Order of S. Dominic is the female version of the Order of Preachers. Nuns wear distinctive habits, usually similar to those worn by the parent Order. The main distinction between Orders of nuns is that between contemplatives (e.g. Carmelites), who live enclosed, rarely or never leaving their convent, and active, mainly teaching and nursing Orders (e.g. Ursulines and Dominicans), and the Sisters of Charity, such as the Poor Clares and the Sisters of S. Vincent of Paul.

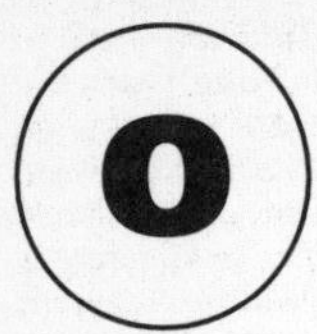

Observants (Osservanza) *See* FRANCISCANS.

oculus (Lat. eye, pl. *oculi*) A round window or opening, which may be glazed or blind.

Ofili, Chris (1968–) A painter born in Manchester to Nigerian parents. Catholic school attendance and serving Mass as an altar boy fed into his art with its iconography and devotional vocabulary. His art foundation course teacher Bill Clarke, he recalls, 'talked about biorhythms, spirituality, and personal energy'. Two art colleges in London furthered his education—Chelsea College of Art and the Royal College of Art. A British Council scholarship made possible a 1992 visit to Zimbabwe, which proved pivotal to his development as an artist. There he discovered both ancient cave paintings and elephant dung as a material. In 1997 he appeared with fellow 'young British artists' in *Sensation* at the Royal Academy. The show went on to the Brooklyn Museum where his piece *The Holy Virgin Mary* became central in Mayor Rudy Giuliani's argument against public funding for American museums, further cementing Ofili's fame and reputation. In 1998 he was the recipient of the Turner Prize, and in 2000 he was made a trustee of the Tate Gallery. In 2003 Ofili was chosen to represent Great Britain at the Venice Biennale. He has been based in Port of Spain, Trinidad since 2005.

OFM (Lat. *Ordo Fratrum Minorum*) *See* FRANCISCANS.

OFMC (Lat. *Ordo Fratrum Minorum Conventualium*) *See* FRANCISCANS.

OFMCap (Lat. *Ordo Fratrum Minorum Capuccinorum*) *See* FRANCISCANS.

oils, holy *See* AUMBRY.

ointment jar The attribute of the *Magdalene (John 12: 3): 'Mary took a pound of costly perfume made of spikenard, and anointed Jesus's feet, and wiped them with her hair.' (But *see* MAGDALENE.) It is also an attribute of SS *Cosmas and Damian, and of the Archangel Raphael (*see* ANGELS), who cured *Tobit.

O'Keeffe, Georgia (1887–1986) An artist whose work discloses 'passionate fascination with the mystery of nature' according to John Dillenberger in *The Visual Arts and Christianity in America* (1989), though her transition from early Abstract Expressionism to complete Abstraction separates her from the Hudson Valley School of landscape painting. She painted abstract versions of the San Francisco de Asis Mission Church in Taos, New Mexico, and was also occupied with a series of crosses painted against abstract natural backgrounds of desert or sea: examples include *Black Cross, New Mexico* (1929) and *Cross by the Sea, Canada* (1931). The iconic image of *Cow's Scull: Red, White and Blue* (1931) also evokes the mystery of the cross. *See also* NORTH AMERICA.

Old Testament subjects Given the great number of people and events recorded in the OT, it is surprising how relatively few subjects were chosen for works of art from the earliest times until at least the late Middle Ages. This was because of the dictum of *S. Augustine that 'the New Testament is concealed in the Old, and the New makes plain the Old', i.e. that the principle of *typology was basic to the interpretation of the Bible, in art as in literature. Hence the very frequent occurrence of Moses as a precursor of Christ, and even the creation of Eve (Gen. 2: 21–3) was seen as a type of the Church, born of the wound in Christ's side. By far the commonest OT subjects were the Fall and Expulsion from Paradise; Cain and Abel; Noah and the Flood; Abraham and Isaac (very frequent as a type of Christ's sacrifice); Moses, especially the Burning Bush, the Manna in the desert, the Brazen Serpent, Moses striking the Rock, and the Tablets of the Law. Other favourites include the Ascension of Elijah; Daniel in the Lions' Den and the Three Children in the Fiery Furnace; Jonah, especially as a symbol of the Resurrection; Susanna and the Elders; Judith and Holofernes less frequently; and Tobias and the Fish. David is rare in paintings, but often occurs as an illuminated initial in psalters, similar to the 'portraits' of Evangelists at the beginning of their Gospels. Although many works have perished, the descriptions given by *S. Ambrose and *S. Paulinus of Nola of church decorative cycles confirm the underlying intention of using OT events only when they make plain that they foreshadow the New Dispensation.

At the Reformation, however, many Protestant bodies began to use the OT in a different way, and artists began to depict scenes which previously had rarely, or never, been illustrated. This is especially the case with *Rembrandt, whose OT subjects account for more than a third of his religious paintings, and for other Dutch 17th-century painters, who represented such obscure subjects as the Levite and his Concubine (Judg. 19: 10–30), painted several times by Eeckhout. It is likely that many such paintings are now unrecognized. This tendency culminated in the 19th century in subjects which are not specific representations of biblical subjects so much as meditations on biblical themes—e.g. C. D. *Friedrich's *Cross in the Mountains*, *Hunt's *Shadow of the Cross* or *The Light of the World*, or *Millais's *Carpenter's Shop*.

olive branch In Early Christian art, in the catacombs, and on sarcophagi, the reference is to Gen. 8: 11 'and the dove came back to him in the evening, and there in its mouth was a freshly plucked olive leaf; so *Noah knew that the waters had subsided from the earth'. An olive branch has always been a sign of peace, and is occasionally shown in the hand of the Archangel Gabriel as a sign of the coming of the Prince of Peace. It is also shown with palms to make a wreath.

Olives, Mount of The site of the Agony in the Garden, with Gethsemane at the foot and the *Imbomon, the traditional site of the *Ascension, at the top. It lies to the east of Jerusalem.

Olivetani (Olivetans) An offshoot of the *Benedictine Order, founded by Bl. (Giovanni) Bernardo Tolomei in 1319 at Monte Oliveto Maggiore, near Siena. Unlike the Benedictines, the Olivetans wear white habits, and the fresco cycle at Monte Oliveto of thirty-six scenes from the life of S. Benedict, by *Signorelli (1497–9) and Sodoma (1505–8), shows him in their white habit.

Omega *See* ALPHA.

omophorion A *vestment worn by bishops of the E. Orthodox Church, corresponding to the *pallium worn by Western archbishops. It is of silk or velvet, about ten inches wide, and about four yards long, embroidered with crosses, and worn over the left shoulder in front, round the neck, and reaching almost to the ground at the back. It is worn over the *phelonion during the Liturgy, and originally was made of wool, to represent the lost sheep brought back to the fold by Christ. At the reading of the Gospel the bishop removed it, since Christ was the true Shepherd of the Flock.

OP (Lat. *Ordo Praedicatorum*, Order of Preachers) *See* DOMINICANS.

operai (Ital.) An *opera pia* is a charitable work or foundation, usually religious, and the *operai* are the lay administrators who run it. The *operai* of major foundations contracted with artists for their works, and such contracts, preserved in their legal archives, are of great importance, not only for identifying artists, but because they show how the *operai* laid down subjects and treatment. The *Operai* of Florence Cathedral had to take the momentous decision to trust *Brunelleschi when he claimed to be able to build the dome of the cathedral without centring, an apparently impossible feat. Their trust was abundantly justified.

opus (abbreviated **op.**: Lat. a work) preceding a name is an assertion of authorship. One of the best known is op. ioh. bell. (opus Ioanni Bellini) on the votive pictures of the Madonna and Child produced by the studio of Giovanni *Bellini: in this case it would not be safe to assume that Giovanni actually painted the pictures with his own hand. *See also* FECIT.

opus anglicanum (Lat. English work) This name for English ecclesiastical embroidery, which was famous throughout the Middle Ages, is found in papal inventories. There are examples in the Vatican and London (V & A), the finest being the *Syon Cope.

opus sectile A form of floor mosaic, made from pieces of variously coloured marbles arranged in a geometric pattern. Opus Alexandrinum is a richer, more elaborate, and expensive form, closer to Cosmati work. The 11th-century floor of the Sanctuary of Westminster Abbey is a rarely seen example, probably made at the same time as the Cosmati tomb of Edward the Confessor.

orant (Lat. *orans*, praying) An orant figure is one in the ancient Eastern position of prayer, standing with arms outstretched sideways, or bent at the elbow, with the hands at shoulder level and palms facing forward. The gesture is still made by the celebrant during the canon of the Mass. On Early Christian sarcophagi and in the catacombs, orants were often representations of the dead, but later they became less common and more symbolic.

orarion A *vestment worn by deacons of the E. Orthodox Church, corresponding to the *epitrachelion worn by priests and bishops: both are versions of the Western stole. The orarion is worn over the left shoulder, hanging straight down back and front. In the West Carthusians wear a similar stole.

oratory This word has several meanings. **(1)** A small chapel, not normally part of a church, and often simply a room set apart in a house or public building, such as a college or hospital, as a place for private prayer. They are not consecrated and the Sacrament is not reserved. They derive from the use of private houses as meeting-places by the earliest Christians.

(2) The Congregation of the Oratory, founded by *S. Philip Neri in Rome. His original followers met in the Oratory of San Girolamo dei Pelegrini or della Carità (of pilgrims or charity) from about 1564, but in 1575 they were formally approved as a religious order and given the old church of San Giovanni, on which was built the Oratorio dei Filippini, where S. Philip founded the concerts of sacred music from which came the term 'Oratorio'. The building was later rebuilt by *Borromini (1637–50). San Giovanni itself was rebuilt after 1575, and has a typically Baroque façade. It was renamed Sta Maria in Vallicella, and is commonly known as the Chiesa Nuova (New Church). The altarpiece is by *Rubens. The basic rule of the Congregation was that it should consist of priests and brothers living in common, but without special vows and retaining their own property. Each house is independent, although new ones are often administered by an established one in the same country. They have been considerable patrons of the arts, especially music. For their main church in London see:

(3) The Oratory, introduced into England by John Newman in 1848, at Maryvale near Birmingham, but a second house was started in London soon afterwards, which is now usually known as the 'Brompton Oratory' in Kensington, with a very splendid Italianate church by *Gribble. This is what is often meant in English by 'the Oratory'. A house and church have now opened in Oxford.

(4) The French Oratory was a similar society of priests, founded in Paris in 1611. It was dissolved during the Revolution, but refounded in 1852, as a teaching order which became famous for scholarship and sanctity.

orb A sphere, like a *globe, but usually of crystal and surmounted by a cross. With the sceptre, it is a symbol of kingly power (cf. the Crown Jewels), and for this reason Christ, the King of Kings, is shown holding one. Sometimes it is held by the Christ Child, as in the painting by *Mantegna in London (NG), where the Child holds an orb in His left hand and an *olive branch in His right, perhaps as the Prince of Peace.

order The various types of classical columns and their entablatures are described as orders. They were Greek in origin: Doric was the severest, Ionic was more decorative, and Corinthian was the most ornate. The Roman forms of the same orders were less strict in their proportions and ornamentation, and a further capital was added—the Composite—as a combination of the Ionic and the Corinthian. The Romans often used highly decorative capitals, not conforming to any pre-existing order, and some were even historiated. Medieval columns stemmed ultimately from Roman, but the period made its own variations in the forms it borrowed. The same term—orders—is used for the number of lesser arches included in the profile of a large Romanesque or Gothic arch.

Orders, Holy These are traditionally seven—three major and four minor—but over the centuries, and between East and West, these have varied. In the Roman Catholic and the Anglican Church, Holy Orders—*sacri ordines*—are held by bishops, priests, and deacons. In the West subdeacons were included among the major orders between 1207 and 1972, but the subdiaconate has always been a minor order in the East. The liturgical roles of priest, deacon, and subdeacon at a High Mass are still found in some Anglican churches and cathedrals; a liturgical subdeacon may be an ordained position or a lay member of the Church community. The other minor orders in the Roman Catholic Church, usually regarded as a step towards ordination, are door-keeper, reader, exorcist, and *acolyte.

In art, the major orders are recognizable either by the appropriate *vestments or by distinctive clerical *dress.

Orders, Religious In common usage, a Religious Order is a body of men, who may or may not be priests, and who may be *monks, *friars, or laymen (*see* THIRD ORDER), or of women, usually *nuns. They live in common under a superior, and are bound by a Rule. Normally they take vows of poverty, chastity, and obedience. From *c.*340 communities of *hermits began to form in the desert, which evolved into monastic communities. In the East they accepted the Rule of S. Basil the Great (*c.*330–79), drawn up between 358 and 364, and still by far the most important in E. Orthodox countries. Many of these monks practised as *icon painters and as scribes and illuminators of manuscripts.

In the West, however, the picture is very different. The Rule of *S. Benedict, *c.*540, is the foundation of Western monasticism, and the Benedictine houses evolved the typical plan for a monastery (*see* SANKT GALLEN). The monastic reforms introduced at *Cluny and at its daughter-houses and affiliated monasteries in the 10th and 11th centuries, and the very different but equally vital and widespread changes effected by the *Cistercians brought *Romanesque architecture to its richest development. They laid the foundations for what, in the 12th century, became early *Gothic.

The next great development came in the early 13th century, with the foundation of the *Franciscan Order of Friars (as distinct from monks). This was in 1217 and was immediately followed by the Order of Preachers, founded by *S. Dominic in 1219, and the *Carmelites in 1245. The importance of the friars in art and architecture lies in their exploitation of Gothic for their great churches adapted to preaching to large congregations in the newly important towns, instead of being in the depths of the country, as were most monastic foundations. This reflected the fact that the friars were in the world, rather than retreating from it. The Franciscans, following the example of S. Francis himself, also promoted a new, much more emotive, iconography—e.g. the painted crucifixes (*see* CROCE DIPINTA), the *crib, and the *Pietà*.

As a result of the Reformation, new Orders founded in the 16th century were in the world rather than contemplative. They included the *Theatines, Barnabites (*see* BARNABAS, S.), and above all the *Jesuits (1540), who are often said, not altogether correctly, to have created a 'Jesuit Style'. The *Oratorians were also active patrons of *Baroque artists, especially musicians. *See also* AUGUSTINIAN CANONS, BRIDGET, S., CAMALDOLENSIANS, CARTHUSIANS, CLARE, S., CONVENTUAL, GESUATI, JERONYMITE, MENDICANT, MERCEDARIANS, MINIMS, MONASTERIES, MONASTIC ORDERS, NORBERT, S., OLIVETANI, PREMONSTRATENSIANS, SERVITES, and URSULINES.

orientation The alignment of a church on an E–W axis, with the altar at the east end and the entrance at the west. In pagan temples this practice was often followed in order to pray to the rising sun, and it was claimed that Christ, the *Sol Invictus, might equally be invoked. This was possible in some early Roman basilicas, since the altar was at the west end, but the celebrant faced the congregation and, therefore, eastwards. Other basilicas had the altar at the east. The most famous of all, *St Peter's, had a west altar, due to the special circumstances of the site. The E–W alignment is usual, but there are many exceptions, especially in towns where the site is restricted.

Original Sin *See* MAN, FALL OF.

Orpheus was a pagan demigod who was celebrated as a lyre-player. His skill was such that he was able to enter the *Underworld in an attempt to rescue his dead wife, Eurydice. In the earliest times he was seen as a *type of Christ, who rescued souls from *Limbo.

orphreys (perhaps Lat. *auriphrygium*, gold Phrygian embroidery) are bands of embroidery on a chasuble (*see* VESTMENTS) or *cope. On a chasuble they are usually arranged as a cross, often Y-shaped. They may originally have covered and strengthened seams. They are always decorative, and are often extremely rich with figurative embroidery.

Orthodox Church *See* EASTERN ORTHODOX.

OSB (Lat. *Ordo Sancti Benedicti*, Order of S. Benedict) *See* BENEDICT, S.

osculatorium *See* PAX.

OSF (Lat. *Ordo Sancti Francisci*, Order of S. Francis) *See* FRANCISCANS.

ostensorium (Lat. *ostendere*, to show) Now usually synonymous with *monstrance, but originally a glass reliquary in which a relic could be exhibited for public veneration.

ostrich eggs The *Madonna and Child with Federigo da Montefeltro* by *Piero della Francesca (*c.*1474: Milan, Brera) has an ostrich egg suspended very prominently above the head of the Madonna. Actual eggs are fairly common in E. Orthodox churches, but their precise significance is unclear. A reference in Job 39: 13–17 to the ostrich leaving her eggs in the sand and forgetting them has been explained as a symbol of the Virgin Birth (since they are hatched by the sun alone), which would be appropriate in a *Madonna and Child*. In the late 13th century *Durandus interpreted the passage in Job as an allegory of man's search for God (perhaps based on the *Bestiaries). This may have been Piero's starting-point, but the question is still open.

O

Ottonian art and architecture *Charlemagne's death in 814 was followed by the problems of succession, which bedevilled Frankish inheritance. His son, Louis the Pious, tried to hold his fissiparous kingdom together, but the great advances of the *Carolingian Renaissance slowly foundered. Over the 9th century the Empire split into three increasingly unstable kingdoms, assailed by marauders on all sides. The papacy, under the control of Roman magnates, fell into increasing disrepute. In 919 Duke Henry of Saxony—'Henry the Fowler'—was elected King of Saxony, and in 929 he forcibly added Lotharingia to his domains; this was the 'Middle Kingdom', originally the kingdom of Lothair, once part of the Merovingian kingdom which became part of Charlemagne's empire. At that time Lotharingia was bigger than the modern Lorraine, which is named from it.

The ambition of his son and successor, Otto I, in 936 was to restore Charlemagne's empire, and he relied on churchmen, as efficient counsellors without hereditary ambitions, appointing them to Countships as well as sees. His vision of Charlemagne's empire drove him to invade Italy in 951, and he was crowned by the pope in St Peter's in 962. The papal estates—the *Regnum Italicum*—had dwindled to their lowest extent, and Otto, after a struggle with the local magnates, created the Holy Roman Empire from the *Regnum Italicum* and his German domains. His negotiations with the Byzantine Emperor, who controlled S. Italy, secured in 972 the prize of the Byzantine Princess Theophanu as wife for his son. Otto II inherited in 973 at 18, died in 983, and when his son Otto III died in 1002, aged 21, the Ottonian line died with him.

Although the Ottonian dynasty had lasted only sixty-six years, a distinctive art had been created which endured well into the 11th century. Otto I encouraged a revival of Carolingian and Early Christian forms, and a renewed Byzantine influence came through the Empress Theophanu's contacts with the Byzantine court. The most important factor was the new wave of Benedictine monastic reform which spread from 933 to reach the furthest frontiers of the kingdom. Everywhere that the reforms spread, learning and scriptoria flourished.

Church building continued to follow the forms set by the Carolingian St-Riquier: basilican naves, apsidal east ends, huge westworks. No churches built during the Ottonian period have survived unaltered, but what was built then, and under the succeeding Saxons, set a type and a compelling example. St Cyriakus, Gernrode, was built in 961–3 on a basilican plan with a high timber-roofed nave, a transept that does not project beyond the aisles, a choir raised over a crypt, and an apsidal east end. There is a second transept at the west end, with flanking towers. A western apse and other small alterations do not affect its austere spaciousness.

Mainz Cathedral was begun under Otto II. It is so strongly influenced by Old St Peter's that the Roman basilica determined its scale and probably also its orientation. It was burnt on its consecration day in 1009, rebuilt with an extra trefoil western sanctuary, increasing its length, was rededicated in 1036, much rebuilt between 1060 and 1137, and vaulted after 1181.

Bishop Bernward (later canonized) was not only a builder, he was also an enlightened patron. His church of St Michael, Hildesheim, a typical double-ender of the Carolingian type, built between 1001 and 1033, uses a module based on the square of the crossing for the proportions of the building. The major works of art which Bishop Bernward commissioned for St Michael are the 12 ft. high bronze column encircled with a continuous frieze with scenes from the Life of Christ, inspired by Trajan's Column in Rome, and the bronze doors, nearly 15 ft. high, made in 1015 for St Michael, but removed in 1035 to the later cathedral by Bernward's successor. Unlike the Byzantine doors which he probably saw in Italy, they consist of eight scenes in each door with vividly expressive figures in relief, the left leaf with scenes from the OT, starting at the top with the *Creation*, and ending with *Cain's murder of Abel*, and the right leaf starting with the *Annunciation* at the bottom, rising to the *Noli me tangere* at the top, with the scenes so arranged that they form *type and antitype parallels of the Old and New Testaments. They were cast in one piece, apparently in a sand mould, a technical triumph of the age. The inspiration probably came from the 5th-century wooden doors of Sta Sabina in Rome.

Ottonian manuscript production had very different aims from those of Carolingian scriptoria. Then the object was to establish correct texts, and the concentration was therefore on bibles and psalters. Ottonian choices were narrower; no great bibles, few illustrated psalters, no classical MSS. The concentration now was on sumptuous Gospel books and books for ceremonial use. They were often written on backgrounds painted like rich brocades, with complex initials in brilliant colour and gold, and the book-covers were elaborate goldsmiths' work set with jewels and ivories. The Egbert Psalter (Cividale, N. Italy) made *c.*977–93 for the Archbishop of Trier has vivid geometric animal figures in gold in violent movement, distinctly Nordic in type, and in the frontispiece of the *Letters of S. Gregory* (Chantilly) is a picture of the Emperor Otto II enthroned with the four parts of the Regnum of *c.*983/5. In these MSS there is a strong influence both from Christian antiquity and Byzantium. There is also a firm understanding of perspective and the ability to create forms in recession. The most sumptuous MS of the period is the Egbert Codex (Trier), a Gospel book with four full-page Evangelist portraits, many gold and coloured initials, and fifty NT illustrations inspired by Early Christian art; there is also a dedication page, with Egbert enthroned with small figures of monks, one of whom presents the book to him.

A more expressive and vehement style followed as the last stage of the Trier scriptorium: the Aachen Gospels of Otto III, which has a frontispiece of the enthroned emperor and twenty-one full-page illuminations of scenes from the NT. In their colour, iconography, technique, and views of cities derived from late Antique types, they all point to a powerful influence from 6th-century MSS from the Eastern Church. This emotional expressiveness appears in the ecstatic *Vision of Isaiah* from a 10th- or early 11th-century Commentary (Bamberg), where the prophet is surrounded by a swirling crowd of seraphim, one of which with a pair of tongs picks up the glowing coal with which the prophet's lips were touched.

Most of the surviving carvings are ivories, usually for book-covers, or for insertion into portable altars. Many of these show influence from Byzantine ivories, but as their material was often whalebone, they were clearly made in the North. None equals the Byzantine-inspired covers of the Lorsch Gospels (Vatican, Museo Sacro) made in the early 9th century, with Christ treading upon the beasts of evil (Ps. 91: 13; Vg. 90: 13), but the Carolingian influence persisted as late as 900/1000 in, for instance, the detached covers probably made for a Sacramentary; one leaf has S. Gregory writing (Vienna, KHM) and the other has the celebration of a Mass (Frankfurt, Bib.), both with strong resemblances to Byzantine work, so that it is possible that they once enclosed a MS made for the Empress Theophanu. Some of the finest ivories of the Ottonian period were made in Milan, among them the panel of *c.*980/3—possibly from a book-cover—with Otto II and Theophanu kneeling at the feet of Christ, holding the infant Otto III. This panel is so close to the treatment of forms in the *Basilewsky Situla* (London, V & A), ordered from Milan in 983, as to make its origin certain. Not only was the effect on patronage of a Byzantine Empress important, but Byzantine Iconoclasm in the 8th and 9th centuries caused a diaspora of skilled Greek artists, so that Byzantine forms continued to be produced in Northern workshops and monastic scriptoria.

Overbeck, Friedrich (1789–1869), was one of the founders of the *Nazarener. With his friend Pforr he founded the Lukasbrüderschaft (Brotherhood of S. Luke, patron of painters) in Vienna in 1809, which later developed into the Nazarener. Their intention was to create a Christian art, based on Perugino and, especially, early Raphael (*compare* PRB). From

1810 Overbeck lived in Rome in the old monastery of Sant'Isidoro. After Peter Cornelius arrived in Rome in 1811, they painted frescoes in the 'ancient manner'. Pforr died in 1812, and in 1813 Overbeck became a Catholic. Overbeck influenced the British PRB through Dyce, and both the Nazarener and the PRB had aims similar to those of the *Oxford Movement.

owl *See* BIRDS, SYMBOLIC.

ox *See* EVANGELIST SYMBOLS.

ox and ass *See* NATIVITY and ASS.

Oxford Movement, the A movement within the Church of England, 1833–45, 'against Popery and Dissent', aimed at returning to 17th-century principles, emphasizing the Catholicity of the Anglican Church. It is usually dated from 1833, when Keble preached a famous sermon on National Apostasy in the University church at Oxford. *Tracts for the Times* followed (hence the alternative name Tractarianism), many by J. H. Newman, whose *Tract XC* (1841) caused such uproar that the series was abandoned. The movement effectively ended in 1845, when both Newman and W. G. Ward were received into the Roman Catholic Church, but it remained influential in High Anglican circles, especially in matters of liturgy and ceremonial. It is often associated with the romantic historicism of the *PRB and *Gothic Revival, as well as the *Cambridge Camden Society.

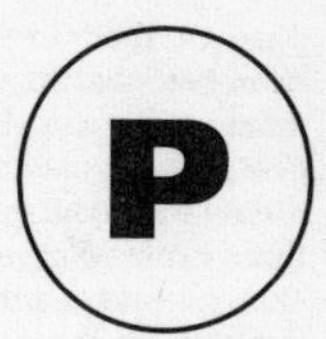

Pacheco, Francisco (1564–1654), was a Spanish painter, working mainly in Seville. He was the master of Velázquez, and later, his father-in-law, and he was also a writer on art. His book, *El Arte de la Pintura* (pub. 1649; a more recent edition is 1956), is important for its detailed instructions for the correct manner of portraying the *Immaculate Conception, which became a quintessentially Spanish subject, painted by himself (Seville Cath.), Velázquez (London, NG), and *Murillo, among many others. Pacheco was unusual at this date in painting Crucifixes with Christ's feet pierced by either four *nails or three; three had been the general usage since the 13th century. He was the painter of a number of the polychrome statues of Juan Montañéz, and his iconography influenced the sculptor who also used four nails in his masterpiece, the *Christ of Clemency* (1603–6: Seville Cath.).

Pacific *See* AUSTRALIA, NEW ZEALAND, AND PACIFIC.

paenula *See* PHELONION.

pala is an Italian word for a large altarpiece, and is used only for a single picture in which the action, figures, and scene are treated as being in one consistent space, and occurring in a single pictorial continuum. It is described as a '*pala* of a unified type' in contrast to an *ancona* (*see* ALTARPIECE), which usually consists of several pictures united in a single frame, but not necessarily consistent between themselves; or a *polyptych, which consists normally of a central picture with a number of smaller pictures—usually figures of saints—grouped round it.

Pala d'Oro The large gold and silver-gilt *reredos of St Mark's, Venice. Doge Pietro Orseolo I is recorded as having ordered, in 976, a new gold and silver *pala* for St Mark's from Constantinople. About 1105 Doge Ordelaffo Falier ordered a new *pala* from Constantinople which was to be placed on the altar (i.e. it was not an *antependium); in 1209 Doge Pietro Ziani had it remade. In 1342–5 it was again remade, perhaps by a Giampolo Boninsegna, who made the gold and silver-gilt framework in a Gothic design, inserting into it all the original Byzantine enamels, the jewels, and a number of new Venetian-made enamels. All the enamels are *cloisonné*; there are over eighty in all, some dating from *c.*1000, and therefore possibly from the first *pala*; many, including some of the finest—notably the *Christ in Majesty* in the centre—date from the 1105 commission; many of those in the 1209 reconstruction were part of the loot brought back from the sack of Constantinople in 1204 by the Venetians (and others; the Venetians were not wholly responsible). The additional Venetian-made enamels are somewhat inferior in quality to the Constantinopolitan ones, and mostly are of incidents from the Life of Christ, and scenes relating the legend of S. Mark, taken from the *Apocryphal Gospels. At the base is an inscription recording part of its history, inserted in the 14th-century reworking on either side of two images of an Empress Irene and one purporting to be of Doge Falier, which is in fact an earlier emperor-figure with the head reworked. Its dazzling effect is from the combination of gold with the brilliant enamels, and over 2,000 gems and pearls, and its artistic importance lies in the incomparable array of Byzantine *cloisonné* enamels from the 10th to the late 12th century, together with the later Venetian Gothic ones.

Palaeochristian A grand word for *Early Christian.

Paleotti, Cardinal Gabriele (1524–97), Archbishop of Bologna. He was interested in the arts, and was a friend of Cardinal, later Saint, Charles *Borromeo at the Council of *Trent, which was concerned with art during its last session (1563). The Council decided that more control should be exercised over the content of works of art so as to counter the Reformed Churches' rejection of art in churches, and to refute their criticisms that much of the art in Catholic churches was at best profane, at worst irreligious. The Council decided to allow the bishops to decide on the fitness of a work of art to be admitted to a church, and Cardinal Paleotti projected a book which should set out guide-lines to be followed. He was a man of wide culture, an art lover, who understood the role to be played by art as an incitement to piety, in its ornamental and didactic potential. His *Discorso intorno alle imagini sacre e profane* (Bologna, 1582; On sacred and profane images) was never finished. Two volumes only appeared, the remaining three being merely summarized at the end of the published work. Vol. 1 rehearsed classical arguments and quotations in favour of art, Vol. 2 dealt with the errors of painters of sacred and profane subjects, since the Church assumed the right to control both. The other books were to have dealt with licentious pictures, a fixed iconography for sacred subjects, and a disquisition on the purposes of art, which he regarded as having a moral didactic function as well as an aesthetic role.

Moral theology is the keynote of the *Discorso*; no works of art are individually criticized. The Council's standpoint may be gauged by their opinion that though the literature of art—Pliny, Dürer, Vasari—should be studied, a quest for perfection suggested vanity, the imitation of the antique suggested paganism, and portraiture suggested improper pride in the sitter. The Cardinal (and the Council) was particularly sharp on obscurity. The pursuit of obscurity for the sake of effect, as in much of Late *Mannerist painting, was condemned as roundly as obscurity through ignorance. He criticized artists who paint subjects they know nothing about, and who crowd too many figures or incidents into their pictures, and he even suggested that an unusual place or in martyrdom the subject should be identified lest the spectator should be confused. He also criticized the artist who tried to depict things which are so mysterious as to be beyond the reach of delineation. But these strictures are nothing compared with those in another work, produced two years earlier, by a lecturer at Leuven University, Jean Molanus, in *De historia sacrarum imaginarum et picturarum* (Leuven, 1580; On Holy Images). In complete contrast to Paleotti's sympathetic approach, it is a cold treatise on religious and biblical exactitude which involves the wholesale rejection of medieval art and the abandonment of most forms of traditional iconography. Even the Life of the Virgin is subjected to this scrutiny for factual exactness, and fails to pass. From the life of her parents, and her childhood in the Temple, to her Dormition, all here as everywhere else, is stripped of any place for the imagination and poetry of expression, and the same treatment was meted out to the saints, to the point that even the tender piety of the Franciscans vanished also. Fortunately, despite the damage that one frost can do, it takes more than that to kill so robust a plant as the artistic imagination. The advent of the Baroque saw to that. *See also* GILIO DA FABRIANO.

paliotto is Italian for an *antependium. It may be a textile hanging in front of an altar, in which case it usually follows the *liturgical colour of the day or season. It may be a more substantial work of embroidery, painted or carved wood, enamels, gilded metal, or even gold, or marble inlays. Some are of great antiquity, the most famous being the Golden Altars in Sant'Ambrogio, Milan, of *c.*850; the Aachen Palace Chapel of *c.*1020; and Basle Cathedral of 1022–4, now in Paris, Cluny Museum. Other notable examples are the painted wooden one inset with gilt-bronze heads, from Sto Domingo de Silos (*c.*1140/50: now in Burgos), the *Pala d'Oro in St Mark's, Venice, those among the elaborate embroideries made for the Baptistery in Florence between 1466 and 1487, from designs by Antonio Pollaiuolo, and the ambitious Silver Altar made for the Baptistery by Verrocchio (1477–80).

pall *See* LITURGICAL OBJECTS.

Palladio was one of the major Italian architects of the 16th century. Andrea della Gondola (1508–80) began as a stonemason in 1524. In 1536 a rich humanist and amateur architect of Vicenza, called Trissino, gave him the name Palladio as an allusion to Pallas, Goddess of Wisdom, and, in 1545, he took Palladio to Rome, where he remained for two years, studying the ruins of antiquity. In a long career as one of the most innovative architects of N. Italy, during which he built palaces and villas in Vicenza and the surrounding countryside, he built only three churches and one church façade, but all are memorable. His earliest church was at Maser (1560?) to accompany the villa built for Daniele Barbaro, Patriarch of Aquileia, and translator of *Vitruvius (Palladio provided the illustrations for it). This church is based on the Pantheon in

Rome: a circular domed building with an entrance portico. His second church was in Venice, where he designed a façade for San Francesco della Vigna (1562), which had been left incomplete by Sansovino. His great innovation was to create the façade from two classical temple fronts, one superimposed on the other, so that the taller temple façade covers the nave and contains the doors, while the aisles are fronted by a lower, wider, façade. The details of each façade supply elements of the other—windows, doorways with Orders, and basements, in a complex but totally harmonious way.

In 1566 he began San Giorgio Maggiore, on the island facing the Doge's palace across the lagoon. The plan of this church, built for the Augustinian canons whose monastery was one of the finest and richest in Venice, takes account of the annual *andata*, or state visit by the Doge, commemorating in this case the Feast of S. Stephen, whose body is in the church. For this reason the church was designed with a dome and apsidal-ended transepts. The deep monks' choir behind the altar is also apsidal ended, and separated from the altar by a screen of columns, so as to achieve the spectacular musical effects of the special Venetian arrangement of 'dispersed choirs'—that is, the provision in the architecture of a modern church for the special choral system evolved in the multi-domed St Mark's, with the apsidal-ended transepts and choir used for the 'dispersed choirs', which, with the band of trumpets, accompanied the Doges on ceremonial occasions. The façade of San Giorgio Maggiore uses the same system of the double temple front, one impacted on the other, as at San Francesco della Vigna.

The same features appear in his third Venetian church, the Redentore, begun in 1576. This more modest church commemorated the cessation of a great plague, and was also one of the churches to which a special *andata* was made on the third Sunday of July, when a bridge of boats was placed across the canal of the Giudecca. Where San Giorgio is of brilliant Istrian stone inside, with red and white marble floors, and the altars have grand altarpieces, several by Tintoretto, the Redentore is a more modest building, with plaster columns and painted cut-outs instead of fine sculpture in the niches, as befits the Franciscans who serve the church. Its beauty derives from the harmony of its proportions and the play of light through the semicircular screen of columns at the back of the high altar, through which the choir can be glimpsed.

Palladio's original design was for a circular church, which he maintained, as Alberti and Bramante had before him, was a more fitting expression of 'the Unity, the infinite Essence, the Uniformity and Justice of God'. The commissioners, however, preferred a long nave.

His *Quattro Libri dell'architettura*, published in 1570, is yet another of the books which set out methods and types of buildings, and which is a synthesis of the lessons to be learned from *Alberti and Vitruvius, and is, incidentally, more accessible and clearer than either. He illustrated it with plans and views of his own buildings, which ensured for them wide dissemination. This was particularly important in England through the advocacy first of Inigo *Jones, and later of Lord Burlington, who, inspired by Campbell's *Vitruvius Britannicus* and Leoni's edition in English of Palladio's *Four Books of Architecture*, went back to Italy to study Palladio at first hand. He bought the major part of his drawings, with the consequent development of Palladian architecture in England in the early years of the 18th century.

It is a fascinating comment on the mutation of taste that in the early 18th century Lord Burlington, no mean judge of architecture, thought San Giorgio Maggiore was 'the most beautiful church in the world', and for George *Street, a passionately *Gothic Revival architect, in Venice in the 1850s, it was the 'most hideous church in the world'!

palladium In Greek mythology, a sacred image of Pallas Athene, sent by Zeus to protect the city of Troy. Its theft made possible the Sack of Troy. Legend says that it was taken after the burning of Troy to Rome, where it was supposed to protect the city, which was, however, sacked by the Goths in 410. Its function was taken over by Christian images—e.g. the Virgin and Child icons of the *Hodegetria or the Virgin of *Vladimir. *See* MADONNA TYPES.

pallium A circular band, two inches wide, with a hanging portion back and front, worn by popes over their shoulders. It is made of wool woven from the fleece of lambs blessed on S. Agnes's Day (21 Jan.) in Sant'Agnese fuori, Rome, while the Agnus Dei is being sung during High Mass; it is then embroidered with six purple crosses. The pallia are then laid for the night on the tomb of S. Peter in the Vatican, and placed in a niche over the tomb before being sent to the recipient. The pallium is given to archbishops, patriarchs (and to some bishops) as a symbol of the 'plenitude of the papal office', and as a sign of participation in papal authority. It has been used since the 5th century, but was originally given as a mark of honour to particular prelates; this created a general desire also to receive the honour, and since the 9th century it has been obligatory for archbishops and patriarchs to petition for it immediately upon being appointed to their sees. Until he receives it, he does not have full authority, and cannot perform certain of the functions of his office, such as ordination, chrism, the consecration of bishops or churches. Pallia are personal and territorial; when the recipient dies it is buried with him, and if he is translated to another see a new pallium must be obtained.

The early history of the pallium is obscure. It derives from imperial insignia, but does not originally have any papal or Roman connection. It appears to have been given at first by the pope to local bishops under his authority, and then spread to ones further out in the provinces, as a major mark of esteem, but it would seem that in the 6th century it was still considered a part of imperial insignia and was withheld pending imperial consent. Finally, by the 8th century, it had ceased to be part of the imperial insignia, and was entirely under papal control, and thus became an essential element in the investiture of a prelate. *See also* OMOPHORION.

palm This begins as an emblem of pagan victory, as may be seen on many classical triumphal arches. In the Christian era it rapidly became a symbol of the victory of faith over the suffering of martyrdom, though it often appears on tombs or monuments which do not commemorate martyrs. Palm Sunday has or has had several names: the Sunday before Easter, Dominica in Palmis or ad Palmas, and in Early Christian times Pascha Competentium, for those who, having completed their catechumenate (and were now *competentes*), were to be baptized on Holy Saturday. On Palm Sunday Christ made His entry into Jerusalem, and the event is commemorated during Mass by the distribution of palms to the faithful, by the reading or the recital by three deacons of the Passion according to S. Matthew, and in some places by a procession. *Etheria describes the Palm Sunday procession in Jerusalem in the record of her 4th-century pilgrimage, and it is also mentioned elsewhere before 472, and by Isidore of Seville (d. 636) as 'a great day'. It was also the day on which candidates for baptism on Holy Saturday were instructed in the whole of the Creed. Very often the Palm Sunday procession began in one church with the blessing and distribution of palms, and continued to another church for the Mass.

The branches of palm blessed on Palm Sunday are now usually dried palm leaves, sometimes plain, sometimes twisted to form a small cross. In some areas the older custom prevails of giving out small branches of box, cypress, olive, willow, or other green branches which commemorate the spreading of palms and other branches before Christ at his entry into Jerusalem, the joyous prelude to the agony of the Passion.

Panagia In the Eastern Orthodox Church *panagia* (Gk. all-holy) has several meanings, all connected with the idea of the sacred. It is often used simply as a title of the Blessed Virgin and may be applied to *icons of her, or to bread solemnly blessed in her honour. It is also used for an *encolpion, a small folding diptych containing an icon of her, and worn on a chain by Eastern bishops. Panagia Nicopoia—'all-holy Bringer of Victory'—also applies to icons of the Madonna and Child Enthroned (*see* MADONNA TYPES). A Panagiarion is a special kind of paten, set on a high foot instead of being flat as in Western usage.

Pantheon (Gk. all the gods) The Pantheon in Rome is one of the few major buildings of antiquity to survive in a reasonable state of preservation. An inscription records that it was begun by Marcus Agrippa, son-in-law of the Emperor Augustus, *c.*27/5 BC; a later inscription of *c.* AD 126 states that it was a work of the Emperor Hadrian, who rebuilt it then, and further restorations were made by the Emperors Septimius Severus and Caracalla. While its exact dedication is unclear its architecture suggests that it was conceived as a symbol of the celestial spheres, associated with the planetary deities. The great opening in the dome allows the sun to penetrate and form a disc of light which moves around the walls like the movement of the planets.

In Early Christian times it was closed, though enough remained to make it worth sacking by the Goths in 410, and it was used as a fortress by warring factions in Rome. In 609–10 it was restored by Pope S. Boniface IV and dedicated to Sta Maria ad Martyres, since he had the remains of martyrs recovered from the Colosseum and the *catacombs re-interred in the church, because the barbarian incursions had made the catacombs unsafe. In the 16th century it became the burial place of eminent artists—Raphael (1520), Peruzzi (1536), Taddeo Zuccaro (1566), and others, and later also of the first two kings of United Italy.

Structurally, the Pantheon is one of the wonders of the world. It is circular, 142 ft. high, with a hemispherical dome of the same width, forming a sphere contained within a cylinder. There is an opening in the top 27 ft. in diameter, which is the only source of light. The brick walls are 19 ft. thick, on a concrete foundation. The weight is distributed by three successive tiers of relieving arches to make the structure strong enough to bear the dead weight of the dome, built outside in steps, and inside in five tiers of 28 coffers of concrete which become progressively smaller as they rise. In front is a large rectangular porch and a portico of 16 Corinthian columns, which were a constant inspiration to Renaissance architects as perfect models of the form. The bronze tiles on the portico were taken by the Emperor Constans II in 663, and replaced with a campanile, built on top of the porch, which was removed by *Bernini, and replaced by two smaller towers, one on each side, which the Romans promptly named 'the asses' ears'; they survived until 1883. Inside, massive blocks of masonry alternate with deep niches with Corinthian columns in front, which appear to support the architrave, above which is an attic with blind windows in coloured marbles, mostly an 18th-century restoration.

The Roman Pantheon remained an inspiring challenge to Renaissance architects from *Brunelleschi in Florence, to *Bramante in Rome, in his original design for the new St Peter's, to *Michelangelo's first designs for the dome of his St Peter's. Though both the original ideas for Florence Cathedral and St Peter's were for hemispherical domes, neither was built in that form since the statics of such a dome were impossible on the substructure proposed for the rest of the design. Bramante's ambition for St Peter's was to raise the 'dome of the Pantheon' on the 'vaults of the Temple of Peace'—the name then used for the Basilica of Constantine. By now, however, the image of a Pantheon had changed. The similarity between the circular domed form and a martyrium or *heroön*, stressed by the new dedication of the Pantheon to martyrs as well as the Virgin, suggested the use of the name Pantheon to describe a building dedicated to the commemoration of the dead. The idea of a hemispherically domed, centrally planned martyrium was the core of Bramante's design for the New St Peter's, and also formed the basis of the church which Michelangelo designed and largely built. Only in the Medici Chapel of the New Sacristy in San Lorenzo, in Florence, did Michelangelo achieve the Pantheon-like coffered dome which he felt appropriate for a burial chapel.

A Pantheon came to be considered as a suitable burial-place for the eminent as well as for saints and martyrs. In León, the 11th-century Panteón de los Reyes was added to the church of Sant'Isidoro as a burial-place for the kings and their families. Another example of a royal Pantheon, though like León, not shaped like the Roman one, is the burial chapel of the kings of Spain which is part of the Escorial. The huge domed Chapel of the Princes tacked on to the choir of San Lorenzo in Florence as the Pantheon of the Medici Grand Dukes of Tuscany was begun in 1602, and building continued until well into the 18th century. It was meant to astonish and overwhelm, and still does though hardly in the manner first intended. Many churches have imitated the design concept of the Pantheon, among them *Palladio's chapel for the Barbaro family at Maser, and also his rejected design for the Redentore in Venice, which he preferred to the church he actually built. Others are Bernini's Church of the Assumption at Arricia, *Fischer von Erlach's St Charles Borromeo in Vienna, and *Gibbs's first design for St Martin-in-the-Fields in London, which was a superb example of a Pantheon adapted to Anglican worship. Unfortunately, the commissioners would have none of it.

In Paris, Soufflot's grandiose church of Ste-Geneviève, begun in 1757 but still unfinished at his death in 1780, was converted into the Panthéon as a burial-place for the heroes of the French Revolution, but few of the memorials, or even graves, of those buried there survived the Restoration. The 'Temple' at Possagno, near Bassano, in the Véneto, which the sculptor Canova began in 1819 as his own burial-place and museum for his sculptures is another imitation. In Washington, the Capitol exercises some of the functions of a Pantheon in that a small rotunda under the dome contains an empty tomb originally intended for George Washington. It is perhaps reasonable to suggest that almost certainly the concept of the two grandest Roman domes inspired Robert Smirke in his construction of the great dome of the British Museum Reading Room in 1857, only two ft. smaller than the dome of St Peter's.

Pantocrator (Gk. *Pantokrator*, all-sovereign, Ruler of all) Originally applied to God, i.e. to all three Persons of the Trinity, it later came to mean Christ as Judge. The figure appears as early as 565–78 on coins of the Emperor Justinian II, but many representations were destroyed by the iconoclasts, including one in Hagia *Sophia, Constantinople. Post-Iconoclastic representations are usually at half-length and overwhelmingly severe, with Christ as Judge, heavily bearded and long-haired, His right hand raised in blessing or pointing to the Gospel Book in His left hand. Behind His head is a cruciform halo, sometimes with IC XC or Alpha and Omega. These mosaics and paintings are predominantly Greek, in domes, apses, or porches: the Pantocrator at Daphni (*c.*1100) is particularly minatory, but at Cefalù in Sicily (*c.*1148) He is noticeably less severe. In the West the type was far less common except in Romanesque *portal sculpture, where a full-length figure of Christ enthroned is usually accompanied by saints and angels.

Paolo, San fuori le Mura (St Paul's outside the Walls) is the basilica of S. Paul the Apostle, who was martyred outside the walls of Rome, on the road to Ostia, during the Emperor Nero's persecution, between 63 and 67, probably in 64. Near by is an antique catacomb, partly pagan, partly Christian, in which S. Paul is believed to have been buried in the tomb of a Christian woman named Lucina. A second catacomb, of Comodilla, is also near, but it contains no record of S. Paul. His remains were eventually transferred to a large basilica, virtually the same size and shape as the original St Peter's, which was begun by the Emperor Valentinianus I *c.*386, and continued by his successors, Theodosius, Arcadius, and Honorius. The most notable surviving parts are the *ciborium*, by Arnolfo di Cambio and Pietro (Oderisi?), made in 1285, and the *Triumphal Arch, with the *Pantocrator and two Apostles, restored by Galla Placidia. The nave was lined with two rows of frescoes, on much the same system as St Peter's. From very early times it was a Benedictine monastery; there still is a beautiful 13th-century cloister, with double twisted columns covered in Cosmati work.

The basilica, with the exception of the *ciborium*, the triumphal arch, and a few remnants of mosaics in the transepts, was burnt on 15 and 16 July 1823. Pope Pius VII was dying in those very days, and the disaster of San Paolo fuori was kept from him. It was rebuilt on the same plan and the same decorative system as before; it was reconsecrated in 1854.

parables (Gk. *parabole*) are short narratives or brief examples taken from life or natural phenomena which Christ told, mainly to his disciples, to teach them moral or spiritual lessons. No firm line can be drawn between any part of Christ's teaching and another, whether it be parables, aphorisms, metaphors, actions, or even miracles, since his whole aim was to teach. In pursuing this aim He used everything which would make the greatest impact on His disciples and His hearers. Who, having once heard the story of the Good Samaritan or the Prodigal Son, has ever forgotten it?

There are, at a conservative count, at least forty parables—perhaps over fifty, according to what is accepted as being a parable—in the three Synoptic Gospels, of which S. Mark has the least and S. Luke the most. Only ten appear in more than one Gospel. There is one in S. John's Gospel. They were not told only to His disciples, since in Matt. 13: 2–3 it is stated: 'Such great crowds gathered round him that he got into a boat and sat there, while the whole crowd stood on the beach. And he told them many things in parables, saying: "Listen! A sower went out to sow seed . . . ".' Later (Matt. 13: 10–17) the disciples asked Him, '"Why do you speak to them in parables?" He answered, "To you it has been given to know the secrets of the kingdom of heaven, but to them it has not been given . . . ".' And He continued by explaining that since the people hear but do not understand, it fulfils Isaiah's prophecy that people will hear and not understand because their hearts have grown dull and their ears hard of hearing (a paraphrase of Isa. 6: 9–10).

Parables are capable of more than one level of interpretation: an immediate level, relating to the circumstances of the moment, as when Christ tells the Chief Priest and the Elders in the Temple the parable (in all three Gospels, Matt. 21: 33–46; Mark 12: 1–12; Luke 20: 9–19) of the man who planted a vineyard, leased it to tenants, and when he sent slaves to collect his share of the produce, they ill-treated and killed the slaves. When he sent his son, they killed him too. Christ asked, what should the landowner do to the wicked tenants? Unsuspectingly, his hearers answered that he should put the wretches to death and let the vineyard to other tenants. Christ then reminded them of Isa. 5: 1–7, where the bad tenants are driven out and the vineyard given into other hands. When they realized that they had fallen into the trap of condemning themselves they were furious and wanted to arrest Him, but did not dare because of the people present. On a larger plane, it is open to all men to pass judgement upon themselves.

Parables have stimulated many works of art; a few examples are given here. Many of them are in Bible illustrations; the 6th-century *Rossano Codex illustrates both parables and miracles. Probably the *Christ separating sheep from goats* (Matt. 25: 32–3) in the upper tier of 6th-century mosaics in the nave of Sant'Apollinare Nuovo, Ravenna, and *The barren fig-tree* (Luke 13: 6–9) in the 6th-century Gospels in Corpus Christi College, Cambridge, are among the earliest parables to be illustrated. *The house built on sand* (Matt. 7: 24–7) and *The seed of corn* (Mark 4: 26–9, John 12: 24) were both in Herrad von Landsperg, Abbess of Hohenburg's *Hortus Deliciarum* (1167–95: destr. but known from copies). *The man who built bigger barns for his harvest* (Luke 12: 16–21) is in the 13th-century portal sculpture of the Porte de la Calende, Rouen; *The wise and the foolish virgins* (Matt. 25: 1–13) was a popular subject in a number of 13th-century carved portals of French cathedrals, one of the finest examples being Strasburg; it was also the subject of Parmigianino's frescoes in Sta Maria della Steccata, Parma, of 1535–9. Two 13th-century stained-glass windows in Bourges Cathedral are of *The Good Samaritan* (Luke 10: 30–7) and *The Prodigal Son* (Luke 15: 11–32). *The Blind leading the Blind* (Luke 6: 39) by Bruegel (1568: Naples) is the most famous rendering of the subject, while the story of *Dives and Lazarus* appears in French portals, 12th-century Moissac for instance, where Lazarus lies in Abraham's bosom while Dives is tormented in Hell, and was also painted by Terbruggen (1625: Utrecht). *The Prodigal Son* is almost certainly the most painted parable; Dürer's tragic etching of the repentant *Son amid the Swine* of *c.*1496 is one of the masterpieces of his early work; the son revelling is a favourite subject of Dutch 17th-century followers of Caravaggio, in that it combined a low-life subject with moral overtones. Honthorst's *Supper Party* (1620: Uffizi) or his *Young man at the procuress* (1625: The Hague, private coll.), and Baburen's *The Procuress* (1622: Boston) are good examples. Murillo painted the subject twice, once in a series of four incidents, *The Departure; The Revels; Ruin; Repentance and Return* (1660–70: Dublin, Beit Coll.) and also in a single picture of the *Return of the Prodigal* (1668: Washington, NG). Rembrandt also painted the subject (*c.*1668: St Petersburg, Hermitage)—one of his late tragic masterpieces. Constantly popular as subject matter, the parables are neatly treated by Christopher LeBrun PRA and by Adrian Wiszniewski (1966) in Liverpool Cathedral. Among modern examples are Van Gogh's *The Sower* (1888: Stedelijk Museum, Amsterdam, the Netherlands); Paula Modersohn-Becker's *The Good Samaritan* (1907: Paula Modersohn-Becker Museum, Bremen, Germany).

Paraclete (Gk. Comforter, Advocate), the Holy Spirit. The word only occurs in John 14: 16, and three more times during Christ's discourse during the Last Supper, and once in 1 John 2: 1. The Biblia Sacra and the Vulgate use Paraclete, AV uses Comforter, meaning the Holy Spirit in the Gospel references, and Advocate meaning Christ in the Epistle reference. NRSV uses Advocate in all references. *See* TRINITY.

Paradise (Gk. *paradeisos,* from Persian, pleasure garden) Originally (as in Gen. 2: 8 etc.), it meant the Garden of Eden and man's happiness before the Fall—the Earthly or Terrestrial Paradise. It later came to mean man's future happiness—the Celestial Paradise—which may be *Heaven or the state of bliss of the righteous before the Last Judgement. *Bosch's *Garden of Delights* (Madrid, Prado) is a picture of Eden, with Adam and Eve, but 14th- and 15th-century pictures of the *Paradise Garden* or *Hortus Conclusus show the Madonna and Child, usually with Virgin Saints (*see* VIRGO INTER VIRGINES) in a beautiful enclosed garden with the *Fountain of Life or the four *Rivers of Paradise. It has been suggested that the water imagery comes from the East. It is rare for Paradise to be represented except as part of the imagery of the Creation or the Fall of Man. Bosch's *Garden of Delights,* for instance, has God presenting Eve to Adam, suggesting the moment after her creation. For the architectural use of the word *see* PARVIS.

Paralipomena (Gk. of things omitted) are the OT books in the Vulgate Bible which are called 1 and 2 Chronicles in the AV, the NRSV, and other Protestant versions of the Bible, because they are considered as supplementary to 1 and 2 Kings.

paraments (Lat. *paramenta*) are *vestments, including copes, and other liturgical garments and altar furnishings, made from textiles. One of the best examples is the *Parement de Narbonne* (*c*.1375: Louvre), an altar frontal with a monochrome brush drawing on silk, with a Crucifixion in the centre flanked by Ecclesia and Synagoga at the top, and portraits of the donors, Charles V of France and his Queen, Jeanne de Bourbon, in prayer below. In a Gothic arcade are six scenes of the Passion. It was not made for Narbonne, where it was found in the 19th century, but must have been made in Paris, as a Lenten frontal for a palace chapel, perhaps the Ste-Chapelle, since it bears the royal monogram in the borders. Such costly and elaborate articles were much sought after, particularly the embroidered *opus anglicanum vestments, which were often given as presents to prelates by English monarchs and were much prized in Rome (a Vatican inventory of 1295 lists over a hundred such vestments, many of which still survive), but they are among the most perishable works of art. Examples are now found in many European museums and some major museums in the US.

p

parclose A screen enclosing a chapel or shrine to separate it from the body of the church, either for the control of crowds or for the security of the contents.

parekklesion (paracclesion) Byzantine churches have only one altar, but large churches needing side chapels with altars had additional small churches, either attached to it, or free-standing alongside. Sometimes, a side chapel would be provided with an altar, flanked by its own *prothesis and *Diaconicon, the whole separated by an *iconostasis, creating a separate church within the original one. Fenari Isa. Camii (Lips Monastery), Constantinople, is an example where the two contiguous churches were built at widely differing dates, the N. church *c*.930, the S. church 1282–1304. Hosios Lukas, Greece, is an example of the two churches close in date: the Katholikon, *c*.1220, and the Theotokos, *c*.1240.

parish church When Christianity was first established in towns in W. Europe it naturally followed the systems developed in Early Christian Rome. Later, as Gaul and other areas were Christianized, presbyters and deacons were sent from the towns into the surrounding rural areas as missionaries (*see* MARTIN, S.). Often, the converted were landowners who built churches for themselves and their dependants, and for proper control bishops ruled that no church could be built without authority, each to be properly endowed with a fully working farm (the origin of the glebe). In England, it is clear from records from the time of Edward the Confessor that many estates and villages had a priest, which presupposes a church, and the Domesday Book of 1086 confirms this, as do the many instances of old churches, particularly rural ones, with Anglo-Saxon remains. It is also clear that, despite the dispossession of the Anglo-Saxon landowners by their Norman conquerors, and the amalgamation of many small estates into the huge estates of both the new Norman landowners and the religious Orders which flooded into the country in their wake to take over the Anglo-Saxon abbeys, the individual parishes changed little in size or number. In England, it was only in the 18th and 19th centuries that a larger population required new parishes to be created, and those were mostly in towns. In London, Acts were passed for the building of fifty new churches in 1711, and a similar act in 1818, for the so-called Waterloo churches, virtually all of which were urban churches. In the first case few churches were actually built, mostly in London, in the second some 260 were built nation-wide.

At its simplest level, a parish church is the main church of a distinct area or district, which may range from a small village to part of a large town. It may vary from a modest structure of a nave and chancel, to a large church of almost cathedral size and elaboration. In fact, many parish churches owe their origins to monasteries or colleges of canons which were dispossessed (e.g. Beverley Minster) or to cathedrals made redundant by the merging of dioceses (Laon, in N. France, one of the grandest early Gothic cathedrals, has suffered this fate). In Italy, when the Franciscans and the Dominicans first arrived in the cities, they were forced to build their large preaching churches (*see* MENDICANT CHURCHES) outside the city confines, and only became parish churches when the city expanded around them; Florence is a good example of this. The only factor which governs size, importance, magnificence is the wealth of the community in which it is situated. In East Anglia the 15th-century 'wool churches' were built or rebuilt from the munificence and prosperity of the local wool merchants; in Venice and Florence community and *guild rivalry encouraged the building and decoration of churches of rich complexity.

In the great fire of London in 1666, almost all the medieval parish churches were destroyed, as well as the cathedral. The parish churches were the first to be rebuilt, since the city was densely populated, and rebuilding of houses as well as churches was begun as soon as the sites could be cleared. *Wren's memorandum setting out his proposals make clear the very great difference between the design of medieval churches adapted for Anglican worship, and the new forms which he designed specifically for Anglican services. Deep chancels, he said, were unnecessary because choirs were not wanted. Pulpits had to be prominent and placed so that everyone in the church could both see and hear the preacher. Many churches had galleries so that a large congregation could be seated within earshot of the preacher and the reader of the large bible which was now in a prominent place. The importance of an easily accessible parish church was essential in an age when everybody went to church, and there was no other legal means of solemnizing a marriage or having someone buried in the churchyard. A loft in the far end was for musicians, eventually replaced by organs, since hymn-singing was normal. The altar was usually a modest affair, and certainly not the important feature that it was in pre-Reformation churches. It was still placed in the east end if possible, but orientation was not essential, only desirable. All these churches had fixed *pews, and it was not until the 19th century Ecclesiological Movement that many of them were modified to increase the importance of the chancel, and for the introduction of surpliced choirs. This movement went hand in hand with the *Gothic Revival. Though the 18th century—and above all the 19th—saw the rise of Nonconformist Churches, and though their chapels and meeting-houses range from the very modest to ones of impressive size, they are not parish churches, and though they baptize, marry, and hold funeral services, the State in the UK insists that a Registrar must be present to record marriages, and the incumbent is responsible for recording baptisms and burials, for the latter of which a Registrar's certificate is essential. The same rule applies to Roman Catholic churches. As the main church—and often the only one—in an area, the parish church will hold the registers of births, marriages, and deaths of those for whom the church and its incumbent were required to officiate; it will contain a font for baptisms, an altar for the celebrant (Roman Catholic churches have two, though the second may be in the sacristy); there is a vestry, or sacristy (often absent in medieval churches), for the robing of the celebrant and for the care of vestments. The bells may be a single one in a simple bell-cote over the door or, in a medieval church, over the chancel arch (as at Preston, Glos.) where it could double as the Sanctus Bell, rung during Mass, or a magnificent and elaborate tower housing a full peal of eight or more bells, or in Italy a separate *campanile. The *font was one of the most important objects in a parish church since the practice of bringing infants to be baptized in the church was once universal in Christian communities. Often family *chapels have been made in, or added to, parish churches, generally to house family tombs, and are common in France and Italy, where services are held on commemorative occasions. In England chantry chapels are usually in cathedrals, but are sometimes built as a separate little structure in the church (the Delawarre Chantry, Boxgrove, West Sussex, for example). Of tomb chapels, the grandest are unquestionably the Chigi Chapel designed by Raphael in 1515 and added to Sta Maria del Popolo in Rome, and the Medici Chapel of San Lorenzo, Florence, begun in 1520 by Michelangelo. Later Medici Grand Dukes built themselves a huge mausoleum also attached to San Lorenzo, of an ostentatious elaboration equalled only by the negligibility of those it commemorates. Memorial chapels exist in, or are attached to, many parish churches in England, with 16th- to 18th-century tombs with elaborate carved effigies of the local magnates. In France, separate tomb chapels are rare in parish churches, and in Spain one of the earliest is for the royal tombs in the 11th-century Panteón de los Reyes attached to Sant'Isidoro, León, and one of the grandest is the Capilla del Condestable (1482–94) at the far end of Burgos Cathedral.

Parmigianino, Francesco (1503–40), was the most famous member of a family of painters in Parma, called Mazzuoli. He was commissioned to decorate the south transept of Parma Cathedral when he was only 19, and

p

in 1522/3 he painted frescoes in three chapels of San Giovanni Evangelista in Parma, with over-life-size figures in fictive architectural settings. After executing a secular fresco cycle in the Castello at Fontenellata (*c.*1523), which shows his assimilation of the art of Correggio, he went to Rome, possibly to escape competition with him. By this time, he had developed into a *Mannerist painter of high refinement and sophistication, his Madonna and Child subjects expressed with studied elegance, with long limbs, finely drawn features, and complicated coiffures. These qualities are shown to the full in the *Mystic Marriage of S. Catherine* and the *Vision of S. Jerome* (both London, NG, 1525–6 and 1527). He was working on this last picture during the Sack of Rome in 1527, and remained oblivious of the battle around him until German soldiers burst into the studio. They were so overawed by the picture that they protected him, and had he not ventured on to the streets, where he was captured by another band of marauders, he would have escaped scatheless. He is said to have ransomed himself by drawing, and eventually he escaped to Bologna, where he remained until 1530.

The works he executed in Bologna show the full development of his aesthetic sensibility in the delicate refinement of features, gestures, and poses in, for instance, the *Madonna and Child with S. Margaret and other saints* (1529: Bologna), and these characteristics are even stronger in the *Madonna and Child with S. Mary Magdalene and S. Zaccharia* (1535: Florence, Uffizi), where a giant S. Zaccharia looms in the front of the composition. This culminates in a work which he appears to have left unfinished: the *Madonna and Child with angels* (1535: Florence, Uffizi) known as the 'Madonna del collo lungo' (. . . with the long neck), where his search for elegant refinement results in an almost surreal elongation of the Madonna and the sleeping Child held in uneasy balance on her lap. In the background is a tiny figure of a prophet at the foot of an extraordinary colonnade, seen in violent perspective.

He returned to Parma in 1530, after a visit to Venice, and resumed working on the decoration of the church of the Steccata, which had begun before he went to Rome. Three tall, elegant young women on either side of the choir arch represent three Wise and three Foolish Virgins. But his extremely neurotic temperament brought him into constant strife with the church authorities, and he also became obsessed with alchemy, believing he could transmute mercury into gold. Finally the authorities lost patience, and in 1539 they dismissed him and sought to imprison him for breach of contract. He fled to Casalmaggiore, near Cremona, where he contracted a fever and died. Vasari records that this former model of sophisticated elegance was now 'bearded, long-haired, unkempt, almost a savage and utterly changed, melancholic and strange'. Before his death he had ordered that he should be buried naked with a cypress cross upright on his breast. This was done.

Parousia (Gk. presence, arrival, particularly in classical usage, of a royal person) In Christian terms it refers to the Second Coming of Christ, His return to Earth at the last day for the *Last Judgement, which will mark the end of the present world order and the entry of redeemed and resurrected humanity into Heaven. Primitive Christianity believed the Second Coming to be imminent, and at various times the belief has been preached, beginning with S. Paul, in 2 Thess. 1 and 2. S. Peter also advances this belief in 2 Pet. 1: 16–18 when he describes Christ in Glory, as he saw Him at the *Transfiguration. He predicts its imminence, when mankind will be confronted with Christ in Glory. Although in Heb. 9: 28, S. Paul uses the words 'So Christ will appear a second time', the definition of *parousia* as the Second Coming is not in the Gospels. It appears first in the Epistles, and then in S. Justin, who was one of the early Christian apologists (Gk. *apologos*, account), that is, philosophers who strove to explain Christianity to the pagan and Jewish world. He wrote two Apologies, the first to refute slanders against Christians, the second to argue the replacement of the Old Covenant by the New. He was martyred under Marcus Aurelius *c.*165, and his importance lies in his having been one of the first converts to come from an educated stratum of society.

The representation of *parousia* in Byzantine mosaics is in the *Hetoimasia, or throne prepared for Christ's coming. The best examples are in the dome mosaics in the 6th-century Baptistery of the Orthodox in *Ravenna.

partridge *See* BIRDS, SYMBOLIC.

parvis(e) In French usage the open space, sometimes colonnaded, in front of a cathedral. In English it is also sometimes used wrongly to mean a room above a church porch. The name is said to be a corruption of Paradise, deriving from the area in front of Old St Peter's in Rome, once called Paradisus.

Paschal Candle, Fire *See* CANDLESTICK and SACRAMENTALS.

Paschal Lamb, the In its origin, this is the lamb eaten by the Jews at the first *Passover (Exod. 12: 1–28), and identified with Christ by S. Paul, 'For our paschal lamb, Christ, has been sacrificed for us' (1 Cor. 5: 7). The only use in the Gospel is in John 1: 29, when John the Baptist declared, 'Here is the Lamb of God who takes away the sin of the world . . .'. The Passover thus itself becomes a *type of the Christian Eucharist, as in D. Bouts's altarpiece of the *Mystic Meals (1464–8: Leuven, St Pieter (Louvain, St-Pierre)). *See also* EUCHARIST.

passio (Lat. suffering) The term is used in the Roman Martyrology for the suffering of martyrs, but, by extension, of the Passion of Christ, which is the major Passion, beginning with His arrest on Thursday evening, and ending with His entombment on Friday evening. This is the central part of the services of *Holy Week.

Passion, Instruments of the A list may be compiled from the **Speculum Humanae Salvationis*, which includes Judas's kiss, the (thirty) pieces of silver, the torches and staves of Christ's captors, Malchus's ear, the open hand that struck Him, the blindfold, the cloak, the spitting mouth, the crown of thorns, the stick striking the crown, the column, ropes, and whips of the flagellation, Pilate washing his hands, the cock which crew at Peter's denial, the cross, nails, hammer, ladder, His clothes and the casting of lots, the reed and sponge, and the lance. Not all of them are always included in images of the Instruments of the Passion. One of the rarest symbols of the Passion in Byzantine iconography is the 'Dreadful Presentation': two archangels show the symbols to the Holy Child sheltering in His mother's arms. A 12th-century example is in the church at Lagoudera, in the Troödos mountains, Cyprus. Botticelli, in the *Lamentation* (*c.*1495: Milan, Poldi-Pezzoli), has Nicodemus holding up the crown of thorns and three nails. Fra *Angelico and his assistants, in the frescoes in the Convent of San Marco in Florence, executed between 1436 and 1446, painted *Christ surrounded by the Instruments of the Passion* for the contemplation of the friars. Only a selection of the major instruments is included. *See also* ARMA CHRISTI.

Passion of the Christ, the *See* FILM.

Passover, the This is the principal Jewish festival of the year, which every spring commemorates the events recounted in Exodus, the second book of the OT (*see* MOSES). The sacrifice of the lamb was also accompanied by the eating of unleavened bread, and this too is part of the Passover observance. Because Christ came to Jerusalem to attend the festival, and because His crucifixion took place on the day before the beginning of the Sabbath of the festival, this fixes the Christian Easter at the same time as the Passover.

The sacrifice of the lamb was discontinued after the siege of Jerusalem and the destruction of the Temple in AD 70. It has been argued that the sacrifice of the lamb, and the eating of unleavened bread were, in origin, aspects of agricultural festivals normal in springtime. This may or may not be true; either way, it does not affect the existence of the festival of the Passover held in springtime as a commemoration of the deliverance of the Jews from their captivity in Egypt. But its concurrence with the Crucifixion fixes the time of Easter for Christians. The analogy of the sacrifice of the Paschal lamb and the Sacrifice of the Lamb of God falls inevitably into the pattern of biblical *type and antitype. An account of the events in Exodus forms part of the liturgy of Maundy Thursday. *See also* MYSTIC MEALS.

pastophorion (Gk.) In the early Eastern Church the pastophorion was a room where the offerings for the Eucharist were received. In many churches this room was at one side of the narthex, but as the design of the *cross-in-square churches crystallized into their later shape, with an apse flanked by two smaller apsidal chambers, the pastophorion in the narthex was superseded by the *prothesis on the north side of the altar. The chamber on the south side is the *Diaconicon.

pastoral staff *See* CROSIER.

paten *See* LITURGICAL VESSELS.

Patmos *See* JOHN, S., THE EVANGELIST.

patriarch A patriarch is a bishop taking precedence over all other bishops. The Pope is the Patriarch of the West, but the title has also been granted to the See of Venice, and of Aquileia, suppressed in 1751. There are Orthodox patriarchs, e.g. of Alexandria, Antioch, Constantinople, and Jerusalem. The title dates from the 6th century, but later patriarchates include Russia, Bulgaria, Serbia, Romania, and Georgia. The symbol of a patriarch's authority is the Patriarchal Cross, wih two crossbars, borne before him.

Patriarchs, the biblical These were the heads or leaders of OT tribes or clans, including those who lived before the Flood, e.g. Noah. The term usually refers to *Abraham, *Isaac, and *Jacob, and to Jacob's twelve sons, who founded the Twelve Tribes of Israel (another name for Jacob). King *David, as an ancestor of Christ, is also so called (Acts 2: 29). The sons of Jacob were Reuben (Vg. Ruben), Simeon and Levi, Judah (Vg. Juda), Zebulun (Vg. Zabulon), Issachar, Dan, Gad, Asher (Vg. Aser), Naphtali (Vg. Nephthali), *Joseph, and Benjamin.

patron saints Patron saints of churches first arose from the Early Christian practice of building churches over the graves of martyrs, or by extending *martyria, the martyr becoming the titular of the church (e.g. St Peter's, in Rome). The body of a saint, buried in a church with an existing dedication might be the reason for changing a dedication (e.g. the Doge's Palace Chapel, Venice, dedicated to S. Theodore, was rededicated to S. Mark when his body, brought from Alexandria in 828, was placed in a rebuilt church in 832). The dedication of a church has to be to a canonized saint, not to a beatified man or woman, but many churches are dedicated to God (in one of His attributes, as e.g. the Hagia *Sophia, the Holy Wisdom), to the Trinity, or to Christ (St Saviour), to the Virgin, or to an event (the Ascension), or to an object (the Holy Cross).

A patron saint is one chosen to be a special advocate with God on behalf of a country, or a place, an association, either lay or religious, or of an individual. The custom derives from the Catholic belief that saints and angels have special activities and concerns—e.g. guardian angels of children—and their aid may be—and often is—invoked, particularly in times of need. Probably the first use of martyrs as the patron saints of a city was by S. Ambrose, who in 386 made SS Gervasius and Protasius the patrons of Milan (they were martyred there). Usually such a dedication was prompted by the possession of relics (often called *patrocinia*), but later the selection was a deliberate choice. Milan later changed its dedication to S. Ambrose. There is no date for the earliest dedication of a church to the archangels Michael, Raphael, or Gabriel, but San Michele, Ravenna, was dedicated in 545. The choice of a patron saint for a country, a place, or an organization is usually because there is a connection between them; e.g. Italy is dedicated to S. Francis of Assisi and to S. Catherine of Siena, because of territorial links; France has adopted S. Joan of Arc, since 1922, before which its patron was S. Louis IX; Ireland is dedicated to S. Patrick, because he converted the Irish. Sometimes the choice derives from a monarch's personal devotion to a saint: S. George displaced S. Edward the Confessor when Edward III founded the Order of the Garter under his auspices *c.*1347, and his arms of a red cross on a white ground became virtually a uniform for soldiers, and 'S. George for England' their battle-cry. A city may have a dedication for varied reasons: Paris to S. Genevieve, because she encouraged the citizens to resist the Franks, and later Attila and the Huns, and also to S. Denis, and to S. Germain, both commemorated by churches in the city, and the abbey outside it. Bury St Edmunds, Suffolk, owes its change of name from plain Bury, because the remains of King Edmund, martyred by the Danes in 869, were finally buried in the abbey there. Guilds, trades, or professions may have patron saints: S. Joseph of carpenters, S. Luke of painters, because he was reputed to have been an artist as well as a physician, S. Cecilia of musicians, SS Crispin and Crispianus of shoemakers, and S. Eligius of goldsmiths because that was their trade. S. Thomas Aquinas as the patron of places of learning is perfectly logical, so is S. Camillo of Lellis of nurses, because he was one. Certain saints may be invoked against certain illnesses or conditions, such as S. Roch and S. Sebastian against plague, S. Agatha and S. Apollonia against diseases of the breast and toothache, because of the manner of their martyrdom, S. Margaret of childbirth because of the legend of her martyrdom. Sometimes the reasons appear logical, at other times merely picturesque: the Madonna of Loreto as the patron saint of airmen is because the Holy House of Loreto is said to have flown through the air, S. Ives of Brittany as patron of lawyers because he was one revered for his honesty suggests disillusioned experience. The list is a long one, and the reasons for choice often obscure. Orsanmichele in Florence was originally the church of San Michele in Orto built in the 8th century, but was converted into a meeting-place for merchants, and to double as the city granary in 1337. In 1380 the arcades which formed the open ground floor were closed in and it became the corporate church of all the guilds of the city (and still doubled as the city's emergency granary).

The feast-day of the titular saint of a church is celebrated in the Catholic Church with the Mass of that saint's official day; the practice has been revived in many Anglican churches since the 19th century.

Paul, Saint and Apostle (d. *c.*65), was the Apostle of the Gentiles. He was born in Tarsus, a Hellenized city in Cilicia (S. Turkey), the son of a Jew who had acquired Roman citizenship, making Paul a Roman citizen by birth. He knew the trade of tent-making, or leather-working (synonymous in Greek), since later he practised it. He was brought up a strict Pharisee, and was sent to Jerusalem to be a pupil of the jurist Rabbi Gamaliel (*c.*10?–80), celebrated for his liberal teaching. Paul was then called Saul, but double names were common among Hellenized Jews. He was a passionate man, with a legalistic mind, and was violently opposed to Christian teaching; his campaigns against those who followed 'the Way', as it was called (Acts 22: 3–7; 26: 9–11), were bitter and energetic. He first appears in the account of the martyrdom of *S. Stephen, who was condemned by the council and was stoned to death (Acts 6: 12–13; 7: 58–60; 8: 1–3) 'and the witnesses laid their coats at the feet of a young man named Saul . . . who approved of their killing him . . . '. After S. Stephen's death Saul 'was ravaging the Church by entering house after house; dragging off both men and women, he committed them to prison.' He 'went to the High Priest and asked him for letters to the synagogue at Damascus, so that if he found any that belonged to the Way . . . he might bring them bound to Jerusalem.' (In fact, he could not have done so.)

As he was nearing Damascus, 'suddenly a light from Heaven flashed around him. He fell to the ground and heard a voice saying, "Saul, Saul, why do you persecute me?" He asked, "Who are you, Lord?" The reply came, "I am Jesus, whom you are persecuting. But get up and enter the city . . . ".' He got up, and though his eyes were open he could see nothing and those with him were speechless; they heard the voice, but could see no one. They led him into Damascus, and for three days he was blind, neither eating nor drinking. The Lord appeared in a vision to a disciple in Damascus called Ananias and told him where to find Saul and to cure him. Ananias protested that he knew the damage Saul had done in Jerusalem, but the Lord insisted saying, 'Go, for he is an instrument whom I have chosen to bring my name before Gentiles . . . and . . . the people of Israel . . . '. Ananias laid his hands on Saul and his sight returned; he ate again, was baptized, and after several days he proclaimed Jesus in the synagogue, saying, 'He is the son of God.' But he met with such hostility that he left Damascus (Acts 9: 1–22).

The Epistle to the Galatians (1: 1–17) extends the narrative in Acts 9 by making clear that after his conversion and his first futile attempt to preach to the Jews in Damascus he went away into the desert, where he remained for a fairly considerable time. He then returned to Damascus and tried again, but the hostility was such that the only way the disciples could save him was to lower him by night in a basket from the walls (2 Cor. 11: 33). Saul returned to Jerusalem three years after his conversion and tried to join the disciples, but no one trusted him except *Barnabas, who told the Apostles about the vision on the road to Damascus, but so few were convinced that those who believed took him to Caesarea and sent him back to Tarsus (Acts 9: 29–30). There he was sought out by Barnabas, and they went together to Antioch in Syria, where they stayed for a year. It was in Antioch that the disciples were first called Christians (Acts 11: 19–26).

Paul's great memorial is his Epistles, which set out his complex doctrinal and ethical teaching; one of the interesting aspects of them is that most, though not all, pre-date the Gospels. There has been widespread disagreement during the last two centuries over which of the Epistles were actually written or dictated by him. While many conservative scholars defend them all, radical ones only accept four—Romans, 1 and 2 Corinthians, and Galatians. A more moderate view admits that the Corinthian Epistles may have had a fair amount of editing, and accepts, with the exception of Hebrews and possibly the pastoral Epistles, that the others are at least partly by Paul himself or written by men in his circle or under his aegis. Romans, the two Corinthians, and Galatians are the heart of Paul's theology, and teachers as diverse as S. Augustine, Luther, and Calvin based their teaching on them. The Epistles to the Ephesians, the

Philippians, the Colossians, and the letter to Philemon are often called the 'Captivity' Epistles. They were written, or drafted for others to write, to churches which he had not founded himself, in response to pastoral and doctrinal crises in the churches, and Paul wrote or drafted them during one or more of his imprisonments, though which ones were written when remains uncertain. He intended churches to exchange Epistles and others probably existed which have not survived. In Colossians 4: 15–16, he writes: 'Give my greetings to the brothers and sisters in Laodicea . . . And when this letter has been read among you, have it read also in the church of the Laodiceans.' Since the two towns are quite near to each other in what is now S. Turkey, and close to Ephesus, this would not have been difficult.

Through the Acts and the Epistles many of Paul's associates are recorded, such as *Mark, Timothy, Barnabas, Silas (called Silvanus in 2 Cor. 1: 19, and 1 Thess. 1: 1), and Titus. In trying to reconstruct Paul's journeys, the Epistles have priority over the Acts, but there is no unanimity of interpretation, only a reasonable reconstruction up to the final, dramatic journey to martyrdom. The Epistles remain the most evocative record of his arduous, adventurous missionary journeys, which lasted to the end of his life. On many of them *Luke travelled with him, as he records from Acts 16: 11 onwards to the end of Acts, a journey which ends in Rome before Paul's martyrdom. In 2 Cor. 11: 24–7 Paul writes 'with far more imprisonments, with countless floggings, and often near to death. Five times I have received . . . the forty lashes minus one. Three times I was beaten with rods. Once I received a stoning. Three times I was shipwrecked; for a night and a day I was adrift at sea; on frequent journeys, in danger from rivers, danger from bandits, danger from my own people, danger from Gentiles, danger in the city, danger in the wilderness, danger at sea, danger from false brothers and sisters, danger in toil and hardship, through many a sleepless night, hungry and thirsty, often without food, cold and naked.' Paul's missionary travels were interspersed by long periods of residence in, for instance, Antioch in Syria, where he stayed for a year on his first and second journeys, and perhaps longer than two years on his third journey. He was in Corinth for a year and a half on his second journey, and the constant nature of his journeying can be grasped from his statement in Galatians 1: 1–24, 2: 1 that between his conversion and his visit to Jerusalem three years elapsed, and his next visit to Jerusalem was fourteen years later.

He travelled through what is now S. Turkey from Antioch in Syria to Greece, to Philippi and Thessalonika, Corinth, and up into Macedonia, by sea, or overland, possibly on foot. His last journey was the result of a riot in Jerusalem, instigated by Jews. He was rescued by the Roman guard and hustled into the Antonia Fortress, condemned to be flogged, but claimed his Roman citizenship which preserved him from such torture. His trial before the Sanhedrin broke up in confusion, but a serious threat to his life caused the Roman commander to send him to Caesarea for judgement by the governor Felix, who evaded the issue by keeping him in prison for the remaining two years of his term of office. The next governor, Festus, invited Paul's accusers to Caesarea and then asked him if he were willing to go to Jerusalem to be tried. Knowing that this would result in his condemnation and death, he appealed to Rome. An appeal to Caesar had to be allowed, and in the autumn, probably of the year 60, he was sent with other prisoners under escort on the long sea journey to Italy. But it was too late in the sailing season, and the ship was caught by terrible storms and finally wrecked on the only beach in Malta. Here occurred the famous incident of Paul, who was helping to gather wood for a fire at which they might warm themselves, being bitten by a snake which clung to his hand. All expected him to die, but he shook it off and was unharmed. They remained in Malta for three months and then sailed for Syracuse, landed near Naples, and after a week started on their journey to Rome on foot. In Rome, Paul lived under house arrest for two years. It seems from his letter to Titus (3: 12) and to Philemon v. 22 that he expected to be released; whether he was and returned to Greece and to Troas (in W. Turkey), and was then rearrested and sent back to Rome (would this explain his remark in 2 Tim. 4: 14 of 'Alexander the coppersmith did me great harm'?) is not known, but his second Roman imprisonment ended fatally during Nero's persecutions. As a Roman citizen, he was beheaded, traditionally at a place now called Tre Fontane on the Via Appia to Ostia. Legend has it that his head bounced three times, and a spring appeared at each place. His body was finally interred in what became the great basilica of San Paolo fuori le Mura—outside the walls—a memorial to the most energetic and powerful advocate of Christianity, who may have come to his vocation later than any other Apostle, but who insisted that his mission was given to him by Christ Himself, and not received from any of the Apostles (Gal. 1: 11–12).

An Apocryphal Acts of S. Paul was written in Asia Minor in the 2nd century by a Christian presbyter who was deprived of his office when the forgery was detected. It circulated widely in Asia Minor and in Italy. It contains a description of S. Paul which, whether accurate or not (and in view of the persistence of oral traditions, it may well be so), is clearly the source of the traditional representation of the Apostle. 'And a certain man . . . when he heard that Paul was come to Iconium, went out . . . to meet him . . . And he saw Paul coming, a man of little stature, thin haired upon the head, crooked in the legs, of good state of body, with eyebrows joining and nose somewhat hooked . . .'. The Apocryphal Acts continues with the story of Thecla, an Iconian girl who was saved from martyrdom by a series of fantastic miracles; her cult gained a great following in Asia Minor, and also spread to Italy (she is the patron saint of Este). The Apocrypha follows many of his journeys, and names a number of his disciples, but often in the wrong order, and also borrows from the equally Apocryphal Acts of Peter, which are as fantastic and incredible a farrago as those of Paul. The Apocryphal Gospels and Acts, like the Lives of many early saints, provide a wealth of vivid detail which fills out the canonical accounts. These stories were for long believed to be true, so that for artists and their patrons they provided a wealth of incidents which furnished subjects.

An account of the martyrdom of S. Paul in a 2nd-century legend seems to have had less effect on the arts than the Apocryphal Acts. There was also a late 4th-century book purporting to be an account of the Apocalypse of S. Paul which had an immense vogue in the West. It was strongly condemned by many church leaders—S. Augustine 'laughed at the folly of someone who had forged an Apocalypse of Paul, full of fables . . .'. But its lasting vogue in the West is attested by its survival in France as late as the 17th century.

Representations of S. Paul are legion, but they usually have one thing in common: they follow an old iconographical tradition that he was thin, had a dark beard and a high forehead and was partly bald. A representative selection of images may begin with the sarcophagus of Junius Bassus (359: Rome, St Peter's Mus.), where the two major Apostles flank the seated Christ. Ravenna is rich in 5th-century mosaic images: in a lunette in the Mausoleum of Galla Placidia are both S. Peter and S. Paul; the procession of Apostles in the domes of the Baptistery of the Orthodox and of the Arians starts from the two major Apostles; the Archbishop's chapel has a roundel of S. Paul in the soffit of an arch; all these images conform to the old tradition of S. Paul with a dark beard and half-bald head. An ivory book-cover relief also shows him like this (1000: Paris, Cluny); an ivory coffer in Tournai Cathedral has Christ (now headless) flanked by Peter and Paul, one with the traditional good head of hair and the other nearly bald; a mid-12th-century wall-painting of *S. Paul and the viper* (St Anselm's Chapel, Canterbury Cath.); a head of S. Paul in a roundel and a scene of his baptism (12th cent.: Palermo, Cappella Palatina) all have the same features; so does a figure in the south portal of Chartres Cathedral (*c.*1215), and the relief of S. Paul in Filarete's doors of St Peter's, Rome (1433–45). Masaccio in a panel from the Pisa polyptych (1426: Pisa) follows the tradition, but Donatello, in the Apostle door of Florence Cathedral sacristy, 1437–43, deviates from it by showing S. Paul with a shock of hair; Dürer in the *Apostle wings* (1526: Munich) follows the tradition. In the cartoons for the Sistine Chapel tapestries, designed by Raphael (1515: Royal loan to V & A Mus., London), and in the tapestries (Vatican Mus.), S. Paul is shown bearded, but with a full head of hair, as he is also in the *Conversion of S. Paul* (1601: Rome, Sta Maria del Popolo) by Caravaggio. This can be explained by S. Paul being still a young man at the time. In the Michelangelo fresco of the *Conversion* (1542–50: Vatican, Cappella Paolina) the artist painted S. Paul with a long white beard, although at the time he was presumably still a young man, in deference to the commissioner, Pope Paul III, who was an old man (Paul's raised arm conceals his hair). The subject became popular in the 16th century, largely because of the fame of the Michelangelo. Bruegel painted a version (1567: Vienna, KHM) with the fallen Saul lost in the escorting caravan; Solimena painted a huge dramatic fresco of the event (1689: Naples, San Paolo Maggiore). There is a miniature of the *Martyrdom of S. Paul* in Pudenzio's *Carmina* (15th cent.: Vatican Lib.), and Rembrandt painted a moving vision of S. Paul, aged, weary, and pensive, writing by lamplight (*c.*1640: Nuremberg) and an equally moving, almost pathetic, *Self-portrait as the Apostle Paul* (1661: Amsterdam). Poussin painted an unusual *Ecstasy of S. Paul* (1649–50: Louvre) showing him raised to Heaven by angels after his martyrdom, evidence of the surviving impact of the *Apocalypse of S. Paul*, and also of Raphael's *Vision of Ezekiel* (*c.*1516: Florence, Pitti) on the artist.

Paul the Hermit, Saint (*c.*230–342), was an Egyptian of birth and education, who fled into the desert of Thebes when he was 22 to escape the persecution under the Emperor Decian, and stayed there until his death at about 90 years of age. He was one of the first hermit saints, and as the first hermit to live in the Theban valley, may be considered as the founder of the *Thebaid which grew up in the area. *S. Antony the Abbot visited him, and on a second visit found him dead, and buried him. The facts of his life, such as they are, are derived from *S. Jerome. Legend has it that he was clothed in skins or leaves, that he was fed daily by a raven, and that lions dug his grave. His cult was stimulated by the Hungarian foundation of the Order of S. Paul the Hermit in 1212 and his body was obtained in 1381 from the Venetians (who had acquired it at the appalling Fourth Crusade in 1204) and transferred to Budapest. His cult also spread into Bohemia (Schlossburg monastery) and to Poland (Czestochova monastery).

In art, he appears with S. Antony Abbot on the Ruthwell cross (7th cent.: Ruthwell, Dumfriesshire); in a four-part icon of King *Abgar holding the Mandylion, with S. Antony Abbot, and four other saints (*c.*945: Mt. Sinai, St Catherine's Monastery); in the *menologion of Basil II (10th cent.: Vatican Lib.); a miniature in a Syrian Psalter (1203: London, BL) shows him clothed in palm leaves, with a bird bringing him food, and flanked by a lion and a bear. The most striking and celebrated image is in the wing of the Isenheim Altar (*Grünewald: *c.*1515/16: Colmar) showing the two hermit saints together. A Ribera of *S. Paul in meditation* (1640: Prado) shows the emaciated saint in a cave clothed in palm leaves.

Paul the Silentiary (Paul Silentiarios) was a wealthy Byzantine 6th-century poet and court official, whose duty was to secure the order and quiet of the palace.

He is notable for his long poem of 563 describing Justinian's restoration of Hagia *Sophia. It provides the fullest description of the church's decoration, including the *ambo, and the materials and techniques used in the work, all of which has disappeared. His other poems, which mingle Christian and pagan themes, are notable for their eroticism.

Paulinus of Nola, Saint (*c.*354–431), was born in Bordeaux, SE France, where his father was a Roman prefect, and a wealthy landowner. By 381 he was made governor of Campania, S. Italy, and there first became associated with Nola (*c.*30 miles east of Naples). By 389 he had been baptized and he became a priest in Barcelona in 395, and then returned to Nola with his wife and a group of friends to lead a life of austere poverty. He was Bishop of Nola by 410 when the city was ravaged by the Goths. After this date little is known of him. He was a notable Christian poet and many of his surviving letters to SS Ambrose and Augustine (394–426) describe the churches he built in Nola and their decoration with paintings and mosaics, explaining the symbolism and justifying them by their influence on the illiterate. They include doves and the Lamb as a symbol of Christ.

Representations of S. Paulinus are few and mostly in France in, for instance, the *predella* of an altarpiece by Luis Borassa in the cathedral of Vich, and also in local churches in Campania.

Paul's, Saint, London The first cathedral of London was built *c.*607 and was burnt down in the great fire of 1087. It was immediately rebuilt, enlarged *c.*1220/40 and again in 1256, and completed *c.*1332, with a spire almost 500 ft. high. It was the biggest building in England, and the spire—destroyed by fire in 1561—was a landmark visible out at sea. This landmark was still a memory in the 17th century and influenced some of *Wren's early projects for the building. Knowledge of the medieval building comes mainly from engravings by Hollar made just before its final destruction in the Great Fire of 1666: by then, it was in a dangerous state, although Archbishop Laud had tried to restore it and Inigo *Jones built the great portico (1634) with Corinthian columns 60 ft. high, which Evelyn recorded in his Diary as perishing (7 Sept. 1666)—'that beautiful portico (for structure comparable to any in Europe)'. In 1666 Wren had made a survey and proposed to recase the nave 'after a good

Roman manner' instead of the 'Gothick Rudeness of ye old Design', but the cathedral was burned down before work started. His first projects were for a long-nave church, without aisles, their space being taken by a promenading area outside, to replace the former use of the cathedral nave as a merchants' meeting-place. These meeting-places were to have galleries above them internal to the church to extend the space for the congregation. Wren managed to get this unsatisfactory scheme abandoned (a model for it is in the cathedral museum). He then prepared designs (two slightly different sets) for a cross-in-square church with a high dome, and a re-creation of the great portico in front. But they were rejected by the church commissioners as 'not sufficiently of a cathedral fashion' though the real reason was probably that they were deemed too close to contemporary Roman Baroque. The cathedral owns a magnificent wooden model of the rejected design large enough to walk into. In 1675 Wren began the new building, having secured from the commissioners authority to vary the authorized design 'by such matters of detail as shall prove beneficial', and he used this device to drive a coach and horses through the authorized design, to the great benefit of the final building. What he finally built was a long-nave church, with a high dome not unlike the one he had planned for his original design, and with a columned portico flanked by two fine towers. It was finished (by declaration of Parliament) in 1711, and Wren finally received his fees, which had been held up pending the completion of the work. The interior contains superb ironwork by Tijou and wood-carvings by Grinling Gibbons as well as grisaille paintings of scenes from the Life of S. Paul in the dome (1716–19) by Thornhill, which were not approved by Wren. Since the late 18th century many statues and monuments have been added, not always to the benefit of the building. The most famous, and simplest, is the slab with Wren's own epitaph: *Lector, si monumentum requiris, circumspice*—Reader, if you seek his monument, look around you. The tomb of Nelson, adapted from a sarcophagus intended for Cardinal Wolsey (in the crypt), and the Wellington Monument by Alfred Stevens (in the nave) are other notable features. Later 19th-century additions include mosaics by Stevens, Watts, and Richmond, which suffer from being no more than traditional oil-paintings made in mosaic, and the second version of *Hunt's *Light of the World* (1851–1900). The Baroque *baldacchino is as recent as 1958, but follows indications in a sketch by Wren himself.

Paul's, Saint, outside the Walls (of Rome) *See* PAOLO, S. FUORI LE MURA.

Pax (Lat. peace) In Early Christian times, and during the early Middle Ages, the Kiss of Peace was a real embrace exchanged between the celebrant (priest) and the deacon, and then given by him to others assisting at the altar. In the congregation it was permissible only if the sexes were segregated. At a Nuptial Mass, the kiss of peace was given by the priest to the bridegroom, who passed it on to the bride. In the 13th century the physical embrace was replaced by the use of a liturgical object called a Pax Brede (or board) or Osculatorium. This was a plate of ivory, metal, or wood with a handle underneath, bearing an image of the Crucifixion, or the Lamb, or a similar suitable subject, which was kissed by the celebrant, and then passed among those present, who kissed it in turn. It was probably of Franciscan origin, and was introduced into England in 1250. It was also introduced in France, Italy, Spain, and Germany, but had to be abandoned because of the dissensions it caused over precedence. In the Eastern Church the Kiss of Peace was given at the offertory, so that it might include the catechumens who then left the service; in the Western Church, it was given after the consecration. In the present Roman Catholic High Mass and in some Anglican churches the embrace is still exchanged by the celebrant and assistants, but among the congregation it has become a handshake, as it is for celebrant and congregation at Low Mass. A ceremonial Kiss of Peace was usually exchanged when contestants ratified a treaty, or agreed to cease hostilities. It was the unwillingness of King Henry II to give the kiss of peace to Archbishop Thomas Becket that convinced the archbishop that the agreement reached between them would not last, and Becket's welcome on his return to England, and his actions in excommunicating some bishops who had sided with Henry, finally led the angry king to his hasty words that resulted in the prelate's murder in Canterbury Cathedral in 1170.

Peace of the Church *See* MILAN, EDICT OF.

peacock *See* BIRDS, SYMBOLIC.

pectoral cross A cross of precious metal, often jewelled, and sometimes containing a relic, worn on a chain round the neck, to hang on the breast. In the Catholic Church it is worn by cardinals, bishops, abbots, and by some canons, but not by the pope. Members of some religious Orders (e.g. *Mercedarians) wear a simple, less valuable cross, which may be of silver or wood and brass. In the Eastern Church it is worn by archimandrates, archpriests, and in Russia by simple priests; bishops wear an *encolpion, which often encloses a relic, but may wear a cross when officiating. In the Church of England it is worn only by bishops.

pediment A gable-like element over a temple front or a window. It may be triangular or segmental, and in Roman classical, Renaissance, and later buildings, pedimented windows were often used in alternation, care being taken to keep to an uneven number so that the central window is flanked by alternating triangular or segmental ones. A broken pediment is one of either form that is split in the centre into two sections, the gap often being filled by a bust, or a decorative feature such as a coat of arms.

pelican *See* BIRDS, SYMBOLIC.

pendentive Where a dome rises from the top of either its supporting *piers or from a drum, the junction between the top of the supports and the base of the drum or dome will be either by *squinches or pendentives. The latter are curved spherical triangles that rise from the tops of the supporting piers to provide the transition from the area of the crossing, or the walls of a chapel, to the drum or the dome. They often became a field for decoration. In Hagia Sophia, huge angels in mosaic were once on the pendentives of the great dome; in S. Giovanni Evangelista, Parma, figures of the Evangelists by Correggio, each accompanied by a prophet, are on the pendentives.

Pentecost (Gk. *pentekoste hemera*, the fiftieth day) is the Greek name of the Jewish Feast of Weeks, celebrating the end of the grain harvest (Exod. 23: 16), which was held on the 50th day after the Feast of Unleavened Bread (late spring or early summer). The Feast was considered by both Jews and Christians as a commemoration of the Giving of the Law—the Ten Commandments—to Moses on Mt. Sinai.

Pentecost is the second major Christian feast after Easter, and is the day on which the Holy Ghost descended upon the assembled disciples, according to Christ's promise that He would send them the Paraclete or Advocate (John 14: 26), and since this was also the day of the Jewish Feast, the name transferred easily to the Christian one, since both took place on the 50th day after Easter and the Passover. 'When the day of Pentecost had come, the disciples were all together in one place. And suddenly from Heaven there came a sound like the rush of a violent wind, and it filled the entire house where they were sitting. Divided tongues, as of fire, appeared among them, and a tongue rested on each of them. All of them were filled with the Holy Spirit and began to speak in other languages, as the Spirit gave them ability' (Acts 2: 1–12). A crowd had gathered outside, and when the disciples spoke to them, though they were of different nations, each one heard them speaking his own language. Some bystanders explained the wonder by accusing them of being drunk, despite its only being nine in the morning, so that Peter quoted the wonderful words of the prophet Joel, 'God . . . will pour out his spirit upon all flesh; your sons and daughters shall prophesy, your old men shall dream dreams, and your young men shall see visions' (Joel 2: 28), and followed them with a peroration on the works, the death, and the resurrection of Jesus as the promised Messiah.

The feast was kept from the earliest times. In the early Church the whole of the fifty days between Easter and Pentecost was also a season for baptism, like the Vigil of Easter, and at that time baptism, except for the sick, was restricted to these two seasons. At first it ranked as a feast after Easter and Christmas, but later displaced Christmas to be the second major feast of the Christian world. In England, Pentecost is commonly called Whitsunday, probably from the white robes worn by the newly baptized.

In art, the interpretation of Acts 2: 1–11 varies considerably, and three forms appeared. Some early MSS place the Virgin in the centre with the Apostles grouped round her, with the dove of the Holy Ghost descending upon them and tongues of fire appearing over their heads, as in the *Rabbula Gospels (586: a Syrian MS, Florence, Laurenziana), in the Shaftesbury Psalter (12th cent.: London, BL), and in a York School Psalter (mid-13th cent.: Glasgow, Hunterian). In the Byzantine *Homilies of the Monk James*

(1081/1198: Vatican) where the Ascension and Pentecost are depicted together, the Virgin is surrounded by the Apostles, and Christ in a *mandorla is raised by angels. In a damaged *Homilies of Gregory of Nazianzen*, painted in Constantinople (880/6: Paris, BN) Pentecost is seen with the *Hetoimasia, the twelve Apostles being grouped in an arc beneath the Throne, from which rays descend upon their heads, while below people look up towards them. In the Pentecost dome of Hosios Lukas (11th cent.) the Apostles alone receive the fiery tongues from the Hetoimasia, and the twelve include S. Paul, recognizable from the traditional image, although the event occurred well before his conversion. In the pendentives of the dome are groups of the people mentioned in Acts 2: 9–12. The Pentecost dome in St Mark's, Venice (late 12th cent.), follows the pattern of Hosios Lukas, with the Hetoimasia in the apex of the dome, but the resemblance is not surprising since the mosaicists were Byzantine. It also contains the traditional images of SS Peter and Paul, and S. Paul is included in many later MSS, though always among the twelve, so that at least one Apostle is omitted. There is no hard and fast rule on whether the Virgin is included or not; in the relief in the cloister of Sto Domingo de Silos, N. Spain (1085–1100), she is omitted, but in the almost exactly contemporary Bohemian coronation Gospels (1085–6: Prague) she is included.

In later Western images, the Virgin is usually present, and the Hetoimasia form disappears almost completely with the waning of Byzantine forms in the West. Although the Acts do not mention the Virgin as being present among the Apostles, her inclusion was really a matter of decorum, as it was in images of the *Ascension, where the texts do not mention her presence. In a few rare examples, the rays descend upon the assembly, which includes the Virgin, from the seated figures of both God the Father and Christ, as in a choir book of 1432 from Mainz, and in a 15th-century Spanish altarpiece (Frankfurt). After about 1400, the image settles into a pattern of the Virgin central to the group of Apostles which often includes the anachronistic S. Paul. Among the most notable of these is the Titian (*c.*1550: Sta Maria della Salute, Venice), an El Greco (1604/14: Prado), and the dome fresco by Franz Anton and Johann Jakob Zeller (1766: Ottobeuren).

personification The use of human figures to represent abstract ideas, e.g. a blindfolded woman with scales to represent Justice, or a winged woman as Victory. The idea is much older than Christianity, but was taken over for e.g. *Ecclesia and Synagogue, *Virtues and Vices.

Perugino, Pietro (*c.*1448–1523), was an Italian painter born at Castello della Pieve, near Perugia, whence the name by which he is commonly known. In his early years he was probably in contact with *Piero della Francesca in Arezzo, and with *Leonardo da Vinci in Verrocchio's workshop in Florence. In 1479 he was in Rome and he was one of the artists named in the 1481 contract for the fresco cycle on the walls of the *Sistine Chapel, devoted to the Life of Christ and the Life of Moses, treated as type and antitype (*see* TYPOLOGY). Perugino painted three frescoes on the altar wall—the Finding of Moses, the Nativity of Christ, and the altarpiece of the Assumption (to which the chapel is dedicated) in the centre, together with figures of, probably, Christ flanked by SS Peter and Paul between the windows above the gallery. These were all destroyed in 1535 to make space for Michelangelo's *Last Judgement.* Perugino also painted the *Baptism of Christ* (with Pinturicchio as his assistant), the *Moses in Egypt*, and the *Charge to Peter* (Christ giving the Keys to S. Peter), which is the finest picture in the series. All the histories have symbolic meanings since the programme was designed to express the role and position of the papacy in the principal chapel of the Vatican, and the place used for conclaves for papal elections. Perugino's share in the work must have ended by November 1483, when he was back in Perugia, and for the next few years he worked there and in Florence.

The characteristics of his art were all present in the *Charge to Peter*—simplicity in design, clarity in narrative, absence of confusion; desirable qualities in late 15th-century Florentine painting, which had become increasingly strained and emotional. Unfortunately these admirable qualities eventually settled into insipidity and vacuousness. He evolved a small number of set patterns, and repeated them for the rest of his life. Only occasionally does he rise above his own mundaneness, as in the *Pietà* (Uffizi) where the dead Christ is stretched across the Virgin's knees, His head and shoulders supported by an angel and His feet by the Magdalene, and in the *Crucifixion with the Virgin and saints* (1496: Florence, Sta Maria Maddalena dei Pazzi), where for once his simple undramatic stereotype figures achieve a deeply meditative quality and there is a beautiful Umbrian landscape as background. Between 1496 and 1500 he was engaged in the decoration of the Sala del Cambio in Perugia (a court for adjudicating commercial disputes), with a mixture of religious and secular themes, during which one of his assistants was the young *Raphael. All his slender repertory is redeployed, and the artist inserted a self-portrait, to which a local humanist added a fulsome inscription to the effect that had the art of painting been lost, and none had revived it, Perugino would have rediscovered it and been the first to restore it. After 1504 he worked only occasionally in Florence, where he was now increasingly old-fashioned, and he had the distinction of being called 'a clown in art' by Michelangelo (whom he sued for the insult). Vasari, in his Life of Perugino, says that he was 'a man of little religious faith, and was quite unable to believe in the immortality of the soul, so that, in words suited to his pigheadedness he obstinately rejected all good ways of life. All his hopes lay in worldly gain and he was willing to do anything for money. He gained great wealth . . .'. This often involved signing contracts promising original compositions, for which he then repeated one of his set designs. When criticized for this he said 'I've used in this work figures which you've praised at other times. If they now displease you, what can I do?'

Peter, Saint, Prince of the Apostles (martyred *c*.64), was born in Bethsaida, a fishing village near Capernaum (Vg. Capharnum) on the Sea of Galilee, probably in the early years of the 1st century. He was the brother of *Andrew, his partner in their fishing enterprise.

The calling of Simon and Andrew varies in the four Gospels. Those of Matthew and Mark are very similar: Jesus, walking by the Sea of Galilee, called Simon and Andrew, and then James and his brother John, sons of Zebedee, who left their boats and followed him (Matt. 4: 18–22; Mark 1: 16–20). Luke leaves the calling until after Christ's fast in the wilderness, yet his account of Jesus in Capernaum going into Simon's house and curing his sick mother-in-law makes clear that He already knew him. He then says that after Jesus had been in Judaea preaching and healing the sick, He returned to the Sea of Galilee, and the crowd so pressed upon Him that He got into a boat, which belonged to Simon, and taught the people standing on the shore. He then told Simon to put out from the shore and pay out the nets. Simon did so, although they had fished all night without success. The result was the miraculous draught of fish, after which Christ promised Simon that he would be a 'fisher of men' (Luke 4: 38–44; 5: 1–11). John tells the story very differently: Simon was brought to Jesus by Andrew when *John the Baptist was baptizing in the Jordan near Bethany. John (1: 35–42) also tells how Jesus changed Simon's name to Cephas (Aramaic for Gk. *petra*, rock, hence Peter). After these, and other incidents, Jesus returned to Galilee. It must therefore be inferred (since John was a witness) that Christ's first meeting with Simon Peter took place well before his being called from his boat.

Peter became the leader of the Apostles, and in the list of the Twelve (Matt. 10: 2–4; Mark 3: 16–19; Luke 6: 13–16) he is always named first. He was a member of the 'inner circle', called by Christ to be present at some of the most dramatic moments of His ministry—the raising of Jairus's daughter, the *Transfiguration, the Agony in the Garden. At Caesarea Philippi, in answer to Christ's question, 'And who do you say I am?', Peter made the great declaration, 'You are the Messiah, Son of the living God', and in return Christ gave the inspiring charge, 'You are Peter, and on this rock I will build my Church . . .', including the awesome right, 'whatever you bind on earth will be bound in heaven, and whatever you loose on earth will be loosed in heaven' (Matt. 16: 13–20; Mark 8: 29; Luke 9: 18–20). John makes no mention of this, but when Christ says 'I am the bread which has come down from Heaven' and that to be saved people must eat His flesh and drink His blood, many who had followed Him were so scandalized that they left Him (John 6: 41–71). When Christ enquired if the Twelve would also leave Him, Peter answered 'Lord, to whom can we go? You have the words of eternal life. We have come to believe and know that you are the Holy One of God' (John 6: 52–69).

Peter is not often specifically mentioned in the Gospels; but one incident stands out. After the miracle of the feeding of the five thousand Jesus told the disciples to cross to the other side of the Sea of Galilee ahead of Him. He went up the mountain to pray, and when evening came the boat was still battling against the wind. Suddenly in the early morning, the disciples saw Him walking towards them on the water. They cried out in fear, 'It is a ghost!', but He reassured them, and Peter cried, 'Lord, if it is you, command me to come to you across the water'. Jesus said 'Come!' Peter started to walk towards Him, but frightened by the strength of the wind he lost heart and began to sink. He cried out, 'Lord, save me!' Jesus stretched out His hand and caught him, '"You of little faith," He said, "why did you doubt?"', and when He got into the boat the wind dropped, 'and those in the boat worshipped Him, saying "Truly, you are the Son of God."'

When Jesus began to tell His disciples about going to Jerusalem, where He would suffer and be killed, and then rise from the dead, Peter protested, 'God forbid it, Lord. This must never happen to you.' Jesus turned on him saying 'Get thee behind me Satan...', accusing him of hindering His work and thinking only in human terms. Then He bade any who wished to follow Him to deny himself, and take up his cross and follow Him. Six days later, He took Peter, James, and John, and led them up a high mountain, where He was transfigured before them with Moses and Elijah. Peter asked if he might make three dwellings for them, and even while he spoke a cloud overshadowed them and a Voice from the cloud said, 'This is my Son, the beloved; with Him I am well pleased; listen to Him.' They fell to the ground in terror, and then Jesus touched them and said, 'Get up, and do not be afraid', and they saw that there was no one there but only Jesus (Matt. 16: 21–3; 17: 1–8; Mark 8: 31–3; 9: 2–8). In Luke, the raising of Jairus's daughter, at which only Peter, James, and John were present, precedes the Transfiguration, and is followed by Christ's charge to the Twelve to go out and proclaim the kingdom of God and to heal (Luke 8: 40–56; 9: 1–6).

Luke says (Luke 22: 8–12) that Christ sent Peter and John to find the ass on which He rode into Jerusalem, and to make the preparations for the Passover. Before the *Last Supper, when Christ washed the *feet of the Apostles, Peter at first refused, but when Christ said that unless He washed him, he would have no part in Him, Peter said impetuously, 'then my hands and my head also' (John 13: 3–11). It was Peter who asked John to ask Jesus who it was at the table who would betray Him, and in response Jesus gave Judas the sop from the dish. When Judas had left, and Christ had given them the bread and wine at the *Communion of the Apostles, He warned them of the disaster which was about to befall Him, and Peter declared 'Lord, I am ready to go with you to prison and to death!', and Christ answered that 'before the cock crows you will have denied me thrice'. All the Gospels record this and subsequent events, though in varying words. After the Last Supper, when they went to the garden, Christ asked Peter, James, and John to watch and pray with Him, during His Agony in the Garden; but when He returned to them, He found them asleep, and reproached them with their weakness in being unable to watch and pray with Him for an hour (Matt. 26: 36–41). When the moment came, and Jesus was arrested, Peter drew his sword and cut off the ear of the High Priest's slave, *Malchus, but Christ reproved Peter, told him to put up his sword, and healed the boy (Matt. 27: 51–3). Peter followed at a distance, and with John's help entered the courtyard where servants and soldiers were gathered round a brazier. Three times he was accused of being 'one of His followers', and three times he denied it. Suddenly the cock crowed, and he remembered Christ's words, and going outside he wept bitterly (Mark 14: 66–72; John 18: 25–7).

After the Crucifixion and the Entombment, on the first day of the week Mary Magdalene and other Holy Women came to the tomb and found it empty. Mary ran to Peter and told him, and he and John ran to the tomb. Peter went in and saw the grave cloths lying on the side, and later, when all the disciples were gathered in the upper room, Christ appeared to them and proved that He was truly risen in the flesh, not as a spirit or ghost, as they had first thought (John 20). The last mention of Peter in the Gospels is when Christ appeared to them on the shore at Galilee and asked Peter three times, 'Simon son of John, do you love me?', and after Peter's assurances, said to him 'Feed my sheep' (John 21).

All the Apostles were present at the Ascension, though none is specifically named. Peter next appears, transformed and heroic, in the Acts of the Apostles. He began with a meeting of over a hundred disciples to decide on someone who had known and followed Jesus to take the place left vacant by Judas's treachery and suicide (Matt. 27: 5), and Matthias was chosen. Often with John, he preached about Jesus and performed spectacular miracles of healing, such as that of the lame man in Solomon's Portico (Acts 3: 1–19), which brought them into direct conflict with the High Priest and Elders. When the Apostles set up a system for almsgiving among the poor of their community, Ananias and Sapphira both lied about their gift, and at Peter's accusation that they were lying to God, they died instantly (Acts 5: 1–11). Such was Peter's fame as a healer that people laid out their sick so that his shadow should fall on them as he walked by (Acts 5: 12–16). Peter and John were arraigned before the council and forbidden to preach in Jesus's name, and when the two Apostles argued their case, the religious authorities plotted to kill them. But a member of the council, the jurist Gamaliel, defended them, pointing out that if their undertaking was of human origin it would fail, as all other Jewish rebellions had done, but if it were 'of God', then it would be impossible to overthrow it, and if they tried then they might be accused of fighting against God. So they contented themselves by having them flogged—the first of many sentences of the 'forty lashes minus one'. Both defied the ban on their preaching (Acts 3: 1–26; 4: 1–22; 5: 17–42).

The first hint of trouble to come was when Hellenist Jews—that is, Greek-speaking Jews from the diaspora outside Palestine—complained that their widows were neglected in the distribution of alms. Seven Hellenists were then chosen, *Stephen among them, to distribute alms, while the Apostles devoted themselves to preaching and proselytizing. Stephen became the first martyr, an event with a dramatic outcome, as it resulted in the dispersion of the disciples to preach outside Jerusalem, and to the whole world (Acts 8: 1–5).

Peter and John are next mentioned in Samaria and then in Lydda, near Joppa (Acts 8: 14–25; 9: 36–43; 10: 9–48), where Peter performed spectacular miracles, and in Joppa he had a vision which made him realize that God did not distinguish between Jew and Gentile, so that it was necessary to abandon the Mosaic laws whereby no Jew might enter a Gentile house, nor eat with a Gentile. Paul had faced the problem in Antioch and also in Corinth, where Gentiles objected to having the Mosaic laws forced on them if they became Christians. The rule against eating together made the Eucharist impossible for a mixed assembly, though it was essential for a truly Christian body. When Paul raised the question in Jerusalem, Peter persuaded the Jerusalem brethren to abandon their insistence on Mosaic laws, but a rumble of resistance remained, which finally surfaced at Antioch when Paul openly upbraided Peter with trimming between the two factions (Gal. 2: 11–14).

Herod began to persecute Christians by executing James, the brother of John, and then arresting Peter, and imprisoning him. But the angel of the Lord awakened him one night, freed him from his fetters and bade him follow until he was outside the prison. In the street the angel left him, and Peter, who imagined that it was a dream, realized that he was really free. He was then helped to escape from the city (Acts 12: 1–17).

The traditional association of Peter with Rome, despite there being no mention of it in the Gospels or the Acts, was established both early and positively. The 1st Epistle of Peter attests it, since he refers to 'Babylon', a common epithet for Rome among Jews and Christians alike. S. Clement, who was probably the 3rd Bishop of Rome, *c.*96, accepted that Peter had been his predecessor as Bishop, and S. Ignatius (*c.*35–107), Bishop of Antioch, who was taken to Rome to be martyred (he was thrown to the beasts in the Colosseum), mentions in one of his letters to the Church in Rome that Peter and Paul had great authority in Rome. *Eusebius states that Peter was crucified head downwards during Nero's persecution, but the belief that the two Apostles were martyred on the same day is an error derived from their joint feast-day (29 June).

The Apocryphal Acts of Peter was written in Greek, *c.*150–200, and includes the usual fantastic stories such as talking dogs, and unlikely miracles. It includes a narrative of the Martyrdom and of the *Quo vadis. The Apocalypse of Peter was written in the early 2nd century and includes a terrifying description of Hell, ending with a vision of Paradise, which includes a re-enactment of the Transfiguration.

In art, Peter is invariably depicted as a stalwart man with white hair surrounding a tonsure, or bald patch, and a dark beard, but the image is not supported, as it is with Paul, by a description in any text either canonical or apocryphal. Only a brief list of representations is appended. Probably the earliest is in the Christian church in *Dura-Europos of *c.*240–50, though it is of an unusual type, but even SS Peter and Paul flanking Christ in the sarcophagus of Junius Bassus (359: St Peter's Mus.) does not follow what becomes the traditional image of either of the two Apostles. By the time of the sarcophagus of Bishop Liberius, later in the 4th century (Ravenna, San Francesco), and the apse mosaic of Sta Pudenziana (Rome, 5th cent.), the conventional images of both Apostles were firmly established.

Often in groups of saints, S. Peter is recognizable from his white hair; one of the finest images is the icon in St Catherine's Monastery,

Mt. Sinai (6th or 7th cent.), painted in Constantinople. *S. Peter dictating the Gospel to St Mark* is seen in the eastern Mediterranean or Egyptian ivory panel (440–670) in the so-called 'Grado chair', Louvre, Paris. The S. Hilda Codex of the early 11th century (Darmstadt Lib.) has a miniature of the *Storm on the Sea of Galilee* with Christ asleep among the frightened disciples, and S. Peter trying to control the boat with the sail blowing away. By now the image is always the traditional one, and has spread over all W. Europe. Probably the most famous figure of S. Peter is the life-size bronze in St Peter's, Rome, which is probably 13th century and by Arnolfo di Cambio, but has been dated as early as the 5th century. The Stefaneschi Altar by Giotto, and his school (*c.*1328–31: Vatican), has images of the *Crucifixion of S. Peter* as well as *S. Peter enthroned* and the Giotto and his workshop *Madonna and Child, with the Archangels Michael and Gabriel, and SS Peter and Paul* (*c.*1325–8: Bologna) has S. Peter with the keys, and S. Paul with the sword of his martyrdom. The frescoes by Masaccio (1425–7: Brancacci Chapel, Sta Maria del Carmine, Florence) include *S. Peter enthroned, S. Peter's shadow healing the sick,* and *S. Peter giving alms*; he is also one of the Apostles in the fresco of the *Tribute Money*. The *predella* of the Linaiuolo Altar by Fra Angelico includes a *S. Peter preaching in the presence of S. Mark* (1453: Florence, San Marco Mus.). Conrad Witz painted *Christ walking on the water* with S. Peter in the boat seeing Him, and then sinking as he tries to walk towards Him (1444: Ghent). On the Ponte Sant'Angelo, Rome, is a statue of S. Peter by Paolo Romano, 1464. One of the principal frescoes in the series in the Sistine Chapel, by Perugino, is of the *Charge to Peter* (1481–2), and in the Stanza dell'Eliodoro, Raphael painted the *Liberation of S. Peter from prison,* 1512. The tapestry cartoons (1515–16: London, V & A, on loan from the Royal Collection) of *The Miraculous draught of fishes, Christ's charge to Peter, The healing of the lame man at Solomon's Portico,* and *The death of Ananias,* and the corresponding tapestries in the Vatican, all illustrate incidents from the Gospels, and the Acts. Michelangelo painted the *Crucifixion of S. Peter* for the Cappella Paolina (1542–50: Vatican), and Caravaggio painted the same subject in the Cerasi Chapel in Sta Maria del Popolo, Rome (1600–1). Tintoretto painted *The washing of the Feet* (1560–5: London, NG). Guido Reni also painted a *Crucifixion of S. Peter* (1604/5: Vatican).

S. Peter's symbols are the keys of Heaven, usually gold and silver, often crossed; also a cock, or (rarely) a fish.

Peter Martyr, Saint (d. 1252), was born in Verona at the turn of the 12th century of parents who professed the Cathar heresy, in which their son was also brought up. When studying at the University of Bologna, he entered the Dominican Order. In 1236 he was in Como and became a vigorous preacher against the Cathars in N. Italy, and as far south as Rome and Florence. He became prior at Como in 1251, and was also appointed by Pope Innocent IV as an inquisitor. He was convinced that he would eventually be murdered because of his anti-heresy campaigns, and this happened when he was on his way from Como to Milan. He and his companions, two friars, were waylaid in a wood by two assassins, one of whom fled in horror at what he had undertaken to do; the other struck Peter on the head with an axe and also stabbed him. One friar escaped, the other was also stabbed so severely that he died six days later. The murderer later repented and became a Dominican lay brother of exemplary piety. The story that in his death agony Peter wrote the word *Credo* in his blood on the ground is a pious legend. He was canonized in 1253, the first Dominican martyr.

Duccio included him in the *Rucellai Madonna* (1285: Florence, Uffizi); he is also represented in the fresco by Andrea di Buonaiuto in the Spanish Chapel in Sta Maria Novella, Florence (1365/6), which is devoted to the *Glory of Thomas Aquinas* and to the Dominican anti-heresy campaigns. He was painted in the works of Fra Angelico (himself a Dominican) among the major Dominican saints in the *Crucifixion with Saints* (Chapter House, San Marco, Florence) and in the *Madonna and Child with Saints* in the corridor of the convent, and in several other frescoes in the series painted between 1437 and 1452. Giovanni Bellini painted the martyrdom twice (both *c.*1509: London, NG and Courtauld Inst.). Sant'Eustorgio, Milan, contains, in the Portinari Chapel, a large tomb/shrine to the saint, by Giovanni di Balducci.

Peter's, Saint, Rome There was a long tradition that *S. Peter had been martyred near Nero's hippodrome below the Vatican Hill and was buried in the nearby necropolis. It is also now certain that, by the early 2nd century, a small *memoria* was built over his grave—some seventy to eighty years after his martyrdom.

*Constantine's decision to build a basilica over this traditional site was taken probably as early as 319–22, when the site was prepared by levelling the ground at the base of the Vatican Hill to create a large terrace. Building began before 324; the little aedicule of S. Peter's *memoria* was left at the west end of the site, the basilica being orientated to the west, instead of the more usual east. The slope made the site difficult to prepare; the west end and the north side were dug out of the hill, and the east end and the south side were built up by about 25 ft. Despite the difficulties, and the size of the undertaking, building proceeded very quickly, so that the structure was basically ready by 329, and mosaic dedicatory inscriptions were placed over the west apse and the triumphal arch separating the nave from the transept.

The church was huge: *c.*390 ft. long, the nave itself being *c.*300 ft. long, and the width across the nave and the four aisles was over 200 ft. Unlike the *Lateran Basilica, the transepts at St Peter's were part of the original construction, separated from the aisles by a columned screen, with the nave separated from the transepts by the *Triumphal Arch. The purpose of the church governed its size: the Lateran was the cathedral of Rome, and built to serve mainly the Romans; St Peter's was a pilgrimage church and had to serve a vast concourse of pilgrims as well as Romans. Moreover, the nave of St Peter's was itself a burial site, a covered graveyard, and when it was demolished in the 16th century to make way for the present building, hundreds of graves, some with sarcophagi, were dug up. The nave also served for funeral banquets (or *agape) until these were discontinued, and the outside walls were lined by mausolea. The front of the basilica was a *narthex running the full width of the building, approached across a large *atrium surrounded by a covered colonnade with a triple portico, and with a *cantharus* in the centre. This was a giant 2nd-century bronze pine-cone under a *baldacchino supported by porphyry columns, and became a fountain for ablutions. The pine-cone is now on the steps of the Belvedere niche, with two of the peacocks from the baldacchino on the balustrade.

The Apostle's tomb, enclosed within a bronze grille, was on the chord of the apse, under a baldacchino resting on four *Salamonic columns. Two more such columns, one either side, carried the architrave of the baldacchino to the corners of the apse, and the openings between them were curtained; a damaged ivory casket from Pola (*c.*400: Rome, Mus. Civico) makes the arrangement clear. The altar, probably portable, was placed in the transept, or perhaps at the beginning of the nave. Unlike churches where the apse contained the bishop's throne, and seats for the officiating clergy, the very different purpose of St Peter's made these unnecessary. Since the function of the basilica was to serve pilgrims to the shrine, and be a burial-place close to a martyr's tomb, the whole building became a giant martyrium, and this aspect of the basilica never changed. The colonnades of the nave were made with columns about 15 ft. apart of various marbles, sizes, and orders, brought from the ruins of antique buildings, crowned by an architrave with a cornice wide enough to serve as a passageway, and surmounted by a wall with two rows of frescoes which survived until the 16th century. Light came from windows above this double row of frescoes. The four aisles were of equal width, covered by a single roof, and with windows in the outer aisle, suggesting that the inner aisle must have been fairly dark. By the time the 16th-century rebuilding began a large two-storey structure open at the bottom had been built on the right side of the nave to cover the bronze statue of *S. Peter enthroned* which still stands in the nave of the present church. The building, in the 4th century, of the basilica of *San Paolo fuori le Mura as a pilgrimage church for a shrine of S. Paul, made Rome the only Early Christian city to have two major martyria.

As was usual with Early Christian churches, the exterior of St Peter's was very plain; all the decorative splendour was inside. Unfortunately only fragments have survived, most of it late, because Rome was so often captured, and sometimes terribly sacked, by invading hordes which included Visigoths, Vandals (the worst until 1527), Ostrogoths, Lombards, Saracens (who sailed up the Tiber and sacked St Peter's and St Paul's), the Emperors Otto I and Henry IV, the Normans, as well as suffering the depredations of innumerable insurrections. One result of continual strife was that the Lateran was no longer secure; Innocent III, between 1198 and 1216, built himself a fortified house on the site of the present Vatican, within the Leonine Walls which had been built by Pope Leo IV in 847–55 for the defence of St Peter's after the Saracen raid. But it was needed for less than a century for in 1305 a French pope, Clement V, abandoned Rome for Avignon, where the papacy remained in 'exile' for seventy years. The Lateran palace was burnt in 1308, and when the papacy returned to Rome with Martin V in 1420, the Vatican was the obvious, if not the only, place to live, though even that was near ruinous.

There seems little doubt that the basilica was in a very poor state of conservation by the middle of the 15th century. By this time, however, the basilica was no longer purely a pilgrim's church; it had become a papal church. Pope *Nicholas V began to build a new choir at the back of the old basilica, but this hardly got further than the foundations when he died in 1455, and the project lapsed. On his election in 1503, *Julius II considered propping up the decrepit walls of the old basilica—they were, so it was said, some three feet out of the true. *Bramante had been in Rome since the winter of 1499, and his known works and projects must have impressed the Pope by his grasp of proportion and scale; by the summer of 1505 Julius had definitely undertaken a complete rebuilding of the basilica, since the foundation-stone was laid on 18 April 1506, and the medal commemorating the event was struck.

This medal and a half ground-plan provide the only ideas of what the design of the church was to be, and what it was intended to look like. It was, apparently, to be centrally planned—in other words, a martyrium—with a dome over the centre and towers at the corners (whether these were to be the four corners, or just the two flanking the façade will never be known). The Apostle's tomb was to be under the centre of the dome, which would be supported by four piers. There were to be four deep apses for the choir, the transepts, and the façade, and an ambulatory round the dome area made from a series of interlocking apsidal spaces. The medal was inscribed *Templi Petri Instauracio* meaning that St Peter's was to be 'restored, revived, brought to completion'—that the Constantinian basilica was to be restored or renewed, rather than destroyed and rebuilt. The central element was the symbolic one: the tomb of the Apostle. Unfortunately, no final plans or projects were drawn up (it was not the custom of the time); work dragged on in years of demolition, and when Julius died in 1513, and Bramante followed him in 1514, there was a workshop containing drawings, most of which were inherited by Peruzzi, a colleague of long standing who continued the work. But once Julius and Bramante were no longer there, efforts were made to have the projects changed to a long-nave church, since this was more acceptable for the clergy for the holding of processions. Raphael, appointed joint chief architect with Peruzzi by Pope Leo X, made a design (or sponsored one) which tacked a long nave on to part of Bramante's central choir. All the architects who ever tampered with the original design changed details and tried to effect compromises; the only useful thing they did was that each one increased the size of the piers which were to support the dome. Raphael died in 1520, the horrific Sack of Rome swept over the city in 1527, Antonio da *Sangallo the Younger took over the work in the 1530s, in an endeavour to repair the damage caused to the unfinished building, with the stark shell of the choir rising over the little aedicule erected to protect the site of the Apostle's tomb, with the two-storey shelter over S. Peter's statue, and the ruined nave stretching out in front of it (there is a vivid drawing of this by Maerten van Heemskerck made during his stay in Rome, 1532–5, in Berlin). Antonio also designed a huge model (Mus. Petriano), which took seven years to make, but fortunately he died in 1545 before he could do more than begin the foundations.

*Michelangelo, then 71 years old, was appointed chief architect in 1547 by Pope Paul III. He and Bramante had been less than friendly, but Michelangelo recognized the brilliance and the power of Bramante's design—and its impracticability. He wrote, 'It was he who laid down the first plan of St Peter's, not full of confusion, but clear, pure, and full of light, . . . whoever departs from this order of Bramante's . . . departs from the truth.' The impracticability lay in the proliferation of small elements, particularly in the apsidal areas forming the ambulatory, and the total insufficiency of the piers to support the projected dome. Michelangelo turned the design round, making it a diamond shape instead of a square, by eliminating the corner elements of the tower spaces, and simplifying the central ambulatory, as well as massively increasing the piers of the dome. The one problem he did not solve was the provision of the essential benediction loggia in the façade. Until the end of his life he laboured on the building, achieving more than had been built since Bramante, and leaving it when he died much as it is known today. The vast scale of the outer walls, the heavy attic storey, the massive drum, and the design of the dome are his. He experimented continually in his drawings, so that sketches for both a semicircular dome and one with a more elliptical profile exist. After his death the elliptical one was chosen; it is easier to build since its more pointed shape exerts less stress on the supporting members.

The dome was built during the short but busy pontificate of Sixtus V between 1585 and 1590 by Michelangelo's pupil, Giacomo della Porta. The problem of the long nave, however, did not go away. In 1603 *Maderno was working on designs for adding to the front of St Peter's, which he did from 1607 to 1612 with the help of *Borromini, supplying among other things a benediction loggia over the narthex (which contains the mosaic of the *Navicella*—the Ship with Christ and the Apostles—from the design attributed to Giotto, originally in the narthex of Old St Peter's). Maderno's setting of the Apostle's *confessio provided the site for *Bernini's baldacchino over the papal altar. The *Cathedra Petri* in the main apse of the choir is also by Bernini and his studio, as are some of the magnificent tombs; others are by Algardi and Canova. The revetment of the interior with coloured marble and gilding, and the covering of the vaulting of the interior spaces with decorative coffering, took place over a long period during the 17th and 18th centuries. The pictures painted for the basilica are now in the Vatican museum; the basilica only has mosaic copies of them. The mosaics in the dome were designed by Cesare d'Arpino, a Late Mannerist painter (1590). The central pair of bronze entrance doors came from the old church and had already been made larger to fit the old church better by Filarete (1433–45), and were again altered to fit the present church; the other three doors were the result of a competition held in 1947, the subjects of them being tenets of the faith. The fifth door is by Giacomo Manzù.

The great open space in front of St Peter's, replacing the original atrium (most of which had already been used by Maderno when he extended the nave), was designed by Bernini (1656–67); the encircling colonnades, four columns deep covering a carriageway, was conceived by the artist as two welcoming arms. Crowning the long architraves are the statues of saints and martyrs as the perpetual witnesses of faith. (*See also* BASILICA.)

Petronilla, Saint, was a 2nd-century Roman martyr buried in the Catacomb of Domitilla, near San Paolo fuori le Mura. She is, apparently, depicted on the wall of one of the chambers of the catacomb. The story which turned her into a totally imaginary daughter of S. Peter is due to the over-enthusiastic compiler of the 5th/6th-century martyrology of SS Nereo and Achilleo (itself otherwise perfectly genuine); it may also have been due to the similarity of name. Her sarcophagus was moved to St Peter's in the 8th century into the Chapel of the Kings of France, because Charlemagne was considered an adopted son of S. Peter, hence the Apostle's 'daughter' became his patroness. The chapel survived until the rebuilding of St Peter's in the 16th century. It was the original site of the tomb of the French cardinal for whom Michelangelo carved the *Pietà*.

pews (Lat. *podia*, Fr. *puye*) are seats for the congregation. Few, if any, early churches had seats, but there was often a long stone ledge or seat, or a row of niches built into the outer walls, hence the saying 'the weakest go to the wall'. Examples are in Wells and Salisbury, Rouen, Amiens, but the practice of providing for the feeble was not universal. People sometimes brought folding stools to longer ceremonies, and to the preaching churches, where sermons could be very long indeed. Pews came into general use in the post-Reformation churches in N. Europe, where long sermons were the rule. Sixteenth-century pews in England often had carved finials, called poppy heads, at their ends, adapted from fine *choir stalls. In the 17th and 18th centuries pews were made like tall wooden boxes with doors to them, called box-pews, and the seats inside were shared by a family, or by a group of parishioners, allocated often according to their standing in the community. A pew-rent was paid to the church. Very few examples of the tall box-pews survive except in small village churches such as Mildenhall, Wilts., and Widford, Oxon. Unfortunately, the now general intrusion of fixed pews or rows of chairs into medieval churches is destructive of the clarity and spaciousness of their naves; similarly, the wholesale removal of Georgian box-pews from 17th- and 18th-century churches which were designed to hold them, is equally destructive of their internal proportions.

phelonion (Lat. *paenula*) is the *vestment in the E. Orthodox Church corresponding to the chasuble in the West, but much fuller and serving as a *cope. It is worn by priests;

bishops wear the *sakkos. It is a cloak-like garment, reaching almost to the ground at the back, but may be much shorter in front. The phelonion may be of any colour, and in rich churches is often of cloth of gold.

Philip, Saint, Apostle. In the Synoptic Gospels he is listed among the Apostles; only S. John's Gospel has facts concerning him. He is also in the account of Pentecost in the Acts of the Apostles. In John 1: 43–51, he is described as from Bethsaida. 'Philip found Nathanael and said to him, "We have found him about whom Moses in the law . . . wrote, Jesus son of Joseph from Nazareth." Nathanael said to him, "Can anything good come out of Nazareth?" Philip said to him, "Come and see."' Jesus convinced Nathanael (Bartholomew) by telling him where he was before he was called. At the first multiplication of the loaves, Jesus said to Philip, when he saw the large crowd: '"Where are we to buy bread for these people to eat?" He said this . . . because he knew what he was going to do. Philip answered him, "Six months' wages would not buy enough bread for each of them to get a little." . . . Andrew, Simon Peter's brother, said to him, "There is a boy here who has five barley loaves and two fish. But what are they among so many people?" . . . Then Jesus took the loaves, and when he had given thanks, he distributed them to those who were seated, and also the fish as much as they wanted . . .' (John 6: 5–11).

The last recorded words of Jesus to Philip were after the Last Supper, when Philip, not having understood Him, asked Him to show them the Father. Philip, like all the disciples, was present at *Pentecost (Acts 2: 1–4), and presumably he was present at the *Ascension. After this there is only tradition, and also confusion between Philip the Apostle and Philip the Deacon. Polycrates, Bishop of Ephesus, in the mid-2nd century, wrote to Pope Victor, 'Philip, who was one of the Apostles, died at Gerapolis, like two of his daughters, the third died at Ephesus.' The Bishop of Gerapolis also knew Philip's daughters, who told him that their father had revived a dead man. He was said to have been martyred, crucified head down, but this may well be part of the tradition. There are Apocryphal Acts of Philip which are the usual farrago of nonsense, including his vanquishing a fire-breathing dragon. His attribute is sometimes a dragon, from the story repeated in the **Golden Legend* with extra details.

He is often represented with S. James the Less. He is among the Apostles in the dome of the Baptistery of the Orthodox, Ravenna. He appears in the polyptych by Taddeo Gaddi, *Madonna and Child, with Apostles* (Florence, Sta Felicità). Other works include a statue by Nanni di Banco (1409–11: Florence, Orsanmichele); Filippino Lippi, *The Exorcizing of the Dragon* (*c.*1502: Florence, Cappella Strozzi, Sta Maria Novella, and also 1504: Rome, Sta Maria sopra Minerva); Gius. Mazzuoli: group of Apostles including S. Philip (1703–11: Rome, Lateran); twelve Apostles also by Mazzuoli, now in the Oratory, London.

Philip the Deacon first appears in the Acts of the Apostles (6: 5–6) with *Stephen and five others chosen to distribute the Apostles' charity so that they could concentrate on conversions. He left Jerusalem after Stephen's death and went to Samaria (Acts 8: 5–13), where he converted and baptized. In Acts 8: 25–39 is the account of his being told by an angel to go towards Gaza; he met an Ethiopian eunuch, treasurer of the Ethiopian Queen, on his way home from Jerusalem. He was puzzled by a text in Isaiah, which Philip explained to him, since he recognized it as one of Isaiah's great predictions about Christ: 'Like a lamb he was led to the slaughter . . . ' (Isa. 53: 7–8). While in the man's carriage, Philip instructed him in belief in Christ, so that when they passed some water the Ethiopian suggested that he should be baptized. Philip did so, and the angel snatched him away, and he found himself on the road to Caesarea. He settled there with his wife and four daughters, all prophetesses. Later, Paul stayed with them. The memorable incident in his career was that of the Ethiopian, but it is rarely represented: there are pictures of the incident by Mathieu Molanus (Antwerp), and Pieter Lastman (Karlsruhe), both Dutch 17th-century painters. He is often confused with the Apostle Philip.

Philip Neri, Saint (1515–95), founder of the *Oratory, was born in Florence. Little is known of his early years; what schooling he had was from the Dominicans of San Marco. In 1532 he was in Cassino, but in 1534 he walked to Rome, then still devastated by the terrible sack of 1527. He lived by teaching, and for more education he went to sermons at the theological University of the Sapienza. He visited sanctuaries and the *catacombs, then almost completely forgotten, where in 1544 he underwent a deep religious experience. In 1548, with friends, he founded a confraternity to care for pilgrims, especially the sick or destitute, and patients discharged from hospital while still unfit to work and in need, and during the Holy Year of 1550 it cared for thousands of pilgrims. During this period he began the devotion of the *Quarant'ore, and in 1551 he was ordained and settled in the community of San Girolamo della Carità in the heart of the city. There he established what developed into the Oratory; it began as a meeting-place for readings and discussions; music was added, first as songs and hymns, and then with instrumental accompaniments. They visited sanctuaries and hospitals, in particular the great hospital of Sto Spirito in Sassia, where some of the group worked daily. In 1575 Gregory XIII gave them Sta Maria in Vallicella, where the rebuilt church known as the Chiesa Nuova (the new church) was eventually flanked by *Borromini's Oratory, which they used for their concerts of sacred music, from which came the term 'oratorio'. A feature of the group was that they took no vows; among them were Cesare Baronius, the ecclesiastical historian and later cardinal; Antonio *Bosio, and Palestrina, who for a time directed the music at the Oratory. No major artist is connected with them, but *Caravaggio's altarpieces show a great debt to Philip Neri's sermons, and his *Entombment of Christ* (1603–4: now Vatican) was painted for one of the side chapels of the Chiesa Nuova. *Rubens painted the altarpiece for the church in 1606. Guido Reni's *Vision of S. Philip* (Chiesa Nuova) was painted after the saint's canonization in 1622, the likeness based on a death-mask. It records his vision of 1544 in the catacombs.

phoenix *See* BIRDS, SYMBOLIC.

phylactery (Heb. *tephillin*; Gk. *phylakterion*, 'safeguards') were small leather cases or cylinders containing strips of parchment inscribed with OT texts on moral laws. They were worn by pious Jews on the forehead and arm during prayers, except on the Sabbath or festivals. Christ criticized the ostentation of those who wore extra large phylacteries (Matt. 23: 5). The custom became Christianized, people wearing invocations or the Gospels round their necks, until it was condemned, particularly in the West, as superstition.

Physiologus (Gk. the Naturalist) is the title of a book by an unknown writer (i.e. not named Physiologus), containing about fifty moral tales concerning the natural world, mainly animals, which are partly factual but largely fantastic. It includes, for example, the pelican feeding her young on her own blood, as a symbol of Christ's sacrifice, or the phoenix, rising from the ashes after three days, as a symbol of the Resurrection. The Greek original was probably written in the 4th century and translated into Latin by the 8th, later becoming transmuted into *Bestiaries.

Picasso, Pablo (1881–1973) A Spanish-born artist active mainly in France, he was the 20th century's most famous, prolific, and versatile artist in painting, sculpture, drawing, printmaking, ceramics, and design. In *A Life of Picasso* (1991) John Richardson gives space in its projected four volumes to the religious themes in the artist's life and work. Many of these come together in his *Crucifixion* (1930), a painting into which many art historical and personal influences flow, and to which Picasso would frequently return in coming decades. Brassaï published related drawings in the magazine *Minotaure* (1933), and in 1993 *The Body on the Cross* exhibition and catalogue (Paris and Montreal) contextualized the painting, drawing on Crucifixion imagery by Bacon, Dix, de Kooning, Guttuso, Sutherland, and Saura. Picasso's sculpture *The Man with a Lamb* (1943), together with others of his works touching on Christian themes, come under Jane Daggett Dillenberger's scrutiny in her forthcoming *The Religious Art of Pablo Picasso*.

Pienza *See* PIUS II.

Piero della Francesca (1410/20–92) was an Italian painter who came from the small Umbrian town of Sansepolcro (then called Borgo San Sepolcro). He was working in Florence in 1439, but returned to his native place by 1442, when he was commissioned by a charitable body to paint a polyptych of which the central part was a *Madonna della Misericordia* (Sansepolcro) showing the members of the confraternity sheltered under the Virgin's cloak. Between 1452 and 1459 he painted his major work, the fresco cycle in San Francesco, Arezzo, of the *Legend of the True Cross* (*see* TRUE CROSS). There are varying accounts of the story in the **Golden Legend*, and the artist has complicated matters by arranging the scenes according to artistic parallels (i.e. the two battle scenes are on facing walls) rather than in strict narrative sequence. The unusual feature of the cycle is an *Annunciation* to the left of the window wall, which must have been included deliberately, since on the corresponding site on the right is the *Dream of Constantine*, which is part of the story. This is logical, if one accepts that the Annunciation, as the moment of the Incarnation, provides the bridge between the pre-Christian scenes, which begin with Adam, and the post-Christian ones, starting with the Dream of Constantine. The Annunciation also forms a direct link between the Queen of Sheba's prophetic vision and the cross itself. Unfortunately, the two prophets at the top of the window wall are unidentifiable, but their youth probably precludes their being OT prophets and makes it possible that they are the two saints John, the Evangelist and the Baptist. Neither image has any positively distinguishing attribute.

The *Flagellation of Christ* (Urbino) is inscribed on Pilate's throne *OPUS PETRI DE BURGO SCI SEPULCR, but not dated: it has been variously dated between the 1440s and 1460s. The interpretations of this small panel are as contentious as its dating. The idea that the three figures represented a murdered Duke of Urbino and two evil counsellors is now virtually abandoned. There was formerly an inscription: 'convenerunt in unum', from Ps. 2: 2 (Vg.: 'The Kings of the earth stood up, and the princes met together'), part of the Breviary readings for Good Friday. It has been suggested that this refers to the Council of Florence in 1439, when attempts were made to heal the breach between the Orthodox Eastern Church and the Western Church, and that the bearded man is a Greek and the robed figure on the right represents the Western Church. That too is improbable, since it still leaves the central figure unexplained. Usually, in Piero's pictures, a simply robed, barefooted figure is an angel, as may be seen in a comparison with the angels in the earlier *Baptism of Christ* (London, NG). There are, in fact, as many interpretations of this small picture as there are scholars to attempt them. None, so far, has fully succeeded. The perspective of the setting fascinated the artist, who has created in the marble floor, where the Flagellation takes place, an ideal reconstruction of the Pavement, Pilate's judgement hall, Gabbatha in Hebrew (John 19: 13) but Lithostratos in Greek. Piero was deeply learned in perspective, and made many drawings for his treatise, *De prospectiva pingendi*. He was also linked, through Urbino, with *Alberti, who was a formative influence on his architectural settings.

Another unusual work is the fresco of the *Madonna del Parto* in the funerary chapel at Monterchi, near Arezzo, painted between 1450 and 1455, and associated with the death of Piero's mother, who was probably buried there. The highly pregnant Virgin stands in a tabernacle-cum-pavilion, with the curtains held back by two angels as she points to her pregnancy. She is the Virgin of Hope, and the Child she bears is the Hope of Salvation. It is an unusual subject in Italy, but more common in Spain.

The *Madonna and Child with Saints, and Federigo of Montefeltro* (Milan, Brera) is remarkable for the very 'modern' treatment of the architectural setting, which was possibly planned to echo the apse of the original church of San Bernardino in Urbino, for which it was painted. This spatial device, designed so that the spectator is drawn into the scene, was used also by Antonello da Messina and *Bellini in their Venetian *Sacre Conversazioni. Above the Virgin's head hangs the mysterious *ostrich egg, which in the Christian East was a symbol of Creation. The spatial arrangement is particularly complicated, since the perspective of the architecture centres on the Virgin's face, which is also the centre of the circle which encompasses both the egg and the Christ Child. Most of the figures have been attributed to various artists working in Piero's studio and the dating varies between 1469 and 1475, with a strong presumption for 1472, the year when the Duke's heir was born and his Duchess later died and was buried in the church. The *Senigallia Madonna* (Urbino) is among the late works, *c.*1470–4, and is, like all his works, notable for the stillness and gravity of the figures. The Virgin, flanked by two angels, holds the Christ Child, with veiled head and with a grave expression, conscious that she is the *Theotokos, and that she holds, not just her child, but the Godhead; yet, as a small concession to popular superstition, He wears a coral necklace with a little coral branch hanging from it—not just a teething comforter, but an *amulet against the Evil Eye.

In the noble fresco of the *Resurrection* (Sansepolcro) the symbolism is stressed by the contrast between the bare trees and earth on the left and the trees in leaf and the sprouting hillside on the right, and the impressive Christ rises by His own supernatural power from the tomb, over the four soldiers—two sleeping, one staring at Him in astonishment, the other hiding his face from the vision, typifying Man's reaction to the Risen Christ. It is never wise to dismiss any aspect of a work by Piero as 'incidental'; he was perhaps the most deeply cerebral of all Renaissance artists, and his subjects have always a theological meaning behind the still, collected, and impassive exterior.

According to Vasari, his fellow-townsman, Piero was blind at the end of his life, which explains why his last works seem to date from almost twenty years before his death in 1492. The unfinished *Nativity* (London, NG) may be his last work, since it shows the influence of Flemish oil-painting, which became known after the arrival in Florence of the Portinari Altarpiece by Hugo van der *Goes.

piers The supports for a dome, in which case there are at least four of them. The term is also used for the supports for arches, used instead of columns so that they can be larger and stronger. It is not uncommon to find that the arcades of a nave are borne on alternating columns and piers. This type of pier often has *colonnettes attached to it, as much for decoration as for greater strength. It is called an alternating system, and the supports are described as 'weak' for a column, and 'strong' for a pier, since they are usually more massive than a column. It is a feature of sexpartite vaulting (*see* VAULTING).

Pietà (Ital. pity, mercy) A *Pietà*, whether in painting or in sculpture, consists of a representation of the dead Christ accompanied by angels, or by the Virgin (sometimes with S. John). It is not the same as a *Deposition from the Cross, or a *Lamentation over the Dead Christ, but is a more reflective, meditative subject, often consisting only of the dead Christ lying on the knees of the Virgin. It developed from the Deposition groups in the 13th and 14th centuries in Spain and in the North, but quickly spread to Italy, with the increase in private devotional images. Yet the subject was sufficiently unfamiliar among Central Italian writers that Landucci, in his *Diary* for June 1482, describes a picture as 'a Virgin seated and holding the dead Christ in her arms, after he has been taken down from the Cross; which is called by some a *Pietà*'. Similarly many artists were unfamiliar with the subject, so that the French cardinal commissioning Michelangelo's *Pietà* described the subject in the contract. Among the various forms are those by a German 14th-century sculptor (*Christ on the Virgin's knees*, Munich); a S. German group (1420–30: Utrecht, Mus.); Donatello (1443: *Dead Christ tended by Angels*, London, V & A); Giovanni Bellini (1460: *Christ upheld by Angels*, Berlin; and 1468: *Christ upheld by the Virgin and S. John*, Milan, Brera); Michelangelo (1500: *Pietà*, Rome, St Peter's). There may be more figures, as there are in Bellini's *Pietà* (Vatican), once part of the Pesaro Altar, where the poignancy is stressed by the interlocked hands of all present, but too many can easily change the meditative character of the work, and convert it into a Lamentation. Further examples are Van Gogh's *Pietà* (after Delacroix, 1889, Amsterdam, Van Gogh Museum); and Käthe Kollwitz (1938 sculpture, Ottawa, National Gallery of Canada). *See also* ANDACHTSBILD, IMAGO PIETATIS.

pilaster In classical buildings a free-standing *column, as in a portico, should be paired on the wall behind it with a pilaster, also called a respond. Pilasters are often used independently to organize a façade into an orderly design.

Pilate, Acts of *See* APOCRYPHAL GOSPELS and PILATE, PONTIUS.

Pilate, Pontius, was the governor—or 'procurator'—of Judaea from 26 to 36, who ordered the crucifixion of Christ. He appears, from the NT narrative, to have begun by trying to dispense justice in a case where the prisoner was accused at first of blasphemy ('I find no case against him'), and only later of the treason (in Roman eyes) of setting himself up as a king. Pilate was afraid of having yet another Jewish religious riot to quell, and afraid also that leniency towards a prisoner whom his subjects were calling a rebel could have serious repercussions if reported in Rome. He took the easy way out, and condemned Christ. Max Beckmann's lithograph (1946) juxtaposes their two heads.

The Apocryphal Acts of Pilate are also known as the Gospel of Nicodemus. The first part, which is 4th century, consists of the story of the Passion and Resurrection more or less as it exists in the Gospels with some lapses into fantasy, and some useful additions. It is the source of the names of the two thieves crucified with Christ—Dismas and Gestas, and also of *Longinus. The account of the Descent into Hell is 5th century, and is a mainly Latin addition which received wide dissemination. The names of the authors are given as Leucius and Karinus, but Leucius Charinus is credited with the authorship of nearly all the Apocryphal Acts of the Apostles, and the name has been transferred to other Apocryphal texts as well. *See also* APOCRYPHAL GOSPELS.

pilgrimage churches

And thrice had she
been at Jerusalem,
She had passed many a strange stream,
At Rome she had been and at Boulogne,
In Galice at Saint James and at Cologne.

(Chaucer, *The Wife of Bath's Tale*, from *The Canterbury Tales*, before 1400.)

A belief that it is necessary to accomplish a deed or journey to a shrine for purification, or in expiation for a grave sin, goes back into distant antiquity, and many religions believe in pilgrimages, as for instance, Jews, for whom journeys to Jerusalem have been an obligation, Hindus to the Ganges, and Muslims to Mecca. In the ancient world, Orestes, Achilles, Alcmeon, and even Heracles, whose Labours were expiatory tasks, are part of the background to journeys made for religious reasons. None of the oracles of antiquity could be approached without a previous rite of purification.

In the Christian world, the veneration of martyrs led to the building of shrines (*Martyria), to commemorate the site of their martyrdom or to house their remains, to which the faithful came on their anniversaries to a celebration, often accompanied by a meal (*Agape). Obviously, the sites of Christ's birth, ministry, death and resurrection were the most important places for veneration. The first pilgrim recorded as visiting Jerusalem was S. Alexander, *c.*230, in fulfilment of a vow. His friend, Origen, also went to the Holy Land. The visit of the Empress *Helena, Constantine's mother, in 326/8, during which she founded the basilicas on the Mount of Olives and at Bethlehem, was recorded in detail by *Eusebius, and according to later traditions she discovered the *True Cross. Her pilgrimage inspired others. An anonymous pilgrim from Bordeaux, whose diary survives, came about five years after Helena, and records the stages of his journeys there and back, giving a detailed account of the sites he visited, both Old and New Testament. Paula, the friend of S. Jerome, whom she followed to Jerusalem in 385 with her daughter Eustochium, made a long pilgrimage in the Holy Land, founded convents for monks and nuns at Bethlehem, and died in Jerusalem in 404. One of the most famous pilgrims, *Etheria, whose account, *Peregrinatio Etheriae*, was found at Arezzo in 1884, was probably a Spanish abbess or nun; she gives a detailed account of her visit to Egypt, the Holy Land, Asia Minor, and Constantinople, in the 4th century. Later, when journeys to Palestine became too difficult because of the Muslim invasions, visits to Rome—'ad limina Apostolorum'—to the shrines of S. Peter and S. Paul became common (they are still obligatory for Roman Catholic bishops). In Anglo-Saxon times a stream of pilgrims followed the visits of Benedict Biscop and S. Wilfred in 653. Rome became even more of a pilgrimage destination in 1300, when Boniface VIII declared a Jubilee and offered indulgences to pilgrims (*see* HOLY YEAR).

Not everyone was in favour; S. Gregory of Nyssa, the younger brother of S. Basil, bitterly criticized pilgrimages in 370, declaring them to be full of moral and spiritual danger in that false confidence in pardon made men careless of sin, and they were pernicious for women who, he maintained, invariably lost their chastity, and that English whores abounded in all the cities on the way. His seems to have been a lone voice. Pilgrims were given legal as well as ecclesiastical protection, both by King Dagobert and by Charlemagne. It was not until the 8th century that a pilgrimage, or a journey to a shrine, was imposed as part of a penance, and was used for certain grave sins for which absolution was delayed, or which were referred to the bishop, or even to Rome for decision. By the 9th century some churches or places had become focuses for pilgrimages—Rome, Jerusalem when possible, but also others less arduous, such as St-Martin at Boulogne, St-Philibert at Grandlieu (destroyed by Norsemen), or St Boniface at Fulda, near Frankfurt. One of the reasons was the belief that intercession would more readily be granted at a shrine, particularly in cures for the sick, one of the chief reasons for pilgrimages. The popularity of such travels, and the attraction, almost the fashion, for such journeys had taken a firm hold from the beginning of the 11th century.

Popular pilgrimages imposed great stress on the town and the church which had to cope with huge crowds. It is also true that they were an enormous source of revenue, so that few cathedrals or large abbeys resisted the temptation to establish shrines which would become pilgrimage centres. In England, the Pilgrims' Way crossed the southern counties from Winchester (S. Swithun) to Canterbury (*S. Thomas Becket), from 1170. Ely (S. Etheldreda) from the 9th century, Durham (*S. Cuthbert) from 998, Hexham and Ripon from the 8th century (S. Wilfred), Westminster Abbey (S. Edward the Confessor) from about the 1240s, and pilgrimages to Chartres, for the veneration of an ancient statue of the Virgin, and to Cologne, for the Shrine of the Three Kings or Magi—one of the masterpieces of *Nicholas of Verdun (1170–1230)—were among the most popular. Pilgrimages imposed changes in the construction of churches, in that most shrines were situated either under the main altar, or in a retrochoir at the east end. The need to regulate large crowds of pilgrims into orderly queues brought about much rebuilding. Abbot Odo of Cluny, in a sermon in St-Martin at Tours in 908, after a rebuilding in 903, refers to the necessity of building churches with aisles as well as wide naves, because otherwise the great press of people overturned the choir stalls and overran the choir. Solutions to this problem of crowd control were either to rebuild with choirs raised above a crypt containing the shrine—this was particularly necessary if the choir was used frequently for monastic services—or to rebuild the apse with an ambulatory round it, or, as at St-Bénigne at Dijon (1000–18) or at Neuvy-St-Sépulchre (1045/6), near Châteauroux, to put the shrine in a rotunda beyond the east end.

Probably the most famous pilgrimage, other than to Rome, was to Santiago de Compostela in Galicia, NW Spain. Pilgrims assembled at gathering places, each one itself an important shrine, and went by fixed stages from one to the next, so that most pilgrims would have visited half a dozen or more by the time the goal was reached. Most of the monasteries on the routes received the pilgrims, who travelled in fairly large parties for safety, since parts of the routes were infested with bandits. Once across the Pyrenees, two routes crossed the north of Spain, though eventually the more southerly, through Pamplona, Burgos, and León, was preferred. The type of church which developed on these routes is typified by the one the pilgrims came to visit: a long barrel-vaulted nave with aisles on either side (sometimes, as at St-Sernin, Toulouse, these were doubled), and galleries above them to accommodate more pilgrims, aisled transepts, a deep choir with an ambulatory and radiating chapels. In front of the church of Santiago (1075–1150) was a huge sculptured portico of the late 12th century—the Pórtico de la Gloria—reached by many steps, and later enclosed in a grandiose 17th-century Churrigueresque Baroque towered façade. At the end of the south transept is a second, earlier, sculptured portico—the Puerta de las Platerías—which gave (and still gives) on to the street of the silversmiths, who made offerings for the shrine.

Of the great churches on the pilgrimage routes, St-Martin at Tours (10th/11th cent.) was destroyed during the French Revolution and a street driven through the transepts; St-Martial at Limoges (1070–95) has also been destroyed, but St-Sernin at Toulouse (*c.*1080) survives, together with Ste-Foi at Conques (1050–1120)—much smaller, but of similar design. Vézelay (1096–1120) had its own independent pilgrimage, to the shrine of the Magdalene, but was on the route to Santiago as a gathering point, and many other minor shrines benefited from the popularity of the great routes through France. Nowadays, huge crowds still assemble on the feast of *S. James (25 July) for the celebrations at Santiago, and the galleries are full of pilgrims—or tourists.

Pilgrimages in Italy—with the exception of those to Rome, to Monte Sant'Angelo on the Monte Gargano peninsula, where a shrine to the Archangel Michael has existed since the 5th century, and to the Holy House at *Loreto since the 13th century—tend to be venerations at local sanctuaries, of which there are a huge number. Some, especially those of the 15th and 16th centuries, are often very important architecturally—Cortona (with two), Todi, Prato, Montepulciano, Lodi, and Sta Maria del Campo, near Pavia, are among the most interesting. In the Catholic south of Germany and in Austria, pilgrimage churches were built in great numbers during the 18th-century Baroque reconstruction of abbeys and shrines destroyed in the Thirty Years War. Most of them are very beautiful, exuberant creations, of novel and imaginative design, full of colour and light, and with sculpture and decoration of exceptional quality. Among the most famous are those built by Johann Michael *Fischer, Balthasar *Neumann (in particular *Vierzehnheiligen), the *Asam brothers, and Zimmerman's Die *Wies.

The greatest English pilgrimage—almost rivalling Rome and Santiago—was to Canterbury, to the memorial chapel of S. Thomas Becket, whose relics were placed in a splendid shrine in 1220. It was completely destroyed by Henry VIII in 1538. The chief pre-Reformation pilgrimage to survive in England, revived in the 20th century by Anglican, Roman Catholic, and Eastern Orthodox Christians, is the one to the Marian shrine at Walsingham in Norfolk. There have been other revivals such as the annual (Anglican) pilgrimage to the restored shrine of Saint Alban in the city that bears his name. A notable survival in Wales is the Shrine of Saint Winifred at Holywell, which has never been suppressed.

Other major Marian shrines which attract huge followings are those of Lourdes in S. France since 1858, Fatima near Batalha in Portugal since 1917, Knock in Ireland, Czestochowa in Poland, Guadalupe in Mexico, and Lisieux in N. France for S. Thérèse of Lisieux. As well as Chaucer, John Bunyan (1628–88) invoked pilgrimage for his main work. *The Pilgrim's Progress, from this World to that which is to come* (1678), a prose allegory in the form of a dream, was illustrated in St Elizabeth's, Eastbourne (1944) by Hans *Feibusch, and in St Anselm's, Kennington 1970–71 by Norman Adams RA.

pinnacle Any tall, usually pointed cresting on the top of a building or on the top of a buttress, or the supporting tower element of a flying *buttress, in which case it strengthens the buttress by pressing down upon it like a weight.

Piper, John Egerton Christmas, CH (1903–92) A British painter of landscapes and abstract compositions, a designer for the theatre and of stained glass, and a writer on the arts. Frances Spalding's *John Piper Myfanwy Piper Lives in Art* (2009) sets out the artist's life, marriage to Myfanwy, their household, family, and hospitality, their much-in-demand place in the arts scene of Britain. They 'did many things very well' (Ruth Guilding), and John's 'studio workbench was the still life of an orderly mind' (Brian Sewell). John placed at the start of his *Who's Who* entry his membership of Oxford Diocese's Committee for the Care of Churches (DAC) for some 38 years—from childhood the architecture, contents, and purpose of church buildings were to become a lifetime's concern, a fellow DAC member recalling 'he seemed to know every church however apparently insignificant ... always full of clear, wise and reasoned advice, given in a mild, but authoritative way' (Tom Hassall). Ecclesiastical works of Piper's deserving special attention are mosaic reredos (1958) St Paul's, Harlow; Eton College windows (1959-63); Coventry Cathedral Baptistery window (1962); Chichester Cathedral tapestry (1966); St Margaret's, Westminster windows (1967); All Saints, Clifton, Bristol (1967); Metropolitan Cathedral of Christ the King, Liverpool (1967); Churchill College Chapel windows, Cambridge (1968); Robinson College Chapel windows, Cambridge (1968); Hereford Cathedral tapestries (1976); Iffley Church window (installed 1995).

Pisano, Nicola (*c.*1220/5 or earlier–before Mar. 1284) and **Giovanni** (*c.*1245/50–after 1314), father and son, were Italian sculptors responsible for the regeneration of sculpture in central Italy; Giovanni was also an architect. Nicola probably came from Apulia, where the Emperor Frederick II Hohenstaufen (d. 1250) had encouraged a revival of Roman classical forms. No works by Nicola can be identified in Apulia; since he dated his Pisa Baptistery pulpit 1260 (1259 modern style) it must be assumed that he left Apulia well before that, to be given so important a commission. It is a marble hexagon, with small figures of Virtues standing on the capitals of the marble columns which raise the structure from the ground. A central column has, at the base, a group of animals and grotesque human figures, possibly referring to the unregenerate world which the Christian message came to reform. Five of the sides have reliefs with scenes from the NT, culminating in the *Last Judgement*; the sixth side is the entrance. In all the scenes, the most striking feature is the Roman classicism of the figures; the Virgin in the *Nativity* and the Holy Women in the *Crucifixion* are Roman matrons; the angels winged Genii; the crucified Christ is a serene Jupiter; the subsidiary figures are taken from Roman sarcophagi, and even the Magi's horses seem harnessed to a quadriga. Some of the corner figures, as well as those in the reliefs, are adaptations from classical models, so that Fortitude is from a Hercules, and the High Priest and his acolyte in the *Presentation* are adapted from a Roman vase actually outside Pisa Cathedral.

The pulpit in Siena Cathedral (1265–8) marks the emergence of Giovanni as a key figure in his father's by now important workshop; the Shrine of *S. Dominic in Bologna was designed by Nicola but carved by his assistants (1264–7). The Siena pulpit is of the same form as the one in the Pisa Baptistery, but octagonal, with larger reliefs. The narrative scenes from the NT are more complex because most of them contain several incidents. The corners between the reliefs now have small figures, and instead of the serene Christus Triumphans of the Pisa *Crucifixion*, the Siena Christ is in the throes of an agonizing death, and the onlookers now recoil in horror. Small figures of Virtues stand on the capitals of the supporting columns, and the base of the central column is surrounded by figures of the Liberal Arts. The *Last Judgement* occupies two panels. Between them is Christ as Judge, and below Him is a cross flanked by angels with the Instruments of the *Passion. Although many of the figures still show Nicola deeply imbued with classical forms, his art has now moved far closer to French Gothic. The figures of the Virgin and Christ, and of some prophets and angels, suggest a knowledge of Île de France portal sculpture.

In the main square in Perugia Nicola and Giovanni made the large fountain finished in 1278 with two basins and with many sculpture reliefs and figures, so alike in style that no decision can be made as to who carved them. Between 1278 and Nicola's death, they carved many of the prophets and saints on the outside of Pisa Baptistery, the first example in Tuscany of sculpture incorporated into architecture. Giovanni later carried the idea further in the design of the façade of Siena Cathedral, of which he designed the lower stages. The free-standing figures of prophets (surprisingly they include Plato and Aristotle) are now, like the Pisa figures, very weather-beaten, but the majestically vigorous Siena ones look forward to the ones by Donatello on the Campanile in Florence.

Two other pulpits by Giovanni followed. The first in Sant'Andrea, Pistoia (1301), is his masterpiece; it is hexagonal with five narrative reliefs separated by single figures which include an Apocalyptic Christ with blood spurting from His side, standing on the lion and serpent with above Him the Hand of God (*see* DEXTERA DOMINI), the dove of the Holy Ghost, and angels, inspired by Psalm 91 (Vg. 90); 'For he will command his angels concerning you . . . You will not dash your foot against a stone. You will tread on the lion and the adder', so that the group is not only a Trinity, but in the words of the Psalm, is also a reference to the Temptation of Christ. The narratives use *Continuous Representation and are more dramatic, as in the Virgin's alarm at the appearance of the angel of the Annunciation and her tender gesture towards the Child in the manger in the *Nativity* scene. The *Crucifixion* includes the two thieves omitted from earlier pulpits, though in many details, such as the Y-shaped cross, the representations of *Ecclesia and Synagoga, and the cringing figures of Christ's executioners, the Siena precedents are followed. The pulpit in Pisa Cathedral (1302–11: 1310 modern style) is larger than the others; it is circular and has nine reliefs, seven on the pulpit proper and two on the stair leading up to it. Most of the reliefs were carved by his assistants; the narrative precedent established in earlier ones is continued, with additions such as the birth and the naming of the Baptist, the Visitation, the Flight into Egypt, the Betrayal of Christ, the Flagellation, and two reliefs for the Last Judgement. Between the reliefs are small statues of prophets, except the one between the Last Judgement panels, which is of Christ. There are now nine supporting columns of which seven are column figures with Theological Virtues, Ecclesia, and Cardinal Virtues, Christ and the four Evangelists, the Archangel Michael, and Samson. Giovanni's interest in the antique survives in the figures of Temperance and Samson—one adapted from the Capitoline Venus, the other from a Hercules.

There are also several Madonna and Child groups of which the most noteworthy are those in the tympanum of the Pisa Baptistery, the one in the Arena Chapel in Padua, where it accompanies the Giotto fresco cycles, one in Prato Cathedral, and a half-length in Pisa Cathedral Museum. He also created a new form for tomb sculpture, in that his monument (now fragmentary) for the Empress Margaret of Luxemburg (1313: Genoa, Pal. Bianco) shows her, not as a recumbent effigy, but raised from the grave by two angels, an idea which fell on barren ground.

It has been reasonably suggested that between *c.*1270 and 1275 Giovanni travelled in France, notably to Reims and Paris, which would explain the apparent influence of French Gothic sculpture, although no specific examples can be adduced—only his more emotional and dramatic quality, which differentiates him from his father, who was, however, receptive to the new ideas emanating from the Île de France. He was also consulted (1287) on the design of the cathedral at Massa Marittima. He was the major Italian Gothic sculptor, able to digest French Gothic, but whose façade of Siena Cathedral has no parallel in France.

piscina (Lat. basin, or fishpond) A niche in the wall, usually on the right, or Epistle, side of the altar, with a bowl-shaped base and a drain to the outside. It was provided for the washing of the vessels used during the Mass—chalice, paten, cruet—and it also usually had a small shelf for the cruet half-way up. They were introduced into churches by Pope Leo IV in the 9th century. Most surviving piscinae are medieval, and they are sometimes very decorative; occasionally they are double (Lady Chapels of Exeter and Salisbury cathedrals). In the NE transept of Salisbury there is another piscina built as a small vaulted recess large enough to have doubled as a font. Their use has been abandoned, since the office of washing the vessels is now done in the sacristy; as only the largest medieval churches were provided with sacristies, piscinae were a necessity. A piscina is often the only surviving indication of the site of an ancient altar.

Pius II, Pope (1405–64). Aeneas Silvius Piccolomini was born near Siena, of a poor noble family. He was educated in Siena and Florence, where he became a highly esteemed humanist. He was secretary to various prelates, travelled widely in Europe, and was sent on a mission to Scotland in 1435. After siding with the anti-papal faction at the Council of Basle (1431–49), and becoming secretary to the Emperor Frederick III, he returned to his papal allegiance, and brought the Emperor over to the papal side. He had never taken religious Orders because of his dissolute life, but he now reformed, took Holy Orders, was made a cardinal, and in 1458 became pope. He struggled to organize a Crusade against the Turks, but failed because of the apathy of European monarchs. Finally, despairing of substantial help, he set off with what forces he had, but died in Ancona.

His most considerable monument (other than his enchanting memoirs) is Pienza, which he built on the site of his native village and named after himself. He built a cathedral, a town hall, a palace for the bishop, and another for himself, and he made Pienza the first deliberate essay in town planning of the Renaissance. He began the work the moment he was pope, since he knew that the money would stop with him. He supervised the design, employing as architect Bernardo Rossellino, who had worked in Florence with *Alberti on the Rucellai palace; it is not surprising, therefore, that his own palace is based closely on the harmonious system of superposed Classical Orders that Alberti had created. The cathedral is quite a different matter; here no Renaissance theories were allowed to appear. It must be one of the last Gothic churches to be built in Italy, and it was based on a German church which Pius had seen and admired. It is three bays wide, the nave bay slightly wider than the aisles, with the transepts projecting by one bay, and has a half-hexagon choir, forming an ambulatory round the central altar. It is quadripartite vaulted throughout and—extreme rarity—is a *hall-church. The back of the church gives on to the steep drop of the hillside, and to prevent any later changes, he left strict instructions that no alterations to structure or decoration were ever to be made.

His palace is in total contrast; it is a Renaissance palace, entirely symmetrical about its central axis, with a colonnaded courtyard, and a large garden at the back reaching to the edge of the hill. A striking feature of the garden front are the three superposed loggie, built because Pius enjoyed the view across the valley to Monte Amiata and the hills beyond. When the place was built, Rossellino had to appear before Pius to explain how he had spent over 50,000 ducats when his estimates were for 18,000. To his astonishment, the pope said, 'You did well, Bernardo, in lying to us about the cost of this work. Had you told the truth you could never have persuaded us to spend so much, and this splendid palace and this church, the finest in Italy, would not be standing. By your deceit, you have built these magnificent structures, which all praise who are not consumed with envy. We thank you, for you deserve a special honour,' and he presented the architect with 100 ducats and a scarlet robe; Bernardo burst into tears of joy (mingled with relief?). His literary output was considerable and includes a history of the Council of Basle, works on biography and topography, including ones based on his European travels, and on Asia, gleaned from other travellers. His *Commentaries* are the account of his life and a summary of his thinking, and are an extremely frank and vivid account of papal politics, unrivalled in interest and insight.

His nephew, Francesco Todeschini, adopted his uncle's name and became Archbishop of Siena (at 22, and still a deacon), and a cardinal a few weeks later. He became pope in 1503, as Pius III, after the death of Alexander VI, it being necessary to find a neutral candidate to bridge the gap between foreign powers endeavouring to influence the election of the new pope, and to counter the threat of interference from Cesare Borgia, the late pope's son. Pius III died ten days after his coronation. He built the library of Siena Cathedral to house his uncle's books in 1495, and had it decorated with frescoes by Pinturicchio with lively scenes from his uncle's life (1502). The library also contains important illuminated antiphonals and other MSS. Pius III also commissioned Michelangelo in 1501 to carve statues for the family altar in Siena Cathedral, but only two figures were carved by Michelangelo, the rest being by his assistants.

plague saints There are some nineteen in all, varying according to country. The most famous are *S. Roch (S. Rocco in Italy), a pilgrim who caught plague and was fed by a dog, which is why he is usually depicted with one; and *S. Sebastian, a Roman soldier ordered to be martyred by being shot with arrows, but who survived. The arrows are equated with plague (Ps. 91: 5–6: 'the arrow that flies by day, the pestilence that stalks in darkness'; Vg. Ps. 90: 6). Others are SS Cosmas and Damian (doctors, who are invoked for other illnesses as well), *S. Antony Abbot (frequently the patron saint of leper hospitals, *see* GRÜNEWALD), S. Charles *Borromeo (because of his heroic work during the plague of Milan in 1575), S. Christopher (invoked in paintings on many English church walls), S. Genevieve of Paris, S. George, and S. Francesca Romana.

Plagues of Egypt *See* MOSES.

planeta A chasuble (*see* VESTMENTS), also described as a large loose mantle covering the whole body (4th Council of Toledo, 663), probably so called from being originally an outdoor garment worn when travelling (Gk. *planetes*, wanderer).

Platytera *See* MADONNA TYPES.

plinth The base of a column or a *pier, usually with a moulding or the masonry base of an exterior wall, which is often a continuous band, interrupted only by doorways. If the plinth of a building changes, this usually indicates alterations to the structure.

pluvial A cope, so called from being originally worn as a protection against rain. *See* VESTMENTS.

polyptych A picture, or a relief, made up of several parts, not less than three (two parts is a *diptych). A polyptych serving as an altarpiece often consists of a large central picture (a Virgin and Child, or a subject such as the Nativity or the Resurrection) flanked by smaller pictures of saints, and often with a **predella* below, and sometimes also with small pictures above or in the pinnacles or the sides of the frame. They were common in Italy from the 13th century and in the North from the 14th, but went out of favour in the 16th. A good example is the S. Columba Altarpiece (Munich) by Roger van der Weyden, with a central Adoration of the Magi and wings with the Annunciation on the left, and the Presentation in the Temple on the right. In Germany from the 14th to the 16th centuries the *Schnitzaltar* was popular, consisting of a carved wooden centre either with painted wings (*see* GRÜNEWALD, Isenheim Altar), or maybe a very grand entirely carved altarpiece with a large central scene and wings with four to six scenes in them, a crowning element, and a *predella*. Such are altarpieces by e.g. Michael Pacher: 1471–81, St Wolfgang; Michael Wolgemut: 1506–8, Schwabach; Veit Stoss: 1477–89, St Mary, Cracow; Tilman Riemanschneider: 1505–10, Herrgotskirche, Creglingen. Other exceptional carved works which may be considered in the same light are the marble panels by Maitani (1310–30) of the *Creation* and the *Last Judgement*, on the façade of Orvieto Cathedral, or the Klosterneuburg Altar by *Nicholas of Verdun (1181), a metalwork *ambo which was converted into a polyptych in the 1330s.

polystavrion In the Gk. Orthodox church, it is a white *phelonion (liturgical cape) with a decoration of black crosses. It is first found in 11th- and early 12th-century mosaics of Church Fathers. It may have been originally limited to patriarchs, but by the 14th century it was also worn by metropolitans. While the phelonion might be of any colour, the polystavrion was always white and the crosses black. The apse fresco of the Hagios Nikolaos Orphanos, Salonika, 1310–20, has the four Patriarchs, SS Athanasius, John Chrysostom, Basil, and Gregory Nazianzus all wearing the polystavrion. A pair of Royal gates (the central gates in an *iconostasis) with SS Basil and John Chrysostom shows them wearing the polystavrion and the *epitrachelion (2nd half 15th cent., Russian Mus., St Petersburg).

pomegranate *See* FLOWERS AND FRUIT.

Pontifex Maximus (Lat. Supreme Pontiff) was originally the title of the Roman Emperor, in his role as chief priest in pagan Rome. From the 5th century it was applied to the pope, as supreme sovereign of the whole Church. In inscriptions the abbreviation Pont. Max. is used. The word 'pontiff' derives from the Lat. 'bridge' and 'maker', i.e. a bridge made between God and man.

pontifical *See* LITURGICAL BOOKS.

pontificals *See* VESTMENTS.

Pontius Pilate *See* PILATE.

Pontormo, Jacopo (1494–1556), was an Italian painter, who trained in Florence under Andrea del Sarto before *c.*1512, when he met *Rosso, with whom he was one of the creators of *Mannerism. In 1518 he painted the *Madonna and Child with Saints*, still in San Michele Visdomini, Florence, which is one of the first Mannerist pictures, with an unease and an agitation which sharply distinguish it from the mainstream painting of the day. He was a profoundly religious painter, whose *Passion* cycle frescoes in the Certosa, Florence (1522–5), are not only Mannerist in their emotional content, but contain un-Florentine borrowings from Dürer's engravings of the *Passion* which help him to express his deep religious vision. His supreme masterpiece is the *Deposition* in Sta Felicità, Florence, painted *c.*1525. The dark chapel possibly dictated the very pale tones and brilliant colour of the picture, but its agonized agitation and crowded composition join with the pale, acid colour and the elongated limbs of the angels holding the body of the dead Christ to stress its emotional effect. He was much influenced by *Michelangelo and the composition reflects the effect of Michelangelo's *Pietà* in St Peter's, Rome. An *Annunciation* on the side wall of the chapel is slightly less emotional, but has the same pale colours.

Pool of Bethesda *See* BETHESDA.

Poor Clares are Franciscan nuns (OSF). *See* CLARE, S.

pope (from Gk. *papas*, Lat. *papa*, father) The title was once used generally by bishops, but in 1073 Gregory VII, in a Roman Council, forbade its use by any Western prelate other than the Bishop of Rome. The title *papas* is used by the Patriarch of Alexandria, and by Greek priests. The pope dresses only in white, with an enveloping black cloak in bad weather. He once wore a voluminous linen garment with a wide sash with long ends, often embroidered or fringed, with over it a loose cape, called a *mozetta*, reaching below the waist, made of red velvet, sometimes hooded or lined with fur. On his head he wore a close-fitting red velvet cap, edged with white, called a *camauro*. Papal portraits through the ages permit one to follow changes in papal dress. His dress nowadays is a white cassock with a short cape over the shoulders, and the traditional sash with fringed or embroidered ends. He no longer wears the *camauro*, or the old papal slippers, but ordinary shoes in the traditional red. One tradition remains: the Fisherman's Ring, new-made for every pope, since it is the duty of the Cardinal Chamberlain to break the ring of a dead pope. The ring is a gold signet-ring, engraved with S. Peter fishing from a boat, with the pope's name round it; it is used for sealing papal briefs.

The papal tiara, or triple crown, is an extra-liturgical head-dress—i.e. it is never worn for, or at, religious ceremonies. It may have originated from a form of Phrygian cap, or Persian royal head-dress much like that of the Doge of Venice, worn as a distinctive papal insignia. It is first mentioned in a 'Life' of Pope Constantine (708–15), and by the 11th century a coronet was added round the lower edge; by the 13th century two lappets were added towards the back. Boniface VIII (1294–1303) added a second coronet, possibly symbolizing the pope's claims to spiritual and temporal authority, and under Benedict IX (1303–4) or Clement V (1305–14) a third coronet was added, and the whole diadem, surmounted by a small cross, was increased in size. Its modern beehive or melon shape was arrived at by the 14th century. The pope is crowned with it, thereafter wearing it only on ceremonial occasions, usually preferring to have it carried before him. It has not been used since the pontificate of Paul VI (1978).

The significance of the triple crown has varied considerably: it has been held to symbolize the Church militant, suffering, triumphant; its powers of ruling, teaching, sanctifying; as emblems of the Trinity; of the triple office of pastor, priest, and prophet. It may have originated from papal claims to spiritual and temporal authority, in the larger sense, the third crown representing the pope's narrower papal authority as ruler of the Papal States. The papal coat of arms is the only one to mix gold and silver, the keys of S. Peter being one gold and one silver.

Images of the popes are legion. Giotto, in the frescoes in the Upper Church at Assisi, represented three popes in the S. Francis series, Innocent III, who authorized the Franciscan Order, Honorius III, who finally approved it, and Gregory IX, who canonized Francis in 1228. All these popes are depicted with only one coronet on the papal diadem. Arnolfo di Cambio, in Rome for the first papal Jubilee declared for 1300, carved a bust of Boniface VIII (St Peter's) which shows the diadem with two coronets, Boniface having added the second one. Martin V, who became pope in 1417, ended both the Schism and the papal exile in Avignon by returning to Rome. A statue of him in Milan Cathedral was erected in 1421, when he was on his way to Rome. This shows him with the diadem with three coronets and the two lappets added by the 13th century.

Papal portraits after this remain consistent: Melozzo da Forlì painted Sixtus IV appointing Platina as Librarian (1475–7: Vatican) and receiving a MS from him. The pope is surrounded by his nephews, with Giuliano dela Rovere, later Julius II, standing facing him. Raphael painted Julius II (*c.*1511: London, NG); Velázquez painted Innocent X (1650: Rome, Doria Gall.); all show the pope wearing a long white robe, a loose *alb over it, the *mozetta*, and the *camauro*. Pompeo Battoni painted Pius VI (1775: Vatican), but this portrait is the first of a pope painted without the *camauro*, which lies on the table, and with a rochet (a short white vestment) over his long cassock, but with the *mozetta* and a stole. Other variations may be seen in the many papal tombs in St Peter's, Rome.

porch *See* NARTHEX.

Porta Clausa, Coeli are titles of *Mary. *Porta clausa* (Lat. a closed door), is from Ezekiel 44: 2—'Then said the Lord unto me; This gate shall remain shut; it shall not be opened, and no one shall enter by it; for the Lord, the God of Israel, has entered by it, therefore it shall remain shut.' It is taken to be a reference to Mary's perpetual virginity, and figures of the Prophet Ezekiel are sometimes shown with a scroll so inscribed. In the *Annunciation* by Piero della Francesca (Arezzo, San Francesco frescoes of the *Story Of the Holy Cross*) he depicts the Virgin under a classical portico, and he also has a firmly closed door behind the Angel.

Porta coeli (Gate of Heaven), like *Regina coeli* (Queen of Heaven), is an honorific. *See also* HORTUS CONCLUSUS.

Porta Santa *See* HOLY DOOR.

portal sculpture From about the 11th century onwards the decoration of church portals with statues and reliefs became an important feature of cathedrals, abbeys, and churches in W. Europe, particularly in France.

In opposition to the destruction of images taking place in the East during *Iconoclasm (which did not end until 842), Charlemagne forbade the destruction of images, and the Council of Paris in 825 (renewing the edict of the 2nd Council of *Nicaea, 787, permitting the veneration of images) ordered their conservation for the instruction of the faithful. Their iconography was to unite religion, history, doctrine, and moral teaching; no separation was to be made between religious and profane knowledge, and all images were to have a symbolic and allegorical meaning. The importance of art is best expressed in the words of Abbot Suger of *Saint-Denis: 'Art leads minds from material to immaterial things'.

The decisions and directives of the various Councils determined the character of art in churches. But the form the decoration was to take was obviously dependent on the architecture of the church and the areas available to the artist, for art in churches has to be understood as a visual extension of religious teaching to which it plays a major supporting role: its didactic function governs its nature and provides its *raison d'être*. For this reason it came to be known as the 'Bible of the illiterate' (*see* PAULINUS OF NOLA). In the early years of Christianity churches were plain, unadorned structures outside; decoration was usually limited to the embellishment of the altar. Early Christian and Byzantine churches adapted *mosaics from their original pagan use as flooring to become the brilliant, costly, and always rigidly controlled didactic decoration inside the church. Fresco decoration followed as a less expensive means of achieving the same effect, but tended to treat subjects more freely.

The areas available to the artist were dependent on the shape of the structure, which could—and did—modify the way in which programmes were set out. This is seen at its simplest in the way in which Byzantine mosaic decoration designed for the domed, cross-in-square church was adapted to the Sicilian long-nave basilicas.

As church architecture in Italy, for example, developed the long-nave basilica with colonnades or arcades, so the area available to the artist was limited to the apse, to the space between the nave arcade and the clerestory, and the walls of aisles or transepts. The purpose of an artistic programme was defeated if the images were too high up, or were confined to the presbytery from which the faithful were excluded. Because Italian churches had, on the whole, large wall spaces suitable for fresco cycles (e.g. *Assisi) exterior sculpture played only a limited role, except for a few grand façades such as Siena or Orvieto. The difference between North and South is also important in that fresco is unsuitable in the northern climate; but sculpture has the advantages of durability and visibility, and could be adapted to didactic programmes. In large northern *Romanesque churches, which were usually long-nave basilicas with arcades supported by piers, columns, or a combination of both, there was little scope for interior decoration, except on capitals, which provided a rich field for instruction, or even merely for fantasy. Porches, doorways, tympana, and lintels offered large, very obvious opportunities, particularly as they presented their themes as much to the passer-by as to the faithful entering the church. In major Gothic churches, which tended to extreme height, capital sculpture was restricted to simple leaf or acanthus designs, but portal sculpture was capable of very extensive development.

The genesis of portal sculpture, which was to develop into one of the leading forms of French art in the 12th and 13th centuries, probably lies in the lintels of modest churches on the Pyrenean frontier, e.g. St-Genis des Fontaines, near Perpignan, *c.*1020, representing Christ in Majesty flanked by Apostles. The earliest surviving portal with carved tympana (in this case two doors, each with a tympanum, and with a structural support between them) is probably the Puerta de las Platerías, at Santiago de *Compostela, of 1090–5. This doorway has been remade twice; all the parts have been moved around, and others added. The loss of two of the major churches on the *Pilgrimage Road (Tours and Limoges) means that evidence is missing, but the tympanum of the Ascension at St-Sernin, Toulouse, of *c.*1118, is probably the next in a Pilgrimage Road church. From the turn of the 12th century the portal with a carved tympanum becomes the norm for churches of any importance. They have multiple archivolts carved with figures related to the theme of the major work, sometimes flanked with figures of prophets, and often with scenes from the OT or the Life of Christ. But hovering over all the grand portals from the 12th century onwards is the ghost of the western portals of *Cluny III, finished *c.*1115. Nothing survived the French Revolution, but they are recorded as a triple portal. The large central door had a Christ in Majesty and the *Evangelist symbols; the subjects of the side doors are not known, but may be conjectured in that they probably established an iconographic system which served as a model. If the portals of Moissac, 1115–20, and Vézelay, 1120–32, are among the most memorable, it is largely because both were Cluniac houses when their portals were carved. In no case is the iconography of a portal ever haphazard; all are governed by a theme to which the various parts add their individual contributions.

The Christ in Majesty in the tympanum at Moissac is a figure of terrifying force, surrounded by the symbols of the Evangelists and the Elders of the Apocalypse, in imagery derived from *Beatus's Commentary on the Apocalypse. The *trumeau*, or central support of the tympanum, is composed of lions and lionesses standing on one another's backs, with two figures, probably S. Paul and Jeremiah, while the lintel is supported by figures of S. Peter and Isaiah. The rest of the deep embrasure has narrative NT panels from the Annunciation to the Flight into Egypt on the right, and on the left scenes from the OT and grim figures typifying Vices.

Vézelay has a triple portal, with new subjects which enlarge the iconography. In the tympanum on the right is an Adoration of the Magi, and on the lintel, scenes from the NT from the Annunciation to the Nativity; in the tympanum on the left is Christ appearing to the Apostles after the Resurrection, and on the lintel the Pilgrims at Emmaus. The tympanum of the central door has Christ sending the Apostles to preach, while the archivolt above and the lintel below are filled with the peoples to whom the message is to be brought; the seemingly disparate scenes have, in fact, a carefully worked out sequence governing the choice of scenes: this is the Incarnation, the Resurrection, and the Ascension, with the Charge to the Apostles: 'you will be my witnesses . . . to the ends of the earth' (Acts 1: 8). The *trumeau* has a badly damaged S. John the Baptist, the forerunner, and on either side of the main door are SS Peter and Paul, and Isaiah and Jeremiah. The central portal at Vézelay thus introduces a new theme. The most vivid Last Judgement portals must be those at Autun, of 1125–35, where the artist, Gislebertus, is one of the few whose name is known, and at Conques of 1130–5; both are gruesomely explicit about the fate of the damned.

Portals with the Virgin are less frequent in the early 12th century; usually she is combined with other subjects, as in an Adoration of the Magi combined with Adam and Eve eating the apple, at Anzy-le-Duc, near Roanne, as an exposition of the First Sin and its Redemption. Saints appear first combined with a grander subject, as at Cahors (1150).

Abbot Suger, in his rebuilding of Saint-Denis, had introduced column figures in the main portal *c.*1137–40 (destroyed in the French Revolution); these had already appeared in Italy as prophets in Ferrara and Verona cathedrals in 1135.

The Portail Royal in the west front of Chartres was made between 1145 and 1155. In 1194 the cathedral was burned down, and only the crypt, the triple west portal, and the two towers survived to provide a starting-point for the new building. The portal is similar to those already existing in Burgundy, except in its size and its more extensive iconographic programme. The central tympanum of Christ in Majesty, with the symbols of the Evangelists, and the Apostles on the lintel below follows the precedents of Cluny III. The right tympanum has a Virgin and Child flanked by angels, with a double lintel below, the lower one with scenes from the Annunciation to the Angel appearing to the Shepherds, and the upper one with the Presentation. In the left tympanum is the Ascension, and the ten Apostles on the lintel below. The sequence is therefore the Incarnation—Christ's appearance on earth, hence the importance given to the Presentation (badly damaged) on the right, and His Ascension into Heaven on the left, with the central tympanum filled by Christ of the Apocalypse. The archivolts round the tympana are filled with small figures of angels, the Signs of the *Zodiac, the Liberal *Arts, the Calendar in the form of the Labours of the *Months—that is, representations of heavenly bodies or symbolic ones. The arches and the lintels are supported by column figures of men and women from the OT, and above the column figures is a frieze of scenes from the Life of Christ. There is a strong horizontal line of demarcation between the tympana and their surrounding personifications, and the historical scenes and figures below. This exemplifies the argument that the OT is not just the precursor of the NT, but also that the NT is the fulfilment of the OT. The programme for Chartres was more complex than any up to that time, and great reliance was placed on contemporary theologians such as Hugo of S. Victor, whose book, *De Sacramentis Christianae Fidei*, expressed the idea that all God's work, whether physical or spiritual, was imbued with symbolic significance.

The huge triple Pórtico de la Gloria at Santiago de Compostela, of 1168–88, combines all the precedents which have already appeared in France and Italy: the column figures (though two column figures were part of the west front sculpture of the Spanish Abbey of Ripoll, of 1160–8), the elaborate iconography of Christ of the Apocalypse, and the *trumeau* for the figure of S. James. Perhaps the grandest of all figures of Christ in Majesty in Spain is in the tympanum of Sant'Iago, at Carrión de los Condes on the Pilgrimage Road, and the most unusual column figures are probably those at Sta Maria la Reál, at Sangüesa, near Pamplona, of *c.*1170, where in a Last Judgement portal SS Peter and Paul are followed by a much smaller figure of Judas hanging.

A number of French portals followed the type set by the Portail Royal at Chartres: Angers of 1150–60, St-Bénigne, Dijon, *c.*1160 (only the damaged tympanum survives in Dijon Mus.); the south portal of Le Mans, before 1158; the south portal at Bourges, *c.*1160, with a *trumeau* of Christ inserted in 1240–50. The first portal entirely dedicated to the Virgin is at Senlis, north of Paris, where the new cathedral was built 1153–84, with a tympanum with the Triumph of the Virgin, in which she sits facing her divine Son. On the lintel are scenes of her death and of her body being carried up to Heaven by angels. The figures on the jambs flanking the door—they are now too detached to be called column figures—are OT typological figures, and the archivolts include a Tree of *Jesse running over three arches, and a final one of prophets. All the portals in or near Paris suffered worse during the Revolution from vandalism than those further away: Paris itself, *Saint-Denis, Senlis, Mantes, Étampes, Meaux, Sens. Most have been restored, often extensively, and not always sensitively. The fascinating variety of scenes and figures in the archivolts—the Life of the Baptist, the Wise and Foolish Virgins, Calendars with the Labours of the Months—these have often fared better, by being less accessible and obvious, and less understood. The Senlis Virgin portal has a wider resonance: Abbot Suger had presented to Notre-Dame in Paris a stained-glass window representing the Triumph of the Virgin (now lost) which provided the subject used at Senlis. The same theme was also used at Mantes, *c.*1180, but when it reappears at Chartres *c.*1205–10, in the centre door of the north portal, it has developed into a Coronation of the Virgin, with the Virgin seated next to Christ, already crowned as Queen of Heaven, and with her death and Assumption in the lintel. At Strasburg the Death of the Virgin with Christ accepting her soul, in the left typmpanum, is matched on the right by her Coronation, with Christ placing the crown on her head. The lintel on the left shows her bier with her body borne to her tomb, and on the right she rises from her shroud to her triumph in the tympanum above. This portal of *c.*1230 is flanked by figures of *Ecclesia and the dejected Synagoga, while between the doors is an enthroned Solomon. Many of these figures have been restored, and Church and Synagogue are copies (originals in the Mus.).

Laon has a triple portal west front, datable 1195–1205, but the order of the portals has changed. The door on the right has a Last Judgement; the left door has a Virgin and Child with the Adoration of the Magi in the tympanum, and the central door has a Triumph (or Coronation?) of the Virgin in the tympanum. All the sculpture at Laon was heavily restored in the 19th century; if the restored Laon preserves its original scheme it is interesting because it presents two different types of Virgin portal, derived from different iconographical traditions.

The first was inherited from Byzantine art and, as in the right-hand tympanum of the Portail Royal at Chartres, Mary appears as the Nikopoia *Panagia, seen frontally, holding the Holy Child centrally before her, enthroned on her knees; she looks neither to right nor left, her role being that of the Theotokos, the God-bearer. She is, however, crowned as Queen of Heaven; this is a purely Western concept, never found in Byzantine art. In the archivolts there are small figures of angels and prophets, and in other Virgin portals these are often the Wise and Foolish Virgins, or the Liberal Arts, portraying her in the forms in which she is addressed in the Litany—Seat of Wisdom, Mirror of Justice, Tower of David, Gate of Heaven, Ark of the Covenant. At Amiens, for instance, the Virgin portal includes an *Ark of the Covenant inside a tabernacle, with the symbolic meaning that as the Ark contained the manna, the bread from Heaven which was the salvation of the Jews in the Wilderness, so she bore within her the Godhead Who was to become the Bread of Salvation for all mankind. The change in the iconography from the hieratic type to the gentler vision of some of the other terms of the Litany: Virgin most merciful, Refuge of Sinners, Consoler of the Afflicted, is due in large measure to the influence of the 12th-century monastic reformers, *Norbert and *Bernard of Clairvaux, and it reaches into the 13th century with S. Francis and S. Dominic, both of whose immensely strong and widespread Orders gave a special place to devotion to the Virgin. As a result the imagery gradually softens to make her less distant, less awesome, and she comes to personify all the virtues, as her imagery widens to include the *unicorn which can only be captured by a Virgin, and the OT Burning *Bush which flamed before Moses, but was not consumed, since her virginity was not impaired by conception and childbirth.

The decision at Chartres, after the fire of 1194, to retain the Portail Royal as the west front led to the decision to add portals to the north and south transepts, probably when they were being built, *c.*1210. They were then expanded from a single door to three doors with a free-standing porch in front of them. The sculpture was not finished before *c.*1235–40. One problem was devising a coherent iconographic scheme to reach over nine doors. The central door of the north transept portal was dedicated to the Virgin, and as the hieratic Theotokos had already appeared in the Portail Royal, a Coronation of the Virgin was a reasonable choice for the tympanum of the central door, with Mary seated next to Christ, and her death and Assumption in the lintel below, and with a Tree of Jesse and prophets in the archivolts. The *trumeau* of the central door is, appropriately, S. Anne, the Virgin's mother, carrying her infant daughter. The tympanum of the door on the left has the Adoration of the Magi, and the Magi's dream in the top half, and the Nativity and Annunciation to the Shepherds below; the tympanum of the right door contains scenes from the OT. The figures in the archivolts tell the stories of Esther, Judith, Gideon, and Tobias; all themes of God's justice, and salvation through faith. An even greater change is in the figures flanking the doors. Column figures have long been abandoned; the left door has three figures on either side, narrative groups of the Annunciation with Isaiah, and the Visitation with Daniel, as major prophets of the Incarnation. The centre door has five figures each side, patriarchs and Melchisedek on the left, and on the right two prophets, Simeon, the Baptist, and S. Peter as Pope and NT counterpart to the OT High Priest Melchisedek. The right door jamb figures are also OT ones, chosen to form suitable counterparts. The porches in front of the portals also have large figures of saints, kings, and bishops, mostly unidentified.

The themes of the south transept portals begin in the centre with the Last Judgement in the tympanum, with lintel and lower ranges of the archivolts given to the Blessed and the Damned. The *trumeau* is an impressive figure of Christ, standing on the beasts of Evil—an image recalling its ancient history from Byzantium onwards, and below Him is a tiny group of the baker who paid for it, together with two of his staff and the baskets of bread of his charity. The other two doors are given to Martyrs and to Confessors, and so are the jamb figures: the Apostles, Martyrs, bishops and Doctors of the Church, and saints. The transept portals of Chartres mark a turning-point; this bald account, which hardly does more than list the subjects and the figures accompanying them, can only indicate the depth of the symbolism of each of the figures. Sometimes the figures remain anonymous due to weathering, which has destroyed inscriptions, or to human agency, more deliberately destructive, but no figure, no incident, was included which did not form part of a programme carefully devised, and scrupulously executed. Chartres is the perfect exposition of the dictum laid down in Nicaea in 787, that 'the churches are of the Fathers who build them' and 'the art alone is of the artist'; it also obeys faithfully all the rules established by the Council of Paris in 825, for the concordance in all the parts is complete.

The triple west front portals of Notre-Dame in Paris, of 1210–20, present a similar problem to those at Laon: to what extent has extensive 19th-century restoration, done to undo the ravages of the Revolution, modified the original programme? The central portal is a Last Judgement. The side portals are both dedicated to the Virgin, a hieratic Theotokos on the right and a Coronation on the left, but most of the main figures are 19th century, and may well have been based on models used elsewhere. The south transept portal is dedicated to the Martyrdom of S. Stephen.

At Amiens, the townspeople refused to damage the cathedral, so for once portals of 1220–35 are virtually entire: a Last Judgement in the centre, with the usual groups of the jubilant and the lamenting, and an unusual number of eight archivolts, with angels, a Tree of Jesse, Elders, prophets and saints, and a *trumeau* of Christ treading on the beasts of Evil. The right door has the Coronation of the Virgin in the tympanum and her death and resurrection in the lintel, and a *trumeau* of the Virgin and Child with over it the tabernacle with the Ark of the Covenant flanked by kings and prophets, as at Paris (which may indicate that the 19th-century restorers at Paris used Amiens as their source). The left door celebrates S. Firmin, a local saint. The jamb figures are intact: Apostles in the centre, groups of the Annunciation, Visitation, and Presentation in the Virgin portal face Solomon and Sheba, Herod and the Magi. The south transept portal was done between 1259 and 1269; S. Honoratus is in the tympanum, and the jamb figures are angels and unidentified saints. The *trumeau* is a Virgin and Child—the so-called 'Vierge dorée', which shows all too obviously her derivation from the smiling figures at Reims. Interesting features of the west front of Amiens are the panels, on the base of the walls on either side of the portals, of small scenes of Virtues, Vices, Labours, and suchlike simple scenes, possibly deriving from the ones which survived Republican destruction at Paris.

Not only are the portals at Reims totally different from their predecessors, but after them nothing was the same again. Reims suffered badly from the Revolution, and during the First World War when it was shelled and set on fire. Four master builders are credited with the building of Reims, though the order in which they worked is still the subject of discussion: they were Jean d'Orbais, Gaucher of Reims, Jean le Loup, and Bernard de Soissons, probably but not definitely in that order. Building started in 1210 with the choir, which was not finished until 1241, but the sculpture of the central portal of the west front is said to have been in place by 1255. It is clear that at least three sculptors worked on these eight figures, since they show marked differences of style: the left jamb of the central doorway has the Presentation of Christ in the Temple, with the figures of the Virgin and Simeon in the centre, carved *c.*1230–3, flanked by S. Joseph on the Virgin's right, and the Virgin's maid on Simeon's left. She is an intrusion into the scheme, and seems to have been included merely to make up the required number of figures, which were carved *c.*1245–55. The right jamb of the central doorway has two groups, the Annunciation and the Visitation. The Angel of the Annunciation is clearly the work of the sculptor who made the S. Joseph and the maidservant, and is believed to have been Bernard de Soissons; the Virgin Annunciate and both the figures of the Visitation are usually dated 1230–3, despite their differences of style, which suggests different sculptors, but both styles can be found in other figures also executed in the big campaign of sculpture of the 1230s, placed in other parts of the west front. The Angel, the maidservant, and S. Joseph all show a characteristic in common: it is a subtle, enigmatic smile, which later, in other less skilled hands, becomes an unpleasing grimace. The triple west front portals have no tympana, the space being filled by stained-glass windows. The central door is a Virgin portal, with her Coronation relegated to inside the top of the sharply pointed gable which surmounts the portal. The side doors also have their main subjects relegated to the gables. The right door has a Last Judgement in the gable, and a variety of saints and OT figures in the jambs, virtually all of them restorations, since they were made headless by being within reach of a vandal. The left door has a Crucifixion in the gable (a rarity in portal sculpture) but now twice restored. The other subjects were all drawn from the Life of Christ and extend into the small figures of the archivolts. The double north transept portals date from *c.*1225–30, and many of the figures are stylistically very close to the Visitation pair on the west front. The tympanum on the right is a Last Judgement with two rows of men and women clambering from their tombs and two rows of the jubilant and the dejected, including a king, a bishop, and a monk. The jamb figures are Apostles, and the *trumeau* is a Christ, headless since the shelling. The left portal is given to events in the life of S. Calixtus, and other saints.

Because of the unusual arrangement of the west portals of Reims, much of the sculpture was carried inside the west front and the lintels of the doors and the spaces between them are filled with niches containing small figures from the Life of the Baptist, or the story of Joachim and Anna. But it is also clear that with Reims, the strict iconographical system has broken down.

The five portals of the west front of Bourges, made from 1240 to 1260, start with a lively Last Judgement in the centre, but drift into celebrations of various saints, and the triple portals of Poitiers, of 1250, present only a collection of themes and subjects often of no more than local significance. Portal sculpture in the mid- to late 13th century is now a long way from the organized theological systems which were the rule from Cluny onwards. Henceforward they appear to be designed with little regard for the theological development of the content and with less scholarship in the relationship of the parts: style also has entered and further diluted the system.

portico The porch of a building projecting from the façade, with columns and a pedimented gable is described as a portico. The columns define it as a tetrastyle, if there are four columns, hexastyle for six, and octastyle for eight. The porticoes of some Greek Revival churches are decastyle—ten columns, or dodecastyle—twelve columns.

porticus *See* ANGLO-SAXON.

Portiuncula (Lat. a small portion) The small ruined church near Assisi which was one of the three repaired by *S. Francis. This was where he received his vocation in 1208, where *S. Clare received the habit from him in 1212, and where he died in 1226. It is now incorporated in the great 19th-century basilica built round it.

Port Royal *See* JANSEN, JANSENISM.

Portugal *See* EUROPE.

Post-Resurrection Appearances *See* CHRIST.

Potiphar's wife *See* JOSEPH.

Poussin, Nicolas (1594–1665), the greatest of French classical painters, settled in Rome in 1624. In 1628 he painted his only 'grand manner' altarpiece, a *Martyrdom of S. Erasmus* for

St Peter's (now Vatican Mus.) with a restraint which does much to offset the horrible details of the saint's death. But Baroque grandeur, inflated gesture, and movement were not his strong suits, and after a severe illness, 1629–30, he abandoned them for good, to work only on smaller pictures for learned and cultured patrons from an increasingly opulent middle class. His great forte lay in the grouping of figures to make a dramatic narrative immediately plain, and among the works which best display this are his two series of the *Seven Sacraments*. The first set was painted between 1637 and 1640 (*Baptism*, Washington, NG; *Penance*, burnt in 1816; remainder, Belvoir Castle, Coll. Duke of Rutland) for Cassiano del Pozzo, a learned poet, classical antiquarian, and secretary to Cardinal Barberini. The second set was painted for the French civil servant Chanteloup, who was Poussin's host during his unhappy stay in Paris, 1640–2, and was painted after his return to Rome (which he never again left). They are now in Edinburgh (NG, lent by the Duke of Sutherland). Both sets show a mature gravity with deep psychological understanding; they also display Poussin's great gift for 'punctuating' the development of his narrative with brilliant colours in the clothes of the protagonists: a golden orange, a strong blue, a deep ruby-red placed exactly so that the eye is led to the core of the meaning of the picture. Nothing in a Poussin is accidental; the related drawings show how carefully he plotted the arrangement of his figures, and the disposition and shapes of his landscape background.

His religious pictures begin early in his Roman career with the unusual *Return from the Flight into Egypt* (*c.*1628–9: Dulwich), a very rare subject, in which the Holy Family embark on a ferry boat to cross a river and the Christ Child alone sees a vision of angels carrying a cross; or the *Lamentation over the Dead Christ* (*c.*1628: Munich), hardly distinguishable except by the subdued marks of the nails on Christ's hands and feet from such secular subjects as *Venus and the dead Adonis* (*c.*1630: Caen). In his middle years he added more turbulent scenes, such as the *Plague at Ashdod* (*c.*1630: Louvre), the *Massacre of the Innocents* (1630–1: Chantilly), or the *Worship of the Golden Calf* (*c.*1636–7: London, NG) to his long series of classical subjects. The finest Madonna and Child subjects come comparatively late in his life, with the magnificent *Madonna on the Steps* (1648: Washington, NG), and the *Madonna with the Basin* (*c.*1650: Cambridge, Mass.). Two versions of the *Annunciation* form an instructive contrast: the one at Chantilly of the late 1620s is full of Baroque movement, with flying putti accompanying God the Father, a pointing angel, a half-swooning Virgin; the London one, of 1657, is totally calm and reticent. The kneeling angel with his two raised and pointing forefingers, the obedient submission of the Virgin, arms spread wide in yielding consent, is the embodiment of her words 'Be it unto me according to thy word.'

Poussin's religious works are never grandiose either in size or feeling. He uses Raphael as his inspiration, as in his *Ecstasy of S. Paul* (1649–50: Louvre), and also as a touchstone for the qualities of quiet devotion and tender feeling. His pictures do not evoke emotion as Caravaggio's do, nor touch the heart as do Rembrandt's; they are works for reflection, meditation, a stimulus to the mind and a challenge to the understanding. His art is best expressed by Bernini, who tapped his forehead and said, 'Signor Poussin works from here.'

Poverello, il Italian for 'little poor man', i.e. *S. Francis of Assisi.

Powers The sixth Order of *angels, thought to be referred to in 1 Peter 3: 22: 'angels and authorities and powers being made subject to Him' [Christ].

PRB *See* PRE-RAPHAELITE BROTHERHOOD.

Preachers, Order of (OP) *See* DOMINICANS.

predella Originally the step at the back of the altar, on which candlesticks were placed, it came also to mean the strip of paintings at the base of an altarpiece. A triptych with wings that open and close needs to stand clear of the altar, so it became customary to introduce a base, up to a foot high, which could then have scenes painted on it. Because *predelle* are much wider than they are high they are suited to narrative scenes, and so it became customary to paint subjects related to the main altarpiece: thus, the *Madonna and Child*, flanked by *S. Peter* and *S. Paul*, would have scenes from the life of S. Peter, with perhaps an *Annunciation* or a *Nativity*, followed by scenes from the life of S. Paul. Because of their narrative character and relative invisibility they are often livelier and more experimental than the more stereotyped image of the main panel. This is the case in what is thought to be the earliest datable example—Simone *Martini's *S. Louis of Toulouse* (1317: Naples, Mus.)—which has scenes from the saint's life at the base.

Premonstratensians An Order of *Augustinian Canons, also called Norbertines or White Canons, from their all-white habit. They were founded by *S. Norbert in 1120 at Prémontré in France, and were influenced by the *Cistercians. They were important in E. Europe, especially in Hungary.

Pre-Raphaelite Brotherhood A movement founded in 1848 by James Collinson (1825–81), William Holman *Hunt, John Everett *Millais, Thomas Woolner (1825–92), and two brothers, Dante Gabriel (1828–82) and William Michael (1829–1919) *Rossetti. The key figures were Hunt, Millais, and Dante Gabriel Rossetti, all students at the Royal Academy. Dissatisfied with the state of contemporary painting, they sought inspiration elsewhere, and particularly in the work of Ford Madox Brown (1821–93), a little-regarded artist who had come under the influence of the German Nazarenes, a group of expatriate painters who sought to reinvigorate art by a return to pre-Renaissance models, religious subjects, and an assertively Realist style. Although Brown did not become a member of the Brotherhood, he remained associated with it throughout his life.

The group announced its arrival in 1849, when Millais, Hunt, and Rossetti exhibited new paintings. Each signalled the existence of the movement by appending 'PRB' to their signatures. More importantly, the paintings they showed were unprecedented in their approach. Characterized by awkward poses, sharp contrasts of light and shade, angular forms, a heightened symbolism, and a close attention to nature, they caused a sensation. A year later, in 1850, the trio exhibited three more paintings, each on a religious theme. Hunt showed *A Converted British Family Sheltering a Christian Missionary from the Persecution of the Druids*, an apparently naturalistic narrative, which was actually packed with symbolism. Rossetti offered *Ecce Ancilla Domini*, an uncomfortable but undeniably original version of the *Annunciation, one drained of colour but freighted with meaning. Most controversial of all was Millais' *Christ in the House of His Parents*, a stylized but highly realist depiction of the *Holy Family in a carpenter's shop.

The critical response to this work was almost uniformly hostile. Millais, in particular, was attacked for producing a painting that was seen by some as crypto-Catholic and others as simply blasphemous. Viewing *Christ in the House of His Parents*, Charles Dickens wrote that observers needed to be prepared 'for the lowest depths of what is mean, odious, repulsive, and revolting'. Shocked by these responses, James Collinson resigned from the Brotherhood, claiming that membership was incompatible with his Roman Catholic faith. To some extent, indeed, the group as a whole broke up, becoming a looser collection of roughly affiliated artists. Nonetheless, the attention they drew also attracted patrons and provoked the influential critic John *Ruskin to write in their defence. Other artists were enthralled by the originality of their work. They soon inspired a growing group of imitators and disciples, including the young Edward Burne-Jones (1833–98), who would perpetuate and develop the Pre-Raphaelite approach—especially its emphasis on symbolism, and his close friend William Morris (1834–96), who applied many Pre-Raphaelite ideals to the design of fabric, stained glass, and tapestry.

As time went on, and as the movement grew larger and more diffuse, so it became harder to determine what Pre-Raphaelitism amounted to. By the 1860s Millais had developed an admiration for the academic art he had once condemned and for Sir Joshua Reynolds, who had once seemed the personification of all that he had rejected. Rossetti, by contrast, moved into a style that can be seen as closer to Aestheticism, with a succession of languorous, rather decadent, and somewhat claustrophobic portraits of beautiful women. Of the founders, perhaps only Hunt remained true to his early beliefs, continuing to produce highly Realist but also strongly allegorical religious works such as *The Scapegoat* (1854), painted near the supposed site of Sodom; his hugely popular *The Light of the World*, which inspired Arthur Sullivan's 1873 oratorio of the same name; and *The Shadow of Death* (1870–3), which returned to an early theme of the Brotherhood, depicting the young Christ in a carpenter's shop.

PRE-ROMANESQUE

This is a useful term for the art and architecture of Western Europe following the decline of Roman imperial power. Christianity, which had followed in the wake of the end of Roman control, developed new forms in art and architecture, reflecting local conditions. Among the problems which it faced were unorthodox doctrines, and although these various heresies, particularly Monophysitism and *Arianism, caused grave political upheavals, they did not affect art and architecture. *Iconoclasm, during the 8th and 9th centuries, mainly in Constantinople and its area, had no effect in the Latin world except to provide work for Greek artists who came west so as to continue to work.

The barbarian hordes from the east, which flooded into W. Europe from the 4th century onwards, as they settled and became Christianized, mostly adopted the Arian heresy. This was introduced by the exiled Bishop Ulfila (*c.*311–83, consecrated 341), who translated the Bible into Gothic, and the liturgy was also celebrated in the vernacular. The Arian Visigoths, after bitter struggles against Byzantium in Greece and Italy, during which they sacked Rome in 410, were driven into Gaul, which they also ravaged. From there, they conquered Spain, driving out the Vandals who had preceded them, and by 484 were in possession of all the lands from the Loire to Gibraltar, and from Biscay to the Rhône. They created a remarkable civilization under the influence of *Isidore of Seville, and the by now Romanized Visigoths achieved a national and religious unity, even assuming Byzantine costumes and customs. In 507 the Frankish King of Gaul, Clovis, who had adopted orthodox Catholicism, defeated them and drove them out of France and back into Spain, where the native surviving Roman orthodox people regarded them with undying hostility. Eventually, the Visigothic King Recared (d. 601) agreed at the 3rd Council of Toledo in 589 that orthodox Catholicism should be the religion of the land, though this was not finally established until 612. In 710 the Berber Tariq invaded at Gibraltar, and a new chapter in Spanish—and European—history opened.

Visigothic, Mozarabic, and Mudéjar art

The architecture and ornament developed by the Visigoths were largely adapted from Roman forms found in the various lands they conquered. They were not an artistically creative race, and only their jewellery and metalwork reached a high level. In Spain, their churches were small and primitive, with roughly executed approximations of Roman work. Most of the survivals from this early period are found in N. Spain, probably because little survived the centuries of Muslim domination in the south. The small church (most are small) of San Juan de Baños, near Palencia, built in 616 on a basilican plan with nave arcades borne on columns with crude Corinthian capitals, is of particular interest in that the arches have the characteristic Visigothic horseshoe shape—their only artistic invention. The 7th-century Quintanilla de las Viñas, near Burgos, built of large masonry blocks without mortar, is as wide as it is long with horseshoe arches and crude reliefs, one of *Christ as the Sol Invictus upheld by angels*, and with (perhaps somewhat later) friezes of birds and tendrils on the outside. The contemporary San Pedro de la Nave has painted friezes and low-relief sculpture imitating classical forms. Iconography in the choir points towards Salvation with scenes showing Daniel, Isaac, Peter, Paul, and Thomas. San Julián de los Prados was built as a palace church some time between 812 and 842, an ambitious timber-roofed basilica with a three-bay nave and aisles and an arcade of round arches on square piers, a transept higher than the nave, and a triapsidal chevet. This shows Byzantine influence, since their churches required apses for the *Diaconicon and *prothesis to flank the main altar (Byzantine forces had established a presence in Hispania from 552 to 628). Restoration at San Julián has uncovered a rich painted decoration, clearly derived from Roman wall-paintings. Sta Maria de Naranco, of 842–50, also in the area, was once the loggia of a palace, and has a tunnel vault borne on transverse arches—the earliest example in Spain.

Following the Moorish conquest, the Visigothic rulers migrated into the unconquered part of N. Spain. The Catholic population that remained enjoyed a period of peaceful coexistence; and for the Jews, who had suffered violent persecutions, it was a deliverance. The subject populations, called 'Mozarabs' (roughly 'would-be Arabs') were taxed and made to pay tribute as 'infidels' but otherwise were left with their own laws, and secular and religious rule; but pressure for the reconquest of Spain never ceased: it became 'crusader country'. By the 9th century Arab religious persecution began, particularly in Córdoba, which caused many Mozarabs to emigrate, and by the 12th century 'convert or emigrate' was the stark choice. It was accompanied by the destruction of Christian shrines, so that Mozarabic art and architecture now only developed in the Christian north, and little survived in the Moorish cities. Monasteries forced to emigrate include those which in 904 built Sahagún, and San Miguel de la Escalada (near León) in 912/3 with horseshoe arches and classical columns in its arcades, and the use of the horseshoe shape even for chapel plans. A lone example of an early barrel-vaulted Mozarabic church is Santiago de Peñalba (founded in 919), near Ponferrada, León, where a high crossing extends upwards into an umbrella dome. Although these churches are in remote areas, they were built by men who trained in highly cultivated centres such as Toledo and Córdoba, where culture and learning in the 10th and 11th centuries were unequalled anywhere in Europe. The brilliant florescence of the Córdovan Caliphate spread northwards into Catalonia to influence, for instance, the Abbey of Ripoll (consecrated in 977), and across the Pyrenees at St-Michel-de-Cuxa (near Perpignan), founded in 878 with the church begun in 955 and consecrated in 974, where Mozarabic influence survives in horseshoe arches and ashlar pillars decorated with rope spirals.

After the 11th century Mozarabic art and architecture vanished entirely; what survived in Spain is Mudéjar ('domesticated'), a Moorish art created by Spanish Muslims who, as a result of the reconquest of parts of Spain by the Christians, adapted the forms they knew to the works required by their new masters. Córdoba was reconquered in 1236, the Great Mosque—the Mesquita—was converted into a Christian church, and a chapel added in 1258 was decorated by Mudéjar artists. Mudéjar art, because of its seven-centuries-long tradition in forms and materials, became virtually a national style, so that Romanesque and Gothic, which eventually entered the country, did so as foreign importations, mostly of French origin.

Few manuscripts of the period have survived. If it could be proved that the *Ashburnham Codex had been produced in Spain in the 7th century, then this would be the most important Visigothic MS; its vivid narrative pictures in their architectural setting, and the strong colour, show Eastern influence. The 10th-century Codex Vigilanus (Escorial) is a history of the Church Councils held in Spain between 600 and 700, and contains stylized 'portraits' of Visigothic kings as well as a self-portrait of Vigila, the scribe. The Arab conquest saw Christian intellectual life rise to new heights, influenced by the brilliance of Arabic culture and science—the first Muslim university was founded in Córdoba. *The Commentary on the Apocalypse* written *c.*776 by *Beatus of Liébana became one of the most copied MSS and versions spread widely in Spain and into France. Its Mozarabic features include strong colour, mainly reds, blues, and yellows, highly stylized figures in bands across the page (Madrid, Bib. Nacional), and in the copy in the Rylands Lib., Manchester, is a vivid vision of the Angel of the Apocalypse hovering over a splendid many-towered Arab palace set in a halo of flames, representing the destruction of Babylon. A 9th- or 10th-century copy of the *Originum seu Etymologiarum Libri*, a compendium of encyclopaedic knowledge by the greatest scholar of the age, S. Isidore of Seville, is illustrated by geometrical and astronomical figures in the usual vivid Mozarabic reds and blues (Madrid, Bib. Nacional; many MSS exist). The work was very important in the choice of subjects of French Romanesque portal sculpture.

The Frankish kingdom: Merovingian art

In Gaul, Germanic tribes of Franks from the Rhineland divided the Netherlands and N. France between them, one tribe under its King Merovech, after whom the dynasty is called Merovingian, eventually becoming the chief one. One of the greatest pilgrimage centres of Merovingian Gaul was the Church of St Martin at Tours, where the small chapel over the grave was rebuilt in 472 by Bishop Perpetuus as a great church to give access to the large number of pilgrims. In 481 Clovis became king at the age of 15. He extended his rule to both Frankish tribes, and ended Roman rule in Gaul by defeating the Roman governor in 486; he became a Catholic in 496, attributing his victory over the Alemanni to Christ, and made Paris his capital. In 507 he again sought a sign of divine support and finally drove the Visigoths back across the Pyrenees, killing their King Alaric II, after which he was named consul by the Byzantine Emperor Anastasius and assumed the title in St Martin's Church. But at his death in 511, his kingdom was divided, according to Frankish custom, between his four sons, who continued to expand their inheritance, until by the mid-6th century most of France had been conquered and the Frankish dominion reached as far as the middle Danube. The kingdom reverted briefly to single rule under Dagobert in 629, again foundered at his death in 638, and in 714 the Merovingians were supplanted by Pepin I and his family, who derived power from their position as 'Mayors of the Palace', and were the real controllers of the kingdom. Pepin I's grandson, Charles Martel 'the Hammer', stemmed the Muslim invasions by defeating them in 732 at the battle of Poitiers. Charles's grandson was *Charlemagne, who founded the *Carolingian dynasty.

Very little survives either of Gallo-Roman or Merovingian building. House-churches, as described in *The History of the Franks* by Gregory of Tours (I.31) had been abandoned when episcopal churches were built in major administrative centres, but since all have frequently been rebuilt in later ages, little is known of them except through excavations and a small amount of literary evidence. Here and there baptisteries have survived—at Poitiers, Auxerre, Marseilles, Aix-en Provence, and Fréjus (once a big Roman port). Marseilles and Aix-en-Provence have ambulatories. In these baptisteries, as in the Abbey crypt at Jouarre (west of Paris), Roman columns and capitals were reused.

The Abbey of *St-Denis outside Paris began as funerary chapel in a Gallo-Roman cemetery over the supposed grave of the martyr Saint Denis, a missionary bishop and first bishop of Paris, buried there in 251. Under Clovis, and it is said under the instigation of Saint Geneviève, it became a royal abbey and a Merovingian dynastic burial-place. At this time it was a very large three-aisled covered cemetery. The church was considerably enhanced by King Dagobert I in the 630s, and it was largely rebuilt by Pepin III 'the Short' after 754. The pope anointed Pepin and his sons Charles and Carloman and invested them as patricians of the Romans at St-Denis on 28 July 754. It was consecrated in 775 in the presence of Pepin's son Charlemagne. The building was based ultimately on Old St Peter's in Rome, which was the model for several churches, now lost.

Very little has survived of the sculpture and artefacts of the Merovingian period: the fine sarcophagus of the first abbess of Jouarre (d. 662) in the crypt of her abbey, carved with two rows of scallop shells and a well-cut inscription; the damaged sarcophagus of 685 which attempts a group of Christ and the Apostles, clearly in imitation of a Roman sarcophagus, but with at its head a finely carved *Christ in Majesty* with the symbols of the Evangelists, clearly based on a Byzantine original (probably an ivory); and Dagobert's bronze throne based on an antique folding chair (Paris, Cluny Mus.).

The main manuscripts of the 7th and 8th centuries are books of theology and liturgy. The most important representative Merovingian MSS are the Luxeuil Lectionary (Paris BN) of the late 7th century, and two 8th-century copies of the Gellone Sacramentary (Vatican Lib., and Paris, BN), both with zoomorphic capitals and decorative flourishes treated quite flatly, with even whole words composed of e.g. fishes and birds, and capitals composed from animals and human limbs. Even when an occasional figure appears, as in the Paris version, the figure is flat and diagrammatic and the simple colours are mostly red, with a few touches of blue and green.

presbytery The part of a cathedral or large church which is normally reserved for the clergy. It lies between the *choir and the *retrochoir, and contains the high altar. It is also called the sanctuary, and the word 'presbytery' may also be used for a priest's house.

Presentation of the Christ Child in the Temple (Purification of the Virgin, Candlemas) According to the Law of Moses a first-born male child must be circumcised on the eighth day and also presented later in the Temple to be dedicated to God and then redeemed by an offering of 5 shekels (Num. 3: 47). In many paintings of the subject Joseph is groping in his purse for the money. However, Mosaic Law also prescribes that the mother must present herself for ritual cleansing forty days after the birth (Lev. 12: 4). When 25 December was fixed as the date of Christmas it followed that the Feast of the Circumcision was on 1 January and that of the Purification on 2 February. For practical reasons it is likely that the Presentation of Jesus to the High Priest and Mary's Purification would have taken place at the same time and so it is common to find two separate actions represented in a single picture. For purification a sacrifice must be offered (Lev. 12: 6–8), 'a lamb in its first year for a burnt offering, and a young pigeon, or a turtledove, for a sin offering... If she cannot afford a sheep, she shall take two turtledoves or two pigeons...'. According to Luke (2: 21 ff.), who tells the story of the Presentation, two turtledoves or pigeons were offered; commenting on this, the **Meditationes Vitae Christi* says that they 'bought two young doves or pigeons to offer, as befits the poor'. The meditation continues with a long description of a procession and the prophecies of *Simeon and *Anna. The name Candlemas is because Simeon called Christ a light to lighten the Gentiles and several of the figures are normally shown holding candles. Mantegna's triptych (Uffizi) seems to show a confusion between the Circumcision and the *Presentation*—the High Priest holds a knife, but the Child looks more than a week old and Joseph carries a basket with two birds in it. In the background are painted reliefs of the *Sacrifice of Abraham* and *Moses with the Law* as OT *types of Christ.

The earliest representation of the Presentation is a 5th-century mosaic in Sta Maria Maggiore, Rome, and the subject is common from the 11th century. There are many 15th- and 16th-century paintings of it especially Flemish, German, and Dutch. Rembrandt's last, unfinished, painting (Stockholm, Nat. Mus.) represents the aged and almost blind Simeon holding the Child in his arms as he recognizes the Messiah.

Presentation of the Virgin in the Temple (not to be confused with the entry above) This is a non-biblical subject, derived from Apocryphal Books such as the Protevangelium of *James and the 'Gospel of the Birth of the Virgin', and repeated in the **Golden Legend*. After *Mary was born to Joachim and *S. Anne her parents dedicated her to the service of the Temple, and, when she was 3 years old, she walked unaided up fifteen steps to the point where *Zacharias, the High Priest, greeted her: 'Around the Temple there were fifteen steps, one for each of the gradual Psalms... And the Virgin, being placed upon the lowest of these steps, mounted all of them without the help of anyone, as if she had already reached the fullness of her age.' Most representations of the subject show a long flight of steps, though not always fifteen as in the fresco by Taddeo Gaddi in his cycle of the *Life of the Virgin* (1332–8: Florence, Sta Croce). As late as 1534–8 the flight of (13) steps was used by *Titian (Venice, Accad.) as a compositional device (there was a door in the way), but he also seems to have followed a variant text which gives Mary's age as 7 since she is a self-possessed little girl half-way up the steps. The same is true of *Tintoretto's more *Mannerist composition (*c.*1552: Venice, Madonna dell'Orto), although he shows the full fifteen steps. Other, rarer, subjects from her life include S. Anne teaching her to read and to sew, which would hardly have been possible had she left home at the age of 3.

The Presentation was especially popular in the East, where it seems to have originated before the 8th century—it is illustrated in the *menologion of Basil II, *c.*984—and it is one of the Twelve Great Feasts of the Orthodox Church. In the West it was established by the 14th century, but was not made a universal feast until 1585.

presepe, presepio (Ital. manger) *See* CRIB.

prie-dieu (Fr. pray God) A wooden seat combined with a kneeler, including a shelf on which a Book of Hours, a Psalter, or Prayer Book can be placed. They are frequently depicted in Books of Hours, together with a portrait of the owner kneeling on one. They also occur often in scenes of the *Annunciation. In Anglican churches a prie-dieu, known as a Litany Desk, may be situated in the central aisle, near the front of the nave, for the use of the Officiant during the recitation of the Litany from the Book of Common Prayer.

primitivism A genre of folk or folk-like paintings characterized by flattened perspective, symmetries of design, emphatic ornament, and simple delight in extraneous detail. Examples from various periods include the early Colonial American funerary limners;

the Peaceable Kingdom series of paintings by the Quaker Edward Hicks; the ex-voto and *retablos paintings in Spanish and French North America, and, in the 20th-century, work by certain African-American artists such as Horace Pippin and by Mexican painter Frida Kahlo. *See also* NORTH AMERICA.

priory A religious house ruled by a prior or prioress. In certain religious Orders, such as the Augustinians, the head of the monastery is a prior; in Benedictine houses, the prior is second in command and serves as a deputy *abbot. In the Mendicant Orders, the convent is ruled by a prior, and priories may also be smaller houses depending upon an *abbey.

Priscilla, Catacomb of, is as early as *c.*150, and the earliest Christian catacomb. It may have the earliest painting of the *Annunciation*. *See* CATACOMBS.

Prodigal Son, the The *parable of the Prodigal Son is one of a series about repentance and forgiveness. It is told in Luke (15: 11–32). A younger son asked his father for his share of his inheritance and went to a distant land, where he wasted it in riotous living. When a famine came he was reduced to hiring himself out as a swineherd and he was so hungry that he would gladly have filled himself with the husks that the pigs were eating. He decided to return to his father and beg forgiveness, asking to be treated as a servant, but his father welcomed him and killed 'the fatted calf' for a banquet. This made his elder brother jealous, complaining that he had worked for their father for years, 'yet you have never given me even a young goat so that I might celebrate with my friends'. The father replied that 'all that is mine is yours . . . this brother of yours was dead, and has come to life; he was lost and has been found'.

The earliest illustrations seem to be in an 11th-century Bible, but the story was popular in the 16th and 17th centuries, especially in the North, where the riotous living provided an excuse for brothel scenes. The so-called 'Merry Company' theme is virtually indistinguishable from the Prodigal in Calvinist Holland (G. van Honthorst, 1623, Munich), but they provide an interesting contrast with the six scenes from the whole story painted by *Murillo (*c.*1675: Beit Coll., Russborough, Co. Wicklow), where the *festivities* are demure rather than riotous.

There is a moving engraving by Dürer, of *c.*1496, showing the Prodigal kneeling in prayer at the trough, with the pigs all round him, and etchings by Rembrandt, as well as a painting of the *Prodigal's Return* (*c.*1668: Hermitage). Further examples include Christian Rohlfs' woodcut with colour (1916); also *Rouault's décor for Diaghilev's ballet *Le Fils Prodigue* (1929); and G. de Chirico (1922, Museum of Contemporary Art, Milan, Italy). Hans *Feibusch treats this subject in All Saints, Iden, Sussex (1950).

Projecta Casket A silver casket, discovered in Rome in 1793 and now in the British Museum, made for the wedding of Projecta and Secundus, *c.*380. It combines a Christian inscription—Secundus et Projecta vivatis in Chri[sto]—with pagan scenes, e.g. Venus is included as appropriate to marriage, not as an actual divinity. The lid has portraits of the couple in a wreath supported by *genii. Late Antique craftsmen were accustomed to mix metaphors in this way, e.g. on *sarcophagi.

Prophets, Major and Minor The Major Prophets are usually agreed to be *Elijah (Vg. Elias), *Isaiah, *Jeremiah, *Ezekiel (Vg. Ezechiel), and, later, *Daniel. Of these, Elijah does not have a Book of his Prophecies, but his life, deeds, and prophecies are recounted in 1 Kings 17: 1 to 2 Kings 2: 11. The other Major Prophets have books in their names. The Minor Prophets wrote the much shorter Books: Hosea (Vg. Osee), *Joel, Amos, Obadiah (Vg. Abdias), *Jonah, Micah (Vg. Michaea), Nahum, Habakkuk (Vg. Habacuc), Zephaniah (Vg. Sophonias), Haggai (Vg. Aggaeus) *Zechariah (Vg. Zacharias), and Malachi. Other OT figures have been regarded as Prophets, including Moses, David, and Solomon. Major Prophets were sometimes regarded as *types of the Four Evangelists, and Minor ones of the Twelve Apostles—even, in a stained-glass window at Chartres, by showing the Prophets carrying the Evangelists and Apostles on their backs. Sometimes they were linked with the *sibyls, the prophetesses of the pagan world 'before the Law' (*ante legem*), whereas the Prophets were part of the Mosaic Dispensation, 'under the Law' (*sub lege*). In both cases they were held to have foretold the Coming of the Messiah, or incidents in Christ's life, by far the most popular being Isaiah, who prophesied the Birth of Christ (AV, 7: 14—'Behold, a virgin shall conceive, and bear a son . . .'), and to have predicted Christ's royal ancestry

(11: 1, 10—'a shoot shall come out from the stump of Jesse, and a branch shall grow out of its roots . . .'). The first is often referred to in representations of the Annunciation and the second in *Jesse Trees, but mostly the Prophets appear as a group of old men with long beards, differentiated only by holding scrolls with key words from their prophecies. What is thought to be the earliest known representation of a prophecy is in the 2nd–3rd-century *Catacomb of Priscilla in Rome, and shows *Balaam pointing to the star—but Balaam is not normally counted as a Prophet. There are certainly representations of Prophets in the 5th-century mosaics of Ravenna (Orthodox Baptistery and San Vitale) associated with the figure of Christ Pantocrator, and they were common in the Middle Ages on church *portals—French cathedrals have 'Kings', stately figures usually serving as Prophets, but the earliest attempts to characterize them individually are probably Sluter's *Well of Moses* (*c*.1400: Champmol, Dijon), followed by the figures by *Donatello (Florence, Cath. Mus.) which have unfortunately been switched, thus confusing their identities. The combination with the sibyls was popular in the Renaissance, because of the fascination of the Renaissance with the ancient world. Perugino's frescoes in Perugia, Pintoricchio's in the Vatican (Appartamento Borgia), and above all *Michelangelo's in the *Sistine Chapel, are the best-known examples.

proskynesis (Gk. veneration, reverence) This word has two meanings. During the *Iconoclastic Controversy it was decided that worship (*latria*) is due to God alone, but a degree of veneration may be paid to people or even things—the Blessed Virgin, saints, icons, relics. By extension, *Proskynesis* describes the act of veneration shown e.g. in an *Adoration of the Magi*, where one of the Magi kneels and kisses the foot of the Child, or even of a donor at the feet of his patron saint: a major example is the mosaic of the Byzantine Emperor Basil I at the feet of Christ *Pantocrator (869/70: Hagia *Sophia, Istanbul). Similar, later, representations of rulers occur in the West. The angels adoring Christ Pantocrator in the dome mosaics of the Martorana, Palermo, *c*.1143–51, are performing a difficult act of *proskynesis*, because of the restricted amount of space.

Protevangelium of James *See* JAMES, PROTEVANGELIUM OF.

prothesis (Gk. preparation) In the E. Orthodox Church this was originally a table for the preparation of the bread and wine for the Eucharist, similar to the *credence in the West. By extension it came to mean a niche or small chamber to the left of the sanctuary (i.e. on the opposite side to the *Diaconicon), where an elaborate preparation is made before the Elements are carried in procession to the altar. This arrangement of two small apses, on either side of the main one with the altar, is basic to the design of Byzantine churches.

Protomartyr The name given to the first martyr, i.e. *S. Stephen (Acts 7: 54–60), or the first martyr in any particular country, e.g. *S. Alban was the protomartyr of England *c*.304.

Prudence One of the Four Cardinal *Virtues, the others being Justice, Temperance, and Fortitude. Prudence is usually symbolized by the figure of a woman looking into a mirror, as in the series by *Giotto in the Arena Chapel, Padua, where she is seated at a desk. The significance of the mirror is said to be that one must 'know oneself', but the Vice of Pride is also often represented as a woman gazing into a mirror. One of the small reliefs on the Loggia dei Lanzi, Florence, 1383, shows Prudence with the mirror, and also a snake, the emblem of wisdom.

Prudentius *See* VICES AND VIRTUES.

psalter A *liturgical book containing the Psalms, in Hebrew (usually for Jewish use), Greek, or Latin. There are two types of psalter; those which have the 150 Psalms in numerical order (biblical psalter), and those in the order in which they are read in the *breviary (liturgical psalter). In the first case the 150 are identical in all versions, but vary in the numeration—thus Ps. 69 in the *Vulgate, both in Latin and in English, is Ps. 70 in the English Authorized and Revised Versions, and there are other similar variations (in this *Companion* both Vg. and AV or NRSV numbers have been given where they differ). Many psalters are illustrated, some Byzantine ones with David scenes as early as the 10th century, and some very literally, such as the *Utrecht Psalter of *c*.816/23. Many have an elaborate initial letter B at the beginning of Ps. 1 ('Beatus vir qui . . .', Blessed is the man who . . .), sometimes occupying the whole page and known as a *Beatus page. The custom of reading all the Psalms in the course of a week (or at least once a month) meant that it was convenient to have them in the order in which they are read in the breviary. From the 11th to the 14th century they were the most popular and important illuminated MSS, but were outstripped in the 14th and 15th centuries by Books of *Hours.

Pseudo-Bonaventura *See* MEDITATIONES VITAE CHRISTI.

Pseudo-Matthew, Gospel of An *Apocryphal Infancy Gospel, claiming to be by S. Matthew, but probably of the 8th/9th century, which is largely based on the Protevangelium of *James and the 'Gospel of Thomas'. It contains the first mention of the ox and the ass in the stable at the *Nativity, as well as legends concerning the Flight into *Egypt. A version of it appears in the **Golden Legend*.

Psychomachia *See* VICES AND VIRTUES.

Pugin, Augustus W. N. (1812–52), was a British architect who was the most intemperate advocate of the *Gothic Revival, which his polemics transformed from a literary and dilettantish architectural vogue into a creed which dominated English architecture for the rest of the 19th century and into the 20th. He was trained by his father, Auguste-Charles Pugin, who came to England as a refugee from Revolutionary France in 1792. Before Pugin senior died in 1832, he had begun to publish *Examples of Gothic Architecture*, and in 1833–4 his son travelled in England and Europe to continue his father's work.

In 1835 he was received into the Catholic Church. Between 1835 and 1837 he published four volumes of drawings of medieval decorative work, and in 1836 the first edition of *Contrasts; Or, a Parallel Between The Noble Edifices Of The Fourteenth and Fifteenth Centuries, And Similar Buildings Of The Present Day; Shewing The Present Decay of Taste*, which portrayed in telling and often bitter forms the differences between his idealized vision of medieval towns, churches, and institutions and the crude utilitarian forms and attitudes displayed in the 19th century. The harsh reviews, emanating mainly from Anglican circles, ensured that the edition sold like the proverbial hot cakes, and he reissued the book with modifications (none of them palliative) in 1841. From 1836 onwards he worked on Barry's competition designs for the new Houses of Parliament, and when Barry won he continued to work for the next ten years on revisions, on the detailing of the building, and on its fittings, ranging from architectural features to umbrella stands. The fame resulting from *Contrasts* brought him three important Catholic patrons: Charles Scarisbrick, for whom he made extensive alterations to Scarisbrick Hall, Lancashire (1837–45), the Earl of Shrewsbury, for whom he altered Alton Towers, Staffordshire (1837–46), and the Roman Catholic Church, beginning with Oscott College, near Birmingham, where he lectured on medieval art and designed the interior of the chapel. During his short career, Pugin designed over forty churches in England and Ireland, including four cathedrals (St Chad's, Birmingham (1839–41), St George's, Southwark in London (1840–52; altered in 1945 after bomb damage), St Barnabas, Nottingham (1841–4), and the now partly rebuilt Our Lady and St Thomas, Northampton (1844–52)), and such major works as St Mary's, Derby (1837–9), St Giles, Cheadle (1840–6), and Ramsgate Abbey (1845–52), next to his own house there. In addition to his increasing labours on the decorative details for the Houses of Parliament, he designed many more houses and churches.

In 1841 he published *The True Principles of Pointed or Christian Architecture*, which restate unexceptionable principles of design such as the subordinate role of decoration, the primacy of convenience, fitness for purpose, and respect for materials. He based his principles on the superiority of Gothic, ignoring the awkward fact that application of the same principles justified classical architecture. In 1843 he followed *Principles* with *An Apology for the Revival of Christian Architecture*, elaborating points made in earlier books, claiming that Gothic was a national, Christian, and beautiful style, and could also be economical and suited to modern materials and methods of construction. By the mid-1840s the climate of Catholicism in England had changed. The resurgence led by John Henry (later Cardinal) Newman, Frederick Faber of the London Oratory, and Bishop (later Cardinal) Wiseman promoted other architectural ideals. Pugin had been in the forefront of the Goths in the *Cambridge Camden Society, but he was disowned by them in 1846. In 1842 the *Christian Remembrancer* commented acidly 'It is utterly absurd to assert, as Mr Pugin has done, and as the Camden Society have re-echoed, that a style of architecture is exclusively Christian and Catholic which was not introduced till twelve long ages of Christianity had lapsed.' Newman maintained that the Oratory, being a Counter-Reformation Order (founded in 1564), was therefore not a medieval Order; the Birmingham Oratory is deliberately Roman and classical, and the London one by *Gribble is in a Baroque style. Pugin himself declared 'I give the whole Order up for ever'.

Pugin's enormous workload finally resulted in mental breakdown, and in 1851 he became insane. His son, Edward Welby Pugin (1834–75), built many Catholic churches, schools, and houses, and for years conducted a bitter polemic over the inadequate and grudging recognition of his father's contribution to Barry's Houses of Parliament.

pulpit and **pulpitum** These two words mean different things, although both come from *pulpitum*, Latin for a raised platform or dais. *Pulpitum* is now used to denote a stone screen in a cathedral or monastic foundation, which separates the *choir from the nave. A pulpit is an elevated structure in the nave, from which sermons are preached. In Early Christian times sermons were preached only by the bishop, from his *cathedra at the end of the church or from a throne in front of the altar. The *ambo was used solely for reading or chanting the Gospel or other parts of the liturgy, but its advantage in audibility soon led to modification in its form—taller and narrower—for use in preaching. Pulpits are not found in E. Orthodox churches, and even in the West sermons were comparatively rare and often preached out of doors (cf. *S. Bernardino), where pulpits were sometimes placed on the exterior of a church, as at Prato Cathedral (by *Donatello and Michelozzo, 1433/8), but this was for the exposition of the relic of the Madonna's girdle rather than for sermons. Early examples of pulpits designed as such include several 12th-century ones in S. Italy, and the four great works by Nicola and Giovanni *Pisano in Pisa Baptistery (1259/60), Siena Cathedral (1265–8), Pistoia, Sant'Andrea (1301), and Pisa Cathedral (1310/11).

The Franciscans, the Dominicans (called specially OP, Order of Preachers), the Reformers, and the *Jesuits attached great importance to preaching and the churches of the Mendicant Orders from the late 13th century onwards all contained pulpits, often elaborate ones, and 17th- and 18th-century pulpits became extremely elaborate, especially in Catholic countries such as the S. Netherlands, with carved wooden supporting figures and sounding-boards (e.g. Antwerp, Brussels, and Malines cathedrals, among many others).

In England in the 18th century the 'three-decker' was evolved, with the parish clerk at the bottom, the officiant reading the service in the middle, and the sermon preached from the top tier—Hogarth's engravings of the *Industrious Apprentice at Church* or *Credulity, Fanaticism and Superstition* show them in use, and a few 'three-deckers' still survive in Dissenting chapels. 'Two-deckers' are normal even nowadays in the Reformed Church. A well-designed modern example of a simple pulpit (1962) is that in St Nicholas, West Thorney, Sussex, faced with slate slabs by sculptor John Skelton.

Purbeck The Isle of Purbeck is a peninsula jutting into the English Channel between Weymouth and Poole. Quarries on the peninsula provide a dense limestone known as Purbeck marble, its colour varying from pale creamy brown to a dark green-grey. It may be very finely cut to give great detail, and will take a high polish; it was exceedingly popular with English medieval builders for tombs, and for *colonnettes, and the *capitals of large columns, often made of a different pale limestone. Among the best examples are the choir of Canterbury Cathedral, where the capitals of the large columns of Trinity Chapel and the colonnettes of the *triforium (all part of the 1175–8 rebuilding) are in Purbeck, perhaps its first appearance in a major church. A favourite device was to contrast a stone shaft with a Purbeck capital, and vice versa, or to surround a stone shaft with Purbeck colonnettes. One of the advantages of Purbeck was that the local craftsmen were very capable, so that Purbeck details could be prepared in the quarry, and carved capitals and polished shafts could be delivered ready-prepared, thus saving the transportation of large blocks of stone. This highly decorative system held no appeal for French masons.

Purgatory is a doctrine that, at death, most people are neither good enough to merit Heaven, nor bad enough to deserve Hell: it is therefore a state of purgation or purification which cannot really be represented in visual terms. The doctrine is held by both the E. Orthodox and the W. Catholic Church, but was rejected by the Reformers, especially *Calvin. The best symbol is probably that of *Limbo or *Anastasis, but the idea that prayers for the dead may relieve the pains of Purgatory, found in 2 Macc. 12: 39–46, was responsible for one very important artistic manifestation;

namely Chantry *Chapels, in which Masses were said for the repose of the souls of dead members of families or corporations such as guilds. Particularly grand examples are Henry VII's Chapel in Westminster Abbey, or *Michelangelo's Medici Chapel in San Lorenzo, Florence. Many hundreds of less elaborate examples survive in English cathedrals and parish churches.

Probably the only serious attempt to represent the idea of Purgatory is the series of drawings by *Botticelli illustrating *Dante's *Divina Commedia*, but these are illustrations to particular images in Dante, rather than an attempt to grapple with the concept itself.

Purification of the Virgin *See* PRESENTATION OF THE CHRIST CHILD.

purple In the ancient world purple was an extremely expensive dye obtained from the mollusc *Murex purpureus* and was therefore the distinguishing colour of emperors (cf. 'born to the purple'). It became the colour worn by bishops and prelates generally—cardinals came much later than bishops and are not necessarily senior to them, so they wear red, even though they are said to be 'raised to the purple'. It is also a symbol of mourning and the *liturgical colour of the penitential seasons of Lent and Advent, as well as for funerals.

Some very elaborate MSS, such as the *Vienna Genesis, were written in gold on purple vellum.

putti (Ital. little boys) Chubby little boys distinguished from *cherubim by their lack of wings. They derive from the classical Erotes and Genii found on Early Christian sarcophagi. Often putti and cherubs are combined, e.g. on the base of the tomb of Illaria del Carretto (Lucca Cath.) by Jacopo della *Quercia, in that the putti have wings.

pyx A small cylindrical box, usually of silver or gold, to contain the Reserved Sacrament (consecrated Hosts to be taken to the sick). They derive from antique cosmetic boxes, often of ivory, but, during the Middle Ages, were often made in the shape of a dove (symbol of the Holy Spirit) and suspended over the altar in place of a *ciborium. Hanging pyxes are uncommon today but are used in some Anglican churches, such as All Saints, Margaret Street, London. *See also* AUMBRY, SACRAMENT HOUSE, TABERNACLE.

Quadrivium *See* ARTS, THE LIBERAL.

quail *See* BIRDS, SYMBOLIC.

Quakers *See* FRIENDS, SOCIETY OF.

Quarant'ore (Ital. forty hours) The Forty Hours Devotion, said to mark the forty hours between Christ's death and Resurrection, began *c.*1556 in Milan and consists of a night and day vigil before the Blessed Sacrament exposed in a *monstrance on the altar, with not less than twelve lights burning around it. The monstrance and candlesticks are often very elaborate pieces of goldsmith's work.

Quarton, Enguerrand (*c.*1415–66 or later), was a French painter active in Provence *c.*1444–66. He came from the North and was influenced by Flemish artists such as Jan van *Eyck, Campin, and Roger van der *Weyden, and, in Provence, by Simone *Martini. Only three paintings are attributed to him, one of which, the *Pietà* (Louvre) is arguably the greatest French painting of the 15th century. It came from Villeneuve-lès-Avignon and was probably painted about 1455–6. What makes Quarton particularly important is that he also painted a large *Coronation of the Virgin* for Villeneuve-lès-Avignon in 1453–4, and the contract for it survives: it is very long and extremely detailed, and on many occasions it expressly provides for Master Enguerrand to use his own judgement. Comparison with the extant work shows how frequently he did so. Since it is so very rare an example of the way in which major altarpieces were commissioned and carried out, extensive quotations follow: 'On the 24th day of April [1453], Master Enguerrand Quarton, of the diocese of Laon, painter, resident in Avignon, made a contract and agreement with the said Dominus Jean de Montagnac . . . for painting an altarpiece . . . First, There should be the form of Paradise, and in that Paradise should be the Holy Trinity, and there should not be any difference between the Father and the Son; and the Holy Ghost in the form of a dove; and Our Lady in front as it will seem best to Master Enguerrand; the Holy Trinity will place the crown on the head of Our Lady. Item, The vestments should be rich; those of Our Lady should be of white damask with a design made according to the judgement of the said Master Enguerrand; and surrounding the Holy Trinity should be cherubim and seraphim. Item, At the side of Our Lady should be the Angel Gabriel with a certain number of angels, and on the other side St Michael, also with a certain number of angels, as it will seem best to Master Enguerrand . . . Item, Beside St Peter should be a martyr pope over whose head an angel holds a tiara, together with St Stephen and St Lawrence in the habits of cardinal deacons, also with other martyr saints as arranged by the said Master . . . Item, In Paradise below should be all the estates of the world arranged by the said Master Enguerrand . . . Item, After the Heavens, the world in which should be shown a part of the city of Rome. Item, On the side of the setting sun should be the form of the church of St Peter of Rome, and before the said church at an exit, one pine-cone of bronze, and from that one descends a large stairway to a large square leading to the bridge of Sant'Angelo . . . Item, Outside Rome the Tiber will be shown entering the sea, and on the sea will be a certain number of galleys and ships. Item, On the other side of the sea will be a part of Jerusalem; first, the Mount of Olives, where will be seen the Cross of Our Lord, and at the foot of that will be a praying Carthusian, and at a little distance will be the tomb of the Lord and an angel below saying: He has risen: He is not here: Behold the place where they have laid Him . . . Item, On the right part will be Purgatory . . . Item, On the left side will be Hell . . . Item, In Purgatory and Hell will be all the estates according to the judgement of said Master Enguerrand. Item, Said altarpiece shall be made in fine oil colours and the blue should be fine blue of Acre . . . and the gold that will be used . . . should be fine gold and burnished. Item, Said Master Enguerrand will show all his knowledge and skill in the Holy Trinity and in the Blessed Virgin Mary, the other parts to be done according to the dictates of his conscience.'

The unusual feature—that the Father and Son should be identical—was scrupulously carried out, and is found in a few other French paintings of the same period. It has been suggested that the arguments between Greek and Latin theologians over the clause in the Creed that the Holy Ghost 'proceeds from the Father and the Son' at the Council of *Florence a few years earlier may have been the reason for this. Another unusual feature is that the cruciform halo, normally reserved to Christ, is given to all three Persons of the Holy Trinity.

Several other contracts for altarpieces, mostly Italian, have survived, but this is perhaps the best example of the give-and-take between patron and artist in which the patron clearly recognizes that it is not possible to put in everything he would like to have, if he is to have a worthy example of the artist's skill.

quatrefoil (from Fr. *quattre feuilles*, four leaves) A pattern shape composed of four lobes, much used in window tracery. The frame round each of *Ghiberti's reliefs in his first set of Baptistery doors in Florence is a quatrefoil. *See also* trefoil.

Quattro Coronati, Santi *See* CORONATI.

Queen of Heaven *See* MARY, THE BLESSED VIRGIN.

q

Queen of Sheba *See* SHEBA.

Quercia, Jacopo della (*c*.1374/5–1438), was an Italian sculptor, born in Siena, whose earliest attributed work is a relief of *S. Agnellus* in Lucca Cathedral, of 1392. He was one of the competitors in the competition for the Baptistery Doors in Florence in 1401, together with *Donatello and *Ghiberti (who won). His competition panel is lost (those by Donatello and Ghiberti are in the Mus. Nazionale), so that his first positive work is the tomb of *Ilaria del Carretto* of 1406 (Lucca Cath.), a work of exceptional beauty. The *putti carrying garlands on the base of the tomb are one of the earliest uses of this Roman classical motive in the Renaissance. A *Madonna and Child* (1406: Ferrara Cath.) was followed by an altarpiece of the *Madonna and Child and four Saints* (*c*.1416–22: Lucca, San Frediano) with the figures, high reliefs rather than free-standing, enclosed in niches in an elaborate Gothic framework. The *Fonte Gaia* (the fountain made for the Campo, Siena, 1408–19) is now preserved in damaged state in the loggia of the Palazzo Pubblico. His part in the font in the Baptistery of Siena Cathedral was limited to one panel, *Zacharias in the Temple*, paid for in 1428–30. He had already contracted in 1425 to make a series of reliefs to decorate the main door of San Petronio, Bologna, but he was always a dilatory worker, and work dragged on while he was forced to go to Siena to finish the relief for the font. In all, there are fifteen reliefs in Bologna, ten of Old Testament subjects and five from the New and in the niche over the main door a *Virgin and Child* and a *S. Petronius*, the remains of a much larger project, which he must have abandoned when he returned to Siena in 1435. He died there three years later. The San Petronio doorway reliefs are his masterpiece, and they exercised a considerable influence on the young *Michelangelo, when he was in Bologna in 1494.

quire is an old spelling of *choir, now rarely used, but it is useful to distinguish between the east end of a church (quire) and a body of singers (choir).

quoins (from Fr. *coins*, corners) The stones at the corners of a building—these may be in a church or its tower, or a secular building—which are carefully cut ('dressed') and have an even, though sometimes an irregular inner edge so that they make a decorative feature on the corners. Stone quoins are often used where the rest of the building is of brick, or stucco, or of a markedly different stone (such as *knapped flint). The corners of Anglo-Saxon church towers (10th–11th centuries) often have alternating long and short quoins making a distinctive and distinguishing pattern, called 'long-and-short work'.

Quo vadis? (Lat. *Domine, quo vadis?* Lord, where are you going?) According to the *Apocryphal 'Acts of Peter', S. Peter, during the persecution under Nero, was persuaded to leave Rome. On the outskirts, he met Christ carrying His cross. When Peter asked where He was going, Christ replied, 'To Rome, to be crucified again', whereupon Peter returned to Rome and to his own martyrdom. The church of Domine Quo Vadis, on the Appian Way, is said to mark the spot. There is a painting of the subject by Annibale Carracci (*c*.1602: London, NG).

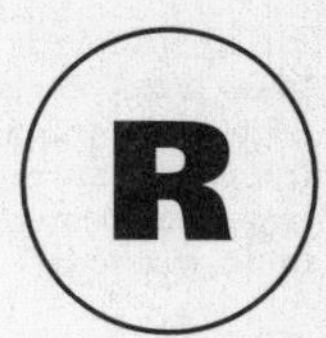

rabbit The rabbit was a symbol of timidity, but also of *luxuria*, as the result of a bad Latin pun. *Cuniculus*, coney or rabbit, and the similar sounding *cunnus*, or 'cunt', caused the rabbit to become a symbol of sexual excess. Pisanello, in a drawing of *Luxuria*, shows her lying on her long hair with a rabbit at her feet (1420/30: Vienna, Albertina). The frescoes in the Palazzo Schifanoia ('Begone dull care'), Ferrara, were painted between 1476 and 1484 and are based on a complicated programme, part astrological, part the labours, pleasures, and pastimes of the months. April, attributed to Cossa, is symbolized by Venus riding on a barge drawn by swans, and accompanied by bevies of young men and women, amorously inclined, around whom a number of rabbits gambol, suggesting that the girls are none too strict in their behaviour.

Rabbula Gospels (Florence, Bib. Laurenziana) A codex written by the monk Rabbula at the monastery of S. John at Zagba in Mesopotamia in 586. It is the earliest known Syriac MS, and the earliest to have a colophon giving the name of the scribe and a date. Its twenty-six illuminated pages, seven of them full-page, are of prime importance for the development of Christian iconography; there are also *Canon tables within arcades on which birds perch, and little marginal illustrations including the Annunciation, the Woman of Samaria, the Baptism of Christ, and the Massacre of the Innocents, as well as lively little animals. This kind of marginal illustration became a feature of later monastic books, such as psalters, and later still of Books of Hours. The full-page illustrations include a Crucifixion, with Christ in a *colobium between two thieves in loincloths, tied to their crosses, not nailed, Longinus piercing Christ's side with his lance, the man with a sponge on a reed, dicing soldiers at the foot of the cross, the Virgin and S. John on the left and three mourning women on the right. Below is the Resurrection, with two women addressed by the angel, the empty tomb in the centre with the guards lying on the ground outside, and on the right Christ appearing to the Holy Women. Thus, as early as the 6th century a complete iconographical model was established. Another important illustration is that of the Ascension, where the Virgin is, for the first time, shown in the centre of the group of Apostles, although she is not mentioned as present in any of the Gospels. This is to make the point that Christ was received into Heaven corporeally, and not symbolically or spiritually; He rose from the dead in His human nature, taken from His mother, something on which He insisted in all His appearances to the disciples after the Resurrection, by bidding Thomas put his hand in His side and in His wounded hands, and by eating in front of them. Rabbula makes the point that as, by His charge to Peter, he founded the Church, so His mother is the mother of the Church. The Rabbula Gospels are written in Syriac, from right to left, and the illustrations may reflect pictures in local churches, particularly in the depiction of Christ in the Syriac form, with short hair and beard, where the usual Byzantine form is with longish hair and beard. Christ crucified in a colobium is another example of Eastern iconography.

Rachel *See* JACOB.

Rahab *See* JOSHUA.

Rainbow, the Noah sacrificed to God when he and his family came out of the *Ark after the Flood, and God placed the rainbow in the sky as a symbol of His promise (Gen. 9: 11–17) that He would never again destroy the world because of man's wickedness. 'When the bow is in the clouds, I will see it and remember the everlasting covenant between God and . . . all . . . that is on the earth.'

Ram, the When God ordered *Abraham (Gen. 22: 1–19) to take Isaac so as to sacrifice him, Abraham obeyed, but as he was about to do so an angel stayed his hand. 'And Abraham looked up and saw a ram, caught in a thicket by its horns. Abraham ... took the ram and offered it up as a burnt offering ... ' The sacrifice of Isaac is a *type of Christ, offered on the cross, and the ram in the thicket is a type of Christ sacrificed.

Raphael *See* ANGELS.

Raphael (1483–1520), properly Raffaello Sanzio, was, with *Leonardo da Vinci and *Michelangelo, one of the creators of the High Renaissance, but was as totally unlike them as they were unlike each other. His early training in *Perugino's workshop led him to produce quiet, well-mannered altarpieces, such as the *Ansidei Madonna* (1505: London, NG), and Vasari even remarked that had Raphael's name not been on the *'Mond' Crucifixion* (*c.*1502–3: London, NG) it would be assumed to be by Perugino. But by 1504, in the *Espousal of the Virgin* (*Lo Sposalizio*) (*see* ESPOUSAL) (Milan, Brera) he had already begun to break free of Perugino's bloodless vacuity, and after he moved to Florence the influence of Leonardo's work revolutionized his vision. There followed a series of small Madonna and Child pictures which combine the intensely human emotion of a mother and child with the exploration of new ideas in composition, and achieve at the same time a very high quality as devotional images of great piety and tenderness. Examples are the *Madonna del Granduca* (1505: Florence, Pitti), and a series of versions of the Madonna and Child with the infant S. John Baptist, including the *Madonna of the Meadow* (1506: Vienna, KHM); the *Madonna of the Goldfinch* (*c.*1506: Florence, Uffizi); and the so-called *Belle Jardinière Madonna* (1507: Paris, Louvre), where the psychological rapport between the Madonna and the two Holy Children is achieved by the device of the look which is exchanged between them.

In 1509 he moved to Rome, where his great career began, to work for two popes, *Julius II and *Leo X, in the series of rooms in the Vatican known as the *Stanze (1509–14). They contain, besides the secular subjects such as the great celebration of pagan philosophy in the *School of Athens*, the *Disputa*, or Discussion on the Holy Sacrament, in the first room, and in the second one, entirely devoted to miracles in defence of the Church, are the *Mass of* *Bolsena (the affirmation of the doctrine of transubstantiation), the *Expulsion of Heliodorus* (the miraculous defence of the threatened Church), the *Liberation of S. Peter* (the miraculous salvation of the Apostle, and the most beautiful of the frescoes through the wonderful effects of moonlight, torchlight, and the glowing aureole of the angel), and the less satisfactory *Repulse of Attila* (the miraculous intervention of SS Peter and Paul in the defence of Rome by Leo I in 452). The remainder of the Stanze, and most of the rest of his work, was achieved with the help of a large number of assistants, of whom only Luca Penni and Giulio Romano were artists of any considerable quality. Despite the importance and complexity of the theological and political themes of the frescoes, no written programme has ever been found for them, although it is unlikely that so important a manifesto would have been left entirely to the artist.

Three major altarpieces are superb examples of his ability to endow his figures with grandeur and to create images of such unforgettable power that they have become virtually synonymous with the personages they represent. The *Madonna di Foligno* (1512: Vatican Mus.) and the *Sistine Madonna* (1512–13: Dresden) have become established as the ideal types of the Madonna and Child. The *Transfiguration* (*c.*1517–20: Vatican Mus.), which Raphael did not live to complete, has superseded all others as the ideal representation of the miracle. It also reintroduces the older use of *Continuous Representation, linking visually the two consecutive aspects of Divine power set out textually in the Gospels.

The tapestries designed for the lower part of the walls of the *Sistine Chapel and woven in Flanders (designed 1515–16: ten tapestries in the Vatican Mus., cartoons for seven in the Royal Collection, on loan to the V & A) were not purely workshop productions; their design and a great deal of the execution of the cartoons are by Raphael himself, though pressure of work meant that much was delegated, to Penni, according to Vasari. The long series of small pictures in the Vatican Loggie are workshop productions, mostly by Penni, but are usually known as 'Raphael's Bible'.

Raphael was the supreme creator of the devotional work, and as such has been the inspiration for many brilliant successors, and the inexhaustible spring for many who have been happy to pillage a greater man's ideas in the production of mediocrities which, in fact, often muddy the wells they draw upon. Even when appointed in 1514 to succeed *Bramante as architect of St Peter's, work for which he had little aptitude, his attitude to the task and to Bramante's imaginative conception shows that he was quite willing to sacrifice the novel use of a central plan by substituting a long-nave design which is always preferred by the clergy, since it gives more room for ceremonial. It required the uncompromising genius of Michelangelo to reinstate Bramante's grand conception.

Raphael, Sarah (1960–2001) A British artist, portraitist, and printmaker. She studied at Camberwell Art School, and her work is often informed by biblical and mythological references. Her Jewish roots contribute a grandeur of ideas to her narrative paintings, while her topographical landscapes, notably of the Cyclades island of Ios and the deserts of interior Australia, are suffused with a (possibly) religious intensity, with shadows of every stone made into marks of reverential beauty. She contributed a series of crucifixions at the behest of her father Frederic for his TV series, *After the War* (1989), her output appropriated by one of the characters based on their family friend, the artist Michael Ayrton. Raphael credits this body of work as being 'neither Christian nor sceptical'. Eschewing the temptation to describe her as an illustrator, despite the legacy of several books containing her bright jewel-like images, notably her father's *Of Gods and Men* (1992), her stylized figures leapt beyond the merely representational. Even her careful choice of titles proposed a timeless, mythic spirit to her family groups and folkloric collages: *Children Fleeing* perhaps nods to dispossession and the evacuation horrors of the Second World War. Despite numerous requests she rarely worked to the constraints of commissions, three exceptions being her portraits of the *Five contributors to the Guardian Women's Page* (1994) and *Chad Varah* (1993), founder of the Samaritans, both for the National Portrait Galley, and *Sir Garfield Sobers* for Marylebone Cricket Club's collection at Lords.

A change of medium from oil paint to acrylic was prompted partly by a greater frequency of migraines she had began to suffer and her penultimate one-woman show, *Strip!* (1998) at the Marlborough Gallery, London was purely abstract, some concepts a homage to the comic strips she loved as a child. Certain academics have proposed a link here with universal visual perceptual experiences, such as the shapes that appear when your rub your eyes too hard, 'seeing stars', prompting her choice of repetitive crowded canvases. Just before her untimely death she created a perspex cube filled with tiny rooms, created with the help of 60 children for the Millennium Dome (2000), which is now owned by the Victoria and Albert Museum and displayed in the Museum of Childhood in Bethnal Green.

SEE WEB LINKS

- The artist's novelist father, Frederic Raphael, evaluates her work.

rason A long, black gown with wide sleeves, which is the distinctive everyday garment worn by E. Orthodox clergy. A tall, black hat with a flat brim at the top called a *kamelaukion* is the usual headgear worn by priests (Russian priests wear it without the brim); monks and bishops wear it with a veil hanging to their shoulders. The name is derived from the camel-hair of which it is made. *See* CASSOCK.

rationale A medieval liturgical vestment or ornament worn on the breast by bishops. It derives from the *pallium, and may be Y-shaped, or H-shaped, or circular, with or without pendants. It is almost always richly embroidered, often with gems or pearls, and with figures and/or inscriptions. The term is also used for a large metal plaque worn round the neck on a chain, or pinned like a brooch. It ceased to be used after the early Middle Ages. It was not unlike a Jewish ephod. *See also* DURANDUS.

raven *See* BIRDS, SYMBOLIC and ELIJAH. SS Anthony Abbot and Paul the Hermit were also said to have been fed, like Elijah, by ravens.

Ravenna and its port, Classe, an estuarine harbour protected by marshes on the land side, was a N. Italian naval base under the Roman Empire. When the Eastern and Western Empires were established, with *Constantinople as the capital of the East, the Western capital was moved from Rome first to *Milan, and then, under increasing barbarian pressure, to Ravenna in 402/4, which became the most important Western outpost of Byzantine rule, and also of *Byzantine art. The Emperor Honorius (395–423) and his half-sister Galla Placidia were responsible for establishing the earliest monuments. However, the barbarians occupied the city in 476 and it was recaptured only in 493, when Theodoric the Ostrogoth, acting for the Byzantine emperor, established his own kingdom in Italy. He reigned until 526, but his rule was bitterly resented by the native Italian population because he was an *Arian heretic, the local people being orthodox Catholics. On his death he was succeeded by his daughter, Amalasuntha, until in 535, when Justinian, who had become Emperor of the East, sent Belisarius and Narses to expel the Ostrogoths from Italy, and Ravenna was established as a province governed by an *Exarch. This lasted until 602 and reinforced in Ravenna the splendour of Byzantium, which had already influenced the later works of Ostrogoth rule.

The buildings surviving from the reign of Honorius are the Cathedral, the Mausoleum of Galla Placidia, and the *Baptistery of the Orthodox. The 5th-century Cathedral (now Sant'Orso) was dedicated to the Resurrection, and was rebuilt in 1734; only the crypt and the circular 9th- and 10th-century *campanile are from earlier times. It is basilican in shape, and probably always was, with a domed crossing (1780–2); it contains the 6th-century *ambo of Bishop Agnellus, reconstructed in 1913, with reliefs of symbolic *beasts—doves, fish, peacocks, deer, lambs, etc.—and two mid-5th-century sarcophagi.

The Mausoleum of Galla Placidia, built between 380 and 450, was more likely to have been a *martyrium rather than a tomb, and only later thought to have been used for the burials of the presumed foundress (who died in Rome in 450) and members of her family. Outside, it is a small, plain brick building, possibly once attached to the now destroyed narthex of the largely rebuilt church of Sta Croce. It has four arms of equal length and a central crossing, and tiny windows 'glazed' with thin plates of alabaster. Inside, the little building is dazzling. The lower parts of the walls are covered with plaques of yellow marble, and above this all the surfaces of the barrel-vaulted arms are covered with *mosaics in excellent condition, Roman rather than Byzantine in style. In the lunette over the door is a representation of Christ as the Good *Shepherd seated amid His sheep and holding an emblematic Cross. This is said to be the last representation of the Early Christian theme of the Good Shepherd—the Saviour amid the faithful. In the lunette opposite is S. Laurence bearing a cross and a book, in the centre is a flaming gridiron, the instrument of his martyrdom, and on the left is a cupboard containing the four volumes of the Gospels. In the ends of the arms of the cross the lunettes are filled with deer drinking from the fountain of life amid acanthus scrolls (Psalm 42, Vg. 41, 'As the deer longs for flowing streams, so my soul longs for you, O God'), and doves drinking from a vase of water amid acanthus vines. The vaulting of these four arms is filled with abstract patterns, those over Christ and S. Laurence having a brilliant blue ground studded with floral and star patterns. Above the lunettes, in each of the lower parts of the crossing vault, are two figures of white-robed Apostles with, at their feet, the symbolic doves drinking from fountains. In the centre of the vault is a cross, set in a field of blue studded with the star and floral motives. The tiny building is rich in symbolism, most of the elements having more than a mere decorative purpose.

The Baptistery of the Orthodox, or of Bishop Neon, of *c.*440–50, is an octagonal tower-like brick building, its only exterior decoration being blind arcades at the top—a characteristic N. Italian Lombard detail, never found in Eastern Byzantine buildings. Inside, there are shallow niches in all the sides and the corners are marked by columns which are now embedded some three metres into the floor, which indicates by how much the ground level has altered. The mosaics which cover the dome and the lower courses of the building have been extensively restored. In the apex of the dome is the Baptism of Christ; surrounding this over-restored central roundel is a marvellous series of Apostles bearing crowns in their veiled hands, and below them a series of symbolic thrones (*Hetoimasia) and Gospels on lecterns (Rev. 5: 1), trellises and *transennae with garlands, and between them decorative elements, such as the candelabra motive derived from Syrian art, in colonnaded niches. Below this, the lunettes between the windows have rich flowing branches and garlands with peacocks (the birds of immortality, which Baptism grants to the soul) and between the windows are panels with stucco reliefs (much restored).

The Baptistery of the Arians (493/526) was built during the reign of the Arian Theodoric, and must have marked the division of the faiths through heresy. It is smaller than the Orthodox Baptistery, but similar in shape and construction. It too has a fine mosaic dome depicting the Baptism of Christ in a central roundel, less restored than the Orthodox dome, with below it a circle of Apostles bearing crowns led by SS Peter and Paul with keys and scrolls in a procession towards a throne. The Orthodox rededicated the Baptistery in 561 to Sta Maria in Cosmedin, a Greek name which refers to its elaborate decoration. Bishop Neon's basilica, built 449–52, was rebuilt in 1000–1261 and rededicated to S. Francesco.

San Giovanni Evangelista, founded by Galla Placidia in 425, was destroyed during the Second World War, but has since been rebuilt. Only the 9th/10th-century campanile is from the older building.

Sant'Apollinare Nuovo was originally built by Theodoric in 500–14, but was rededicated in its present name in 560. It is, like all the buildings of Ravenna, in brick, with a colonnaded portico or *narthex on the front, and a circular 9th-century campanile. Inside, the nave arcades are borne on twenty-four marble columns with Byzantine-type Corinthian capitals. The most striking feature of the interior is the superb mosaics; at the highest level on the left side of the nave are small panels of the Life and Passion of Christ, separated by panels with decorative motives of shells bearing a cross and two columns; on the right there are post-Resurrection scenes. These scenes of the Life of Christ are the earliest most complete surviving series, and the representations of Christ are notable for the variations in His appearance—bearded in the Passion scenes, but beardless in those after the Resurrection. The differences attest to the different sources of the imagery: the bearded Christ is derived from influence from the East, while the beardless Christ is Roman in inspiration. The next, lower, range between the windows is of single figures of prophets and saints, and the lowest range on the left side consists of a procession of twenty-two regally robed female martyr-saints carrying their crowns, issuing from the port of Classe and preceded by S. Martin and the three Magi in Phrygian dress, advancing towards the enthroned Madonna and Child with four angels. On the right side is a procession of twenty-six male martyr-saints, crowns in their hands, proceeding from Theodoric's palace and the city of Ravenna towards the enthroned Christ with four angels. Part of this decoration was made during the time of Theodoric, but all traces of the hated Arian king and his court have been removed and replaced by curtains, except for bits of an arm and some hands which survive on the columns of the palace. The two great processions of saints date from the second half of the 6th century (*c.*561) and replace whatever else had been made in Theodoric's time. The original apse and its mosaics were destroyed by an earthquake in the 8th century.

San Vitale was begun by Amalasuntha (Amalaswinta), Theodoric's daughter, and paid for, like many of Ravenna's churches, by the banker Julianus Argentarius, and is said to have cost the enormous sum of 26,000 gold *solidi*. It was dedicated in 547/8, after the end of Ostrogothic rule, by Archbishop Maximianus, who stands next to the Emperor Justinian in the two mosaics in honour of the Emperor and the Empress Theodora, which are the only parts of the mosaic decoration executed after the establishment of the Exarchate. The complex shape of the church follows the Byzantine model of SS Sergius and Bacchus in Constantinople (*see* BYZANTINE ART), but is unlike its prototype in two respects: the openings, each with two columns, between the piers which rise from the floor to support the dome, are all curved both on the ground floor and in the galleries of the upper floor, whereas in SS Sergius and Bacchus they are alternately curved and straight, and the dome, to save weight, is made not of brick but of 'chains' of earthenware jars inserted each into the next. The shape is one used for martyria, which is supported by the dedication to S. Vitale, said to have been martyred there in the 2nd century, and by the apse mosaic. The lower parts of the walls are covered with plaques of variegated marble, and the floor (several times raised) is inlaid with marble. The complex capitals, with carved imposts and deeply undercut carving of the capital itself, are of the type used in Constantinople and unlike those in the other Ravennate churches, being richer, more complex than those in Sant'Apollinare Nuovo.

The mosaics which cover the upper parts of the walls are among the most splendid examples of the art of the early 6th century. The presbytery is flanked by two chapels, doubling as martyria and *pastophoria, one of the earliest appearances of apsidally ended side chapels. The semi-dome of the main apse contains a mosaic of Christ enthroned on the globe of the Universe flanked by two angels, with the four *Rivers of Paradise issuing from beneath the globe. He gives the crown of martyrdom to S. Vitale on the left, while the earlier Bishop Ecclesius on the right presents the church. On the side walls are the two later (mid-6th-century) mosaics of the Emperor Justinian and his court on the left, and the Empress Theodora and her court on the right, both making offerings. These images symbolize the change of rule; neither Emperor nor Empress ever visited Ravenna, and they are in a very different style from the earlier apse mosaic, more eastern, more hieratic than the Roman beardless Christ of the main apse. In the lunettes over the columns on either side of the presbytery are, on the left,

Abraham and the three angels, and the Sacrifice of Isaac; and on the right, the Sacrifices of Abel and Melchisedek. The lunette with Abraham is flanked by the prophets Jeremiah and Moses receiving the Law, and the lunette with Abel and Melchisedek is flanked by Moses feeding Jethro's sheep, and taking off his sandal amid multiple burning bushes—all symbolic OT prefigurations of Christ and the Virgin Birth—and Isaiah. Over both lunettes are angels holding roundels with the cross, a Christianized form of the winged Genii common on classical triumphal arches. The upper storey has mosaics of the four Evangelists and their symbols. In the apex of the vault is a roundel with the Sacrificial Lamb, supported by four angels. There are also decorative motives and details such as birds feeding from baskets of fruit, doves drinking from vases, vines heavy with grapes—all subjects rich in symbolism, justifying the words of the 9th-century chronicler Agnellus: 'Nowhere in Italy is there a church like it as a building or in manner of construction.'

Sant'Apollinare in Classe was built between 532 and 536 by Julianus Argentarius, but was consecrated in 549 after the establishment of the Exarchate by Archbishop Maximianus. It is a typical N. Italian basilica, with a narthex, nave, two aisles with an arcade borne on columns with Byzantine capitals of a type similar to those in Sant'Apollinare Nuovo, an open wooden roof, and an apsidal east end. The circular campanile is 10th century. The church has been heavily restored, the narthex and all the nave mosaics being modern. The marble plaques which once covered the interior were removed by the town's overlord Sigismondo Malatesta in 1449 for the decoration of the Tempio Malatestiana in Rimini. Inside, the small central altar (restored in the 18th cent.) is the one erected by Maximianus, and several of the 6th-century sarcophagi in the aisles have reliefs of doves, peacocks, vines, crosses, sheep, palms—all imagery of the Resurrection and Paradise.

The apse, with steps to allow for the insertion in the 9th century of a crypt beneath it, has magnificent mosaics begun during the Visigothic period: in the upper part of the semi-dome is the Transfiguration, symbolized by a Latin Cross on a star-studded blue field, flanked by half-length figures of Moses and Elijah, and with the Hand of God blessing (*see* DEXTERA DOMINI), on a gold ground flecked with small clouds. Beneath this are the three Apostles, Peter, James, and John, who were present, represented by three sheep. In the lowest part of the apse, in the centre of a flowery meadow—Paradise—stands S. Apollinare in prayer, wearing a bishop's vestments, with six sheep on either side representing the faithful. Above the semi-dome is a roundel with Christ blessing, flanked by the *Evangelist Symbols, and on either side of the apse are representations of Jerusalem and Bethlehem from which issue twelve sheep symbolizing the Apostles. In the remaining narrow spaces below are the palms of martyrdom. The mosaics above and around the apse are probably 7th to 10th century, but the four figures of the early bishops between the windows are part of the earlier Arian work. The small remaining sections of wall on either side have 7th-century representations of, on the right, the Sacrifices of Abel, Melchisedek, and Abraham, and on the left, the Emperor Constantine IV and his brothers granting privileges to the Church in Ravenna. The heads of these figures were later altered. On the return wall of the apse on either side are figures of the Archangels Michael and Gabriel, with below them half-length figures of the Evangelists Matthew and Luke.

The Archbishop's palace, built in the 5th and 6th centuries, has been much reworked, so that little remains of its antique splendour. The museum contains the 6th-century ivory throne of Bishop *Maximianus, made probably in Constantinople and the finest surviving example of its kind. It is said to have been given in 1001 by the Doge of Venice to the Emperor Otto III, who restored it to Ravenna. The Chapel of St Peter Chrysologus (also called the Oratory of St Andrew) was built by Peter II, Bishop from 491 to 519, whose monogram is in the mosaics. It is a Greek *cross-in-square building with a semicircular apse and semi-dome, built like the domes of San Vitale and the Baptistery with terracotta tubes. The walls are covered with marble plaques and in the vaults are fine 6th-century mosaics, the crossing vaults with four angels supporting a roundel with Christ's monogram, and with other roundels with the Symbols of the Evangelists. Many have been heavily restored. The chapel is preceded by a rectangular antechapel with barrel-vaulting covered with mosaics of lilies and birds on a gold ground. In the lunette over the door is a mosaic with the rare image of *Christ as a Roman Soldier*, standing on the lion and serpent of evil, young, beardless, with shoulder-length hair, wearing a tunic and breastplate. Instead of a sword He holds an open book with the words *Ego sum via veritas et vita* (I am the way, the truth, and the life [John 14: 6]).

In spite of the restorations, Ravenna remains one of the most important monuments of early Church art, and one of the finest examples of Byzantine art in Italy.

Rebecca *See* ISAAC.

Recollects are a branch of the *Franciscan Order, dedicated to the rule of poverty, to detachment from the world, and prayerful recollection of God. After three centuries of dissension over the interpretation of the rule of poverty, and the separation of the friars of the Observance from the Conventuals in 1517, they established themselves in France in 1597 and were called Recollects. They were suppressed at the French Revolution, but after re-establishing themselves in France they were grouped in 1897 with other Observants as Friars Minor. Other branches of the Franciscans who follow the strict observance are Capuchins and *Minims.

red *See* LITURGICAL COLOURS.

red hat *See* HAT.

Red Sea *See* MOSES.

refectory, the This is the area in any monastery, convent, school, or other establishment housing many people, where they eat in common. In Cistercian monasteries, which have the best organized plan (in that the design of Cistercian houses was almost always the same no matter where it was built), the refectory gave off the cloister, with the long trough for washing in the same arm of the cloister. The kitchens adjoined one end of the refectory, and above it was the dormitory. It was customary for there to be a reading desk or pulpit on one side, for an edifying reading to be given during meals. If the walls had paintings, as they often did in Italy, the normal subjects were the *Last Supper*, or the *Feast in the house of Levi*, the latter particularly favoured in Venice.

Reformation, the The Reformation started, not with the intention of breaking completely with Rome, but with—as its name implies—reforming the government of the papacy and correcting its abuses. *Luther, with whom the movement began and who was its driving force, moved from opposition to a form of papal fund-raising to an eventual total break on doctrinal grounds. The spark which started the blaze was the decision of Pope Leo X to have a campaign in Germany for the sale of indulgences to raise money for the building of the new *St Peter's in Rome. Similar campaigns had already met with much opposition because the people believed that the often considerable sums raised were not used for the promised purposes, drained local religious foundations of money, and were used to keep the papal court in luxury. Luther's violent opposition stemmed from his objections to indulgences because of what he held to be their equivocal character, and from his experience of Rome in 1510, when he was shocked by the laxity and worldly luxury of the life of Roman clergy. The result was the nailing of the ninety-five Theses to the castle church door of Wittenberg in 1517. The outcome was explosive. He slowly moved from the reform of abuses through the stages of the rejection of papal and episcopal authority, and the abolition of monasteries, to the doctrinal changes of justification by faith alone, and the rejection of all sacraments except Baptism and the Eucharist. Luther's reforms became popular with the German princes, since they justified their taking entire control of what had hitherto been the powers of the Church in their territories, the cessation of all subsidies to Rome, and the appropriation of monastic land. Their lead was followed by many of the Free Cities of Germany, and the kings of Denmark and Sweden. When one of the results was a popular uprising, Luther was appalled by the terrible excesses of the burning and looting of churches and monasteries, and he sided with the princes in the horrible Peasants War which followed. This cost him a great deal of his popularity, but ensured him the essential support of the rulers. The Lutheran 'Augsburg Confession' of 1530 was presented to the Emperor Charles V in an attempt to achieve a settlement between the Catholic and Protestant parts of his domains, but was rejected, and after the two sides had failed to find any agreement, a further effort was made in 1548, and a partial compromise was reached between the Catholic and Protestant parts of the empire. The princes and the Free Cities were finally left to control their own religious affairs, though this left a further internal conflict between the Lutheran and Calvinist areas.

In Switzerland, *Zwingli, who held beliefs similar to Luther's, gained in 1523–4 the support of the civic authorities of Zurich for a series of anti-papal and anti-monastic moves, and these changes were adopted rapidly in most N. Swiss cantons and parts of SW Germany. War ensued with the Catholic cantons, and in 1531 Zwingli was killed in battle. Leadership of the Reformation in Switzerland moved to Geneva, where in 1536 *Calvin succeeded in bringing in a theocratic rule of a more doctrinal and revolutionary character. A short exile because of clashes with the more powerful city of Berne was followed by Calvin's return to Geneva in 1541. His rule was then absolute and all citizens were required to make a profession of faith, refusal being punished by exile, and active opposition by draconian methods. Calvinism became the religion of Scotland, and flourished also in France among the Huguenots, and in Holland Calvinism inspired the bitter but eventually successful struggle against the Spanish domination of the Netherlands.

In England, the anomalous position of the crown made for a very different attitude towards reformers. Henry VIII had begun by being a vigorous opponent of Luther, but the long-lasting difficulties with Rome over his divorce from Catherine of Aragon, and the eventual failure in what was called 'the King's matter', soured his relations with Rome. These difficulties made him receptive to ideas that meant, in fact, that he could extend monarchical control in the kingdom by eliminating papal authority, achieve thereby his need for divorce, and, by dissolving the monasteries, acquire at the same stroke enormous riches and huge amounts of land. The Reformation therefore had a distinctly secular quality, though the religious ideas which had swept across the Continent were well supported in England. In 1531 Henry was declared to be the 'protector and only supreme head of the Church and clergy in England', and despite the hesitation of the clergy, they finally accepted the clause. Cranmer became Archbishop of Canterbury in 1532, and all the bishops of the realm accepted Henry as the head of the Church and abjured the papacy, except John Fisher, Bishop of Rochester, who paid for this by being beheaded for treason in 1535, and was followed to the block by the Chancellor, Sir Thomas More. The death of Henry VIII, and the brief reign of Edward VI, was followed by the accession of Mary, daughter of Catherine of Aragon, who immediately undid as many of her father's acts as she could. With some violent suppression of Protestant reformers, she restored Catholic worship and papal supremacy, but died five years later. The reign of Elizabeth began the Protestant restoration, and in 1559 the Acts of Supremacy and Uniformity were passed. The first made her 'supreme governor' in all spiritual, ecclesiastical, and temporal causes, and the second re-established the use of the English Prayer Book of Edward VI, a modified version of the one originally compiled by and under the aegis of Thomas Cranmer and which, with substantial revision in 1662 and some later modifications is still the Book of Common Prayer of the Church of England. It contains much pre-Reformation material, especially from the Sarum Missal that Henry VIII had made mandatory for the English Church as part of his programme of centralization. There followed prolonged and violent persecution of Catholics, exacerbated by plots inspired by support for the imprisoned Catholic Mary, Queen of Scots, and bedevilled by violent measures in the staunchly Catholic Ireland. Eventually executions died out, and the threat of Calvinist rigour, made real by the Cromwellian victory in the Civil War of 1642–9, was removed at the restoration of Charles II, but most of the disabilities attendant upon being a Roman Catholic remained until 1829 when the Act of Emancipation was passed. As an ultimate result of the Reformation no European Christian country now professes publicly any form of religious discrimination.

The Reformation had a very powerful effect on the arts. In countries in which the new forms of worship became the rule, churches were stripped of their pictures and statues, and where sculpture was part of the structure it was often defaced or broken. Secondary altars being forbidden, they were either broken up or taken out and burnt or buried. Vestments, carved choir stalls and confessionals, illuminated missals, choir books and antiphonals, were added to the bonfires fuelled by the works of art, and where it was impossible to remove wall-paintings, they were whitewashed over. Many stained-glass windows were smashed. But, especially in more remote areas of the countryside, Catholic practices and church furnishings sometimes survived. For some English churches the 18th century proved more destructive than the years of the Reformation; Salisbury Cathedral kept its medieval stained glass until 1793.

In the early years of the Reformation, up to the late 16th century, large numbers of polemical caricatures were produced, often of an obscene character, of—according to which side was favoured—the pope or Luther, and when the *Counter-Reformation got under way, art was propagandist rather than controversial. Religious painting became a matter of private patronage and no artist in any of the Protestant areas who had any care for his livelihood or even his life could paint a picture of the Virgin Mary except in the most humble and domestic setting—as Rembrandt did in a number of his most beautiful small works, which might, except for a sudden blaze of light enveloping the figures, have been any cottager with a small child.

Only where a now reformed faith was in charge of very grandiose buildings, as happened in England with the cathedrals, did some of the art survive because in many cases removing it was virtually impossible without causing grave damage. Thus the stalls of the Lady Chapel of Ely Cathedral survived the Reformation, but fell victim to the urge to destroy which animated the more ardent soul of the Parliamentarian who systematically beheaded every figure in the delicate carvings round the nodding arches over the stalls. The destruction of the shrine of S. Thomas Becket in Canterbury Cathedral produced twenty-four cartloads of treasure, much of it superb works of medieval goldsmithy, melted down for Henry VIII's treasury.

The Revolution of 1789 in France produced similar depredations for political reasons fuelled by anticlericalism so that works of art paid the price for social and political wrongs, and innumerable figures in magnificent sculptured portals now have 19th-century heads, and some were almost totally destroyed. Reliquaries, gold altar furnishings, and ciboria were also consigned to the melting-pot. A by-product of what may be called the death of religious painting for churches is that subjects drawn from the OT were commissioned by private people for their houses, and genre, landscape, still life, and in the Netherlands, marine subjects and, of course, the inevitable portraits, became the artists' staple. Two subjects that, if not popular, at least have a covert religious content are the *Vanitas still-life, and the simple still life of a goblet of red wine, a water jug, and a loaf on a plate, with perhaps a few adjuncts of the Vanitas type—an hourglass, a book, some oysters, or an unstrung violin. In England, religious painting revived during the late 18th and early 19th century, but not to any great extent; religious sculpture was usually confined to funeral monuments. A renaissance in English religious art began with the Catholic revival in the Church of England and the work of the Pre-Raphaelites and the Arts and Crafts Movement, and further flourished in the 20th century.

In architecture, the Reformation resulted in few churches being actually destroyed; it was sufficient to denude them (in some cases) of their Catholic ornamentation, or to tone it down, and to insert a pulpit in a prominent position. Where new ones were built, as in the Netherlands, a *central plan was favoured, and churches became auditoria, in that their main emphasis was on the pulpit rather than the altar, as for example at *Charenton. In his rebuilding of the churches of London after the Great Fire, *Wren based many of his City churches on the central plan, and his High Church beliefs ensured that most were adorned by a splendid carved *reredos. *St Paul's Cathedral, too, has very fine carving; he disapproved of the painting of the inside of the dome, though it may be doubted if this was purely for religious reasons. *See also* COUNTER-REFORMATION, and TRENT, COUNCIL OF.

Regina Coeli (Mary, Queen of Heaven) is an anthem in honour of the Virgin, sung during the Easter season. A charming legend is attached to it: in the last year of the pontificate of Pelagius II a terrible flood in 590 left Rome in the grip of bubonic plague, and Gregory the Great, who had just been elected, ordered an image of the Virgin to be carried in procession. When the crowds reached the bridge across the Tiber near Hadrian's mausoleum angels were heard singing the anthem, and the pope made the response, 'Pray for us, Lord, Alleluia'. The angel of death was seen on the top of Hadrian's tomb sheathing his sword, and ever since it has been called the Castel Sant'Angelo, and on its summit stands a bronze statue of the Archangel Michael. *See* CORONATION.

Reichenau is a small peninsula, whose links with the larger peninsula of Constance are so exiguous as to make it virtually an island. It is famous for three sites, Unterzell, Mittelzell, and Oberzell, which were Benedictine monasteries with important scriptoria, and Carolingian wall-paintings. Many of the MSS are now in Karlsruhe. *See* ROMANESQUE.

relics, reliquary Reliquaries are receptacles in which relics are kept. A relic may be the body of a saint, or part of it, clothing or any object connected with the saint, or it may be an object venerable in itself, the commonest examples being fragments of the True Cross. The instinct to keep a relic of a loved or revered person is universal. Jews hold that contact with dead bodies render a man ritually unclean, so relics were not kept, but pagans in antiquity preserved relics. Christians—as early as S. Ignatius, Bishop of Antioch, who was thrown to the lions in the Colosseum in 107, or S. Polycarp, Bishop of Smyrna, who was martyred at the age of 86 and his body burnt—gathered what could be found of the remains of martyrs and regarded them as 'more precious than jewels'. The Church honours the relics of martyrs because their deaths witness to faith, and in the *catacombs Mass was said over the tombs of martyrs. In the 5th century the veneration of relics was attacked by Vigilantius, an Aquitainian priest, and defended somewhat intemperately by *S. Jerome, arguing that martyrs' relics are honoured for Him for Whom they died. The 2nd Council of Nicaea in 787 anathematized those who rejected relics, and ordered that no church should be consecrated without them. During the Middle Ages the desire to possess a relic reached fever-pitch and they were accordingly manufactured to meet the demand. The 4th Lateran Council, 1215, in an effort to curb the proliferation of bogus relics, forbade any not authenticated by a bishop, or their exhibition outside the receptacles in which they were kept. The Council of Trent forbade the sale of relics, and excommunicated sellers of bogus relics. Belief in the authenticity of relics is a matter of choice.

The earliest surviving reliquaries are probably the silver *ampullae (Monza Cath. and San Columban, Bobbio), given to Queen Theodolinda of the Lombards by Pope Gregory the Great *c*.600, and a small box (Vatican, Mus. Sacro) painted with scenes from the Life of Christ in which a pilgrim put stones, earth, and pieces of cloth that he had collected during his journey to the Holy Land, though these are not so much relics as evidence of his piety. The importance attached to relics is attested by the 6th-century Byzantine ivory (Trier Cath.), depicting the translation of a reliquary carried in procession to its new home, attended by many clerics and with crowds filling every vantage-point.

Relics of Christ, the Virgin, the Baptist, and Apostles are often claimed. For instance Trier (Cath.) and the parish church of Argenteuil, near Paris, both claim to have Christ's seamless garment for which the soldiers cast lots. Both are 12th-century traditions. It is claimed that the Holy *Shroud of Turin is Christ's winding-sheet, but recent scientific tests date it no earlier than the 14th century.

Many reliquaries were made to contain fragments of the True Cross, notably the magnificent enamel, silver-gilt, and jewelled one in Limburg-an-der-Lahn, datable 964/5. The Ste-Chapelle in Paris was built by S. Louis, King of France, in 1243–8, to house a reliquary (destroyed in the French Revolution) for a thorn from the Crown of Thorns.

Relics of the Virgin include the Holy House of *Loreto, claimed to be the house in which the Annunciation took place. The cathedral at Prato, near Florence, claims to have the girdle which the Virgin is said to have thrown down to S. Thomas at her *Assumption, and which appears to have been brought to Prato during the 13th century. Perugia Cathedral claims to have the Virgin's wedding-ring. Santiago de Compostela is claimed as the final resting-place of the Apostle *S. James the Great, but the tradition is not earlier than the 11th century, though it became one of the major *pilgrimage churches, as did Vézelay when the legend of S. Mary *Magdalene became popular and they claimed to have her relics. So do several other places.

Reliquaries come in various forms. Caskets, portable altars, which often doubled as reliquaries, and burse-shaped ones, are usual from the 8th century onwards. Reliquary crosses are less common, the most important being the enamelled cross of 817–24 from the Lateran Sancta Sanctorum (Vatican, Mus. Sacro). Amulets are rare, the principal survival being Charlemagne's of the late 8th century, now in Reims Cathedral. Reliquaries were made in the form of busts, heads, or arms, including one of S. Lawrence (now in Berlin: Staat. Mus.) and of one of the Apostles (now in Cleveland, Mus., though whose arm is uncertain). A richly enamelled reliquary of 977/93 shaped like a large nail, and made to contain a nail which is claimed to have been one used in the Crucifixion, is in Trier Cathedral, and a large staff, richly jewelled, of 988, at Limburg-an-der-Lahn, is claimed to enclose S. Peter's staff, while the great Cathedra Petri in the apse of St Peter's is claimed to contain S. Peter's chair.

Conques in the south of France was one of the major pilgrimage churches and has a notable treasure, which fortunately survived the Revolution during which so many priceless objects were lost. A 'lantern' reliquary of S. Vincent, of *c*.860, its shape based on a classical Roman tomb, has a clear glass centre in which the relic could be exposed, but the most important reliquary is the cult image of S. Foi, a full-length seated figure of a 3rd(?)-century 12-year old girl martyr, a piece of whose skull is enclosed in the back of the figure. Her head is a remarkable 5th-century Roman parade helmet with enamelled eyes inserted, and the figure is encrusted with jewels. Her cult was extraordinarily widespread; there is a chapel dedicated to her in Westminster Abbey, and a stained-glass window in Winchester Cathedral, and cities called Santa Fe are said to be named after her, though more probably with the meaning of the words 'Holy Faith' in its Christian sense, since all the cities so named were originally Spanish. From the 11th century onwards, the usual shapes of reliquaries were as house-shrines, that is, a shrine made in the form of a small church with a very rich sculpture. In French, these are often called *châsses*. The most famous are those of S. John the Baptist and S. Pelagius of 1059, and S. Isidoro of 1063, both in Sant'Isidoro, León, given by King Fernando and Queen Sancha; S. Godehard, of *c.*1132, at St Michael, Hildesheim; S. Heribert, of 1150/60, in Cologne-Deutz; and the most famous northern one of all, the Shrine of the Three Kings (Cologne Cath.) and others by *Nicholas of Verdun. The most famous painted reliquary is the shrine of S. Ursula (1489: Bruges, Mus.) by *Memlinc. Tower reliquaries were also popular e.g. the shrine of S. Mary (*c.*1205: Tournai); a variant form is the domed church shrine, such as the Hochelton Reliquary (*c.*1170: London, V & A), and a similar one in Berlin (Mus.), in silver-gilt with engraving and enamels on the 'structure' of the centrally planned church, and walrus ivory figures round the 'dome' and the 'walls' of the church.

Very large and rich reliquaries were commissioned in 1347 from the Sienese goldsmith Ugolino di Vieri by the cathedral of Orvieto, one to contain the corporal of the miracle of *Bolsena, and the other for the relics of S. Savino; both are still in Orvieto, but the number of grand reliquaries which survive in Italy is small compared with the number known to have existed.

The great age of reliquaries was the 10th to the 14th centuries. After that their number and value—and variety—diminishes. The great enemy of their survival is their very considerable value, as booty, and even more often, changes of fashion.

Religious Orders *See* ORDERS.

Rembrandt van Rijn (1606–69) was the greatest religious painter in the Protestant tradition. In his early years, though working successfully as a portrait painter, he also painted religious subjects—a group of Passion scenes which were bought by Prince Henry of Orange (1633–9: Munich) and various OT scenes treated in an exuberantly Baroque manner, e.g. the *Belshazzar's Feast* (*c.*1635: London, NG), or the horrific *Blinding of Samson* (1636: Frankfurt). Some of his early etchings also combine Baroque drama and his concern for strong effects of light—e.g. the *Raising of Lazarus* (*c.*1632) or the etched version of his *Descent from the Cross* (1633). His most famous and most acclaimed etching is probably the *Christ healing the sick* (1639–49: the 'Hundred Guilder Print') which he continued to work on for many years, as he did on the *Three Crosses* (1653–60), of which several Print Rooms have varying versions.

In the later years of his life, after the disasters of the death of his wife Saskia in 1642, his bankruptcy in 1656, and the ostracism meted out to Hendrickje Stoffels, who lived with him and brought up his sole surviving child Titus, he painted and etched religious works with a quieter, deeper feeling, creating a Protestant iconography, suited to a society which rejected religious painting in churches, and traditional Catholic religious iconography. Such subjects, for instance, as *Peter denying Christ* (1660: Amsterdam, Rijksm.) or the *Prodigal Son* (late 1660s: Leningrad), though well within the canon of Catholic subject-matter, are given a new humanity and depth of feeling, while his Virgin and Child subjects and Nativities are consistently unhieratic and adapted straight from the type of simple domestic genre subjects (*Nativity*, 1646, London, NG; and *Holy Family with Angels*, 1645, Leningrad). His new treatment of old themes is not so much secularization as making a story from the OT or the Gospels new and vividly memorable; for instance, in *The Risen Christ appearing to the Magdalene* (1638: Royal Coll.) where instead of a vision of Christ in Glory after the Resurrection He is seen in an accurate transcription of the words of S. John's Gospel (21: 14–17), where Mary Magdalene at the empty tomb turns and finds Christ standing behind her, and blinded by her anguished tears believes Him to be the gardener. There are rarely haloes or aureoles in Rembrandt's religious works; if there is any such stress on the figure of the Virgin or Christ it is achieved by what might well be no more than an 'accidental' lighting effect, as in the striking *Christ at Emmaus* (1648: Louvre, and Copenhagen). Only in a few etchings is this rule broken, notably in the 'Hundred Guilder Print' and in the *Christ preaching* (*c.*1652). Certain subjects, which could be considered particularly Catholic, such as the martyrdoms or visions of saints, are totally absent. The subjects he chose are nearly always biblical and adhere strictly to the text. His genius lay in investing them with new and powerful meaning.

RENAISSANCE

(Fr., and Ital. *Rinascimento*, rebirth) The *Oxford English Dictionary* defines it as 'the revival of art and letters under the influence of classical models in the 14th to the 16th century'. First applied in 19th-century art theory, the term was used to convey the conscious 'rediscovery' of antiquity through a vigorous and creative reinterpretation of classical literature and art. The term is also used more generally to denote those periods in European history when there was an attempt to return to the spirit of classical antiquity, and to study its cultural and intellectual legacy. This can be seen, for example, in the Carolingian *renovatio* (9th century), when the Palatine court of Charlemagne at Aachen became a centre for classical learning, and later in Medieval France with the establishment of cathedral schools (most famously at Chartres) seeking in various ways to assimilate classical philosophy, mathematics, and geometry with theological thought and Christian cosmological principles. In these examples, however, the plural term 'Renascences' has been used to distinguish them from the Renaissance of the 15th and 16th centuries, thereby underlining their significance as 'intermediary' phases in which classical antiquity was never systematically rediscovered and interpreted (Panofsky).

In Italy, unlike in other parts of Europe, the classical past continued to exert a powerful influence throughout the Middle Ages, on account of its more visible legacy and the prevalence of its greater continuity of classical culture in literature and the visual arts. From a regional perspective, this continuity is most clearly evident in Tuscany, during the 11th and 12th centuries, where a particular form of Romanesque style emerged that was much truer to its classical predecessor, with its more conscious use of classical elements such as columned screens in polychrome marble. Exemplified in the church of S. Miniato al Monte, this Tuscan Romanesque has even been described as a 'proto-Renaissance' building.

The Renaissance in Italy can be divided into two distinct periods: the Early Renaissance and the brief but highly productive period of the High Renaissance. The dates of each period have been fiercely debated by historians, but here the assumption is made that the Early Renaissance began fully at the opening of the 15th century and lasted until its end, while the High Renaissance proper occurs during the first two decades of the 16th century.

As indicated in the definition of the term in the OED, the early manifestations of Renaissance art can be found before the 15th century, most notably in the paintings of *Giotto and the Lorenzetti, with their evidence of a new perspective rendering of space not previously found in the Middle Ages (Edgerton). While preceding the establishment of a formal theory of perspective (*perspectiva artificialis*) in the 15th century, the work of Giotto (in particular) exemplifies a mode of representation that gave a new sense of drama and individual emotion to figures.

The importance of Giotto in the early development of Renaissance painting was already recognized by *Vasari in his *Vite* (1550), where the author uses the Italian term *rinascita* (meaning 'rebirth') to explain a form of art that was modelled more on nature.

For Vasari, the Renaissance was a uniquely Italian phenomenon (or more specifically one rooted in Tuscany), and only later, and rather haphazardly did it extend its influence to northern Europe—to France, the Netherlands, and parts of Germany. This assertion was closely allied to a view, cultivated by Humanists in the early 16th century, that Italian art and culture were superior to the rest of Europe, a claim that was to underpin an emerging proto-nationalist sentiment in some regions of Italy—or 'Italianità' (Ilardi).

The idea of Italy as the 'bearer' of the classical tradition is underlined by the association of the term 'Gothic' with the Dark Ages, when savage and uncivilized barbarians north of the Alps laid waste to parts of Italy. This derogatory term explains the status of *Gothic architecture (or what Vasari calls *maniera tedesca*) as an inferior style to its classical counterpart; indeed that the demise of the former was necessary for the success of the latter, through its Renaissance reformulation. In a letter to Pope Leo X, Raphael (or a member of his circle) identifies among the architectural styles that of the Goths ('*Gotti*'), a form of architecture which he characterizes as '*goffa*' (from which our modern pejorative term 'goofy' derives), to distinguish it from '*la maniera cosi bella*' of the age of the emperors.

Running parallel with the artistic developments of the Renaissance, from the 14th century, was the emergence of Humanist thought that is chiefly credited with the rediscovery of ancient literature (Greek and Latin), but a form of scholarship that was not merely a revival. It signalled a decisive change from Medieval Scholasticism by emphasizing man's central place in the universe, his free will, and ultimately his superiority over nature. These qualities, which were drawn directly from ancient literary sources and inspired more by Aristotle than by Plato, provided Humanists with a model of how man could seek answers to questions of goodness and truth.

The dissemination of Humanist principles throughout the Renaissance was facilitated by the use of a specific form of Latin (called 'Ciceronian') as a universal language that consciously differentiated itself from the 'impure' or corrupted Latin used in medieval cathedral schools and monasteries.

The new insight into ancient textual sources could be said to underpin many of the artistic and architectural initiatives of the Renaissance. It should be remembered that in the courts of the ruling families and institutions of Italy—such as the Gonzagas in Mantua, the Medici in Florence, the Sforzas in Milan, the Montefeltros in Urbino, the d'Estes in Ferrara, the popes in Rome, and the doges in Venice—the elevated status of artists and architects in the social hierarchy of the Renaissance meant that they were largely free to mix with princes, courtiers, and Humanists. Exchange of ideas between arts and letters inevitably occurred formally and informally. This influence occurred alongside the fertile exchange of ideas between artists within the competitive environment of the workshops (*botteghe*), and by means of direct observation and interpretation of classical works of art and architectural ruins as they came to be discovered.

Accompanying the new pictorial understanding of painting and sculpted relief was a growing interest in the use of mythological allegory and the 'moral tradition of iconography' to convey venerated Christian themes. While part of an already established tradition found in the Middle Ages, allegory during the Renaissance provided a moral lens through which exemplary human qualities could be represented and communicated to a Humanistic audience.

Likewise, in architecture the influence of Humanist thought was pervasive, exemplified in the reception and interpretation of the famous architectural treatise, *De Architectura libri decem* ('Ten Books of Architecture') by *Vitruvius, an ancient and venerated work, the oldest treatise on architecture to have survived from antiquity, and the model for subsequent architectural treatises of the Renaissance, best exemplified in *Alberti's celebrated *De re aedificatoria*.

An over-riding ambition of Humanists during the Renaissance was to reconcile pagan and Christian principles, and philosophical and scriptural sources, by presenting Greco-Roman and Judeo-Christian traditions as essentially part of a common eschatology. Echoed in the conscious emulation of the classical past in the visual arts, this Humanist enterprise was soon to be undermined by dissenting voices within and outside religious circles that presaged the Reformation.

Anticipations of the Renaissance

Even before the period of Giotto and the Lorenzetti, the first stirrings of a new vision came towards the end of the 13th century, when the powerful Byzantine formalism that inspired the *Ravenna mosaics of the groups of Justinian and Theodora and their entourage gave way to a more spontaneous treatment of figures, and to efforts to achieve a greater degree of naturalism—an effort to achieve, in other words, a naturalism redolent of antique Roman art, known from sarcophagi and portrait busts, and present from the late 4th century in Roman mosaics, such as the apse of Sta Pudenziana, in the 5th-century doors of Sta Sabina, and which emerged strongly in the late 11th- and early 12th-century *Romanesque sculpture of Wiligelmo in Modena, and Antelami at the end of the 12th century in Parma and Fidenza.

The stirrings of greater change came in the 13th century, with the Florentine *Cimabue and the Sienese *Duccio, who were producing large altarpieces distinctly different from late Byzantine inspired ones of the 1260s to 1280s. Cimabue was in Rome in 1272, where contact with Early Christian mosaics is likely. He is credited with being the master of *Giotto, with whom the earlier tentative moves towards greater naturalism were finally so successful that they opened a new era. Giotto was in Rome at the turn of the century (he is attributed with the famous altarpiece of St Peter's Basilica, showing scenes of the martyrdoms of St Peter and Paul), which suggests that he was probably in contact with Cavallini, the major Roman painter of the day, whose now mutilated masterpiece, the *Last Judgement* (Sta Cecilia in Trastevere), was painted about 1293. The other major artist in Rome for the 1300 Jubilee was Arnolfo di Cambio, sculptor and above all architect of Florence Cathedral, and pupil of Nicola *Pisano.

In the frescoes of Giotto and the Lorenzetti the timeless (transcendent) world of the Middle Ages is transformed by a new interest in temporal matters. Humanity, rather than the divine, takes centre-stage, and the acts of pious figures (principally saints) are measured in relation to their personal experiences—expressed through such emotions as mercy, love, adoration, and mourning. Examples can be found in the frescoes depicting the Life of St Francis in the Upper Church of the Basilica of St *Francis of Assisi, and in the fresco cycle of the Life of the Virgin *Mary in the Arena (Scrovegni) Chapel in Padua.

In a different vein the fresco *Effects of Good Government*, in the Palazzo Pubblico in Siena by the Lorenzetti, is a masterpiece in secular painting presaging the 15th century, with a strong emphasis on *landscape as an allegory of the just and merciful state. The cultivated and well-maintained countryside is mirrored in the fresco by a well-ordered city, whose representation (in the form of a walled Medieval city) conveys a civilized and law-abiding community enhanced by scenes of dancing figures. Hence, the fresco communicates a double message; that society is the custodian of nature, and that abundant nature constitutes an emblem of good government.

These significant artistic developments were parallelled by a new appreciation of classical literature in the 14th century, exemplified in particular by the work of Francesco Petrarch, scholar and poet laureate. Disillusioned with the corruption and moral decay of his own age, Petrarch sought to draw upon the culture and language of antiquity to provide a model of spiritual reform. Along with the work of Giovanni Boccaccio, Petrarch's understanding of the classical past inaugurated the age of Humanism in the Renaissance which was to underpin much of the artistic achievements of the 15th and 16th centuries.

Early Renaissance

Probably the earliest evidence of the flowering of the Early Renaissance in the 15th century can be found not in painting but in bronze relief, highlighted in the famous competition for the bronze doors of the north entrance to the Baptistery of Florence Cathedral in 1401. The jury from the *Arte di Calimala* (Cloth Importers Guild) selected two finalists; the young (and little known) *Ghiberti and the older and more established *Brunelleschi. Each artist was required to produce a bronze relief panel depicting the story of the Sacrifice of *Isaac, both entries attempting in varying ways, to give greater temporal expression to a religious scene, earlier anticipated in the paintings of Giotto, by conveying the triadic relationship between the action of Abraham (at the moment of sacrificing Isaac on an altar) and the intervention of the angel. What differentiates the two artists, however, was their treatment of ancient models: for Brunelleschi the medieval past served as a visible point of departure, in his strong gestural (even contorted) treatment of figures, especially Isaac; for Ghiberti, on the other hand, it is the more fluid and refined composition of polished bronze figures (consciously alluding to classical precedents) that stands out. In the latter, in particular, the defining break is with the medieval past, and at the same time an anticipation of a new mode of representation. As the winner of the competition, Ghiberti undertook one of the most important artistic commissions in 15th-century Florence, which became known as the 'Gates of Paradise' for the Baptistery.

As this competition confirms, the Early Renaissance was primarily focused on the city of Florence, a rich mercantile and banking centre in Europe, often described as the 'birthplace' of the Italian Renaissance. Through the generous patronage of Lorenzo de Medici, Giuliano de Medici, and other influential families, Florence became a magnet for artists aspiring to achieve recognition and status in a fiercely competitive environment. It was also from here that many famous artists, such as *Leonardo and *Michelangelo, were to seek their fortunes in other parts of Italy, such as Milan and Rome.

An important aspect of Ghiberti's work is his attempt as a writer to articulate the structure and meaning of linear perspective, which he applied to the bronze relief panels for the Florence Baptistery. Preceding *Alberti's later 'codification' of *perspettiva artificialis* in his influential *De Pictura* (also translated into Italian as *Della Pittura*), Ghiberti's interpretation of perspective was partly influenced by medieval theories of optics; claiming indeed that perspective itself was not based on strictly geometric but luminary properties. In this sense, Ghiberti's interpretation could be said to bridge the transition between medieval *perspettiva naturalis* and Renaissance *perspettiva artificialis*.

Brunelleschi, too, explored linear perspective, but in his case through more practical experiments within the actual city itself, in his famous one-point perspective construction of Florence's Baptistery (from the south entrance of the cathedral) and his lesser-known two-point perspective view of the Piazza della Signoria. More familiar, however, is his daring and innovative design for the dome of Florence Cathedral (the first completed dome since antiquity) and his numerous architectural projects in Florence (Santo Spirito, San Lorenzo, Ospedale degli Innocenti, Rotonda di Santa Maria degli Angeli, and Cappella de'Pazzi).

The achievements in bronze relief, evident in Ghiberti's *Gates of Paradise*, were soon equalled in painting with the arrival on the scene of *Masaccio in Florence in the early 15th century, whose frescoes (the *Trinity* at S. Maria Novella and the *Tribute Money* in the Brancacci Chapel in S. Maria del Carmine) express for the first time the use of perspective rendering in painting (in the former), and a conscious attempt to model painted figures using contemporary sculpture (in the latter). Masaccio's short life, however, and the propensity of patrons to settle for the more accessible charm of *Masolino and Gentile da Fabriano's International Gothic, might have delayed the vital changes which developed in the 15th century, had it not been for the spur provided by the inventive genius of Brunelleschi, referred to earlier, and of Alberti's underpinning of the new trends with learned literary argument and classical architectural precedents, influenced by his humanistic background. The vigour of *Donatello's sculpture, the softer more sinuous—even Gothic—rhythms of Ghiberti, Luca della *Robbia's tender simplicity, and Fra *Angelico who, despite his deceptive tenderness, fully grasped the implications of Masaccio's heroic style, all united to create the new expressiveness. The generations that followed Masaccio's premature death include most of the great names of Florentine art: Uccello, Fra Filippo *Lippi, Castagno, *Botticelli, the Pollaiuolo brothers, Ghirlandaio, Verrocchio, Filippino Lippi, and the list culminates in Leonardo da Vinci.

Florence's reputation as the source of the best available talent is borne out by Florentines being recruited for the 1481 fresco cycle in the *Sistine Chapel, and for the papal tombs by the Pollaiuolo brothers. Florence also attracted artists from other areas, who came either to study, like *Piero della Francesca and, later, *Raphael, or to share in Florentine commissions, like *Perugino and *Signorelli; all these men had an important Florentine period either before returning to their own cities, working in various other centres to which they were summoned because of their reputation, or like Raphael, achieving his greatest fame in Rome. Some of the most famous Florentines worked in N. Italy: Uccello in Venice and Padua, Donatello in Padua where he had a formative influence on the young *Mantegna, and through him affected Giovanni *Bellini in Venice. Piero, trained in Florence, exercised in Urbino as decisive an influence on the young *Bramante as was Mantegna's on Ferrara and Bologna. Bramante's first architectural work was produced in Milan, while Leonardo was also there; though they were both artists of the High Renaissance rather than of its first phase, their works there were not being produced before the last years of the 15th century.

High Renaissance

The true High Renaissance lasted barely more than two decades, and begins with Leonardo, proceeds to its period of Roman greatness, its brief moment of classical harmony and balance, with Bramante and Raphael, and ends virtually with Raphael's death in 1520, by which time Bramante was also dead. Unlike the Early Renaissance, the period of the High Renaissance was centred primarily in Rome, thanks to the new-found confidence and ambitions of the popes as patrons. Furthermore, unlike the previous century in Florence, which was largely dominated by a literary (rhetorical) perspective of Humanist thought, 16th-century Rome drew more direct influence from the material legacy of antiquity, the basis of epigraphic and archaeological interests. The discovery and appropriation of remains of Roman antiquity was not a uniquely Renaissance phenomenon, as evidenced by the abundant reuse of ancient *spolia* in the construction of churches from the period of Early Christianity. But by the early 16th century, examination of the material legacy of antiquity becomes much more intrusive and systematic, supported by Humanistic and antiquarian scholarship. Architectural and artistic interest in Rome's classical legacy effectively begins with the visit of Brunelleschi and Donatello to the papal city in 1402 to uncover and record its ancient remains. This was followed by the work of Alberti who, as a papal secretary to Nicholas V (1447–55), was commissioned to undertake a major survey of the topography of Rome (*Descriptio Urbis Romae*) that was probably influenced by the earlier study of Rome's ancient topography by the 15th-century antiquarian Flavio Biondo (*Roma Instaurata*). By the beginning of the 16th century, this interest in the physical topography of the city contributed to a more conscious monumental architectural vocabulary that sought to emulate the legacy of the imperial Roman past.

Anticipated in the largely unrealized urban projects of the 15th-century Pope Nicholas V—to transform Rome from a decaying medieval city to one that sought to emulate the legacy of the imperial past—by the beginning of the 16th century the city witnessed a bewildering series of transformations reflecting an urgent expectation of things to come. Besides responding to the increasing demands of the Jubilee celebrations, whose frequency had increased from 50 to every 25 years during the pontificate of Sixtus IV (1471–84), this motivation to transform Rome was also partly due to a belief, prevalent among Humanists, clergy, and artists, that the papal city had arrived at an auspicious moment in its history when a new 'golden age' would emerge that could be compared to those of the biblical past.

The theme of the golden age becomes prevalent during the pontificate of Julius II (1503–13), and continues—albeit less pervasively—during subsequent papacies until Clement VII (1523–34) and the sack of Rome in 1527. Architectural manifestations of this vision can be seen in Bramante's famous Tempietto of San Pietro in Montorio, on the Janiculum (*c.*1502), which has been described as the first building of the High Renaissance.

With the urban transformations of Rome, including the insertion of Via Giulia and Via della Lungara (Bramante), the design of the new St Peter's Basilica (Bramante, Giuliano da Sangallo), the Cortile del Belvedere (Bramante), and the unfinished Palazzo dei Tribunali (Bramante), and at the same time the commissioning of fresco cycles for the ceiling of the Sistine Chapel (Michelangelo) and the Papal Apartments (Raphael), the pontificate of Julius II constituted an unrivalled period of artistic and architectural production on a scale and complexity not seen since antiquity. Here, the *renovatio* of classical antiquity is accompanied by a propitious portrayal of papal Rome as the *altera Jerusalem*. Aspects of this ambition continued under Leo X, but with a less coherent vision and scale of operation.

Other architects of importance during the High Renaissance include Baldassare Peruzzi (Rome), Antonio da Sangallo the Younger (Rome), Raphael (Rome), Vignola (Rome), Jacopo Sansovino (Rome and Venice), and *Palladio in the Veneto, all of whom in varying ways were inspired by the architectural legacy of Imperial Rome. At the same time, artistic and architectural creativity develop towards greater complexity, dominated by the towering figure of Michelangelo, whose output included sculpture, painting, and architecture. It should be remembered that his first Roman works are of the late 15th century, most notably the Pietà sculpture. He bestrides the scene in Florence and Rome for the next 70 years in all three major arts. A testimony to the changing priorities and fortunes of the 16th century in Rome can be seen in the vast and complicated project for the new St Peter's Basilica, whose vicissitudes and prevarications resulted in a rather unsatisfactory scheme. The product of many contributors during the 16th century—Bramante, Fra Giovanni Giocondo, Giuliano da Sangallo, Peruzzi, Raphael, Antonio da Sangallo the

Younger, Michelangelo, and Giacomo della Porta—the project for the new basilica absorbed huge amounts of funds and extended over a period of more than a century.

In painting, the soft luminosity of *Correggio in his easel pictures and his bold use of perspective in his dome frescoes looks forward to the *Baroque, while the *Mannerism that evolved after the death of Raphael takes over in Florence and other cities in the 1520s. Assisting Raphael on the frescoes in the Stanze in the Papal Apartments, Giulio Romano stands out in the High Renaissance and Mannerism, as his work in Mantua shows. In Venice the Renaissance is prolonged to the end of the 16th century by *Titian, *Veronese, and *Tintoretto, whose principal outputs, in the form of large-scale oil paintings on canvas (rather than fresco), was a unique feature of High Renaissance art in the Veneto.

The Renaissance outside Italy

North of the Alps, 14th-century art was characterized by *International Gothic, where the emphasis was on naturalism of detail—landscape, portraiture, animals, genre—rather than on the Italian striving for structure, proportion, perspective, and the relationship of forms in space. International Gothic had considerable influence in Italy, and represented an opposing trend to Masaccio's heroic style, since it was a softer, more accessible art for its charm and beauty.

In the Netherlands its counterpart lies in the naturalistic qualities of such artists as Jan van *Eyck, Roger van der *Weyden, and Hugo van der *Goes. Details such as swags, putti, and bits of classical architecture were evidence of an artist's up-to-dateness, as in Gerard *David. In the 16th century, Italian art became a hunting-ground from which artists of undoubted ability, such as Quentin Massys, Mabuse, Floris, and Martin van Heemskerck, all of whom actually went to Italy, brought home their ill-understood, superficial gleanings. These they married to borrowings from van Eyck, van der Weyden, Dürer's engravings, and the ever-present influence of the Raphael cartoons for the Sistine Chapel tapestries, woven in Flanders, where the cartoons remained for many years. The results were not always very happy.

The French invasions of Italy, which began in 1494 and lasted until 1525, resulted in the importation of Italian artists into the North, so that the High Renaissance and Mannerism and their outward forms, rather than their intellectual basis, were merged into local practice, not always to its immediate advantage.

In architecture, the Renaissance first crept in by the use of various classical details in a curious mixture with Gothic ones, since these were regarded purely as decorative fantasy elements to be added freely to familiar structures. A more serious interest in Renaissance architecture came after the French invasions of Italy, and from a theoretical standpoint, the dissemination of Renaissance architectural principles into France was due in part to the work of Sebastiano Serlio, whose dedication of Book 3 of his famous architectural treatise (*I Sette Libri dell'Architettura*) to Francis I resulted in an invitation to the court at Fontainebleau.

The importation of Leonardo into France by Francis I did not come about until his real course in Italy had been run, and for the French king he was, perhaps, the most striking trophy of his Italian forays, but despite the aura with which his name invested Francis's artistic patronage his work was limited. The attempt to create a distinctly French style of classicism had to await Philibert Delorme's famous architectural treatise, *Le premier tome de l'architecture* (1567).

In England the major Renaissance artist was *Holbein. In sculpture, the importation of Torrigiano from Italy produced, in Westminster Abbey, the double tomb of Henry VII and his Queen, Elizabeth of York, and that of his mother, Lady Margaret Beaufort. In architecture, the usual use of Renaissance detail to decorate late Gothic structures continued until some French ideas began to appear in the 16th century, such as symmetry, to be combined with a modernized version of the familiar—the old tower gatehouse, Netherlandish strapwork ornament, huge windows, and the traditional great hall. The very grand country houses built by men enriched by the dissolution of the monasteries offer a conspectus of these features—Longleat, Burghley, Wollaton, Montacute, and Hardwick—which continued until the end of the century. Painting languished after the death of Holbein in 1543, and except for the brilliant miniaturists, Nicholas Hilliard and his pupil Isaac Oliver, need was satisfied by importing talent, usually from the Protestant Netherlands, to fill the demand for the essential portraits. There was no religious painting, and sculpture was for tombs.

In Germany, the Renaissance was not a growth with either roots or branches: it was an imported exotic plant from which decorative florets could be plucked to deck Gothic structures with novel ornaments—much as it was treated in the rest of N. Europe. In painting, its greatest exponent was *Durer. *Cranach, and later in the century, Altdorfer, show little enthusiasm for more than the most superficial aspects of Italianism; Cranach may have used descriptions of Venetian paintings—Giorgione or Palma Vecchio, for instance—for his simpering, titillating Venuses, decked out in large hats and jewellery, but little else, but they can hardly be laid at the door of the Renaissance. Altdorfer's landscapes, which begin as backgrounds to his religious subjects, finally become the most important element in his pictures, and in such works as the *S. George in the forest* (*c.*1510: Munich) are part of the Northern development of landscape as an independent subject. *Grünewald was very different in his approach to Renaissance art, in that he uses its technical devices in the Isenheim Altar to heighten the emotional impact of his late Gothic vision.

In Spain, Renaissance architecture begins by suffering the same fate as it does in N. Europe: it furnished 'modern' details for Gothic buildings. Charles V had a palace begun on the Alhambra, Granada, with a grandiose circular courtyard full of reminiscences of Raphael and Giulio Romano, but the project was abandoned in 1586. Philip II's *Escorial, and parts of the cathedrals of Granada and Valladolid, borrow certainly from Italian precedents but are merely the prelude to a totally national style developed in the next century. Alonso Berruguete was the son of Pedro, court painter to Ferdinand and Isabella of Spain, who is believed to have worked in Urbino. Alonso was made painter to Charles V, and worked mainly as a sculptor in wood, on choir stalls in Toledo Cathedral (1529–32), and in his paintings he is close to Rosso, but with influences from Leonardo, and Raphael. Luis Morales is first recorded in 1547. He practised an ecstatic style of Mannerist religious art laced with a blend of Massys and Leonardo known at second hand, preceding El Greco as a Mannerist painter in Spain. But when this painter of genius settled permanently in Toledo in 1577 Philip II disliked El *Greco's Mannerism and would not employ him, because he preferred the Titians that he imported. He also disliked the crucifix by Cellini, made for the Escorial. Torrigiano, after finishing the Tudor tombs in Westminster Abbey, went to Seville, but came to a miserable end at the hands of the Inquisition in 1528. It was not until the next century that a truly great Spanish art emerged, which was able to profit from the Renaissance.

Reparata, Santa is the original name and dedication of the 11th-century Florence Cathedral, demolished to make way for the present cathedral, dedicated to S. Maria del Fiore (S. Mary of the Flower). Recent excavations under the floor of the present church have revealed much of the older structure. The saint herself is something of a mystery. She appears in Bede's *Martyrology*, and is said to have been a girl martyred at Caesarea during the Decian persecution, 250–1. Eusebius, Bishop of Caesarea, does not mention her, nor is she recorded in any Eastern martyrology. She is mentioned in the **Golden Legend*, and in the *Catalogus Sanctorum* of de Natalibus, and he conflates her with S. Margaret, with the story that being forced to marry she fled on her wedding day dressed as a boy and took refuge in a monastery under the name Pelagius. She was later accused of immorality, her innocence only being revealed after her death. From this to being a martyr was a short step. But the same story is told of a S. Pelagia of Jerusalem, with the suggestion that the three are a conflation of a single girl, the name 'Reparata' being 'reparation' of the injustice done to her. Legends of this type have long been associated with extreme ascetic sects which have practised and encouraged male and female celibacy, and which promoted such legends to counter pagan worship of Venus. Arnolfo di Cambio included

S. Reparata in a group of the *Madonna with SS Zanobius and Reparata*, both additional patron saints of Florence, and Andrea Pisano also made a figure of the saint, both of which were once part of the façade of Florence Cathedral, and are now in the Museo dell'Opera. Bernardo Daddi's *Madonna and Child with saints* contains a S. Reparata in one of the compartments (Uffizi).

Repose, Altar of *See* ALTAR OF REPOSE, and EASTER SEPULCHRE.

repository art is, like *bondieuserie, a pejorative description of over-sentimentalized and highly coloured works commercially produced for sale in shops selling devotional articles. Such shops were called Repositories, and the name survives for the small areas in many Catholic churches which sell rosaries, holy pictures, statuettes, and prayer books.

repoussé (Fr. 'pushed out') A term used to describe metalware, usually silver or gold, where the surface design is raised above the background.

reredos, the This is usually an immovable adjunct to an altar, though not a *liturgical object properly speaking and neither is it a necessary adjunct to an altar. It developed slowly from paintings on the wall against which the altar was placed. From wall-paintings or mosaics, carved or painted panels followed, which were usually fixed to the back of the altar. Over many years these developed into often very large paintings or carved works of art, as for instance, Grünewald's Isenheim Altar. The subjects represented ranged from the Life of Christ, in particular, the Last Supper and scenes of the Passion, and may also include the Virgin and subjects relating to the saint or saints to whom the church, chapel, or altar is dedicated. Sometimes they are quite small—many older parish churches can provide examples—but sometimes they are huge carved screens with rows of niches for small statues of saints, as at Winchester Cathedral, and the Chapel of All Souls, Oxford. Unfortunately, most of the English ones have lost their medieval statues, and if the niches now have statues they are usually 19th century.

Rest on the Flight into Egypt *See* EGYPT.

Resurrection The Resurrection of Christ is attested by all four Gospels, not as a spectral apparition, a hallucination, a vision, or a supernatural appearance, but as a factual, physical event. The first scenes to be represented after the Entombment are of the guards watching over the tomb (Matt. 27: 62–6). This appears first as a wreath encircling the sacred monogram, above a cross, with two guards below (4th-cent. sarcophagus, Catacomb of Domitilla), and in a detail on the Basilewsky *Situla (980: London, V & A). In one of the ivory reliefs on the casket (420/30: London, BM) the door of the tomb is shown open, the guards inattentive or asleep, with two of the Holy Women. The early mosaics in Sant'Apollinare Nuovo, Ravenna (before 526), have a scene with two Holy Women meeting the angel outside the tomb. The number of Holy Women varies according to the Gospel, sometimes two, sometimes more; only John 20: 1–18 says Mary Magdalene came alone, to find the stone rolled back. She ran to tell the disciples, and Peter and John came running, found the tomb empty, and John 16: 10 says they then went home. Mary stayed weeping, stooped to look into the tomb, and saw two angels, one of whom asked her why she was weeping. She said 'They have taken away my Lord, and I do not know where they have laid him.' She turned and saw a man, whom she thought was the gardener. He too said to her, '"Woman, why are you weeping? Whom are you looking for?" She said "Sir, if you have carried him away, tell me where you have laid him, and I will take him away." Jesus said to her "Mary!"' and then she recognized Him. This is the moment Rembrandt chose (1638: Royal Coll.), with the two angels sitting on the tomb. More than one angel is rare: there are two in a miniature in the Farfa Bible (11th cent., from Catalonia, now Vatican) and four women; a relief in the church wall at Dax (12th cent.: SW France) has two angels and three women. A relief on the font (12th cent.: Modena Cath.) has the rare scene of three Holy Women buying spices to embalm Christ's body (Mark 16: 1–8) although John 19: 39–40 says plainly that these were brought by Nicodemus, and a capital from the old cathedral, Pamplona (12th cent.: Mus.), shows Mary Magdalene trying to convince the incredulous disciples of what she has seen. In Byzantine art, the Resurrection is followed by Christ's standing in triumph over the forces of Evil, represented by the snake, or a dragon-like beast, and the *lion: this type of figure of Christ is in the mosaic in Ravenna (500: Archbishop's palace chapel); or standing on the beasts, as in the *trumeau* of the south portal at Chartres (13th cent.); but sometimes enthroned with the beasts beneath his feet (13th cent.: Mainz Cath. tympanum). The *Anastasis*, or the Harrowing of Hell, when Christ descended into the underworld to free the souls of the just who have been awaiting liberation, since they had died before the age of Grace—*ante legem* or *sub lege* instead of *sub gratia*—is the usual Byzantine form in which the Resurrection is represented. Christ grasps Adam by the wrist and drags him out of Hell, closely followed by Eve and by the prophets (1025: Hosios Lukas tympanum mosaic; 12th cent.: Torcello Cath. *Last Judgement* mosaic; early 14th cent.: Constantinople, Kariye Camii wall-painting). The subject was always part of Western art, since it is one of the surviving examples of Anglo-Saxon sculpture (Bristol Cath.), and continues to Donatello (*c.*1460: ambo relief, San Lorenzo, Florence), Dürer (1510: Great Passion), and Tintoretto (1568: San Cassiano, Venice).

Among the frequent representations of the Resurrection is that of Christ either actually emerging from the tomb, or having just done so. This appears in illustrations such as that in the Utrecht Psalter to v. 5 of Ps. 19 (830: Utrecht) where Christ accompanied by two angels 'comes out like a bridegroom from his wedding canopy'; or more usually Christ is stepping out of the tomb, as in works by Nicholas of Verdun (1181: Klosterneuberg Altar), or Piero della Francesca (1460–4: *Resurrection*, San Sepolcro), both with sleeping guards below. After the Council of Trent it is rare to find Christ stepping on the top of the tomb, and the type presented by Bellini (1479: Berlin), with Christ in the sky above the tomb, and astonished guards gazing up at him or cowering terrorstruck below, is more usual, as in the Michelangelo drawing (1532: London, BM) which was an early project for what eventually became the *Last Judgement* in the Sistine Chapel, or the El Greco (1595: Prado). *See also* CHRIST.

Resurrection of the Dead *See* JUDGEMENT.

Resurrection of Lazarus *See* LAZARUS.

retable, retablos A retable began, like a **predella*, by being a shelf (Lat. *retabulum*, rear table) at the back of an altar, used for ornaments. It progressed to being part of the framework of panels forming a *reredos, and finally became another name for an altarpiece, either painted or carved, which was made up of one or more panels which were fixed together, i.e. not hinged like a *triptych. A good example is the Pisa Polyptych by Simone Martini (1319: *Madonna and Child with Saints*). Retablos, also known as *laminas* in Mexico, are small paintings on tin, wood, or copper, used chiefly at home altars to venerate a great number of Catholic saints, similar in scale to the ex-voto, or *votive painting, prevalent in Spanish and French North America. In the 20th century, the form was appropriated by Frida Kahlo and provided some inspiration for the Mexican muralists. *See also* NORTH AMERICA.

retrochoir The part of a cathedral or major church, lying behind the *presbytery, which can be reached from the choir aisles. It fulfils the same function as an *ambulatory, in that it gives access to chapels, usually including a *Lady chapel. If the church possessed a shrine which was the object of pilgrimages (and most major churches had one) the separation of the presbytery from the retrochoir enabled pilgrims to gain access to the shrine without interrupting the services in the choir.

Return of the Holy Family from Egypt *See* EGYPT.

Revelation, Book of *See* APOCALYPSE.

Revelations of Saint Bridget *See* BRIDGET, S.

Reyntiens, Patrick (1925–) A stained-glass artist with numerous commissions of his own as well as interpreting other painters' designs into stained glass (notably and frequently John *Piper's), head of Fine Art 1976–86 Central School of Art and Design, London, educator, writer, and international lecturer. Upbringing, education, and war service gave him an experience and cultivated knowledge of art and architecture especially from a Catholic viewpoint. Marriage to painter Anne Bruce (1927–2006) brought about a professional collaboration at Burleighfield Art Centre, High Wycombe, Buckinghamshire, set up in 1960 and attracted a wide range of students from abroad for work in a variety of media. Piper drew Reyntiens in on the window for Oundle School, and among others Coventry Cathedral's Baptistery window, and windows in Eton College, Churchill College, and Robinson College Chapels, Cambridge, and St

Margaret's, Westminster. At Derby Cathedral and Liverpool Metropolitan Cathedral Blessed Sacrament Chapel he worked with Ceri Richards; and at All Saints, Basingstoke, with Cecil Collins. His own work can be found in the Hall of Christ Church, Oxford; in Southwell Minster, Nottinghamshire; in Washington National Cathedral, USA; and in the Abbey of his alma mater, Ampleforth College, York.

Ribera, Jusepe (José) (1591–1652) was a Spanish painter, born near Valencia, who passed his working life in Italy. He is first recorded in Rome in 1615, but was almost certainly in N. Italy (then a Spanish possession) and in Parma before that. In Rome, he was very strongly influenced by *Caravaggio and his Flemish and Dutch followers. He was in Naples in 1616, also a Spanish possession, where he married the daughter of an artist who employed him as an assistant; and he rapidly became very successful, working for many Spanish viceroys, some of whom took their purchases back to Spain. He is recorded as saying that in Spain native artists were poorly regarded, 'whereas here I am highly regarded and my works paid for in a way which I find very satisfactory'. He visited Rome occasionally, once to receive the Cross of Knighthood of the Order of Christ in 1626, and at the same time he probably became a member of the Accademia di San Luca, since only after 1626 does he refer to himself as *Academicus Romanus*. In 1644 his 14-year-old daughter Margarita married a magistrate who died in 1651 leaving her to bear a posthumous child; this ends the romantic tale of her supposed seduction by Don John of Austria, who only arrived in Naples in 1648. From 1644 to 1648 he suffered a form of paralysis in his right arm, followed by a stroke, but recovered sufficiently to finish some works before his death.

His first recorded works were etchings—studies of ears, eyes, mouths, for the use of students. Half-length 'portraits' of Apostles or Saints followed, popular subjects in the 17th century, also painted by artists such as El *Greco and *Zurbarán, as well as *Rubens and other Northern painters working in Spanish-dominated areas. Large pictures of Crucifixions, Depositions, and martyrdoms display his striking use of light and shadow, and also his gift for portraying the more horrifying aspects of suffering and torture. This is particularly true of the *Martyrdom of S. Bartholomew* and mythological subjects such as the *Flaying of Marsyas* (Brussels and Naples Mus.). Most of the major painters of his time visited Naples and were known to him, in particular Velázquez.

Ribera had a large studio of assistants, since many of his pictures exist in as many as nine to twelve versions.

ribs The projecting elements that mark out the areas of vaulting, separating the cells or severies of the vault. Where there is a central rib running along the length of the vault, it is called the ridge rib and is common in English Gothic vaulting, but uncommon in French vaulting. In Gothic vaulting, the ribs often join with columns or *colonnettes and run down the walls to the ground. These are called wall ribs or formerets.

rings *See* SEALS AND RINGS.

Ripa, Cesare, was the author of *Iconologia*, first published in Perugia in 1593 and Rome (1603), and in many later editions. It is an encyclopaedia of personifications of abstract concepts for the use of artists. The allegorical figures are not exclusively Christian, but include general concepts—Chastity, Eternal Felicity, Divine Wisdom—as well as pagan personifications. Many of the allegories are so obscure that they could not be understood without the book: nevertheless, it was influential throughout the 17th century and was translated into Latin and most European languages. There was an English edition in 1709, and a second one as late as 1778–9. Bernini's *Truth* (1646–52: Rome, Borghese) is based on it, and there are probably many more allegories awaiting identification. (*See also* ATTRIBUTE, EMBLEM.)

Rivers of Paradise, the four These are the four rivers which watered the Garden of Eden, and flowed from there into the land to which Adam and Eve were banished. They are named as Phison (or Pishon), Geon (thought to be the Nile), Tigris, and Euphrates, of which only the last named are now identified. They have, however, gathered a wealth of allegorical meanings, since they are frequently shown issuing from Christ's throne or from below His feet (Rome: apse mosaics in Sta Costanza, SS Cosmas and Damian, Sta Prassede, Sta Pudenziana, San Clemente, San Giovanni Laterano; Ravenna: apse mosaic, San Vitale). S. Ambrose interpreted them as referring to the Four Gospels, flowing from the word of

Christ to bring salvation, and also as the four Cardinal *Virtues. Often, two stags are found quenching their thirst at these streams, personifying Christians revived by the Gospels and the Eucharist, and also a reference to Ps. 42 (Vg. 41): 'As the deer longs for flowing streams, so my soul longs for you, O God.'

The four rivers are personified at Chartres, north portal (13th cent.), by four young men bearing vessels from which water flows. Van *Eyck in the *Adoration of the Lamb* has four springs of water flowing into a fountain—the Fountain of Life—below the altar of the Lamb, to which all the processions are advancing. The allegory of the Water of Life is a constant one throughout the Early Christian and the medieval world.

Robbia, Luca della (1400–82), was a Florentine sculptor and inventor of glazed ceramic sculpture. His first major work was the marble *Cantoria* (Singing Gallery) for Florence Cathedral (1431–8: Mus. dell'Opera) for which *Donatello made the companion gallery two years later. Luca also made a pair of bronze doors (1464–9) for the Sacristy.

At an early date, Luca discovered a method of applying a coloured vitrified lead glaze to terracotta figures and this laid the foundations of the della Robbia workshop enterprise, which engaged the whole family in a very profitable business. Examples of the early types of relief are the plain white *Visitation* group (Pistoia, San Giovanni Fuorcivitas) or with blue details as in the *Madonna and Child* (Florence, Innocenti Hospital), or the *Resurrection* with white figures on a rich blue ground in the lunette over his own cathedral doors. Among those involved in the workshop was his nephew Andrea (1435–1525), who made the endearing roundels of babies in swaddling bands later inserted into the façade of the orphanage of the Innocenti in Florence. Eventually several other colours were introduced, particularly by Giovanni, Andrea's son, who exploited the technique to exhaustion in the production of large groups, multicoloured garlands for coats of arms or heraldic devices, and the business continued well into the 16th century.

In its origins, Luca's discovery encouraged the creation of simple figures with a restraint and dignity which puts them among the formative influences of the High Renaissance. They also encouraged the production of devotional images of great beauty and tender feeling, and the popularity of his glazed terracotta groups in no way derogates from Luca's qualities as an artist. *See also* APOCALYPSE.

Roch, Saint (*San Rocco* in Italy) He was believed to be one of the most efficacious of the *plague saints, invoked in France, Germany, and Italy. He came from Montpellier (S. France), and lived *c.*1350–*c.*1380. He became a pilgrim to Italy, caught the plague, and was reputed to have been fed by a dog. He is said to have worked miraculous cures, eventually returned home, and was repudiated by his family and perhaps even imprisoned as an impostor. Another story has him be arrested as a spy in Lombardy, die in prison, and have miracles claimed at his tomb. His fame spread rapidly, his relics were removed to Venice in 1485, but his cult subsided during the late 16th century. He is usually shown wearing a short tunic, exposing a sore on his leg, and accompanied by a dog. Images are: Quentin Massys: *S. Roche* with the plague spot, and his dog (late 15th cent.: Munich); Tintoretto: *S. Rocco curing the plague stricken*, 1549, and *S. Rocco in prison, comforted by an angel*, 1567: church of San Rocco, Venice. *See also* SEBASTIAN, S.

Rococo A movement or style, parallel with the late Baroque and the emerging Neoclassicism, and not, as is sometimes believed, a separate historical epoch. The term 'rococo' is derived from the dominating form of ornament—*rocaille*; its origins are in France around 1730, preceded by a short period of Regency (1715–30), and so Rococo is also very often described as 'style *rocaille*'. In contrast to the main characteristics of the late Baroque, both Regency and Rococo are mainly an introverted art of interiors, and primarily found in secular buildings. Emerging after the death of Louis XIV, they are part of the fundamental change in French culture as the centralized and hierarchically organized, theocentric culture of the state came to be transformed into a more individualized, enlightened, and progressively secularized way of life. In the sphere of art and its iconography, the myth of Apollo and Hercules is replaced by the cult of Venus and Pan. The art of Regency and Rococo was strongly influenced by the move of Philip, Duke of Orleans (the regent of Louis XV) and his court from Versailles to the Palais Royal in Paris, and the move of the aristocracy into private town mansions.

The heavy interiors of the Baroque were replaced by rooms with light plasterwork and subtle cornices contrasting with plain ceilings and paintings above door panels. Mirrors were used generously and with great freedom. Stucco and tiles came to replace wood. Coloured marble or imitation marble was quite often used for floors and chimney-pieces. Walls were often covered with the same material that was used for chair upholstery and curtains. This new interior decor was praised as delicate, comfortable, private, and intimate, but the critics spoke of it as asymmetrical, exuberant, and frivolous.

Among the leading architects and designers of the art of the Regency Gilles-Marie Oppenord (1672–1742) should be mentioned for his decoration of the interiors of the Palais Brion (1715), along with François Antoine Vasse (1681–1736) and the interiors and monumental Galerie Dorée that he designed in the Hôtel de la Vrillière-Toulouse (1718). The nature of Regency art is best summarized and illustrated in contemporary paintings of Jean Antoine Watteau (1684–1721).

Watteau is credited with inventing the genre of '*fêtes galantes*'—scenes of bucolic and idyllic charm, inspired to a high degree by theatricality drawn from the world of Italian comedy (*Commedia dell'Arte*) and ballet. However, his most accomplished painting, *The Embarkation for Cythera* (1718) shows that its surface conceals a serious message about the transformation of the inherited world into an idyllic picture, in which the traditional gods are replaced by cold statues, celebration of life and love by gallant play, and the poetics of art by aesthetics. The most authentic form of French Rococo flourished 1730–50. The main protagonists were the architect and designer Juste-Aurèle Meissonnier (1695–1750) who built Maison Bréthous (1732) in Paris and designed interiors, including furniture in France and abroad as far as Poland. His main contribution was the book of *rocaille*, *Livre d'ornements* (1734), a collection of the most radical forms of *rocaille*, whose influences were of international extent. Other contributions are the drawings and etchings of Jacques de Lajoue (1687–1761) and the work of Nicolas Pineau (1684–1754), who became responsible for the decoration of the interiors of the Hôtel de Matignon (1732), the Hôtel de Villars (1732–1733), the Hôtel de Mazarin (1735), and several others in Paris and in St Petersburg. The most complete examples of pure French Rococo are the interiors of the Hôtel de Soubise designed by Germain Boffrand (1735–1740) with over-door paintings by François Boucher (1703–70).

There is a temptation to speak about international Rococo particularly in view of certain similarities in the development of art in France and England, Spain and Italy, but such similarities should be seen as no more than parallels. The exception is South Germany and in particular Bavaria. There had been a long tradition of close links between Bavaria and France. Many members of the Munich court and artists, travelled, studied, and sometimes stayed for several years in France. The appropriation of the French *rocaille* was based on a deep resonance with the long tradition of decoration and ornament in the local architecture. *Rocaille* was seen as a continuation and synthesis of this tradition. Furthermore, this was reinforced by the genuine religious faith of the population, and by interaction with the neighbouring Protestant faith. As a result, the appropriation of *rocaille* was not passive. It had undergone a transformation of its meaning in light of the traditional richness of the Catholic culture and it played a different role from its French counterpart. The interiors of the German Rococo churches are not defined by architecture alone. In most cases, the same if not the more decisive role is played by painting. The relation of architecture to painting creates a space of illusion in which the celestial and terrestrial worlds communicate by their contrast or, as it is very often the case, by their continuity. It is in the domain of communication that *rocaille* plays its most important role.

The main elements of *rocaill*—acanthus, shells, and rock crystals—preserve the memory of their origins in the tradition of grotesque (from *grotto*, associated with the creative powers of earth). As ornament, *rocaille* has pictorial qualities, but it is not a picture, it is only like a picture. The same is true of its sculptural and architectural qualities. This Protean character of *rocaille* makes and keeps it a creative medium of mediation in the mediating and unifying of space. The best examples of Rococo churches are those not only decorated but also built with the same creative intentions. The first to mention is the collaboration of the brothers Cosmas Damian (1686–1739) and Egid Quirin (1692–1750) Asam on the building and decoration of the Benedictine abbey church in Weltenburg (1716–1724), which shows the slow emergence of the Rococo characteristics of the interior—the unity of the central space dominated by the fresco above and the elaborate treatment of the relation between the dome and the nave. The most interesting is their later collaboration in the St Johann Nepomuk Church (Asamkirche, 1733–46) designed as a private chapel of their own house in Munich. The purest examples of the South German treatment of Rococo space are the churches in Steinhausen (1727–33) and Die Wies (1745–54) both built and decorated by the brothers Dominikus (1685–1766) and Johann Baptist (1680–1758) Zimmermann. In both cases the centralized oval space culminates in the ceiling fresco, but in such a way that architecture, stucco, and fresco are fused in a space dominated by pastel colours and natural light. The result can be described as naturalized spatial illusion. The role of the stucco ornament (*rocaille*) in the articulation and unification of space can best be appreciated in the late example of the Abbey in Zwiefalten (1739–47), designed by Johann Michael Fischer (1692–1766), the most accomplished architect of the South German Rococo, and stuccoed by Johann Michael Feichtmayr (1709–72) of the large family of stucco artists, and from the so-called Wessobrunn School, the centre of the region's stucco works. The crowning example of the tradition of Rococo in Germany and central Europe is Vierzehnheiligen (1743–72), designed by Johann Balthasar Neumann (1687–1752) and stuccoed by Johann Michael Feichtmayr. After 1750 Rococo is slowly transformed and eventually replaced by Neoclassicism.

Roger van der Weyden *See* WEYDEN.

ROMANESQUE ART AND ARCHITECTURE

may be broadly defined as the art of Western Europe from the 10th to the 13th century, varying according to local circumstances and influences.

From about the year 900, the approach of the year 1000 was regarded with apprehension. Some may have dismissed this as superstition, but fear of the millennium resulted from a misunderstanding of prophecies in Revelation, particularly of ch. 18, with its fearful description of the destruction of Babylon, and 20: 2–7, with the reiteration of 'one thousand years'. Despite S. Augustine's explanation in the *City of God* that S. John's 'thousand years' was only a metaphor for the duration of the world, not an actual time limit, many believed that the end of the world would come with the millennium. After the fateful year had passed, energy in art as well as life was renewed with a vigour in which thankfulness and relief played a large part.

Romanesque architecture is not simply a derivative from Roman architecture. Its ambiguous name was invented by a 19th-century French archaeologist to describe an architecture which he felt corresponded to the development of Romance languages from Latin. Neither is it a set of solutions applied either over the area or the period in which it flourished. Changes in rite required new forms, and these were created through art, architecture, and learning, in the use of mathematics and sophisticated systems of proportion in design and in new methods of construction. The most consistent features of Romanesque are simplicity in planning, the creation of sequences of spaces within larger elements, solidity of materials, and grandeur of scale and effect. Of the greatest importance was the development of church music, in particular of Gregorian chant, which is best heard in a vaulted church.

France

The first wave of Romanesque church building stemmed from the *Carolingian St-Riquier in N. France, which set an example of vast size and a many-towered silhouette. Violent Viking raids—in one of which St-Riquier was destroyed—as well as fires caused by lightning and accidents, prompted experiments in vaulting of which St-Bénigne, Dijon, was one of the early efforts. It was built in 1001–18 by the Italian William of Volpiano, and was based on the Holy Sepulchre in Jerusalem, but technical problems resulted in such a forest of piers that it was difficult for the congregation to see or hear the service. The only surviving part of the church is the crypt under the large rotunda for the shrine of the saint built at the end of the choir. Another solution which was not tried again is transverse vaulting (that is, vaulting which goes from side to side of the nave bay by bay, instead of being a continuous element). This was an experiment used at Tournus, begun *c.*950 and vaulted during the 11th century and completed *c.*1120. It was the final refuge in Burgundy of the abbey of St-Philibert-de-Grandlieu, near Nantes, also a victim of a Viking raid. Tournus also has a large two-storey *westwork with a vaulted *narthex and a huge tower over it—almost a defensive bastion. The thrust of the transverse vaults is taken by the diaphragm arches of the nave walls to allow clerestory windows and direct light without compromising the verticality of the walls. The apse has an ambulatory with radiating side-chapels to create the model Romanesque *chevet* in response to new liturgical developments and a growing number of pilgrims. The relics of Saint Philibert were below the high altar in the crypt and the tomb of Saint Valérien was in the central radiating chapel of the ambulatory.

By the 11th century France had split up into large feudal units such as Aquitaine, Burgundy, Provence, where energetic prelates and religious Orders built large churches and monasteries. The first major architectural problem was created by the rapid development of pilgrimages. From the 10th century onwards it must have seemed as if all Europe was on the move, not only to local shrines, but over great distances. One result was that choirs and east ends were rebuilt so that pilgrims could be marshalled into orderly processions which did not interfere with the services in the usually monastic choirs. These changes of design are characteristic of *pilgrimage churches, which also show the rapid introduction of vaulting and the new forms of east ends.

It was at *Cluny in Burgundy that the full development of one of the major forms of Romanesque was created. Cluny was the largest monastic foundation in the North, and its example, and that of its many daughter-houses spread across Europe, set the standard. Autun, of *c.*1120–32, and Paray-le-Monial, of *c.*1100, are among the most perfect Cluniac churches. Cluny had three major phases in its development, with Cluny III, built by Saint Hugh who was its abbot for more than 60 years, being the largest church in medieval Europe. It was a measure of the order in every way, paced out by frequent processions and filled by the chant of the *laus perennis*. The next important force was the *Cistercian Order, which reached even wider distribution and influence. There were many churches, however, outside both Cluny and Cîteaux, which created new forms.

Among them are the aisleless domed churches of Aquitaine and the Saintonge in SW France, such as Angoulême Cathedral, begun *c.*1105, with a sequence of four domes on pendentives which run down into massive piers, and the cathedral of Périgueux, of the 1120s, formally related to St Mark's in Venice, with a Greek Cross plan with five domes. Another variation is in the cathedral at Angers, begun in 1010, where the aisleless nave was covered *c.*1150 by three large bays of domical vaulting—steep rib vaults separated by high, pointed transverse arches which carry the weight of the very high vaults.

The first pilgrimage church at Vézelay was sacked by the Normans, and in 878 was rebuilt on the top of the hill. In the 11th century it claimed to have the relics of S. Mary *Magdalene, based on a fantastic popular legend. The new church was built to accommodate thousands of pilgrims, to whom were joined those on the way to Santiago de Compostela, for which it was a staging post for pilgrims going from Germany and E. France to Spain. The nave was rebuilt from 1120 to its completion and dedication in 1132, with groin vaults, and the capitals of the columns were carved with figures and stories. The great *portal with its three-bay vestibule was finished by *c.*1150. The Gothic choir and transept were rebuilt, 1185–1215. The Hundred Years War (1338–1453) ruined the country and pilgrimages died out; the Religious Wars of the 16th century left Vézelay delapidated, the Revolution even more so. By 1840 when it threatened to collapse, the French Historic Monuments Commission undertook to restore it, and *Viollet-le-duc here began his long career.

In the Loire area, the major survivor is the Abbey of St-Benoît-sur-Loire, once called Fleury, dating from the mid-11th century to *c.*1130. Its most unusual feature is the huge square porch, with massive piers with carved capitals on the columns. The choir is raised above the level of the nave to accommodate a crypt for the relics of S. Benedict, dug out of the ruins of Monte Cassino left desolate after a Lombard raid in 585. Provence shows strong Burgundian influence since St-Gilles-du-Gard was once a Cluniac pilgrimage church, begun after 1077. The triple portal was being made by 1142, and was finished *c.*1195. St-Trophime, Arles, is a partly 10th-century basilica, with exceptional portal sculpture, and a cloister which, with Moissac, is among the finest in France.

The Norsemen, so destructive from the 8th century onwards, finally became colonists in N. France, and the last effective Carolingian monarch, Charles the Bald, in 911 granted Rollo (Hrolf) land round the mouth of the Seine as a fief, which was eventually called Normandy after them. Rollo became a Christian in 912, as Robert, but the history of the Duchy is chequered before William dispossessed his brothers and eventually, in 1066, conquered England. In 1002 monks from St-Bénigne, Dijon, came to reform Norman monasteries; Bernay is probably their first work. It was built between 1017 and 1040, was as large as Cluny II and much the same in design. During the French Revolution it became a barn, but is now in proper care. Following the influence from Dijon and Cluny came the Lombard Lanfranc who founded the Abbey of Bec (Le Bec-Hellouin, SW of Rouen, built between 1066 and 1077), which became a centre of learning. (Lanfranc later was Archbishop of Canterbury, which he also rebuilt.) Jumièges, now a ruin, on the Seine downstream from Rouen, had been founded in 654 but suffered the usual fate, and was entirely rebuilt from 1037; it was awaiting the presence of Duke William for its dedication in 1067, but he was then busy conquering England. The abbey's architectural links are with *Ottonian forms, in the huge westwork with upper chamber, and massive towers which are part of the façade, reflecting the influence of Strasbourg, the first Saxon-built church to incorporate towers in the west front. It is an early example of a more harmonious Romanesque west façade. The east end had a vaulted *ambulatory following the latest pilgrimage church designs. Besides the two towers of the westwork, there was a wooden tower over the crossing, recalling St-Riquier. Most of its features were important for later developments in England.

The two great abbeys in Caen, founded between 1062 and 1067 by William the Conqueror and his wife Matilda—St-Étienne, or the *Abbaye aux Hommes*, and La Trinité, or the *Abbaye aux Dames*—have been much rebuilt. Both churches were originally timber-roofed, and have massive west towers as part of their façades, those of St-Étienne now crowned by beautiful Gothic spires. The severity of the façade of St-Étienne, with its rows of tall round-headed windows, are what English Romanesque church façades were probably like before the almost universal intrusion into them of huge Perpendicular Gothic traceried windows. The three tiers of choir windows in La Trinité are also found at the very dámaged Cerisy-la-Forêt, near Bayeux. Lessay, N. of Coutances, founded from Bec, was built between about 1030 and 1091 on the normal Cluniac design of Bernay, with a long nave, a three-storey elevation of nave arcade, *triforium, and *clerestory, and the earliest rib-vaulting in France, of *c.*1100. It was destroyed during the Second World War, but because of its archaeological importance it has been reconstructed. These churches are important in view of the pre-Conquest appearance of some of these forms in England, particularly in King Edward the Confessor's rebuilding of Westminster Abbey, and particularly for later developments in England after 1066.

French MS painting was backward-looking during the 10th and 11th centuries, so that Carolingian forms persisted. A mid-11th-century *Christ in Majesty* from a missal produced at St-Denis (Paris, BN) repeats formulas of Carolingian illumination current two centuries earlier. Some English influence percolated into N. France through the Abbey of St-Bertin, near St-Omer, where English artists in the *scriptorium introduced the vivid movement and fluid drawing of drapery current in Canterbury. MSS from the Abbey of St-Vaast, Arras, also show the mixture of a still-living Carolingian tradition with Anglo-Saxon influence. After the Norman Conquest the currents flowed both ways, since English scriptoria were now more open to Continental influence.

Even Cîteaux, the major Cistercian monastery founded in opposition to Cluniac opulence, was influenced by Anglo-Saxon art in that one of its founding abbots was the biblical scholar and hymnologist S. Robert Harding. In the early years the scriptorium of Cîteaux concentrated on texts for their monastic life, including Robert Harding's Bible of Cîteaux (Dijon, Bib. Municip.) of 1109–33, which contains figures in lively drawing and decorative scrolls full of the birds and beasts that inhabit English MSS of the period. But the burgeoning artistic life of the Cistercians was stifled by *Bernard of Clairvaux who, when he became abbot, campaigned effectively against the intrusion of any art into the churches of the Order; he regarded it as an expensive distraction.

Few examples of free-standing sculpture have survived, in comparison with the wealth which has survived as part of a building, either as carved capitals or as the very important *portal sculpture. St-Sernin, Toulouse, one of the major pilgrimage churches on the road to Santiago de Compostela, was begun *c.*1060 and the choir was dedicated in 1096. Round the ambulatory are seven marble reliefs; in the centre is a *Christ in Majesty* with the Evangelist Symbols, two reliefs of angels, and two of Apostles. They are derived from ivories of Byzantine and Carolingian origin and are also evidence of the survival in the South of France of its classical past.

It is in the carving of capitals that the richest vein is found of biblical illustration, moralizing themes, and pure fantasy. The capitals of the great porch and the choir of St-Benoît-sur-Loire, carved at the end of the 11th century, have very mixed themes. Old Testament themes such as the Sacrifice of Abraham, Daniel in the Lions' Den, and Jonah and the Whale, which are *types of Christ, and of the Entombment and Resurrection, Gospel narratives from the Annunciation to the Flight into Egypt, and the story of S. Martin of Tours, are mixed with purely decorative fronds. From the choir colonnade of Cluny III only eight capitals and two from adjacent pilasters have survived, and among these are such themes as the tones of music, the Liberal *Arts, the *Rivers of Paradise, as well as biblical themes such as Adam and Eve after the Fall. They were probably carved in the early 12th century. The capitals at Autun, from *c.*1120–32, are famous because the sculptor's name, Gislebertus, has survived. Again, the themes are the didactic ones, which teach by the representation of Gospel narratives and selected typological examples from the OT, or are admonitory as in the Combat of *Virtues and Vices, or the dire results of sin. They are indeed sermons in stone and were designed as such. Sometimes purely classical themes appear—Ganymede carried off by an eagle, or the Personification of the Winds at Vézelay, 1120–40, or purely secular themes such as the Labours of the Month, or two-tailed Mermaids. Occasionally a statue has survived; a 12th-century *Virgin and Child* in wood (Louvre) or an enthroned *Virgin and Child* in painted wood and metal at Orcival, near Clermont-Ferrand in central France, and great cult images, such as the figure of Ste Foi (Foy) at Conques, part devotional image, part *reliquary. The abbey also has a wonderfully carved tympanum of *c.*1124 over the west door, showing Christ in Majesty, Heaven and Hell, reminding pilgrims on the road to Compostela of the reason for and the ultimate end of their pilgrimage.

England

Edward the Confessor was the son of the luckless Aethelred the Unready and Emma, daughter of Richard I of Normandy. When he was deposed in 1014, Aethelred fled to Normandy, where he died in 1016. Edward, then 13, remained in Normandy when his mother returned to England in 1016 to marry Canute, King of England and Denmark. Canute's line failed in 1042, and Earl Godwin of Wessex secured Edward's election as King. When Godwin died in 1053 his power was inherited by his son Harold. Edward's main interests were hunting and the rebuilding of Westminster Abbey on a Cluniac plan, to be larger and more splendid than anything in England. Building began *c.*1045/50, and enough was finished for a dedication in 1065, a few weeks before Edward died in January 1066. The Bayeux Tapestry shows Edward's death and funeral procession to the abbey: there are no west towers, but a nave and a large, complex crossing tower, and that the building is unfinished is indicated by a man on a ladder fixing a weathervane on the choir, though that part must have been complete.

In 1064 Harold was in Normandy, and a prisoner of Duke William, who forced him to swear a solemn oath on relics that he would support his, William's, claim to the English crown, which he said Edward had promised to him (they were cousins and Edward was childless). Harold, elected to succeed, repudiated the oath and was crowned by Stigand, Archbishop of Canterbury. He was killed at the Battle of Hastings in October 1066. What the Bayeux Tapestry documents is William's side of a dynastic struggle, and it endeavours to legitimize his invasion by stressing the moral side of the story of a perjured man who swore a sacred oath, betrayed it, and was punished for his sin. William was crowned on Christmas Day, 1066, in Westminster Abbey; Stigand was deposed in 1070, and Lanfranc, Prior of Bec and Abbot of St-Étienne in Caen, became Archbishop of Canterbury. The pacification of the kingdom included the expropriation of the Anglo-Saxon landowners in favour of William's followers and the replacement of all Anglo-Saxon bishops except Wulfram of Worcester with Normans, who immediately set about replacing the modest Anglo-Saxon churches with new cathedrals and abbeys built according to Norman style. The pace was fantastic. In 1067 William ordered the building of Battle Abbey to commemorate his victory (it was said to have had an altar over the spot where Harold was killed); its apse with an ambulatory and radiating chapels was consecrated in 1076, and must have been the first such church in England. Lanfranc began rebuilding Canterbury in 1070, with a triapsidal plan like Westminster. Bury St Edmunds was begun in 1070, Lincoln and Gloucester in 1072, S. Augustine's Abbey at Canterbury, in 1073, Rochester and St Albans in 1077, Winchester in 1079, Ely in 1083, and Worcester in 1084, when Wulfram wept to have to replace his Anglo-Saxon church with a new-style Norman one. Durham was begun in 1093 and set an entirely new form; the choir aisles were built between 1095 and 1100, and are the first use of rib-vaulting. While these great churches follow precedents set in Normandy they are of far greater size—naves from eight to fourteen bays long—and the choirs are usually of two forms: apsidal, with or without flanking aisles, or triapsidal, the central apse being flanked by lesser apses. Norwich and Peterborough had ambulatories, and Norwich also had one round the apse at both choir and gallery level. None of these churches has survived unaltered, and even where the wide curve of the apse survives, with the three storeys of windows like La Trinité in Caen or Cerisy-la-Forêt, the later addition of retrochoirs has changed the original forms. Perhaps the most striking features of all these churches is that, though they have their roots in Bernay, Jumièges, and Caen, they are far larger, higher, grander than anything built in Normandy or France, and with the exception of Cluny III, before the great building campaigns of 13th-century Gothic. In scale, their affinities are with contemporary German churches. They are an architecture imposed by an alien, dominant clergy, who rejected the Anglo-Saxon which they replaced, and which owe nothing to the older churches they despised and superseded.

Almost nothing has survived of the contents of the treasuries of pre-Reformation abbeys and cathedrals. The twenty-four cartloads which, between 1536 and 1540, carried the treasures of Canterbury to the Royal Mint are proof of the zeal of Henry VIII's commissioners, and the same tide of despoliation spread over the whole country. MSS suffered less; once their precious covers had been removed they had no further intrinsic value. Many have, therefore, survived, but only a few three-dimensional works. Church carvings—capitals, fonts, portals, were not affected at this time; their destruction came with the Puritans of the Commonwealth. Among the larger pieces of pre-Conquest sculpture are the *Christ in Majesty* in Barnack church, near Stamford, the Bristol Cathedral *Harrowing of Hell*, the huge *Crucified Christ* at Romsey Abbey, probably of the early 11th century, and the *Crucifixion*, with the Virgin and S. John, of similar date, at Langford, near Burford (Oxon.), which unfortunately was reassembled wrongly when it was moved to its present position. Smaller works include a book-cover in silver, gilded metal, and gold filigree (New York, Morgan Lib.) with a *Christ in Majesty* flanked by seraphim above a *Crucifixion* with the Virgin and S. John. It was made for Judith, daughter-in-law of Earl Godwin, and is therefore obviously before 1066. The Gloucester candlestick, made between 1104 and 1113 (London, V & A), was probably made in England since the convoluted inhabited scrolls with which it is decorated are English in type; the high quality of the bronze casting makes even more tragic these lone survivals of a lost art.

Among the larger pieces of sculpture are the two panels in Chichester Cathedral, probably of *c.*1150, with *Mary and Martha at the feet of Christ*, and the *Raising of Lazarus*. An unusual work of great technical virtuosity is the carved whalebone panel of the *Adoration of the Magi* (London, V & A), the origins of which probably lie in the cross-influences of England, N. France, and Liège.

The great richness of Anglo-Saxon MS illumination as, for instance, in the Winchester *benedictional of S. Aethelwold (London, BL) of the late 10th century, survived also in the scriptoria of Ely and Canterbury, and for even longer in Winchester itself in luxuriant frames and borders. But after 1066 there was an obvious gap while William consolidated his grip on the country. The upheavals caused by the removal of the Anglo-Saxon bishops and abbots from their churches (most English cathedrals were either monastic or communities of Augustinian canons) and the years during their rebuilding more to Norman taste, were not ones which favoured MS production. The most famous is the Domesday Book, begun in 1086, which is not a religious MS, but a register of property for the purpose of tax-gathering. As Anglo-Saxon illumination had been in the front rank in Europe, it was the church buildings, not the books, that the Normans changed. But one result was the opening up of English scriptoria to influences from Carolingian, Ottonian, and Italian sources.

At Canterbury, with the newly appointed Archbishop Lanfranc and the Norman monks he brought with him, little changed, since it had always had the most contacts with Continental forms. After 1070, more MSS were produced with historiated initials, a Norman taste which stemmed largely from Carolingian examples. Some are so large that they are no longer subsidiary to the text, but are the main illuminations, often taking up most of the page (although some of the most extravagant examples of these are in Irish and English MSS of the 7th to 9th centuries, so they were hardly a new form). In the 12th century new sources of inspiration arrived with increased contacts with the Mediterranean, through the connections of the Normans in the North with those who were carving out new kingdoms for themselves in S. Italy and Sicily, and also from the First Crusade, preached in 1095. Byzantine influences are reflected in the bold characterization of figures set, like mosaics, firmly in a frame, and this shows in the Canterbury Psalter of the scribe Eadwine, *c.*1150 (Cambridge, Trinity Coll.), who used a *Utrecht Psalter type of vividly drawn outline illustrations translating the incidents of the psalm into literal renderings. In the Bury Bible (Cambridge, Corpus Christi Coll.) of 1121–48, illuminated by a 'Master Hugo', a secular artist who was also a goldsmith, the illustrations are rich in colour with firm outlines and much gold, and are influenced by Sicilian mosaics, though retaining the traditional twisting branches and exotic birds in many of the initials. The Winchester Bible (Cath. Lib.) probably of 1160–70 and commissioned by Bishop Henry of Blois, brother of King Henry I, is the major work of the period.

Wall-paintings have survived at Canterbury, notably the restored 12th-century *S. Paul* in St Anselm's Chapel in the crypt. There is also *stained glass at Canterbury from the time of the rebuilding of the choir after the fire of 1174.

Germany

When Otto III died in 1002, leaving no male heir, the crown passed successively to Henry II, Conrad II, Henry III, IV, and V, the last dying childless in 1125. The prestige and influence of the Church was increased by the preaching of the First Crusade in 1095 in a long-delayed—but enthusiastically received—response to the appeals of the Byzantine Emperor after Jerusalem had been taken by the Seljuk Turks in 1071, and access to the Holy Places became impossible. Among the churches founded in the early 11th century are Strasbourg Cathedral of *c.*1015, which set a precedent for towers forming part of a west front; Worms Cathedral, 1000–25, though most of it is late 11th and 12th century; and Maria Laach, 1093, mostly 12th/13th centuries. For sheer scale, Mainz and Speyer cathedrals exceed any other church of their time. Speyer was founded in 1030 as a royal burial-place, but only part of the crypt of that campaign survives. It was enlarged by Henry III and IV, vaulted in 1100, and given multiple towers, but it was extensively rebuilt after having been burnt by the French in 1689. St Maria im Capitol, Cologne, was built 1048–65 with an unusual trefoil east end, possibly influenced by San Fedele, Como, a towered façade, and a tower over the crossing (now demolished). Two important churches were converted from late Antique buildings—Trier Cathedral from a square assembly hall, to which an apsidal east end and a characteristic westwork were added in 1050, and St Gereon, Cologne, an oval *martyrium to which a long nave was added in 1067–9. The great monasteries of Hirsau and Hersfeld, influenced by Cluny, are now huge ruins, but with Speyer, they were in the vanguard of the full development of Romanesque.

Eleventh-century Worms survives in the present church only because the foundations determined its size and shape; the rest is later. Among the largest churches, now in Belgium and Holland but which were then in Saxon lands, is St Gertrude, Nivelles, an 11th-century church with a huge turreted westwork. It was burnt during the Second World War, but has been restored. Tournai Cathedral was begun *c.*1110, and has a groin-vaulted nave with a nave elevation of four storeys, by the insertion of a second *triforium below the *clerestory. The original three apses of the east end were begun in 1165 with rib-vaulting, but the choir has since been rebuilt in Gothic. Tournai is outstanding for the fine grouping of its towers—a massive crossing tower, and four transeptal towers. Maastricht, in Holland, has two important churches, both with huge westworks: St Servatius, begun in 1087, when it became a royal monastery, and the Lady Church begun in 1000 and much worked on from 1150 onwards.

The patronage of Henry II was outstanding. To him are due two great *antependia—the so-called Golden Altar (Paris, Cluny Mus.) of *c.*1022–4: Christ the King in the centre flanked by three archangels and S. Benedict, and a second golden one, made *c.*1020, for the royal chapel at Aachen, later altered into a *reredos. Ten scenes of the Life of Christ surround a figure of Christ in Majesty. He also gave a carved marble *ambo to the chapel at Aachen, *c.*1002–14, shaped and ornamented like Bishop Agnello's 6th-century ambo in SS Giovanni e Paolo in Ravenna.

The Golden Gospels (Nuremberg), made for Henry III in the 1st half of the 11th century, are written in gold, with a full-page *Christ in Majesty*; two other MSS (Escorial Lib.) of 1045–6, made for Speyer, have, in one, Conrad II with his Empress Gisela crouched at the feet of a *Christ in Majesty*, and in the other Henry III with Empress Agnes presenting Speyer to the Virgin, both following a Byzantine form. Among the larger sculptures of the period are the wooden doors, about 15 ft. high, of St Maria im Capitol, Cologne, of 1050–65, and finely carved with scenes from the Life of Christ. The imagery ranges from the *Annunciation* to the *Baptism of Christ* on the left door, and from the *Entry into Jerusalem* to *Pentecost* on the right door; only three of the nine saints once at the base survive.

In 1100 the Bishop of Paderborn paid for a portable altar (Paderborn, Cath. Treasury) made by Roger, a monk of the nearby monastery of Helmarshausen, who is believed to be the monk *Theophilus, author of *De diversis artibus*, the most famous medieval technical manual on the arts. A *font, now in St-Bartélemy, Liège, is attributed to Rainier de Huy, who came from a town famous for metalwork. He is also believed to have carved some ivory book-covers; one, of the *Crucifixion with the Holy Women*, in Notre-Dame, Tongres, near Liège, has affinities, despite its small size, with the font, in the ease and grace of the figures, and the naturalism of the Crucified Christ, carved in high relief against a plain ground. Another, with the *Crucifixion* (Brussels, Mus.), of *c.*1150, so closely resembles a *Crucifixion* on a book-cover made for the Abbess Theophanu of Essen (now Essen Minster), of *c.*1050, that it seems probable, not that one is a copy of the other, but that they derive from a common source. That the two ivories were produced in different workshops a century apart is indicative of the long-lasting influence exerted both on design and iconography by an Early Christian or Byzantine original.

Scriptoria in the Meuse valley produced notable MSS, also strongly influenced by Italian and Byzantine art in style and iconography. The *Stavelot Bible* (London, BL) of 1093–7 has most of the illustrations compressed into the initials, but it contains an impressive full-page *Christ in Majesty* with roundels of the Evangelists. The bold and vivid characterization reflects Ottonian models, and the figure is given greater power by being compressed within its Greek key frame. It also reflects the energy and power of Rainier de Huy's font. Influence from Italian and Sicilian mosaics can be found in many MSS and wall-paintings: the vault in the crypt of St Maria im Capitol, Cologne, painted with late 12th-century scenes from the *Life of the Baptist* and the 13th-century apse painting in the church at Saeby, near Frederikshavn, N. Denmark, of *Christ in Majesty* show how widely their influence was felt. The expository qualities of Byzantine art appear in works such as the *Crucifixion* in the Floreffe Bible (London, BL) of *c.*1160 where the scene under the cross is of the sin-offering of the calf—OT and NT *type and antitype. This Italian and Byzantine influence spread through most German scriptoria and workshops during the whole 12th century and operated on the subject-matter, and also on the techniques used, in that *champlevé* enamels were used to imitate the more costly *cloisonné* enamels used in 11th-century court art. The gilt-bronze antependium of *c.*1120–30, in the church at Gross-Komburg, near Schwäbisch Hall, has a central Christ in an enamelled mandorla flanked by the Apostles each framed by bands of enamels. The nearest comparison is with the Golden Altar of Henry II (Paris, Cluny Mus.) of 100 years earlier. The other major work at Gross-Komburg is the circular candelabrum of *c.*1130, over 15 ft. wide, in pierced bronze with towered gates as the candle-holders, each with figures of saints and angels, representing the Heavenly Jerusalem as described in the Apocalypse. It follows the design of the candelabrum at Hildesheim Cathedral, made between 1054 and 1070, and in turn became the model for the larger candelabrum given by the Emperor Frederick Barbarossa to Aachen Cathedral in 1166.

When the last Saxon emperor, Henry V, died childless in 1125, the electing princes and bishops refused to elect his nephew for fear of making the empire hereditary. Two emperors later, after a bitter civil war between the factions of the Welf and the Weiblingen (a Hohenstaufen castle)—factions known elsewhere as Guelf and Ghibelline—the choice fell on the only man who belonged to both families. Frederick I of Hohenstaufen, better known as Frederick Barbarossa (Red Beard), became emperor in 1152. The magnificent golden Shrine of Charlemagne was made between 1165 and 1215 for Aachen as the coronation church of the German emperors. On it the face of Charlemagne bears the features of Emperor Frederick Barbarossa who had Charlemagne canonized, unfortunately by the anti-Pope. His forays into Italy began in 1154 in pursuit of his claim to be the new Charlemagne, and continued until he was defeated by the Lombard League in 1176 at the battle of Legnano.

His son, Henry VI, pursued the same megalomaniac ideas as his father, but where his father was a man of honour, Henry was cruel and treacherous. He raised the empire to great power externally, but Germany remained politically unstable. He married the heiress of Sicily, pacified the island, and was crowned in Palermo in 1194. Despite Barbarossa's failure to make the empire hereditary, when Henry died in Sicily in 1197 his only child, Frederick, was accepted as emperor.

One consequence of the fervour with which the Hohenstaufens pursued their Italian ambitions was the influence on German architecture of Lombard forms. The triple apses of St Maria im Capitol (*c.*1040–1219) and of the Holy Apostles (from *c.*1190), both in Cologne, have strong Lombard features, the latter with small arcaded galleries under the eaves—virtually a Lombard trademark—and on the built-up exterior of the later high central tower, and these features are even more marked in Gross St Martin, Cologne, of 1185 onwards, where the massive central tower, its flanking turrets, and the triple apses all have the decorative arcading, as well as gables with oculi surrounded by blind round windows. Murbach, near Colmar, but then in Germany, is only a fragment of its original size, but is still an impressive late 12th-century choir with a double-towered transept—a form adapted from Sant'Abbondio, Como, built fifty years earlier. Lombard decorative features are present in Worms, Mainz, Maria Laach, Andernach, reaching into the 13th century, as for instance at Limburg-an-der-Lahn, of 1235, where the exuberant tiers of arcading and blind windows, central wheel window, and oculi are in brilliant contrasts of light and dark stone, and inside offers the first virtually French Gothic interior based on Laon, while the many-towered silhouette looks back to Tournai. By the end of the 13th century, instead of being a source of inspiration, Germany is a net receiver of new ideas.

The greatest master of metalwork and enamelling of the late 12th century was *Nicholas of Verdun, who in 1181 finished, for the Abbey of Klosterneuburg, outside Vienna, a pulpit or ambo in *champlevé* enamels, which was later converted into a *retable (still *in situ*). He is also credited with the design and much of the work on the Shrine of the Three Kings in Cologne Cathedral, also still *in situ*. From the late 11th century onwards, Italo-Byzantine influence was strong in S. Germany and Austria. The major centre was Salzburg, where there were flourishing workshops of goldsmiths, carvers, and painters, producing many

MSS with initials and figures of Italo-Byzantine and Ottonian type. One of the grandest MSS is an *Antiphonary* (Vienna, Hofbibl.) with flowing tinted outline drawings which in their clarity and fluidity combine the incisiveness of metalwork with a rhythm and feeling for the solidity of bodies beneath the flowing draperies. An outline drawing of *Christ in Majesty* (Vienna, Hofbibl.) is as monumental as any of the great figures from mosaics, either in Greece or Sicily.

Italy

The links between late Classical, or Early Christian, and Romanesque architecture come to the fore in N. Italy. In *Milan Sant'Ambrogio, founded by S. Ambrose in 385, San Lorenzo Maggiore and San Simpliciano, both also 4th century, were built during the brief period *c.*285–395, when Milan was the capital of the Empire of the West. Barbarian invasions compelled the removal of the capital to the safety of the Adriatic marshes, where *Ravenna was founded in the early 5th century. Skill in building had continued in the area between Lakes Como and Lugano known as the Isola Comacina. During the 9th and 10th centuries Lombard builders—*Maestri Comacini*—spread across N. Italy, and into France and Spain, and their characteristic building forms can be traced over these areas and into the Rhineland and Switzerland.

When Sant'Ambrogio was rebuilt in 824–59, as Milan emerged from its political troubles, the forms were those of its Lombard builders. San Lorenzo Maggiore is also one of the most important Early Christian churches to survive from Milan's brief period as an imperial capital. It was built in the mid-4th century, was restored in the 12th century, partially collapsed in 1573, and was restored by Cardinal *Borromeo. The building which has survived is the largest centrally planned Early Christian church, built on a classical Roman scale, for which the only comparisons are the Hagia Sophia in Constantinople, and Michelangelo's project for St Peter's. No architectural details remain to link it with the Lombard builders whose masterpiece it was, though the tower to the south is one of the earliest remaining, dating from the 10th century. San Simpliciano has suffered so much reworking over the centuries that little survives but its basilical form.

Arcaded external galleries are a striking feature of 12th-century N. Italian churches such as the cathedrals of Parma, Piacenza, and Modena. Most of these N. Italian churches are basilical with domes borne on squinches over the crossing, covered with an octagonal tower-like structure, called a *tiburio*, often with a blind arcade under the eaves of its roof. The most unusual church is San Fedele, Como, where a short nave leads to three semi-domed apses round the crossing dome, all with ambulatories leading from the aisles. The plan is probably 11th century, although the church was not finished until the 12th, raising interesting parallels with St Maria im Capitol in Cologne, of similar form and date, particularly as the Cologne church has such obvious Lombard features in its blind arcading. The other major church in Como is the Abbey of Sant'Abbondio, built from 1063 and dedicated in 1095, with double aisles to the nave, and tall towers rising above the transepts and flanking the apsidal end. This church was very influential in Germany; for instance, at Murbach near Colmar, St Gereon, Cologne, and Maria Laach.

All these major churches, particularly Parma and Modena, are very high, and usually have a three-storey elevation. Parma and Modena have deep crypts under their elevated choirs, and high domical vaulting in the nave. Parma also has one of the largest baptisteries, begun in 1196; an octagonal structure with a high-arched base, four storeys of colonnades above it, and an attic. Inside is an octagonal dome, with frescoes from 1260 onwards, with a *Deësis at the top, and Old and New Testament scenes below. There are also sculptures by Antelami and his followers. Modena was begun *c.*1099 by a Maestro Lanfranco described as *mirabilis artifex, mirificus aedificator* (wonderful craftsman, astonishing builder), though work continued into the next centuries, since the huge *rose window is 13th century and the vaulting is 15th century.

Other notable features of these Lombard and Emilian churches are the porches borne on columns which rest on the backs of *lions. The symbolism of these lions, which often hold in their claws a man or a serpent, is obscure but of ancient origin, and has been variously interpreted as watchfulness, from the belief that lions sleep with their eyes open, or from their common use as symbols of strength and courage. The man is not seen as being devoured, while the serpent is being attacked and vanquished, hence also the idea that the man is defended or warned, and the serpent or beast of Evil is being destroyed. The frequent use of lions under the columns which support pulpits (e.g. those by the Pisani) is also part of the mythology of the lion equalling strength, vigilance, and truth, and owes much of its power to the story of Daniel, and to being the symbol of S. Mark, and the companion of S. Jerome. Also notable are the huge towers which flank the churches; Sant'Ambrogio, Milan, has one either side of the nave, of the 11th and 12th centuries, and among the most impressive are those of Parma and Modena cathedrals, San Zeno, Verona, of 1045–1178, and the Abbey of Pomposa, over 150 ft. high, built in 1036. Most double as campaniles, but their size outstrips this function.

Like Ravenna, *Venice is a place apart, but some cities in the Véneto, such as Verona, fall within the scope of Lombard Romanesque. San Zeno, arguably the finest Romanesque church in N. Italy, was rebuilt twice from its 5th-century origins and was completed in the early 13th century. The columns of the porch, as usual, rest on lions, and the front has important sculpture as well as bronze *doors. At the end of the very high nave, the apsidal choir is raised above a deep crypt. Its most celebrated altarpiece is by *Mantegna.

Romanesque in Tuscany is very different, for 10th-century forms persist to blend with Gothic in the 14th century. Pisa Cathedral was begun in 1063 by an architect called Buscheto, and continued building into the 13th century. It is one of the largest churches in Italy, cruciform, with an oval dome over the crossing, with no *tiburio* to conceal the domical shape. Unlike N. Italian churches it is built of white marble, with the characteristic Pisan decoration of multiple columns and inlays of coloured marble. The separate baptistery is similarly decorated, and has sculpture by both the Pisani. The complex is completed by the famous Leaning Tower and the *campo santo with the cloister surrounding the cemetery, also built in the 13th century. The prolific use of coloured marble, so that the piers of the tribunes and the arches of the aisles are striped dark grey-green and creamy white, increases the decorative quality in complete contrast to the more austere character of Romanesque in Lombardy and Emilia. The sculpture of Nicola Pisano in the baptistery pulpit is, in its classicism, entirely Romanesque, but that of his son, in both the baptistery sculpture and the cathedral pulpit, reaches forward to Gothic.

The oldest surviving building in Florence is probably the baptistery, which may go back to the 5th century, but was much reworked; the interior of the dome contains mosaics of the 13th and 14th centuries probably executed by Venetian mosaicists or by artists trained by them. They include a *Christ in Majesty*, with a *Last Judgement*, *Prophets*, and the *Hierarchies of Angels*. The strong Byzantine influence exerted by these mosaics had a powerful effect on the development of 13th-and 14th-century Florentine art. The three sets of bronze doors are of the 14th and 15th century (*see* GHIBERTI). The cathedral opposite was rebuilt by Arnolfo di Cambio at the end of the 13th century. Both buildings are covered with a revetment of coloured marbles in green-grey and creamy white, which is the characteristic Tuscan decorative system. On the hillside above the town, San Miniato al Monte was begun in 1018. It has the early Romanesque deep crypt under the apsidal east end with the high altar on the bridge-like system over the crypt reached by steps from the aisles. The nave arcades are spanned by transverse arches which support the open timber roof. The striped marble decoration of the outside is repeated inside.

Siena Cathedral was begun in 1196, and the cruciform building with a hexagonal dome on large squinches continued being built well into the late 13th century when Giovanni Pisano began the façade. The whole building, inside and out, is in coloured marble stripes, as is the tall campanile. The baptistery lies under the main apse, which it supports, and is a 14th-century building, notable for the sculptors employed on the font, who include *Donatello. But with Siena, despite its round-headed arches and its starting date, the move into Gothic is clear. It is also clear for Orvieto, begun in 1290, as a commemoration of the miracle of *Bolsena. It is Romanesque in its general form, though most of the building was 13th and 14th century and executed in stripes of dark and light stone. The façade has remarkable sculpture, with bronze symbols of the Evangelists and marble panels, probably by Maitani, one of which portrays with graphic force the horrors of Hell, though these are

Gothic rather than Romanesque. In the 12th century churches in *Rome were still the Early Christian ones, though some were rebuilt in the 11th century after disasters. Outside Rome, the majority of 11th- and 12th-century churches were rebuilt by the cardinals and princes in whose estates they lay.

S. Italy was bedevilled by the struggles between the Byzantine Empire and invading barbarians who settled it in the 6th century, leaving only the extreme south to the Byzantines. The country remained a prey to war, bandits, pirates, marauding Saracens, and the campaigns of the German emperors, chiefly Otto I and II. The Byzantines regained control at the end of the 9th century but oppressive rule and taxation brought rebellion in 1009–12, during which the Normans came to the fore. They had come from the 10th century as pilgrims to the shrine of S. Michael Archangel on Monte Gargano (a shrine in a cave founded in the 490s), and many remained as mercenaries. They soon realized that the land was an 'empty quarter', and they set about conquering it. By the end of the 11th century William of Hauteville took the title of Count of Apulia. In 1054 Pope Leo IX was defeated by the Norman Robert Guiscard, who made himself Duke of Apulia and Calabria and in 1059 a later pope invested him with the fief, and promised him the Kingdom of Sicily 'if he could expel the Saracens'. He controlled most of the south by 1071, and between 1071 and 1091 the Normans completed the conquest of Sicily. Early in the 13th century S. Italy and Sicily passed to the Hohenstaufen emperor Frederick II (1220–50). Soon after his death control passed to another northerner, Charles of Anjou, who transferred his capital to Naples.

In 1087 a force from Bari went to Myra in Greece and stole the relics of *S. Nicholas (d. 326) and brought them back to Bari, where the cult resulted in the large basilica of San Nicola, completed in 1197. The cathedral, of 1170–8, is like San Nicola—nave and two aisles, very wide transept, and three apses in the east end. All up the coast are austere churches; Trani, for instance, standing immediately on the shore, is composed of two churches one over the other, and the upper church has magnificent figured bronze doors of 1175–9 by Barisano, who also worked at Ravello and Monreale in Sicily. The sanctuary of S. Michael at Monte Gargano is not a normal church, but is a cave closed by bronze doors made in Constantinople in 1076. At Otranto in 1080–8 the Norman Bohemund built the cathedral, which has one of the largest pictorial mosaic floors in Italy.

Sculpture and Architectural Decoration

The finest sculpture in N. Italy is in the small chapel of Sta Maria della Valle, in Cividale del Friuli beyond Udine in the far NE of Italy. The chapel was built by a Visigothic king, and some sculpture from his time—the 9th century at latest—is still in the chapel. There are also six magnificent, life-size figures of female saints in stucco which may well be of Ottonian date, i.e. of the 10th century, since their grave nobility is consistent with other examples of Ottonian art, though there is no similar sculpture except ivories to which they can be related. So much controversy has surrounded their dating that it seems reasonable to begin this section with them, in case they are—as has been averred—Byzantine-inspired Venetian work of the 12th century or later.

Sant'Ambrogio, Milan, has a 12th-century pulpit with a low-relief panel with a grave, stiff *Last Supper* with an elaborate table setting, and below it a relief of stylized animals and beasts. Reliefs of this kind, with odd mixtures of secular and religious type, remain common, particularly in the carved jambs of church doors. The major works of the 12th century by the sculptor Wiligelmo on the façade of Modena Cathedral are reliefs from Genesis and figures of prophets, contemporary with works in S. France, and French influence on him is strong. Two of his assistants worked at San Zeno, Verona, on the panels flanking the main door, creating scenes from Genesis and the Life of Christ. The bronze doors of San Zeno were made in two stages; the older reliefs, from the 11th-century doors, fairly crude in execution, are of OT and NT subjects and are now in the lower parts of both doors. When the church was enlarged in the 12th century the doors were remade, incorporating the older panels, but with new panels of OT subjects, and the Life of S. Zeno.

At the end of the 12th century and the beginning of the 13th, Benedetto *Antelami dictus* (called Antelami), who probably came from the Lombard Alps, worked at Parma. He was influenced by classical sculpture, and certainly knew Provence, perhaps having been trained there, possibly at St-Trophime in Arles. 1178 is the first fixed date for his work in Parma Baptistery, where he carved a *Deposition*, with very expressive figures—particularly the soldiers dicing for Christ's seamless garment—and unusual features such as *Ecclesia* and *Synagoga* standing on either side of the cross. His baptistery doors include the 'Door of Redemption', of 1196, with the *Madonna and Child*, and the Shepherds and the Three Kings in the tympanum; on the lintel are scenes from the Life of S. John the Baptist; the *Last Judgement* door has an impressive Christ as Judge, and angels holding the Instruments of the Passion. These are French rather than Italian themes. In a niche in one of the blind arcades are the figures of Solomon and the Queen of Sheba. Another tympanum has an *Allegory of Life*, depicting Man's futile effort to escape the consequences of sin and folly. This subject travelled to the West through Byzantium, and like the same allegory in a panel at Ferrara, it shows that the moral and philosophical subjects which had already appeared in French portal sculpture were also now appearing in Italy. In the 11th century *Venice had no definite artistic personality, but by the 12th century Venetian taste turned to Byzantine art as a source, leaving it distinct from the rest of Italy.

In central Italy, decorative stonework, such as intarsia floors and *transennae were general. Larger pieces of sculpture include fine *pulpits, such as the one in Pisa Baptistery by Nicola *Pisano, and a font in San Frediano, Lucca, with the story of Moses. Bonanno made two pairs of bronze doors for Pisa Cathedral in 1180. One pair was destroyed in a fire, but the pair with the *Life of Christ* survives. The revival of sculpture in Tuscany came with the work of Pisano and his son Giovanni.

In S. Italy, a mixture of Byzantine and Arab art comes mainly in the form of decorative pavements, pulpits, and altar fittings worked in intarsia or Cosmati techniques, of which the finest are those of 1155–88, in Salerno Cathedral, built by Robert Guiscard. Many doorways have porches on columns with lions and griffins much like those in N. Italy. At Ravello, San Pantaleon has bronze doors by Barisanus of Trani, in which some of the reliefs used in the doors he made for Trani, and Monreale in Sicily, were reused. But no sculptor of any great note has been identified; there is, however, the suggestion that Nicola Pisano originally came from Apulia, and migrated to Tuscany, and the very classical head of a young woman personifying Divine Wisdom, which is over the stair leading to the pulpit in Ravello, is suggested as evidence for this.

Painting and Mosaics

There is little point in trying to separate the two arts. In Rome, the tradition of mosaic decoration was inherited from Early Christian example; in Venice, it came from Byzantium. The cost of mosaics meant that they were only created where cost did not matter, but in less affluent communities wall-paintings were originally an acceptable substitute, to become with the passage of time the unquestioned choice.

In general, wall-painting was not a favourite form in Tuscany, as decorative marble wall revetments were popular before the 14th century. Painting was used for the large crucifixes (*see* CROCE DIPINTA) and for retables, particularly of the Madonna and Child (*see* MADONNA TYPES), or for pictures of saints. Byzantine influence remains the major influence on both painting and mosaic decoration until the very end of the 14th century.

Manuscripts

In the 11th and 12th centuries the main centres for manuscript production were in the scriptoria of Benedictine monasteries, especially at Monte Cassino, and—for N. Italy—at Bobbio. A fine *Vita S. Benedicti* (Vatican Lib.) was made in 1070 for Abbot Desiderius of Monte Cassino, and also a lectionary in 1072 in which the Abbot, with the square halo denoting a living man, is depicted presenting the book to S. Benedict. Since Desiderius imported Byzantine artists, Byzantine influence pervades all the arts which were inspired from Monte Cassino. In S. Italy, the scriptoria of Troia and Benevento, influenced by Monte Cassino, were among the main sources of *Exsultet rolls. Of the very large bibles, known from their size as Atlantic bibles, one of the finest is the Pisa Bible made in 1169 for the cathedral (now at the Certosa di Calci, Pisa), in four volumes. An interesting 13th-century MS made in 1259 by Giovanni Gaibana is a lectionary (Padua, Cath. Treasury) containing a *Dormition of the Virgin*, dark in colour and entirely Byzantine in its treatment of the subject. There was also a strong cross-current between N. Italy and S. Germany, largely due to the Hohenstaufen emperors.

Spain and Portugal

In the early Middle Ages, the Mediterranean border between France and Spain did not exist. There is, therefore, no demarcation between the architecture north and south of the Pyrenees. Influences from Lombardy dominated church building probably well before the 10th century, since Lombard masons were then established in Barcelona, and many churches have the blind arcades under the eaves which are almost a hallmark of Lombard work. They are found at Ripoll, in N. Catalonia, a Benedictine monastery on the scale and plan of Old St Peter's, of *c*.1020–32, where the west front has sculpture on an iconographic and doctrinal programme made between 1160 and 1168, spread over a third of the façade; it is the earliest such portal in Spain. The abbot who rebuilt Ripoll was also Bishop of Vich, N. of the Pyrenees; he built St-Martin-du-Canigou perched on its crag, between 1001 and 1026, and rebuilt the 9th-century St-Michel-de-Cuxa, both near Prades, SW of Perpignan; both have the massive square towers like those at Ripoll, which are also a feature of Lombard churches.

In the rest of Spain, as the crusade against the Moors progressed, building was strongly affected by Mudéjar, Mozarabic, and Moorish influences (*see* PRE-ROMANESQUE: Visigothic) according to the background of the masons. San Vicente de Cardona, near Manresa, of 1020–40, is distinctly Lombard; Jaca Cathedral, E. of Pamplona, begun *c*.1060/70, is less so, but was not finished until the 12th century; and the cathedral of Seo de Urgel, near the Andorran border, of 1131–75, is the last major church of Lombard type. Tarragona Cathedral was begun in 1171, and was not finished until 1287. It has a Burgundian cloister which blends Cistercian form with Cluniac sculpture. The major Cistercian house in N. Spain was Poblet, of 1180–96, built with the usual pointed tunnel vaults of Cistercian Romanesque, and on a huge scale.

The progressive reconquest of Spain from the Moors, as Alfonso VI (1065–1109) enlarged and consolidated his kingdom, resulted in an influx mainly of French, since there were not enough Spaniards to fill the new territories and the newly founded religious houses. The king was a lavish patron of Cluny and Santiago, and in his reign the Abbey of Sahagún, near León, was refounded as a daughter-house of Cluny. A remarkable example of Moorish forms is in the church of the Holy Sepulchre at Torres del Rio, near Pamplona, of the late 12th century, where the dome of the small octagonal church is built in complex interlaced arches supporting the central lantern.

In León, a narthex was added in 1054–67 to an older church (rebuilt by 1063 as Sant'Isidoro), as a royal pantheon. It recalls the burial porch of the Carolingian St-Riquier and the first *St-Denis in idea, and in form the tower porch of St-Benoît-sur-Loire. The domical vaulting of the Panteón de los Reyes is covered in frescoes painted *c*.1175, and the capitals of the short and heavy columns and pilasters have a mixture of figurative and foliage carvings. The rebuilt Sant'Isidoro is an example of the influence from the *pilgrimage churches on the road to Santiago de Compostela, as happens all along the thirteen stages of the Spanish part of the route. Santiago itself is a major example of the form.

Zamora Cathedral, near the Portuguese border, was built between 1152 and 1174, and the dome over the crossing was inspired by the Church of the Holy Sepulchre in Jerusalem. The sixteen segments of the ribbed dome show a mixture of French and Muslim work; the roofs of the dome, and of the turrets and gables added later, are covered with rounded stone tiles like giant fish scales. These are also a feature of the crossing tower of the Old Cathedral at Salamanca, built after it was wrested from the Moors in 1050. The town was colonized by a Burgundian ruler, and the Old Cathedral (the new one is 16th cent.) is a mixture of various French forms. It has a ribbed dome of sixteen segments crowned on the outside with a conical roof covered with stone 'fish scales' as at Zamora. A third church, Sta Maria la Mayor, at Toro, near Zamora, dates from 1160 and is perhaps the finest Romanesque church in Spain.

A number of fine cloisters have carved capitals, usually double on twin columns. Sto Domingo de Silos, S. of Burgos, dates from 1085 to 1100, and has a two-storey cloister, with decorative capitals on the ground floor carved with scenes such as the *Annunciation to the Shepherds* and the *Flight into Egypt.* The records of names suggests that many of the sculptors were of Moorish origin. The lower ranges also have exceptional corner piers with panels carved with scenes from the Life of Christ—an *Annunciation* combined with a *Coronation of the Virgin* is most unusual, a *Tree of Jesse,* and scenes from the Passion. Piers with carved narrative panels had already appeared at the cloister of Moissac by 1100, and the spread of the idea is part of the influence of the Pilgrimage Road. Pamplona once had a Romanesque cloister of 1127–45, from which a few surviving capitals (now in the Museo de Navarra) include a very graphic *Story of Job,* and a *Passion* series from the Betrayal to the Resurrection, including a very rare scene of the Magdalene telling the incredulous Apostles about the Risen Christ. Other fine cloisters are those at Sta Maria de l'Estany, near Manresa, of the early 12th century; Gerona of *c.*1150, with narratives from Genesis; and Santillana del Mar, near Santander, of the late 12th/early 13th century.

The Capilla de San Miguel, of 1165–75, which is the antechamber to the Cámara Santa at Oviedo, has six columns each side, and carved as part of them are pairs of Apostles, each pair grouped as if in conversation. On the west wall is a fresco of the *Crucifixion* with Christ's head carved in high relief. Two unusual *Depositions,* both of the mid-12th century, carved in wood as free-standing groups of five life-sized figures were, one at San Juan de las Abadesas, near Ripoll, the other high in the mountains near Andorra at Erill-la-Vall: the one at San Juan is still *in situ,* the one from Erill-la-Vall is split up between Vich (Museo Episcopo) and Barcelona (Mus. de Arte de Cataluña). Both have reminiscences of Lombard art, and are similar to the *Deposition* groups in the cathedrals of Volterra and Tivoli, both early 12th century.

When Sant'Isidoro, León, was built in 1063, Fernando I and Queen Sancha presented a reliquary made in 1059, still in the church Treasury. In another reliquary of 1063, with scenes from Genesis of the *Creation,* and the rare subject of *God clothing Adam and Eve before the Expulsion,* there is some evidence that the carver knew Ottonian ivories—quite possible in view of the influx of French abbots into the newly recovered lands. Another royal gift was an ivory altar cross (Madrid, Mus. Arqueologico) carved on both sides, one of only three early medieval ivory crosses to survive; it is unusual in having below Christ's feet a tiny figure of the redeemed Adam, and above His head a *Risen Christ* with the dove of the Holy Spirit and two angels.

The Cámara Santa of Oviedo was wrecked in 1934 during the Spanish Civil War. The Arca Santa, a reliquary the size of an altar, of *c.*1075, was covered with silver panels embossed with figures. The damaged front panel (now heavily restored) has a *Christ in Majesty* flanked by saints, the top is engraved with a *Crucifixion,* and the sides have scenes from the *Nativity* to the *Flight into Egypt* on the right, and the *Ascension* with Apostles below on the left. Much of the imagery of this and other reliquaries derives from the sculpture of churches on the Pilgrimage Road, and there is good evidence that some of the highly skilled ivory carvers and metal-workers from the Moorish south moved to the north to work; for instance, the front panel of the Arca Santa in Orviedo is framed in a long decorative inscription in Kufic script.

The MSS and mural paintings produced in the 11th and 12th centuries inherit many features from the Visigothic and Mozarabic art of the preceding *Pre-Romanesque period. This appears in the copies of *Beatus of Liébana's *Commentary on the Apocalypse,* of which over twenty exist, surely only a part of the original number. In the mid-10th-century Beatus MS from San Millán de la Cogolla (Madrid, Acad. de la Historia) the Evangelist Symbols in the *Vision of the Lamb* swirl with huge outspread wings round the central Lamb, in dark, violent colour, while the monks personifying the Elders are clustered like so many Noah's Ark figurines. A Beatus of 1220 from Las Huelgas (New York, Morgan Lib.) has the *Four Horsemen of the Apocalypse* riding like elegant huntsmen amid a field of dead and dying, the scorpion tails of their lion-headed horses flailing to kill their victims. The Ripoll Bible, of *c.*1040 (Vatican Lib.), is the most lavishly illustrated bible of the period, and its illustrations relate to the sculpture on the west front of the Abbey.

The survival of so much Romanesque painting in Spain is due to the relative poverty of the area. Where Northern patrons presented rich antependia and jewelled altar furnishings which later fell prey to reversals of fortune or fashion, or to pillage, Spanish frontals and retables were usually painted and were thus not reusable assets. One of the most unusual antependia to survive is that of Sto Domingo de Silos, which is partly painted and partly enamels, but with the heads of Christ and the Apostles, and some decorative details in high relief in gilded copper. The greater part of the surviving mural paintings are in the NE of Spain, mostly in Catalonia, and there is a very strong influence from Byzantine art derived from N. Italy, coming into Spain with the Lombard builders. The paintings in San Clemente at Tahull, of *c.*1120–50, are clear derivations from Byzantine models. The paintings in the vaults of the Panteón de los Reyes in León made between 1167 and 1188 are among the most notable survivals. They include a *Christ in Majesty* with the symbols of the Evangelists in human form, and with the wings and heads of their symbols, and each not only named but the symbolic creature named too. A *Christ of the Apocalypse* is accompanied by the Book of Revelation, S. John, the Seven Seals, and the Seven churches of Asia. The *Last Supper* is also in the form taken from S. John's Gospel, with Christ giving the sop to Judas. Sta Maria, Tarrasa (near Barcelona), has a fresco of the *Murder and Burial of S. Thomas Becket,* which must date after 1173, the year he was canonized. It is not a remarkable work of art, but the widespread occurrence of this subject across Europe testifies to the horror which the event evoked.

Portugal was reconquered from the Moors between 1055 and 1064 and the repopulation was mainly by French and other adventurers. The main influences on the form of churches, other than the simple N. Spanish types, was from Burgundy and the Pilgrimage Road. Lisbon was retaken by English and Flemish pilgrims in 1147, and the cathedral was built by an Englishman from 1150 onwards in the same form as was customary in Spain. The Old Cathedral of Sé Velha, Coimbra, was begun in 1162, with a Moorish battlemented top, a deep porch, and two square corner towers. Almost always the simplest form of tunnel vaulting was used for naves, and groin vaults for the aisles with tribunes over them. The principal Cistercian house was the remote Alcobaça, N. of Lisbon, of 1158–1223, almost a *hall-church. Perhaps the most interesting church is the best surviving Templar's church in Europe—the Convento do Cristo, Tomar, built from 1162 as a fortified church on the Moorish frontier. The original rotunda has an added nave built in Gothic and the fantastic Manueline style.

There is no Romanesque in the south of either country. By the time the Moors had finally been defeated Gothic had become the norm.

Romano-British While there is good evidence that Christianity was established in England before the 6th century, the only surviving objects of Romano-British art are the tessellated pavement (probably 4th cent.) found at Frampton Villa (Dorset, but now inaccessible); the frescoes in the presumed chapel at Lullingstone Villa (Kent), where an underground room has two *Chi-Rho symbols painted on the walls; a fine pewter dish with Chi-Rho symbols, found in the Isle of Ely (Cambridge, Mus. of Archaeology); and silver from the Traprain Law (East Lothian) hoard (Edinburgh, Nat. Mus. of Antiquities), which may originally have been loot from Gaul.

Rome, Early Christian and Medieval Tradition says that S. Peter came to Rome *c.*42, and that S. Paul wrote the Epistle to the Romans *c.*58 in expectation of coming to Rome, but was brought there from Caesarea *c.*60, and that both were martyred during Nero's persecution, between 64 and 68.

In Acts 18: 1–4 is the first mention of Aquila and Priscilla, or Prisca, Jews forced out of Rome by Claudius's expulsion, who were already Christians, and whom S. Paul first met in Corinth. In Rom. 16: 3–5, he mentions them, saying 'Greet also the church in their house'; they travelled with him to Syria, but probably returned to Corinth since in 1 Cor. 16: 19 and 2 Tim. 4: 19, they are again mentioned. Pudens he mentions in 2 Tim. 4: 21. Prisca, Pudens, and Praxides (Prassede), Pudens's sister, are all said to have founded churches in Rome (Prassede and Pudenziana are also said to have been Pudens's daughters), and the churches which have these dedications claim their origin in them. The great apse mosaic of *c.*400 in Sta Pudenziana names the church as Pudens's. Certain other churches are of great antiquity—San Pietro in Vincoli (once *titulus Apostolorum* and later *Basilica Eudoxiana*, from the Empress who presented the reputed chains of S. Peter), SS Quattro Coronati (once *titulus Aemilianae*), Sta Sabina (once *domus Sabinae*), Sta Maria in Trastevere, founded by S. Callixtus, pope from 217 to 222, who also founded the church of San Callisto nearby. There must also have been others, but these at least have been excavated and found to have Roman houses under them which were possibly the original *domus ecclesiae*. It is not unreasonable to believe that the memory of the original *domus* might have survived in a city which changed its shape but little over its first four Christian centuries.

The semi-clandestine nature of the church changed with the advent of Constantine. The *Lateran seems to have been the first of his foundations, *St Peter's the second. There followed rapidly the funerary *basilicas outside the city walls, San Sebastiano, San Lorenzo, Sant'Agnese, and city churches such as Sta Croce in Gerusalemme, founded by Constantine's mother, S. Helena, SS Cosmas and Damian built out of two Roman temples, with fine 6th-century mosaic in the apse and over the triumphal arch, and near by another church, San Lorenzo in Miranda, built into the Roman temple of Antoninus and Faustina in the 9th century. The first San Clemente and Sta Maria Antiqua are no longer used, the first because it has been rebuilt over the site, the second because the remains of very old frescoes render it more a museum than a church. There are also buildings which began as Roman secular ones, or as cult buildings, such as Sta Costanza, which has very fine possibly pre-Christian mosaics, and is believed to have contained the tomb of Constantine's daughter, and San Stefano Rotondo, a converted pre-Christian circular building, once much larger than it is now. Sta Maria Maggiore was named by its founder, Pope Liberius (352–66) and called after him the *Liberian basilica.

Churches in Rome are very numerous; there are some 470 in the latest compendium of the city's churches, including those which were outside the walls when they were built, and are now well within the city area, but this does not include religious houses, hospitals, institutions, or private chapels. This is a very small advance on the 414 listed in the Turin Inventory of 1300.

First in rank are the basilicas, of which there are seven major and a number of minor ones. The major basilicas are the Seven Pilgrimage Churches of Rome: St John Lateran, the cathedral of Rome, with the nearby Scala Santa, which was always included among the major pilgrimage sites, St Peter's, Sta Maria Maggiore (the Liberian Basilica), Sta Croce in Gerusalemme, Sta Maria in Trastevere, *San Paolo fuori le Mura, and San Lorenzo fuori le Mura. The other two basilicas outside the walls, San Sebastiano, and Sant'Agnese, which were also, like San Lorenzo, always known to have been built above *catacombs, were also important, but in early times were always visited in large groups for safety. Adjoining Sant'Agnese is the circular Sta Costanza. Sta Croce in Gerusalemme, despite its ancient origin, only has a small chapel in the crypt and the pillars of the nave remaining from its early foundation.

The minor basilicas include some of Rome's most interesting churches. Some have been rebuilt after disasters. San Clemente was destroyed when the Norman Robert Guiscard besieged Rome in 1084, and from 1108 onwards was rebuilt on the same site, reusing parts of the old church which now lies beneath it (and has a piece of older Roman history beneath that, since the excavations have revealed a Mithraic temple). The *schola cantorum, the *Paschal candlestick, and the two *ambones are from the Early Christian church, as probably also are the antique columns of the nave. The bishop's throne in the centre of the apse, the ciborium over the altar, and a large part of the superb mosaic of the *Triumph of the Cross* in the semi-dome of the apse are of the 12th century. Part of the mosaic is probably remade from the original Early Christian apse. SS Quattro Coronati was also burnt by the Normans in 1084 and rebuilt in 1111, and a fine cloister was added in the 13th century. SS Giovanni e Paolo on the Coelian Hill was built probably in the 4th century to commemorate two men martyred by Julian the Apostate in 361. The church was rebuilt after being destroyed by Alaric the Goth in 410 (when its founder, Pammachius, was killed by the invaders) and again destroyed by Robert Guiscard in 1084, and rebuilt so many times over the centuries that no part of the antique structure can be found except by excavation. San Gregorio Magno near by was built in 575 by S.

Gregory before he became Pope Gregory the Great, rebuilt during the Middle Ages, and again in the late 16th century.

San Bartolomeo *ad insula*, on its island in the Tiber, was a 10th-century church built by the Emperor Otto III, restored in 1113 and 1180, as well as many times later, usually because of flood damage. Sta Maria in Aracoeli is on the site of the Roman Temple of Juno, the sacrificial 'Ara' where legend says the Sibyl predicted to Augustus the coming of Christ. It stands at the top of a long flight of steps beside the Campidoglio, and probably dates from the late 8th century. In the 9th century it changed from Greek monks to Benedictines and was rebuilt in 1250 when it became Franciscan. 'It was in Rome', Gibbon recorded in his *Autobiography*, 'on the 15th October 1764, as I sat musing amidst the ruins of the Capitol, while the barefooted friars were singing vespers in the Temple of Jupiter' (as he thought) 'that the idea of writing the decline and fall of the city first started to my mind'. Sta Maria sopra Minerva is an 8th-century church built on the remains of a Temple of Minerva Calcidica, rebuilt in 1280 to be the only Gothic church in Rome. It lies almost behind Sta Maria ad Martyres, better known as the *Pantheon.

Many campaniles were built, or rebuilt, between the 10th and 13th centuries. There are still some thirty-six of the towers in Rome, all much alike in design: brick built, usually square, and from four to seven storeys high, with small colonnaded windows increasing in number as the tower rises. The finest flank Sta Maria in Cosmedin, a 12th-century tower seven storeys high, beside a 6th-century church, enlarged in the 8th century when it was given to Greeks, refugees from Iconoclasm; and Sta Maria Nova (Sta Francesca Romana), where the 12th-century tower is *c.*135 ft. high.

After the struggles over investiture which threatened papal authority over the Church in the whole of Europe during the 11th century, Rome was poor and it was not until the 12th century that some restoration of churches was undertaken. Mostly, other than basic repairs, this took the form of what is now called *Cosmati work—altars, floors, *ambones, Paschal candlesticks, thrones—with inlays of varied marbles and mosaic tesserae—made by families of marble-workers practising the same style. Sometimes in the 13th century a work of sculpture in the round was made, such as the Paschal candlestick for San Paolo fuori le Mura, by Pietro Vassaletto, with reliefs of the Passion, or thrones such as the one he—or his son—made for the cathedral at Anagni. Wooden sculpture must have been common, but little has survived. A fine *Madonna and Child* at Alatri, near Frosinone, in polychromed wood, treated with Byzantine formality, may be as late as the end of the 13th century, and the cathedrals of Tivoli, outside Rome, and Volterra, near Siena, have 12th-century groups of the *Deposition*, similar to those in Catalonia.

Rome contained a large number of Early Christian mosaics, from the mid-4th century (or perhaps earlier) ones in Sta Costanza, to the 9th-century ones in Sta Prassede and San Marco. Virtually nothing was produced from the 9th century to the 12th, and it would seem that the art had died out (possibly because no one could afford it), and had to be reintroduced in the mid-11th century by the importation of mosaicists from Byzantium by the Abbot Desiderius of Montecassino, to such good effect that the most outstanding works of Romanesque art in Rome are the mosaics, which continued to be the preferred form of decoration. The most notable are the apse mosaic in San Clemente, and the two in Sta Maria in Trastevere. The *Triumph of the Cross* in San Clemente is dated by inscription to 1127. In it, the cross of the crucified Christ grows out of an acanthus, from which also sprout scrolling branches. The twelve doves on the cross represent the twelve Apostles, and on either side are the Virgin and S. John. The scrolls are inhabited by birds, nests with fledgelings, *amorini*, some blowing trumpets, some riding dolphins, named saints, Fathers of the Church, a monk, a group of people, and a cage of birds with the inscription that Christ is imprisoned by our sins. At the base of the acanthus is a tiny deer encircled by a jewelled band. This suggests that the artist was using the Early Christian mosaic in the original church, either actually incorporating parts which could be recovered when the church was rebuilt from 1108 onwards, or was inspired by it, but no longer understood its classical allusions. The image of the deer eating the snake comes from the 3rd- or 4th-century *Physiologus*, and is an image of the Resurrection, for it says that the deer eats the snake to grow new antlers and thus be reborn. The symbolism of the verdant acanthus and the branches springing from it is because the cross standing on it is the source of all life, while the scrolls of branches are the Church in which all life finds shelter and sustenance.

At the bottom of the apse are the four *Rivers of Paradise, with deer about to drink, a conflation of Ps. 42: 1 (Vg. Ps. 41) with Isaiah 35: 6, 'then the lame shall leap like a deer', since further along is a man supported by a crutch minding sheep. There are peacocks, quails, a snail, a pheasant, and on the wall above the apse on the left is S. Peter with S. Clement, and on the right is S. Paul with S. Lawrence; in both the inscription is 'agios' for saint, indicating that the mosaicist was a Greek. Below the two Apostles are *Isaiah and *Jeremiah with prophetic scrolls, and below them Jerusalem and Bethlehem. In the top of the apse is the traditional representation of the tabernacle with the Hand of God emerging from the clouds.

Sta Maria in Trastevere is a 3rd- and 4th-century basilica, restored by Innocent II in 1140 on his return to Rome from France, where he had been a guest of Abbot *Suger at St-Denis during a schism. A stained-glass window (now destroyed) in Notre-Dame, Paris, given by Suger, was the first use of the theme of the *Triumph of the Virgin*, the theme of the apse mosaic of Sta Maria in Trastevere. The central figures of the Virgin and Christ are flanked by saintly popes, over Christ's head is the tabernacle and the Hand of God and the dove of the Holy Ghost. Below the main mosaic are the twelve sheep—the Apostles—with the *Agnus Dei in the centre. On the *Triumphal Arch above the apse are the symbols of two Evangelists, SS John and Matthew, and the prophets Isaiah and Jeremiah with the scrolls of their prophecies, as in the San Clemente mosaic, as well as the caged birds. Here they have a double reference: to the two doves brought to the Presentation as the offering for Christ, and to the words 'Christ is imprisoned by our sins', which also accompany the motive in San Clemente. The façade also has a fine mosaic of *c.*1190: a frieze of robed and crowned Wise Virgins with their lamps approaching an enthroned Virgin and Child from either side. Some of the Virgins are of the late 13th century. The apse mosaic of Sta Maria Nova (now Sta Francesca Romana), of *c.*1160, represents the enthroned Virgin and Child flanked by SS Peter, Andrew, James, and John, each framed in an arch. Above the Virgin is the usual tabernacle with the Hand of God, like the ones in San Clemente and Sta Maria in Trastevere. The sacristy contains a rare 5th-century icon of the *Madonna*. The church itself was originally built to replace Sta Maria Antiqua, and incorporated an oratory of SS Peter and Paul, made in the 8th century out of the west portico of the Temple of Venus and Rome. The rest of the temple, one of the largest in Rome, lies behind the church.

Among some fragments in San Paolo fuori le Mura is a mosaic icon of the *Virgin and Child* of *c.*1210 which survived the disastrous fire of 1823. Other survivals are the elaborate *ciborium made in 1285 by Arnolfo di Cambio, who had an assistant who may have been Pietro Cavallini; and at the back of the apse is the huge mosaic made from *c.*1220 representing *Christ blessing, with SS Peter and Andrew, Paul and Luke*. Under the altar is the Apostle's tomb, preceded by the *confessio.

The mosaic by Jacopo Torriti in the apse of Sta Maria Maggiore, of 1296, is of the *Coronation of the Virgin*, a subject which grew out of the earlier subject of the *Glory of the Virgin* and, like it, was French inspired. Torriti's apse mosaic in the Lateran was remade in the 19th century. Both his work, and that of Cavallini in his series of the *Life of the Virgin* in the lower part of an apse in Sta Maria in Trastevere, and also in the impressive surviving parts of his *Last Judgement* of 1293 in Sta Cecilia in Trastevere, show how powerfully Byzantine imagery continued to inspire early medieval art in Italy, even when the actual subject was adapted from France.

The Jubilee proclaimed by Boniface VIII for 1300 saw the last blossoming of art in Rome for well over a century. *Giotto's *Navicella*, remade after a fashion for the atrium of the present St Peter's, Arnolfo di Cambio's grandiose bronze of S. Peter, in the nave of the basilica, his ciborium for San Paolo fuori, Torriti's mosaic in Sta Maria Maggiore, Cavallini's *Life of the Virgin* and his *Last Judgement* in Sta Cecilia were followed by the bitter consequences of internecine strife.

The abduction of Pope Boniface at Anagni by French knights, followed by his death in 1303, the brief papacy of Benedict XI, and the troubled eleven months which it took to elect Clement V finally decided Clement (who was French) to remove the papacy to Avignon, where it remained for seventy years. An attempt at a return to Rome was made by Urban V in 1376; he stayed for three years, but found continued residence impossible and returned to Avignon. His death in 1389 was followed by a disputed election and the great schism, which lasted until the surrender of the last schismatic, John XXIII, and the election of Martin V in 1417. When Martin returned to Rome in 1420, the Lateran had been burnt, St Peter's was in advanced decay, the Vatican barely habitable, the treasury empty, the Papal States overrun. He began by recovering the Papal States, which gave him the money to begin the restoration of Rome, but after his sudden death in 1431 and the lingering aftermath of the schism, which continued to trouble Europe until the election of Nicholas V in 1447, there was no real peace.

By this time, the *Renaissance was in full flood in Florence. Nicholas V was the uncle of *Alberti, and was, therefore, well aware of developments in architecture, sculpture, and painting in Florence. Though it was probably his predecessor Eugenius IV who commissioned the frescoes in the pope's private chapel from Fra *Angelico *c.*1446–9, it is now known as the chapel of Nicholas V. The Great Chapel of the Vatican—the *Sistine Chapel—was preceded by an earlier chapel, but was rebuilt and redecorated by *Sixtus IV. The ceiling was painted early in the 16th century by *Michelangelo, who later also painted the *Last Judgement* on the altar wall. *Raphael was also concerned with the decoration of the Sistine Chapel.

Architecturally, the 16th century opens with *Bramante, who built the cloister of Sta Maria della Pace, and followed it with the *Tempietto, in San Pietro in Montorio. The beauty of this design must have drawn him to the notice of Julius II, for whom he drew up the first designs for a replacement for Constantine's St Peter's, which lingered on for many years, with abortive projects by Antonio da *Sangallo the Younger, before being brought into being by Michelangelo, who died before completing the basilica. The dome was finally erected under *Sixtus V, by Giacomo della Porta, and other work was done by *Vignola, who built other important churches in Rome. The unfinished front was extended by *Maderno, who changed the character of Michelangelo's St Peter's by altering his centrally planned church into one with a long nave. Other important architectural work in Rome by Michelangelo was the design of the city civic centre, the Campidoglio. Painting and sculpture in the 16th century were dominated by Michelangelo, though little of his sculpture is to be found in Rome, except for his early masterpiece, the *Pietà* in St Peter's, and his painting was exclusively in the Vatican. *Vasari's frescoes in the Cancelleria point the difference between Michelangelo and himself, but his greatest achievement was his important book, the *Lives of the Painters, Sculptors and Architects,* published first in 1550, and in an enlarged and amended version in 1568.

Painting in the second half of the 16th century dwindled into vapid *Mannerism until new energy was infused into it at the end of the century and the beginning of the 17th from Bologna, with the *Carracci, and with *Caravaggio in Rome. The major and enduring influence on all the arts in the 17th century was from *Bernini, whose long life and prolific output in architecture and sculpture revitalized the artistic scene and created the *Baroque, and with it the art of the *Counter-Reformation. He was not, of course, the only man in the field, in that he could never have created as much as he did without his very large studio. The other major architect of the period was Maderno's nephew, *Borromini, who never worked on Bernini's scale, and whose genius—though equal—was more individual and his career far shorter. Bernini's only real competitor as a sculptor was *Algardi. The most important painters of the century, after the deaths of Caravaggio and Annibale Carracci, were *Poussin, and Claude, though the latter was entirely a landscape painter, despite the literary titles of his works. The development of illusionism in decorative painting was carried to amazing heights by Pietro da Cortona, who was also an important architect, Baciccio, who painted the ceiling of the *Gesù, and Andrea Pozzo, whose ceiling of Sant'Ignazio is perhaps the ultimate extreme of illusionism. The next century saw a turning away from the energy, movement, and excitement of the Baroque, and the creation of a more placid, tepid, art, striving for classical elegance and restraint rather than for the expression of fervour and drama. Its protagonists were Canova and Mengs, both of whom worked on an international as much as on a Roman scene. The Baroque was the last great artistic movement generated by Rome, and the last great outpouring of religious art in any country, with the exception of the very late *Rococo form of Baroque in S. Germany and Austria. Since then there have been religious artists generally outside Rome—Caspar David *Friedrich, the *Nazarene, *Rouault, and *Gill, for example—and the occasional creation of a modern religious work of art, such as Graham Sutherland's huge tapestry design for Coventry Cathedral, or Henry Moore's *Madonna and Child* in St Matthew's, Northampton. Churches have been built to replace the losses occasioned by two world wars, and to cater for the growth of populations, such as, for instance, those in the new Roman quarter of the EUR. But nowhere in the modern world have the signs of interest in religious art yet amounted to a revival. Happily, however, more is done now to conserve what remains from the ages of Faith. *See also* BASILICA and STATION CHURCHES.

Romuald, Saint (*c.*950–1027), was born in Ravenna, the son of the duke, and as a result of a family quarrel in which his father killed a relation, he entered the monastery of Sant' Apollinare in Classe. He was soon dissatisfied with the easy life, and became a disciple of a hermit called Marino with whom he went to Venice, where they met the Abbot of St-Michel-de-Cuxa, in the Pyrenees; they joined him, and with the Doge, and two other Venetians, went to St-Michel and lived an austere hermit's life. When he heard that his father, who had entered Sant'Apollinare in Classe, had left the monastery, he returned to Ravenna, persuaded him back into the cloister, and then lived in a hut in the marshes of Classe. He finally settled near a monastery in the hills at Verghereto, near Forlì, but when the monks heard that Conte Ugo of Tuscany was to provide for a hermitage, they drove him out. He moved restlessly from place to place, founding small monasteries or hermitages, seeking solitude, but gathering disciples instead. He was summoned from the last, an island in the Po, by the Emperor Otto III to reform the house at Sant'Apollinare in Classe, but his rigour upset the monks and he could not tolerate their laxity, so he fled to Montecassino, where he again settled as a hermit. He was then in Rome, living as a hermit, but when the city rebelled against Otto he decided to go and convert the Slavs. He went to Poreč (Parenzo), but after three years and founding another monastery, he returned to San Benedetto in Alpe, near Forlì, to live as a hermit. He received news of the martyrdom in Poland of former disciples, immediately proposed going as a missionary, but the difficulty was to reconcile his desire to lead a mission with his yearning for solitude. After living for a while near Arezzo, he again came to Classe to struggle with a simoniacal abbot who tried to murder him. He returned to Istria for a short time, then came back to two of his earlier foundations, and so disrupted the second that the abbot persuaded him to leave. The Emperor Henry II put all the monasteries in the area under Romuald, with the idea of subordinating the monastic houses to the hermitages. Such were the difficulties, that Romuald was given first the monastery of Monte Amiata, and then Camaldoli, where the hermitage he founded still exists. Once a prior was chosen, he abandoned the place to return to his early creation of Val di Castro, where he died alone in his hut in June 1027.

S. Romuald is usually painted in white robes, as a Camaldolensian, but occasionally in black as a Benedictine. He figures in a triptych by Nardo di Cione (1365: Florence, Accad.) of the *Trinity, with SS Romuald and John the Evangelist* in the wings, and a *predella* of three scenes from the life of S. Romuald, including his vision of Jacob's Ladder; Andrea del Castagno: *Crucifixion with Saints*, including S. Romuald (1440–5, fresco, Florence, Sta Maria Nuova Hospital); Andrea Sacchi: *Vision of S. Romuald* (17th cent., Vatican).

Ronchamp *See* LE CORBUSIER.

rood The word is derived from Anglo-Saxon, meaning cross, and was used for a large crucifix standing on the pulpitum or on a screen dividing the nave from the *chancel; it was usually flanked by figures of the Virgin and S. John to represent Calvary. In pre-Reformation England, the pulpitum or screen would always have supported a rood, and normally a narrow gallery called the rood loft would have run along the top. Access to it was gained from a stair from the aisle to one side of the chancel arch, and in many country churches a gap in the aisle wall shows where access to the rood loft was obtained. In some fairly isolated country parishes the original rood screen has survived, but few roods have survived the Reformation. The purpose of the rood loft was to enable a deacon to chant the Gospel on great feasts, and also during the Easter ceremonies for Holy Saturday; the readings, and in particular the *Exsultet roll, and some of the prayers were chanted from the rood loft.

In French churches, the rood sometimes stood on the pulpitum or *jubé*, sometimes on a separate arch or beam within the choir area. Although fragments of these richly carved screens exist in museums in Paris and Bourges, and although they, and the roods which once stood on them, are known from descriptions (mostly 17th cent.), no early rood and no early medieval screen has survived. It is recorded that *Suger's great cross at St-Denis once stood on the pulpitum there. Only three complete later screens exist: an elaborate late Gothic carved stone screen at La

Madeleine, Troyes; a fine 16th-century stone screen with Renaissance ornament at Arques-la-Bataille, near Dieppe; a surprising one in St-Étienne-du-Mont, Paris, of 1545, with late Gothic and Renaissance ornament and a double stone staircase coiled round the supporting piers on either side.

In Germany, more than one pulpitum, and occasionally roods also, have survived (e.g. at Gelnhausen, near Frankfurt, and the Marienkirche, Lübeck, N. of Hamburg). In Italy, the custom was to hang a huge crucifix (*see* CROCE DIPINTA) with the Virgin and S. John in roundels at the ends of the arms of the cross over the arch of the main altar, but in most cases these crosses have now been removed to the sacristy (or to a museum).

As a result of the Ecclesiological Society's efforts (*see* CAMBRIDGE CAMDEN SOC.) to revive medieval forms in English 19th-century church building and to reorder the interior of old churches which had been altered in the 17th and 18th centuries, many screens have been rebuilt across the chancel arch, though they no longer serve any function except to divide the nave from the chancel. But it was left to the 20th century to introduce a rood into a Wren church, fixing it to the wall at the end of the chancel above the altar where it is a total anachronism (St Mary le Bow, rebuilt after bomb destruction during the Second World War).

The palace of Holyrood House, in Edinburgh, grew out of the guest-house of the Abbey of Holy Rood, i.e. Holy Cross, and has retained the name, although all but the nave of the abbey was destroyed at the Reformation. It is now the Canongate parish church.

r

rosary A rosary is a string of beads used for counting prayers said in sequence. Basically, any string will do if the number of beads or knots in the string is known. The normal Catholic rosary in common use consists of five sets of ten beads, each group separated by a single bead. This is the original form joined into a circlet, but a small metal plate at the join of the circlet with a tail of a single bead, three beads, a single bead, and a small crucifix, has been added to the circlet. In use, the sequence of prayers is an Our Father and ten Hail Marys, and when the sequence ends at the little plate to which the tail is attached, this part permits of personal variations. The practice of counting prayers on sets of stones, or on devices such as beads or a wheel, is very ancient and probably pre-Christian. The legend that the rosary was presented to S. Dominic in a vision by the Virgin is a pretty one; the Dominicans have a particular devotion to the Office, which they popularized, and which they may well have introduced as a regular devotion. The word 'rosary' is derived from rose garland, or garden (Lat. *rosarium*); in French a rosary is called a *chapelet*, or wreath.

The full rosary consists of a threefold repetition of the five sets of the ten Hail Marys, with the appropriate Our Fathers and Glorias, but it is unusual for this to be recited at one Office. The three rosaries are each dedicated to one of the Mysteries of the Rosary, which should be the subject of a meditation while the prayers are being recited. There are various other rosaries, such as S. Brigid's, the Servite devotion of the Seven Dolours, the Immaculate Conception, the Crown of Our Saviour, attributed to a Camaldolese monk of 1516, and the Rosary of the Five Wounds, approved in 1823. All these use a variant number of Hail Marys. There is no truth in the story that the rosary was invented by the Venerable Bede; this is merely a piece of bad etymology: bead from Bede.

Mysteries of the Rosary: there are three Mysteries of the Rosary: the Joyful Mysteries, which consist of meditations on the Annunciation, the Visitation, the Birth of Jesus, His Presentation in the Temple, and His discovery after being lost for three days. The Sorrowful Mysteries are the Agony in the Garden, the Scourging, the Crowning with Thorns, the Carrying of the Cross, and the Crucifixion. The Glorious Mysteries are the Resurrection of Christ, His Ascension, the Descent of the Holy Ghost, the Assumption, and the Coronation of the Virgin.

All fifteen Mysteries are depicted in medallions above a *Madonna and Child with Saints* by Lotto (1539, San Domenico, Cingoli, near Macerata), and below the *Madonna and Child, with S. Dominic and angels*, in an odd order, but all present (Guido Reni: 1596–8, San Luca, Bologna). Barent van Orley painted two panels with *The Seven Joys* and the *Seven Sorrows* (*c.*1518: Rome, Colonna Gallery) in small roundels surrounding a Madonna. In the Joys, there is a Madonna and Child in the centre, with a unicorn (presumably, but really a goat with one horn). In the Sorrows, there is a *Mater Dolorosa in the centre. The Joys and the Sorrows do not conform to the usual list, and appear to conflate some of the three Mysteries, with extra subjects from the Life of the Virgin.

On the hillside leading up to the pilgrimage church of Monte Berico outside Vicenza is a covered portico with a staircase 700 m. (*c.*2,300 ft.) long built in 1746–78, with 150 arches, one for each bead of a full rosary, with a small chapel every ten arches dedicated to one of the Mysteries, plus one at the beginning. A chapel half-way is dedicated to Christ and one at the end is dedicated to the Madonna, making seventeen in all.

rose *See* FLOWERS AND FRUIT.

rose windows are large circular windows in medieval church façades, transepts, and choirs. They are so called because the segments of tracery composing them can be likened to the unfolding petals of a full-blown rose. They are almost invariably filled with stained glass.

Their origin is in the *oculus*, or circular opening of classical buildings such as the Pantheon in Rome, or smaller domed buildings lit from above. Round windows occur sporadically in Carolingian churches and are common all over Europe from the 11th century onwards. By the 12th century they developed into large windows with 'wheel' tracery formed as slim colonnettes radiating from a central roundel set into a church façade. Sometimes, like the three in the façade of Assisi Cathedral, the central circular window has, round the edge, figures of angels and the Evangelists, or as in the eight-lobed oculus at St-Étienne, Beauvais, the figures round the edge symbolize the Wheel of *Fortune, as they rise to triumph and then fall again.

The development of Gothic art made the large round window increasingly popular, and the heavy divisions of the early wheel window evolved into the more delicate tracery of the rose window, which became a prominent feature of French and English Gothic cathedrals and major churches. Usually, they are sited in the façade and transepts—Laon, in N. France, originally had four rose windows, but one was destroyed in the 14th century. Notre-Dame in Paris has one in the south transept, begun in 1258, and a second smaller rose in the attic storey, where it could light only the roof timbers. Their height from the ground makes the incidents portrayed in the stained glass difficult to read; and at Reims the attraction of colour and light resulted in a double rose window, one in the façade proper, the other, smaller one replacing the sculpture normally in the tympanum of the portal. Lincoln has two of the largest transept windows in England, one being an early 13th-century rose with a complex Christological iconography.

Rossano Gospels, or **Codex Rossanensis** (Rossano, Calabria, Mus. Diocesano) This MS belongs to the small group of 6th-century luxury MSS (the *Vienna Genesis and the Codex *Sinopensis are others) written in Greek in gold and silver letters on purple vellum. Although Calabria ceased to be part of the Byzantine Empire in the 12th century, Rossano remained Greek-speaking. The MS contains nearly all Matthew and Mark. There are fifteen illuminated pages, three of which are full-page; the rest have pictures at the top, and the bottom of the page has prophets, with prophecies relating to Christ. The full-page illustrations are a 'portrait' of S. Mark at the beginning of his Gospel—a prototype for the Evangelist portraits which so frequently precede Gospels—and two scenes from the Life of Christ. This is one of the first to have the *Entry into Jerusalem*, with the boys climbing the palm-tree, the *Last Supper* (with Judas putting his hand in the dish), and the *Institution of the Eucharist*, with Christ giving bread to each of the remaining Apostles. The other full-page picture shows *Christ before Pilate* at the top and the *Repentance of Judas* below, with Judas casting the 30 pieces of silver at the feet of the High Priest and then hanging himself. The only earlier example of Judas's suicide is in an ivory plaque (BM) of the Crucifixion, which can be dated to 420/30, and is of Roman inspiration. Also new is a scene in which Pilate tells the Jews to choose between Christ and Barabbas. Among other illustrations are some of Christ's miracles: the *Healing of the Blind Man* and the *Raising of Lazarus*, and parables such as the *Good Samaritan* and the *Wise and Foolish Virgins*. The *Canon tables have a decorative frontispiece. It is clear from these 6th-century MSS (and also from the *Rabbula Gospels) that the models they provide are only departed from when totally different subjects are introduced. Moreover, the image of Christ is established by the Eastern instead of the Roman type. Christ is a mature, bearded, dark-haired man of commanding dignity.

Rossetti, Dante Gabriel (1828–82), was the son of an Italian political refugee in London. He was both poet and painter, undecided as to which was his true vocation. After various false starts, he was helped by Holman *Hunt, through whom he met *Millais, and with them was a founder-member of the *PRB (which see). He painted two religious pictures, *The Girlhood of Mary Virgin* (1848–9) and *Ecce Ancilla Domini* (1849–50: both London, Tate), which contain new iconographic inventions, the *Girlhood* picture being very heavily loaded with symbolism, explained in two sonnets intended to be attached to the frame. The *Ecce Ancilla Domini* (an Annunciation), like Millais's *Carpenter's Shop*, was so badly received that he abandoned purely religious subjects altogether. Both, however, were sincere attempts to recast traditional iconographies. His *S. George* subjects are not religious pictures, but 'chivalry' subjects, and his *Blessed Damosel* pictures are partly romantic musings and partly dictated by his troubled emotions over the death of Elizabeth Siddal.

Rossi, Giovanni Battista de' (1822–94), is the archaeologist chiefly responsible for the excavation and study of the Roman *catacombs. His interest in Early Christian remains began when he was a boy, and was confirmed by the Jesuit Giuseppe Marchi, who took him to a catacomb. He began his studies by compiling a compendium of Early Christian references from Patristic writings, inscriptions, early calendars (which record the days on which saints are commemorated, and often, in the case of Early Christian martyrs, where they were buried), and from the writings of earlier scholars such as Cyriaco d'Ancona, a merchant who travelled in the E. Mediterranean in the 14th century, and Onofrio Panvinio, an Augustianian monk who wrote the literary history of catacombs in the mid-16th century, but who believed them to be totally lost. The first to devote himself to the discovery and exploration of the catacombs was Antonio *Bosio. In 1782 Séroux d'Agincourt began a history of art based on early monuments, actually went into a catacomb and then had several reopened, but set the dreadful precedent of removing the ancient paintings from the walls. This led to new protective measures and the sites were closed. In 1840 Giuseppe Marchi began *Monumenti delle arti Cristiane*, and with the young de' Rossi found the tomb of the martyr Hyacinthus in the cemetery of S. Hermes, which determined de' Rossi to pursue excavations. Marchi believed the subject to be possible only theoretically, through literary sources, but not possible in practical terms. De' Rossi persisted, and as a result of his discoveries he gained the enthusiastic patronage of Pope Pius IX, who gave all such investigations into his hands. He pursued them for the rest of his life, and made spectacular discoveries, in which he was much helped by the studies of the soil and subsoil of the areas round Rome made by his brother Michele Stefano, a geologist. He published, under the name *Roma sotterranea*, which he used in honour of Bosio, three massive volumes (1863–77) which detailed his discoveries in the catacombs and burial-places, with settled dates of sites and the epigraphy of inscriptions. He also wrote on Early Christian mosaics in Rome, and published an iconographic plan of Rome in 1879, on the location of catacombs and early cemeteries.

Rosso, Giovanni Battista ('Rosso Fiorentino') (1495–1540) He was a fellow student with *Pontormo in Andrea del Sarto's studio, and worked in Florence, 1513–21, but with little success, since his commissioner rejected his *Madonna and Child with saints* (Uffizi) on the grounds that the saints looked like devils. In his *Deposition* (1521: Volterra) the figures are distraught, and the body of Christ being lowered from the cross is livid. *Moses defending the daughters of Jethro* (*c.*1523: Uffizi) is filled with large figures in strained poses, violent foreshortening and movement, and sums up the tension and strains of early *Mannerism. He was in Rome until the Sack (1527), when he was lucky enough to escape, wandered about Italy, and finally reached Venice, where Aretino drew him to the notice of Francis I of France, who engaged him to work, with Primaticcio, on the decorations in the Gallery at Fontainebleau in 1530, where the use of high-relief stucco figures in the frames of the pictures and on the chimney-pieces was unique at that date. He painted a last striking *Deposition* (now Louvre), memorable for Christ's livid mauve body and red hair. In view of his troubled career, it is not the quantity of his works that makes him an important Mannerist, but their intensity and emotional charge.

rotulus (Lat. roll) Originally, books were written as rolls on strips of papyrus, canvas, parchment (or vellum), which unwound as they were read. This type of book still survives in synagogues, and also in mosques. As early as the 2nd century, Roman law distinguished between rolls and codices, or books as we know them. Rolls were superseded in general use about the 4th century, when it became more convenient to use individual leaves of parchment, as pages, though they survived in ecclesiastical use in the form of *Exsultet rolls.

Rouault, Georges (1871–1958), was born in a cellar during the bombardment of Paris at the time of the Commune. He trained in a stained-glass window workshop, and in 1890 became a student at the École des Beaux-Arts. From 1891 to 1895 his teacher was Gustave Moreau, who at first influenced him towards his own powerfully symbolic style. Rouault had painted religious subjects, much influenced by Rembrandt, while still strongly under Moreau's spell, but Moreau's greatest legacy to his pupil was posthumous, since Rouault became the curator of the Musée Moreau, which opened in 1903. This relieved the artist of pressing money burdens and enabled him to concentrate on the subjects which he made particularly his own: clowns and circuses, prostitutes, and—influenced by Forain—judges and prisoners, and religious subjects, his main stimulus towards the first three being the result of his emotional response to poverty and human misery, and the fourth his strong Christian faith.

His style changed little once he had left the influence of Moreau behind; it is the early experience of his training in stained glass that dominates in his use of the powerful dark outlines that enclose simple blocks of colour. He adapted the visual effects of stained glass to painting and graphic work, but he added nothing new iconographically. It is the deep religious feeling of his many heads of Christ (the long series of *The Holy Face*, the *Crucifixion*, and *Christ mocked*) that have placed him among the most important religious artists of the 20th century, e.g. *Ecce Homo* (1938–39 State Gallery, Stuttgart, Germany). Some of his stained-glass windows (1939-48) can be seen in Notre-Dame-de-Toute-France, Plâteau d'Assy, Haute Savoie, France.

Little honoured or commissioned by the Church during his lifetime (though his works were much sought-after subsequently for the Vatican Gallery of Modern Religious Art), Rouault was made Commander of the Légion d'Honneur in 1952, and the Centre of Catholic Intellectuals in Chaillot celebrated his eightieth birthday.

His work is also seen in the 1929 décor for Diaghilev's ballet *Le Fils Prodigue*.

Rubens, Sir Peter Paul (1577–1640), was the foremost Northern painter of grand Counter-Reformation Baroque altarpieces, comparable with Bernini in Italy. He trained in Antwerp and went to Italy as court painter to the Duke of Mantua in 1600. In 1603 he accompanied a Mantuan embassy to Madrid, which gave him the chance to see the Titians and Raphaels in the Spanish Royal Collections. In 1606 he painted the altarpiece for the Chiesa Nuova (Sta Maria in Vallicella) in Rome, where hung the *Entombment* by Caravaggio, whom he greatly admired and whose rejected *Death of the Virgin* he bought in 1607 for the Mantua Collection (now Louvre). In Italy, he studied the works of Michelangelo, Titian, and other Venetians, as well as absorbing the influence of Caravaggio and the Carracci. On his return to Antwerp he was appointed court painter to the Spanish Governors of the Netherlands. His first great commissions were for Antwerp Cathedral—the *Raising of the Cross* (1610) and the *Descent from the Cross* (1611–14). Both pictures display his vehemently dramatic style, his grasp of narrative, movement, chiaroscuro, composition, and executive genius. After these triumphs, he was inundated with commissions, and founded his prolific workshop, which was based on the system of himself preparing the *modelli*, or preliminary sketches, and then (if the commission were sufficiently important) finishing the pictures executed from them by his assistants. He employed only the best: Jordaens, Van Dyck, and Snyders all began their careers in his studio.

He did not seek to be iconographically inventive; he painted the traditional aspects of his commissioned subjects, whether a miracle (*S. Ignatius Loyola healing the possessed*, 1619: Genoa, Sant'Ambrogio), a martyrdom (*S. Livinus*, 1635: Brussels), an *Adoration of the Magi* (1624: Antwerp), a large group of saints such as the *Mystic Marriage of S. Catherine* (1628: Antwerp, St Augustine's), where the saints are the fourteen Auxiliary Saints, or *Vierzehnheiligen, invoked by those in distress, an *Assumption* (1626: Antwerp Cathedral), which as clearly acknowledges the influence of Titian's Frari Altarpiece as his *Last Judgement* (1616: Munich) is inspired by Michelangelo.

He also painted some smaller religious works with deep sensitivity to character and incident, such as the *Christ and the Doubting Thomas* (1613–15: Antwerp), the tiny *Flight into Egypt* (1614: Cassel) so reminiscent of Caravaggio and Elsheimer, or the *Lamentation over the Dead Christ* (1614: Vienna, KHM), where the breadth of the composition and the intensity of the emotion belie its tiny size. These smaller pictures are generally by his own hand.

His decoration for the Jesuit Church in Antwerp, consisting of thirty-nine ceiling paintings, commissioned in 1620, is known only from the *modelli* which, unusually, he was allowed to keep. The three altarpieces also survive since they had already been removed from the church before it was burnt in 1718.

His style and fame were also spread by prints. Many of his large compositions were engraved and widely disseminated, which in turn increased the demands on him and on his workshop. The series of fifteen engravings for the *SS Apostolorum Icones* (Images of the Holy Apostles), engraved mainly by Cornelius Galle the Elder, were published between 1646 and 1650 from designs known from drawings and paintings which he had executed *c.*1615. Early in his career he also made versions of the *Holy Face*, the *Mater Dolorosa*, and *Christ as Salvator Mundi*, which too were engraved. It may well have been these 'portrait heads' which prompted his series of 'portraits' of the Apostles, each one strongly characterized, painted between 1610 and 1612, and sent to Spain (Madrid, Prado).

From 1623 onwards he was employed by the Spanish Governors of the Netherlands on diplomatic missions, because, as a painter however eminent, he was not an 'official' ambassador, and could, if it suited the rulers, be repudiated without breaking diplomatic conventions. These journeys took him to Holland, Spain, and England, and on one of these visits he was knighted by Charles I for whose father, James I, he had painted the ceiling of the Banqueting House, Whitehall, his only grand decorative commission to survive.

Rublev, Andrei (*c.*1360/70–*c.*1430), was a monk whose icons and frescoes are in the Byzantine style. His early works show knowledge of those of *Theophanes the Greek, who was painting in Moscow in the 1390s. In 1405 they worked together in the Cathedral of the Annunciation in the Kremlin on frescoes and the *iconostasis, from which some icons have survived. This was the prototype of the Russian form of iconostasis, which is much larger than the Greek form. Rublev collaborated with Theophanes, but was probably not his pupil, since his own style is more linear and gentle. About 1408 he painted frescoes in the Cathedral of the Dormition, Vladimir, where the iconostasis is the largest to survive, though not completely—some icons are ten ft. high. The *Ascension* is in Moscow, Tretyakov Museum, which has other works by him, including the *Trinity* (*c.*1411?), which is nowadays perhaps the best known of all icons.

rubrics (rubricated initials) The ordinary use of the word rubric means an instruction at the head of a document or for the conduct of a rite, which was written in red (Lat. *ruber*) to distinguish it from the text. The word comes from Roman law, in which instructions were written in red. The custom transferred from there to the Church, where the rules for the conduct of Mass, special feast-days, or other rites were defined in red, to distinguish them from the rite itself, and such rubrics had to be observed by the celebrant. The red letter was also used in calendars of church feasts to mark them off from ordinary days, hence the phrase 'a red-letter day'.

Rubricated initials were purely ornamental, and appeared at the beginning of a text—a Gospel, a chapter of the Bible, a prayer. They appeared in MSS at a very early date, and developed fairly quickly into *historiated initials, which sometimes, as in the Book of *Kells, came to occupy most of the page. The custom of rubricated initials survived the change to printed books, and usually continued to be printed in red.

Ruskin, John (1819–1900), was Victorian England's most influential art critic. He was a polymath—teacher, reformer, artist, collector, who wrote on painting, sculpture, and architecture, political economy, religion, cultural history, the natural sciences, and many other subjects. Through his narrow Evangelical upbringing, he came to know the Bible thoroughly; his father's collection of English watercolours included many by Turner, and he also accompanied him on his business travels, so that he saw churches and great houses. After a private education, he began studies in Oxford (1838), but fell ill and travelled in Europe to recuperate in 1840–1. The first volume of *Modern Painters* (1843) is a defence of Turner's art. His prose, vivid, fluent, lucid, attracts two reactions: to some, it is a magnificent expression of truth and feeling; to others, a sequence of purple passages in which he praised what he admired, and denigrated artists and art which he disliked.

Modern Painters, volume II (1846), explored the relationship between art, nature, and the divine; volumes III to V (1856–60) are even broader in sweep. His Italian tour of 1845 deepened his knowledge of Italian Christian art; he admired Italian Gothic as the full flowering of medieval culture in *The Seven Lamps of Architecture* (1849), yet while he described the Renaissance as 'the Fall', and his admiration for *Veronese and *Tintoretto increased, so did his detestation of Renaissance architecture, particularly *Palladio. He dismissed 17th-century art, including Rubens, Rembrandt, Claude, and Poussin, with contempt, and described Dominichino and the Carracci in the *Stones of Venice* (1851–3) as 'the Scum of Titian'. He also wrote disparagingly of *Pugin.

His aim was to teach his readers to 'see clearly', and he drew so as to educate his eye, and that of others. His books were admired for his Romantic critique of industrialization and urbanization, his idealization of the Middle Ages, and his appeal to modern painters to work from nature. He defended the PRB in pamphlets, letters to the press, and entries in his *Academy Notes* (1855–9, 1875), including memorable explanations of *The Light of the World, The Awakening Conscience*, and *The Scapegoat* (all by Holman *Hunt). His unhappy marriage to his cousin, Euphemia ('Effie') Gray (1848–54), annulled for non-consummation, did not affect his admiration for *Millais, despite Effie's marriage to him in 1855. He was also a generous patron to Dante Gabriel *Rossetti, a fellow teacher at the Working Men's College.

After his 'unconversion' from Evangelical dogma in Turin in 1858, and his recognition that Catholic Italy had produced the greatest art the world had ever seen, his focus turned to political economy, mythology, and social issues. He inherited a fortune when his father died in 1864, which he used to support the Oxford drawing school, and the Guild of St George's Museum in Sheffield. He was elected the first Slade Professor of Fine Art at Oxford in 1869, and several series of lectures were published, on themes of religious art, and the relationship between ethics and aesthetics, but after the death of his mother in 1871, and of his beloved Rose La Touche in 1875, he suffered severe mental breakdowns in 1878 and the 1880s. In 1878 he won a libel action brought by Whistler, against whom he had made an intemperate outburst. His travels to France, Italy, and Switzerland continued, and he wrote on Christian art and architecture again (*Mornings in Florence*, 1875–7, *St. Mark's Rest*, 1877–84, *The Bible of Amiens*, 1880–85, on the cathedral's portal sculpture), despite increasing difficulties resulting from his mental decline. For the last twenty-eight years of his life he lived at Brantwood in the Lake District, and *Praeterita* (1885–9) is the fragmentary autobiography of a critic of art and society for whom theory and practice were indivisible. His legacy is the clarity of his observation of the art and architecture that he admired, and of natural forms—rocks, rivers, trees, ferns—in his drawings, and the power of the most arresting non-fictional prose of the Victorian age.

RUSSIAN ART AND ARCHITECTURE

It is no accident that the conversion of Russia to Christianity in the 10th century was inspired by the richness and sensuality of Byzantine art and architecture. Accordingly, the art and architecture of the Russian Orthodox Church continues to function as a fundamental expression of its religious beliefs and principles to this day.

According to legend, Vladimir I (*c*.956–1015), Prince of Kiev, sent envoys in 988 to sample the religions of his neighbours—Orthodox (Eastern) Christianity, Catholic (Western) Christianity, Islam, and Judaism. On the strength of the heavenly beauty and power of Hagia Sophia in Constantinople, capital of the Byzantine empire, he chose the liturgy, architecture, and spirituality of the Orthodox Christianity of Byzantium. Orthodox prelates, monks, builders, and painters were brought to Kiev (capital of ancient Rus, in present day Ukraine) and the earliest surviving Christian monuments reflect their heritage directly. While the first Christian edifices were built of wood, in keeping with local traditions, the earliest substantial remains to survive were built in brick and were based on the imperial church, which originally led to the Christianization of Russia. Churches dedicated to Hagia Sophia (Holy Wisdom) were built in Kiev before 1037 and in Novgorod in 1045–50, the capital of ancient Rus until 988. Their centralized plan, a rectilinear grid surmounted by a central drum and a dome, was a definitive characteristic of Byzantine churches. It appeared in innumerable variations in subsequent Russian churches, differentiating them from the longitudinal, cruciform model of the medieval West.

The earliest churches were decorated by immigrant Byzantine artisans, who brought their techniques, styles, and above all, their beliefs with them. While the Church of Hagia Sophia in Kiev was decorated in the typically Byzantine technique of mosaic, the rarity in Russia of the raw materials that were necessary for this medium ensured that it did not prosper further. However, fresco painting made use of local materials—mostly minerals and vegetal dyes, accounting for the earthiness of their colours—and it did therefore become common, covering the interiors of many whitewashed brick churches from floor to ceiling with images from the Old and New Testaments, and the liturgy and the lives of the saints. But the material that was most available to the ancient builders of churches in Russia was wood, and for many centuries the vast majority of churches, and almost all other buildings (and even domestic utensils), were made of this material. As it is impossible to apply frescoes to a wooden surface, these churches were hardly ever decorated on the inside. Very few examples survive, the earliest dating from the 15th century.

The most distinctive manifestation of Christian art in Russia is undoubtedly the icon, (literally in Greek an 'image', but now the word is used to refer to the sacred imagery of the Orthodox Church). By the time the tradition of icon painting was brought to Russia, the theological status and visual language of icons were very fully developed. Whereas Byzantine icons, however, had tended to be made from the diverse materials that were available throughout the empire—gold, ivory, enamel, steatite, and painted wooden panel—in Russia they were almost invariably made of wood. Moreover, where icons in Byzantine churches had been leant against a low rail that divided the sanctuary of a church from its congregational area, Russian icons were, by the 14th century, assembled on a tall and wide screen of images, called the iconostasis, which reached to the ceiling and entirely obscured the sanctuary from the layman.

The theological status of icons was confirmed at the Triumph of Orthodoxy in 843—before the conversion of Russia to Christianity—when the Iconoclastic Controversy (726–843), which doubted the legitimacy of sacred images, came to an end. The iconoclasts (against the use of images) had maintained that 1) the Old Testament decreed against the use of 'graven images' and that to produce them was therefore blasphemous; 2) the ancient pagans of Rome erected idols to their gods, and to make images was to follow in their idolatrous footsteps; and 3) the iconoclastic religion of Islam was coming into prominence at this time, at the expense of Christianity, and perhaps it was because this new religion was iconoclastic that God was showing it favour, in which case should Christianity not do the same? The iconodules (supporters of icons) countered these arguments by maintaining that God's choice to incarnate himself as Jesus Christ was itself a form of divine representation and could therefore serve as a legitimizing precedent for the entire tradition of icon painting. On this basis, icons constituted an extension of the incarnation of Christ and, as such, were considered to be sacramental—rather than decorative, didactic, or emotive—objects. Although the iconodule position eventually prevailed, icon painters did make some concessions to the iconoclasts, establishing practices that became central to the tradition of icon painting in Russia. Firstly, it was considered idolatrous to represent God the Father in Russian icons, as there was no sacred precedent on which to base the image (unlike images of God the Son); in order to refer to the Trinity without representing God the Father as an old man with a beard, as in the Western tradition, icon painters depicted the three angels, the 'Old Testament Trinity', who visited Abraham and Sarah (Gen. 18. 2). Secondly, images of the Resurrection of Christ were outlawed because this episode in Christ's life was not actually witnessed by human beings, therefore, there was no precedent for visualizing it; the ubiquitous image of Christ descending into Hell (the Anastasis) was used instead. And thirdly, three-dimensional sculptural icons were never made because they were seen to resemble pagan idols, unlike two-dimensional pictures.

Because icon painting was considered to be a sacramental art, it was not subject to the self-expressive and aesthetically self-conscious agendas of Western European art (from the 15th century onwards). Artistic originality was never commodified; on the contrary, the role of the painter was to perpetuate the tradition in which sanctity had been invested. For this reason, the style and subject matter of icons rarely changed; it was not meant to change. By the 14th century, for instance, the subject matter of the iconostasis had crystallized into a standardized format comprising (in descending order, from the top): a row each of patriarchs and prophets; a smaller row of church feasts (including the Annunciation, Entry into Jerusalem, Crucifixion, etc.); a large row of primary saints, including Saints Peter and Paul, the Archangels Michael and Gabriel, John the Forerunner (John the *Baptist), and the Mother of God, converging on a central icon of Christ in Majesty; a row of local icons, including one of the saint to whom the church in question was dedicated, and a pair of 'royal doors', usually presenting images of the four Evangelists.

Despite the ostensible lack of desire or scope for development, the appearance of Russian icons did change over the centuries. From the 13th to 15th centuries, the Mongol invasions of most of the territory of Rus led to a disintegration of the kingdom and the weakening of its links with its sources in Byzantium. The territory of Kievan Rus eventually became reconfigured around, firstly, the principalities of Vladimir-Suzdal and then Muscovy, which shook off the 'Tatar yoke' in 1480. In the same years Muscovy absorbed the city-states of Novgorod, Tver, and finally Pskov, whose independence was reflected in the idiosyncratic styles of their icons. Together with the fall the Byzantine empire to the Ottoman Turks in 1453, these developments led to the celebration of Moscow by its rulers, as the 'Third Rome', inheriting the mantle of the early and 'authentic' Christian Church. The political successes of Muscovy coincided with a period of religious intensity and monastic revival, considered by many to be the heyday of icon painting. The purity and quality of the icons of this period are epitomized by those attributed to Andrei Rublev, the only icon painter whose name is well known, and is thought to have worked in Moscow, and Vladimir under the guidance of *Theophanes 'the Greek' (ie. Byzantine). His best-known work, considered to be exemplary since the 16th century, is his icon of the Old Testament Trinity.

Although Russia did not experience a Western-style 'Renaissance' in the 15th and 16th centuries, the influence of the West did eventually register in its art and architecture. The 15th-century churches in the Kremlin in Moscow—for instance, the Church of the Dormition (1475)—include classical details introduced by the Italian architect Aristotele Fioravanti. It was not, however, until the 17th century that Russian culture began to reflect the powerful influence of Western European culture and values. Icon painting became more naturalistic at this period, departing from the stiff, graphic, and 'spiritualized' style of Byzantium; its styles became more aesthetically self-conscious and decorative, and painters such as Simon Ushakov (1626–86) began to sign their icons, reflecting an unprecedented interest in self-expression. In many cases, their iconography also became more cerebral and less contemplative than their medieval counterparts' work. Contrary to the ancient dictates of traditional Orthodox theology, icons showing both God the Father and the Resurrection of Christ were also produced at this time.

Under Peter the Great, the Westernizing tendencies of the 17th century were subjected to the most rigorous systematization, epitomized by the founding of the city of St Petersburg in 1703. As a sign of his intention to make the new city a 'window on to the West', the first church that Peter had built there (the Peter and Paul Cathedral, from 1712) was given a longitudinal plan and a tall spire in the manner of a 17th-century English Protestant Church. The interior, which reflects the Catholic influence of its Swiss-Italian designer Domenico Trezzini, is in a more opulent Baroque style and includes such un-Orthodox features as a pulpit and large three-dimensional sculptures. Churches built in the city in the middle of the century continued to use the thoroughly Western Italianate Baroque style, despite their return to the traditional plan with a large central dome and four smaller domes at the four corners (the Smolny Convent by Francesco Bartolommeo Rastrelli, 1748; St Nicholas by Savva Chevakinsky, 1753).

The first signs of a re-evaluation and revival of traditional Russian styles occurred towards the end of the 18th century—after a hundred years of Westernization. The Gothic detailing of the Chesme Church (1780) in St Petersburg is a further example of European influence; although the building has a Greek cross ground plan, it copies the revival of a medieval style that had no history of its own in Russia. It was not long before the principle of romantic, nationalistic historicism (the rationale of the Gothic revival in the West) developed its own roots in Russian soil, as reflected in the first churches to return to a fully Byzantine model—which had no precedent in the West. The Church of the Redeemer, designed, significantly, for Moscow after the retreat of Napoleon in 1812 and commenced in 1839, is the most significant example of this trend. This monumental building (destroyed by Stalin in 1931 for ideological reasons and rebuilt in the 1990s, also for ideological reasons) captured the spirit of the contemporary Slavophile movement. This trend, which gathered momentum throughout the 19th century, attempted to revive Russian traditions in every area of cultural life to serve as precedents for the consolidation of a 'truly Russian' cultural identity. By the end of the century, fully Russified adaptations of the traditional Byzantine church-type were being designed; for instance, the Church of the Spilled Blood, built, somewhat incongruously, in St Petersburg (to commemorate the assassination of Tsar Alexander II in 1881) in the exuberant, colourful, and barbarous style of St Basil's Cathedral in Moscow (1555).

Icon painting was subjected to the same process of Westernization and revival as architecture. In the 18th century, icons for prestigious churches were largely painted in a classically naturalistic manner, which was universally seen to be more sophisticated and appropriate than the naïve and 'backward' Orthodox tradition. In the 19th century, however, icons came to be appreciated for their spiritual intensity, which informed the art of several 'realist' painters; for instance, that of Nicolas Ge (1831–94) and Ivan Kramskoi (1837–87). These artists, inspired by the renunciate example of Leo Tolstoy (1828–1910), highlighted the moral implications of the life of Christ at the expense of the ritual conventions of the Church, which they believed to have become ossified and institutionalized. It was not, however, until the end of the century that initiatives were taken to revive the religiosity and intensity of icons as well as their stylistic and metaphysical characteristics. In the 1880s, the initiative to build a new church in a traditional style on the private estate of Savva Mamontov at Abramtsevo inspired several contemporary artists and designers to research the folkloric dimension of Russian art that had been neglected by the rhetoric of the Realists. While icons were used in this context as an instrument with which to revive the traditional values of the Russian people, they were also used as a precedent for the development of anti-classical and anti-bourgeois styles in art that constituted the avant-garde. While some artists adopted the proto-modernity and populism of icons at the expense of their religiosity, others (for instance, Natalia Goncharova, 1881–1962) recycled their religious imagery for the sake of its poetics of simplicity, immediacy, and sincerity. Kasimir Malevich (1879–1935) took the revival of interest in icons to the most extreme level by attempting to capture their absolute sanctity at the expense of all other features, including their subject matter. When he first exhibited his Black Square in Petrograd (St Petersburg) in 1915, he hung it provocatively across the corner of the room, in the manner in which Russian icons are displayed in traditional Russian homes.

In the Soviet Union, both religious imagery and avant-garde styles were in effect banned. Thousands of Orthodox churches and icons were destroyed. Many icons, considered to be worthless at home, were also exported to the West, initiating a commercial market for icons that enabled many otherwise vulnerable examples to be saved. It was not until the fall of the Soviet Union in 1990–91 that the taboo on sacred art in Russia was lifted and that an appreciation of the artistic, historical, and spiritual value of icons was developed, resulting in the reacquisition of many exported examples by Russian individuals and institutions. Although Christianity itself has seen a revival of interest since 1991, the state of many historical churches in Russia continues to be precarious. *See also* EUROPE.

Ruth The Book of Ruth, which is only four chapters long, tells the story of Ruth and Naomi. Naomi and her husband fled to the land of Moab because of famine. He died, but their two sons had married Moabite women, Ruth and Orpah. Ten years later both men died and Naomi decided to return to her native Bethlehem. Ruth and Orpah both accompanied her, but she advised them to turn back and Orpah did so. Ruth said: 'Do not press me to . . . turn back from following you. Where you go, I will go; . . . your people shall be my people, and your God my God. Where you die, I will die—there I will be buried . . . ' (1: 16). In Bethlehem, Naomi's kinsman Boaz (Vg. Booz) allowed Ruth to glean in his fields of barley and wheat. Naomi told her to go and sleep in the barn where Boaz slept, and he discovered that they were kin. Under the Law, a widow should marry the nearest kinsman of her late husband, but he renounced his right, and Boaz married her. Their son Obed became the father of *Jesse, who was the father of *David and therefore an Ancestor of Christ.

In the *Sistine Chapel *Michelangelo painted one of the lunettes of the Ancestors, inscribing it *Salmon. Booz. Obeth*, but the woman and child represented are probably Ruth and Obed, and the old man Boaz. Salmon was Boaz's father. The subject is extremely rare in Italian art, but there is a Bassano in the Royal Collection. It was, however, popular in 17th-century Holland, especially among Rembrandt's followers—there are several by G. van den Eeckhout, as well as by B. Fabritius, P. de Grebber, Jan Victors, and W. Drost (Oxford, Ashmolean), and A. de Gelder. Poussin painted Ruth and Boaz in the harvest field as *Summer* in his *Four Seasons* (1660–4: Louvre), and the subject was popular as a genre scene in the 19th century.

Ruthwell cross *See* CROSSES, STANDING.

Ryder, Albert Pinkham (1847–1917) An American painter, largely self-taught, with an impressionistic style tending toward abstraction, perhaps due to an ocular condition that limited his ability to focus on detail. His highly imaginative paintings evoke a sometimes dreamlike, often mystic and unsettling depiction of the natural world. Robert Hughes in *American Visions: The Epic History of Art in America* (1997) makes the point that although 'he was never in his own view a Modernist, a succession of American artists ... would look up to him as an emblem of esthetic purity, a holy sage, and the native prophet who linked tradition to Modernism'. His striking treatments of religious subjects include *Christ Appearing to Mary* (1885), *The Way of the Cross* (date unknown), and *The Resurrection* (1885). *See also* NORTH AMERICA.

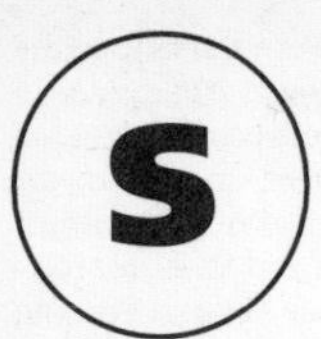

Sabina, Santa Sta Sabina is a church on the Aventine Hill in Rome, begun in 422/32, and referred to as *titulus Sabinae* in the 5th century. Sabina was probably therefore a real woman, but there is no evidence for her being a saint, although later legends make her a Roman martyr. A *schola cantorum was added to the church in the 9th century and the whole church was restored in the 1930s to give a good idea of the appearance of an Early Christian *basilica. Its greatest treasure is a pair of olive-wood doors, datable *c.*432, with eighteen (out of twenty-eight originally) OT and NT scenes in relief. One represents the Crucifixion, and, with the contemporary ivory in the British Museum, is the earliest known representation of the Crucifixion. This shallow relief shows Christ with arms not fully extended as they would be if He were actually hanging from the cross, but almost in a symbolic gesture with His arms with bent elbows holding them out in front of the mouldings in the relief, as if they were to represent the cross. There are nail marks in His hands, but He stands firmly on the ground. The artist of the ivory relief makes no such concessions to Early Christian squeamishness. The other panels include miracles and OT scenes.

saccos *See* SAKKOS.

Sacra Conversazione (Ital. holy conversation) One of the most popular forms of *Madonna and Child with Saints.* It may be seen in the evolution of groups of saints and angels around the Enthroned Madonna in the work of Giotto and his followers, but is really established in 15th-century Florence (Fra *Angelico, Domenico Veneziano, Fra Filippo *Lippi). In earlier polyptychs the individual saints occupied separate panels, usually with gold backgrounds. The basic notion of a Sacra Conversazione is a single space, a room or a landscape, in which several saints, donors, or angels, are grouped together around the Madonna and Child—some talking, some gesturing, but usually all aware of the presence of Christ and of each other, though in some of *Bellini's large altarpieces the figures are more meditative and detached. The type has been popular ever since, and was soon perfected by Giovanni Bellini, *Piero della Francesca, *Titian, and *Raphael.

Sacrament, the Blessed In ordinary usage this refers to the Eucharist, and specifically to the consecrated Host, as in the Catholic devotion of the Exposition of the Blessed Sacrament in a *monstrance. It also refers to the consecrated Host given by the priest to the communicant and to the consecrated wine, if communion in both kinds is being given, as it always is in the Anglican Rite, but not always in the Catholic one. In the Catholic Church the consecrated sacrament may also be reserved: that is, kept in the *ciborium either in anticipation of another Mass to be celebrated, or so that the Last Sacraments of confession and the Blessed Sacrament may be administered as the Viaticum (Lat. provision for a journey) to a sick or dying person. The Last Rites may be given at any time of the day or night, without any requirement of previous fasting.

According to the Thirty-Nine Articles, reservation of the Sacrament is not permitted in the Anglican Church, nor is its exposition in any form, nor may it be carried about. The rule against its being carried, and against its reservation has, however, been relaxed considerably in recent years. *See* SACRAMENTS, THE SEVEN.

sacramentals Originally, this term was used freely as an equivalent for *Sacraments, particularly in the Eastern Church, but from the 13th century the word was restricted to acts or objects, not specificially instituted by Christ, which accompany the Sacrament, or are necessary for its administration. They are covered roughly under six headings: praying, anointing, eating, confessing, giving, and blessing. They therefore include such acts or objects as the sign of the cross, the oil or chrism used at Baptism or for anointing the sick, grace at meals, the general confession during Mass, alms given in a consecrated place, such as a poor box, but not in furtherance of a private charitable purpose, such as a donation to a street collection, and such things as palms on Palm Sunday, candles on an altar or lit as part of an invocation, holy water, vestments, incense and the censer or thurible, the fire at the Easter Vigil Mass, and the ashes used at the Ash Wednesday Mass. Sacramentals also cover devotions such as the *rosary, the *Stations of the Cross, the litanies, and the angelus.

Sacrament house, as distinct from a *ciborium or a *tabernacle, may be one of two things: an *aumbry or cupboard usually near the altar, used for the reservation of the Sacraments; or a very tall, elaborately carved shrine-like structure used for the same purpose. The finest medieval example is the one in St Lorenz, Nuremberg, of 1493–6. Their use for the reservation of the Sacrament was forbidden in Roman Catholic churches in 1863, but the practice has been revived in recent years. Modern examples are also found in Anglican churches, such as St Mary-le-Bow in London. *See also* AUMBRY, CIBORIUM, PYX, and TABERNACLE.

Sacraments, the Seven They are Baptism, Confirmation, Communion (or the Eucharist), Penance (or Confession), Matrimony, Ordination, and Extreme Unction. While there has never been any argument that Christ instituted Baptism, the Eucharist, Penance, and Ordination, all of which can be justified by Christ's words or acts in the Gospels, some theologians have argued that Confirmation, Matrimony, and Extreme Unction do not have that final authority. In the Catholic Church all seven are accepted unequivocally; three of them are held to be unrepeatable, in that their effect is indelible. These are Baptism, Confirmation, and Ordination. Should there be any doubt whether they have or have not been given, then they may be repeated, but only 'conditionally', i.e. in case they might not have been administered properly.

In the Orthodox Church all seven Sacraments are recognized, and have been since 1267; before then the list varied. Byzantine liturgical books do not distinguish between sacraments and sacramentals, reserving the term *mysteria* specifically to the Eucharist. Some Reformed Churches only recognize Baptism and the Eucharist, the Anglicans recognize all seven, and Quakers and the Salvation Army do not accept any.

Roger van der Weyden painted an altarpiece with a *Crucifixion with the Virgin and S. John* set in a church, with Mass being said at an altar in the background. The wings have the remaining *Six Sacraments* (*c.*1445: Antwerp). The so-called Cambrai Altarpiece, produced in Roger's workshop (*c.*1459: Madrid, Prado) has a *Crucifixion in a church with the Virgin and S. John*, also with Mass being said at an altar at the back, where the priest elevating the Host mirrors the Crucifixion depicted at the front. There are scenes of the *Passion* round the arch enclosing the central part, and the remaining six Sacraments are depicted, three on either side.

Poussin painted two series of the *Seven Sacraments*, the first series finished in 1642; *Baptism* is now in the National Gallery, Washington, *Confession* has been destroyed, and the remainder are in Belvoir Castle, Rutland. The second series, larger in size, was painted between 1644 and 1648, and is complete: it belongs to the Duke of Sutherland and is on loan to the National Gallery of Scotland, Edinburgh. They are perfect examples of the artist's theory that a picture should convey the maximum of moral content in a composition which shall also convey intellectual meaning and that the sensuous charm of colour should not be allowed to diminish its intellectual and moral power. The artist's theoretical intentions in no way, in this case, diminish the impact of the beauty of the pictures. There is also a set of the *Seven Sacraments* (1712: Dresden) by G. M. Crespi.

In Eastern art, the Sacraments are often depicted in Bibles and in *menologia. From the 6th century onwards the Eucharist was only represented on liturgical vessels, until in the 11th century it began to appear in apse mosaics. In all cases, however, it is the *Communion of the Apostles at the Last Supper—the Institution of the Eucharist—which is depicted, never communion given to the faithful. In hagiographical books, other Sacraments may be depicted, such as Baptism, Ordination, or Extreme Unction, and in the rare instances when Marriage is depicted, it will be Christ joining the couple, not a priest; this rule pertains only to representations of the Sacrament *per se*, not to incidents when they are administered on specific occasions. Hence, pictures of the Marriage of the Virgin show the High Priest performing the rite. Confession, or Penance, and Confirmation appear only when the Sacraments are being represented as themselves, as they are in the Poussin and Crespi series, not for incidents involving specific occasions or persons.

Sacra Rappresentazione (Ital. sacred drama), an Italian *mystery play. From about 1500 many were printed, preserving the texts, but they represent much older forms of sacred drama performed by guilds and confraternities. It is not clear how far they influenced the visual arts or were influenced by them, but Vasari's Life of Piero di Cosimo (1568) shows how important such productions were for painters.

Sacra Via or **Via Sacra** (Lat. Sacred or Holy Way) In the Rome of Antiquity, the Via Sacra was the street running through the Forum Romanum, between the Velia at the east end and the Palatine Hill at the west end, and led to the Capitol. It was so called because it passed near the Temple of Vesta and its adjacent Atrium Vestae and the Regia, the seat of authority of the *Pontifex Maximus, and was the last stage of Imperial Triumphs.

In Christian terms, the Sacra Via is the Via Dolorosa (the Road of Grief), or the Way of the Cross in Jerusalem, the streets trodden by Jesus as he carried the cross to Golgotha, outside the city wall. Incidents on the way are commemorated in the *Stations of the Cross. *See also* SACRO MONTE.

Sacred Heart *See* HEART.

Sacred Monogram *See* NOMEN SACRUM.

Sacred Name *See* NOMEN SACRUM.

Sacrifice of Abraham *See* ABRAHAM.

sacristy, sacristan (Lat. *sacristia, sacrarium,* or *secretarium*) A sacristy is a dependency of a church in which are kept the *vestments and the *liturgical vessels used in the Mass or other services. Sacristies were attached to the apses of Syrian churches from *c.*400, and in medieval churches they were often built behind or on either side of the presbytery. In cathedral or conventual churches where there might be accumulations of vestments, several sacristies might be provided for higher and lower clergy, acolytes, choristers, and servers. Sacristies are normally provided with a crucifix, cupboards, chests, often special cope chests, a table on which vestments may be laid out by the sacristan for the priest's use, a *lavabo* for the priest to wash his hands before celebrating, and a secure silver cupboard for the liturgical vessels. Most Roman Catholic sacristies also contain an altar, either for the reservation of the Sacrament or for use from Good Friday to the first Mass of Easter morning. In Italy, sacristies are often richly decorated.

The sacristy is also the place where the registers of baptisms, marriages, and burials are kept, and is often used for the signing of the marriage register. In E. Orthodox churches, two chambers, one on either side of the apse, are the *prothesis on the left and the *Diaconicon on the right, which are the equivalent of sacristies. The sacristan, who in smaller churches is usually a layman, but in cathedrals or major churches may be in Orders, is responsible for the care and ordering of the vestments and liturgical vessels, and for the maintenance of the church.

In Anglican churches, the room where the clergy vest is usually called the vestry, and was once also the place where the parishioners or a parish council met to arrange the business of the parish, secular and religious. In cathedrals with an elaborate ceremonial, many officiating clergy, and large choirs, which need many vestments, and which have a large number of liturgical vessels, the vestries are termed sacristies, and cathedral chapters usually have a Canon Sacristan in charge of them.

Few English medieval parish churches have proper vestries. The custom was for the priest to arrive, already vested, by the priest's door in the chancel, with or without his server. Many nowadays make do with a disused chantry chapel, a curtained-off part of one of the aisles, or the area under the bell-ringers' chamber in the tower.

Sacro Monte (Sacri Monti) (Ital. Holy Hill or Hills) There are several in N. Italy, mostly on the hills of the lower ranges of the Alps. Among the most notable are those at Oropa, Varese, Varallo, Orta, Crea, and Locarno in Switzerland. Oropa, above Biella, is dedicated to the Virgin, and is one of the oldest pilgrimage sites in the West. It was founded, traditionally, by S. Eusebius, Bishop of Vercelli, in 369, and the original modest chapel contained a wooden statue of the Virgin, brought from Jerusalem, and reputed to have been carved by S. Luke. All subsequent rebuildings of the sanctuary church have conserved the original chapel with its image of the Virgin, blackened by the passage of time, now largely covered with gilding. The very large modern church is part of a complex of nineteen chapels, twelve of which are dedicated to incidents in the Life of the Virgin, and the others to saints.

Varese, in Lombardy above Como, has a double sanctuary, the Madonna delle Tre Croci (... of the Three Crosses) and, more important, Sta Maria del Monte, from where, on the road down the hillside, are fifteen small 17th-century temples dedicated to the Mysteries of the *Rosary. Unusually, the pilgrimage to Sta Maria del Monte begins at the top, from an image of the Virgin in the church, which is held to be miraculous.

Varallo, like Oropa, is in Piedmont, and compared with the others is huge. It climbs the steep side of a hill called, like that of the *santuario* of Varese, delle Tre Croci; a long winding path is flanked by forty-four chapels or small booths open to the pathway. It was first founded in 1491 by a Franciscan, Bernardino Caimi, who called it the New Jerusalem, and it was executed mainly by Gaudenzio Ferrari, who had many assistants. It was continued and enlarged in the last quarter of the 16th century, with architecture by Galeazzo Alessi, and paintings by Morazzone and Tanzio da Varallo, as well as a number of other painters and sculptors, and was not finished until 1765. The booths contain over 600 painted statues and 4,000 figures, arranged as 'tableaux', beginning with Original Sin, and continuing from the Annunciation through the Life of the Virgin. At the 12th booth the Life of Christ takes over with the Baptism, until at the 41st the narrative ends with the Holy Shroud with 19th-century replacement figures of the Dead Christ, the Holy Women, S. John, Joseph of Arimathaea, and Nicodemus. The 42nd contains the Death of S. Francis of Assisi, the 43rd the Holy Sepulchre, which was the first built by Fra Bernardino. The last is dedicated to S. Carlo Borommeo. The last scenes surround the open piazza in front of the Basilica of the Assumption, of 1641–9, which contains an *Assumption* designed by Antonio Tempesta, consisting of *c.*140 painted statues and figures. The Sacro Monte of Varallo was much promoted by both Cardinal S. Carlo and Cardinal Federico *Borommeo as a Counter-Reformation devotion, and is one of the major pilgrimage sites of N. Italy.

Also just S. of Varallo, at Civiasco, is a sanctuary dedicated to the Madonna of Loreto, of the end of the 15th century. The small church is surrounded on three sides by a portico with late 15th-century frescoes mostly by Antonio Zanetti, but with some by Gaudenzio Ferrari, and inside the church, by Ferrari and Luini. There are many pilgrimage churches in N. Italy, most of them dedicated to the Virgin. Caravaggio, in the province of Bergamo, includes a Holy Fountain, and has a pilgrimage dedicated to the Magdalene as well as the Madonna. *See also* STATIONS OF THE CROSS.

Sacro Speco (Ital. Holy Cave) *S. Benedict, unhappy at the loose life he saw around him in Rome, retired *c.*500 to Subiaco, about 20 miles from Rome. He lived there in a cave for three years, devoting himself to meditation and prayer. The cave communicated with a monastery, originally separate and above it, but of which it now forms part, by a staircase (the Scala Santa: Holy Stair) which follows the steep and stony path by which the saint reached his hermitage. A small community grew up round him, for whom he composed the Benedictine Rule; they moved with him to a permanent home at *Monte Cassino, where the Order was finally constituted after his death. In the cave there is now a statue of the saint by Raggi (1657). The whole complex is adorned by a wealth of 13th-, 14th-, and 15th-century frescoes, including also an 8th-century Byzantine fresco.

Saint-Denis is a cathedral in a suburb of Paris, but was originally an abbey, founded by King Clovis as a royal mausoleum in 507. Odilon of Cluny was abbot until his death in 1049, and the abbey adopted the 'Customs of Cluny', introducing a taste for splendour which reached a climax under its most famous abbot, *Suger. From his school-days there he had nourished the ambition of rebuilding the abbey. He became abbot in 1122 and died in 1151.

The abbey was a place of pilgrimage to the shrine of *S. Denis, a national saint, and the royal burial-place; the town also had three important yearly fairs, which brought great crowds. In his account of his work Suger describes the result: 'Through ... the number of faithful the basilica suffered grave inconveniences. Often on feast-days, completely filled, it disgorged through its doors crowds moving in opposite directions ... At times ... the crowded multitude offered so much resistance to those who strove to enter ... that no one could move a foot, or do anything but stand benumbed like a statue, or as a last resort, scream ...'.

The original west front had two towers which Suger says 'threatened ruin'; he removed the cramped porch, rebuilt the towers and west front, opened three large doors to the nave and the aisles, and designed the three portals with sculpture. Over the main door was a Last Judgement in the tympanum, and the door jambs had small figures of the Wise and Foolish Virgins in niches. The arches of the portal had figures, probably of the Elders of the Apocalypse, and there were also Signs of the *Zodiac and Labours of the *Months. Of the two side doors, the tympanum on the right had the Last Communion and martyrdom of S. Denis and his companions, and the left one had a mosaic executed by Italian artists. Between the doors were column figures, carved in one with the column, representing OT kings and queens, patriarchs, and prophets. Portals with columns were not unusual in late 11th/early 12th-century churches; and the Moissac portal, of 1110–20, had figures of S. Peter and Isaiah on either side of the door; but so far no one had combined the two. Suger also had gilded bronze doors made with scenes of the Passion, Resurrection, and Ascension for two of the portals, using the existing doors in the door with the mosaic. They carried an inscription expressing his feelings about art in church: 'The dull mind is awakened to truth through the material, and in seeing this light, is revived from its former dejection.' His love of colour, enamels, mosaics, stained glass, gold and jewelled altar furnishings is part of his belief, derived from the mystical doctrines of the Pseudo-Dionysius, as translated by John Scotus Erigena, that by overcoming the senses and the powers of reason, the soul may ascend to God through the effulgence of inner light to which one path was the beauty and splendour of colour and light in works of art.

The sculpture was badly damaged in 1771 at the hands of 'enlightened' clergy, who removed many of the column figures; and at the Revolution the kings and queens were destroyed, because they were thought to represent French royalty. The tympana were also damaged, not only by Revolutionary fervour, but by ill-conceived restoration. Suger's doors have also vanished. The triple portal was, however, the first in a church in the Île de France, and its scheme lies behind the grand series of *portal sculptures of the 12th–15th centuries, attached to Gothic rather than *Romanesque churches such as Vézelay. The work took from 1130 to 1140.

Suger's account also records the rebuilding of the choir: 'We also changed to its present form . . . the choir . . . and we endeavoured to enlarge it. Moreover, we caused to be painted . . . by many masters . . . the splendid variety of new windows, both below and above; from that first one . . . with the Tree of *Jesse in the chevet of the church to that which is installed above the principal door in the entrance. Because of their value on account of their wonderful execution and the expenditure of painted glass and sapphire glass, we appointed a master craftsman for their protection and repair'—possibly the first record of the appointment of a maintenance staff. In its original arrangement, the choir was ended in an apse and was elevated over a crypt in which a passage encircled the saints' shrines; Suger rebuilt the choir with an *ambulatory using rib-vaulting borne on columns, and with seven radiating chapels which almost formed a second ambulatory, creating the first Gothic church. He filled his new chapels with stained-glass windows, and the *clerestory of the choir itself also had large stained-glass windows to achieve the light which he felt was so spiritually important. Rib-vaulting had been used in the areas behind the triple portal, but in the choir it was more skilfully managed, though only the ambulatory and the chapels survive from Suger's work, completed between 1140 and 1144.

After Suger's death no new work was begun until 1231, when the transepts and the nave were rebuilt by order of Louis IX—S. Louis—who wanted royal tombs in the transepts. These were built with aisles so that the east end of the church became almost a central plan extended by a long nave. The king installed sixteen effigies to commemorate his predecessors; fourteen survive, though they are purely conventional 13th-century figures. The chief architect of the work was Pierre de Montreuil until his death in 1267, and under him Suger's choir was also rebuilt, though the ambulatory and radiating chapels remained as Suger had left them, except that they were re-roofed; the work was not completed until 1281.

Royal burials continued until the Renaissance, when two funerary chapels were projected. The first, for the Valois dynasty, by Catherine de Medici for her husband Henry II and their three sons, successively kings of France, was begun in 1572 but not completed; it was demolished in 1719 and the tombs brought within the church. The second, for the Bourbon dynasty, was designed by François Mansart on a scale which would have dwarfed the church, but was never begun.

The tombs form a gallery of French sculpture from the 12th century onwards, since many were later brought from demolished churches, and they change slowly from purely conventional images to more realistic figures based on death-masks. Many of the tombs were damaged during the Revolution, but restored later, and many were saved from destruction by Alexandre Lenoir, who set up the Musée des Monuments Français during the Revolution to preserve monuments from churches and houses sequestrated by the state. Most of what he saved was later removed either to the Louvre, or, in the case of royal effigies, they remained in St-Denis. The 16th century created a new form of tomb: tomb-chests with an effigy of the dead lying on it were a normal form, but the idea of the *gisant or images of the corpses of the dead, placed within an arched structure, on the top of which the living monarchs were shown in prayer, was a new arrangement of the old form of the medieval *gisant*. Such were the tombs of Louis XII and Anne of Britanny by Jean Juste (Giovanni di Giusto Betti), Francis I and Claude de France, with three of their children, by Philibert de l'Orme, the bronze figures of Henry II and Catherine de Medici, kneeling in prayer, with their grimly evocative white marble *gisants*, all by Germain Pilon, in the colonnaded temple below them. These are the only monarchs to have two tombs; the second, also by Pilon, shows them lying in state in royal regalia.

The religious wars of the 16th century brought havoc. The library was pillaged, Suger's great cross disappeared, the community was dispersed, and the abbey demoted to a priory. The Revolution was even worse. The rest of the treasure was melted down, including Suger's Golden Altar, although a painting by the Master of *S. Giles (London, NG) shows part of it and is the only record of the church *c.*1500. The tombs and the west front were mutilated, the lead was stripped from the roof. The abbey became successively a Temple of Reason, a grain store, a military hospital, and in 1806 Napoleon made the abbey buildings into a school for the children of holders of the Legion of Honour, and proposed also to make the church a mausoleum for his dynasty. Incompetent restoration started, under an architect who burdened the north tower with a badly built spire which was destroyed by lightning, bringing the tower itself down in its fall in 1837. He was dismissed in 1846, and replaced by *Viollet-le-duc, who destroyed the area of the shrine in the crypt to make room for an imperial tomb for Napoleon III, who died in exile in England and is buried there.

Saints, All This major feast has been celebrated since the 4th century in honour of all known and unknown Christian saints. It was given a fixed date on the first Sunday after Pentecost, still observed on that day in the Eastern Church. In the West, the date was moved to the 13 May, to coincide with the dedication in 609 of the Pantheon in Rome as Sta Maria ad Martyres. Pope Gregory IV (d. 844) moved the date to 1 November when on that day he dedicated a chapel in St Peter's to 'All the Saints'. In the Catholic Church All Saints Day is followed on 2 November by All Souls Day (unless that is a Sunday, when the commemoration of the dead is held on 3 November). All Saints Day is recognized in the Church of England, and in the most recent revised prayer book 8 November is dedicated to the Saints and Martyrs of England. *See also* ALLERHEILIGENBILD.

saints and beati (Ital. Blessed) The term 'saint' was first used for holy people, or just all Christians, as S. Paul uses the word in e.g. Rom. 1: 7, or 1 Cor. 1: 2. It is probable that it was always used of the Apostles and the Virgin, and the first veneration of martyrs from *c.*156, and accompanied by a cult of their relics, at their memoria (*see* MARTYRIUM). The appellation 'saint' first appears officially in the 5th century, when precise designations were first found desirable, for instance, the Virgin was not finally designated *Theotokos—'the Mother of God', instead of Christotokos, 'the Mother of Christ'—until the Council of Ephesus in 431. Early canonization was generally accorded to martyrs, without any formalities, because they were particularly venerated for their courage and perseverance in suffering and for their willingness to die for their faith. Martyrologies were written from the 4th century—for instance, the Roman Calendar of 354—and all culminate in the *Martyrologium Romanum* of 1584. The Eastern Church has a similar compilation in the *menologium of Basil II, illustrated in the 10th century. When persecutions ended, canonization was usually by acclamation because of the way in which the recipient of the honour had performed his office, or for the outstanding quality of his or her devotion. Gregory the Great, for instance, was canonized by acclamation immediately after his death in 604.

The term 'canonization' in the Roman Catholic Church means that the pope declares a man or woman, who must be dead, and who may have been dead for a very long time, to have entered into glory in the eternal life and to be worthy of veneration, and of 'being raised to the altar'; i.e. a picture or statue of the saint may be placed on an altar for veneration by the faithful, and that prayers may be made to the saint asking for his or her intercession on behalf of the faithful. Canonization brings in its train a number of honours: the new saint is entered in the catalogue (the canon) of saints, public recognition is enjoined, and the new saint may become one of those publicly invoked by the faithful; churches may be dedicated to God in memory of the saint and named after him or her, a festival may be instituted in his or her memory, and the Mass and Office may be offered to God in memory of the saint. Pictures may be painted in which the saint is represented in glory, and his or her relics may be revered in a shrine, or be enclosed in an altar stone inserted into an altar at which Mass is said.

The process for a canonization takes the form of a long inquiry into the life, works, character, and piety of the man or woman on whose behalf the process has been instituted, and in particular, inquiries are made whether any miracles have taken place as a result of acts by, or intercessions to, the person. Nobody may be presented for canonization who has not previously been beatified; in about 1170 Pope Alexander III asserted that no one should be venerated without the authority of the Church in Rome, and this was inserted into the canon by Gregory XI (pope from 1170 to 1178). Beatification is, therefore, an essential preliminary stage (or hurdle) before canonization can proceed, in the course of which many of the same inquiries will be made. The beatified man or woman will then be described as 'Blessed', but may only be publicly venerated locally, or in a particular diocese, or by a religious Order of which the beatified one was a member. Very occasionally, the pope may extend the public veneration of a beatified one to the whole Church. Before the 17th century, it was possible for a bishop to beatify within his own diocese, but no longer.

Saints are invariably depicted with an aureole or *halo round their heads, and the Beati or Blessed with rays. Saints usually have one or more *attributes, and while saints in the Eastern Church tend to have more generalized attributes, such as a mitre, a breastplate, or a staff, in the West attributes tended to be more characteristic of the saint. Paintings of groups of Apostles are known from before 313 in *catacombs, and Apostles also appear on *sarcophagi, and on *gold glass. By the 4th century the Apostles Peter and Paul had a virtually standardized iconography. The Evangelists are sometimes represented writing their Gospels, at others they appear in their symbolic form in the *Tetramorph. OT figures also have specific attributes, as does S. John the Baptist.

In the Eastern Church, canonization followed much the same system as that followed in Rome. The leaders of the *Reformation rejected canonization with varying force, on the grounds that it was unscriptural. *Zwingli and *Calvin rejected it totally, *Luther did not interfere with the dedications of existing churches, but new ones were either not given dedications, or were dedicated to Apostles. Far earlier, heretical sects such as the Bogomils and the Waldensians rejected canonizations. The Church of England rejects canonization in the Thirty-Nine Articles, but the Annunciation, the Purification of the Virgin, S. John the Baptist, and the Apostles are all specially commemorated in the Book of Common Prayer. The modern Calendar of the Church of England, updated from time to time with the approval by the General Synod, includes ancient and pre-Reformation saints and martyrs of the Western and Eastern Churches, as well as the commemoration of holy people of post-Reformation times; these must have been dead for 50 years, with the exception of martyrs, e.g. Janani Luwum (1977). The dedications of churches in England have been altered only where the original dedication (e.g. to the Assumption of the Blessed Virgin Mary) is unacceptable to Anglicans. In some of these cases the original dedication has been revived, e.g. The Assumption, Attleborough in Norfolk (on the Walsingham Way).

While there are a certain number of churches dedicated to prophets and other important OT figures (Venice has ones dedicated to Moses, Job, Samuel, and Jeremiah: S. Moisè, S. Giobbe, S. Samuele, S. Geremìa) only the Maccabees have a feast-day in the West, which was kept in the early Church to commemorate the seven Jewish brothers and their mother who were martyred with total barbarity for their refusal to abandon the precepts of their Jewish faith. Their heroism and their nearness to the Christian era (2nd cent. BC), and the example they showed commended them to the Early Christian Fathers, such as S. Gregory Nazianzus and S. Augustine. *See also*, for individual Saints, AGATHA, AGNES, ALBAN, AMBROSE, ANDREW, ANTONINUS, ANTONY, AUGUSTINE, BARNABAS, BARTHOLOMEW, BENEDICT, BERNARD, BERNARDINO, BONAVENTURA, BOROMMEO, BRIDGET, BRUNO, CATHERINE, CECILIA, CHRISTOPHER, CLARE, CLEMENT, CLIMACUS, SANTI QUATTRO CORONATI, COSMAS and DAMIAN, CUTHBERT, DENIS, DOMINIC, DOROTHY, ELIGIUS, ELIZABETH, EUSTACE, FRANCIS, GEORGE, GILES, GREGORY, HELENA, HUBERT, HUGH, IGNATIUS LOYOLA, ISIDORE, JAMES, JEROME, JOHN, JOSEPH, JUDE, LAURENCE, LEONARD, LONGINUS, LOUIS, LUCY, LUKE, MAGDALENE, MARGARET, MARK, MARTIN, MARY THE BLESSED VIRGIN, MATTHEW, MATTHIAS, MAURICE, MONICA, NICHOLAS, NORBERT, PAUL, PETER, PHILIP, ROCH, ROMUALD, SEBASTIAN, SIMON, STEPHEN, SYLVESTER, THERESA, THOMAS, URSULA, WILGEFORTIS, ZENO, ZENOBIUS.

sakkos (saccos) (Gk. sack) A *vestment worn by archbishops and metropolitans in the E. Orthodox Church, and frequently by bishops as well, instead of a *phelonion. It is a short tunic, perhaps derived from the Byzantine imperial *tunica* with half-sleeves, not unlike the Western *dalmatic, but fastened at the sides and richly embroidered.

Salome Two women called Salome are referred to in the Gospels. The first one is mentioned by Mark in 15: 40, as being among the women who 'from a long way off' watched the Crucifixion, and who in 16: 1 was among the women who came with spices to the sepulchre, found it open, and were told by the angel that Christ had risen, and to go and tell the Apostles, but were so terrified that they fled and told no one. Matthew in 27: 55 also mentions the women watching the Crucifixion 'from a distance', and calls one of them 'the mother of the sons of Zebedee', i.e. James and John. John, in his narrative of the Crucifixion, says in 19: 25 that with the Virgin near the cross was Mary, the wife of Clopas (AV, Vg. Cleophas), and the Magdalene. This would suggest that Clopas and Zebedee are the same person, and that it was his, John's own, mother who stood with the Virgin. Luke 24: 10 names the women as Mary Magdalene, Joanna, Mary the mother of James, and 'the other women'. The Holy Women with the Virgin appear in most representations of the Crucifixion, but with the exception of the Magdalene and Zebedee's wife their identities remain very vague.

The second Salome is named, not by Matthew in 14: 6, but by Josephus, the Jewish historian of the period, as the woman described by Matthew as the daughter of Herodias who danced before Herod, and who, prompted by her mother, asked as a reward for the head of S. John the Baptist. The same story is told in AV, Mark 6: 17–29. Representations of *Salome with the head of John the Baptist* appear in a panel in the 9th-century bronze doors, Verona, San Zeno; in a miniature in Luithar's Evangeliary, 990, Aachen Cath.; by Donatello: bronze relief for the Baptistery Font, Siena, 1425–7; in a fresco by Fra Filippo Lippi, in Prato, Duomo, finished *c.*1465; by Sebastiano del Piombo: 1510, London, NG; Lukas Cranach: 1510, Lisbon; Caravaggio: 1607/8, London, NG; Guido Reni: 1630/5, Rome, Gall. Naz.; in 1635, Sarasota; in 1635/40, Chicago. There are also rather gruesome images of the Baptist's head on a platter; one is a late antique chalcedony dish with the Baptist's head in gold and enamel inserted into it *c.*1430/40, now in Genoa Cathedral; Dieric Bouts painted one now in Oldenburg, and there are replicas by the studio (one in Barnard Castle); there is also one by an anonymous follower of Leonardo da Vinci: *c.*1511, London, NG. Caravaggio's masterpiece of the *Decollation of the Baptist* (1608: Malta, Valletta Cath., Oratory of St John) depicts Salome bending to receive the head of the Baptist.

The attempt by Italian Early Renaissance artists to render Salome dancing led to the adoption of the Classical motif of a Maenad, used in the Donatello relief in Siena, and Fra Filippo's Prato fresco. *See also* DECOLLATION, and JOHN THE BAPTIST.

Salome the Midwife The Protevangelium of James tells the story of the Nativity, adorned with the tale of the two midwives. After the birth of Jesus, one of them went out of the cave in which the birth had taken place, and met the second midwife, to whom she said, 'Salome, Salome, . . . A Virgin hath brought forth, which her nature alloweth not'. Salome would not believe her, so they returned to the cave, Salome examined Mary, and immediately her hand withered. She cried out, beseeching God to pardon her, and an angel appeared and told her to pick up the Child.

S

She did so and immediately she was healed. The *Golden Legend* repeats the story. This scene is often represented in 15th-century Flemish and German painting, and is part of a series of apocryphal events connected with the *Nativity. The most notable examples are the painting by Robert Campin: Dijon, before 1434, and one derived from it by Jacques Daret, datable 1434, Thyssen-Bornemiza Coll.

Salomónica is the Spanish and Portuguese form of Solomónica, a spirally twisted Corinthian column, derived from an antique column preserved in St Peter's, Rome, which is said to have come from Solomon's Temple. This type of column is known to have been used in Old St Peter's, and *Bernini used the form (1624–33) to support the *baldacchino over the papal altar in St Peter's, where they are decorated with vines and gilded. English examples are rare, but there is an undecorated pair supporting the south porch (1637) of St Mary's, Oxford, wrongly attributed to Inigo *Jones. They are much used in Spain and Portugal for Baroque altars and *reredoses. In the Tapestries for the Sistine Chapel designed by *Raphael (1515), for which the cartoons are in London, V & A (on loan from HM the Queen), highly ornate Salomonic columns are represented as part of the Beautiful Gate of the Temple, where the miracle of the lame man took place, as recorded in Acts 3: 2–11; this gate is also referred to as Solomon's Portico, hence the name given to this type of column.

saltire An X-shaped cross, said to have been the shape of the cross on which *S. Andrew was crucified. A white saltire on a blue ground is the national flag of Scotland.

S

Salvator Mundi (Lat. Saviour of the World) is a devotional image of Christ blessing, and in some instances holding an orb in His left hand.

There are examples by Antonello da Messina (1465: London, NG); Mantegna (1493: Correggio, Congregazione della Carità). The subject was also popular in the North both as *Christ blessing* and variants of the theme such as *Christ crowned with thorns*, and either blessing or not. Roger van der Weyden (1451: the Braque Altar, Paris, Louvre) has Christ blessing, between the Virgin and S. John; Dieric Bouts painted a number of heads of Christ, blessing or not, some (e.g. Rotterdam, Boymans) as the *Vera Effigies* (True Image), many of *Christ crowned with thorns* (Kansas; New York, Met. Mus.; Historical Soc.; London, NG). There are also some by Memlinc and Gerard David. Benedetto Diana (d. 1525) also painted a *Christ blessing* (London, NG).

Samaria, the Woman of The story of the meeting between Christ and the Woman of Samaria is told only in John 4: 4–41. On his way from Judaea to Galilee, Jesus passed through Samaria, and sat by Jacob's Well to rest. A woman came to draw water and Jesus asked her for a drink. She was astonished that a Jew should ask anything of a Samaritan, because of the ancient feud between the nations, but He told her of the living water which it was in His power to give, and when she asked for it He told her to fetch her husband. She said she had none, and He told her that the man she was living with was not her husband, and that there had been five others. He then told her that 'God is spirit and those that worship him must worship in spirit and in truth'; she replied that when the Messiah came, he would proclaim all things to them. He said to her 'I am he, the one who is speaking to you.' When the disciples returned, they marvelled that He should be talking to a woman, but she left her water-pot and ran to the town to fetch people, saying that she believed the Messiah was by the well. The Samaritans came and listened to him, and then asked Him to stay with them; He did so for two days, 'And many more believed because of his words'.

The subject appears as early as the Catacomb of S. Callixtus, 3rd century; in the throne of *Maximian, 545/53; in the *Rabbula Gospels, 586; in a mosaic in Sant'Apollinare Nuovo, 6th century; in many MSS from the 9th to 13th century; in a Duccio *predella* panel from the *Maestà*, Washington, National Gallery. The subject was not popular during the Early Renaissance, but reappears in the 16th/17th century with Lukas Cranach: 1525/37, Leipzig; Veronese: 1560, St Louis, Missouri; Annibale Carracci: 1595, Milan, Brera; G. B. Crespi: 1605, Toledo Cathedral; Baciccio: 1676/7, Rome, Spada Gallery; and a modern version by Mario Sironi (1947–8) in the Vatican Collection of Modern Religious Art, Rome.

Samaritan, the Good This is one of Christ's most memorable parables, recorded in Luke 10: 25–37. A lawyer asked 'Who is my neighbour?', and Christ replied with the story of the man who 'fell among thieves', was robbed, beaten, and left by the roadside. Two men came past, a Levite and a priest, who passed by on the other side. A Samaritan found the injured man, took pity on him, tended his wounds, set him upon his ass, took him to an inn and paid the innkeeper to care for him, promising that if it cost more than what had been given, he would repay it when he returned. 'Which of these three, do you think, was a neighbour to the man who fell among the robbers?' Christ asked. He said, 'The one who showed him mercy.' And Jesus said, 'Go and do likewise.' The sharp point of the story is that Jews and Samaritans had a long history of enmity, and the men who passed by on the other side were Jews of the most godly sort.

Among the earliest representations are ones in the 6th-century *Rossano Codex, and in an 11th-century fresco cycle in Sant'Angelo in Formis (near Capua), both Byzantine rather than Western. In these and other such early representations of the subject, Christ personifies the victim and an angel personifies the Samaritan, a motif linking the Samaritan's action with the Seven Works of *Mercy which disappears in later Western treatments of the subject. These include a miniature in the 10th-century Evangeliary of Otto III (Munich Lib.) and one in the 11th-century Evangeliary of Henry III (Escorial). The theme was revived in the 16th century with Jacopo Bassano (London, NG, and Hampton Court); Rembrandt? (London, Wallace Coll.) and etching, 1633 (Cambridge, Fitz.); Delacroix, 1849 (Paris, private coll.); Daumier, 1856–8 (Glasgow, Burrell); Van Gogh, 1890, copy after Delacroix (Otterloo). *See also* PARABLE.

Sampietrini (Ital. Men of St Peter's) are a body of craftsmen engaged on the maintenance and repair of the basilica of St Peter's in Rome. Formerly, they actually lived with their families on the roof of the building. They were instituted by Pope Clement VIII in 1600 as a result of a suggestion made to the Board of Works by one of the masons, that instead of casual labourers being employed on repairs, a special body of men should be set up; he trained the first thirty men to be employed on the huge fabric, who now number hundreds of specialists in all the necessary crafts. The jobs are virtually hereditary, in that sons are trained in whatever craft they may show a bent for—masons, stuccoists, gilders, glaziers, plumbers, carpenters, or mosaicists—and from an early age they learn the complicated geography of the building. One of their duties is to fix the damask hangings used to decorate the pilasters of the interior for great ceremonial occasions. Another is, quite literally, to weed St Peter's, because—like most of Rome—the church is built of travertine, a stone with many minute fissures in which seeds, blown by the wind or dropped by birds, lodge, germinate in the rain, root and grow, and if left frost cracks the stone.

Samson (Heb. 'like the sun') was an OT Hebrew warrior and hero, whose history is in Judg. 13–16. At that time the Israelites were subject to the Philistines. His father was *Manoah (Vg. Manue) and an angel appeared to his wife and told her that though she was barren, she would bear a son, that he was to be a *Nazirite from his birth, and would deliver Israel from the Philistines. The angel also appeared to Manoah and told him to obey the commands he had given to his wife. His wife bore a son and named him Samson. When Samson grew up, he went to a Philistine town where he saw a woman who pleased him; he told his parents to get her for him as a wife. Their protests were useless. When on his way to the town to visit her he was attacked by a lion, which he killed with his bare hands, and when he was returning to marry her, he found that bees had built a hive in the carcass. He did not tell his parents either about the lion or the bees, and at the marriage feast he made a wager with thirty guests of the bride that they could not solve his riddle: 'Out of the eater came something to eat. Out of the strong came something sweet.' The wager was for thirty festal garments, but the men persuaded Samson's wife to find out the answer. She did so, and in anger at having been cheated, Samson said to the thirty guests, 'Had you not ploughed with my heifer, you would not have found out my riddle!' and he went to Ashkelon in Philistia, killed thirty men, took their spoils and gave them to the wedding guests. When he went to claim his bride, he found that her father had given her to another. In revenge, Samson caught 300 foxes, tied them together by their tails, stuck a burning torch between the tails and loosed them into the Philistine harvest which was burnt, with their vines and olive groves also. In revenge, the Philistines burnt the bride and her father, whereupon Samson 'smote them hip and thigh, with great slaughter'. They then invaded Judah, and the Israelites in panic promised to deliver up Samson, but when the Philistines came with rejoicing to take him, he burst his bonds and with the jawbone of an ass, he killed a thousand of them. He was then thirsty, and called to the Lord for help, and God split open a rock and water gushed out.

Once he went to Gaza to a prostitute, and the men of Gaza lay in wait for him, believing that he would stay until dawn, but he left by midnight, and finding the gates shut, he took hold of them and the gateposts and carried them away. Then he fell in love with a woman called Delilah, and the Philistines promised her money if she would beguile him into telling the secret of his strength. Three times she persuaded him, each time he told her a false story, and when the Philistines burst in he snapped the bonds. The fourth time, he told her the truth, and when he was asleep she had his hair cut off, the Philistines burst in and, his strength gone, they blinded him and took him to the prison to grind corn. But his hair grew again, and when they were holding a great feast in honour of their god Dagon, they had him brought from the mill and put between the two pillars in the centre of the house to amuse them. He asked the boy who led him to let him rest against the pillars, and when he felt them he prayed 'Lord God, remember me and strengthen me only this once ... and let me die with the Philistines.' God gave him strength and he strained with all his might, and the house fell on the lords and the people, 'so those he killed at his death were more than he had killed during his life'.

Several incidents in the story of Samson are prototypes of Christ. His birth, like that of Isaac, was predicted by an angel, and was miraculous in that it was to a barren woman. The lion is an ancient symbol of sin: Samson killed the lion and from its carcass came the sweetness of honey; Christ trampled on sin, and from His victory came the sweetness of salvation. God split the rock so that Samson might drink and be saved as Moses struck the rock and saved his people; Christ saves by the water of baptism.

The oldest representation of *Samson killing the lion* is in the Catacomb of the Via Latina, 4th century; there are also: *Samson and Delilah*, relief on the Perugia fountain (Nicola and Giovanni Pisano: 1278); *Samson holding a column* (Ghiberti: 'Gates of Paradise', 1425–52, Florence, Baptistery); *Samson buckling the column in the house of Dagon*, statue (1480: Karlsruhe); *Samson with the jawbone of the ass* (Guido Reni: 1611, Bologna); Rubens: *Samson captured by the Philistines* (1609: London, NG); Rembrandt painted several incidents from the story of Samson: *The angel ascending in the smoke of Manoah's sacrifice* (1641: Dresden); ... *posing the riddle at the wedding-feast* (1638: Dresden); ... *threatening his father-in-law* (1635: Berlin); and a horrific *Blinding of Samson* (1636: Frankfurt).

Samuel (Heb. name of God, or heard of God) was the last of the OT Judges to rule Israel. His father came from Ephraim, his mother was childless, and when they came to Shiloh to the Temple, she prayed that God would give her a son. The High Priest, Eli, said, 'Go in peace; the Lord God grant your petition ...'. Hannah bore a son, and named him Samuel. A few years later, she brought him to the Temple and said to Eli, 'My Lord, ... for this child I prayed, and the Lord granted my petition ... Therefore ... he is given to the Lord.' Hannah sang a song of gratitude to God and rejoicing which may be compared to the Virgin's *Magnificat*, since several phrases have the same import.

Now Eli had two sons, both priests who, because Eli was old, ruled in his name, but they were greedy scoundrels. One night when Samuel was sleeping in the Temple before the Ark, he heard a voice calling, 'Samuel, Samuel'. He got up and went to Eli and said 'Here I am, for you called me'; Eli said 'I did not call. Lie down again.' This happened three times, and Eli realized that it was God who was calling, so he told Samuel to answer, 'Speak Lord, for your servant is listening'. God answered, predicting disaster for Israel and in particular for Eli's house. Next morning, Samuel was afraid to tell Eli what God had said, but Eli begged him not to hide the word of God from him, so Samuel told him the truth. Years passed and Samuel became known as a trustworthy prophet. The Philistines attacked the Israelites, and after a first defeat the Israelites brought the Ark of the Covenant into their camp, hoping that it would help to defend them, but they lost the next battle also, and the Ark was captured and Eli's sons were killed. When the news reached Shiloh, Eli fell from his chair and broke his neck. The Philistines put the Ark into the Temple of Dagon, but so many disasters afflicted them that they returned it to Israel. Eleazar became its priest, but Israel was ruled oppressively by the Philistines for the next twenty years, until Samuel told the Jews that unless they repented and threw out the idols they now worshipped God would not deliver them. They did so, and then they defeated the Philistines, and there was peace while Samuel ruled them, not as a king but as a judge. But when Samuel was old, the elders complained that his sons were oppressing them, and they demanded to be ruled by a king, like other nations. Samuel argued that God was their king, and an earthly monarch would oppress them more, but they still demanded one. God told Samuel to listen to the voice of the people, but to warn them that evil would come of it. Samuel consecrated *Saul and at first all went well, but then Saul defied God's orders about the Amalekites, God rejected him, and told Samuel to anoint *David in his place.

David was only a boy, but after he killed the giant Goliath, Saul took him into his service, but some years later Saul began to hate David because he saw him as a threat to his kingship. David fled, and long years of strife followed. Samuel died, and soon after Saul was at war again with the Philistines. Before the battle of Gilboa Saul went to the Witch of Endor, who summoned Samuel from the Shades, and Samuel told him that he would lose the battle and that he and his sons would be killed. This happened and David became king.

There are few illustrations of Samuel's life except in bibles and portal figures: the Winchester Bible (12th cent., Winchester Cath.); the Bury Bible (1140: Cambridge, Corpus Christi Coll.). There is dramatic painting of the defeat of the Israelites and the death of Eli's sons at Gilboa in Jean Fouquet's *Antiquités Judaïques* (*c.*1470, Paris, BN).

Examples in portal sculpture are at Senlis: 1170, probably the earliest, with Samuel holding his identifying attribute of a sacrificial lamb; others are at Chartres: N. transept portal, centre door, left jamb, Samuel with the sacrificial lamb, 1205–10; Reims, right portal, left jamb, Samuel holding the sacrificial lamb 1245–55; Amiens: S. transept portal, archivolt, right side, Samuel anointing David, 1259–69. A painting by Gerbrand van den Eeckhout (1621–74): *Samuel as a child in the Temple*, is in Oxford, Ashmolean.

sanctuary may refer to either that part of the choir of a large church which contains the high altar, or in a small church, the part inside the altar-rails. The term may also be used of a shrine. In Byzantine churches the sanctuary is the part of the *bema*, enclosed within the *iconostasis. Sanctuary is also a term referring to a claim to safety (usually meaning freedom from arrest) claimed by men or women who take refuge in a church. While the police rarely take such people forcibly, much effort is used to persuade them to give themselves up. Once it was a sure means of escape from an enemy—for instance, the great knocker on the door of Durham Cathedral was a 'sanctuary', since few cared to incur the wrath of the Church by violating it. The Church no longer affords sanctuary of this nature; nowadays one takes one's chance on the Law. *See also* SANTUARIO.

Sangallo A family of Florentine architects. The main members were:

Giuliano (*c.*1443–1516). His chief contribution to church architecture—other than his undistinguished project for the rebuilding of *St Peter's (*c.*1514)—is Sta Maria delle Carceri at Prato (begun 1485), a Greek cross design (*see* CROSS) with a dome of the type Brunelleschi built on the Old Sacristy, San Lorenzo, and the Pazzi Chapel at Sta Croce, both in Florence. His Prato church has an elegant coloured marble revetment on the outside, unfortunately not completed. The interior provided the first solution to the problem of using the Orders correctly when pilasters meet at the corners. His only other church is Sta Maria dell'Anima, the German and Netherlandish church in Rome. Giuliano was a close friend of *Michelangelo.

Antonio the Elder (1455–1534) was Giuliano's brother. He built the pilgrimage church of San Biagio, Montepulciano (*c.*1518–45), one of the major centrally planned domed churches of the Renaissance, and the most important derivation from *Bramante's projects for St Peter's. It is a Greek cross design, with the interior and the lower storeys of the exterior built according to Vitruvian principle, adapted by Bramante in the Tempietto, of using the severe Doric Order for a church dedicated to a male martyr saint. In Rome he is credited with the façade (1500–23) of the older church of Sta Maria dell'Anima, the church of the Germans and at one time also of Netherlanders and Dutch, which is usually attributed to a Northern designer, because it is virtually a *hall-church.

Antonio the Younger (1485–1546) was their nephew. He was an assistant of Bramante, and, after his death, of Peruzzi and Raphael on the St Peter's projects, and later made his own designs to supersede Bramante's. He built part of the choir, and designed the huge wooden model (in St Peter's Mus.) embodying his ungainly compromise project for converting Bramante's central plan to a long-nave design. It was rightly castigated by Michelangelo, who succeeded him in 1546/7, and who demolished all his work on the site. He also built most of the Farnese Palace.

Sankt Gallen (Saint-Gall), near Lake Constance, owes its origin to the Irish missionary S. Gall (*c*.550–645), who accompanied S. Columbanus on his mission to Gaul from their monastery in Co. Down, Ireland; he remained to live as a hermit in what is now Switzerland when S. Columbanus continued his journey into Italy. The present Benedictine monastery was founded at least a century later, but claims a connection with the hermit-saint. From the end of the 9th century it was famous for its scriptorium, and its library and collection of MSS is still one of the finest monastic libraries in existence.

The Sankt Gallen plan for a monastery is famous as the earliest of its kind to survive. It was made *c*.820, probably as a result of a council held in 816 which was attended by S. Benedict and Einhard (or Eginhard), a historian who was a member of Charlemagne's court, and possibly also by Beseleel, the director of the imperial workshops and the emperor's building projects. It must be assumed that S. Benedict would have expressed views on a design for an ideal monastic foundation, with all the necessary dependencies from a novitiate to cattle pens, and from the abbot's house to the poultry yard. The plan was sent to Abbot Heito of Reichenau and to Abbot Gozbert of Sankt Gallen, neither of whom attended the council—Abbot Gozbert was only elected in 816—as a pattern, or exemplar, of how the parts of a monastery should be arranged. It is not an architect's working drawing—no allowance is made for the thickness of walls—but an ideal system to guide a competent master mason and which he could adjust according to the size of the monastery required, and to the terrain on which it was to be laid out. It is very informative about the design of a great abbey and also of an up-to-date monastic church: a long nave, aisles with side chapels, wide transepts, a deep, raised apsidal choir, and a *westwork with a second apse. Both apses have semicircular areas around them, called 'paradius', the west one being larger than the east one, and having a colonnaded walkway round it, like an atrium, flanked by detached staircase towers, isolated from the rest of the building. The interior of the church was to contain a font, which implies that the abbey was expected to serve a local community, and there was a guest-house and a hostel for travellers. The choir and the transepts were separate from the public areas of the church, as was essential for monastic life. The ideal plan was not followed when the monastery church was built, and the extent to which this ideal layout was followed for the rest is not known, since it has been totally rebuilt. Some idea of the size of buildings in the ideal plan can be estimated: the site was some 500 by 700 ft., the church from east to west was to be *c*.325 ft. long and some 90 ft. wide, with transepts of 120 ft., and a cloister over 100 ft. square. These dimensions are not unusual, if one considers the size of Maria Laach. The ideal plan follows a traditional monastic layout with guests to the north, menial or service areas to the south, service courts to the west, with the east part of the site reserved to the monks and novices. The towers, attached here to the large atrium-like area of the 'paradius' rather than to the church itself, often had chapels at the top, and many had a light. One would have expected the enclave to be surrounded by a wall, but when the Hungarian raiders attacked it in the early 10th century, it was an open site and suffered accordingly.

The abbey was rebuilt between 1748 and 1767 by Peter Thumb and Giovanni Gaspare Bagnato of Como, master mason of the Teuronic Order at Lake Constance. The church was rebuilt on the now usual German Baroque plan with nave and chancel of equal length on either side of an impressive rotunda, and with six side chapels on a half-oval plan. The complex was finished, including the decoration, in 1760, except for the semicircular apse at the east end, built by J. M. Beer between 1761 and 1768. From its original plan the church retains the apse at both ends, the west one contributing to the fine two-towered west front. The library was rebuilt by Thumb between 1758 and 1767.

Santa Sophia, Constantinople *See* SOPHIA.

Santiago *See* COMPOSTELA and JAMES, S.

Santo, il (Ital. the Saint) The popular name for the great basilica dedicated to *S. Antony of Padua in that city. The church itself was begun soon after the saint's death in 1231, and construction lasted until well into the 14th century. It has six hemispherical domes, the central one with a curious conical '*tiburio*', two detached campaniles, and other small towers which give the building a very exotic silhouette. The choir has eight radiating chapels with, in the centre, a large Treasury. The High Altar is by *Donatello, but has been dismembered and reconstructed. It contains some of his most important and influential works. There are also three paintings of 1511 by *Titian in the nearby *scuola.

santon (Fr. dialect, 'little saint') A clay figure in a Christmas *crib.

santuario (Ital. sanctuary, holy place) is usually used for a church containing relics or a particularly venerated object. It is also used for places of pilgrimage, such as *Loreto, or the *Sacro Monte at Varallo, or the basilica of S. Francis at Assisi. Italy is dotted with pilgrimage churches dedicated to the Madonna, such as those at Cortona, Lodi, or Monte Berico near Vicenza, all of which qualify for the title.

Sarah *See* ABRAHAM.

Sarah The wife of *Tobit.

sarcophagus (Gk. *sarkophagos*, flesh-eating) Stone or terracotta coffins for the bodies of important people were common in Greece, Etruria, and Rome, long before Christianity, e.g. the Alexander Sarcophagus, of the 4th century BC. Greek sarcophagi are usually carved in high relief on all four sides, Etruscan ones often have a reclining figure of the deceased on the lid (cf. *gisant), and Roman ones are usually carved on three sides only, the fourth side being placed against a wall. On the whole, pagan Romans cremated their dead, but some were buried in *catacombs, and it is thus difficult to distinguish Christian sarcophagi from pagan, especially as the Christians, during periods of persecution, did not want to be conspicuous. The simplest form of such sarcophagi is the strigilated, with a plain S-pattern on most of the front and a central space with an inscription, an *imago clipeata with a bust of the deceased, or an allegorical scene which could be interpreted in several ways ('neutral' iconography). Another form consists of a series of reliefs across the whole width of the long side of the sarcophagus, sometimes in two layers to get more symbolic scenes into the space. From the 4th century, after the Edict of *Milan (313), when the persecutions ceased, until they revived in the short reign of Julian the Apostate (361–3), more elaborate forms were introduced, with the columnar type, framing separate scenes between classical columns, and the City-gate type, with an elaborate architectural background. From the 4th century also Passion scenes are represented, though still symbolically, the earliest known being Vatican 171, with the *Chi-Rho surrounded by a wreath of Victory and sleeping soldiers symbolizing the Resurrection.

The earliest Christian sarcophagi were made by workshops which also made for various pagan religions, so that the style is constant and only slight variations in iconography distinguish them. In addition, many sarcophagi were made in Asia Minor and exported in an unfinished state so that, for example, a bust would be roughly blocked out and finished from a death-mask when the time came. Thus we find philosophers holding scrolls or a *Hermes Kriophoros which can be turned into Christ giving the Law (*Traditio Legis) and the *Good Shepherd respectively; or Bacchic scenes with Cupids gathering grapes might be taken to be the True Vine. Pagan and Christian burial sites were often adjacent in cemeteries and catacombs, so that even when the original site of a sarcophagus is known it is not proof of its owner's allegiance. After 313 it was no longer necessary to adopt such ambiguities and we find such specifically Christian symbols as the Chi-Rho, itself originally an arcane symbol of Christ.

Many examples from this period have survived, principally in Rome (Vatican, St Peter's, Museo Cristiano and elsewhere), and in Milan, Ravenna, and a distinct subgroup in S. France (Arles). Among the most popular subjects were *Jonah, *Moses striking the Rock, S. Peter striking the Rock (a non-biblical parallel to Moses, probably based on the Water of Salvation dispensed by the Church), and other Old and New Testament scenes which could be read as *types and antitypes. Among the most splendid examples are the sarcophagus of *Junius Bassus, the Prefect of Rome, who was converted in 359 and died in that year (Mus. of St Peter's), another in the Lateran Museum (No. 174), or the so-called Sarcophagus of Stilicho, in Milan (Sant'Ambrogio: late 4th cent.). The Junius sarcophagus has ten scenes on the front: *Sacrifice of Abraham, Arrest of S. Peter, Christ giving the Law, Christ arrested, Christ before Pilate* and, below, *Job, Adam and Eve, The Entry into Jerusalem, Daniel in the Lions' Den*, and *S. Paul going to Martyrdom*. The scenes may, at first sight, seem haphazard, but they in fact follow a very carefully worked out sequence, of type and antitype, and OT/NT parallels.

Sargent, John Singer *See* NORTH AMERICA.

Satan *See* DEVIL.

Saul (Heb. loaned) was the first OT king of Israel, anointed by *Samuel against his will because the people, who had hitherto considered God as their king, asked to be ruled by a king 'like other nations' (1 Sam. 8: 4–9). There are two accounts of how Saul was chosen. One is that God indicated to Samuel that Saul was His chosen man, and Samuel anointed him, but Saul kept this secret from his family until a violent attack by the Ammonites from across the Jordan on the city of Jabesh-gilead drove him to assume publicly the leadership for which he had been chosen. He gathered a force together and routed the Ammonites, establishing himself as a military leader. Samuel then proclaimed him as king. The other account is that when Samuel was forced to agree to a king, lots were drawn to choose from which tribe he should come. The tribe of Benjamin was chosen, Saul hid, but was found and Samuel presented him to the people most of whom cried, 'Long live the king!' (1 Sam. 10: 20–5). Then came the victory over the Ammonites, after which Saul's kingship was uncontested.

After another two years, Saul led an army against the Philistines, a difficult undertaking since the Philistines never allowed the Israelites to possess arms nor to have a smith, so that they were armed only with pitchforks, scythes, and sickles. They attacked the town of Geba and killed its garrison. The Philistines attacked them with horsemen, chariots, and infantry, but Jonathan, Saul's eldest son, who had been the real victor at Geba, by another daring move, spread panic among the Philistines who fled, and the Israelites, who were so terrified that they had hidden themselves in caves and crevasses, came out and killed the fleeing enemy. This victory at Michmash reduced the pressure from the Philistines, so that Saul could turn his attention to other foes who harassed him: Amorites and Zobahites from the north, Ammonites from Transjordan to the east, and Amalekites from the south.

Samuel had never been reconciled to God's choice of Saul, and when he did something wrong, attacked him fiercely. Offering the sacrifice before the battle of Michmash, instead of waiting for Samuel, was one offence, the second more serious one was that God ordered Samuel to tell him to attack the Amalekites and to spare nothing—the whole population, and all their cattle and sheep. Saul disobeyed, and after his victory he brought back the king, Agag, and the herds claiming that they were to be a sacrifice. Samuel retorted that obedience came before sacrifice, killed Agag himself, and never saw Saul again. He had already anointed *David. Then came the episode of Goliath.

Saul's increasing fits of depression were relieved by David's playing the harp, but Saul turned against him, fearing that the people's praise of David because of Goliath was a threat to himself. His enmity eventually drove David into exile, and then into alliance with the Philistines, who attacked Saul, but would not allow David to join them lest he change sides during the battle. Samuel was now dead and in desperate hope of guidance, Saul went with two aides to Endor, where he sought out a woman famous as a medium, but she protested that witchcraft was punishable with death. He insisted that she summon up Samuel, but when she did so Samuel told him that he would lose the battle, and that he and his sons would be killed. The battle of Gilboa went against Saul; his sons were killed, and he was badly wounded, and when his armour-bearer refused to kill him to prevent his falling alive into the hands of the Philistines, he fell on his sword, and his armour-bearer did likewise. The Philistines found their bodies on the battlefield, cut off Saul's head and hung his body with those of his sons on the walls of their city of Bethshean, but they were recovered by a force from Jabesh-gilead, the city which Saul had saved at the beginning of his reign. When David heard what had happened, he gave vent to his grief in a poignant lament (2 Sam. 1: 19–27) for Saul and for Jonathan, who had been his friend from the beginning, had tried to reconcile his father and David, and had several times saved David's life.

Saul's reign had lasted about twenty years, and during it he had turned Israel from a cowed and captive race into a warlike people ready and able to defend themselves. His troubles stemmed from his wilful defiance of Samuel's authority as the word of God, and from his sense that God had then abandoned him, which caused his violent and unpredictable behaviour.

Jean Fouquet, in *Les Antiquités Judaïques* (1470, Paris, BN), illustrates David lamenting the deaths of Saul and Jonathan in the battle of

Gilboa; there is a painting attributed to Rembrandt, *David playing the harp before Saul* (?1650/60, The Hague, Mauritshuis); and Julius Schnorr von Carolsfeld depicts *Samuel anointing Saul* in *Schnorr's Bible Illustrations* (1860).

Saul was the first name by which *S. Paul the Apostle was known. He is first mentioned in Acts 7: 58, as present at the stoning of *S. Stephen. Acts 9: 1–31 recounts the story of his conversion. Acts 13: 9 is the last time he is mentioned as 'Saul also known as Paul'.

Savonarola, Girolamo (1452–98), was famous as a preacher of reform in morals and conduct, and for calling for a Council which would impose the reform of the papacy. He was born in Ferrara, entered the Dominican Order in Bologna in 1475, and was sent to preach in Ferrara and then to Florence in a general dispersal of the monks of his convent because of war. He first preached Lenten sermons in San Gimignano in 1484/5, speaking about the corruption of the Church and the punishment to come. In 1486 he was preaching in Lombardy on the same themes, and in Brescia predicted the terrible results of failure to repent—words which were remembered in 1512 when the city was sacked and about 6,000 were killed by the French. He was in Padua in 1489, when he was sent to Florence at the request of, to his astonishment, Lorenzo de' Medici, at the suggestion of Pico della Mirandola. He preached for the first time in Florence in his convent church of San Marco in 1490, to such crowds that in the following Lent he preached in the cathedral. His sermons were a fiery diatribe about the corruption and greed of the clergy, on the unchecked immorality and dishonesty of the rulers and richer citizens, on the venality of judges, and the widespread degeneracy of the people. He could find many texts in the OT to provide a theme for his hell-fire oratory; he also predicted that Lorenzo de' Medici, Pope Innocent VIII, and the King of Naples were about to die.

In 1491 he was elected Prior, but refused to make the customary courtesy call on Lorenzo, who was furious at being so slighted. He then tried to placate Savonarola with rich gifts, which the Prior gave away. By early 1492 Lorenzo was dying at his villa at Careggi, about five miles north of Florence. On his death-bed in April he sent for Savonarola to hear his last confession, but the friar demanded that Lorenzo, as a prerequisite, should free the people. Lorenzo turned his back, Savonarola left, and Lorenzo died a few days later. Although Florence was not a hereditary possession, he was succeeded by his son Piero, a foolish, arrogant, and hasty young man. He was less tolerant than his father of the friar's sermons and had him silenced, so far as Florence was concerned, by getting the General of his Order to send him back to Bologna. In July of the same year Pope Innocent VIII died, to be followed by the election of Rodrigo Borgia, as Alexander VI. Savonarola returned to his convent after his Lenten sermons in 1493, was re-elected Prior, and made a Provincial of the Order, which gave him control of all the Dominican houses in Tuscany. He reformed the convent of San Marco by enforcing the original rule of poverty.

Meanwhile, Lodovico Sforza, Regent of Milan, hard pressed by the accusations of the mother of his nephew, the legitimate heir, that he had usurped her son's state, and threatened by many enemies, had suggested to the French king, Charles VIII, a feeble, vainglorious young man, that he should reclaim the Angevin kingdom of Naples. The French army crossed the Alps and invaded Italy in 1494. Savonarola hailed the French king as the long-promised scourge which should cleanse Italy of the Borgia pope, and Florence of the Medici. Piero de' Medici, cowed by the size of the French army, agreed to surrender important fortresses; Florence rose in revolt, drove him from the city, opened its gates to the French, but had grave misgivings when they saw an invader march through their city, accompanied by a large quantity of very purposeful-looking artillery. Charles made it clear that he considered the city as captured, and a large subsidy was paid to persuade him to continue his march. Savonarola's third prediction had already come true when Ferdinand of Naples died in January 1494.

Savonarola established political control over the city ruled nominally as a republic by a council, but which he controlled as a theocratic dictatorship through the power of his impassioned oratory and the violent partisanship of his followers, which provoked such demonstrations of fanaticism as the 'Bonfire of the Vanities' in which men and women threw on the flames books of secular poetry, pictures and sculptures of profane subjects, ornaments and brightly coloured clothes. But his rule also provoked much opposition, and the city was divided between the partisans of the Frate, called 'fratisti' or more derisively 'piagnone' (moaners, snivellers), and a couple of opposition parties, one called 'arrabiati' (furious, die-hards), who opposed every effort at creating a new constitution, and 'bigi' (grey ones), conciliators who tried to tread a middle way. A feature of his sermons which aroused concern was his claim that his prophecies and visions were of Divine origin; the pope ordered him to appear before him in 1495 to explain these claims. Savonarola refused on grounds of personal danger and ill-health. He was then forbidden to preach; he continued to attack the Curia and Alexander personally, and in 1497 he was excommunicated. This also he ignored. Alexander now threatened an interdict, but his opponents were too wily to use force to hand him over. He had first to be discredited. At this point one of the Frate's disciples, Fra Domenico da Pescia, proposed an ordeal by fire, which he would undergo to prove the Divine origin of Savonarola's visions. He had always been opposed by the Franciscans, one of whom was persuaded to accept the challenge. The supine city authorities set the stage for the ordeal by preparing the pyre through which the contestants were to walk on 7 April, but one objection after another was made, dusk fell, and the authorities postponed it, and believing that Savonarola had refused, the crowd turned against him. The convent of San Marco was stormed by a mob, Savonarola was dragged out with his two companions and thrown into prison. Under torture he admitted that his visions were the result of his pride and ambition, but immediately on being returned to his cell he retracted his confession. Because he was a cleric, his judges had to obtain papal permission to execute him. The pope sent two commissioners to review the trial, which involved fresh examination under torture. He was condemned to death as a heretic and schismatic. On 23 May 1498, with his two followers, he was hanged on the piazza in front of the Signoria, and their bodies were then burnt, the ashes of the pyre thrown into the Arno so that no relics could survive.

Fra *Bartolommeo painted two portraits of Savonarola, one of which is in his cell at San Marco, kept as it was in his lifetime. Many medals were struck, bearing his head in profile, adapted from the Fra Bartolommeo portrait. There is also a grim record of the terrible end of the saga in an anonymous picture of the great piazza in Florence with the three bodies hanging from the gallows and the pyre flaming up beneath them (London, NG). On the reverse is a profile portrait of the Friar, made probably from the medal.

Savonarola had a considerable effect on the art of his day. *Botticelli is not said to have been a 'piagnone' himself, but his brother Simone was and so were other members of his family and household, and other well-known Florentine artists such as the della Robbia family, Lorenzo di Credi, and the architect Cronaca. Certainly after 1495 Botticelli's art changes character, developing a darker more dramatic quality, expressed in the *Mystic Crucifixion* in the Fogg Museum and in the two emotional *Lamentations over the dead Christ*, but is this not reasonable in such troubled times? The theory has also been advanced that *Signorelli, in the *Last Judgement* which he painted in 1499 in the cathedral of Orvieto (a papal city), 'portrayed' Savonarola as the Antichrist preaching, inspired by the Devil, not as a portrait, but as a symbol. The only portraits in the frescoes are those of himself and Fra Angelico, who began the work in 1447.

Scala Santa *See* LATERAN.

scamnum (Lat. bench) *See* SYNTHRONON.

scapulars (from Lat. *scapulae*, shoulder-blades) are part of S. Benedict's Rule for the monastic habit. They are pieces of cloth, about 12 to 18 inches wide, according to the habit of the Order, which hang down, back and front, to the hem of the habit. S. Benedict originally said that they were to be worn by monks working in the fields, but later they were universally adopted because of their symbolism, with small variations in their form and colour according to the Order. They symbolize the 'yoke of Christ' (Matt. 11: 28–30) in the verses ending with His words, 'Come to me, all you that are weary and are carrying heavy burdens, and I will give you rest... For my yoke is easy, and my burden is light.'

The 'smaller scapulars' are worn by Catholics in the world who have joined a religious Order as a Tertiary, and also in modern times by members of sodalities such as the Children of Mary, reserved to women and girls, and the Guild of the Blessed Sacrament, reserved to men and boys.

Scapulars originated with the Carmelites, and are claimed to have resulted from a vision of the Virgin by the General of the Order, *S. Simon Stock, at either Cambridge or Aylesford in Kent in 1251. It was said that this vision was recorded by his secretary, Peter Swannington or Swaynton, held in records at Bordeaux. But S. Simon died in 1265, and the first mention of the vision was in 1398, and the identity of Swaynton has long been controversial. The reports of the vision, and the great spiritual benefits held to result from the wearing of the brown smaller scapulars led to a considerable increase in devotion and adherence to the cult. Despite the controversy, many popes have granted privileges to the Orders wearing scapulars, and great preachers such as Bossuet (1627–1704) have proclaimed their virtues as symbols of devotion. Other Orders (about 17 in all) have also adopted scapulars; the Trinitarian priests wear a white linen one with a red and blue cross; the Servites have a black woollen stuff one for the 'seven dolours of the Virgin'; a light blue cloth one was given by the 16th-century Theatines in honour of the Immaculate Conception; and the Vincentine Fathers of the Society of S. Vincent de Paul, founded in 1833, give their members a red scapular. The wearing of scapulars, of any Order, is not a decoration, but involves continuous devotion to prayer and observance of the obligations assumed at the taking of the relevant vows.

Scapular medals are granted by some Orders, and may be worn instead of the cloth scapulars; they have an image on one side of the Sacred Heart and of the Virgin on the other.

schola cantorum (Lat. school of singers) This title describes two different things: the body of trained singers, and also that part of the church where the singers were placed. Such, for instance, is the Schola Cantorum in San Clemente, in Rome, which is an enclosed area of the basilica reserved to the choir and situated in the nave near the high altar, and between it and the congregation. The introduction of choirs into churches inevitably meant that a special place in a church had to be planned for them. In the Sistine Chapel, the Schola Cantorum is in a gallery with a slightly projecting balustrade on the right side of the chapel above the level of the screen which once divided the presbytery from the lay area (the screen has since been moved so that the gallery for the choir is now within the presbytery area). In England, most cathedral choirs are placed in the area separated from the congregation by the screen or the altar-rails; on the Continent screens are rare and the choir is placed either in the presbytery or in an enclosure in the nave which, in fact, is a *schola cantorum*. Examples are in St Peter's, Rome, and Florence Cathedral. In smaller churches there is often a choir loft at one end of the church, or a balcony above the nave. Many choirs occupy the choir stalls, as, for instance, in King's College Chapel, Cambridge.

Scott, George Gilbert (1811–78), was an English architect famous as much for his restorations as for his own buildings. He built his first church in 1838, and in 1841 won the competition for St Giles, Camberwell, London, which, like all but one of Scott's works, was in a Gothic Revival style. In 1847 he obtained his first commission as a restoration architect for Ely Cathedral, succeeding his friend Edward Blore, who recommended him for similar work at Peterborough Cathedral and Westminster Abbey. In 1840 he won the competition for the Martyrs' Memorial in Oxford, using the form of the Eleanor Crosses as the basis for his design. In 1842 he joined the High-Church *Cambridge Camden Society despite his evangelical background, but this association was disrupted when he began a church for the Lutherans in Hamburg. He also built the Nikolaikirche in Hamburg. In 1856 came the 'Battle of the Styles', when Lord Palmerston rejected Scott's winning Gothic design for the Foreign Office in Whitehall, and gave him the option of building in the Italianate style or losing the commission. Scott, it is said, spent a holiday in Bognor deciding on his reply to the ultimatum, and then built the Foreign Office in the required Classical style.

In 1864 his designs for the unpopular Albert Memorial in Hyde Park were selected and built from 1864 to 1872, after which he was knighted by Queen Victoria—in a total reversal of opinion, most modern critics now admire the monument. He was the professor of architecture at the Royal Academy Schools, 1868–73, and from this period became more concerned with restoration. An anecdote, which even if apocryphal, supports stories of his huge work-load, tells that once, on arriving at a provincial city, he telegraphed his office saying: 'Am in x... Why am I here?' There is scarcely a major medieval church or cathedral that he did not work on, which eventually prompted William Morris to found the Society for the Protection of Ancient Buildings in 1877 in protest against his often insensitive alterations. His *Autobiography* was published in 1879, and reveals the depth of his dislike of Renaissance architecture, which he saw first hand on his sole trip to Italy.

His son, George Gilbert Junior (1839–97), was overshadowed by his father, but was one of the important church architects of his time. He rejected his father's concentration on 13th-century Gothic, and with his partner Bodley, turned to late Gothic and to 17th-century classical styles. He died insane. His son Giles Gilbert (1880–1960) won the competition for Liverpool's Anglican Cathedral in 1903, and worked on the project for the rest of his life. It was eventually finished, on a much reduced scale, in 1980. He also built many Roman Catholic churches, and important secular works.

Scourging *See* FLAGELLATION.

screen *See* CHOIR and ICONOSTASIS.

scriptorium (Lat. *scriptum*, written) A room in, or part of, a monastery in which manuscripts were written and illuminated. Sometimes part of the cloister would be used in good weather. Most of the major monasteries had a scriptorium.

scroll A curved element of architectural decoration, such as the more elaborate forms of broken *pediment or decorative volutes.

scuola (Ital. school) The ordinary citizens of Venice had no say in the government of their State, and served it only in subordinate capacities. They took no part in the election of the Doge, which was managed by Counsellors drawn solely from those patrician families who had been members of the Great Council in 1297. From this tight oligarchy was created in 1355 the Council of Ten, which had supreme powers. To offset this deprivation of any civic role, the State encouraged the charitable confraternities founded by the Dominicans and the Franciscans after their arrival in the 13th century. Their idea was the creation of groups of citizens who would teach—hence the name 'scuole'—Christian ideals and the practice of charity towards their less fortunate fellow citizens. At one time they were also flagellants, particularly in processions on penitential occasions. While at first all ranks of society might belong to a scuola of their choice, an edict later forbade nobles to become members, because the State did not allow close contacts between patricians and the citizens, any more than it allowed contacts between nobles and foreigners.

Originally, there were six major confraternities: the Scuole di San Marco, San Rocco, Sta Maria della Carità, San Giovanni Evangelista, Sta Maria della Misericordia, San Teodoro, and the late addition of the Scuola dei Carmini. There were also lesser scuole, generally confined to nationalities—Albanians, Slavs, Armenians, or Greeks, as well as certain trade guilds or *fraglie* (brotherhoods) such as the gondoliers, the workers in the Arsenale (the shipbuilding yards), and a very late one for the painters. The Armenians still have a church and monastery on the Island of San Lazzaro, and the Greeks since the end of the 15th century have had their own church celebrating the Orthodox Rite in San Giorgio dei Greci.

The governors of the scuole were rich bourgeois; their function was threefold: religious, charitable, and spectacular, conforming to the Venetian love of pageantry and piety. The granting of girls' dowries, the issuing of sacks of flour to the poor, caring for the sick, giving pensions to the aged and to widows, providing for orphans, and in general serving as friendly societies and an early and effective social security system was the role they filled. All members paid into the funds, according to their wealth, and while the rich who filled the honorific positions were not expected to profit from their position, the funds they contributed and managed enabled the Scuola di San Marco, for instance, to be the first provider of a free public health authority in Europe which was civic, instead of monastic.

The great scuole all had splendid headquarters, of which the surviving example is the Scuola di San Rocco, the richest of them all. The ground floor is a large assembly hall with a nave and two aisles; a grand staircase leads to the first floor where there is a second large hall with an altar at one end, and a smaller hall called the *Albergo*, which was the committee room of the governors. The Scuola di San Rocco is famous for the painted decoration by *Tintoretto, and also has paintings by *Titian and *Tiepolo. The Treasury, despite losses sustained during the Napoleonic occupation, contains goldsmiths' works of the 15th and 16th centuries, and some 13th-century Byzantine ones.

The Scuola di San Marco is now part of the city hospital. Its façade retains the reliefs with extraordinary perspective effects by Tullio Lombardo in a Renaissance setting of characteristically Venetian idiosyncrasy by Pietro Lombardo and Mauro Coducci. The upper floor over the fine entrance hall, and the *Albergo*, have been restored. Sta Maria della Carità is now part of the Accademia Gallery, with one of the original Titian decorations still *in situ* and with a courtyard by *Palladio. The fine building of the Scuola di San Giovanni Evangelista was saved in the mid-19th century by a group of citizens to become a Centre for the Building Arts. It originally possessed a reliquary with a fragment of the Holy Cross, and the great hall was decorated with a series of paintings (now in the Accademia) by Carpaccio and Gentile *Bellini, depicting one of the Scuola's grand processions with their reliquary in the Piazza San Marco, and also the fascinating series recording the occasion during a procession with the reliquary when the press of spectators caused the collapse of a bridge, and the reliquary fell into the canal, to be rescued by the Grand Guardian. The Scuola della Misericordia functioned mainly as a funeral society, and the Scuola dei Carmini still exists and owns works by Tiepolo.

seals and signet-rings Before *c.*200 AD it is virtually impossible to identify any specifically Christian artefact, but the use of distinguishing seals and signet-rings in commerce seems to have led to Christians using symbols of their religion on their seals, not necessarily identifiable as such by outsiders. Many such seals and rings exist (e.g. in the BM), and their justification can be found in Clement of Alexandria (*c.*200): 'Our seals ought to be a dove or a fish or a ship running before the breeze or a tuneful harp or a ship's anchor. And if there should happen to be a fisherman, he will call to mind the apostle [Peter] and the children drawn up from the water . . .', an allusion to Baptism. All the objects mentioned are well-known Christian symbols, and may have a connection with the word 'seal' in Rev. chs. 5–7.

seasons *See* MONTHS, LABOURS OF THE.

Seat of Mercy (Mercy-Seat, Throne of Grace) In the OT numerous references to the Jewish Temple describe the Mercy-Seat as the golden cover of the *Ark of the Covenant, on which the High Priest sprinkled blood once a year as an atonement, where God is enthroned between the cherubim (Exod. 25: 17–22; 26: 34; 30: 6; 37: 6; Lev. 16: 13–15; Num. 7: 89; and 1 Chron. 28: 11). In the NT (Heb. 9: 5), Paul contrasts the Old Dispensation sacrifice with that of the New, Christ's sacrifice on the Cross. In *Luther's German Bible he used the word *Gnadenstuhl* (Throne of Grace), where the NRSV has 'mercy-seat'. Nineteenth-century German art-historians adopted *Gnadenstuhl* as a term to describe representations of Christ crucified, supported by God the Father, with the dove of the Holy Spirit, usually over Christ's head. This is a special type of *Trinity, and is sometimes still so described, but the emphasis on the sacrifice of the Cross is greater than is usually found in representations of the Holy Trinity, although it is not always easy to distinguish them. The earliest known representations of the Seat of Mercy are early 12th-century (e.g. a German portable altar, before 1132: London, V & A). Others are the Trinity fresco by *Masaccio (Florence, Sta Maria Novella), an Austrian 15th-century altarpiece (London, NG), the panel by Hugo van der *Goes (Royal Coll., on loan to Edinburgh, NG), and an engraving by *Dürer of 1516. The church of St John Nepomuk, Munich, by the *Asam brothers, 1733, has a Seat of Mercy of great virtuosity in the ceiling.

Seat of Wisdom *See* SEDES SAPIENTIAE.

Sebastian, Saint The only document for the saint is the brief record of a *deposito Martyrum*, 'XIII Cal feb. Fabiani in Calliste et Sebastiani in Catacumbas' (deposit of Martyrs; 13 Feb. Fabian in Callixtus and Sebastian in the Catacombs) and a commentary by S. Ambrose on Ps. 118, appropriate for a martyr. Sebastian may have been born in Narbonne, but is said to have come from Milan, but all that is known of him is that he went to Rome and was martyred there. Since there was virtually no persecution in Milan, but Maximian was very violent in Rome, it may be suggested that he was, like some members of devout communities, eager for martyrdom. What S. Sebastian has, in very large measure, is a legend, probably composed in Rome towards the mid-5th century by a skilled writer who placed his martyr very carefully in a Rome he knew and described accurately. The legend is a historical romance, with many marvels, conversions, sermons on the faith, and grisly descriptions of martyrdoms.

The author brings Sebastian to Rome to join the Pretorian Guard. By rising in favour through his loyalty, he was appointed to the personal imperial guard where his favoured position enabled him to succour many imprisoned Christians and to spread pro-Christian propaganda among men in power, making many converts. Such zeal did not pass unnoticed, and after burying the SS Quattro Coronati he was caught and condemned to the military execution of being shot with arrows.

He was taken into a field, tied naked to a post, and shot so full of arrows that 'he looked like a hedgehog'. His executioners left him for dead, and that night Christians, led by S. Irene, a martyr's widow, came for his body to bury it. He was still alive, so she took him back to her house and nursed him until he recovered. Instead of leaving Rome, as he was begged to do, he presented himself at the Temple of Hercules, where the two emperors, Diocletian and Maximian, were performing a rite, and proclaimed his faith in Christ. Diocletian had him flogged to death in the Palatine hippodrome, and his body flung in the sewer to prevent its being found. The saint appeared that night to a Lucina, told her where he was, and asked her to bury him near the tombs of the Apostles Peter and Paul on the Appian Way. She obeyed and placed his body in the Catacomb of S. Callixtus.

This idealized figure is grouped with a number of martyrs, many well known, but from different periods. The story-teller links them in a totally invented complex family group. Only the fact that Sebastian was a soldier might be true, if one discounts the fact that the military life was one from which Christians were discouraged. As late as the 3rd century the Catacomb on the Appian Way was famous for a *memoria Apostolorum* (memorial of the Apostles) and in the 4th century the church built near by was called the *ecclesia Apostolorum* (church of the Apostles), until the dedication was changed to San Sebastiano. His remains had been tidied up in his *arcosolium, but no dispersal occurred until some were begged for the abbey of St-Méard at Soissons (of which only the crypt remains) and installed in 826. The rest of the body was taken to San Gregorio in the Vatican and the head was moved in a precious reliquary to the SS Quattro Coronati. In 1218 all the Roman relics were returned to San Sebastiano.

The saint was very popular in Rome, and he was joined with S. Anthony, S. Christopher, S. Roche, and the Fourteen Holy Helpers as a protector against plague. In S. Sebastian's case, this was because of his death from arrows, since being struck by the plague was equated with being struck by the arrow of death. He survived, therefore in him lay the hope of a cure.

He was popular also with artists. There is a 6th-century mosaic in Sant'Apollinare Nuovo, Ravenna, a 7th-century one in San Pietro in Vincoli, Rome, and a 13th-century one in St Mark's, Venice. A very rare image, of the saint fully dressed, with hat, sword, and spurs, is by the Catalan school of Mazzan de Sas (15th cent.: Mus. Lázaro Galdiano, Madrid). Most of the finest 15th-century Italian representations are because it was one of the few subjects which allowed the painter or sculptor to depict a nude male body in the pride of life and beauty. The roll-call is endless but it is headed by Piero della Francesca (1445–58: *Misericordia Polyptych*, Sansepolcro), Giovanni Bellini (1464–8: *S. Vincent Ferrer Altar*, SS Giovanni e Paolo, Venice), Antonello da Messina (1476: Dresden); Mantegna, who painted three (1470: Vienna, KHM; 1480: Paris, Louvre; 1490: Ca' d'Oro, Venice), each utterly different and equally splendid; Botticelli (1473: Berlin). The subject spread to the more timorous North with Memlinc painting two (*c.*1470: Brussels; 1490: Paris, Louvre), and Q. Massys (1518: *Trinity Altar*, Munich). After mythologies became popular, permitting as they did the depiction of Venus, Adonis, Apollo, and similar figures, S. Sebastian as a way in which the artist could depict the nude other than in Crucifixions, *Pietàs*, or martyrdoms lost much of its urgency. An exception is the Georges de la Tour *S. Sebastian tended by S. Irene* (1649–50: loan to Louvre). In the 16th and 17th centuries works by Rubens, Van Dyck, the Carracci, meant that the subject no longer had the attraction of a dangerous novelty in religious art, since the taste could easily be accommodated or gratified in other ways.

Second Coming *See* PAROUSIA.

Sedes Sapientiae (Lat. Seat of Wisdom) In 1 Kings 10: 18–20 it says 'The king (Solomon) also made a great ivory throne, and overlaid it with the finest gold. The throne had six steps. The top of the throne was rounded in the back, and on each side of the seat were arm rests and two lions standing beside the arm rests, while twelve lions were standing, one on each end of a step on the six steps. Nothing like it was ever made in any kingdom', and vv. 23–4 say 'Thus King Solomon excelled all the kings of the earth in riches and in wisdom. The whole earth sought the presence of Solomon to hear his wisdom.'

Solomon is equated with eternal wisdom, and is thus a *type of Christ, since Matt. 12: 42 says 'The Queen of the South will rise up at the Judgement with this generation and condemn it, because she came from the ends of the earth to listen to the wisdom of Solomon and see, something greater than Solomon is here!' The place of the throne of Solomon is therefore the House of Wisdom, and is a prophecy relating to the Church. During the 11th and 12th centuries Divine Wisdom is portrayed as Ecclesia, a woman crowned and sceptred, and Ecclesia is also associated with the Virgin, who bears the Divine Son of Isaiah's prophecy. From the mid-12th century onwards she becomes the *Sedes Sapientiae* in which the Logos is made flesh, and the most powerful image is of the hieratic *Theotokos seated on the Throne of Wisdom holding the revealed Logos on her knees. Such, for instance, is the image in the right portal of the west front of Chartres. Often she is accompanied by prophets who foretold the coming of the Messiah, and in representations of the Annunciation Mary is often portrayed as seated or standing within a regal canopy; that is, she is already portrayed as being in the House of Wisdom (Rhenish ivory relief, *c.*1100: Berlin; Jacopo Torriti, mosaic, 1295, Rome, Sta Maria Maggiore). In the relief on the doors of Sta Sabina, Rome, of 430–2, of the *Adoration of the Magi,* Mary is seated on a throne raised by six steps from the approaching Magi; in the mosaic on the Triumphal Arch of Sta Maria Maggiore, Rome, of 432–40, the Holy Child is seated on a large throne, richly cushioned like one of the thrones of the *Parousia in the Baptistery of the Orthodox in Ravenna, raised above His mother's lesser throne. In the mosaic in Sant' Apollinare Nuovo, Ravenna, of *c.*520–60, of the Magi approaching with their gifts, she is enthroned with the Child on her knees, the throne being raised on a wide step. Also, in all the late 13th/early 14th-century *Madonna and Child enthroned with Angels* (and sometimes also with prophets) by Cimabue, Duccio, Giotto, and Simone Martini, and by Masaccio in 1425, the Virgin is the Theotokos seated on the Throne of Wisdom holding the Incarnate Logos.

The Queen of Sheba's visit to Solomon is seen in the **Speculum Humanae Salvationis* as an antitype of the Magi's coming to Bethlehem to worship the enthroned Divine Wisdom. After the end of the 14th/early 15th century the imagery of the Throne of Solomon united to the *Sedes Sapientiae* disappears in favour of the less formal, unhieratic forms of the Franciscan-inspired Virgin of Tenderness—the Panagia disappears into the Glycophilousa more readily in the West than she does in the East. The title Seat of Wisdom is one of the titles given to the Virgin in the Litany of Loreto. She was also referred to as such by S. Anselm and S. Bernard of Clairvaux.

Thrones of the Virgin are sometimes depicted with lion heads on the arms: there is an *Enthroned Madonna and Child* by Lorenzo Monaco (Edinburgh, NG of S); Jan van Eyck: *Lucca Madonna and Child* (Frankfurt), with four lions on the throne; Roger van der Weyden: *Madonna and Child standing before the throne* (Vienna, KHM), with lions on the arms of the throne. *See also* MADONNA TYPES.

Sedia Gestatoria is, or was, since its use is now discontinued, the papal processional carrying throne borne on the shoulders of the *sediarii* (chair carriers). It was derived from the antique Roman imperial processional carrying throne.

An example is in the Raphael fresco in the Vatican Stanze of the *Expulsion of Heliodorus* where Julius II, seated on the *Sedia* with his court around him, witnesses the miracle.

sedilia (Lat. *sedile,* seat) Seats, usually three in number (but in large churches there may be as many as five), were built into the thickness of the chancel wall on the Epistle side, for the use of the celebrant, the deacon, and subdeacon during the sung parts of the High Mass, Lauds, and Vespers. They are common in the chancels of medieval churches in England, where the central seat is often higher than those for the deacons, and all three may have decorative traceried arches over them. Their use has long been discontinued and a movable bench or seats (*scamnum, scamna*) used instead. However, a number of Gothic Revival churches have had *sedilia* built into the sanctuary wall. *See* GOSPEL SIDE.

Sens, William of, was a 12th-century French master mason who designed and built part of the choir of Canterbury Cathedral. He may have been trained at Reims, but most likely at Sens itself during its rebuilding in the 1140s–1160s. The story of the Canterbury choir is told by the monk Gervase in his vivid chronicle of the disastrous fire which destroyed Archbishop Anselm's 1170 choir in 1174. Several masons were consulted about its rebuilding, and finally William of Sens was chosen because of 'his lively genius and good reputation'. He began at the west end of the choir, had reached the choir transepts by 1178 and was working on the crossing vault over the high altar when he fell from the scaffolding. He was so badly injured that he returned to

France, and the work was continued by William the Englishman. He may either have had experience of Sens, since he used one of the main characteristics of its choir—the coupled columns—in the arcades of the Trinity Chapel (as it now is, which is to the east of the choir transept and was to become the shrine of S. *Thomas Becket), or plans, and perhaps materials, for this unusual feature were already in the masons' lodge. William the Englishman finished the choir by 1184.

Sepulchre, Easter *See* EASTER SEPULCHRE.

Sepulchre, the Holy, is the place venerated as the tomb in which Christ's body was laid after the Crucifixion, and from which He rose on Easter morning.

*Constantine conquered the Western Empire by 312, but did not extend his rule over the Eastern Empire until he had defeated Licinius in 324. This gave him control over Palestine and Jerusalem, with the Holy Places. His mother, the Empress Helena, came to Jerusalem and 'discovered' the Holy Sepulchre and the 'True Cross'. There was great controversy over the actual site, and in 326 Constantine determined the site, and an eyewitness of this was the historian Eusebius, who gives an account which has always been accepted. S. Helena built the first church of the Holy Sepulchre, or rather of the Anastasis, or Resurrection, dedicated in 335. The Eastern Church preferred to celebrate the Anastasis instead of Christ's sacrifice on the cross because crucifixion was a shameful, criminal death, so that it was not until the mid-5th century that any representations of it became common (the earliest are on the doors of Sta Sabina in Rome, and on the ivory plaque on the casket in the BM, both of *c.*430, and Roman, not Eastern). The Resurrection was a joyous miraculous celebration, the antithesis of the stark tragedy which preceded it—triumph instead of disaster.

The Persians invaded Palestine, took and sacked Jerusalem, and destroyed S. Helena's church in 614, but in 626 a second church was built, which survived until in 1010 the Caliph Hakeem had all the buildings on the site demolished. A third church was built during the First Crusade, *c.*1100. This church was in turn replaced by a fourth church built after the Second Crusade, 1147–9. The enclave was made so large that it covered the most important holy sites in Jerusalem and also a part of the Via Dolorosa, the 10th to the 14th *Stations being brought within the enclave of the Holy Sepulchre. This was again rebuilt in 1310, was partly burnt in 1808, so that after another rebuilding by 1810, little remains of any older part but an early bell-tower and the lower walls of the Constantinian rotunda.

The enclave contains two main areas, a domed rotunda containing the rock cave of the Holy Sepulchre itself on the west, and the church on the east. There are also numerous chapels surrounding the Holy Sepulchre and the church, one being the site of the Crucifixion, which is also now within the enclave. S. John's testimony (John 19: 17, 20) that Christ carried the cross and went 'out to what is called the Place of the Skull', and 'because the place where Jesus was crucified was near the city', and the words in Heb. 13: 12, 'suffered outside the city gate' seem to have been overridden. This is because the city was largely rebuilt by Hadrian in 132–5 after a disastrous Jewish revolt, and the Romans deliberately altered its topography to destroy both Jewish and Christian religious sites. The ground on which the cave-tomb stood was levelled, and then built up to make a site for a temple of Venus, and Eusebius, who was an eyewitness of Constantine's recovery of the site which, though obliterated was still remembered, recorded the event in his *Life of Constantine*. There was another witness who, though only a boy at the time, never forgot that he had seen Christ's tomb restored to light. This boy was Cyril, who later became Bishop of Jerusalem.

Many Christian Churches claim the right to space for their services in the Holy Sepulchre. The strife between them caused so much trouble that in 1852 the Ottoman government decreed the 'Law of the Status Quo', which determined who should have which areas, and this law is still maintained despite the passing of Ottoman control. The Holy Sepulchre and the rotunda, and the Stone of Unction, belong to the Patriarchates of Constantinople, Alexandria, Antioch, and Jerusalem, the Armenians, and the Roman Catholics; individual chapels belong to the Copts, the Syrians, and the Ethiopians. All the Churches exercise their right to hold services on Sunday mornings, and in Holy Week and Easter Sunday, many of them at the same times and with their choirs. The Orthodox have granted the Anglicans the privilege of using the Chapel of the Skull beneath Golgotha. The Stone of Unction, on which Christ's body was prepared for burial, is a replacement (1810) commemorating the destroyed original, and many of the areas perpetuate long traditions; for instance, the Chapel of the Skull claims to contain the skull of Adam, and this fits the medieval typology of the First Adam being buried beneath the place where the Second Adam was crucified, so that the man who committed the first sin is buried beneath the place where the Man died to redeem mankind.

Seraphic Order Another name for *Franciscans. *S. Francis was given the title of the 'Seraphic Doctor' by *S. Bonaventura because he had received the Stigmata from a seraph. Sometimes the title is given as 'Seraphic Father'.

seraphim *See* CHERUBIM.

serpent In Gen. 3 is the account of the meeting between the serpent and Eve: 'Now the serpent was more crafty than any other animal that the Lord God had made. He said to the woman, "Did God say, 'You shall not eat from any tree in the garden'?" The woman said ... "We may eat of the fruit of the trees in the garden, but God said, 'You shall not eat of the fruit of the tree that is in the middle of the garden, nor shall you touch it, or you shall die.'" But the serpent said to the woman, "You will not die; for God knows that when you eat of it your eyes will be opened, and you will be like God, knowing good and evil." So ... she took of its fruit and ate; and she also gave some to her husband ... and he ate. Then the eyes of both were opened, and they knew that they were naked ...' Later, when God questioned Eve saying, '"What is this that you have done?" The woman said, "The serpent tricked me, and I ate." The Lord God said to the serpent, "Because you have done this, cursed are you among all animals ... upon your belly you shall go, ... and I will put enmity between you and the woman, and between your offspring and hers; he will strike your head, and you will strike his heel."'

The serpent is equated with the Devil, as having provoked the *Fall of Man, and is also equated with sin, since Adam and Eve in taking the forbidden fruit were guilty of the first sin of disobedience. In representations of the *Immaculate Conception, Mary is seen as treading on the serpent, as the symbol of sin, since she was born sinless, and in the Incarnation she is the bearer of the One who is the ultimate conqueror of sin, and as God promised at the moment of cursing the serpent, there would be enmity between the serpent and her 'offspring'—that is, Jesus Christ.

An indirect result of God's condemnation of the serpent for its craftiness is its adoption as a symbol of wisdom, as in the saying 'as wise as the serpent', i.e. as underhand, secretive, and sly. In fact, Christ himself says (Matt. 10: 16), 'See, I am sending you out like sheep into the midst of wolves; so be wise as serpents and innocent as doves.' And, strangely, Moses hung a brazen serpent on the pole as the symbol of salvation. There is also the classical symbol of Time or eternity in the form of a snake eating its tail, though this is subject to contradictory interpretations.

Caravaggio, in the *Madonna and Child with S. Anne* (1605–6: Rome, Borghese Gall.) has the Christ Child treading on His mother's foot as she treads on the head of the snake, depicting Him as the Devil-destroying fruit of the Incarnation, and her as the Immaculate one. *See also* BRAZEN, DRAGON, EDEN, and MOSES.

Servites are members of the religious Order of Servants of the Blessed Virgin Mary, founded in 1240 by seven wealthy Florentine city councillors who had joined together seven years previously to devote themselves to the service of the Virgin. They follow the Augustinian Rule, with some Dominican modifications, and wear a black habit. The Order spread rapidly, and by the time they received papal recognition in 1304, an Order of Servite Nuns had also been founded. Their most influential member was S. Filippo Benizzi who, after several years as a lay brother, joined the Order in 1259 and became its fifth General in 1268. Under him, the Order spread widely, sending out missionaries as far as India and founding many convents in France and Germany. He died in 1285. There is also a Third Order of Lay Sisters, founded in 1306 by S. Giuliana Falconieri, who devote themselves to nursing and to the education of children.

There are five frescoes in the atrium of the SS Annunziata in Florence (the Servite church) of incidents from the life of S. Filippo, one by Cosimo Rosselli (1476), and four by Andrea del Sarto of which one is dated 1510. Romanino painted an imaginary portrait of the saint (*c.*1530/50: London, NG) as part of an altarpiece of *The Nativity, with five saints*.

Seth (Heb. founder) was the third son of Adam and Eve (Gen. 4: 25), born to them after Cain killed Abel. Seth was the great-great-great grandfather of Enoch, who was the father of Methuselah, who was the grandfather of Noah.

The *Golden Legend* has the following story in the account of the Invention of the Holy Cross: when Adam was ailing, his son Seth went to the gate of the Garden of Paradise and asked for a few drops of the oil from the tree of Mercy, that he might anoint his father's body and thus repair his health. But the Archangel Michael appeared to him and said: 'Nor by thy tears, nor by thy prayers mayest thou obtain the oil of the tree of Mercy, for men cannot obtain this oil until five thousand five hundred years have passed', which is to say, after the Passion of Christ. Another chronicle relates that nevertheless the Archangel Michael gave to Seth a branch of the miraculous tree, ordering him to plant it on Mount Libanus. Still another history adds that this tree was the same that had caused Adam to sin; and that when he gave the branch to Seth, the angel told him that on the day when this tree should bear fruit, his father would be made whole. And when Seth came back to his house, he found his father already dead. He planted the tree over Adam's grave, and the branch became a mighty tree, which still flourished in Solomon's time.

Piero della Francesca, in the fresco cycle of the story of the *True Cross* (1452–9: Arezzo, San Francesco), depicts Seth and the sick Adam before his departure on his errand of mercy, and bewailing the dead Adam on his return with the branch of the tree. *See also* TRUE CROSS, LEGEND OF THE.

Seven Basilicas *See* ROME.

Seven Deadly Sins *See* DEADLY.

Seven Dolours *See* SORROWS.

Seven Gifts of the Holy Ghost *See* GIFTS.

Seven Joys *See* JOYS.

Seven Liberal Arts *See* ARTS.

Seven Sacraments *See* SACRAMENTS.

Seven Virtues and Vices *See* VIRTUES.

Seven Works of Mercy *See* MERCY.

Sheba, Queen of In the OT, she was the ruler of an Arabian or African country, which was perhaps part of Ethiopia. She heard of the wisdom, and the wealth, of Solomon, and came on a state visit to him (1 Kings 10: 1–13) in Jerusalem travelling 'with a very great retinue, with camels bearing spices, and very much gold, and precious stones'. She came prepared with many riddles and questions, and found that he could answer them all. She was astonished at the state in which he lived, his house, his food, his servants and their clothes, and she told him that what she had seen far surpassed all that she had heard. She presented him with 120 talents of gold (if no exaggeration, the fabulous weight of about 4½ tons), jewels and 'never again did spices come in such quantity as that which the Queen of Sheba gave to King Solomon . . . Meanwhile King Solomon gave to the Queen of Sheba every desire that she expressed . . .'. From this it has been inferred that he also gave her an heir. The Ethiopians to this day maintain that Menelek, their king, was this son, who thereby gave them a dynasty descended from David. By a strange and very old tradition, the Queen is reputed to have been web-footed, and in French is called 'La Reine pédauque'. This odd disfigurement appears on figures of the Queen on several French 12th-century portals, some known now only by drawings made by the Benedictine Dom Plancher in the 18th century. Such for instance is the portal of Bénigne, where the column figures flanking the doorway included the Queen of Sheba, clearly recognizable from the deformed foot. Legend tells that when she went to meet King Solomon in his throne room, the floor was so highly polished that she thought it was water and lifted her skirts, thus revealing her deformity. Her inclusion on so many French portals from Chartres onwards is because she represents pagans of the OT world coming to honour the Law, just as the Magi symbolize the pagan, or Gentile, world coming to worship Christ.

Lorenzo Ghiberti represented the meeting between Solomon and the Queen of Sheba in one of the reliefs in his second pair of Baptistery doors (1425–52: Florence) and Piero della Francesca devoted one large fresco, divided into two sections, in his series of the *True Cross* (1452–9: Arezzo, San Francesco), to the Queen recognizing the tree and her reception by Solomon. *See also* TRUE CROSS, LEGEND OF.

sheep are one of the commonest symbols of the faithful, deriving from Christ's charge to Peter (John 21: 4–17) to 'Feed my sheep'. Isaiah 53: 6 says, 'And we like sheep have gone astray'; and in Matt. 25: 32 Christ says, 'He will separate them . . . as a shepherd divides his sheep from the goats . . .'; and in the general confession of the Book of Common Prayer are the words, 'We have erred and strayed from thy ways like lost sheep.' The Apostles themselves are often represented by sheep in Early Christian mosaics, as, for instance in Sant' Apollinare in Classe, outside Ravenna, 6th century, and in SS Cosmas and Damian, Rome (*c.*530), and St Mark's, Venice, 9th century. *See also* SHEPHERD.

Shem Noah had three sons, Shem, *Ham, and *Japhet. After the Deluge, Noah drank the new wine from the replanted vines and it made him drunk. When Shem was told by Ham that Noah was lying exposed in his tent, he and Japhet took a garment and entered the tent backwards and covered their father. When Noah awoke he blessed Shem and Japhet, and cursed Ham for his offence (Gen. 9: 20–6). Shem was the father of Eber, and through him father of the Semitic race, including those that later became the people of Israel. Michelangelo in the fresco *The Drunkenness of Noah* in the Sistine Ceiling portrays Shem with averted gaze covering his father.

Shepherd, the Good The Good Shepherd is a title of Christ based on John 10: 1–16. Christ begins by telling the disciples that anyone not entering the sheepfold by the gate is a thief and a robber, and that the shepherd enters by the gate; he calls his sheep and they follow him, because they know his voice. When the disciples do not understand his meaning, He continues by saying that He is the gate for the sheep, and whoever enters by Him will be saved. He continues with the words 'I am the good shepherd. The good shepherd lays down his life for the sheep. The hired hand . . . sees the wolf coming and . . . runs away. I know my own and my own know me, just as the Father knows me and I know the Father. And I lay down my life for the sheep. I have other sheep that do not belong to this fold. I must bring them also, and they will listen to my voice. So there will be one flock, one shepherd.' Luke 15: 3–6 tells a different story: 'The Pharisees and the scribes were grumbling, "This fellow welcomes sinners and eats with them." So he told them this parable. "Which one of you, having a hundred sheep and losing one of them, does not leave the ninety-nine in the wilderness and go after the one that is lost until he finds it? When he has found it, he lays it on his shoulders and rejoices. And when he comes home, he calls together his friends and neighbours, saying to them, Rejoice with me, for I have found my sheep that was lost. Just so, I tell you, there will be more joy in heaven over one sinner who repents than over ninety-nine righteous persons who need no repentance."'

In Heb. 13: 20, there is the phrase, ' . . . our Lord Jesus, the great shepherd of the sheep, . . .' and in 1 Pet. 2: 25, S. Peter says 'For you were going astray like sheep, but now you have returned to the shepherd and guardian of your souls.'

The vivid simile of the loving shepherd lasted as a glowing image for those that heard it, and remained so, since the image of the Good Shepherd caring for his flock has echoes from the OT in Ps. 23 (Vg. 22) and also from Homeric times. It is common in pastoral peoples, as exemplified by the classical image of the Hermes Kriophoros, a Tanagra figure by Calamis, of Hermes bearing a sheep on his shoulders, which doubled very easily as a figure of the Christian Good Shepherd, particularly during the times of persecutions. The theme appears in numerous catacomb paintings (SS Domitilla, Callixtus, Pretextatus, and Pietro e Marcellino), often combined with the growing vine. It also appears on some sarcophagi, one in the Lateran combining the 'vine allegory' (John 15: 1, 5: 'I am the true vine, and my Father is the vinegrower . . . I am the vine, you are the branches') with the Good Shepherd. There are two 4th-century sarcophagi in the Vatican and Lateran Museums with depictions of this allegory.

The image of the sheep appears again in John 21: 4–17, where 'Just after daybreak, Jesus stood on the sea-shore', and when the disciples returned from fishing, having caught nothing, He told them to cast their net again and they made a huge catch. John said 'It is the Lord!', and after Jesus had given them bread and roasted fish He asked Peter, ' . . . do you love me?' three times, receiving each time a more anguished response, 'Lord, you know I love you!' and each time He then said 'Feed my lambs', 'Tend my sheep', and 'Feed my sheep'. This charge to Peter also echoes, and in its memorable poignancy reinforces, the earlier charge of the *Traditio Clavium—the giving of the keys of Heaven—in the words (John 20: 23) 'Whose sins you shall forgive, they are forgiven; whose sins you shall retain, they are retained.' Possibly the last appearance of the Good Shepherd is in the Mausoleum of Galla Placidia, Ravenna, of the 5th century. In the Council of 692, which applied only in the Eastern Church, not in the West, the image of the Lamb as a prototype of Christ was forbidden, lest it should lead to accusations of animal worship.

An Order of nuns, which began in 1641 as 'Sisters of Our Lady of the Good Shepherd of Angers', was founded for the conversion and care of prostitutes, and was refounded in 1835 as the 'Order of the Good Shepherd Sisters' with the same objects, to which was joined work in hospitals and on missions. They now have convents world-wide, and in N. and S. America have the care of women's prisons.

Shepherds, Adoration of *See* NATIVITY and CHRIST.

Ship of the Church The immediacy of a ship as a symbol of the Church is easy to understand. Christ called fishermen from their boats, promising that He would make them 'fishers of men', and Himself taught the crowds from one of their boats.

The symbolism of the ship as the Church journeying on the waters of life, bearing the cargo of human souls and steered by Christ, goes back as early as Justin Martyr in the 2nd century and is part of the oral teaching of the early Church. There are a number of allegories of the ship with the cross-rigging of the mast as a symbol of the cross, and elaborations in which the ship sails in violent storms and is saved by Christ as steersman. Noah's ark also serves as an image of the great ship with its cargo of souls moving towards salvation, so that the ship is both a sign of hope for eternity, as well as a symbol of the certitude of salvation for those who sail in her. Even Jonah thrown from the ship and swallowed by the whale can serve as an example of the ship with its cargo of souls saved by the sacrifice of one Man, and his three days in the belly of the whale from which he was cast upon the shore becomes the symbol of Christ's three days in the tomb and His resurrection. The very shape of the church, with a long *nave*, i.e. *navis*, ship, and with, in the early forms, an apse at one end with the bishop's throne in it, may be likened to a ship with the helmsman steering it.

The symbol of the ship was frequently used in the *catacombs. Tiles sealing *loculi have ships painted or scratched on them: one in the cemetery at Ostia has a ship with the name Eusebia on the prow; two in the Catacomb of Domitilla, one with a dove with a sprig of olive in its beak on the prow, the other with a ship with a dove and over it the inscription *Genialis in pace.* One tile in the Catacomb of Priscilla has a ship in port with an anchor, and a painting in the Catacomb of Callixtus shows a ship in a storm with a figure standing on the prow praying while another half-figure in a cloud holds him by the arm, while amid the waves another figure sinks, lost by lack of faith. Funerary steles and gems also were often carved with such symbols: a stele in Spoleto has a ship with three named Evangelists (Matthew has been broken away) rowing, while Christ standing in the prow steers them towards a lighthouse, and a gem has S. Peter, who, having jumped from the ship, sinks as he tries to walk on the water and is saved by Christ.

Perhaps the most significant image of the Ship of the Church is the (much over-restored) mosaic of the *Navicella,* in the atrium of St Peter's, Rome, which is the one designed by Giotto for the atrium of Old St Peter's, and removed to the new church when the present atrium was added to it by *Maderno.

shrine (Lat. *scrinium,* chest or coffer, and Germ. *Schrein,* a casket or house-altar) A shrine implies a holy place, relic, or object, and also a special day of veneration or a *pilgrimage. The most famous English shrines, all of which had popular pilgrimages, were Canterbury for S. Thomas Becket, and Winchester for S. Swithin, between which ran the Pilgrims' Way, a large part of which still survives as a Kentish country lane. Westminster Abbey was the shrine of S. Edward the Confessor, Durham of S. Cuthbert, Ely of S. Etheldreda, and Ripon of S. Wilfred. The most famous Marian shrine and most popular pilgrimage site in England was at Walsingham in Norfolk, where a replica of the Holy House of Nazareth was built in the 11th century. Like all the other great pilgrimage shrines of medieval England, it was destroyed at the Reformation in 1538, but the pilgrimage to Walsingham has been revived. Most of the major churches to which pilgrimages were—or still are—made contained a shrine which housed relics of the saint in whose honour the pilgrimage was made. *See also* PILGRIMAGE CHURCHES, and RELICS, RELIQUARY.

Shroud of Turin (Sacro Sindone) The Holy Shroud has been in Turin since 1578. It can be traced back as far as 1360 when it was at Lirey or Liré in the diocese of Troyes. It has no earlier documented history, but in 1389 the Bishop of Troyes petitioned Pope Clement VII in Avignon to stop the veneration of a so-called relic purporting to be Christ's shroud, which he maintained was a cloth painted with imprints which a local painter had admitted making. The priest exhibiting the 'shroud' was ordered to make clear to pilgrims that it was a representation of Christ's shroud, not the actual thing. Nevertheless, the object caused bitter controversy. Many maintained that it was genuine, and that it had come into the possession of a French noble family after the destruction of the Knights Templar, its original owners, by King Philip IV of France in 1312, and the burning at the stake of the Grand Master, Jacques de Molay, in 1314. It eventually came into the possession of the House of Savoy, and with them went to Turin, to become the major relic of the cathedral.

No one has ever been able to explain to universal agreement how the image was made, but it fits the body of a man crowned with thorns, and crucified, not through the hands, as Christ crucified is always depicted, but through the wrists. The argument for this is that the hand is too weak to stand the weight of a body hanging from it, and its weight would tear it away from the nails. By the time the first images of Christ crucified were made, nearly a century after crucifixion ceased to be a penal punishment, memory of the actual method seems to have been lost. The image on the shroud is a negative image, and was not properly recognized until it was photographed in the 1890s, and on the developed photographic plate the negative image became clear. The explanations advanced for it are that contact between Christ's blood and the aloes and other spices used (John 19: 40) by Joseph of Arimathaea in the shroud in which His body was wrapped, created a chemical compound which impregnated the shroud with the marks of His wounds which it displays so convincingly.

Recently, however, after long pressure, the Bishop of Turin consented to the shroud being subjected to a Carbon-14 test. This produced a result inconsistent with a 1st-century origin, and tending more towards the 14th, but gave no help towards a reasonable explanation of how it had been made. No credible miracles have ever been adduced as the result of any contact with the shroud, nor of veneration of it, and no works of art are connected with it, except the special chapel in which it is housed at the back of Turin Cathedral. This was completed by *Guarini between 1667 and 1690 with an astonishing pyramidal tracery spire through which the light filters down upon the black marble shrine below. The shroud is, however, still—and probably always will be—the subject of fierce argument; it is either believed in, or it is rejected. It joins several other similar miraculous images: the so-called portrait of Christ sent to King *Abgar, the *Mandylion, and the Vernicle or image on *Veronica's veil, and a number of 'miraculous' images of the Virgin, and similar things.

sibyls In the ancient world there were women inspired by Apollo, who uttered prophecies through them. They were associated with particular places from which they derived their names. The first was the Erythraean, followed by the Cumaean, Samian, Delphic, Libyan, Persian, and Tiburtine, followed by Cimmerian, European, Agrippan, Hellespontic, and Phrygian, making twelve to match the number of Minor *Prophets and *Apostles. In fact, in the earliest times there were only two or three, and the list given by Varro (d. 27 BC) has only ten, but the names known in later times come from the Christian Lactantius, writing in AD 305/13. The *Oracula sibyllina* (the Sibylline Oracles), a collection of their sayings, were kept in various cities and were consulted in Rome as early as 496 BC—and for the last time officially in AD 363. The original collection was burnt in a temple fire in 83 BC and a new set was collected and preserved in the Roman Temple of Apollo. This also was destroyed, perhaps by the Byzantine general Stilicho *c.*410. This set, however, was extensively interpolated by Jewish and, later, Christian writers so that the fourteen books of copies which have survived are historically worthless. During the Middle Ages the only two sibyls to be represented were the Erythraean, who was associated with Virgil and thought to prophesy the Last Judgement, and the Tiburtine, who was also associated with Virgil (*see* AUGUSTUS and THE SIBYL), and foretold the coming of Christ. During the late 15th century, in accord with the new interest in Antiquity, they became much more popular, especially as men felt that the great pagan philosophers must have been divinely inspired and so were a revelation to the Gentiles parallel to the Jewish Prophets. In 1481 Filippo Barbieri's booklet on them was published in Rome and the end of the century saw several cycles representing some or all of them, including Filippino Lippi's fresco cycle

S

(1488–93) in the Carafa Chapel of Sta Maria sopra Minerva, the main Dominican church in Rome (Barbieri was a Dominican). There is a miniature by Jean Fouquet of *c.*1460 in the so-called *Hours of Adelaïde de Savoie* of six sibyls. The final seal of approval came with their inclusion in the *Sistine Chapel together with the Prophets. *Michelangelo represented only five—Delphic, Cumaean, and Libyan on one side, and Erythraean and Persian on the other. There are seven Prophets because the two ends, above the altar and the door, have Jonah and Zechariah respectively.

Signorelli, Luca (*c.*1441/50, perhaps 1445–1523), born in Cortona, was probably a fellow-pupil of *Perugino under *Piero della Francesca *c.*1470, but his mature style has nothing in common with the hieratic calm and monumentality of Piero's figures, and is closer to contemporary Florentines, such as Antonio Pollaiuolo, who, like Signorelli, was interested in anatomy and the rendering of violent movement. Signorelli probably took part in the decoration of the *Sistine Chapel, *c.*1482 (*Death and Testament of Moses* is credited to him), where Perugino was apparently the chief master. Signorelli's own masterpiece is the fresco cycle in Orvieto Cathedral, begun in 1499 and perhaps finished by 1502 (last payment, Dec. 1504). This cycle had been begun, in 1447, by Fra *Angelico, with ceiling paintings of the Last Judgement, and Saints, Prophets, and Martyrs, completed by Signorelli. In 1494 Orvieto was bypassed by the French armies on their way to Naples (much the same thing happened in 1945 during the German retreat), and this salvation probably spurred the *operai—who had been negotiating with Perugino—to complete the chapel as a thank-offering. This commission suited Signorelli's dramatic talents very well, and he extended the Last Judgement theme down to the walls of the chapel from 1499, with the *Signs of the end of the world over the entrance arch, and the story of *Antichrist in the first bay to the left of the entrance (it has been plausibly suggested that Antichrist was inspired by *Savonarola). This fresco includes portraits of Angelico and Signorelli himself, in front of the picture-plane and pointedly disregarding the temptations offered by Antichrist. Opposite the Antichrist fresco is the *Resurrection of the Flesh*, with fairly realistic-looking skeletons emerging from their graves. The second bay on the left has the *Calling of the Elect* (i.e. they are on the right of Christ in the *Last Judgement*), which leads into the *Entry into Paradise* on the altar-wall: opposite is the fresco of the *Devils seizing the Damned* and driving them into Hell. It is particularly noticeable that the demons are not the grotesque animal-like creations of medieval fantasy, but all too human creatures, but in the livid colours of decaying flesh, taking sadistic pleasure in their brutal task. This scene extends on to the right altar-wall and has figures of Charon and Minos from classical mythology, who recur in *Michelangelo's *Last Judgement.*

The sources for the cycle, apart from the Gospels of Matthew, Mark, and Luke, and the Apocalypse (cf. Antichrist), are the **Golden Legend*, the visions of *S. Bridget, and apocryphal writings such as the 'Apocalypse of Thomas', and the great sequence of the *Dies Irae*.

This cycle is Signorelli's undisputed masterpiece, and, although he was in Rome in 1508 and again in 1513, by then his fame had been eclipsed by that of *Raphael and Michelangelo. He returned to his native Cortona and maintained a provincial workshop until his death. His dated works continue until 1521.

Signs of the end of the world According to the accounts in Matt. 24: 29–31, Mark 13: 4–27, and Luke 21: 7–27, before the Second Coming of Christ, the *Parousia, and the Last *Judgement, there will be signs in Heaven and on earth of the impending end of the world. These dire events are also less explicitly described in the Book of Revelation, as well as in the Apocrypha of Thomas. They amount to about fifteen signs, which include the appearance of false prophets claiming to be Christ (*see* ANTICHRIST), Christians led into apostasy, and also earthquakes, famine, war, and pestilence. The sun will be darkened, the light of the moon will fail, and stars will fall from the heavens. The last sign will be the Son of Man in the Heavens, with angels blowing trumpets.

The best examples of this subject in art are in the fresco cycle by *Signorelli (1499–*c.*1504: Orvieto Cathedral), where in the fresco over the entrance arch he depicts the wrath of God falling from the sky upon the earth below. In an adjacent fresco he depicts the Antichrist preaching, while his followers demand money, and swagger insolently, and the faithful are murdered by bravoes. In the background, the wrath of Heaven falls like thunderbolts on the wicked, and believers are martyred. The cycle proceeds with the joyful resurrection of the elect, and the blessed in Paradise, while the damned are carried away by devils. That the cycle was painted immediately after the fall of Savonarola in Florence, and during the violent campaigns waged by Cesare Borgia in his attempt to carve himself out a private fiefdom from the Papal States, accentuates the immediacy of Signorelli's vision of the world he felt was crumbling about him.

Simeon An aged prophet who, together with the prophetess *Anna, recognized the infant Christ during the *Presentation in the Temple (Luke 2: 22–32) and proclaimed Him as 'a light to lighten the Gentiles, and for the glory of thy people Israel'. Then Simeon blessed them, and said to His mother Mary, 'This child is destined for the falling and rising of many in Israel, and to be a sign that will be opposed so that the inner thoughts of many will be revealed—and a sword will pierce your own soul too.' Nothing more is known of either Simeon or Anna.

Simon of Cyrene *See* STATIONS OF THE CROSS.

Simon, feast in the house of There are accounts of a feast in the house of Simon in all the Gospels, but they seem to relate to two different men, and three separate incidents. The account in Matt. 26: 6–13 tells how, two days before the Passover, Christ went to a banquet in the house of Simon the Leper in Bethany (who must have been cured of leprosy, either by Jesus or by one of his disciples, otherwise he would have been an outcast) and a woman came with a jar of costly ointment and poured it on His head as he sat at table. There were murmurs about the waste and how it might have been sold and the money given to the poor. Christ's reply was, 'Why do you trouble the woman?... For you always have the poor with you, but you will not always have me. By pouring this ointment on my body she has prepared me for burial... wherever this good news is proclaimed... what she has done will be told in remembrance of her.'

The account in Mark 14: 3–9 is virtually identical, both placing the incident immediately before the Passover, and Christ's prediction of his forthcoming death.

The account in Luke 7: 36–50 is different. This time the moment is before the death of John the Baptist, and Christ had been asked to eat at the house of a Pharisee called Simon. A woman, hearing that He was eating there, came and stood weeping behind Him, bathing His feet with her tears, kissing them, and drying them with her hair; she then anointed His feet with the costly ointment in her jar. There were murmurs about the waste, but He silenced them by telling the parable of the two debtors who were forgiven, one who owed much and one little, asking which would love the creditor more? Simon answered, the one who had been forgiven more. Jesus then pointed out to him that no water had been poured on His feet when He entered, no kiss had been given Him, no ointment had been poured on His head, but she had never ceased to do all these things to His feet. Simon, within himself, had said that Christ, if He were a prophet, should have known that this woman was a sinner, and have repulsed her. But He ended His reproof by saying that '... her sins, which were many, have been forgiven; hence she has shown great love. But the one to whom little is forgiven, loves little.' Then He said to her, 'Your sins are forgiven', and when those at table protested by what right He forgave sins, He said to her, 'Your faith has saved you, go in peace.'

The account in John 12: 7, 8 is different again, and would appear not to be a banquet given by Simon, in that the time is after the raising of Lazarus and six days before the Passover, and the occasion was a banquet in the house of Martha and Mary in Bethany at which Lazarus was present. But the anointing with perfume is a feature of this banquet also, in that Mary took a pound of costly perfume made of spikenard, anointed Jesus's feet with it and wiped them with her hair, so that the house was filled with the fragrance. The murmurer against waste was Judas Iscariot, but as S. John scathingly remarks, this was not because he cared about the poor, but because he was a thief and stole from the common purse. Jesus merely said, 'Leave her alone. She bought it so that she might keep it for the day of my burial. You always have the poor with you, but you do not always have me.'

Most of the medieval illuminators who painted this incident in their Gospels seem to have settled on the account from S. John's Gospel rather than the ones in SS Matthew, Mark, or Luke, obviously because it follows on so well from the raising of Lazarus. It appears in a *Homilies* of S. Gregory Nazianzus of 867–86, painted in Constantinople; and in 1015–22 on the bronze column of Bishop Bernward at Hildesheim. A miniature in a psalter of *c.*1260 from the Upper Rhine, now in Besançon, has an odd duplication of the scene, with one woman pouring the perfume on Christ's head, while another wipes His feet with her hair. The subject did not find much favour during the Renaissance, except with Veronese, who painted it twice, once in 1560 (Turin), and again *c*.1572 (Louvre), and there is a Tintoretto of 1562 in Padua. An 18th-century treatment of the subject by Antonio Gabbiani is in Dresden.

Simone Martini *See* MARTINI.

Simon Magus, as the name implies, was a magician, whose story is in Acts 8: 9–24. After the death of Stephen, Philip—not the Apostle, but Stephen's fellow deacon—went to Samaria to preach the Messiah to the Samaritans. A man called Simon practised magic there, and the people believed in him and called him 'the power of God that is called Great'. Philip preached with great success, and even Simon believed and was amazed at Philip's miracles. When the Apostles in Jerusalem heard of the success of Philip's mission, they sent SS Peter and John to baptize the converts with the Holy Spirit, since they had only received baptism in the name of the Lord Jesus. When Simon saw that the Spirit was conferred by the laying on of hands by the Apostles, he offered them money for the same power to be granted to him. S. Peter cursed him, and Simon appeared to repent. (This is the sin of 'simony': the offering of money for a spiritual benefit, or for a benefice.) According to the Apocryphal Acts of Peter, Simon went to Rome before S. Peter did, and continued his magic there. The Apocryphal Acts recount fantastic stories of the contest between S. Peter and Simon Magus and the magician's eventual defeat. He undertook to fly over the Sacred Way (presumably the Sacra Via) in Rome, but he fell and broke his leg in three places as S. Peter had prayed. He was carried out of the city to Aricia (Ariccia?) and died there.

S

Simon Stock, Saint (*c*.1165–1265), also called Simon Anglus and Simeon Stock, became General of the Carmelite Order at a great age (*c*.1247). He joined the Order when it arrived in England, and when he became General he obtained papal approbation for the changes in the Rule which the Order made when it left Palestine after the failure of the Crusades. He reorganized it on the lines of the mendicant Orders, after which it spread rapidly, particularly in England. An Order of enclosed nuns was founded in the Netherlands in 1452, which had great success in France, Italy, and Spain. During the 16th century the discipline was much relaxed, but was re-established by S. Teresa of Avila and S. John of the Cross.

One of Tiepolo's most splendid ceiling paintings is of the *Virgin appearing to S. Simon Stock* in the Scuola Grande del Carmine (1739–44), and granting him the scapula which is one of the emblems of the Order. There is also a relief by Ignaz Günther (1748) on the high altar of the Carmelite convent church in Reisach.

Simon Zelotes, Saint, or **Saint Simon 'the Less', Apostle,** was called by Matt. 10: 4 and by Mark 3: 18, 'the Cananaean', and by Luke 6: 15, 'Simon who was called the Zealot', inferring that he had been a member of the Zealots, a Jewish party of revolt which Josephus mentions as having resisted Roman rule in Galilee, and which later moved to Jerusalem. There seems to be little justification of the name as applied to Simon, and it may well be no more than a personal description of him as zealous. He is always associated with another Apostle, S. Jude, and they are invariably coupled together in dedications. In the Eastern Church he is misidentified with Nathanael (*see* BARTHOLOMEW). According to the **Golden Legend*, Simon and Jude were brothers of James the Less, and sons of Mary of Cleophas, wife of Alphaeus. Jude was sent on a mission to Agbar at Edessa, while Simon preached in Egypt, and then both went to Persia, where they confounded local soothsayers, who revenged themselves by having them martyred. The *Golden Legend* says that Simon died in Edessa, but according to other texts, he returned to Jerusalem after being in Egypt, and on the death of James the Less was made bishop. The later histories of both saints are very confused; it possibly was Simon, son, rather than grandson, of Cleophas, Joseph's brother, who became bishop, which is confirmed by *Eusebius. Simon is said to have been martyred by crucifixion, at a great age, by Trajan, during the conquest of Jerusalem in AD 70, but by others to have been sawn in two in Persia at an unknown date.

He is commemorated in Venice in the church of San Simeone Piccolo, which contains a 17th-century painting of his martyrdom, by Bortoloni, and an 18th-century picture of him preaching by F. Penso. He is represented in the cloister of Moissac; with S. Jude in a mosaic in the right aisle of St Mark's, Venice, and also by a bronze figure by Dalle Masegne in St Mark's. He is in a series of eleven Apostle heads by Ribera (1615–30: Prado); a head by Rembrandt in a series of Apostles (1661: Zurich) has him holding his attribute, a saw (but also a falchion in Greek images, or a book), and he is included in paintings of the extended family of the Virgin by the Master of Frankfurt (15th cent.: Frankfurt), and Quentin Massys (1509: Brussels). *See* KINSHIP OF CHRIST.

Sinai, Mount, is in the desert between Egypt and Palestine, and is held to be sacred to God. It was the site (Exod. 19: 3 ff.) of the encounters between *Moses and *JHVH (God), when He gave Moses the Law, which the prophet was to lay down to the Jews, after God had liberated them from slavery in Egypt. Moses had been in the area—or close to it—before (Exod. 2: 15–22; 3: 1 ff.) when in flight from Egypt he had taken refuge in Midian, and had tended there the flocks of his father-in-law Jethro. It was during one of his forays for pasture below Mt. Sinai that JHVH spoke to him from the burning bush, and commanded him to lead the Jews out of their captivity in Egypt.

In the valley below Mt. Sinai is the convent of St Catherine, which grew out of a fort built by the Emperor Justinian in 530, to protect hermits who had settled on the holy mountain. It is the smallest independent community of the Othodox Church, proclaimed so in 1575, with its own archbishop who is also the abbot. The collection of early icons is famous, and the library contains a celebrated collection of early MSS, from which came the late 4th-century Codex Sinaiticus, once in the Imperial Museum, St Petersburg, but sold in 1933 to the British Museum.

El *Greco painted two versions of *Mt. Sinai and S. Catherine's convent*, taken apparently from a popular engraving sold to pilgrims to the convent (*c.*1567: Modena, and Hatvani Coll., Budapest). They are among his earliest Venetian works.

Sindone *See* SHROUD.

Sinopensis, Codex This 5th/6th-century MS was found at Sinope in Turkey and is now in Paris (BN). It consists of part of the Gospel of Matthew with illustrations: the miniatures are smaller than those in the *Rossano Codex, and all are at the base of the 43 pages, following the words they illustrate. Each has a prophet on either side with texts related to the scene. These include new scenes of *Herod's Feast* and the *Beheading of the Baptist*, the earliest to show Herod with a gesture of revulsion at the sight of the ghastly trophy. The MS was probably made in Asia Minor, and the figures are expressive and lively characterizations, though with less nobility than those in the Rossano Gospels. Although they introduce new subjects they are not as important iconographically as the Rossano or *Rabbula Codices. Sinopensis is one of the very few MSS written in gold and silver on purple vellum, which suggests that it was made for a Constantinopolitan patron.

Sins, Seven Deadly *See* DEADLY.

Sippe, die heilige *See* KINSHIP OF CHRIST.

Sisera *See* JAEL.

Sistine Chapel The principal chapel of the Vatican. The Great Chapel, now called the Sistine Chapel, was preceded by an earlier chapel which, as is the custom with palace chapels, was entered from an upper floor, in this case through the Sala Regia, and therefore had a vaulted substructure with its own windows and doors. It was not a chapel for daily use, its function being to provide a venue for those ceremonies at which the pope would officiate, when the papal court and, usually, the ambassadors of foreign powers and eminent foreign visitors would be in attendance. It also served as the place in which Conclaves were held for the election of a new pope. Nowadays, Conclaves overflow into the Sala Regia.

Its builder, Pope *Sixtus IV (hence its name), is usually credited with destroying the building of his predecessors, but it is clear that he—or his architect Giovannino de' Dolci—used as much as possible of the preceding structure, since some of the irregularities of the building would be impossible to explain in any other way. The present chapel is a rectangular brick structure, some 115 ft. long by 40 ft. wide, and about 65 ft. high, with a depressed barrel-vaulted ceiling, above which is a guardroom. The dimensions were not chosen haphazardly, but endeavour was made to conform to those of Solomon's Temple as they are given in 1 Kgs. 6: 1–38. Construction lasted from 1477 to 1481, with the painting lasting until 1483, when Sixtus attended a service for the first time. The chapel was divided into two equal parts by a marble screen or **cancello* with fine carved details. Above it on the right side was the slight projection of a marble balustrade which fronted the recess for the Sistine Choir. The 15th-century floor is of the type derived from the *Cosmati workmanship of the Romanesque period, known as Opus Alexandrinum, a complex pattern of inlays of various coloured marbles which mark out the processional way across the area reserved for the laity with large whorls of inlays, and that reserved for the clergy beyond the *cancello* with smaller islands of mosaic. Later the *cancello* was moved to increase the area reserved for the clergy, so that its position no longer marks the centre of the chapel, and no longer falls exactly in the centre of the choir balcony, neither does it match any longer the division of the chapel marked by, for instance, *Michelangelo in his divisions of the ceiling decoration. The walls and ceiling have series of frescoes, executed for Popes Sixtus IV, *Julius II, and Paul III, which are among the most important works of art created during the Renaissance. They include the series on the walls commissioned in 1481 by Sixtus IV from, notably, *Perugino, *Botticelli, *Signorelli, and Ghirlandaio, of the concordance of the *Story of Moses* with the *Life of Christ* as *type and antitype. They have the additional theme of papal supremacy, particularly important for the place where Conclaves for papal elections were held, and exemplified by Perugino's *Christ giving the Keys to S. Peter* (*Traditio Clavium). Below them, the walls are painted with fictive hangings, over which the tapestries designed in 1515 by *Raphael were hung on great feast-days. Between the twelve windows are full-length figures of popes by the artists of the 1481 frescoes, and below the windows runs a narrow walkway.

The ceiling was painted in 1508–12 by Michelangelo with the *Story of the Creation* to the *Drunkenness of Noah* in a series of nine histories to complete the story of the world told in the series on the walls below; the world before the Law on the ceiling, under the Law in the *Story of Moses*, and in the Age of Grace in the *Life of Christ—ante legem, sub lege, sub gratia*. On the curve of the vault are seven prophets and five sibyls, and in the lunettes over the windows are the Ancestors of Christ. Across the corners are the four divine deliverances of the OT—*David and Goliath, Esther and Ahasuerus, Judith and Holofernes*, and *Moses and the Brazen Serpent*. The wall above the altar is filled by Michelangelo's *Last Judgement*, of 1536–41.

The painting of the *Last Judgement* involved considerable modification of the existing scheme of the paintings: two windows in the altar wall had to be filled in, and all the existing paintings on that wall were obliterated. This meant destroying *Christ between SS Peter and Paul* in the first series between the two windows, which would have been what Jonah was pointing down to from the series of prophets, two of the scenes from the Moses and Christ series—*The finding of Moses* and the *Nativity of Christ*—and the Ancestors of Christ in the lunettes of the two lost windows. There was also an altarpiece on the wall, possibly an *Assumption* by Perugino (the dedication of the Chapel), damage to which by Lutheran soldiery during the Sack of Rome in 1527 may have been one of the reasons why the repainting of the altar wall was carried out.

The last work undertaken in the chapel was because the collapse, in the 17th century, of the lintel of the entrance door from the Sala Regia badly damaged the two paintings from the Moses and Christ series on that wall, and they were replaced by the same subjects, *S. Michael protecting the body of Moses* and *The Resurrection*, by two inferior painters, Hendrick van der Broek, known as Arrigo Fiammingo, and Matteo Perez de Alesio, known as Matteo da Lecce. The tapestries (the cartoons for seven of which are in the Royal Coll. and are exhibited in the V & A) are now in the Vatican Museum.

Sistine Madonna, the A painting by *Raphael (now in Dresden) was executed for the Benedictine church of San Sisto (S. Sixtus) in Piacenza in 1512/13. The Virgin, grave, barefoot, with veiled head and dressed in the simplest robe, bears the Christ Child in her arms as she walks on clouds—i.e. she is a vision. She is attended by two saints, Pope Sixtus II, a 3rd-century martyr, whose papal tiara stands on the parapet below him, and *S. Barbara, believed to have been martyred *c.*303, relics of whom were in the church. The picture is called the Sistine Madonna, not because of any connection with the Sistine Chapel, but because of Pope Sixtus, and because it was commissioned by the nephew of Sixtus IV, Julius II, to whom the figure of Sixtus bears a strong resemblance. He had been a patron for the rebuilding of the church for which he presented the altarpiece.

situla (Lat. urn) A small ivory bucket to hold holy water, for use on state occasions, e.g. the entry of the Emperor Otto into Milan in 980 (Milan Cath. Treasury), or the Basilewsky Situla, also used for Otto (London, V & A). Others are in Aachen Cathedral Treasury and New York (Met. Mus.).

Sixtine Chapel/Madonna *See* SISTINE.

Sixtus IV, Pope (1414–84). Francesco della Rovere was born into a very poor family in Savona (Liguria) and became a Franciscan friar; he was sent to the Universities of Padua and Bologna, acquiring a reputation as a theologian. He became General of his Order in 1464, was made a cardinal in 1467, and was elected pope in 1470. One of his first concerns was to promote a crusade, and he actually managed to gather enough money for a fleet, but received little practical help. The fleet took Smyrna, but quarrels between the Neapolitan and Venetian contingents resulted in the city, which should have served as a base for operations, being sacked and set on fire, and the Crusade then petered out.

Sixtus IV had numerous relations; his nephews were all given either rich worldly or ecclesiastical benefices, and members of the Ligurian community also received great benefits from him. When Sixtus became pope, before the year was out, two nephews, Giuliano della Rovere (later Pope Julius II) and Pietro Riario were made cardinals. By 1472 relations between Rome and Florence had become strained, and by 1478 were so bad that the pope supported a conspiracy by the Pazzi family to overthrow Lorenzo de' Medici. During the Sunday High Mass the conspirators fell on Giuliano and Lorenzo de' Medici; Giuliano was killed, but Lorenzo managed to reach safety behind the bronze doors of the sacristy. The conspirators rushed into the streets, trying to rouse the people against the Medici, but failed. The Archbishop Salviati, his brother, his nephew, and Francesco Pazzi were all taken at once and hanged from the windows of the Palazzo Vecchio, and anyone remotely connected with the conspiracy was also killed. War between Rome and Florence followed, with Florence also being attacked by an interdict, which the city ignored.

Eventually there was peace between the pope and the Medici, but the remainder of his reign was passed in a succession of struggles with Naples, and Venice, as well as with constant depredations by the Turks, who captured Otranto in Apulia in 1480, and slaughtered hundreds of the inhabitants in the cathedral. A long war between Venice and Milan, which also involved Naples, was further complicated by a violent feud between the Orsini and the Colonna families, both very powerful in Rome. In the summer of 1484 Sixtus died.

The thing most remembered (and unfairly so) about Sixtus is his nepotism, but when he became pope he had no Roman following to which he could turn for support in papal politics; he could rely only on his family. His achievements were considerable, however; he rebuilt the Sistine Chapel and the Lateran palace, he enormously increased the Vatican Library, appointing the Lombard humanist Platina (1421–81) as his librarian, he promoted the collection of antiquities for the Vatican collections. He founded the Sistine Choir, patronized art, and during his pontificate the series of frescoes in the Sistine Chapel—the 1481 series on the walls—was executed by artists imported from Florence. His patronage of humanists made Rome a centre of learning rivalling Florence.

His court artist was Melozzo da Forlì, who painted, *c.*1477, the fresco of the pope presiding over the founding of the library, surrounded by his nephews and with Platina kneeling before him. His splendid tomb by Antonio Pollaiuolo (Museum of St Peter's) celebrates his patronage of learning, and is a masterpiece of the bronze-caster's art.

Sixtus V, Pope (1525–90). Felice Peretti is another example, like Sixtus IV, of a poor boy entering the Franciscan Order virtually as a child, and rising through his talents to become pope. He was born near Montalto in the Marche, a poor farmer's son, and entered the local Franciscan convent when he was 12. He became a preacher, particularly powerful against heresy, and in Venice he was an active Inquisitor before becoming one in Rome. He was sent to Spain with the papal legate concerned with the affair of Archbishop Carranza of Toledo, who had been accused of heresy and whose case had dragged on for over ten years. On his return he found that his chief patron had become pope as Pius V, and the pope immediately appointed him as his confessor, and made him a bishop. In 1570 the pope made him a cardinal, but after Pius's death in 1572 Cardinal Boncompagni, whom he had accompanied when he was legate in Spain, became Gregory XIII, and their relations, strained during their Spanish visit, were very poor, and consequently he lived a very retired life in his villa on the Esquiline Hill. However, he enjoyed the friendship of S. Ignatius Loyola and S. Philip Neri. When Pope Gregory died in 1585, Cardinal Peretti was elected pope, taking the title of Sixtus V in honour of his Franciscan predecessor.

As pope, he was a man of great energy and determination, impetuous, with a violent temper, severe, prudent, respected, feared, but neither loved nor popular. He determined to curb banditry in the Papal States, promoted chiefly by the private armies of the Orsini and the Colonna, and he largely succeeded. He restored order in the Papal States with often ruthless vigour, and introduced important reforms in the government of the Church, such as the obligation for bishops to make visits every one or two years to Rome (the 'ad limines' visits) to render an account of their sees, and the establishment of the various 'Congregations' of the faith (bodies that inquire into heresies, are concerned with canonizations, etc.; originally, there were fifteen such Congregations, there are now nine). He reformed the curia, and fixed the number of cardinals at seventy (there is now no limit). He also restored the finances by creating new classes of honorary offices for sale which enabled him to spend on his public works. His artistic works, in view of his short reign, also testify to his energy. His first undertaking was the erection of the obelisk in front of St Peter's, which was done by Domenico Fontana over several months, but eventually with total success in September 1586. This was followed by the erection of other obelisks by Fontana: one outside the Lateran, another outside Sta Maria Maggiore.

Fontana was then employed to complete the Lateran palace (which is the one seen to this day). He also worked on the Scala Santa, moving one of the staircases to make the chapel more accessible. Sixtus ordered the statues of Trajan and Marcus Aurelius to be removed from their columns and replaced by SS Peter and Paul. He commissioned the grandiose tomb of his patron Pope Pius V for Sta Maria Maggiore, and also his own, no less imposing, on the opposite wall. He was enthusiastic about the enlargement of the Vatican Library, building for the purpose the wing which crosses the Belvedere courtyard, not only because more room was needed for the removal of the library from a damp part of the Vatican, but because he wished to prevent for ever the old custom of holding tournaments in the great courtyard.

In 1589 another of Fontana's major works for Sixtus was completed: the opening of the Aqua Felice, the aqueduct which brought new water, which he called after himself, from near Palestrina to Rome along the line of the ruined aqueduct of Alexander Severus of 222–5. The pope bought the water source from the Colonna family, and planned that it should supply the Esquiline, Viminal, and Quirinal Hills with a virtually inexhaustible water supply. He also negotiated the purchase of the Quirinal palace from the Este family as a summer residence for the papacy, the Vatican lying lower and less healthily in the great Roman summer heat. His grandest undertaking was the completion of St Peter's, by finishing the dome, work on which had stopped at the top of the drum when Michelangelo died in 1564. The work was begun in 1588, by Giacomo della Porta, and finished in 1590, the pope saying the first Mass in the completed basilica on 14 May 1590. The lantern, the mosaics inside the dome, and the lead covering, and the façade with the Benediction Loggia, still remained to be done. Unfortunately, for as many churches as he restored, he irretrievably damaged others by removing parts of their original construction, believing that he thus 'restored' them to their Early Christian appearance. His one failure was his new edition of the Vulgate, which required extensive correction before it could be used.

There is a fine portrait of Sixtus V by Scipione Pulzone, 1588, in the Corsini Gallery, one in the Vatican Library, probably by Pietro Facchetti, and another by Ottavio Leoni. There is a bronze statue of Sixtus in front of the sanctuary at Loreto by Antonio Calcagni (1589), who had once been in Michelangelo's studio.

SJ *See* JESUITS.

Slavophiles *See* RUSSIAN ART AND ARCHITECTURE.

snake *See* SERPENT.

Snow, Miracle of the This is a legend connected with the foundation of the basilica of Sta Maria Maggiore in Rome. A rich man, called Giovanni Patricio (the Patrician), prayed to the Virgin for guidance how best to use his wealth, since he and his wife were childless. That night, 5 August 352, she appeared to him, to his wife, and to Pope

Liberius (352–66) and told them to build a church in her honour where next morning they would find snow. Snow was found on the Esquiline Hill despite its being high summer, and all went in procession to the site. The pope outlined the shape of the church in the snow with his pastoral staff, and it was built there. According to another version of the legend, Giovanni was told in his vision to go to the Esquiline Hill, where he found the snow arranged perfectly in the shape of a church. The title Sta Maria ad Nives (St Mary of the Snows) has often been used for churches dedicated to her, because of her purity.

Sta Maria Maggiore was very badly damaged in riots after the election of Pope Damaso in 366, to whom the Romans objected because he was a Spaniard. The basilica was rebuilt by Sixtus III (432–40), after the Council of Ephesus in 431, which finally decided that the Virgin was the *Theotokos and not the Christotokos.

There is a rare representation by Masolino (*c.*1427/3: Naples) of Pope Liberius marking out the plan of the church in the snow. It is part of a dismembered altarpiece of which other parts are in Philadelphia and London (NG). One of the London panels has been attributed convincingly to Masaccio. Two semicircular canvases by Murillo (1662–5: Prado) also depict the story. They once hung in Sta Maria la Blanca in Seville, became French booty during the Peninsular War, and were restored to Spain after Napoleon's defeat.

soffit The flat part underneath an arch or window frame.

solea (Gk. high, royal place) There are a variety of interpretations, but it probably refers in early Eastern Christian and Byzantine churches to the raised enclosed platform or steps serving as a processional way from the *iconostasis to link it with the *ambo, or linking the apse with the nave. After *Iconoclasm it was no longer used, so that the term was applied to the portion of the *bema outside the iconostasis. It is also used for the semicircular step(s) outside the Holy Doors in a Byzantine church, virtually the same thing. Communicants kneel at this place to receive communion.

Sol Invictus (also **Sol Justitiae**, and Gk. **Helios**) was the Sun God worshipped in pagan Rome as the source of heat and light. The 'unconquered Sun' and the 'Sun of Justice' were terms sometimes applied to Christ. Excavations below St Peter's have revealed a 3rd/4th- (perhaps mid-3rd) century mosaic of Christ recognizable by His cruciform halo, in the chariot of the sun. The symbol sometimes appears on rings or seals.

Solomon was the third OT king of Israel, preceded by *Saul, and his father *David. He was the son of Bathsheba, whom David married after he had had her husband Uriah murdered; she persuaded David to give her son preference over his brothers, Absalom and Adonijah, the sons of other wives. Absalom rebelled against David and was killed; Adonijah was supported by Joab, whom David had deposed from his rank as general, and after David's death and Solomon's succession, Adonijah tried to obtain David's last concubine for himself (to obtain a king's wives or concubines implies victory or rights over him). It cost Adonijah and Joab their lives (1 Kgs. 2: 19–34).

Solomon obtained his wisdom as a gift from God, for when God asked him in a dream what he would most desire, he asked that he should have 'an understanding mind to govern your people, able to discern between good and evil; for who can govern this your great people?' (1 Kgs. 3: 5–15). It was because of his reputation for wisdom and splendour that the Queen of *Sheba came to visit him. Perhaps the greatest test of his discernment was his ability to distinguish between the true mother and the false one in the story of the two babies (1 Kgs. 3: 16–27).

Two women, both prostitutes, who lived in the same house, had both given birth to boys, but during the night one overlay her child and when she saw that he was dead she took the other woman's son and put her dead son in the other woman's bed. When the second woman looked closely at the dead child she saw that it was not her son. Both claimed the living child. Solomon said, 'Bring me a sword', and when one was brought, he said 'Divide the living boy, and give half to one, and half to the other.' The woman whose son was alive cried out to the king not to kill the child, but rather to give it to the other woman, while the other woman wanted the child divided. 'Give the first woman the living boy. Do not kill him. She is his mother.'

God made a solemn covenant with Solomon and promised him that if he obeyed His commandments, and kept His statutes, then He would maintain him on the throne of Israel, him and his house for ever, but that if he turned aside from His laws, and set other gods before Him, then He would cast him out, and his house would become a place of desolation (1 Kgs. 9: 3–9).

Despite Solomon's great reputation he remains a more shadowy figure than David. The impressive state he kept is evidence of the wealth his country derived from straddling one of the major trade routes in the Middle East between Mesopotamia—the Great Kingdom on the Euphrates—and Egypt, and trade provided the money he spent on building a magnificent Temple for the Lord, in the belief that a truly impressive capital would seal his position as a great king. In the Temple he is supposed to have included the ornate twisted columns known as *Salomónicas. He used Hiram of Tyre to sail the Mediterranean for him, and obtained from him timber, skilled craftsmen, and smiths for his building projects. But he was obliged to use levies to pay for them, and forced labour for the work, and also to pledge some of his cities to Hiram to finance them, and Hiram found them but a poor return for his gold. He cemented his trade treaties with foreign marriages—a Pharaoh's daughter, and women from foreign lands—and this ultimately was his undoing, because they led him into idolatry. For them, he built altars to strange gods, and kept these festivals with them, and so angered God that though He kept Solomon on his throne, the next reigns were all beset with troubles. Rehoboam, who succeeded him, did not have a peaceful reign, and only inherited part of the kingdom.

Solomon is credited with Odes, which he clearly did not write, or have written, since they were either in Greek or Syriac originally, and may be a Christian version of a Jewish text as late as the 1st or 2nd century. Solomon is also said to have written eighteen psalms, but these also are much later—probably from the time of the Roman invasion of Pompey, between 70 and 40 BC. They speak of a land overcome by divine retribution for sin, and two of them predict the coming of a Messiah of the house of David, who will save his nation and rule justly. There are two, however, which are credited to Solomon in the Psalter—72 (Vg. 71), which begins 'Give the king your justice, O God . . . May he judge your people with righteousness . . . ', and later (v. 15) says, 'May the gold of Sheba be given to him . . . ', and 127 (Vg. 126), which begins 'Unless the Lord build the house, those who build labour in vain . . . ', both of which are reminiscent of Solomon's prayer for wisdom, and his building of the Temple.

'The Song of Solomon' is also known as 'The Song of Songs', or the 'Canticles', and is an OT book included in the Hagiographa (Gk. sacred writings), that is, books not belonging to the Law or the Prophets. It appears to be a collection of love poems ascribed to Solomon and his beloved, the Shulammite, and their courtiers. Its language, which is frankly erotic, suggests that it probably dates from about the 3rd century BC, but it may include earlier poems. From an early date, Christian, as well as Jewish, textual critics have interpreted the work allegorically—it could hardly be included among sacred writings otherwise. In the Talmud it is held to be an allegory of God's love of the people of Israel. Christian writers have interpreted it as God's relationship with the Church or with the faithful soul. Such commentaries exist from the 2nd and 3rd centuries, and it has been much favoured by mystics, receiving one of its most famous commentaries in the 86 *Homilies on the Canticles* of S. Bernard of Clairvaux. Other mystics who have written on them include S. Teresa of Avila and S. John of the Cross, particularly in his *Spiritual Canticle*.

Yet another book has been ascribed to Solomon: the Book of Wisdom or, as it is more generally called in the Bible, the Book of Proverbs. These are a mixture of advice, admonition, warnings, encouragements to good behaviour, and heartfelt counsels against temptation, such as 'a prostitute's fee is only a loaf of bread, but the wife of another stalks a man's very life'. Or such as 'Go to the ant, you sluggard, and consider its ways . . . '. They were ascribed to Solomon because of his reputed wisdom, and so might carry more weight, but they were a mixture of Jewish religious teaching and Greek philosophy of the Alexandrian type, and date in all probability from the 1st century BC. They were important in Christian teaching because of their strong morality, and appear to have influenced S. Paul, and the epistles of SS James, Peter, and John as well.

There are Christian prototypes in the story of Solomon. He rode into Jerusalem on an ass, to be anointed by Zadok the priest, a foreshadowing of Christ riding into Jerusalem before the Passion. When Solomon received Bathsheba he did her the greatest honours, rising to meet her, bowing before her, and seating her at his right hand. This is held to be a prototype of Christ seating the Virgin at His right hand and crowning her.

There is a figure of *Solomon enthroned* in the synagogue of Dura-Europos, *c.*230; a 10th-century enamel of *Solomon entering Jerusalem* in Vienna, KHM; *Solomon's Dream* (11th cent.: Arras Bible, Paris BN); Nicholas of Verdun: *Solomon and the Queen of Sheba* (Klosterneuberg Altar, 1181); a figure of Solomon on the Virgin Portal of Amiens Cathedral, 14th century; Sebastiano del Piombo: *The Judgement of Solomon* (*c.*1509: Kingston Lacy, National Trust); Raphael: *The Judgement of Solomon*, ceiling panel in Stanza della Segnatura (*c.*1509: Vatican); Pietro da Cortona: *Solomon*, fresco cycle (1625: Rome, Pal. Mattei di Giove).

Sophia, Santa (Gk. *Hagia Sophia*, Holy Wisdom), was one of the greatest churches in the world, which began as a Byzantine church, was briefly westernized during the Crusades, Byzantine again, and then finally for nearly five hundred years a mosque, before being secularized in 1934. It was built by the Emperor Justinian to replace the preceding cathedral, burnt down during the Nika riots in January 532 which turned from a battle between rival sporting factions into a full-scale anti-government riot lasting eight days, burned the heart out of the city, and nearly cost Justinian his throne—and which probably would have done had it not been for the courage of his Empress Theodora.

He had two architects: Anthemios of Tralles, of whom little is known except that he was a mechanical and structural engineer practised in geometry and mathematics, who died probably in Constantinople before 558 (the traditional date of *c.*534 is wrong), and Isidore of Miletus, held to have been both architect and mathematician, who also died before 558, since Isidore the Younger rebuilt the dome after the collapse in 558. Neither is known for any other architectural work.

The church was the second on the site. The first Hagia Sophia ('Divine Wisdom', that is, Jesus Christ) was burned down during riots after the second banishment of S. John Chrysostom in 404 and rebuilt by 415; the second was destroyed during the Nika riots, with Hagia Irene, the Chalke or entrance of the Palace, the baths of Xeusippos, and part of the Senate House on the Augustaion. Justinian began the rebuilding of the city, and especially of the cathedral, immediately after the wreckage of the rioting had been cleared away. Work started in December 532, and lasted five years from start to dedication on 27 December 537. Procopius, twenty years afterwards, wrote a history of the building of the church, in which he records Justinian offering the building to God and adding the words, 'Solomon, I have excelled you!'

The church is unique: it combines the central plan with the longitudinal axis by being a single vessel under a huge dome 107 ft. across with 40 windows round the base. This dome was buttressed by semi-domes at either end, but with vaulted aisles on either side visually separated from the central space by colonnades and the huge piers which uphold the dome. While the centre is a single space, rising without interruption from floor to apex of the dome, the four massive columns on either side bear six lighter columns, so that on either side of the central space there are spacious vaulted galleries at first-floor level. The entrance is through a double, vaulted *narthex: the narrower, plain exonarthex with a fountain in the centre is entered through five doorways from the forecourt, while seven entrance doors give into the inner, or esonarthex, much wider and grander than the exonarthex. The imperial entrance was at the far south end, and as the emperor entered he faced a mosaic of the *Donations*, showing the Virgin receiving the city from Constantine and the church from Justinian—though this mosaic was late 9th/early 10th century, like the one over the main door representing *Leo VI kneeling before Christ*, dating from the late 9th century (Leo VI reigned from 886 to 912), thus Justinian himself would never have seen either, though many of his successors did. The imperial entrance was the central larger doorway of the group of three in the middle of the esonarthex, from where the full splendour of the central domed space opens out. To immediate left and right there are small apsidal shapes with two columns bearing four columns and a semi-dome, and overhead is part of the first-floor gallery surmounted by a huge semicircular window which lights the interior. On either side are the piers and the columns which serve both to conceal the aisles and support the galleries on the upper floor. In 558 there was a partial collapse of the dome, repaired by Isidore the Younger, who raised it by over 20 ft., giving it extra stability by changing its profile slightly. After the rededication five years later, *Paul Silentarius wrote his descriptive poem. The church has also endured earthquake damage more than once, and in 989 the main arch in the west collapsed with its semi-dome and part of the main dome.

Massive buttresses have also been added to the outside. When the Turks took Constantinople in 1453 they converted the church into a mosque and added a minaret to each corner; they defaced the mosaics, and also added the forest of hanging lamps which are such a feature of early representations of the interior.

The interior was covered with multi-coloured marble revetment, all the capitals were intricately carved and pierced, and parts of the walls were covered with marble inlays, but there was little mosaic decoration. There were later emperor and empress votive mosaics on the walls of the galleries, a marvellous late 12th-century *Deësis*, a huge cross (now gone) on the central dome, and enormous archangels on the pediments, now only partly surviving. The centre of the church was reserved to the clergy, and to processions along a raised *solea to and from the *bema to the *ambo. The emperor had a special 'box' on the left side of the apse; he was the only layman who ever entered the bema. The empress and her court used the gallery facing the apse, the rest of the gallery was the *gynaeceum, and men found what space they could in the aisles. The altar and the ciborium were of gold, and across the apse were twelve columns which bore curtains to screen the altar from view. Perhaps the church is best summed up by the description the Russian envoys sent back to Prince Vladimir of Kiev which decided him to make his country follow the Eastern rather than the Western Church rite: 'We knew not whether we were in heaven or on earth. For on earth there is no such splendour or such beauty, and we are at a loss how to describe it. We only know that God dwells there among men, and their service is fairer than the ceremonies of other nations. For we cannot forget that beauty.'

S

Sorrowful Mysteries *See* ROSARY.

Sorrows, Man of *See* MAN.

Sorrows of Mary Often called the Seven Sorrows, or Seven Dolours, the number varies, but they are usually (1) *Simeon's prophecy at the Presentation (Luke 2: 35; 'And a sword shall pierce your own soul too'); (2) the Flight into Egypt; (3) the absence of Christ for three days, disputing with the Doctors in the Temple; (4) the Way to Calvary; (5) the Crucifixion; (6) the Deposition; (7) the Entombment. The hymn 'Stabat Mater' describes Mary grieving at the foot of the Cross. *See also* ROSARY.

Soudarion *See* MANDYLION.

soul, symbols of the The classical symbol of the soul was normally the butterfly, and it appears also in many catacomb paintings, where it is derived from classical sources. A new-born child is also an image of the soul, particularly if borne up to God in a napkin, which represents Abraham's bosom, a frequent form for the depiction of bliss. A bird is also considered to be a symbol, since a dove was said to have left the body of the Virgin, and some saints, at the moment of their deaths. The peacock was believed to have incorruptible flesh, and thus to be immortal, and the cry of the peacock during the night was believed to be the souls of the dead crying for mercy. Birds, either drinking from a fountain or pecking at bread, represent the soul seeking the Eucharist for its nourishment. The skull is the commonest emblem of death, rather than the soul, but it serves as the constant reminder of the soul's need of perfection, as the emblem of hermits and mystics.

Souls, All, is a very ancient commemoration of the 'faithful departed', probably linked with the Feast of *All Saints, and held on the next day (i.e. 2 Nov.). It was certainly known by 837, but its popularity arose through Odilo of *Cluny, who ordered all Benedictine houses of the Cluny congregation to keep it in 998. From them it spread to become universal. The great Latin sequence of the *Dies Irae* has inspired many composers, but there seem to be no works of art specifically associated with it, other than the dedication of many churches and colleges.

soutane French for *cassock.

Spain *See* EUROPE.

spandrel The triangular space between two arches or across the corner of a vaulted space—for instance, in Michelangelo's Sistine Chapel ceiling, double spandrels cross the corners of the ceiling where it meets the walls.

Spanish missions *See* NORTH AMERICA.

Spasimo, lo (Ital. agony) The term is sometimes used to describe a representation of the Virgin fainting beside the Cross, or on the way to Calvary. *Lo Spasimo di Sicilia* is a title given to Raphael's *Christ falling beneath the Cross* (*c.*1516: Prado), originally in Sta

Maria dello Spasimo in Palermo, Sicily. According to Vasari, the ship carrying it to Sicily was wrecked near Genoa, but the case containing the painting floated safely to shore and the Genoese did not want to give it up, and it required the intervention of Leo X to get it to Palermo. It was subsequently taken to Spain for the collection of Philip IV in 1662. *See also* SWOON.

Species, the Sacred The consecrated bread and wine of the *Eucharist. Also called the Elements.

Speculum Humanae Salvationis (Lat. Mirror of Human Salvation) Together with the **Biblia Pauperum*, this was one of the most important *typological books of the later Middle Ages—about 350 MSS are known, together with *block-books and early printed editions. It was written *c.*1324, probably by a Dominican, but the author is also sometimes identified as *Ludolf of Saxony. Unlike most typological books, which have one OT subject, or sometimes two, to each NT subject, the *Speculum* has three types to each NT antitype. Because of the difficulty in finding suitable subjects the types are occasionally taken from Jewish or secular history. Like Ludolf's *Vita Christi* the *Speculum* was very popular in N. Europe, but less so in Italy.

A *Heilspiegelaltar* (Mirror of Salvation altar) was commissioned from the Swiss painter Konrad Witz *c.*1435, but only twelve fragments have survived, mostly in Basle Museum. Unfortunately the large central panel is lost and it is not known what the subject was, or even if it was a painting rather than a relief. However, two of the surviving panels represent the extremely unusual subjects of *Julius Caesar's general, Antipater, showing his wounds* and *King David with the Three Heroes*. Both these subjects occur in the *Speculum*, as types of Christ interceding for humanity, and of the Adoration of the Magi.

Speculum Majus (Lat. The Great Mirror) The greatest of the late medieval encyclopaedias (cf. ISIDORE OF SEVILLE), compiled by the Dominican Vincent of Beauvais (*c.*1190–1260), who settled in Beauvais *c.*1229 and wrote the *Speculum* 1247–59 in three parts, the *Speculum Naturale, Speculum Doctrinale*, and *Speculum Historiale*: the fourth, *Morale*, was probably planned by Vincent, but is not his work and is based on *S. Thomas Aquinas's *Summa*. The *Speculum Majus* attempted to codify all human knowledge, and it has been estimated that it summarizes the work of some 450 authors, pagan and Christian. It was certainly the source of much medieval art, especially *Bestiaries, and had a specially powerful influence on French Gothic art, e.g. cathedral portal sculpture and stained glass.

Spencer, Sir Stanley, RA (1891–1959) An English painter whose *The Resurrection: Cookham* (1924–6, Tate) was claimed by the critic of *The Times* to be 'the most important picture painted by any English artist in the present century ... the combination in it of careful detail with modern freedom of form. It is as if a Pre-Raphaelite had shaken hands with a 'Cubist'' (1927). Something of the villager about him (his father played the organ at the parish church) brought him home to Thames-side Cookham in Berkshire each day from the Slade School of Art, London, which he attended (1908–12), winning a composition prize. At one level the village (its streets, houses, characters, boats, swans, and gardens) occupied his imagination, but art and literature invaded it, too. These pressures collided, cohabited, and combined. So Giotto's fluttering curtains, uniting the twin *Annunciation* scenes in the Scrovegni Chapel, Padua, multiply and form a backdrop to Spencer's *Christ carrying the Cross* (1920). Spencer's religious sensibility was often nurtured by this 13th-century Italian source: his comprehensively planned and executed programme (1928–9) of altarpiece and friezes for the War Memorial Chapel at Burghclere, Hampshire give a serviceman (on the home front, and then in Macedonia) the space to reflect on war. True to form (and in line with epic, too) Spencer attended to the detail of daily military life in the lateral friezes, but then went on to lift up the horror of the innumerable crosses delivered in quiet ecstasy back to the Christ figure in the large reredos mural. The same detailing, relish in patterning and texture, varied palette, and united atmosphere is found in reredos as in frieze, as it was to be in rendering front gardens, bedrooms, still-lifes and, later, portraits and landscapes. Pevsner's European viewpoints on Burghclere (in *Hampshire and the Isle of Wight* 1967) corrects any estimate of Spencer as 'rustic' or quaint:

> the Burghclere paintings are England's prime contribution to European Expressionism and ought to be visited by foreigners and Englishman alike ... He painted the interior from 1927 to 1932, but based

S

> his work on sketches made immediately after the war ... he was twenty-seven in 1919 and thirty-six, and at the summit of his art when he started in the chapel.

Pevsner elaborates the European reference in his writing about the east wall *Resurrection of the Dead*:

> we are looking at all this at an odd angle, as if from the air. This device to combat everyday normality was familiar to the Mannerists of the C16 ... yet no one in England in 1932, let alone 1919, knew about Mannerism ... parallels with Casorati and even de Chirico, and also the German *Neue Sachlichkeit* ... one must be grateful to the church authorities for having tolerated a cycle as silent about organized religion as about the glories of a won war.

When his Slade contemporaries graduated they scattered home and abroad, but Spencer was always journeying inwards. Readings *en famille* had filled his mind with imagery from the Bible and from spiritual writers: he portrayed *John Donne arriving in Heaven* (1911), and in the following year came *The Nativity* and *Joachim among the Shepherds*, works which startled his Slade teachers into admiration. This tormented, shifting spirituality emanated from a religious background that was 'a hybrid nonconformist-evangelical Anglicanism, and the emphasis was on God's omnipotent goodness and love rather than on His wrath and the perils of hell fire' (Farr). For the artist's own thoughts on paintings completed and envisaged, and on his bumpy marital and erotic relationships, Adrian Glew's *Stanley Spencer Letters and Writings* (2001) offers a good selection. The 'villagey' nature of the artist's life is well captured in John Rothenstein (ed.) *Stanley Spencer: The Man, Correspondence, and Reminiscences* (1979).

S

spire, steeple A spire is a tall, slender cone or pyramid, often octagonal, which is erected on a *tower as a decorative feature. A steeple is a combination of a tower and a spire.

Spires appear early in the West and develop from the elongation of conical roofs. One of the commonest, yet most complex, forms is the broach spire, which starts either directly from the top of the tower, or from inside a parapet, as four triangular bases, and continues as a slender, higher octagonal spire. It is one way of raising a spire without having to go to great height. In Germany, the triangular bases are often still part of the tower, so that the spire rises from a tall, pointed attic storey; this type is known as a Rhenish helm. Other types of spire rise inside the parapet of the tower, some with corner pinnacles for added decoration, some with small flying buttresses from the pinnacles to brace the spire, some just as a tall sharp, needle-like form. Many German, and German-inspired, churches have very high, open-work spires—*tours de force* of delicate masonry—and a late Gothic example such as Freiburg im Breisgau has three such spires. A *flèche* (Fr. arrow, no English equivalent) is a slender pinnacle perched over the crossing or the choir of a church. They are rare in England, though there is a fine one on the roof of St Edmund, Southwold; they are also found in Germany, and the one over the choir at Reims is an excellent example. They do not appear to serve any vital function, but mark a change in the roof line.

After the Renaissance, spires died out, but were popular again during the Gothic Revival of the 19th century. The most fantastic spires of modern times are those by Gaudí on the Sagrada Familia (Holy Family) in Barcelona, of which so far only the nave has been consecrated.

Spirit, the Holy *See* TRINITY, THE HOLY.

Spirit, Seven Gifts of the *See* GIFTS.

Spiritual Exercises, the, were written by *S. Ignatius Loyola during the period he spent in retreat in the cave at Manresa before he began his mission as a religious. They consist of a series of meditations—mental exercises, rather—spread over a period of retreat, during which the mind is directed first to the nature and consequence of sin, and to the Four Last Things—Death, Judgement, Heaven, and Hell. In this initial stage, however, Heaven is temporarily put aside, and the mind is directed to the consequences of the other three, and particularly, to the awful consequences of Judgement. The nature of death, the trappings and surroundings of death, and therefore of both its inevitability and the irrevocability of its aftermath, are vividly presented to the mind. The events of Christ's earthly life from the Incarnation, His penurious birth in a stable, the hazards of His childhood spent in flight and as a refugee in Egypt, the recognition at His baptism of the moment when His mission on earth had begun, His preaching (above all, the Sermon on the Mount) and His miracles, their nature and their purpose, are all to be evoked and visualized as nearly as possible as personal experiences. Eventually His betrayal,

His trial, Passion and His agonizing death, are all to be pictured, felt, experienced mentally and as nearly physically as possible, so that these events are considered not as sufferings undergone in the past, but eternally re-created, re-inflicted, by the fact of mankind's continued sinfulness. Finally, the mind is encouraged to consider the joy of the Resurrection, the bliss of the Ascension, and the nature and power of God's love of mankind, with the overriding question 'What have I done to be worthy of this?' All through these meditations, the role of the Virgin, as the mother of Christ and as the Mother of the Church, is paramount in bringing home the nature of the sacrifice made for mankind and the price paid for redemption.

Many who have not been members of religious Orders have undergone the mental discipline of the *Exercises*, difficult though they are. Above all, it is their visual realism, almost it might be said, their tactile quality, which is impressive. It is known, for example, that *Bernini practised the *Exercises*.

SPIRITUALITY AND CHRISTIAN ART

Spirituality, understood broadly but within a Christian frame of reference, may be said to take its origin and character from a verse from the opening chapter of Genesis, a verse pregnant with meaning—'and the Spirit of God moved upon the face of the waters'. The Hebrew word, here translated as 'Spirit', could as easily be rendered 'spirit' or 'wind', and 'moved upon' could perhaps be better translated as 'was hovering over,' for the process continues: spirituality is the experience (or study) of how the invisible but real divine wind or spirit engages with the raw, unformed chaos of life and matter, bringing forth identity, order, meaning, and purpose. In Genesis, this process includes the creation of human beings in the divine image and likeness, with a special responsibility for their fellow-creatures. In the New Testament, Saint Paul takes this process further still: spiritual life is our willingness to allow ourselves to be changed into the likeness of Christ, who is 'the image of the invisible God' (Col. 1:15). Hence 'all of us ... seeing the glory of the Lord as though reflected in a mirror, are being transformed into the same image from one degree of glory to another; for this comes from the Lord, the Spirit' (2 Cor. 3:18). So spirituality becomes that process by which the divine Spirit changes those it invades into the image and likeness of Christ, and so sets them free from any kind of slavery (which Paul calls life 'according to the flesh') to be a part of the transfiguration of the entire creation, until it too is set free for 'the freedom of the glory of the children of God' (Rom. 8:21). Four key words outline this process, with particular reference to art: the role of *images*; the means by which we see the *glory* of the divine; the attraction or *beauty* of God; and the way art can nurture a spiritual life which is in itself an act of *resistance* to all that enslaves and destroys.

Images

If human beings are in some respect images of God, however defaced by sin, then the use of images in Christian art assists in the process of being restored to a lost likeness by becoming more Christ-like. The Bible is, however, ambivalent about images (*see* JEWISH AND CHRISTIAN INTERACTIONS), using the same word for image as is used in Genesis 1:26 to describe our creation in the divine image. The Septuagint, or Greek translation of the Hebrew scriptures, translates the Hebrew with a Greek word 'icon', so introducing a word that will have a significant future in the development of Christian art. It is important to note that both the Hebrew and the Greek denote something real, not simply a Platonic shadow or external appearance of an inner spiritual reality (Heb. 10:1). And in the New Testament Epistles, icon is used to describe Jesus: '... those whom [God] foreknew', writes St Paul, 'he also predestined to be conformed to the image of his Son' (Rom. 8:29). The use of images in the Bible is not, of course, restricted to humans; and Christian spirituality's pervasively visual component takes much of its origins in the Psalms, which deploy a vast array of images, overwhelmingly (though not exclusively) drawn from the natural world, and which use visual language extensively. The teaching of Jesus is also rich in imagery: indeed he almost invariably uses images, not concepts, and stories (rather than abstract philosophy) in his teaching.

It is therefore not surprising to discover the importance of images and the language of image in Christian thought and art. In general terms, theologians recognized the power of images as complementary to verbal formulations in conveying truth, though Western Christian thinkers, following Augustine, tended to be anxious about the potential of artistic images to mislead the unwary. And even in Eastern Christianity the ambivalence about the visual made itself felt. In the 8th and 9th centuries of the Christian era, especially (though not only) in the Byzantine empire, a fierce dispute (which came to be known as the Iconoclastic Controversy) arose about the use of images in Christian art and worship. Hitherto, at least from the end of the 2nd century of the Christian era, representational art had flowered among Christians as it did across the Roman world generally. The controversy was eventually settled in favour of the use of images, although Reformed theologians (notably *Calvin) disapproved of their use. Thereafter the use of images in art (and especially the icons of the Orthodox tradition whose composition is in itself an act of contemplative prayer) was important in making spiritual truth accessible to those who could not read, as declared by Saint *Gregory the Great and so making accessible the God who became incarnate in Christ. In Christian spirituality, the use of the imagination is a powerful resource, but it needs educating and directing appropriately. The use of images in religious art, from paintings in great cathedrals to Victorian drawings in Sunday School manuals, helped to inspire and to direct imaginative prayer; and this finds expression in the language of liturgy, in meditative prayer (such as the rosary), in hymnody, in charismatic choruses, and in countless other ways.

Seeing the Glory

Contemplating images is not only or primarily a physical process. In a society saturated with images of every kind, the act and art of seeing differ from those of a pre-Enlightenment society. Early Christians, following Plato, became like what they contemplated: hence really to see anything was to come close to it (not spatially but spiritually), and to participate in what was seen. The rich programmatic decoration of a church either with icons (in the *Byzantine tradition) or with paintings, stained glass, and carvings (in the Western tradition) had one overriding purpose above all others: to make the one who worshipped or visited there into a participant of the mysteries depicted. To enter one of these buildings is to be invited to become a participant in the truth of its story.

But for this to happen the one seeing had to be willing to be changed by what was being contemplated. There is space to suggest only a few of the many approaches to this in the Christian spiritual tradition. For Plato and those who were influenced by him, this required a willingness to discern the spiritual (that is, non-physical, or strictly speaking, metaphysical) reality (or 'form') that lay behind it, just as an icon on a modern computer both points beyond itself and offers access to a larger program that lies beyond. Others took a different view, involving a radical devaluation of the physical that was ultimately incompatible with the Christian doctrines of creation and incarnation. The 20th-century Orthodox theologian Sergei Bulgakov argued instead that the unique role of human beings, created in the divine image, is to see the unity of the beautiful, and its implication as pointing to a divine artist, without devaluing the physical universe around us:

> One common aesthetic function exists for humanity: the creation of beauty, art. Although art is reserved for creatively gifted individuals, it ... is rescued from atomistic multiplicity, irreducible to one revelation of beauty, by the fact that it has a common language, that beauty is accessible in the entire multiplicity of its forms. Thus this unity of beauty also presupposes a transcendental subject of beauty, a universal artist, and a common source of beauty: Beauty itself.

The 20th-century French philosopher Simone Weil believed that art seeks to make evident 'the infinite beauty of the entire universe': unlike Plato, she believed that, rather than seek the really real beyond the material, we must instead strip ourselves of the illusion that we are at the centre of the universe, in effect taking the place of God: this renunciation of self allows us to be transformed inwardly by what we look at. More recently, John Drury, in his *Painting the Word* (1999), reflecting on how we look at Christian art, has expressed this process of 'unselfing' in terms of sacrifice.

Sallie McFague has suggested that we must reject a Platonic approach that exalts the spiritual at the expense of the physical, and seek instead to see things, neither as signs nor as objects but as fellow subjects, resisting the temptation to remain outside and in control, and instead, as participants rather than spectators, come close to what we see in the manner (and with all the attendant risks) of a genuine encounter.

So in practice, for example, Leonardo da Vinci painted his *Adoration of the Magi* (1481, Galleria degli Uffizi, Florence). As Professor Martin Kemp has pointed out, Leonardo has represented Christ's arrival on earth as a profoundly unsettling event: the painting combines 'the balanced symmetry suitable for the ritual of worship with a tangled turbulence which expresses extremes of spiritual agitation'. Strange faces depicting a wide variety of emotions are staring at the scene while the three kings reverence the child. Two mysterious figures flank the composition, probably representing the viewer, who is invited to consider how the birth of this child might be understood, its import for the world, and its ordering if kings worship a child born in poverty. In the final analysis the Christian response to such a mystery can only be that of the magi: adoration. And adoration means doing what they did, and what on Good Friday Christ did: giving unconditional love and reverence to God. Adoration effects a change in viewers, lifting them out of self, into a larger sphere, at once more demanding and more generous, in fact the mirror-opposite of a narrowly utilitarian, profit-oriented worldview. Contemplating art thus elicits a response of adoration and wonder, as this painting is designed to do, it begins to change both the viewer and the viewer's world.

The beautiful

Art manifests the beauty and the attractiveness of the divine, which is also manifested in nature. Hence the Wisdom of Solomon declares that 'from the greatness and beauty of created things comes a corresponding perception of their Creator' (13:5; cf. Rom. 1:20–23); and in the Christian spiritual tradition, beauty and goodness were for centuries inseparably linked. In the New Testament, the same word can mean both 'beautiful' and 'good': thus, in the Septuagint translation of the opening chapter of Genesis, which describes God creating the universe, the words translated 'and God saw that it was good' could as accurately be rendered 'and God saw that it was beautiful' (Gen. 1:10). Beauty (one might say) made goodness attractive; one of the Latin words for beautiful describes something that is finely formed, that has form and purpose and meaning. It was one of Augustine's great contributions to Christian life and thought to recognize that beauty could be found not only in what was formally attractive, or what might be believed to reflect Plato's 'forms' or eternal realities, but in the seeming degradation of human suffering:

> In what sense was [Christ] fair of form on the cross? Because God's foolishness is wiser than human wisdom, and God's weakness more powerful than human strength [1Cor. 1:25]. Let us therefore, who believe, run to meet a Bridegroom who is beautiful wherever he is . . . Beautiful he is as a baby, as the Word unable to speak . . . beautiful in his miracles but just as beautiful under the scourges, beautiful as he invited us to life, but beautiful too in not shrinking from death, beautiful in laying down his life and beautiful in taking it up again, beautiful on the cross, beautiful in the tomb, and beautiful in heaven.

But the links between physical objects and metaphysical realities, between beauty and goodness gradually dissolved, uncoupling ethics from aesthetics to their mutual detriment. George Steiner has pointed out that the Holocaust took place in a country that was heir to some of the finest art and culture the world has seen. Hans Urs von Balthasar has attempted to restore the link between beauty and goodness by looking at the beauty of the divine revelation in creation, to see the glory not only in creatures as images of their Creator but in the ultimate, degrading extremities to which the divine love is willing to go in order to reveal its character and transforming power (which is why for Balthasar the Christian doctrine of Jesus' descent into hell is so important).

This is no academic point: countless depictions of the suffering Christ, in churches and medieval wayside shrines, reflect this. In Mexico (*see* NORTH AMERICA), the Day of the Dead (celebrated around the feast of *Todos Santos* or All Saints at the beginning of

November) is marked by an outpouring of artistic creativity to accompany the traditional ceremony of offering food and drink for the dead, praying for them, and asking them to pray for the living. Flowers, candles, *papier mâché* tableaux, children's art, painted pottery, and images of Our Lady of Guadalupe (the patron saint of Mexico) festoon households, cemeteries, and streets in celebration of the resurrection of the dead. The beauty of this celebration lies precisely in its transience and fragility: death, often violent and random, disrupts and abbreviates earthly life; but in this great annual festival it is itself both subverted and, so to speak, out-imagined, so that even in the midst of death indestructible love and beauty can be glimpsed.

Spirituality and Resistance

In this way art—both the 'high' art of cathedrals and great painters, and the popular art of family and community—continues to nurture a spirituality of resistance to all that enslaves and destroys human life. Two examples of many may illustrate the point. During the Second World War, about 15,000 Jewish children were transported to the Nazi concentration camp at Terezín. Of the hundred survivors, some responded to their terrible fate by drawing pictures and writing poems, in which prayers and religious imagery are mingled with observations of the beauty of the world around them and beyond.

The second example, in St Andrew's Metropolitan Cathedral, Glasgow, is Peter Howson's painting of the Martyrdom of St John Ogilvie, the Scottish Jesuit priest who was tortured and killed at Glasgow Cross on 10 March 1615 for refusing to accept the king's spiritual jurisdiction. Howson depicts the saint, standing calmly, even serenely, with a noose round his neck, staring directly at the viewer. You are not looking at him. He is looking at you. Here in this powerful work of art is the epicentre of any authentic spirituality: here, the divine Spirit is bringing to birth meaning and hope even in—in fact precisely in—the midst of the most terrible evil and fear.

Spiritual Works of Mercy There are seven: (1) to convert the sinner, (2) to teach the ignorant, (3) to counsel the doubtful, (4) to comfort the sorrowing, (5) to bear wrongs patiently, (6) to forgive injuries, (7) to pray for the living and the dead. *See also* CORPORAL WORKS OF MERCY.

Sposalizio, lo *See* ESPOUSAL.

springing The springing of an *arch is the point at which it starts from its supporting element—a pier, or the plinth at the top of a column. A stilted arch is one in which the beginning of the curve of the arch is well above the point where it springs from its support—it could be described as having a 'delayed' springing. It is a common feature of the choirs of Romanesque and Gothic churches where the arcade turns to form a semicircle in the apsidal end.

squinch The alternative and earlier method to a *pendentive in reaching across the corner between two walls or two arches to create a surface on which a dome or a drum may be raised. It consists of building a succession of arches from one wall to the other, one above the other, each projecting further forwards than the one below so that with a similar arrangement rising from the other walls, it will form an octagon at the top, which may easily be bridged. It is only suitable for fairly small domes, and is frequently found in the crossing of Romanesque churches. Conques, one of the pilgrimage road churches, is a good example. It was superseded by the pendentive, though these were used in Hagia Sophia in Constantinople five centuries earlier.

squint Some medieval churches may sometimes be found with a hole or slit cut through the wall which would enable someone to see the altar from outside the church. It is usually believed that this device was made in order that a leper might attend Mass without mixing with other people, but there is no evidence for this. A hole in a pier, or even in an interior wall, was sometimes made to enable the altar to be seen for the elevation of the Host. The device is also known as a *hagioscope*.

SRE (Lat. *Sancta* [or *Sacra*] *Romana Ecclesia*) Holy Roman Church, usually as part of a cardinal's title e.g. Johannes Smith SRE Card. on a tomb or title-page.

staff *See* CROSIER.

stag *See* HART.

STAINED GLASS

As a means of incorporating the windows into the decoration of churches, stained glass may have begun with the Byzantine use of *transennae of wood or stone with the interstices filled with pieces of coloured glass; one has been found at the 7th-century Sant'Apollinare in Classe, outside Ravenna. Pieces of glass embedded in calms (H-shaped strips of lead used to join the pieces) sufficient to make a small window have been found with objects of the late 8th or 9th centuries in France. Glass windows are recorded in the 9th-century annals of the cathedral of Auxerre, in Burgundy, and the Romanesque cathedral of 1076 records windows for which special maintenance provisions were made, similar to those of Abbot Suger at *Saint-Denis. The oldest surviving examples of Western stained glass are the head of Christ, of 1050/1100 from Wiessenburg, Alsace (now in Strasburg, Frauenhaus Mus.), four full-length, life-sized figures of prophets made for the nave of Augsburg Cathedral between 1050 and 1150, and the lower part of an *Ascension* of *c.*1140–50 in Le Mans Cathedral. Older stained-glass windows rarely survived the rebuilding of their churches, the glass itself was reused, as for instance at St-Denis when the choir was rebuilt in the 13th century. Sometimes older windows were incorporated into new work, as at Chartres, when the large *Virgin and Child* recovered from the ruins of the church burnt in 1174 became the *Notre Dame de la Belle Verrière* (Our Lady of the beautiful window) inset into a window of the rebuilt church, and clearly distinguishable by its lighter blues from those of the 13th-century window which now frames it. The iconography of stained-glass windows is never inventive; they served as vivid illustrations of the Bible, the Gospels, and the lives of the saints for those who could not read.

The technique described by *Theophilus in the early 12th century varied little over the centuries, except in the colouring of the glass. The design was usually drawn out on a white board the size of the window and the pieces of coloured glass were cut to shape and inserted into the lead calms, which followed the major outlines of the design, though the drawing of details—faces, hands, hair, draperies—would be done with a black pigment which was given a light firing to fix it, and shading of forms was by a brown pigment in three depths of colour, used as a wash and then fired in. The joins in the calms were soldered together with tin, and wires were soldered in to hold the windows to strengthening bars called saddle-bars; a strong iron armature was embedded in the window frame and the saddle bars were fixed to it to prevent wind damage. The armature was an important part of the design since one of rectangular panels would have straight bars where a design with circular panels would have an armature to match.

The glass in early windows is usually of strong colours, but in Cistercian churches only plain glass was allowed, with the slightly greenish tinge of the natural glass, and the calms were always arranged in abstract, never figurative, designs. The colours were made by mixing various iron and copper oxides to the molten glass, which might be coloured all through—'pot metal'—or applied by dipping pieces of white glass in the coloured glass. This process, called 'flashing', was always used for red, because red pot metal was so dense in colour that light could not penetrate it effectively, and the beauty—and the point—of stained glass is its translucence. In the early 14th century the discovery that chloride of silver, applied to glass, produced a yellow stain which could be varied from a pale to a deep amber resulted in the development of new colours by flashing the silver yellow on to the limited primary range. Technical improvements also removed the greenish tinge to make clear glass almost colourless.

The great period of stained glass was from the late 12th to the mid-15th century with the windows of Chartres, Bourges, Sens, and Auxerre in France, and Canterbury, York, Gloucester, and Tewkesbury in England. By the late 15th century the flat, two-dimensional character of the early windows was lost through the imitation of three-dimensional painting, with its chiaroscuro and perspective effects. This led to groups of windows being treated as a single unit, as at King's College Chapel, Cambridge (1515–*c.*1531), with small rectangular panels less dependent on pieces of glass joined by calms than on the grid of saddle-bars, and the narrative ignoring the boundaries set by the stone transoms. Eventually the technique itself was abandoned, as at St Jans, Gouda, in Holland, where large narrative windows were rectangles painted with vitreous enamels (1555–1603).

Stained glass, being predominantly a religious art, suffered first from the Reformation, then from changes in architectural taste, and from its rejection by the 'Enlightenment' in France, when many Gothic windows suffered the same fate as medieval sculptured portals. Its main secular use was in heraldic glass; for this the later vitreous enamel technique was more common. During the *Gothic Revival, stained glass returned to favour, forming an essential part of the decoration of new buildings inspired by enthusiasm for the romance and sanctity of the Middle Ages. Firms active at this time included: Clayton and Bell; Burlison and Grylls; Heaton Butler and Bain; Charles Eamer Kempe; and finally Ninian Comper. Truly original work was produced from 1860 onwards by Edward Burne-Jones and William Morris, whose values fired the burst of creative energy known as the Arts and Crafts movement. In stained glass from 1900 to 1930, the key practitioner was Christopher Whall, whose teaching influenced Louis Davis, Karl Parsons, Douglas Strachan, and Henry Payne, as well as women artists in glass Wilhelmina Geddes, Margaret Aldrich Rope, and Mary Lowndes. Of particular merit are the First World War memorials to be found in many places of worship.

In response to the Second World War, in the United Kingdom the reassertion of traditional values allowed surviving Victorian firms a period of prosperity (Goddard and Gibbs, Clayton and Bell, Whitefriars). Basil Spence's Coventry Cathedral was the most dynamic and inspiring building of this post-war period, with stained glass by John *Piper, Patrick *Reyntiens, and the Royal College of Art team (Keith New, Geoffrey Clarke, and Lawrence Lee), and revolutionary engraved glass by John Hutton. Fine work within the figurative tradition continued to be made by Christopher Webb, Francis Skeat, John Hayward, John Lawson, David Hillman, and the brilliant Hungarian artist Ervin Bossanyi during the slow process of reconstruction that continued into the early 1960s.

New stained glass in France (*see* EUROPE) was fostered by the Dominican monk Father Marie-Alain Couturier, who encouraged renowned artists and architects to collaborate with glass studios in the production of inspiring new images for the medium. Marc *Chagall, Georges Braque, Henri Matisse, and Le Corbusier all created stained-glass designs for churches with his support.

Meanwhile in Germany (*see* EUROPE), architects and glass artists were using stained glass as an uncompromising architectural material. The influence of Georg Meistermann, Ludwig Schaffrath, and Johannes Schreiter was especially important in bringing clarity of design to the medium during the 1970s and 1980s. The fashionable, intellectual, and highly skilled windows produced at this time deeply affected many students including the young British artist Brian Clarke. His dramatic, colourful windows showed the beauty of stained glass as a medium for modern architecture (Victoria Quarter, Leeds).

By the 1990s, however, screen-printed, kiln-formed, and laminated glass had become the techniques of choice for glass artists such as Alexander Beleschenko and Martin Donlin. The Church continued to commission interesting work from Tom Denny (Hereford Cathedral and Durham Cathedral), Alan Younger (St Albans), and Graham Jones (Westminster Abbey). Probably the most permanent memorials to Queen Elizabeth II's Diamond Jubilee in 2012 were stained-glass windows by Douglas Hogg (Queen's Chapel of the Savoy) and Leifur Breidfjord (Southwark Cathedral).

stalls *See* CHOIR STALLS.

standing crosses *See* CROSSES.

Stanze, le (Ital. rooms) These are rooms on the third floor of the Vatican which lie over the Appartamento Borgia, painted and decorated by Pintoricchio for Pope Alexander VI, which Pope Julius II refused to use, so great was his detestation of his predecessor, whose arms and emblems of the Borgia Bull were everywhere in the decoration.

Three rooms make up the Stanze, painted between 1509 and 1517 by *Raphael and his assistants. The first is the Stanza della Segnatura (... of the sealing), and was where papal briefs were signed and sealed. It was also Pope Julius's study and private library, and where final appeals were heard in causes in which the Pope exercised the *Signatura Gratiae* and the *Signatura Justitiae*, the two *swords of Spiritual and Temporal Justice, and documents with the papal seal confirmed the findings.

The second room is the Stanza d'Eliodoro, and the third is the Sala dell'Incendio. The ceilings of all the rooms are vaulted and painted, and because of their shape, all the walls meet the vaulting in such a way that the tops of the paintings which cover the four walls are wide hemispheres. At the base of the paintings there is a deep dado which is now painted, but which originally was covered by intarsia bookcases. The themes which governed the three rooms were worked out with great care, and in the case of the Segnatura were strictly appropriate to the function of the room.

The walls and the ceiling of the Segnatura are covered with roundels relating to *Justice*, *Theology*, *Philosophy*, and *Poetry*, and between them and lower towards the walls are rectangular panels with subjects relating to those in the roundels nearest to them on either side, so that each rectangular picture has two points of reference. Justice and Theology are accompanied by the *The Fall of Man* and Justice also joins with Philosophy in the *Judgement of Solomon*. Philosophy and Poetry are united with *Urania*, who symbolizes the intellectual power and divine harmony of the Universe, while Poetry and Theology are joined in *Apollo judging Marsyas*, with a double reference to art and the punishment for flouting divine authority. The four rectangular panels are painted with a fictive gold mosaic background, and are partly by Raphael and partly by Sodoma, who served as his assistant. The walls have huge frescoes with Raphael's first masterpieces, the *Disputa* and the *School of Athens* facing each other. The first, despite its ambiguous title, is not a 'dispute', but a 'disputation' on the Holy Sacrament, which stands exposed on the altar around which the whole concourse is gathered. In the sky filled with angels is God the Father; below Him, God the Son in a wide aureole, and below Christ, God the Holy Ghost, a dove floating in an aureole, completing the Trinity. Christ holds up His hands to show the wounds of the crucifixion, and is flanked on either side by the Virgin and S. John the Baptist (the traditional Deësis) and by the Elect, a gathering of Patriarchs, Apostles, and Saints, seated on the clouds of Heaven and accompanied by angels holding the Gospels. The earthly gathering round the altar which is conducting the disputation consists of Fathers and Doctors of the Church, Theologians and Philosophers. The *Disputa* corresponds to the ceiling roundel of Religion. The wall opposite has the fresco of the *School of Athens*, corresponding to the roundel of Philosophy. It is a gathering of the most celebrated philosophers of antiquity: in the centre at the top of the steps are Plato and Aristotle, who stand with gestures characterizing their philosophies, Plato pointing up to the celestial regions, Aristotle down to the material world. Round them stand other luminaries including Socrates and there are also groups of teachers, such as Pythagoras and Euclid, Ptolemy, and Zoroaster with their students, who include (apparently) Bramante, which is not unlikely in view of the very grand architecture of the rooms in which they are assembled. There is a striking figure of Diogenes sprawled on the steps and in the foreground a solitary figure of Heraclitus, leaning on a block of stone, and generally identified as a portrait of Michelangelo. Raphael included himself, with Sodoma, in the far right side. The other frescoes correspond with the roundels above them: *Poetry* with *Parnassus*, where the Muses surround Apollo, and *Justice*, with below three of the four *Cardinal Virtues*—Fortitude, Wisdom or Prudence, and Moderation or Temperance (Justice is missing, but may be inferred from the two frescoes below). In spaces below the Cardinal Virtues are two scenes concerning Justice; these are commemorations of legal events: *The Emperor Justinian granting the Pandects*—his code of civil law—and *Pope Gregory IX granting the Decretals*—the recently codified body of canon law. Pope Gregory is clearly a portrait of Julius II. There are also some fill-in frescoes of lesser importance below *Parnassus*.

The second room is the Stanza d'Eliodoro (... of Heliodorus), which is dedicated to subjects portraying Divine intervention on behalf of the Church: *Heliodorus prevented from robbing the Temple*, *The Liberation of S. Peter*, *The Mass of Bolsena*, and *Attila repulsed at the gates of Rome*. The ceiling has frescoes of four major divine interventions in the OT—*God appearing to Noah*, *Moses and the Burning Bush*, *The Sacrifice of Abraham*, and *Jacob's Ladder*. This is the last room decorated for Julius II, who is portrayed seated in the *Sedia Gestatoria, surrounded by his court. Opposite is the Attila fresco, painted for Pope Leo X, seen confronting the invader, who recoils before the vision of SS Peter and Paul in the sky above the Pope. The other two frescoes are among Raphael's greatest masterpieces: *The Mass of Bolsena*, with Julius kneeling before the altar where the doubting priest witnesses the miracle of the Blood on the corporal. Below the praying Pope is a splendid group of the Swiss Guards in their full uniform. The remaining fresco is of *The Liberation of S. Peter* (Acts 12: 3–17), with, in the centre, the Apostle freed from behind the prison bars by the angel in an effulgence of light, on the right side the angel guiding the bemused S. Peter through the gates of the prison, and on the left, the guards stunned by the light sprawling across the steps. A striking feature is the way the contrasts of light are managed: moonlight shining through a cloudy sky, the blaze of light from the prison, and the flickering torchlight from the brand the soldier is holding.

The Stanza dell'Incendio (. . . of the fire) was painted for Pope Leo X; the subjects are miracles on behalf of the Church: *The Fire in the Borgo*, when the fire was halted at the intercession of Pope Leo IV; *The Battle of Ostia*, when Leo IV's victory over the Saracens saved Rome; *The Coronation of Charlemagne* by which the pope claimed temporal as well as spiritual power; and the *Oath of Pope Leo III*, which he took to refute a slander and to establish an important rule of Canon Law. It follows very closely the design of the *Mass of Bolsena*. Except perhaps for the designs, the last three frescoes have little to do with Raphael. The fourth room, the *Sala di Costantino*, is entirely given up to battle pieces by Giulio Romano painted after Raphael's death.

The first two rooms, and the *Fire in the Borgo* in the third constitute one of the major works of Raphael, and established him among the great artists of the High Renaissance.

S

Star of Bethlehem *See* MAGI.

Station churches, days Pope Gregory the Great (590–604) decreed that certain Roman churches would have fixed ceremonies on more solemn days, called *statis diebus*—Station days. These involved fasting, and the Station was usually on a Wednesday or a Friday. It is probable that the Pope first encountered the custom in Constantinople, since he does not appear to have invented it. A Station consisted of meeting at a church near the Station church, forming a group or *collecta*, and then going in procession, usually with hymns and prayers, to a Mass which, if it were held at one of the major basilicas, would be said by the pope or his representative. These Stations were marked in the old Roman Missal: there were 84 in all, held at 40 different churches, but only 45 were at major basilicas. Many Stations, even at major basilicas, were on less important days, and many were held at less important churches. Station days clustered in Advent, and from Christmas to Epiphany, during Lent and the Easter season, and ended at Pentecost.

The custom still survives, despite changed conditions in modern Rome, at least for the Lenten Stations, some of which are held in the early morning, others in the afternoon. The pope only officiates at one Station, the Ash Wednesday one at Sta Sabina.

Stations of the Cross This is a Catholic devotion, of Franciscan origin, and of particular importance during Lent, as a rehearsal of the Way of the Cross or *Via Crucis* which Christ trod on His way to His death. Once they were erected only in Franciscan churches, but were extended to all Catholic churches in 1731, and the Stations are marked with a cross (this is essential) and a number on the walls, but no more, in their most basic form; otherwise, accompanied by a painting or relief depicting the particular scene. The number is now fixed at fourteen, but when they were first devised and the number and incidents had not been fixed, there were often as many as twenty-two, and in some churches even more. The cross on the wall is the essential sign, because in Jerusalem the sites from which the custom of following the *Via Crucis* arose were marked on house walls with small crosses.

While from the earliest times pilgrims to Jerusalem visited the places where Christ suffered, in so far as they could still be recognized, the various points on His last journey were included in a general visiting of sites. When the *Via Crucis* was first walked, about 1285–91, it was followed in reverse, starting with Golgotha and working back to Pilate's seat of judgement. By the 13th century, a legend had grown up, elaborating a story recorded by a Syriac writer as early as the year 34, that the Virgin used every day to visit the places where her Son had carried His cross, and also other places such as the site of His baptism. Eventually the Franciscans, who were recognized by the Turkish authorities as the Guardians of the Holy Places, appear to have established a route. When

Turkish restrictions on the movement of pilgrims became harsher, such pilgrimages inside the city took place as near dawn as possible, to avoid friction between Christian pilgrims and the local inhabitants. William Wey, a fellow of Eton College, visited Palestine twice—in 1458 and 1462. Under the guidance of the Franciscans of Mount Sion he did the tour round the holy places like all the other pilgrims, and he refers to them as 'Stations', but he does not give this name to any of the holy places outside Jerusalem. The reason for calling the devotion a 'Station' is because it was—and still is—always made standing. Another early sign of a fixed route dates from 1480, with a pilgrim called Felix Fabri, who left a long account of the Virgin's daily walk covering the ground of her Son's journey to Calvary, but he too walked in the reverse direction. His description of his pilgrimage makes clear how difficult it was to visit the Holy Sepulchre in the face of the obstruction of the Muslim key-holders, and it must largely have been because of the desire of those who never attempted such a journey to have a similar type of 'domestic pilgrims' way' that the idea of the Stations of the Cross arose.

The first were those set up in Nuremberg by Martin Ketzel as a result of his pilgrimage about 1468, which were carved by Adam Krafft and completed probably before 1490. There were only eight, known as the Seven Falls of Christ, since all except the last, which was a Deposition, were illustrations of Christ either falling under the cross or struggling to rise. Other sets at Leuven dating from 1505, and at Bamberg dating from 1507 are also recorded. Although called the Seven Falls, they usually comprised eight scenes, and many had actual distances marked between them—so-many steps or double steps—and a writer who describes the Leuven ones in 1666 says that it was the custom to follow them on a devotional pilgrimage, particularly in Holy Week. By the 17th century, Calvaries, as they were called, were a common feature of French (particularly Breton) churchyards, and spread to S. France, Italy, and Germany. From later devotional works it is clear that the Seven Falls cover other incidents as well, since the Falls coincide with the meeting with His mother, the incidents of Simon of Cyrene, Veronica and her veil, and the meeting with the women of Jerusalem.

The devotion that emerged from the numerous accretions accumulated by the end of the 17th century bore no resemblance to the actual experience of walking the *Via Crucis* in reality, so that their eventual systemization into the present series of fourteen is a logical solution to what otherwise could have become a muddle. The choice of incidents, like the number of them, is far more due to 16th-century writers of devotional works than to any route actually trodden by pilgrims. The incidents were chosen and codified into the fourteen by a Franciscan, S. Leonardo of Porto Maurizio (1676–1751) in the 1720s as (1) Christ is condemned by Pilate, (2) Christ is laden with His cross, (3) Christ falls for the first time, (4) Christ meets His sorrowing mother, (5) Simon of Cyrene is forced to help Christ with the cross, (6) Veronica wipes Christ's face with her veil, (7) Christ falls for the second time, (8) Christ meets the women of Jerusalem, (9) Christ falls for the third time, (10) Christ is stripped of his garments, (11) Christ is nailed to the cross, (12) Christ dies on the cross, (13) Christ's body is taken down from the cross, (14) Christ is laid in the sepulchre.

The spread of the devotion was slow. S. Alfonsus Liguori adapted the Stations for his Redemptionist Fathers (which he founded in 1732) and with them it spread into Austria and thence into France and England, although the Stations were not said in the Oratory Church in London until 1854. Some very extensive Stations exist in a number of churches, usually in the grounds leading up to them, as at the pilgrimage chapel on the hill outside Würzburg, or in the very elaborate Italian ones at, for instance, the *Sacro Monte at Varallo, or the long covered arcade climbing the hill to the pilgrimage church of Monte Berico outside Vicenza.

It would be invidious to try to select examples for particular notice since every Catholic church has a set, but a fine set by Eric *Gill is in London, Westminster Cathedral. Giandomenico Tiepolo made a set of paintings of the Stations for San Polo, Venice, in 1747–9, and from them a fine set of etchings in 1749. There are 16 plates in all, 14 for the Stations, plus a frontispiece and a dedication, and the series is entitled *Via Crucis*, following the devotion written for the sacramental by S. Alphonsus, which is the one still in common use. Others exist, notably one by Cardinal Newman.

In recent years the freedom of treatment given to artists commissioned to design these scenes has led to renderings of great diversity. These examples are worthy of note: Angel Zarraga (1936, Saint-Ignace-de-la-Cité-

Universitaire-de-Paris, Gentilly, France); Henri Matisse (1949–52, Chapelle du Rosaire, Vence, France); Bertin Ahrin (mid-20th century, Benin); W. T. Monnington (1966, St George's, Brede, Sussex); John Keating (1953, St John's, Tralee, Ireland).

stave church A form of church, specific to Norway, of which thirty-four still exist, out of a known 322. They are entirely timber built, and the construction is derived from shipbuilding. They are also called 'mast' churches, because they are built from tall pine masts, arranged as a frame to uphold the steeply sloping roofs rising in tiers one above the other. The high nave is open to the roof, the aisles are narrow, and the walls are thick timber planks held together with diagonal crossbeams. They are the earliest form of Christian church in Norway, built from the 11th century onwards, and even as late as the 16th century. Typical examples are at Urnes and Borgund, near Alesund, and Torpo, on the Hallingdal, near Oslo. Urnes is probably the oldest, of *c.*1100; the masts of the nave are double, with the lower columns having cubic capitals and a second tier of masts rising from them. The carved decoration at Urnes is very rich, giving its name to the type of interlaced, twisted tendrils and elongated beasts which decorate columns and doorways. Borgund dates from *c.*1150, with an apse added *c.*1175 with its own circular roof. Round the church is a covered walk, so that the silhouette is of three tiers of roof crowned by a three-tiered steeple, and the corners of the roofs are ornamented by dragons. There is a separate belfry similarly built. Borgund does not have the rich decoration of Urnes, but the masts rise uninterrupted for about 50 ft. Gol, now at Bygdøy near Oslo, of *c.*1200 is very fine, with an apsidal end with its own roof, and like Borgund has its covered walk, which only survives in part at Urnes. The most probable origin of the form is in Viking ceremonial halls.

steeple *See* SPIRE.

Stephaton The man holding up a sponge filled with vinegar on a reed in scenes of the Crucifixion (cf. John 19: 29), as a counterpart to *Longinus. He first appears in the *Rabbula Gospels of 586, but becomes a common feature of Byzantine images of the Crucifixion. He also appears with Longinus on standing *crosses in Ireland, Scotland, and England, indicating that the form developed from Byzantine example rather than European.

Stephen, Saint, was the first deacon and the first martyr. He was chosen, and six others were joined with him, to be the men appointed to distribute alms evenly among the widows whom the community supported. This would allow the Apostles to teach and preach, without being distracted by any other duties. Stephen was informed against to the High Priest and the elders—it is to be noted that (according to Acts 6 and 7) the instigation came from Cyrenians, Alexandrians, and others from Cilicia and Asia; in other words, not Jerusalem Jews—and Stephen was brought before the court. In his speech before them he finally accused them of killing 'the Righteous One', and cried out that he saw '. . . the heavens opened and the Son of Man standing at the right hand of God'. Thereopon they cried, 'Blasphemy!', dragged him out of the city, and stoned him to death. The witnesses laid their coats at the feet of a young man called Saul, who approved of their killing him. This Saul, of course, became the Apostle Paul. A church commemorating the place of his martyrdom outside the Damascus Gate was built by the Empress Eudoxia (455–60). His relics were later transported to Constantinople, and from there to Rome, where they were placed in the same tomb as those of S. Laurence, in San Lorenzo fuori le Mura. They are therefore usually coupled together in art, as they are in the Vatican Chapel of Nicholas V.

S. Stephen is usually shown wearing a dalmatic, as a recognizable attribute of his diaconate. Thus he appears in the Fra Angelico frescoes in the Chapel of Nicholas V (1447: Vatican); in the Fra Filippo Lippi frescoes of the *Life of S. Stephen* (1460–4: Prato Cath.); in the Giulio Romano *Stoning of S. Stephen* (1523: San Stefano, Genoa); and in a tapestry of the *Stoning of S. Stephen* woven for the Sistine Chapel series (Raphael School: *c.*1515: Vatican).

sticharion A *vestment worn by priests and deacons of the E. Orthodox Church, corresponding to the Western *alb, but, unlike it, a sticharion may be of any colour.

Stigmata (Gk. marks) are the marks of Christ's five wounds from His crucifixion: one to each hand, one to each foot, and one on the right side. Certain saints have been granted the imprint of the Stigmata, none before the 13th century, when the first was *S. Francis of Assisi, during his fast on Mt. Alvernus, in 1224. A few other saints have been granted the same privilege, notably *S. Catherine of Siena, who besought Christ that hers should be invisible, so that she experienced only the pain, but not the outward signs.

The Stigmata are very rare: of the 330 men and women recorded as having received the Stigmata, only 60 have been saints or *beati*, and no one has ever been canonized solely because of the Stigmata. The majority of recipients have been women. The most recent, well-attested, case is that of Padre Pio, a Capuchin friar of San Giovanni Rotondo, in Apulia (Puglia), S. Italy.

stipes (Lat. a post) The stone support of the altar *mensa* or table, either a central block or detached uprights, firmly cemented to the *mensa*. The plural *stipites* is sometimes italianized into *stipiti*, to describe upright members like pilasters, used to frame doors or windows, but not subject to the laws of proportion applying to classical pilasters, in that they often taper so that the top is wider than the base.

stock In the Catholic Church, one of three small metal vessels containing the holy oils—of catechumens, of the sick, and chrism—kept in an *aumbry, when these are still used, but otherwise in the sacristy.

Stock, Saint Simon *See* SIMON.

stole A long, narrow strip of cloth worn by the priest at all rites. *See* VESTMENTS.

stoup, holy water Jews attached much importance to ritual ablutions, and in Early Christian rites the worshipper washed his hands, face, and sometimes feet in a *cantharus or *fountain at the entrance to a church. By the 9th century this practice was abandoned in favour of the Asperges, or sprinkling of the congregation with holy water. In all churches of the Latin Rite and in many High Anglican and Episcopalian ones, there is a basin (stoup) holding holy water at the entrance to the church, not to be confused with the *font, for worshippers to sign themselves with the sign of the cross. Stoups are normally of stone or metal set into a niche or standing on a base or colonnette, often elaborately decorated, as in the pairs in St Peter's, Rome, which are held by putti larger than a human being.

Street, George Edmund (1824–81), was an English architect who was a powerful exponent of the *Gothic Revival. He entered *Scott's office in 1844, and was absorbed into the most energetic and vital Gothic Revival centre of the time. The form of Gothic advocated by *Pugin was already in retreat by the mid-century in favour of the more exuberant and eclectic High Victorian Gothic. In 1849 Street established himself in Oxfordshire, where he was diocesan architect from 1850 until his death. He moved to London in 1856 and slowly his work reflected less of the early forms of ecclesiastical Gothic Revival. He moved towards a more popular secular style, a less strait-jacketed Early English Gothic, and a freer use of French Gothic and Ruskin's Venetian Gothic. He travelled extensively abroad, and published a book on N. Italian Gothic in 1855, and one on Spanish Gothic in 1865, as well as recording his journeys in France and Germany. The result is that his Gothic is permeated by the experience of numerous Continental developments, creating an eclectic style. By the 1860s the taste for High Victorian Gothic modulated to an acceptance of the newly emerging taste for the 'Queen Anne' style, influenced by his own pupils, Philip Webb, Norman Shaw, and William Morris. His major state commission, as a result of the competition for the new Law Courts in 1866–7, shows how much his style had evolved in the direction of the now more popular, picturesque and colourful aspects of French 13th- and 14th-century Gothic, although the design was much modified (1879–81) before its final execution. One of his last works was the Neo-Romanesque American Presbyterian Church in Rome, 1872–6, and the American Church in Paris, finished after his death, which was hastened by the strain resulting from the Law Courts commission, finished a year after he died.

string course A horizontal moulding running across a building, often marking off one storey from another.

subdeacon *See* ORDERS, HOLY.

Sudarion (Sudarium) *See* VERONICA.

Suger (1081–1151) was Abbot of St-Denis, near Paris, from 1122 until his death. He rebuilt the abbey, which he had entered at the age of 10, and reformed the Benedictine monastery. In the early 11th century the abbey was strongly influenced by Odilon of *Cluny, and

Cluniac rule was briefly adopted. Suger believed that the glory of God could only worthily be served by magnificence in the building of a church and splendour in its decoration—ideas which also inspired Cluny. St-Denis was a small, dilapidated 8th-century building, which in Suger's rebuilding became the first example of Gothic architecture with, in the choir, the first use in the Île de France of rib-vaulting. Between 1130 and 1140 he built a porch, or narthex, with chapels over it, and a façade with three deep portals flanked by twin towers. The portals at St-Denis contained the earliest column figures—the west front of Chartres was only begun in 1145—but Suger's were destroyed in 1771, and the 19th-century restoration completed the ruin of the portal sculpture, of which only fragments survive. His choir, with an ambulatory and radiating chapels, dates from 1140 to 1144, but the choir itself was later rebuilt. A great deal of his work was altered by his successors, and during the Revolution the church suffered appalling damage because, as the royal mausoleum, it attracted the violence of popular fury, becoming successively a 'Temple of Reason', a granary, and a military hospital. All Suger's fabulous treasure, including the huge gold cross and the golden altarpiece (known to us from a picture in the NG, London, by the Master of S. Giles) was melted down. In the stained glass of the choir is a portrait of Suger. What we know of the glories of St-Denis is mainly from Suger's own account of his work in *De Sancti Dionysii Liber* (Book of Saint-Denis).

Sun of Righteousness *See* SOL INVICTUS.

superscription *See* TITULUS.

Supper, the Last, was the last occasion on which all the Apostles were together with Christ before the Passion. The account in Matt. 26: 17–35 is brief and to the point: 'On the first day of Unleavened Bread the disciples came to Jesus, saying, "Where do you want us to make the preparations for you to eat the Passover?" He said, "Go into the city to a certain man, and say to him, 'The Teacher says, My time is near; I will keep the Passover at your house with my disciples.'" The disciples did as Jesus had directed them, and when it was evening, He took his place with the twelve. While they were eating, He said, "Truly I tell you, one of you will betray me." They were greatly distressed and began to say to Him one after another, "Surely not I, Lord?" He answered, "The one who has dipped his hand into the bowl with me will betray me. The Son of Man goes as it is written of him, but woe to that one by whom the Son of Man is betrayed! It would have been better for that one not to have been born." Judas, who betrayed him, said, "Surely not I, Rabbi?" He replied, "You have said so." While they were eating, Jesus took a loaf of bread, and after blessing it he broke it, gave it to the disciples, and said, "Take, eat; this is my body." Then he took a cup, and after giving thanks he gave it to them, saying, "Drink from it, all of you; for this is my blood of the covenant, which is poured out for many for the forgiveness of sins. I tell you, I will never again drink of this fruit of the vine until that day when I drink it new with you in my Father's kingdom."'

The account in Mark 14: 12–25 is so similar that it contributes nothing to the story; it even omits the part about Peter being told that before the cock crew he would have denied Him three times, which Matt. includes. Luke 22: 7–38 is a little fuller, but differs mainly in details. Only the account in John 13: 1–38 includes the Washing of the *Feet, and differs considerably in detail, inasmuch as S. John elicited from Christ the identity of the betrayer, and records Christ's words to Judas, bidding him, 'Do quickly what you are going to do', so that Judas left the gathering before Christ instituted the Communion, and therefore never received it.

All the accounts concentrate on the principal event of the Last Supper, which is the *Communion of the Apostles—the Institution of the Eucharist, the central event of the Mass, and of all Communion services of no matter what denomination.

Illustrations of the *Last Supper* are only exceeded in number, importance, and distribution, by those of the *Crucifixion*. The earliest representations are not, as might have been expected, in the Catacombs, where such images are in fact of Eucharistic banquets—one for instance in the Catacomb of Callixtus of the early 3rd century has only seven figures. It seems clear that for the Early Christians the whole imagery of the Passion seems to be of subjects which they preferred to avoid. Among the earliest representations is a 6th-century mosaic in Sant'Apollinare Nuovo, Ravenna, where Christ and only eleven Apostles recline on classical *triclinia* with some fish on the table before them. The illustration in the *Rossano Gospels, of later in the 6th century, is more factual, since there are twelve Apostles, and on the table in the centre of the *triclinia* is a large bowl, closer to the text.

The selection of examples here is made so as to show how the conception of the scene changed. In many of the Northern examples, in MSS such as a N. French one (9th cent.: Prague), or the early 11th-century Gospels of Bishop Bernward (Hildesheim), Christ points out Judas by giving him a piece of bread, and the tradition of his being on the wrong side of the table is established as early as the 9th century, and possibly earlier. The subject also merges quite naturally into the Communion of the Apostles, which may sometimes be distinct, but is generally implicit.

One interesting coupling of subjects occurs in Nicholas of Verdun's Klosterneuburg Altar (1181), where the *Last Supper* is placed with *Melchisedek offering bread and wine* and *Aaron placing manna in the Ark*, all as examples of sacrificial meals. There is also a pair of less usual representations in the Dieric Bouts *Mystic Meal (1464–8 St Pieter, Leuven) and another grouping of sacred meals by Hans Brüggemann in a set of wooden *predella* carvings (1515–21: Bordesholm Altar, Schleswig) representing *Abraham and Melchisedek, The Last Supper, with Christ washing the disciples' feet, An Early Christian commemorative feast,* and a *Passover meal.* Despite Dürer's having made several series of the *Passion,* he only represents the *Last Supper,* and not the Communion of the Apostles, and in one, dated 1523, the bread is still in the basket on the floor and only a single cup—or chalice—stands on the bare table.

Among the Italian examples, *Duccio in the Siena *Maestà* and *Giotto in the Arena Chapel frescoes both depict the *Last Supper* and the *Washing of the Feet* separately. Fra Angelico in the little panels on the Silver Cupboard doors (*c.*1450: Florence, Accad.) includes the *Washing of the Feet, The Last Supper,* and the *Communion of the Apostles* in three separate scenes. It was the custom to depict the *Last Supper* on monastery refectory walls, as straightforward treatments of the subject. Examples in Florence include ones by Castagno (1457/8: Sant'Apollonia Mus.) and Ghirlandaio (1450: Ognissanti). Titian painted two as altarpieces, one now in Urbino Palace, 1522/4, and another now in the Escorial, of 1564 (version in Milan, Brera); Tintoretto painted many, all for churches: Sta Marcuola, 1547; San Simeone Grande, 1560s; San Polo, late 1560s; San Trovaso, *c.*1560; Sto Stefano, *c.*1580; San Giorgio Maggiore, 1594. There is also one in Lucca Cathedral *c.*1592. Of these, the most outstanding, because they exploit different artistic problems of interpretation, are the ones in San Marcuola, San Trovaso, and San Giorgio Maggiore, this last paired with the *Gathering of the Manna.* Veronese was at his best in grand banqueting scenes, and one, intended as a *Last Supper* for the refectory of the monastery of San Giorgio Maggiore, was, because of the strictures of the Inquisition, converted into a *Feast in the House of Levi* (1573: Venice, Accad.). The others were all feasts mentioned in the Gospels, but none was intended for a *Last Supper.*

*Poussin painted three important versions of the *Last Supper,* two in his sets of the Sacraments, as the *Eucharist*: both sets were painted in Rome, the first in 1642, the second between 1644 and 1648. Both sets interpret the subject as Roman classical meals, with the Apostles reclining on classical banqueting couches. The third version (1641: Paris, Louvre) has the Apostles standing round Christ, while He distributes the bread of the Eucharist among them. In all his versions, the painter manages to separate Judas from the other Apostles without breaking the intensity of the moment in which Christ institutes the Sacrament.

The most celebrated painting of the *Last Supper* is, without doubt, the one by *Leonardo da Vinci, in the refectory of Sta Maria delle Grazie, Milan, commissioned about 1495, and abandoned in 1499 when the artist left Milan. Supreme in its interpretation of the moment when Christ says He is to be betrayed, it is also catastrophic in its defective technique. It nevertheless remains, even in its mutilated restored condition, the touchstone by which all other representations of the subject are judged, and justly is the most admired for its penetrating psychological insight into the effect His statement had upon the Apostles, and the outward simplicity with which this effect is achieved.

surplice A later version of the *alb, ampler and slightly shorter, with long wide sleeves, worn by servers at Mass, members of the choir, as well as priests. *See* VESTMENTS.

Susanna(h) and the Elders The story of Susanna comes from ch. 13 of the Greek version of the Book of Daniel, and is now included in the Apocryphal books of the OT. The story, which is not in the Hebrew text, is in two different versions: the one in the Septuagint celebrates the virtue of a young Jewish woman, falsely accused by two corrupt and lustful old men, with her trial taking place in the synagogue, and the young Daniel inspired by an angel to defend her; the version in Theodotion (a 2nd-cent. Christian who translated and edited the Septuagint into a new Greek version) is more vivid, and in it Daniel is inspired directly by God to defend the innocent Susanna. The story itself is one of the most engaging in the Bible.

Susanna was the virtuous and beautiful wife of a rich Jew called Joakim, who had a fine house and garden in Babylon. Many Jews came to his house, because he was a leading member of the community. Among them were two elders, both of whom were corrupt, unjust judges, who lusted after the lovely Susanna. When all the visitors had left, she was in the habit of walking in the garden, and one day they hid themselves there, hoping for an opportunity to seduce her. She came into the garden with two maids and told them to shut the garden doors and to fetch the things she needed, for as it was a hot day she intended to bathe. When the maids had gone, the two judges came out of hiding, and threatened that if she did not lie with them, they would declare that they had found her with a young man, and would accuse her of adultery, for which she would be sentenced to death. She cried for help, and they shouted their wicked story, so that she was taken to be tried, and because they were elders and judges their story was believed. Susanna cried out to God for help, and as she was being led to execution, a young man called Daniel was inspired to cry out that he would have no part in shedding her blood. When he was asked why, he declared that the evidence against her was false. She was taken back to the court, and Daniel had the two elders segregated, so that he might examine them separately. He asked each in turn under what tree they found Susanna with the young man, and each one named a different tree, thus exposing the lie they had told. The two elders were then condemned for bearing false witness, and the virtuous Susanna was vindicated. According to the Law, as laid down in Deut. 19: 16–21, the false witness is to be punished with the same punishment as would have been the fate of the one against whom the false testimony was given. In the case of Susanna, the punishment for adultery was to be stoned to death; this therefore was their punishment.

The story has long been a popular one, the first representations being in the catacombs from the late 3rd and early 4th centuries: in the Pietro and Marcellino, in the Domitilla, in the Coemeterium Maius, and with Daniel in the Callixtus catacomb. The popularity of the story is because Susanna is seen as an exemplar, or emblem even, of the virtuous soul saved from the clutches of the Devil. Often the scene with Susanna and the exposure of the elders appears in representations from the story of Daniel as in the Bible of S. Isidoro, of 1000. The full story of Susanna and the elders is set out in eight episodes in the Lothar Crystal of *c.*865 (London, BM) cut to commemorate the vindication of Lothar II's Queen against the false accusations of two archbishops who supported the King's attempt to divorce her, aided by papal legates sent to see that justice was done, but who were bribed to support the King's accusations. Pope Nicholas I was so incensed at the injustice being done to her that he quashed the proceedings, forced the King to reinstate her as Queen, deposed the two archbishops, and disgraced the corrupt legates. Pictures of the elders with Susanna bathing are by Tintoretto (1555–60: Louvre; 1560: Vienna, KHM); Veronese (1560s: Vienna, KHM; 1575: Genoa, Doria Coll.); Rubens (1635/8: Munich); Van Dyck (1618/20: Munich); Piazzetta (*c.*1720: Florence, Uffizi); Sebastiano Ricci (1713: Chatsworth), and *Susanna before the Judges* (1725/6: Turin); Ricci also painted a virtual copy (now at Chatsworth) of the Veronese of the subject now in the Louvre. *See also* DANIEL.

Sutherland, Graham (1903–1980) A British painter, printmaker, and designer, who began his large contribution to art in churches with *Crucifixion* (1946) (*see* PICASSO, PABLO) commissioned for St Matthew's, Northampton, and hung opposite the *Madonna and Child* (1934) (*see* MOORE, HENRY). Other paintings of this subject followed together with a *Noli me tangere*, Chichester Cathedral (1961). His *Christ in Glory in the Tetramorph* (1962) for the new Coventry Cathedral, a tapestry measuring 74 by 38 ft woven in France by Pinton Frères at Felletin near Aubusson, was preceded by nearly a decade of experiment with different design treatments. The final head of Christ derived, said Sutherland, 'from a hundred different things—photographs of cyclists, close-ups of people, photographs of eyes, Egyptian art, Rembrandt, and many others'.

swag A form of festoon imitating a piece of cloth or a garland draped from one support to another. They are classical in origin, and became a frequent feature of Renaissance, Baroque, and Rococo decoration, and may be painted in pictures, carved, or made of plaster or wood, painted and often gilded.

Swedenborgianism *See* NORTH AMERICA.

Swoon, the The Virgin's swoon beneath the cross was a feature of pictures of the *Crucifixion*, particularly during the 14th and early 15th century. In a few cases the Virgin lies on the ground, tended by the Maries, but more often she is supported in a fainting condition but still standing. The devotion was bitterly attacked by *Molanus, whose harsh attitude to non-scriptural expressions of feeling and emotion finally resulted in the Church banning the motif, on the grounds that S. John (John 19: 25–7) says specifically that the Virgin stood beneath the cross, as in the words of the anthem *Stabat Mater Dolorosa* probably of the 13th/14th century. The Virgin is also said to have swooned when meeting Christ during the procession to Calvary, and a place is indicated for this moment in some old itineraries of the Passion. It is not accepted in the imagery of the *Stations of the Cross. After Molanus's diatribe the incident disappears from the imagery of the Crucifixion. It may be said in his defence, however, that the Byzantine and early Western medieval tradition always shows the Virgin standing beneath the cross.

Illustrations of the Virgin's swoon are in Queen Mary's Psalter (*c.*1300: London, BM); in the *Crucifixion* (1333: Antwerp) by Simone *Martini from the Orsini polyptych; in the central panel of the Berswordt Altar (*c.*1397: Dortmund) by a Westphalian Master; and by *Masolino in his fresco of the *Crucifixion* (*c.*1428: San Clemente, Rome). It survives as a motif as late as 1444 in a work by Parri Spinelli in Arezzo, Conservatorio di Sta Caterina, and was probably always inspired by Franciscan devotion and the influence of the **Meditationes Vitae Christi*. Two paintings of the *Procession to Calvary* by Raphael, one of *c.*1506 (London, NG), the other, *Lo Spasimo di Sicilia* (*c.*1516: Prado), show the Virgin in a fainting condition, supported by the Maries.

sword The sword is an attribute of saints who have been martyred either by being beheaded or by being pierced with a sword; chief among them is S. Paul, for whom it is not only the emblem of his martyrdom, but refers to his preaching, since according to Eph. 6: 17, he urges his readers to 'Take the helmet of salvation, and the sword of the Spirit, which is the word of God'. Among many other saints martyred with the sword are S. James the Great, Bishop of Jerusalem and the first Apostle to be martyred, S. Matthias the Apostle, S. Denis or Dionysius, patron saint of France, S. Thomas of Canterbury, S. Catherine of Alexandria, S. Agnes, and S. Cecilia.

When the infant Jesus was presented at the Temple, He was held by the aged Simeon, who said to the Virgin that '... a sword will pierce your own soul too'. Seven swords, therefore, represent the Seven Sorrows, or the Seven Sorrowful Mysteries of the *Rosary.

The sword is also the emblem of Justice, together with a pair of scales, and symbolizes also authority. This is expressed clearly in the *Stanza della Segnatura in the Vatican. The room doubled as Pope Julius's private study and library and the place where he presided in the final court of papal justice: the *Signatura Gratiae*, and the *Signatura Justitiae*, the two swords of spiritual and temporal justice, and where the documents which confirmed the findings were sealed, hence the name of the room—the Sealing Room. Papal justice was based on the Bull 'Unam Sanctam' issued by Boniface VIII in 1302, in which he enunciated the doctrine of the 'two swords': that the pope as the supreme head of the Church possessed final jurisdiction in both spiritual and temporal law. The basis for this doctrine is in Luke 22: 38: 'They (the disciples) said "Lord, look, here are two swords." He replied, "It is enough."' In the window embrasure of the wall of the Stanza della Segnatura on which the *Cardinal Virtues* (Fortitude, Prudence, and Temperance) are painted, Christ is depicted with His disciples, pointing to two swords which lie crossed on the ground.

On the remaining wall spaces below the *Cardinal Virtues* are *Justinian granting the Pandects* (civil law) and *Pope Gregory IX granting the Decretals* (canon law). Pope Julius himself is said to have indicated the subjects to be represented, so that the choice of themes indicates a total continuity in papal thinking on the subject of spiritual and temporal law, difficult as it was to enforce the latter in the 16th century, three centuries after its first promulgation.

Sylvester, Pope (314–335). Little is recorded that is not legendary. He is said to have baptized the Emperor Constantine in the Baptistery of the Lateran, the palace given to him by Constantine as the site for the see of Rome, where he built the first Lateran basilica as the cathedral of Rome. He is also reputed to have received the so-called Donation of Constantine, which gave him wide temporal rights, and enabled him to claim primacy over the patriarchates of Antioch, Jerusalem, Constantinople, and Alexandria. Despite its having been fabricated in the 8th–9th centuries in the Empire of the Franks, the Donation had great influence until it was finally proved to be a falsification in the 13th century. The legends connected with Sylvester are fantastic in the extreme and include such stories as curing Constantine of leprosy by baptism (he was not in fact baptized until he was on his death-bed in Nicomedia), reviving a dead bull killed by having the secret name of Yahweh whispered in its ear, closing the jaws of a dragon which was killing people by breathing on them, and resuscitating two dead priests, predicting the death of a pagan governor who was endeavouring to extort the property of a martyred Christian; the man choked on a fishbone that very night at dinner. He was, apparently, the pope who began the wearing of a tiara. These legends were all painted by Maso di Banco in a series of frescoes (1335–45: Florence, Sta Croce).

symbol, symbolism (Gk. *simbolon*, mark, token) The *OED* defines 'symbol' as 'Something that stands for, represents or denotes something else . . . especially a material object taken to represent something immaterial or abstract'.

For the Early Christians, the use of images as symbols was very difficult, so difficult that Tertullian (*c*.160–*c*.225), an African Church Father, regarded all images and representations as dangerous and forbade their use, declaring that for a people newly escaped from idolatry they presented the greatest danger of relapse—of worshipping the symbol itself instead of what it represented. The fear of idolatry (or the accusation of it) almost certainly accounts for the paucity of sculptured figures in Early Christian times. The twin strands of the development of Christianity—the Hebrew strand emanating from Jerusalem, where the use of images of any kind challenged the old Hebraic prohibition expressed in the First Commandment, itself a reaction to the Jewish experience in Egypt, and the Hellenic strand emanating from the first proselytizing Apostles and disciples, particularly SS Paul and Mark, in the Graeco-Roman world, where images were a normal aspect of life—had to be reconciled before the use of symbols, much less images, became acceptable. It was the Western that became the dominant strain, in that after the destruction of Jerusalem by the Romans in AD 70, the main field of Christianity lay in the West; the Jewish strand was dispersed into a non-Jewish world. Even the Jews themselves, in a non-Jewish world, accepted images and representations, as may be seen in the Synagogue in *Dura-Europos, and in Jewish catacombs in Rome from the Augustan to the Constantinian period.

The use of symbols was important during the periods of the sporadic but violent Christian persecutions as a means by which believers declared their affiliation to fellow believers, yet at the same time, was close enough to innocuous or even to pagan imagery as to render them harmless. *Clement of Alexandria (d. *c*.215) lists the dove, the lyre, and *Ichthys, Origen (d. 254) refers to Christ as *ichthys*, and the catacombs have many such as the vine, grapes, the winepress, symbolizing the Passion, derived from Christ's words in John 15: 1–6, 'I am the vine . . .', yet which could refer to Bacchus; the Good Shepherd refers to Christ's words in John 10: 11–16, 'I am the Good Shepherd . . .', yet it could refer to *Hermes Kriophoros. Others were the anchor and the ship, symbols of hope to a Christian, the fish of *ichthys*, a fountain or vase with deer or a dove drinking from it, the peacock, the lamb, a man amongst lions for Daniel, the palm of martyrdom, a dove for the Holy Spirit, or with an olive branch as in Noah's ark, the triangle for the Trinity, the keys of S. Peter, an *orant, the *Sol Invictus, a pagan image taken over by Christians, the *Chi-Rho, all with no significance to a pagan, yet full of meaning to a Christian. The one potent symbol for later generations—the cross—was absent from Early Christian symbolism, because of the reluctance to accept that Christ had died the shameful death of criminal execution. The narrative scenes of the Life of Christ in Sant' Apollinare Nuovo, Ravenna, which are probably the earliest (6th cent.) NT cycle, do not include the Crucifixion.

The Bible is, of course, the fountain-head of symbolism and allegory. Eve's apple (*see* ADAM), *Noah's ark, the rainbow after the Deluge, *Jonah's whale, *Moses's burning bush and brazen serpent, *Balaam's ass, *Gideon's fleece, are all subjects that Christians, who viewed the NT as the fulfilment of the OT, treated as symbols and allegories to be interpreted in terms of the events of Christ's life and the message of His teaching. In the NT, the journey and adoration of the *Magi, the changing of the water into wine at the marriage at Cana, the feeding of the 5,000, the miraculous draught of fishes, all have a deeper significance underlying the plain narrative of the events: they all have symbolic meaning. Possibly the most familiar symbols are those of the *Tetramorph of Ezekiel for the four Evangelists.

Later Christian use of images and symbols was a convenience of teaching, particularly among illiterate and semi-literate people who could be effectively instructed by their use. This was, basically, the *raison d'être* of mosaics, fresco cycles, stained-glass windows, and later, when the fear of sculptured figures was overcome, of sculptured portals and statues. Symbolic construction, too, plays its part. The symbolism of the *martyrium, either as the tomb of a martyr, or a *memoria* over the place of martyrdom, exercises a powerful symbolic effect, since the shape becomes expressive of a type of church building, and influenced, for instance, the design of the new *St Peter's in Rome. The cruciform shape of the later long-nave medieval church with transepts forming the arms of a cross was not originally designed with any symbolic aim; the shape resulted from the need for extra space at the choir end of a church, but it soon given a symbolic meaning as an image of the crucifixion. The most completely symbolic use of architecture and decoration is in the *cross-in-square domical churches of the Eastern Rite, where every part of the church was given a symbolic meaning, from the lowest part for the congregation with marble revetment on the walls, symbolizing the world, rising through the region of paradise with mosaics of saints on the upper parts of the walls, to the celestial regions in the upper domical parts where the great feasts of the church were portrayed—the Annunciation, the Nativity, the Baptism of Christ, the Transfiguration, the Crucifixion, the Resurrection (or rather the *Anastasis* or Harrowing of Hell), with the Virgin in the apse, and Christ as the Pantocrator in the top of the dome. The Eastern system became a rigid one, while in the less highly organized West no such rigid system was ever imposed.

During the Middle Ages in the West symbolism reached its high-water mark. Everything in Nature and in daily life was invested with a symbolic meaning, and people were encouraged to see symbolic meaning in even the meanest event—the hen lifing its head to swallow the water in its beak was raising its eyes to Heaven in thanks and worship; the lioness licking its new-born cubs did so for three days to give them life, as Christ had risen after three days in the tomb. Bestiaries are full of such symbolic inventions. The use of allegory gives extra meaning to a narrative account, a description of an event, or a subject in which a different matter is in fact offered to the reader or spectator—as for instance, Bunyan's *Pilgrim's Progress* recounts a journey which is an allegorical account of the soul's journey towards Salvation, or Hieronymous *Bosch's painting of the *Hay-cart* in its passage through the world is an allegorical exposure of human folly and sin, or *Bruegel's painting of *The Blind leading the Blind* is an allegory of human stupidity leading to destruction. The step from symbolism to allegory is a small one; the main difference is that the symbolic is usually more succinct and more immediate. *See also* ALLEGORY, DURANDUS, and EXEGESIS.

Synagoga *See* ECCLESIA.

synagogue The synagogue is the meeting-place for worship of the Jewish community in any place where they have settled, and where ten adult men can be found to constitute a quorum. The foundation of synagogues dates back, apparently, to the Babylonian exile of the 5th/6th century BC (recorded in 2 Ks. 24 and 25: Vg. 4 Kings; and in Ps. 137: Vg. 136), which lasted seventy years. The Temple in Jerusalem was destroyed and the people forcibly removed to Babylon; synagogues then became the focus of Jewish life, but no sacrifices could be offered, only prayers and the reading of the scriptures. This tradition survived after 538 BC when they were permitted to return to Jerusalem and to rebuild the city and the Temple (Ezra 5 and 6: Vg. 1 Esdras 5 and 6; and Neh. 2, 3, 4: Vg. 2 Esdras 2, 3, 4, 5). Many Jews did not return, so that the synagogue remained a feature of Jewish communities wherever they settled. The role of the synagogue once again became important when the Temple at Jerusalem was destroyed by the Romans under Titus in AD 70 (the catastrophe predicted to the weeping women by Jesus on his way to Calvary: Luke 23: 27–33), and even more when Hadrian in 130 made Jerusalem a Roman city which Jews might enter only on one day a year to bewail the destruction of the Temple by Nebuchadnezzar at the time of the Babylonian exile. Before the Edict of Milan in 313, Judaism was a 'tolerated' religion, but under Roman rule although they were exempted from the obligatory oblation to Roman deities and the Emperor, their position was always precarious because of the frequency of Jewish rebellions in Palestine. These were usually provoked by Roman prohibitions of such Jewish religious rites as circumcision, for instance, by Hadrian, rescinded by Antoninus Pius, but severely prohibited for non-Jews, which stopped Jewish proselytizing. After the triumph of Christianity, the position of Jews deteriorated markedly, and shamefully.

Some synagogues are, or have been, magnificent buildings, such as the one at Cologne, the Amsterdam Synagogue of the Portuguese Jews built in 1676, the Bevis Marks Synagogue in London, rebuilt after the fire of London in 1666, and the one in the Buda part of Budapest founded in the 15th century, which was the first in Central Europe. It is now undergoing extensive restoration. In shape they were, and are, basilical, with a central prayer hall, important *matronea, and with the Ark of the Covenant containing the rolls of the Torah in the same position as the high altar of a Christian church. Large synagogues often had a lawcourt, a library and rooms for study, a treasury, and even guest rooms. One of the finest surviving is at Sardis in Turkey. The synagogue at *Dura-Europos on the Euphrates, built *c.*250, was extensively decorated with wall-paintings of biblical subjects, evidence that Hellenized Jews outside Palestine did not have the same repugnance for imagery as Jews in Palestine.

synthronon is the semicircle of seats round the apse of a Byzantine church, reserved to the clergy. In the centre was the bishop's throne, placed usually a little higher than the other seats. In some instances, the steps up to them were high enough for a passage, the purpose of which is unknown, to run underneath them. A surviving Western example is in the apse of the cathedral of Torcello, outside Venice.

Syon Cope This late 13th-century *vestment, now in the Victoria & Albert Museum, London, is one of the finest surviving examples of *opus anglicanum. It belonged originally to the Syon Convent near London, founded for *Brigittine nuns in 1414/15 by Henry V and secularized by Henry VIII.

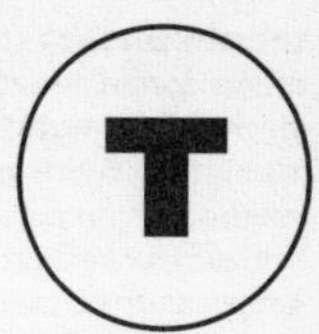

tabernacle (Lat. *tabernaculum*, tent) (1) Jewish; (2) Christian; (3) the Feast of Tabernacles.

(1) The original OT tabernacle was a portable shrine to contain the *Ark of the Covenant, made under the direction of Moses, following the instructions he had received on Mt. Sinai, and described in great detail in Exod. chs. 25–31; 33: 7–10; and 35–40. It was in two sections, the outer being the Holy Place containing the seven-branched candlestick (*Menorah), the table for the shew-bread (the twelve loaves of the offering), and the altar of incense. The inner part, the Holy of Holies, contained only the Ark. The Tabernacle was carried by the Israelites on their wanderings, marked by the Pillar of Cloud by day and Fire by night. The Tabernacle was repeated in Solomon's *Temple, but subsequently destroyed by Nebuchadnezzar.

(2) In Christian usage a tabernacle is a receptacle for the Blessed Sacrament. *Constantine is recorded as having given a golden tower to Old St Peter's and other similar towers are recorded; they were the predecessors of the Sacrament-house of the Middle Ages, popular in Germany and France, one of the few survivors being the enormous open-work stone tabernacle in St Lorenz, Nuremberg, by Adam Kraft (1493–5). Another form was a *pyx in the shape of a dove suspended over the altar. The usual form of pyx, however, is a cylindrical or rectangular box with a domed or pyramidal top, usually elaborately decorated, but with a tabernacle veil completely covering it. The veil is usually of silk and may be of cloth of gold or silver, or white, or matching the liturgical colour of the day. A light (white in the Anglican Church, white or red in the Roman Catholic Church) is kept burning nearby to indicate the presence of the Sacrament. At various times in the (Roman) Catholic Church the tabernacle has been placed in the centre of the high altar or in a special Sacrament Chapel, but from the 16th century to the 1960s it was on the high altar, except in cathedrals, generally, and in some convents, where separate chapels were provided. In the Anglican Church, the Sacrament is most often housed in an aumbry.

(3) The Feast of Tabernacles is the last of the three great Jewish feasts in the year (cf. *Passover and *Pentecost). It lasts for eight days in the late autumn, after the corn and wine harvests, and is a thanksgiving for them. It is also a reminder of the Israelites' wanderings in the wilderness, since the tabernacles from which it is named were booths made from branches, in which the Israelites once lived for the duration of the festival. The tabernacles signify the tents of the Jews' nomadic life. The Feast is described in Exod. 23; Lev. 21; Num. 29; and Deut. 16: 13–15.

Tabitha, Raising of Tabitha, the Aramaic form of the Greek name Dorcas, was a benevolent woman living in Joppa who made clothes for the poor. She died, and was laid out for burial, when two men from the Christian community who had heard that S. Peter was at Lydda, not far away, went to him for help. He went to Joppa, found that Tabitha was being mourned over by women who showed him the clothes which she made for them. He sent them out of the room, knelt and prayed and then said, 'Tabitha, arise.' She opened her eyes and sat up, he gave her his hand and helped her up, and then called the women into the room, and they saw that she was alive. The miracle caused a sensation and many became Christians as a result. The story is told in Acts 9: 36–42, and parallels the story of the raising of Jairus's daughter in Matt. 9: 18, 23–6; Mark 5: 22–4, 35–42. It was S. Peter's first miracle of raising the dead to life.

The scene is represented by *Masolino in one of the frescoes in the Brancacci Chapel in the Carmine church in Florence, when he was working there with Masaccio in 1425–7.

Tablets of the Law *See* MOSES.

tabula ansata (Lat. *ansa*, handle) A horizontal rectangle with handle-like projections on the short vertical sides, used to frame an inscription. Many examples exist in the catacombs and on Early Christian and Byzantine ivories. The fashion was revived in the Renaissance, as a conscious classical allusion, e.g. the tablet held by a putto in Raphael's *Madonna of Foligno* (Vatican Mus.).

Talents, Parable of *See* PARABLES.

Tamar *See* DAVID and JUDAH.

Tau cross *See* CROSS.

Temperance One of the four Cardinal *Virtues, the others being Fortitude, Justice, and Prudence. Temperance is usually symbolized by a woman holding a bridle, or pouring water into a goblet of wine, but the allegorical figure by *Giotto in the Arena Chapel, Padua, is a woman holding a sword bound into its scabbard.

Tempietto, the (Ital. little temple), is the tiny circular chapel built by *Bramante as a *martyrium in the courtyard of the monastery of San Pietro in Montorio in Rome, to mark the spot where it was wrongly supposed that S. Peter had been crucified. It has been dated variously between 1502 and 1512, but was probably planned and begun at the earlier date though its completion may well have been at or by the later one. It is the earliest High Renaissance building in Rome, and the perfection of its design and proportions may well have been what drew Julius II's attention to Bramante as a competent adviser on the restoration of St Peter's.

Templar, the Knights An Order of military knights founded in 1118 by Hugo de Payens who with eight companions formed themselves into a military body to protect pilgrims to the Holy Land from bandits. At first they were based at Solomon's Temple in Jerusalem and lived on charity, until in 1127 Hugo returned to the West to obtain recruits and help from the Church. In 1128 the Council of Troyes approved the Order's rule, which was believed to have been written by S. Bernard of Clairvaux, who dedicated to Hugo a treatise 'in praise of the new militia'. There were four ranks: knights, serjeants, squires, and chaplains. Their main counterparts were the Knights Hospitallers of S. John of Jerusalem, founded at the end of the 11th century, who eventually became the Knights of *Malta. After their formal accreditation the Templars increased rapidly in wealth and power, and spread to all parts of Christendom. They acquired property, since knights had to prove eight generations of nobility (four for each parent) and bring a dowry of land or money into the Order. The fighting forces of both Orders played an increasingly important role in the wars with the Turks, who were the rulers of the country from the moment when the Caliph Omar rode victorious into Jerusalem in 638. The First Crusade of 1095, fought to regain the Holy Land for Christendom, resulted in the capture of Jerusalem in 1099, the foundation of the Latin Kingdom of Jerusalem ('Outremer'—Overseas, as it was called), and the crowning of Baldwin of Bouillon as king of Jerusalem on Christmas Day 1100. But the Christian success resulted in virtually continuous war, during which the Templars fought with the allied European powers in the various Crusades almost as allies, rather than as auxiliaries. They provided, as they expanded in numbers and prestige, a regular army of trained fighting men, possibly numbering as many as 15,000 over the years, although they were a force over which no monarch or local commander had any control: they answered only to the pope and their Grand Master. They were also the main banking and money-lending enterprise in 'Outremer', and as they became powerful so they became rapacious, and their bitter hostility to the Hospitallers rendered them unreliable. Also, as the principal bankers in 'Outremer'—not an activity which made them popular—they came into closer contact with Muslims (whom they frequently found were easier to deal with, and often more honest, than their fellow Christians) and many Templars, from long residence in 'Outremer', had Muslim friends, and became interested in Muslim learning, religion, and medicine, which was far more advanced than that of the primitive Western doctors.

The position was not improved by the arrival of the Teutonic Knights who, although fine fighters, added yet another intransigent element to the already divisive rivalry of the Hospitallers and the Templars, each behaving as independent states in the territories they controlled. Jerusalem was lost in 1187, and the Christians were limited to the coastal fortresses, but in 1291 the last of them, Acre, fell after a fierce defence conducted by the Grand Master of the Templars, who was killed in the battle. The Templars retired to Cyprus and many returned to their countries of origin to await events. In 1306 the new Grand Master, Jacques de Molay, went to France to discuss a projected Crusade with Pope Clement V at Avignon. He then heard of the charges being made against the Order—heresy, sodomy, and blasphemous initiation rites. Chief among them was the accusation that to prove their total obedience to the Order, the ceremony included desecrating the cross presented on the Grand Master's order. These horrible accusations were supported by the testimony of two knights who had been disgraced and expelled from the Order, but it was eagerly accepted by King Philip IV of France who was determined to suppress the Order in order to despoil them of their great wealth, which was lodged in their houses in Paris and London.

Suddenly in October 1307 the king ordered the arrest of the Grand Master and all the knights in France. Over the next seven years travesties of trials took place in which torture was freely used to obtain confessions. The pope suppressed the Order in 1312, and assigned their property to the Hospitallers, but so high were the 'expenses' the crown claimed the trials had cost that little money accrued to the Hospitallers, though they obtained much property. Many knights died under torture, many confessed and then retracted their confessions, producing new sessions of torture; the trial of Jacques de Molay was prolonged by these means until his final condemnation. With two of his principal officers he was burnt at the stake in March 1314. The story is told that from the flames he protested his innocence, and summoned the king, the pope, and the principal judiciary at the trials to meet him before the throne of God within fifty days. Both Philip and Clement V died within this time limit.

In England, Edward II in 1310 at the pope's request had all the Templars in the country arrested, and though they were condemned to be imprisoned on the flimsiest evidence, the trials were not so inhumane as the French ones. The king, however, confiscated their property. In Spain and Portugal, they were arrested but all were acquitted because of their part in the struggle against the Moors. Modern scholarship has produced evidence very much in favour of the Order. Their churches were always circular, like the Temple in Jerusalem from which they took their name. Two survive in England: one dating from 1185 (a nave was added in 1240) in their former property in London, now the Inner and Middle Temple off the Strand. A second circular church, in Cambridge, dating from *c.*1130, is probably but not certainly a Templars' church, although it was built for a 'fraternity of the Holy Sepulchre', of which nothing else is known.

temple This is not normally a name for the churches of Christian denominations, though it is used by some Nonconformist or Pentecostal sects. However, *Alberti, in his treatise on architecture, consistently refers to churches as temples, but this is possibly because the work was originally written in Latin, and to a scholar of such deep classical learning such language may well have come naturally.

Temple, le *See* CHARENTON.

Temple of Jerusalem The account in the OT of the building of the Temple at Jerusalem by Solomon is in 1 Kgs. 6–9, and also in 2 Chron. 3: 3 ff. 'In the 480th year after the Israelites came out of the land of Egypt, in the fourth year of Solomon's reign . . . he began to build the house of the Lord.' There follows a long and detailed description of the Temple, which has been very influential in later ages, in that many efforts have been made to use the proportions of Solomon's Temple in the construction of Christian churches. At 60 cubits in length and 20 cubits wide, by 30 cubits high, a cubit being the length of a forearm from fingertip to elbow, about 18 inches, this would equal about 90 ft. long by about 30 ft. wide. by about 45 ft. high. These are given as the dimensions of the Temple, but there also are extra spaces, described in 1 Kgs. 6: 3 as a vestibule in front of the house, 20 cubits wide and 10 cubits deep, and in vv. 5 ff. as 'structures against the wall of the house, running round the walls of the house, both the nave and the inner sanctuary; and he made side chambers all round'. These chambers (1 Kgs. 6: 10) were 5 cubits high (7 ½ ft.). But as the description continues in v. 6, it seems clear that this series of side chambers was in fact three storeys high, and projected more as they rose; in vv. 8–10 entrances to these upper chambers are described. Allowances have to be made for the thickness of walls and floors, so that at a conservative estimate one would have to reckon that the side structures were about 20 to 22 cubits high (say, 30 to 35 ft.). It seems that the measurements given in 1 Kgs. 6: 2 can only refer to the

Temple itself, not to the whole building of which the Temple was one element. But difficulties arise from the statement in 2 Chron. 3: 4, that in front of the Temple was a vestibule 20 cubits long with a height of 120 cubits (180 ft.), and another statement in 2 Chron. 3: 9 that he overlaid the 'upper chambers' with gold. In 2 Chron. 3: 15, he is said to have placed in front of the house two pillars 35 cubits high with capitals of 5 cubits on top of each of them, about 60 ft. high. It would seem sensible to limit one's conjectures to the dimensions of the actual Temple area, which included a sanctuary 20 cubits square.

Churches built therefore in the proportions of 3 : 1 in plan, and at 2 : 1 in elevation would emulate the inner element of Solomon's Temple. The interior also has been influential for later Christian generations, in that it sets a standard for very lavish decoration, one feature of which is the so-called *Salomonic columns. One other interesting point about the detailed description in the Bible, is that the cherubim in the inner sanctuary were 10 cubits high, which interprets the Mosaic prohibition of images in a manner consistent with later Christian practice: that images were permissible provided that they were only decorative.

2 Kgs. 24 (Vg. 2 Paralip. 35) tells how Nebuchadnezzar first captured Jerusalem, against King Jehoiachin, who surrendered himself and his family. He does not appear to have done more damage to the Temple than to loot it. The population of Jerusalem was taken in captivity to Babylon, and Jehoiachin's uncle Zedekiah (Vg. Sedecias) was made king in his place. But eleven years later Zedekiah rebelled against the Chaldeans, with disastrous consequences. Nebuchadnezzar returned (2 Kgs. 25; 2 Paralip. 36) and besieged the city, and after four months, there being no food left, Zedekiah escaped, but was captured, and the Chaldean vengeance was frightful. The city was taken, the Temple was destroyed, and the remainder of the population taken into captivity, leaving only the poorest to work the land. But a later rebellion resulted in the remainder of the people fleeing to Egypt, so great was their fear of the Chaldeans. 2 Chron. 36 (1 Esdras) tells how even the might of the Chaldeans fell before Cyrus of Persia, when the prophecy of Jeremiah was finally fulfilled. The Jews returned to Jerusalem and were able to begin rebuilding the Temple which had been a desolate ruin for seventy years.

The return under Cyrus is thought to have been *c.*538 BC, but does not seem to have been very successful, possibly because of opposition from the Samaritans. A second effort was made under Darius, who reigned from 521 to 485, with encouragement from the prophets Haggai and Zechariah (Vg. Aggeus and Zacharias). Darius returned many of the Temple vessels which Nebuchadnezzar had looted. A third period under Artaxerxes (464–423 BC) came under Nehemiah (Vg. Nehemias; the books of Ezra and Nehemiah are very confused, and form a continuous text, since parts of one are mixed with parts from the other). The Temple was apparently then completed, but with none of the splendour of its state under Solomon.

The second Temple was desecrated in 167 BC by Antiochus Epiphanes, a member of the Seleucid dynasty, which came to power after the death of Alexander the Great. They tyrannized over Jerusalem (1 Maccabees) and established a brutal garrison, but two years later it was rededicated by Judas Maccabeus of the Hasmoneans, but continuous war with the Seleucid commanders followed. The major restoration of the Temple was by Herod the Great, more as a bid for popular approval, since he was an Edomite who had been appointed by the Romans and his only link with the Hasmoneans was by his marriage with Mariamne, granddaughter of Hyrcanus, the last of the Hasmoneans. He was astute, ruthless, but an able ruler. The Temple which he rebuilt was splendid, but built not through any genuine religious feeling, only as a means of consolidating his position. During his reign Jesus was born, and he is the Herod of the Gospels (Matt. 2). When the Jews revolted against the Romans in AD 70, Jerusalem was taken and the Temple was destroyed. Temple worship ceased because sacrifices were only possible in the Temple. One result was the growing importance of *synagogues as the centre of Jewish religious and social life.

templon *See* ICONOSTASIS.

temptation *See* MAN, FALL OF.

Temptation of Christ Christ was tempted three times by the Devil, immediately after his *baptism by *John the Baptist in the Jordan. The account is in Matt. 4: 1–11, and also in Mark, who merely refers to His having been tempted, and Luke 4: 1–13, but his account differs from Matt. 4 in a reordering of the sequence of temptations, and also in his location of the event. Jesus had been led by the Spirit to retire to the wilderness, where He fasted for six weeks, after which He was hungry. The Devil said to Him, 'If you are the Son of God, command these stones to become loaves of bread', to which He retorted, 'Man does not live by bread alone, but by every word that comes from the mouth of God.' The Devil then took Him to Jerusalem to the pinnacle of the Temple, 'If you are the Son of God, throw yourself down,' reminding Him that angels would prevent His even dashing His foot against a stone, to which He retorted, 'Do not put the Lord your God to the test.' For the third temptation the Devil showed Him all the kingdoms of the earth, and said that they would all be His if He worshipped him, to which His answer was, 'Get thee behind me, Satan! for it is written, Worship the Lord your God, and serve only Him.' The Devil recognized defeat, and left Him, and angels ministered to Him. (NRSV has 'Away with you, Satan'.)

The Temptation of Christ is represented in two forms. Either He and the Devil stand before each other as two men (ivory relief, *c.*850, book-cover with the Temptation in the centre, surrounded by scenes from the Gospel, Frankfurt) or He is confronted with a monstrous creature, with wings, claws, and of a daunting hideousness. The artists' temptation is to present the Devil in the most terrifying and repellent guise, and most have succumbed to it, particularly during the Middle Ages, and even as late as the 16th century some still felt it necessary to equip the Devil with a pair of horns. Of such is, for instance, a MS illumination in an early 9th-century Psalter, Stuttgart, where the Devil is a horrific creature, as he is in one of the capital reliefs by Gislebertus in St-Lazare, Autun, of 1120–30, and even in the Duccio *Maestà* of 1308–11, Siena. The wing of the altarpiece by Jacob Cornelisz of 1520/30, Aachen, makes his Devil recognizable only by his horns. Both Titian, in his *Temptation*, *c.*1540–5, Minneapolis, and Tintoretto in the *Temptation* scene in the Scuola di San Rocco, Venice, 1564–88, reject these easy horror formulas. Titian makes Satan a beautiful boy, and Tintoretto paints him as a resplendently beautiful 'fallen angel'. The Ary Sheffer oil painting (1857) of this scene is in the Walker Art Gallery, Liverpool. *See also* CHRIST.

Ten Commandments *See* COMMANDMENTS.

Tenebrae candlestick A triangular stand for fifteen candles, used during Holy Week. *See* HEARSE.

Ten Thousand Martyrs *See* MAURICE, S.

Teresa *See* THERESA, S.

Tertiary A member of one of the *third orders of religious, who take modified vows and live in the world.

tesserae (Lat. dice) are the small cubes of stone, marble, or glass used in making *mosaics. It seems also to have been a sign of recognition between Christians in times of persecution, much as a seal or ring: in modern Italian *tessera* is a season-ticket—i.e. a pass.

Tetragrammaton The abbreviation *JHVH or *YHWH. *See* NOMEN SACRUM.

Tetramorph (Gk. four forms) The OT Prophet *Ezekiel, in his vision (1: 4–11; 10: 14) described winged creatures with four faces: 'a stormy wind came out of the north: a great cloud with brightness round it and fire flashing forth continually, and in the middle of the fire, something like gleaming amber. In the middle of it was something like four living creatures . . . they were of human form. Each had four faces and each of them had four wings. Their legs were straight, and the soles of their feet were like the sole of a calf's foot . . . Under their wings on their four sides they had human hands. And the four had their faces and their wings thus: their wings touched one another; each of them moved straight ahead without turning as they moved. As for the appearance of their faces: the four had the face of a man, the face of a lion on the right side, and the face of an ox on the left side, and the face of an eagle; such were their faces. Their wings were spread out above; each creature had two wings, each of which touched the wing of another, while two covered their bodies.' Ezek. 10: 14 describes the *cherubim—'Each one had four faces: the first face was that of the cherub, and the second face was that of a man, the third that of a lion, and the fourth that of an eagle.' These bafflingly obscure descriptions apply to the Tetramorph, but Rev. 4: 6–8 describes 'four living creatures full of eyes, in front and behind: the first . . . like a lion, the second . . . like an ox, the third had a face like a man, and the fourth like a flying eagle. And the four living creatures, each of them with six wings, are full of eyes all around and inside. Day and night without ceasing they sing, "Holy Holy, the Lord God the Almighty, who was and is and is to come."'

As individual figures, with bodies corresponding to their faces, they became the *Evangelist Symbols: a man (or angel), for Matthew, a lion (often winged, like the lion of Venice) for Mark, an ox for Luke, and an eagle for John. Sometimes a figure of the Evangelist as a scribe is pictured writing his Gospel, with the relevant symbol close by him, as in the opening to Mark in the 8th-century *Ada Gospels* (Trier) or the 9th-century *Book of Armagh* (Dublin, Trinity Coll. Lib.), in which each Gospel is prefaced by a single page with only the symbol of the Evangelist, as interpreted by the Irish scribe, who clearly had never seen a lion.

Various attempts to represent the Tetramorph as described by Ezekiel have been made e.g. in a 5th-century mosaic in Hosios David, Salonika, or in the 6th-century *Rabbula Gospels (Florence, Bib. Laurenziana), where the Tetramorph supports Christ's mandorla; or the 9th-century mosaic with Ezekiel and the Tetramorph in Sta *Sophia, Istanbul. Another version, with the body of a lion but with four heads and four different feet, ridden by the allegorical figure of *Ecclesia, occurred in a MS of *c.*1170, now lost, and in a 14th-century statue on the façade of Worms Cathedral. By far the best-known attempt at representing Ezekiel's vision is the small painting by Raphael (*c.*1517: Florence, Pitti), but this hardly reflects the text; rather, as Vasari noted, 'a uso di Giove', like a *Jupiter Tonans*.

Thaddaeus *See* JUDE.

Theatines The Clerks Regular of Divine Providence, an austere religious Order, founded in Rome in 1524 to combat the abuses which were giving rise to Protestantism. One of the founders was G. P. Carafa, Bishop of Chieti (in Latin Theate, hence Theatines), later Pope Paul IV. The Order, active in the *Counter-Reformation, included the architect *Guarini.

Thebaid In the Upper Nile valley, near Thebes, a Christian community flourished in the 3rd century. The first to come there was *S. Paul the Hermit, and S. *Antony Abbot visited him, and eventually buried him. Other reclusive men joined S. Paul, living as hermits, but eventually, under the government of S. Antony and S. Pachomius, they joined in communities, founding the first monastic settlements. They were known as the Desert Fathers. The idea was often taken up in later times, for example by the hermit monks of *Camaldoli.

Paintings of the Thebaid are by Mariotto di Nardo (*c.*1390: Estergom, Christian Mus.), and by an anonymous Cologne master (1500: Munich) who included a meeting of SS Antony Abbot and Paul, and several Temptations of S. Antony. The 14th-century frescoes by ?Traini in the Campo Santo, Padua, depicting the *Triumph of Death contain a Thebaid as a representation of holy peace and happiness, in contrast to a worldly scene of pleasure.

Theban Legion *See* MAURICE, S.

Theoderich was a German monk, probably from Hirsau in the Rhineland, who visited the Holy Land *c.*1172 and wrote a guide to the Holy Places, especially the Holy *Sepulchre. He had some knowledge of architecture and gives a detailed description of the church as it then was, including the stone of *Unction, as well as accounts of other sites in the city. He visited all the places in the vicinity of Jerusalem associated with Christ, says he went to the Sea of Galilee, and its cities, describes Mt. Tabor which he says was the site of the Transfiguration, Naim, and Nazareth. Then (rather improbably) comes mention of Damascus and Antioch, Sidon, Tyre, and Tripoli, and he has already mentioned Hebron and Abraham's Oaks of Mamre. At the end of his account he admits that much of what he recounts comes not only from his own experience but also from the reports of others. Where he writes from experience he is clear and engagingly descriptive; where he repeats from others, his account is confused and ill-ordered.

Theological Films: Ingmar Bergman, Robert Bresson, Andrei Tarkovsky *See* FILM.

Theological Virtues (Faith, Hope, Charity) *See* VIRTUES.

Theophanes the Greek ('Feofan Grek') was a Byzantine icon and fresco painter who went to Russia in the 1370s, being recorded in Novgorod in 1378 and Moscow in 1405, where he probably died 1405/10. With *Rublev, he was one of the two great Russian artists of the Middle Ages. The two are known to have worked together, but Rublev was probably not his pupil as their styles are so different—

Theophanes used a sketchy, 'impressionistic' technique which derived ultimately from Late Antique wall-paintings. His first recorded works were frescoes in the Church of the Transfiguration, Novgorod, of 1378, parts of which survive and which influenced the Novgorod School. In Moscow with Rublev he worked on the Cathedral of the Annunciation in the Kremlin (1405), of which some damaged icons survive. He and Rublev introduced the Russian form of *iconostasis, which is much larger than the Byzantine-Greek three-tiered type. Some illuminated MSS have also been attributed to him.

theophany A manifestation of the divine. *See* EPIPHANY.

Theophilus was a monk, priest, and craftsman who wrote *De diversis artibus* (Of various arts), probably in the first half of the 12th century. He may be identical with Roger, a monk of Helmarshausen, who made a portable altar for the Bishop of Paderborn in 1100. The identification depends upon a note in one of the copies of the treatise (the original MS is lost), which reads: 'Theophilus . . . qui e[s]t Rugerus'—(who is Roger). The treatise itself is one of the most important on the arts of MS illumination and wall-painting, glass-making, and, especially, all forms of metalwork, obviously written by an expert craftsman.

If Theophilus is the Roger who made the portable altar now in Paderborn Cathedral, then there are strong links between his work and that produced in the Meuse valley in the Low Countries, but the most important influence was from Byzantium, transmitted through *Carolingian and *Ottonian examples coming from Italy. In his treatise Theophilus makes it clear that he knew 'Greek' works, as well as Italian, Russian, and Arabic techniques. 'Greek' was the term commonly used to describe Byzantine art.

The few pieces that can reasonably be ascribed to Roger include two altars in Paderborn, with engraving, niello inlays, and figures in relief—all techniques described in detail by Theophilus—as well as two altar crosses in Frankfurt and Cologne with large rectangles at the ends of the arms and engraved backs, and a book-cover for the *Helmarshausen Gospels* (Trier Cath.) of *c.*1100, with a silver-gilt cross set with gems enclosing four copper-gilt reliefs of the *Evangelist Symbols, each with six wings—telling evidence of the influence of Early Christian ivories and mosaics.

The same shape of cross characterizes the large ivory altar cross of *c.*1100–30 in New York (Met. Mus.). The cross is carved on both sides; on the front it is made in the guise of a 'ragged staff' like a budding branch to represent the *lignum vitae*, the Tree of Salvation. The figure of Christ is missing. The corners have Passion scenes, and at the bottom of the staff are Adam and Eve released from Limbo. On the back of the cross there are Evangelist Symbols (John is missing), and the shaft and arms have Prophets. There are also roundels on the front, of *Moses and the *brazen serpent*, and on the back the *Agnus Dei*. Although undocumented, it is likely that this masterpiece came from Roger's workshop.

Theotokos (Gk. God-bearer. Lat. *Deipara, Dei Genetrix*) A title of honour of *Mary the Blessed Virgin as Christ's mother. It was upheld and confirmed at the Councils of Ephesus (431) and Chalcedon (451), which refuted the Nestorian heresy which denied the Divine nature of Christ, claiming that she was no more than the Christotokos—the Christ-bearer. *See also* MADONNA TYPES.

Theresa of Avila, Saint (1515–82), was one of the great mystics and is a patron saint of Spain. She was the foundress of the reformed, or Discalced, *Carmelites. She was born in Avila, in Castile, into an aristocratic family, and in her childhood showed a strong religious bent. Her decision to become a nun was inspired by reading the letters of S. Jerome when recovering from an illness, and after gaining her father's unwilling consent she entered the Carmelite convent of the Incarnation in 1535. From 1536 to 1539 she lived at home during an illness, but then returned to the cloister. Her convent was of the relaxed discipline, and she began to practise mental prayer. In 1555 she experienced an inner conversion which profoundly changed her spiritual life. Her visions and mystical experiences became known, and led to much unhappiness and some persecution. She was encouraged by S. Peter of Alcantara, a Franciscan of extreme asceticism, who for a time was her confessor, and eventually in the teeth of opposition from religious and civic authorities she founded her first reformed convent in 1562. The thirteen nuns of this small foundation were bound to a life of strict enclosure, poverty, manual labour, and prayer, depending on what they could grow in their garden and on unsolicited alms. Mother Theresa's reformed houses eventually numbered seventeen. The struggle for reform in her Order was paralleled by that of S. John of the Cross, whom she advised and encouraged in his efforts at similar reform of the Carmelite Friars; they met with opposition and persecution from the unreformed branches of both their Orders, until finally they were given independent status.

S. Theresa was commanded to write her autobiography and an account, which is full of practical common sense, of her foundations; she also wrote *The Way of Perfection*, a manual for her nuns, and *The Interior Castle* on prayer and contemplation. She was canonized in 1622 (on the same day as *S. Philip Neri, *S. Ignatius Loyola, and *S. Francis Xavier) and in 1970 was made a Doctor of the Church with *S. Catherine of Siena, the first women to be so honoured. The only contemporary portrait is at Avila, painted by a friar in 1570, showing her with her vision of a dove, but the most famous image is the *Bernini *Ecstasy of S. Theresa* in Sta Maria della Vittoria in Rome, which represents her transverberation (piercing through) as the subject of the meditations of members of the Cornaro family. She was particularly popular in the late 16th and early 17th centuries, before and after her canonization, and there are paintings by Rubens and sculpture by Cano and Günther among others.

Third Order The name given to men, and women, who are associated with certain religious Orders, but do not take the full vows of profession in the Order. They are called Third Orders to distinguish them from the First and Second Orders of fully professed monks, or friars, and nuns. The inspiration behind Third Orders began with *S. Francis of Assisi who, after founding his own Order, and after the Order of Poor Clares (the Minorites) under S. Clare had been established in the Rule he prescribed, founded a Third Order in 1221 as a kind of 'middle way' between profession in a religious Order and living in the world. He named them 'Brothers and Sisters of Penance'; they served a year's novitiate, were bound by the Rule to live soberly, to practise their religion assiduously, and to be active in works of charity and mercy. Very many people in all walks of life were attracted to the Third Order, including S. Louis of France, S. Elizabeth of Hungary, S. Bridget of Sweden, S. Catherine of Siena, and S. Roch. Sometimes they lived in communities as Regular Tertiaries, following the Rule and wearing the habit of their Order, though rarely in public, and all wearing a *scapular under their ordinary clothes. They could retain their property, as did, for example, the Béguines in Flanders, and the Oblates of the Tor de Specchi, founded in Rome about 1425 by S. Francesca Romana. Many combined the disciplined life of the Order with a lay existence, usually working in charitable enterprises, or in teaching and nursing. Houses of Regular Tertiaries were founded from the late 13th century, and are often, particularly in the case of Sisters, almost as strictly disciplined or enclosed as fully professed members of the Orders. The Franciscans and Dominicans have the most important Third Orders, concentrating particularly on charitable and social work, teaching, and missionary work (for example, the Franciscan Missionaries of Mary); other Orders to found Tertiary branches are the Carmelites, the Servites, and the Augustinians.

The oldest association of this type antedates S. Francis's foundations by some forty years—they are the Béguines, mentioned earlier. They were started by a zealous priest of Liège about 1180, who founded an institution for widows and single women who wished to live a religious life, but who did not want to be in an enclosed Order. They called themselves after their founder Lambert le Bègue, which soon became Béguines, and the communities in which they lived Béguinages. This was not a convent, but a *laura*, or collection of cottages in which the women—one or two to a cottage—lived running their own little households. It was surrounded by a wall and had a chapel in the centre served by a priest to whom each woman made a vow of chastity and obedience. She could leave at any time, and could reclaim her property if she did so, but for as long as she lived there, she engaged in charitable work, particularly in Sunday schools for girls, and in the Divine Office. They also took in pensioners, who did not belong to the community, but paid for their upkeep. They still exist, in Ghent, Bruges, Antwerp, and Mechlin (Malines). Similar communities for men called Béghards were founded in the early 13th century, but most of them eventually entered the Third Orders of the Mendicant friars.

'Thomas, Gospel of' (Infancy Gospel, 'Acts of Thomas') *See* APOCRYPHAL GOSPELS.

Thomas the Apostle, Saint, was one of the Twelve Apostles, and is mentioned in all the Gospels, though not in the lists in the Synoptic Gospels. In John 11: 16 he is named as the 'twin' (Gk. *didymus*), and when Jesus proposed to return to Bethany because Lazarus was dead, despite the threats made by the Jews against His life, Thomas said to the other disciples, 'Let us also go, that we may die with him.' He is next mentioned during the Last Supper, when he interrupts Jesus (John 14: 4–5) because he cannot understand what He means by the words 'And you know the way to the place where I am going' by saying, 'Lord, we do not know where you are going. How can we know the way?' This is when Jesus answers with the words, 'I am the way, the truth, and the life . . . '. The last mentions of Thomas in the Gospels are after the Resurrection; first, when he was not with the other disciples when Jesus appeared among them, and refused to believe them (John 20: 24–9) 'Unless I see the mark of the nails in his hands, and put my finger in the mark of the nails and my hand in his side, I will not believe.' A week later Christ again appeared among the disciples, and Thomas was there. Jesus said to Thomas, 'Put your finger here and see my hands. Reach out your hand and put it in my side. Do not doubt but believe.' Thomas answered 'My Lord and my God!' Jesus said to him, ' . . . Blessed are those who have not seen and yet believe.' Second, he is mentioned as among those (John 21: 1–3) on the shore of the Sea of Galilee (S. John says Sea of Tiberias, but they are the same) when they all went fishing, but caught nothing. This is the occasion for the Miraculous Draught of Fish. The only really memorable thing about Thomas is his incredulity, because it was only the second time any disciple had specifically declared a belief in His divinity (the first time was Peter, when he said 'You are the Messiah, the son of the living God', Matt. 16: 13–20) and also because it gave Jesus the opportunity to stress the overwhelming importance of faith for the disciples themselves, and for those to whom the disciples would be sent.

According to *Eusebius, Thomas evangelized the Parthians, east of Mesopotamia; another source says that he evangelized India, and he is claimed as the origin of their Christian beliefs by the people of Malabar, and that he was martyred at Mylapore, near Madras. Later his body was removed to Edessa, N. of Palestine, in the 4th century, and is said to have been moved again to Ortona, on the Adriatic coast S. of Pescara. There is a wealth of apocryphal literature attributed to S. Thomas, or attached to him, such as the Acts of Thomas, dating from before the middle of the 3rd century, relating his missionary work in India, where he went as an architect recommended in that capacity by Jesus himself, to build a palace for the king. He is also said to have worked in a neighbouring kingdom where he was martyred.

There is also an apocryphal Gospel of Thomas written in Greek, found in Upper Egypt in 1945/6, and dating from about 150. It claims to have been written by 'Didymus Judas Thomas' (Judas is a second name also found in the apocryphal Acts but not in the Gospels). It consists not of a narrative, but of a series of sayings and parables attributed to Jesus, some of which resemble matter found in the Gospels of Matthew and Luke, but to which they are no more than a secondary source which does not warrant the fuss made over it when the book became generally known in 1959.

The remaining apocryphal book is the Infancy Gospel of Thomas, which professes to record the 'miracles' performed by Christ when a child. It exists in all the languages current in Early Christian literature (Greek, Aramaic, Ethiopic, Latin, Georgian, and Syriac). Most of the incidents are exhibitions of supernatural powers with no moral or theological significance, and often showing the Christ Child as cruel and vindictive. It derives probably from folklore; there is no evidence for its date. The *Golden Legend* is full of fantastic stories of Thomas being sent to India by Jesus, his deeds, conversions, and martyrdom there, and in the account of the Assumption of the Virgin records how he, once again being absent from the event, refused to believe the miracles which occurred at the burial of the Virgin, and the Virgin's girdle fell from Heaven into his hands to convince him of her bodily assumption. Much of the material is derived from the apocryphal Acts. The saint's attribute is a spear, or an architect's set-square, the latter because of his Indian legend.

Most of the representations of S. Thomas concentrate on his incredulity. The earliest is a 10th-century ivory in Berlin, and there is an 11th-century mosaic in Daphni, a 12th-century one in Monreale, a 12th-century relief in the cloister of Sto Domingo de Silos, in which—as at Monreale—Christ guides Thomas's hand towards the wound in his side. The most famous is the Verrocchio bronze in the niche of Orsanmichele in Florence, of 1483, and there are at least four copies of a Caravaggio of *c.*1598/9, of which two are in Potsdam and the Uffizi, and a third in the parish church of Thirsk (attributed to Carracci). Among the finest representations are those by Guercino (1621: London, NG), Passeri (1675–86: Rome, Sta Croce in Gerusalemme), and Rubens (Antwerp). Prato Cathedral claims to have the Virgin's girdle as a relic, and it is exhibited once a year from the outside pulpit made for the purpose by Donatello and Michelozzo in 1439. The cathedral has a chapel dedicated to the relic, the Cappella del Sacro Cingolo, with a fresco cycle by Agnolo Gaddi of 1392–5 of the *Assumption* with the Virgin giving her girdle to Thomas, and also recounting the story of Michele Dagomani, a citizen of Prato, who found the relic in the Holy Land and presented it to his native city. Other representations include: Orcagna: the carved panel of the *Assumption with S. Thomas receiving the girdle* (1352–60: Florence, Orsanmichele); Benozzo Gozzoli: *Assumption, with S. Thomas receiving the girdle* and *predella* panels with the *Life of the Virgin* (Vatican Mus.), which was once the altarpiece of the high altar in San Fortunato, Montefalco, where Gozzoli painted the fresco decoration dated 1450; frescoes now in the public library of Castelfiorentino, S. of Florence, which once were part of a roadside tabernacle and include an *Assumption with S. Thomas receiving the girdle*, datable 1484; and lastly, Matteo di Giovanni: *Assumption with S. Thomas receiving the girdle* (1474: London, NG). *See* APOCRYPHAL GOSPELS; ASSUMPTION.

Thomas Aquinas, Saint (*c.*1225–74), was a Dominican philosopher and theologian, who was declared a Doctor of the Church by Pius V in 1567 and given the title of 'Angelic Doctor'. His great monument is his *Summa Theologica*, and Leo XIII in 1879 enjoined its study on all students of theology. It is now obligatory for all students of theology and philosophy in Catholic universities.

Many facts of his life are unclear. He was the youngest son of Count Landulf of Aquino, and was born at Roccasecca d'Aquino, probably about 1220/5, and was educated at the neighbouring Abbey of Montecassino from the age of 8, where his parents intended him to become abbot. He left the abbey, why and exactly when is unknown, but probably about 1240 and went to the University of Naples, where he first became acquainted with Aristotelian philosophy. There he joined the recently founded Dominican Order because it offered him the opportunity to dedicate himself to an intellectual apostolate, but his family was so bitterly opposed to the idea of his joining a Mendicant Order that they held him prisoner at Roccasecca for about a year, but he still persisted. The exact details of this period of his life are very obscure, but in April 1244 he either joined or rejoined the Dominicans and after being in Rome for a short time he was in Paris until 1248, where the Dominican theologian Albert of Lauingen (later S. Albertus Magnus) encouraged further his study of Aristotle, Plato, and other Graeco-Arabic sources. In 1248 he followed Albert to Cologne to study at the newly founded *studium generale* there. The story is told that because he spoke very little, and was naturally corpulent, his fellow students called him 'the dumb ox', but some notes of his on a difficult proposition argued by Albert were passed to him by one of the students, and he was so impressed by their acuity and intellect that he arranged a disputation on the thesis, after which he said, 'We call him the dumb ox, but with his learning he will utter a bellow which will resound the world over.' In 1252 Thomas was back in Paris, where he wrote his first treatise in defence of the Mendicant Orders, and after taking his Master's degree in theology in 1256 he moved from centre to centre over the next ten years, from Anagni, Orvieto, Rome, Viterbo, Paris, and Naples, while working on his *Summa Theologica*. On the way to the Council at Lyons in 1274 he died at the Cistercian monastery of Fossanova (near Priverno, about 50 miles from Naples).

He was a prolific writer, author of many other treatises, including ones on the Gospels, the Epistles, the Psalms, Job, Isaiah, Jeremiah, and one against the Islamic philosopher Averroes. He was the most famous commentator on Aristotle during the Middle Ages, whose teaching was known in Catholic Europe from about 1220, and had considerable influence particularly in the universities of Paris and Padua, and in Rome. After deep study, mainly by Albert, his views on the eternity of God, on the immortality of the soul, and on free will were found to be destructive of Catholic doctrines, and his teaching, from being prescribed in Paris, was then proscribed. Thomas Aquinas's thesis was directed at one of Averroes's chief defenders who proposed that things might be true philosophically, though not in conformity with Catholic faith. This doctrine, of 'double truth' was particularly unacceptable. These works preceded the *Summa*, which he did not live to finish. His philosophy was characterized by his distinction between reason and faith, that while certain beliefs may be held by faith, yet they are not therefore contrary to reason, and their acceptance by believers is through personal revelation and decision. But there are also things where reason is the principal argument for their acceptance, and these require no revelation. In this he follows the Aristotelian argument that since man is both corporeal as well as intellectual, things that are intellectually conceived must also first be realized by the senses. Some of his tenets were later condemned by the Church; a story connected with the rejection of some of his views tells that in grief he knelt before a crucifix and exclaimed, 'Lord, was ever a man treated with such injustice!', and the Crucified replied, 'And I, Thomas?' This story is illustrated in one of the frescoes in the Strozzi Chapel. He remains one of the greatest Christian thinkers and teachers, and was accorded particular honour by the Council of *Trent, and the greater part of his teaching is revered as the true expression of Christian doctrine.

In person, he was a tall, corpulent man, with a pale face and a bald head. His powers of concentration when he was working were so formidable that he is said to have been able to dictate to four secretaries simultaneously on different subjects, and his periods of deep contemplation and prayer reached often to ecstasy. Even before his canonization in 1323, his body was being dismembered for relics, so that many places, even non-Dominican, claim to have one, and although he died in N. Italy, his body—or what remained of it—was taken to St-Sernin, Toulouse, in 1368, where it remained until it was moved to the Dominican church of the Jacobins in Toulouse in 1974.

Images of S. Thomas Aquinas are legion. The oldest and the only one possibly painted in his lifetime was in Sta Maria in Gradi, Viterbo, but has been destroyed. Among the most interesting are *The Triumph of the Church*, by Traini (14th cent.: Siena, Sta Caterina); Sassetta, *The vision of S. Thomas* (Vatican), and *S. Thomas praying in a chapel* (1423/6: Budapest). Quite often painters have changed his appearance, making him slim, instead of his recorded substantial figure. Other representations are by Andrea Bonaiuti (and assistants): in *The Triumph of S. Thomas Aquinas* (*c.*1368: Florence, Spanish Chapel in the cloister of Sta Maria Novella; this fresco shows S. Thomas with Averroes, and heresy, beneath his feet); Filippino Lippi: *The Triumph of S. Thomas Aquinas* (1488–93: Florence, Strozzi Chapel, Sta Maria Novella); Zurbarán: *Apotheosis of S. Thomas Aquinas* (1631: Seville).

Thomas of Canterbury, Saint (*c.*1118–70). Thomas Becket is one of the handful of archbishops who have been murdered in their own cathedrals. He came of a Norman family settled in London, and was sent to study in Paris. About 1141 he entered the household of Archbishop Theobald of Canterbury, who sent him to Bologna and Auxerre (then a leading legal school) to study canon law. The subject had gained new importance from the production in 1140 of the first complete collected edition of canon law known as the Decretals which had been compiled by Gratian, who was then teaching canon law at Bologna. On his return Thomas joined the considerable body of jurists in the entourage of the archbishop, who ordained him a deacon and made him archdeacon of Canterbury in 1154. In 1154 King Stephen, who had since 1135 been waging a totally destructive civil war against Henry I's daughter Mathilda, whom Henry had appointed to succeed him, finally died and was succeeded by Mathilda's son Henry II.

The new king, who was aged 21, had inherited a ravaged and lawless land, which he was determined to bring to order and justice. As a result of the changes which had taken place since the reign of Pope Gregory VII (from 1073 to 1085), who began the struggle against a host of ecclesiastical abuses, many of them stemming from lay investiture (appointment to church offices by secular rulers or magnates), there was increasing friction between Church and State. Archbishop Theobald, therefore, proposed to the king that he should take Thomas as his Chancellor, since he knew him to be learned, wise, and incorruptible. Thomas was about 34, a fine horseman, with a love of hunting, and also convivial, with a taste for splendour—very like the king himself. The appointment was a great success; the king and his chancellor hunted together, feasted together, and Thomas's advice and management of king, court, and affairs of state seemed to be perfect, even to the point that on a number of occasions, Thomas sided against the Church in rulings on lay investiture.

In 1152 Henry had married Eleanor of Aquitaine, the divorced wife of Louis VII of France; she brought with her the Duchy of Aquitaine, which was then lost to the French crown. This embroiled England in wars with France, and in 1159 Henry was forced to fight to gain Toulouse, part of his wife's apanage. Thomas accompanied the king and joined in the fighting. In 1161 Archbishop Theobald died, and Henry determined to make Thomas his successor, believing that his projects for moves against the Church would be more easily achieved were Thomas, his friend and boon companion, archbishop. Although Thomas warned him that if he became archbishop their friendship would be destroyed, since as head of the Church in England he would not tolerate the incursions the king proposed into ecclesiastical privileges, Henry insisted, refusing to believe that their close relationship would not survive Thomas's elevation. Realizing that resistance was useless, Thomas unwillingly acquiesced. Up to now he had only been a deacon; he was ordained priest on the day before his coronation in 1162. He then resigned his chancellorship, to the king's chagrin, and totally reformed his life. He gave up hunting and other sports, and the luxury and profusion of his former life, and very soon it became clear that the king and the archbishop would soon be at loggerheads. The first instances were over 'benefit of clergy', whereby priests and others in orders could only be tried by an ecclesiastical court, even for civil offences. More serious conflicts soon arose and the king summoned all bishops to meet him at the royal hunting lodge of Clarendon, near Salisbury, where the Constitutions of Clarendon were drawn up. At first Thomas refused to accept them, but many bishops and magnates pressed him to agree to them, and Thomas finally gave in, afterwards blaming himself bitterly for having done so. The king then determined to force Thomas to resign his archbishopric, and after an abortive meeting at Northampton, Thomas fled the kingdom, beginning a voluntary exile in 1164 which lasted until his return to Canterbury in 1170. The pope, Alexander III, was himself an exile at that time, having been forced to flee from Rome by the Emperor Frederick Barbarossa, and was living at Sens, in N. France. The envoys of Henry and of Thomas met to argue their case before the pope, and Thomas himself appeared and surrendered his archbishopric into the pope's hands. The pope refused to permit Thomas to resign, and Thomas retired to the Cistercian abbey of Pontigny, and wrote to the king with mounting severity, finally resorting to solemn excommunication in 1166, which was confirmed by the pope. Then Henry made a cardinal blunder; it is the privilege of the Archbishop of Canterbury to crown the king, but Henry determined to have his son Henry crowned and the Archbishop of York performed the ceremony. The pope and the King of France were furious, the King of France because young Henry had been crowned without his wife Margaret, the king's daughter. The pope threatened to interdict Henry's French provinces. This was so serious a turn of events that Henry capitulated, and the two contestants met and were outwardly reconciled in July 1170, but Thomas would not return until all the confiscated estates of the see of Canterbury had been restored. One of the most important proofs of the genuineness of a reconciliation is the exchange of the Kiss of Peace, but the king always evaded it, so that when Thomas returned to Canterbury on 1 December, things were still at danger point. He was received with acclamation by the monks and the people, and with equal acclaim when he came to London to salute young King Henry, whom he had known since his childhood. When this was reported to Henry he was furious, and whether or not he said the fateful words attributed to him is uncertain: 'Who will rid me of this upstart priest?' He cannot have intended what happened next because it meant the ruin of his whole policy of gaining control over the Church, but believing it would win them favour, four knights left secretly, and met at Saltwood Castle, near Hythe. From there they rode to Canterbury on 29 December, together with a force they had collected, had a violent argument with Thomas who, when they left, went to the cathedral, to be followed by the knights who struck him down near an altar and killed him. The whole party then pillaged the palace, taking everything they could find, even the horses from the stables.

His body was interred in the crypt where it remained until July 1220, when it was removed to the shrine in the cathedral. The murder of an archbishop in his cathedral was sensational, and the king when told of it fell into paroxysms of grief and lamentation. The pope threatened interdict, and to avoid this Henry swore on the Gospels that he had no part in the outrage and promised full penance, since he recognized that his enmity had provoked the crime. He made (almost) full restitution of all the estates of the see, abrogated the obnoxious Constitutions of Clarendon, agreed to go on a pilgrimage, and in May 1172 was pardoned for his part in the murder.

In February 1173 Thomas was canonized as S. Thomas of Canterbury, and in July 1174 Henry performed his final expiation by being scourged by the monks before S. Thomas's tomb, and spending a day and a night in prayer before the relics of the saint.

That year the choir of Canterbury Cathedral was destroyed by fire. The splendid new choir was designed by William of *Sens, and the shrine of the saint was placed in it, to be eventually despoiled and destroyed by Henry VIII in 1538.

The earliest representation of S. Thomas Becket is before 1182 in Monreale, but only as a bishop, and his cult seems to have been propagated from Monreale: William II of Sicily's wife was the daughter of Henry II of England. A MS illustration in Harley 502, of *c.*1190–1200 (London, BM), is probably the first picture of the murder. A 12th-century fresco of the murder is in Spoleto, SS Giovanni e Paolo; and very soon the subject spread all over Europe and into Armenia. Canterbury Cathedral has a fine 13th-century stained-glass 'portrait' of Becket, in the choir ambulatory. A MS by the Boucicaut Master, *c.*1405–8, Paris, Musée Jacquemart-André, has a large miniature of the murder.

Thomas More, Saint *See* MORE, SIR THOMAS.

three *See* TRINITY.

Three Holy Children The OT story is in Dan. 2 and 3, which recounts how King Nebuchadnezzar, who greatly favoured Daniel, had appointed at his request Shadrach, Meshach, and Abednego over affairs in the province of Babylon. The king had made a giant golden statue and commanded at the dedication that when the people heard the music of the pipe, drum, lyre, and other instruments, they should all fall down and worship the idol. If they did not, they would be thrown into a fiery furnace. Some Chaldeans came forward and denounced the Jews because they had not worshipped according to the king's order. The king, enraged, ordered Shadrach, Meshach, and Abednego to be brought before him, and told them that if they did not worship the idol, they would be thrown into a fiery furnace. They answered him: 'If our God, whom we serve, is able to deliver us from the furnace of blazing fire and out of your hand, O king, let him deliver us. But if not, be it known to you, O king, that we will not serve your gods, and we will not worship the golden statue that you have set up.' The furious king ordered the furnace to be heated seven times more than usual, had the three men bound and, still wearing their normal clothes, they were thrown into the furnace. The king said to his counsellors, 'Was it not three men that we threw bound into the fire?' They answered, 'True, O King.' He replied, 'But I see four men, unbound, walking in the middle of the fire, and they are not hurt, and the fourth has the appearance of a god.' The king then approached the door of the furnace and said, 'Shadrach, Meshach, and Abednego, servants of the Most High God, come out! Come here!' They came out of the fire, and not a hair of their heads had been singed, and nor had their garments. Nebuchadnezzar said, 'Blessed be the God of Shadrach, Meshach, and Abednego, who sent his angel and delivered his servants who trusted in him . . .'. The king decreed that no one should blaspheme the God of the three under pain of the most terrible punishment.

The interpretation of this miraculous deliverance is seen as the grace of God protecting the elect, like the deliverance of *Susanna, and *Daniel himself in the lions' den. The angel is interpreted as a symbol of Christ descending into Limbo to rescue the souls of the just. The scene was represented in the 3rd-century *Catacomb of Priscilla, and on a 4th-century sarcophagus (Louvre), where they are dressed as Persians, as they were considered as a prefiguration of the Three *Magi. They are also in the *menologium of Basil II (10th cent.) and the Virgin Portal at Laon (12th cent.), and though not a popular subject, appear in some medieval *portal sculptures, but are rare after the end of the 15th century. In some texts they are named as Ananias, Azarias, and Misael.

Three Kings *See* MAGI.

Three Living and Three Dead *See* MEMENTO MORI and TRIUMPH OF DEATH.

Three Maries at the Sepulchre *See* MARIES.

Throne, Preparation of the *See* HETOIMASIA, PAROUSIA.

Throne of Grace *See* SEAT OF MERCY.

Thrones *See* ANGELS.

thuribile, thurifer *See* CENSER.

tiara, triple, is the form of diadem used by the pope. Its early history is obscure; it seems that the first distinctive head-dress was called the *camelaucum* (the name suggests a Byzantine origin) and is recorded in his *Vita* as worn by Pope Constantine (708–15) as a papal prerogative. It was shaped somewhat like the later Doge's diadem, in order to distinguish it from the crowns worn by temporal rulers. Thereafter its changes of shape and design may be traced somewhat irregularly in papal tombs, but it is described as white, and shaped like a candle snuffer. A damaged wall-painting of a pope officiating at the translation of the relics of S. Clement, in the narthex of the lower church of San Clemente, Rome, of 1085/1115, shows him wearing a tall, conical diadem with a band, probably jewelled, round the base. In a MS of *c.*1150 of the *Letters of S. Gregory* (Paris, BN) the pope wears a soft, low head-covering with a band round the crown and another running back across the top. The damaged tomb slab of Pope Lucian III (d. 1185, Verona, Duomo), shows him wearing the tall conical diadem with a ?band round the base, but also a knop at the top, and the effigy of Clement IV (d. 1268: Viterbo, San Francesco alla Rocca) shows him wearing a conical diadem of modest height, with the now customary band round the base and across the top, with a knop. In the 13th century two lappets were added towards the side or back which usually lay over the front of the pope's shoulders. The diadem on the effigy of Adrian V (d. 1276), in San Francesco, Viterbo (badly damaged in the last war), shows that it had a jewelled band round the base. The effigy of Pope Honorius IV (d. 1287: Rome, Sta Maria Aracoeli) shows him with a single crown round his conical diadem. Pope Boniface VIII (d. 1303: St Peter's crypt) had a second crown over the jewelled band on his diadem, because he claimed temporal and spiritual dominion, and this appears on his tomb, and Pope Clement VI (d. 1346: Abbey of La Chaise-Dieu) wears three crowns round his diadem in his tomb-effigy (or what survives of it after its desecration during the Wars of Religion in 1562). By this time also, the diadem had increased in bulk to a beehive shape, which it still has. The knop continued to exist, varying in size from pope to pope, and finally became a small cross. The three crowns were because the pope was a temporal ruler in the Papal States, and claimed temporal power over the secular rulers of Europe, by reason of his spiritual dominion, the whole symbolizing his triple jurisdiction. Since Clement VI three crowns have remained the normal form. The three crowns have also been given symbolic meanings: the Trinity; the Church militant, suffering, and triumphant; the three roles of the Church: teaching, ruling, and sanctifying; and the pope as pastor, preacher, and prophet.

One of the unusual representations of the papal tiara is in images of the Trinity, and of the *Seat of Mercy, where God the Father is shown wearing a papal tiara. An example is in a MS by the Boucicaut Master in the Musée Jacquemart-André, Paris, *c.*1405–8.

Tiepolo, G. B. (Giambattista) (1696–1770), was the last of the great Venetian decorative painters, equally at home in oil-painting and in fresco—a rarity among Venetian artists. He was also one of the last painters of religious subjects on a grandiose scale, and the finest exponent of *Rococo in Italy. His early works were influenced by the dark tonality of Piazzetta, and it was his first major frescoes, of Abraham and Jacob (1725–8) for the palace of the Patriarch of Aquileia in Udine, NW of Venice, that probably suggested a lighter use of colour in oil-painting. The Udine frescoes show his virtuosity allied to his perception of character and a rare sense of humour. His system of composition in his ceiling paintings, secular as well as religious, depended on his creating a wide and open field in which his figures could float, and placing major figures in sharp perspective round the edge of the picture while a visionary group soared overhead, a system current in Roman Baroque painting early in the previous century, and used in Venice by *Veronese and Piazzetta. He gave it a new twist by pushing the extremes of contrast between darker 'border' figures and the effulgent vision overhead, filling the sky with smaller figures floating in a limitless ethereal region; an example is the *Institution of the Rosary*, with the adjoining panels of the *Glory of S. Dominic* (1738–9: Venice, Gesuati), or the *Coronation of the Virgin* (1755: Venice, Pietà). In his altarpieces he achieves a quality of remoteness for the celestial figures by his exploitation of sharp perspective angles, and a low viewpoint which enables him to give to the figure of the Virgin or a saint a quality of exaltation, to emphasize the supernatural nature of a vision, and also by the opulent beauty of his figures as in *The Virgin and Child with SS Catherine of Siena,*

Rose of Lima, and Agnes of Montepulciano (1748: Venice, Gesuati). His *Last Communion of S. Lucy* (1748: Venice, SS Apostoli) shows him translating this lavish beauty into pure, but highly improbable, drama and this reaches its apogee in his last great Venetian religious work, *S. Thecla interceding for the plague-stricken of Este* (1758–9: Este, Cathedral), where the drama reaches an operatic intensity (indeed, it was once described as 'S. Thecla, soprano; God the Father, bass'). This huge picture, commemorating the plague of 1638, is one of the last great 'plague' pictures in Western art, and is replete with all the appropriate long-established iconographical features of the genre—the intercessory saint, the celestial Saviour, in this case God the Father, the crying child reaching for the breast of its dead mother, the grief-stricken man and horrified witnesses, the figures carrying away the body of a victim. His last religious works were painted in Spain, where he went in 1762 to fresco ceilings in the Royal Palace, Madrid. Of the seven altarpieces commissioned for the church of San Pascual Baylon, near Aranjuez, in 1767, only five *modelli* (four in London, Courtauld Inst., one in Dublin, NG) and some fragments of the dismembered paintings survive. By the time of his death taste had changed and his ethereal and visionary style had been swept away by the deadly chill of Neoclassicism. The five *modelli* show that in his old age Tiepolo could create works of deep spiritual feeling. In this he was equalled by his son, Gian Domenico (1727–1804), who painted a series of the *Stations of the Cross for San Polo, Venice, in 1747–9, and made a set of fourteen etchings, entitled *Via Crucis*; his subjects are the same as those chosen by S. Alphonsus, *c.*1750, or later. Gian Domenico also made etchings after his father's pictures, e.g. *The Virgin and Child with S. Dominic and an Abbot* (1750–60: Banbury, Upton House, National Trust).

Tiffany Studios *See* NORTH AMERICA.

Tintoretto, Jacopo (Robusti) (1518–94), claimed to have been a pupil of *Titian's, and certainly emulated him, although his style, technique, and workshop practice differed totally from Titian's. He was far more influenced by Central Italian Mannerism and by Michelangelo, whose works he may perhaps have seen early in his career. Unlike Titian or Veronese, he painted very few secular subjects, except for the political allegories and votive pictures for the Doge's Palace where such subjects were virtually obligatory, concentrating almost exclusively on religious works and portraits, mostly of men.

He frequently used architectural settings and backgrounds of a classical character, derived possibly from the architectural treatises of Serlio, as in his early masterpiece, *S. Mark rescuing a Slave* (1547–8: Venice, Accad.). He also used steep perspective settings so designed that the subject 'climbs', so to speak, the picture plane. An example is *S. George and the Dragon* (*c.*1560: London, NG). He combined this rising perspective with the unusual and novel device of the 'exploding centre'; for instance in the *Last Supper* (*c.*1559: Venice, San Trovaso) at the table placed cornerwise to the picture plane, Christ remains a still, calm centre amid the Apostles who stretch, lean, thrust away from Him. The same device of steep perspective and exploding movement was used in the huge compositions of the *Last Supper* and its OT parallel, the *Gathering of the Manna*, both about 12 ft. by 18 ft. (1592–4), flanking the high altar of San Giorgio Maggiore, and in the poignant *Entombment of Christ*, of the same date and in the same church.

His major work was the decoration of the *Scuola di San Rocco, a grand religious confraternity of which he was a member, and to which he devoted a large part of his energies from 1564 to 1588. There were a number of such confraternities in Venice (and Tintoretto worked for several of them), which were encouraged by the State. He received a regular stipend from the Scuola, which was paid with greater regularity than the State pension he was given for his work in the Doge's Palace, where he painted many of the replacements for the Bellinis and Titians lost in the fires of 1574 and 1577. He decorated almost the whole of the Scuola, starting with the three ceiling panels in the *Albergo*, or governors' meeting room, where he circumvented the original project of a competition to select an artist by painting the central picture and inserting it in the ceiling—a *fait accompli* which gained him the work at the cost of making many enemies. The paintings in the *Albergo* consist of the four huge scenes of the Passion, the central *Crucifixion* being 17ft by 40ft. There are thirteen ceiling paintings in the Upper Hall, an altarpiece, ten huge scenes of the Life of Christ on the walls, and a ceiling painting on the staircase. In the Lower Hall are eight very large scenes from the Life of the Virgin.

Tintoretto's apostles and saints are humble, often ragged men; the Last Supper takes place in an ordinary inn, with only the simplest fare, the plainest table settings, and the crudest peasant furniture. Even the opulent Susanna emerging from her bath (*Susanna and the Elders, c.*1555: Vienna KHM) has only a few trinkets, and the Empress Helena (*The discovery of the True Cross, c.*1561: Venice, now in Sta Maria Mater Domini) wears no more than the plainest circlet and simple 'antique' robes. The result of this deliberately plebeian emphasis is that he holds the spectator's attention, not by any outward show like Veronese, but by his concentration on the significance of the action.

Unlike Titian, he did not confine his assistants (and he had a large studio, without which so great a volume of work could never have been accomplished) merely to the preparatory stages of his works, or to copies, but also employed them on versions, enlargements, or much altered variants. His paintings in the Doge's Palace are perhaps his least successful, because they are heavily dependent on the workshop, but they include the enormous *Paradise,* 23 ft. high by 72 ft. long. All were based on his designs, but the workmanship is very variable.

His consistent avoidance of luxury and opulence, his insistence on portraying the incidents of the Gospel narrative as expressing Christ's choice of his disciples among the poor, the humble, and the obscure, was perhaps influenced by the ideas flowing from the Council of *Trent. He did not have any immediate successors; his ideas found their most striking echo in *Caravaggio, who seems to have known Tintoretto's work, since he uses the device of the 'exploding' composition and also concentrates on the poverty and simplicity of Christ, the Virgin, and the saints, as well as of the votaries who people his religious works.

Tissot, James, Doré, Gustave, and other artistic influences *See* FILM.

Titian (Tiziano Vecelli) (*c.*1487/90–1576) was supreme among Venetian painters, excelling his older rival Giovanni *Bellini, and his immediate contemporary Giorgione, whose early death in 1510 removed the one artist who might have challenged his position. His very long life—not the 99 years which would result from accepting his own varied claims about his age, made when trying to extract payment for works painted for Philip II of Spain—enabled him to produce a body of work of unrivalled range and variety, of which his religious subjects form an important part.

Among the earliest is his votive picture of *S. Mark enthroned with SS Cosmas, Damian, Roch, and Sebastian* (*c.*1509/11: Venice, Sta Maria della Salute), which, since the saints represented are the two doctor saints on the left and the two plague saints on the right, is probably connected with the virulent outbreak of plague of 1506–7 or the one of 1510–11 which carried off Giorgione. His lovely early essays in the Madonna and Child theme (the so-called *Gypsy Madonna, c.*1510: Vienna, KHM) are superb continuations of the type of devotional image set by Bellini's Madonnas. His first truly grand religious work was the *Assumption* (1516–18: Venice, Frari) which, partly from its enormous size (some 22 ft. high), partly from the way in which he composed the work in relation to the surrounding framework and its overall impact in the huge church, and partly because he created for the subject a totally new iconographic scheme which has the Virgin rising to glory supported by a host of angels from a tomb surrounded by the astonished and clamouring Apostles, was vital and novel and above all was so composed that it raised the subject to a new level of grandeur. Strangely, it did not at first meet with the approval of its Franciscan commissioners. All his marvellous gifts as a colourist, his skill in designing, so that the figure of the Virgin, projected from the tomb to join the welcoming Godhead above her, is still linked by the gestures and the concentrated gaze of the Apostles to the world which she so triumphantly leaves behind, are fully displayed here. His grand altarpiece of the *Madonna di Ca' Pesaro* (1519–26: in the same church)—a votive picture celebrating the naval victory of the donor Jacopo Pesaro, Bishop of Paphos, over the Turks in 1502—created a vital new model for such works in the asymmetry of the design, because the position of the altarpiece on a side altar on the left side of the nave demanded that, since the spectator also approached from the left, the composition should be based on a rising oblique movement. It also follows, and expands, the type of composition established by Bellini's *S. Giobbe* and *S. Zaccaria* altarpieces, by suiting the composition to the architectural system and the scale of the church—though in this case the huge stone columns in the picture hardly concur with the brick Gothic piers of the church. Devotional works—i.e. not altarpieces painted for a church, but rather as more intimate private devotional pictures—abound in his *œuvre*—examples are possibly the *Entombment* (*c.*1525/30: Paris, Louvre) despite its size, with its novel and intricate use of light and shadow, and its rich colour; or such a tender and affecting treatment of the Madonna theme as the *Madonna and Child with SS John the Baptist and Catherine* (*c.*1530: London, NG), set in a wide landscape backed with the mountains of his native Cadore region of N. Italy; or the evocatively sensual handling of the *Penitent Magdalene* (*c.*1530/5: Florence, Pitti), clothed only in her abundant auburn hair, yet at the same time expressive of ecstatic devotion. By the 1540s his vision had turned towards darker subjects: the *Ecce Homo* (1543: Vienna, KHM) sets the composition in the most unusual form. At the top of a huge flight of steps, and pushed into the extreme left of the picture, is the Victim and his Roman judge, while the condemning crowd, backed by mounted men at arms—one Western, one Turkish—surge up the steps. This is closely followed by the first version of the *Crowning with thorns* (*c.*1542/5: Louvre), where, again on a flight of steps leading to a dark gateway surmounted by the bust of a Roman emperor, the soldiery with violent brutality force the agonizing crown on to the head of their Victim. The influence of new formal ideas, emanating from Central Italian Mannerism, can be seen in the use, here as in the *Ecce Homo*, of the spectator seen from the back—a typically Mannerist compositional device of using a foreground figure seen from the back, so as to push the central group further back in the picture space.

The effect of Mannerism is at its most evident in his religious works, particularly in his altarpieces, where perhaps he felt a greater need to create more adventurous compositions, because of their more public nature. The *Martyrdom of S. Lawrence* (*c.*1548/9: Venice, Gesuiti) is a truly horrific vision of the saint held down on the flaming brazier of his gridiron under the lurid glimmer of torchlight and the moon piercing the storm clouds overhead. The second version of the *Crowning with thorns* (1570–6: Munich) is close in composition to the first, but totally different in handling and intensity of feeling. Here, the simple architectural background is now replaced by a group of flaring, smoky torches, the carefully detailed muscular forms of the executioners are less obtrusive, yet in essence are more elemental in their violence; Christ's agony is less histrionic, more passive, more withdrawn. The emotion is more intensely tragic. The picture was among those unfinished at his death, like the final *Pietà* (*c.*1570/6: Venice, Accad.) which was intended for his own tomb in the Frari and was completed by Palma Vecchio. The Virgin supports the body of the dead Christ on her knees, with the lamenting Magdalene on one side, opposed to the pathetic kneeling figure of Titian himself on the other, crawling piteously towards the body of the dead Redeemer—the complete allegory of faith.

Among the many works commissioned by Philip II of Spain was a later version of the 1525/30 *Entombment* (1559: Prado), where the supporting figure of Joseph of Arimathaea is a portrait of the artist in his old age, and where the intensity and poignancy of grief animates all the figures and renders any local detail almost irrelevant.

titular church *See* TITULUS.

titulus (Lat. title) The word has four different meanings: it is the 'title' of Christ, affixed to His cross at His Crucifixion. This was written by Pilate as *Iesus Nazarenus Rex Iudeorum*, and when the chief priests objected that he should not have written, 'Jesus of Nazareth King of the Jews' but 'This man said, I am the King of the Jews', Pilate retorted: *Quod scripsi, scripsi*—'What I have written, I have written' (John 19: 21–2). It was also common practice to include the nature of the crime committed; Matt. 27: 37 and Mark 15: 26 give a different version of what Pilate wrote, but John was there beside the cross. The oldest representation of the Crucifixion, an ivory which is part of a series on the Passion of Christ (*c.*430: London, BM), has on the top edge of the plaque over the cross the letters REX IVD, and usually the full text was inscribed on a plaque at the top of the cross. The abbreviation now commonly in use, INRI, does not appear much before the middle of the 12th century, but both forms can be found well after that: there is no marked change as there was for the use of three *nails or four.

(2) From the 3rd century certain of the oldest churches in Rome were known as 'titular' churches. Many had existed in private houses before the Edict of *Milan, and after the recognition of Christianity became the oldest parish churches. Each had clergy appointed

to serve it, all with revenues established as part of their 'title', and this title was given at their appointment. Otherwise they were at the charge of the pope or the bishop. The titular churches were also the appointed churches of cardinals, so that a cardinal's title would be, as in the case of Pope Julius II, the Cardinal of San Pietro in Vincoli. In 499 a Roman synod identified thirty titular churches; there are now reckoned to be twenty-five. *See also* ROME.

(3) The title of a church is the name by which it is known and in which it has been dedicated. This dedication may be one of five kinds: (*a*) to a Divine person, i.e. Christ the King (Catholic cathedral, Liverpool); (*b*) to a mystery: the Holy Trinity (Dreifaltigkeitskirche, Salzburg; SS Trinità, Florence); (*c*) to a saint (St Peter's, Rome; St Paul's, London; St Patrick's, NY); (*d*) to a sacred or sanctified object, or a relic, such as the Holy Cross (Sta Croce in Gerusalemme, Rome; the Santa Casa, Loreto); (*e*) a sacred event (the Church of the Nativity, Bethlehem; the Holy Sepulchre, Jerusalem; the Chapel of the Ascension, Jerusalem (an 8th-cent. octagonal chapel on the Mt. of Olives, now a mosque)).

A fixed altar in a church must also be given a title and this cannot be changed without papal authority. Two altars in the same church cannot have the same title, or dedication. No altar, except by papal authority, may be dedicated to a *beatus* (one not yet canonized). Altars may only have one of the dedications listed above.

(4) The 'titulus' of a church implies that it can provide a living for the priest, either because it has land which he may cultivate, or because there is an endowment. A priest may not be ordained unless he can be appointed to a benefice sufficient to support him. Churches without a titulus must be supported either by the congregation, by a religious Order, or by the diocese.

t

Tobit The Book of Tobit is one of the Apocryphal books of the OT and tells the story of a pious and charitable Jew and his son Tobias, and the object of the story is to inculcate strict adherence to Jewish law and customs, and the exercise of heroic virtue. The story was written by a Jew, probably between 225 and 175 BC, in Hebrew or Aramaic (both versions are known), and placed after the fall of Jerusalem to the Assyrians (*c.*922 BC; the author's grasp of historical facts is unreliable). Tobit and his family were taken captive at the fall of Jerusalem, and lived at Nineveh. He was favoured by the king, who sent him on buying missions into Media (the N. part of modern Iran), and on one of these he deposited with a fellow Jew called Gabael ten talents of silver. Tobit fell from favour under the next king, because an informer told that he buried the bodies of Jews whom the king had killed and thrown over the wall. Tobit fled, but the king was murdered by his sons, and the next king appointed Tobit's nephew over his affairs, so that he recovered his property. One day when he was about to eat, Tobit sent his son Tobias to find a poor Jew to share his feast, but Tobias returned to tell him of a Jew strangled and his body thrown into the market place. Tobit left the table and went to bring the dead man's body to his house, so as to bury him later after dark. Only then did he eat. Later he buried the man, and the night being hot he lay down in the garden to sleep. On the wall were sparrows, and their droppings fell in his eyes and blinded him. For four years while he was blind, Anna, his wife, worked as a seamstress, and one of her clients gave her a kid, but Tobit accused her of stealing it. In anger, she demanded to know how much good his charity had done them.

He decided to send Tobias to collect the money deposited with Gabael, and he told Tobias to find a reliable guide. Tobias found a man, not knowing that it was the Archangel Raphael, who had taken the identity of a relative called Azariah, and together with Tobias's dog they left for Media. At the Tigris, he caught a large fish, and was told to cut out the liver, gall, and heart, and then they ate some and salted the rest. When they reached Ecbatana in Media, 'Azariah' told Tobias that Raguel his kinsman there had a beautiful daughter, Sarah, whom he was to marry, but she was cursed by a demon who had killed all her previous seven husbands when they entered the bridal chamber. Tobias was alarmed because he was an only son, and if the demon killed him then who would care for his parents? 'Azariah' assured him that if he did as he was told all would be well. When they reached Raguel's house they were welcomed, and doubly so when Raguel was told who Tobias was. 'Azariah' explained to Raguel about Tobias's wish to marry Sarah, and all was soon arranged, a marriage contract signed, and a bridal room prepared. When Tobias entered it, he remembered 'Azariah's ' words, and put the heart and liver of the fish on the incense and the smoke so stifled the demon that he fled. Raguel meanwhile made arrangements to bury Sarah's unfortunate eighth husband,

and the next morning sent to discover if he were alive, and the maid returned to say that they were sleeping together peacefully.

Tobias then sent 'Azariah' to Rages where Gabael lived who had the money, and he returned with Gabael to join the wedding celebrations, and afterwards Tobias, Sarah, and 'Azariah' set out for home. Tobit meanwhile, had begun to fear for Tobias's life, in which Anna joined weeping and lamenting. When the returning party neared Nineveh, Tobias was told to have the gall from the fish ready, and to come as an advance party to tell Tobit of the approach of a daughter-in-law, and they went, together with the dog. Tobias greeted his father, smeared the gall on his eyes, and the white film fell off, and he could see again. When the renewed wedding festivities were over, Tobit discussed what reward should be made to 'Azariah', and they decided on half of all they had brought back from Ecbatana, but when they told 'Azariah' this, he told them that he was really the angel Raphael. He explained that it was because of Tobit's charitable goodness, that he had even left his dinner on his plate to go and bury the dead, that God had sent an angel to reward him. And he then ascended to heaven in front of them. The book ends with a long prayer of thanksgiving and praise, and with the wonderful description of the heavenly Jerusalem with 'gates of sapphire and emerald, and walls of precious stones, and towers of gold and streets paved with ruby and the stones of Ophir'. Much later after Tobit and Anna were both dead, Tobias, Sarah, and their children joined Raguel in Ecbatana, for Tobit had prophesied the destruction of Nineveh and said that they would be safe in Media. And in Media they lived happily ever after.

The story has attracted a large number of pictures; Botticini (1446–98) painted the subject three times: one in the Uffizi has Tobias and his dog walking in company with three archangels, Michael, Gabriel, and Raphael, and the other in Florence, Accademia, has him carrying his fish, and with his dog trotting alongside, walking hand in hand with Raphael, who holds the small jar with the entrails of the fish. Below the two figures is the kneeling child donor, and it was a custom at the time that such votive pictures should be offered by a child. A third is in Bergamo. Others are by Pollaiuolo, and Filippino Lippi (both in Turin), Verrocchio (*c.*1460: London, NG); Matthias Stomer (*c.*1600–*c.*1650: seven known in all, one of *Tobit cured of blindness* in Catania, Mus. dei Benedettini, others in private colls.); Domenico Feti (*c.*1589–1623: Berlin; early work: *Healing of Tobit*); Adam Elsheimer's *Tobit and the* Angel (1602–03, Städel, Frankfurt am Main, Germany); Bernardo Cavallino (1622–54): *Tobias taking leave of his parents* (Rome, Gall. Naz.); Rembrandt: *Tobit accusing his wife* (1626: Moscow) and *Raphael leaving Tobit and Tobias* (1634: Louvre).

Francesco and Gian Antonio Guardi, probably in collaboration, painted a series of the *Story of Tobias and the Angel* in the organ gallery of the church of the Archangel Raphael, Venice, 1750. The carved wooden figures by Ignaz Günther of an *Angel and a child*, usually described as a Guardian Angel, may in fact be (though there is no dog or fish) of Tobias and the Archangel Raphael (1763: Munich, Bürgersaal). Eric Gill carved *Tobias and Sara* (1926) for St John's College, Oxford. *See also* ANGEL.

tomb of the BVM From the 4th century a tradition existed that a church on the Mt. of Olives enclosed the tomb of the Virgin Mary. During the period of the Crusades, *c.*1130, another church was built, presumably to replace the original one, and the Byzantine crypt of this church claims to contain the tomb. *See* DORMITION.

Tondal *See* TUNDAL.

tonsure The shaving of the crown of the head in a circle, as a distinguishing mark of a cleric. In some monastic Orders the head was shaved so as to leave only a circle of hair round the head, considered as a symbol of the Crown of Thorns, but the tonsure of secular priests is only a small patch on the top of the head, and even that is not done in countries where the custom is unusual.

In the early Church, the practice was unknown, no more being enjoined on all Christians than to avoid ostentation in dressing their hair, and to keep it short. Clerical tonsure was in use in Gaul in the late 5th and 6th centuries, and spread generally in the Church, though the extent of the tonsure varied considerably over the centuries, and provoked violent controversy during the Synod of Whitby in 663, when the so-called Celtic tonsure was questioned. This consisted of shaving all the front of the head from a line drawn from ear to ear. It was worn in Celtic monasteries both at home and abroad. In the late Middle Ages the difference between monastic and secular tonsure was usual, and at one time the size of the tonsure increased with each rise in rank within the ministry. In the Eastern Church, a monk's tonsure is a cruciform cutting of the hair. In the case of children dedicated to the priesthood, the tonsure was given with the office of Reader, but it consisted normally of no more than the cutting of some snippets of hair from the top and sides of the head. This form was also used for laymen admitted to minor orders, and enabled them to claim, if necessary, 'benefit of clergy' (trial in an ecclesiastical court rather than a lay one). Since it was the outward distinguishing mark of a cleric, tonsure was not given before admission to some minor office, for instance that of Reader, and now it may be given only to those who propose to become priests.

Torcello is an island in the Venetian lagoon, first colonized in the 7th century. It was the seat of a bishop until the 18th century, and the cathedral was founded from *Ravenna in 639. The remains of a baptistery and some mosaics date from the 7th century, but the cathedral was rebuilt in 1008 and subsequently altered. It has an 11th-century carved *iconostasis, and a huge mosaic of the *Last Judgement* (12th/13th cent.) which is purely *Byzantine in style, with characteristic Byzantine subjects such as the *Anastasis, *Parousia, *Deësis, and *Hetoimasia, and the Resurrection of the Dead (see below).

In the main apse is a huge, grave, *Virgin and Child* (of the Hodegetria type; *see* MADONNA TYPES) floating in the gold field, with the Apostles below. In a side apse is a *Christ Blessing*, between angels, with four saints below, and on the arch above is the *Mystic Lamb* with angels. The entrance wall is covered by the *Last Judgement*. At the top is a traditional Harrowing of Hell (Anastasis), with a giant figure of the Risen Christ grasping Adam by the wrist, with the Baptist, the Forerunner, by His side as the last person of the Old Dispensation needing the same deliverance from Limbo as the Just of the pre-Christian age who acclaim their Saviour. On either side stand angels in rich Byzantine dalmatics. In the register below is a Last Judgement with much smaller figures—Christ in a mandorla, flanked by the Virgin and the Baptist, with six Apostles on either side (Deësis). Below them is the Preparation of the Throne (Hetoimasia), and trumpeting angels summoning the dead with the unusually explicit Byzantine details of the Earth giving up its dead in the guise of wild beasts bringing the limbs of their victims, and the Sea, personified by a woman, with marine beasts belching out the bodies of the drowned. Below this is the Archangel Michael with the scales, with on one side the saved, clothed in rich garments; and on the other devils claiming their due and angels driving the damned into Hell. At the bottom is the Virgin flanked on one side by Abraham with the souls of the Just and a martyr, and on the other by S. Peter with the keys of Heaven opening the gates of Paradise. On the other side of the doorway are the naked sinners lamenting in Hell, and grim heaps of skulls and heads amid flames and worms. The door has an *orant Virgin in the tympanum. While the imagery is entirely Byzantine, the workmanship of what is probably the largest and most elaborate *Last Judgement* of the medieval world shows a strong admixture of local assistants' work, and has also suffered from restoration.

The early 11th-century church of Sta Fosca, is a *martyrium, internally a Greek cross and externally an octagon. Legend says that it commemorates two martyrs, Fosca and Maura, both from Ravenna, martyred during the persecution by the Emperor Decius, their bodies recovered from the sea and buried in N. Africa, at Saqratha, whence they were taken by a Christian to Torcello. While the church positively exists, the legend is generally believed to be just a legend, though it does go back to the 12th century. The church is firmly within the Ravennate architectural tradition, although this was no longer a very vital force by the 11th century.

Totentanz *See* DANCE OF DEATH.

tower Until bells became common, about the 6th/7th century, there was little reason for church towers except security. Early churches in Rome did not originally have towers; Old St Peter's had a tower with three bells in the 6th century, but in most of the other early churches the tower—or *campanile—was added in the 8th to the 10th centuries. The 5th- and 6th-century churches in *Ravenna have towers mostly of the 9th/11th centuries or later. Byzantine church forms did not include towers.

In N. Europe, by the 6th or 7th centuries bells were known in Gaul and England, and the combination of a tower for safety with a bell which could be a call to Mass, or a tocsin to warn of danger, seems common sense. The origin and purpose of the round towers of Ireland are obscure, but they are probably

Christian in origin, and are usually hollow tapering stone shafts, 100 to 150 ft. high, with a low pointed roof, dating from the 6th to the 13th centuries. They rarely communicate with the churches near by, and were probably defensive rather than bell-towers, since their windows are very small and the door to them high up.

In the North towers were common by the 8th century. The *Pre-Romanesque church of St-Denis, near Paris, and the Abbey of St-Réquier in N. France both had towered fronts. The development of *westworks in Carolingian churches encouraged the proliferation of towers, so that by the 11th century they were an essential feature and were part of the aspiration to a nine-towered silhouette (two on the front, two on either side of the transepts (i.e. four in all), two on either side of the choir, and a crossing tower in the centre), although no church ever achieved this ideal. Many of the massive twin-towered façades of *Romanesque churches were later given extra stages to achieve the rich decorative effects of the *Gothic silhouette, as at St-Étienne at Caen, or Durham and Lincoln cathedrals. Towers are a feature of major Gothic churches, and the twin-towered west front is often accompanied by a large decorative crossing tower, as at Canterbury and Lincoln.

In the campaign of major church building in N. France during the 12th–14th centuries, the towered façade seemed to revive the desire for a multi-towered effect. Laon has an elaborate twin-towered façade and two towers (out of the four projected) flanking the transepts; Chartres, with a twin-towered west front, was also to have had towers on either side of the transepts, and further towers flanking the choir, though these only exist in their lowest stages and do not affect the skyline. It was possibly the site itself which inspired these ambitions since both Laon and Chartres stand on hilltops, and they reflect the long-lived ambition which was achieved in Germany in the seven-towered silhouette of the 13th-century Limburg-an-der-Lahn, perched like a diadem on its hill above the river. Another crowning feature in France is the *flèche* (arrow), the thin, light, open-work pinnacle over the crossing (Paris, Amiens, and Cologne), or on the choir (Reims). This form of tower or *spire is so rare in England that there is no English word for it. In S. France, the most impressive tower is the single one of Albi Cathedral, standing like a fortress against the heresy which it was built to suppress. In the West the huge 14th-century open-work single spire of Strasburg is a form popular in Germany, as at Freiburg im Breisgau, Ulm, and Vienna.

Towers and steeples continued to be built with the classically inspired churches of the 17th and 18th centuries, despite objections that classical or Palladian models did not admit of steeples combined with columnar porticoes. Most of the towers of *Wren's City churches were built later than the churches themselves and many were designed with spires of inventively varied design—no two are alike. Towers which double as belfries have a clear function, connected with the church: spires have none, and therefore steeples, which combine a tower with a spire, are an elaboration which may be, as Wren wrote in 1708, 'an ornament to the town', but can also suggest a spiritual aspiration, which may have been their purpose from their first appearance. In Europe, the influence of the Renaissance, encouraging the centrally planned domed church, diminished the importance of towers in favour of a small lantern, and eventually the classical revival of the late 18th and early 19th centuries tended to eliminate towers altogether. In 19th-century England they were so much a part of church design that their survival, either as classically inspired forms or *Gothic Revival ones, continued. Towers on modern churches, if they exist, are hardly more than functional structures to carry a bell.

Tower of Babel *See* BABEL.

tracery The pattern made with the stone ribs that fill the upper part of Gothic windows, and into which the glass, either plain or stained, is inserted. Plate tracery is the earliest type, the pattern made by the stone ribs being not unlike a flat plate cut out in simple *quatrefoils or other shapes. As the bars of the ribs became thinner and more complex, bar tracery superseded plate tracery, and eventually the extreme richness of highly variegated patterns was reached, such as the windows of Exeter Cathedral, where almost every window is filled with a different tracery pattern. It is an almost infallible indication of the date of the window, which is often later than the structure into which it has been inserted, as is the case with most large Romanesque churches that have had later west windows inserted, as at Tewkesbury Abbey or Winchester Cathedral. Experience taught that it was useless to introduce stained glass into elaborate tracery. Tracery was also found in blind windows and arches, and is a common decorative device in panelling or in 14th-century picture frames.

Tractarian Movement *See* OXFORD MOVEMENT.

Trades, Christ of the Christ was reputed to have been a carpenter, and the image of Christ of the Trades may be likened to a secular form of the *Arma Christi* where Christ showing His wounds is surrounded by the tools of various trades and crafts instead of the symbols of His Passion. It symbolizes the dignity of labour and of craftsmanship.

A wall-painting of *c.*1400 at Rhäsüns, Grisons (Switz.) shows Christ standing, as in an *imago pietatis*, surrounded by depictions of the tools of various trades and occupations. Another, of similar date, at Ormalingen (Switz.) shows Christ surrounded, and pierced even, by various instruments and tools. The idea of a religious aspect of everyday labour is symbolized by the Chapel of Industry, Coventry Cathedral (from 1952).

Traditio Clavium (the Giving of the Keys) Christ giving the Keys of the Kingdom of Heaven to S. Peter is in Matt. 16: 13–20, the actual words of the donation being in v. 19. Jesus asked the disciples '"Who do people say that the Son of Man is?" And they said "Some say John the Baptist, but others Elijah, and still others Jeremiah or one of the prophets." He said to them, "But who do you say that I am?" Simon Peter answered, "You are the Messiah, the Son of the living God." And Jesus answered him, "Blessed are you, Simon son of Jonah! For flesh and blood has not revealed this to you, but my Father in heaven. And I tell you, you are Peter, and on this rock I will build my church, and the gates of Hades will not prevail against it. I will give you the keys of the kingdom of heaven, and whatever you bind on earth will be bound in heaven, and whatever you loose on earth will be loosed in heaven." And he sternly ordered the disciples not to tell anyone that he was the Messiah.'

The curious answer that some believed Him to be John the Baptist, whom Herod had already killed, is because of a belief in the reincarnation of prophets. It also explains the references to Elijah and Jeremiah, particularly since Elijah, who had been taken up to heaven alive, was expected to return to earth as a presage of the restoration of Israel and its deliverance from its foes. Jeremiah, who is believed to have been stoned to death by Jews enraged by his repeated calls to repentance, predicted the fall and destruction of Jerusalem and wept over the city he loved, but knew was doomed. He is seen now as an OT prefiguration of Christ, and the Roman conquest of Palestine would have predisposed thoughtful Jews of that time to equate Jesus, as a new and very powerful prophet, with one of the great prophets of antiquity. The subject appears in Early Christian art mainly in sarcophagi, and in the mosaic semi-domes of some of the early churches in Rome. The sarcophagus of Junius Bassus (359: St Peter's Mus.) is one of the earliest, and shows Christ, seated over Coelus, a personification of the Heavens, giving a scroll both to S. Peter and S. Paul. The sarcophagus of Probus (395: Grotto of St Peter's) shows Christ holding a jewelled cross, and with a scroll in His hand, standing between SS Peter and Paul. The dome of the Arian Baptistery, Ravenna, *c.*500, has a mosaic of the Throne of God with S. Peter one side holding keys, and S. Paul the other side, holding a scroll. A miniature in the *Golden Evangeliary* of Henry II (1002–14: Munich) shows Christ handing an object, presumably keys, to S. Peter with the other disciples standing behind him. In a miniature in the *Sermons of S. Anselm of Canterbury* (1130: Verdun) Christ, with sheep at His feet, hands two large keys to S. Peter. A relief by Donatello (1428–30: London, V & A) shows Christ giving the keys to S. Peter at His Ascension. The Sistine Chapel has—or had—two important representations of the donation: the Perugino in the fresco series of 1481 has Christ giving the keys to S. Peter kneeling before Him, and the Raphael tapestry of 1515/16, now in the museum, but made for the Chapel, combines the scene on the seashore of 'Feed my Sheep' with S. Peter kneeling before Him holding the keys in his hand. These two images, in the Chapel which was the place where conclaves for the papal elections were held, were powerful visual assertions of the Petrine Primacy, and reminders of Christ's words, '...and upon this rock I will build my Church'.

Traditio Legis (the Giving of the Law) This is the counterpart of the preceding Giving of the Keys. Representations of the scene appear mostly in Early Christian sarcophagi. In one (350/60: St Peter's, Grotto) Christ is seen in the centre, with SS Peter and Paul on either side of Him; He hands a scroll to S. Peter. A damaged sarcophagus fragment (370: Rome, San Sebastiano) has the same treatment of the scene. The apse mosaic of Sta Costanza, Rome, *c.*350, has Christ, with sheep at His feet, between SS Peter and Paul, handing S. Peter a scroll. The same treatment of the theme appears in 4th- and 5th-century sarcophagi in Arles, St-Maximin; Ancona; Milan (Sant'Ambrogio); and several in Ravenna.

The scroll of the Law is that of the New Covenant which Christ gives as the counterpart of the Old Covenant given to *Moses, which the New Covenant supersedes. It is given to S. Peter, with S. Paul standing by, although he was not present at the Giving of the Keys, because S. Paul, as the upholder of the old Mosaic Law, was converted to the New Covenant, and became one of its most forceful and heroic advocates.

transcendentalism An influential philosophical movement that was primarily a literary one in America, but it also inspired many painters of the 19th century. It now serves as a lens through which the epic landscapes and nature paintings of much of that century can be understood, as in the case of Thomas *Cole and Asher B. Durand. It might also be seen to influence the romantic mysticism of painters such as Albert Pinkham Ryder, Elihu Vedder, and Henry Ossawa Tanner. *See also* NORTH AMERICA.

transennae are small balustrade panels, often made with slabs of marble, pierced or carved, or with marble inlaid with mosaic decoration of the *Cosmati type, which are frequently found in Byzantine and Early Christian churches, as enclosures for parts of the church not open to the laity. They were also used to enclose shrines of martyrs from incursion while allowing a view inside, and even the passage of a handkerchief or napkin called a *brandea* to be pushed through to come into contact with the shrine. There are fine examples in the *schola cantorum of San Clemente, Rome, in Sant'Apollinare Nuovo and San Vitale, Ravenna, of the 6th century, Aquileia Cathedral of the 11th century, St Mark's, Venice, in the choir and galleries, of *c.*1063, and the altar enclosure of the Martorana, Palermo, 1143. There is a good early example in the Victoria & Albert Museum, London, and there are good modern versions in some of the side chapels of Westminster Catholic Cathedral, London.

transept The part of a church which crosses, at right angles, the area between the nave and the choir. Originally, *basilicas had no transepts, but these began to be introduced in the Western church between the nave and the apse about the 5th century when more clergy needed extra space adjacent to the altar. The introduction of transepts, which usually projected beyond the nave and aisles, changed the shape of churches from a basilican to a Latin *cross plan. They provided space for extra chapels, and for extra doors and *portals. The third Abbey church of *Cluny was the first church to have double transepts, the smaller second one crossing the nave at the level of the choir, and the first one three bays further west along the nave. Double transepts were not, however, popular in France or in Italy; in England they became general in major *Gothic churches, the smaller second one crossing the *chancel between the *choir and the *presbytery, the first, larger, one across the nave being usually covered by a crossing *tower. In early Romanesque churches, particularly in Germany, the *westwork usually incorporated a transept, but once the westwork was no longer a dominant feature this form of second transept disappeared.

Transfiguration The Transfiguration is one of the twelve great feasts after Easter itself. In the Byzantine Church it was at first an optional feast, but was widely observed before 1000. In the West it was observed, for instance, by Peter the Venerable, Abbot of Cluny, by 845, and Pope Gregory IX (1227–41) speaks of it as a current feast. It was not made official in the West until 1457 by Pope Callixtus III, and its feast-day changed from 14 July to 6 August as a commemoration of the defeat of the Turks before Belgrade on that day.

The account of Christ's Transfiguration is in three of the Gospels: Matt. 17: 1–13; Mark 9: 2–13; Luke 9: 28–36. The one in Matt. 17 is the best: 'Six days later, Jesus took with him Peter and James and his brother John and led them up a high mountain, by themselves. And he was transfigured before them, and his face shone like the sun, and his clothes became dazzling white. Suddenly there appeared to them Moses and Elijah, talking with him. Then Peter said to Jesus, "Lord, it is good for us to be here . . . ". While he was still speaking, suddenly a bright cloud overshadowed them, and from the cloud a voice said, "This is my Son, the Beloved; with him I am well pleased; listen to him!" When the disciples heard this, they fell to the ground and were overcome by fear. But Jesus came and touched them, saying, "Get up and do not be afraid." And when they looked up, they saw no one except Jesus himself alone. As they were coming down from the mountain, Jesus ordered them, "Tell no one about the vision until after the Son of Man has been raised from the dead." And the disciples asked him, "Why, then, do the scribes say that Elijah must come first?" He replied, "Elijah is indeed coming first, and will restore all things; but I tell you that Elijah has already come, and they did not recognize him, but they did to him what they pleased. So the Son of Man is about to suffer at their hands." Then the disciples understood that he was speaking to them about John the Baptist.' John 1: 14 is an elliptical reference to the vision: '. . . and we have seen his glory, the glory as of a father's only son, full of grace and truth.' 2 Pet. 1: 16–18 reads 'we have been eyewitnesses of his majesty. For he received honour and glory from God the Father when that voice was conveyed to him by the Majestic Glory, saying, "This is my Son, the Beloved, with whom I am well pleased." We ourselves heard this voice come from heaven, while we were with him on the holy mountain.' Here the Divinity of Christ was affirmed, in that His innate glory which lay concealed in the humanity He had accepted by His human birth, blazed out as He was acknowledged by the two major prophets of the OT as the One who superseded the Law which they had brought, and was proclaimed by God as His Son. His redeeming mission was confirmed, and the 'cloud' which swept Him from the disciples' sight was, like that which later enveloped Him at the Ascension, the glory of God Himself.

The apse mosaic of Sant'Apollinare in Classe is interpreted as a symbolic representation of the Transfiguration, in that the large cross at the top, above the figure of S. Apollinare, is flanked by two half-figures emerging from clouds, and the three sheep beneath represent the three disciples present at the vision. The apse mosaic of St Catherine's Monastery, Mt. Sinai, of 565–6; the Triumphal Arch of the apse in SS Nereo e Achilleo, Rome, *c.*800; the apse of the monastery church at Daphni, *c.*1100, are other mosaics of the subject. An Anglo-Saxon ivory of *c.*900, and a magnificent 15th-century embroidered dalmatic, the so-called dalmatic of Charlemagne, Rome, St Peter's Sacristy Treasury; Giovanni Bellini: *c.*1460, Venice, Correr, are other treatments of the theme.

It is usually accepted that the 'holy mountain' was Mt. Tabor, which lies about 10 miles SE of Nazareth. Other sites suggested are Mt. Hermon, on the S. flank of which is Banyas, once Caesarea Philippi well to the N. of the Sea of Galilee, and the Mt. of Olives. After the vision, Jesus passed through Galilee to Capernaum, which suggests that Mt. Tabor was the true site. An example of this theme can be seen in a Russian icon of the Novgorod School (15th-century) from the Holy Theotokos Church on the Volotovo Field near Novgorod.

In all three accounts, the Transfiguration is followed by the story of the man with the epileptic son who besought Jesus to cure him, telling Him that the disciples had tried but failed. In Mark 9: 19 Jesus rebukes them all: 'You faithless generation . . . How much longer must I put up with you?' The boy had convulsions, and the father begged Him, '. . . if you are able to do anything, have pity on us . . .'. Jesus said, 'If you are able! All things can be done for the one who believes.' The father cried out, 'I believe; help my unbelief!' Jesus healed the child, but the disciples asked why they could not do it, and He answered that it could only be done through prayer. Raphael's last major work, 1518–20, unfinished at his death, and completed by Giulio Romano, is of the *Transfiguration* with the rare scene of the healing of the epileptic boy below the vision on the mountain. Further examples can be seen in Carel Weight's versions (1963, in Manchester Cathedral) and (1965 in St Aidan's, East Acton, London). Binoculars are required to study the fine but densely drawn *Transfiguration* (2011) window in Durham Cathedral by Tom Denny. *See also* CHRIST, Life and Miracles of

Transito *See* DORMITION.

transi tomb *See* GISANT.

Transitus Mariae *See* DORMITION.

Transparente (Sp. **Trasparente**) This extraordinary piece of illusionism was devised by the Spanish architect and designer, Narciso Tomé, for Toledo Cathedral and was completed in 1732. Its origins lie in the illusionistic devices of Bramante in Sta Maria presso San Satiro in Milan, Bernini's two exploitations of illusionism in the Scala Regia of the Vatican and the Cornaro Chapel in Sta Maria della Vittoria, Rome, for the vision of the Transverberation of *S. Theresa, and Borromini's use of sharply accelerated perspective in the staircase of the Palazzo Spada, Rome, to enlarge its apparent size. No example which remotely compares with the Toledo *Trasparente* has ever been attempted since.

Toledo Cathedral is a Gothic building of traditional 13th-century French type, begun in 1227 and finished in 1493, with double aisles extending into a double ambulatory. The high altar in the Capilla Major has a vast Late Gothic reredos rising to the vaulting. Strict Spanish observance objected to people being able to walk in the ambulatory at the back of the reredos without respecting the Sacrament within it. Tomé devised an ingenious system which would allow the Sacrament to be seen—and therefore venerated—from both sides of the reredos. This involved opening the reredos to provide a hollow receptacle, glass-fronted on both sides (hence the term *trasparente*) in which the Sacrament was placed. From the ambulatory highly decorative columns linked by curved cornices to other very decorative larger columns draw one's attention to the Sacrament and give the illusion of a deep chapel, and the glass-fronted 'ciborium' is surrounded by angels that conceal the structural elements. The angel figures draw one's eyes upwards to a polychrome marble representation of the *Last Supper*, above which the Virgin soars into Heaven. To complete the illusionistic effect of a vision, the whole thing is flooded with light from an invisible source somewhere behind the spectator, and when one turns to discover the source of the illumination a vision of Christ seated on clouds and surrounded by the Heavenly host is seen beyond the vortex of angels.

What the architect has done is to remove a section of the inner ambulatory vaulting, which it was safe to do because of the strength of the Gothic structure, and to erect a huge dormer shaped like a ship's ventilator and to insert a large window into it which would flood the sculpture with golden light, but which, because of its dazzling effect, would enable the sculpture to be seen, while the source of the illumination remained virtually invisible. The device is entirely successful within the conventions of a Late Baroque theatrical illusionism rarely employed in church decoration.

Transverberation *See* THERESA OF AVILA, S.

tree About thirty trees are mentioned in the Bible, of which some have achieved a certain fame. The first is the Tree of Knowledge (see below) which is not specified as being an apple tree, but the apple is the fruit generally associated with the *Fall, because it is the commonest fruit tree in the West. The fig-tree is the first tree named in the Bible, in that when Adam and Eve, having eaten the fruit of the forbidden tree, knew themselves to be naked they sewed fig-leaves to make themselves loincloths (Gen. 3). The fig-tree also figures in the NT; in Matt. 21, Jesus being hungry, went to a fig-tree to find some fruit, but it was barren, and He cursed it whereupon it withered on the spot. Also, in Matt. 24: 32 Jesus uses the fig-tree in a parable, that since one can recognize the approach of summer from the state of the fig-tree, so when the signs of the end of the world begin to appear, then one can recognize the coming of the kingdom of God.

Noah's ark (Gen. 6: 14) was made of cypress wood, and when he tried to find out if the waters of the flood had dried up, he sent out a dove, and it returned with an olive-leaf in its beak. The ark of the Covenant which God ordered Moses to have made (Exod. 25, 26, and 27) was of shittim wood, as were its carrying poles, the altar for the sacrifice, and the table for the shewbread. It is so named in the AV, and in the Vg. as setim, but botanically is the *Acacia seyal*, which NRSV correctly translates as acacia.

The cedars of Lebanon are famous, but no longer exist there: Solomon used them for the Temple, but they are members, though the most splendid, of the family of fir-trees, which includes the cypress, mentioned several times in Isaiah, notably in 55: 13, where the prophet says, 'Instead of the thorn shall come up the cypress, instead of the briar shall come up the myrtle . . .'.

Oak is important in that Abraham lived near the Oaks of Mamre (Gen. 13: 18) in Hebron. Two trees easily confused are the sycamine (Luke 17: 6 in AV), which is another name for the mulberry, and the sycamore (Luke 19: 4), which Zacchaeus climbed so as to see Jesus as He passed, and from which he was summoned to become Jesus's host in Jericho, and which is in fact not the sycamore of the West but a species of large evergreen fig-tree. The palm-tree is one of the commonest trees of the coast of Palestine, and the olive needs no other comment but to recall its importance as the Mt. of Olives (where now none grow) where

Jesus walked and taught His disciples, and which was the site of the opening moments of His Passion as well as the place from which He ascended into Glory. The vine is a constant subject, most memorably in Christ's own description of Himself (John 15: 1–6) as the Vine of which the disciples are the branches. The gourd which sheltered Jonah is also a species of vine, known as the 'vine of Sodom': the colocynth, which is a drastic cathartic, and in quantity a violent poison. Then there are the two trees which saved the innocent Susanna whom the elders accused of adultery: one said it was a mastic-tree, which is an evergreen bush, mentioned only this once in the Bible, the other said it was an evergreen oak, or holm-oak, also only mentioned here. The major difference is one of size; the mastic-tree is quite small, the holm-oak is a majestic tree.

The psalms also have trees mentioned in them. The most poignant is the pathetic lament of the exiles in Babylon: 'By the rivers of Babylon... we sat down and wept ... On the willows there we hung up our harps...' (Ps. 137); the *Salix babylonica* is the 'weeping willow'. In Ps. 104 birds build their nests 'in the cedars of Lebanon, and ... the stork has its home in the fir-trees'. In Ps. 107 'they sow fields and plant vineyards', and Ps. 148 lists fruit-trees and cedars. In Ezek. 27 is a lamentation for the destruction of Tyre, with a list of the things that made the city great: fir-trees from Senir, cedar from Lebanon, oaks of Bashan, pine from Cyprus, and the goods traded between Tyre and her neighbours included ebony, cassia, and sweet cane. Other trees mentioned here and there are the almond (which blossoms before it leafs, which allows Jeremiah (1: 11, 12) to make an unexpected pun on the Hebrew word for it which also means 'hasten' or 'watch'), the ash (which is not the N. ash-tree, but the Aleppo pine, a species of fir-tree), the bay in Ps. 37: 35 (in AV 'the wicked... like a green bay tree'; both Vg. and NRSV have 'cedar of Lebanon', because a bay-tree means a green tree growing in its native soil, not any specific kind of tree), box, citron, elm (mentioned only once, which is not the N. elm, but the terebinth, which looks like a small oak-tree). Hazel is in fact the almond, juniper is a desert bush like broom, and poplar is the white poplar which the North also calls the aspen, but can be a resinous shrub about 20 ft. high.

The *Arbor Vitae* or Tree of Life is a symbolic term for the wood of the cross, and is linked to the rite of the Veneration of the Cross, which is part of the Good Friday rite, recorded as early as the 4th century in Jerusalem by the pilgrim *Etheria. Its counterpart is the *arbor mortis*, tree of death, the tree on which Judas hanged himself. The so-called Judas Tree, which blooms at Eastertide with red blossoms on the bare wood, is popularly believed to be the *arbor mortis*. The Apostle Jude, in his Epistle v. 12, describes slanderers as 'autumn trees without fruit, twice dead, uprooted'.

Trees are often represented in catacomb paintings, and on sarcophagi, but they are symbolic rather than recognizable images of identifiable species. A contemporary *Tree of Life* mural (2003) by Mark *Cazalet can be seen in Chelmsford Cathedral.

Tree of Jesse *See* JESSE.

Tree of Knowledge The Tree of Knowledge and the Tree of Life were in the middle of the Garden of Eden (Gen. 2) and God commanded Adam that he should not eat the fruit of the Tree of Knowledge of Good and Evil. In Gen. 3: the serpent tricked Eve into disobedience, causing the *Fall, and when they had both eaten of the fruit of the Tree, they knew that they had done wrong. For this, they were expelled from the Garden, and an angel with a flaming sword was set to guard the Garden, lest Adam should eat the fruit of the Tree of Life, and live forever. *See also* MAN, FALL OF, and SERPENT.

trefoil A decorative shape of three equal lobes, much used in *tracery windows or blind tracery patterns as in the Angel Choir of Lincoln Cathedral.

Trent, Council of The 19th Ecumenical Council, held at Trento, in the Tyrol, between 1545 and 1563. Its importance lay in defining the differences between the Roman Church and the various Protestant bodies of the 16th century, as well as imposing new discipline on the Roman Church itself, especially concerning clerical education. For the arts, the most significant session was the last (3–4 Dec. 1563), when the decision, in 787, of the Second Council of *Nicaea concerning the legitimacy of images, and against *iconoclasm, was reconfirmed: 'Moreover, let the bishops diligently teach that by means of the stories of the mysteries of our redemption portrayed in paintings... the people are instructed and confirmed in faith. If any abuses have found their way into these holy and salutary observances, the holy council earnestly desires that they be completely removed . . . so that no representation of false doctrine or occasion of grave error be exhibited. Such zeal and care should be exhibited by the bishops . . . that nothing may appear that is disorderly or unbecoming . . . nothing that is profane . . . The holy council decrees that no one is permitted to erect . . . any unusual image unless it has been approved by the bishop; also that no new miracles be accepted . . . unless they have been investigated and approved by the same bishop'.

This decree was partly the result and partly the justification of much 16th-century aesthetic controversy over the place of painting and sculpture in the Church, which had been attacked by the more extreme Protestants (*see* DECORUM). The Council of Trent also asserted the authenticity of the Latin Vulgate *Bible and admitted into the *Canon of Scripture several books rejected by, e.g., Anglicans. For the arts, this meant that subjects such as Daniel in the Lions' Den or Susanna and the Elders were admissible in churches.

Trials of Christ *See* CAIAPHAS, PILATE.

triangle An equilateral triangle is a symbol of the Trinity, God the Father, God the Son, and God the Holy Ghost, each being represented by one of the equal sides of the triangle. With an eye inside the triangle, it becomes the symbol of the All-Seeing Godhead.

Pontormo: *Supper at Emmaus* (1525: Uffizi) is unusual in having the triangle with the Eye of God over the head of Christ.

tribune *See* TRIFORIUM.

Tribute Money There are two separate references to Tribute Money—i.e. tax—in the NT. The first is recorded only by Matthew (17: 24–7) and refers to the annual tax payable by every adult male Jew to maintain the Temple at Jerusalem. When the collectors approached Peter for the money for himself and for Jesus, Jesus asked Peter 'From whom do kings . . . take toll or tribute? From their children or from others?' Peter said, 'From others'; Jesus, 'Then the children are free' (or should be exempt), 'However, so that we do not give offence to them, go to the sea and cast a hook; take the first fish that comes up; and when you open its mouth, you will find a coin; take that and give it to them for you and me.'

This miracle is represented in its entirety in one of the main frescoes by *Masaccio (*c.*1425: Florence, Sta Maria del Carmine), but is otherwise rare, and its significance in this connection is not clear. The other Tribute Money is the much better-known account (Matt. 22: 17–21; also in Mark and Luke) of the attempt by the Pharisees to trap Christ, by asking whether it was lawful to pay tax to Caesar? He asked to be shown a coin, and, having established that it had Caesar's head on it, He said 'Give therefore to Caesar the things that are Caesar's, and to God the things that are God's'. Apparently this incident does not occur in art before *c.*1500. There is a painting by Titian of 1568 in London (NG), another in Dresden, and several replicas, as well as Baroque examples.

tricerion *See* TRIKERION.

trichora (Gk. tri-conch) describes a building, usually a church, of which the east end, or altar area, is designed with three apses placed round a central domed space. Of such a form was the altar end of the Church of the Nativity in Bethlehem, of between 560 and 603, though whether there was a central dome leading to the nave is doubtful. An example of the type is the Catholicon of the Great Lavra on Mt. Athos founded in 963, and a Romanesque example of the form is at Germigny-les-Prés, near the Abbey of St-Benoît-sur-Loire. Both Palladio's great 16th-century churches in Venice, San Giorgio Maggiore and the Redentore, exploit the same motif. *See also* CELLA TRICHORA.

Tridentine The adjective from *Trent, Council of.

triforium A triforium is an arcaded passage in the interior elevation of a nave, lying above the colonnade or arcade and below the *clerestory. The simple basilican form had no triforium, but with the introduction of *gynaecea in early Byzantine churches space had to be made for galleries or tribunes over the main arcades or colonnades of the nave. This was done—for instance, at St Demetrios in Salonika (422–32)—by creating an extra storey, usually in the form of an arcaded area under the aisle roof between the nave arcade and the clerestory. Access to this gallery was normally directly from the *narthex.

Similar matronea (the Latin term for gynaecea) were built in some Italian Romanesque churches, for instance in San Nicola in Bari. Even where tribunes existed, they do not appear to have been similarly used in N. Europe, but many pilgrimage churches have such tribunes to accommodate large congregations, as for instance at Santiago de Compostela. There are also wide galleries in some English Romanesque churches, such as Ely, Peterborough, and Romsey, but whether they were ever used for pilgrims is doubtful since access to them is difficult. Some major northern Romanesque churches have them because they were also pilgrimage churches—for instance St-Rémi at Reims in France, Sant' Ambrogio in Milan (where there are tribunes but no clerestory). The large ones at Santiago de Compostela are used at the great festival of S. James.

A three-storey elevation, without tribunes, led to a narrower triforium masking a passage under the aisle roof. Sometimes it is no more than a narrow strip of arcaded masonry below the clerestory—a blind triforium—as at the Abbey of La Trinité at Caen, in Normandy, and this feature sometimes coexisted with tribunes beneath it, as at Laon in N. France, creating a four-storey elevation. In N. High Gothic churches, the triforium is rarely more than a decorative screen in front of the aisle roofs. With the revival of classical forms during the Renaissance, the triforium disappeared except for instances of deliberate revivalism, mostly in 19th-century Gothic Revival churches.

trikerion (tricerion) A candlestick with three lights, to symbolize the Trinity. It is used by Greek bishops to bless the congregation. *See also* DIKERION.

Trinities, the Two This is a representation of the Trinity, as defined below, combined with the Christ Child with the Virgin and S. Joseph. The finest example of this rare subject is by Murillo, of the late 1670s, in London, National Gallery. There is a second example by Murillo in the Louvre, and two examples by Zurbarán, one of which is in Sta Maria, Zafra (near Badajos, W. Spain).

Trinity, the Holy God the Father, God the Son, and God the Holy Ghost. The dogma of the Trinity, which is central to Christian theology, maintains that the One God exists in Three Persons and One Substance. In the strict sense this is a Divine Mystery, in that it cannot be understood by reasoning, unless it is divinely revealed, and it cannot be demonstrated even were it to be revealed. Although it is beyond the power of reason to explain it or demonstrate it, yet it is not beyond reason to believe it, since it is not incompatible with rational thought. The dogma is set out with admirably succinct clarity in the Nicene Creed, and with even more precision in the Athanasian Creed, and its finest classical exposition is by S. Thomas Aquinas.

In art, the ideal depiction of the Trinity is in the simplicity of the *triangle, exemplified in the triangle of the Gk. letter 'delta'. In early Byzantine art, God was never portrayed in human form, but as the *Dextera Domini, as in the 4th/5th-century ivory of the Ascension (Munich) where the Hand of God grasps that of the Ascending Son, or in the 9th-century apse of St Mark's, Venice, where Christ, flanked by saints and the square-haloed Pope Gregory IV, stands below the Hand of God and above a dove, below which is the nimbused Lamb of God, with the 'sheep' of the Apostles on either side. The earliest representation of God the Father as a man does not appear to be before the late 13th century, and it is possible that some of the ruined frescoes in the Upper Church at Assisi are in fact by Cimabue, and one of them portraying Noah building the ark, and the Deluge, has a figure of God the Father. In the Arena Chapel in Padua (1306), Giotto portrayed God the Father, enthroned amid angels, deciding on the Annunciation, which is portrayed below. After this date, He is frequently placed in a roundel over a Christ in Majesty or a Virgin and Child. Examples of both are attributed to Giotto.

The three figures of the Trinity are also fundamental to the portrayal of the *Seat of Mercy. An icon by Andrei Rublev, of the Trinity in the figures of *Abraham and the Three Angels* (after 1422: Tretyakov Gall., Moscow), is one of the most memorable depictions of the theme. The *Coronation of the Virgin* by *Quarton, of 1453, has two identical men, with a dove, crowning the Virgin. A strange mid-15th-century representation of three mens' heads, joined as if on one body, is on a lavabo, now Museo Bardini, Florence (wrongly attributed to Michelozzo), and an identification with the Trinity has been suggested as an interpretation of its meaning. There are also some MSS with miniatures by Jean Fouquet (*c.*1420–*c.*1481), one of the major French painters of the 15th century, representing the Trinity as three identical figures seated on identical thrones (*Hours of Étienne Chevalier*, *c.*1470: Chantilly) In one, a *Coronation of the Virgin*, one of the figures has descended from the row of Gothic thrones on which He had been seated, to crown the kneeling Virgin; in another MS, the *Hours of Diane de Croy*: *c.*1465, Sheffield, Ruskin Museum, the three figures are seated in virtually identical positions on identical thrones. Another representation is by Barent van Orley, in the *Dormition of the Virgin*, 1520: Brussels, Municipal Hospital. Here the Trinity is represented as three identical figures, crowned with papal tiaras, enthroned above the Assumption of the Virgin, who lies on her death-bed below. This type of representation of the Trinity is said to have been prohibited by Pope Urban VIII because the Holy Spirit was not to be depicted as a man but only as either a dove, or as the tongues of fire which descended upon the heads of the disciples at Pentecost.

One of the grandest representations of the Trinity is the *Disputa* by Raphael, in the Stanza della Segnatura in the Vatican, 1509–11. This is a Renaissance version of the earlier vertical arrangement, from God the Father's triangular halo, through Christ who shows his wounds, to the dove of the Holy Ghost floating over the monstrance with its host, stamped with the Crucifixion. Even the design of the frontal of the altar on which the monstrance stands is a single line with no beginning and no end, stressing the theme of Eternity. The *Gloria* by Titian, of 1551–4, Madrid, Prado, depicts God the Father and Christ, and the dove of the Holy Ghost, presiding over the prelude to the Last Judgement. S. Augustine likened the Trinity to the essentials of being, the sun, light, and heat, which could be visualized as interlinked rings. Chichester Cathedral of the Holy Trinity houses the tapestry (1966) by John *Piper: its scheme has the four outer and narrower panels showing *The Elements* and *The Evangelists' Symbols*. The central three larger ones project an equilateral triangle with a white disk symbolizing *The Father*, a Tau cross for *The Son*, and a flame-like wing for the *Holy Spirit*, all in vibrant colours.

triptych A painting which is made up of three parts, usually with a central portion and two wings, often made so that the wings close over the centre. Sometimes, there is also a **predella* below the central part, to enable the wings to swing to easily. The outside of the wings may also be painted, sometimes with the portraits of the donors (if the work is given to a church) or coats of arms, and sometimes with the patron saints of the commissioners or donors. One of the largest triptychs is the *Ghent Altar, Bruges, St Bavo, but a more modest example is the *Linaiuoli Madonna*, by Fra Angelico, of 1433 (Florence, San Marco), where the central panel of the Madonna and Child has wings with saints on both sides. The marble frame, designed by Ghiberti, has a roundel with God the Father in the pediment over the centre, and there is a *predella* below. This type of triptych went out of fashion in Italy with the development of the *Sacra Conversazione, and surviving examples tended to be in fixed frames, such as the Bellini *Frari Madonna*, Venice, Frari church.

The triptych survived in the North, particularly in Germany, where the 'schnitzaltar' remained popular well into the 16th century. This is a triptych where the centre is a large carved wooden altarpiece with wings which are sometimes painted, but may also be reliefs. The finest example is *Grünewald's Isenheim Altar (1515/16: Colmar), with multiple painted wings which close over the central wooden carved altarpiece, with a divided painted *predella* which also closes over the carved one. *See also* DIPTYCH, POLYPTYCH, PALA.

Triumphal Arch This term describes two utterly distinct things. One is a large, imposing arch, built usually by a Roman emperor to commemorate a military conquest. Of such are the Arch of Titus, of Septimius Severus, and of Constantine in Rome, the Arches of Benevento, Rimini, and Orange (S. France). Modern examples include the Arche du Carrousel and the Arc de Triomphe, Paris, and the Marble Arch and the Constitution Arch, London, all 19th century. The characteristic of the usual form, such as that of the Arch of Septimius Severus, is a large central arch flanked by a smaller one on either side. Even when there is only one arch, as in the Arch of Titus, this does not alter its status as a Triumphal Arch.

The other type describes either the portion of wall over the arch which divides the nave from the chancel, or the portion of wall over the apse itself. In most Early Christian churches they are usually decorated with mosaics. An example of the first form is the Triumphal Arch of Sta Maria Maggiore, Rome, which has mosaics of *c.*435, with incidents from the childhood of Christ, some of them of apocryphal incidents. The chancel and choir of the church lie well beyond it. The 9th-century mosaic apse of Sta Prassede, Rome, is enclosed in a Triumphal Arch with processions of Apostles and martyrs approaching the heavenly Jerusalem. This type is more usual because in most churches the apse with the high altar gives directly off the nave and is not separated from the nave by transepts.

Triumph of Death This is a secular allegory of the transitory nature of human life. Among the most striking examples are the frescoes in the Campo Santo, Pisa, attributed to Francesco Traini, a Sienese painter recorded from 1321. This series was largely destroyed in 1944, during the Second World War, but the underlying drawings—the *sinopie*—reveal a draughtsman of rare energy and imagination. The subjects range from the pleasures of courtly life to the spiritual rewards of religious retirement from the world in a Thebaid, to the degradations and miseries of the poor, the blind, and the crippled, who cry out for the welcome relief of death which would end their sufferings. A cavalcade of nobles and ladies with their suites of huntsmen suddenly come upon stinking decayed corpses in their open coffins, against which they hold their noses and cover their mouths as they hurry past. The series ends with an Ascension and a traditional Last Judgement with two particularly striking groups, the cleric who has crept into Heaven, but is detected and forced to join other false religious in Hell, while an angel rescues a girl who has somehow strayed into the wrong group, and another group of women who continue their violent worldly quarrelling even in Hell. *See also* DANCE OF DEATH and MEMENTO MORI.

Trivium *See* LIBERAL ARTS.

Trophy of the Cross A cross surmounted by a *Chi-Rho monogram encircled by a wreath (of victory), the whole forming an allegory of the Crucifixion and Resurrection, as on a sarcophagus of *c.*350 in Rome (Lateran Mus.). *See also* CRUCIFIXION.

True Cross, Legend of the This is a long story in the **Golden Legend*, which was adapted by Agnolo Gaddi for his frescoes in Sta Croce, Florence, and which *Piero della Francesca also used for his fresco cycle in San Francesco, Arezzo. The frescoes by Piero are in the apse of the church, and the major part of the cycle is arranged in three tiers on each of the side walls, and on the lower part of the altar wall. They are now in a damaged state, and have been extensively restored. The cycle starts on the right side in the top lunette with the Dying Adam sending Seth to the gates of Paradise to ask the angel for some oil from the Tree of Mercy, so that he might live. Seth is repulsed by the Archangel Michael, who gives him some seeds from the Tree of Sin, and tells him to place them in Adam's mouth when he is dead. Seth returns to find Adam dead, and buries him with the seeds in his mouth. They grow into a mighty tree which lasted until the time of Solomon, who cut it down to use it in building the Temple, but the craftsmen found it useless and threw it out to be a bridge over a stream called Siloam. The second fresco tells how when the Queen of Sheba came to visit Solomon and was about to cross the bridge, she saw in a vision that from it would be made the Cross upon which the Saviour would die, and she fell on her knees and worshipped it. Solomon, surrounded by his courtiers, received her and her ladies, and she told him about the wood of the bridge, adding that He who would be crucified on it would destroy the kingdom of the Jews. Solomon had the wood buried deep in the earth. When Constantine faced his enemy Maxentius at the Milvian Bridge, he feared to lose the battle, but when he was asleep in his tent an angel appeared to him and said, Raise your head. He then saw in the sky a cross made of light, with the text *In hoc signo vinces*—'In this sign shalt thou conquer'. He had a cross made and carried before his army, and he prayed that his hand would not be stained with Roman blood. Maxentius had deliberately weakened the supports of the bridge, and himself fell into the trap he had set for Constantine. He charged across the river, the bridge broke, and he was drowned.

Helena, Constantine's mother, summoned the Jews in Jerusalem to find out where Christ's cross had been buried. No one would tell her, but when she threatened to burn them, they pointed out one man, called Judas, who knew. When he refused to tell her, she had him thrown into a dry well, and after a week, being ravenous, he told her where it was, and the diggers unearthed three crosses, but nothing to say which was the True Cross. A body being taken for burial came past, and each cross was tried in turn, and when the third cross touched the dead man he sat up on the bier. The cross was then taken to the Basilica of the Holy Sepulchre.

Three centuries later, King Chosroes of Persia stole the cross and encased it in his throne beside which he kept a cock. The Emperor Heraclius defeated him and offered him his life if he would become a Christian. He refused, so Heraclius killed him. The Emperor took the cross in procession to Jerusalem, but as he was about to enter the gate, its stones fell in his way and welded themselves together so that they could not be moved. An angel appeared to him, reminding him that Christ carried his cross through this gate in humility. Heraclius took off his robes and his shoes, and barefoot carried the cross to the church. The remaining frescoes are of an *Annunciation* (which is also a *Porta Clausa) and half-lengths of now unidentifiable saints.

trumeau *See* PORTAL.

Tundal (Tundale, Tungdal), sometimes wrongly called Saint, was an Irish poet active *c.*1149. His *Vision* contains a lurid and disgusting description of the tortures of Purgatory and Hell (it also has a description of Paradise). The *Visio Tundali* was translated into several vernacular languages in the 12th/13th centuries, but enjoyed a marked popularity in the 15th. The only known illuminated MS is a French version in the Getty Museum, California, but French translations are also reflected in the famous MS of the *Très Riches Heures du Duc de Berri* (*c.*1410–15) or the *portal of St-Maclou, Rouen. A Dutch version (1484) was known to *Bosch, and its influence can be found even as late as El *Greco's *Adoration of the Name of Jesus* (*c.*1580: Escorial).

tunic, tunicle *See also* DALMATIC.

Turin, the Holy Shroud of *See* SHROUD.

turris (Lat. tower) A *pyx or *reliquary in the shape of a tower.

TWENTIETH AND TWENTY-FIRST CENTURY CHURCH ARCHITECTURE

In 1897 Anatole de Baudot built the first reinforced concrete church at St-Jean-de-Montmartre, Paris. Using one of *Viollet-le-duc's Gothic designs, the structure looked so fragile that building work was prolonged until 1904. At the opening of the 20th century, there was a competition to build Liverpool Anglican Cathedral. Giles Gilbert Scott, Sir George Gilbert *Scott's grandson, won the competition at the remarkable age of 21, so G. F. Bodley was appointed to supervise the work. When Bodley died in 1907 the emphasis in Scott's work changed.

He abandoned the Gothic refinement of his Lady Chapel and his work became more powerfully articulated and rational, even Rationalist. This was a new departure for the period around the Great War, as can be seen by contrasting the cathedral and the churches published in Sir Charles Nicholson and Charles Spooner's *Recent English Ecclesiastical Architecture: A Series of Illustrations of Notable Modern Work* (published *c.*1910), where Spooner wrote:

> A new church is in essentials very like an old one. The Christian faith is the same today as it was at the beginning, though possibly our understanding of it has grown and developed. The central act of worship, the offering of the holy eucharist, is the same as when the Church emerged from the Catacombs ... and I suppose it will remain the same as long as the Church militant is on earth. The buildings used for that worship obviously have certain characteristics of plan and arrangement which survive in spite of great differences of style and detail.

This makes the reassuring claim that the problem for ecclesiastical architecture was essentially a matter of style, rather than planning – 'It is unnecessary in the planning of a church to be guided by the type of service which happens to be the custom in the particular parish', he continued. A wide array of architectural styles was allowed, from the Byzantine brick of Bentley's Westminster Cathedral to the powerful Gothic stone of the early work at Scott's Liverpool Cathedral.

The cathedral occupied the whole of Scott's career, and when he died in 1960 it remained unfinished, taking another nineteen years to complete. Scott was also an industrial designer, with Battersea and Bankside power stations to his credit, but he thought their Modernism was inappropriate for church architecture, where a more traditional style should be used.

Rationalism had already begun to affect the design of churches, including Antonio Gaudi's Güell Chapel near Barcelona, built between 1898 and 1915, and Theodore Fischer's Church of the Redeemer in Munich from *c.*1900 and dedicated in 1901. The former was in a stripped-down Gothic that was shaped as a kind of diagram of the structural lines of force, while the latter was an exercise in a strict economy of ornament within a Romanesque idiom. In 1907 Fischer was one of the original members of the German Werkbund and in 1910 he produced St Paul's, Ulm, where he left the concrete structure radically exposed. The sweeping arches of St Paul's and the parabolic granite arches of Lars Wahlmann's Engelbrekt Church (1914), Stockholm, would be echoed in the developments of the 1920s and 1930s. After the dreadful experience of the First World War, Otto Bartning published *Vom neuen Kirchbau* (on New Church Architecture) in 1919, which rejected timid historicism. He began exploring the possibilities of centrally planned churches to focus community, resulting in the remarkable 'Sternkirche' project (1922) and the round steel and concrete Church of the Resurrection in Essen. It had a central font with the altar behind and a set of three radically modern windows by Johan Thorn Prikker. It was a functionalist liturgical arrangement to reflect the gathered worshipping community, but the expressive qualities of the structure still recall the soaring rhythms of the Gothic.

In Britain the question of appropriate style increasingly divided the architectural profession during the first three decades of the 20th century, and in ecclesiastical work the traditionalists were very much in the ascendant. The first two decades were dominated by traditionalists such as Nicholson, Temple Moore, and Ninian Comper. In France Auguste Perret completed the iconic concrete Church of Notre-Dame du Raincy on the outskirts of Paris in 1923. It is an aisled basilica where the walls have been dissolved into an array of stained-glass panes designed by Maurice *Denis, set in a pre-cast concrete frame. His last building was St-Joseph, with a tremendously tall tower as a landmark in the reconstruction of Le Havre. Meanwhile in Germany, as early as 1923 Domenicus Böhm designed the parish church of St Peter and St Paul, Dettingen (Karlstein) and in 1930 Rudolf Schwartz produced the uncompromisingly modern Church of Corpus Christi in Aachen. In The Hague in 1925/26 H. P. Berlage, the grand old man of Dutch architecture, built the First Church of Christ, Scientist, heavily influenced by Frank Lloyd Wright's Unity Temple (1906) near Chicago.

Before 1936 stylistic refinement and Modern architectural form appeared in the work of Francis Xavier Velarde at St Gabriel, Blackburn; H. S. Goodhart-Rendel at St Wilfrid, Brighton; N. F. Cachemaille-Day's St Nicholas, Burnage; Edward Maufe's St Thomas, Hanwell; and Giles Gilbert Scott's St Francis, Terriers; all published in *New Churches Illustrated* (Incorporated Church Building Society, 1936). The U-shaped Burnage (1931–32) bears a strong resemblance to Böhm's (1931) Church of St Camillus, Mönchengladbach. In the face of considerable opposition, Böhm had also produced a remarkable circular church, St Engelbert, Cologne. But the only evidence of new planning coming to the fore in this group of English churches was at John Keble Church, Mill Hill, London, built by D. F. Martin Smith in 1936 where he placed the Choir in the middle of the congregation and brought the altar well forward. New liturgical ideas embedded in experimental architectural form had only begun to appear in England the year before with J. H. L. Langton's Church of the First Martyrs, Bradford. The plan is octagonal and the altar was forwards with the pulpit directly behind on the axis. It was admired by Eric Gill who designed the Roman Catholic Church of Gorleston-on-Sea in 1939. Even by 1947 and the publication of *Fifty Modern Churches*, the only liturgically adventurous church illustrated was Cachemaille-Day's centrally planned St Michael and All Angels, Wythenshawe of 1937. Two interlocking squares produced a star-shape and the altar was intended to be in the centre. Like Böhm, he met with opposition, which unlike Böhm he was unable to overcome, and in the event, the bishop insisted it be pushed back into one of the points which was completely framed in the glare of traceried windows. A successful example of a centralized altar was J. N. and J. B. S. Comper's St Philip, Cosham, Portsmouth, of 1938. Theological and liturgical developments combined with architectural and artistic experimentation meant that new Anglican churches and their design became less and less clearly distinguishable from Roman Catholic and even Non-Conformist buildings such as the Unitarian Chapel at Mill Hill, Leeds, though some aspects of design—such as Ninian Comper's English Altar—could hardly be more traditional, historically rooted, and distinctively Anglican.

The devastation of the Second World War in Britain and across Europe, combined with shifts in population and suburbanization, resulted in a huge amount of church building. Increasingly, the issues became focused on the question of visible continuity or discontinuity with the historical tradition, and secondly (at least in British priorities) on new architectural planning for a reformed liturgy. Yet, at the same time, this period also witnessed the closure of a large number of churches. In England, in the period between 1940 and 1980, the Methodists alone closed 5,000 churches—disposing of a quarter of their stock in a single decade. From 1969 to 1980, the Church of England made 1,434 churches redundant. These were turned into homes, shops, or clubs, or simply demolished. Whether this movement reflects the terminal decline of the Church—or simply another stage in its development—remains open.

In 1951 the Festival of Britain had a 'Live Architecture' section, which featured Trinity Congregational Church, Poplar, London, by C. C. Handyside and D. Rogers Stark. Its planning was particularly interesting because Congregationalist worship, mission, and organization required spaces for a wide range of religious and secular activities. This approach was evident in *Fifty Modern Churches* of 1947 (aptly referring to Wren's 50 churches in the redesign of London after the Great Fire), and was explored by the Congregationalist architect Edward Mills in *The Modern Church* of 1956. In that book he places his own work in the context of the worldwide architectural community and the worldwide Church of all denominations. He includes his own Methodist Church in West Greenwich, London, alongside Handyside and Rogers Stark's Congregational Church in Poplar, Spence's experimental Anglican parish churches in Coventry, and Maguire's project for a Roman Catholic Church.

The story was similar in the United States; in *Religious Buildings for Today*, a book of 1957 compiling a series of articles on religious architecture, a basic assumption was made absolutely clear:

> It is one of the axioms of the architectural profession that architecture always tells the truth about the society in which it takes form. However much an age might try to disguise itself, its real nature is disclosed because architecture is the most social of all the arts.

Clearly the historical disguises of the historical styles would have to be dropped in favour of an honest expression of contemporary religious life. Another article in the book optimistically predicted that in the coming decade, 'some 70,000 churches and synagogues will be constructed or substantially altered'. The photographs reveal formal experimentation in the architecture, and even radicalism in the arts, but the plans reveal conservatism in liturgical arrangements. That extends to the transatlantic examples cited and to Le Corbusier's Chapel at Ronchamp, and the design for Coventry Cathedral, which won the open competition for Basil Spence. A similar approach based in the sociology of religion was taken up in 1972 in Reinhard Gieselmann's *Contemporary Church Architecture* with a text in both English and German. It opens with the words:

> A discussion of church architecture must involve a discussion of religion. Yet the church is not only the home of a religious congregation but, more than that, a building belonging to society at large.

The conservative, and increasingly the radical interpretations of what that might mean filled the book. Architects represented included Antonio Gaudí, Rudolf Steiner, Domenikus Böhm, Frank Lloyd Wright, Otto Senn, Le Corbusier, Alvar Aalto, Martin Purdy, Oscar Niemeyer, and Aldo van Eyck. Designing a church had become an exercise in sociological reflection in an international language. Not only was it relevant, it was vital.

In Britain, the most high profile 20th-century examples of new churches were the competitions for the new cathedrals, but new churches could be found everywhere. In England, by the early 1960s, over a thousand new structures had been erected, 400 of which were churches, and, showing the same social concerns as in America and Europe, the remainder were dual-purpose buildings or church halls. Even with increasing secularization, considerable momentum was sustained. For example, from 1969 to 1993 the Church of England alone built 400 new churches, many of which were large and architecturally important. Many were significant architectural statements in their own right—and they continued to possess a wider cultural importance. Coventry Cathedral, as the historian Gavin Stamp observed, was 'the last modern building in Britain *of any type* that ordinary people have queued to see inside. That was quite an achievement.'

An overview of 20th-century developments in England can be seen in its new cathedrals, including F. Bentley's Westminster Roman Catholic Cathedral, Sir Edward Maufe's Guildford Cathedral begun in 1936 and consecrated in 1961, the already-cited example of Giles Scott's Liverpool Anglican Cathedral (with an interesting parallel in the Gothic St John the Divine, New York, with later designs to complete the crossing tower), Sir Basil Spence's Coventry Cathedral (1951–62), which replaced the medieval building bombed during the Second World War, and Sir Frederick Gibberd's Roman Catholic Metropolitan Cathedral of Christ the King built in Liverpool in the wake of Vatican II. It was built on the enormous vaulted crypt of the cathedral designed by Edwin Lutyens in 1929, begun in 1933 and abandoned in 1941.

In terms of the stylistic debate, this series of cathedrals conforms to the pattern already established. Westminster Cathedral was a historicist *tour de force*. Liverpool Anglican evolved stylistically from the winning design in 1901 to completion in 1979. Guildford was stylistically advanced at its inception and liturgically conservative. Lutyens' Liverpool Metropolitan similarly was stylistically an imperial blast relating to his design for the Viceroy's House in New Delhi of 1912, and intended to rival St Peter's itself, but it was inappropriate in changing historical circumstances.

Interestingly, when Scott was initially invited to provide a design in 1942 to replace Coventry's cathedral, destroyed on 14/15 November 1940, his proposal as developed by 1944/45 showed a dramatic use of Modernist form and lighting, and also a liturgically advanced central altar. His plan was rejected and a competition arranged. This dispute, explicitly focused by the competition and its aftermath, queried continuity or discontinuity with historic architectural and liturgical forms. National and international interest produced no fewer than 219 competition entries of every conceivable type, including an entry by Colin St John Wilson that reconfigured the function and architectural form of the cathedral. Another by Peter and Alison Smithson was formed by a huge hyperbolic paraboloid roof structure that allowed the functional elements of the cathedral, including a cuboid Trinity Chapel and a Choir in the form of an 'ark' rather like the ancient *schola cantorum*, to be deployed freely within the three dimensions of the structurally unencumbered interior. The winner of the competition was Basil Spence with a rather traditional plan integrating great works of modern religious art. His later proposal to bring the altar well forward to serve a more modern liturgy was firmly suppressed. Spence's Cathedral was the embodiment of the Festival of Britain 1951, where he had himself designed the 'Ships and the Sea' Pavilion. Centralized liturgical planning reached its definitive statement between 1958 and 1960 with the building of St Paul's Bow Common, London, by Robert Maguire and Keith Murray.

The last of the series of cathedrals, Gibberd's Liverpool Metropolitan, is the embodiment of Vatican II thinking. Already in 1962 at a conference in Liverpool, Gibberd said of his centralized plan: 'This is a complete and decisive break from the traditional cathedral plan.' This sense of rupture with historic tradition has only recently been 'corrected' with Benedict XVI restoring the possibility of the Latin Mass *ad orientem*. The Vatican is now promoting an interpretation of Vatican II in terms of continuity rather than discontinuity. The polarized debate continues.

However radical some of the changes brought about by Vatican II and their effects might appear, they were explicitly couched in terms of continuity with the tradition, and 'the liturgical norms of the Council of Trent have in many respects been fulfilled and perfected by those of the Second Vatican Council' (General Instruction on the Roman Missal). As noted, Benedict XVI re-emphasized this aspect of continuity in Vatican II and even showed favour to the reintroduction of the Latin Mass.

There was, however, an intention to involve the laity more in the celebration of the liturgy in the vernacular. The reforms regularized and aligned much of the work by the Liturgical Movement over the course of half a century at least. The involvement of the laity had architectural ramifications to enable their full participation, and to create a new set of relationships within the community united around the altar. The sanctuary was no longer to be the distant preserve of the clergy.

Since the early 20th century, the combined work of the Liturgical Movement and the Modern Movement in architecture had been experimenting with architectural form that would promote the involvement of the laity. The renewed liturgy was to provide the brief for a renewed church architecture. Between 1922 and 1923, Auguste Perret had built Notre-Dame du Raincy in Paris in naked concrete and huge areas of glass in the walls to bathe the celebration in light. The thin shafts supporting the vault allow clear visibility for the celebration of Mass, in its way perfecting the visual participation intended by the Tridentine reforms. Just as the Gesù had similarities to Protestant hall churches, so Perret's Catholic church achieved in concrete what Otto Bartning achieved in steel for the German Evangelical Church. The *Stahlkirche* was designed as a kit of parts and built for an exhibition in Cologne in 1928, then disassembled and rebuilt in Essen in 1929. It, too, wrapped a glass wall round a huge space punctuated by sinewy steel columns. It was in Germany that both the Liturgical Movement was most strongly rooted and the greatest church architects of Modern Movement flourished. The architect Rudolf Schwarz was in close contact with the theologians of the movement for liturgical renewal, in particular Romano Guardini, who was an active collaborator on some of his projects. Corpus Christi, Aachen, built by Schwartz between 1928 and 1930, has cool, crisp, sculptural forms, an impressive numinous white interior, and a visually accessible black marble altar raised on seven steps, and suitable for celebration facing the people.

The Liturgical Movement in France was led by the *Centre de Pastorale liturgique* wielding influence through its many publications. Another important point of contact between the Church in France and the arts, including architecture, was the journal *Art Sacré* whose editor was Fr Marie-Alain Couturier. He knew Le Corbusier well and frequently visited his studio when the pilgrimage chapel at Ronchamp was being designed (between 1952 and 1955). He died before it was complete but his last article, dictated in his last illness and left unfinished, concerned Ronchamp.

Despite being championed by Couturier, Ronchamp has had a mixed reception, both formally and in terms of fitness for the liturgy. It is certainly highly unusual, even for a pilgrimage chapel, but it does provide well for visibility, and there are exciting possibilities for outdoor liturgy between the east end and the brow of the hill. It is actually the expressive qualities and the use of materials that are often at issue with architectural critics. Couturier also cites Matisse and the chapel of 1952 he designed and Auguste Perret built at Vence. It is a beautiful white space flooded with Mediterranean light, the walls covered in drawings by the master. There is a small nave and a single transept for nuns. The altar is turned at 45 degrees to the axes so that the religious and laity are equally addressed by the priest who must celebrate facing those who are gathered for worship. Every last item was designed by Matisse, including the cross and vestments, creating a stunning unity. Other churches where art again gave voice to Catholic teaching included the Chapel of St Pierre at Villefranche-sur-Mer by Jean Cocteau, and Fernand Léger's Church of the Sacred Heart, Audincourt and Notre-Dame de Toute-Grace at Assy consecrated on 4 August 1950. There he produced a mosaic on the façade, George *Rouault did the stained glass, André *Lurçat provided a huge tapestry of the Apocalypse for the apse, and there were also works by Pierre Bonnard, Braque, and Matisse. The architecture was in the vernacular, but was the bearer of content that spoke magnificently of contemporary Catholicism. All this preceded the Constitution on the Sacred Liturgy by more than a decade, creating further pressure towards reform.

While the Second Vatican Council was meeting, and during the publication of the Conciliar documents, the Roman Catholic Metropolitan Cathedral in Liverpool was being designed and built. It has become the iconic architectural statement of the transformation of the Church. Its designer, Sir Frederick Gibberd, approached it as a functional problem in terms of the aspirations of the Second Vatican Council.

With a circular plan and central altar, Gibberd 'found it possible to place three thousand people within 70 feet of the sanctuary'. Here again the cathedral was intended to be a framework for the arts, both structurally with stained glass by John *Piper and Patrick *Reyntiens, and for later commissions over time. This was a radical departure in both liturgy and architecture, and Vatican II has long been associated with the radical reform of Catholicism. Now, however, with Benedict XVI having begun to stress the continuities of Vatican II, the insights of Pope Francis are awaited. *See also* EUROPE: 20TH- AND 21ST-CENTURY PAINTING, SCULPTURE, STAINED GLASS.

tympanum (Lat. a drum, or wheel of a pulley, Gk. *tympanon*) The area above the lintel of a doorway, or the base of a pediment, which is enclosed below an arch or below the segmental or triangular top of a pediment. It became a useful field for mosaics (i.e. over the door of the entrance into Hagia Sophia), or for medieval portal sculpture (i.e. at Vézelay, for the relief of *Christ sending out the Apostles to preach*). The available space in a tympanum was often increased by making the arch very large, and having the lintel supported by a *trumeau. Classical temples usually had important sculpture in the tympana of their pediments.

type, antitype, and typology (Gk. *typos*, mould, figure) The method of biblical interpretation by which persons or events in the OT are understood as prophetic symbols of persons or events in the NT. Christ Himself spoke of Jonah as a prophecy (or type) of His Resurrection (Matt. 12: 40, 'For as Jonas was three days and three nights in the belly of the sea monster, so for three days and three nights the Son of Man will be in the heart of the earth'), and the Brazen Serpent was a type of the Crucifixion (John 3: 14, 'And just as Moses lifted up the serpent in the wilderness, so must the Son of Man be lifted up'). Typology is very common in Early Christian art in catacombs and on sarcophagi, especially Jonah as a symbol of the Resurrection, and the Ark floating on the Flood symbolizing the waters of Baptism and salvation. In the 4th century S. Augustine summed it up: 'Novum Testamentum in Vetere latet: Vetus in Novo patet'—The New Testament is hidden in the Old, the Old is made clear by the New. The best medieval examples are the **Speculum Humanae Salvationis* and the **Biblia Pauperum*, which were designed as typologies. Stained glass is often typological, as in twelve windows at Canterbury, but sculpture less commonly so. In the 15th century there is an important document, the contract of 1464 for the altarpiece of the *Mystic Meals* by *Bouts: 'In this altarpiece . . . on the centre panel the Supper of our Blessed Lord with His twelve Apostles, and on each of the inner wings two representations from the Old Testament: (1) the Heavenly Bread [i.e. Manna], (2) Melchizedek, (3) Elijah, (4) the Eating of the Paschal Lamb as described in the Old Covenant . . . To make this altarpiece to the best of his ability . . . in such order and truth as the Rev. Masters Jan Vaernacker and Gillis Bailluwel, Professors of Theology, shall prescribe to him with regard to the aforementioned subjects.' Perhaps the most important of all typological cycles is also 15th century—in the *Sistine Chapel in the Vatican, where the walls were frescoed in 1481/2 with the Life of Moses opposite the Life of Christ. Nicolas of Verdun is thought to have been the first, in his Klosterneuburg Altar of 1181, to divide the OT into scenes *ante legem*, before the Giving of the Mosaic Law, and *sub lege*, after and under the Law. In the Sistine Chapel *Michelangelo completed this scheme with his frescoes on the ceiling which are *ante legem* (1508–12) and the tapestries designed by *Raphael (1515–16), with scenes from the Acts of the Apostles, to hang on the walls below the frescoes, are *sub gratia*, i.e. under the New Covenant.

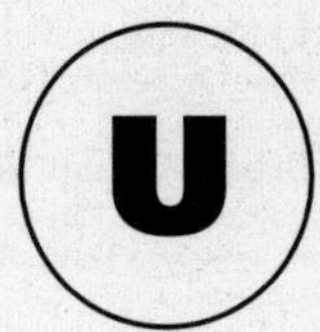

Ultramontane (Lat. *ultra montes*, beyond the mountains i.e. the Alps) The term was applied to anyone supporting the centralizing tendency and papal authority in the Roman Church, e.g. the *Jesuits, against nationalistic tendencies. In 19th-century England Cardinal Vaughan and the London *Oratorians deliberately chose Italianate rather than *Gothic Revival forms in art and architecture as an expression of Ultramontanism.

Umiltà, Madonna dell' *See* MADONNA TYPES (Madonna of Humility).

Unction, Extreme The anointing with oil of a dying person: the Last *Sacraments.

Unction, the stone of According to S. John's Gospel (19: 39–40), *Joseph of Arimathaea and *Nicodemus took the body of Jesus and anointed it with myrrh and aloes 'according to the burial custom of the Jews'. An 11th-century *icon shows the body laid out on a stone slab—the stone of Unction. This is the earliest known representation of the stage between the Deposition and Entombment, and is very rare in Western art. The 'red stone' on which the body was laid out has been venerated since ancient times and was taken to Constantinople in the 12th century before being returned to the Church of the Holy Sepulchre in Jerusalem, where its replacement still is. This is probably the scene represented in the painting by Carpaccio in Berlin, and maybe also in the one by *Holbein (1521/2: Basle). In the East the scene is almost never represented directly, but is symbolized by the *epitaphios—a Byzantine example of the 12th/13th century in Venice (Mus. di San Marco) may have inspired Carpaccio.

Uncumber *See* WILGEFORTIS.

undercroft A *crypt. A vaulted chamber, usually below the choir of a church, but sometimes sufficiently above ground to allow of natural lighting from windows at ground level, as at Canterbury Cathedral.

Underworld In classical mythology, Hades and the Afterlife. Hades was the ruler of the dead, and, by extension, became the name of his kingdom, usually thought of as underground and beyond the rivers Styx and Acheron. The dead were shadows; or, in other versions, the good went to Elysium and the wicked to Tartarus. From this, it was easy to arrive at the Christian conceptions of *Limbo, *Purgatory, *Heaven, and *Hell, and the ancient reverence for the dead became the Early Christian *agape. Charon who, in Greek myth, ferried the souls of the dead across the Styx, became so familiar that he actually features in Christian iconography, most notably in *Michelangelo's *Last Judgement*.

unicorn A mythical *beast, like a white horse with a single horn growing from the middle of its head, perhaps based distantly on the rhinoceros. According to the *Bestiaries, it can be caught and tamed only by virgins. In several OT references it is called strong, e.g. Num. 23: 22; 24: 8, and especially in Job and the Psalms; hence it was a *type of Christ. A 5th-century mosaic in San Giovanni in Fonte, Ravenna, may be the earliest representation. It was also thought that the horn of the unicorn, dipped in water, could nullify the poison from serpents, as Christ purified the world from sin. This may be the meaning of the unicorn on the font in the Baptistery at Pisa, of 1246. Since only a virgin could tame it, it became a symbol of the Incarnation, and some curious Unicorn Hunts were produced in the 15th and 16th centuries, until the Council of *Trent prohibited them in 1563. They showed the unicorn with its head in Mary's lap, as a symbol of the *Virgin Birth, accompanied by the Archangel Gabriel and various hunting dogs (said to be Mercy, Truth, etc.), in a *Hortus Conclusus. *Honorius claimed that, by allowing itself to be captured by a virgin in this way, it was a type of Christ's betrayal.

Urban VIII Maffeo Barberini, who became Pope Urban VIII (1623–44), consecrated New St Peter's in 1626 after it had been extended by *Maderno, and was active in patronizing *Bernini and beautifying Rome. As Pope, and as head of the powerful Barberini family, he commissioned many statues and busts of himself and members of his family, the Barberini palace, and many works for St Peter's, including his own tomb (1628–47), the *Longinus* (1629–38), and the *baldacchino over the Confessio (1624–33), with its huge twisted columns of bronze, mainly taken from the portico of the Pantheon. This barbarous act was the occasion of a lampoon 'Quod non fecerunt barbari, fecerunt Barberini'—What the barbarians did not do, the Barberini did.

Uriah *See* DAVID.

Uriel, the Archangel One of the four chief Archangels. *See* ANGELS.

Ursula, Saint The legend of this saint and her companions begins with a Latin inscription of *c.*400 in St Ursula, Cologne, recording the burial of some local virgin-martyrs. By the 9th century this had grown into the story of a princess and her companions who suffered in the persecutions of the emperors Maximianus and Diocletian. A misreading of a text which said XIMV (eleven virgin-martyrs) was probably corrupted into XIM V: *undecim milia virgines*—11,000 virgins. In this form the story grew in popularity until it reached its apogee in the **Golden Legend,* where Ursula becomes the daughter of a British (or, more likely, Breton) Christian king betrothed for political reasons to a pagan English prince. She obtained a respite of three years during which she and her betrothed went on a pilgrimage. They sailed down the Rhine to Basle and thence went on foot to Rome, were received by the pope, the pagan prince was baptized, and they set off for home. Accretions to the legend made Pope Cyriacus join the pilgrims, but when they reached Cologne they were all martyred by the Huns, who had meanwhile captured the city. The Huns under Attila did overrun much of Europe during the mid-5th century, and the awkward fact that the register of popes does not record a Cyriacus was got round by saying that because he left Rome his name was deleted.

In 1155 a quantity of bones was found at Cologne which, despite their including skeletons of men and children, probably from a forgotten cemetery, then became relics of the princess and her companions. All this fantasy was added to by the 'revelations' of a visionary, Elizabeth of Schönau, so that the Rhineland, the Low Countries, N. France, and, later, Venice, became centres of the cult. Among the pictorial cycles devoted to her, there is a series of eight scenes by the anonymous Master of the Ursula Legend, probably painted *c.*1486 for a convent in Bruges (now in the Mus.), but the outstanding ones are on the Shrine painted by *Memlinc with its faintly absurd crowds of pilgrims jammed into tiny cockleshell boats, and suffering martyrdom with mildly deprecatory expressions; and the series of nine large pictures (1490–5) by Carpaccio once in the Scuola di Sant'Orsola in Venice (now in the Accademia). The Scuola was a charitable institution devoted, among other things, to looking after young girls, Ursula being their patroness. The series has charming genre scenes of 15th-century Venetian life masquerading as early medieval in N. Europe. There is also an altarpiece by *Tintoretto in San Lazzaro dei Mendicanti, Venice. Holy Trinity, York, has a 15th-century stained-glass window with Ursula sheltering her votaries under her cloak, in the manner of a *Madonna della misericordia, but otherwise she is little regarded in her supposed native country.

Ursuline nuns A teaching Order of women, founded in 1535 by Sant'Angela Merici, dedicated to the education of girls. It became the largest such Order, especially in France and Canada, and has made an enormous contribution to the education of women. Their patroness is *S. Ursula, but there is no direct connection.

Utrecht Psalter An illustrated *psalter, now in the University Library, Utrecht, but probably written and illustrated in Reims, in N. France, about 816/23. It has a series of lively pen-drawings in brown ink, illustrating, very literally, the Psalms. The drawings are in an expressive style, based ultimately on Late Antique models, perhaps transmitted through Byzantine MSS. It is the masterpiece of *Carolingian book-illustration and has some 166 drawings, each with several scenes, extending across the full width of the page.

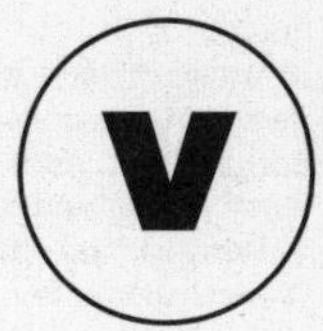

Van Eyck *See* EYCK.

Vanitas still-life From early times *Memento mori was a favourite theme for meditation, represented by S. Jerome with a skull, the **Ars Moriendi*, or the *Dance of Death, all serving as reminders of the brevity of human life. In the 17th century in the Protestant North, where church patronage was non-existent and the demand for domestic religious paintings was small, a fashion developed for moralizing paintings with no overt theme, but with symbolical content. In the Calvinist university town of Leiden there developed a form of still-life painting, known as Vanitas, from Ecclesiastes 1: 2—'Vanity of vanities; all is vanity'. It consists of emblems of transience and mortality—a skull, a guttering candle, an hour-glass, a butterfly, soap bubbles, even a cankered flower—juxtaposed to objects of vanity, wealth, or power—a mirror, an *objet de vertu*, even books (learning) or musical instruments (the pleasures of the senses). The principal painters include W. C. Heda (1594–1680), P. Claesz (*c.*1597–1660), J. D. de Heem (1606–83/4), and perhaps D. Bailly (1584–*c.*1657). An example of the genre is in London (NG), by the Delft painter Herman van Steenwyck (1612–after 1655).

Vasari, Giorgio (1511–74), is most famous as the author of the *Lives* of Italian painters, sculptors, and architects, first published in 1550, and, in an enlarged and revised edition, in 1568 as *Le Vite de' piu eccellenti Pittori, Scultori e Architettori*. It is the foundation of Italian art history, and, apart from its value as a source for the biographies of artists, gives a very clear idea of the approach to Christian iconography in the period of the *Counter-Reformation by a conforming artist. His descriptions of Byzantine works and those by Giotto or Angelico, as well as those by Michelangelo, whom he idolized, give an insight into 16th-century taste.

As a creative artist Vasari was a much better architect than painter, but his altarpieces are important as reflecting the ideals of the Council of *Trent. For example, in his *ricordi* he notes that on 10 August 1540 he was commissioned to paint an altarpiece for the Altoviti Chapel in SS Apostoli, Florence (still there; sketch in Oxford, Ashmolean Mus.), 'showing the Tree of the Fall, to which are attached Adam and Eve and many Patriarchs and Prophets, and above them Our Lady . . . treading on the head of the Serpent, coiled around the Tree'. His most famous building is a secular one—the Uffizi in Florence, a consummate piece of urban scenography, despite its flouting of the Vitruvian canons of proportion.

Vasconcellos, Josefina de (1904–2005). A sculptor trained under Emile-Antoine Bourdelle, who gained early recognition for her religious images. *Repentance of St Hubert* was accepted for the Royal Academy Summer Exhibition in 1926, the year she gained her majority, and two years later she had looked across to Normandy to provide a statue of the patron saint for St Valerie, Varengeville-sur-Mer. It was the *Prince of Peace* by Vasconcellos, standing over 2.5 metres, that provided the focus of the Hero's Shrine and Memorial at Aldershot in 1950. Penetrating another shrine was the *Virgin and Child* (1957) for St Paul's Cathedral. Yet wider appeal was sought for sites of such public concentration of attention as Coventry Cathedral's *Reconciliation* (1995) bronze, versions too, for Hiroshima's Peace Park, for the Berlin Wall, and for Stormont Castle.

The arresting yet tender authoritativeness of her best figurative works brought both balm and tonic to the generation whose faith had been jarred or destroyed by the First World War. In her sacred figures, French urban poise married with a sturdy British lustiness, startled into life many an aisle or transept. Her Crib, welcomed yearly in Trafalgar Square, London, offered its providing parish church of St Martin-in-the-Fields some emblem of its ministry among the outcast and needy. Margaret Lewis's *Josefina de Vasconcellos: Her Life and Art* (2002) chronicles the many rebuffs and difficulties that nevertheless did not hold the sculptor back from taking new initiatives on into old age.

Vatican, the Mons Vaticanus, one of the Seven Hills of ancient Rome, just outside the city walls, is the traditional place of the martyrdom and burial of *S. Peter (*c.*64?). In this belief (which now seems confirmed by excavation), the Emperor *Constantine built Old *St Peter's from *c.*324/30 over the Apostle's grave, and a papal residence seems to have been established there by *c.*500. The Lateran Palace in Rome, however, next to the cathedral, was the principal papal palace until the return of the papacy from *Avignon in 1377. Since then, and especially since *c.*1420, when Pope Martin V definitely took up residence, the Vatican has been the main seat of the popes. The Vatican Library, Michelangelo's Sistine Chapel, Raphael's Stanze, and the huge collections of Early Christian antiquities, as well as the collections of paintings and sculpture in the Vatican Museums make it one of the world's greatest treasure-houses. It suffered terribly during the Sack of Rome in 1527, a six-week-long horror launched against the city by the forces of the Emperor Charles V, during which the palace was pillaged by his Lutheran troops, who among other depredations burnt all the bookcases and their contents from the Stanze to keep themselves warm during the harsh winter which followed. The architects who have left the greatest mark on the buildings are the otherwise unknown Giovannino de' Dolci, who rebuilt the Sistine Chapel for Pope Sixtus IV in 1473–84, and *Bramante, who began the main inner courtyard, the Cortile di San Damaso, with its series of superposed loggie where later Raphael's pupils painted the biblical sequence known as 'Raphael's Bible'. He also built the long ranges of buildings on the courtyard leading up to the Belvedere, which he also built in the uppermost part of the garden, and which was much altered by Pirro Ligorio and by *Michelangelo, who added the grand staircase from the courtyard and placed on it the ancient bronze pine-cone which had stood as a fountain in the atrium of Old St Peter's. This huge courtyard was once used for tournaments to which the intolerant Sixtus V so objected that he had the new wing for the Library built by Fontana in 1589–90 across the middle, and in 1817–22, since the grand vista was already spoilt, Raffaele Stern built a second wing with a fine gallery to house part of the Vatican collection of antique statuary. In the gardens, the so-called Casino of Pius IV was in fact built for Paul IV by Pirro Ligorio from 1558 to 1561, with rich stucco decorations. The fine state staircase, the Scala Regia, was built by *Bernini in 1663–6, and leads to the older Sala Regia, which was decorated by Vasari, among others, with frescoes commemorating the Battle of Lepanto (1571), and forms the state entrance to the Sistine Chapel. Further rebuilding was done by Fontana, the favourite architect of Pope Sixtus V, who rebuilt the papal apartments, still used by the pope. In modern times a huge underground audience chamber has been constructed, where the pope receives large groups of pilgrims.

Since 1929 the Vatican Palace, St Peter's Basilica, the Piazza di San Pietro, and also the papal villa at Castel Gandolfo, outside Rome, have constituted the Vatican City State, an independent sovereign State recognized by most nations.

vault, vaulting An arched roof or ceiling, generally built of stone, brick, or in concrete, but sometimes in plaster or wood, to imitate earlier forms. (Wren used such a device in more than one of his City of London churches, rebuilt after the fire in 1666.) The earliest forms of vaulting are *barrel* or *tunnel* vaults, where the vaulting is continuous and, because of its great weight, has to be borne on very strong walls or massive piers. Most of the 10th-century pilgrimage churches have this type of vaulting. Barrel vaults with a right-angle intersection, meeting in a *cross vault*, were used by the Romans in some of their great buildings such as the Thermae, but in the early Romanesque period experiments with making the barrels slightly pointed helped to reduce the thrust or pressure on the side walls, which could then have small windows cut into them, with arcades below borne on strong piers. Cluny Abbey was a case in point.

Gothic *rib vaulting* was first experimented with in the late 11th century (Durham Cathedral), and rapidly became the most general form, in ever-increasing complexity as the number of ribs was increased. At first, in quadrilateral rib vaulting, there were four ribs rising, one from each pier at the corners of the bay to the boss on the ridge rib in the centre of each bay, creating four cells, webs, or severies to each bay. In sexpartite vaulting there were six ribs, four ribs rising to a central boss from strong piers at the corners of the bay, and two ribs rising from weaker supports, such as columns between the piers, permitting an alternating system of strong and weak piers or supports and therefore two arches to each bay (Bourges and Laon cathedrals). There were then six cells, webs, or severies to each bay of the vaulting. Most French Gothic churches continued to use the simple quadrilateral form (though there are important instances of sexpartite vaulting), but in England vaulting systems became far more complex, with the development of *tierceron ribs* rising in a cluster from the pier to the ridge rib which they meet at various spaced out points (as at Lincoln). Later extra *transverse ribs* were introduced, running across the bay from an extra boss on the central tierceron rib to the arch on either side (Bristol choir). When the tiercerons were themselves joined by shorter ribs, called *liernes*, which joined all the ribs in a central pattern (Canterbury nave), all the elements of the most ornate forms of vaulting were in place, leading to star vaults where the patterns are at their most complex (Tewkesbury choir). This was part of the English love of surface decoration that went hand in hand with the development of elaborate window tracery. Exeter Cathedral is perhaps the extreme example, with eleven tiercerons per bay on each side, together with the most elaborate of all window tracery. The next development was a return to barrel vaulting decorated by a lattice of small lierne ribs (Wells retrochoir), followed by the introduction of cones covered with tracery rising from each corner of the bay to meet in the middle of the bay in a diamond pattern. With *fan vaulting* (Gloucester cloisters), as it is called, from the late 14th century onwards, the last forms of vaulting had been created, and after the long life of this form, which lasted into the 16th century (Westminster, Henry VII's Chapel), the next move was to abandon Gothic altogether in a return to classical forms.

veil *See* HUMERAL, VERONICA.

Venice and Saint Mark's The barbarian invasions which swept into N. Italy during the 5th and 6th centuries resulted in refugees from the ravaged mainland seeking safety in the islands of the lagoon. They settled first in *Torcello and other islands, and in the 8th century some moved to the islands of the Rialto, draining them with canals, securing the mud-flats with piles, to lay the foundations of the present city. They were fishermen and sailors, ruled at first from *Ravenna and later, in theory, from Byzantium, which granted them the right to a *dux* (leader), or Doge in Venetian dialect. On one small island a fort had been built in the 5th century, and a church later dedicated to S. Peter. This, San Pietro in Castello, became the seat of a bishop and remained the cathedral until 1807, when the patriarchate—as it had become—was transferred to St Mark's.

Much of Venetian history is legendary. The see of Aquileia was reputed to have been founded by S. Mark, and when the Evangelist was travelling back to Rome by sea, his ship put in at the islands. An angel appeared to him, saying 'Pax tibi, Marce, evangelista meus. Hic requiescet corpus tuum' (Peace unto you, Mark, my Evangelist. Here your body will rest). S. Mark travelled on to become Bishop of Alexandria and died there. Despite the inconsistencies of this story, when two merchants returned from Alexandria in 828, bringing with them the body of S. Mark, which they claimed to have acquired from the custodians of his shrine, the relic was received with acclamation. Instead of placing it in the cathedral a chapel was built in the garden of the Doge's palace, thus associating S. Mark with the political centre of the State, which adopted him as its patron, displacing the former patron, S. Theodore. The winged *lion of the Evangelist's symbol became the arms of Venice, and the angel's prophecy its motto.

By the mid-9th century Venice had become a powerful maritime state, only nominally subject to Byzantium, and treating as equals with the Empire, which controlled Italy and dominated the papacy. The original chapel built by 832 was damaged in a fire which destroyed the palace and a large part of the city. The next Doge restored and largely rebuilt it. It was consecrated in 978 and was the church for which the *Pala d'oro was commissioned. Increasing wealth resulted in 1062 in plans for the replacement of the church with one which would be worthier of the relic they owned and reflect greater credit on the city. The church of St Theodore, which pre-dated the arrival of S. Mark, was demolished and a new basilica was begun in 1063 on the plan of the Holy Apostles in Constantinople (which was later destroyed by the Turks). It was a grand form of *cross-in-square church, with a

central dome and a dome over each of the four arms of the cross. The structure was completed by 1073, and the long programme for the marble revetment of the lower walls and the mosaic decoration of the five domes, their supporting arches, and the conch of the apse, was begun. The design of the basilica itself was Constantinopolitan, as were also the builders, though there is evidence that Lombard builders were brought in. Most of the structural material came from outside Venice, and most of the mosaicists came originally from Byzantium: they were experts working in Italy after *iconoclasm had destroyed their livelihoods in their own lands. Many of the mosaics have suffered from restoration, and also from intrusion into a Byzantine decorative system of mosaics designed by Renaissance artists who rejected a system they did not understand and intruded perspective and naturalism into an art which rejects such pictorial effects.

Eleventh-century Venice had no developed artistic personality, and Lombard works were not current in the city, though they were in the Venetian mainland. Either Venice imported works of art from Byzantium or it imported the artists. Distinct from the rest of Italy, not only was figure sculpture determined by these importations, but also the ancillary arts—*transennae, pavements, pulpit decoration, book-covers, *antependia, as well as the long process of the mosaic decoration of St Mark's. The badly eroded figure of *Christ blessing* on the façade of St Mark's, despite its exaggerated proportions, the low relief of the *Angel of the Annunciation* on the façade of SS Giovanni e Paolo, the superb *Deësis* inside St Mark's, are all evidence of the power of Byzantine ivories as models. Other ideas were also at work. Some of the doors of St Mark's are framed by arches with very different sculpture—subjects such as the Labours of the Months, the Trades and Occupations—subjects alien to Byzantine thought—inhabited scrolls with wild fantasy figures, and even a group of *Joseph's Dream* show that the influence of Antelami and his followers in Parma, Ferrara, and Verona, and also of French *portal sculpture, could penetrate here, even if it took until the late 13th century.

In front of the basilica there was once a canal, and beyond it an orchard and a church dedicated to S. Giminiano. Doge Sebastiano Ziani, in his short reign (1172–8), filled in the canal, rebuilt San Giminiano at the far end of the area, and opened up the whole area as a paved piazza. The famous exterior view of St Mark's, so well known from Canaletto's and Guardi's views of Venice, is dominated by the silhouette of the domes rising above the late 12th-century Gothic arches which frame the mosaics on the façade. Above the atrium were the four gilt-bronze horses looted from Greece by the Romans, removed to Constantinople either by Constantine or Theodosius II, and taken as part of the loot from Constantinople after the sack of the city in the appalling Fourth Crusade of 1204. They have now been removed to preserve them from pollution.

The *Dominicans and the *Franciscans both arrived in Venice in the 1230s and were granted land for their churches—the Dominicans built SS Giovanni e Paolo (San Zanipolo in Venetian dialect) from 1246; a huge brick Gothic church, with nave, two aisles, and a deep apsidal choir flanked by two small apsidal chapels on either side. The later façade with an impressive portal is flanked by the tombs of 13th-century Doges. Inside, the church is filled with monuments to Doges and notables, and the ceiling painting of the *Glory of S. Dominic* is by Piazzetta, before 1727, with striking perspective effects. Next to the church is the Scuola di San Marco, once the seat of one of the six major *scuole, but now part of the main hospital of the city. Outside the church is the monument to the *condottiere* Bartolommeo Colleone, begun by Verrocchio *c.*1479, and completed by Leopardi in 1495. It is one of the major equestrian monuments of the Renaissance.

Near the Dominican church is San Francesco della Vigna, built by Sansovino, with a façade by *Palladio. The church was built on the site of a vineyard which once had an old church in which S. Mark is said to have spent the night when his ship touched at the islands on his way to Rome.

The Franciscans settled at the other end of the city, and their first church was replaced from 1338 by one similar to SS Giovanni e Paolo, but even larger. Sta Maria Gloriosa de' Frari is brick-built, with a wide nave, two aisles, a deep apsidal choir flanked by three apsidal chapels on either side and a *coro* with splendid carved choir stalls at the head of the nave, over which hangs *Titian's early masterpiece (1516–18) of the *Assumption of the Virgin*. The Frari, as it is generally known, is the largest church in Venice after St Mark's, and is also filled with the tombs of Doges as well as with celebrated works by Titian (the Pesaro Altar) and Giovanni *Bellini (the *Frari Madonna* in the sacristy). Next to the Frari is the

Scuola di San Rocco, the only one of the major scuole to retain its original form, though not its function: for it, *Tintoretto, who was a member, painted the series of forty huge pictures for which it is famous.

Few churches in Venice show anything of the exuberant Gothic characteristics of the secular late Gothic of such buildings as the Doges' Palace, the Ca' d'Oro, or the Palazzo Giovanelli, all 15th-century works built at a time when the Renaissance had already superseded Gothic in Florence. Sta Maria de' Miracoli (1481–9), by Pietro Lombardo, is one of the first Venetian churches to show the influence of the Renaissance, but the typical Venetian taste for exquisite decoration shows in the polychrome marble inlays in the façade. By now there was no longer any connection with Byzantium—Constantinople had fallen to the Turks in 1453—and the 15th century saw Venice committed to a mainland empire reaching to Lombardy, while still striving to maintain its maritime trade in the face of Turkish naval opposition. The 15th century ended disastrously; the 16th began worse. Columbus's ships from the Caribbean brought syphilis with them, a scourge which spread like wildfire across Europe; in 1499 Vasco da Gama reached from Lisbon to India via the Cape of Good Hope. The discovery of this new sea-route ended the commercial supremacy of Venice as the main port of entry for Oriental trade into Europe. The fruitless attempts of the French to conquer Lombardy, and Venetian efforts to increase their land empire at the expense of the Papal States, embroiled all Italy in war. Eventually, Venice recovered her mainland possessions, largely because her rule was preferable to anyone else's, but no further attempts at expansion were made.

Nevertheless, it was the 16th century that saw the flowering of Venetian art, architecture, music, and printing. The Bellini and Vivarini families, Carpaccio, Lotto, Giorgione, Titian, Tintoretto, and *Veronese, the Bassano family, and Pordenone were among the painters, and sculptors and architects included the Lombardo and Buon families, Vittoria, Palladio, Sansovino, and Sanmichele, the last two being refugees from the Sack of Rome. They brought new glory to their city and rendered the traditional themes of Christian art in more brilliant and expressive ways, continuing into the 17th century with architects like Longhena, whose Sta Maria della Salute is the supreme Venetian Baroque church. Painters like Piazzetta and *Tiepolo in the 18th century continued to produce religious works, alongside the secular artists like Canaletto and Guardi, until the advent of Canova's Neoclassicism, and the final downfall of the Venetian State itself at the hands of Napoleon in 1797.

Verdun, Nicholas of *See* NICHOLAS.

Vermeulen *See* MOLANUS.

Vernicle *See* VERONICA.

Veronese Paolo Caliari (or Cagliari), called Veronese (*c.*1528–88), was born in Verona, but went to Venice *c.*1553 and became the greatest Venetian decorator before *Tiepolo. He painted numerous religious subjects, including a large number of his finest in the church of San Sebastiano (1563 onwards), but his art tends to be dismissed as mere excuses for sumptuous decorations. This is not entirely fair (cf. the *Crucifixion*, Louvre; and the *Baptist preaching*, Rome, Borghese), but his natural gift for opulent display was the occasion of a celebrated encounter with the Inquisition in 1573. Veronese had painted a *Last Supper* for the refectory of the monastery of San Giorgio Maggiore in Venice (now in the Accademia), but as it was some 40 ft. wide he filled up the space with elaborate architecture and scores of figures, thus contravening a basic principle of *decorum and the spirit of the Council of *Trent. The record has survived, and the Inquisitor wanted to know why, in a *Last Supper*, Veronese had introduced 'buffoons, German soldiers, and similar scurrilities'. His defence was that he had a large space to fill, and artists had a traditional licence to paint as seemed best in the circumstances. He was ordered to amend the painting, but all that actually seems to have happened was a change of title, inscribed on the parapet, to the *Feast in the House of Levi*, dated 22 April 1573. His most brilliant decorations were secular—in the Doge's Palace and the Villa Maser.

Veronica, 'Saint' According to legend, the woman who wiped Christ's face with her veil (or a napkin), as He was carrying the Cross. The cloth (also called Vernicle or Sudarium) was imprinted with a miraculous image, similar in type to the *Mandylion (*see* CHRIST, Portraits of). This *vera icon*, or 'true image', probably gave rise to the name Veronica. The episode is represented in the 6th *Station of the Cross and was popularized by the Franciscans, but is not recorded in the NT. It occurs, not before the 4th century, in the *Apocryphal Acts of Pilate (part of the Gospel of Nicodemus), where Veronica is also identified with the *Woman with the Issue of Blood, whom Christ had cured. She has also been identified with other women who were disciples. Another, later, version of the story is in the **Golden Legend*. What is said to be her veil has been in St Peter's, Rome, perhaps since the 8th century, and was kept in one of the tabernacles made by Bernini in the main piers, with a huge statue of her by Francesco Mochi, of 1629–40, in the large niche in the pier below. She is invariably represented as holding the veil and displaying the image, which may be realistically shown as bleeding and crowned with thorns, or purely symbolically with the cruciform halo.

vesica piscis (Lat. bladder of a fish) A *mandorla, an upright almond-shaped glory, or aureole, enclosing a figure, usually that of Christ Enthroned or the Virgin, as in the Porta della Mandorla of Florence Cathedral.

Vesperbild *See* PIETÀ.

vessels, liturgical *See* LITURGICAL OBJECTS AND VESSELS.

vestments are special garments worn by the clergy and their assistants during liturgical ceremonies. They should be distinguished from clerical dress and the habits worn by members of religious Orders, which are their everyday dress. Although elaborate vestments were and are part of Judaism (cf. Exod. 28), there seems to be no direct connection with Christian usage. From the beginning Christian priests used ordinary garments, of the best quality and normally white, but sometimes with *clavi* or stripes, purple or reddish in colour, as may be seen in the 6th-century mosaics of San Vitale, Ravenna. In the course of time these ordinary upper-class Roman garments ceased to be normal civilian wear and were preserved as the distinctive garb of priests for liturgical purposes. By the 10th century they were established in both East and West, and the Roman and Byzantine forms were broadly similar, in that deacons, priests, and bishops have separate vestments, all based on the ancient *tunica alba* and *tunica dalmatica*. These have remained essentially unchanged to the present time. At the Reformation, the Calvinists and other extreme Protestant groups abandoned vestments and the ministers wore only a preaching gown, similar to an academic gown, with or without white neck-bands, similar to those worn by lawyers. These also have remained essentially unchanged, but are rarely represented in art. Two exceptions are the portraits by Rembrandt of the English-born Calvinist Johannes Elison (1634: Boston) and the Remonstrant Uytenbogaert (1633: private coll.): both men wear black gowns and white ruffs, not bands. The Anglican and other episcopal churches, while retaining clerical dress, gradually abandoned Eucharistic vestments. In the Canon law of the Church of England the cope has been permitted since 1604, and in some Anglican churches this is still worn instead of the chasuble at the Eucharist. Eucharistic vestments were reintroduced at Wilmscote, Warwickshire, in 1845, and in other places under the influence of Tractarianism and the Catholic Revival, but were the cause of great controversy for the rest of the century. The Eucharistic vestments of chasuble and stole for the priest, with dalmatic and tunicle for the deacon and subdeacon at High Mass, are now worn in many Anglican churches, though some clergy wear cassock, surplice (or cassock alb), and stole. Eucharistic vestments are broadly divided into 'Gothic' and 'Roman' shapes, the chasuble of the former being ample and tent-like (based on the Roman *paenula*), while the later forms, originating in the Baroque period, are considerably cut down to allow greater freedom of movement. In particular, the Roman chasuble is fiddle-shaped and far smaller than the Gothic form. In the late 20th and early 21st centuries, the Gothic style has been more popular.

The strict observance of *liturgical colours for vestments is a 19th-century revival of earlier practices and confined to the West—the E. Orthodox Church allows any colour without restriction.

The Eucharistic vestments are those most frequently represented in works of art. In the West they are the *alb, *amice, chasuble (worn by priests and bishops), *dalmatic (worn by deacons), *girdle, maniple, stole, and *tunicle (worn by subdeacons). Bishops, and some abbots, also wear mitres, gloves, and sandals, or stocking-like buskins. Other Western vestments include the *almuce, chimere, *cope, *cotta, hood and tippet, *humeral veil, mozzetta, *pallium, rochet, *surplice, and the *tiara worn by the pope alone. Marks of rank include such things as the red hat of a cardinal or the gaiters and apron formerly worn by Anglican bishops, but these are not vestments. Strictly speaking, the alb, amice, girdle, rochet, surplice, and cotta are, like the *cassock, robes and not vestments.

In the Byzantine Rite the *epigonation and *epimanikion have no Western equivalents. The other E. Orthodox Eucharistic vestments are the *sticharion, similar to the alb; *epitrachelion or *orarion, stoles; *zone, a belt corresponding to the girdle; *sakkos, dalmatic; and *phelonion, chasuble. The *omophorion is similar to the pallium, and Orthodox bishops wear a gilt crown in place of a mitre. *See also* LITURGICAL COLOURS.

vestry, sacristy A room or chapel, usually leading off the main body of a church, in which the vestments and liturgical vessels are kept. Old churches—i.e. pre-Reformation—often have no sacristies; the priest entered by the 'priest's door' in the chancel, ready vested. The cope originated in the garment used to protect him from rain and cold.

The vestry in an Anglican church was also a meeting-place where discussions were held, and decisions made, concerning the civic problems of the parish—the state of the roads, the maintenance of a bridge, an almshouse, a school, as well as, obviously, problems over the maintenance and management of the church and its graveyard. Most of these duties are now undertaken by civic authorities and the Parochial Parish Council is only concerned with matters pertaining to the church and its fabric.

Via Crucis, Via Dolorosa (Lat. Way of the Cross/of Sorrow) Traditionally, the route taken by Christ from Pilate's house to *Golgotha. From very early times there has been a custom of following the route, meditating on the events of the Passion. The Franciscans, as guardians of the Holy Places, established this as a series of devotions, varying from seven to fourteen, which eventually became the *Stations of the Cross. *Via Crucis* is also the title of a series of paintings by Gian Domenico Tiepolo in the Chapel of the Crucifix in San Polo, Venice, of 1747, from which he made the series of etchings, published in Venice in 1748, which is an early example of the fourteen Stations in their final form. These are found, in the form of paintings or sculptures, in Roman Catholic churches and in many Anglican ones, and they are used devotionally in Lent and especially in Holy Week. Occasionally a Via Crucis may be found out-of-doors, as at the (Anglican) Church of St John the Baptist, Frome in Somerset. *See also* SACRO MONTE.

Vices *See* VIRTUES.

Vienna Genesis (Vienna Staatsbibliothek) This is an OT MS, which probably emanated from one of the Eastern centres of the Byzantine Empire in the 6th century. It is written in Greek in silver uncials on purple vellum and is one of the most important of the small surviving number of 6th-century MSS. It consists of 52 pages, 48 of which contain part of Genesis, from the Fall of Man to the death of Jacob, although there are gaps. There are 48 illustrations, sometimes in two registers, though a few, such as the *Deluge* and the *Establishment of the Covenant*, are single pictures, so that it is really a narrative Bible picture-book with a text which explains, and is sometimes shortened to fit, the illustration below. The arrangement of the scenes suggests that the codex may be derived from an older scroll in which text and illustration would have formed a unit, but when scrolls were superseded by codices, the scribes simply wrote the text over several scenes grouped together so that the illustrations use the system of *Continuous Representation. Wall-paintings found in the synagogue at *Dura-Europos are of incidents in the Pentateuch arranged in rows one above the other, and may well have provided another source for books with illustrations in several registers. The iconography of the Vienna Genesis is simple and direct, telling the story vividly, but it did not have much influence except as an example of narrative power and in its early use of Continuous Representation.

Vierzehnheiligen, (Ger. Fourteen Saints) also known as the Auxiliary Saints and the Fourteen Holy Helpers in Need. The term has two meanings: (1) the saints themselves, who are usually identified as George, Blaise, Erasmus, Pantaleon, Vitus (Veit), Christopher, Denis, Cyriacus, Acacius, Eustace, Giles (Egidius), Margaret, Barbara, and Catherine of Alexandria, although there are local variations, for instance Sebastian is often substituted for one of the others. They are invoked in aid of most human ills—Blaise for sore throats, Margaret for troubles in childbirth, Barbara for protection from death by lightning, Sebastian against plague, are among the best known.

(2) It is also the dedication of one of the most famous German *pilgrimage churches, built by Balthasar *Neumann between 1743 and 1772 near Banz in Franconia. As a pilgrimage church it has a large and elaborate altar in the central oval as the focus of the building, but this altar (1764) was not designed by Neumann, although his Baroque spatial planning allowed for it. Like Die *Wies, it is one of the masterpieces of 18th-century German religious art.

Vignola, Giacomo Barozzi da (1507–73), was the major Roman architect of the 3rd quarter of the 16th century. He built only three churches, all in Rome, but all were innovatory in planning. The first was the little Sant'Andrea in Via Flaminia, 1550–3, to accompany the Villa Giulia which he was building for Pope Julius III. It is a simple rectangular block, with an oval drum above, almost totally concealing the curve of the oval interior dome. The front has a flat classical temple façade, articulated by pilasters in an irregular system which uses classical forms without conforming to traditional rhythms of façade design. The interior is very plain, and arranged on the long axis of the oval dome, the first use of this form. His second church was the mother-church of the Jesuit Order, the *Gesù, by far the most important of his works.

The third was the little Sant'Anna dei Palafrenieri, just inside the Vatican enclave, planned in 1565, but finished after his death by his son, with a façade by a later hand. It is the first church built on an elliptical plan, as well as having an oval dome, and it inspired many Baroque architects building chapels and oratories during the next century. Vignola's other major work was a book, *La regola delli cinque ordini dell'architettura*, 1562?, which became one of the most influential architectural treatises, along with those of *Vitruvius, *Alberti, Serlio, and, a few years later, *Palladio. His own architectural style reaches back to the order and regularity of *Bramante and avoids the wilder aspects of *Mannerism, which was why he was a major influence on later French architecture.

Villard de Honnecourt was a 13th-century mason, draughtsman, and possibly sculptor, from N. France (Honnecourt is near Cambrai). He compiled a sketchbook (Paris, BN) probably in the late 1220s, which is the only such medieval text of its kind to survive. It illustrates masons' workshop constructional practices, traditional principles of applied geometry, mechanical devices for surveying, measuring, stone-cutting, war machines, schematic diagrams for designing human and animal figures, a lion described as 'drawn from life' which is still a purely heraldic figure, portraits, figures which may be designs for portal sculpture, as well as drawings from *Bestiaries and ivories. Among the plans and elevations of notable churches are those of the Cistercian abbey of Vaucelles (near Cambrai, now destroyed), the towers of Laon, several of the windows of Reims, Chartres, and Lausanne, where he says he designed the rose window, the plans of Cambrai and Meaux cathedrals. On one of his drawings he writes 'Once when I was in Hungary, where I spent a long time', which possibly was at Pilis, a Cistercian house; otherwise all we know of his life is what can be deduced from his book, neither can any building be definitely ascribed to him. He was a man of education as well as of practical ability, who wrote a beautiful script, knew Latin and *Vitruvius, the only surviving ancient text on architecture, known from Carolingian times onwards. Because his book contains nothing on Amiens or Beauvais it is assumed that he died, or stopped working, in the late 1220s or early 1230s.

Vincent of Beauvais *See* SPECULUM MAJUS.

vine The vine, or a vineyard, occurs as a metaphor both in the OT, e.g. Ps. 80 (Vg. 79), Isa. 5, and in the NT (John 15: 1–6), where Christ speaks of Himself: 'I am the true vine, and my Father is the vinegrower. He removes every branch in me that bears no fruit. Every branch that bears fruit he prunes to make it bear more fruit . . . Just as the branch cannot bear fruit by itself unless it abides in the vine, neither can you unless you abide in me.' This was, with the Good *Shepherd, one of the commonest Early Christian symbols and is found from the earliest times, e.g. in the catacombs (Domitilla and others) and on sarcophagi. There are good examples in the vault mosaic of Sta Costanza, Rome, and the sarcophagus, thought to be that of the Emperor Constantine's daughter, Constantina, now in the Vatican but said to have come from Sta Costanza. Both are early 4th century. Like the Good Shepherd, the vine was an image familiar to pagans from Bacchic scenes, and might therefore pass unnoticed, just as the Good Shepherd might be read as *Hermes

Kriophoros. By about the 6th century the vine was less popular, but it was revived as a reference to the Eucharist, grapes and wheat becoming symbols of the Bread and Wine. *See also* WINEPRESS.

Viollet-le-duc, Eugène (1814–79), is famous as a restorer of Gothic churches, including most of France's major cathedrals, and of secular buildings such as the Château de Pierrefonds and the town of Carcassonne. His other claim to fame, which sprang from his work as a restorer, is his 10-volume *Dictionnaire raisonné de l'architecture française du XIe au XVIe siècle*, 1854–68, which is a polemic in favour of Gothic architecture as an early expression of the argument that 'form follows function'. It is also the expression, as a reflection of his deep anticlericalism, of Gothic representing the rise of civic power, the product of urban effort, the development of secular institutions, owing nothing to religious inspiration, patronage, or fervour. One of the most useful—and most beautiful—elements of the *Dictionnaire* is in the detailed sectional drawings illustrating, for example, the buttressing systems of Amiens Cathedral, the hammer-beam roofing of Westminster Hall, or the construction of a vaulting rib by 'exploding' the stone blocks to explain how they are put together. His career as a restorer began when he became the right-hand man of Prosper Mérimée, the first Inspecteur Général des monuments historiques, and his first major work was the restoration of the church of the Madeleine at Vézelay, 1840–9. There followed Notre-Dame, Paris, 1844–64, Amiens Cathedral, 1852–8, Reims Cathedral, 1860–71, *St-Denis, outside Paris, 1860–8, and a host of others. While in some cases he can be accused of being heavy-handed and of allowing his passion for imaginative reconstruction to outpace the evidence provided by the building itself, there is no doubt that his twenty-five years of indefatigable labour secured the survival and stability of many Gothic masterpieces. His attitude to Gothic is the opposite of *Pugin's highly religious, Romantic passion, and far more deeply scientific than the practitioners of the *Gothic Revival in England. Viollet-le-duc's two volumes of *Entretiens* (1863–72), published in English as *Lectures*, 1877–81, range from Roman to modern, and are important for his correlation of Gothic structural methods with 19th-century use of cast-iron framework and constructional engineering technique.

Virgin, the Blessed *See* MARY.

Virgin Birth of Christ The fundamental Christian doctrine that Christ was born of the Virgin Mary, conceived of the Holy Ghost, and without a human father, is based on Isa. 7: 14, 'Ecce virgo concipiet et pariet filium' (AV: 'Behold, a virgin shall conceive, and bear a son'), Matt. 1: 18–25, and Luke 1: 26–38. (NRSV has 'Look, the young woman is with child and shall bear a son'.) From the earliest times non-biblical writings such as the *Protevangelium of James added picturesque details which inspired artists. Evidently, the dogma itself, like that of the *Trinity, is not susceptible of visual representation, but can be symbolized by oblique references in representations of e.g. the *Annunciation or the *Nativity. In Annunciations a ray of light streaming through a window (Jan van *Eyck, Washington, NG), or through a glass vessel filled with water (Fra Filippo *Lippi, Florence, San Lorenzo), accords with *S. Augustine's observation that the Holy Spirit, like light through glass, can pass without changing the nature of that through which it passes. Sometimes the ray, with the Holy Ghost in the form of a dove, is directed at Mary's ear (as in the van Eyck in Washington), since it was argued that she conceived at the moment of hearing Gabriel's words, and accepting her mission.

In Nativities, the obvious reference is where the figures of the midwives, *Salome and Zelomi, are shown (e.g. J. Daret, Thyssen Coll., Lugano), or where the vision of *S. Bridget was the source used by the artist (R. van der *Weyden, Bladelin Altar, Berlin). Some other references, less obvious, are to the Song of Songs—the sealed *fountain, the *Hortus Conclusus, the *Porta Clausa—or to *typologies such as the Burning *Bush or *Gideon's Fleece.

Virgins, Eleven Thousand *See* URSULA, S.

Virgins, Wise and Foolish *See* WISE.

Virgo inter Virgines (Lat. virgin among virgins) A type of devotional image, popular in the 15th century, showing the Virgin and Child seated among a group of female virgin saints—Agatha, Agnes, Catherine, Dorothy, Lucy, and others—often in a garden setting (*compare* ANDACHTSBILD and HORTUS CONCLUSUS). A good example is the painting of 1509 by Gerard *David (Rouen, Mus.), which is unusual in containing the portraits of himself and his wife. It was painted for the convent where their daughter was a nun. The Virgo Master is the name given to an unknown Dutch painter (*c.*1470–1500), from his picture of this subject in the Rijksmuseum.

Virtues The third hierarchy of *angels. They are warrior-angels, often wearing armour and carrying weapons, sometimes with four blue wings.

Virtues and Vices The Cardinal Virtues, so called from Lat. *cardo*, a hinge, are Fortitude, Justice, Prudence, and Temperance, since all others depend upon them. The Theological Virtues are Faith, Hope, and Charity, of which S. Paul said (1 Cor. 13: 13), 'And now faith, hope, and love abide, these three; and the greatest of these is love.' These seven virtues have seven corresponding vices—the Seven Deadly Sins—Pride, Anger, Lust, Avarice, Envy, Gluttony, and Sloth. In pre-Christian times moral qualities were frequently personified—Minerva as Wisdom, Mars as Martial Valour—and so the Vices and Virtues soon became symbolized by female figures. Prudentius (348–*c.*410), a Spanish lawyer who became a writer of hymns and the author of the *Psychomachia* (Battle of the Soul), described the contests between pairs of Virtues and Vices—Faith and Idolatry, Chastity and Lust, Patience and Anger, and so on—and his poem had a vast influence on later medieval literature. There are many illuminated MSS of it, and the first illustrations may go back to the 5th century, since the MS in Paris, Bibliothèque Nationale, of the 10th century, is clearly based on a much older model. The combat was a favourite subject for Romanesque church portals in France and elsewhere, but by the 13th century artists no longer followed Prudentius closely. The pairs of figures became more symbolic, and the cathedrals of Paris and Amiens have figures no longer derived directly from Prudentius. In the early 14th century *Giotto established a series of seven virtues and seven vices in the Arena Chapel in Padua, representing Prudence, Fortitude, Temperance, Justice, Faith, Charity, and Hope, with Despair, Envy, Idolatry, Injustice, Anger, Inconstancy, and Stupidity (*Stultitia*) on the other side.

His personifications are memorably vivid.

Visigothic *See* PRE-ROMANESQUE.

Visitation, the Only Luke (1: 39–42) tells how, after the Annunciation, 'In those days Mary set out and went with haste to a Judaean town in the hill country, where she entered the house of *Zacharias (Zechariah), and greeted *Elizabeth. When Elizabeth heard Mary's greeting, the child leaped in her womb. And Elizabeth was filled with the Holy Spirit and exclaimed with a loud cry "Blessed are you among women, and blessed is the fruit of your womb . . . ".' *See also* MARY.

Vitruvius (Marcus Vitruvius Pollio) was a Roman architect who had an immense influence in post-Classical times, particularly in the Renaissance. He is known to have worked from *c.*46 to 30 BC, and to have built the basilica of Fano (now destroyed) near Pesaro. His main claim to fame is that he composed a treatise on architecture in ten books, *De architectura*, which he dedicated to the Emperor Augustus. It is the only composition on architecture to survive from antiquity, and MS copies of it were known, for instance, to Alcuin at the court of Charlemagne. A copy was found in 1414 in the library of the monastery of Sankt Gallen, and was thereafter regarded as an exemplar of classical architectural orthodoxy by Early Renaissance architects. The first text was not printed until *c.*1486 in Rome, and an illustrated edition was made in 1511. Italian translations were made *c.*1520 and in 1521 with an extensive commentary and illustrations, and another was published in Venice in 1556 with illustrations by Palladio, intended for practising architects as well as for the general reader. His appeal to the Renaissance architect and learned patron was because he enunciated the doctrines of 'utility, strength and beauty', and for him—and those who followed his precepts—beauty was derived from mathematics and, very important, from the use of the proportions of man as a scale for the proportions of a building. Although the surviving text is often obscure, these principles were in total accordance with Renaissance feeling and aims. Both Alberti and Palladio were encouraged—if not inspired—by his arguments in favour of architecture as an imitation of nature, and based therefore on rational principles. His concept of 'decorum', emphasized the importance of site and weather conditions, and his view of the architect as a man of universal culture fitted in with Renaissance ideals of the artist as a creative being. His descriptions of the Orders, based on the proportions of column, capital, and entablature of the three types, Doric, Ionic, and Corinthian, though they were regarded as a 'canon', were nevertheless not adhered to slavishly, and neither Alberti nor Michelozzo felt themselves bound by them, claiming for themselves the liberty to invent and create independently. Bramante, in the Tempietto in the courtyard of San Pietro in Montorio in Rome, begun in 1502, obeyed Vitruvian principles in using the Doric Order for a male martyr (S. Peter), but Raphael, and above all, Michelangelo felt free to do much as they pleased with the elements of classical architecture, and to use them creatively. After the first flush of Renaissance enthusiasm, Vitruvius ceased to be a strait-jacket, and provided merely a classical framework which might be interpreted as the creative architect thought fit. He was important in providing an impetus for architects to produce learned tomes, in which they followed his models of divisions into various 'books'—'Ten Books' (Serlio), 'Five Orders' (Vignola), 'Four Books' (Palladio).

Vladimir, Our Lady of The holiest Russian icon, the *palladium of Vladimir, and, from 1315, of Moscow. It is actually a Byzantine work, painted in Constantinople *c.*1131, when it was taken to Russia. It is a Glycophilousa *Madonna type, and is now in the Tretyakov Museum, Moscow.

Volto Santo (Ital. Holy Face) Any representation of the face of Christ, but normally meaning the over life-size crucifix in Lucca Cathedral. It shows Christ standing against the cross, rather than hanging from it, and He is clad in an ankle-length tunic or *colobium* (*see* CRUCIFIX, CHRISTUS TRIUMPHANS). The cedar-wood carving is said to have been in Lucca since 797, but the style of the statue is that of the 11th/12th centuries, possibly Byzantine. It has been suggested that the present carving is a replacement for the original, much older, statue, which, according to legend, was carved by *Nicodemus. Certainly there are many copies throughout Europe, especially in Spain, and it is mentioned by Dante and in Langland's *Piers Plowman*. The image of the Holy Face, like *Veronica's Veil, is common in E. Orthodox icons.

Voragine (Voraigne) *See* GOLDEN LEGEND.

votive chapel, church, painting, picture, offering, (Lat. *votum*, a vow) also called an ex-voto. An offering in gratitude for a favour, e.g. recovery from grave illness. The practice was common in pre-Christian times and is probably as old as humanity. Offerings range from flowers, candles, and small tokens—wax limbs, models of crutches, and similar things—up to major works of art, like *Palladio's church of Il Redentore, solemnly decreed by the Venetian government in 1576, after the cessation of a terrible plague. A form prevalent throughout the history of Spanish and French North America, is a small devotional painting on canvas, tin, or some other material, which offered thanks and prayers to a particular saint for intervention in a specific situation, distinct from retablos, also called *laminas* in Mexico. *See also* NORTH AMERICA, RETABLE.

voussoirs Wedge-shaped blocks of stone, wide at the top, narrowing as they descend, which make up the structure of arches. The central one in each arch is called the keystone, since it holds all the others in position.

'Vox clamantis in deserto' (Mark 1: 3; The voice of one crying out in the wilderness, Prepare the way of the Lord) Often written on a scroll held by *John the Baptist. *Compare* ECCE AGNUS DEI, where the Baptist is usually shown as an older man.

Vulgate The Latin text of the *Bible, prepared from 382 by *S. Jerome, to supersede the Old Latin text which existed in many variant forms. His text became the common one (*editio vulgata*) in the West, but it differs in some ways from the Protestant versions, e.g. the Authorized Version of 1611, in the numbering of the Psalms and in other instances. It is therefore quoted here (as Vg.) when the difference is significant—*see* HORNS OF MOSES. The Codex *Amiatinus is the earliest surviving complete text of the Vulgate.

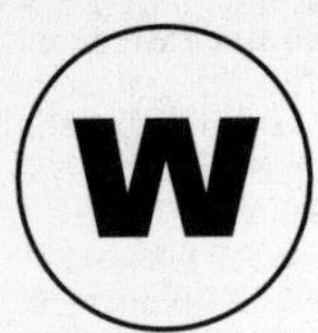

Wallfahrtskirche The German word for a *pilgrimage church, usually in a remote spot. The design of such churches is influenced by the need for an altar or shrine commemorating the miracle which gave rise to the church as the centre, with space around it for the pilgrims. Two of the most famous German examples, both of the 18th century, are *Vierzehnheiligen and Die *Wies.

Warhol, Andy (1928–87). An American painter, printmaker, sculptor, and filmmaker, archetypal pop artist. His recognizable silk-screen prints received cult attention, and his religious subject matter worked inventively on Leonardo's *Last Supper* and images by Uccello, Piero della Francesca, and Raphael. Skeletons, skulls, the electric chair, and suicide occupied him too. Pittsburgh's Andy Warhol Museum houses the single largest collection of his work. His near-contemporary Robert Rauschenberg wrote of his fellow artist 'he befuddles critical history'. Jane Daggett Dillenberger's *The Religious Art of Andy Warhol* (1998) provides a sensitive and faithful account of the charismatic life style threaded through with religion (he was Catholic of the Byzantine rite). *See also* NORTH AMERICA.

Washing of the Disciples' Feet *See* FEET and CHRIST.

Water, Christ walking on Two versions of this miracle are given by Mark and Matthew. Mark (6: 45–56) says that, after the Miracle of the Loaves and Fishes, the Apostles embarked in a boat to cross the Sea of Gennesaret, and Jesus went alone to pray: 'When he saw that they were straining at the oars against an adverse wind, he came towards them early in the morning, walking on the sea . . . they thought it was a ghost and cried out'. He stilled the waves and the wind. Matthew adds to this (14: 27–33): 'they cried out in fear . . . Peter answered him "Lord, if it is you, command me to come to you on the water." He said, "Come." So Peter got out of the boat, started walking on the water, and came towards Jesus. But when he noticed the strong wind, he became frightened, and beginning to sink, he cried out "Lord, save me!" Jesus immediately stretched out his hand, and caught him'. This miracle is not often represented, but there is a fine Tintoretto in Washington (NG), and a painting of 1444, by Konrad Witz (Geneva), is unusual in conflating this with the Miraculous Draught of *Fishes. Delacroix also painted the subject in 1853.

web Another name for a cell or severy of a vault.

Weighing of Souls *See* JUDGEMENT, THE LAST; ANGELS (the Archangel Michael); WEYDEN, R. VAN DER.

West, Benjamin *See* NORTH AMERICA.

westwork is an adaptation from Ger. *Westwerk*. It is a feature of *Carolingian church architecture from about the mid-8th to mid-10th centuries and consists of a tall building, flanked by towers containing staircases. The central block consisted of several storeys, with a low entrance hall leading into the west end of the church and supporting a large room above which opened directly into the nave. This room often had an altar and was usually surrounded by further rooms, the access to all being by the tower stairs. The exact purpose of these structures has been debated, but the commonest explanation is that they were an imperial tribune, from which the Emperor and his retinue could attend services in the main church, but which could also be used independently for secular ceremonies. The Benedictine abbey at Corvey in Lower Saxony, Germany, has a surviving westwork, of 873–85, so has Tournus, 950–1120, Gernrode, St Cyriakus, 961, and the Abbey of Maria Laach, as late as 1093–1156.

Weyden, Roger van der (1399/1400–64), was a younger contemporary of Jan van *Eyck. He shared the same technical skill, but his influence was greater than van Eyck's; where Jan tended to create a closed world of dispassionate observation even when dealing with tragic subjects, Roger is emotional and dramatic. There are no signed pictures, or solidly documented ones, and the records are confusing. He was born in Tournai in the then Duchy of Burgundy (now in Belgium), was in the Tournai workshop of Robert Campin 1427–32, and in 1436 became the City Painter of Brussels.

The crucial attribution to Roger is a *Deposition* (Prado) known as the *Escorial Deposition* from its being recorded there as by him in 1574. A date *c.*1435/7 has been guessed at. It shows the qualities which differentiate it from earlier Netherlandish art: an emotional charge, deep feeling, and skill as great as that of van Eyck. It is also a meditative treatment of the subject, and although the detailing is intensely realistic, the 'closed' background, with the figures arranged as a frieze in front of a plain stone wall, changes the impact of the work by using its realism for unrealistic purposes.

In the *S. Luke painting the Virgin* (two versions, in Boston and Munich) he challenges van Eyck, since the composition is a reversed image of van Eyck's *Madonna of Chancellor Rolin* (Louvre), with a similar background, but less formal and hieratic, and with a new tenderness. For Chancellor Rolin's Hospital in Beaune, founded in 1443, he painted the altarpiece of the chapel (dedicated in 1451) at the far end of the great *salle* occupied by the sick: the huge polyptych of the *Last Judgement.* The portrayal of the Last *Judgement has a long history, from portal sculpture to the paintings of 'Dooms' on the west walls of churches, as a grim reminder to those leaving the building, but Roger's version breaks new ground. In the large central panel, Christ in Majesty, with the lily and the sword which have issued from His mouth, is seated on a rainbow with the globe beneath His feet. On either side at the top are angels with the instruments of the Passion. A long ribbon of texts flow from Him with the words of judgement: 'Come to Me, blessed ones . . .' and 'Depart from Me, ye wicked . . .', and below Him stands the *Archangel Michael with the scales of judgement. At the base of the rainbow are the Virgin and S. John the Baptist, as the Intercessors, and on either side of them are ranged the twelve Apostles with three saints behind each group. The gold ground is suffused by delicate rosy clouds. Below, the dead rise from the ground, and on the left—that is, on Christ's right hand—the blessed are ushered into Paradise, and on His left the lost souls in tears and misery stumble to their fate in Hell. All this conforms to the traditional Last Judgement, from the great mosaic in *Torcello to the various French Gothic portal sculptures which portray the subject, except for one detail. In Torcello, S. Michael holds the scales level, perhaps following Job 31: 6: 'Let me be weighed in a just balance, and let God know my integrity', but in all the French portals which show Michael as the weigher of souls it is the soul of the saved which sinks, while that of the damned rises, according to Dan. 5: 27: 'You have been weighed in the scales and found wanting'. Roger's good soul rises, whereas the bad soul, weighed down by its sins, sinks, and in grief and rage goes to his reward. The same idea is occasionally found in Italian 14th-century painters, in individual representations of S. Michael. Roger's interpretation—if indeed it be his—is more in conformity with the rational view of Classical Antiquity, where in the symbolism of the scales, victory was not of good over evil, but of life over death.

Bartolommeo Fazio (1456) says that Roger was in Italy for the Jubilee of 1450. Two pictures support this statement: an *Entombment* (Uffizi; formerly in the Medici collections) with Christ upheld by Joseph of Arimathaea and Nicodemus in front of a square-cut rock tomb, and mourned by the Virgin, S. John, and the Magdalene, for which the prototype is an *Angelico School work now in Munich. The second is a *Madonna and Child with four Saints* (Frankfurt, Städel). The saints are Peter and John the Baptist, patrons of Piero and Giovanni de' Medici, and Cosmas and Damian, the two doctor (*medici*) saints, adopted by the Medici because of the pun on their name. The Baptist is also the patron saint of Florence. On the plinth at the base of the picture is a Medici emblem—a red fleur-de-lis. That the two doctor saints are portraits of well-known Burgundian officials, one of whom was often in Italy, does not invalidate the attribution.

In the *Seven Sacraments* triptych (Antwerp, Mus.) the Crucifixion in the central panel is placed in the nave of a Gothic church, with the Eucharist being celebrated at the altar in the choir behind. The other sacraments are shown in various parts of the church, seen on the wings. The tiny angels hovering between the columns of the aisles, the draperies fluttering round the sagging body of the crucified Christ, the fainting Virgin upheld by S. John, the grief-stricken Holy Women at the foot of the cross, all indicate that this is not just a representation of the central acts of the Christian faith—Christ's sacrifice of Himself for the redemption of mankind, and the perpetual re-enactment of that sacrifice in the Institution of the Eucharist—but a meditation on the event, just as was the *Deposition*. The triptych of the *Crucifixion* (Vienna, KHM) has the same meditative character. A pastoral landscape stretches across the full width of the triptych, and two donors kneel at the foot of the cross. That this is a meditation, not a vision, is made clear by the cleft in the rocky ridge which divides the donors from the objects of their devotion.

The diptych of *Calvary* (Philadelphia, Mus.) and the single panel of *Calvary* (Escorial) are variations on the same tragic theme. In both, there is a return to the symbolism of the *Deposition*—a blank stone wall over which hang backcloths with carefully painted creases, and against which the cross with its burden stands out starkly; the visionary effect is heightened by the realism with which it is portrayed.

The triptych of the *Adoration of the Kings* (Munich) is more traditional, since it follows the **Golden Legend*, a precedent followed by many artists. The Virgin is seated with her son on her lap in a crude shed with ill-thatched roof, built into a massive ruin. The ox of the NT gazes attentively, the *ass of the OT looks only to the trough. One of the royal worshippers is Charles the Bold, who became duke in 1467, and whose death in 1477 ended the Duchy of Burgundy. The outstanding figure in the Presentation scene on the right wing is the young maidservant, carrying the basket with the offering of two turtle doves; she turns her head to look out of the picture, drawing the spectator into the scene, something which is a commonplace in Italian art, but very unusual in the North. The central panel also introduces something rare if not new in the North, but usual in Italy; behind the royal worshippers is a long train winding its way along the road, and at its head is a Jewish High Priest, expressing that cherished hope of the Christian that the Jews too would recognize the Christ as their Messiah. The emptiness of that hope is anachronistically portrayed by the tiny crucifix on the pillar above the serene Virgin's head.

Roger's influence on Flemish and German art of the later 15th century was immense, but his closest immediate follower, *Memlinc, never rose to his expressive heights. Only Hugo van der *Goes approaches him in drama and emotional force.

Whale, Jonah and the *See* JONAH, and LEVIATHAN.

wheat, from which bread is made, is a symbol of the *Eucharist, as when the Christ Child is shown with ears of wheat: in conjunction with grapes or wine the symbolism is even more evident (e.g. Botticelli, *Madonna and Child with an Angel*, Boston, Gardner Mus.). Many Northern still-life painters of the 17th century depict bread and wine, which may be covert references to the Eucharist.

wheel The attribute of *S. Catherine of Alexandria, who was meant to be martyred on a wheel. It broke, and her executioners were injured. *See also* FORTUNE.

white *See* LITURGICAL COLOURS.

White Canons *See* NORBERT, S.

White Friars *See* CARMELITES.

White Monks *See* CISTERCIANS.

Whitsun *See* PENTECOST.

Whore of Babylon Chapter 17 of Revelation is a sustained diatribe against 'the great whore who is seated on many waters ... I saw a woman sitting on a scarlet beast ... and it had seven heads and ten horns ... The woman was clothed in purple and scarlet, ... holding in her hand a golden cup ... And I saw that the woman was drunk with the blood of the saints and the blood of the witnesses to Jesus ... the seven heads are seven mountains on which the woman is seated.' Originally intended to refer to pagan Rome on its seven hills, proud, cruel, and persecuting Christians, it was simple for the 16th-century Reformers to transfer the allegory to papal Rome. Polemical writings and popular woodcuts make this identification with the papacy (*see* REFORMATION).

Wies, Die (Ger. meadow) A famous *pilgrimage church in the countryside below the Bavarian Alps, and one of the masterpieces of German Rococo architecture. It was built by Dominikus Zimmermann (1685–1766), who was also responsible for the decorative plasterwork and the pink and green, white and gold interior. The origin of the building was a miraculous statue of the Christ of the Flagellation, which occasioned a pilgrimage from 1738; and the penitential theme was taken up by Zimmermann's brother, Johann Baptist, in his frescoes. The ceiling has a *Judgement* which includes the *Preparation of the Throne of Judgement*, or *Hetoimasia, an unusual Byzantine subject. The church was closed in 1803, during the Napoleonic suppression of churches, but demolition was prevented by local opposition and Wies was reopened in 1831.

Wilgefortis (Uncumber, Liberata, Kummernis) is a striking example of a non-existent saint, whose legend was invented in the late Middle Ages (probably in Flanders, late 14th cent.). According to the legend, she was the daughter of a pagan king of Portugal, who betrothed her to a Sicilian prince; she, however, became a Christian and refused to marry him. She prayed to become ugly and grew a beard, at which the prince backed off. Her father was furious and had her crucified (cf. *S. Barbara). She was popular among women with bad husbands, who made an offering of oats at two images of her in Norfolk, in return for which she was supposed to 'uncumber' them. The origin of the legend is supposed to be the unfamiliarity, in N. Europe, of the type of Crucifix represented by the *Volto Santo of Lucca, where Christ is represented as alive and standing against the cross, rather than hanging from it, and also wearing a *colobium. Several images of her were in English pre-Reformation churches, but the only survivor is a statue in Henry VII's Chapel, Westminster Abbey.

windlass *See* ERASMUS, S.

winepress From the 14th century a winepress became a symbol of the Eucharistic sacrifice, with the beam of the press representing the Cross and Christ crushed beneath it. By the late 15th century it symbolized Christ's Blood in the Eucharist, but by the 16th century, in Protestant countries, the symbol was that of Christ's suffering, and this gruesome image was widely employed on both sides. In the OT there are several references to winemaking and vineyards, e.g. Isaiah 63: 3, which was held to prefigure Christ's sacrifice and also the wrath of God; or Num. 13: 17–30, where Moses sent two spies into the land of Canaan and they returned bearing a huge cluster of grapes as a symbol of the richness of the land, later interpreted as the wine transmuted into the Blood of Christ. The Chapel and Confraternity of the Holy Blood (Saint-Sang) at Bruges claimed to have drops of Christ's actual blood, and other places made similar claims. In France there are many representations which resemble the *imago pietatis, and the *Fons Vitae, which shows the Crucified Christ's blood pouring into a fountain, giving salvation to assembled worshippers.

winged lion The symbol of *S. Mark, and therefore also of Venice. *See* EVANGELIST SYMBOLS.

Wisdom, in Greek Sophia, and in Latin Sapientia, is a theological term which may apply to Christ (1 Cor. 1: 24, and elsewhere), or to one of the Seven *Gifts of the Holy Spirit. This philosophical abstraction, which was intended by the dedication of Hagia *Sophia (Santa Sophia) in Constantinople, became personified as a crowned woman, and, by about 600, was transmuted into a female martyr in Rome—Sta Sofia—who was martyred with her three young daughters, Fides, Spes, and Caritas, i.e. Faith, Hope, and Charity, the three Theological *Virtues. It is not clear whether such a person ever existed, but Faith, Hope, and Charity are not uncommon as girls' names.

Wise and Foolish Virgins The *parable of the Wise and Foolish Virgins is told in Matt. 25: 1–13. The five wise virgins had oil for their lamps and awaited the coming of the Bridegroom, but the five foolish ones allowed their lamps to go out for lack of oil. This was interpreted as a sign of the Last Judgement and the need to be constantly on the watch for the Second Coming. In Early Christian times the subject was already connected with the *Virtues and Vices, or the contrast between *Ecclesia and Synagoga. The Virgins frequently formed part of Last Judgement scenes in Gothic portals and were also represented separately, e.g. in Schongauer's engravings of *c.*1480, as well as occurring in the **Biblia Pauperum* and **Speculum Humanae Salvationis*. An example on this theme by Frederic, Lord Leighton (1864) is found in St Michael and All Angels, Lyndhurst, Hampshire.

Wise Men, the Three *See* MAGI.

wolf The wolf, especially in N. Europe, was a dreaded predator, and so became a symbol of many evils—lust, rapine, greed, and other vices—so that a wolf in sheep's clothing became a potent symbol of hypocrisy, and, in Reformation polemics, usually referred to the clergy, who were faithless guardians of the sheep, i.e. Christ's flock. Compare John 10: 12–15: 'The hired hand who is not the shepherd . . . sees the wolf coming and leaves the sheep and runs away . . . I lay down my life for the sheep.' The fresco by Andrea da Firenze in Sta Maria Novella, Florence, shows the Dominicans (*Domini Canes*, hounds of God) protecting Christians from the wolves of heresy.

One of the best-known incidents in the life of *S. Francis of Assisi is the taming of the Wolf of Gubbio. The wolf had killed many inhabitants of Gubbio, but Francis made a pact with it, drawn up by a notary, that the citizens would provide it with food and it would cease to prey upon them. The wolf became a pet of S. Francis.

Woman clothed with the Sun *See* APOCALYPTIC WOMAN.

Woman of Samaria *See* SAMARIA.

Woman taken in Adultery This is recorded only by S. John (8: 3–11). Under Mosaic Law the punishment for adultery was death by stoning, so when a woman was caught in the act, the Scribes and Pharisees, anxious to destroy Jesus, asked Him whether she should be stoned, knowing that if He said 'No', He would repudiate Moses; and if He said 'Yes', He would break Roman law, which allowed only Roman judges to sentence to death. 'Jesus bent down and wrote with his finger on the ground . . . He straightened up and said to them, "Let anyone among you who is without sin be the first to cast a stone at her." . . . When they heard it, they went away, one by one, beginning at the elders . . . Jesus . . . said to her, "Woman, where are they? Has no man condemned you?" She said, "No one, sir." And Jesus said, "Neither do I condemn you. Go your way, and . . . do not sin again."' John does not record what Jesus wrote on the ground, but, in the fairly rare cases where He is represented as doing so He usually writes 'Qui sine peccato est vestrum, primus in illam lapidem mittat' (Who among you is without sin, let him be the first to cast a stone at her) or its equivalent in the vernacular (e.g. in Flemish in Bruegel's grisaille of 1565, London, Courtauld Inst.), but a medieval legend claims that He recorded the sins of her accusers.

Woman with the Issue of Blood One of the miracles of *Christ recorded in Matthew, Mark, and Luke—'Now there was a woman who had been suffering from haemorrhages for twelve years. She had endured much under many physicians, and had spent all that she had; and she was no better; but rather grew worse. She had heard about Jesus, and came up behind him in the crowd and touched his cloak, for she said, "If I but touch his clothes, I will be made well." Immediately her haemorrhage stopped; and she felt in her body that she was healed of her disease' (Mark 5: 25–9). This miracle was a fairly common subject in Early Christian art, in *catacombs (2nd–4th cent.: Praetextatus; Petrus and Marcellinus), on sarcophagi, and in mosaics (Ravenna, Sant'Apollinare Nuovo). *Eusebius, in his *History of the Church*, has a fascinating account of a statue in Caesarea Philippi: 'On a tall stone base at the gates of her house stood a bronze statue of a woman, resting on one knee and resembling a suppliant with arms outstretched. Facing her was another of bronze, an upright figure of a man . . . his hand stretched out to the woman . . . This statue, which was said to resemble the features of Jesus, was still there in my own time [i.e. before *c.*340], so that I saw it with my own eyes when I resided in the city . . .'. Later writers attempted to identify the woman with *Veronica, or, in the **Meditationes Vitae Christi*, with Martha, the sister of Mary Magdalene and Lazarus. The bronze statue seen by Eusebius was probably an ancient representation of a city surrendering to its conqueror.

Works of Mercy, the Seven *See* MERCY.

world, end of the *See* SIGNS, and JUDGEMENT.

Wounds, the Five Sacred *See* ARMA CHRISTI.

Wren, Sir Christopher (1632–1723), architect and astronomer, was born into the High Anglican church, his father being a clergyman who became Dean of Windsor and his uncle was the Bishop of Ely, who was imprisoned by the Puritans for eighteen years during the Commonwealth. The young Wren was described when he was a student at Wadham College, Oxford, by the diarist Evelyn as 'that miracle of a youth' and his interests were originally scientific. One of his first buildings, the Sheldonian Theatre, Oxford (1664–9), was a combination of the ancient Roman Theatre of Marcellus (known to Wren only from engravings) with a ceiling covering a 70-ft. span, derived from contemporary mathematical investigations. This combination of ancient Roman architectural principles, as transmitted by Italian Renaissance theorists, with the constructional principles made possible by 17th-century science, is the essence of his art. In 1665–6 he made his only trip abroad, to France, staying mainly in Paris, for eight or nine months. There he saw buildings in the classical style, including domed churches, which were unknown in England at that time. He bought engravings and met *Bernini, who was then briefly in Paris, and became more interested in architecture. He returned just before the Great Fire of London (1666), as a result of which the entire City—including about 100 churches and *St Paul's Cathedral—needed to be rebuilt. There had been no need for new churches since the Reformation, so his rebuilding of some fifty-two, mostly on their original cramped sites, to suit the new Anglican liturgy involved great ingenuity in planning. The new liturgy, with its stress on preaching, needed new forms such as the *auditory church, while continuing to have a vestigial choir and an altar at the east end. Calvinist churches, on the other hand, needed neither chancel nor fixed altar. Wren's greatest achievement was to provide a specifically Anglican compromise between the altar and the pulpit in his City churches. They were built in two stages; first the actual body of the church and, later, when money became available, the spires. Most were begun *c.*1670 and many were executed by local craftsmen under Wren's general supervision, but among those certainly by him are St Bride's, Fleet Street (1671–1703), St Mary-le-Bow, behind St Paul's (1670–97), and especially St Stephen Wallbrook, the Lord Mayor's parish church (1672–9).

The rebuilding of Old St Paul's meant the creation of the first cathedral in England for the new liturgy, and here Wren was decidedly on the side of those in favour of splendour for the greatest church in the capital city—he deliberately used elements of St Peter's in Rome, even though he knew it only from engravings (e.g. by Lafreri and Dupérac) and plans (by A. da *Sangallo the Younger and *Michelangelo), and his Great Model of 1673 (a huge wooden model still preserved in the cathedral itself) was his own favourite, although it was never executed. It was a complete break with pre-Reformation Gothic church design—some thought it 'not enough of a cathedral fashion' (i.e. not Gothic), and others were unhappy about its evident relationship to St Peter's—and Wren was forced to make a compromise design, to 'reconcile as near as possible, the Gothick to a better Manner of Architecture'. This received the Royal Warrant and work began in 1675: over the years Wren used a small provision in the warrant that he might vary it in such manner as to render it more beautiful, and he used this as a means of driving a coach and horses through the warrant to enable him to modify it very greatly. Built largely on the foundations of the destroyed Old St Paul's, it is one of the finest Baroque buildings in Britain (1675–1710).

In 1708, in his old age, he set out his views on the building of churches in a *Memorandum* for the Commissioners for building fifty new churches in London: 'Fronts as shall happen to lie most in View should be adorned with Porticos, both for Beauty and Convenience; which, together with handsome Spires, or Lanterns . . . may be of sufficient Ornament to the Town . . . If the Churches could hold each 2000, it would yet be very short of the necessary Supply. The Churches therefore must be large; but still, in our reformed Religion, it should seem vain to make a *Parish-church* larger, than that all who are present can both hear and see. The *Romanists*, indeed, may build larger Churches, it is enough if they hear the Murmur of the Mass, and see the Elevation of the Host, but ours are to be fitted for Auditories. I can hardly think it practicable to make a single Room so capacious, with Pews and Galleries, as to hold above 2000 Persons, and all to hear the Service, and both to hear distinctly, and see the Preacher. I endeavoured to effect this in . . . the Parish Church of *St James's, Westminster*' (St James, Piccadilly). He was buried in his great cathedral which he lived to see finished, and his memorial is of the simplest: 'Si monumentum requiris, circumspice'—If you seek his monument, look around you.

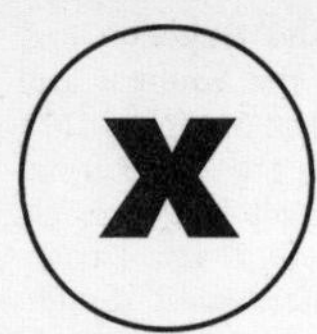

xenodochium (Late Lat. from Gk. stranger and guest house) That part of a monastery which served as a guest-house for travellers and pilgrims. Several existed in Rome by the 6th century. The word was also used for the place where strangers were detained for a period, to ensure that they were not suffering from the plague. Such a place existed, for instance, on the outskirts of Milan in the 16th century.

XPC, XPS, XC *See* MONOGRAM and NOMEN SACRUM.

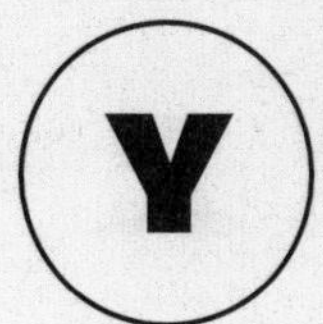

Year, the Liturgical In the West, the Church's year begins with Advent, the first Sunday on or after 30 November, and continues through Christmas, Epiphany, Lent, Holy Week, Easter, and Pentecost (Whitsun). In the Church of England, the Sunday after Pentecost (White Sunday), Trinity Sunday, begins the season of Sundays after Trinity (in accordance with the Book of Common Prayer Calendar). Since 2000, the last four have been replaced in the *Common Worship* Calendar by Sundays of the Kingdom, leading to Advent Sunday. The last of these, also observed in the Roman Catholic Church, is the Feast of Christ the King.

The Easter season in medieval times lasted for 40 days, from Easter Day to Ascension Day, but now in modern Calendars it runs for 50 days, From Easter Day to Pentecost.

Each season has its own *liturgical colour, which is used unless a feast day takes precedence.

yellow Formerly a *liturgical colour, and sometimes used as a substitute for cloth of gold, or even white.

YHWH (Yahweh: often rendered, wrongly, in English as Jehovah) *See* TETRAGRAMMATON and NOMEN SACRUM.

Yevele, Henry (1320–1400) A master mason at work in late medieval England. He is best known for his work on the nave of Westminster Abbey (from 1376) and the nave of Canterbury Cathedral (from 1377) amongst other projects.

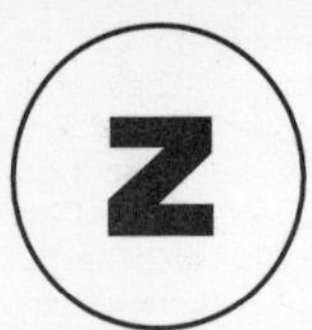

Zacchaeus (Luke 19: 1ff.) was a rich tax-collector (i.e. 'publican'), who wanted to see Jesus, but was too short to see over the heads of the crowd. He climbed a sycomore tree, where Jesus saw him and said He would visit him. 'All who saw it began to grumble and said, "He has gone to be a guest of one who is a sinner",... Then Jesus said to him, "Today salvation has come to this house, because he too is a son of Abraham. For the Son of Man came to seek out and save the lost."' The narrative detail of the man in the tree is found in mosaics and paintings, and may be confused with the *Entry into Jerusalem, with the people cutting palm branches (Matt. 21: 7–9; Mark 11: 8; John 12: 13).

Zacharias (Zachariah, Saint Zachary, Zechariah) One Zacharias (Vg. Zachary) was the father of *John the Baptist; the other was an OT Minor Prophet, also called *Zechariah (see below). Zacharias was a priest serving at the altar of incense, and was the husband of *S. Elizabeth. Luke (1: 5–25 and 57–80) tells how the Archangel Gabriel appeared to Zacharias in the Temple and told him that the childless Elizabeth would bear a son who was to be called John. Zacharias was struck dumb, but recovered when the child was born and he wrote on a tablet that his name was John. Cycles of the Life of the Baptist often contain this scene—e.g. the fresco by Domenico Ghirlandaio (1490) in Sta Maria Novella, Florence. According to the *Apocryphal Book of James, Zacharias was the priest who presided over the *Espousal of the Virgin, and was later murdered by Herod.

Zack, Léon (1892–1980). A painter, illustrator, designer of tapestries and windows, and sculptor, who was born in Russia, but left in 1920 for Paris. In painting, from figurative beginnings he oscillated between lyrical and geometric abstraction. The latter is represented in his numerous commissions for stained-glass windows, where geometric networks of fine black lines delicately stand out from the walls, diffusing a gentle light (1955, Notre Dame des Pauvres, Issy-les-Moulineux). He also completed numerous sculptures in a simple, allusive style: liturgical furniture (1953, Agneaux), high altars (1959, Sacred Heart, Mulhouse), crucifixes in bronze (1951, Urschenheim) or other material, several Stations of the Cross (1950, Carsac, in ceramic), a crucifixion tapestry (1960, Pantin), and altar candles. He completed the gates for the pool at Lourdes (1955) with Maxime Adam-Tessier, his collaborator since 1953.

Zadkiel, an *angel, leader of the Dominations (Dominions) of Angels.

Zebel According to the *Golden Legend*, the believing midwife present at the *Nativity. *See* SALOME.

Zechariah (Zachariah, Zacharias) was an OT Minor Prophet, whose OT Book contains prophecies of the rebuilding of the Temple, and the coming of Christ—e.g. 12: 10, 'when they look upon the one whom they have pierced', and 13: 6, 'What are these wounds on your chest?' (Vg. 'in the midst of thy hands'.) The answer will be 'The wounds I received in the house of my friends'. He is therefore represented as a prophet in e.g. the van *Eyck Ghent Altar and in *Michelangelo's Sistine Ceiling.

Zelomi *See* SALOME.

Zeno (Zenone), Saint, was Bishop of Verona and died *c.*372. He was apparently of African origin, but was not a martyr. He was made patron saint of Verona in the 8th century (and also of Pistoia); his body was transferred to the church of San Zeno in Verona in 807. This is now one of the most important Romanesque churches in Italy, rebuilt from 1118. It has famous bronze doors, also 12th century, with scenes from the OT and NT as well as some from his Life. He also appears in *Mantegna's S. Zeno Altar (1456–9) in the church. Other representations of him occasionally show him as an elderly bishop with a fish, but it is not clear why.

Zenobius, Saint, patron saint of Florence, was Bishop of Florence *c.*420. He was buried in Sta Reparata, now the Cathedral, and his relics are in a bronze casket made in 1432–42 by *Ghiberti, with reliefs of his miracles. He is frequently represented in Florentine works of art, as an elderly bishop, often with the Florentine lily on his crosier, mitre, or vestments. There is a series of four scenes from his life by Botticelli (Dresden, London NG, and New York, Met. Mus.), and other artists who represented him include Orcagna, Lorenzo Monaco, Gozzoli, Domenico Veneziano, Filippino Lippi, Verrocchio, Ghirlandaio, and Albertinelli.

Zodiac, Signs of the *See also* ASTROLOGY and MONTHS, LABOURS OF THE. The astrological signs of the Zodiac are not Christian, but they occur so frequently (e.g. in cathedral portal sculpture and calendars, usually in conjunction with the Labours of the Months) that they may be listed here. They correspond roughly with the twelve months and are, beginning from January: Aquarius, the water-carrier; Pisces, the fish; Aries, the ram; Taurus, the bull; Gemini, the twins; Cancer, the crab; Leo, the lion; Virgo, the virgin; Libra, the scales; Scorpio, the scorpion; Sagittarius, the archer; and Capricorn, the goat.

zone (Gk. girdle) A girdle worn by priests of the Byzantine rite, confining the *sticharion and the *epitrachelion.

zucchetto (Ital. *zucca*, the top of the head) A black skull-cap worn by priests. It is purple for bishops, scarlet for cardinals, and white for the pope.

Zurbarán, Francisco de (1598–1664), settled in Seville at the invitation of the City Council in 1629. His most productive years were from 1635 onwards, when his distinctive talent for simple, austere pictures of saints, painted mainly for religious houses, flourished. Doctrinally straightforward, they have a majestic solemnity, strong chiaroscuro, and restrained colour, which owes little or nothing to the influence of the Tenebrism derived from Caravaggio or Ribera, but stems from traditional southern Spanish unidealized naturalism. His altarpieces are often of the most undramatic, even prosaic, aspects of the lives of his subjects, but treated with such simple realism that they achieve a remarkable quality of mysticism, and conform to the strictest canons of Counter-Reformation artistic theories of the aims of religious painting: they concentrate on the 'witness' aspect of their subjects. This was always helped by the directness of his technique. Many of his works (particularly his workshop productions) were sent as trading ventures to Spanish possessions in S. America, notably Peru, but were not always attended by commercial success. In the 1640s he found himself forced to compete with *Murillo, which brought about changes in his impasted technique in favour of sweeter colour and softer handling, which did little for his art except to make it a more conventionally conformist aspect of Counter-Reformation Baroque. In 1658 he moved to Madrid in search of commissions, renewing his contact with Velázquez, which first began in 1634.

Among his noblest works are the *Martyrdom of S. Serapion* (1628: Hartford, Conn., Wadsworth Atheneum), unforgettable in its simplicity, its dignity, and its avoidance of any effects of horror or bloodshed, despite the terrible nature of the martyrdom, one of a series of martyrdoms of members of the Mercedarian Order. A gentler image is the *S. Margaret* (*c.*1631–2: London, NG), where the saint is seen as a charming young woman in a large straw hat, dressed like any housewife going to market with her shopping bag over her arm and her fingers tucked inside her Missal, identified only by the shadowy dragon that accompanies her much as might a pet dog. Both the pictures of *S. Francis,* also in London, National Gallery (1635–40 and 1639), are more dramatic, and the pair of *S. Bonaventura at the Council of Lyons* and the *Saint on his bier* (1629: Paris, Louvre) include an unusual gallery of sensitive portraits. While his gifts as a colourist are fully developed in the *Adoration of the Magi* (1638: Grenoble), he is at his most impressive in his magnificent management of white, as in the robes of his Mercedarian and Carthusian saints. Several of the *Twelve Tribes of Israel* are in the Bishop's Palace at Bishop Auckland, near Durham.

Zwingli, Ulrich (1484–1531), was a Swiss Protestant Reformer who disagreed with *Luther, but was responsible for the conversion of Zurich, where he was elected People's Priest at the Great Minster in 1518. By *c.*1524 he succeeded in abolishing all images and paintings in churches, as well as church music, and, in 1525, he finally succeeded in abolishing the Mass. He was killed in battle with dissident Catholic peasants in 1531.

Web links of general interest

UK

British Museum
Contains word art and artefacts. **Collection Database Search** of the Museum's two million records available for researchers.

Courtauld Instiute of ArtGallery
European arts, including paintings, drawings, prints, sculptures and decorative arts from 14th to 20th centuries.

National Gallery
Western Art from 13th to 19th centuries.

Royal Academy of Arts
British art and artefacts from 18th century to the present day.

Tate Britain
British art from the 15th century to the present day.

Tate Modern
Modern international art from 1900 to the present day.

Victoria and Albert Museum
Museum of art and design from the medieval to the present day.

Birmingham - Barber Institute of Fine Arts Gallery
Gallery of Birmingham University containing works from the 13th to the 20th centuries.

Cambridge - Fitzwilliam Museum
Includes collection of prints, paintings, and drawings from Europe, America, and Asia from the 13th century to the present day.

Edinburgh - Scottish National Gallery
Collection of fine art from the early Renaissance to the end of the 19th century.

Glasgow - Kelvingrove Art Gallery and Museum
Selection of religious art from its large and varied collections.

Liverpool - Walker Art Gallery
Collection of paintings and sculpture from the 13th to 20th centuries.

Oxford - Ashmolean Museum of Art and Archaeology
Paintings and drawings with online access to its collections.

EUROPE

Amsterdam - Rijksmuseum
Dutch paintings from the 15th to 19th centuries and other European masters.

Athens - National Gallery
Collection of European and Greek art from the 14th to 20th centuries.

Berlin - Alte National Galerie
19th and 20th centuries sculpture and paintings.

Berlin - Gemälde Galerie
European art from the 13th to the 18th centures.

Bruges - Groeninge Musum
Flemish and Belgian art from the 15th century to the present day.

Copenhagen – Danish National Gallery,
Danish and Western paintings, drawings, and sculptures from the last seven hundred years.

Dresden - Gemäldegalerie Alte Meister. Zwinger Complex
Especially strong in Renaissance Italian painting and 17th-century Dutch and German.

Dublin - National Gallery of Ireland 15,000
European and Irish works of art from early 13th to 1950s.

Florence - Uffizi Gallery
Italian art works from all centuries but especially strong in paintings from the 12th to 17th centuries.

Madrid - Prado Museum
European art from the 12th to 19th centuries, especially strong in Spanish paintings.

Munich - Alte Pinakothek
German and European painting from the 18th and 19th centuries.

Paris - Louvre Museum
Art and artefacts from the 12th to 20th centuries; the Atlas database contains details of 30,000 items.

Rome - Vatican Pinacoteca and Museum
Art gallery and museum in the Vatican City containing sculpture, paintings, and tapestries from the 12th to 19th centuries, including Sistine Chapel paintings.

Siena - Palazzo Pubblico (Town Hall)
Gothic building containing Sienese frescoes and early Christian art.

St Petersburg - Hermitage Museum
Western European art from the 13th to 19th centuries and Byzantium art collection.

Vienna - Kunsthistorisches Museum
Contains an art gallery of 16th- to 18th-century European paintings.

Zürich - Kunsthaus
Collection of paintings and drawings from the 15th century to the present day.

ELSEWHERE

Art Abstracts - Access via subscription - academic or public libraries
This database provides comprehensive indexing and abstracts from more than 450 international art publications, including periodicals, yearbooks, and museum bulletins. *Art Abstracts*' international coverage encompasses periodicals published in English, French, German, Italian, Spanish and Dutch, focused on a broad range of art topics, including advertising, archaeology, crafts, folk art, graphic arts, interior design, video, film, architecture, and art history. Indexing from 1984 to the present.

Index of Christian Art
The website of the index founded in 1917 by Professor Charles Rufus Morey (1877–1955) and now containing records of 80,000 works of Christian art with more than 100,000 colour and black and white images divided into two sections: 1. Medium and location. 2. Subject file.

Art History Resources
Art history resources on the web includes a section on Early Christian Art. Text and images of architecture and art works with authors cited at the end of each entry.